THE WRITER'S HANDBOOK

The Writer's Handbook

Edited by

SYLVIA K. BURACK

Editor, The Writer

Publishers   THE WRITER, INC.   Boston

CONTENTS

BACKGROUND FOR WRITERS

HOW TO WRITE—TECHNIQUES
GENERAL FICTION

CONTENTS

vii

CONTENTS

Background
for Writers

>> 1

BEGINNING

BY KELLY CHERRY

I AM A WRITER. I WRITE THOSE WORDS—"I AM A WRITER"—JUST LIKE that, as if it were as easy as that, or as if it mattered. It has not, in truth, been easy, but it does matter. I *trust* that it matters *literarily,* but I *know* that it matters *literally.*

The house in which I am writing is set in the middle of an arboretum; if you don't know to look for it, you're not likely to find it. The postman refuses to deliver packages to the door: too long a hike, too many mosquitoes. I don't mind. I welcome the solitude, the temporary lull in my life.

Why do I sit here writing? What earthly purpose does my writing serve? For a moment, let's set aside the conventional answers. The conventional answers include communication (as of an idea), aesthetic gratification (the reader's, or just the writer's), even art for art's sake. Let's even set aside the work's own demand to be brought into being. All of these are true answers but do not go beyond the specific case. We're seeking something deeper, something broader on which the whole of literature is based. Well, as you can guess, it's not for money. Some few writers do earn newsworthy incomes, of course; not very many serious ones do, and hardly any innovative ones do. A few more earn sufficient incomes because they were brought along by publishers when the publishing industry was willing to think of an advance not as a down payment on subsidiary rights but as an investment in an author's career; these writers were given time to develop a steady readership. Most of us, if we depended on our writing for an income, couldn't keep body and soul together.

Not long ago, as I was feeling very tired, I decided to figure out how many words I'd written in the past ten years alone. It came to one million finished words, or minimally five to ten million draft words, or

3

one million draft words every one to two years, not counting personal and professional correspondence and research notes. I teach full time. When I teach fiction writing, I average, per semester, three thousand pages of student manuscripts to read and mark in sentence-by-sentence detail. That is excluding non-degree students, independent study tutorials, and the odd novel in the anonymous knapsack. Like most writers, I also give readings, serve on panels, do workshops, apply for grants—a series of time-consuming steps that might be called The American Literary Soft-Shoe Shuffle.

Looking at those figures made me proud, but also tireder. I kept thinking how, if I were a different kind of writer, or perhaps Joyce Carol Oates, they would have added up to 730 books, all published, instead of 9½, of which 4 have been published and 5½ are in my desk drawer. But my case—this specific case that is mine—is no different from any other writer's; what I do and experience professionally is no different from what other writers do and experience. This is not just my life; it's a writer's life, and after all, a writer doesn't just choose it; clearly, she does anything she can to be allowed to live it, including—frequently with the secretly compelling sense of being a bit of an adventurer—throwing the rest of her life completely out of alignment.

So. The question returns. Why?

Why does anyone consent to the emotional, financial, spiritual, and even physical contortions that are necessary in order to lead the writer's life in America today? There are almost no grants. Only a few serious writers receive large advances; often, there are no advances at all. But we are blockheads, Dr. Johnson, who would write, who do write, for free! We would give our work away! Yet all too often, manuscripts filed in our desk drawers remain in our desk drawers. We write, most of us writers, without hope of publication or comprehension, happy and grateful when they come but not daring to assume either. We give our lives to our work. Even my dog, who wishes I'd stop this thing I'm doing and come play with him, puts his front paws in my lap and looks up at me, asking, Why?

The answer's as close on the question's heels as Duncan is on mine.

The answer is, *For the same reason I am telling you what my life as a writer is like.*

You had, most probably, no idea who I am; now, like it or not, you're stuck with an idea of me. Not necessarily—though possibly also—an

4

idea of mine, but necessarily an idea of me. You now know that there exists at least one person with the inner dimensions I have described. You may or may not be interested in my life, but that's not the point; and I might have lied—but I haven't. The point is simply that you are now obliged to recognize the writer of this piece as a conscious being.

We are all of us poets and storytellers, making literature of our lives, and when we listen to one another, we learn, through that exercise of the imaginative faculty, that this planet is a reality in at least more than one mind.

A writer is someone who makes the tracks of her mind's thinking visible for anyone who wants to follow her. This doesn't mean she is limited to autobiography; far from it. She *can* imagine the imaginations of others, even the imaginations of imaginary people, called characters or personae.

Critics, we may say, are census-takers.

But the writer knows that these imaginary constructs are dependent for their being on language. Therefore she agonizes over her verbs; she frets over her nouns; she restructures her sentences, paragraphs, scenes—and still she can't help knowing that no matter what she finally decides, everything hinges on whether it's Tuesday or Wednesday, and what she ate for breakfast. The only way I can say I sit *here* writing is *by* writing. Writing locates the *here,* and by unavoidable implication, a *there.*

I stand and stretch, look out the kitchen window. With the porch light on, I can see black oak, white oak, bur oak, black cherry, and shagbark hickory. Arrowwood and elderberry bushes are clumps of shadow; flowering raspberry surrounds the house. Asleep or skittering at the edges of the lawn are possums, foxes, rabbits, woodchucks. I can hear the shy whistle of the phoebe and the evening flute concerto of the woodthrush, and in the distance, the low thrum of Beltline traffic.

I turn back to the kitchen. The lighted fish in the aquarium are living their silent lives. Do you know that the female swordtail has no tail? That, deprived of a mate, she may change her sex?

Black oak, white oak, bur oak, black cherry, and shagbark. These trees, whether or not they grow *really,* independent of perception, now grow in your brain. I've planted them there; my words are seeds. We are rooted in our language. Whether or not this world exists independently of our consciousness is a question for the idealists and the empiricists still to debate; but your consciousness of my consciousness has unquestionably grown. It buds; it will leaf.

The world is populated by people who become human through their imaginative awareness of others' inner lives. It is the writer who works hardest to heighten, provoke, prod, even create, germinate and engender that awareness. What joy, what privilege!—to be so essential to existence. This is the writer's earthly purpose and her cause, which she serves gladly, in any circumstances, with a sense of its utter and transcending importance. That's why I said "matters." That's why I said "literally." In the beginning *is* the word.

➤➤ 2

SUPPOSE? AND WHAT IF?

BY MARY HIGGINS CLARK

WHEN I WAS LITTLE, THE MOST THRILLING WORDS IN THE LANGUAGE were "once upon a time." When I heard those words, I snuggled up and waited, eager to be transported to castles with magic gardens, or deep, dark caves where wicked giants dwelled.

As I grew up, I traded fairy tales for mystery stories and spent blissful, totally absorbed hours shivering over telltale hearts, footsteps in the dark, and piercing screams resounding through empty houses. The more I read, the more discerning I became. Soon I realized that certain characters stayed with me long after I had finished reading their stories. I began to see that some suspense writers are quite simply in a class by themselves—their plots are unique; the scenes they conjure up are always vivid and alive. They made me sense the danger, urge the detective to work more quickly, beg the intended victim to take greater care. That is the essence of storytelling—to involve the reader (or listener) so vividly in the story that he or she virtually is there, not as a spectator but as a participant in the ongoing adventure.

In my first writing class, I was given the most valuable advice that a young writer could receive. The professor said, "Take a situation that intrigues you and ask yourself two questions: *Suppose?* and *What if?* Then turn the situation into fiction."

I've been following that advice for more years than I care to count. But when I turned to suspense writing, I added another question: *Why?* I believe that no matter what the action in a suspense story, the *why* has to be satisfied. Four people may have strong reasons to commit a crime, but usually only one will go over the edge and actually do the deed. *Why* was his or her motivation stronger?

I've always believed that reading a suspense story can be compared to taking a ride on a roller coaster: Your heart begins to pound when you buy the ticket. You are terrified as the car starts to chug-chug up the first steep climb. Your breath quickens as you anticipate the first steep drop, the hairpin turns. Delicious fright. And then, when the brake trips, the car slows, and you arrive safely back at the starting point, didn't you always feel a sense of release?

Sometimes a story builds slowly, not unlike a fire that begins in the basement and then stealthily spreads through the walls and ceilings of the house until that terrible moment when it bursts into a no-exit inferno.

When you read a good suspense story, I think you experience something similar: You begin with a sense of apprehension. You are involved from the get-go. You are the protagonist. You know more than the detective. You fear for the victim. You share the emotions of fright, discovery, panic. If it's a particularly good story, you start to hear noises in your own house—the staircase creaking, the wind outside, the furnace settling. And when the story concludes, you feel a catharsis of released emotion.

➤➤ 3

THE WRITING LIFE

BY DIANE COLE

RECENTLY I WAS ASKED TO GIVE AN "UPBEAT" TALK ABOUT "THE writing life." But after I thought about all the great writers whose work had been neglected and rejected during their lifetimes, I wasn't so sure just how upbeat my talk would be.

As a working writer myself, I would be the first to agree that all writers face a terror when they sit down in front of a blank page—or more likely these days, a blank computer screen. It's hard to be as nonchalant as the great sports writer Red Smith, who said: "It's easy to write. You just open a vein and bleed."

My mind raced with thoughts about the writing life: The good. The bad. And the stuff you really don't want to hear about. Finally, I decided to tackle a few popular myths about "the writing life."

Myth #1: Writing is glamorous.

Reality: Only if your idea of glamour is staring at your computer screen for long stretches at a time each day.

Myth #2: Writers make scads of money.

Reality: Only a very small handful of writers sign multi-million-dollar contracts. A recent survey by the National Writer's Union found that a writer's median annual income hovered somewhere between $6,000 and $10,000 a year. About 30 percent made less than $2,000. Only the top 15 percent earned more than $30,000 a year.

I'm not going to tell you my writing income—it would be too embarrassingly paltry—but I will say that my first paid writing assignment was writing book reviews for the *Baltimore Sun* at the princely sum of $20 apiece. As a writer friend of mine advised: "I always tell students, if you want to be a writer, marry rich."

Myth #3: Writers need to suffer. Besides, the Bohemian life is romantic! And after all, you *do* need interesting, unusual, heart-rending material to write about!

9

Reality: It's not that writers *need* to suffer, but they often do because they don't have money, and one reason they don't have money is that they receive so many rejections.

Given all these grim facts, why does a writer take all this on—and write?

George Orwell wrote: "All writers are vain, selfish and lazy, and at the very bottom of their motives there lies a mystery. Writing a book is a horrible, exhausting struggle. . . . One would never undertake such a thing if . . . not driven on by some demon whom one can neither resist nor understand."

Which leads me to examine my own motives. What about the demons that have driven—and that continue to drive—me?

I've been scribbling things down for as long as I can remember. As a child, I would listen to my parents and their friends converse and carry away with me not the sense or substance of what they said, but the rhythm, the accent, the music of their different ways of expressing themselves. Without realizing it—and perhaps this is the only way you *can* cultivate this—I was developing what my fourth-grade teacher would tell me was a feel for language and an "ear" for dialogue. And when she encouraged me to keep on writing, I thought: Maybe it's possible, maybe I can become a writer some day.

And there was also the desire—maybe the need—to leave my mark, by writing something that would somehow be of use to others, whether it entertained, gave solace, provided practical information, or simply made another person smile.

Finally, in 1979, my husband and I moved to New York, and I decided to try my hand at writing fulltime. The rejections started pouring in immediately. But, gradually, I started getting acceptances, too. Writing on a variety of subjects for an increasing number of publications, I slowly began to build a career as a writer.

All that is more about *how* I got to be a writer than *why* I write and what gives meaning, for me, to "the writing life." So let me be very specific about *why* I wrote my book, *After Great Pain: A New Life Emerges.*

My own experience of loss and threatened loss lies at the core of *After Great Pain.* First there was the death of my mother, from cancer, when I was twenty-two. Only the year before, while still a college senior, I had helped my boyfriend Peter (now my husband) through

10

his bout with radical cancer surgery, radiation treatments, and chemo-
therapy. Coming one on top of the other, these battles—one successful,
the other not—had left me raw and numb, utterly weary, but perhaps,
I hoped, also a little wiser.

Then, one spring morning less than two years later, I faced the possibility—what seemed at that moment the probability—of my own bizarre and violent death when an armed band of Hanafi Muslims seized
the B'nai B'rith Building in Washington, D.C., where I worked, and
held more than one hundred of us hostage there. During those thirty-
nine hours of captivity, I grieved for myself and for all I had left undone, but I also came to a new understanding of life's peculiar resilience even amid terror and anguish.

With that new wisdom, Peter and I married. But then, even as I
began to formulate my book, there came the increasingly apparent
reality that I would not be able to bear a child.

Was it difficult to write about such painful experiences? How could
it not be? But it was also carthartic. Each experience of loss, I realized,
had also led to a transformation. After great pain had come numbness,
anger, guilt, and all the other stages of grief. And finally, each time, a
new self had emerged, one with a different vision of who I am, a
different sense of what I could do or even wanted to do, and a different
perspective on what my future might hold. And there was a happy
ending—or should I say beginning—to my story: the adoption of our
wonderful son, Edward.

Writing about these experiences began as a therapeutic necessity—
a way of trying to make sense of things that seemed to lack sense.
Moreover, it was my hope that my story could help others by giving
voice to their pain and perhaps easing them through their grief to a
sense of renewal.

What started as journal entries eventually became the seeds for
personal essays and articles. Those personal essays eventually grew
into my book, *After Great Pain,* in which, I see in retrospect, I did
accomplish many of the things I had set out to do: To use my love of
language to deliver what I believe is an important message about life
and loss and love—and also about endurance and resilience, and, finally, faith and renewal.

And ultimately, I discovered, writing is itself an act of faith and
renewal in the unending story of every writer's writing life.

11

>> 4

CULTIVATING THE LIBRARY HABIT

BY JOHN JAKES

LIBRARIES ARE MAGICAL PLACES. THERE'S NOTHING QUITE LIKE strolling the hushed aisles, letting your eye rove along dimly lit shelves. Each spine, each title, seems to beckon with a promise of incredible wonders, surprises and adventures.

Libraries not only take us into new and exciting realms, but also help us grow. They answer questions, solve problems, enable us to better ourselves. If I did not have the library habit—which is passed on by families—I certainly couldn't research and write the first chapter of a historical novel.

Whatever the need—from simple escape reading to learning gourmet cookery, or evaluating mutual funds, or confronting dire illness—as my son, Mike, said in his 20s, when he set out to master the handling of small boats: "There's always a book."

I've never forgotten those words. A majority of Americans know how true they are. According to the American Library Association, 66 percent of us use one of the nation's 15,000-plus public libraries annually. And the usage numbers go up each year.

But finding the books we need or want, when we want them, is getting harder. Our libraries are in trouble. And we'd better take notice and remedy the situation before one of our nation's most precious assets becomes a skinny, starving shell of its old self.

With today's tax dollars stretched to the limit, states and towns facing a budget crisis find the library a tempting target. But when they do, bad things happen. Services are curtailed, hours shrink. Worst of all, libraries are closing all over the country. Even in the Great Depression, I don't know of *one* library going out of business.

It's a terrible situation—and here's the paradox: Americans as a whole don't want it to happen! Individually, we want our libraries to succeed. We want *more* for them, not less.

12

So what's wrong? I'm afraid we must round up the usual suspects—politicians and their Frill Mentality. This is a mindset that perceives public libraries as less important than unfilled potholes.

The Frill Mentality is sometimes bolstered by the assertion that libraries are dinosaurs, doomed to extinction by the computer age. I doubt it. I suspect it will be many years before every home has a computer and the money and expertise to use it.

And will we then give up the children's story hours? Book discussion groups? The librarian who helps us find exactly what we're searching for?

But the Frill Mentality is widespread and insidious. It attacks the very life blood of our nation—information, knowledge. Because a library isn't just some pleasant, dusty building under the trees that's nice to have but not really essential. I believe passionately that the library is one of the cornerstones of a healthy community. It gives us the opportunity to encounter great ideas, great minds, great art.

And spare me the argument that reading is declining because of TV. It may be true in some quarters, but I've seen TV adaptations of my novels drive hordes of new readers straight *to* the libraries, hunting for Jakes books. Some of those readers send me letters saying mine is the first novel they've ever read.

What, then, can you or I do as individuals do to protect and promote our public libraries?

• First, get the facts and figures. Is your library adequately funded? If not, what's a reasonable higher goal to work toward? If you have a good local or county library board, its members can be helpful here.

• Second, watch for elected or appointed officials who exhibit symptoms of the Frill Mentality. If one of them starts blathering about "unnecessary" library hours and "expendable" services, jump on that person with calls or letters. If he or she is unreasonable, elect someone else next time.

• Third, for muscle in your own locality, it helps to have an organized Friends group. If there's one where you are, join it. If there isn't, start one. Friends of Libraries U.S.A. (1700 Walnut St., Suite 715, Philadelphia, PA 19103) will be glad to help.

Finally, as a strategic objective, work to have the library operating tax removed from the general tax fund, and always put it to a public vote separately.

"There's always a book," our son said. That's a promise we absolutely have to keep.

➤➤ 5

TALKING ABOUT WRITING

BY URSULA K. LE GUIN

PEOPLE COME UP TO YOU IF YOU'RE A WRITER, AND THEY SAY, I WANT to be a writer. How do I become a writer?

I have a two-stage answer to that. The first-stage answer is this: You learn to type (or to word-process). The only alternative is to have an inherited income and hire a full-time stenographer. If this seems unlikely, don't worry. Keyboards are easy to learn.

Well, the person who asked, How do I become a writer, is a bit cross now, and mumbles, but that isn't what I meant. (And I say, I know it wasn't.) I want to write short stories, what are the rules for writing short stories? I want to write a novel, what are the rules for writing novels?

Now I say Ah! and get really enthusiastic. You can find all the rules of writing in the book called *Elements of Style,* by Strunk and White, and a good dictionary—I recommend the *Shorter Oxford*; Webster's is too wishy-washy. There are only a very few rules of writing not covered in those two volumes, and I can summarize them thus: Your story may begin in longhand on the backs of old shopping lists, but when it goes to an editor, it should be typed, double-spaced, on one side of the paper only, with generous margins—especially the left-hand one—and not too many really grotty corrections per page.

Your name and its name and the page number should be on the top of every single page; and when you mail it to the editor it should have enclosed with it a stamped, self-addressed envelope. And those are the Basic Rules of Writing.

I'm not being funny. Those are the basic requirements for a readable, therefore publishable, manuscript. And, beyond grammar and spelling, they are the only rules of writing I know.

All right, that is stage one of my answer. If the person listens to all that without hitting me, and still says All right all right, but how *do* you become a writer, then I can deliver stage two. How do you become a writer? Answer: You write.

It's amazing how much resentment and evasion this answer can arouse. Even among writers, believe me.

The most frequent evasive tactic is for the would-be writer to say, But before I have anything to say, I must get *experience.*

Well, yes; if you want to be a journalist. But I don't know anything about journalism, I'm talking about fiction. And of course fiction is made out of experience, your whole life from infancy on, everything you've thought and done and seen and read and dreamed. But experience isn't something you go and *get*—it's a gift, and the only prerequisite for receiving it is that you be open to it. A closed soul can have the most immense adventures, go through a civil war or a trip to the moon, and have nothing to show for all that "experience"; whereas the open soul can do wonders with nothing. I invite you to meditate on a pair of sisters. Emily and Charlotte. Their life experience was an isolated vicarage in a small, dreary English village, a couple of bad years at a girls' school, another year or two in Brussels, and a lot of housework. Out of that seething mass of raw, vital, brutal, gutsy Experience they made two of the greatest novels ever written: *Jane Eyre* and *Wuthering Heights.*

Now of course they were writing from experience; writing about what they knew, which is what people always tell you to do; but what was their experience? What was it they knew? Very little about "life." They knew their own souls, they knew their own minds and hearts; and it was not a knowledge lightly or easily gained. From the time they were seven or eight years old, they wrote, and thought, and learned the landscape of their own being, and how to describe it. They wrote with the imagination, which is the tool of the farmer, the plow you plow your own soul with. They wrote from inside, from as deep inside as they could get by using all their strength and courage and intelligence. And that is where books come from. The novelist writes from inside.

I'm rather sensitive on this point, because I often write science fiction, or fantasy, or about imaginary countries—stuff that, by definition, involves times, places, events that I could not possibly experience in my own life. So when I was young and would submit one of these things about space voyages to Orion or dragons or something, I was told, at extremely regular intervals, "You should try to write about things you know." And I would say, But I do; I know about Orion, and dragons, and imaginary countries. Who do you think knows about my own imaginary countries, if I don't?

But they didn't listen, because they don't understand. They think an artist is like a roll of photographic film: You expose it and develop it and there is a reproduction of Reality in two dimensions. But that's all wrong, and if any artist tells you "I am a camera," or "I am a mirror," distrust them instantly; they're fooling you. Artists are people who are not at all interested in the facts—only in the truth. You get the facts from outside. The truth you get from inside.

O.K., how do you go about getting at that truth? You want to tell the truth. You want to be a writer. So what do you do?

You write.

Why do people ask that question? Does anybody ever come up to a musician and say, Tell me, tell me—how should I become a tuba player? No! it's too obvious. If you want to be a tuba player you get a tuba, and some tuba music. And you ask the neighbors to move away or put cotton in their ears. And probably you get a tuba teacher, because there are quite a lot of objective rules and techniques both to written music and to tuba performance. And then you sit down and you play the tuba, every day, every week, every month, year after year, until you are good at playing the tuba; until you can—if you desire—play the truth on the tuba.

It is exactly the same with writing. You sit down, and you do it, and you do it, and you do it, until you have learned how to do it.

Of course, there are differences. Writing makes no noise, except groans, and it can be done anywhere, and it is done alone.

It is the experience or premonition of that loneliness, perhaps, that drives a lot of young writers into this search for rules.

Writing cannot be shared, nor can it be taught as a technique, except on the most superficial level. All a writer's real learning is done alone, thinking, reading other people's books, or writing—practicing. A really good writing class or workshop can give us some shadow of what musicians have all the time—the excitement of a group working together, so that each member outdoes himself—but what comes out of that is not a collaboration, like a symphony performance, but a lot of

17

totally separate, isolated works, expressions of individual souls. And therefore there are no rules, except those each individual makes up.

I know. There are lots of rules. You find them in the books about The Craft of Fiction and The Art of the Short Story and so on. I know some of them. One of them says: Never begin a story with dialogue! People won't read it; here is somebody talking and readers don't know who, and so they don't care, so—Never begin a story with dialogue.

Well, there is a story I know, it begins like this:

"*Eh bien, mon prince!* so Genoa and Lucca are now no more than private estates of the Bonaparte family!"

It's not only a dialogue opening, the first four words are in *French,* and it's not even a French novel. What a horrible way to begin a book! The title of the book is *War and Peace.*

There's another Rule I know: Introduce all the main characters early in the book. That sounds perfectly sensible, mostly I suppose it is sensible, but it's not a rule, or if it is somebody forgot to tell it to Charles Dickens. He didn't get Sam Weller into the *Pickwick Papers* for ten chapters—that's five months, since the book was coming out as a serial in installments.

Now you can say, all right, so Tolstoy can break the rules, so Dickens can break the rules, but they're geniuses; rules are made for geniuses to break, but for ordinary, talented, not-yet-professional writers to follow, as guidelines.

And I would accept this, but very grudgingly. Put it this way: If you feel you need rules and want rules, and you find a rule that appeals to you, or that works for you, then follow it. Use it. But if it doesn't appeal to you or work for you, then ignore it; in fact, if you want to and are able to, kick it in the teeth, break it, fold staple mutilate and destroy it.

See, the thing is, as a writer you are free. You are about the freest person that ever was. Your freedom is what you have bought with your solitude, your loneliness. You are in the country where *you* make up the rules, the laws. It is a country nobody has ever explored before. It is up to you to make the maps, to build the cities. Nobody else in the world can do it, or ever could do it, or ever will be able to do it again.

Absolute freedom is absolute responsibility. The writer's job, as I see it, is to tell the truth. The writer's truth—nobody else's. It is not an easy job. You know how hard it is to say to somebody, just somebody you know, how you *really* feel, what you *really* think—with complete honesty? You have to trust them, and you have to *know yourself*, before you can say anything anywhere near the truth. And it's hard. It takes a lot out of you.

You multiply that by thousands; you replace the listener, the live flesh-and-blood friend you trust, with a faceless unknown audience of people who may possibly not even exist; and you try to write the truth to them, you try to draw them a map of your inmost mind and feelings, hiding nothing and trying to keep all the distances straight and the altitudes right and the emotions honest. . . . And you never succeed. The map is never complete, or even accurate. You read it over and it may be beautiful, but you realize that you have fudged here, and smeared there, and left this out, and put in some stuff that isn't really there at all, and so on—and there is nothing to do then but say O.K.; that's done; now I come back and start a new map, and try to do it better, more truthfully. And all of this, every time, you do alone—absolutely alone. The only questions that really matter are the ones you ask yourself.

>> 6

BETWEEN THE REAL AND THE BELIEVABLE

BY CHARLES McCARRY

SOME TWENTY YEARS AGO I PUBLISHED A NOVEL IN WHICH ONE OF the characters, a pathologically jealous young woman, was so obsessed with her husband, an American spy who kept his operational life secret from her, that she embarked on a series of joyless adulteries in order to accumulate secrets of her own, and so become his romantic equal.

Soon after this work appeared, I found myself at a dinner party in Northampton, Mass., seated next to an agitated feminist, who, like my unhappy character, was young and beautiful and a recent bride. Throughout dinner, she told me how much she hated the girl in the book, whose behavior she had found to be utterly unrealistic and an insult to women—"male chauvinist propaganda," she called it.

I was not surprised by the onslaught. For a writer in America, going out to dinner is like living as an American in Europe: Total strangers think they can say anything they like to you. Still, I had trouble grasping the point. Why did a 1950s fictional character have to conform to an ideological model that had not yet been invented at the period in which the novel took place?

I asked my critic to tell me in plain English why she disliked and distrusted my character so. After a moment of angry silence the woman threw half a glass of California burgundy on my best gray suit and replied, "Because I used to be just like her!"

On the way home, my wife wisely told me I should take this happening as a compliment. But there was more to it than that, as is perhaps demonstrated by the fact that I have never even considered using the wine episode as a scene in a novel. Truth in life and truth in art are not the same, and for the reader—that passive collaborator who must complete the author's work by developing it in his mind as if it were

20

a strip of exposed film—suspension of belief is quite different from believing what one is expected to believe.

Unlike speech, which slips into the consciousness obsequiously through the ear, the written word clambers into the mind through the window of the eye. It is more likely to be welcome if it wears the mask and costume of a harmless guest at a masked ball than if it carries the blackjack and clinking tool kit of a real burglar. People do not like to be surprised, but fiction that abjures the element of surprise is mere bedtime story.

Over the years I have moved back and forth between novels and nonfiction, including collaborations on the memoirs of well-known public figures—"like a polygamist moving from bedchamber to bedchamber," as a friend, monogamous in literary matters, put it. Others have suggested that what I learn from writing about the real world must be of direct use to me in writing novels.

Not really. For one thing, writing is famously a cure: By the mystical process of transforming the invisible contents of the mind into black ink on a white page, you get rid of the damn stuff forever. For another, though reality checks are part of the process, no true novel can be made from anything but the imagination and its silent partner, experience, which is not at all the same thing as research.

Knowledge of the world of affairs does confer certain secondary benefits on the novelist: He learns for a fact that the great are only the small made large. But there is very little he can carry back and forth between the two forms, though they are much alike from a technical standpoint—he uses the technique of fiction (action proceeds from character, dialogue reveals inner meaning, surprise is the soul of narrative) to write about real people in real life, and the fundamental problem is the same in both forms: The greater the verisimilitude, the greater the will to resist it.

For a decade at the height of the Cold War, I worked abroad under cover as an intelligence agent. After I resigned, intending to spend the rest of my life writing fiction and knowing what tricks the mind can play when the gates are thrown wide open, as they are by the act of writing, between the imagination and that part of the brain in which information is stored, I took the precaution of writing a closely remembered narrative of my clandestine experiences. After correcting the manuscript, I burned it.

21

What I kept for my own use was the atmosphere of secret life: How it worked on the five senses and what it did to the heart and mind. All the rest went up in flames, setting me free henceforth to make it all up. In all important matters, such as the creation of characters and the invention of plots, with rare and minor exceptions, that is what I have done. And, as might be expected, when I have been weak enough to use something that really happened as an episode in a novel, it is that piece of scrap, buried in a landfill of the imaginary, readers invariably refuse to believe.

>> 7

THE JOURNEY INWARD

BY KATHERINE PATERSON

DO YOU KEEP A JOURNAL?" NO, I ANSWER A BIT RED-FACED, BECAUSE I know that *real* writers keep voluminous journals so fascinating that the world can hardly wait until they die to read the published versions. But it's not quite true. I do make journal-like entries in used schoolgirl spiral notebooks, on odd scraps of paper, in fairly anonymous computer files. These notations are all so embarrassing that I am hoping for at least a week's notice to hunt them down and destroy all the bits and pieces before my demise.

I write these entries, you see, only when I can't write what I want to write. If they were collected and published, the reader could logically conclude that I was not only totally inept as a writer but that I lacked integration of personality at best, and at worst, was dangerously depressed.

If I had kept a proper journal, these neurotic passages would be seen in context, but such is not the case. If my writing is going well, why would I waste time talking about it? I'd be doing it. So if these notes survive me, they will give whatever segment of posterity might happen upon them a very skewed view of my mental state.

The reason I am nattering on about this is that I have come to realize that I am not alone. As soon as my books (after years of struggle) began to be published, I started to get questions from people that I had trouble answering in any helpful way: "Do you use a pen and pad or do you write on a typewriter?" (Nowadays, "computer" is always included in this question, but I'm talking about twenty years ago.)

"Whatever works," I'd say. Which was true. Sometimes I wrote first drafts by hand, sometimes on the typewriter; often I'd switch back and forth in an attempt to keep the flow going. The questioner would thank me politely, but, looking back, I know now that I had failed her.

"Do you have a regular schedule everyday or do you just write when you feel inspired?" the person would ask earnestly. I am ashamed to say, I would often laugh at this. "If I wrote only when I was inspired," I'd say, "I'd write about three days a year. Books don't get written in three days a year."

Occasionally, the question (and now, I know, all these were the same question) would be framed more baldly. "How do you begin?" "Well," I would say, "you sit down in front of the typewriter, roll in a sheet of paper and . . ."

If I ever gave any of you one of those answers, or if any other writer has ever given you similar tripe, I would like to apologize publicly. I was asked, in whatever disguise, a truly important question, and I finessed the answer into a one-liner.

How *do* you begin? It is not an idle or trick question. It is a cry from the heart.

I know. That's what all those aborted journal notes are about. They are the cry when I simply cannot begin. When no inspiration ever comes, when neither pen, nor pencil, nor typewriter, nor state-of-the-art computer can unloose what's raging about inside me.

So what happens? Well, something must. I've begun and ended over and over again through the years. There are several novels out there with my name on the cover. Somehow I figured out how to begin. Once the book is finished, the memory of the effort dims—until you're trying to begin the next one.

Well, I'm there now. I have to begin again. What have I done those other times? How have I gotten from that feeling of stony hopelessness? How do I break through that barrier as hard as sunbaked earth to the springs of creativity?

Sometimes, I know, I have a conversation with myself on paper:

What's the matter?
What do you mean "what's the matter?" You know perfectly well. I want to write, but I can't think of a thing to say.
Not a single thing?
Not a single thing worth saying.
You're scared what you might say won't be up to snuff? Scared people might laugh at you? Scared you might despise yourself?
Well, it is scary. How do I know there's still anything in here?

24

You don't. You just have to let it flow. If you start judging, you'll cut off the flow—you've already cut off the flow from all appearances—before it starts.

Grump.

Ah yes, we never learn, do we? Whatever happened to that wonderful idea of getting up so early in the morning that the critic in you was still asleep?

How do I know it will work this time?

You won't know if you don't try. But then, trying is risky, and you do seem a bit timid to me.

You don't know what it's like pouring out your guts to the world.

I don't?

Well, you don't care as much as I do.

Of course I do. I just happen to know that it is so important to my psychic health to do this that I'm willing to take the risk. You, my friend, seem to want all the creative juices inside you to curdle and poison the whole system.

You're nothing but a two-bit psychologist.

Well, I've been right before.

But how do I begin?

I don't know. Why don't we just get up at five tomorrow, come to the machine and type like fury for an hour and see what happens? Could be fun. Critic won't be up, and we won't ever have to show anybody what we've done.

Now you understand why I have to burn this stuff before I die. My posthumous reputation as a sane person of more than moderate intelligence hangs in the balance. But living writers, in order to keep writing, have to forget about posthumous reputations. We have to become, quite literally, like little children. We have to remember our early griefs and embarrassments. Talk aloud to ourselves. Make up imaginary companions. We have to play.

Have you ever watched children fooling with play dough or fingerpaint? They mess around to see what will emerge, and they fiddle with what comes out. Occasionally, you will see a sad child, one that has decided beforehand what he wants to do. He stamps his foot because the picture on the page or the green blob on the table falls short of the vision in his head. But he is, thankfully, a rarity, already too concerned with adult approval.

The unspoiled child allows herself to be surprised with what comes out of herself. She takes joy in the material, patting it and rolling it and shaping it. She is not too quick to name it. And, unless some grownup interferes, she is not a judge but a lover of whatever comes from her heart through her hands. This child knows that what she has created is marvelous simply because she has made it. No one else could make this wonderful thing because it has come out of her.

What treasures we have inside ourselves—not just joy and delight but also pain and darkness. Only I can share the treasures of the human spirit that are within me. No one else has *these* thoughts, *these* feelings, *these* relationships, *these* experiences, *these* truths.

How do I begin? You could start, as I often do, by talking to yourself. The dialogue may help you understand what is holding you back. Are you afraid that deep down inside you are really shallow? That when you take that dark voyage deep within yourself, you will find there is no treasure to share? Trust me. There is. Don't let your fear stop you. Begin early in the morning before that critical adult within wakes up. Like a child, pour out what is inside you, not listening to anything but the stream of life within you. Read Dorothea Brande's classic *On Becoming a Writer,* in which she suggests that you put off for several days reading what you have written in the wee hours. Then when you do read it you may discern a repeated theme pointing you to what you want to begin writing about.

Begin, Anne Lamott suggests in her wonderful book *Bird by Bird,* in the form of a letter. Tell your child or a trusted friend stories from your past. Exploring childhood is almost always an effective wedge into what's inside you. And didn't you mean to share those stories with your children someday anyhow?

While I was in the midst of revising this article, my husband happened to bring home Julia Cameron's book, *The Artist's Way.* Cameron suggests three pages of longhand every morning as soon as you get up. I decided to give the "morning pages" a try and heartily recommend the practice, though these pages, too, will need to be destroyed before I die.

When I was trying to begin the book which finally became *Flip-Flop Girl* (and you should see the anguished notes along the way!), I just began writing down the name of every child I could remember from the fourth grade at Calvin H. Wiley School. Sometimes I appended a note that explained why that child's name was still in my head. Early-morning exercises explored ways the story might go, and I rejected most of them, but out of those fourth-grade names and painful betrayals a story began to grow. Judging from the notes, it was over a year in developing and many more months in the actual writing. But I did begin, and I did finish. There's a bit of courage for the next journey inward.

Now it's your turn. Bon voyage.

REINVENTING YOUR WRITING CAREER

BY TOM PEELER

MY COMEBACK AS A FREELANCE WRITER HAS BEEN NOTICEABLY LESS dramatic than George Foreman's in boxing—more like the little engine that could. Maybe I had it too easy at first. Over a ten-year period I sold more than 100 articles and wrote a weekly column for a major daily newspaper for a year and a half. After not writing for about ten years, I discovered upon my attempts at reentry that America's editors had learned to get along without me.

I have had to reinvent my approach to free-lance marketing to conform to the system, needs, and demands of the current market, which have changed greatly over the last decade. The things I have learned in the process can benefit new writers as well as those whose careers may need some retooling. Here they are:

1. *Organize.* Most people who have taken personality tests have been told that they are either organized or creative. That won't work anymore; a successful free lancer has to be both, even if getting organized feels like trying to write left-handed if you are not. I use a loose-leaf notebook to record my queries by date, subject matter, and publication to which I have sent them. In a separate section of the notebook, I record the same information for finished articles. In a filing cabinet, I keep track of article ideas, writing tips, magazine guidelines, and subjects that I have researched. Any magazine that I can get my hands on goes into a vertical file, in alphabetical order.

With this system, I know what I've sent where, so I won't suffer the embarrassment of sending the same query to the same editor. I have learned how long it customarily takes different markets to respond, and I know who hasn't paid me yet.

2. *Automate the details.* Paying attention to necessary details can be even more tedious than organizing, but just as essential. Anyone

who has ever received a barely legible note scribbled on a query saying, "Send it in, and we'll look at it," knows that editors don't like details either. Would an overworked editor really reject a promising query just because I omitted a stamped, self-addressed envelope? I don't want to find out.

To reduce the boredom of tending to the mundane, for about $40 I get 1,000 self-addressed envelopes printed in a size slightly smaller than those in which I submit my manuscripts or queries, to accommodate a letter-size return.

I used to work on a portable typewriter, but I can't imagine trying to compete in today's market without a computer or word processor.

3. *Know the market.* Overkill is impossible here. I like to see two or three recent issues of any magazine I consider a promising market, *and* get writers' guidelines from the magazine, if available. To hold down the cost, I browse through the magazine section of my library. For my files, I might make a photocopy of the masthead and perhaps of an article typical of the magazine's style.

Even if I have already studied the market lists in books and magazines that specialize in such information, I usually pick up a useful tidbit or two from the guidelines. For instance, though I was aware of the general rule at *Modern Maturity* that unsolicited manuscripts will not be considered, I learned from the guidelines that the rule does not apply to essays, fiction, puzzles, and tips. The *Country America* guidelines include the names of the editors assigned to special sections of the magazine.

4. *Submit quality queries only.* I was so anxious to get back to writing that at first I played the law of averages: I figured that twenty-five queries would net me five or six go-aheads. But editors do not observe the law of averages. Twenty-five poorly drafted queries will net a return of zero. What I was overlooking was the fact that these editors don't know me. In the past, those who did could count on a finished product that would satisfy their needs, regardless of how hurried my query might have been. But this is not so for the unknown free lancer. The query must address the three whys: why this subject, why me, and why now? Jack Lowry, Editor of *Texas Highways,* says that he places more emphasis on how well the query is written than he does on published clips, since he cannot tell from the clips how much of the

work was done by the editor. Even if it means researching most, even all, of your story before writing your query, it's worth the effort.

5. *Specialize.* Perhaps the most dramatic change in the magazine market from ten years ago is the concentration today on narrow, specific areas of interest. Previously, a reader interested in an article on fishing would flip through the pages of *Sports Afield* or *Field & Stream* in search of an article on scaly creatures among features on turkeys or deer. Now there are magazines devoted to freshwater, saltwater, and fly fishing. Within the freshwater category there are publications that concentrate on bass, catfish, and crappie. Geographically, freshwater enthusiasts can focus on Pennsylvania, Oregon, Minnesota, or Texas.

In other words, concentrate on the area that interests you, and if you're not an expert now, you may become one. And even if the area of interest still requires consultation with recognized professionals, specialization will allow you to develop regular sources and will give you credibility with the pros who know you can speak the language.

6. *Establish your credibility.* Since most editors prefer to see queries first, rather than finished articles, you have to convince them that you will deliver what you promise; you can't simply tell the editor that you know what you're talking about and will always meet a deadline. If you have had other articles within your specialty published by respected magazines, this is the credibility you need. If you have established your expertise in other ways (through a hobby or a blue ribbon at the state fair), let the editor know. If you lack expertise yourself, identify your prospective sources and document their credentials.

7. *Submit timely ideas.* Even if you're able to convince an editor that you have a good idea and know what you're talking about, you still have to deal with "why now?" Most magazines have longer lead times than they did in the past; it's not unusual today for magazines to plan their contents eight months to a year in advance, some even longer.

If food is your specialty, submit your plum pudding query in January if you want it considered for the next Christmas issue. For an article on the 50th anniversary of a special event, look for something that happened 48 or 49 years ago.

8. *Be patient.* A quick response to a query is not necessarily good news; it may simply mean that you did not make the first cut. Many

magazines have a person who screens submissions and sends back those that lack potential. Those that make the first cut may be sent on to a senior editor, or even to a committee of editors, a process that can easily take two or three months.

Since the process can be so painstakingly slow, and since queries must be well-timed, some writers send multiple queries. While this is more common now than it used to be, I do not feel comfortable with sending multiple queries. I do not want to be in the position of having an editor remember that after spending time considering and finally giving me a go-ahead on my query, a competitor wound up with the article. I would rather send a single query, far in advance, and then follow it up with a courteous self-addressed stamped postcard request for a response.

9. *Don't take it personally.* Only rarely will an editor tell you why your submission was rejected. The rejection may reflect upon the quality of your work, but in many cases, it may mean that you simply do not understand a particular market. A query or an article can be top-quality but wholly unsuitable if written from the wrong angle or even in a style different from that preferred by the editor. Free-lance writing success is like any sales effort—while quality queries are essential, if a writer is trying to reach new markets, the rejection slips will always outnumber the go-aheads.

$\ggg 9$

BUILDING SELF-CONFIDENCE

BY MAIA WOJCIECHOWSKA

OVER THE YEARS OF TEACHING CREATIVE WRITING COURSES I HAVE encountered many talented writers, a number of whom share a common complaint: they'd wished, for years, to start writing.

"What stopped you?" I ask.

Their answers and excuses range from "my family," "my job," to "lack of time." The one hardest for me to understand, especially with talent, is: "lack of self-confidence." Having never accepted that excuse as valid, I would like to offer some possibly helpful advice.

First of all, what haven't you written? a novel? a short story? an article? a nonfiction book? a play? a poem?

If you hope to become a published writer, you definitely need confidence. It's as important as guts and knowing how to bluff. Bluffing is part and parcel of the whole game of getting published, and you must view it as the equivalent of playing poker. If you are afraid of losing, don't sit in on the game, and if you can't bluff, you will be dropping out too many times to have any fun. Without having fun, playing poker or writing wouldn't be worth the effort.

Drop into your neighborhood bookstore. You should feel a surge of confidence merely by looking at what seems like an avalanche of books. Books seem to be getting published and presumably even read, in greater numbers than ever before. Of course there is more to fiction than just today's best sellers and yesterday's unsuccessful blockbusters selling at one tenth their original price.

The field of nonfiction has enlarged its scope beyond the usual categories, with shelves of inspirational and motivational books overflowing. Doesn't it stand to reason that a talented, still-to-be-published writer would find comfort and self-confidence in the very fact that more books are being published than ever before?

32

Find the section in the bookstore where whatever you have written, or want to write, would belong. It should be invigorating for you, a talented writer, to look over the competition. There is little there that cannot be improved upon; you can do much better, can't you? Of course you can! The question is, will you? And when? Is your confidence rising?

Keep in mind that it is the writer who provides ideas. Without a writer there is no story, no play, no poem. Without writers there would be no need for librarians or libraries, publishers or bookstores.

Writers are entitled to the confidence that comes with the writer's central position in a civilized society or even semi-civilized society, such as ours. Whose life have you failed to enrich by *not* writing? Your own, or someone who has been deprived of what you have to give? What do you have to say, that nobody has said before? It's all been said before, you may think—perhaps, but not in the way that you can say it. There is nothing new under the sun, yet the sun comes up each day, and every day there is someone waiting to be talked to in a book, in that special way that Hemingway described best:

All the good books are alike in that they are truer than if they had really happened and after you've finished reading one you will feel that happened to you and afterwards it all belongs to you; the good and the bad, the ecstasy, the remorse and sorrow, the people and the places and how the weather was.

There is something else that he said about writing that might get you started, if you have talent and want to go into this second oldest profession that does not always pay for what you do:

When you first start writing stories in the first person, if the stories are made so real that people believe them, the people reading them nearly always think the stories really happened to you. This is natural because while you were making them up you had to make them happen to the person who was telling them. If you do this successfully enough you make the person who is reading them believe that the things happened to him, too. If you can do this you are beginning to get what you are trying for which is to make the story so real beyond any reality that it will become a part of the reader's experience and a part of his memory. There must be things that he did not notice when he read the story or the novel which without his knowing it, enter into his memory and experience so that they are a part of his life. This is not easy to do.
—From an unpublished manuscript in the Kennedy Library collection. Roll 19. T 178

It's not easy to do. But what, after all, is easy, besides falling in love?

33

>> 10

GERTRUDE STEIN'S SECRET

BY HELEN MARIE CASEY

"AND THAT IS ALL THERE IS TO GOOD WRITING," GERTRUDE STEIN wrote, "putting down on the paper words which dance and weep and make love and fight and kiss and perform miracles."

Who can argue with a description that creates its own miracle of synopsis, that uses action verbs to show as well as tell, that mirrors the magic of words at work?

Without explicitly mentioning stories or poems, Stein's collection of highly charged, extraordinarily visual action words takes us to the realm of imaginative writing, to poems, plays, and novels we love.

We know what she is talking about because we know where words in the hands of an artist can take us. We've been there. We've been in that magic kingdom where "Let's pretend" ends by taking us deep into meanings we didn't know we could find.

Stein's words focus us on the raw power of language, of even the simplest words: *dance; weep; make; love; fight; kiss; perform; miracles.* At the same time, they humble and they energize us. These words are choreographed. They are alive. They are in motion. They sing. They are compelling.

Is it the content of what she has to tell us that arrests us, or is it the phrasing itself? Does the magic, in fact, lie in the way she has placed her words on the page?

We look again and are struck by the cadence she has achieved by the balanced use of that small word *and*: "And that is all there is to good writing, putting down on the paper words which dance *and* weep *and* make love *and* fight *and* kiss *and* perform miracles." There's a lilt in the movement of the sentence that rises with each succeeding action word. This is no accidental arrangement of thoughts. The statement

34

has the economy of a tightly crafted short story at the same time that it has the grace of a lyric poem.

What do we learn from so brief—and eloquent—an observation about good writing? We're reminded all over again that words work. They do not achieve their effect by serendipity. They cannot be selected at random. All words are not equal. After they are selected, words must be properly shaped and chiseled if they are going to leap when they must.

Words cannot be partnered willy-nilly. Strong, simple verbs do not want to be overpowered. They must be trusted to carry their full weight.

Words that the tongue savors require time for the savoring. Duration. They want pauses around them, pauses created by other words that slow us down and pauses created by careful line breaks and intelligent punctuation.

The hard work of writing is not the initial setting down of words but the listening to them to hear what they are telling us about themselves, about how they want to work, how they want to go about saying what they want—and know how—to say. Words in fresh combination, words in patterned repetitions, words doing work they've never done before: All have their own requirements.

In a sense, each word or image becomes a hinge. That word-hinge has dictates of its own about precisely what may follow. The heft of each word must be taken before it can be entrusted with carrying on its work on the page.

What Gertrude Stein knew about language she tried to tell us. She wrote and spoke about language. She experimented with language, spending a lifetime letting words play through her fingers to the page. She listened to words with the intensity of an artist who, while moving away from conventional approaches, is listening all the while for new direction. Her ear became her great ally in writing. It taught her to follow the rhythm of language; it taught her the importance of repetition, particularly nuanced repetition; and it taught her to create and value the dense linguistic texture created by words—often seemingly devoid of meaning—reverberating off each other.

Gertrude Stein was thoroughly unconventional in her writing. She broke syntactical rules. She thumbed her nose at traditional approaches to narrative. She created new patterns in every genre she touched. She left us an immense body of work, and she shared her secret: *If the communication is perfect, the words have life, and that is all there is to good writing, putting down on the paper words which dance and weep and make love and fight and kiss and perform miracles.*

>> 11

Do the Writing Only You Can Do

By Christopher Scanlan

TWENTY YEARS AGO, WHEN ONE OF MY RELATIVES WAS IN THE MIDST of a painful divorce, I found myself wondering how children react to their parents' separation. What came to mind was one of those "What if" questions that drive many writers, in this case, "What if a little girl made an inventory of every item in her father's study the day before he moved out of the house?"

I made some notes, wrote drafts, discarded them, and tried again. The piece sat in my desk drawer, off and on, for years. I wrote other short stories, but always found myself returning to that one.

Many, many drafts later, I finally reached a point at which I was willing to send it out. A long list of publications rejected the story, including *Redbook,* and I can't say I blame them. I knew that it still wasn't good enough. But in my heart, the story never died. I kept at it: reading books about children and divorce, rewriting draft after draft. A newsroom colleague who had written award-winning fiction suggested that the story ended on page 10 of my 12-page manuscript. I made the cut and sent it around again. This time, the editors at *Redbook* liked the story.

Many people say they want to write, but they don't know what to write about. Looking back at the stories that I am proudest of, I can detect a central fact about each of them: They are pieces that only I could have written. That realization led me to a rule I try to live by: Do the writing only you can do.

Keeping the faith

How many times have you said to yourself, "That would make a great story," but then let the idea succumb to the doubts that plague most writers. Novelist Gail Godwin believes the writer must ignore the carping and criticism of the inner voice (she refers to it as "the

37

watcher at the gates") that tells many of us that we have no talent, that our ideas are worthless, and that there is no point in trying.

My short story ends after Emily, a precocious 12-year-old, has faked an upset stomach to stay home and record every item in the den occupied by her departing father, just as I had dreamed it all those years ago:

She imagined making a scrapbook, like the one Mrs. Markham had everyone make of their class trip. She would paste in the list of everything in his den, all the books, the pictures, the furniture. Paste in the pictures she'd taken. Write captions underneath. That way, even if her father took everything away, she would always remember what it looked like. And when he finally came home, she would surprise him. He would return, carrying all his boxes back into the den, and he would try to remember where everything went. He'd be standing there, rubbing his chin, when she walked in with the scrapbook. "Daddy, your books go here. Schoolbooks on the top shelf, paperbacks on the next one. That chair? Put that right over there. No, no, your diploma goes on that wall. Here, let me show you," Emily would say, taking charge.

A friend describes me as "sports-challenged" because I have so little interest in sports. I like to point out that I might care about the World Series or the Super Bowl "if my coach had given me a full uniform when I played Little League."

For years, hearing people laugh when I recounted my comic adventures as an uncoordinated, pint-sized athlete, I used to wonder if it might make a good story, but then the "watcher" at my gate would whisper, "no one cares" about my life on the bench. That was before I resolved to do the writing only I can do. I sat down and put the anecdotes on paper. On the day Super Bowl XXIX was played, my essay, "Stupor Bowl," appeared in *The Boston Globe Magazine*. It recalled the days three decades before when "I was small and scrawny, a clumsy flop at tennis, golf, backyard football, you name it. I lagged behind the pubescent progress of my friends, whose voices were deepening, whose chins were sprouting hairs, who really needed to wear jockstraps."

Silence the watcher at the gate to your imagination by keeping the faith in your ideas, because those are the ones that will set you, and your stories, apart.

Every writer has a territory, a unique landscape of experience and emotional history. Like any landscape, there are safe havens and dangerous places. I could easily write a light-hearted piece about being the father of three girls. But the topic that needed exploring was my darker side: my temper with my kids. The essay I wrote begins with this painful scene:

It's late at night, and I'm screaming at my kids again. Yelling at the top of my lungs at three little girls, lying still and terrified in their beds. Like a referee in a lopsided boxing match, my wife is trying to pull me away, but I am in the grip of a fury I am unwilling to relinquish. "And if you don't get to sleep right now," I shout, "there are going to be consequences you're not going to like."

First published in *The Boston Globe Magazine,* the essay has been reprinted many times. Some of my friends had cautioned me against publishing this piece; people might get the wrong idea about me. But writing it helped me understand myself and, more important, treat my family better. Judging from the letters and phone calls I've received from readers grateful to see a painful issue in their life aired publicly, it's helped others, too. Explore a dangerous region of your writer's territory by writing a piece nobody can write but you.

Letting the story speak

It was a dream assignment. *The Washington Post Magazine* assigned me to write a profile of the first Vietnamese graduate of West Point. Tam Minh Pham was a young man who marched with the long gray line of cadets in 1974, returning home just in time for the fall of his country and six years imprisonment. But his American roommate never forgot him, and twenty years later marshaled his classmates to cut through bureaucratic red tape and bring their buddy to America for a new life.

It didn't take much reporting for me to decide that this was a powerful story, worthy of the length of a cover piece. The only problem: The top editor didn't agree, and I was advised to stick to the prescribed limit. But when it came time to write, I had trouble holding back. I decided to write the first draft for myself and worry about length later. I began this way:

As usual, bribes loosened the guards' tongues. Another transfer was coming. By this time, after four years in jungle camps guarded by the North Vietnamese army, the inmates were going to a prison run by the Cong An, the security police. When he heard the rumor, Tam Minh Pham knew what to do. For years, he'd heard the stories about the cruel men in yellow uniforms who took people

39

away in the dead of night, about the torture, the killings. He waited for the camp to quiet down and the night air to fill with the scent of cooking fires, and then he crept out of his bamboo hut to the garden.

That opening scene went on for another 500 words, much too long for the kind of story I knew the editor was expecting. Fortunately, he was willing to take a look. The next day, word came back that some changes were needed; the piece, now scheduled for the cover, needed to be longer.

The quickest way to lose editor's interest is to give them something different from what they expected. At the same time, writers need to let the story speak if they are going to produce stories that break barriers for themselves and their readers.

Tapping your private stock

We were on our honeymoon in Europe, a month-long trip that had already taken us to Germany, Holland and Paris. Now with a week left before we headed home, we were making good on a promise to a friend: to visit the grave of a man we had never met, who had died in a war fought before my wife and I were born. Pfc. John Juba, the half-brother of our friend back home, had died in the 1944 Normandy invasion, but no one in his family had ever seen his grave. Finding it took two train trips, four cab rides, and visits to three cemeteries, before we finally stood in front of the marble tombstone in the Brittany countryside where the soldier was buried. In my hand was a bouquet of white roses that an elderly farmer had let us cut from his garden. Beside us stood a man named Donald Davis, the cemetery's superintendent. In "The Young Who Died Delivered Us," the account of our search, I described the moment this way:

The graves at Brittany lie beyond the Wall of the Missing—4,313 white crosses and Stars of David lined up on a manicured field like a marching band at halftime. Five varieties of grass keep it green all year round. The cemetery was empty and so quiet we could hear the rain falling on the flower beds bordering the graves. . . . I laid the flowers in front of the cross and knelt to take a picture for his mother.

"Wait." Davis bent down and turned the bouquet around so the flowers faced the camera. "Otherwise, all you'll get is a picture of the stems." Every trade has its secrets.

"Rest in peace, John," I said under my breath.

Readers are deluged today by clichés, commonplace descriptions, and derivative plots. Search, as you write and revise, for the telling details and observations that give resonance and meaning to your story, that set it apart, and your chances of producing a piece with universal appeal are strong. Draw on your individual experiences by tapping the "private stock" of experience, memory, and feeling that is inside you. The story of that pilgrimage to a soldier's grave has paid off with publication of "The Young Who Died Delivered Us" in six different newspaper magazines, as well as a reprinting in a popular textbook. But most rewarding were the letters from readers who saw themselves in our search. Wrote one man who helped lay out the cemetery where John Juba is buried: "You seem to have caught the feelings experienced by us who were there."

Spreading the word

It was an offhand comment by an interview subject. I was reporting a story for Knight-Ridder Newspapers about guns and children, when Mary Steber of Liverpool, N.Y., told me that she and her suburban family had never worried about guns until their 14-year-old son, Michael, was shot to death while watching a football game at a classmate's house. The friend's father, a retired policeman, kept a collection of firearms in an unlocked closet.

"You warn your kids about sex and drugs and alcohol and getting in a car with a stranger," Mrs. Steber said. "Yet guns were never mentioned in our house. We never thought of it as a problem."

Now whenever Michael's siblings visit a new friend, they make a point of reassuring their parents, "Don't worry, they don't have guns."

When I heard that, I thought, "What a great message for parents." Our own daughters had just reached the age of sleep-overs and visits to their friends' homes. Before we let them pay a visit, we started asking parents of our kids' friends, "Do you have guns in your house?"

Almost every day, it seems, the news reports yet another shooting of a child with a gun left unattended. Perhaps the Steber family's common-sense approach, if heeded by enough parents and gun owners, might save a life. To spread the word, I wrote an essay I called, "It's 10 p.m.: Do You Know Where Your Guns Are?" and began sending it around to newspaper op-ed pages. So far, its child-protecting message

41

has reached readers of *The Christian Science Monitor, St. Petersburg Times,* and *The Orlando Sentinel.*

We all have stories that only we can tell. How we dealt with the loss of a parent, coped with an out-of-control emotion, why we cheered getting fired, the time your sister nearly burned the house down, the way your children's school deals with a social problem, retracing a memorable trip, recreating a haunting memory.

List the stories only you can write. Then write them.

➤➤ 12

RHETORICALLY SPEAKING

By LouAnne Johnson

I PEEKED IN THE WINDOW. THIRTY FRESHMAN HONOR STUDENTS SAT waiting, pens poised above their brand-new notebooks. They were ready. I wasn't sure I was, but I decided to go ahead and give my plan a shot. If they got it, fine. If they didn't, I'd think of something.

"Good morning, ladies and gentlemen!" I shouted as I marched across the floor and slammed my briefcase down on the instructor's desk. Silence. "As you know," I went on, "this is an honors level composition course. You are here because you have high grade-point averages, and your high school teachers think you are good writers. Perhaps you are. I intend to find out." One boy in the back of the room put his head down on his desk. I ignored him.

"My name is Miss Johnson. I've been a writer for the past thirty years. I am also a former officer of the United States Marine Corps. I'm not used to taking any crap, and I don't intend to take any from you. If you expect to get an A in this course, you're going to have to earn it. If you aren't ready to work, the door is open. Make your choice, and make it now."

I could tell from their expressions, and their glances toward the door, that every student in the class wanted to leave. But they were smart kids, smart enough to know that walking out of a required course on the first day of college would not be an intelligent move. They sat still. Without saying anything further, I made a quick turnabout and marched out of the room, letting the door slam behind me. Before they had a chance to recover, I swung the door open again and sashayed daintily back inside.

"Hi," I said, as I giggled and patted my hair. "My name is, like, LouAnne, and I'm, like, your instructor, and I want everything to be, like, really cool, so everybody can, like, express himself or herself without, like, being afraid of any put-downs or anything. Oka-a-ay?"

The boy who had put his head down on the desk during my drill sergeant routine sat up straight and glanced at the girl beside him. She raised her eyebrows and shrugged. A few small smiles showed me that some of the students were starting to catch on. But most of them sat, staring at me, clearly confused. I giggled again and ran out of the room.

The third time I opened the door, I walked in and smiled pleasantly. "Good morning. I am your instructor. My name is LouAnne Johnson, and I hope that we will accomplish two things in this class. Number one, we will meet the requirements for this course. Number two, you will actually learn something about writing."

I picked up a marker and drew two vertical lines, dividing the white board behind me into thirds. I labeled the sections #1, #2 and #3, then asked the class members to vote which of my three different introductions represented "the real Miss Johnson." I recorded their votes on the board. The boy in the back voted for #1, but the rest of the class voted for #3.

"Why did you pick the third one?" I asked. "Anybody? Just speak up."

"I could just tell," one young woman said.

"You seemed real," somebody added from the far corner. "Genuine."

"But why?" I insisted. "Can somebody try to explain it?"

There was such a long silence that I almost gave up. Then a young man in the front row adjusted his glasses and cleared his throat. "I believe there was some element in your voice that matched the expression on your face and the look in your eye. They all matched, so to speak. I didn't sense any incongruity."

"Thank you very much," I said, and I meant it. His explanation was even better than the one I had planned. "Just as you can sense that a person is pretending, acting insincerely, you can also sense dishonesty in writing. I'm sure you've all read pretentious prose that put you off because it tried to impress you. And it's quite likely that you've thrown down some article or essay you'd started to read that may have contained a brilliant idea, but was so poorly presented and illogically organized that it wasn't worth the effort it would have taken to read it." A few nods encouraged me to continue.

"When you write compositions for me, don't try to sound like a textbook, or your high school English teacher, or your favorite author. While I'd encourage you to use techniques and writing styles that you

44

admire, I don't mean for you to try to copy them. Learn how to use them; make them your own. Write in your own voice. Each of you has a particular combination of vocabulary, tone of voice, facial expressions and gestures that creates a distinct, individual personality when you express your ideas during a conversation. But when you write, you can rely only on language—word choice, sentence style, punctuation—to communicate your personality."

It worked. They got it. Instead of deluging me with the standard five-paragraph essay, written entirely in passive voice, using the longest possible words, these students learned to use language either to show or hide their personalities, depending upon the assignment. To project a sense of objectivity in her research paper, for example, one young woman, Suzette, chose relatively formal language and complex sentence structure:

College campuses can be misleading, with their tree-lined walkways, stately lecture halls, and dormitories. Statistics have repeatedly demonstrated that America's colleges and universities are not the safe havens many parents believe them to be.

Later, Suzette wrote a personal essay on the same topic, but the voice was completely different.

My parents think I'm safe here at NMSU. They don't know about the date rapes and muggings. And I'm not going to tell them. They would just worry about me, because they don't realize how much the whole world has changed since they went to college.

In this essay, colloquial phrases, first-person voice, and simpler sentence structure gave a good sense of Suzette's personality and attitude: She's young and scared, but she's determined to be independent.

Although all of my students agreed that finding their own voices was necessary, some of them needed extra time and practice before they finally "got it right." One young man became frustrated when his peer critique group pronounced that he was almost, but not quite, there.

"How do they know whether it's my voice or not?" he challenged me.

"Other people can critique your writing for form and content," I said, "but no one else can know whether you have said what you wanted to say, whether the message the reader receives is the one you meant to send."

45

"How will I know when it's right?" he asked.

I was tempted to say, "How do you know when you're in love?" But I realized that my voice might not be the one this particular student needed to hear. So I quoted from journalist Marya Mannes's essay, "How Do You Know It's Good?" Mannes's answer? "When you begin to detect the difference between freedom and sloppiness, between serious experimentation and egotherapy, between skill and slickness, between strength and violence, you are on your way. . . ."

My student frowned for a moment, digesting this new idea, then smiled. "Why didn't you say that before?"

>> 13

Choosing a Writers Conference

By Shirl Thomas

FROM MY OBSERVATIONS AS A CONFEREE, AS WELL AS A SPEAKER AND workshop leader at writers conferences, I have found that those who attend often feel shortchanged, for a variety of reasons: They may find speakers uninterested, hard to approach, or disappointing; are unclear about a conference's procedures and available services; or feel that they don't get the most out of workshop sessions, particularly when writers at varying levels of competence are in the same group.

There are countless writers conferences—local, regional, and national; they can be as short as one day or as long as one week. The conference locale, cost, and theme or focus can vary greatly; subject matter may be geared to beginners or cover advanced writing or marketing techniques. So, how do you decide if a particular conference is worth the time and money? One important factor to consider is your motivation. Are you writing for love of the written word, or striving for a professional career? Prospective goals can make a difference in your determination.

If you write primarily for self-expression, speakers who deal extensively with the literary marketplace or small presses would be of interest. These "little" magazines often publish only experimental works and poetry, and usually offer modest compensation—sometimes, "payment in copies only." However, they are receptive to beginning writers who can gain valuable experience from contributing to these markets and have a better chance of getting published.

If you have professional goals, attending workshops on business and marketing would be beneficial, along with hearing speakers from the more prestigious magazines and publishing houses, as well as literary agents who could be helpful in placing your work later on.

In any case, some research is necessary before making an informed

47

decision about attending one conference over another. Here are some guidelines:

1. Does it fit your needs?

You should have a direct interest in the market categories represented. Most conferences will offer a range of several different fields, while others are organized around a specific theme or topic, such as "Writing for Children" or "Articles in the Making." Find out in advance what market categories will be covered. Do they match your writing interests?

For example, if workshops and seminars emphasize "whodunits" and you're concentrating more on "how-tos," you may want to choose a different conference. (There is much to be said, however, for mixing fiction techniques with nonfiction styles.)

2. What type of help will be offered?

There are four popular conference formats: lectures; workshops; writer discussion groups; and speaker roundtables, or a combination of two or three. Choose the one most appropriate to your taste and needs, taking into account whether a conference is geared to your level of writing. Ask yourself these questions: Will discussions include beginning fundamentals or be restricted to more advanced techniques and the business side of writing? Will detailed instruction be offered? Will there be an opportunity to have your manuscript critiqued at the conference? By whom? Other conferees, or workshop leaders—editors, publishers or agents? May manuscripts be sent in advance and appointments set up so that you can be sure of being able to discuss your work with a professional? Should you bring a writing sample— or a portfolio?

Determine the level of your participation well in advance, and be prepared to take advantage of these opportunities.

NOTE: Make sure any material you do bring with you is professionally typed and ready for the market. No first drafts!

3. Who are the speakers?

Research the qualifications of speakers and the genres and specific areas they will cover, and decide whether they warrant your time and effort. Will appointments for private consultation be available? If not, ask whether speakers will have question-and-answer sessions or will mind being approached by participants at the conference. And when the time comes, remember: Don't be too timid or too pushy.

4. How much will it cost?

In addition to the registration fee, will the costs for food, lodging, and travel fit your budget? Conferences at luxury hotels may be prohibitive, so you may want to consider going to a conference held on a college campus. (Don't expect to recoup expenses with the money you'll make from your writing!)

5. What are the proposed schedules?

Will there be a conflict in the schedules for the lectures or workshops in which you have a special interest? If so, will you be able to buy tapes of the overlapping seminars? Do you object to early-morning or late-evening sessions?

NOTE: If you are restricted by time or finances, you may want to check to see if you can be a part-time participant.

Attending the right conference at the right time can open doors of opportunity for a writer, provide an often needed change of scenery, a fresh point of view, and insight into how others are pursuing the craft. Although some writers may find the prospect of being around professional authors intimidating, keep in mind that successful published writers were once beginners, too, and are usually sensitive to newcomers' trepidations. Though some speakers' egos may interfere with the goal of addressing writers' concerns, most are dedicated to assisting writers and are prepared to help—otherwise, they would not agree to participate.

If you leave a conference feeling only that it provided entertainment or perhaps a diversion, then there may have been little merit in having attended. But if the time spent at a writers conference helps you improve, or has given you a push in the right direction, then it was a worthwhile endeavor—whether you write for the love of the craft or with the goal of becoming a professional. In any case, it's a personal choice. Decide what you want to derive from the experience, and then go for it.

>> 14

THE FRUSTRATION FACTOR

BY GARY A. CROW

WHEN I GAVE A COPY OF MY NINTH BOOK, *THE FRUSTRATION FACTOR: How to Manage People Who Drive You Up A Wall* (Glenbridge Publishing Limited), to a friend, I was asked the now familiar questions: "How long did it take you to write it?" "Is it hard to write a book?" "Where did you get the idea?" "How did you get a publisher?" Then came the even more familiar rationalization, "I'm thinking about writing a book, but I really don't have the time. You know how it goes."

Those questions leave me simply speechless. Even after writing nine books, I still have no idea how to reply. . . . No, that's not quite right . . . I *do* know, but I was taught to be polite. I think I will say here what I was tempted to say to my friend.

First, it took me thirty years to write this book, with the eight that preceded it serving as practice. This is not to mention the newspaper columns I did week after week for free and those articles and other books that never made it into print. This book is the latest iteration of my writing career and the most recent culmination of what talents I have.

Here is another truth: "It took about an hour per page to write the book and another few hours per page to edit and rewrite." I also was tempted to say, "About half as much time as you spent watching TV during the last two years," but I'm not sure it actually took that long.

Is it hard to write a book? No, not particularly. You can do it like this: Write one sentence a day for ten years, retype it so that all the paper is white, not yellowed from aging, give it a title, and tell all your friends that you have finished your book and are looking for a publisher. You don't have to do anything else. You have written a book.

If you're asking me if writing *The Frustration Factor* was hard work, that is a much more complex question. Now, with a copy of the published book sitting on my shelf, as I think back to the process, it seems as if it just magically appeared. I remember bits and pieces of the process, but I am unable to connect the book's reality with anything I would now call work. There were the hours and weeks at my keyboard when I would drift into that mental space where sometimes interesting but more often trivial and empty mind games are played, where the occasional burst of energy and productive output emerge. There were the fun times, when I made time to read articles about strong openings, dialogue, pace and flow, how to submit a manuscript, the secrets of successful writers, and anything else I could find about what I cannot help doing: writing. There also were the seemingly endless days of writing and rewriting and then rewriting again. Now that was seriously hard work.

It seems I have found the answer to your question: It was hidden in that mental space where some good ideas linger among the unimportant ones. Writing the book was a curious mix of fun, tedium, and persistence. From that point to finishing a book that the publisher was willing to invest in was very hard work, as are most things worth doing.

As for the next question, where did the idea come from? I don't have a clue. I never did just get the idea. At some point in the thinking/writing process, the idea was simply there. It is sort of magical after all.

When it comes time to find a publisher, I follow almost all the rules. If a publisher requires a query letter, that is what I send. If the complete manuscript is requested, it goes out, neatly typed, double-spaced, grammar and spelling checked, with no staples or fasteners, and in a box. Sufficient return postage is a must, too, but only a return envelope for a reply letter. This costs less than printing another copy, especially since the one I sent may come back with editorial comments written on it or not looking fresh.

Now for the rule I do not follow. I send a query letter to anyone I think may be interested. The same goes for anyone who asks to read the manuscript. "No simultaneous submissions" is someone else's rule. Most publishers are going to turn down the book, no matter how good it is. The worst thing that can happen is that more than one publisher may want to see the manuscript and decide to accept it. If so, I have to say, "No" to some, and they may be upset. But it also is upsetting for me to get one of their rejection letters.

I can handle having a publisher upset with me because I sold my project to another company, especially since it usually takes two or three months per rejection. At that rate, it could take years to find the one publisher who can and will work successfully with my book manuscript. That may be fine for those who have completed "the work of their lifetime"; but I have other books to write and need to get on with it.

I think the real key is to listen and learn. Remember that you are looking for an editor who likes your book. Among those who reject it are the few who will take time to make a cryptic comment, like the editors who rejected *The Frustration Factor* with, "There is a problem with the order of things"; "Interesting idea, but where is the how-to information"; "Too short"; "Great, wish I could publish it"; and the best of all, "Interesting; give me a call when you have time, and we can talk about it." When I have time? What a wonderful sense of humor that editor has! Is this very instant too soon?

How did I get a publisher? I was persistent, and lucky that Glenbridge's editor found my query in the pile on his desk on a day when he was experiencing his own frustrations. Or, possibly, my first sentence—"Do you ever have to work with people who absolutely, totally, and unequivocally drive you up the wall?"—caught his attention and he kept turning the pages to see what happened next.

The other equally important point is this: The publisher believes that the book will sell. That's the publisher's business—selling books.

Now you know what I would have liked to tell my friend; but what did I actually say? "It took some time." "It was hard work at times, but not all that bad." "The idea evolved over time." "Getting a publisher was a combination of persistence and good luck."

As for, "You know how it goes." Sure, I know how it goes. One word at a time, at least 50,000 times. It's easy to see why you haven't gotten past just thinking about it.

➤➤ 15

"I" Is Not Me

By Margaret Maron

RECENTLY, AN IRATE READER TOOK ME TO TASK FOR MY NOVEL, *Shooting at Loons*. Offended when my first-person narrator remarked that someone was "not much taller than me," the reader acidly inquired if grammar were no longer important.

"It is clear that you don't know any better than to let your character—a judge with a law degree, for heaven's sake!—use bad grammar," he fumed, "but why didn't your editor catch it? Don't editors edit anymore?"

Fortunately for me, my editor is more astute than that particular reader. She knows the stylistic difference between an author's formal voice and a character's narrative voice and would never try to smooth away my "I" character's verbal idiosyncrasies. Nevertheless, that letter did make me stop and reconsider how, as writers, we often do use a first-person voice as a shorthand method to convey character and personality without actually having to spell them out.

The omniscient author's voice pays strict attention to the laws of grammar and punctuation; the narrative voice pays strict attention to the character of the "I" who is telling the story.

As someone who reads Fowler's *Modern English Usage* for sheer pleasure, I do know the difference between subjective and objective pronouns; and yes, I do try to use them correctly when writing third-person or formally. (Actually, Fowler prefers "Not much taller than me" over "Not much taller than I," which "strikes the reader as pedantic.") But that is neither here nor there. The truth is that when I write first-person fiction, I deliberately mimic language that will let my readers know this person's social class, present emotional status, and whether he is likeable or mean-minded, brave or timorous, a whining pessimist or a cheerful optimist.

This is especially useful in the short story form, where every word counts.

In my short story, "Deadhead Coming Down," no third-person description of an easily bored trucker can match the immediacy of his own voice saying,

> There's not one damn thing exotic about driving a eighteen-wheeler. Next to standing on a assembly line and screwing Bolt A into Hole C like my no-'count brother-in-law, driving a truck's got to be the dullest way under God's red sun to make a living. 'Specially if it's just up and down the eastern seaboard like me.

The trucker speaks in short blunt words and his coarse denial of his brother-in-law's worth foreshadows his truly callous actions in the story.

Conversely, when I wrote "On Windy Ridge," I hoped that the slower, dreamlike pacing and choice of elegiac language would help convey the image of a middle-aged mountain woman who possesses both intelligence and a slightly psychic sensitivity:

> Waiting is more tiresome than doing, and I was weary. Bone weary . . . but my eyes lifted to the distant hills, beyond trees that burned red and gold, to where the ridges misted into smoky blue. The hills were real and everlasting and I had borrowed of their strength before.

In *Shooting at Loons,* the novel that so exercised my overly pedantic reader, my narrator is Deborah Knott, a district court judge in her mid-thirties. Even though she knows better, Deborah is a breezily colloquial Southerner who makes grammatical slips because she is the daughter and sister of semiliterate dirt farmers who will use dialect, split infinitives, double negatives, sentence fragments, dangling participles, and a host of other colorful grammatical errors till the day they die. True, she has a law degree; true, she is a judge. Neither has turned her into a grammarian. (I was once sent to the principal's office because I would not agree when the English teacher insisted that *it's* was the possessive of *it.* She, too, possessed an advanced degree.)

With one foot in North Carolina's agrarian past and the other firmly planted in its high-tech present, Deborah is never going to "get above her raising." Not if I have anything to say about it.

After all, I have a classic precedent for claiming the right to a narrative voice that is not necessarily my own.

54

In a preface to one of his books many years ago, a certain writer used his formal voice to explain the technical side of creation: "In this book a number of dialects are used . . . . The shadings have not been done in a haphazard fashion, or by guesswork, but painstakingly, and with the trustworthy guidance and support of personal familiarity with these several forms of speech." Then switching into his first-person narrative voice, that same author wrote, "You don't know about me without you have read a book by the name of *The Adventures of Tom Sawyer,* but that ain't no matter."

Had Mark Twain written the whole book as omniscient and highly literate author, *The Adventures of Huckleberry Finn* would be a forgotten piece of 19th-century esoterica. Instead he gave us Huck's distinctly ungrammatical *"I"* voice and the book remains a living, breathing masterpiece a hundred years later.

>> 16

MIXED SIGNALS

BY NANCY SPRINGER

THE YOUNG MAN ENTHRONES HIMSELF ATOP A CLASSROOM DESK, FAC-
ing me, swinging his combat-booted feet. He is holding a copy of one
of my novels; I have just signed it for him. "So how do you do this,
anyway?" he asks, keeping his voice deep and casual. "How do you
get a book published?"

He is a student in the writing class I teach at a post-secondary school
attended mostly by youngsters who are not academically inclined. He
wears a lot of leather, always dresses entirely in black, has a bizarre
haircut, some tattoos, a ring in one nostril. He wrote his how-to paper
on "How to Throw a Hand Grenade" and his "If I Had Three Days to
Live" paper on suicide-bombing his former employer. He is muscular
and struts when he walks; other male students get out of his way. He
is rowdy in class. Yet whenever I ask him to please shut up, he smiles
with genuine sweetness and does so—for a few minutes. He is always
in attendance, always on time, he writes unusually well, and a lot of
what he says—out of turn and between Elvis impersonations—is off-
the-wall funny and brilliant. He upstages me constantly. I like him, yet
feel deeply unsure about him—mixed signals put me off balance, keep
me thinking about him. A friendly, intelligent youth who dresses like
death incarnate and is fascinated by weapons? What is he really like?
I can't tell.

Now, though, I recognize the glimmer nearly hidden deep in his
wise-guy eyes. Or maybe I merely think I recognize it. Maybe I'm
just hoping.

How do you get a book published? I have a dozen glib responses at
the ready to provide me with quick escape in social situations, but for
this young man I think a moment, trying to give him a good, true
answer. He waits. "It's a twofold process," I say, "and most people
concentrate too much on one aspect or the other."

56

He is listening attentively, his mouth firmly shut.

"First you have to write something good," I say, "which means you really have to learn how to write. That part usually takes years. And then, once you have something worthwhile, you need to market it. Go to conferences, meet people, learn your way around publishing. I see people who write great stuff and stick it in a drawer, and I see a lot more people who write crap and think that if they could just find an agent they could get it published. It doesn't work that way. You have to write good stuff first."

My student nods seriously. I remember he called me at home one evening about an assignment—"Hi, this is Jason." For a moment I couldn't place him; I needed a surname, so in a light tone I asked, "And which Jason might that be?" "The good Jason," he said. This response, as bizarre as his haircut, gives me a shadowy feeling—presumably I have always experienced "the good Jason"? What is the other Jason like? I'm not sure I want to know.

Now, back in my classroom, he says shyly, "I'm writing this book. It's about this kind of hero-type guy, they killed his girlfriend, he's gonna get revenge. He was Army Intelligence, and now he's a bounty hunter. He knows weapons and explosives, he knows how to track people, he can do everything. But I don't want him to be just, you know, a stereotype."

I knew it, I knew it, I knew he was writing a novel! That glimmer deep in his eyes was pure writerly yearning. But I do not inflict any effusions upon him. I try to be as casual and low-key as he is trying to be. "The last book I did with a hero-type guy in it," I say, "I made him short, fat and bald."

"Yeah!" He sits straight up, his face alight with childlike enthusiasm above his metal-studded black-leather jacket collar. "That's what I mean, I need to do something unexpected. Surprise people. I mean, like real life, like me. The way I dress, people don't expect me to be nice."

I nearly laugh out loud, mostly at myself. It is so simple now that he has given me the key. "Jason," I say, "I have hopes for you." He might just do it. He might really be a writer.

"Why?" he asks anxiously, as if my opinion can make it happen.

"You're a twofold person," I say. And maybe that's what a writer has to be. A layered person. The private, hidden person who writes. And the public person who sells what the other has written.

He's a rebel as well. A rebel against appearances and conventional expectations. One who defies What People Think. One who ascribes to secrets and complexities. One who tries to surprise. And maybe a writer needs to be those things, too.

He smiles; we talk awhile longer. I silently and gratefully note that he does not ask me to read his novel manuscript. He has the right instincts: He will do this on his own. I tell him to let me know when he is ready, and I will help him plug into the publishing network. He thanks me, hops off the desk and swaggers out, turning at the door. "Thankyouvermuch." He bows over an imaginary microphone, going into his Elvis routine. In addition to all the rest of it, he's a clown.

A clown obsessed with weapons and combat.

After he is gone, my warm and happy sense of sureness about him deserts me, and doubts shadow me again. Who or what is he? He is built in layers like an onion, and I hope he is not bitter at the core.

Or if he is, I hope writing can help him.

I hope he really is a writer. He is a layered person, and writing is a layered process, draft upon draft upon text upon subtext upon symbol upon subconscious self-expression; it is fitting that writing might be his calling. I hope so. I hope he is writer, because someday I want to read his book. I hope he is a writer, because I want to know what's at the core of this particular onion. I hope he is a writer, because I hope writing will save him from the other Jason.

>> 17

TWO TRUTHS AND A METAPHOR

BY ROGER MARTIN

I JUST FINISHED READING A GOOD BOOK. I MEAN A *GOOD* BOOK. Dreadfully good. Excruciatingly good. A book with a story as large as the galaxy and characters that won't stop living in my mind. A book about love and struggle, pain and hope.

And while the book thrilled me as a reader, it also broke my heart. You see, this is a book I could not write.

Call it inferiority, if you have to label it, slamming into your own limitations like running smack into a glass door you didn't realize was closed. Anyone who writes knows the feeling.

Writers aren't the only ones who suffer the slings and arrows of their own inadequacies. Writers suffer more than most, though, because the very act of writing takes great ego.

The idea that we writers have something to say, something worth saying, something only we individually can say, is insane arrogance. Nevertheless, it's an insanity we must have to keep hammering year after year.

Then one day we discover someone is out there writing words more powerful than anything we can conjure up. Someone is doing what we do, and doing it better. We lose our energy and sink into depression because the realization hurts. The more we strive to write well, the more we hurt.

Most of us, being at least marginally rational, respond the only way possible. We throw in the keyboard and swear we'll never write another line. The promise lasts for a week or three months or a year. Then one day we begin writing again. We've girded up the rags of our self-esteem and returned to the fray.

Every writer I know has quit at least once, some a dozen times. What sends us back?

Hope drives some. Above the frustration, it gleams like a white angel. The chance for a bestseller, for a prize, or for that happy day when the letter that comes isn't a rejection slip.

Habit masters some. They write because writing gives rhythm to their lives. Writing is how they make sense out of life. They don't write as a substitute for living, they write as a response to living.

Truth motivates some. They pursue it in all its forms, stalking it with their notebooks. Like Hemingway, they're hunting that "one true sentence," and when they capture it, they start the chase for the next one.

Some need to tell a story, to tell it true and straight, and the telling is the thing.

Whatever our motivation, the work isn't easy and the odds for success are poor. Writers inhabit a narrow strip between the rising tide of mass entertainment and the shrinking literacy of the general population.

For all of us self-stranded exiles, I offer two truths and a metaphor. The first truth is this:

Writers write. Whatever the circumstances. Whatever the odds.

They write when they feel good. They write when they don't. They write when they're elated, and when they're depressed. They write when the muse strikes them, and when it doesn't, they bolt their backsides to a chair and write anyway. Good words or bad, writers define themselves by writing.

That's what makes a writer. Not prose quality or keen insight or deft plotting. There's not some magical standard that determines when we're "good enough," and we suddenly become writers. We're writers when we write.

Here's the other truth:

Writers read continuously. They gorge themselves on words like starvelings at a banquet, and never have their fill. They read widely, stuffing their heads with words, because they believe nothing read is ever wasted.

Reading fills the well of imagination. It makes us rich in experience by infusing us with the lives and experiences of others. Other than writing itself, reading is the single greatest teacher of writing. We're all imitators, and there's no shame in that. The words and ideas of

60

others are the lumber and brick we use to build words and ideas of our own.

And when we read that impossibly good book, that's when it's the best. When a book breaks our heart, it's stretching us. That's when we see what words can do and how much room we have to grow.

Growth is neither easy nor painless, but it is necessary. That's why writers keep reading.

Now for the metaphor.

Writers are the torchbearers of civilization. They throw light on the bewildering occurrences we call life. Flaws and all, what the light reveals is our common humanity. Writers explain us to ourselves, and try to wrest order from what seems like chaos.

Some of us are searchlights, able to cast a beam into the far reaches of the human soul. Some of us are candles, barely able to sustain a glow against the darkness. Except within limits, we don't get to choose the size of our light. Few of us will stand with Shakespeare, Hemingway, or Tolstoy. We can only stoke the spark we have, making the most of whatever talent the muse allots us.

That's our duty as writers. Each of us has a unique place in the world. We're set in a corner only we can illuminate, to whatever degree our skills allow. I can't write the great book; I just read it. I can write only what I know, feel, and understand. Nevertheless, the words I write are important because light is additive. Another's light doesn't diminish my own. Our lights together make us stronger.

So I keep working, guided by two truths and a metaphor.

⪼ 18

BOOKS ON TOP

BY E. ANNIE PROULX

EVERY OTHER WEEK SOMEONE SAYS THAT BOOKS ARE DEAD OR DYING, that just around the corner is the black hour when they will be curiosities like stereopticon slides or milk stools—probably the same thing they said when radio was invented, when television flickered its way into our living rooms.

To some the phrase means sluggish book sales in the recent and lingering recession; to others it means that the old gray novel ain't what it used to be. Not a few associate the obliteration of distinguished literary houses and imprints in the age of the corporate takeover as synonymous with the inevitable disappearance of books. The hearse followers mournfully announce that no one reads these days, can't read, won't read. It doesn't strike them as peculiar that there is a fierce scramble among corporate interests to buy the publishing houses that put out these dying books.

It's possible that the premature obituaries merely cover our confusion about the clouded direction of change in the culture. As the big publishers try for bestsellers at the expense of serious books, it is increasingly the small publishers and university presses that are finding and publishing the books of interesting new writers.

Books once rather scornfully considered grist for the small publisher's mill are catching the reading public's interest. Among the new books published last year were important works of fiction from Arab-Americans, African-Americans, Chinese-Americans, Mexican-Americans, Caribbean-Americans, Native Americans, and others. The so-called gay and lesbian novel is beginning to escape the genre closet and stand on bookstore shelves alongside traditional works.

Book groups, an old idea, are everywhere. Books are moving into motel and hotel rooms, where a year ago one could find only a single title in a black binding. Now thousands of copies of Joel Conarroe's *Six American Poets* engage travelers in lonely rooms across the continent. There are guidebooks to used bookshops, and a few imaginative independent booksellers thrive in the shadow of ever-increasing numbers of superstores.

Those who say the book is moribund often cite the computer as the asp on the mat. But the electronic highway is for bulletin boards on esoteric subjects, reference works, lists and news—timely utilitarian information, efficiently pulled through the wires. Nobody is going to sit down and read a novel on a twitchy little screen. Ever.

In a curious way, the computer emphasizes the unique virtues of the book:

The book is small, lightweight and durable, and can be stuffed in a coat pocket, read in the waiting room, on the plane. What are planes but flying reading rooms?

Books give esthetic and tactile pleasure, from the dust jacket art to the binding, paper, typography and text design, from the moment of purchase until the last page is turned.

Books speak even when they stand unopened on the shelf. If you would know a man or woman, look at their books, not their software.

>> 19

THE POWER OF A BOOK

BY MARY WARREN

I ALMOST MADE THE BIGGEST MISTAKE OF MY LIFE AND ABANDONED the juvenile field . . . until a book arrived in the mail that carried me back to my childhood.

A prodigious reader, I discovered that books like *Heidi* and *The Secret Garden* and *Emily of New Moon* could carry me far away to different lands and different centuries.

My favorite books were Laura Ingalls Wilder's Little House series. Each year a new one appeared under the Christmas tree with my name on the gift tag. There came an autumn, however, when it looked as if no further Wilder book would be there. *The Little Town on the Prairie* seemed to finish off the story of Laura and Mary's childhood years. Surely Laura would marry Almanzo Wilder because that was the author's name, wasn't it?

One stormy November day, I sat down at my desk to write to my favorite author, telling her how much I enjoyed each book, and how I wished she could write one more to end the series with Almanzo's courtship. I already knew that I wanted to be a writer when I grew up, but I was far too shy to admit that to Mrs. Wilder.

Instead, I asked her how to make sourdough. Back came a letter from the Wilder farm in Missouri, written in Laura's handwriting on lined stationery. In addition to telling me exactly how to make sourdough, she assured me that the book I'd requested, *These Happy Golden Years,* was going to be on the bookstore shelves in time for Christmas.

Although Laura Wilder never lived to see my work in print, she has always remained my role model. When I teach or lead workshops, I use her carefully detailed descriptions of prairies, blizzards, and warm family life as examples. I have read her books countless times, as I struggle over my own depictions of characters and scenes.

When Laura needed a long sentence, she crafted one. When a short one worked best, that is what she used. At least one of her sentences in *The Long Winter* is 42 words long. Another is only three: "Pa's nose purpled." Those were the only words necessary to show how cold it was.

One day, a 12-year-old boy growing up on a midwestern farm wrote to me, telling me why he liked my books. He wrote about his pets, the farm animals, and his hobbies. At last he got around to what he *really* wanted to say. "P.S. I want to be a writter." (The spelling is his.)

That farm lad reminds me of the little girl growing up in Brooklyn many years ago. But at least he set *his* shyness aside long enough to confide: "I want to be a writter." I am glad he liked my books. I hope his dream of being a published author has come true.

What about the book that arrived in the mail the other day and stirred me to take another look at the direction I wish to take? *Dear Laura* (compiled by HarperCollins editor, Alix Reid) is a charming collection of over 100 letters written to Laura Ingalls Wilder from the 1930's into the early 1950's. A copy of my letter to Laura Wilder is on page 44, and her return letter to me, with directions on how to make sourdough, is on the very next page!

I had forgotten about the warm way youngsters respond to books that touch them until I sat down and laughed and wept over every page of *Dear Laura*. It reminded me of the meaning books can bring to children's lives, how a special book may act as a rudder to steer them, fostering hope and understanding.

Not long ago, I went to my files and leafed through the letters and the crayoned illustrations of scenes from my books that children had sent to *me*. Many of them begged me to write more books.

Yes, I've changed my mind. I want to begin writing for a young audience once again.

How To Write—
Techniques

➢➢ GENERAL FICTION

➤➤ 20

PITCH-PERFECT DIALOGUE

BY SHELBY HEARON

I'M AN INVETERATE EAVESDROPPER. NOTHING IS MORE FUN THAN GO-ing out for an early-morning muffin or a late-night plate of fried eggs and listening to the couple or the family in the booth behind you. A few lines of conversation, scraps of talk, and you know at once what the relationship between the people is, what the problem is, where they're coming from. All without even turning your head.

Achieving the same instant sense of "knowing all about" fictional people is more difficult. For one thing, you don't have the tone of voice, which is so revealing. In real life, the transaction—"I think I'll have the pancakes" and "I'm looking at the waffles"—can be heard with several different undertones, inflections, nuances. But on the page it's hard to convey what the listener knows is the subtext. Yet, the secret of pitch-perfect dialogue begins there: with trying to figure out what you know and how you know it when you're listening in on other lives.

Private eyes and spies provide unbeatable "eavesdropping" opportunities on the printed page. Who could confuse a character from P. D. James saying, "That was preternaturally slow," with one from Elmore Leonard asking, "Wha' took you so long?"

But in addition to these obvious clues in vocabulary and syntax, I always start on a new character by asking myself what I want to tell the reader first about the person. How to tell something is not nearly as difficult as deciding what is the crucial trait to reveal. But, say you decide to show right at the start how your character (let's take a father-type of guy) feels about his body and how he feels about authority: If you're dealing with men, you know they spend a lot of time wishing their bodies were different, and a lot of emotion on their relation to the guy in charge.

So you decide—two birds with one stone—to have your father-type in the hospital about to have his gallbladder out. He's prepped, waiting on that tight, white-sheeted bed, and in comes John Archer, abdominal surgeon.

Your man says:

"Hey, Arch, watch out when you're messing around down there below the belt you don't remove anything I may need. Ha ha."

Or he says:

"Jeez, Dr. Archer, I'm scared blue. I can't help it, look at me, I'm cold as a fish. My old man, he flat out died from this same trouble. Younger than me."

Or he says:

"Morning, John. I guess I'm as ready as I'll ever be. Maybe taking some of my gall out will make me easier to live with. I know a few who'd agree with that."

Or he says:

"Well, Doc, don't take this as lack of confidence, but my law partners, malpractice litigators par excellence, will be looking over your shoulder when you pick up that knife."

Let's take another example. Say you want to show that the way a young woman feels about her man goes right back to how she feels about her mom. So maybe you start with her having lunch with him in a public place.

She says:

"The pastrami was O.K., I don't care all that much, the corned beef probably isn't any better, but just once I'd like to order for myself. Just once I'd like to open my mouth and say exactly what I want."

Or she says:

"You're sure? Gosh, you're always paying for everything. Lunch, the trip to Cancun, that totally gorgeous pink sweater. Really, I mean it, you make me feel really special."

Or she says:

"Here, I'll read it for you. I think you left your glasses on the dashboard. You like that soup, remember? The sort of borsch. It agrees with you, you said last time."

From here, it's just a matter of a phone call to Mom, in which we overhear a few snippets of conversation, to make your point that history, at least in our love life, always repeats.

An aid to writing convincing dialogue, and one you'll unconsciously pick up when you're listening in, is to give your character her or his own special metaphors. I often do this, as an exercise, just to get new voices clearly in my head: Have each character say, "It's hot as ———," "I'm mad as ———," "It's time to ———," "No point in ———." And I always have my ear out for phrases I have never heard before. One I picked up when I moved to Vermont (writers love to move around to new places for this reason!) and I'm sure to put to use soon is: "He may not be the sharpest knife in the drawer, but ———." And almost anything can follow—"he's a true friend," "steady as night and day," "somebody you can trust," etc. I jot down every sentence like that I overhear.

Another choice the writer can make in deciding how to reveal character through dialogue is selecting who gets to say what lines. My own preference is to "cast against type," to use a film term. For example, listen to a couple fighting: One of them wants to get married, the other doesn't. One of them has been hurt to the quick by the cavalier attitude of the other. Readers will be more apt to hear the fight and really feel they have come to know these two people, if you do the unexpected. *He* wants to get married; *she* wants to play around. He's been wounded by her; she has grown tired of all the talk about commitment.

"I want marriage. I want the whole baggage. The dirty socks and pink toothbrush and recycle bins."

"Place an ad."

"Do you know how comments like that hurt? Do you have a clue how words can bruise?"

Read them with *she said* and then *he said,* then reverse it and read *he said* and *she said,* and you hear the impasse between them in a new way.

Or try a parent and child.

"I never know where you are or when you're coming home."

"Lighten up. What are my options in this burg, anyways?"

Spoken by a parent to a child, the reader doesn't really hear the words, because expected scenarios get in the way. But spoken by a twelve-year-old boy to his forty-five-year-old mother, the two lines seem fresh, and a new situation is suggested. The reader is drawn into the story.

A lot of times, real life suggests these switches on the expected. I can recall when I was a young mother, driving to the trailhead in the Rockies to pick up my backpacking son, gone sometimes for days at a time. Then, three years ago, I went back to Aspen after a long absence, to see if I could do the day hikes I'd done years before. (To prove that if I wasn't the sharpest knife in the drawer, at least I wasn't rusty.) And there my son was, grown, driving me to the trailhead, setting a time when I had to return, checking to be sure I had a windbreaker in case of a summer storm, and proper gear. And I'm sure our conversation mirrored the ones we'd had in the past, with the roles reversed.

Go back to the thrillers I mentioned earlier. What if Elmore Leonard's guy on the lam in Florida says, "That was preternaturally slow," and P. D. James's man in London asks, "Wha' took you so long?" There would be a sense of having met someone unexpected and the surprise would engage the reader.

In my current novel, *Footprints,* I have a couple whose daughter died in a car wreck, and her heart is transplanted into a southern preacher's chest. The father (a brain scientist) is devastated; he clings to the belief his daughter is still alive, and becomes very mystical about the transplant. His wife, in turn, becomes quite scientific in her handling of loss, exploring in a cool, investigative manner the theories of what life is, what the mind or self really is, considering the transplant almost akin to Frankenstein's borrowed life.

But why not imagine you are listening to them talk over coffee in the booth behind you. What does she say to him? What does he say to her? What does the reader overhear?

>> 21

STRATEGIES FOR REVISING SHORT STORIES

BY GEOFFREY BECKER

REVISION IS GOOD. ON THE OTHER HAND, YOU CAN ALWAYS TRY TO write it right the first time." This provocative statement from a professor I had in graduate school seemed obvious. We all knew that the initial writing of a story was only about twenty percent of the ultimate effort involved. After that came the hours of cutting and pasting, crossing out paragraphs, scribbling in the margins.

But those words kept me thinking for years. While I still believe he oversimplified things, I've also come to understand the truth of what he said. Do things "right"—or close to "right"—the first time and revision is easy and a pleasure. Write a story that has problems at some basic level, and no amount of cosmetic surgery is likely to save it.

Paradoxically, in order to reach the level where one does things "right" the first time, it's usually necessary to do things "wrong" quite a lot. Experienced (or unusually gifted) writers are already at a place where they don't make beginner's mistakes.

In my own teaching experience, I've been amazed at different people's notions of what constitutes a revision. I've had students tell me they've done seven drafts of a piece, only to discover that each rewriting involved making a few changes to a hard copy, entering those on the computer, then printing the story out again. Version seven isn't noticeably different from version one. Perhaps the problem is with the word "draft," since in the computer age, the old meaning—a new, completely retyped set of pages that involved some human being fingering each keystroke—is completely dead. We need to be careful about confusing the two: One involves interaction with a manuscript, the other pressing a button. Truman Capote joked about Jack Kerouac, "That's not writing, that's typing." But it's not a joke that some people actually confuse rewriting with printing out a new copy.

To revise a first-draft short story, it's important, first, to recognize how close you are to having achieved what you want. If you are very close, great; you can set about the business of fine-tuning and editing. But if you don't know what you've got, it may be a good idea to view the piece as an experiment. Consider beginning again from scratch, using the same materials, but this time with the benefit of experience that comes from having told the story once before. Perhaps you chose the wrong point of view. Perhaps you chose the wrong scenes to dramatize. This is the most drastic kind of rewriting, but it can also be the most rewarding. Too many beginning writers approach their fiction as finished once an initial draft exists. It has a beginning, an ending, a middle—it must be a story. They are unwilling—understandably, considering the work that was involved in the writing—to start over. Instead, they change a little dialogue here, remove an adverb there. The story changes, but doesn't improve.

If only we knew the rules, we wouldn't make mistakes! We *would* write it right the first time. But there are no rules. The best writers are constantly violating, with gleeful impunity, what they think *might* be the rules. They play around with the point of view, shift tenses all over the place, and they *still get published.*

The only real rule is this: Anything that works is O.K. It's not that the goalposts keep getting moved; they aren't even there. A good story succeeds on its own terms.

All of which can be, well, frustrating. The following suggestions may help you avoid some common writing traps, and also guide you toward ways of looking at your finished story and seeing it in a new light. Most new writers working on short stories have difficulty with revision. We'd rather be potters: Throw a pot, glaze and fire it, sell it. But it's a rare first-draft short story that is strong enough to be sent out into the world without further attention.

Try to avoid writing a story that:

• *Begins in a static place with a character staring at something (often a photograph), then remembering something that took place in a different time and place.* This is the classic "frame" device, but unless something is going to happen in the frame itself, why not look in on the story at a more compelling moment?

• *Is all dialogue.* This can certainly be done, and has been. But in stories by beginners, it's often a sign that the author hasn't done the extra work necessary to imagine an interior life for the characters and is simply observing them. Another story to avoid is the one that takes place entirely over the phone. This is not particularly dramatic, since phone conversations usually recount things that happened elsewhere. Essentially, what you'd be giving the reader is a person alone in a room holding a receiver. Yes, there are two characters, but they are miles apart. (Point-of-view shifts can seem really odd in these stories.)

• *Has a narrator so vile and unpleasant that there is no reason for readers to want to spend time in his or her company.* We read because we want to learn about other people, even ugly ones. If you're going to give readers a mass-murderer-serial-rapist (every college-level creative writing instructor gets two or three of these stories a semester), you'd better have really imagined an interior life for him and not have shown him simply as the sum of his actions.

• *Hangs together only by virtue of some huge metaphor.* A married couple has a garden they enjoy working in. As the years go by, it goes to weed. One night, they have a terrible fight. It looks as if they may divorce. In the morning, the two of them go out and start putting the garden back in shape. This ends up being more about the garden than about the people (not to mention that it's terribly obvious and cliché).

• *Gains all its momentum through gradually revealing to the reader information that the main character had access to all along.* Play fair: If you're writing a third-person story from the point of view of Tom, who is home from college and acting distant and strange and can't relate to anyone, but you don't let us know until page fifteen that it's because he figured out two weeks ago that he's gay, you've cheated.

• *Simply follows the decline of a character with a serious illness and ends with his or her death.* The most emotional thing that can happen to us in real life can be predictable and unengaging on the page.

You've got a completed draft, with a title. It's got the shape of a story, but you know it's not finished. How do you take it further?

Try asking these questions:

Where does the story really start? Go back and look at your opening. Have you done significant "pre-writing"? I've learned that the first drafts of my own stories rarely begin until somewhere around the middle of page two. What seemed like a beginning (and was, in the sense that it got me going) is not always the place that the story kicks into gear. You may be able to cut more than you thought possible. Look for those places. Remember, cutting is *good*. To paraphrase Jay Leno in those old Doritos ads: "Cut all you want—you can always write more."

Are there too many characters? Can you justify them? Are there people given stage time who have no bearing on the story at all?

Have you included more than is necessary? While you create, you're figuring out for yourself what's going on as well as explaining it to the reader, which is why things don't just get neatly onto the page in perfect order. Paring down to the essential comes later, and, if you were writing well to begin with, such tightening can be a real pleasure. Which scenes are doing nothing (except perhaps showing off how good you are with language)?

Is your dialogue doing something? Does it develop character? Move the plot? Ideally, it should do both. Dialogue gives fiction transparency and breaks things up rhythmically, too. Watch out for dialogue that exists solely to give the reader information, or is merely chitchat. Also, look out for "Ping-Pong" dialogue, with the speakers constantly referring to each other by name. Try to avoid unnecessary "tagging" of dialogue with adverbs, or elaborate ways of getting around the word "said."

Do you know what the story is about? Now that the story exists, you can read it with a critical eye. Writing is a process of discovery, and your story is certain to have grown in ways you hadn't planned. Where can it be developed to explore further what you've so far only touched on? Have you shown the crucial moments of decision and discovery? The crisis action? Is what you've written original, or have you fallen into some cliché? Don't have your characters and situations develop in a way you think they *ought* to; let them surprise you. Life is, after all, surprising.

Have you paid attention to the most simple details? Sometimes, in their attempts to achieve loftier, more literary goals, writers overlook the mundane, everyday things that help make fiction believable. Have you committed technical errors? Sent someone to a Vikings game in May? Had them put a pot of water on to boil, then go off to pick up the kids after school? A lot of fiction writing is about keeping track of the little things, moving people across rooms, etc. What time is it? What's the weather like?

Have you really cut all you can? You've worked and worked and you still hate what you've done. Circle *everything* that strikes you as boring or nonessential. Cut until you can cut no more. See what's left. For instance, scenes that do nothing more than transport a character from one place to another can often be dispensed with. Does your character spend pages three and four on a bus?

When you think there's nothing else to be done, put the story away. Don't send it out. It will change (well, you will, anyway) over time. Wait two weeks. Then reread it, and see what you did.

Finally, cultivate a couple of people in your life to show your work to. It's good to have someone who loves and accepts everything you write as brilliant, but in addition, see if you can find someone a little tougher, whose opinion you trust, and bounce your story off that person, too. In the end, the best thing you can do is develop two sides of yourself: one that's experimental, risk-taking and imaginative, another that is tough, no-nonsense and ruthless. Trust them both, but not at the same time.

>> 22

THE MAKING OF A NOVELIST

BY BARBARA TAYLOR BRADFORD

I AM GLAD TO KNOW THAT THERE ARE PEOPLE OUT THERE WHO WANT to torture themselves as I do every day of the year trying to write fiction. But, before I tell you how I do it, I must share with you a little anecdote about what happened to me a couple of summers ago when I went on an eight-week, fifty-odd-city tour. In St. Louis, a very nice elderly gentleman came to a book signing with two copies of *Everything to Gain*. He told me the names of the ladies that he wanted me to inscribe them to, which I did. As I was writing, he said, "I love your books."

I thought, "Oh, a male reader." So, I looked up and said, "I am glad you like the books I write. What other books of mine have you read?"

"I haven't read any," he said. "I never read your books, but you do write marvelous books, and I love you for it."

I looked at him strangely.

"You see," he went on, "when my mother-in-law comes to visit every year, I buy your new book, and I give it to her. She doesn't speak until she leaves, when she says goodbye."

* * *

When I was seven, I started to write. By the time I was twelve, I sold my first short story. I wanted to be a journalist because I was smart enough by the age of fifteen or sixteen to know that at that age you really don't write novels that you can sell. Anyway, I worked on the *Yorkshire Evening Post*. I was a reporter for two years, became "Women's Page" Editor at eighteen, and moved to Fleet Street when I was twenty. I was on a number of different newspapers and magazines. Then, in 1963, I married Robert Bradford and came to live in the States. He is the person who makes all the miniseries of my books.

Anyway, I worked here as a journalist for a number of years, but I'd never, ever lost that desire to write fiction.

Between about 1968 and 1975, I started four novels that I never finished. As I look back on those manuscripts, which I kept and didn't throw away, I realize that with all those attempts, I was teaching myself how to construct a novel and write dialogue. I think the reason I never finished them was that I lost my nerve. So, my first tip to you is: **Don't lose your nerve. Keep going.** There was nothing really wrong with any of those unfinished novels; I just panicked. I would put one away, and a few months later, because I had that tremendous urge to write fiction, I would start another.

In late 1975, I had the idea for *A Woman of Substance.* I had just read an interview with the British novelist Graham Greene, in which he said that character was plot; in other words, what makes a person tick, his qualities and flaws, is what is going to tell the story. From that moment on, I knew how to write fiction, and my protagonist Emma Harte came rushing into my mind. I also understood that I should write about what I knew, so, of course, I set the story in England because I am English, and in Yorkshire because I come from there. I created the story of a woman who started with nothing and achieved greatness through her own ability, because I have always been attracted to and fascinated by strong women who were accomplished and either acquired power politically or made a great deal of money or had big careers, whether it was a woman like Madame Curie or Elizabeth I, one of the great queens and politicians in history.

With all these things running through my mind, I sat down and wrote an outline. That is my next tip: **Start with an outline.** I still do an outline for each of my novels, though I do it slightly differently from the way I used to. I also break my books up into parts, because it really helps shape a story: What you're doing is organizing a lot of material and people. Each part becomes a number of chapters, and I make a note of how much of the story I have to tell in that chapter; I've got it down now to a fine art. A lot of writers go off on a wrong tangent because they have not organized themselves, the characters, the story, or the material. In writing *A Woman of Substance,* I created six parts and broke each part into so many chapters, and then said, "All right. In Chapter 1, I must do this. In Chapter 2, I have to tell this part of the story." It became a natural progression. So, in a way, it's organization.

You must have what I call the six "D's": "D" for *desire,* the desire to sit down in the first place to do it; "D" for *discipline;* "D" for *drive, dedication,* and *determination.* If you don't have all those qualities or traits when you start to write a novel, you are never going to finish it, because it is hard. It's the hardest work I have ever done, far harder than being a journalist. You have to want to write that novel more than you want to do anything else. The last "D" is for *distraction,* which means that you have to want to write that novel more than you want to go to the movies, the theater, out to dinner, or have some free time. For me, it is a long process. I keep very long hours. You need a lot of physical stamina to be able to keep those hours, but the rewards are wonderful: When you finish a novel, you have the great satisfaction of having accomplished something that you hope is going to be a best-seller.

It's the hardest thing for me to tell you how to write a novel. I told you about not losing your nerve and about creating an outline, structuring the book and breaking it down into parts. You must also have the characters pretty clear in your head; they are going to change, because people change when they are under stress or have problems to cope with. So, if a character is static, then the book is going to be static.

I begin on page one. A lot of writers don't; they get ideas and will write a chapter and put it aside. I can't do it that way. I start with page one, and I finish Chapter 1 before I move on to Chapter 2. Eventually, I do get ideas that can work somewhere else in the book. I make a notation and put it in a folder. But when I work on Chapter 1, I do it over and over again until it is right. I work on a typewriter. Why don't I use a computer? Because typing is easier for me. The easiest way for me to write is in longhand; then I type that up, and keep typing. I write all over it, and retype it. In that process, I put things in, take things out; I refine, I cut, I edit. I add again. At the end, when I'm satisfied, I send a hundred pages to a typist, who puts it on disk.

As an aside, my editor in London told me recently that she knows when a book has been written on a word processor or when it's been written in what she calls the "old-fashioned" way. "When a person writes a novel by hand, then types it up, cuts it, edits it, and revises it," she said, "the book is very, very rich. It's like walking through a landscape, a cityscape or wherever. You smell the sea. You see the sky. You hear the birds. You get all those details of atmosphere and all the things that should be in a novel, as well as the characterizations. People who use word processors drive through that landscape and so much is missed." I am not knocking word processors, but, for me, my way is simpler. Perhaps there are writers who don't miss any details. That brings me to another point—details.

What is a novel? To me, it is a monumental lie that has to have the absolute ring of truth if it is going to succeed. Although a lot of readers have written to say they *were* Emma Harte, there never was an Emma Harte—except in my head. Her whole life story was an invention. I cut her from whole cloth; I created a woman's life. That's what I do. I am a storyteller, and I created a marvelous character, her life, all the family members, and people involved with her. So, it was a lie, but in actuality, what gave the book that ring of truth was the research and the details. I went to the Imperial War Museum in London, and I researched the First World War. In a way, I was a reporter again. I talked to older people in Yorkshire, and I asked them what it was like working in the mills. I talked to my uncle who had been in the Second World War, and to older members of the family who had been in the First World War. I acquired all of those details either by firsthand information or by doing research. I think that's what gives a lot of my books that fundamental ring of truth, because while they are all invented, they do have that sense of reality.

Several years ago, I wrote a novel called *Remember,* which began in Tiananmen Square when the students were demonstrating in 1989. How could I reconstruct that? I really knew nobody I could talk to. So, I called a reporter in California who had been in Tiananmen Square. He was happy to tell me what I needed to know. What was it like? Why were the satellite links cut off? Why did this happen? Why did that? He gave me a lot of information, and I went out and bought books on that particular incident in Chinese history. The picture books were the best, because they gave me visuals that helped me write that part of the book. Keep in mind that it's the research and getting to the truth about something that counts.

When I sit down to write, I am really juggling a lot of balls in the air. First and foremost, I am telling a story, but that's not enough. You have to create a mood and atmosphere; you must know that the story takes place in Manhattan on June 14, 1996, or Leeds in 1904; it must have a sense of time and place, mood and atmosphere. You can do that with weather, with furnishings and with people's attitudes. You're structuring the story; you're telling the story. You're doing mood, atmosphere, a sense of time and place.

Then there's dialogue. Dialogue isn't just people talking. I write dialogue over and over again, because it has to delineate character, to move the plot along, tell more about the person. It also has to sound real, authentic. If you recorded people having a conversation and listened to it on a tape recorder, you'd hear a lot of ums and ahs and digressions and pauses, because that's how people talk. But when you write dialogue in a novel, it must be very, very precise.

In addition, you have characterization. What is the protagonist of the book like? Is she or he a good person? A bad person? What are the other characters like? What are their favorite things? What is their history? What baggage have they brought to the story at the point in time when you are telling it? I often start with a blank postcard. I put the name of the main character, his or her age, and all of the details, as if I were a psychiatrist. I even create the birthdate, the sign of the zodiac, the hair color, where he or she was born, whether he or she has brothers or sisters, and what he or she likes or dislikes. I think the character lives because I've invented a person that's real to me. As I go along, I'm always making notations about my characters, how they change, and how they respond to incidents and to things that happen in their life that I have created. As a novelist, what you're really doing is playing God, moving your characters around and making them do what *you* want them to do.

You also have to entertain. If you write popular fiction, as I do— commercial fiction, primarily—it's your responsibility to be entertaining, to involve the readers in a world that doesn't exist except in the writer's imagination, but is so engaging, so compelling that they are pulled into it. That, to me, is real entertainment.

I try to show life as I see it through my angle of vision and, perhaps, pass my own opinions along about many things. I try to touch and move my readers, because I think people empathize then.

A publisher in England once said to me, "You know, you make people cry, and people love to cry."

I said, "I am not quite sure what you mean by that."

"Well, what I mean is you must touch people," he said.

I do think people want to be touched and moved and to identify and understand that the problems they have and things they have to face in their lives are also faced by others. That's what I try to do in all of my novels.

>> 23

WHOSE VIEWPOINT?

BY GAIL RADLEY

ONE OF THE FIRST DECISIONS YOU'LL HAVE TO MAKE WHEN WRITING a story may seem like the simplest: in whose viewpoint to tell it. Many writers grab instinctively at "I" or "he" or "she" without giving the matter much thought. There is a variety of viewpoints from which to choose. You may even, with care, use more than one viewpoint. Each choice casts the story in a different light, offering distinct advantages and disadvantages. While your instinctive choice may be the best one, it should be backed by knowledge.

The once-popular omniscient viewpoint gives all-seeing writers the chance to drop at will into the minds and hearts of any character. The advantage of omniscience is that readers can see the big picture, with its web of conflicting emotions and goals. But, like most big pictures, it has to be seen from a distance, and readers may not have focused anywhere long enough to care. When reader empathy is missing, the story goes out the window.

Some viewpoints are rarely used—second person, for example, which seems quirky and may annoy the reader:

You phone your mother. She starts nagging again, and suddenly you don't care if you ever see her again. You slam down the receiver.

"Wait a minute," the reader protests. "I *love* my mother. We get along fine." And then, if the reader continues reading, there may be a battle of assertions on your part and protests on the reader's for the rest of the story.

The objective viewpoints—first and third—in which the viewpoint character acts as observer and reporter, are used more often. With the objective approach, the only feelings and thoughts revealed are the narrator's. A first-person objective narrator might say:

86

I sat nearby as George phoned his mother.

"How are you?" he asked. There was a stretch of silence in which George grimaced. He slammed down the receiver. "Nagging as usual," he told me. "I don't care if I ever see her again."

Here George reveals his feelings and thoughts to the narrator, who relays them to the reader. Though readers are a step removed from the hero, they get some insights into George's make-up from the narrator's "report."

The first-person objective narrator—who is observing the hero—may not only speculate about George's feelings, but offer his own opinions:

George's stomach is probably churning uncomfortably, I thought. I couldn't count the times I'd seen him reach for the antacids after a conversation with his mother. I'd often thought George took her too seriously. What he considered nagging, I'd have taken as expressions of concern. I wished I'd had a mother who'd taken as much interest . . .

Now the narrator is in danger of wresting the story away from George; suddenly readers are more concerned about the sort of mother the poor narrator had! Within limitations, the objective first-person can give a fairly intimate view of the hero. You may have a problem, however, if George decides to storm off, leaving the narrator alone in an empty room to speculate.

This problem can be resolved by using the third-person objective viewpoint. As with the first-person objective, the style is that of observer/reporter:

George phoned his mother. "How are you?" he inquired.

"I wish you'd call earlier," she complained. "I've been sitting here all morning wondering what you're doing. I've told you time and again . . ."

George listened a moment, his face contorting. Then he clapped down the receiver. "Nagging as usual," he mumbled to Rover.

Not knowing George's innermost thoughts and feelings may help build suspense; it's hard to know what he'll do next. On the other hand, knowing George only through observation may hold the reader at a distance.

For this reason, most writers settle on a *subjective* point of view, either first or third. In first-person subjective, the hero tells his own story. Readers know exactly what he thinks and feels moment by moment. It's a sure way for the writer to build reader identification and give the story authenticity. Of course, there are drawbacks. Readers may tire of the incessant "I," and the story may be overly melodramatic, particularly when the hero or the situation is very emotional. It is hard to present a picture of the protagonist without the clichéd device of having him gaze into a mirror, a puddle, or a store window! Also, when the writer uses a first-person narrator, shifting to another viewpoint can be very awkward.

All of these problems can be resolved with the third-person subjective viewpoint. Here, the writer "becomes" the viewpoint character, relating his thoughts and feelings, but no one else's. The degree of limitation the writer accepts, however, is flexible. The character may not be able to see himself, but the writer can choose to step back to allow description and commentary on the character. Additionally, when writing in third person, it is much easier to change viewpoints from one character to another.

But changing viewpoints must be done with care. Early versions of my juvenile novel, *Odd Man Out* (Macmillan 1995), were met with skepticism. The story is about eleven-year-old twins, Kit and Jordy, who befriend Oakley Duster, a mentally challenged man in their rural community. Eventually, they are called upon to make a public stand in support of this man, a decision each twin finds difficult, but for different reasons. The story belonged to both of them, and though it would have been simpler to tell it in *one* twin's viewpoint, I felt strongly that showing the perspectives of both twins would help reveal the complexity of their problem and allow me to develop their changing relationship more fully, without casting either twin as the bad guy. Just when readers might be annoyed with Kit for blowing up at Jordy, I'd take them into *her* mind to help them understand *her* struggles. In addition, telling the story from both male and female viewpoints is likely to attract more readers.

How could I keep the readers' empathy? I'd have to spend sufficient time in each twin's viewpoint for readers to get to know them both. Then, when I wanted to change viewpoint, I'd do it at chapter breaks, a point when readers are ready for change. (A shift of viewpoint within a chapter could be indicated by leaving an extra space between passages.) I mentioned the viewpoint character's name within the first two or three sentences to orient the reader. Thus, one chapter begins:

Awkwardly, Kit set the overstuffed laundry basket on the basement floor. She pulled the chain that lit the bulb dangling above the washing machine and glanced around the basement. Its gloom suited her.

A "Jordy" chapter begins:

Kit was quiet as they walked home from the bus stop Tuesday, Jordy noticed. He himself felt restless and discontented.

I also took care to divide the number of chapters equally between the twins, for the most part alternating, giving each character equal time for development.

Paul Zindel used a similar technique in *The Pigman,* in which classmates John and Lorraine alternately tell the story of their encounters with Mr. Pignati. Using the first-person for each, Zindel was able to develop truly distinctive voices. Chapter 1, with John as the viewpoint character, begins:

Now I don't like school which you might say is one of the factors that got us involved with this old guy we nicknamed the Pigman. Actually, I hate school, but then again most of the time I hate everything.

Chapter 2 shifts to Lorraine's viewpoint:

I should never have let John write the first chapter because he always has to twist things subliminally.

These two characters not only have different problems and personalities, but different vocabularies, as well. Notice, too, how Lorraine's mentioning John's name helps orient readers. In the first-person, shifts in viewpoints are rarely used. Zindel handles it here by giving the characters the task of writing their story jointly.

It is possible to shift viewpoints successfully, but proceed with caution! Avoid bouncing from character to character; change viewpoints only when necessary, and allow each viewpoint character uninterrupted time. Develop characters fully, so that readers perceive their individuality. Signal the shifts through chapter or line breaks, use of

89

the characters' names, and distinctive vocabularies and manners of speech.

When selecting the viewpoint for your stories, don't gloss over the choices. First, understand the differences; then trust you instincts. The result will be a richer, more complex and memorable story.

>> 24

CREATING VILLAINS YOU HATE TO LIKE

BY EILEEN GOUDGE

LADY MACBETH HAS A SPOT. SHYLOCK FEELS PERSECUTED. MRS. Danvers is obsessed. Hannibal Lecter is fastidious. Even Frankenstein is more misunderstood than monstrous. But these fictional villains all have one thing in common: They're memorable. Why? What *is* it about these characters that makes them stand out in a crowd of men in black hats? What makes their crimes so compelling?

It's simple, really. What makes a villain—or any character—unforgettable is dimension. Most writers know that for a hero or heroine to be interesting, he or she must be more than a one-note Pollyanna. A touch of angst, a shameful past, a dark side—all of these devices serve to contour and shade what might otherwise be the literary equivalent of cream cheese. But often, the same skilled writer will make the mistake of painting the villain of the piece all in black, a sociopath with no redeeming features and all the staying power of a tabloid headline.

Yes, such misfits *do* exist in real life . . . but unless we know what makes them tick, what makes them human, what to some extent explains their actions, they're not terribly interesting. Witness Truman Capote's chilling nonfiction tour de force, *In Cold Blood*. Had Capote not portrayed his subjects as men to be pitied as much as abhorred, would the book hold quite the same fascination for us? Instead, we find ourselves squirming as the date of their execution approaches, unable to beat a safe retreat into our own righteousness. These young killers clearly have no place in civilized society—but they are human. Through them, we begin to see ourselves in a different light, a kind of there-but-for-the-grace-of-God view that tends to be thought-provoking, and even disturbing as it cuts a little too close to home.

Fictional predators, when richly drawn, can come alive in the same way. By behaving in less than predictable ways, and by virtue of past actions that might cast them in a gentler light, they become not only less evil, but more interesting. Let's face it, pure evil is boring. You can pretty much predict what the man in the black hat is going to do, because he has no conscience to get in his way. It's even kind of comforting, because you don't have to worry too much about anticipating his actions; all you have to do is root for the hero to escape his clutches. All well and good for Spiderman and the Green Hornet, but don't we look for more in novels than the stuff of comics? And doesn't a worthy protagonist deserve more than a good chase? Give me a villain with a higher purpose, a soupçon of remorse, a dash of leading man in him, and I'll guarantee you a duel you won't want to miss.

Ken Follett's *Eye of the Needle* is a good example of how a multi-faceted villain can help build pulse-pounding suspense. In Chapter One, Faber, the Nazi spy known as *Die Nadel,* is discovered with a short-wave radio by his landlady, whom he then feels he has no choice but to kill. Upon stabbing her to death, he throws up. At once, our interest is piqued. Who is this cold-blooded killer with so weak a stomach for blood-letting? Might there be more to him than meets the eye? Indeed there is. More than a threat to Western civilization, someone whose actions could drastically alter the outcome of World War II, Faber is a man with a soft spot for a particular woman—a man capable even of gallantry. In the cat-and-mouse chase that ensues, Faber's conflicted nature leads us down a path far more circuitous than any traveled by a stock spy in a standard thriller. Nearing the climax, we almost root for him, while hating ourselves for doing so. Faber, of course, falls victim to his own Achilles heel, while forever securing a place for himself among the Great Villains of Modern Fiction.

In my own novels, I strive to make my antagonists complex, and yet easily fathomable. Often, they come dangerously close to being *likable.* I wouldn't go so far as to say that David Sloane, in my novel *Garden of Lies,* is anyone you'd want your daughter to bring home, and especially not the kind of person you'd want as your gynecologist. But by my weaving in strands of memory from David's childhood and adolescence, readers can sympathize with, if not forgive, the actions of a man who has not escaped the long shadow of his abusive alcoholic father, or his own shame about his roots. In the courtroom climax, when David is publicly humiliated by the woman he set out to destroy, he evokes pity even while no one would deny there is poetic justice in his comeuppance.

The same applies to Rudy in *Such Devoted Sisters*. For all his Machiavellian grotesqueness, he is in many ways a more engaging villain than his handsome, self-serving half-brother, Val, because Rudy is motivated, even *twisted,* you might say, by his obsessive love for his niece Laurel. At the dark heart of his evil machinations lies the tender ache of knowing he can never possess the kind of beauty and purity embodied in a young woman like Laurel. Trapped within his own ugliness, he is nearly driven mad by his yearning.

While writing the scenes in which Rudy plots to gain custody of Laurel's illegitimate baby, I found myself remembering how I'd felt reading "Rumpelstiltskin" for the first time, when I was eight or nine. How could I have pitied the princess when her baby was taken from her and at the same time, have felt a little sorry for Rumpelstiltskin at being thwarted in the end? Such is the dichotomy that defines the very best fiction, and makes it as timeless as a Grimms' fairy tale. For in art, as in life, the real story is often told between the lines and in the subtle shadings between black and white. In reflecting on the eternal puzzle of what makes good people do bad things and vice versa, we learn to know ourselves better.

How, you might ask, can you achieve this uneasy balance in your own antagonists? The answer is: not easily. It's a juggling act, and too heavy a hand in either direction can end up looking like something that came out of the oven too soon—in other words, a soggy mess. In rendering David Sloane (*Garden of Lies*), I realized that he needed a motive in addition to his tortured past for turning so nasty in the end. He needed to feel justified—and not entirely without reason—for his vicious attack on Rachel. And so I gave him a motivation that would make almost any man, nice or nasty, squirm. Early in the novel, after Rachel has told him she's pregnant with his baby, and he's insisted that she have an abortion, she informs him that the only way she'll even consider such a thing is if *he* performs it. This isn't as farfetched as you'd think. David is a doctor, after all, and ob/gyn is his specialty. Pushed into a corner, he reluctantly acquiesces—and becomes impotent in the years that follow. Imagine his rage at Rachel then! In a way, who could blame him for lashing out?

Oddly enough, in writing *Blessing in Disguise,* the shadings of gray

I had given Cordelia in my earlier drafts eventually transformed her from an antagonist into a protagonist. She was never really bad to begin with, but through her willfulness, as well as her stubborn avoidance of the truth, she had managed to alienate one grown daughter and make a spineless lump out of the other. What differentiates Cordelia from Rudy and from David Sloane is that Cordelia, at some point, sees that her old methods aren't working and finds the courage to strike out into the new and frightening territory of self-discovery. She and her daughter Grace manage a reconciliation of sorts, but as in real life, it's both less than it might have been and more than either of them had dared hope for. Cordelia even finds true love in the form of her poetic gardener.

But without Cordelia, a reader could say that *Blessing in Disguise* has no real villain. Which brings me to my next point: Not every novel *needs* a villain. When mining for conflict, I often find the richest dramatic ore lies in situations, particularly family situations, rather than in one particular person, or a cat-and-mouse chase. Broken promises, shameful deeds, dark secrets—these are the ingredients that can make a plot simmer, as well as light a path to the villain that lurks in the heart of all of us. In Peter Benchley's novel *Jaws,* you could say the shark is the bad guy—but is it? The shark has no personality and no motive for killing other than to fill its stomach. The real evil in *Jaws,* as I see it, is the town's inertia and the pig-headed avariciousness of petty bureaucrats. The hero, in bucking the system, finds himself up against an antagonist more formidable—and, in a way, unbeatable—than any snack-happy shark. After all, it's a lot easier simply to stay out of the water than to remove oneself from life situations rife with conflict!

But let's say you've already written your novel. Maybe you've sent it out to a few publishers who rejected it. You've been told it has a terrific plot, but the characters are somewhat flat. You're prepared to rewrite it, but you don't know where to begin. So let's start with your villain, since the chances are good that this is where artificial resuscitation is most needed. You've done your job in most respects. Your villain's modus operandi is well established: He's clever; he's ruthless; he's a perfect foil to your hero. But is he a little too perfect? You might want to season him a bit by introducing a new strand—a past injustice, a tortured memory, a dysfunctional family—but feel that it would alter the plot in an adverse way or require you to start all over from scratch. If at all possible, you absolutely *should* do what is necessary to make this the best character and the best book it can be. But maybe the same goal can be achieved in another, less tricky way. This is where odd quirks and unlikely characteristics can be used in fleshing out cardboard villains.

Take Hannibal Lecter, in *The Silence of the Lambs.* Who would imagine a cannibal could be a dilettante? A deranged sociopath who also happens to be brilliant and, yes, even gentlemanly. This study in contrasts is part of what makes him so fascinating, far more so, in fact, than the main villain, whose most interesting feature is his penchant for human hides.

Hard Fall, by Ridley Pearson, is another example of how life can be breathed into a villain. I was privileged to read that novel in an early draft, in which the antagonist, Kort, came dangerously close to appearing like a character from Central Casting. On the advice of his agent, Pearson added an extra dimension, giving Kort not angst or some moral quandary, but a toothache! Imagine plotting to blow up an airplane full of passengers while in the throes of a throbbing toothache. Desperate to get to a dentist, Kort becomes human to us in a very immediate way, someone we can relate to whether we want to or not.

In *Such Devoted Sisters,* I gave Rudy a similar weakness: He's allergic to chocolate. What makes it ironic is that Annie, the object of his ire, is the owner of a successful chocolate shop. I used this device in *Blessing in Disguise,* as well. Teen-aged Hannah (more a wannabe than a real villainess) has an allergy to nuts—which she uses to her advantage in the opening chapter, when her father's girlfriend, Grace, accidentally serves her a piece of chocolate-nut torte.

And who could forget Don Corleone, the patriarch of *The Godfather,* tending his garden and playing so sweetly with his grandson? This, from the mafioso responsible for chopping off a horse's head and having it placed in a man's bed. Contradictory? Yes, but such is the stuff of real life. People are seldom what they appear to be on the surface, and in some cases, they can surprise even themselves. Part of what made *Schindler's List,* the novel and the movie, so compelling was the duality of Schindler's nature. He was a far-from-perfect man, a philanderer and opportunist, who found himself cast in the unlikely role of savior—a role that bewildered Oskar Schindler himself as much

95

as it did anyone who knew him. Fate had brought his sterling qualities to the fore and made him a hero. It follows then that the same war (as the story suggests) made monsters out of ordinary men who might otherwise have led uneventful lives. Allow this uneasy stretch to apply to your fictional villains and you could come up with something that will have readers turning the pages even as they scratch their heads.

Recently, at Stratford-on-Avon, I had the matchless experience of seeing *Macbeth* performed by the Royal Shakespeare Company. I had never seen the play on any stage, and was overwhelmed by something that somehow had escaped my notice in reading it: Lady Macbeth, one of the most ruthless villainesses of all time, isn't *all* bad. She's a snake—but she has a conscience. O.K., so it isn't *much* of a conscience. In fact, it's about the size of—well, a *spot.* In her famous closing speech, as she scrubs at her palm in a vain attempt to remove the imaginary spot, she becomes, for a singular, nearly poignant moment, vulnerable, an object of pity rather than contempt.

What would Lady Macbeth have been without her spot? Not nearly as enduring, I can assure you. In its marvelous complexity, hers is a role that any actress would kill for, but which few can carry off. Not because they aren't talented or skilled, but because it isn't easy to project, or even to imagine, the spot of warmth that lies at the core of even the coldest heart.

As writers, we must bring empathy into our craft along with our imaginations. For in the very best fiction, every larger-than-life hero has a small devil on his shoulder, and every villain wears, if not a tarnished halo, then at least a hat more gray than black.

>> 25

WHAT YOU NEED TO KNOW ABOUT NOVEL WRITING

BY SIDNEY SHELDON

Q. *Do you feel that fiction should teach a lesson, or even indirectly convey a message to readers?*

A. Fiction is primarily for entertainment, but if there is a moral to the tale without interrupting the story it's a plus.

Q. *If you had to recommend one of your novels to someone who had never read any of your work, which one would you pick? Why?*

A. *The Other Side of Midnight* or *If Tomorrow Comes.* I enjoyed doing the research on both of them.

Q. *Do you have a specific reader in mind when you're writing?*

A. It would be impossible for me to have a specific reader in mind when I write. My novels are sold in 100 countries in 64 languages. My readers range from truck drivers to physicists to housewives to teachers. I would have no idea how to write a book that would entertain a truck driver in Croatia *and* a teacher in Madrid.

Q. *How do you come up with titles for your books? How important do you think titles are? What is your favorite novel title, excluding your own work?*

A. Titles for my books come to me at various times. Sometimes in the beginning or while I am in the middle or at the finish. To make the title fit the story I make up quotes at the beginning of my books. I've done this with all my books. For example, in *Morning, Noon & Night* there's a beginning quote:

Allow the morning sun to warm
Your heart when you are young
And let the soft winds of noon
Cool your passion,
but beware the night
For death lurks there,
Waiting, waiting, waiting.

Arthur Rimbaud

Actually, Rimbaud never said it. I did.

Q. *What (if any) is your typical "routine" when you sit down to start a new book?*

A. When I begin a book I go into my office at about 9:00 a.m. and work until 6:00 p.m. Very often if I can't sleep at night I go into my office for a few hours and then go back to bed. When the draft of a novel is finished I start to do rewrites, sometimes up to a dozen, until it's as good as I think I can make it. Then I send it to my publisher.

Q. *What do you see in terms of your future writing? Are you working on a new novel now? How does it differ basically from your earlier novels?*

A. I've just started on my fifteenth novel. It differs from my other novels because the protagonist has a different occupation and the characters are individuals I've never written about before.

Q. *You do several drafts of a novel—how do you decide when your work is finished? When your book is in type, do you ever feel that you could still make changes in it?*

A. Even though I do many rewrites on each book, when I see the printed copy I always want to do one more.

Q. *Has an unsolved true-life case involving a serious crime—murder, rape, arson, for instance—ever been the jumping-off place for one of your novels? Or have you ever felt that the "solution" of a real-life crime was wrong, and you wanted to solve it in your own way?*

A. Many writers get their ideas for novels from the front pages of the newspapers, and there is nothing wrong with that. Drama is always the basis of an exciting story. However, I prefer to work from within and let the story develop from my character.

Q. *Can an author "fall in love" with a character to the point that he makes him or her behave as he hopes or wants, instead of as the plot or interaction with other characters requires?*

A. In *Bloodline,* old Samuel completely ran away with me and before I realized it, I had devoted 150 pages to him. In the last rewrite I had to eliminate most of them.

Q. *Have you ever had a novel go off in a direction you didn't foresee or didn't want? If so, how did you get the book back on track— or did you instead let it lead you?*

A. All of my novels go off in directions I never anticipate. When I begin a novel I start with a character. I have no plot, no beginning, no middle and no end. I start dictating to a secretary and then the fun begins. The character takes over and at the end of the day there are situations that did not exist in the morning. So, in a sense, I am the reader as well as the writer. I can't wait to see what happens next!

Q. *Which writers did you admire at the outset of your career? How did they influence your writing?*

A. Long before I began writing novels I read Sinclair Lewis, Thomas Wolfe, James Thurber, Dickens, Tolstoy, Twain and many other great authors. I hope I learned something from them.

Q. *The publishing world has changed so much over the past ten years. What advice do you have for today's aspiring writer, for whom it's more difficult than ever to get published?*

A. Today more than 1,000 titles are published every week. There is so much competition for floor space in bookstores that it is almost impossible to get a book published unless you have a name. Yet, new writers are published every year, so someone is succeeding! My advice is never to give up. If other people can do it, you can do it.

➤➤ 26

EMOTION: THE DRIVING FORCE IN YOUR STORY

BY MADELEINE COSTIGAN

STORY IDEAS CAN COME FROM ANYWHERE—A SNATCH OF CONVERSA-tion, an intriguing character, a pivotal event in a person's life. But what makes these ideas come alive on the page is the emotion they generate in the mind of the reader—not the writer. The writer may need to feel deeply to communicate emotion, so deeply that Tennessee Williams felt it necessary to warn, "Don't let anybody see you at your typewriter." Yet in fiction it's what's on the page that counts.

Norman Mailer tells of the young writer who came home from an evening in which he had met the most wonderful woman in the world. He was so transformed by the experience that he decided to write a story about it and immediately sat down at his desk. "I love you," he wrote. "I love you." The words recreated the entire evening in his mind, and he spent hours reliving every moment. His reader, however, was left with nothing—except perhaps a vague suspicion that he had interrupted the start of a love letter.

So how is it done? Why is it that one writer can graphically describe a character's blood, sweat, and tears, yet leave the reader unmoved, while a writer such as John Galsworthy can deliver in one sentence an emotional punch that leaves the reader reeling?

After publishing short stories in major magazines for several years, it became clear to me that just when I thought I'd made a breakthrough, I'd soon discover that what I'd actually come up with was at best an efficient, perhaps even powerful way to evoke a particular emotional response—germane to one story.

Later, as assistant fiction editor at *McCall's,* I added a new dimension to my understanding of fiction and had a unique opportunity to work with many fine writers and editors. But I can't claim to have ferreted out any trade secrets or magical clues that simplify the complex process of fiction writing. I did, however, make a few interesting discoveries: Every writer struggles. Even those who constantly improve their skills don't find writing easier. And the quality of a story is usually in direct proportion to the number of drafts it has been put through.

Before a story is accepted by any magazine, it must pass muster with several editors. Because editors endure the same pressures and traumas as anyone else, a story that is written close to the bone has a better chance of acceptance, particularly when it happens to connect with the editors' perception of human experience. To be effective, the story will deeply involve the reader with the characters and what is happening to them. The writer sustains this involvement through emotion. Emotion must drive every element of the story: characterization, plot, theme, and setting. Each scene must further the plot, disclose significant aspects of the characters, contribute to the theme and be anchored in such a way that the reader has a sense of place.

In everyday life, most people mask their emotions a good bit of the time. In fiction, your characters may conceal themselves from one another but not from the writer. The writer sees beyond the mask. To reveal a character in crisis, the writer has to be more than the fly on the wall. It's fine to see what the character does and hear what the character says, but the reader wants to know how the character feels in this particular life crisis. And why. The writer must draw the reader not just into the story, but so deeply into the characters that the reader is likely to speculate about what the characters would or would not do, even after the story ends.

Now back to writing full time, I am once again engaged in unraveling the mystery that is fiction writing from yet another vantage point. How does the writer communicate authentic emotion? Each story is new territory, and there are no easy answers that will guarantee a story's success. Yet, having read numerous manuscripts from new and established writers, there are a few commonplace snares I caution you to avoid:

1. *Don't play it safe.*

The writer can't skate on the surface of a problem and hope to portray genuine emotion. Go to a character's deepest level, reveal the character intimately. There's a catch to this. In revealing the character, the writer also gets revealed, even though the material is in no way autobiographical. When you write fiction, you tell more about yourself than about any character. There's no place to hide. So, if you find yourself shying away from a scene, or attempting to gloss over a crucial event, stop where you are and work it through. In doing so, you'll come to a greater, more thorough knowledge of your characters and their situation, which will lead you to the compelling truth at the heart of your characters' fear, love, anger, grief, or joy. Thus enlightened, you can rewrite the scene drawing from the landscape of your own psyche. But don't expect to be comfortable; if you are, you probably won't be convincing. Or, as an editor once wrote to me when returning a manuscript—"Nice writing, but it didn't get me in the heart, which is where I like to be got."

Before sending a story out, ask yourself this question: Will it get the reader in the heart? If it doesn't, revise.

2. *Beware of sentimentality.*

If playing it safe is one extreme, mawkish sentimentality is the other. Early on, the fiction writer is wise to relegate sentimentality to Valentine's Day. How do you know if you're getting maudlin? If you find yourself describing choking sobs, churning stomachs, pounding hearts, pulsating bodies, and other clichés, you're mired in sentimentality. Readers will reject such off-the-top-of-the-head writing. Go back and concentrate on more relevant details. Impact comes from images that conjure up appropriate feelings in the reader.

Real emotion is simple, but there is nothing simple about creating emotional response in the reader. To avoid having a strongly emotional scene turn saccharine, I find it helpful to inject a note of humor, or a tangential thought to cut tension.

In my story, "The Second Son" (*Good Housekeeping*), the emotion I was working with was grief and the way different members of a family deal with it. Joanna's fourteen-year-old son, Jamie, has died of an aneurysm. While grieving for Jamie, Joanna relives the time shortly after her brother Charles's death when he was two years old and Joanna was four. Unless handled with care, such a scene can get very sloppy. I rewrote it several times before I decided on the following paragraphs:

She remembers the sprays of white flowers, her father crying on the way to the cemetery. Was it all right to notice? Or was it like reminding Uncle Rob that he always told the same jokes? Grown-ups didn't cry, especially fathers. Her sister, Emily, caught her father's fingers and said, "I'll give you all my pennies if you'll just stop crying."

What a silly thing to say! But the next minute her father stopped crying and put his arm around Emily, leaving Joanna wishing she'd thought to say it.

Sometimes, knowing what to play down or leave between the lines is as important as knowing what to emphasize. Which details most affected the character? Was the character's thinking process logical or disjointed?

Space is so limited in a short story that I find it best to spend little time on physical description and concentrate on what's inside. Try to brush in enough of the concrete and specific to illuminate your character; yet leave enough space for your reader's imagination to operate. Waste no words on the banal; search out the detail that is unique, telling.

In "The Second Son," I needed to portray Emily, Joanna's sister, without having her appear in the story. My way of handling this was to give a brief glimpse of Emily in Joanna's thoughts.

Emily, with her penchant for taking people in hand! Joanna imagined herself becoming one of Emily's projects—doing laps in the pool at the Y, volunteering.

3. *Never trivialize real problems with unreal solutions.*

Nothing is more discouraging to an editor than seeing a promising story fall apart at the end. If the ending is predictable, unbelievable, ambiguous, contrived, or out of sync with the actual story, the reader will feel cheated, no matter how fine the writing.

A real conflict doesn't just disappear or get resolved by a fortunate turn of events. As the story unfolds, characters and plot progress toward a realistic resolution that is both inevitable and unanticipated.

Sometimes it's a matter of focus. Should your focus be from a wide angle? Or quite narrow? It makes a difference. And only you can decide. The short story has been called "the art of the glimpse." But there are no absolutes.

How to stay focused, yet keep the reader off center at the same time? Arturo Vivante has said that a little inconsistency in a character can help to make the character more interesting.

In the above-mentioned story, Joanna longs to talk about Jamie.

Elizabeth, her mother, can't bear to and resorts to silence or to changing the subject whenever Jamie is mentioned. Then Mark, Joanna's younger son, is accidentally confronted with a pipe and package of tobacco Jamie had hidden. Joanna is speechless. Mark has practically canonized Jamie and isn't prepared to deal with such hard evidence of his brother's frailty. With effort, his grandmother finds the words to tell Mark of an incident involving Joanna's deceased brother Charles and reminds him of the importance of remembering the actual person, not just the idealistic fragments that memory conveniently selects.

Much moved, Joanna tells her mother how much her response has helped Mark:

"Mm," her mother says. "Do you think there's enough celery in the potato salad?"

What did she expect? Joanna asks herself. That her mother would start organizing support groups for bereaved parents? Talking about Charles seems to have exhausted her. *Living requires enough energy, never mind reliving,* Joanna thinks. Still, she knows her mother's words will come back to her.

For now she does what Emily would do, the sensible practical thing that will erase that unfamiliar gray tinge from her mother's face. She pronounces the potato salad to have just the right amount of celery.

"Good," her mother says. "I was hoping you'd say that."

The intensity of the moment forces Elizabeth to step somewhat out of character during her conversation with Mark. Yet, it is clear that at the end of the story she is the same reticent person she was at the beginning. What has changed is Joanna's perception of her. And it is this change in perception that deepens the relationship between mother and daughter and resolves their conflict.

Fiction writing remains an elusive process that demands a fusing of disparate elements. Exploring the chemistry of these elements when filtered through the writer's imagination yields infinite possibilities. Sometimes this pursuit can seem as futile as the alchemists' quest. But when the elements converge in a story that portrays truth, the experience can be most satisfying.

>> 27

TITLES

BY BARNABY CONRAD

ASIDE FROM MAKING YOUR LITERARY PRODUCT UNIQUE AND SERVING as sort of a trademark, the primary function of a title is to lure unsuspecting readers into your story. Although titling is one of the most imprecise, capricious, and subjective components of a story, most people have definite ideas of what a good title is or should be.

In hindsight, and after millions of copies of a book have been sold, it is easy to say that *The Catcher in the Rye,* for example, is a great title. But suppose you were the first person to hear J.D. Salinger propose, as the title for his first novel, that peculiar juxtaposition of words. Would you rush out to buy a book called *Pansy?* That was one of the many titles Margaret Mitchell came up with for *Gone With the Wind* before it was published by Macmillan. Other suggested titles included *Tote the Weary Load, Tomorrow Is Another Day, Milestones, Ba! Ba! Black Sheep,* and *Jettison.* It has been said that eighteen titles in all were considered before the author came up with *Gone With the Wind* from Ernest Dowson's poem "Cynara." Would we even now think the phrase "gone with the wind" so memorable a title if the novel had sold, say, only hundreds of books instead of multimillions?

As Somerset Maugham said so accurately: "A good title is the title of a book that's successful." The title of one of Maugham's many successful novels, based loosely on Paul Gauguin, was *The Moon and Sixpence.* "People tell me it's a good title, but they don't know what it means. It means reaching for the moon and missing the sixpence at one's feet."

To be good, it's not always necessary for a title to be understood.

Maugham had originally titled his masterpiece, *Of Human Bondage, Beauty and Ashes,* but ultimately discovered it had been previously used.

Walker Percy said that a good title "should intrigue without being too baffling or too obvious." Some titles baffle us until we have read the book—and sometimes even afterward: *A Clockwork Orange, Catch 22, Kaputt, Shibumi, The Milagro Beanfield War, Like Water for Chocolate, The Unbearable Lightness of Being*, et cetera. Their very unfamiliarity and strangeness are calculated to lure readers into finding out what the story is about.

Just where do titles come from—and when?

"The title comes last," said Tennessee Williams.

Hemingway said: "I make a list of titles *after* I've finished the story or book—sometimes as many as a hundred. Then I start eliminating them, sometimes all of them."

It is often startling to hear of the terrible first choices of famous novels. Charles Dickens originally wanted to call the classic novel that ended up as *Bleak House, Tom-All-Alone's The Ruined House*. His *Hard Times* started out as *Two and Two Are Four*.

When Charles Dickens planned to write an exciting serial, he immediately encountered title trouble. His first titles were:

Time!, The Leaves of the Forest, Scattered Leaves, The Great Wheel, Round and Round, Old Leaves, Long Ago, Far Apart, Fallen Leaves, Five and Twenty Years, Years and Years, Day After Day, Felled Trees, Memory Carton, Rolling Stones, Two Generations. Later he jotted down other possibilities: *One of These Days, Buried Alive, The Thread of Gold, The Doctor of Beauvais*.

And then, on March 11, 1859, he wrote a friend: "I have got exactly the name for the story that is wanted; exactly what will fit the opening to a T: *A Tale of Two Cities*."

Where does the imagination for a great title come from?

Many writers find their titles in the body of the work itself, perhaps in the dialogue. Margaret Mitchell's title idea *Tomorrow Is Another Day* was a cliché taken from Scarlett's thoughts.

Many titles have come from nursery rhymes, such as *When the Bough Breaks, The Cradle Will Fall*, and so forth. Ed McBain has written a dozen crime books with titles like *Cinderella; Mary, Mary; Jack and the Beanstalk*.

Over the years, Shakespeare has been one of the most tapped, and seemingly inexhaustible, sources of titles. For example, *Something Wicked This Way Comes, Cakes and Ale, Remembrance of Things*

Past, The Sound and the Fury, The Dogs of War, The Winter of Our Discontent, To Thine Own Self Be True.

Thomas Wolfe's title *Look Homeward, Angel* came from a line in Milton's "Lycidas," but only after such titles as *They Are Strange, They Are Lost,* and *The Exile's Story* were rejected by his renowned editor, Maxwell Perkins. (Wolfe's wonderful title *You Can't Go Home Again* came not from a poem but a chance remark by a friend.)

Lines from songs have provided many good titles, such as: *Blue Skies, From Here to Eternity, Body and Soul.*

The Bible, of course, has been a gold mine, especially Ecclesiastes (*The Sun Also Rises*) and The Song of Solomon (*The Sound of the Turtle*), and many more.

Common phrases can make good titles:

I Can Get It for You Wholesale; They Shoot Horses, Don't They; You Could Look It Up; Born Yesterday; Fun While It Lasted. Simply using the hero's or heroine's name as a title was more common in the past than it is today; for example: *Pamela, Tom Jones, Emma, Madame Bovary, Jane Eyre, David Copperfield, Nana, Tom Sawyer, Ivanhoe, Ethan Frome, Jude the Obscure, Anna Karenina.*

Nor have single-name titles gone totally out of fashion in more modern novels: *Rebecca, Laura, Lolita, Mrs. Bridge, Elmer Gantry, Youngblood Hawke,* and *Forrest Gump.*

More common are variations using a name, such as:

The Prime of Miss Jean Brodie, Sophie's Choice, Henderson the Rain King, Portnoy's Complaint, and *What Makes Sammy Run?*

Place names are frequently used in titles either alone—*USA, Middlemarch, Wuthering Heights, Winesburg, Ohio, The Cruel Sea, The Big Sky, The Secret Garden*—or in conjunction with other words—*Babylon Revisited, Manhattan Transfer, Barchester Towers, Brideshead Revisited.*

Appomattox would be an adequate title; Bruce Catton's *A Stillness at Appomattox* is a great one.

So when all is said and done, we see that the art of titling is a curious and mercurial and mysterious one.

To show the disparity between some original titles and the ones ultimately published, here is a list of well-known works:

Previous Titles	Published Titles
With Due Respect	A Moveable Feast
The Sentimental Education of Frederick Henry	A Farewell to Arms
Catch 19	Catch 22
Twilight	The Sound and the Fury
Blanche's Chair in the Moon	A Streetcar Named Desire
Finnerty's Ball	The Man With the Golden Arm
They Don't Build Statues to Businessmen	Valley of the Dolls
Tenderness	Lady Chatterley's Lover
All's Well That Ends Well	War and Peace
Four and a Half Years of Struggle Against Lies, Stupidity, and Cowardice	Mein Kampf
Pumphrey	Babbitt
The Last Man in Europe	1984
The Mute	The Heart Is a Lonely Hunter
Before This Anger	Roots
The Birds and the Bees	Everything You Always Wanted to Know About Sex (But Were Afraid to Ask)
The Kingdom by the Sea	Lolita
No Safe Harbor	Ship of Fools
To Climb the Wall	The Blackboard Jungle
The Whale	Moby Dick
Too Late, Beloved!	Tess of the D'Urbervilles
Private Fleming, His Various Battles	The Red Badge of Courage
Something That Happened	Of Mice and Men
The Sea-Cook	Treasure Island
The Man That Was a Thing	Uncle Tom's Cabin
Bar-b-que	The Postman Always Rings Twice
A Day of Fear	Matador

➤➤ 28

PIQUING THE READER'S CURIOSITY

BY JOAN AIKEN

ONCE WHEN I WAS SITTING IN A PACKED LONDON UNDERGROUND train, I heard the following snatch of conversation between two men who were standing close by me, but I never saw their faces among the crowd of rush-hour passengers. The first voice, the sort that alerts you at once to listen, asked, "Did I ever tell you the story of the mushroom?"

"No, what was it?" the other voice asked.

"Well, there were only two officers in charge. A couple of days before this happened they had vacuumed the parade ground. Lord, those Germans are thorough! You could have rolled out pastry on that parade ground."

"But what about the mushroom?"

"I was coming to that. There was this white flagpole in the middle of the parade ground. . . . Ah, Charing Cross, here we are."

The train stopped, the two men got out, taking with them forever the secret of what happened to the mushroom. That was about thirty years ago, but I still wake sometimes in the small hours and occupy myself with speculations as to where and in what circumstances the mushroom turned up.

Curiosity is the main characteristic that divides human beings from other animals. Of course some animals are inquisitive, too, but not to the ruinous degree that has brought the human race to its present precarious clutch on atomic development and other undesirable areas of knowledge. If only our earliest ancestor had not rubbed two sticks together and discovered how to light a campfire. . . . But here we are, congenitally inquisitive, and there is no going back. We long to find out what began it all, and what happened in the end. Ancient myths and folk tales give warnings about the perils incurred from prying into

109

other people's business: Prometheus stealing fire from the gods; Psyche spilling hot oil from the lamp on Cupid in her eagerness to discover the identity of her nightly visitor; the terrible revelations of Bluebeard's chamber.

Magic—a dangerous force, like electricity, like radiation—is unleashed by attempts to discover what lies ahead, to divine the future, to skip all the tedious intervening chapters and turn on to the very last page. Why do we read stories? Because we long to find out what happened next. Any writer who can evoke this curiosity is sure of an audience. But how is it done? How can you keep your readers atwitter with suspense? Some authors can relate the most wonderful, hair-raising events in such a flat, disinterested manner that they might just as well be recounting the annals of the local archaeological society, while others make the most trifling event full of entertainment and surprise. The important factors are who is telling and who is listening.

One way to arouse curiosity, and a very good one, is to imply that there is a secret waiting to be revealed. What kind of secret? Well, it must be an important, a crucial one, or it would not have been kept secret in the first place. The revelation must then be postponed for as long as possible. This is a matter of judgment, for if you delay the revelation *too* long, the reader may become impatient, and close the book, or turn on to the end; or, even worse, when the disclosure comes, it comes as an anti-climax and the disappointed reader may feel that it was not worth waiting for.

Dickens was a very shrewd hand at delayed-action disclosure: A main part of his technique was to provide half a dozen subplots, each with its own mystery, so that, in *Our Mutual Friend,* for instance, there is the mystery of the dead man found in the Thames, the mystery of Silas Wegg's evil hold over Mr. Boffin, and Mr. Boffin's peculiar behavior, the involved goings-on of the Lammles and Veneerings and their financial dealings, the paranoid behavior of Bradley Headstone, and the very odd, inscrutable relationship of Fledgeby and Riah—and a wealth of other oddities. The reader is given continual short glimpses of all these strange connections, enough to whet curiosity. But it is not until well after the halfway mark of the book that any explanations are forthcoming, and, as fast as one mystery is unravelled, another is brought back, to keep the reader turning the pages until the very end. Dickens's work had to be planned in installments for serial publication, so there was an obligation to provide a cliffhanger for the end of each part.

Fiction writing in Dickens's day had undergone a total change from the tranquil pace of the eighteenth century, before the Industrial Revolution, when readers, living mostly in the country, had unlimited reading time and were prepared for a novel to begin in a leisurely manner.

Writers then had all the time in the world to convey their message, and readers could settle down comfortably for a nice peaceful three-volume reading orgy in the long lamplit winter evenings.

All this came to an abrupt end in 1859 with the publication of Wilkie Collins's *The Woman in White,* which appeared serially in *All the Year Round.* A mass audience of middle-class readers had arrived. They wanted action. Stories had to begin with a bang: the Dover coach on a foggy night brought to a halt by a lone horseman; an escaped convict confronting a terrified boy in a lonely churchyard; wills, legacies, deathbed dramas. Wilkie Collins was a master hand at a gripping beginning. The protagonist in *The Woman in White* is first seen fleeing from her persecutors across Hampstead Heath. *The Moonstone* (not actually a moonstone, but a yellow diamond) opens with the storming of Seringapatam and the theft of the jewel from the forehead of the Brahmin god.

The only problem with such a rousing start is that not every writer has the ability to maintain the tension at this pitch for the rest of the story. Wilkie Collins at his best could do so, but he was not always *at* his best, and sometimes the tension began to sag as the plot became almost too formidably complicated.

How can this kind of lapse be avoided—apart from having a simpler plot? Keep your tale peppered with odd, unexplained episodes. You can have characters behave seemingly out of character, turn nasty, be seen in unexpected places in unlikely company. Your hero, for instance, meets an old friend who greets him with a blank stare, with no sign of recognition; a faithful hound growls at his master of ten years; two old women are seen in a village street looking at photographs, and one of them suddenly shrieks in astonishment.

To keep the reader's attention focused on your hero (who is engaged in a struggle against apparently insuperable odds), it can be useful to endow him with an unexpected minor attribute that will stand him in good stead in confronting a vital crisis. He is a qualified tea-taster; or she has perfect musical pitch; he speaks ten different African languages; she is an expert on the kind of paint Velasquez used. The reader must, of course, have been previously informed of this specialized knowledge or skill, but in a passing, offhand way. If it comes as a complete surprise to the reader at the moment of crisis (he was the only man in England who could undo a particular knot), the reader could be justifiably annoyed. "Author's convenience" must be avoided at all costs. The author's real skill lies in creating the type of situation that would require the hero or heroine's unique expertise to be brought into play. There is a folk-tale model based on exactly this pattern: The hero is sent into the world on a seemingly hopeless quest, accompanied by six friends. One can run faster than anyone in the world; another is a champion archer . . . and so on. Here, of course, the pleasure for the reader lies in anticipating the triumph of the hero and his friends.

I had a good time writing my children's book, *The Whispering Mountain,* in which the hero, a short-sighted, delicate, unathletic boy, has to contend with a gang of local bullies and with a couple of London criminals. He always carries with him a tiny *Book of Knowledge,* which invariably provides him with the precise bit of know-how to meet each emergency. I happen to own such a book, and so was able to tailor the emergencies in the story to fit the information it provided. The idea, of course, is not new: I adopted it from *The Swiss Family Robinson,* in which the calmly competent mother of the family is always able to produce from her reticule the necessary ball of string, pair of pliers, or sticking plaster to deal with a problem.

Naturally, a story need not be presented on such a simplistic physical level to keep the reader's curiosity stimulated. Jane Austen arouses and maintains interest easily and spontaneously with her basic problem situations. How will the Bennets ever manage to marry off all those five daughters? How will Anne Elliot manage to endure the painful ordeal of encountering her lost lover again after eight years of heartbreak? What is the mystery attached to Jane Fairfax? Why wouldn't she go to Ireland? How will poor little Fanny Price make out when she is sent to live among those rich scornful relatives?

A tremendously important element of readability is the solid basis of the plot. A well-balanced, strong story generally has one or perhaps two crucial events in it. One, fairly early on, is to give you a foretaste of what the writer is able to provide. Charlotte Brontë whets your

112

appetite by telling about Jane Eyre's incarceration in the Red Room and the consequent ghostly terrors. Then the story settles down to sober reality until the second explosion with the mad Mrs. Rochester in the attic. Mystery novelist Reginald Hill, in one of his Detective Dalziel mysteries, teases the aghast reader early on with a wild description of a crazed gunman and mayhem in a village street; then he rewinds the story to an earlier point of time, and so keeps readers on tenterhooks, waiting while he leads up again to the moment when all hell is going to break loose. And then he deals the expectant reader another shattering surprise.

Readers today are much more sophisticated than they used to be. They are accustomed to fictional trickery, guessing games, speeding up and slowing down of action, even unresolved questions and crises. They have only to walk along the street or into a supermarket or bookstore to see racks and racks of paperbacks and hardbacks, all screaming their messages of drama and sensationalism. But it is still possible to find a simple straight-forward story that will keep the reader breathless, attentive, and compulsively turning the pages. The novels of Sara Paretsky, Tony Hillerman, Reginald Hill, Dick Francis, and Rosamund Pilcher are good examples.

Fiction today has to compete with television, videotapes, films, rock music, virtual reality; and the horrors and crises in world news, exciting discoveries and inventions, and human deeds and misdeeds.

Sometimes a story depends for its momentum on a single character, or on the relationship between two characters. We love Character A and would like to see him on good terms with Character B, but they have always been at odds. How can an agreement between them be brought about? The relationship between Beatrice and Benedict in Shakespeare's *Much Ado About Nothing* is a fine example of such a story.

In *Little Lord Fauntleroy*, Frances Hodgson Burnett accomplishes this in a domestic setting. Character A won't love B, but B wins him over. The crusty old Earl of Dorincourt is unwillingly obliged by law to accept his unknown American grandson as his heir; how long will it take the gallant little fellow and his gentle gracious American mother to win their rightful places in the old aristocrat's rugged heart? Of course, it does not take very long, but the course of the story is pure pleasure for the reader all the way, even with the end so clearly in view.

Another heroine who achieves her end by possessing startlingly unexpected attributes and winning hearts all the way is Dorothy Gilman's Mrs. Pollifax, a senior citizen spy. Often teamed with tough male colleagues who at first deeply mistrust and resent her, she breaches their defenses by candor, practical good sense, humor, courage, and a touch of mysticism that is irresistible. We all love to read about good triumphing over evil, and to be given the certainty that it will do so, with a touch of humor thrown in, is an unbeatable combination.

Unrecognized love must always command the fascinated attention of readers, and Rebecca West makes tantalizing use of this knowledge in her magnificent novel, *The Birds Fall Down.* In this story, the clever but repulsive double agent Kamensky is infatuated by the teenage heroine Laura, but she is wholly unaware of this from first to last, believing that he intends to assassinate her. The unacknowledged duel between them builds up to an almost intolerably suspenseful climax, heightened by the fact that most of the other characters, Russians, are given to immense, loquacious, red-herring monologues on every conceivable topic, always just at the moment when some catastrophe seems imminent, or a train is about to leave.

Virginia Woolf had an idea for a play, never actually written: "I'm going to have a man and a woman . . . never meeting, not knowing each other, but all the time you'll feel them coming nearer and nearer. This will be the really exciting part, but when they *almost* meet—only a door between—you see how they just miss." Perhaps not surprisingly, she never did put the idea into a play or story. But Mary Wesley, in her novel, *An Imaginative Experience,* used a similar plot, except that she does finally permit her couple to meet. This kind of scheme for a story clearly displays that fiction is a kind of teasing game carried on between writer and reader, a game like Grandmother's Footsteps, in which I, the writer, try to steal up on you, the reader, without allowing you to find out beforehand what I intend to do.

And the theme of *curiosity,* dangerous, misplaced, unwarrantable curiosity, takes us, by way of myth and folklore, to ghost stories and the supernatural. "A Warning to the Curious" is the title of one of M.R. James's best-known ghost stories, and a very terrifying story it is, yet entirely convincing. Who could resist the possibility of discovering one of the legendary three royal crowns, buried somewhere, long ago, on the Suffolk coast "to keep off the Danes or the French or the Germans." But the surviving crown has a ghostly guardian, and the fate of the inquisitive rabbity young man who goes after it is very awful indeed. All the details in this story are exactly right: the foggy, sandy countryside, and the character of Paxton, the silly young man who has dug up the crown and now wishes he hadn't. The narrator and his friend try to help, but "all the same the snares of death over-took him," James states, but then proceeds to describe a harrowing chase through the fog, poor Paxton pursued by a creature "with more bones than flesh" and a "lungless laugh." Paxton is finally found with his mouth full of sand, his teeth and jaws broken to bits. . . .

Operas have overtures, in which snatches of all the best arias are beguilingly introduced, giving the audience a taste of the pleasures to come. In the same way, the shrewd writer will, by an opening sentence, sound the *voice* of his story, suggest what is likely to happen, and so whet the reader's appetite: "The marriage wasn't going well and I de-cided to leave my husband," says Anne Tyler at the start of *Earthly Possessions;* "I went to the bank to get cash for the trip." And so she set the style and tempo for a wildly free-wheeling and funny plot.

Your voice can be humorous or terrifying, sad, wild, or romantic; only *you* can give it utterance, only you can lead your reader by a cobweb thread through the windings of your own particular story. What did happen to the mushroom? Each of us has his own theory as to that.

115

➢➢ 29

MAKING THE READER CARE

BY MARJORIE FRANCO

EMOTION, OR A STATE OF FEELING, IS SOMETHING WE ALL EXPERIence, and for most of us our persistent memories are of situations or happenings that aroused a powerful emotion. When writing a story, the author uses a variety of emotions, trusting the reader to experience them along with the character. The character needs to be convincing enough to cause the reader to recall his or her own emotions, though not necessarily the specific experience that aroused them.

A friend once told me that her brother's favorite memory of childhood was of a summer night when he and the other members of his family stood around in the kitchen eating ice cream cones. Happiness, no doubt, was the emotion he connected to the scene, and this simple emotion resulted from many factors, including the summer night, the kitchen, the cold sweetness of the ice cream on his tongue, and above all, the sharing of pleasure with a loving family.

Although this memory from real life is different from the world of fiction, it is an example of how we remember moments that affect us. Our storehouse of memory continues to grow from childhood on, providing us with ideas for characters, setting, and conflicts, which, with the help of imagination, craft, and an appropriate tone, we weave together to create a story we hope will make the reader care.

Not an easy task, and one that beginning writers sometimes sidestep by having emotion occur off scene, or by simply stating it in narrative.

In *Lectures on Literature,* Vladimir Nabokov writes that memory causes the perfect fusion of past and present; that inspiration adds a third ingredient, the future. The writer, he believes, see the world as the potentiality of fiction.

An observant writer once saw a woman getting off a bus, and was so struck by something about her appearance and manner, she became the inspiration for a character in his story.

Henry James, sitting next to a woman at a dinner party, listening to her describe an event that actually took place, began thinking along fictional lines, sowing the seeds for what would become his novella *The Aspern Papers.* Once the idea had formed in his mind, he didn't want to hear the woman's entire story, for he was already creating his own.

We may begin creating a fictional character with a real person in mind, but the end result is never a duplicate of that person, because it's impossible to get inside another person's head, no matter how well we may know him or her. But it is necessary to get inside our characters, to know their personalities, strengths and weakness, what will make them feel love, hate, joy, anger, fear and pain; what experiences will affect their lives, and how they will deal with their problems. Much of this is revealed by showing them interacting with other characters in particular situations; with scene and dialogue; and with conflict.

The idea for my story "Between Friends" (*Good Housekeeping*) began with a real person in mind, but the character of Janet quickly took on her own personality and became fictional. The protagonist, Alison, welcomes new arrival, Janet, to the neighborhood, and they become friends. The conflict begins with Janet's casual criticism of Benny, Alison's son. Gradually, it escalates to the point where Janet says, "Maybe you've put your job before the interests of your child. Maybe if you'd stayed home more things would have been better." Words are exchanged, and the friendship ends with bitter feelings on both sides.

I believe the reader can relate to this confrontation, for we have all experienced criticism, as well as the hurt and feeling of rejection that accompany it. And when the critic is a friend, we may feel doubly rejected. Alison, who has gone out of her way for Janet, feels she's been treated unfairly, just as the reader may have felt at some time, even though the situation might have been different. Here, again, I trust the reader to tap into emotions that may be latent and experience them vicariously with the character.

The climax of the story occurs when a desperate Janet comes to Alison for help. Alison is about to leave for an important job interview, but when Janet says, "It's Andy, he ate a whole bottle of aspirin," she is horrified, and putting aside their differences (as well as her interview), she immediately drives Janet and Andy to the hospital.

117

Here, Alison has to make a quick decision, and the one she chooses says something about her character, her sense of right and wrong. Another person, unwilling to sacrifice an important interview for someone who has treated her badly, might have called an ambulance and left Janet and her son to wait for its arrival.

In addition to trying to show insight into the main character, I was also trying to establish empathy for Janet, the antagonist. Janet has her own problems. Perhaps she regrets having given up her job to stay home with her children; perhaps her criticism of Alison is grounded in envy; and, most important of all, perhaps she feels responsible for placing her son in danger, guilty of an act of negligence, the same kind of negligence of which she had accused Alison's son. Anger, envy, and guilt are emotions that have touched us all.

In our attempt to make the reader care, I believe we must keep in mind the difference between identifying with and relating to characters. The definition of identify is "to be, or become the same." Writers who create unique characters shouldn't expect the reader to identify with them. I take the view that though there is a universality in human beings, still each of us is different in a unique way. In contrast, the definition of relate is "to have a relationship or connection," a better goal, I think, for making the reader care.

As important as characters are to a story, they would not hold the reader's attention without some form of conflict. Conflict moves the story and keeps the reader interested while waiting to discover what happens next. Conflict generates emotion and requires the character either to solve the problem or to deal with it in a satisfactory way.

In my story "Midnight Caller" (*Good Housekeeping*) Dianne, a teacher and recently divorced mother of an infant son, is receiving anonymous phone calls, usually at midnight. She lives on the second floor of a three-story building; her friend Greta lives upstairs with her teenaged son, and another friend, Hank, lives on the first floor. Safety is of great importance to Dianne: On her own, and responsible for her infant son as well as for herself, she has tried to protect herself by choosing to live near friends. When the phone calls begin, she persuades herself that her name was picked at random from the phone book; still, they represent a threat to her feeling of safety and cause her a sense of unease. Then one snowy night, with all the roads blocked, all feelings of safety vanish and unease gives way to outright fear.

"What are you wearing?" the voice on the phone says. "Is it the yellow nightgown with the ruffles, or the white one with the lace?" Slowly, as if in a dream, she touches the neck of her nightgown and runs her fingers over the yellow ruffles. She hangs up, heart pounding, wide awake after being startled out of a sound sleep, and goes to her son's room.

The setting contributes to the tension—the apartment building surrounded by snow "thick on the rooftops and the bare trees, high where it had drifted against fences in backyards"—and so does the detail: the nightgown with the ruffles, her son's room "small, shadowy and warm, smelling of baby powder and freshly washed blankets. Clean."

Dianne's desire for safety is in conflict with the outside threat, the fact that she is interacting with an unknown person. By using certain words, abstractions are made concrete: "pounding" and "startled" contrast with "warm," "baby powder," and "clean."

In the end, Dianne discovers the identity of the midnight caller. It is not Hank, her neighbor, or one of her students at school, possibilities she had considered. It is Greta's son, who has often baby-sat for her. Like Alison in the first story I mentioned, Dianne is faced with a difficult and very important decision.

In these two stories, I've tried to show how characters, conflicts, and settings can generate emotion in the reader. But the emotion expressed through the character must first be felt by the writer who uses memory, experience and observations together with creative imagination to write the story and present it with clarity so the reader will understand.

Readers don't need to have conscious memory of events in their lives that aroused certain feelings in order to imagine a fictional situation and relate to it either positively or negatively. But those feelings can be touched by the characters in a story and the events in their lives, and when that happens, readers begin to care.

>> 30

IT REALLY HAPPENED

BY CHET VITTITOW

AT A RECENT WRITERS CONFERENCE, EIGHT OF US WERE GATHERED in a small room, reading manuscripts aloud and analyzing them. I was about to comment on a story that had just been read when the writer said, "The man was my grandfather . . ." and I knew what was coming next. She went on, "It really happened."

Writers seem to consider those three words—*it really happened*—as a kind of incantation, as if by uttering them a bad story could be elevated to Pulitzer Prize status. In this case, however, the writer did not take our well-intentioned criticism lying down. Instead, she fired back a question worth more than all the comments that had been made so far in the session.

"Tell me," she demanded. "Why is it that everyone tells you to write from your experiences, then criticizes you when you do?"

She had a point. Moreover, it is a basic question, a fundamental question. Reiterating fundamentals is as important to developing writing skill as mastering any new technique.

Write from experience. Write what you know. Do such self-evident statements demand explanation? If they lead to *it really happened* criticism—then, yes, they do.

To write *from* experience is not the same as writing *about* your experiences. At the most basic level, we have all experienced a different variety of words. I know words that you do not; you know words that I do not know. I grew up in the marginally southern state of Kentucky, and I speak fluent Hillbilly. I am not familiar enough with Cockney English to try to pull it off on the page.

I have stood in front of a jury and cross-examined witnesses. I have never given birth. I can play several musical instruments, but I cannot draw a recognizable picture of a dog. I believe that I can act, but I am mistaken.

These are the experiences I use to enrich my characters. If my heroine plays the violin, you can bet the strings will appear in the correct position. If she gets herself pregnant, she will have a "difficult labor." I will not try to give a blow-by-blow account.

"Oh?" you ask. "So I can't write science fiction unless I've been on a spacecraft? And just how many people, on the average, do you have to kill to write a mystery story?"

Well, of course you can write science fiction. If you need to describe a shuttle launch, there are plenty of firsthand accounts. Use them. See if the descriptions match anything you *have* experienced. Just be careful not to force it.

Actually, I did stumble across a corpse once, though I was not responsible for the demise of the person. When my character found a body, his reaction was the same as my own:

Priding himself on his composure, Ozro began making his way back to the Castle to phone the police. He was halfway there before he realized that he was running as fast as he could.

I used only that, a reaction. All the other circumstances were different. I did not try to plug my own story into Ozro's life. No one who has read it has criticized me for it. I have never had to say, "It really happened."

But what is so wrong with, "It really happened"? What is wrong with using the events in my life to craft a story?

Maybe nothing. Maybe there are episodes in your life that need only be mildly "fictionalized." Maybe your entire life is so glittering a series of vignettes as to warrant an autobiography. Maybe. For those writers who simply wish to insert the more interesting chapters of their lives into a story, I have found four stumbling blocks, one or more of which will occur when "it really happens":

The first is *improbable coincidence*. Life is full of improbable coincidences. An old friend and mentor told the tale of being mustered out of Korea the day before Christmas Eve. Upon arriving in Seoul, he met an old high school buddy, who put him on the next flight to the Philippines. There, he met *another* old buddy who got him to Hawaii, where he met *another* old buddy who got him to San Francisco. . . .

You get the point. He "old buddied" his way back to Georgia in time for Christmas Eve. Who is going to believe it? Moreover, such a coincidence, if merely related, is simply curious. An author's job is to further the plot, not just relate amusing anecdotes. In advancing that plot, the writer must make it show that it's *essential* that the character arrive home by Christmas Eve. Once the plot is shown to turn on the event, the coincidence becomes not just fortuitous, but completely unbelievable.

To be sure, there are writers who do use improbable coincidence, and use it to great effect. Clive Cussler piles coincidences one on top of the other, until they all become part of a grand, adventurous roller-coaster ride. The reader doesn't think of them as coincidences, and just enjoys the trip. But as the writer you must be deft, confident, and—most of all—aware of what you are doing. Do not throw in a coincidence just because it made an impression on you at the time.

Did I say, "made an impression"? It must have been a segue into what I call *the honeymoon effect.*

My wife and I honeymooned in New Orleans. What a city! What people! Oh, what a great time we had! Well, what do you expect? We were on our honeymoon! Every memory is affected by the event itself. But what was a profound emotional experience for me may not come across as such for the reader.

Should I abandon these experiences, throw them in a sort of literary lock-box, never to be used? No. I like to think of them as photographs, rather than as a videotape. We have all seen those interminable videos Uncle Fewmet took on the trip to Disney World, complete with a shot (and narrative) of the place where Aunt Dewlap got that corndog, and a riveting explanation of what happened to it on Space Mountain. The point is, such films are boring. They ramble; they evoke memories only for the participants, not the viewer. A still photo seeks to capture the moment in one frame. You should try to make words do the same. A single image will serve better than a four-page description. The reader does not need to know every detail of a trip—only that it was fun.

In a worst-case scenario, the writer's emotional memory of an event may simply not mesh with even the most objective recitation of events.

When my first wife left me—listen up, this *really happened*—she did so out of the blue. I came home, no wife. The next day she left a sort of "Dear John" message *on my answering machine.* I was devastated.

A year later, I was watching *Buffy the Vampire Slayer* with the woman I would later marry. At one point, Buffy blurts out incredulously: "You mean you broke up with my *answering machine?!*" We howled. Time had passed. What had been subjectively agonizing was objectively funny.

I do not worry about answering machine breakups these days. That would not be my wife's style. It would be an *incongruous action.*

Sometimes a writer has a wonderful experience that warrants telling, but does not have a character suitable to carry the story effectively. Do not force it. Your personal experience may be as pointless to the plot as it is incongruous to the character. A pointless vignette in the middle of an otherwise logical story does nothing but show a lack of narrative skill. No matter how funny—or sad, or moving, or frightening—an event may be, make sure it is something the character would do, and make sure it advances the plot.

Which brings me to the final pitfall. I call it the *reality defense.* You could also call it *hiding behind your life.*

In this case, the event described will usually be painful. It will also be improbably coincidental, "honeymooned," or incongruous. When challenged, the writer tosses out those three magic words: *It really happened.* By questioning the validity of the writing, is the validity of the writer's life being questioned? Think of the reality defense as a sort of literary guilt trip. Fortunately, there is a two-word response to the reality defense: *So what?* This may sound cruel, but it's not. It is literally "tough love."

Perhaps your writers group wants to bare its collective soul. Sobs will be sobbed. Tears will fall. I think such emotional feeding frenzies are fine! Exorcising the painful parts of your life is wonderful. It is therapeutic, but it will not produce good writing. Do not be afraid to give tough criticism, and do not be upset when it is offered. Do not hide behind your hurt; use the experience to make the reader see that your *character* is hurt.

Remember, when you push your manuscript from the proverbial nest, it must fly on its own. You will not be there to nurture or protect it. You will not be there to defend it. You can't call every potential reader and say, "It really happened."

>> 31

FIVE BEGINNERS' PROBLEMS
AND HOW TO SOLVE THEM

BY MONICA WOOD

FIRST, THE BAD NEWS: DESPITE A DAZZLING VARIETY IN THE STORIES they choose to tell, beginning fiction writers are easy to spot. Their efforts are thwarted by the same problems: inconsistent point of view; wooden dialogue; too many modifiers; autobiography masquerading as fiction; and trick endings. The good news is that once they recognize these problems and learn to solve them, their writing leaps almost instantly to another level. Nothing is more satisfying to any writer, beginning or otherwise, than learning to use new fiction-writing techniques.

One: Inconsistent point of view

Many beginning writers make the wise choice of first person for telling their first stories. The "I" narrator helps to keep a story focused and the narrative consistent. Not all stories work best with an "I" narrator, however, and this is where third person comes in.

Most beginners don't discover the complications of point of view until they begin writing in the third person. When writing in the third person, you have two choices: *omniscient point of view* and *third-person limited consciousness point of view*. Understanding the differences between these points of view will help you gain control over your own writing in a way you never thought possible.

The omniscient narrator is usually all-knowing, letting the reader in on the thoughts and feelings of any or all of the characters. (Look to any fairy tale or nineteenth-century novel for an example.) The omniscient narrator can see what the characters can't see and hear what the characters can't hear:

124

Irritated, Larry stood on the corner wondering what had become of Iris. He adjusted the cuffs of his shirt, as he listened to the gonging of the town clock. Across town, in the confines of her drawing room, the object of Larry's irritation was petting her Siamese cat and humming an aria whose rhythm exactly matched Larry's fretful pacing.

Here we have two characters as seen by one narrator. The omniscient narrator has the authority to set us down on a street corner to look at Larry, and then whisk us uptown to see Iris, all in the space of a paragraph. This is not as easy as it looks. Unless your prose has the pristine consistency of tone that comes with years of writing experience, the omniscient narrative quickly deteriorates into a muddle of shifting viewpoints:

Larry stood on the corner, wondering what was keeping that dratted Iris. Ten minutes late already, but of course she wouldn't bat an eye over a measly ten minutes. Across town, in the confines of her drawing room, the object of Larry's irritation was petting her Siamese cat and humming an aria whose rhythm exactly matched Larry's fretful pacing.
Darn that Iris, Larry thought. Isn't this just like her . . .

In this example, a colloquial tone ("dratted," "bat an eye," "Darn that Iris") jars against a more formal, genteel tone ("In the confines," "object of irritation," "fretful pacing"). This is not an omniscient narrative; this is a narrative that shifts abruptly from Larry's viewpoint to Iris's and back again. In short order, the story will begin to unravel and the hapless reader will be left to wonder who the main character is supposed to be.

One effective technique for avoiding the shifting point of view syndrome is to write the story in a *third person, limited consciousness* point of view. With this technique, the reader is privy to the thoughts and feelings, or consciousness, of only *one* character:

Irritated, Larry stood on the corner, wondering what was keeping Iris. The town clock gonged ten times. Perhaps she had forgotten him—again. Perhaps at this very moment she was ensconced in her drawing room, running an idle hand over the pampered pelt of her Siamese cat.

In this version, we are allowed inside only one character—Larry—which gives the story a consistency that the earlier, shifting version lacked. We see Iris as Larry imagines her, not the way she really is. As a result, the reader will feel more anchored to one character, and

125

the story will seem more focused and polished. At first you might resist the limitations of this technique, but with practice you'll discover its capacity for unifying your narrative and deepening your characterizations. Sticking to one character's viewpoint offers you ample opportunity to explore the complications of his personality, because everything that happens in the story is filtered through his experience.

If you *must* give another character a viewpoint, try alternating point of view in sections—write two or three pages in Larry's viewpoint, leave a couple of blank lines, then start a new section in Iris's viewpoint. You can go back and forth like this if the story is long enough. Most short stories run nine to fifteen pages, however, which doesn't leave much room for two characters' viewpoints.

Two: Wooden dialogue

Writing dialogue is a tricky business, but there are several techniques you may use to avoid having your dialogue sound like a beginner's.

Avoid hellos and goodbyes. Beginners often waste precious pages with the beginnings and endings of conversations. "Hello." "Jack, is that you?" "Yeah, it's me." "Well, what do you want?" This kind of ambling paralyzes the story's forward motion. When the phone rings, skip the pleasantries and get to the point:

Jack picked up the phone. It was Jill, with a song and dance about why she couldn't make it to the ball game.
"You know how Mother is," she said. "I can't leave her for one second."

And when it's time to hang up, dispense with the farewells:

"Mother was fine when you wanted to go to the auction last Saturday," Jack said.
"Are you going to start on me? Don't start on me, Jack."
They went on like this for twenty minutes before hanging up. Jack hauled on his coat and started up the hill.

Similarly, when characters are meeting one another, skip the introductions and get to the real conversation:

Felix ushered me into the room and made some introductions. "You're a *philanthropist*?" a woman in green said to me. "I've never met a philanthropist who was still living."

126

Use contractions. Nothing ruins a line of dialogue like an uncontracted verb. "I *do not* want you to come" sounds stilted, whereas "I *don't* want you to come" sounds natural. Can'ts, don'ts, won'ts, and couldn'ts almost always read better than cannots, do nots, will nots, or could nots.

Don't use dialogue to fill in the plot. Beginners' dialogue often seems staged for the reader's benefit:

"Rachel," Bob called, running to her. "I haven't seen you since your father's computer-graphics company burned down three months ago."

In this line of dialogue, *computer-graphics company* sticks out as unnatural, as does *three months ago.* Rachel already knows what happened, so Bob has no reason to state the obvious. (Besides, he's out of breath from running and couldn't get all those words out in one take anyway!) If you must convey information about the plot, use a combination of dialogue and narrative:

"I haven't seen you since the fire," Bob said. Three months had passed, but he could hear it still, that magnificent popping and sparking, and finally the handmade sign—SINCLAIR COMPUTER GRAPHICS—crashing into a flaming heap on the sidewalk. "How's your father, anyway?"
"You've heard of a man without a country?" Rachel said. "Sometimes I think a man without a company is worse."

Avoid dialogue tags like "he chortled" or "she sneered." Elaborate dialogue tags mark a beginner. A simple "he said" or "she asked" should suffice in most cases.

These techniques take the wooden quality out of dialogue. You might try reading dialogue aloud, to yourself or to a friend, in order to catch trouble spots. If it doesn't sound right, it isn't going to read right.

Three: Autobiography disguised as fiction

Most of us write to share something of ourselves—our outlook, our family history, a personal trauma or triumph, a turning-point event that altered our lives. Sharing and recording our lives is a worthy purpose, and that's what autobiography is for. Unfortunately, many beginners write fiction that is only thinly disguised autobiography. Their "fiction" suffers from the constrictions of real life—if the real character had a Caddy with blue pinstripes and whitewalls, then the

127

car takes up space in the story, whether it's relevant or not. The result is a story that takes forever to begin, because the author spends too much time being accurate.

Good stories require something more than the truth. Real life doesn't have the urgent shape of fiction; it has far too many detours and irrelevancies to make a story by itself. You must alter the truth, often dramatically, in order to make stories. If your storyteller is an "I" narrator who looks like you, thinks like you, and acts like you, then your story is headed for trouble. Narrators are characters, not authors. If you, the author, are skinny, make the narrator stout. If you have a pet dog, give the narrator a pet llama. Once you separate yourself from the narrator, you are free to invent in ways that the "real" story, no matter how interesting in itself, would never allow. This is no time to be faithful! Cheat on the truth; that's how stories are born.

Four: Too many modifiers

Test yourself by going through one of your stories and circling all the adjectives and adverbs (especially those ending in "ly"). You may be surprised at how many there are. Adverbs and adjectives can add luster to your prose, but their overuse can be deadly. Many beginning writers, unsure of their storytelling powers, rely too heavily on modifiers to set a scene or create a character. Ironically, too many modifiers serve to muddy rather than clarify description, as in the following story excerpt:

> Alice deftly sprayed the antique mahogany table and fiercely wiped it down, her first meaningless chore of the muggy August day. The other chores, dashed onto a scrap of bright white monogrammed paper in Mrs. Delano's self-consciously elegant hand, would have to wait. Mrs. Delano liked this handsome table to shine brilliantly. Alice rubbed and rubbed, stopping just short of meeting her own meekly subservient reflection. Wincing, she stood up, put a hand to her permanently aching back and arched like an old, arthritic cat. Her simple blue cotton uniform with the starched white collar had once fit so neatly, but now it pulled slightly at the waist, a sign that she had been in Mrs. Delano's beautiful Tudor-style house much too long.

The author wants to convey a sense of Alice's hopelessness, but the barrage of modifiers is not much help. The most important and telling detail—the too-small uniform—is all but lost in the clutter. Look how much more poignantly you can convey Alice's plight by removing the modifiers and letting the detail shine through:

128

Alice sprayed the table and wiped it down, her first chore of the day. The other chores, dashed onto a scrap of paper in Mrs. Delano's elegant hand, would have to wait. Mrs. Delano liked this table to shine. Alice rubbed and rubbed, stopping just short of meeting her own reflection. Wincing, she stood up, put a hand to her back and arched like a cat. Her uniform strained at the waist, a sign she had been here too long.

Removing modifiers can help you find the story you want to tell. Beginners tend to rely on adjectives and adverbs to do the hard work of description. Don't fall into that trap. Using modifiers is not a short-cut to characterization. Don't be content to tell us that Character A speaks "airily"—give us some airy dialogue instead.

Five: Trick endings

Beginning writers somehow have the idea that a story's ending must be a grand surprise. Stories of the supernatural rely on the element of surprise, of course, as do mystery and suspense stories, but in contemporary, literary fiction, the "trick" or "surprise" ending is a sure mark of a beginner. For example, the narrator turns out to be a pig or a car; the main character puts a gun to his head and fires; the real-estate agent turns out to be the homebuyer's long-lost daughter. Variations on these last-minute strategies occur dismayingly often in first fictions.

One way to test the integrity of an ending is to ask yourself if the resolution comes from within the character or from an outside element. A character who changes his mind, or "comes to realize" or takes Path A over Path B should do so as a result of his own actions, not someone else's. Never allow someone to come in at the last minute to get the character out of a jam. Take the gun from the character's head—now what does he do? He has to solve his problem in some way, doesn't he? If the real-estate agent and the homebuyer are not long-lost mother and daughter, then something else (something more interesting) must be binding them. Surprise or trick endings let the writer off far too easily. Stories that come to rest as a result of the characters' own motivations and behavior are the hardest to write but the most sat-isfying to read.

If you recognize your own writing in some or all of these examples, do not despair. Addressing yourself to the task of solving these com-mon problems means you are no longer a beginner!

>> 32

How Hobbies Shape Your Characters

By Fraser Sherman

What do your characters do when they're not saving the world, winning the girl, exploring new planets or resolving personal crises? Have you the slightest idea?

You should; the best fictional characters have lives that go on even when we're not reading about them. Rex Stout fans know detective Nero Wolfe spends his time between books growing orchids; Robert Parker's Spenser boxes and cooks gourmet meals; the *Enterprise's* Captain Picard reads Shakespeare and detective thrillers. They aren't "just killing time," they're making themselves more believable.

Giving characters hobbies can do a lot more than just flesh out their lives: Hobbies can enhance characterization, give your books a colorful, intriguing background, spark plots, and even symbolize your theme. Whether your characters' passions are ballet, fine jade, or collecting a complete set of Happy Meal toys, giving them a hobby can make a better, more salable story.

Characterization

Characters' hobbies don't automatically give them a personality. Nero Wolfe grew orchids, but so can CEOs and axe murderers; Hannibal Lector liked a good chianti, but you could also write about a living saint who knows her wine. Hobbies can, however, *show* personality by the way your characters approach their pastimes.

Suppose your protagonist is a chess player. Does he overwhelm his opponents with aggressive play, or cautiously wait for them to make a fatal mistake? Does he use bizarre gambits to make people laugh, or because he's arrogantly convinced he can win with any handicap? If the game goes against the character, will he give in too soon? Sulk? Knock the board over?

Showing characteristics in a small matter like chess makes the big matters believable. Once readers see your hero move his pieces without thinking, they'll accept his acting recklessly even when doing so threatens his marriage, his career, or his efforts to infiltrate the militia movement. ("Talk about a bad decision—but that's the kind of thing he does, isn't it?")

On television, Murphy Brown's fondness for classic rock reminds viewers that she's a staunchly liberal child of the sixties, an attitude that's affected events in many episodes. In print, Raymond Chandler's Philip Marlowe puzzles out chess problems between solving crimes; this shows not only his intelligence but the isolation—he plays alone, rather than against a human opponent—that's so much a part of his character.

Revelation

Hobbies can also bring out traits hidden from everyone else in your story (and perhaps from your readers). You've presented your hero's antagonist as a bitter, workaholic CEO who collects classic comic books as an investment, but then you show him rereading them endlessly every weekend, the one pleasure left in his life. This can turn him from a one-dimensional creep to a tragic figure (he hates who he is, but can't figure out how to change), or can foreshadow his eventual redemption when he rejects the man he has become.

Developing a character in this way requires careful work. Readers may accept inconsistent behavior in real life, but in fiction, people are supposed to make sense. If you want your readers to believe that the comic-reading dreamer and the pitiless executive coexist in the same person, you have to show them enough of how the man thinks to make him believable.

Anne Rice does this well in *Vampire Lestat*, when her title hero decides to take up rock-and-roll. It seems like a complete departure from Lestat's sinister ways in *Interview With a Vampire*, but Rice uses Lestat's new hobby to explore his character, showing us his arrogance and his eagerness to thumb his nose at convention. By the end of the novel, the author has shown how Lestat's arrogant wit is the key to all the sides of his personality.

Tags

Not every role in a story should get the same amount of attention. For minor walk-on characters, often all you need is a "tag," a trait that makes them distinctive enough for readers to remember. It's particularly useful if you have such traits show up more than once, so your readers won't wonder, "Who?"

Hobbies make a good tag. A husband who tapdances, a best friend who takes part in Civil War reenactments, a police informer who collects Beatles memorabilia—their hobbies help make them memorable, even if you don't delve deeply into their character.

If you want your minor character to serve as comic relief, a break in an otherwise serious story, make the tag a truly outrageous hobby. For instance, nobody takes an Elvis impersonator seriously.

Mood

Just as hobbies can set the tone of a comic-relief character, they can help set the tone for your novel. In Lawrence Block's *The Thief Who Couldn't Sleep* and its sequels, Evan Tanner belongs to the Flat Earth Society; to a group for the restoration of the Stuarts to the English throne; and to several other crackpot or fringe organizations. Once readers know he's such a flake, they won't take his tongue-in-cheek adventures seriously.

Background and setting

Good fiction can take your readers into worlds where they've never been and probably never will go—and that includes the worlds of different hobbyists. John Dunning's mysteries, *The Bookman's Wake* and *Booked to Die,* take place in the world of rare-book collecting. And several children's series have hooked horse-loving young girls with stories about riding academies and horse clubs.

Even if a hobby doesn't take center stage, it can give readers a feel for your setting. Mrs. Madrigal's hobby of pot-growing helps Armistead Maupin capture the laid-back mood of mid-seventies San Francisco in his *Tales of the City*; gladiatorial combat in the movie epic *Spartacus* shows Rome's arrogance and callousness toward slaves.

If you do make a hobby a key part of your story's background, remember to "write what you know"—or at least what you can research. If you have no idea what a grandmaster chess rating means, or how to store old comic books, or how to trace a family tree, find out before you use them in your story.

In science fiction and fantasy, the world you create will often be truly alien to your readers. Hobbies can help give them a feel for it.

Larry Niven's "Dream Park" series centers on a holographic Dungeons-and-Dragons-style game; Piers Anthony's *Blue Adept* gives us "the Game," an elaborate, Olympic-scale competition on the planet Proton. Watching the books' heroes play, readers learn about these characters, their world, its culture, and technology. They also have a good time—both games are colorful, imaginative creations.

Plotting

Let's say your protagonist is in a neo-Nazi fortress, and you can't figure out how to make her escape believable. One possible solution is to give her a hobby, such as martial arts, weight-lifting, computer-hacking, or any other skill she may need.

Consider the movie *Psycho*: Few men, however crazy, would know how to stuff and preserve their mother's corpse, but early on, the movie establishes that Norman Bates is a skilled taxidermist. Or consider Richard Connell's classic, *The Most Dangerous Game*: The hero's skill as a world-class hunter is what keeps him alive when the murderous hunter General Zaroff chooses the hero as his latest quarry.

Zaroff's obsession with hunting also shows how hobbies can provide motivation: What drives a character can shape or start a plot, no matter what genre you work in. In a number of mystery novels, for instance, the killer/thief/blackmailer is motivated by his love for stamps, rare coins, or books—like the autographed Kipling manuscript that triggers murder and theft in Lawrence Block's *The Burglar Who Liked to Quote Kipling*. Likewise, Jonathan Gash's detective/antique dealer Lovejoy solves (and occasionally perpetrates) shady dealings involving antiques.

How about romances? In Amanda Quick's best-selling historical romance, *Mistress,* the hero is a brilliant amateur scientist; he falls in love with the heroine when she talks knowledgeably about his research and tells him it's his mind, not his wealth or looks, that attracts her.

Fantasy? I'm writing one about a woman who gains superhuman powers, but, initially, I couldn't decide what she'd do with them. When I made her a comic-book fan, her motivation and goals became obvious: She'd live out her childhood fantasies as a crime fighter, like Wonder Woman and Batgirl.

Theme and metaphor

In Theodore Sturgeon's award-winning *Slow Sculpture,* a scientist's passion for bonsai becomes more than a character trait. Embittered and cynical about the possibility of human improvement, the scientist finally realizes that to improve society he has to shape it gently, the same way he sculpts his tiny trees. Bonsai symbolizes the story's theme.

Alas, Babylon, by Pat Frank, uses keeping tropical fish to create a metaphor. With electric power gone after a nuclear war, the fish-keeper can't keep the tank hot enough for the more delicate fish, but the hardy guppies survive. The protagonist takes it as a reminder: To survive in the ruined world, he and his friends will have to be strong, determined and tough.

If you use a hobby thematically, don't confuse personal feelings with symbolism. You may think of hunters as sadistic, but your readers may think of them as men who love the outdoors, or guys engaged in male bonding. Show what your hunter symbolizes either by stating the theme explicitly (Sturgeon spelled his bonsai metaphor out) or implicitly (parallel the hunter's kill with a drive-by shooting).

Making the most of hobbies

I've found it useful to keep a list of hobbies (sailing, rose-growing, bee-keeping, juggling, etc.) so that if I'm stuck figuring out how my characters spend their spare time, I have a source for ideas. I may look for a hobby that *fits* their personality, or use a hobby to *determine* their personality. In the fantasy I'm writing, I had a much clearer image of my hero's best friend after I made her a self-published poet.

Whether you create jazz musicians, UFO-watchers, or quilt-makers, your novel will be the better for the hobbies you choose.

134

>> 33

WHAT EVERY GOOD STORY NEEDS: URGENCY

BY SHERRI SZEMAN

IF I HADN'T FALLEN OFF THE MOUNTAIN, I NEVER WOULD HAVE BE-lieved it. Actually, I did believe it before I fell off the mountain, but the first sentence of this article is an example of what writers need to have in their fiction in order to have vibrant, intriguing, publishable work: URGENCY. When a piece of fiction has urgency, the reader can't wait to keep reading. He doesn't want to eat dinner or do the dishes or even go to sleep! All he wants to do is read! All writers can learn to put urgency in their work, improving it and making it more publishable.

Before the twentieth century, not many writers worried about keep-ing their readers' attention, so urgency was not a question writers necessarily had to deal with. Now, however, writers are competing with television, videos, and movies for their audiences, so their task is more challenging than their predecessors'. Urgency cannot be "pasted on" or simply attached to the piece of writing. It must be an integral part of it, inseparable from the plot or the characters. It is urgency that will keep the readers clamoring for more, so it must be honest urgency, that is, it must evolve naturally from the characters, the plot, and the circumstances of the short story or the novel you are writing.

Take, for example, the first paragraph of my novel *The Komman-dant's Mistress,* the story of a Nazi commander of a concentration camp who forces a Jewish inmate to be his mistress during the war. Part One of the novel is narrated by the Kommandant, while Part Two is narrated by the girl, Rachel. Not only does the opening sentence present urgency, but other sentences of that paragraph reinforce that initial urgency. I've italicized these sentences for emphasis:

Then I saw her. There she stood, in the village store, her hair in a long braid down the center of her back, her skin white in the sunlight, and *my hand went*

135

to my hip, seeking the weight of my gun. As the girl spoke, I stumbled back against one of the shelves, my fingers tightening at the leather around my waist. While the shopkeeper arranged the food in the bag, the morning sun glinted on the storefront windows, illuminating the girl. The wooden shelves pressed into my shoulder and back. *Sweat dampened my forehead and ribs.* Another shopper spoke, frowned, pushed aside my arm to reach a jar on the shelf behind me, *but I didn't move. My hand slid down over my hip and leg. No, I'd forgotten that I no longer wore my gun.*

The reader now wonders: Who is this girl, and why is this man looking for her? Why did he have a gun, and why does he want to shoot her? What's happened between them that he seems afraid to confront her? And, finally, what happened that he no longer wears his gun?

Urgency must be maintained throughout the piece of fiction to be effective, however. It doesn't keep your readers' attention if you present them with urgency in the opening sentence and paragraph, but then lapse into long-winded, overblown scenic descriptions. If it takes your readers 50 pages before they come to the next instance of urgency, you'll lose them before they get to it. For urgency to be effectively maintained, it must be integral to the plot or to the character. In *The Kommandant's Mistress,* for example, after the war, the Kommandant is intent on finding the girl (for reasons which he does not reveal) before he is arrested and tried for war crimes. Though at various times he spots the girl for whom he searches, he is not courageous enough or physically near enough to confront her, while at the same time being pursued and sometimes ambushed by the men who are chasing him so that they can bring him to trial. Thus, the Kommandant is desperate to find the girl before his pursuers find him, so that he can give his version of what happened before he is executed for his war crimes. These two levels of urgency keep the reader turning pages. (In fact, when I was on tour and met some of my readers, they "complained" to me that my book kept them awake all night because they "couldn't put it down.")

In Part Two of *The Kommandant's Mistress,* when Rachel gives her version of the events, the urgency is different, though related to the urgency in Part One. Rachel constantly thinks she sees the Kommandant, and, naturally fearing him, she keeps moving in order to avoid him. Her husband David has had enough of this constant moving and is threatening divorce, unless she becomes less "obsessed" with the

136

Kommandant. Rachel, therefore, needs to deal with her experience in the camps before it destroys her relationship with her husband and, some might say, before it destroys her own sanity. Here is a passage from her version which illustrates the urgency (once again, I have italicized the pertinent passages):

Now it was quiet, and *I didn't hear the noise that had woken me.* I went to the front door; yes, it was locked. I moved the curtains.
The car was there again.
I raced upstairs, my heart pounding. I yanked open the bottom dresser drawer and *grabbed the pistol.* It was already loaded. *It was always loaded.* I readied it for firing as I rushed back down the stairs, to the window beside the front door. Breathing heavily, I pushed the curtains aside.
The car was gone.
After an hour I went upstairs, pulled a blanket from the cupboard, and *returned to my post* by the front door. I sat there, my face next to the glass, my hands tense around the gun.
The car did not come back that night.
The gun and I did not sleep.

Urgency moves the Kommandant and Rachel through their respective stories. It gives them a "reason" for telling their stories; it also gives the reader a reason for reading them.

I didn't always use urgency in my writing, and I don't think it's a coincidence that before *The Kommandant's Mistress,* which was when I first became aware of the concept of urgency, my fiction was constantly rejected, sometimes with the criticism to eliminate the "dry descriptive passages" and to "get on with the story." After I realized that these criticized passages didn't contain urgency, I eliminated them. Now I use this technique in all my fiction, and whether or not they call it "urgency," so do other successful writers. Here are some opening lines from some of my stories to give you an idea of the different ways you can impart urgency. Notice that your titles can also be used to develop urgency effectively:

In the beginning, God created Nebraska, and boy, did he make a mistake. ("Dismal, Nebraska")

The day I learned to fly, I was three years old. ("Learning to Fly")

When I was seven years old, the rock on which the Church had stood for almost two thousand years trembled, collapsed, and crumbled into dust. ("Dancing for the Blind")

137

We weren't always living in the Ice Age, Eddie and me. ("Love in the Time of Dinosaurs")

It's true, I admit it: I'm a freak. ("Hunchback of the Midwest")

This is how the plan to kill your husband could begin. ("Naked, With Glasses")

Open any book of award-winning short stories, and you'll find the same thing: urgency in the opening sentence that compels the reader to continue reading:

I'm not trying to flatter myself, but I was the first colored woman he ever seriously considered loving. (Kathleen Collins' "Stepping Back")

I am not a lucky traveler. (C. W. Guswelle's "Horst Wessel")

Later we will tell how we happen to be here in the first class lounge of the *United States,* but for the time being: there are three of us, and we are, incredibly, the only persons seated in a space that is at least fifteen meters wide and perhaps twenty-five meters long. (Robley Wilson, Jr.'s "The United States")

The woman who can't dance moves in with the Arthur Murray Studios dance instructor. (Mary Peterson's "To Dance")

As to Caesar's health, there seems to me no cause for alarm. (John Gardner's "Julius Caesar and the Werewolf")

She had kept the bottle stuck down inside a basket of clothes that needed ironing, and throughout the course of the day whenever she had a chance to walk through the back room where the basket was kept, she would stop for the odd sip or two. (Gerald Duff's "Fire Ants")

The examples of urgency in quality published fiction are endless. Some writers call it by different names; John Jakes, for example, calls this element "intrigue," but the concept is the same. As you write, you should ask yourself questions such as these: "Where's the urgency in this chapter?" "Why does this character have to tell his story now?" or "When's the last time I put some urgency in here?" Last year, just as an experiment, I gave my freshman composition students the traditional first-person story assignment, but told them they had to include urgency. I simply told them that the first sentence, the first paragraph, and various sentences or paragraphs throughout the narrative had to make me keep reading. In class, I made them all write the first sentence of a proposed story, which, of course, they were allowed to change when they wrote their real stories. Most of the sentences were similar, but all showed a grasp of the concept:

By the time the gun went off, it was too late.

He tried to warn his brother, but he'd already grabbed the gun and headed out the door.

When I saw Stephen with that girl, I knew exactly what I had to do.

I might have spent the rest of my life in jail if it hadn't been for that one night.

For the actual assignment, the students not only turned their practice sentences into real opening sentences with wonderful urgency, they managed to keep the urgency through their entire narratives.

If beginners can so easily impart urgency to their narratives, then it should be an even simpler task for creative writers, published or not. Urgency is one of the most vital things new writers need to learn. Without it, your fiction is likely to put readers to sleep; even worse, after reading the first sentence, readers may never even buy your novel. Notice how many people browsing in a bookstore pick up a book and read the opening before they decide to buy it, and how many of those books get put back on the shelves. It's a good exercise for writers at all levels: Go to the bookstore and spend an hour or so reading the opening lines in novels. How many of them impart urgency? How many keep you turning pages, right there in the bookstore? How many do you buy so that you can finish reading? If a work of fiction can't pass the urgency test, it isn't very likely to have either a large or an enthusiastic audience. Never assume you have a captive audience: You don't. As a writer, you have to earn your audience. Whether you want to write bestsellers or masterpieces (or both), the best way to attract an audience and to keep it is through urgency.

>> 34

TELLING DETAILS

BY MARCIE HERSHMAN

WRITERS, BY NATURE, LOVE DETAILS. THERE'S SOME PART OF US that's gotten trained to notice and hold on to them, even in the midst of our own personal tumult. *This detail,* we might say to ourselves upon entering a room, *this fact of X's eyelids lowering, and her slow, seemingly casual half-turn away as I walk through the doorway, unannounced, means she's ashamed by what she did last month to me. This slight flutter of her pale eyelids—yes; the half-turn of her torso, begun with a twitch of the narrow shoulders—yes.* In times when we later need a boost, we might call up the particulars of X's apparent embarrassment to give ourselves the energy to explore some other feeling we have, as yet inexplicable. Or perhaps we summon these details in order to begin moving in a new direction, to push ourselves more confidently along a path that will lead us to the next necessary interaction.

In professional terms, we also hold on to and use details in our work. Sometimes we hold on to one or another of the darn things for years. The process might start when we're working on an early draft of a story or chapter—and we "discover" the detail in the attempt to show the sudden lurch in our main character's gait, say, at the moment he spies his ex-wife coming toward him as they cross the same busy street. In our second pass at the story, however, we realize that as brilliantly put as the descriptive detail about Mr. XX's physical stride originally seemed, it's no longer right for his emotional stride—now that we've finished the story and have come to understand XX in all his complexity. So, we edit. The detail that struck us in the first run-through is itself struck: Out it goes.

Only trouble is, it doesn't leave, not all the way. It might be excised from the page, but it's taken up a whispering residency in our mind.

140

If, out of weakness or love, we try to reinsert it into the same story, it will make only a semi-honest fit. Why? Because it's a bit of rhetoric now, just bunched-up words, empty as the jacket some stranger threw onto our doorstep on a day grown too warm for its use or comfort. Again, the editing pencil comes out.

Denied a place to lodge, this detail might float back into view at odd moments. "A sudden hitch in an effortlessly long, loose-legged gait" might be exactly what we need to have in another tale—the one we haven't written yet. It might serve as the grain of sand that irritates our literary imagination long enough so that thin layers of gleaming substance adhere to it. The sand that makes the pearl; the pearl that makes the story.

Well and truly used, a detail is indissoluble.

But.

But of course I've been going on here about a certain kind of detail. The *telling* detail. One of that company of absolutely select particulars that possesses not only enough self-assurance to reward both writer and reader with a further insight into a character, but also enough physical reality to push that person a bit farther along in the outside world. In other words, the telling detail is versatile; it can speak to both theme and plot. It reveals a sly, inward-gazing intentionality (character and theme) in addition to a more public purpose (action and plot).

The telling detail is the essential detail. It wastes nothing. It is crucial, rather than self-important. Instead of just filling up space on the page, it takes what might seem *plausible* and hammers it down as *inevitable*.

I'd like to illustrate this with the first sentence from a short story by the writer, Lynne Sharon Schwartz. "Mrs. Saunders Writes to the World" (1978) was among the first stories Schwartz published. Even at this early stage in her career, Schwartz exercised great selectivity in her details.

You need to know the plot that follows to understand how *telling* the details are. "Mrs. Saunders Writes to the World" concerns a widow who longs to hear someone call her by her first name; but those who would have been intimate enough to do so have died or moved away, and the young people in her apartment complex don't think to ask. Mrs. Saunders is from a generation "too polite" to make any such direct request. What happens after that? She takes to spray painting

141

her name on the sly. Her name, as graffiti, appears all over the building; but, of course everyone assumes it's the work of a youngster, until. . . .

But back to the lead sentence:

> Mrs. Saunders placed her white plastic bag of garbage in one of the cans behind the row of garden apartments and looked about for a familiar face, but finding nothing except two unknown toddlers in the playground a short distance off, she shrugged, gazed briefly into the wan early spring sun, and climbed the stairs back to her own door.

Now that you, too, have the writer's advantage of knowing the sweep of the plot, you can see how each seemingly casual action speaks to the work as a whole. Since Mrs. Saunders will feel discarded in life, Schwartz shows it first by having her disposing of inessentials—trash. Since she will remain outside of reciprocal friendships, here she sees "toddlers"—those who are not only unequal to her but are also "unknown"—that is, unnamed. And "having a name" will prove to be Franny Saunders' central struggle. The sentence ends with a climb "back to her own door." In fact, she shuts both a real and a metaphorical "door" seventeen pages later.

All this—*told* in the first sentence. It's a sentence that most likely got reworked once the story was completed. After all, an author can make a character do anything in the world. Mrs. Saunders could have been introduced singing in the shower; she could have been watching TV. But Schwartz searched for the best details. Without giving the story away, she subtly gave it shape, with each and every word.

There are those who argue you can't write solely with *telling* details. More often you need—they assert—common detail.

Well, sometimes you do need the merely factual common detail. But sometimes comes, in my experience as a writer of literary fiction, rarely.

Here's a way to explore this argument. You may have noticed how writers-in-training often begin a story with a character's eyes opening from sleep to focus on the numbers on the alarm clock. The next sentence says that it's eight-fifteen, one-twenty-six, or five o'clock, precisely. A common use of common details.

Can a writer forgo using these blandly efficient numbers about time of day, and instead use *telling* details to speak more to the internal and external action of the story, right off the bat? Also, is it possible to avoid the usual next part of the problem—where the writer takes up the better part of the same page to get her character, XXX, over to a bathroom mirror, in order to give the reader an accurate description of XXX's face?

Since we know that most people leave bed in the morning and trudge over to the bathroom, the choice this writer has made just to use common details (clock numerals, bathroom mirror) yields for the reader the picture of a generic person, rather than a unique, specific individual—a character already caught, let's say, in the middle of some unique situation. The unique situation? Well, that's surely the start of the story-to-come. So, even from the first moment, the *telling* detail—the non-generic or non-common detail—will hold more potential.

Let me offer now some of my own ways of addressing the above technical challenges. The next two paragraphs are taken from the beginning of my novel, *Safe in America,* and focus the reader on a main character, Evan Eichenbaum:

First, his left arm stiffened, though he hadn't been sleeping on it, at least not that he knew; he'd awakened on his back. Slowly, he raised the bare arm above his head. No pain, just the cool air bathing it. Second, he began kneading the area that didn't hurt, his neck and shoulder. As he worked these muscles over hard, the few hairs on the back of his hand caught the low light in the room. The day had only just started; the creamy slats of the venetian blinds were edged pink. Evan was then sixty-seven years old, and of course he knew what to do with his own body's aches and pains. Third, lowering his arm, he slipped his hand just under the sheet, where the best heat was trapped.

Vera was sleeping on her stomach. When he ran his fingers along her spine, the silky nightgown rippled. By habit she turned toward him, eyes still closed, and sighed. She didn't yet know that during the night mostly everything had unraveled. The tiny crossed swords of her black bobby pins had slipped from the curls she'd hoped to keep coiled; a piece of the tissue paper wadded to support the waves of her hairdo now beat loosely against the pulse in her neck. Her disarray and abandon were full of trust. He watched her, breathing. He cuddled into her and could smell part of the secret between them: the warm skin on her neck, the beautiful Vera-is-here perfume. How long did he stay like that? Fourth, his chest tightened with a fierce warmth. It was true, nothing hurt him.

These two paragraphs are paced not by a clock, but by a man's movements, as he tries to determine what has awakened him. From the start, we understand something is not quite right with Evan because he slowly raises one bare arm into the cool air, as if seeking some kind of relief; we see him kneading the muscles, quietly, gingerly. These are details that tell something about him (how methodical he is, how cautious) and they're details that foretell, too: There's a heart attack to come.

Yet even when the focus isn't on Evan, but on his sleeping wife, Vera, the details in her description underscore our uneasiness. Take the detail of the "tiny crossed swords" and supporting tissue paper, all coming undone in Vera's hairdo—the point being made that despite the care being taken, "during the night mostly everything had unraveled." Telling details, and foretelling, too. They give us insight into the characters' personalities, and make Vera and Evan particular individuals; they also move the action along in the current situation, and hint of the situation to come.

Finally, let's go back and address the first problem, that of the alarm clock. Which sentence of the following is more telling in terms of establishing that Evan has awakened in early morning? "The numerals of the clock read: 5:23"; or: "The creamy slats of the venetian blinds were edged pink." My decision when rewriting was to cut the former and keep only the latter. Why? Because with the blinds' slats limned with dawn, the reader enters the sleeping couple's room, and gets not only a sense of its decor, but an awareness, too, of the world outside as it fills with the quivering color signaling the start of a process that is large, quiet, natural, unstoppable.

My hope is that these two paragraphs yield more than what I can take up the space here to explain. But that's what using details—carefully chosen, essential, versatile, telling details—can do: give us a vivid sense of the larger picture.

The truth is: In terms of our writing, we must not only be drawn to details, we must sweat them.

>> 35

WHEN REAL LIFE IS TOO REAL FOR FICTION

BY ALYCE MILLER

"HAVE I GOT A STORY FOR YOU!" SAYS THE PERSON I'VE JUST MET. "Tell me what you think. You can write it if you want to. Or maybe some day I'll write it down, and it will be a best seller."

There are numerous myths about fiction writing, and one of the most commonly heard is that writing is the act of transcribing events found in real life. If a real-life story is interesting, the thinking goes, then just imagine how amazing it will be as a story!

Oddly, the opposite is often true. While writers frequently borrow from "real-life" events, they work in the realm of imagination, piecing and patching and inventing. Their primary tool is language; in other words, how something is said, or what Flaubert called *le mot juste* (the right word). They have choices about the order of telling, not being bound by journalistic notions of chronology or time. A story can be set in the present, even if it took place thirty years ago, as long as it includes convincing details. Writers are free to change locations, adapt the idea to other environments, introduce other plot points, etc. A death by cancer in real life may be transformed into a heart attack. A small town in New York may become a medium-sized city in Ohio. A vacation to Hawaii may become a business trip to Indonesia. The resulting story may feel more like a collage of the real and the imagined, and characters may end up being composites or entirely made up.

This freedom to allow the story to breathe and unfold on its own terms is at the very heart of fiction. To write "real life" exactly as it happened can be limiting, even boring. Coincidences in real life may not play out as believable in fiction. "But," says the beginning writer, defending her story about a close friendship with a new neighbor, "my neighbor and I really were born on the same day, and our two children

145

really do have the same first names. And we both grew up in Colorado and married computer scientists."

While all this may be true in real life, it may translate as "unrealistic" in fiction, unless it is written as satire or parody. Often coincidence in real life is used instead of the details required by fiction. In this case, the similarities between the two women's lives should not be a substitute for the development of their friendship.

Much experience is felt through the senses, and it is often sensory detail that helps fiction writers get at the truth. Marcel Proust, of course, is a marvelous example, reconstructing as he does ordinary childhood events through the use of powerful sensory details. Assuming that readers have had the same experiences in real life can make a writer lazy and unwilling to particularize the experience she is writing. Take an emotional real-life event, the death of a loved one. Many beginning writers, when describing it in fiction, will fall into the trap of assuming, say, that the reader will automatically share her sorrow. But this is not true. If a person standing face to face with you says, "I lost my child in a tragic accident," that can be a very powerful moment. Through physical proximity, you as the listener can perceive inflection, body language, and facial expressions that particularize and personalize that moment. But look how flat that same emotionally charged moment could go on the page:

My friend Mary burst into tears when she said, "I lost my son in a tragic accident." I couldn't believe my ears. I felt so bad for her. Tears rolled down my face as I reached out to comfort her.

The expression of the emotion may be truthful, but it will not move the reader. The reader is given a fairly generic and predictable description of sadness (feeling bad, tears rolling down the face, reaching out to comfort) inherent in an undeniably sad event. How could that same event be rendered through the use of texture and detail, and even subtlety? This is where the transformation into fiction takes place. What if the same moment were rewritten like this?

Mary turned away from me and toward the open window beyond which her niece was playing on the tree swing out in the green yard. It was difficult at first to hear her words, but when I did I was struck by the flatness of her tone. "I lost my son in a car crash. It happened five years ago." From the open

146

window came the delighted shrieks of the niece. Mary cleared her throat. "I don't really like to talk about it," and she closed the window.

Several more dimensions have been added to this scene. The presence of the very-alive niece enjoying life serves as a counterpoint to Mary's sorrow. The reader begins to get a clearer picture of Mary, a woman torn apart by grief, who remains very self-contained. Her gesture of closing the window indicates she is shutting out the joyful sounds of her niece at play because, presumably, they remind her at the moment of her dead son.

A real-life event is transformed to follow its own set of truths. And this brings me to a very important point. Of course writers always take ideas from real life, but it is generally the powers of observation that they bring to bear on their writing, and not the stories themselves. Very little in real life is lost on writers. The world is made up of images and words, and even the most mundane and trivial moments interest writers, because the best writers pay attention to everything. It might be the argument they overhear on a New York subway or the weeping of a child at the end of a school hallway that engenders a story idea. It might be a photograph or a piece of music or something as seemingly negligible as a piece of paper blowing in a gutter.

But those finely honed powers of observation allow the writer to imagine Mary turning away and closing the window. By downplaying the emotion and allowing the careful accumulation of details to speak for themselves, the writer focuses not on "a portrayal of grief," but specifically on "Mary's grief."

The move from real life to fiction involves particularization and intense looking. Remember, you can't follow your doubtful reader around and periodically tap him on the shoulder and say, "But it really happened that way."

Another problem with "true stories" is that they are often either overly complicated or too event-filled. For example, in real life I know three sisters who have led lives that really do bring new meaning to the word "unbelievable." A short list includes kidnapping, murder, bank robbery, incest, infidelity, prison sentences, alcoholism, drug abuse, etc. And that's only a start. Needless to say, their lives have been fodder for lots of local gossip in my home town. But as fiction, all the events of their lives would stretch any reader's credibility. Because those events are so overwhelming and emotionally charged, it would be too easy for the writer to overlook the subtleties, and rely solely on transcribing a litany of traumas. For example, the older sister's self-destruction by alcoholism could in and of itself be a story. The youngest sister's incarceration for murder and the birth of her third child—fathered by a prison guard—in the prison hospital could make a novel.

The point of good fiction is not merely to shock or titillate: It is often a means for accessing and assessing the world by another set of truths.

This is one of the major distinctions between journalism and fiction: Journalism relies on verifiable facts. Fiction sets its own terms and devises its own truths. We've all read real-life profiles and scandals that are entertaining and intriguing, and frequently the more preposterous real life is the more we enjoy its improbabilities.

"I don't believe it!" we love to say when we read an article in the newspaper, amused or outraged by some twist on human behavior. In fiction, though, the reader is not satisfied simply with facts.

So often my beginning writing students start off on their first story with great assurance. "I'm going to write a story about all the times my parents were down in Mexico, and I was left behind with my crazy aunt. I mean, she was so nutty, you won't believe the weird things she did. I always knew I'd have to put her in a story." Several pages later the story begins to run out of steam. The writer is so focused on telling things exactly as they happened that she forgets the flexibility available in fiction. The aunt's antics become episodic and anecdotal, as in "first she did this, then that." The story gets flatter and flatter, the more examples there are of "see how crazy my aunt was." Soon that's all the story is.

Let's take a look at the premise for this story. It's certainly an intriguing idea. For starters, let's say that in reality the parents have gone off to Mexico five times and left the young girl all five times with her crazy aunt; reading about each episode would become repetitive. The writer has the option of compressing time, perhaps setting the story during only one of the parents' absences, and maybe covering only a week instead of months so the story can be more focused. Let's say in real life the girl was in her late teens. The writer might decide that thirteen would be a more interesting age for the girl to develop a relationship with the crazy aunt. The girl would be less judgmental at thirteen, maybe more willing to go along with the aunt's antics. Perhaps in real life the aunt was a religious fanatic who prayed over the girl night and day. The writer might recognize the difficulties of portraying such extremes without falling into clichés (after all, this has been done so much), and so develops less predictable passions in the aunt. Maybe the aunt makes her own beer in the cellar and wants the girl to help her sell it. Or does the aunt go out and play her violin in the subway while the girl sings? In other words, rather than starting a story with a finished idea in mind, the writer begins to depart from the "truth of real life" and explores avenues of invention that perhaps reveal the aunt in a new way.

I often talk to my students about the "shape" of their stories, the way a sculptor might consider a piece of wood or stone. Where does the light fall? What angles are exposed? Where does the eye naturally want to travel? It is the same with making a story. If you force a story to fit certain expectations, driving it rapidly toward a pre-set conclusion taken from real life, it could easily go limp.

There is no question that fiction is transformative. Stories develop in the writer's imagination, but their invention, while drawing on memory and fragments of real life, is never fixed or static. Often the story will begin to shape itself, to begin to go in unexpected directions. This is one of the most exciting things about writing fiction: the sense of discovery.

Another difficulty in transcribing "true stories" onto the page is the writer's tendency to control, because he or she already knows how events turned out. So often I hear beginning writers say, "I'm going to write a story about my sister and how her boyfriend went out with her best friend and when my sister found out she was so mad, she let the air out of his tires so he was stuck. Then she broke up with him, and three weeks later she married this guy who is really rich."

The problem with this kind of certainty in beginning a story is that it leaves the writer nowhere to go: The ending, so to speak, is already written. The story, if it unfolds as the teller has suggested it might, runs the risk of being episodic, as in "First she did this, and then she did that." There may not be enough attention paid to character development and scene and dialogue.

In addition, it would seem that the writer has already decided from whose point of view the story will be told—probably the sister's. What if the story were told from the point of view of the best friend? Or the boyfriend? Or the younger sister? Or an invented narrator, like a neighbor or a brother?

If the story is already "written," the writer would find herself restricted. And frequently, when the story is based on real-life events, the writer uses her own point of view. This makes it more difficult to develop any kind of psychic distance or irony, and the story may end up as a preachy, single-voiced rationalization. To avoid that you may try to let another character tell the story.

Another approach to "true stories" might be to abandon all but the barest premise. Try distilling the idea to "My sister's boyfriend once went out with her best friend." From there, where do events go? How are the characters developed? What has happened before? What if the boyfriend is unlikable or lies about the incident? What about the parents? What other family dynamics might be at work? As quickly as possible, move into your imagination to let the story unfold itself. There may actually be another, more interesting story that you come up with along the way. The business with the boyfriend may end up being secondary, or it may disappear altogether.

Keep in mind that there really are "no new stories," only variations on themes, so the trick to fiction writing is not just to come up with a good plot. *Romeo and Juliet* is a love story, and so is D. H. Lawrence's "The Horse Dealer's Daughter." So are Yukio Mishima's "Patriotism," Marguerite Duras' *The Lover,* and James Joyce's novella *The Dead.* Given such variety, one realizes that "love story" tells us very little about these works, because while that might have been the starting premise, all of them are about other things as well. It is their execution, the form they take, the style, the point of view, the rich details that make them so specific, while enlarging the vision of the world they describe. In other words, their telling comes from the writers' imagination and speaks to universal concerns.

A question I'm repeatedly asked is, "Did those things in your book really happen to you? Do you really know people like the characters in your stories?" I have two responses, "yes" and "no," but never one or the other.

What I mean is that the characters and events that develop in my imagination are both drawn from real life and made up. Writers come

150

at the truth from one angle, then they weave in a little of this and a little of that.

At what point does real life stop and fiction begin? There is no clear boundary. Fiction writers are travelers. They cross back and forth over the border, collecting, selecting, arranging, and transforming.

➤➤ 36

PLOTTING YOUR NOVEL

BY M. K. LORENS

I'VE ALWAYS SUSPECTED THAT THE OLD DICTUM "WRITE WHAT YOU know" would be far better expressed as "Know what you write."

Maybe you're one of those disgustingly organized writers who works out plots in advance and carefully inscribes each scene on a file card or stores it away in the memory bank of your PC. Or maybe, like me, you are that almost-extinct critter, the Blank Page Writer, and you simply throw your unsuspecting characters into ice-cold water and yell, "Swim, damn you!," as you hammer out your novel on the old manual Remington you bought in 1964.

However you do it, you still have to fulfill the basic responsibility of any storyteller. You have to start your story, move it forward, and keep it moving to the end.

Profluence.

That's the fancy word for it. "Character isolated by a deed / To engross the present and dominate memory" is what the poet William Butler Yeats called it. What I have always thought it meant is that the kind of story you write depends upon the people who inhabit your imagination, the intensity of their fictional life. Character isolated by a deed.

But the practical fact is that unless you know what sort of plot your characters are suited for, you're likely to come out with a chaotic mass of incidents instead of a forward-thrusting plot. Suppose, for instance, that Mary Shelley had written Victor Frankenstein and his Creature into a neat little social comedy like *Pride and Prejudice,* or that Jane Eyre somehow turned up not in Mr. Rochester's country house but in that inn on the road to London where Tom Jones had so much fun.

Mary Shelley, of course, began with the plot already dictated, more or less. She wrote *Frankenstein* on a sort of dare from her husband

Percy's intellectual pals to come up with a better Gothic novel than they did. But what if you have no preconceptions about the kind of plot you want to write? Where do you start, and how can you be sure you're doing it right?

The answers are simple. You start with imagination. (Not self-expression, please. Leave that for your diary.) And there's only one way to tell if you're doing it right. Do it, and see if it works.

Right, then. Let's try a little experiment. Suppose we begin with a simple statement that could belong in any sort of modern novel, with almost any cast of characters.

"The bus pulled away without them."

Chapter One, Page One. Point of Attack.

As the beginning of our plot, the line assumes that some things have happened before the bus pulled away and that some other things will happen now that it's gone, and we're standing there in the dust.

What these things are depends entirely upon who "they" may be. We now have to decide who our main characters will be, and I choose to make one of "them" a woman. She needs a name straightaway. Andrea? Elizabeth? If I want to write a romance, maybe. Those names are elegant and a bit remote, and they have nothing to do with the woman whose somewhat bony, rumpled figure I have already caught a glimpse of, standing in the dust, inhaling exhaust fumes of that departing bus.

No, no! No Andreas or Elizabeths. Let's call her Jimmy.

That choice of name gets our plot up and running. Because this woman, my Jimmy—whose name is almost certainly not *really* Jimmy—is carrying a lot of baggage already, and I don't mean suitcases. It's a small-town name—as a matter of fact I happen to have had a female cousin named Jimmy—and you don't bump into a lot of women called Jimmy on Park Avenue.

Besides, I've decided that her real name is Germaine, and being Jimmy was better than what the boys called her in school. She's heavily freckled, with reddish-brown hair, and everybody called her Germaine Measles.

There she is, my Jimmy, standing on the dusty shoulder of a back road at the edge of a small midwestern town. Blue Creek, Kansas. Why? Why not? I once lived in western Kansas, and almost nothing there was blue, including the sky when the oil refineries were running.

153

Jimmy's wearing a Toronto Blue Jays baseball cap—high treason in Kansas City Royals country—and her luggage consists of a bulging backpack and two plastic shopping bags. Has she been to Toronto, or is Canada a cool, blue dream to which she hoped that bus would take her?

But the word isn't "her." It's "them." She's traveling with a little boy, scrawny, bratty, but real. Named? Weasel Karloff. You guessed it. Real name Boris.

Now, then. Jimmy and Weasel have missed the bus. We have opened the plot—not the story, because that's what we've just been fishing out of my nefarious subconscious—in the middle of things. *In medias res*. In the middle of events that will be built upon and will grow into a climax.

We have begun our plot at the point at which something has to happen. Our characters have to go on or turn back, fight or sink into the dust and be defeated. They have to make a choice, and so do I, as the writer. Write what you know. Know what you write.

What kind of novel is this likely to become?

That depends on what Jimmy and Weasel do next. If they go back to the place next to the mortuary where Jimmy keeps house for her eighty-seven-year-old mother, and Jimmy marries Pete Redwing, the half-Sioux Vietnam vet who runs the filling station, and they adopt Weasel and live happily ever after . . . then we've got a romance, though not the kind in which Andrea or Elizabeth would feel at home.

But suppose Pete has flashbacks and patrols his gas pumps with an M-1 and shoots the social worker who's headed for Jimmy's house to take custody of Weasel?

Tragedy? Mystery? Melodrama?

Or suppose Jimmy and Weasel, having missed the bus, hitch a ride with a crazy half-Sioux named Pete Redwing, and light out with him for Canada, experiencing on their journey all the virtues and brutalities of modern America at the end of the twentieth century?

This is a picaresque, an episodic novel about a rascal off to seek his fortune, in the manner of Huckleberry Finn.

Or suppose that instead of Jimmy, we focus on Weasel, watch him grow up under Jimmy's care, go to school, become a politician, run for the Senate, and at last run for President, to be defeated and return at last to Blue Creek, Kansas, as the bus he came home on leaves him standing—what else?—in the dust. This time we've got what's sometimes called a growth-and-education novel, like *David Copperfield.*

The point of the exercise is that the combination of characters and setting dictates the profluence of plot. They begin as separate elements, but they quickly merge to establish a line of scenes or episodes of mounting intensity. One cardinal law of plotting—which most of us break at some time or other—is that the line of story must never be confused, muddied up or twisted to fit some external factor, like the need to preach a sermon or put in another sex scene or chop up a few more body parts. Everything must move the plot forward to its inevitable climax. In *The Fugitive,* Lieutenant Gerard *must* catch Richard Kimball. Henry the Fifth *must* fight the Battle of Agincourt. Subplots, flashbacks, everything you use must in some way contribute to the inevitability of that climactic scene.

> Character isolated by a deed
> To engross the present and dominate memory.

Most of the time, when I sit down to write a novel, I know only two things about the plot—where it starts and what that great crucial scene will have to be. Sometimes I even dream it. But that is because by that time, I know the characters far better than I know myself.

Far too well to leave them standing in the dust of Blue Creek, Kansas, while the last bus to their future pulls away.

➤➤ 37

LET DIALOGUE DRIVE YOUR STORY

BY SONIA LEVITIN

"LET ME TELL YOU A STORY," SHE BEGAN, "ABOUT ONE OF THE MOST fascinating, bizarre, and evil people I have ever met." Such a beginning is bound to charm a listener or a reader into paying attention, asking for more. Dialogue is a powerful tool for the writer. Used well, it will define your characters, move your plot, and amplify your theme—and it is fun to read.

Something about a line set between quotation marks adds life and realism to a scene. A few lines of narrative can do wonders in moving the time and place of your story and doing it quickly. But dialogue infuses fiction with emotion and action, and sustains the tension better than narrative can.

Characters joined in action naturally speak to one another. When they speak, readers learn not only what is going on, but how each person reacts to the events and, further, how he or she either disguises or admits true feelings.

What makes good dialogue?

In a word, I believe it is intensity. A few well-chosen, carefully honed words of dialogue work better than several paragraphs of explanation. For example, in my historical novel *Escape from Egypt,* I chose dialogue to open the story, having decided that it was the most efficient and immediate way to show not only time and place, but also the very strained circumstances of my hero Jesse's life:

"You! What are you carrying in that basket?"
"Only a few vegetables from our garden, my lord. Would my lord like some for his table?"
"What poor harvests you Israelites produce, and after we give you everything you need! It's disgusting."

156

Immediately we see the fear and servility of the slave pitted against the arrogance and authority of the master. From the dialogue, we can well imagine the resentment of our hero, and indeed, the following narrative emphasizes what the dialogue has begun. It affirms that Jesse is an Israelite slave in ancient Egypt, mistreated and miserable, but still vital.

Thus, dialogue can lead adroitly into several paragraphs of description, making the narrative seem less boring, less pedantic. Our goal as fiction writers is to avoid pedantry, to create the illusion of an effortlessly flowing tale unfolding before the reader's very eyes. To do so, we must offer information smoothly, so the reader gains knowledge almost without realizing he has acquired facts he needs to know.

It is much better to describe a character's looks, disposition, and station through dialogue than merely to chronicle this information. So, to show Jesse's age, status, and physical features, I used brief dialogue with a woman who, like him, is run down by a gang of Egyptian teenagers with their horses:

"Let me dress that cut for you," the woman said. "It's a shame to scar that fine face of yours."

And, she goes on:

"Jesse, son of Nathan and Devorah! Why, you've grown a hand's breadth since I last saw you!"

Thus, the reader knows the names of Jesse's parents, that he is probably in his mid-teens, having experienced a growth spurt, and that he is handsome. When the woman asks Jesse, "Where have you been keeping yourself?" Jesse replies,

"I've been working in the home of In-Hop Tep."
"Ah, In-Hop Tep," says the woman, much impressed, "you're coming up in the world. No wonder you don't have time to work in our small garden."
"I do my share, Ima. At night I weed and make furrows. . . ."

From this small bit of dialogue, readers learn that Jesse is privileged to work in an illustrious household, and that he is a person who takes responsibility seriously. He becomes immediately heroic through these traits, first by being specially privileged and then by being humble.

157

A good deal of the tension in a story has to do with the actions and reactions not only of the main characters, but also of minor characters and what I call the "Greek chorus."

Sometimes the impact of events that occur in a story needs to be put into focus for the reader. That's where the Greek chorus comes in. Basically, this "chorus" is a bit of generalized dialogue or "mob reaction":

"Kill him . . ."
"Don't let him go . . ."
"He is evil . . . evil!"

Likewise, in a scene of joy, we can expect the chorus to augment and elucidate the prevailing emotion:

"Happy father! Happy mother! Joyous reunion!"

I used a similar technique—bits of dialogue uttered by various unnamed people—in my book *Adam's War,* after the tragic outcome of a mock battle:

"It's a miracle one of the children wasn't shot."
"They say that rifle was pointed toward the swings."
"A good thing Adam jumped on that boy."
"People shouldn't keep guns. You see what happens."

Adam is not a direct participant in this scene. The effect of this talk is powerful; it shows how the tragedy has affected everyone in the community, not only Adam and his friends. The "chorus" can also serve as a bridge between scenes, finally narrowing in on a specific character, who continues the action.

Dialogue in a story is very different from real dialogue—but the trick is to make it *appear* realistic. Real dialogue is repetitive, boring, and often inconclusive. The famous dialogue in the movie *Marty* comes to mind as an example of dialogue that is static, but is for that very reason funny and affecting.

"What do you want to do tonight?"
"I don't know, what do you want to do?"
"I don't know—what do you want to do?"

158

Obviously, one cannot go on this way too long. In a story, one or two repetitions of a word or a phrase are enough to indicate a pattern. Suppose you have a character who is not truthful. To highlight this trait you have decided, like Shakespeare, to use protestations to prove the opposite. When this liar speaks, he is apt to preface his remarks with, "Well, to be totally honest. . . ." Two or three repetitions are enough to alert your reader to this character's machinations. Likewise, any other speech perversion or mannerism should be used judiciously, sparingly, just enough to make the point. This also goes for dialect, incorrect grammar, or foreign words. To suggest a mere flavor of the exotic, it must not dominate, or it becomes intrusive, overwhelming the plot.

One way to make dialogue appear realistic is to offer digressions—just a few. Remember, characters do not always answer questions directly.

"What are you asking for that old Samovar?"
"My grandmother brought it over from Russia, you know."
"It's lovely—I've seen them in antique stores."
"So have I. Many are very valuable indeed."
"What are you asking for it?"
"Well, suppose you make me an offer."
"I don't know—I'm not really into antiques."

A certain amount of verbal fencing goes on, especially in a negotiation. The inquirer attempts one tactic and, failing to get what he wants (the price), he tries another. Negotiation applies not only to money matters; every time one character wants something from another, negotiation takes place. Thus, to help your dialogue come alive, think of it as a contest. In his book, *The Art of Dramatic Writing,* Lajos Egri explains that good dialogue shows truth revealed *under pressure.* Don't make it too easy for your character to get answers or solutions. By presenting evasion, misunderstanding, exaggeration, and even downright lies, you keep the pressure on. Then, when true facts and feelings are finally revealed, the character and the reader experience a literary high—catharsis.

Novelists can learn a great deal from reading plays. A good playwright must move the plot and express all the emotions through dialogue, with only minor action to accompany the words. In a successful dramatic scene, the pitch of the dialogue rises gradually, each line intensifying the stakes, the conflict, until a climax is reached. Then, in an outburst of emotion, resolution is achieved, the truth is finally told, the scene ends. That is the best and most satisfying use of dialogue, to bring a highly charged scene to fruition by doling out the revelations little by little, then letting the "point" explode.

A couple of "don'ts" about dialogue are in order. First, don't repeat in dialogue what has already been explained in narrative. It is much more effective to let your reader in on the surprise *as your character reveals it to another person* than to broadcast the character's intention in advance.

For instance, one might say in narrative: Veronica decided to tell Stan that she did not want to see him again.

Stan came to the door. "We're through, Stan," said Veronica.

This is a complete flop, because there is no tension, no surprise.

Consider, however, Veronica getting dressed, fixing her hair, listening to her favorite CD, making herself a drink, pacing, pondering, remembering their times together while she waits for Stan. The doorbell rings. She answers.

"Hi, gorgeous."
"Hi, Stan."
"What's wrong? Aren't you glad to see me?"
"Sure, I'm glad to see you."
"You don't look it. Come here. Give us a kiss."
"Stan—don't."
"What's the matter, baby? Aren't you feeling well?"
"I can't—I don't want to see you anymore, Stan. Please don't say anything. I mean it this time. We're through."

Another "don't": Don't have too many dangling speeches. People do interrupt, they do speak at cross-purposes, but a sequence of dialogue must be easy to follow, and too many unfinished phrases cause confusion and become annoying to readers.

As you practice writing dialogue, keep in mind that every person's speech is unique. Just as we know our friends by their voices on the telephone, we also know them by the content of their talk, by their speech rhythms, and the peculiar ways in which they use words.

An old-fashioned character, for example, uses old-fashioned words, a homespun style, a slow cadence of speech. "He's slow as molasses." Or, "I packed me a grip and left."

A hip teenager speaks quickly, incorporating slang and references to pop culture. "Hey, I'm not into dancing—let's go grab a Starbucks."

A Swiss college professor sounds different from a Portuguese gardener. A child's speech differs from an adult's. Some speech differences reflect status and education, others interests and lifestyle. A horse-trainer will speak in terms of horses and the out-of-doors; the seamstress describes things in terms of close, careful concentration; the sailor's speech reflects his visual and emotional connection with the sea. We need to know a great deal about the characters speaking, and be able to put ourselves visually, emotionally and psychologically in their place before we can accurately portray their speech.

In my novel, *The No-Return Trail,* when a young husband who is an unschooled Kentucky woodsman compliments his wife by saying, "Your hair shines just like a blackbird's wing," he speaks in terms of what he knows and loves, reflecting his experience and his status. Were he a professor or a cabinet maker, surely his comment would be different.

It is interesting and creative to produce dialogue that provides a clue to your characters' personalities. It deepens your story to know how characters speak, and why. The boss who laughs too much is unknowingly revealing his own insecurities. A doctor who speaks mostly in monosyllables has trouble articulating his feelings. A boy who always argues is probably in desperate need of attention. The mother who constantly scolds may be masking her deep anxiety and concern.

Consider carefully who your characters are, what they know, and what they reveal—both consciously and unconsciously—by the way they speak. Make their revelations come about in a lively give-and-take, under pressure, remembering that dialogue drives your story.

➤➤ 38

ON LOCATION: YOU ARE THERE!

BY WINIFRED MADISON

OBVIOUSLY, A STORY HAS TO HAPPEN SOMEWHERE. READERS WANT TO feel that they are right where the action takes place or they will suffer disappointment, or even a sense of displacement, if the location is undefined. One of the joys of reading is that it takes you somewhere else or, by comparison, makes the place where you live more understandable.

More important, characters and plots are so deeply influenced by where the story takes place that they cannot be divorced from it, even though the themes are universal. Can you imagine *Wuthering Heights* taking place anywhere but on the lonely moors of England, or *Tom Sawyer* and *Huckleberry Finn* far from the Mississippi River? While Shakespeare's *Romeo and Juliet* is clearly set in Italy—more exactly, in Verona—*West Side Story,* based on the same theme, could take place only in New York City.

Choosing the setting is a tremendous pleasure for the writer who has a love for place. Certain cities, such as Venice, Paris, New York, New Orleans, or Los Angeles, act as magnets for writers. However, the temptation to choose a background about which a writer may dream romantically—perhaps the French Riviera or the American Southwest or a village in the English countryside—is chancy if you do not know the area well. You run the danger of sounding like a travel brochure, which will be immediately clear to those who do know the place. Even with maps and research, it's all too easy to make the kind of mistake that will lose your reader's confidence. For example, if you choose to write about San Francisco although you have seen it only in the movies, you might slip up by confusing the Bay Bridge with the Golden Gate Bridge, and will immediately lose your credibility. Creating a place realistically is as tricky as committing the perfect crime.

Write about places you know. "But the place where I live is so *dull!*" you may complain, or, in the words of Gertrude Stein, "There is no there there." Be assured there is, but you may have become so accustomed to it, that you cannot "see" it any more. You may rediscover your home by leaving it for a day, a week, or even a year, and viewing it from a distance.

The prairies were considered dull until Laura Ingalls Wilder's *The Little House on the Prairie.* Monterey was once a sleepy California coastal village until John Steinbeck brought it to life in *Cannery Row.*

A location need not be dramatic or bizarre or unusual; what matters is how you view it and what understanding you bring to it. A fast-food restaurant, a supermarket, or an ordinary suburban home may have as much emotional drama in it as the secluded estate of a billionaire or a grand hotel in Venice, depending on what you do with it. Experience any place, even one you know well, as though you were seeing it for the first time. Let the air brush against your cheek, and listen to the sounds—whether it's the distant crowing of a rooster or the impatient horn-blowing of a traffic jam—and soon it will come alive.

To make the most of a setting, *be there.* Use all your senses. Your first gut reaction is important. Does the place make you feel elated or gloomy, strange, bored or excited? What does it do to your plot and characters?

1. *See it as a painter would.* Is the tone of the place light, dark, or grayish? What are the colors that come to mind? Is the landscape predominantly mild, with the easy rises and falls of a rural setting, with fields and woodlands? Or is the skyline harshly geometric with the architectural complexities of a modern city?

2. *Consider the climate.* A fiercely hot atmosphere will produce characters who speak, move and act differently from those in a temperate climate, just as the colors of Arizona or New Mexico with their hot pinks, terra cottas, and turquoise skies will vary markedly from the cool greens and cloudy blues of the Northwest.

3. *Make the weather work for you,* bringing out the emotional quality your story needs. It's possible to orchestrate it. A continual rain may be soothing and gentle, or the same rain may become increasingly depressing. A sunny day may be sparkling and light, yet too much sun can be harsh and punishing.

4. *Odors play a part in the scene.* A street in a large city with

163

garbage piled up will not smell like a field of newly mown hay. The tempting whiff of baking bread from a bakery, the familiar smell of chlorine from a swimming pool, the medicinal smell in a hospital, the scent of perfume on a woman passing by . . . the list is endless, and each olfactory detail will help bring your setting to life.

5. *Atmosphere is filled with sound,* even the sound of silence. Heavy traffic with the screech of brakes, the incessant repetition of horns and the terror induced by sirens may be only part of the background, but they will say a great deal about the mood of your story. Use different kinds of noise, like a soundtrack underscoring the spirit of the scene: a loud rock band, the noise of children at play, a student practicing a violin or a saxophone, the lapping of water against a boat, the intermittent roar of a plane flying overhead, the sudden silence in a lonely room.

6. *Become a sky watcher,* and see how this will increase your repertory of atmosphere; skies are theaters in which all moods may pass at one time or another. Bright sunlit skies with a few puffs of cloud may suggest a playful mood, just as a glowering sky with blackening clouds will foreshadow danger or violence. Skies may be one of a hundred shades of blue, each with a different emotional message. But blue is not the only color. Sometimes all traces of color disappear from the sky, leaving it seemingly blank. Let a flock of black crows fly across this colorless sky, or have a single plane leave a diminishing white trail.

Beware of the predictable. It is easy to think of a funeral on a cold dreary day, but on a bright day, when the earth becomes alive and joyful with spring, death may be even more poignant. Describe a garden wedding caught in a sudden storm that drenches everyone. Have a gale of wind come up at an outdoor concert, throwing the music off the stands into the audience.

Location. Focus on environment—buildings, houses, and rooms, as well as a geographical area. A character's immediate surroundings are of prime importance. Houses, whether grand or humble, carry intense emotional weight. Among those "fictional" houses that play unforgettable roles are Tara, in *Gone with the Wind* (Margaret Mitchell) and Manderley in *Rebecca* (Daphne Du Maurier).

Lofty structures like bridges, towers, churches, lighthouses, and nuclear reactors are important symbolically as they rise into the sky and dominate the landscape, either elevating, as the spires of Oxford, or threatening, as the nuclear reactors in P. D. James's novel, *Devices and Desires*. Conversely, settings hidden from daylight—caves, cellars, tunnels and basements—suggest the dark underground of mind and spirit.

Falling in love with a place is an experience so common to many writers that stories seem to rise out of it. During the year I spent in Vancouver, I frequently rode the ferry through the Gulf Islands, and this led to my writing a novel that takes place there—*The Genessee Queen*. Here is a paragraph from it:

> At the moment it is a blue day, everything blue, so blue that Monica feels herself drenched in blueness. She leans on the rail of *The Genessee Queen* as it leaves the mainland and wonders that she has never tired of the trip, though she has made it many times. She knows exactly how on this day the cool northern light will bathe the islands that rise in the distance a chilled gunmetal blue. She has also seen on other days the water gleaming in the sun. A ferry sailing in the distance and the gulls screeching mournfully as they circle above, remain insistently white. But it can change. In the north, the sun lurks in a furrow of moody clouds and possibly all the blueness will drain away in a matter of minutes, becoming colorless, as if the whole view were an overexposed film.

Names. Collect names of places; they can be magical in setting a mood to your story. If you wish to avoid naming a particular place because you do not really know it, you can make up a name, but most readers will want to know the general location of your story, whether it's the Arctic circle, Los Angeles, or an island in the Mediterranean.

Being a name freak or a map junkie will help writers in pursuit of exactly the right name. Among my favorites are Illyria (in Greece) or Elyria (in Ohio and Kansas) and the Isle of Skye, which actually are as poetic as they sound. Such names as the Firth of Forth, Lands End (in England or San Francisco), or Giggleswick in England have a style about them and suggest different emotional moods. Among the many names in Northern California are Cool, Rough and Ready, Shirttail Canyon, and Fiddletown. I also admit a fondness for the name of Boring, Oregon. Unless you know these places, it would be unwise to set your story there, but knowing such names may help you choose exactly the right one for the location of your story or novel.

A last word. Be careful. You may fall so in love with your setting that you will want to go on and on about it. Don't. You may lose a reader who is not ready to wade through page after page of description. Your reader wants to get on with the plot. Catch the mood of the setting; ask yourself if it is right for your story; find the telling details; and do whatever you can to make the reader believe he is actually there, and that's all you need to do.

➣➣ Specialized Fiction

$\succ\succ$ **39**

WRITING THE DISASTER NOVEL

BY RICHARD MARTIN STERN

DISASTERS, MAN-MADE OR OCCURRING IN NATURE, ARE OBVIOUS SUB-jects for fiction. I refer to such events as wars, hurricanes, floods, fires, avalanches, earthquakes and the like, all of which are the stuff out of which memorable fiction can be fashioned.

They offer scope for heroics, self-sacrifice, crisis, love, hate, all of the conflicts and emotions of which men and women are capable.

But in writing them there is one danger that must at all costs be avoided if a successful story is to be achieved: allowing the disaster itself to overwhelm your tale, instead of remaining in the background as it should. Let me illustrate.

A Tale of Two Cities is set against the backdrop of the French Revolution and the reign of terror and could have been set in no other time or place. But it is not *about* the Revolution; it is about the characters Dickens invented and the story he contrived for them.

The single scene in which the woman does not even drop a stitch in her knitting as she watches the severed heads fall from the guillotine is the only scene I can remember that actually shows the reign of terror in action, but the strain and horror of the times permeate the entire novel through the thoughts and actions of Dickens's characters. It is this concentration on the characters and *their* story that makes the tale as memorable as it is.

In a like manner, *Gone With The Wind,* a story of our own Civil War, is not about the war, the battles, the ebb and flow of the huge forces involved, but about the characters Margaret Mitchell depicted and how they are affected by the war and react to it and to one another. The war is the background, the setting against which the tale is told, and the emphasis is on the characters alone.

The truism, of course, is that there is no substitute for characterization, the invention and presentation of people the readers can identify with, and with whom they can suffer, or fear, or love, or despair, whether the action takes place in a drawing room or in temporary shelter from a blizzard out on the frozen tundra.

A novel of mine called *Snowbound Six* is about winter Search & Rescue in the mountains of New Mexico. In the book, the snow is always there, and the cold, hypothermia which can kill, an avalanche, struggle for survival in an ancient cave and the S&R team's attempts to reach the victims. But the emphasis is on the individuals, victims, rescuers, and interested bystanders alike, and the effects of the disaster on them, how under great strain they react and how in various ways their lives are affected. The disaster, in short, is the background; the people are the story, which is as it must be.

In writing about disasters, it is easy to forget this basic fact and to be carried away by the fascinating complexities or the factual dangers of the situation, to invent ingenious mechanisms for survival and concentrate on them, to get lost in the sheer magnitude of whatever disaster you are dealing with and make all this the central body of your tale. Not madness, but failure lies in that direction.

During World War II, the British were successful in stealing German coding machines called collectively Enigma, and with them they were able to intercept and decode German messages, orders, and actual battle plans.

All this was done in the greatest of secrecy by an isolated group of cryptographers and mathematicians. At times it even became essential that lives be sacrificed because saving them might let the enemy know that their codes had been broken.

All of this is a tremendous story that can now be told, and it has been written—as nonfiction. The writer of a successful *fictionalized* tale against this setting would have to ignore the actual workings of Enigma, however fascinating the details might be, to concentrate instead on the men and women involved and show the *effects* of Enigma—its successes and failures—on them, as for almost the entire duration of the war they dwelt under enormous strain and in such secrecy that the existence of the organization was never known except in top governmental circles.

There would be ample scope for jealousy, love, agonizing decisions, the pressures of day-and-night labor in order to keep up with events,

170

and internal conflicts inevitably arising under such clandestine and painstaking demands.

The machines would always be there, and the war itself would be ever-present as the messages were intercepted and their meanings laboriously extracted. But, to repeat, the story would be about the people, the characters.

Too much of today's disaster and action fiction tends to ignore this basic principle and concentrates instead on gunfire or explosions or careful, detailed descriptions of avalanches or buildings collapsing in earthquakes—in short, special effects that may be ingenious, but are scarcely satisfying to the reader. The writers forget that what the reader identifies with are the characters.

When I set out to write *The Tower*, one of the two books on which the film *The Towering Inferno* was based, I had only the basic idea of people trapped by fire on the top floor of a gigantic skyscraper.

The possibilities for disaster were almost endless, and the material I managed to assemble was both vast and fascinating. The World Trade Center in New York was then under construction, and I managed to get a schematic wiring diagram of the entire complex, including the electric substation that was built solely to provide electricity to the Trade Center. There were numerous magazine articles about the complexities and difficulties the builders were encountering. I had accounts of skyscraper fires that had actually taken place both here and abroad, and accounts of elevator failures in them (the basis for signs now in every hotel telling guests to use only the stairs in case of fire). I had geologic studies of the bedrock upon which the twin towers would rest seven stories beneath the surface, along with studies on the near impossibility of evacuating modern high-rise buildings if disaster struck, and so on.

I could, and did, use almost all of the material in the book, but neither it nor the fire was paramount. The story was, as it had to be, about the people involved—who they were; how they came to be on the scene, either trapped inside or outside trying to help; how they reacted during the crisis, some growing in stature, some diminishing in panic.

The temptation to describe the design and structure of the building in detail, or the intricacies of the wiring, the way the elevators worked and how because of smoke they could become inoperable—in short,

171

the temptation to include the physical makeup of the disaster—was enormous, but it had to be resisted. Page after page went into the wastebasket because the description was not germane to the story.

Readers do not identify with concrete and steel or with wiring and ingenious mechanisms. Readers identify only with people, their personal problems, their loves and dislikes, their heroism or the lack of it, their speech and mannerisms, their fears and their strengths, and above all, with their interactions with one another. This is the basic fact that must be kept in mind in writing a disaster novel or indeed, any fictional tale.

Your goal should be that long after the facts of the story have faded in memory, at least some of your characters in the tale will remain in the readers' minds, and if you have done your job well and made the story powerful enough, you can hope that the readers may find themselves wondering how they might have behaved under similar circumstances.

Then, and only then, will you have succeeded in what you set out to do.

40

THE HOWS AND WHYS OF WRITING MYSTERIES

BY SUSAN KELLY

A GLANCE AT THE SHELVES IN YOUR LOCAL BOOKSTORE WOULD SUG-
gest, by the sheer weight of numbers, that there are more crime writers
practicing their craft than there are criminals practicing *theirs*. (Not,
unfortunately, quite true.) But despite the huge number of mysteries
being produced today, publishers are still eager to hear from new writers. All they require is that their voices be fresh, exciting, and talented.

Say you've got the freshness, the excitement, and the talent on tap.
What can you do to enhance your chances of grabbing the brass ring,
otherwise known as a publishing contract? Perhaps my experience can
make yours easier.

I started writing, or trying to write, mysteries in 1979. The first
three book manuscripts I produced, all featuring Liz Connors, free-
lance crime reporter and former college English professor, were rejected. Now I'm glad they were, although at the time, of course, I
wasn't. Back then I really didn't have a grasp on what I was doing.

But you can learn from trial and error, and I did. Whatever success
I've achieved was a result of, number one, paying serious attention to
the reasons my first three "books" were rejected. One editor said that
Liz needed more motivation (other than just curiosity) for investigating
a crime. This may seen obvious, but as a teacher of writing, I've
read several potentially interesting manuscripts in which the detective
didn't seem to have a really valid reason for trying to solve the crime
on which the book was premised. Cops, private eyes, and reporters
have a built-in motive—they get paid to do what they do. With an
amateur detective (which is actually how Liz started out) some other
rationale is necessary. More on this later.

Plot is clearly important, but as one top mystery editor once told me, a problem with plot is the easiest thing in the world to fix. But lending themselves less easily to remedy are writing style, characterization, theme, and dialogue. Until you master these elements, you can't write a successful mystery.

What makes a good writing style? To begin with, it has to be literate and readable. Beyond that, if it works, it works. Compare P. D. James and Robert B. Parker: totally different, but equally successful. Dialogue should sound as if it were spoken by real people. And the theme must be interesting and important enough to engage the reader's sympathy and attention. Usually, what is timeless tends also to be topical. Conflicts in human relationships of whatever kind—man/woman, parent/child, brother/sister, friend/friend, the list is endless—always work, because they're always new to the person experiencing them.

Beyond those general principles, here are some guidelines:

1. *Love your detective.* I'm serious. Dead—so to speak—serious. The best mysteries written today are character-driven rather than plot-driven, so you want to create a protagonist who's not only real but intensely likable, to you and to your readers. And since most likely you'll be creating a series detective—publishers prefer series to single-shot novels—you'll want to create a detective whom you'll be able to live with and grow with for the succeeding five, ten, or twenty novels.

Before you do anything else, write a biography of your detective. This will serve as a reference tool and inspiration. It doesn't have to be a polished piece of writing; no one will see it but you. Update it as fresh notions occur to you about the protagonist's interests, appearance, tastes, background, education, etc. Don't worry if the bio seems incomplete. More about your detective will invariably emerge, the longer you think about it. Provided, of course, that you love him or her.

2. *If you are planning a series, work up similar bios for your recurring secondary characters.* Follow the process described above.

3. *Outline your story.* This is torture for me, but it's necessary and helpful. Even if you're not happy with the finished product (*I* never am), at least you'll have a framework on which to hang successive better ideas, which, trust me, will come to you. Also, a publisher may ask you to submit an outline of the book before asking to see the whole manuscript. It's best to have one ready to go.

4. *Research, research, research.* This is especially important for the beginner. Luckily, there are scads of excellent books available on police procedure, methods of investigation, forensics, and other related matters. Read them, and take notes. Create a file of newsclips on interesting and unusual criminal investigations, arrests, and trials. Study court documents—easily obtained from most law libraries.

5. *If your local police department has a civilian "ride along" program, sign up for it.* Even if you're not writing a procedural, you'll want to have the experience of directly observing how law enforcement professionals work. Apart from that, it's fun. And, oh—offer to spring for the coffee and doughnuts.

6. *Attend a criminal trial.* They're nothing like most television dramatizations; they're better.

7. *Listen for spoken dialogue that you can reproduce in your fiction.* Most good mysteries are notable for the great talk between the characters. "Great talk" here equals "realistic talk," as well as witty or thought-provoking talk. Carry a small notebook with you *always,* so that if you happen to overhear a funny/bizarre/poignant snatch of conversation in the subway/restaurant/office/classroom/grocery, you can write it down for future use. Some truly fantastic vignettes can later emerge from such notes.

8. *If you have an area of expertise, use it in your mystery novels.* You've been involved in television production? Fabulous. Give your detective experience in this area. Set your mystery against that backdrop. You've worked in health care? Great. Mysteries and thrillers with a medical angle do very well. (Read novels by Robin Cook and Patricia Cornwell.) You know about the law? (Do I have to mention George Higgins, Scott Turow, John Grisham, and Jeremiah Healy?) Fishing is your hobby? Cooking? Travel? Astronomy? Art history? Paleontology? Use them.

The list of vocations and avocations is endless. If you write about what you know thoroughly and are good at, you'll lend authenticity to your fiction, so vital to a successful mystery.

And remember, too, that people enjoy learning things, especially if they're not being force-fed the information and quizzed and graded on it.

175

9. *Motive is paramount.* If you're contemplating writing a series featuring an amateur detective, give that character a compelling reason to investigate the crime. The most compelling motivations are often the most personal: The detective, or someone very close to him or her, has been falsely accused of a heinous crime, and no one—except, of course, the detective—believes in his or her innocence.

10. *Setting is paramount.* In a good mystery, the setting—whether urban, rural, suburban, foreign, or domestic—functions almost as a character. By that I mean it is fully developed and three-dimensional, as pulsing and breathing as its populace. Set your book in a place you know thoroughly—down to which little side streets are one-way or dead ends. Walk around the town; take photographs and keep them in front of you as you work on your descriptions. Make whatever that place is *live* on the printed page.

11. *Expand your horizons with each book.* Don't repeat crimes, or the exact method of investigation. First, because you won't want to keep writing the same book. And second, because different circumstances and situations create an environment in which your detective can grow. Editors—and readers—love this process of evolution and development.

➤➤ 41

WRITING THE SUPERNATURAL NOVEL

BY ELIZABETH HAND

I'VE ALWAYS THOUGHT THAT THE OLDEST PROFESSION WAS THAT OF storyteller—in particular, the teller of supernatural tales. A look at the cave paintings in France or Spain will show you how far back our hunger for the fantastic goes: men with the heads of beasts, figures crouching in the darkness, skulls and shadows and unblinking eyes. Take a glance at the current bestseller list, and you'll see that we haven't moved that far in the last twenty thousand years. Books by Anne Rice, Stephen King, Joyce Carol Oates, and Clive Barker, among many others, continue to feed our taste for dark wine and the perils of walking after midnight. But how to join the ranks of those whose novels explore the sinister side of town?

First, let me distinguish between supernatural fiction and its tough (and very successful) younger cousin, the horror novel. Horror novels depend heavily upon the mechanics of plot, less-than-subtle character-izations, and shock value—what Stephen King calls "going for the gross-out." In spirit and execution, they aren't that different from the "penny dreadfuls" of a century ago, crude but effective entertainments that tend to have a short shelf life. Unlike more stylized works such as *Dracula, The Turn of the Screw* or *The Shining,* most horror novels lose their ability to chill the second time around—they just don't stand up to rereading. As Edmund Wilson put it, "The only horror in these fictions is the horror of bad taste and bad art."

In the wake of Stephen King's success, the 1980's was a boom dec-ade for horror fiction. But the market was flooded with so many books—and so many second-rate Stephen King imitators—that pub-lishers and readers alike grew wary. With the dwindling reading public, it's far more difficult today to get a supernatural novel into print.

But the readers *are* there. And they're quite a sophisticated audience, which makes it both more challenging, and more fun, to write the sort of novel that will appeal to someone who prefers *The Vampire Lestat* to the *The Creeping Bore*.

More than other genres, supernatural fiction is defined by *atmosphere* and *characterization*. By atmosphere, I mean the author's ability to evoke a mood or place viscerally by the use of original and elegant, almost *seductive* language. Science fiction and fantasy also rely heavily upon unusual settings and wordplay, often against a backdrop of other, imagined, worlds. But the most successful supernatural novels are set in *our* world. Their narrative tension, their very ability to frighten and transport us, derives from a conflict between the macabre and the mundane, between everyday reality and the threatening *other*— whether revenant, werewolf, or demonic godling—that seeks to destroy it.

The roots of supernatural fiction lie in the gothic romances of the eighteenth and nineteenth centuries with their gloomy settings, imperiled narrators and ghostly visitations. Even today these remain potent elements. Witness Anne Rice's vampire Lestat during a perambulation about prerevolutionary Paris:

> The cold seemed worse in Paris. It wasn't as clean as it had been in the mountains. The poor hovered in doorways, shivering and hungry, the crooked unpaved streets were thick with filthy slush. I saw barefoot children suffering before my very eyes, and more neglected corpses lying about than ever before. I was never so glad of the fur-lined cape as I was then. . . .

Much of the pleasure in Rice's work comes from her detailed evocations of real, yet highly romanticized, places: New Orleans, Paris, San Francisco. It pays to have firsthand knowledge of some desirable piece of occult real estate: Readers love the thrill of an offbeat setting, but they also like recognizing familiar landmarks. So, Stephen King has staked out rural Maine as his fictional backyard. The incomparable Shirley Jackson (whose classic "The Lottery" has chilled generations of readers) also turns to New England for the horrific doings in *The Haunting of Hill House, The Bird's Nest* and *We Have Always Lived in the Castle*. Daphne du Maurier's novella "Don't Look Now" gives us a tourist couple lost amidst the winding alleys of Venice, a notion creepy enough to have inspired Ian McEwan's nightmarish *The Comfort of Strangers*. Just about any setting will do, if you can imbue it

178

with an aura of beauty and menace. My neo-gothic novel *Waking the Moon* takes place in that most pedestrian and bureaucratic of cities, Washington, D.C. But by counterpointing the city's workaday drabness with exotic descriptions of its lesser-known corners, I was able to suggest that an ancient evil might lurk near Capitol Hill:

> From the Shrine's bell tower came the first deep tones of the carillon calling the hour. I turned, and saw in the distance the domes and columns of the Capitol glimmering in the twilight, bone-colored, ghostly; and behind it still more ghostly buildings, their columned porticoes and marble arches all seeming to melt into the haze of green and violet darkness that descended upon them like sleep.

Style, of course, is a matter of taste and technique, and as with all writing, your most important tools should be a good thesaurus and dictionary. (Good taste in reading helps, but is probably not necessary.) A thesaurus can transform even the oldest and most unpalatable of chestnuts. "It was a dark and stormy night" becomes "Somber and tenebrous, the vespertine hour approached."

The danger, of course, is that such elevated diction easily falls into self-parody. But when well-done, it can quickly seduce the reader into believing in—well, in any number of marvelous things:

> Last night I dreamt that I woke to hear some strange, barely audible sound from downstairs—a kind of thin tintinnabulation, like those coloured-glass bird scarers which in my childhood were still sold for hanging up to glitter and tinkle in the garden breeze. I thought I went downstairs to the drawing room. The doors of the china cabinets were standing open, but all the figures were in their places—the Bow Liberty and Matrimony, the Four Seasons of Neale earthenware, the Reinecke girl on her cow; yes, and she herself—the Girl in a Swing. It was from these that the sound came, for they were weeping.

This is from Richard Adams's superb *The Girl in a Swing,* to my mind the best supernatural novel I've ever read. One of the problems in writing supernatural fiction stems from the fact that "ghost stories" are nearly always better when they are really *stories*, rather than full-length novels. Indeed, many of the classic works of dark fantasy—*The Turn of the Screw,* Charlotte Gilman's "The Yellow Wallpaper," Oliver Onions's "The Beckoning Fair One"—are novellas, a form that particularly suits the supernatural, but which is a hard sell: too short for publishers looking for meaty bestsellers, too long for a magazine mar-

179

ket that thrives on the 5,000- to 7,000-word story. It is very difficult to sustain a high level of suspense for several hundred pages. Chapter after chapter of awful doings too often just become awful, with the "cliffhanger" effect ultimately boring the reader.

Characterization is one way of avoiding this pitfall. If your central characters are intriguing, you don't need a constant stream of ghoulish doings to hold a reader's attention. Think of Anne Rice's Lestat, whose melancholy persona has seen him through several sequels. Or the callow student narrator of Donna Tartt's *The Secret History,* a novel which has only a hint of the supernatural about it, but which is more terrifying than any number of haunted houses:

> Does such a thing as "the fatal flaw," that showy dark crack running down the middle of a life, exist outside literature? I used to think it didn't. Now I think it does. And I think that mine is this: a morbid longing for the picturesque at all costs.

The Secret History is told in the first person, as are *The Girl in a Swing,* Rice's *Vampire Chronicles,* and *Waking the Moon.* In supernatural fiction, it is not enough that the protagonist compel our interest. Readers must also be able to truly *identify* with him, to experience his growing sense of unease as his familiar world gradually crumbles in the face of some dark intruder, be it spirit or succubus. That is why the first-person narrator is so prevalent in supernatural tales. It is also why most uncanny novels feature individuals whose very *normalcy* is what sets them apart from others. Like us, they do not believe in ghosts, which makes it all the worse when a ghost actually does appear.

But "normal" does not necessarily mean "dull." Richard Papen, the narrator of *The Secret History,* is drawn into a murderous conspiracy when his college friends seek to evoke Dionysos one drunken winter night. In *The Girl in a Swing,* Alan Desland is a middle-aged bachelor whose most distinguishing characteristic is his extraordinary *niceness*—until he becomes obsessed with the beautiful Kathe, who may be the incarnation of a goddess—or of a woman who murdered her own children. And in C. S. Lewis's classic *That Hideous Strength,* an entire peaceful English village is besieged by the forces of darkness.

As with all good fiction, it is important that the central characters are *changed* by their experiences, whether for good or ill. Lazy writers often use mere physical transformations to effect this change: The

180

heroine becomes a vampire. Or the heroine is prevented from becoming a vampire. Or the heroine is killed. Far more eerie is the plight of the eponymous hero of Peter Ackroyd's terrifying *Hawksmoor,* a police detective who finds himself drawn into a series of cult murders that took place in London churches two hundred years before:

> Hawksmoor looked for relief from the darkness of wood, stone and metal but he could find none; and the silence of the church had once again descended as he sat down upon a small chair and covered his face. And he allowed it to grow dark.

While he is very much a twentieth-century man, Nicholas Hawksmoor's unwanted clairvoyance gives him a glimpse of horrors he is unable to forget, and forever alters his perception of the power of good and evil in the world and in his work.

In many ways, the intricacies of *plot* are less central to supernatural fiction than is *pacing* (another reason why short stories usually work better than novels). A careful balance must be achieved between scenes of the ordinary and the otherworldly. Usually, a writer alternates the two, with the balance gradually tipping in favor of the unreal: Think of Dracula moving from Transylvania to London, and bringing with him a miasma of palpable evil that slowly infects all around him. In *Waking the Moon,* my heroine's involvement with the supernatural parallels her love affair in the real world. However you choose to do it, don't let the magical elements overwhelm your story completely.

Especially, don't let the Big Supernatural Payoff come too *soon.* (The only thing worse that killing off all your werewolves fifty pages before the end is penning these dreadful words: IT WAS ALL A DREAM.) Think of your novel in musical terms: You wouldn't really want to listen to one Wagnerian aria after another, would you? Well, neither would you want to read page after page of mysterious knockings, stakes through the heart, and screams at midnight.

Finally, dare to be different. Does the world really need another vampire novel? How about a lamia instead? Or an evil tree? As always, it's a good idea to be well-read in your chosen genre, so that you don't waste time and ink reinventing Frankenstein's monster. In addition to the works mentioned above, there is a wealth of terrific short supernatural fiction that can teach as well as chill you. *Great Tales of Terror and the Supernatural* (edited by Herbert A. Wise and Phyllis Fraser) is perhaps the indispensable anthology. There are also collections by great writers such as Poe, Robert Aickman, John Collier, Edith Wharton, Isak Dinesen, Sheridan Le Fanu, M. R. James, and many, many others. Jack Sullivan has written two books that I refer to constantly: *Elegant Nightmares* and *Lost Souls,* classic studies of English ghost stories that can serve as a crash course on how to write elegant horror. These, along with Stephen King's nonfiction *Danse Macabre,* should put you well on your way to creating your own eldritch novel. Happy haunting!

>> 42

WRITING HISTORICAL FICTION

BY WILLIAM MARTIN

NEVER LET THE FACTS GET IN THE WAY OF A GOOD STORY."

I can't remember where I heard that remark for the first time, but it's my favorite wiseguy answer whenever anyone asks me what the most important rule is for the historical novelist. And it's true.

No matter how many interesting facts you may have collected about, say, the battle of Midway, no matter how many fabulous events cry out for dramatization when you decide to write your Civil War epic, remember this: Character and plot are master and mistress of the historical novel, just as they are of any genre of mainstream fiction. *And you have to do all that research.*

But if you write a historical novel, you'll have a good chance of catching a publisher's eye, because there's always an audience for historical fiction. And you'll find that historical fiction has built-in advantages for any writer:

(1) There's no such thing as writer's block when you write historical fiction, because you always have your research to keep you working. *Blocked? Me? No way. So what if I've been reading old diaries for a week. I may read them for another week, too, and well, yeah . . . eventually I'll have to write, but . . .*

(2) History gives you character. History books and primary sources—old newspapers, diaries, ship's logs, and the like—are filled not only with details, but with the power of personality, and personality breathes life into fiction. And after you've spent time looking at an era through the eyes of those who lived it, you realize that beliefs, manners, and human trappings may change, but human nature doesn't.

(3) History gives you structure. It's always offering you another set of beginnings, middles, and ends, whether you're talking about something as specific as a single battle or as expansive as a century.

183

This means you always have structure. And structure means story. And the hard facts of life in mainstream popular fiction is that readers want story.

Interesting characters inhabiting a world that has no suspense, no drama, and no payoff, will not pay your bills. But there are plenty of stick figures walking through best sellers, simply because the authors knew how to pack their tales with conflict, movement, and climax.

The ideal, of course, is to create characters driven by strong personalities and motivated by strongly-held beliefs, then test the personalities and challenge the beliefs, so that conflict, movement, and climax rise inevitably from the decisions the characters make. This is true whether your fiction is set in the present or past. But it never hurts to have a single strong plot element to keep your characters focused.

When I wrote my first novel, I looked to the past, to the history-soaked turf of Boston, where I found the facts from which to fashion a good story: In the nineteenth century, Boston was a peninsula surrounded by tideflats; the tideflats were filled with trash and gravel, and the twentieth-century city took shape. In the upscale Back Bay neighborhood, you can still dig down through the basement floors and into the muck below to find artifacts tossed into the landfill a century ago. What if there was buried treasure down there, too?

And what would the treasure be? How about something that itself was rooted in Boston history, something made from gold and silver, perhaps? And who was Boston's most famous silversmith? Once you start asking yourself the right questions, the answers can flow with the logic of a good story.

A tea set crafted by Paul Revere would have been valuable when it was made and is priceless today, especially if it had passed through famous hands before disappearing into the Back Bay. The most famous hands in America during Revere's time? George Washington's.

Initially, I planned to write a short historical prologue following the tea set's journey from Revere to the President's mansion to the Back Bay, then get on with my treasure hunt—modern characters digging through the modern city. But my opening scenes changed all of that.

I had decided to begin with a historical event—a banquet held in Boston in 1789, when the gentlemen of the city honored the new President. It would be a perfect place for Revere to give America's greatest hero a gift. But a banquet can make for a boring scene, even if the

184

guest list includes Washington and Revere. I knew the facts. I had to give them a good story.

That was when the character of Horace Taylor Pratt took shape—a Yankee shipper modeled after several hard-headed shippers I had read about. He watched the far horizons for the return of his ships, but always kept one eye on the pennies in his pocket and would see a ceremonial tea set as a grand waste of money.

Here is the first paragraph:

Horace Taylor Pratt pulled a silver snuffbox from his waistcoat pocket and placed it on the table in front of him. He hated snuffboxes. They were small, delicate, and nearly impossible for a man with one arm to open. Whenever he fumbled for snuff, Pratt cursed the two-armed world that conspired against him, but when he wanted a clear head, he had to have snuff. This evening, he wanted wits as sharp as a glasscutter.

The opening tells us a lot about Pratt in a small space: He is short-tempered, self-pitying, and about to cause trouble. Perhaps the most telling phrase in the paragraph is *wanted wits as sharp as a glasscutter.*

Every scene you write should create conflict. And the best conflict flows from the character. In every scene, no matter what genre you're exploring, always ask yourself: *What does the main character in this scene want, and who's in his way?* When you find the answer, you'll understand your scene. Keep asking, and eventually, you'll understand your novel.

After introducing Pratt, I reveal the room and the historical giants who fill it, but my focus remains on Pratt and his young son, who is mortified to see his father taking snuff in the presence of George Washington. We are, as I like to say, looking at history from ground level, focused as much on details like the snuffbox and the emotions of Pratt's son as on the new President.

Readers of historical fiction love to come into the company of historical giants, to imagine what they would do in the presence of a George Washington. Your characters, in scenes like this, are the stand-ins for your readers. You must always try to see the giants of history, or grand historical events, through your characters' eyes, colored by your characters' emotions and brought to life by the tactile details of their surroundings.

And always look for the conflicts within the conflict. In that opening

185

scene, Pratt wants to make his opinions known: He thinks the tea set is a hypocritical waste of money, commissioned by the gentlemen of Boston to curry favor with the new President. That's the main conflict. But a scene that has smaller conflicts popping off within it will be richer and more textured, especially if the conflicts are built around details specific to the era in which the book is set. So, Pratt wants snuff, but he lost an arm at Bunker Hill, so he has to fumble with the snuffbox. *Conflict.* He takes his snuff and sneezes boorishly, angering the gentlemen around him. *Conflict.* His son is embarrassed. *Conflict.* Pratt tells the boy he'll curry favor with no man and take snuff in front of any, even the President. Then Revere brings in the tea set and all hell breaks loose.

Cut to the present. A history graduate student named Peter Fallon is studying Pratt's old ledgers and finds a strange note, written to Pratt from the White House on the night in 1814 that the British burned Washington. It mentions a tea set, arriving in the Back Bay "ten to fifteen days hence." It's signed by someone named DL. Fallon ends the scene wondering, who is DL?

I decided to answer that question in the next scene, and that decision made *Back Bay* a best seller. I cut back to the White House in 1814 and the character of DL, Dexter Lovell, a Pratt agent who engineers the theft of the tea set from under Dolly Madison's nose. With that scene, history became more than a mere set-up for the modern treasure hunt. The movement of the tea set through history *became the story*.

By alternating chapters throughout the book, I was able to propel the story along on converging tracks, past and present, that finally meet. Writing *Back Bay* became like writing a serial, with a cliffhanger at the end of every chapter. I would leave my characters twisting in 1814, jump forward and move on to characters twisting in the present, then jump back, and do it again. The reader who might want to skip chapters wouldn't dare, because every chapter was focused on that tea set—stealing it, losing it, hunting for it, finding it, and losing it again.

There is a term in screenwriting called the *through-line*: the idea that keeps the story moving. What does the character want and how is he drawn along?

Think of your novel as a journey. Your readers want to be taken along with your characters through time, across space, toward a conclusion that satisfies them—and may teach them something, too. A plot element like that tea set can cut through your story like the white line down the middle of the road, whether you're traveling across a thousand years of history or a few weeks.

With *Cape Cod,* I attempted a novel that was broader in scope than anything I'd written before. I decided once more to set historical and modern stories on converging tracks, and even though *Cape Cod* is thirty percent longer than *Back Bay,* covering ten centuries instead of two, I found a plot element to hold it together—the lost log of the *Mayflower.* The log—and the knowledge it may contain—gives every chapter and every character a focus, past and present.

In my new novel, *Annapolis,* I have written another multi-generational saga. This one follows an American naval family from the early eighteenth century to the present, while telling the story of the U.S. Navy from the Revolution to Vietnam. It's not a buried treasure story, but I find that the things I learned in *Back Bay* and refined with *Cape Cod* still help me to organize great spans of time.

Annapolis is ninety percent history (compared with fifty percent in *Back Bay* and seventy-five in *Cape Cod*), but I still employ that past-and-present converging-track structure, because in a book like this, modern characters provide an important perspective. As they attempt to understand the mysteries of the past, they demonstrate for the reader how directly past affects present, whether we're discussing grand political movements or the misguided decisions of ancestors who lived two hundred years ago.

But in order for their perspective to have dramatic meaning, the modern characters need that plot element to tie them directly to the historical characters. In *Annapolis,* I've built an old Annapolis mansion, so all the characters will have something to fight over when they're not sailing off to war. But the book is really unified by a thematic element rather than a physical object.

I know that starting with a theme and tacking on a story is going back-end-first. Still, a little thematic control may be the best way to find a through-line in a book that covers nine historical eras, eight wars, six battles, about two hundred characters, *and* is a book-within-a-book, to boot.

A modern character, Jack Stafford, is writing the story of his family in the Navy. His theme is the evolution of honor. But he cannot confront the last, most painful chapter, in which honor is sacrificed in

Vietnam. So he asks another character to read his book from the beginning. Through the nine interconnected stories, each sustaining suspense and providing a climax of its own, his characters wrestle with their visions of honor, and the story travels inexorably back to the Mekong Delta, a dark night in 1968, and a final clash between honor and chaos.

Jack Stafford never worries about facts getting in the way of *The Stafford Story,* his book within the book, because he knows that the facts of history provide some of the best stories. And he learns, as he confronts Vietnam, that sometimes it is as important to be true to the spirit of history as to the letter.

And that's something I've been learning since I wrote about that 1789 banquet. Know the facts, use them because they bring the past to life, but remember why your readers are there. They want to see history before it became history, when nobody knew what was going to happen next.

In my *Annapolis* research, I read a riveting war patrol report by the commander of the submarine *Nautilus,* the first U.S. vessel to find the Japanese fleet at the battle of Midway:

0824: The picture presented on raising the periscope was one never experienced in peacetime practices. Ships were on all sides moving across the field at high speeds and circling away to avoid the submarine's position . . .

There is a sense of awe in that passage that you can almost feel, a sense of fear that you can almost smell, because you know that some of those Japanese ships are going to come after the *Nautilus.* Do the commander and the fictional lieutenant that I put aboard fight or run? Live or die? We know who won the battle of Midway, but for the reader who goes aboard that cramped little submarine, the only question is, what happens next?

Even in a submarine, I look for the ground-level perspective on history. I ask myself, what does it feel like in my characters' shoes? How are they changed by their confrontation with history? How do they change history as they go through it? To a reader of fiction, the answers to these questions are as important as the facts of history . . . maybe more so, because they tell the human story embedded in history.

188

➤➤ 43

THE CRAFT OF THE ESPIONAGE THRILLER

BY JOSEPH FINDER

WHEN I WAS IN MY MID-TWENTIES AND STRUGGLING TO WRITE MY first novel, *The Moscow Club,* I got to know another aspiring writer, a cynical and embittered (but very funny) man, and told him I was immersed in the research for a spy thriller I hadn't begun to write. He shook his head slowly and scowled. "That's a sign of desperation," he intoned ominously. "Research is an excuse for not writing."

This ex-friend has given up trying to write and is working at some job he despises, while I'm making a living writing novels, so I think there may be a moral here. That old dictum writers are always accosted by—"Write what you know"—is, in the espionage-thriller genre, at least, a fallacy.

Obviously, research is no substitute for good writing, good storytelling, or the ability to create flesh-and-blood characters. But even the masters of the spy novel plunge into research for the worlds they create. John le Carré (the pen name for David Cornwell) was for a short while a spy for the British secret service, but nevertheless, he assiduously researches his spy tales. In the extensive acknowledgements at the end of *The Night Manager,* he thanks numerous sources in the U.S. Drug Enforcement Agency and the U.S. Treasury, mercenary soldiers, antiques dealers, and the "arms dealers who opened their doors to me." The novel only *reads* effortlessly.

I suppose you can just make it up, but it will always show, if you do, and the spy thriller must always evoke an authentic, fully realized world. Readers want to believe that the author is an authority, an expert, an insider who's willing to let them in on a shattering secret or two.

But no one can be expert in everything. My first novel was about a

CIA analyst who learns of an impending coup attempt in Moscow and is drawn into the conspiracy. In the first draft, however, the hero, Charles Stone, was instead a ghostwriter for a legendary American statesman. Luckily, my agent persuaded me that no one wants to read about the exploits of a ghostwriter.

Transforming Charlie into a CIA officer took a lot of rethinking, but fortunately, I had sources: While a student at Yale, I'd been recruited by the CIA (but decided against it), and I had some friends in the intelligence community. They helped me make Charlie Stone a far more interesting, more appealing and believable character.

The best ideas, I believe, spring from real-life events, from reading newspapers and books, and from conducting interviews. Frederick Forsyth came up with the idea for his classic thriller, *The Day of the Jackal* (a fictional plot on the life of Charles de Gaulle), from his experience working as a Reuters correspondent in Paris in the early 1960s, when rumors kept circulating about assassination attempts on de Gaulle. Robert Ludlum was watching TV news in a Paris hotel when he happened to catch a report about an international terrorist named Carlos; this became the seed for one of his best novels, *The Bourne Identity.*

When I first began thinking about writing the novel that later became *The Moscow Club,* I was a graduate student at the Harvard Russian Research Center, studying the politics of the Soviet Union. I remember reading Forsyth's *The Devil's Alternative,* which concerns intrigue in the Kremlin. Why not try my hand at this? I thought. After Mikhail Gorbachev became head of the Soviet Union and began the slow-motion revolution that would eventually lead to the collapse of that empire, I began to hear bizarre rumors about attempts in Moscow to unseat Gorbachev. The rumors didn't seem so far-fetched to me. But when *The Moscow Club* came out at the beginning of 1991, I was chided for my overly active imagination. Then, in August of that year, the real thing happened: The KGB and the military banded together to try to overthrow the Gorbachev government—and suddenly, I was a prophet!

My second novel, however, was a significant departure from this political background. *Extraordinary Powers* concerns Ben Ellison, an attorney for a prestigious Boston law firm (and former clandestine operative for the CIA). He is lured into a top-secret government experiment and emerges with a limited ability to "hear" the thoughts of others. This sprang from a reference I'd come across in a study of the KGB to some highly secret programs in the U.S. and Soviet governments that attempted to locate people with telepathic ability to serve in various espionage undertakings. Whether or not one believes in ESP, the fact that such projects really do exist was irresistible to me. I sent *Extraordinary Powers* to a friend who does contract work for the CIA; he confided in me that he'd received a call from a highly placed person in a government agency who actually runs such a project and had used psychics during the Gulf War. He wanted to know whether I'd been the recipient of a leak.

With this seemingly fantastic premise at the center of my novel, it was crucially important that the world in which this plot takes place be a very real, very well-grounded one. Because I wanted the telepathy project to hew as closely to reality as possible, I spent a great deal of time talking to patent lawyers, helicopter pilots, gold experts, and even neurologists. I was relieved to get letters from a world-famous neurobiologist and from the editor of *The New England Journal of Medicine* saying that they were persuaded that such an experiment was within the realm of possibility.

In one crucial scene in *The Moscow Club,* Charlie had to smuggle a gun through airport security, but I had no idea how this might actually work, so I tracked a knowledgeable gun dealer, and after I'd convinced him I was a writer, not a criminal, he became intrigued by the scenario and agreed to help. It turned out that this fellow had a friend who used to be in the Secret Service and had actually taken a Glock pistol and got it past the metal detectors and X-ray machines in security at Washington's National Airport and onto a plane to Boston. He then showed me exactly how he'd done it, so I could write about it accurately. (I left out a few key details to foil any potential hijacker.)

Can readers tell when a scene or a detail is authentic? I believe so. I'm convinced that painstaking research can yield a texture, an atmosphere of authenticity, that average readers can feel and smell. (There will always be a few experts waiting to pounce. In *Extraordinary Powers,* I mistakenly described a Glock 19 as having a safety, and I continue to get angry letters about it.)

The longer I write, it seems, the more research I do. For my forthcoming novel, *Prince of Darkness,* whose hero is a female FBI counter-terrorism specialist, I managed to wangle official cooperation from the FBI, and I spent a lot of time talking to several FBI Special Agents. I also interviewed past and present terrorism experts for the CIA, asking them such questions as, would they really be able to catch a skilled professional terrorist—as well as some seemingly trivial ones.

Since the other main character in *Prince of Darkness* is a professional terrorist-for-hire, I thought it was important to talk to someone who's actually been a terrorist. This was not easy. In fact, it took me months to locate an ex-terrorist (through a friend of a friend) who was willing to talk. But it was worth the time and effort: My fictional terrorist is now, I think, far more credible than he'd have been if I'd simply invented him.

I've done interviews with a convicted forger for details on how to falsify a U.S. passport; with a bomb disposal expert about how to construct bombs; with an expert in satellite surveillance to help me describe authentically how the U.S. government is able to listen in on telephone conversations. I've often called upon the expertise of police homicide detectives, retired FBI agents, helicopter pilots, pathologists, even experts in embalming (or "applied arts," as they are called).

Since an important character in *Prince of Darkness* is a high-priced call girl, I spent a lot of time interviewing prostitutes, expensive call girls, and madams. As a result of this groundwork, I think this particular character is more sympathetic, more believable, than I'd have drawn her otherwise.

Because international settings are often integral parts of spy novels, I strongly believe that travel—really being there in Paris, say, or Rome, or wherever—not only can help you create plausible settings, make them look and smell and feel real, but can suggest scenes and ideas that would otherwise never occur to you. But not everyone can afford to travel (or likes to; ironically, Robert Ludlum, whose plots traverse the globe, abhors traveling). No doubt you can get by tolerably well consulting a good guidebook or two.

Gathering research material is a strange obsession, but it's by far the best part of writing thrillers. I will admit, however, that this passion can go too far. In Rome, I was pickpocketed while standing in a *gelato* shop. When I realized that my passport and all my cash and travelers checks were gone, I panicked. I searched for the perpetrator and came upon a man who looked somewhat shifty. I approached him and pleaded, in my pathetic Italian, *"Per favore, signore! Per favore!* My passport! *Per piacere!"* When the man responded by unzipping his travel bag to prove he didn't have my belongings, that he was innocent, I knew I'd found my man. I told him quietly: "Look, I'm on my honeymoon. If you give me back my passport and my money, I promise I won't turn you in."

He looked around and furtively put my passport and wallet back in my bag.

At this point any sane tourist would flee, but, I went on, "One more thing. If you'll agree to be interviewed, I won't call the police."

He looked at me as if I were out of my mind. "I'm quite serious," I said. "Let me buy you an espresso."

He sat down at a table with me as I explained that I was doing research for a novel partly set in Rome. Flattered that a writer would take an interest in his life, he began to tell me all about how he got into this line of work, about his childhood in Palermo spent snatching purses, about how he travels around Europe frequenting international gatherings of the rich and famous, how he lives in hotels and is often lonely. He explained how he spots an easy mark, how he fences passports, which travelers checks he has no interest in. He demonstrated how he picks pockets and handbags, and taught me how to make sure it never happened to me again.

Much of the information I gleaned from this pickpocket later turned up in the Italy sequence in *Extraordinary Powers.*

I'm certainly not suggesting that a committed espionage novelist must go out of his way to get his pockets picked in Rome, or consort with convicted forgers, assassins, or terrorists. But the longer I write espionage fiction, the more strongly I'm convinced that if you're going to write about unusual people and circumstances in a compelling and plausible way, there's really no substitute for firsthand experience.

>> 44

CREATING MEMORABLE ENDINGS

BY PETER ROBINSON

JUST AS YOU HAVE TO HOOK READERS AT THE BEGINNING OF YOUR story, you have to hook them again at the end. The final hook is different in kind from the opening one—after all, you are not trying to make someone turn the pages faster at the end—but last impressions do count a lot.

Writers trying to get published are far more concerned about making their openings, plots, characters, and narrative structures so strong that an editor will actually read their manuscripts all the way to the end. Beginnings get all the polish; endings are often just left to fizzle out. Yet if you plan to write more than one novel, a powerful ending can be an important way of building up a loyal readership. And if your beginning and middle are so good, then why should you skimp on your ending? Imagine how an audacious and unusual final page or paragraph might just sway an editor who already likes the manuscript enough to have read that far.

Many endings, particularly in the crime field, are trite and conventional. This is partly because mystery fiction often demands some variation of the "Golden Age" ending, in which the detective explains to the suspects assembled in the vicarage drawing-room how he solved the crime.

But mystery fiction—or any other kind of fiction, for that matter—doesn't have to end like that if you remember that every book can have *two* endings: The first ties up the strands of the plot, whereas the second presents some powerful image, action, or dramatic scene, leaving the reader with something to think about after finishing the book. If you are lucky, of course, both endings merge into one.

The first ending is relatively easy to handle if you keep in mind one or two basic points. After all, if you have spent so much time working

194

out your plot, planting the clues and red herrings, you must not leave anything hanging. Keep a written record of all your clues and tick them off as you tie them up. Make sure you explain all your red herrings away. Your ending should stem logically and naturally from situations and events you have already set up in the narrative, with no new material thrown in at the last minute.

The most interesting decision with the first ending is whether you should tie up *all* the loose ends. This depends very much on how close to reality you want your story to appear. In real life, few loose ends are tied up; threads are left hanging; important events may remain unexplained, and we can rarely see a person's motives with the clarity of a novelist.

I recall something P. D. James said some years ago about the modern mystery: Justice may be done and order may be restored at the end of the story, but the cost, in human terms, is often very high. Some characters' lives have been so contaminated by their contact with the criminal investigation that they will never be the same.

Modern mysteries can and do reflect this duality. Often, the guilty go unpunished, and the innocent suffer. Many mysteries have just and logical solutions that, nonetheless, leave a legacy of misery and disruption behind. Occasionally, the villain gets away, which we know happens often enough in real life. Patricia Highsmith created an interesting villain in her "Ripley" novels—a character who literally gets away with murder. Whether this kind of first ending is for you or not depends on how morally complex your plot is. It is no mean feat to write a book in which your villain escapes, and your readers praise you for it.

In writing a series, you also have the option toward the end of introducing a twist in the lives of one or more series characters. An affair begins, perhaps, or seems about to, and the reader has to wait until the next book to find out exactly what happens. This loses its effect if you overdo it, but a few subtle hints that there are changes in store for your series characters next time around certainly won't be amiss.

The second ending has not so much to do with plot and loose ends as with leaving the reader *something to remember you by*. It may consist of your final sentence, paragraph, or a brief scene, and it involves taking risks and daring to be unconventional.

When I came to the end of writing *The Hanging Valley,* I wanted to avoid the conventional gathering of suspects and explanation of the

195

crime, so I took care of all that obliquely in an earlier scene and ended, instead, with dramatic action. That ending has always been associated in my mind with the final piano chord of The Beatles' "A Day in the Life." It comes with a loud crash and reverberates long after.

Most readers responded positively to my ending, but one person told me she took the book back to the shop because she thought there must be some pages missing from the end. That's what happens when you take risks.

Sometimes you don't finish your story until, literally, the last sentence. To illustrate what I mean, I will give away the ending of my book *Past Reason Hated.* For those who haven't read it, this won't ruin the plot element because it deals more with theme and subtext.

Throughout *Past Reason Hated,* my series character, Inspector Banks, is at odds with a new police image being foisted on the public. It is a paternalistic image of bobbies on the beat and your friendly neighborhood copper showing you the way, telling you the time. This false, nostalgic image is symbolized for Banks by the antiquated blue light outside the police station.

At the end of the book, Banks is walking back to the police station on an icy night after solving a particularly tragic murder and explaining the ironies of the case to the bereaved lover. Earlier, he had confiscated a catapult (British term for slingshot) from a teenager who was using it to shoot pebbles at the ducks on the river:

About twenty yards beyond the station, on Market Street, he stopped and turned. That damn blue light was still shining above the door like a beacon proclaiming benign, paternal innocence and simplicity. Almost without thinking, he took the catapult from his pocket, scraped up a couple of fair-sized stones from the icy gutter, put one in the sling and took aim. The stone clattered on the pavement somewhere along North Market Street. He took a deep breath, sighed out a plume of air, then aimed again carefully, trying to recreate his childhood accuracy. This time the lamp disintegrated in a burst of powder-blue glass, and Banks took off down a side-street, the back way home, feeling guilty and oddly elated, like a naughty schoolboy.

And so the book ends. While I make no claims for this as a great ending, it does illustrate some points I want to make about the often overlooked *second* ending.

First, it is *unusual.* We don't normally expect our fictional police heroes to go around acting the way Banks does here. Secondly, though this ending is not essential to the plot, it ties in strongly with one *theme,* that of the difference between public image and reality, and it reveals the main character's reactions to this.

Thirdly, it ends the book on a note of *action,* an image rather than a dry statement. It proffers a strongly *visual* scene that is likely to stick in the reader's mind. Fourthly, it adds something to our understanding of the *character.* We have never seen Banks act this way before. He is a policeman, not a common vandal, but here we watch him destroy public property and, I hope, sympathize with his motives. Because in fiction you can be with someone even when he is alone, you see Banks here in a private moment, when he thinks nobody is watching. Usually he is the responsible, if slightly irreverent, cop, but here you get some insight into the mischievous child inside him.

Most writers, and some readers, know that characters in a novel have no life beyond what they are given on the page. If it were important for readers to know what happens to someone after the narrative, then the author would have to add an extra chapter or write a sequel.

On the other hand, anyone who loves books knows that characters can live on in the imagination and haunt a reader long after the story is over. In the same way, fictional events can often resonate well beyond the pages in which they were "lived." If you follow this line of thinking, you will see that the more memorable you make your ending, the more a scene of action reverberates like a piano chord; and the more strongly a visual image is lodged in the reader's mind, then the more chance you have of hooking readers into buying your next book, and the one after that.

197

➤➤ 45

WHY HORROR?

BY GRAHAM MASTERTON

FEW PEOPLE UNDERSTAND THAT WRITERS ARE WRITING ALL THE time.

To think that a writer is writing only when he or she is actually hammering a keyboard is like believing that a police officer's job is "arresting people."

Even while they're not sitting down at the word processor, writers are writing in their heads. Inventing stories. Playing with words. Thinking up jokes and riddles and metaphors and similes. These days, I write both historical sagas and horror novels. Most people relish historical sagas, but I'm often asked, "Why do people like horror?"

I think they like horror novels because they depict ordinary people dealing with extraordinary threats. They like to imagine, what would *I* do if a dark shadow with glowing red eyes appeared in my bedroom at night? What would *I* do if I heard a sinister scratching inside the walls of my house? What would *I* do if my husband's head turned around 360 degrees?

I've found my inspiration for horror stories in legends from ancient cultures, and my research into how these demons came to be created by ordinary men and women is fascinating. Each of them represents a very real fear that people once felt, and often still do.

There are beguiling men who turn into evil demons. There are monsters that suck your breath when you're asleep. There are gremlins that steal children. There are horrible gorgons that make you go blind just to look at them, and vampires that drain all of the energy out of you. There are zombies who come back from the dead and torment you.

My favorite Scottish demons were the glaistigs, hideous hags who were supposed to be the ghosts of women haunting their former homes.

They were frequently accompanied by a child who was called "the little plug" or "the whimperer." If you didn't leave out a bowl of milk for the glaistigs, they would suck your cows dry or drain their blood. Sometimes a glaistig would carry her little whimperer into the house, and bathe it in the blood of the youngest infant in the house, and the victim would be found dead and white in the morning.

Now, this is a legend, but you can understand what genuine fears it expresses. A woman's fear of other women intruding into her home, as in the film, *Fatal Attraction*; a man's fear of losing his livelihood; parents' fear of losing their children to malevolent and inexplicable illnesses, such as crib death. What I do is take these ancient demons, which are vivid and expressive manifestations of basic and genuine fears, and write about them in an up-to-date setting, with modern characters.

The very first horror novel I wrote was called *The Manitou*. A manitou is a Native American demon, and in this novel a 300-year-old medicine man was reborn in the present day to take his revenge on the white man. I was inspired to write that by *The Buffalo Bill Annual, 1956*.

Since then I have written books based on Mexican demons, Balinese demons, French demons and Biblical demons, two dozen in all, and I'm working on another one about the Glasgow woman who makes a pact with Satan so that her house disappears every time the rent collector calls.

I started writing horror novels at school, when I was 11. I used to read them to my friends during recess. Reading your work out loud is always invaluable training. When I met one of my old school friends only recently, he said, "I'll never forget the story you wrote about the woman with no head who kept singing 'Tiptoe Through the Tulips.' It gave me nine years of sleepless nights, and I still can't have tulips in the house."

Horror books seem to sell well all over the world, with some notable exceptions, like Germany. The French love horror, and the Poles adore it. In France, *Le Figaro* called me "Le Roi du Mal," the King of Evil. I was the first Western horror novelist to be published in Romania, home of Dracula. I received a letter from a reader this week saying, "I have to write to congratulate you on a wonderful book, rich with ideas and shining with great metaphors. Also very good printing, and excellent paper, which is appreciated here because of bathroom tissue shortage."

How extreme can you be when you write horror? As extreme, I think, as your talent and your taste permit, although gruesomeness is no substitute for skillful writing. I had several complaints about a scene in my book *Picture of Evil*, in which the hero kills two young girls with a poker. People protested my graphic description of blood spattering everywhere. In fact, I never once mentioned blood. All I said was, "He clubbed them to death like two baby seals." The reader's imagination was left to do the rest.

It is catching the mood and feel of a moment that makes your writing come to life. Most of the time you can dispense with whole realms of description if you catch one vivid image; catching those images requires thought and research. When I write historical novels, I frequently rent period costumes which my wife and I try on so I can better understand how my characters would have moved and behaved when wearing them. How do you rush to meet your lover when wearing a hobble skirt? How do you sit down with a bustle?

We also prepare food and drink from old recipes, using cookbooks by Fannie Farmer, Mrs. Beeton, and Escoffier. One of the least successful period drinks we prepared was the King's Death, drunk by King Alfonso of Spain in the Men's Bar of the Paris Ritz. The King's Death is made with wild strawberries marinated in Napoleon brandy, then topped up with half a bottle of champagne—each! We served it to some dinner party guests, and they became incoherent and had to go home.

Whether you're writing history or horror, thrillers or love stories, the most important technique is to live inside the book instead of viewing it from the outside. Your word processor or typewriter is nothing more than a key that opens the door to another world. When I'm writing, I step into that world, so that it surrounds me. So many writers as they write look only forward at the page, or screen, forgetting what's all around them.

Think of the rain on the side of your face and the wind against your back. Think of what you can hear in the distance. Think of the fragrances you can smell. Most of all, *be* all your characters: Act out their lives, act out their movements and their facial expressions, and speak their dialogue out loud. Get up from your keyboard sometimes, and do what you've imagined; then sit down and write it. The Disney artist Ward Kimball used to draw Donald Duck by making faces in the mirror. You can do the same when you're writing about the way your characters act and react.

Your best research is watching real live people living out their real lives. Watch every gesture, every nuance, listen to people's conversations and accents. Try to propel your story along at the pace that *you* would like to read it. Avoid showing off in your writing; all that does is slow down your story and break the spell you have been working so hard to conjure up. How many times has your suspension of disbelief been broken by ridiculous similes, like "her bosoms swelled like two panfuls of overboiling milk."

Two similes that really caught my attention and which I later used in novels were an old Afrikaner's description of lions roaring "like coal being delivered," and the hideous description by an Australian prisoner of war of two of his fellow prisoners being beheaded: "the blood spurted out of their necks like red walking-sticks."

To my mind, the greatest achievement in writing is to create a vivid, spectacular novel without readers being aware that they are reading at all. My ideal novel would be one that readers put down, and discover that they're still in it, that it's actually come to life.

The other day I was reading *Secrets of the Great Chefs of China,* and apart from the eel recipe, where you throw live eels into boiling water and have to clamp the lid down quickly to stop them from jumping out of the pot, the most memorable advice the book gave was, "A great chef prepares his food so that it is ready for the mouths of his guests; it is both a courtesy and a measure of his professionalism." That goes for writing, too.

>> 46

WRITING CRIME FICTION

BY GWENDOLINE BUTLER

YOU MUST ENJOY READING DETECTIVE AND CRIME STORIES OR YOU should not think of writing one. It is work, of course, sometimes hard work, but always enjoyable. Don't wait for the ideal day, the ideal moment; there isn't one. And don't worry too much about the perfect beginning—you can always go back and rewrite. Just begin. If you wait, you may never start.

Do not let the story go dead on you. I try to write about a thousand words a day, but every writer must set her own quota. When I do more than my usual thousand, I regard it as money in the bank for the days (and they come, believe me) when creation is a real slog.

Do not wait for inspiration; you may not get it if you just sit looking at a blank page. Start typing, and it will come. The mere act of putting words on paper will oil the wheels and get your imagination working.

Some writers know their plot in detail before they begin writing; others, of whom I am one, know the beginning and the end and let the story grow in between. It does not matter which school you belong to—and indeed it may change from book to book—but keep notes on names, times of day, days of the week on which events take place. You can fall into a hole if you are not careful, and discover as you check your manuscript that two events cannot happen on the same day as your plot demands, unless you create a day with thirty-two hours!

I always keep a notebook with me and one by my bed for ideas, useful bits of dialogue that I can jot down at once, because otherwise they never can be recalled in quite the neat, clever way in which they first popped up.

A study of the different genres of crime writing is important, too: the so-called cosies, the police procedurals, the female private investigator or police detective, the horror and blood crime story. Not long ago, the "gothic" was immensely popular. (Its popularity has waned a little.) The genres are not always clearly distinct, and one may merge into another. I enjoy trying different types; I won a Dagger from the CWA for a story about a girl in late-Victorian Oxford that was almost a gothic, but tougher and less romantic.

You may also feel drawn more to one genre than the others. But study the market, read the competition; trends go up and down.

Now that you've made your choice, the first thing I want to say may not sound much like encouragement, rather like the surgeon saying this may hurt but you will be the better for it. Crime writing is demanding. It will take energy, dedication, professionalism. You'll need stamina, because unless you strike luck with first-time publication (say film or TV rights sold), you'll need to build your career up by writing regularly, a book a year. You owe this not only to your publisher, who has invested money in you, but to your readers. And there is another, more personal reason for regular writing: As you write you will develop, you will hone your skills.

Beginning each day can be a hurdle to a writer who lacks confidence, but there are various tricks for getting around this. At the end of their writing for the day, some authors leave a sentence hanging in midair so they know where to start the next day. I tried this and found it did not help me; experience has taught me that I have to write myself out for the day. In the morning, I plunge straight into writing, knowing that if necessary, I can cut. Somehow this seems to get my mind working so that after a short time, I find sentences coming easily. Similarly, there are points when you sink into the slough of despond. For me, this usually comes about two-thirds of the way through. Don't despair, just write on, one word after another, as if you're climbing a staircase.

You have a story to tell, so where will it come from? The story is made of several parts: *plot* or storyline; *character*; and *background*. Of course, you cannot separate these three elements, because your characters are rooted in the background, and the plot derives from the interaction among the three. But suppose, determined to start your crime story, you draw a blank as to a plot? How do you start assembling one? Remember that you are writing a crime novel, which demands straightaway a victim, an aggressor, an investigator, and of course, a crime.

Is there only one victim, or several? When you have decided this, you have taken your first step. What sex will your victim be? If a woman, then love and jealousy may account for her death. If more than one woman is involved, you may have started on a serial-killer crime. I always find writing these interesting. If the victim is a man or if here, too, you have several victims, then is it an organized crime killing?

The characters are beginning to have faces. Name your main character at once, remembering that certain names suggest certain personalities and backgrounds. An Ada, for instance, is not likely to be an adolescent, but an older woman from a working-class family. I am going to give a bit of advice that I learned the hard way: MAKE A LIST OF YOUR CHARACTERS' NAMES, and keep it pinned on the wall in front of you. Believe me, it will do away with many frantic searches with you wondering, Did I call the detective's sidekick—or the police surgeon, or the victim's best friend—George or Dr. Curzon or Fiona?

When the principal character is named and his or her fate is clear in your mind, your plot starts to build. On occasion—and this is a gift from the gods—a plot idea will fall, fully formed, into your mind. Welcome it, but take care, because when this happens, character tends to take a secondary place to mechanics of the plot. There is a natural reason for this: Your imagination has not been gripped by the characters, but by the working of the plot. So you will need to do extra work, taking care to create live, believable characters. The background, too, the world in which your plot will play itself out, must be real, but it is people who will drive the plot forward.

It is hard for readers to take in a large cast all in one gulp, so introduce your characters with care, not all in the first chapter, even though you may mention them or hint at their existence. In this way you catch readers' attention and make them turn the page. Remember that you don't have to reveal everything about your characters in narrative; it is more interesting and amusing if you do so through dialogue. No need to say that Henrietta is clumsy; instead her friend Alice can cry out: "Oh, Hetty, you really have to be more careful. You nearly knocked that table over." Readers like to work things out from hints. Here dialogue is very important, and the language and rhythm must suit the speaker.

I don't like to use dialogue for its own sake. I use it to move the action, or make a plot point. Having a character in the wings, a surprise, is also a good idea.

Where do I get my plots? Sometimes from air; I start writing and it grows, almost of its own accord, and it can surprise me as much as it does my readers. Sometimes I get a beginning from something I saw, as when in Rome I went to the oldest, most rundown little waxwork show, which later gave me the beginning for a novel set in Windsor. Drama is all around you; some days you will find that you hardly need to invent: Look across the road. There is a woman standing on the corner; you can see her from your worktable in the window. (Do have a worktable and window; a blank wall is no help to the imagination.) Do not believe those who say the story must come from inside you: It is the interaction between your mind and the outside world that will give your story life.

In crime fiction you have to provide clues. The detective who is working on the case will need what I call "top clues," that is, clues that are pointed out in the text for the detective to follow, and the reader, too, of course. Such clues as a pair of men's shoes—not the victim's—beside the victim. Are they the killer's? If so, then the reader assumes the killer is a man. But why leave the shoes? The wily reader and the sharp detective have to ask if the shoes are false clues, planted by the killer to turn the suspicion toward a man. But is the killer actually a woman?

There is one more point: When the shoes are first mentioned, they are described as black and white. This description comes up again in the next paragraph. After this second mention, experienced readers will say, "That means something," and as they turn the pages, they'll begin to look for what it is. This is what I mean by a hidden clue put in to intrigue readers.

As you write, you may discover, as I often do, that you have to go back to plant clues that are necessary as your plot develops. A bit of deception and double dealing comes in useful here. I like writing a sentence that appears to mean one thing, but at the end, will have the reader saying, "So that's what it meant!"

Of course, you will have moments of crisis: Don't draw back from them. When your self-confidence seems to collapse with the credibility of your plot, you may well end up with that extra element your plot needs: a new character to lend a twist to the action in another chapter.

Sharp observation skills are necessary for any writer of fiction, but perhaps especially for the crime writer, for whom it is vital to create a believable world with all the details of setting, behavior, and dialogue accurate and fresh. Keep in mind that you have invented a possibly hard-to-believe plot that you must buttress by accuracy in every particular, so your reader will willingly suspend disbelief.

TELL THE READER WHERE IT HURTS

By George C. Chesbro

DOES YOUR HERO OR HEROINE HAVE A PROBLEM? NO PROBLEM. LIKE a grain of sand in an oyster, something out of place in a fictional character—a constant irritation, a character flaw, inconsolable sorrow, a physical disability—can often result in something gleaming, rare, and of great worth. For an author, this means the creation of a fictional character who is three-dimensional and, well, "rounded," who moves around on the pages and through the plot instead of just sitting there; also a person whose welfare the reader may come to care about as much as the resolution of whatever game is afoot, and perhaps even more. This burden borne by the character may be an essential part of the plot, but not necessarily—unless, of course, the theme is revenge, where pain and rage are the driving forces. The point of the "problem" is that it gives the heroine or hero a unique perspective on life and events, which can then be shared with the reader. People who know serious suffering often feel empathy with the underdog, and pain compels them to swim naturally—and believably—in ever deeper and darker waters that more balanced and less haunted people would certainly avoid.

Literature, especially mystery fiction, abounds with examples: alcoholics, compulsive thieves, the lame, lonely, paralyzed and blind. However, for the purposes of this discussion, I will limit my observations to my fictional creation, one Dr. Robert Frederickson, aka Mongo the Magnificent, who is an achondroplastic dwarf.

When the notion of a dwarf as private investigator first occurred to me, I vigorously opposed the idea. I was searching for a "different" kind of series character, but this was ridiculous. I couldn't see how anybody would take him seriously—not prospective clients, and, even more dreadful to contemplate, not editors, who would scoff at the exploits of such an unlikely character and reject my efforts. I would be wasting my time.

This constant specter of rejection and humiliation was, of course, precisely the point, and is at the core of what makes Mongo such a rich human being. But it took me a while to realize this.

Fortunately for me, Mongo is tough, and he would not be denied. Try as I might to conjure up a more "suitable" candidate who would be easier for me to work with, the damn dwarf just kept tapping at the back doors of my mind, insisting that I give him a chance to live, grow, and show me what he could do. Well, what was I to do?

I still didn't believe I could sell this guy, but in order to get him off my mind's back porch, I let him in, looked him over a bit more carefully, sat down at my typewriter, and sent this wounded but incredibly resilient man out into the world. Almost immediately Mongo began to touch me in a myriad of odd and mysterious ways. Regardless of how he was treated by prospective clients and editors, *I,* at least, would afford him the dignity and respect he deserved. I could feel his pain to a level matched only by his brother, Garth, who had abruptly materialized at his side.

The observation is frequently made that Mongo does not in any way consider himself handicapped, and the fact that he is a dwarf is irrelevant. This is true for Mongo and (one hopes) the reader. But Mongo's dwarfism is never irrelevant to the author, nor to Garth, whose bottomless love for and ferocious devotion to his brother, whom he nurtured and protected in childhood, has led him into those same dark and dangerous waters, where he has been permanently damaged, albeit in a radically different manner. Their strong bonding dates back to a time when Mongo's dwarfism *was* a problem, and it's important for me as the writer to know that, and also that a key to Mongo's character is that he has always been driven to overcompensate for his slight stature, to excel at every challenge he undertakes. This he has done, as a circus headliner, martial arts expert, criminologist, college professor, and, finally, as a private investigator.

Ordinary people do not lead extraordinary lives. If Mongo had not been born a dwarf, it's quite possible that he and Garth would have ended up as dairy farmers on their family's ranch in Nebraska. Then where would *I* be?

Let me give some concrete examples of how Mongo's "problem" has been invaluable to me as an author in both characterization and plotting.

In his debut, we met a man who was determined to achieve the same measure of success in the private arena as he had in the worlds of the circus and academia. Then, Mongo's problem was not that he was a dwarf, but, rather, who was going to *hire* a dwarf private investigator. No Maltese Falcons for Mongo. Only the people who knew Mongo *personally,* who appreciated just how effective he could be, would seek out his help. *I* knew that Mongo's being a dwarf was going to cause him problems, and so the plots of both *Shadow of A Broken Man* and *City of Whispering Stone* have their roots in academia. In *City of Whispering Stone,* Mongo is hired by his former boss in the circus. Being a dwarf did not define what Mongo could do, but it did define the manner in which I could initially unleash him against his foes.

See how useful this "problem" business can be, and how it works? It focuses the minds of both the author and reader.

Then came *The Beasts of Valhalla.* Here, in the first book of what I would come to think of—after the fact—as an epic trilogy (including *Two Songs This Archangel Sings* and *The Cold Smell of Sacred Stone,* with *Second Horseman Out of Eden* as a kind of coda), the lives of the brothers undergo sea changes. As Mongo returns home to Nebraska after an absence of many years to attend the funeral of a favorite nephew, he is haunted by memories of his childhood. There, the reader finally gets an insight into just how tortured those early years were for a dwarf growing up in a rural community in the heartland of America. Mongo had to battle not only evil forces that literally threaten to destroy humankind, but also personal ghosts and demons that threaten to drain his resolve, resources, and courage by once again making him feel small.

The brothers emerge victorious from this great adventure. Garth, however, has been seriously damaged psychologically; now their childhood roles have been reversed, and it is Mongo who must keep a cautious eye on Garth, who, in certain situations, can turn into an avenging angel who takes no prisoners. Again, while Mongo's dwarfism plays only a marginal role in the plots of these books, the *pain* of his past is very evident, and permeates the atmosphere of all the novels. One hopes it has deepened the character and enriched the plots.

And now *Garth* has a "problem," multiplying the possibilities for characterization, new perils, plot twists and turns. While Mongo's "problem" was the heart of *The Beasts of Valhalla,* it is Garth's spiritual pain that throbs at the center of *Second Horseman Out of Eden.*

By the end of the trilogy and coda, the brothers have become world-famous, retained by Fortune 500 companies and government agencies. They are wealthy and comfortable. The devices that launched the plots of my early books are no longer required, indeed, they would not work. Mongo, who has taken his brother, once a cop with the NYPD, on as a partner, has more work than he can handle. His cases can come from anywhere. The fact that he is a dwarf is now even less relevant to plot, but not to *character.* And surely not to the reader who has been following Mongo's exploits, for they understand how the dwarf became father to the giant.

All of this information about Mongo and my insight into what makes him tick did not come to me full-blown. In the beginning I knew only that he was a dwarf. Fiction writing is a spooky business, truly a dark art. Novels, like mushrooms, grow in dark places. There is an absolutely marvelous and magical process I call "discovery" that is a gift to the author when character and story become organic, living things. First you start, and then you find out things as you go along, sometimes in one book, other times over the course of many books. Mongo and Garth are very real to me, *alive,* and so they keep growing and changing in ways that often surprise and delight me. (Fiction writing can be thought of as dreams becoming words, a kind of controlled madness.)

I believe that any success enjoyed by the series is a result not so much of the plots (which have been accurately described as ranging from the bizarre to the very bizarre), as of the character of Mongo. The very first discovery I made about him, apart from his dwarfism, was that *everything* he did was part of a quest for dignity and a desire to be taken seriously—just as every one of us, at one time or another, has felt very small in a world of giants that threatens to crush us. *Voilà*: Reader identification and a willingness to trek with Mongo into some very strange worlds. In exchange for my granting Mongo's request for dignity and to be taken seriously, he has given me a number of rich rewards, including a modicum of success that allows me to make a living doing exactly what I want to do—dream. And it all began with my reflection on one man's pain, and where it might take him.

Telling the reader where a character hurts can often lead to considerable pleasure, satisfaction, and success for an author.

>> 48

WHAT HAPPENS NEXT?
WRITING FOR PLOT

BY KARIN MCQUILLAN

IT WAS A GREAT SHOCK TO ME, WHEN EXAMINING THE FIRST DRAFT of my first novel, to realize that after half a lifetime of reading books and watching movies, I still didn't understand what a plot was well enough to create my own. I'd come up with a solid framework for the story, a mystery called *Deadly Safari*: The heroine, Jazz Jasper, is a spunky American woman who has started her own safari company in Africa, and the story begins as a murder occurs on her first trip with a group of important clients. I'd filled each chapter with exciting events involving clues, wild animals, Maasai warriors, and a vivid set of characters. And yet it didn't hold together, at the end of each chapter you could close the book with a satisfied sigh, instead of reading on till two in the morning. Something was missing: a plot.

I spent the next year on a quest to discover how to write a tight, gripping plot. I analyzed successful novels; I took copious notes on how to create suspense, how to structure scenes; and I tore apart and put together my own book over and over. By the end, I had distilled a few basic principles of excellence and methods of applying them that worked for me.

A strong plot is not a mystical achievement of inborn talents, but like ninety percent of writing, one more element of craft that can be broken down into comprehensible parts, practiced, and eventually mastered. Even after three published works, I don't claim that plotting is the easiest part of writing, but it is often the most satisfying. Nothing equals that wonderful feeling when you get it right, and your story flows from that first paragraph that hooks readers until you let go of them in the final pages.

The three essential elements of creating an excellent plot are the three C's: causality, character, and complication.

Causality: Everything happens for a reason

The key to plot is causality, without which the events of your book are essentially static. What you want to create is a game of billiards, where the initial action sets off a chain of events, A leading to B and C, C ricocheting off D, and B off E, until the last ball falls into the pocket. Since each event has an effect, you create in readers' minds the question, "Given this event, what will happen next?" Will readers keep turning the pages to find out? Without causality, after a given event anything or nothing could happen, and your reader would likely not go on reading.

You can and must make each step seem logical and believable by using foreshadowing, a powerful tool that prepares the reader to accept plot development by planting information earlier in the book that makes later action believable. The foreshadowing may be an object, a fact, a character's values or personality, or an event. As Chekhov said, if you show a gun in Act One, it must go off in Act Three. Conversely, if a gun goes off in Act Three, you must have brought it on stage in Act One. No matter how unusual or heroic the events are, if your foreshadowing is skillfully done, your readers will be willing to suspend disbelief and stay within the fantasy of the story.

Near the beginning of my novel, *The Cheetah Chase,* Jazz Jasper goes to a fancy party in the capital city where she meets a visiting Saudi princess who is presented with a tiny cheetah cub. Jazz is appalled that an endangered wild animal is being used as a pet. She finds out that the princess and her husband are in Kenya on a camping safari in the northern desert. Later in the book, when Jazz is flying in a two-seater plane to a remote part of the northern desert, retracing the last days of the murder victim in an effort to find out what information he might have stumbled on that led to his murder, the reader is prepared for her to discover some place that is secret and dangerous. Her small plane has to make an emergency landing, and Jazz has to trek to her destination—a tribe of nomadic warriors and herders recently visited by the murder victim—where she discovers that the Saudi camp is nearby, and is involved in illegal hunting.

213

This series of events gives readers one surprise after another, but nothing they haven't been prepared for earlier in the story. I foreshadowed the plane crash with a chapter in which Jazz takes a test flight at the airport and finds that the airplane had not been fixed properly. Therefore, although readers are shocked when the fuel tank springs a leak, they believe it could happen, because the plane was badly maintained. Coming upon the Saudis would have seemed a mere coincidence if readers had not already learned in the party scene about the existence and location of the camp. Through foreshadowing, the plot elements are linked in a meaningful chain of events: The victim's murder after a visit to the desert leads Jazz to retrace his steps; poor maintenance leads to a plane crash; searching in the desert leads Jazz to find the Saudi camp, which the reader already knew was in that area. The reader will happily give in to the adventure, and be carried along.

No matter how many dramatic surprises you spring on your readers, if you have included the necessary links in the chain of causality, you will give them the feeling of an inevitable working out of fate. This inexorable rightness is one of the reasons people read novels: It gives the comforting illusion that our crazy world can make logical sense, that things happen for a reason! In the real world, fate is capricious, and random events happen all the time, but in the fictional world, coincidences will make your story seem artificial. Because something really happened that way can never justify its use in a story. The story has its own requirements in order to seem believable, and the primary one is causality.

The unity of character and action

E. M. Forster, in *Aspects of the Novel,* distinguishes between a story and a plot this way: "The king died and then the queen died" is a story. "The king died and then the queen died of grief" is a plot. What makes a plot is causality, which relates the first death to the second death. The queen dying of grief is obviously characterization as well, which brings us to a second key element of plot: the unity of character and action.

Every event in a novel must grow out of and simultaneously build character. The characters are known through their actions; the prime adage of fiction is show, don't tell. At the same time, actions are believ-

214

able because of who that character is, given her history, personality, and relationships with the other characters.

Readers know that my heroine Jazz is impulsive, brave, and passionate in defense of wildlife. Furthermore, the reader has seen Jazz's barely controlled outrage when the Saudi princess is given a cheetah cub as a pet. Still, would she seem a believable character when I later have her steal the cub from the princess's tent? I needed even more preparation to convince the reader that Jazz would risk her life to save an animal. So when the princess shows off the cub to Jazz in the desert chapter, I make the cub look miserable and sick, wearing a tight diamond collar and showing signs of severe dehydration. To bring matters to an emotional head, the cub wriggles to escape the princess's grasp, and she slaps it around.

Identifying with Jazz, the average reader will be incensed and want her to do anything to get that cub away from captivity, abuse, and certain death. Given Jazz's character, she has to try and rescue that cub, and the playing out of this action not only shows new levels of bravery and resourcefulness in Jazz that the reader didn't know she had, it also brings her up against the most severe physical and moral challenges she has ever faced.

If you force a character to act "out of character" just to serve your plot, you will lose plausibility. If it is vital for a given character to take a particular action, then you must prepare the reader to accept and understand why this character would do such a thing by providing convincing motivation earlier in the book. Solving problems like this will make your characters more complex and unique.

If at any time you throw in an irrelevant event because "the character took over," you have lost control of your plot. Instead of A leading to B and C, suddenly readers are wandering down Y, wondering how they got there and what it has to do with anything. It is wonderful when your understanding of a character gives you ideas for the next logical step in the plot; it is a disaster when meandering after a character muddies and even destroys the chain of causality. Actions must be true to character, but they grow out of and lead to other actions.

Complication

Perhaps the most famous definition of plot is: Boy meets girl, boy loses girl, boy gets girl. But this definition is inadequate, because it

215

leaves out causality. It does a good job, however, of capsulizing the basic building blocks of plot: problem, complication, resolution. This little trio repeats itself over and over, from the small scale of every scene to the large scale of the entire book. It is the engine that moves the plot. Your protagonist is confronted with a problem, which arises from his or her goal meeting either internal or external opposition, or both. The most common form for the complication is conflict within and between characters, but it can also be shown in a confrontation with an outside force of circumstance or nature. In meeting the initial problem, the protagonist faces further complications that create an even worse problem, building up to a climax of complete disaster. In the climax, the protagonist meets this seemingly unsolvable problem head on, and either fails or succeeds.

The goal and the conflict will be more meaningful and have greater impact if they are personalized rather than abstract. Instead of having Jazz fight impersonal forces endangering cheetahs, I have her fight for the life of one particular cheetah cub named Comet. The villains are not a generalization about people who buy wild animals as pets, or hunters who bribe officials so they can kill endangered wildlife, but specific characters with faces and names and personal quirks. The idea that saving wildlife requires determination and self-sacrifice on everyone's part is embodied in Jazz's heroic qualities.

The structure of your plot can be drawn as a staircase leading to the climax. Each stair is made of a goal, complication, and partial resolution leading to the next goal. In my book, *Elephants' Graveyard,* the wealthy head of an organization that fights ivory poaching is murdered. One of the first people Jazz wishes to question is Joseph, the victim's confidant, but here the first complication arises: Joseph has abruptly quit his job as family butler, and disappeared. In trying to find him, Jazz is faced with a series of obstacles that are circumstantial, human, and cultural. A relative who is taking care of Joseph's apartment refuses to say where Joseph has gone despite Jazz's most persuasive efforts. When Jazz tries to question neighbors, the relative loudly announces that a juju (magic charm) will harm anyone who talks about Joseph's whereabouts. Jazz and her partner, Inspector Omondi of the Nairobi police, manage to discover that Joseph is driving a cab, and after scouring various colorful Nairobi neighborhoods, trace him to the city's most dangerous shantytown. Just as they are being led to

216

him, Jazz and Omondi are attacked by a gang of thugs with machetes, and Joseph takes off. This is the climax of the sequence: A minor setback has led to a deadly threat, and Jazz's quarry has escaped just as she thought she'd found him.

Through her sense of humor and quick thinking, Jazz turns the thugs into allies, and in a reversal of fortune, the thugs help her nab Joseph. Joseph mistakenly thinks Jazz and Omondi have saved him from attack, and in recompense, is willing to talk to them. But he will tell them only so much, giving them a clue that will lead them into further adventures. And so the next goal—and the next series of complications—are set in motion. Notice that to overcome each difficulty, Jazz and Omondi have to take positive action, which moves the plot forward.

Often a plot falters because the writer has not put complication into a scene. After you have finished the first draft, make an outline that analyzes each chapter: State the goal; the obstacle to achieving that goal; and the partial solution that results from action the protagonists take, leading to a new goal. Read authors whose plots move well, and identify the conflict/resolution sequences that build up to the climax.

Causality, character, and complication: Keep a firm grasp on these principles and you will create tight, dynamic plots that will keep your satisfied audience reading into the wee hours of the morning.

➤➤ 49

WRITING THE FRONTIER NOVEL

BY JOHN EDWARD AMES

NOVELS SET ON THE AMERICAN FRONTIER ARE OFTEN DISMISSED AS formula fiction, quaint "horse operas" about the long-gone past. But in fact they continue to attract and hold readers because their courageous, decent, tough-but-seldom-mean protagonists satisfy an enduring need for homegrown heroic myths—prose versions of the original epic-heroic poems that eventually evolved into modern literature.

"Frontier fiction" is a general category that includes short, action-oriented Westerns (averaging 50,000 to 60,000 words and most often set in the 19th century—what Elmer Kelton calls the familiar "utility Western") as well as series novels and many but not all of the more ambitious, less rigidly defined historical novels. While this category enjoys fewer best sellers than do most other genres, it is certainly enduring.

One reason for this longevity is the loyalty and enthusiasm of the readers drawn to frontier and historical fiction. They expect the basic elements of all good fiction, of course: believable characters, intriguing dialogue, compelling plots and vivid settings. But writers who understand these readers also understand some important conventions of the frontier genre.

1) *Obscure research is less valuable than accurate and interesting details about everyday life.* Just as students of a foreign language start by memorizing the most important, high-frequency words, frontier writers need to compile basic details about daily life in the past: details about foods and beverages, leisure activities, occupations, household objects and furnishings, medicine and doctors, monetary systems and typical prices for common items.

Your editor may or may not know that Indians mounted their horses from the right side, white men from the left. But you had better know it, because some of your readers surely will—and they will resent your ignorance of such basic details. They also expect you to know such things as the value of a double-eagle gold piece or the various steps involved in loading and firing a percussion rifle. Too many writers don't respect the genre enough to go beyond the television clichés from the days of *Bonanza* and *Gunsmoke.*

Nor should you treat "the past" as one vague, fuzzy, undifferentiated period. It's not enough, for example, to know what a hoop skirt is: Do you know exactly when the hoop skirt was all the rage last century, and in what diameters during which decades? Nineteenth-century fashions changed dramatically from decade to decade, and a woman dressed for the theater in 1820 looked very different from her counterpart of 1860.

One good reference source is Marc McCutcheon's *Everyday Life in the 1800's.* Other more general sources for good details include David Lavender's *The Great West* and Mark Twain's *Roughing It.*

2) *Convey research indirectly.* Even though period information is essential, it should never take over or interrupt the dramatic flow of your story. Beginning writers often over-research, sometimes to postpone the more difficult task of composition. Thus armed with stacks of notecards, they produce prose that matches the narrative cadence of a parts catalogue.

One good strategy to help you avoid this pitfall is to skip exposition, when possible, and let your characters inform the readers more naturally in dialogue. Writers tend to report too much when they use exposition; dialogue, in contrast, forces them to select only the most germane details, just as taciturn cowboys are famous for uttering terse sentences stripped down to their bare semantic bones.

In an early draft of my first historical novel, *Unwritten Order,* I included an expository paragraph about the hazards posed by the Comanche penchant for making arrow points out of metal instead of flint. This information was useful, but during revision I realized that a more logical way to convey this relevant information was in the words of the contract surgeon who removed such an arrow from my hero:

"See there?" Enis Hagan said, holding a palm-size iron triangle out in the fading light. "Cut from white man's sheet iron. I'd rather get hit by a flint arrowhead any day over one of these. See there how it bent and clinched when

219

it hit bone? Made it a sonofapup to extract. I had to hook it with a looped wire and pray the shaft didn't come loose."

3) *In frontier fiction, setting itself often assumes the status of a character, usually an antagonist.* This basic rule is necessitated by geography and history, not by the laws of drama. One stark and important fact defines not only the American West, but the main focus of much writing about that vast region west of the hundredth meridian: "The West can count only a very few rivers," wrote Donald Worster in *Under Western Skies,* "all well distanced from one another and many of them drying up by summer's end."

Don't dismiss that quiet sentence as too obvious or irrelevant for writers. The aridity and other harsh physical features of the American West caused far more suffering than gun slingers, the Cavalry, and wild Indians combined, and writers of frontier fiction should reflect this important fact. Indeed, man against nature is a crucial element in much good frontier fiction: The ability to cauterize a wound, find water and shade in the desert, or interpret the warning calls of birds could mean the survival edge in a harsh and unforgiving environment.

4) *Diction or word choice is especially important.* A strong sense of time and place is crucial to frontier fiction. One way writers satisfy this requirement, besides providing vivid descriptions and apt topical references, is through mastery of historically accurate diction.

I've found it useful to remain aware of three major influences on 19th-century frontier diction, each distinct though often overlapping the others: a) the fur-trapping era (circa 1800 to 1850); b) the brief but important cowboy era (circa 1865 to 1890); c) words used by or traditionally associated with Native Americans. I recommend that writers "collect" frontier words and phrases in notebooks, learning the differences among the three main influences and noticing which characters would logically speak which words.

The nomadic fur traders who explored the intermountain West also left perhaps the most colorful influence on frontier speech. Characterized by an earthy directness and a quirky taboo against saying "I" or "me," this mountain-man argot dominated frontier speech during the first half of last century. Three fascinating American novels showcase this unique language and are must reading for frontier writers: *The Big Sky,* by A. B. Guthrie, Jr.; *Lord Grizzly,* by Frederick Manfred; and

Mountain Man, by Vardis Fisher (basis for the movie *Jeremiah Johnson*). Excellent nonfiction sources include Osborne Russell's *Journal of A Trapper* and Irving Stone's *Men to Match My Mountains.*

While the speech of the fur traders has been neglected, cowboy-era lingo is more familiar to many of us. Even so, much of its original color and power have been lost and trivialized by over-reliance on pat words and phrases associated with utility Westerns. The plot of Owen Wister's classic novel *The Virginian* has aged somewhat, but his book is rich with authentic cowboy-era speech. So are the novels of Zane Grey and Frederick Faust (a.k.a. Max Brand). Excellent nonfiction sources include Andy Adams' *Log of A Cowboy* and E. C. "Teddy Blue" Abbott's *We Pointed Them North.*

Diction used by or related to Native Americans poses more problems, especially because many North American Indian languages were never recorded in writing and thus have been lost. Others are too typographically complicated to print; many "Indian" words conventional to frontier fiction are either English translations or mistaken permutations.

All this confusion suggests that would-be frontier writers are well advised to familiarize themselves with the Native American point of view as a precursor to apt word choices for expressing it. One logical place to begin is with the title voted number one on the Western Writers of America's list of the best Western nonfiction books: Dee Brown's *Bury My Heart at Wounded Knee,* a history of the West from the Native American point of view (it includes an excellent bibliography of further sources).

5) *Innovate or evaporate!* Those who don't read frontier novels believe this genre is a crusty old codger, hidebound and resistant to change. They are wrong, but their attitude is understandable. For most of this century Western movies and fiction have been dominated by what Bernard DeVoto called "the cowboy on a pedestal" mentality. The relatively brief cowboy era was certainly important. But it has been vastly overblown, distorting our perception of the larger history of the frontier.

Variety has always been there for readers who sought it out. Indeed, fans of Western movies and fiction have shown strong interest lately in the Indian point of view and in other previously "marginalized" characters and perspectives. My *Cheyenne* series was intended as a six-book project to test the market; twenty books later, reader interest shows no sign of flagging. Curiosity about Native American culture and history has never been stronger, in part because more and more writers are seriously recognizing the practical and inspirational value of such study. Editors welcome well-written alternatives to the standard plots and heroes. Judy Alter's *Libbie* offers a thoughtful new look at George Armstrong Custer from his wife's point of view, reminding readers that the West was far more complicated and diverse than the dime novels and shilling-shockers will allow. Pete Dexter's *Deadwood* provides a fascinating version of the Wild Bill Hickok story, as told from the point of view of such hitherto "peripheral" characters as Chinese laborers. Cormac McCarthy's haunting *Blood Meridian* depicts the violent conquest of Apacheria with uncompromising grace and power. It has also convinced even the most dubious critics of "shoot-'em-ups" that innovative frontier fiction can be important literature, too.

Every genre features conventions that endure and help define it for loyal readers. But only a dead fish swims with the stream. Frontier fiction that pleases readers will survive and even flourish in the 21st century if we writers show true pioneer spirit and continually breathe new life into it.

>> 50

A Mystery in Three Acts

By Stephen Greenleaf

In writing a mystery novel, I've found that it is helpful to follow the basic structure of the play in three acts, a foundation that has been central to dramatic prose since Aristotle.

Act I introduces the crime and the mystery to be solved; the sleuth who will solve it; and the setting in which the crime occurred. Act II describes the investigation that points to a conclusion, but later proves erroneous. Act III depicts the final confrontation between the sleuth and the villain, reveals the deductions that led to the true solution, and suggests the ramifications of the secrets that have emerged along the way. If supported by the persuasive prose and imaginative incident that make for a well-crafted novel, this approach to plotting will produce a good book.

To this end, you should begin your story dramatically. Since the premise of a mystery is that the crime to be solved has already taken place and the sleuth (the point-of-view character) didn't witness it, your opening requires imaginative improvisation.

There are at least three ways to achieve a beginning that will engage the reader at once: One is to open with a prologue that describes in vivid detail the crime as it occurs, narrated either in the third-person omniscient point of view or in the voice of the victim or villain. The second is to begin with the sleuth in a devilish predicament, then flash back to show how he got into such a fix. The third is to have the person who reveals the details of the crime do so in such a way that the reader feels as if he or she were there when the crime took place.

Once the crime is set forth, you must establish several plot elements within the first few chapters, first and foremost revealing the voice of the sleuth and making his personality sufficiently unique and engaging that readers will want to spend several hours with him.

Your sleuth must be, in Raymond Chandler's phrase, a person "fit for adventure," which should be established quickly. In the opening pages, the hero should say something and do something so clever and unexpected to reveal him as unusual and in some ways unique. All aspects of the hero's personality need not be revealed at the outset, of course; some should remain an enigma until well into the heart of the novel. The job of Act I is merely to establish the existence of a complex and compelling and credible person.

The crime that propels the story—the mystery the sleuth is to solve—must be a serious one; it doesn't have to be murder, but it has to be the moral equivalent of murder—kidnapping, child abuse, sexual assault, etc. It must also be intriguing in and of itself: committed in an unusual way, in an unusual place, or involving an unusual person—or all three. Also, readers should learn enough about the victim to care that the perpetrator is brought to justice.

To be most effective, the opening scenes should include a symbol—a person, an object, a natural phenomenon—that can serve as a metaphor for what is happening in the overall setting. Having his symbol reappear at the end will give the story a sense of closure. For an example, see the way Ross Macdonald used the forest fire in *The Underground Man*.

The opening crime should generate two essential aspects of the plot. First, it should provide two clues to a solution—physical and psychological. Some clues obviously point in a specific direction; others aren't recognized as clues until later, e.g., the hound that didn't bark (as in Sherlock Holmes' "Silver Blaze," from *Memoirs of Sherlock Holmes*). You should include a variety of clues in your story so that the clever reader can solve the mystery by analyzing the details that you have supplied.

The opening crime also suggests a line of investigation in which the suspects and motives will carry the sleuth to the end of Act I. Chapter 2 is the logical first step the sleuth would take to solve the crime described in Chapter 1: If a wife is dead, the first thing you must do is talk to the husband. How do you come up with other suspects? Make a chart of the people who touched the victim's life, personally and professionally. Then select those characters who would be believable and powerful suspects—a jealous lover, an envious sibling, an ambitious rival—and have the sleuth question them. Editors say they want "character-driven" rather than "plot-driven" novels, so choose a few well-rounded suspects to enliven your story.

The major suspects who appear in Act I should reappear later in the novel, after the sleuth has learned that they are not as disinterested as they seemed. A good plot is often circular, bringing the reader back to the beginning of the quest but in an atmosphere that has been redefined by the work of the detective. One of the suspects who appears in Act I must turn out to be the real villain; it's not fair to discount him, or to have the solution depend on luck or coincidence or information that the sleuth knew but the reader didn't.

After the investigation is underway, it is time to introduce the subplot. While your plot carries the story, the subplot carries the theme. This means that the subplot is where you move the tale from the particular to the universal—where the events in the novel correspond with the events in the reader's life.

Most subplots arise from two sources: a crisis in the sleuth's private life—divorce, alcoholism, unemployment; and the fact that the investigation causes the sleuth to confront issues of courage, honesty, or fidelity, creating dilemmas that call into question his sense of himself or his purpose in life. An important part of the dramatic arc of the novel is the change that takes place within the sleuth as the subplot is resolved.

The subplot also offers a way to alter the pace of the story by moving back and forth between the personal and professional obstacles the sleuth encounters. It is also a way to broaden the author's canvas by introducing scenes of romance or pathos or humor that are not part of the main investigation.

At the mid-point of Act I, something happens that indicates the crime may be more complicated than it first appeared. There is no elucidation, just hints that there are depths and densities still to be revealed—for example, a hint that the victim was not the upstanding citizen he was reputed to be. At this point the reader may see the hints more clearly than the sleuth does.

At the end of Act I there is a change in the focus and scope of the inquiry. The initial line of investigation proves unproductive: The major suspect dies or the crime turns out to be other than it first appeared—a murder instead of a disappearance, a kidnapping instead of a runaway. The story takes a new direction, plunging into the heart of Act II, in which the following things should happen:

a) A sense of urgency must be developed. If the crime is not solved soon, even worse things will happen.

b) The investigation should expand to include other characters from different walks of life. Every scene, whether an interview or a fist fight or the discovery of physical evidence, must yield a fact that points toward the solution, even though the relevance is not always obvious at the time.

c) As the subplot evolves, the sleuth's backstory is revealed: how he got to be the way he is, what's lacking in his life, what's kept him from achieving his goal previously.

d) The writer reveals that the sleuth has a personal stake in the case—because his life has been threatened, or his investigation may expose issues that disturb him, or a suspect is emotionally linked to him in some way.

e) Hidden motives proliferate as the result of the discovery of secret relationships—love affairs, business shenanigans, family feuds. The depths and densities only hinted at in Act I become clear in Act II.

f) At the mid-point of this Act, the sleuth is stymied; a solution seems impossible.

g) By the end of Act II, the force of logic and the elimination of alternatives point to a conclusion—a villain and a motive emerge from the uncertainties, and the sleuth reveals the results of his investigation. But he still hasn't got it quite right.

His mistaken conclusion can take various forms. He may have incorrectly identified the villain, but his reasoning may be right: The prime suspect actually turns out to be a victim who has been framed. Or he points to the perpetrator, but his reasoning is wrong: The case is more complex than it had appeared, which presupposes that others are involved in ways previously unknown to him. Or the sleuth has misinterpreted a clue and needs to retrace his steps to find out where he went wrong.

In contrast to the end of Act I, where the error was obvious to all, at the end of Act II the error is known only to the sleuth (and perhaps to the clever reader), who finally recognizes the scheme that provoked the crime. The crucial clue turns out to be some action or event that seemed innocuous in Act I, but now takes on new meaning because of information obtained by the end of Act II.

In Act III, the sleuth reevaluates what he has learned and resumes his quest. The subplot resolves itself; the sleuth is stronger for his private ordeal and strengthened for the final drive toward the true solution. The story climaxes in a confrontation between the sleuth and the villain—a meeting of the forces of good and evil.

The climactic scene should be a memorable conflict in which the villain's own weapons are turned against him, and the sleuth triumphs against what had appeared to be all odds. The case is solved, the client is satisfied, the closing symbol tells us that the story has ended, and even the clever reader has been outwitted.

It's easier said than done, of course. Plotting is hard work, a feat of imagination, a riff of theme and variation, a game of "what if" played out in the clever corners of the mind. Some writers work it out ahead of time; others improvise along the way. You'll sleep better if you work it out, but you probably won't have as much fun.

>>51

A Novel by Any Other Name . . .

By Elizabeth George

I'VE FOUND THAT ONE OF THE BENEFITS OF ACHIEVING THE STATUS of published writer is that I've been able to meet and talk with hundreds upon hundreds of readers and unpublished writers since my first novel hit the bookstores in 1988. My role when asked to speak to neophyte writers is to give a shot-in-the-arm discourse about persevering through doubts and dead ends that go hand in hand with completing a project, as well as weathering the maddening frustrations of trying to get someone to read, to represent, to believe in, and—*mirabile dictu*—to purchase their work.

But every so often, a conversation develops that carries me in another direction, prompting me to evaluate what I do when I sit down in front of my word processor every day and, more important, why I do it.

I had such a conversation not long ago with a psychologist-cum-novelist who told me that he intended to write mystery novels only until such a time as he became good enough to write "a real novel." The fact that a mystery (or thriller or crime or suspense or psychological) novel is indeed "a real novel" possessing all the requirements of "a real novel" appeared to escape him. As far as he was concerned, writing a mystery was going to be a way to practice his craft, rather like baking cookies in the hope that one day he could work himself up to the challenge of a layer cake.

Let's ignore the questionable sense our psychologist displayed in sharing this peculiar literary plan of action with a mystery-suspense writer. Instead, let's examine what he failed to realize about the well-crafted mystery. First, it *is* a novel of character, of plot, of setting, of dialogue, of metaphor, of allusion, of landscape, of drama, of conflict, of love, of death, and most important, of imagination. And second, to

228

deny the mystery-suspense its place among the world's "real novels" is to deny a place among "real novelists" to such writers as Thomas Hardy *(Desperate Remedies)*, William Faulkner *(Intruder in the Dust)*, Charles Dickens *(Bleak House)*, Wilkie Collins *(The Woman in White)*, Edgar Allan Poe *(Murders in the Rue Morgue)*, Dorothy L. Sayers *(Gaudy Night)*, George Eliot *(Silas Marner)*, Nathaniel Hawthorne *(The House of the Seven Gables)*, and more recent writers like Alice Hoffman *(Turtle Moon)*, Scott Turow *(Presumed Innocent)*, Kem Nunn *(Pomona Queen)*, and a host of others whose mysteries and suspenses have stood and will stand the test of time.

This is not to argue that there are no deplorable mystery-suspense novels being written. On the contrary, dozens of writers seem to turn them out on an annual basis. But the novelist who commits herself to the process, the product, and the passion of writing is, believe me, writing "a real novel" from start to finish.

The mystery-suspense novel provides the writer with a natural structure, and it is perhaps because this structure exists in the first place that the uninformed neophyte writer might evaluate the mystery-suspense as a lesser creature in the world of literature. The natural structure is generally the same: A situation of grave import (like a murder) has occurred or is threatening to occur or a dramatic question is presented to the reader; this situation or this dramatic question must be resolved in some way by the final pages of the book. But it is what the individual writer does with this natural structure that can, and often does, alter the tiresome label "piece of genre fiction" to "literary classic."

Because a given structure exists, the writer of the mystery-suspense can choose to provide her readers with little more than a skeleton of a novel and still get away with constructing a whodunit that not only entertains, but also stimulates the reader's perspicacity. In this sort of novel, the hero or heroine—be the character a spymaster, a police detective, a private investigator, an FBI agent, or an amateur sleuth caught up in unexpected circumstances that try the intellect if not the soul—marches fairly directly to the conclusion of the story, encountering the expected road blocks, clues, red herrings, and conflicts along the way. Or the writer can take that same skeleton and hang upon it the organs, muscles, and flesh of subplot, theme, character development, exploration of social issues, and the complex psychology

229

of human relationships. It's my belief that the novels that stand the test of time, that move out of genre because of their refusal to be bound by the mundane rules of genre, follow this latter course of action.

To write a mystery-suspense that is "a real novel" is to write largely about character. In these novels, the characters and the circumstances engendered by those characters drive the story forward, and not vice versa. Characters do not exist to be set pieces in a contrived drama whose value is ultimately revealed in a single indecipherable clue or a "gotcha" ending whose sole purpose is surprise rather than provocation of thought. Mystery-suspense novels that are "real novels" end where they begin: with an examination of the human heart—in conflict, in despair, in peace, in anguish, in love, in happiness, in fear.

When a writer decides to create a novel of character within this genre of mystery-suspense, she challenges herself to move beyond the simple mechanics of plotting, to drive from her mind the temptation to adhere to a formula, and to take a risk. She decides to begin with character and to use character as the foundation for the hundreds of pages and thousands of words that will follow that character's creation.

This is what I have attempted to do with my novels, which are sometimes called literary mysteries, sometimes novels of psychological suspense, sometimes detective stories, sometimes police procedurals, sometimes British novels, but are always—at least to my way of thinking—"real novels" from start to finish. I begin with a kernel of killer, victim, and motive. I plant that kernel into the soil of imagination, and I begin to people a world in which killer and victim move.

In peopling the world of the novel, I create individuals. I begin with their names, knowing that the name I give to a character will have a large influence upon the way a reader feels about him. So when I wanted the victim in *Missing Joseph* to be seen as a gentle and thoughtful country vicar, I named him Robin Sage, just as when I wanted the schoolboy bully in *Well-Schooled in Murder* to be believable as a mutilator of self and others, I gave him the name Clive Pritchard with the hard sound of that initial *C* and the surname reminiscent of a farming tool.

Once I have named my cast of characters, I begin the process of making them real. Each is given a personality that has—as we all do—a core need in life. Perhaps the core need is to be seen as competent, perhaps it is to be in control of self and others, perhaps it is to belong,

230

to be of service, to be perceived as authentic. The character's personality arises out of his backstory, which may or may not become part of the novel but is indeed part of the groundwork that leads up to the writing of the novel. The character's backstory includes his family relationships, his growing up, any pivotal events that shaped him, his friendships or the lack thereof. Within this backstory is woven the character's interior landscape: what his agenda is with other characters, what his throughline is for the entire novel, how he reacts to stress, what he experiences as joy or pleasure. To this are added the telling details that will appear in the novel and act as a means by which the reader can view the character in a more direct light: that peculiar article of clothing worn by a teen-aged boy but once belonging to his absent father; that bullet-like line of ear studs and the silver nose ring donned by the girl who always wears black; the hairlip covered inadequately by a mustache; the perfect sitting room with no mote of dust floating in the air; the bitten fingernails; the choice of artwork; the music listened to; the car driven; the condition of the curtains hanging at the windows; the collection of tea cups lovingly displayed. The character is given a place of birth, a place in society, and a place within his individual family. He is described physically, mentally, psychologically, and emotionally. And when that is done, he stands on the brink, ready to come to life in the manuscript itself.

But my preliminary work does not end here. Because the novel will not exist in outer space, I must create an inner space for it. This is its setting. The setting may be a place as simple to construct as was the Yorkshire village of Keldale in *A Great Deliverance* where a farmer met a hideous end in an old stone barn. What was required of that little village: two pubs, an inn, a churchyard containing the grave of an abandoned newborn, a huge ruined abbey with a legend descending from the time of Cromwell. Having seen many such villages and abbeys during my time in Yorkshire, I needed only to assembly my photographs and map out my locations.

Or setting may be as challenging as the creation of Bredgar Chambers, the public school founded by Henry VII that sat in West Sussex and served as the setting of *Well-Schooled in Murder*. Here I needed all the accouterments of the English public school—the great chapel, the dining hall, the houses of residence, the quadrangle, etc.—and the only way to make them authentic was to blend myself into the world of the English public school for a period of time until I knew it well enough to create my own, from its prospectus to its architecture.

Or setting may require that I bring a real place to life, jockeying its streets and buildings a little in order that it might accommodate just one more college. This was the case in *For the Sake of Elena,* where St. Stephen's College was slid into the new space I created between Trinity College and Trinity Hall. But to make it real—and thus to integrate it into an atmosphere that felt authentic to the reader—St. Stephen's had to be a place of architectural significance, for such is the case of every college in the city of Cambridge.

With setting and characters well in hand, I begin to outline the plot. Sometimes I use a step outline only, creating a preliminary list of scenes with fragments of information to guide me in the construction of those scenes. Sometimes I use a running plot outline, in which entire sections of the novel are outlined in depth, including description, narration, and dialogue. And sometimes I have to feel my way slowly into the novel, allowing an initial scene or the glimpse of a character to dictate what will follow.

The story I ultimately tell grows out of all of this: these characters who have been created in my imagination from that initial kernel of killer, victim, and motive; this setting that I have labored over like a loving god; this plot that I am always unsure of, partly in terror of, but determined to carry onward. And when that story has reached its conclusion, if it's successful and not a tosser, it comprises plot and subplot, internal and external conflict, theme, drama, moments of reflection and evaluation, landscape, setting, metaphor, and allusion.

It is, because of how it has been written, in every way a real novel.

232

➤➤ 52

WHAT MAKES A GOOD SPY THRILLER?

BY MAYNARD ALLINGTON

I RECENTLY HEARD A JOURNALIST WHO SHOULD KNOW BETTER GIVE some bad advice to a group of aspiring writers who wanted to know how to write a novel. Pounding his fist on the podium, he replied, "Put a sheet of paper into your typewriter and start writing!" That's a bit like telling someone interested in bullfighting to grab a cape and go into the ring. The bull, of course, has his own theory about what will ensue.

Writing a novel is not so different from going into battle. You are facing a long campaign. Before you mount your first offensive, certain logistics have to be in place.

Amateur writers generally ignore this. In their eagerness to write, they lay down a barrage of words on the computer screen the moment an idea strikes. You may produce four or five good chapters before the screen goes blank from writer's block—the battle fatigue of amateur novelists.

What essentials must be in place before you begin writing? The three most important are premise, plot, and character.

The critical first step common to all novels has to be the selection of a *premise*. Not just any premise, but one strong enough to carry a story line through three or four hundred manuscript pages. Don't confuse premise with theme. The theme of *The Caine Mutiny* (perhaps the most *technically* perfect novel in 20th century literature) is of a young man coming of age in war. The premise is far more sweeping. A naval crew at sea finds itself under the command of a paranoid captain whose instability leads to a mutiny during a typhoon, and to the subsequent court martial of the officer who relieved him of his post.

Novels that bore the reader invariably lack a strong premise, and they end up as rejects, so choose your premise carefully. Ask yourself two questions: Is your premise *big* enough to carry a novel, and is it *believable*?

The premise of my novel *The Grey Wolf* builds out of an abortive military coup by a cadre of senior Soviet officers against Stalin in 1942. What would be the consequences if British Intelligence were secretly involved in the conspiracy?

Clearly, this premise is big enough to support a multitude of chapters and a large cast of characters. But is it credible? A strip search of history isn't required, only a simple frisk. It yields some relevant facts: There was, indeed, a failed assassination attempt on Stalin in 1942 in Moscow; the fact that political commissars could, and often did, countermand orders in the field caused deep discontent in the Soviet officer corps; and finally, it is known that Churchill was an outspoken and bitter enemy of communism from the time of the Bolshevik Revolution.

All of this evidence is enough to validate our premise. Time to move on to the next step in the process: plot.

I am often asked, "Do you start out with characters, or with a plot?" The truth is, these generally develop at the same time. A plot in its purest form is a story line choreographed along what Truman Capote has called that "great demanding arc" of beginning, middle, and end. Obviously, you must have some idea of your key characters before you can construct your plot.

At this juncture in *The Grey Wolf,* I knew the lead character would be a British Intelligence officer. Waiting for him in Moscow would be his Soviet NKVD counterpart. I had a vague idea for a heroine who would play a role in the assassination attempt on Stalin. I knew the assassin would be a staff briefing officer who would have routine access to the Soviet leader inside the Kremlin. I had no idea what these characters looked like. They were only mock-ups standing in for the real characters who had not yet reported to the set.

The plot, too, was still unformed. I had yet to figure out how to get Churchill and the British SIS (Special Intelligence Service) involved in the conspiracy. The action, I knew, would move from London to Murmansk, then on to Moscow by rail. The coup would, of course, fail. At that point the Churchill government would abandon its agent, who would be captured, interrogated in Lubyanka prison, and would later escape. The last long section of the novel would involve a chase north to Archangel where the climax would take place after a German air raid.

234

Now there is a certain form to what I have just described—the shadow of a beginning, middle, and end—but it is far from a plot. It resembles more the sequences of a film script, which must be broken down into scenes, or in the case of a novel, into chapters.

The next step, then, is to develop a chapter outline showing exactly how and where your events will unfold. Having an outline doesn't mean you won't encounter small diversions that force you to improvise on your plan, but it embodies your strategic vision.

As you work on a chapter outline, never forget that conflict is the fuel of a novel. It may be physical conflict, goal-oriented conflict, sexual conflict, or even self-conflict, but it *has* to be there in some form. Even in the planning stage you must measure every chapter against that standard. If conflict is not evident, eliminate the chapter.

Now that you've finished your chapter outline, you're ready to start writing, right? Wrong. Your characters aren't in place. Remember those cardboard characters we left stranded in the plot? Time to summon the real cast for a dress rehearsal.

Inept spy novelists have a tendency to draw their heroes and villains from a roster of clichés. How many CIA and KGB agents in fiction are duplicates of each other? In a setting where the focus is on action, it's easy to lose track of the human factor.

This brings us to a classic model of spy fiction—Graham Greene's *The Ministry of Fear,* set in London during the blitz. After half a century in print, it's still a prototype to be studied for all the elements I have mentioned so far, especially character.

Chapter One finds Arthur Rowe drawn to a small street fair in Bloomsbury. Rowe is a troubled man. The *fête* holds comfortable childhood associations for him, so as dusk approaches, he lingers among the stalls and bunting. Some women have baked a chocolate cake with real eggs and butter (a rarity in wartime Britain) to raise money for war relief. It will go to the person who can give the closest estimate of its weight. A guess costs sixpence. What we don't yet know is that the cake contains a capsule of microfilm.

Rowe enters a fortuneteller's booth to have his palm read. In the course of their talk, he innocently blurts out a phrase that is, in fact, a coded response. The fortuneteller informs him it is the cake that he wants, and gives him the weight. Rowe acquires the cake about the time the real spy is rushing into the fortuneteller's booth. Rowe has walked off with microfilm in a cake meant for a German spy.

An ordinary novelist would have let the action take over from there. But Greene is no ordinary novelist. Now we learn why Arthur Rowe is a troubled man. He has killed his terminally ill wife, whom he loved, and has never come to grips with his own actions. This is his *psychological* characterization, an element many writers overlook. It is what sets Arthur Rowe apart from the standard hero in the standard thriller. He is a complex figure who could have stepped out of a literary novel.

Another model worth examining is *The Spy Who Came in From the Cold,* arguably John Le Carré's best novel. The opening sentence jerks us to attention. Alec Leamas is waiting at a West German checkpoint in Berlin for an East German defector to come across. It's a dark, icy October night, the zone lit by arc-lamps. Finally, the defector, Karl, appears, walking his bicycle across the no-man's-land between the checkpoints. Midway, sirens peal and powerful searchlights come on. Karl tries to run but is cut down as Leamas watches. Leamas knows that his man has been betrayed by an East German agent named Mundt. Karl is the last agent in Leamas's network, all of whom have been eliminated by Mundt. Leamas is through, and realizes it.

Chapter Two opens with Leamas on a plane bound for London. Le Carré now gives us a physical description of Leamas and tells us a great deal about him, this in third-person narrative from the novelist's point of view. It's the technique an amateur might use, but Le Carré makes it work. How? Because of the selectivity of the information. He uses no clichés. Then, through Leamas's own self-reflection, we get a picture of a tough, embittered, burnt-out spy who is all but finished. Finally, we see him through the eyes of a stewardess serving him a drink. Three views of Alec Leamas—each different, but giving the reader a three-dimensional character.

I have used these two examples because they illustrate such opposite approaches to characterization. Arthur Rowe's physical description is deliberately vague. His character is projected through his psychological frame of mind. So are the background description and action. Greene forces the reader to experience everything through the eyes of a man tortured by his own role in the mercy killing of his wife. Premise, plot, and character were never more masterfully entwined.

The facets of character I have discussed here so far must be set in

236

your mind before you write the first sentence of your novel. Until you have absorbed your characters totally, you can't make them act and speak credibly. Don't forget that dialogue, apart from moving a story forward, can also serve to *develop* the character you have created in your mind. For example, an early scene in *The Grey Wolf* has an SIS officer named Rosewall trying to recruit the lead, Antony Ryder, into British Intelligence. The scene takes place in a London Pub:

> "That's the problem," Rosewall went on. "Your file doesn't tell me anything. A chronology of events, that's all it is. I don't really know much about you at all. Nobody does. I find that rather curious . . ."
> "How?"
> "Because most people leave clues behind in their relationships with other people. You appear to have had no relationships. Would it interest you to know that most of your instructors at university didn't remember you?"
> "It wouldn't matter to me one way or the other."
> "What does matter to you?"
> "Nothing in particular."
> "I rather imagined you were a bit young to be that cynical."
> "It's not cynicism."
> "Then what would you call it?"
> "I wouldn't call it anything."

This is only a small excerpt of dialogue, but it illustrates how well this device can work. Rosewall is telling us a great deal about Antony Ryder. And in the *tone* of his responses, Ryder is telling us a great deal about himself.

Premise, plot, and character. Once you have them in position, you're ready to begin your novel. You may still have problems to solve as you write, but you will have launched a successful plan of attack.

But wait! I almost forgot. I wanted to tell you how a spy thriller differs from a literary novel. Answer: It doesn't. Every great thriller has the architecture of a literary novel. The best of these works transcend category. They soar away from a specific genre into that mysterious landscape of great literature where books never die.

➤➤ 53

SERIES CHARACTERS: LOVE 'EM OR LEAVE 'EM

BY ELIZABETH PETERS

CONAN DOYLE LEARNED TO LOATHE HOLMES SO INTENSELY, HE TRIED to murder him. At the opposite end of the spectrum are such writers as Dorothy Sayers, whose affection for Lord Peter Wimsey has prompted a certain amount of rude speculation. What is it about series characters? Is there a happy medium between loving and loathing them? Do the advantage of series characters outweigh the disadvantages? Should you, if you haven't done so already, consider starting a series?

In addition to the non-series Barbara Michaels novels, I write three different series, featuring Jacqueline Kirby, librarian; Vicky Bliss, art historian; and the notorious Amelia Peabody, Victorian gentlewoman Egyptologist.

None of the novels in which these three characters first appeared was intended to be the beginning of a series. The reason the series developed is simple and crass: There was a demand. I don't know why publishers suddenly decided that series characters were "in." They had always been popular, as witness Holmes, Poirot, Wimsey, et al., but it was not until ten or fifteen years ago that interest resurfaced. Now, many mystery writers have a series character, and those who do not are being pressured to create one.

The demand of the market is important. If publishers aren't buying a particular type of book, there is not much point in writing it, except for your own satisfaction. However, it is a big mistake to write only for the market, and a bigger mistake to do something you detest simply for the sake of sales.

There are certain disadvantages to a series. It does limit the author to some extent; a given plot may not be suitable for your character.

Another disadvantage is that you have to reintroduce the character in every book, and it requires some skill to tell a new reader what he needs to know without boring those who have read earlier books and without slowing the action. Publishers want series, but they also insist that each book stand on its own. This may not be literally oxymoronic, but it's darned hard to do.

However, this last problem is simply one of craftsmanship, and I find that the advantages of a series character far outweigh the disadvantages. Over the space of several books, you can develop the character far more richly and convincingly than is possible in one book, and I believe character has become increasingly important in the mystery novel. Readers are no longer satisfied with stereotypical robots—the Young Lovers, the Detective, the Sinister Lawyer, and so on. The most successful writers of the New Golden Age have succeeded in large part, not so much because of the ingenuity of their plots, but because readers like their characters and want to know more about them.

And, in my opinion, the author should feel the same way about the characters. If, as you hope, the series is a success, you are going to live with these characters for a long time. If you don't like them, they will get on your nerves, and you will either loathe them or become horribly bored by them. (Readers are less likely to become bored than you are. If they do lose interest in your characters, you will know about it; they will stop buying the books.) But there's no reason for you to take on a task you despise when, with a few relatively simple tricks, you can learn to enjoy your characters and look forward to the next visit with them. After writing seven books in the Amelia Peabody series, I am finding her and her family more fascinating every time around.

The most important thing is to begin by creating realistic characters. This may sound paradoxical when applied to Amelia, but in fact she is far less of a caricature than some readers believe. I had read an enormous number of contemporary novels, biographies, social histories, and travel books before I began writing the series, and there are many real-life parallels to Amelia's career, opinions, and behavior, as well as those of her eccentric husband, Emerson. Even Ramses, their catastrophically precocious son, is based to some extent on actual Victorian children, and, to an even greater extent, on normal boys of all eras who exhibit similar tendencies.

If the protagonists of the novel are properly conceived, they will behave consistently and comprehensibly. Of course this requirement is true of character development in general, but it is particularly important with series characters, whom the reader comes to know well. One useful result of consistently drawn characters is that you will find their personalities often determine the way the plot is going to develop. By now I am so familiar with the behavioral patterns of the Emersons that I have only to set up a situation and describe how they will inevitably react.

Just because a character is consistent, however, doesn't mean his behavior should always be predictable. In fact, seemingly irrational behavior makes a character more realistic; real people don't always behave sensibly either. Yet, if we examine the true motives that govern their behavior, we find it is not inconsistent, that we ought to have anticipated it. It is the author's task to establish this. The reaction you want from a reader is a shock of surprise, followed immediately by a shock of recognition: "Oh, yes, of course. I ought to have realized . . ." that despite her constant criticism of her son, Amelia would kill to protect him; that though Emerson complains about his wife's recklessness, he is secretly amused by and appreciative of her courage; that while Ramses sounds like a pompous little snob, he is as insecure as are most young children.

The best way of establishing character is through actions rather than words. This is particularly true if you are writing in the first person. Amelia describes herself as hard-headed and unsentimental, but it should be apparent by page ten of the first book in the series that she is a soft touch who acts on impulse, and then has to scramble desperately to find logical reasons for her actions.

But the smartest thing I did with the Amelia series wasn't done deliberately; it was pure serendipity, or luck, or as I would like to believe, "a writer's instinct."

Crocodile on the Sandbank, the first book in the series, ended like any conventional romantic mystery novel, with Amelia happily married to the hero. This should have been the end of the story; conventional literary wisdom maintains that the protagonist of a series should remain single and therefore open to further adventures, amatory and otherwise. But when I decided to resurrect Amelia, I had to resurrect Emerson as well. I mean, there he was. Worse—he and I had got

Amelia pregnant. Emerson may have done it on purpose, but I certainly didn't. The demands of a husband interfere considerably with a heroine's activities as a detective; the demands of a baby are almost impossible to dismiss.

If I had intended *Crocodile* to be the first in a series, I wouldn't have been as specific about dates. Not only did Amelia inform the reader of her age (curse her!), but historical events mentioned in the book tied it to a particular year. As the series continued, there was no way I could get around this, or fudge the date of Ramses' birth, or keep him and his parents from aging a year every twelve months.

I decided to regard these developments not as limitations but as challenges. Could a spouse and a baby be advantages to a heroine, instead of the reverse?

There are two ways of dealing with a detective's spouse. The first and perhaps most common method is to make the spouse a minor character (babies are particularly useful in keeping wives in the background). I chose the second alternative: husband and wife operating as equal, active partners in a genuine team. Note that word *equal*. I wanted my readers to feel that it would be inconceivable for either Amelia or Emerson to function independently of the other.

Insofar as the romantic element was concerned. . . . Well, that was another challenge. I couldn't see any reason husband and wife shouldn't be enthusiastic lovers as well as affectionate, supportive mates, but in order to maintain the "sexual tension" editors are always demanding, the marriage had to be questioned, even threatened, periodically. Rivals who crop up from time to time keep both Amelia and Emerson on their toes (so to speak). In the Amelia novel *The Snake, the Crocodile and the Dog,* I resorted to an even more drastic expedient, which resulted in a severe, potentially destructive strain on their relationship. However, the real conflict stems from the personalities of the major characters themselves. Amelia's air of smug self-confidence conceals a painful inferiority complex, particularly with regard to her personal appearance. She'll always be jealous of more beautiful women, and Emerson will never stop wondering what *really* happened when his wife was in the clutches of her devoted admirer the Master Criminal. Their marriage will never be boring and neither of them will ever take the other for granted.

The birth of Ramses presented even greater difficulties, and more provocative possibilities. In the second book of the series, I hadn't quite come to grips with the difficulties, so I did what most writers do with inconvenient babies: I left Ramses at home and allowed his parents to continue their activities without him. By the third book, *The Mummy Case,* I was ready to cope not only with Ramses, but with the tripartite relationship.

During this novel, Ramses developed into one of the most perniciously obnoxious children in all of mystery fiction—or so I have been told. I'm rather fond of the poor little devil myself, and I do not respond politely to readers who want me to drown him. However, by the fifth book I decided he was getting a little out of hand, so I copied a device by another writer, and introduced two children who were so awful they made Ramses look sympathetic by comparison. They also forced Amelia to reevaluate her feelings for her son. He becomes a full and active participant in his parents' adventures, supplying both comic relief and much-needed assistance in critical situations. His participation stems naturally and inevitably from his own character traits, which are the result not only of heredity but of upbringing; as he matures he will undoubtedly play a larger and quite different part. His relationship with his parents will change as well; a young adult can't (or shouldn't!) be treated like a child.

So the baby, who might have been a liability, is developing into an individual with considerable future potential. Ramses is about to enter adolescence, and I await this development with much interest.

The minor characters who populate a series are almost as important as the protagonists, and this, I think, is another way in which the New Golden Age mysteries differ from those of the first Golden Age. Instead of a single sidekick or bumbling foil from Scotland Yard, the Emersons have acquired a group of friends, enemies, and hangers-on who form a pool from which I can draw: Gargery, the cudgel-wielding butler; Kevin O'Connor, the brash young reporter; Abdullah, the loyal foreman; Evelyn, Amelia's sister-in-law; Nefret, the golden-haired beauty who has won Ramses' adolescent heart; and above all, Emerson's hated rival, the Master Criminal. The utility of a cast of supporting characters should be obvious. Like the major characters, they have changed and developed during the course of the books, and their occasional reappearances add to the reader's feeling that these are real people with decided personalities and distinctive foibles.

This is why I do not anticipate ever becoming bored with my series characters. Like real people, they change. Like real people, they are not always predictable. I have a rough idea of what is going to happen to them, but I could not emulate Agatha Christie and write the last book in the series now. I don't know what the Emersons are going to do until they do it—but when they do it, I am not really surprised. "Of course. I should have known. . . ."

From a purely practical viewpoint, there is one simple way to avoid being bored by your series characters: Don't confine yourself to a single series. Some writers can do this; I don't believe I could. The Barbara Michaels novels give me the opportunity to use plot ideas that don't fit any of the series characters, and the two other series I write as Elizabeth Peters allow me to employ themes and interests unsuited to Amelia and company.

To a lesser extent—probably because I have written less about them—Vicky and Jacqueline are also maturing and changing. Jacqueline has become a best-selling writer of romances, a development she regards with a distinctly jaundiced eye, and somewhere in her background there is a Mr. Kirby. Who is he and what happened to him? Some day I may find out.

As for Vicky, she's not getting any younger, and when I began *Night Train to Memphis,* I decided it was time for Vicky to sort out her feelings, not only for the dashing Sir John Smythe, but for her exasperating but engaging boss, Herr Direktor Schmidt. By the time I finished the book, I was a trifle surprised, and decidedly intrigued, to discover how Vicky, as well as John and Schmidt, have changed since they first appeared on the literary scene.

And that, dear Reader (to quote Amelia), is the real trick. Let your characters grow; allow them to mature and develop; put them into situations that will force them to exhibit hitherto unsuspected aspects of their personalities. The other day I was talking with a friend who inquired interestedly, "Is Vicky going to get pregnant in this book?" My reaction was instantaneous, spontaneous, and, I am afraid, typical of the generation in which I was raised. "Pregnant?" I squawked indignantly. "She isn't even married!"

I am fairly sure Vicky's reaction would be, if not identical, equally indignant. But one never knows. At least *I* never know, and that's why I like writing about my series characters.

If you don't like yours and can't make them into people whose company you enjoy, be brutal. No, not that brutal; I do not recommend killing off major characters, no matter how much you detest them. You can be sure some of your readers have become attached to them and will resent you for bumping them off. Just ignore them for a while. Shrug and smile politely when readers ask when you are going to return to Harry or Jennifer or whoever. Start another series, with characters who do appeal to you. You may find, after enough time has elapsed, that Harry and Jennifer aren't as repellent as you thought. If they still don't appeal to you, let them languish in the limbo of forgotten literary figures. The bottom line is simple: Enjoy your characters or leave them alone.

>> 54

BEFORE YOU WRITE YOUR
HISTORICAL NOVEL

BY THOMAS FLEMING

THERE IS NO SUBSTITUTE FOR RESEARCH WHEN A WRITER TACKLES A historical novel. The first and most important reason is the commitment every writer, both in fiction and nonfiction, has to the truth. Another reason, seldom grasped by beginning writers, is how much impact research can have on a novel's development.

In the course of publishing 17 novels, most of them in that category amorphously described as historical (I prefer to call them novels of the historical imagination), I have found that research can deepen an imaginary character, transform a key scene, and even alter a novel's plot.

In my novel *Loyalties,* about an American who becomes involved in the German resistance to Hitler, I have a scene in which the main American character, Jonathan Talbot, must rescue from Nazi hands the German woman, Berthe von Hoffmann, who is trying to make contact with the Americans on behalf of the resistance. The encounter takes place in the deserted palace of the Alhambra, in Granada, Spain. The American, disguised as a German businessman, must choose a moment to murder the Nazi SS Oberfuhrer, who is close to forcing Berthe to reveal the identity of the leaders of the resistance.

I knew little about the Alhambra Palace when I started the book. After considerable research, I acquired a lot more knowledge, but something remained missing in my sense of the appropriate place to commit the murder. I went back and did more research. I discovered that there was a palace within the palace, an ugly monstrosity built by one of the Spanish kings after the Moors fled. On the wall of one of the central rooms was an immense painting depicting the expulsion of the Jews from Spain in 1492. At its center was a tragic column of refugees winding over the horizon.

Here was the detail I wanted. As the SS Oberfuhrer gazes up at the painting and smugly tells Talbot he plans to persuade General Franco to let him bring it back to Berlin and hang it in the Reichchancellery, Talbot whips a silk cord around his throat and begins strangling him. That painting transformed more or less ordinary hugger-mugger into a symbolic scene of great power.

In researching my previous novel, *Over There,* I discovered on a dusty shelf in the stacks of the Yale Library about forty memoirs of women who had gone to France during World War I. No one had looked at these volumes for fifty years. In many, the pages were still uncut.

By the time I finished devouring these books, I had completely re-plotted the novel. Instead of a drama about an eccentric general and the men in his division, I created one of my best women characters, Polly Warden, a feminist who, like most of these women, goes to France to prove that a woman can face the horrors of the western front as courageously as a man.

In one of those Yale memoirs, I discovered an entire scene describing the author's arrival at a French hospital just behind the front lines in the middle of the night. Without an iota of training as a nurse, she found herself giving tetanus injections, bandaging desperately wounded men. I transplanted that scene into Polly's story, making it her defining moment in France.

Historical novel research is not something "extra"—a lot of facts that embroider or support the central imaginary story, sort of the way a frame surrounds a painting. In a good novel, the imagination blends the imaginary and the factual into the very warp and woof of the story. They become a single element—the narrative flowing through the landscape of the past.

A novelist does not look for the same sort of facts that historians need to buttress claims of authenticity or arguments. Historians are seldom interested in personal emotion. For a novelist, that is the essence of his search. For my novel, *The Spoils of War,* I spent months researching the Republican theft of the presidency in 1876. I acquired enough information about this famous scandal to write a good history book—or at least a solid article—on it. But I did not find what I wanted until I uncovered the astonishing fact that the managing editor of *The New York Times,* then the Republican Party's flagship paper, was the man who orchestrated the plot. The same paper that had won the moral admiration of the world for uncovering the machinations of Boss Tweed and his corrupt Tammany henchmen in New York!

For the first time, I was able to portray my main character, Jonathan Stapleton, who carried some of the money south to bribe electors in key southern states to switch their votes, as a man who saw himself performing a moral mission. He was preventing the Democratic Party—the party of secession and rebellion, responsible, in his (and the managing editor's) mind, for the million deaths of the Civil War— from regaining the presidency. That discovery enabled me to give that part of the book a spiritual depth that led directly to the tragic development of the next phase of the story: the breakup of Jonathan Stapleton's marriage because his southern-born wife could not accept his reason for participating in the scandal.

As a writer gets into a historical novel, he or she has to keep feeding the imagination fresh facts. I favor doing about sixty percent of the research at the start and then completing the rest as the ongoing narrative tells you what you need. Often small details can play a tremendous part in a later scene. In my research for *Time and Tide,* my novel set in the Pacific during World War II, I came across an incident in which American sailors discovered a huge Japanese torpedo washed up on Guadalcanal. It was far superior to any torpedo then in use in the U.S. Navy.

I fed this fact into my narrative. My main character, Captain Arthur McKay, commander of the imaginary ship that sails through the book—the *USS Jefferson City*—reports the discovery of the torpedo to his superiors. But the Navy bureaucracy ignores him, and in the next battle, a flotilla of Japanese destroyers wreaks havoc on the American fleet, firing these torpedoes from long range. McKay's disillusion with the Navy deepens, and the reader watches him plunge into a drinking bout that almost wrecks his career.

How do you do such research? Often, by rummaging around in diaries or oral histories of the participants in the history you are writing about. Research for a novel covers some of the same ground as research for nonfiction—you need to know the big picture—but in the novel the focus is on what fits into your smaller picture, on things that intensify the emotional dimensions of your story.

If your novel involves the politics and social life of a period, like my

247

book, *The Spoils of War,* which is set in New York in the decades after the Civil War, newspapers of the day provide another source of background information. These are available on microfilm in many big public libraries, or may be borrowed through interlibrary loan.

I could not have written *Over There* without the 1918–19 issues of the *Paris Herald,* which contained fascinating, day-by-day coverage of Americans in Paris and at the front during World War I. Reading the reactions of people who were in Paris when the Germans were shelling the city by day and bombing it by night was like a trip in a nightmare time machine.

Biographies or memoirs of minor figures, generals of the second rank, diplomats, and politicians provide another valuable source of material for historical fiction. These are often full of the minutiae you need to bring scenes to life. You can often transplant one of these characters to your story under another name, bolstering your novel's authenticity.

Even better are interviews with some of the people involved in the events you use in your novel, if you can locate them. I spent a fascinating weekend with the late General Albert Wedemeyer (who was 91 at the time) discussing the leak of Rainbow Five, the top-secret U.S. plans for World War II. On December 4, 1941, this story created blazing headlines in papers across the country. Wedemeyer was suspected of leaking the plans and for a while was threatened with a firing squad. I attributed much of this experience to my novel's main character, Jonathan Talbot.

For *The Officers' Wives,* I interviewed at length two Army wives who had followed their husbands through Korea and Vietnam, which gave me priceless insights into a woman's reaction to the turmoil these wars created in the Army. Neither woman resembled even faintly the three women I later created as main characters in the novel. That is not the way the historical imagination works. It does not literally copy, but transforms the research facts as required by the plot into the blend of imagination and history that the writer is creating in the novel.

Sometimes, as you work on a novel, you find the research-writing process reversing itself: Instead of research helping you create a character, the character inspires you to do more research, which often adds a whole new dimension to your book.

The historical novelist's ultimate challenge is to discover a new interpretation of a major aspect of the past. Here the novelist is brushing shoulders with the historians, and he must be very very sure of the available facts. At the same time, he is more free to deal in probabilities. In *The Spoils of War,* I decided from my research that the battleship *Maine,* which blew up in Havana harbor in 1898, was almost certainly not sunk by the Spanish, as the history books long told us. Nor did its magazines explode accidentally, as recent historians have suggested, influenced by a study of the event written by Admiral Hyman Rickover. Far more probably, the ship was sunk by the Cuban revolutionaries, who despised the Americans and had no compunction about manipulating them into the war on their side.

To bolster this conclusion, I hired an expert on naval architecture, who wrote me a devastating critique of Rickover's book. My expert told me that after reading the Admiral's so-called evidence, he was convinced that the *Maine* had been sunk by a mine. With this reassurance, I made the destruction of the *Maine* by the Cuban revolutionaries part of the final scenes of *The Spoils of War.*

In *Loyalties,* I encountered an even more momentous reinterpretation. I started the book with the assumption that Franklin D. Roosevelt never made a major mistake during World War II. As I dug deeper into the unexplored world of wartime Washington, I slowly began to perceive a very different president, a fatally ill, even dying man who nursed a pathological hatred of all things German, to the point of refusing to negotiate with the decent Germans who were trying to overthrow Hitler. I spent six months confirming this interpretation from dozens of sources, eventually writing a 50-page essay with over 100 footnotes. I showed this to several historian friends before including this characterization of Roosevelt in the novel.

These experiences have taught me that a historical novelist should take nothing for granted in the so-called history of even the recent past. Every writer should approach his story with the skepticism of the reporter, looking for the truth about men and measures, about events great and small, in the maze of yesterday. At the same time, historical novelists must never forget that they are storytellers, struggling to shape a narrative into the novel's demands as art.

➤➤ 55

SCIENCE FICTION THAT SELLS

BY MICHAEL A. BURSTEIN

SCIENCE FICTION DIFFERS FROM ALMOST EVERY OTHER FORM OF LIT-erature in that the writer cannot make any assumptions about the reader's expectations. When you begin to write a mainstream story set in contemporary times, or a story set in a known historical period, you can safely assume that the reader has some familiarity with the background of the world, and you can build your story on that background.

But as a writer of science fiction, you have no such luxury. Almost by definition, you can set your story anywhere or "anywhen." Even if you set the story in "the future," different readers will have different ideas as to what the future will hold. How, then, can a writer create such a world? What kind of characters can be placed in that world, and how can we possibly write stories that will seem authentic to our readers?

I am a relatively new science fiction writer, with only two published stories and two more sales to my credit. But I turned a critical eye to my first published story, "TeleAbsence," to try to discern exactly what made it a contender. What I discovered were some nearly universal principles for constructing good science fiction.

"TeleAbsence" is about an inner-city child named Tony who sneaks into a telepresence school using a pair of Virtual Reality glasses—or "spex," as I call them—that he's stolen from another student. When Tony puts on the spex, he takes on that student's image and persona as far as the rest of the class is concerned. The school is heavenly, compared to the dilapidated school Tony attends in New York City. Students can "jack in" from all over the country and experience a classroom environment that can be manipulated almost by pure thought. Textbooks automatically adjust themselves to a student's reading level, and the teacher can shake up the classroom to simulate an earthquake. Tony is desperate to stay, but knows that it is only a matter of time before the teacher and the other students discover the truth.

From this description, you may already have ascertained what I consider the first and most important step in constructing good science fiction, and that is to start with a good *idea*. Science fiction is more idea-based than anything else. The idea for this story came from a comment I heard at a science fiction convention, that by the year 2000 everyone would have an electronic mail address. I wanted to point out that the recent explosion of the Internet into many people's daily lives did not mean free access to information for everyone. But, the basic concept I was interested in, the Internet, was no longer science fiction; it was real science.

So I extrapolated. Instead of the Internet, I created a system of Virtual Reality schools, which had originally been designed as a solution for violence in schools. Instead, the public money to fund them never materialized, and the technology was adopted by private school systems that could afford them. The analogy was solid, but subtle enough for the reader not to feel beaten over the head with my message.

Once I had my idea, I needed to develop the *characters* and *plot* that worked best for this idea. I tend to feel that plot and characters must always be developed together, and in science fiction they must be thought of in the context of the scientific or technological advance your story is about. As a general rule, when writing science fiction, you can get the characters out of your idea by asking the question, *Whom does this hurt?* No one cares to read about someone whose life is made happy by scientific advances; good science fiction comes from stories of everyday people dealing with technological developments being thrust upon them.

To illustrate the power of asking the question posed above, let me tell you about my original idea for character and plot. I briefly considered writing about a scientist who has a friend, a teacher, who is killed because of school violence. The scientist then goes on to develop the technology for telepresence schools, and all ends happily. I abandoned this idea after less than a page of writing, not only because it says the opposite of the message I wanted to get across, but because the story

251

of a scientist solving a problem is a very old tradition in science fiction, bordering on cliché. Instead, I asked myself who would be hurt by the technological development of VR schools and realized that it would be those same students who were supposed to benefit from it. Not only did I have a better story, but I had dramatic irony and the ability to show the reader what these schools would be like—all by asking one simple question about character.

Also, in a good science fiction story, the characters should always be comfortable in their world, accepting situations that seem fantastic to the reader. The classic example is from the opening sentence of a Robert Heinlein novel: "The door dilated." None of the characters in this world of the future is surprised at the thought of a "dilating" door. Such doors are as commonplace in that world as hinged swinging doors are in ours. When we turn on a television set, we don't react by saying, "My God! Moving pictures and words are coming out of that little box!" Nor should your science fiction characters react to the everyday technology of their world.

In the same way, Tony in "TeleAbsence" understands exactly what the telepresence school is all about. Yes, he does have the thrill of discovering new things when he sneaks into the school, since he's never been to one before, but he is familiar with the concept. When the story begins, he is completely cognizant of the existence of the telepresence schools. He has heard about them all his life; they are as ubiquitous in his world as a jet airplane is in ours.

The overriding principle in creating a plot is that it must be based on the science fictional extrapolation of the story. In true science fiction, the story would fall apart if the science were removed.

There is no way that "TeleAbsence" could be about a child who sneaks into a regular school.

Beginning writers often commit this plot error in writing what is sometimes called a "space western." In such a story, a space patroller (sheriff) rides his spaceship (horse) around the galaxy (town), having shootouts with space pirates (outlaws), firing his laser pistol (six-shooter). *If a story does not need to be science fiction to work, then it is not science fiction and should not be written as such.*

Although the same should not be said about the way one works *conflict* into a science fiction story, putting elements of science fiction into it can make the conflict much more powerful. In "TeleAbsence,"

252

Tony is scared of being found out, but imagines he is safe because the student whose spex he is using can't jack in without them. Then Tony is confronted in a manner very suitable to science fiction, as is seen in the following:

Tony was interrupted by a sharp buzz, and he looked up. At the front of the classroom appeared an older man with thick grey hair. He headed straight for Tony, a scowl on his face, and Tony looked down again, in fear.

He heard Miss Ellis speak. "Mr. Drummond, what are you doing here?"

The man didn't answer Miss Ellis. He went right up to Tony and said, "Give them back! They're mine!"

Tony shivered. It had been too good to last; now he was going to be found out. This man was obviously Andrew's father, come to get the spex back.

"Mr. Drummond!" said Miss Ellis, with an angry tone that was familiar to Tony. "I would appreciate it if you would not interrupt my class to talk with your son! Can't this wait until later?"

"This is not me—I mean, this is not my son!" Mr. Drummond shouted.

There was silence for a moment. Tony felt Miss Ellis move next to him and Mr. Drummond. "What's going on?" she asked.

"This kid stole my—I mean, my son's spex!"

Tony looked up at Miss Ellis and saw her smile. Facing Mr. Drummond, she said, "That's you, isn't it, Andrew?"

For the first time since he appeared, "Mr. Drummond" looked uncomfortable. "Ummm, yeah, Miss Ellis. I had to use Dad's spex to jack in. Whoever this is—" he pointed at Tony—"stole my own spex."

"Ah-ha. Andrew, go home. I'll take care of this."

"Ummm. You won't tell my Dad, will you? I don't want him to know that I've been careless."

"No. I won't tell him. Now go. I'll contact you later."

The image of Andrew's father vanished, and Miss Ellis turned to Tony. He was on the verge of tears.

We've seen how to develop the idea, plot, and characters for a science fiction story, but how do you explain the background of your world so readers will understand and appreciate it? Above all, *avoid the infodump,* an expository lump that does nothing but provide information. When contemporary characters make phone calls or fire guns in a mainstream story, they don't stop to contemplate and explain the technology to the reader. When characters avoid taking the subway or walking through certain neighborhoods, they don't stop to deliver a treatise on the sociological development of their hometown.

But what about a science fiction story? I like to call the technique *painting tiny brushstrokes.* I must admit that I cheated a little, as "Tele-Absence" is set in a classroom, and therefore I can have the teacher explain things to her students; that's a lot more logical than having a 22nd-century police officer deliver an interior monologue on the mechanics of his laser pistol while in hot pursuit. And even in the classroom, I tried to keep such explanations to a minimum. For example, here is an excerpt from a scene where the students are discussing their hometowns in class:

> Since he knew Los Alamos better than East Lansing, Brian chose to talk about his original hometown instead of where he was now. Tony barely paid attention as Brian talked about the joys of small-town life and then displayed some pictures from a family photo album that he was able to pull up using his computer. Miss Ellis then discussed the arid mountainous area where the town was located, and how there had been a scientific laboratory there until the year 2010.
>
> Janice went next, and again Tony was too scared to pay attention. Janice described San Francisco, and, possibly still thinking about lunch, mentioned the delicious seafood and sourdough bread. Miss Ellis talked about other things, such as the earthquakes that San Francisco had experienced, and the Golden Gate Bridge, which she said had been one of the longest suspension bridges in the country until the earthquake just last year that destroyed it. She showed three-dimensional video images of the earthquake, and even made the classroom shake up a bit, so the students could experience a bit of what an earthquake was like.

Notice the details that are merely implied. What kind of future has the closing of a major scientific laboratory? Why hasn't Miss Ellis mentioned an attempt to repair the bridge? These little details can make the world more realistic. Here's another example, later in the story:

> The following Monday afternoon, Tony took the subway down to Greenwich Village. He had to show a pass at 96th Street in order to continue under the fence, but Miss Ellis had arranged everything.

That's all that's mentioned. Tony doesn't ruminate over recent history, nor does he explain to the reader why the fence is there and why he needs a pass to go downtown. But the frequent reader of science fiction can draw the appropriate conclusions.

There are two more important points for writing good science fiction. First, make sure you puzzle out all the consequences of the idea you are extrapolating before you sit down to write, or else some astute reader will wonder why, if there is a cure for death in your story, no one seems to mention the overpopulation problem. This is a major problem in TV science fiction such as *Star Trek*: If replicators can create anything people might need, why does there still seem to be a capitalist-based economy? Don't be guilty of this error.

Finally, if you want to write publishable science fiction, try to end on a positive note without losing sight of the story you're trying to tell. I wanted Tony to end up in the telepresence school, which would have been a happy ending, but that wouldn't have made my point. And the obvious, unhappy ending was for him to return to his old school. Instead, Miss Ellis takes him on as a private student in the afternoons. They don't have the advantages that the technology might give them, but the reader feels hopeful for the future. And that's the best way for a science fiction story to end.

>> 56

BUILDING CONFLICT IN THE
HISTORICAL ROMANCE

By Patricia Werner

CONFLICT, SET IN A COLORFUL BACKGROUND, IS WHAT DRIVES THE historical romance. Here are some of the techniques for weaving threads of conflict into a complex tapestry that will appeal to readers.

Plotting opposites

History itself offers barriers an author can use to create obstacles between lovers. One popular technique is having the hero and heroine on opposite sides of two warring factions (such as the North and South during the Civil War or the British and the Colonists during the American Revolution).

Another possible choice could be to make the main characters members of feuding families. Or they might be from different social classes or ethnic backgrounds. By using incidents in the story to show the characters' personal goals, you can bring them into conflict with each other. Such incidents move the plot forward.

For example, a railroad baron may want to buy a widow's land to lay track through the mountains. But the widow wants to hold on to her land because it's her son's birthright, and she promised her father she would never sell it. Or perhaps the land offers her a chance to prove that she can be a successful rancher.

In this plot, the railroad baron and the widow have different ideas for proper use of the land. But if, in spite of this conflict, the baron and the widow are attracted to each other, you have the set-up for a valid historical romance plot. Your challenge as the author is to let those two characters work out their conflicts and acknowledge their love by the end of the book.

Motivation and purpose

Motivation provides the reason your characters take certain actions.

256

Although in life people sometimes seem to do things for no apparent reason, your characters must act *with* reason, and their actions must be consistent with their personalities. Plant these reasons, or motives, either in the thoughts of the character, or in dialogue in which the character confides hopes, dreams, and secrets to another character. This will reveal your characters' motives and show the reader how and why the hero's and heroine's purposes are truly in conflict.

For example, in my historical romance *The Falcon and the Sword,* set in the early barbarian kingdoms of what later became known as France, the heroine, Judith, has attached herself to her childhood friend, a princess who has just married the king of Neustria. (Neustria, Austrasia, and Burgundy were Frankish territories in 567 A.D.) Judith's purpose is to protect the newly married princess from an evil, jealous concubine. Thus Judith's friendship with the princess *motivates* her to keep watch over her friend.

The hero, Marcus, is an envoy from the kingdom of Austrasia and his political purpose is to serve *his* king. The two kings are warring brothers. Judith finds herself in a position to act as a spy for Marcus. It would have been easy to end the book there and have him take her back to Austrasia. But being people bound by the moral code of the Franks called for a blood feud. Hence, when the princess is murdered, Judith's moral code *motivates* her to avenge her friend's death, keeping her apart from Marcus, whose purpose is to wage a war for his king.

Your characters' motives must be believable, and to achieve this credibility, you must put yourself into your characters' thoughts and get to know them. Try to live the scene as you write it, so you will know which motives are logical for each character. Ask yourself, does this character have a reason for his or her actions? Don't write anything that seems vague to you, or it will certainly seem even vaguer to your readers.

Emotional conflicts

Let emotional conflicts provide an undercurrent for the larger historical issues. Emotions draw the reader into a story. The characters react emotionally to the need to meet the social or political challenges of the plot, and this advances the story.

Here is how I showed social conflicts arousing emotions in *Velvet Dreams*: The impoverished Duke of Sunderland goes to America to

257

seek an American heiress to pay his bills. He doesn't intend to marry for love. Socialite Amanda Whitney wants to marry only for love, so from the start their actions are at cross-purposes. Amanda's mother threatens to kill herself if Amanda marries the ne'er-do-well American whom Amanda is secretly pledged to, thus putting her under emotional pressure.

But Amanda has misjudged her American suitor, who jilts her. Her anger at the Duke's overt desire to marry her for money and her desire to prove her mother wrong motivate her to rebel and turn to a French scholar for solace. She is in conflict with the Duke, with her mother, and with the societal values with which she was raised. All of these conflicts provide excitement, danger, and action, which hold the readers' interest.

One man, one woman

When your hero and heroine fall in love with each other, they must be free of all ties. The one woman-one man historical romance is standard for the genre, which has well-defined conventions when it comes to love—though both hero and heroine may have had previous relationships or even marriages. They must not, however, indulge in romantic dalliances with anyone else *while their relationship is developing,* especially not after they have gone to bed together. Timing here is the key to emotional entanglement.

In some circumstances, it is permissible for the heroine to become romantically and physically involved with another man before falling in love with or consummating her relationship with the hero. This adds to the original conflict and makes the reader turn the pages to find out which man will win. But this should always be very carefully done and well motivated, or it will offend readers.

In *The Falcon and the Sword,* Judith takes a barbarian lover for protection. Though she cares for him, according to the conventions of historical romance, he has to leave or die before she can form a relationship with Marcus. Her barbarian lover is killed in battle; Judith grieves; Marcus rescues her from the Saxons. Only then, after a slow, emotional build-up, does their love take root, and they finally consummate their relationship.

Setting

Setting can provide another wedge between characters. Perhaps the heroine is in a place she despises, but she has to be there to carry out her mission. Or the place represents something from her past that must be avenged or purged. Her resentment of the hero may stem from the fact that he is so much a part of that place that he could never think of leaving. Or perhaps he cannot leave because he has responsibilities there.

In a historical romance, the characters may be sent on journeys, thus separating the hero and heroine for several chapters. In a novel this long, there is room for adventures. It is a convention of this genre that when hero and heroine are apart, they should continue to think of one another.

Complications

Complicate the conflicts wherever possible. Carefully weave together the historical, romantic, and goal-oriented conflicts. Every step the heroine takes toward *her* goal should inadvertently antagonize the hero or frustrate *his* goal. This action and reaction will advance the plot, but at the same time, you must draw the hero and the heroine deeper and deeper into their relationship. In spite of all their conflicts, make them care about what will happen to the other person if their own goal is met.

Push your heroine into such a tight corner that she has few choices that would help to get her out. Use motives that make for difficult choices. And the result of each choice should throw her back into the path, or arms, of the hero.

Secrets

Give either the hero or heroine a secret: One can wear a disguise to obtain information or to hide something. Here the conflict stems from the fact that the disguised character must pretend to be another person, at the same time wishing deeply to reveal the truth.

In my novel, *Cimarron Seductress,* Roslyn Dwayne, an ex-outlaw named Cimarron Rose, decides to leave the outlaw life. She goes to live in Indian territory with distant relatives who know nothing of her past. There, she is attracted to Marshal Luke McBride. But she learns to her horror that he is looking for Cimarron Rose, a woman he believes can lead him to the Doolin gang, who accidently killed his sister in a shootout during a bank robbery at Southwest City.

Can Roslyn admit that she is Cimarron Rose? No. Because by this

259

point in the story, her uncle, who's lost his wife, has come to depend on her to take care of his sons, her cousins. If she tells the truth, she'll not only lose Luke but will also disappoint her new family. But she cannot live the lie forever. When an old crony of Doolin's shows up, saying that Doolin's been hurt, is nearby, and needs help, the old loyalty tears at her. The Doolin gang took her in when she was small—orphaned when her parents died in a train wreck. Bill Doolin taught her how to survive in a tough situation. Surely she owes him something, too.

Build the conflicts one on the other. You are not simply retelling a well-known historical event; you must entangle the central characters deeper and deeper into multiple plot conflicts. It must appear as if they cannot escape but of course they must. How does the author achieve this without jarring the reader or making one of the characters do such a sudden about-face that it appears ridiculous?

Make your characters undergo change. Plant the seed early on that the character actually wants to change, so that when it occurs, the change will be motivated. For example, Roslyn had already decided to become a law-abiding citizen *before* she met Marshal McBride. He had already decided to give up his badge and turn to ranching once the culprits were caught. So their resolution at the end seems convincing.

At the resolution of the story, self-revelation brings hero and heroine to accept their mutual love in spite of the difficult conflicts. Luke realizes that Roslyn really is no longer a woman on the wrong side of the law, that she acted as she did because of loyalty, not cowardice. He would want her to be no less loyal to him. Love conquers all? Yes, but it must do so in a believable and well-motivated way.

What about sex?

Make the passion sizzle while the conflicts grow. These two characters burn for each other, but they are in conflict with one another because of their opposing goals. Their inner conflict keeps them from acknowledging their love at first. Their passion for each other should be followed by denial, or a feeling of guilt, or anger. Sexual encounters as well as their arguments must ring true.

Most editors leave the number of love scenes and the degree of explicit sex up to the author. Historical romances are categorized by editors as sweet, spicy, or sensual. Sweet romances do not lack in sexual attraction that leads to passionate embraces; the characters may even go to bed together near the end of the novel—but the curtains are drawn.

Spicy romances take time out from plot developments and other adventures to present a few steamy scenes. Sensual romances have many explicit love scenes, but even so, they should be well integrated into the story line; each love scene—justified and well motivated—should intensify the conflict.

Length

Most historical romances run from 100,000 to 135,000 words. The novel must have a happy ending, otherwise it will be classified as a saga or mainstream historical novel. Your manuscript will be from 400 to 550 typewritten double-spaced pages, producing a book that will run from about 364 to 474 printed pages.

Do enough research to make the setting and story come alive in your mind, and to write a salable book, keep the conflict going till THE END.

>>57

THE PLOT'S THE THING

BY REGINALD HILL

IT IS A TRUTH UNIVERSALLY ACKNOWLEDGED THAT EVERYBODY'S GOT one good novel in them.

It is a delusion generally untested that everybody can write it. Which is just as well for us writers who can go about quietly cannibalizing our friends' lives and experiences for our own plots.

I want to talk here about plotting, the process by which we take the raw materials of our fiction and serve them up in a digestible mode. Get it wrong, and what you planned as soufflé may turn out as scrambled eggs.

Of course, when that happens, professional writers don't blow their brains out; they start looking for a market for scrambled eggs. But if what they've got is cold porridge, they feed it to the pigs and start again.

So let's start with what a plot is not. It isn't just narrative, not even moving narrative. Tell your friends that you got mugged in the elevator, and they'll be truly shocked and sympathetic, but that's because they're your friends, and even your nearest and dearest will show signs of irritation if you're still going on about it the following week. To turn it into the kind of anecdote that people ask you to repeat to others who haven't heard it takes a bit of art, which, as Sir Thomas Browne said, is the perfection of nature. So, if you were on your way to an important job interview when the mugging happened, and you put the experience behind you and went straight in anyway, forgetting that the mugger, attracted by the handsome gold buckle on your belt, had made you remove it . . . . Now it's a funny recyclable story, but still a long way from a plot. At best there might be the germ of a short story there, but so what? Great short stories are made by concentration, not expansion.

What I'm laboring to stress is that plot and story are not the same thing. A plot is both the structure in which the narrative takes place and a function of that narrative. To describe the way I see plot, I'm going to take the writer's easy way out and resort once more to metaphor.

Think of it as a house: A conventional arrangement would be a living room, a dining room, and a kitchen on the first floor, and three bedrooms and a bathroom on the second. Of course, if people are to live comfortably in the house, there must be access to each room from a common area—a hallway downstairs and a landing upstairs, plus a stairway connecting the two floors. There will probably be an attic, possibly a cellar. Some of the rooms may interconnect directly—say, the kitchen and dining room, or two of the bedrooms, one of which is a nursery. Each of the rooms will have specific functions with occasional variation, as when you have the living room serve as a bedroom when you have too many overnight guests. Some rooms, like the bathroom, may be locked without causing surprise. But a locked bedroom may, in certain circumstances, cause unease, and a locked kitchen, downright alarm. There are certain areas in which the presence of certain people is expected, but others in which their presence will require explanation. Some windows are more private than others: One window looks into the back garden, while another looks out onto the street. People living outside the house use these windows, too: sometimes to see in, sometimes to get in.

Corbusier's definition of a house as a machine for living in works only if we see people as the machine's moving parts, and so it is in my analogy. You start your story with a shell, and your characters move in. The shell they move into is going to direct and restrict their activities, but your characters are the forces that will shape the way the shell comes to life, sometimes dramatically. When I started writing decades ago, I thought it was pretty easy, especially once I'd opted for the conventionally structured crime novel. I could decide whether I wanted a country cottage or a town house, a gothic castle or a condo. Narrative was linear: People moved in at the start of a book, and the survivors arranged themselves photogenically at the end.

But pretty soon I began to realize that art is harder, not easier, than life; that having total control is no soft option; that being the Mighty Oz requires a hell of a lot of huffing and puffing from that small man behind the curtain. With control over your house—your plot—you can knock down walls as well as open doors and build extensions if you find you're short of space. Like Faustus, you'll find that your dominion can stretch as far as the mind of man.

Now I realize that all I'm doing here is telling you what it's like, not how to do it. To be honest, I feel that to give practical advice, I really should have written this article years ago, before I learned just how complicated it all was. If you yourself have reached that happy stage at which it all seems pretty simple, then don't let me discourage you. It may be that you are one of the really lucky ones who can construct a flow chart on paper or in your computer that will keep your plot straight as a ploughman's furrow. If you have this gift, treasure it, refine it; don't distract yourself with the wildflowers growing at the edge of the field.

But if once you start writing a story you never stop thinking about it no matter what you're doing, not even after you've finished it; and if your idea of making notes is to scribble things in margins, on the backs of envelopes, under your watch strap—then you need more than a flow chart to plot your story. If you're happy to spend half an hour tracking the right word through a thesaurus or dictionary and another half hour tracking all the other lovely words you chance upon; if you can read the hundred pages you've labored over for a week and accept what your sinking heart tells you and go back to the beginning and write them all again—then you, too, are tempted by the freedom in plotting I've been talking about. If you feel that in holding a mirror up to life, fiction may have to select but must never simplify; if you think a typewriter and a stack of paper are the best company in the world— then here for you alone are the few crumbs of anything resembling practical advice I can give:
• The simpler the plot, the subtler the plotting.
• Girl meets boy is not the same as boy meets girl.
• The three touchstones of plotting are pace, point of view, and continuity.

Pace doesn't mean speed; it means the *right* speed. Diagnosis and cure are simple. If you've reached where you want to be in your story too quickly, ask yourself what you've left out. If you've come to a certain point too slowly, ask yourself what kept you so long. When Charlotte Brontë wrote, "Reader, I married him," in *Jane Eyre,* it was enough. But if Herman Melville had written, "Reader, it killed him," when Captain Ahab finally confronts Moby Dick, he would have left readers dissatisfied. Always try the most direct route first. If it works, it works, and the 50 pages of explication you'd planned are superfluous. On the other hand, because I generally find I need to know far more about my characters and their context than my readers do, I spend a great deal of revision time paring away unnecessary detail.

Point of view is obviously of prime importance in plotting. If you go for the single eye (or I), then you limit your options in a way that can either be attractively simple or simply frustrating. If you want to let the reader know what's going on in the bathroom, you can't just tell it; you've got to put your I's eye to the keyhole, which is only a partial *view,* or have another character describe what's happening, which is a partial *version.* But if you go for godlike ubiquity in your viewpoint, then you give yourself a much greater problem of selection. This must be related to pace: Are you going at a gallop or taking a stroll? But it also relates to tone. The temptation of first-person narrative is to take on the tone of a smart-mouth, as with the traditional hard-boiled P.I., for example. The tone taken with the omniscient narrator can be one of patronizing preachiness. Some Victorian writers were particularly prone to having an uplifting chat with their readers. In writing my novel, *Pictures of Perfection,* I was faced with the problem of how best to introduce information about the past: flashback? straight history? character reminiscence? I opted for excerpts from a history of the local parish written by a former vicar. This device allowed me not only to give information, but also to make the kind of general observations I wanted to make without (I hope) sounding pompously *ex cathedra.* Throughout the book, in fact, I confronted the same problem. What happened in the fairly distant past was essential to an understanding of what was going on in the present, and I indulged in many experiments before I settled on the version that was finally published. All the versions were, of course, subject to the tests of pace and point of view. Some leeway and difference of opinion may be permissible here, but the last of my three touchstones—continuity—permits no compromise.

Put simply, no matter how well paced your plotting is or how clever you are with your point of view, without continuity, the overall effect is a jerky and disjointed novel. By continuity I do not mean making sure your hero's shirt doesn't change color between scenes. Instead, continuity means wholeness, "hanging togetherness," integrity. I enjoy the interweaving of complex plots, I love tying and untying knots, but I'm always aware that one false move could result in a messy tangle rather than a pleasing pattern.

Plotting is not the story you want to tell, it is finding the best way of telling that story. And if, as you write, the reference books and scribbled notes to yourself and last month's mail pile up around you, then you are probably capable of enduring the uncertainties, mysteries, and doubts necessary to tell that story, without any irritable reaching after fact and reason (that quality Keats called *negative capability*). You will be able to because you are confident your unconsciousness or intuition will show you the way. If you're my kind of plotter, then the best advice I can give you is, don't let anything go till you feel it's right.

>> 58

WRITING EFFECTIVE DIALOGUE

BY JEREMIAH HEALY

LET ME ASK YOU BEFORE YOU BEGIN THIS PIECE TO READ THE FOLlowing exchange:

Beginning Draft

John Jeffers walked into the room. He saw Mary Edwards standing at the window. John exclaimed, "Mary, what are you doing here?"

Mary turned to him. "Aw, John, I am just so upset about Martha," she blurted.

John walked across the room, taking her in his arms. He whispered, "Aw, Mary, I am sorry about Martha, too, but we cannot let it ruin our lives."

Mary held him tightly. "I know, but it is all just so hard," she murmured. "And besides," she added, "I think I know where Geoff hid the knife."

If you feel the above passage represents good dialogue, then stop reading this article. On the other hand, if you don't like the John/Mary exchange, but you recognize in it, uncomfortably, some of your own tendencies as a writer, then the following may be helpful to you.

Though I write mystery novels, most of my comments will apply to many types of fiction. As a premise, let's assume that dialogue should serve three purposes: story advancement, character development, and writing style. I'm going to spend a little less time here on the first two purposes and a little more on the third.

In order to use dialogue to advance the story in a mystery novel, you have to have some idea of what information must be communicated to the reader in each chapter. In my opinion, the best example of a writer who uses dialogue to inform the reader about the story is Elmore Leonard. Pick up any of his street thrillers (*Glitz, Stick,* etc.), and notice how he tells the reader most of his plot through dialogue. Leonard's high point is the opening chapter of his Edgar Award novel, *LaBrava,* in which the entire setting of the story is explained by a two-character exchange of dialogue.

Does the passage I use at the beginning of this article advance the story? Hard to tell, since we don't know what information the writer wants to communicate to the reader or where in the story line the passage appears. At the very least, though, we know the male character is surprised to find the female character in the setting; the female character is upset about someone else; there is some pre-existing relationship between the male and female characters; and, somehow, another character and a knife are involved in a sinister way. Let's say, then, that the story has been advanced by the John/Mary exchange.

The second purpose of dialogue is character development. The reader has to see your characters as more than just ciphers or the novelistic version of operatic spear-carriers for the plot. Here, we know that the female character is upset; that the male character is empathetic ("I am sorry . . ."), yet forward-looking ("We cannot let it ruin . . ."); and that the female character is also troubled by a secret she believes she's discovered. While there is some overlap with the story advancement purpose, the writer has done a credible job with character development, too. Read any of Mary Higgins Clark's novels for other examples of the use of dialogue to develop character.

I think, then, that the major failing of my first exchange is in writing style, and I'd like to focus upon this third purpose of dialogue. Reread my opening passage. Stylistically, what's wrong with it? Answer: technically nothing. The characters in the exchange speak perfect English in perfect sentence structure, with thesaurus "cue" words like "exclaimed" and "blurted" (and "whispered" and "murmured") that tell the reader exactly what intensity of emotion the author meant the characters to reveal.

However, judged from a novelist's standpoint, the dialogue is dreadful. It's stilted and unnatural, because people in the real world having actual conversations don't speak in complete sentences and do use contractions. Also, through the dialogue *itself,* a writer ought to be able to convey the intensity of expression without thesaurus cues. The word "said" is virtually the only expression cue you should ever need, and even that often isn't necessary, since in a two-character scene the break in paragraphs "cues" the reader that the other character is now speaking, and the character action (stage directions of "she turned" or "he walked") usually can cover the rest.

Now, let's rewrite the opening passage using just the foregoing suggestions (incomplete sentences, contractions, and stage directions, but no cues other than "said"):

First Revision

Walking into the study, John Jeffers saw Mary Edwards standing at the window and stopped short. "Mary, what are you doing here?"

Mary turned to him. "Aw, John, I'm just so upset about . . . you know." She turned back to the window. "Martha."

John walked across the room, taking her in his arms. "Aw, Mary, I'm sorry, too. But we can't let it. . . . We have to go on with our lives."

Mary held him tightly. "I know. It's just so . . ." In a different tone, she said, "Besides, I think I know where Geoff hid the knife."

An improvement? I think the answer is clearly yes. Are we there yet? Clearly not. Why?

A couple of subtler, even subliminal problems. The writer has named the male character "John Jeffers." There's nothing wrong with a common first name like "John," or an alliterated surname like "Jeffers." However, the writer has used up or "burned" the possibility of another character with the first name "Jeff" by having a surname with that "root" in it. Otherwise, the reader would be subliminally confused in the dialogue by references to the "Jeff" sound in a name, and thus "Geoff" in the last phrase would have to be changed. In my private investigator novels, the protagonist's name is "John Francis Cuddy." If I were to have another character's first or last name sound like or contain "John" or "Francis," I'd subliminally confuse even longstanding fans of the ten-book series.

This reasoning also applies to the similarity of "Mary" and "Martha." I try to avoid even the same first *initials* for more than one of my characters, and I keep an alphabet of first and last names, listed vertically, when I begin any novel, to be sure I don't accidentally have several characters with a first name beginning with a specific letter. Though not technically related to dialogue, the naming of characters does affect dialogue directly.

A continuing problem with names in our first revision of the opening passage is that John, Mary, *and the author* use the names themselves too much. To get around this, the author can inject a last name in stage direction prose, while the characters in dialogue occasionally address each other by first name (or even better, nickname). Pronouns, also, if the antecedent is clear, provide the reader with both variety and necessary cues.

Finally, the author should give a pet phrase to only one character, so that for the reader the phrase becomes that character's subliminal signature. Therefore, Mary and John should not both use "Aw" as a pet phrase.

Let's do a second revision of the opening passage, cumulating these last observations (different names, different initials, nicknames, and different pet phrases) into the first revision:

Second Revision

Walking into the study, John Jenkins saw Mary Eberson standing at the window and stopped short. "What are you doing here?"

Eberson turned to him. "Oh, Jack, I'm just so upset about . . . you know." She turned back to the window. "Karen."

Jenkins walked across the room, taking her in his arms. "Hey-ey-ey, Mary, I'm upset too, but we can't—Look, we have to get on with our lives, right?"

Eberson held him tightly. "I know, it's just so . . ." In a different tone, she said, "Besides, I think I know where Geoff hid the knife."

Better? I think so, though we still have some stylistic problems, as in the two usages of "walk." However, in fixing some problems we've created others. For one thing, I don't like the way the author's use of the surnames in stage directions "feels" in this scene.

How can I be writing an article implying that you can and should revise dialogue mechanically, even suggesting some "tricks" on how to do it, when some of the best writers have told me they don't revise at all? Simple. Mechanical revisions showing how *not* to write will improve many authors' dialogue immediately, but while I can "tell" you how some of the best do it, I can't "teach" you that method. Each writer learned his or her own "tricks" intuitively by writing.

I come down midway between the mechanical model and the intuitive one. To write what I hope will be natural, effective dialogue, I first imagine a real person with the characteristics of a given character. I try to imagine that person/character having an actual conversation with another person/character in some real-world setting (people speak differently in bars from the way they do in doctors' offices). Then, instead of *creating* the dialogue as an author, I just *transcribe* it as a stenographer would. I key into my computer what I "hear" each person/character saying to the other during this scene in my head. I

270

would, of course, already have done some planning to determine how the dialogue must advance the story and develop the characters, as suggested earlier. Then, with just a little revision, I can make the dialogue stylistically smooth, and thereafter, I can read the exchange aloud, as a quality control for "natural sound."

So the opening passage again, as a third revision:

Third Revision

Entering the study, John Jenkins saw Mary Eberson standing at the window. "Mary, what the hell are you doing here?"

She turned to him. "Jack, I've just been . . ." Back to the window. "I'm still upset about Karen."

He crossed the room, closing his arms around her gently. "Hey-ey-ey, you got the right, o.k.? But don't let it run your life."

"Or ruin it?" Mary put her left hand on his right forearm. "Good advice. It's just . . ."

"What?"

"The knife."

"The knife?"

"Yes, I think I know where Geoff hid it."

Is this third revision the best yet? I think so. The story is advanced, the characters are developed, and now even contrasted as well. (The reader may be curious about why John and Mary seem to be close when he "sounds" less well educated than she does.) When read silently, the writing is "stylish." When read aloud, the exchange sounds "natural."

Of course, I may like the third revision best because it's *my* way of doing the scene, "transcribing" what I "hear" the characters saying to each other. Accordingly, I'd advise you to use the hints in this article as vehicles for immediately improving your dialogue. Then, slowly develop your *own* way of writing effective dialogue thereafter.

271

➤➤ NONFICTION: ARTICLES AND BOOKS

>> 59

Do's and Don'ts of Magazine Article Writing

By Donald M. Murray

THERE ARE EXCEPTIONS TO EVERY RULE IN WRITING: THE BEST WRITing often occurs when the experienced writer cuts across the grain of tradition. Most of us, however, have to know the "rules" and traditions to bend or break them. Here are some of the basics of magazine article writing that should be mastered *before* you bend them or break them.

Point of view

Your magazine article should have a strong point of view, express a vigorous opinion, important news, a revelation, an argument, an edge that answers the readers' questions: "Why should I bother to read this?" In writing magazine articles—unlike writing news stories—you shouldn't try to be on all sides of the subject, but should make clear to the reader what side you're on. Everything in your article should reflect that view.

The lead

A good magazine article doesn't need an introduction, so don't begin with the background of your subject, how you happened to get interested in it, why the reader should read it, or how you obtained the basic information for it. Begin your article with conflict that produces tension, often revealed by including a brief example or anecdote and problem that will be resolved at the end. It's a good rule to start as near the end as possible and then plunge your reader into the central tension. When you've involved your reader in this way, weave in background facts or information as you think the reader needs it to understand the purpose and point of your piece.

Authority

Early in your article, you should—briefly—establish your authority by revealing your connection with the theme of your article, including some specific, accurate information that will persuade your reader that you know your subject and have the right to be heard and trusted. A calm, confident voice will help you achieve this and will make the connection with the readers so they will say, "Yes, that's the way it is."

Voice

The voice of your article should be conversational: It's not a lecture, a sermon, or an attack, but rather, the voice of a friend discussing an issue you want to share with the readers. The intensity and tone of your voice is tuned to the subject and to your readers.

Selection and development

Don't include all the facts you've gathered in the course of your research, but make a careful—and ruthless—selection of the details that will fulfill the promise of your lead. Then develop your lead fully so your readers will recognize its significance. You can't get away with writing "it was a disturbing experience," but must explain in detail what disturbed you, how and why and what it means in the context of your article. You have to do more than summarize: You must show why and how it was disturbing and what is the importance of the shock or surprise.

Exposition and pace

Keep readers moving forward so they won't lose interest, but slow the pace when you feel that the readers need time to absorb and reflect on what has been written. You can achieve this variety of pace by weaving necessary exposition into the text, tucking factual sentences into your paragraphs. But don't ladle the facts or information you think necessary onto the readers in huge servings; dole it out in spoon-sized portions.

Sequence

Through your narrative, take your reader on a journey from lead to ending. The sequence or order of your narrative depends on your knowing how to make the article most effective. This will not necessarily follow the order in which you experienced the events or story you are relating. Magazine articles distort time for effect. If you are using chronological order, you should not record what you say evenly—sixty minutes to the hour, twenty-four hours to the day. Sometimes you

276

have to recount the events of a war, for example, describing weeks of boredom, punctuated by seconds of terror. As an article writer, you should skip over the boredom—unless *that* is the subject—and develop and expand the moments of terror.

Transitions

Use as few transitions as possible. Give readers the information you think they need when you think they need to know it. Anticipate and answer the readers' questions when you feel they would be raised. I used to write articles one paragraph to a page, and later rearrange them in the order the reader would need to know them. I never had to write a transition like, "Meanwhile, back at the ranch. . . ."

Faces

Readers like to read about people who express ideas, theories, concepts, issues. They walk on the page, talk, confront each other, engage in dialogue; they reveal themselves through physical actions—not "he was fat," but "the floor sagged when he stepped into the room," and vocally through direct quotes: Not, "he talked about the problems of school funding," but, "I was learned by chalk and blackboard. I don't need no computer to help my kid graduate from high school."

Sources

Use live as well as written sources. When you bring those authorities on the page, they speak directly to your readers and help convince them of the validity of your article's theme.

Endings

Don't end your article with a formal conclusion that tells readers what you've said, what the article means and how they should react. It's too late at this point to explain the significance of your article, too late to command readers to think or feel a particular way. The most effective ending gives readers information—a quotation, a statistic, a fact, a scene, an anecdote—that will make them think and feel.

>> 60

WRITING THE FIRST-PERSON ARTICLE

BY MARY ALICE KELLOGG

WHEN DOES SOMEONE BECOME A WRITER? HOW DO YOU KNOW THAT that's what you want to do? Everyone has some particular, pivotal moment when the answer to that question becomes clear, and for me, it was at the tender age of ten. I wrote a letter to the editor of *The Western Horseman,* recounting in my best ten-year-old prose what it was like to ride horses in the desert outside my hometown, and how happy it made me. To my delight—and total surprise—the magazine published my effort, and my writing course was set.

Without realizing it, I had published my first first-person story. And, also without knowing it, I had followed one of the most important rules of writing: "Write what you know." That's what we do, after all, when we write an essay or first-person piece. But even with no characters to invent, no endless interviewing, the first-person piece, ironically, is one of the hardest things to write. But in more than twenty-five years of professional writing, I've found that the first-person form is the one place I can be myself as a writer, let my thoughts and observations go where they will. It's the form I love the most, but it's also, even after all these years, still difficult.

Why? Because having a great first-person story to tell is only the beginning. Take the first-person piece I wrote about my Aunt Mary, who died recently. For 35 years we'd exchanged letters—I saved every one—and I wanted to do a story about what she taught me through our correspondence. While the experience meant a great deal to me, would people who didn't know me or my Aunt Mary want to read it? That's the first question I ask myself when thinking about writing any essay. In this case, I decided that the key to the piece would be how generations can reach out to one another, learn from one another—an element that would touch many families, not just mine.

Your first-person essay is on solid ground if you follow three basic rules: 1) You should feel passionately about the subject; it should make you laugh, see red, contemplate the human condition in ways large or small. Passion—an enthusiasm for what you are saying—is not only *a* starting point, it's the *only* place to begin. You must have a point of view, and sell that point of view, that particular experience, to others.

2) Your first-person piece must have a point that is applicable to others, a focus that gives what happened to you a universal quality. It's not enough, for example, to experience being discriminated against because you're over fifty; you have to take that experience and make others feel what you felt, and along the way offer some insight into how others might react or change. Yes, you have something you want to say, but *why* do you want to say it? Whom do you want to reach? What do you passionately want to tell them?

And 3) you must write in your own voice. That's the whole point of any first-person effort. If you admire Dave Barry's prose, the worst thing you can do is try to write like him. Writers who succeed do so because they have something to say in a way that can't be said by anyone else. Listen to how you speak, the phrases you use that mark your speech, the way you organize your thought patterns, the way you tell a story or anecdote. Then sit down and write that way, and continue to do so. No one finds his or her writing voice right off the bat; the key is to stick with it so your first-person style is as natural as your being there in person. The highest compliment readers can give me is to say that in reading an article of mine, they can *hear* my voice.

As with any article, the first-person piece must tell a story, with a beginning (including a grabbing lead), a middle to develop your views, and a strong end. A couple of years ago, I did a first-person piece about growing older (something I feel passionately about). I decided to have a makeup artist age me 25 years, then spent a day as an older woman to see what fears about aging might crop up (the universal here: many members of my generation are afraid of getting gray). Here's how I began the piece:

As a member of the baby-boom generation, I've tried not to think about growing older. When I am old and gray, I will be blonde, I trill. But if truth be told, at 45 I am frightened of growing old, which is why I decided to conduct this generation-bending experiment.

279

My experiences that day made up the middle of the piece: people's reactions to me, how I felt in my new "skin." And, at the end, I told what I had learned:

I was encouraged by what the woman within had shown me: that I am invisible only if I allow myself to be. . . . I look forward to meeting that woman in the mirror again. I know now how very much I will enjoy being her someday, for real.

It's true that life is the best source material. It is for me. And there are as many opportunities for first-person expression, as many places to begin, as there are experiences to relate. It's up to you to decide which way to go. Here are some basic jumping-off points that I use to get started:

• *An incident that happened to you.* Make the reader care about it. Did the airline lose your luggage? It happened to me a few years ago, and not only did I get mad, I got even, writing an essay about what was in that suitcase, how much I felt the loss, and what I learned about taking irreplaceable items on the road in the future.

• *A unique experience you've had*: Surviving a plane crash or earthquake; helping a loved one through an illness or divorce; raising a Down's Syndrome child; or learning to write with your left hand after breaking your right arm—all perfect first-person material. The key is to examine in a personal way not just the experience itself, but the aftermath. How did it change you? Your loved ones? What did you learn that might help others? In my case, searching for and finding my father after many years and discovering I had an entirely new batch of relatives gave me the opportunity to examine the issues of tolerance, forgiveness, and personal growth. The article appeared in *Glamour* and received a national writing award.

It also taught me a lot about patience, which is important when writing in the first person about a life-altering event. I had tried for years to write this story—in first person, as a reporting piece, and as third-person fiction. But it never quite worked out the way I wanted it to. Finally, when the time was right, first-person won out. I joked with my editor that the story took me 15 years and an afternoon to write, but in this case, I simply needed time to put all the issues—and my thoughts—into perspective:

280

I've learned to accept things. I saw that finding someone is never a simple proposition, even on the best of terms. Nothing is the same. I can accept my father, too. When his father died recently, he called me and we settled down to talk as I had always hoped a father and daughter could. Our exchange wasn't an insight-filled sensitivity session, but it was something basic and of value. And, at the end of it, he signed off as he always does: "I love you, hon. Thanks for finding me."

• *Life stages.* Turning 40, being a newly divorced dad with custody of the kids, losing your job. If Gail Sheehy can make a career out of this, surely you can find a new angle in the tale you have to tell others going through the same thing.

• *Humor.* You say you're a klutz? A bad housekeeper and proud of it? The only one whose dog flunked obedience class? Then tell it with a smile.

• *A trend that touches you.* I broke into *TV Guide* by noticing that there were few blonde role models on television (I'm blonde). I not only wrote about how that made me feel, but also interviewed and took to task the programming executives who create TV shows. (No surprise: They were all brunette.) We're all touched by societal issues, from blaring radios in cars, to worries about health care, to kids who behave badly in restaurants. Take a trend or issue, show how it affects your life, and offer some first-person observation and advice along the way.

• *Family.* Everyone's got 'em; the trick is to find something unique that makes your reminiscence of interest to the reader. An essay I sold to *Diversion* was a tribute to my mother, who taught me from childhood how to travel "first class." I spoke of what I learned from her, what made our trips memorable, and how her legacy lives in me in a particularly special way. I'm a travel writer who's reported from 64 countries so far; much of my interest in the world came from my mother's enthusiasm about new places.

Once you have the subject and framework for your first-person piece, *know your market.* A lively or moving first-person piece can never see the light of day, no matter how well-written, unless it finds the appropriate publisher. And there are more outlets today than ever before: the editorial pages of your local newspaper (yes, a reasoned and passionate letter to the editor is a good start, and could lead to an op-ed piece . . . or in my case, to a career); general magazines; women's

281

magazines; men's magazines; publications for every hobby and special interest. I turned my experience of breaking my foot and being in a cast into a light piece for *Weight Watchers Magazine.* I wrote about how the experience taught me patience, not to mention ingenious ways of keeping the weight off when I couldn't jog.

Marketing is all-important. A careful reading of several issues of the magazine you are aiming for will tell you the kinds of subjects and treatment they give to first-person pieces. Check the length (a 2,000-word piece won't fly if the magazine runs only 750-word, one-page essays), note whether all the first-person pieces are by men or women, and if the magazine is hospitable to humor or never uses it.

But in your marketing, be careful not to try to adapt your writing *voice* to those that have appeared in the magazine. Your unique voice is your key to selling; your research will simply tell you what magazines publish first-person and what kinds of subjects are of interest to them. If you want to write a piece on being a klutz in your all-woman aerobics class, *Family Circle,* for example, would be a better place to submit than *Esquire.* Your experiences working in a senior center would find a more receptive home in *Ladies' Home Journal* or *Modern Maturity* than in a Generation X-type publication like *Details.*

Writing the first-person piece can be one of the most satisfying and rewarding—and yes, *fun*—writing you may do. Just keep your own voice and perspective in the forefront, and remember that what happens to you is important and may be important to a reader as well, if written with passion and enthusiasm.

➳➳ 61

Picking A Victim: A Biographer's Choice

By Carl Rollyson

One of my readers recently wrote to me that she had not "picked a victim" yet, but she was giving serious thought to writing a biography. How did one go about it? she wanted to know. I relish the idea—I must admit—of thinking of the biographee as a victim. The biographer, after all, has enormous power, picking and choosing what aspects of a life to emphasize, what parts to leave out. Like a novel, a biography is a story in which characters are manipulated and moved about to suit the biographer's point of view. My attraction to the form derives from this urge to reconstitute a life within the covers of a book.

I don't blame anyone for feeling victimized by the "biografiend." In miniature, a biography is rather like having to sit still for a photograph that you do not want taken of yourself. You're robbed in some way of your substance. And you are probably not consoled by the "biografriend's" insistence that he or she admires you and must have a picture. At the same time, in my role as biographer I am like a reporter or a novelist who has few, if any, scruples about getting the story.

I subscribe, in other words, to a conflict of interest theory of biography. There is my interest in writing a book about, say, Susan Sontag. And then there is Susan Sontag's interest in herself. These interests are mutually exclusive. Susan Sontag is the subject of my book, whereas Susan Sontag is the subject of *her* life. Biographers often ignore this fundamental point or won't admit it—at least they won't own up to it when they are writing about writing biographies. If you've read biographers on biography, you know they sound like a very noble lot—especially Leon Edel. You'd never guess he was a snoop just like the rest of us, trying to get the low-down on Henry James. Do you think Henry James would have given Leon Edel permission to write a biography about him?

I like the feeling of working against my subject, of trying to find out things that he or she has tried to bury or to obfuscate. I have learned to be wary of my subjects. I find them enormously entertaining. I learn a great deal from them, but I don't trust them. Not because they're all liars, but because they want to have it their way.

It may sound as though I take a hostile attitude toward my subjects. No, I'm just skeptical, and I like to turn over their lives from many different angles to see what I can shake loose for my narrative. Without this sense of resistance, of friction, I wonder whether biography would be quite so appealing. As much as most kids growing up, I liked digging for buried treasure, and when there was no buried treasure to be found, I buried some myself for later discovery. I think of my subjects the same way: They like hiding things, and they may even have a sneaking admiration for the one who finds them out. I know I have conducted more than one interview in which the interviewee was not forthcoming until it was made clear that I had already done some digging and had turned up some pretty tantalizing items.

I think the biographer is ultimately his or her own authority. I borrow that phrase from R. G. Collingwood. He has in mind the fact that any genuine work of history is more than the sum of its evidence; it depends, in fact, on the interpreting mind of the historian, who must bring together disparate materials and insights—rather like a detective—into a unified, organic whole. That whole is, essentially, a story, a narrative of meaning. Otherwise, Collingwood argues, there is only scissors-and-paste history, in which the historian slaps together fragments of evidence and testimony from his sources or authorities. This quilt of fact and speculation might make a rather gaudy design, but it would not be a work of history.

The biographer, I would argue, does much the same thing. For example, for my biography of Lillian Hellman (published in 1988), I assembled the following raw material for Chapter 17: a letter from Walter Jackson Bate (at one time chairman of Harvard's English department); a journal kept by Ken Stuart (a student in Lillian Hellman's Harvard writing class); interviews with faculty members who knew Hellman during her Harvard stay; an interview with her physician; and a few newspaper articles. All of these materials would not have added up to Chapter 17. First of all, I didn't use all of the evidence; some was redundant. Though some was fascinating, there was too much to fit

284

into my narrative, already burdened with significant detail. I knew that readers would stand for only so much on this phase of Hellman's career. To relate all of it would have seriously damaged the shape of my book; it would have placed too much emphasis on that period of Hellman's life.

Considerations of this kind I call esthetic. I wanted to write a good book and knew I would have to be selective. Just as important, however, were the selections I had already made in previous chapters, where I emphasized Hellman's contentiousness, her pride in her work, her attraction to young people, her generosity, and her tendency to be high-handed. All of these qualities I found in my evidence for Chapter 17—although as individual bits of evidence, these sources contradicted each other. Bate, for example, was offended by an incredibly demanding and insensitive bitch, while Ken Stuart was charmed by her shrewd and patient handling of young writers, including himself. In the chapter as published, I hope these seeming contradictions are resolved—that is, that they are understandable, given the different contexts Hellman found herself in. With students she would never behave the way she behaved with Bate. He was supposed to be the red carpet man, the one who should have fawned over her. With Ken Stuart, it was just the opposite: Hellman knew she was there to give him something. Nowhere in Chapter 17 do I make this comparison between Hellman's treatment of Bate and Stuart, but I believe it is there in the configuration of my narrative, and that it can be found by readers who have been following the whole story of my book.

While I was writing the biography of Hellman, I often had a sense of her struggling for possession of my book. There was no doubt in my mind that she did not want me to write it my way. Not just because I would find out things—like her Communist Party membership—but because, like a dramatist, I was setting her up in scenes that were not of her own making. I was questioning her memoirs and producing an alternative version of her life.

Biographers worry when they are cut off from some of the evidence. When I began my research on Hellman, I did not know that she had restricted her archive. That piece of shocking news was announced by Richard Wilbur during an interview. "I hope the unavailability of the Texas material does not pose too great a problem for you," he remarked in his characteristically understated way. "What?" I gulped.

"Oh, I hear that Lillian restricted everything for the use of her author-ized biographer," Wilbur casually noted. "Oh, yes," I said, with as much of a knowing air as I could assume. I had a good sweat over this setback. I remember announcing it to a colleague in the street—my way of admitting the worst and taking it as a challenge. Somehow I forced myself to feel good that Lillian Hellman was going to make things hard for me. I wanted to write about her so badly, it may not have made a difference if I had gotten the word about Texas earlier. Still, I am grateful for having begun in ignorance of this fundamental fact.

I knew I had to reconstruct the Texas archive. I reasoned that through a long career, Hellman would have left papers, letters, and various traces all over the country—especially in New York and Holly-wood—and I was not wrong. Not only was I able to locate nearly everything that was in Texas in the Academy of Motion Picture Arts and Sciences, the University of Southern California Library, Boston University Library, the Wisconsin Center for Film and Theatre Re-search, and in the hands of her friends all over the country, I found new material—hundreds of letters, a screenplay Hellman never ac-knowledged, her husband's diary, and many, many other items that were not in the Texas archive. I also consulted half a dozen excellent dissertations written during the years the Texas archive was open, and this doctoral work proved invaluable in reconstructing my understand-ing of Hellman's working papers.

For me, the most important thing is the overwhelming desire to write about a particular figure. That usually means I already have—even if I can't articulate it yet—a vision of my subject. I have already decided I'm right for the biography. Everything else, then, will have to fall in line, no matter what obstacles I encounter. To prospective biographers I recommend that you know why you want to write about so-and-so. When you have convinced yourself—or as I like to say, deluded yourself—that you are the best person for the job, then it is time to take on all the other troubles you will surely face. I'm reminded of Brenda Maddox, who has written a splendid biography of Nora Joyce. She went to Richard Ellmann, generally acknowledged to be *the* Joyce biographer. "A biography of Nora?" Ellmann asked incredulously. "What for?" There was no new material worth writing about. Besides, hadn't he, *the* Richard Ellmann, done the definitive biography of James

286

Joyce? There was nothing left to be done. And Maddox, the Joyce scholar apparently observed, was only a journalist. Thank heavens Brenda Maddox went ahead—discovering, by the way, much new material and no doubt changing the way James and Nora Joyce will now be viewed.

Speaking only for myself, I hope to tell a good story. Because it is a story, I have to deal with everything—not just my subject's public face. I want the gossip, the intimacies, everything that I can find out that made that person what she or he is.

Writing biography is a shameless profession, an exercise in bad taste, a rude inquiry. Most biographers I have met prefer not to say so in public. We are journalists and sometimes scholars who try very hard to be accurate. But is it any wonder that the biographer's choice gets expressed as the picking of a victim?

➣➣ 62

BECOMING A BOOK REVIEWER

BY JOANN C. GUTIN

TEN YEARS AGO, I WAS MIRED IN AN ENDLESS PH.D. DISSERTATION. Every morning I trudged to the library; every afternoon I trudged home. In between, I shuffled index cards.

A book review saved my life. One day I woke up convinced that if I didn't write something short, manageable, and finite, I was doomed: So I wrote a book review and mailed it off to a local paper. I was innocent of the prescribed procedures—hadn't ever heard of a query letter, in fact—but I got lucky. Though the editor who got my unsolicited review didn't publish it, she remembered it, and asked me to review something else several weeks later.

That review produced a clip that got me other reviewing assignments; those assignments gave me the courage to try longer pieces. In a sense, that 750-word review was the springboard to my writing career.

Book reviewing, you see, is a good way to get into print. And you shouldn't have to make the same mistakes I did at the outset. There is, in fact, a systematic way to go about becoming a book reviewer and writing reviews that you will be proud of.

1. Pick the right book.

Go to the periodicals room of your library and get the latest copy of *Publishers Weekly,* the publishers' trade magazine. (*Library Journal* and *Booklist* are good, too.) The "Forecast" section of *PW* contains pithy reviews of books due out in the next few months, organized by category. Anything there by a novelist whose previous work you know? Any nonfiction title on a subject in which you have expertise?

You need this familiarity because unless you know something about the book, you won't be able to do it justice. And if you don't know anything about the subject, why should anyone assign you the book for review?

2. Get the assignment.

Query the book editor of your local paper (or another small paper, or a small magazine): Convince her or him that you'd bring something special to a review of this book. If you have clips, send them. If you don't, make your letter that much more persuasive. If the editor is interested, he or she will arrange to have bound galleys of the book sent to you, and give you anywhere from a week to a month to write the piece.

If you're dying to review a book that's already out, skip the query and write a review, keeping it to 750 words, max. Then send it to the editor of choice with a brief note describing your credentials. She probably won't publish it—more than likely the book has already been reviewed—but she may think of you when a similar book comes up.

3. Read the book.

Sounds obvious, right? But reading for review is an entirely different process from reading for pleasure; it is a constant process of taking your own mental temperature. I think of my reviewing persona as a tiny intruder perched on my shoulder, a sort of Tinker Bell in horn rims. Whenever I get lazy and start floating along on the tide of words, she tugs smartly on my earlobe and reminds me that my job is to figure out why this book makes me feel the way it does, not to have fun.

So read the book twice, minimum, never in bed and never without a pencil in hand. Make notes as you go. I use the inside cover and the half-title page to write a word or phrase and a page number. These notes are often cryptic, as in, "p. 131—Oh, I'm *sure!*"—but they remind me of what I need to go back and ponder.

4. Read a lot of other things.

How does this book compare to the writer's earlier work? Read— or at least skim—the writer's published works. You can even read the old reviews, as long as your own ideas have jelled enough, so that, unaware, you won't parrot what someone else thinks. Check the writer's entry in *Contemporary Authors.* A little biographical information can deepen your understanding, even give you an interesting angle for your piece.

If your book is nonfiction, the writer will be arguing for a particular point of view. There's bound to be another; discover it. You may not include any of this research in your review, but understanding the intellectual background of any book will strengthen your all-important critical backbone.

5. Think about what you've read, then begin to write.

Of course, what you write and how you write it are up to you; all the usual precepts of good writing apply. But one task is not optional: You must figure out what the author was trying to accomplish, and tell your readers—convincingly and entertainingly—whether or not he did it. Anatole France once said that the role of the critic was to tell of his mind's adventures among masterpieces; sounds grandiose, but it sums up the process.

Don't produce a long and dreary plot summary; that's always the mark of a novice. Your aim is to distill the book for your reader so he can understand your reactions to it and judge whether he wants to take the plunge himself.

Don't lambaste a book for failing to accomplish what it never set out to do: Such reviews provoke justifiable howls of protest in the "Letters to the Editor" column in book sections. So *K is for Killer* isn't *Crime and Punishment*. So what?

Don't use the review to show off how much you know; nobody cares, except for your mother. If you are an expert—and if you've done your homework, you'll be an expert of sorts—your confidence will shimmer between the lines. But your review is the book's moment in the sun, not yours.

6. Tell the truth.

As is the case in any writing, this is the hardest part. You're a reader, so you love books; you're a writer, so you know how hard it is to make books. But as a reviewer, you need to put those other roles aside. Your primary responsibility is to *your* reader, not to the book publisher, or the author, or the author's undoubtedly large and loyal circle of friends.

Think about it: If you hedge, or exaggerate a book's virtues out of some misguided sense of politeness, what happens? Your readers will buy the book, discover, all by themselves, it's a turkey, and learn to mistrust both you and the paper you're writing for. Nobody wins.

Obviously, a responsible reviewer doesn't ridicule a book or take cheap shots or ooze gratuitous nastiness all over the page. But a responsible reviewer isn't mealy-mouthed, either. With a reviewing assignment, you've jumped feet first into the marketplace of ideas. There's a lot of pushing and shoving out there; it goes with the territory.

Some books deserve negative reviews because they're not very good. If you don't have the stomach to write a legitimate pan, don't write it. Don't write anything at all: Call or write the editor and explain that this book needs a different reviewer. But if you've done the research and the thinking that will enable valid criticism to stick, then you have the right—indeed, the responsibility—to speak your mind.

7. Hold your head high.

Those of you with business smarts may have wondered how much book reviewing pays. In purely financial terms, it pays peanuts. With the hours of homework you have to do, even a fast writer will make less money reviewing for the Sunday book sections of the big papers—which pay several hundred dollars for a review—than he or she would make flipping burgers. Small papers pay much less; little magazines may just let you keep a copy of the book.

Book reviewing can be good for your career. People may read your reviews and ask you to write articles. If you've been reviewing books about things you love, then editors may ask you to write about things you love. This is a very good thing; in fact, for a writer there's nothing better.

But there's another, less solipsistic way to think about the process of reading and writing about books: The thoughtful, informed book review contributes to our national conversation about ideas. You're a writer; you care about ideas; and hundreds of books are published every month.

What are you waiting for?

>> 63

WRITING ARTICLES
THE PROFESSIONAL WAY

BY RUTH DUSKIN FELDMAN

THERE ARE THREE KINDS OF WRITERS: THOSE WHO WRITE SOLELY FOR self-expression, those who are published occasionally, and those who make writing a career. Many aspiring writers think you begin in the first category and gradually move into the second and then the third. But my observation and experience tell me that people in the third category—those who strive to make a living as writers—approach their work very differently from those who don't.

Many would-be writers separate the process of writing from the process of marketing what they write. They struggle to perfect their craft, to say what they want to say as well as it can be said. That's certainly a worthwhile goal. But if you want to sell what you write, you must play by the rules of the marketplace. Your writing—from the start—must be aimed toward publication.

Professionals who write for magazines normally write on assignment. Writing on assignment means that all of your writing time is spent in remunerative activity. Equally important, it means that you know exactly who your audience is and how to focus your article. Unfortunately, it's hard to get an assignment without credits (previously published work), and you can't get credits without writing on speculation. But whether you're writing on assignment or "on spec," the same marketing principles apply. You need to sell an editor on your idea and your ability to carry it out. The best way to do that is to write a query.

A query is a letter intended to find out whether an editor wants to see your article. The response you're seeking is a go-ahead to submit the full article. The query should include salient information about the subject, succinctly and provocatively stated. Within one single-spaced page (or, at most, two), your query must show that your topic is timely, that it will "turn on" the magazine's readers, and that you can deliver what you promise: a well-researched, well-written, publishable article.

A query can be written before or after the article. A query written in advance can help you shape the finished piece; often the lead paragraphs are almost identical. More important, in constructing a query you force yourself to think through the form the article should take: what information to include and what main points to cover in what order. When you sit down to write the article, instead of staring at a blank sheet of paper, you have a blueprint to follow.

Here's how I led off one query (and later, the published article in *Chicago Parent*):

Dear (Editor's Name):

Let's Bring Back Grandma-Care

Everybody talks about the day care crisis, but hardly anybody mentions one solution that can be beneficial for the child and the entire family: part-time care by a grandparent.

As a busy professional writer, I never expected to be minding my baby grandson two days a week while my lawyer daughter works; but I've been doing just that for the past year, and loving it. My daughter and I call our arrangement "shared parenting," and we've uncovered several other families that are doing the same.

My query continued with some facts that appeared in expanded form further down in the body of the article:

"Grandma-care" is an old idea whose time may have come again. With more than half the mothers of babies and preschoolers in the work force, nearly one out of four of their young children, if not supervised by the father, are spending the day with Grandma, and another 10 percent with other relatives. And a recent Harris poll shows that the average working parent would prefer to have a family member mind the kids.

I went on to mention the length I had in mind (a fairly standard 2,000 words), sources I planned to tap (studies on the importance of the grandparent-grandchild relationship, as well as interviews with families engaging in "grandparent-care"), and a brief summary of my relevant professional experience. I enclosed a few clips of published work. (But don't let a lack of credits and clips deter you: A recent survey of 32 national magazine editors, conducted by Lee Jolliffe of the University of Missouri, found that the writer's experience carried less than three percent weight in editors' judgments of queries. The most important criteria were writing skill and the merits of the idea itself.)

Both the query and the article should be targeted at a specific magazine and its audience. The topic, the choice of words, the suggested length, all must be appropriate. Does that mean if one editor rejects a query you have to start from scratch? Of course not. I often recycle queries among magazines with similar audiences—for example, *Woman's Day* and *Family Circle*—or adapt a query to a magazine with a different audience.

Some writers find it easiest to write for a few magazines they read regularly and know well. I prefer to be more eclectic. I've sold articles to a wide variety of national, regional, local, women's, in-flight, and travel magazines. First, I decide on a topic I want to write about. Then I look for one or more markets it's likely to fit. Sometimes I've sold an article two or three times, each time revising and refocusing it with a different audience in mind.

Tailoring your writing to different audiences is not as difficult as it may seem. Do you speak to a child the same way as to an adult? Of course not. Successful oral communicators adjust their speech to the person they are communicating with. Successful writers do, too.

I began my adult career as a teacher. I've never forgotten the advice given to beginning instructors: Start where your students are; don't assume knowledge they don't have. For writers, that advice translates into: Get inside the reader's head. Make sure you're talking his or her language.

Often all that's required is a slight shift of viewpoint. For example, after my article on grandparent-care appeared in *Chicago Parent,* I sold a somewhat different version to *New Choices for the Best Years,* (now called *New Choices: Living Even Better After 50*), a national magazine for the 50-plus age group. *New Choices* pitched it toward grandparents rather than parents by reversing the opening paragraphs—emphasizing the experience of a grandparent-caregiver more than the need for good day care.

It's a good idea to study several issues of the magazine you intend to approach and send for its editorial guidelines (enclosing an SASE). The more familiar you are with the publication, the more readily you can put yourself in the place of its readers. Are they predominantly men or women? How old and how educated? What are their occupations and interests? What are their problems? What do they want and need to know?

My article on rafting Utah's Green River first appeared (after many rejections) in *Utah Holiday*. I later recast it (and cut it almost in half) for the *Chicago Sun-Times* travel section. Still later, *Going Places,* a magazine of the Montgomery Ward Travel Club, bought a third, even trimmer version.

The "hook," or focus, of the original *Utah Holiday* piece—what sold the editors on running yet another article on whitewater rafting in a state where that activity is practically de rigueur—was gender. The article, "Nine Women on a Raft," ran in a special section called "Summer and Self." It was a reflective reminiscence of an adventurous bonding experience among the all-female participants, several of whom had left nervous husbands at home, and of the interplay between the women and our strapping young male guide. It was also a story about age and the fulfillment of dreams. I began with a quotation from the philosopher Søren Kierkegaard:

"It is very dangerous to go into eternity with possibilities which one has oneself prevented from becoming realities. A possibility is a hint from God. One must follow it."

The first few paragraphs briefly recounted how, ten years earlier, I had begun writing for brochures from rafting companies, only to be discouraged by my acrophobic spouse. Then I wrote:

Reaching the half-century mark forces the realization that possibilities are not forever. So, the August after my fiftieth birthday and my daughter Laurie's law school graduation, we kissed her still-dubious father goodbye and set out on a ninety-six-mile journey down Utah's Green River with Adventure Bound, Inc., an outfitter that has run river excursions for nearly a quarter-century in Utah and Colorado.
Our route lay through Desolation and Gray canyons, which stretch end to end on the site of an ancient lake. The rapids increase gradually in turbulence—numerous and rough enough to challenge novices, yet not too dangerous to paddle.

Next came a paragraph about the region's discovery and about the fur traders, beaver trappers, gold miners, cattle ranchers, and dam promoters who had "failed to tame that wilderness." Then I launched

295

into a selective chronological narrative of our journey (including my being thrown from the raft by the force of a particularly nasty rapid) and the women's varied reactions. In the final paragraphs, I returned to the opening theme:

> While my comrades headed for a washroom and a change of clothes, I stripped off my pedal pushers and wet sneakers and swam into the current until my strength was spent, then sank onto a wooden float, breathing heavily and contemplating the brilliant blue sky. My arm was bruised from my baptismal spill, and my coccyx bone was saddle-sore, but I never had been more content.
>
> I recalled the correspondent in Stephen Crane's "The Open Boat," who, cast adrift with three shipmates, knew at the time that it was the best experience of his life. Our situation had been far less perilous, the finish unmarred by tragedy. But we too had escaped a certain danger and experienced exhilaration in following our possibilities down river.

In the *Going Places* version, which was aimed at men *and* women considering rafting for the first time, I dropped the literary references, played down the feminine angle, and wrote shorter, declarative sentences. In the opening paragraphs, I pared down the introductory explanation and the historical material and added this:

> I was in good physical shape, yet by no means an athlete. But there was no need to be. Adventure Bound has taken first-time rafters ranging in age from 10 to 83 on river trips.
>
> . . . . The canyon walls—more than 5,000 feet deep at one point—guard a near-virgin wilderness. Since we would be far from civilization for four days, it was reassuring to know that the raft would be inspected by park rangers, that guides were Red Cross trained, and that no passenger had ever been seriously injured.

I included more specifics about how rivers are rated for difficulty and about clothing and equipment, and eliminated the final paragraph, ending with "I had never been more content."

Did these changes cramp my writing style? Although I prefer the *Utah Holiday* version, the *Going Places* piece retains much of the feeling of the original. Making the changes was the necessary price for presenting my message to a wider audience.

A market-oriented approach to article writing can make it more likely that *your* words will reach an audience. In my book, that is what writing is about.

➤➤ 64

CREATIVE NONFICTION: WHERE JOURNALISM AND STORYTELLING MEET

BY MARK H. MASSÉ

A DEDICATED FIFTH-GRADE TEACHER GIVES HER STRUGGLING STU-dents hope in a depressed New England mill town (*Among Schoolchildren,* by Tracy Kidder). A power-hungry Southern sheriff clashes with a proud African-American community leader in rural Georgia (*Praying for Sheetrock,* by Melissa F. Greene). Innovative crisis workers in Oregon help clients battle mental illness as they heal their own emotional pain in my book, *FRONTLINE.*

These may sound like fictional narratives, but they are factual accounts—products of extensive research and reportage, combined with dramatic storytelling techniques. Welcome to the exciting world of creative nonfiction. In the 1960s and 1970s, when Truman Capote *(In Cold Blood),* Gay Talese *(Honor Thy Father),* and Tom Wolfe *(The Right Stuff)* were melding in-depth reporting with literary writing, their work was called New Journalism. Currently, the term "creative nonfiction" is increasingly popular. The good news for today's writers is that this genre offers new, expanding opportunities to craft distinctive, evocative stories using a combination of fiction and nonfiction techniques.

To produce successful creative nonfiction, you must have a credible and compelling story to tell. It should inform and enlighten the reader and be based on verifiable facts. Yet, a good creative nonfiction writer will transcend the conventions of fact-based journalism by portraying characters with psychological depth, providing riveting details and descriptions, and presenting a true story that uses dramatic scenes to engage the reader's interest and emotions.

297

A telling comparison

Compare the following two treatments of a scene from a 24-hour crisis hotline. First, a straight news approach:

> Pat, a veteran crisis worker, sits in one of the clinic's cluttered offices and answers another call.
>
> "I got a .45 here on my lap, and I've spent the last week convincing myself that I shouldn't pull the trigger," the man on the line says. "But I've run out of reasons. I'll give you five minutes to convince me that I shouldn't kill myself."
>
> "That's not going to work," Pat says firmly. "You could give me five minutes or five years, and I still might not have an answer that I could give you. What I can do is help you to find you own reasons to go on living—if that's what you want to do."

The same scene in creative nonfiction style (from *FRONTLINE*):

> A dozen steps away in the cluttered buckstopper office, which overlooks the wide, sagging front porch, Pat instinctively takes a deep breath and plants his bare feet firmly on the scruffy brown carpet before answering the phone.
>
> "I got a .45 here on my lap, and I've spent the last week convincing myself that I shouldn't pull the trigger. But I've run out of reasons." The voice on the other end is deep and gruff-sounding, the craggy voice of a longtime pack-a-day man. His words are flat, emotionless. "I'll give you five minutes to convince me that I shouldn't kill myself."
>
> The first thing that pops into Pat's mind is the one-liner that he told the crisis team at last Monday's group debriefing session: "Suicide is our way of telling God—you can't fire me, I quit!" But Pat isn't smiling. The familiar queasy feeling of fear is welling up inside him.
>
> "That's not going to work," he tells the caller. "You could give me five minutes or five years, and I still might not have an answer that I could give you." He pauses, not knowing if he'll hear the click of a receiver. "What I can do is help you to find your own reasons to go on living—if that's what you want to do."

By including concrete details and sensory imagery to describe the scene (e.g., bare feet on a scruffy carpet; craggy voice of a longtime pack-a-day man), I tried to evoke a mood and make an impact on the reader. The use of extended dialogue and internal monologue—other techniques of creative nonfiction—heightened the tension in this life-and-death drama. Through numerous interviews, oral histories, and months of "participant observation," I learned firsthand about the demanding life of a crisis worker. Tom Wolfe calls this approach "saturation reporting," getting to know people, settings, and story background in sufficient detail to craft a literary journalistic tale.

Extensive research into the inner world of crisis intervention enabled me to write the kind of dramatic scene typically found in fiction. In the excerpt from *FRONTLINE,* I was able to "get inside the head" of the crisis worker and share his thoughts, feelings, and fears with the reader. Ultimately, this scene worked because of the same dynamic that drives successful short stories and novels: a sympathetic protagonist confronted with a complicated problem, conflict, and crisis in which the outcome is uncertain.

To write creative nonfiction successfully, focus on these fundamentals:

1) An appropriate subject
2) Research
3) A dramatic story

Choosing an appropriate subject

The first consideration in approaching a creative nonfiction project is the author's interest in and connection to a given subject. An appropriate topic is one that can be presented with sufficient scope to achieve the intimacy, insight, and drama required of a well-written work of creative nonfiction. In my study of the Eugene, Oregon, crisis intervention team, access to crisis workers' personal and professional lives over several months gave me the opportunity to compile detailed material that I would later rely on when writing my nonfiction narrative.

There is a wide range of subjects suitable for creative nonfiction treatment. Here is a list of possible categories for your consideration:

- Adventure
- Biography
- Business
- Communities
- Crime stories
- Family sagas
- Government & politics
- History
- Institutions
- Personal experience
- Popular culture
- Science & technology
- Sports
- Travel

Before embarking on a work of creative nonfiction, ask yourself: What is this story going to be about? What are the broader themes

299

and/or ramifications of this subject? How can I marshal the facts, the emotions, and the deeper meanings of this story?

For example, in telling his story of friendships in a Massachusetts nursing home (*Old Friends*), Pulitzer Prize-winning creative nonfiction writer Tracy Kidder examined a much larger landscape: aging in America. My tale of Oregon crisis workers on the "front line of pain" isn't merely about mental illness; ultimately, it is a universal story of heroism in everyday life—how "ordinary" people (caregivers) are capable of extraordinary achievements in serving others in need. This theme is appropriate for any good story, whether fiction or nonfiction.

Research

Maybe you don't fancy yourself as brilliant a chronicler of popular culture and the American scene as Tom Wolfe. Perhaps you aren't as renowned for your powers of observation and reporting as John McPhee. Do Joan Didion's remarkable insights into the seemingly ordinary events of everyday life intimidate you? Don't despair. In deciding whether to tackle a work of creative nonfiction, go back to the basics of what makes a writer in the first place.

Are you a good people watcher? Observe the particulars of how a person dresses, walks, eats, gestures. Train your ear to hear the subtleties of a conversation—the trace of an accent, the tone of a voice, an inflection. By putting gestures and conversation together, try to detect any underlying meaning to the dialogue. Concentrate on the recurring details of the environment you are studying, such as "official or unofficial" norms, customs, and rituals.

As a careful and sensitive observer of individuals and groups, you may be able to conduct the saturation reporting that is the foundation of creative nonfiction. Excellent interviewing skills will be vital to your research. In studying people over an extended period of time, you must be adept at gaining their confidence and cooperation. This is achieved by your personal credibility and persuasiveness, combined with sensitive, creative interviewing techniques. Your ability to converse with rather than interrogate your sources will determine how successful you will be in portraying your characters accurately and with the detail required of a fully developed, complex story.

Creative nonfiction has been called the "literature of fact" for good reason: Writers in this field depend on information to generate a story.

In addition to observing and conducting interviews, you must immerse yourself in your subject by reading voraciously, using electronic information retrieval services (computerized databases) and contacting experts. When collecting facts, you must "sweat the details."

Creative nonfiction writers must not violate the rules of accuracy and honesty. In the words of Gay Talese, "All that we write should be verifiable." Before you write a single line of internal monologue for a character, make sure you have in your interview notes the actual words from the person about what he or she was thinking at a given time.

A dramatic story

The years I have spent as a fiction writer—honing my narrative skills, structuring dramatic scenes, developing complex characters, drafting realistic dialogue—gave me the confidence to write creative nonfiction. Before you attempt a work of creative nonfiction, you must know the difference between such basics as narration, description, and exposition. Once you have mastered these storytelling techniques and acquired research and reporting skills, you may have the tools to produce vivid, innovative nonfiction narratives.

A creative nonfiction story begins with sound research. Cull your notes for scenes with dramatic potential (e.g., arguments, crises, confrontations, discoveries), including names of the characters involved, a description of the complication, and the resolution—if there was one. Also, list your scenes chronologically—a valuable aid when it comes time to plot your story.

Selecting the appropriate narrative structure is just as essential for a work of creative nonfiction as it is for a novel. Review your material carefully, and remember that form should follow function. How can you best present this story in a way that informs, enlightens, and engages the reader? If there is a natural progression to the story, then a chronological structure may be appropriate. But even with a chronological structure, you may choose to begin the story *in medias res* (in the middle of the action) with a dramatic opening, before flashing back or forward to resume the story.

When chronicling the accounts of several individuals in a creative nonfiction story, you may find it helpful to use parallel narratives that converge at a climactic point in the "plot." Another tried-and-true

301

method is the quest or journey story, in which characters pursue a dream, destination, or goal and the plot develops accordingly.

Like the fiction writer, the author of creative nonfiction must decide on the proper point of view of his or her story. The best approach is to let the strength of your material determine whether you use first- or third-person viewpoint or a combination of the two. Another key decision you must make is how much of a role (if any) you will play in the story: Remember, the presence of the writer as a character may detract from the story's dramatic action.

Although a creative nonfiction story uses a mixture of narrative techniques, it remains a fact-driven literary form, emphasizing concrete, verifiable details about characters, events, settings, and dialogue. Unlike the fiction writer, who can rely solely on his or her imagination to weave a story, the creative nonfiction writer is bound by facts, opinions, observations, and other information collected during the research phase. But, the imagination of the dramatic nonfiction author plays an important role in the creative and persuasive "telling" of a true story.

⪼65

Writing Opportunities in the Great Outdoors

By Brian McCombie

With over 120 million Americans participating in outdoor activities each year, it's no wonder that there are dozens of national and regional magazines serving this market. Add the scores of tabloids, hundreds of newspaper features and columns, plus the many general-interest magazines that publish outdoor-related pieces, and there are significant opportunities for the writer with outdoor experiences.

My first success with outdoor writing came about eight years ago, when a small hunting and fishing magazine published a humorous essay of mine about a canoe/camping trip gone awry. Since then, I've written how-to pieces, essays, interviews, and book reviews for a variety of outdoor publications.

Am I a specialist in any of the areas in which I write? No, though I have broad knowledge in a number of areas—conservation, natural history, various wildlife issues, hunting, and fishing. When I get an idea for a query or receive an assignment, I immerse myself in the activity and record my experiences as they happen. If the piece is issue-oriented, I do the necessary research at a library or interview experts in the field. Only after I feel fully comfortable with my level of knowledge is it time to write.

Hooks and bullets?

With approximately 75 million people hunting and fishing every year, magazines devoted to these sports activities represent over 60% of the outdoor writing market. The backbone of these publications is the how-to article that provides useful information for the practicing hunter and fisherman, but there are also openings for many more types of writing than the standard "hook-and-bullet" piece (as insiders refer to

303

how-to fishing and hunting articles). Study this market's Big Three—*Sports Afield, Outdoor Life,* and *Field & Stream*—and you will discover articles and essays on conservation, wildlife laws and regulations, history, camping, backpacking, and emergency outdoor medicine. The mid-sized and smaller magazines don't have this range of coverage, but they still publish humor, interviews, personal essays, and breaking news.

Then there are the dozens of outdoor magazines devoted to a specific non-hunting or non-fishing activity. *American Hiker, Backpacker Magazine,* and *Canoe & Kayak Magazine* are good examples. Some cover a range of outdoor activities, like *Silent Sports,* which uses articles on cross-country skiing, backpacking, camping, and cycling. A number focus on outdoor sports within a specific region. Articles that inform, share experiences, and give practical advice are the editorial focus of these publications. New product reviews are becoming increasingly popular, as are "destination" articles about places where outdoor activities take place, opinion pieces, essays, and interviews.

Finding your niche

Outdoor writing is a market of niches, and you'll need to find yours. Start by making a list of your outdoor experiences, noting how many times a year you participate in the activities; where and with whom you participate in them; and events that may have occurred.

Next, read a number of magazines in your field of interest, and make a note of the following:

• How many of the feature articles fall into the how-to category? What other types of writing does the magazine publish?

• Is the focus of articles first-person (writer's personal experience) or third-party (experts in the field)? A mixture of the two?

• What columns are open to free lancers? To determine this, see if they are written by the same person each issue; if not, they are probably open to free-lance contributions.

• Pay special attention to the back page—often a place for short, first-person essays by a variety of writers.

Read the letters to the editor, too. There's no better place to discover the concerns and interests of the readership. And, as always, request and study writer's guidelines, if available.

Now, review your list of outdoor experiences. What types of articles and essays are you reasonably qualified to write? For instance, if you have canoed a number of times, but not regularly and always with your much more experienced friend as guide, you aren't ready to write for an audience of seasoned canoeists. Don't be discouraged. You can always become more familiar with an activity; but your present knowledge may be enough for certain types of articles. Remember that every form of recreation has many more novices than masters; perhaps you can write a short do's and don'ts piece for the first-time canoeist; interview three canoeing instructors on the basic ways to hold and use a paddle; or write a humorous essay (as I did) from a beginner's point of view.

Even if you are fairly experienced, increase your knowledge with some more research before you query a magazine. The more you know, the easier it is to make your first sale.

High-impact queries

It's not enough to become well-versed in an activity or subject before you query the editor of an outdoor magazine; you also have to find a new twist to the material. As an example, bass fishing is a very popular topic in many outdoor magazines, with literally hundreds of articles published every year. This strong demand, however, produces an endless recycling of the same article ideas. If an editor needs yet another 2,000 words on "The Secrets of Summer Bass," he is likely to use regular contributors.

The good news for writers is that editors and their readers become bored with the same old material. How to get an editor's attention? Break out of the rut. Query with an article or essay centered on a new technique; a unique method; a way to solve a common problem; a novel use for a product; or a way to do something less expensively.

As you participate in the activity and do research, you'll discover what is already standard practice and knowledge. Then, improve upon what is known. Experiment (when it's safe to do so, of course). Ask others what approach or technique they have used successfully. Find out what tactics or methods were popular ten years ago, and see how they can be revived and updated.

Present your great new idea in the first sentence of the first paragraph of your query. Follow up with a few specifics. Now that you've piqued

305

the editor's interest, explain why you're the person to write the article. With a little luck, you'll be well on your way to making a sale.

Photos

Most outdoor publications insist that photos accompany articles (and sometimes essays, too). Though the magazine may actually use only a few (usually 2 to 6 per article), editors like 15 to 20 to choose from. Some will want all color or black-and-white; others a combination of the two. Many magazines include photo payment in the total fee; others pay extra for the photos they print, ranging from $10 and up for a single black-and-white shot, $30 to $250 for color, and $200 to $700 for a color photo that appears on the cover.

You don't have to be a professional photographer to sell your work. But you do have to take clear, well-lighted shots that reinforce some element of your text. Best advice: Have people doing something in your photos, because magazine editors hate static shots. For example, don't take a picture of an empty bike trail; instead, show two or three bicyclists peddling. Similarly, rather than telling readers how to set up a tent, include a series of step-by-step photos showing a person going through the procedure.

A 35-mm camera is standard equipment. New models do just about everything automatically, from focusing to selecting the correct lens opening for the right lighting. Most magazines have photo guidelines that will tell you not only the types of photos desired and how much they pay, but other important information, such as the preferred type and speed of film.

Take many photos, especially when you're starting out. Film is relatively cheap, and more photos mean you have more of a chance of taking publishable ones. You will also need to provide captions and get permission from the people in the photos to use their likeness.

Solid knowledge, a compelling twist, and strong photographic support: These are the elements for success in outdoor writing.

>> 66

WHY I WRITE NONFICTION

BY BETTINA DREW

THE EXQUISITELY SHAPED EMOTION OF POETRY IS TOO PAINFUL FOR A steady diet, fiction seems dauntingly contrived, plays suffer from the same problem, and I suppose these are some of the reasons I write prose that is not of the fictional kind. Literarily speaking, nonfiction is an unglamorous genre, its patched-together name suggesting only what it isn't. But I know I have far more in common with the literary person than with the scholar or journalist because I write out of emotion.

When I look at the evidence of a past time or the detritus of a spent life or a man-made landscape, I often have an emotional response that I can't explain right away, but which is far too visceral to be dismissed. Why, for instance, do I find Disney World so horrifying when so many people seem to find it fun? Why do I despise what has been done to the city of Stamford when many people find it clean and pleasing? I write to answer these questions, and in so doing I identify, understand, justify, and think through my own perceptions.

I also write to explain certain mysteries to myself. How did slave-holders in Charleston become so emotionally bifurcated they could whip a woman till her back was striped and then serenely turn to talk of Paris fashions? These things are so complicated, have so many facets to them, that I know I can understand them only by writing about them—i.e., by ordering their different parts very deliberately, so that they make sense and lead into each other and fuse into what might approach the truth, were the truth apprehensible.

This is not so far from saying that I write to make sense of life; otherwise, it rushes by me in a constantly moving overload of experience and emotion and vision and sound and trivia. If I can stop and better understand one little piece of it, follow one little drop on its course, then I can begin to hope that the entire experience could actually *be* understood.

It is impossible for me to write without imagining a reader. For me, the act of writing is inextricably connected to other people. When I refine a composition, I am always thinking about how a phrase or a sentence will "sound" to others. In some sense, writing is like a gift that I offer to others. But on a deeper level, I write so that my opinion will be included as part of the larger human response, and axiomatically so that I can be included in humanity. In the real world, there are many reasons for a person's perceptions to get counted out: The person is considered too young, or too neurotic, or too exuberant, or too dirty, or too pretty, or too sexy, or too intense, or is the wrong color or the wrong sex or the wrong class or, for whatever reason, was stuck in the wrong goddamn envelope. I find it wonderfully reassuring that by writing nonfiction I can communicate with other people, mind to mind.

Moreover, I want to be judged on the basis of what I think and believe expressed at its best. And that's in my writing. To me, it's no surprise that so many writers have been bitter, cranky, seemingly incomprehensible people. The best writers devote themselves to doing their utmost to create something that will outlive them—something more profound than their arbitrary envelopes. The best writers feel compelled, in the words of a writer I once knew, "to give of themselves"—to bring their insides out. "That's where the beauty is," novelist Robert Stone once said to me, pausing at the thought in the middle of a flight of stairs in one of the best conversations of my life, and that's it. Writing is the painstaking working out of thoughts and ideas that are deeply pondered and deeply felt. In that sense it offers us the one opportunity to be who we really are. The callousness of everyday life often prohibits the expression of the most vulnerable and beautiful parts of us. Writing doesn't. And so writing offers me, without compromise, the possibility of being the best that I can be—and that is what I want to leave as evidence of my brief tenure among other human beings.

What to write

The choice of *what* to write is to some degree random, changing with the effects life experiences—so many of them random—have on a writer. That choice is always going to be subjective—sometimes even

308

I myself don't understand why a subject attracts me. Being subjective has something to do with my particular personality and complexities. So whether I attempt to understand what happened to me—to write my life, as it were—or whether I write about the experiences of others, the writing still ends up satisfying my emotional need.

That need is to prove, over and over and over again, that we aren't all stuck in our envelopes, that we're not all alone here, and that life in what is—American fundamentalists notwithstanding—a completely secular age does indeed have meaning, even if that meaning is contained only in our attempts to understand it.

$\gg\!\!\gg 67$

WRITING TRUE CRIME:
A TWELVE-STEP PROCESS

BY SUSAN KELLY

BOOKS ABOUT TRUE CRIME HAVE BEEN POPULAR—AND SOUGHT AFTER
by publishers—ever since Truman Capote's *In Cold Blood* became
one of the major bestsellers of 1966. Having recently written and published a true crime book myself, let me share with you some of my
experiences, translated into advice.

1. *Choose a contemporary criminal case as your subject.* By this I
mean a recent crime, one still fresh in the public's memory. Publishers
aren't looking for so-called historical crime—and by "historical crime,"
they mean a crime that occurred not two hundred, but twenty years
ago. (The national attention span seems to be getting shorter and
shorter.) There are some rare exceptions to this rule (Lizzie Borden;
Jack the Ripper), but in general, the only ones who can break it are
name-brand authors.

2. *Pick a case that's been solved, or one that you have the solution
to.* Publishers want stories that have resolutions—in other words, a
beginning, a middle, and an end. Again, there are some exceptions to
this rule, but editors almost always make them only for authors who
are already household names.

3. *Find out which houses publish a lot of true crime.* Consult the
nonfiction review section of *Publishers Weekly,* and check the shelves
in the bookstores to see who's doing what. There's little point in trying
to interest a publisher that specializes in self-help, gardening, and cat
books in a tale of murder and mayhem.

4. *Read and learn from the acknowledged masters in the field:* Capote; Norman Mailer *(The Executioner's Song);* Joe McGinniss *(Fatal*

310

Vision); Ann Rule (The Stranger Beside Me); Peter Maas (The Valachi Papers); Shana Alexander (Anyone's Daughter); Vincent Bugliosi and Curt Gentry (Helter Skelter). Every word of Dominick Dunne's trial reportage on the Menendez and Simpson cases is worth study.

5. *Write a winning proposal.* This includes not just a detailed synopsis of the crime, but some explanation of why it would interest a wide reading public. Emphasize any credentials you have that would make you well, if not uniquely, qualified to write this story: a background in law enforcement or criminal investigation; experience as a reporter; or special relationships with victims or witnesses. Furnish a bibliography of sources actual or potential. State your plans for research.

6. *Collect every press account of the crime you can find.* This requires spending lots of time poring over the yearly indexes to newspapers, *The Readers' Guide to Periodical Literature,* and other such sources. I assure you this is time well spent. In the first place, you will need the information these newspaper and magazine articles contain. Also, you will want to interview some of the reporters who originally worked the case, and you'll need their names.

7. *Interview as many people involved in the case as you can.* It goes without saying that you'll talk to the principals on both sides—as many of them as are willing to speak to you. But you should also interview those on the periphery. Even if they don't contribute hard information, they often can provide a different or off-beat slant on the case. And they may be able to suggest other sources you'll want to investigate— sources who might not turn up in the usual or obvious ways, but who could potentially furnish you with critically important data.

8. *If the case goes to trial, and it's being held while you are researching or writing the book, attend the trial.* You can get transcripts of the proceedings afterward, and I encourage you to do so, but nothing beats your own impressions, recorded day by day. Remember that what appears in the transcript may not be all of what was actually said in court. Certain parts of the testimony may be stricken from the record. Beyond that, you will want to observe the demeanor of prosecutors, defense attorneys, witnesses, defendants, judge, and jury. Attending the trial will give you the opportunity to see physical evidence that may have been kept under wraps before the trial.

9. *Immerse yourself in local color.* This is especially true if you're not already familiar with the area in which the crime took place. Research local history, politics, social modes, customs, and traditions. This kind of background adds essential flavor and depth to your narrative. One of the reasons John Berendt's *Midnight in the Garden of Good and Evil* scored such tremendous success was that it gave a fly-on-the-wall account of a city (Savannah, Georgia) and a way of life.

10. *BYOC.* This means Bring Your Own Camera. It doesn't have to be a four-thousand-dollar Hasselblad—just one that takes good, sharp images. (I love my old Nikon with the rubber band around the body to hold the battery compartment cover in place.) Load that camera with the best quality black-and-white film. Take as many pictures as you can of the people, places, and things connected with the crime. The developed photos will keep fresh in your mind those people, places, and things while you write about them. Also, if the pictures are sharp enough, you may be able to use them as illustrations for the book. And you'll want to use as many of your own photos as possible, since it is horrendously expensive to purchase them from newspapers or other sources, and publishers generally require authors to absorb this expense.

11. *Remember that it's always better to over-research rather than under-research a subject.* If you do an ultra-thorough investigation, some of the information you acquire will ultimately prove either repetitive or unnecessary. *But*—you won't know this till after you've finished writing the book.

12. *Even if you transfer all of your research and interview material to computer disks—keep the originals of everything.* When I say everything, I mean everything: tape recordings, handwritten interview notes, letters requesting interviews, letters responding to those requests, newspaper and magazine clippings, etc. Most publishing houses retain lawyers to read nonfiction manuscripts and vet them for possible legal problems. These lawyers like to know—for very sound reasons—that you can back up any claims that you make in the book,

312

that a quote you attribute to a source can be verified. And even if you have to rent storage space, don't ever dispose of any of this material. If you've been a careful researcher and a responsible reporter, the chances you'll be sued are remote. But . . . we live in a litigious society, and it's wise to protect yourself.

>> 68

EXPANDING YOUR FEATURE ARTICLES INTO BOOKS

BY ROSEMARY WELLS

TAKE A LOOK AT SOME OF YOUR PUBLISHED ARTICLES. HOW MUCH research did you undertake for each one? Many times you will have a large file of surplus material. Perhaps you reslanted this material for submission to other publications and are beginning to make regular sales. Some editors are even commissioning your work. So where do you go from here?

A few years ago I was in this position, when a reader's chance remark—"Why don't you write a book about this?"—made me stop and think. My article, published in *Good Housekeeping* Magazine, was about helping bereaved children, a vast subject. During my research, I had made numerous contacts and amassed a thick file of material. I began to wonder how I had confined it all into 1,500 words. Within days of that remark I had embarked on the busy but enjoyable journey toward my first nonfiction book. Perhaps my experiences could steer you on a similar path.

First, choose the article you think most suitable for expansion, perhaps one on a subject you specialize in. As an elementary teacher and widowed mother, I chose a subject close to my heart: children and how to help them.

I then had to consider how much relevant information I could accumulate, and whether I could explore the theme further. I soon realized that many of the issues raised in my interviews deserved their own chapters, so I felt confident there would be plenty of information to work on. I began by getting back in touch with the many professionals I had talked with and quoted in the original article. All were cooperative, and many gave me introductions to others who might be helpful: I met teachers; doctors and nurses; ministers; experts and consultants in child psychiatry, mental retardation, and pediatrics; counselors and social workers. Their expert advice and encouragement were invaluable. The same happened with the families I had interviewed previously, who introduced me to friends. I soon had more contacts than I could possibly visit. I had also received several letters from parents after the *Good Housekeeping* article, and I would suggest that any of your published pieces that have produced reader feedback would be worth considering for expansion into books.

At this stage I asked myself four vital questions:

1) Are there other books on this topic?
2) Is another needed?
3) Who would want to publish it?
4) Would it sell?

Publishers will want to know how many books already exist on your subject, and how yours will be different, more up-to-date, present a new angle or an unusual viewpoint. My angle was to look at bereavement from the child's viewpoint and to help adults understand that view.

My local librarian helped me draw up a preliminary list of relevant titles, and I could trace many references on file, tape, or microfiche. Although there are many books on bereavement, and a few concerning children, most of them were written by professionals for professionals. Was there a place for a book on the subject by an author like me?

Among the letters I received following my article was one from Cruse, an organization in Britain that cares for the widowed and their children, asking if they could use my article in their journal *Bereavement Care*. When I visited their offices, I was allowed to browse in their library. To my surprise, a staff member told me there was a need for a book on bereavement, written "in the style of a women's magazine." This gave me the encouragement I needed.

The lesson here is not to be discouraged by the number of books already published on *your* subject; their authors may not have tackled it in the way *you* intend to, and they may not appeal to readerships *you* want to attract.

Families coping with grief had generously shared their experiences with me, and I knew such families would be among my readers. But as a result of my research I had come to realize how many adults have had to attend to a grieving child at some time in their working lives:

315

police officers, ambulance crews, schoolteachers, hospital workers, and, of course, ministers. This market research would, I felt, be useful when I approached a publisher.

Now I had to sift through my enormous mass of notes, files, tapes, and clippings. I learned (during moments of slight panic) that if you are researching for a book-length work, you will need to keep an alphabetical index from day one. Double-check quotes, titles, addresses (and their spellings), phone numbers, the date of each call, the source of every contact. Note where and from whom you borrowed books and papers, plus the page numbers of every reference and quotation. You may think you will remember, but you won't! Even with the most sophisticated database you will be in trouble if you forget to store that one, vital reference. Not being a computer buff, I used cards secured in sturdy elastic bands. Yes, old-fashioned, but useful to pop in your pocket to take to interviews.

I knew I had to start by organizing everything into chapters. The problem was, where to begin? This is where my original article became my guide. I had opened it with a story that compared bereavement with the other significant family loss—divorce—and suggested that, like children of divorce, bereaved children have special problems. I then quoted a child psychiatrist who confirmed that children under ten who suffer the loss of a parent have a high risk of depressive illness in adulthood and that such a risk can be lowered if the child is encouraged to express grief at the time of loss.

So I knew the opening chapter of my book must discuss the seriousness of parental loss to a child, and I titled it "Grief in Childhood." From attending a lecture by a top child consultant at a London hospital and meeting with a compassionate founder of a children's hospice, I was able to outline the typical reactions children have to grief; to alert parents or caregivers to what *could* occur; and to point out that such reactions are normal. Also, it was vital to mention a child's own perception of death, depending on his or her age.

I had used short paragraphs and subheadings in the article, and decided to use the same format for the book. My first subheading had been "Emotional Disturbances," and from readers' comments I knew that anecdotes and true stories from children were always appreciated. I used many from families I met (changing names for those who wished

316

to remain anonymous) and in that way described the wide range of behavior patterns that young people exhibit.

By Chapter 2 I felt it was time to help adults cope with a bereavement crisis. I titled it "Do You Want to Help a Bereaved Child?" and used for my first two headings, "Breaking the news" and "How to get children to talk." Some counselors told me of many experiences that would help readers understand the difficulties involved. All of this made me realize that I must include advice on when and how to seek professional advice for children.

The next subheading in my article had been "Obsession with Death," and I found it hard to sort out the profusion of stories I had in my files about children with fantasies, fears, and misunderstandings. Finally, I divided them into the various causes of death, and Chapters 3 and 4 became "Terminal Illness" and "Unexpected Death." The first involved visits to hospices, and the second concerned families who had been involved in car accidents or other incidents leading to sudden death. Even families in which a member had committed suicide were anxious to tell me their tragic stories.

This led me to Chapter 5, specifically for and about "The Surviving Parent." I began by stressing that bereaved children are often left with a parent who is in deep shock and possibly quite unable to comfort other family members just when they most need it. Because this chapter had to cover so much—parents who were divorced prior to death; children without fathers or mothers; when both parents die; the feelings of a child who had never known one, or possibly either parent— subheads were invaluable.

In the article I had discussed only the death of a parent, but I felt that the book should also cover "Death of a Sibling," and this became Chapter 6, including such issues as crib death, stillbirth, children's hospices, funerals, and sibling jealousy.

As a teacher, I have noticed strangely old-fashioned attitudes in some schools toward bereaved children. Bereavement-training programs for teachers are now being set up in many countries, but there are still those who believe death should not be mentioned in a classroom! Since I had many stories to recount, some from my own pupils, I knew the whole of Chapter 7 could be devoted to"School Attitudes."

"The Role of Religion" was the next heading in my article, and in four short paragraphs I had been able to touch on the subject only in general terms. In the book I would have the luxury of covering many beliefs and cultures, but this was no small task. I met with leaders and ministers of about ten major religions and heard their varying methods of handling grief in families. So "Religious Attitudes" became Chapter 8.

The article had ended with a paragraph headed "A friend in need," in which I offered advice for anyone faced with a grieving family: how keeping the routine of a child's life as ordinary as possible is helpful; how much children need to talk to "a listening heart"; and how bereavement *can* bring a family closer together.

I knew I would need a chapter that offered the same encouraging lines, but in my research I had found yet more themes to cover, and many facets to those themes. Often when you expand a theme you will find yourself in totally unexpected territory. For instance, I discovered families who had been *relieved* by the death of a family member—perhaps that of a violent or abusive parent or older sibling. This involved more research and advice from counselors in different faiths and it became a short Chapter 9: "When a Family Death Brings Relief."

The counselors had also explained "How Bereavement in Childhood Affects Adult Life," and this became my final chapter 10.

In the last few paragraphs, I used my "friend in need" ideas, and so was able to conclude the book on an upbeat note.

One of the hardest aspects of this type of work, especially for book lengths, is knowing when to stop researching and start writing. When writing my second book, I became more selective and learned to write as I went along.

When you are finally ready to approach a publishing company, first go to the library and look for the publishers who publish the type of book you are writing. Examine these carefully to find out what length they seem to prefer, whether the style is academic or informal, the usual length, number of chapters, and whether they have chapter numbers and/or titles. Do they use footnotes, or are such references all at the end of the book? Are there any diagrams or illustrations? Send for their current catalog to see what they are bringing out. I chose a publisher of a series of books on "Overcoming Common Problems," which sounded appropriate for the book I had written. Having studied several of their books, I concluded that mine was close to their style.

From market listings, you will learn whether they require a query letter, outline, or simply prefer a brief covering letter with one or more sample chapters. Some may wish to see the complete manuscript.

A good query letter is a chance to sell yourself. I suggest you include a copy of your original article. It is the pivot from which you are working; what you wrote then was important to you, it sold, was published, and you believe it will make an interesting book. It could give your initial inquiry the edge over another writer who sends a vague query.

Reading through your published articles may provide you with more than one possible subject for a nonfiction book. By this time, you should know which ideas are worth pursuing. Where there is not enough material, or you don't feel strongly about the subject, forget it. Never waste time on a non-starter, although some pieces that will not quite stretch to a book could provide another couple of features.

⇉ 69

WHEN A BIOGRAPHER'S SUBJECT IS LESS THAN PERFECT

BY DAVID ROBERTSON

RECENTLY, I HAD THE PLEASURE OF READING IN A NATIONAL NEWS-paper a favorable, front-page review of my first biography. The book's subject is James F. Byrnes, a former U.S. Secretary of State, who was an unrepentant segregationist, a firm advocate of the atomic bombings in Japan, and the architect of the Republican "southern strategy" that has given us such leaders as Newt Gingrich. Stating that I had chosen a "sometimes wholly unsympathetic subject," the reviewer praised the book as a "balanced, deeply researched and sympathetic history of the man."

My first reaction to the review was like that of a boy who had learned how to aim a pellet gun, but who then shot and killed a songbird: I felt pride in my skills, but was appalled at the results. What had I done by raising in public memory the life of such an apparently unsympathetic figure? And if I, as the biographer, had been found sympathetic to such a life, what did that say about me, and the uses to which I had put my life and literary work?

Upon reflection, however, I decided to accept the praise for what it is. Even unsympathetic subjects deserve an accurate accounting of their minor virtues, as well as their major vices. If nothing else, such a biographical account can help explain to the reader how the subject failed to achieve a good, or at least decent, life by choices taken or not taken. And, frankly, for a biographer searching for a modern subject, twentieth-century history offers far more major figures whose lives will provide shock and disapproval than admiration and self-identification. Think, for example, of the number of twentieth-century leaders who were "great" in the sense that Stalin was great, rather than that Eleanor Roosevelt was a great leader.

Whether in dealing with a public or a private figure, with a sympathetic or unsympathetic subject, the writing of all biographies is, I believe, a deliberate grappling with the "other," an entity different from us, a person whose life we cannot fully comprehend or approve. The first biographer to learn this hard lesson was the biblical Jacob, who spent all night wrestling with an angel in an attempt to learn the other being's true name. (Jacob got his hip broken for his trouble.) But the resulting struggles, particularly with an unsympathetic subject, can strengthen a biographer's skills, just as I feel mine were strengthened by my struggles to determine whether Secretary Byrnes led an admirable or unadmirable life.

Currently, I am grappling with my own dark angel; I am writing a second biography of a man who, unlike Byrnes, is largely an admirable figure, but whose personality and actions are disturbing to me. The subject is Denmark Vesey (1767?–1822), a former slave who purchased his own freedom and then attempted the largest slave insurrection in the history of the United States at Charleston, South Carolina. In many ways, we are similar: Vesey, like me, was in his late forties when he attempted his uprising; we could have spoken in several foreign languages; we both spent much of our free time as manual laborers, and have no illusions about the horrors of American slavery. But as I walk the nineteenth-century streets of Charleston at night, passing Vesey's carpentry shop where he had planned his revolution, one thought is inescapable to me: I am a white southerner. Had Vesey's plot succeeded, his followers were under his strict orders to kill *every* white person at Charleston, including men, women, and small children, before burning the city and seizing ships at harbor to sail for Africa. Hence, although I am Vesey's biographer and intend to write sympathetically of his life, there is no doubt that, had we chanced to meet, Denmark Vesey would have cut David Robertson's throat.

My experience in writing and researching lives of subjects whose actions appear malevolent or whose historical image resists a biographer's self-identification has led me to adopt certain techniques. I offer these techniques to other biographers struggling with a less-than-sympathetic subject.

Write the life your subject lived. Some subjects, as disparate and attractive as Alice James or Adlai Stevenson, engage a biographer's admiration for what they could not or did not do. But frequently in writing of public or famous figures, the biographer is tempted to scold or rebuke the subject for not living the life the biographer expected. This can be great fun at the expense of the dead, of course, as Lytton Strachey demonstrated in *Eminent Victorians.* But recent biographies of John Kennedy and Lyndon Johnson have been marred, in my opinion, by the biographers' refusal to consider the historical and political limits to their subjects' actions and their personal failings. Byrnes, for example, as a Supreme Court Justice, U.S. Senator, and the "Assistant President" during World War II, did far less than he should have to protect civil liberties for blacks and the rights of organized labor. But in researching the careers of other prominent southern politicians—including Justice Hugo Black of Alabama, who served with Byrnes on the Supreme Court—I discovered that Byrnes often did more than his contemporaries expected of him, and sometimes did so to his personal disadvantage. Justice Black chose to remove himself from electoral politics and try to do what was right; Jimmy Byrnes chose to remain in politics and to do what was possible. I chose to write the life of the politician, not the jurist.

Such a decision means that the biographer must emphasize historical context as well as personality. Expect to do far more research in history and social sciences if you choose to write on an unsympathetic subject. (My bibliography and endnotes to the Byrnes biography ran to 69 small-type pages.) That research helped me comprehend—if not fully approve—the planned ferocity of Denmark Vesey's attempted revolt. I discovered that during Denmark Vesey's lifetime, South Carolina contained more African-born people in bondage than any other slave-holding state at the time. These proud men and women considered themselves to be *African,* not African-American, and in a type of "ethnic cleansing," their masters were attempting to destroy their ties to marriage, parenthood, their religion, and their nations. Vesey, who probably had traveled to Africa, preached to these first-generation slaves that he was attempting to liberate not only them, but also their right as a people to exist unmolested in their own homeland. Considered historically as an armed struggle against physical and cultural genocide, Vesey's actions appear more expedient. Do we blame the Cheyenne for taking no prisoners at Little Big Horn?

Don't be surprised by surprises. In writing a biography of an unredeemably selfish or cruel individual, don't be surprised by occasional acts of generosity or sentimentality. Include them, not as unaccountable surprises, but as further evidence for your case. Sentimentality is the weakling brother of brutality. Even human monsters will occasionally show pity or indulgence as if to convince themselves, if not the reader of their biographies, that they really *aren't* monsters. Hitler, an acquaintance told me, was very fond of lighthearted movies and large, friendly dogs. Stalin, with his baggy-seat trousers, his beloved pipe tobacco, and his crinkly brown eyes, could appear as Uncle Joe from the Old Country. The contiguous existence of pity and brutality within one uneasy individual is a concept as twentieth-century as Freud, who warned us that inside each sadist is a powerless child terrified of becoming a victim, and as ancient as Tacitus, who wrote of one cruel Caesar that if we could see his soul at night, we would see a face self-lacerated in fear.

Occasionally, a subject acting against type can illuminate the larger personality the biographer wishes he had been. Byrnes, who after his retirement from the Department of State spent much of his life frustrating efforts to put civil rights legislation into effect in the South, was outraged when a black friend of his was denied the use of a public restroom in South Carolina in the 1960s. Byrnes wrote angry letters, and considered all sorts of political retribution, in an effort to convince a white segregationist that Byrnes' black friend was "special," and therefore deserving of all the civil liberties and rights of any U.S. citizen. Yet Byrnes seemed never to have considered that, legally and morally, all individuals are special, regardless of their skin color. Byrnes' failure to make an intuitive and ethical leap toward all U.S. citizens, regardless of his good intentions in this single episode, illuminates both his possibilities and his limitations as a national leader.

Shake hands with your dark side. "If Hitler could have had any friends, I would certainly have been among his close friends," Albert Speer tells us in his memoirs of the Third Reich. Speer's account of how he became Hitler's chief architect and armaments minister is in many ways also the "best" biography of Hitler, but it is in no way an *apologia* for the madness and unadulterated evil of Adolf Hitler. Speer's book is, rather, a disturbing account of how a possibly decent

323

individual came in his writing to identify with such an evil person. Speer's account is plainly self-serving. But it offers a statement *in extremis* of the final temptations and difficulties besetting the biographer of an unsympathetic subject.

Leon Edel has warned us of what he called "transference," whereby a biographer's subject becomes an idealized self-portrait of the biographer. Transference occurs most commonly when the subject is considered admirable. Conversely, when writing of an unsympathetic subject, the biographer is in danger of being unnerved by recognizing his own baser impulses in the actions of the subject. I began to be concerned with my own past untruthfulness, for example, after years of seeing in Jimmy Byrnes' life how easily a lie can advance a career. Similarly, I have never felt the lash of slavery; but what if I had? And what if I had then met Denmark Vesey, a man of biblical presence and authority, who secretly handed me a weapon and told me, as he told his other followers at Charleston, "And they shall utterly destroy all that was in the city, with the edge of the sword"?

In recognizing the parts of our personality we wish to deny, we can to a degree control them or change them. In writing about an unsympathetic subject, you must expect to learn as much about your own darker side as about your subject's. When the subject's baser motives hit too close to home, the biographer can be tempted to write an overlong justification of the subject's actions, or be cowed into an embarrassed silence. But if a biographer is honest about his or her own strengths and weaknesses, then that biographer can write about an unsympathetic subject with uncommon honesty and strength.

All of which brings us back to Jacob struggling with his angel at night. Jacob, you will recall, never learned the angel's true name. But in acknowledgement of Jacob's struggles, and the wound he received, the angel told Jacob *his* true name. Jacob became a better, and different, person for knowing it. Similarly, the struggles and personal wounds a biographer sustains in writing about an unsympathetic subject can, at the end of the subject's life, leave the biographer with a different and better identity: as a researcher, biographer, and as literary artist.

➤➤ 70

CONDUCTING THE "SENSITIVE" INTERVIEW

BY KATHLEEN WINKLER

A DAUGHTER WHO WAS STALKED AND KILLED BY A FORMER LOVER. Surgery that left impotence in its wake. An abortion kept secret for years. A past that includes painful abuse.

Occasionally in your writing career you may find yourself interviewing people about topics that are very hard to talk about. Sometimes it's because they are physically unpleasant or embarrassing. Sometimes it's because they are emotionally wrenching. In either case, you as the writer have a great challenge: to make your subjects feel comfortable enough to share sensitive, intimate experiences with you so your readers can benefit from them.

An awkward interviewer, trampling on the subject's sensibilities, will not only not get a good story, but can also do great damage to the subject, who may never again trust anyone enough to open up.

A skilled and sympathetic interviewer, on the other hand, will not only elicit a moving story from the subject, but may actually help him or her come to terms with an experience kept hidden or repressed for years.

It all depends on how you go about it.

As a medical writer for fifteen years, I've interviewed people on such intimate topics as sexual function, emotional responses to physical scars from surgery, and life-threatening illness. In the course of writing *When the Crying Stops: Abortion, the Pain and the Healing* (Northwestern Publishing House), I interviewed twenty women about their abortion experiences and subsequent reactions. Some of these women had never told their stories to anyone before the interview.

As a result of these often painful interviews, I've developed an approach to sensitive interviewing and some helpful ways to make such interviews easier for me and for the subject, and more productive.

325

I believe that the number one rule for interviewing on any topic, especially a sensitive one, is respect for the person sitting across from you. Always keep in mind that he or she doesn't *owe* you anything. In most cases your subject is telling his or her story out of a simple desire to help others cope with the same or a similar problem, with no expectation of any kind of reward. The subject, therefore, has the right to decide how much to share. While as the interviewer you can encourage the sharing and make it as free of stress as possible, you must not try to force the person to reveal more than he or she is willing to. The subject has the right to end the interview at any point, or to say, "I don't want to talk about that"—and you must respect that decision.

There are some things you can do to make a sensitive interview as tension-free as possible for the subject, and, at the same time, get the information you need to write an honest and moving piece.

• Since it's absolutely essential to use a tape recorder during the interview—especially if there are likely to be any legal aspects to the project—ask the subject for permission to do so, explaining that you want to be sure your quotes are accurate. But get the permission on tape before you begin.

• Preparation is important. Never try to "wing" an interview. Learn as much as you can about the person in advance. If the story is likely to have a psychological or medical slant, do your research: Familiarize yourself with the problem and the various treatments and side effects. In dealing with a social problem—child abuse, spouse battering, etc.—read current background material on all aspects of it.

• Prepare your questions carefully ahead of time. Start with the general, less threatening questions and move on to those dealing with the more difficult, personal aspects of the experience. Begin by asking about the subject's childhood and the events that led up to the traumatic experience. This will help relax your subject and get the dialogue flowing.

• When you arrive at the interview, the subject is likely to be nervous. A warm smile, a handshake, and a friendly comment—"I'm so happy to meet you; I think it's wonderful that you are willing to share your experience with others"—will go a long way toward putting the subject at ease.

• If your subject is especially nervous, confront that fact—don't ignore it—saying, "I know this may be difficult for you. That's understandable. Many people are uneasy at first, but it won't be as hard as you may think."

• Start with a disclaimer, if you think it will help. Say, frankly, "I hope you will want to share your thoughts and feelings, but I won't pressure you to say any more than you want to." If you have agreed to anonymity for the subject, emphasize at the outset that you will not, under any circumstances, break that promise.

• Use broad, general questions at first, asking such non-threatening questions as, "Tell me a little about yourself: Where are you from? What was it like growing up in your family? How did you get along with your siblings? Parents?" If this leads to an appropriate opening, you might follow the answer with, "Can you tell me a little more about that?" Obviously avoid questions that can be answered with "yes" or "no." Have a summary question ready for the end—"What's the most important effect this experience has had on you? What is the most helpful thing you would like to share with the readers?"

• Move gradually, in chronological order, through the part of the person's life that is relevant to the story. If the subject wanders and gets off track, bring the interview back to the main topic by saying something like, "We're going to get to that in a minute, but right now I'd like to hear more about—." A little humor never hurts: "Hold on a bit; we're getting way ahead of ourselves."

• When you are ready to deal with the sensitive topic, warn the person by saying, "We've come to the point where I need to ask you some more specific questions about what happened." If the subject becomes emotional, confront that directly, saying, "Go ahead and cry if you feel like it. I certainly understand. I would have cried, too, in that situation." Don't try to hide your emotional reaction; if you actually do respond with tears, that's O.K. I've never done a sensitive interview in which the subject cried and I didn't shed a few tears, too.

• Give your subject plenty of time to respond to your questions. If she or he stops at a critical point, pause, too, and then make a casual comment to start the conversation flowing again: "That must have been very hard for you. What happened next?" Keep your voice warm and sympathetic.

• Never make a judgmental comment. Obviously, remarks like, "How could you have done that!" are taboo, but so are even subtle gestures

327

or verbal responses, no matter how repellent you may find what the subject says.

• Get on tape the subject's wishes about using real names in your feature.

• When you have finished the interview, thank the person warmly, and leave your card so she or he can reach you if she wishes to give you some additional information. Don't be reluctant to call her back for clarification or more details. Store the tapes in a fireproof safe. It is not advisable to show the subject a transcript of the tape recording or the manuscript prior to its publication.

Though telephone interviews on sensitive subjects can be done, they do present a different challenge. Sometimes the anonymity of the phone allows a nervous subject to talk more freely, but it can, in some instances, be inhibiting.

• Always tell the person that the phone interview is being tape recorded. I usually say, "I'm taping this, so you don't have to worry about talking slowly enough for me to take notes."

• As in a face-to-face interview, you must establish a personal relationship over the telephone, which presents some difficulties. Chat casually at first, in a warm, friendly tone, asking about the weather, how the person likes living in his or her hometown, how he or she spent the weekend. Get to know the subject a bit before jumping into the interview.

• Schedule your phone interview at a time when you are not likely to be interrupted. Disconnect your call-waiting! Late night often works best for me. There's something about quiet houses and low lights that encourages the flow of conversation.

Talking to people about their most intimate, personal problems and experiences can be exhausting and emotionally draining, for you as well as for your subject. Don't schedule too many such interviews back to back or you may find yourself on overload. Allow time for a break between interviews.

Some of your subjects may well be in need of professional counseling and may try to put you into the role of therapist. Remember that your job is only to ask the questions and listen—which may in itself be therapeutic for the subject. Never offer advice. It may in some instances be appropriate to ask, "Have you ever had professional help in dealing with this problem? You might find it helpful."

Sharing the darker side of pain often helps the teller and the reader to know that they are not alone, that other human beings have had similar experiences and survived.

As writers, we have a tremendous responsibility in doing sensitive interviews. We have a responsibility to our subjects not to betray their trust. And, in addition, we have a responsibility to our readers to present these stories as honestly and with as much empathy as we can. Conducting ourselves with the utmost professionalism is the only way to live up to it.

Writing a Life

By Linda Simon

"Biography works in mysteries," wrote Leon Edel, the masterful biographer of Henry James. "That is its fascination." Many biographers have likened themselves to detectives trying to find a missing person—their subject—by searching for clues in letters, diaries, photographs, and whatever other artifacts survive as evidence of their subject's life. Working in public archives and private collections, biographers read intimate revelations, discover secrets, and ultimately come to know their subjects better, perhaps, than they know their own friends and family. The work of a biographer can be difficult, frustrating, and time-consuming; but, as Edel tells us, biography has many rewards. Biographers learn not only about the particular details of their subject's life, but also the historical, cultural, and social context in which they lived; not only about the particular problems and decisions that their subject faced, but something about human nature, about the dreams and desires that we all share. As a result of their search into someone else's life, biographers often learn something about themselves.

Choosing a subject

Who makes a good biographical subject? If we look at library shelves, we find that in the past biographies were written about famous men—and a few women. The biographical subject usually was a hero: someone who had accomplished some great feat, held an important political position, or made a lasting contribution to the arts. The biographer paid homage to this person's greatness by portraying his life as exemplary. Catherine Drinker Bowen, who wrote biographies of such great men as Justice Oliver Wendell Holmes and John Adams, tells us that writing about heroic figures was, for her, an uplifting experience:

To spend three years or five with a truly great man, reading what he said and wrote, observing him as he errs, stumbles, falls, and rises again; to watch his talent grow . . . this cannot but seize upon a writer, one might almost say transform him. . . . The ferment of genius, Holmes said, is quickly imparted, and when a man is great he makes others believe in greatness. By that token one's life is altered. One has climbed a hill, looked out and over, and the valley of one's own condition will be forever greener.

Biographers today, however, are not likely to share Bowen's belief in heroes. Experience, observation, and a dollop of Freudian psychology has disillusioned many of us. We tend to believe that all people have their weaknesses, flaws, and dark sides. We look for complexities and contradictions—and we find them, even in men and women who have enacted great deeds.

Although many biographies are written about famous men and women, increasingly we find biographies about those who lived relatively ordinary lives. Jean Strouse, for example, decided to write about Alice James, a minor historical figure compared with her brothers, the novelist Henry James and the philosopher William. Alice James, Strouse wrote, "made no claim to have carried on an exemplary struggle or to have achieved anything beyond the private measure of her own experience. To make her into a heroine (or victim-as-heroine) now would be seriously to misconstrue her sufferings and her aims." Still, Strouse believed that Alice James's experiences could illuminate for readers the context of women's lives in the nineteenth century. She believed that writing about "semi-private lives" helps us to enter the world of ordinary men and women—the world, after all, in which most of us live.

If biographers today have a wide range of subjects to choose from, how does one decide? Who is a good subject? Simply put, a good subject, like an interesting friend, is someone whose stories we like to hear, someone we would like to introduce to other people. A good subject is not always likable, but never dull. It is someone whose story has not yet been told, perhaps, or in any case, has not yet been told the way we understand it. We may feel a connection with this subject because we share similar experiences or sensibilities; or we may feel admiration, even envy, for the subject's life. We may be attracted to someone who lived in an exciting time and place, even if that person did not contribute greatly to the excitement. Always, we feel that there is a mystery to be solved: Something about this person is not yet known, and we want to discover it.

I had been reading books by and about American expatriates in Paris, simply for the pleasure of it, when I noticed that Gertrude Stein emerged again and again in memoirs of the period. Surely Stein is an interesting historical figure: an experimenter in poetry and prose whose unconventional appearance and personality made her the center of attention wherever she went. I liked Stein's raunchiness, self-confidence, and literary daring. As I read biographies of Stein—again, simply for the pleasure of immersing myself in the period—I noticed that her companion, Alice B. Toklas, seemed to be a mysterious figure. Was she a kind, protective supporter of Stein? Was she a cold-hearted manipulator? Most biographers portrayed Stein as a dominant force in the household, but was Toklas really in charge? These questions motivated me to see Toklas as a potential biographical subject: She presented a problem for me; she was a mystery.

Although Alice Toklas lived a "semi-private" life in comparison with Gertrude Stein's, still she lived an extraordinary life in comparison with, say, my grandmother or uncle, who did not cavort with the likes of Ernest Hemingway, Pablo Picasso, and F. Scott Fitzgerald. But anyone's grandmother or uncle might be a suitable biographical subject. If your grandmother was an immigrant who kept diaries and sent letters to relatives in her native land, if your uncle was a health food guru who traveled the world teaching new ideas about nutrition, they may be interesting subjects for a full-length biography or a shorter study: an article in a historical journal, for example, or a chapter in a collection of biographical sketches. As a potential biographer, however, you need to ask the same questions about these subjects that you would ask about anyone else: Would my grandmother or uncle interest other people? Is there sufficient source material to give me enough biographical information for my study? Is there a mystery about this person that I want to solve?

Finding clues

Once biographers find a subject, they need to assess whether sufficient biographical material will be available to them. Biographers can write only about someone who has left a paper trail, including letters, journals, creative writing, works of art such as films or paintings, interviews. The biographer must have access to material that can document the subject's life.

If you have chosen a subject who has been written about before, existing biographies can help you to locate archives where there is material about your subject. I knew from biographies of Gertrude Stein that the Stein archives were housed in the American Literature collection at Yale University's Beinecke Library. Many of Toklas's letters were housed there as well. But to find other material, I began a search in the reference room of my local library. There, I examined such sources as the *National Union Catalogue of Manuscript Collections* and the *Directory of Special Libraries and Information Centers* to locate other archives where I guessed that I might find Toklas correspondence or other material. I wrote to these libraries, visited some, ordered photocopies, and began to assemble my own files of source material.

The reference room of a good library contains many directories that lead researchers to archival material. Some of these directories are specialized—focusing on women's history, science, or art, for example. Reference librarians are helpful and knowledgeable about these sources. I have discovered these professionals to be a biographer's best friend.

If you find few sources in library archives, the search becomes a bit more complicated. If your subject has survivors, you need to find out whether material that you need may be in private collections: the attic of your subject's grand-niece or the basement of your subject's ex-wife. Sometimes, survivors are cooperative; sometimes, however, they feel threatened by an interloper who may discover information about the family's life that they wish to be kept private. Although many biographies have been written in the face of survivors' hostility, some biographers find such a situation uncomfortable and stressful. If you are among them, you may want to choose another subject.

Doing it

Researching and writing a biography is not a quick project. It takes time to locate material, time to assemble sources, time to track down clues. You may find yourself spending years formulating a chronology of your subject's life. Anyone beginning a biography needs to have developed strong research skills. Historical writing is good practice, and so is newspaper reporting. Gradually, biographers develop a sense of intuition about their subject, discovering that they can anticipate their subject's reaction to a new acquaintance or a new experience.

Suddenly, they feel it is time to write. When I was working on a biography of Thornton Wilder, I went to visit a charming man who had been a close friend of Wilder's. He began to tell me some stories about Wilder's life—his experiences in the theater, his days as a soldier, his literary friendships—and I found that I could finish sentences: These were stories that I knew in even more detail than Wilder's friend. When I returned home, I began to write the book.

Some biographers write as they research, sketching in the parameters of a life, filling in details as they find them. Some biographers spend twenty years involved in their subject's life, although not all of those years are spent researching and writing. Few writers are able to work on a biography full time, so other tasks—teaching, translating, even doing the laundry—intervene in the research and writing process. Yet biographers admit that even when they are not actually conducting research or writing, their subject becomes a companion, someone they think about often. They begin to see events in their own lives through their subject's eyes; they reflect on their own experiences in light of what they learn about their subject. Biography invites introspection. Personal introspection—thinking about why people behave as they do, about the forces that shape us and the way we affect other people—is good training for the biographer's work.

Biographical problems

In the past few years, biographers have come under attack as being nothing more than burglars, rifling through lingerie drawers and laundry bins, looking for the worst about their subject. Joyce Carol Oates coined the term "pathography" to apply to biographies that present subjects as neurotic, psychotic, depressed, incestuous, alcoholic, or suffering from other antisocial maladies. But these biographies reflect our current intellectual climate more than they reflect the craft of biography.

Certainly the kinds of questions that biographers ask about their subjects have changed over time. Biographers have been influenced by the work of psychologists and social scientists; they examine their subjects from different perspectives, depending on their own ideas

334

about personality development and the cause and effect of behavior. A biography of John Kennedy, written in the 1960s, would have ignored questions about family rivalry and sexual infidelity that biographers feel free to ask twenty years later. A burgeoning interest in biographies of women, beginning in the 1970s, changed both the kinds of questions that biographers asked and the subjects that they chose to write about. In creating a sense of the reality of someone's life, biographers have come to see that the superficial interactions and daily routine may not define an individual. This delving deeply into another personality may seem to some an invasion of privacy. But responsible biographers take their task seriously: They want to find a missing person. Without their efforts, their subject would simply disappear, fade from memory, be lost to history. Biographers keep spirits alive.

>> 72

TURNING A PERSONAL EXPERIENCE INTO AN ARTICLE

BY KATHRYN LAY

HAVE YOU EVER READ AN ARTICLE THAT HAS TOUCHED YOU IN A special way? You think, "That happened to me" or "That's the way I feel" or even, "Maybe I could write about my experience with . . ."

Someone else's story has communicated a feeling or emotion that relates to your life, or has shown you how to solve a similar problem. Personal experience articles can be humorous, sad, informative, or thought-provoking. They remind readers how they felt in a similar situation, or they warn others how to avoid a problem. Many times, readers learn how to cope with or overcome similar events. And most often, personal experience articles offer hope.

If something special has happened in your life that you think would touch others, there are several ways in which you can turn it into a publishable article. Personal experiences can be written in as few as fifty words or run to several thousand. Here are the three most popular types:

1) *Your story.* This is an account of something you or someone close to you has experienced that will interest other people—something they can relate to or identify with.

After I went through a false pregnancy following years of infertility, I wrote the article, "No Less A Woman," which has been published four times. Many readers wrote to say it touched, encouraged, helped, or educated them.

2) *Real-life drama.* Most people have not had the experience of being mauled by a bear or surviving a plane crash, but the fact that someone else went through this adventure or trauma and survived can make compelling reading. "As told to" articles are one way to write

someone else's dramatic story. You must first, of course, get the person's permission. Also, it's important to capture the emotion and descriptions as if you were there when it happened.

3) *The how-to.* In this type of piece, you share what you've experienced emotionally and/or physically while you were pursuing a particular goal, and show others how they might achieve a similar goal.

For instance, has an experience with your children, friends, relatives, or even strangers, or your success in a new venture, given you insight and information that would be valuable to others? Use anecdotes, emotion, and firsthand experience to write your how-to personal experiences.

In "Make a Date to Plan Together," I described how my husband and I set up planning sessions that helped us reach our goals and strengthened our relationship. The article was originally published in *Sunday Digest* and has been reprinted many times.

Once you have found a personal experience you want to write about, study different magazines to find where your story would fit best; each publication has its own needs and style. For example, women's magazines have specific preferences, most often dealing with women's or parenting issues. An article on how you or someone you know overcame bulimia might find a home in *Family Circle* or *Woman's World*. And a personal experience how-to about your camping trip through the Rockies would have a good chance of acceptance at a travel, outdoors, or regional magazine, as long as you give it an unusual twist. Inspirational magazines could be the market for a personal experience piece on a battle with cancer, domestic abuse or violence, or the death of a family member.

Personal experience articles aren't necessarily about momentous events. They might deal with a more common experience, such as your relationship with your mother-in-law. Or in an informative article you may explain how your runaway dog gave you an idea for a new business. Humorous personal experience pieces are always in demand. Most people can relate to the problems of moving; in an article I wrote about my own moving experience, there was nothing deep or life-threatening, yet readers could understand and laugh along with my misadventures.

337

There are four basic steps that will help you write a successful personal experience piece:

1) *Hook your readers immediately.* My article "No Less A Woman" began in this way:

"You are about six weeks pregnant," the doctor informed me. After two years of waiting to hear those words, I wanted to laugh, to cry!

This tells readers at the outset what the piece will be about. If it concerns your struggle with a disease and readers are facing the same problem or know someone who is, there is a good chance they will want to read about your experience.

2) *Follow the hook with a statement that explains what the article is about.* In "Make a Date . . ." I let the reader know right away what to expect:

Four times a year my husband and I spend time alone planning creative ways to meet common goals. There are five steps to setting up such goal-planning sessions.

Once you have captured your readers' attention, or stirred their memories or longings, they will want to know whether your article will give them a story of hope, or solutions to a problem.

3) *The body of the piece must be well organized and interesting.* Get your experience down on paper first. During the rewrite see if it can or should be structured differently. Describe your experience as it happened; leave out unnecessary details, but include emotion and tension. Did you reach a point of no return? Did you give up hope at any point? Readers who may have struggled with the same problem want to laugh or cry with you; they want to see that someone else feels as they do. Imagine how you would tell your story to a special friend, not to a reporter who wants "just the facts."

4) *Wind your article up by returning to your beginning idea.* Give your readers something to think about after they've finished reading your article—an idea, a feeling, or a plan of action they can follow for a similar problem. I ended "And Baby Makes Three," a piece about our daughter's adoption, by bringing readers back to a common emotion.

338

When others see Michelle, they speak of how wonderful it is that she has parents who love her. But I always correct them. We are the ones who have been blessed.

At the end of "No Less A Woman," I went back to my original problem of infertility and the emotional change I'd experienced:

Does my infertility make me less of a woman? It may seem to, if I allow the world to tell me what a woman should be. I know, however, that in the eyes of my loving husband, I am no less a woman.

Everyone has had at least one personal experience, perhaps many, that would make good articles. Keep a journal. Reflect on events of the day or week. If you think something has the potential for a personal experience piece, ask yourself these questions:

• Can others relate to my experience?
• Could an article about it encourage, teach, warn, or help others, or is the audience too limited?
• Can I write it with emotion, yet step back from it so that it won't become a "self-portrait account" or a "soap-box tirade"?
• Is there a market for this? Even more than one?

These questions can later be used as guidelines when you begin to write. Once you know your target audience and what you hope to give your reader, the piece will flow more easily.

How do you submit personal experience articles? Although many magazines will accept unsolicited manuscripts, some prefer query letters first. For several reasons, this may be the better approach for the writer. If there is a limited market for your personal experience, you may not want to spend time writing the complete article. And if, after reading your query, an editor does ask to see the manuscript, you will be able to gear it toward *that* magazine's audience. An editor may ask to see your article and give you ideas of what slant or information she prefers. Your chances of selling your article will increase if you know in advance what the editor expects.

As with your article, begin your query with a "grabber" sentence, stating what your piece will be about. If it is humorous, say so in a funny way. If it is meant to be dramatic, make sure the opening sentence is intriguing. Make sure your query reflects whatever emotion you expect your article to evoke in your readers.

Your query should also stress the unique angle of your article, mention expert sources, if any, and why your personal experience may help or make a difference in the lives of the magazine's readers. Show the editor that you will give its readers accurate, authoritative information, and that what you have to say will touch them. If you have had articles published previously, send tear sheets, especially if they were personal experience pieces.

Even after you receive a go-ahead to your query, your article may not sell to that magazine . . . but don't panic. Submit it to the next magazine on your list of possible markets. Some of my personal experience articles have sold the first time out; others have sold after ten or more rejections. As with all writing, persistence and market research will increase your chances of selling.

If you enjoy reading personal experience articles, there is a good chance you'll enjoy writing them, and get satisfaction from touching readers' hearts and lives.

≫ 73

WRITING COMPELLING ARTICLE LEADS

BY STEVE WEINBERG

AFTER RESEARCHING THE LIFE OF CONTROVERSIAL TYCOON ARMAND Hammer, it was time for me to write a magazine profile. Like many writers, I had countless possibilities for openings, thanks to hundreds of anecdotes I had collected, representing every phase of his long life. If, on the other hand, I decided against opening with an anecdote, I could choose among leads relying on direct quotations, imagery, atmosphere, or jokes told about him.

So, facing the blank page, I felt confident I had enough material for a successful article. Yet, simultaneously, I felt paralyzed by all the possibilities of how to begin.

Then I remembered the writer's main mission in composing profiles, as well as exposés, how-to articles, personal experience vignettes, travelogues: to tell interesting *stories* while informing readers.

Over my decades of free lancing, I have learned a formula for effective storytelling in articles: the tension-resolution model. Many articles lack tension (call it suspense or mystery or even foreshadowing, if you prefer). As a result, many readers find no reason to stay with the writer until the end.

Creating tension is the difference between writing "The king died, then the queen died" and "The king died, then the queen died of grief." The first version does nothing but present the facts. The second version suggests a plot with inherent tension: What in the queen's relationship with the king led her to become a grieving widow? Exactly how did the grief kill her?

Using the tension-resolution model myself, I found the opening for my profile fell into place. It read like this:

To the casual observer, it appeared that Armand Hammer's amazing career had come to an end. In fact, it appeared he was about to die.

341

The date: March 4, 1976. The place: the Los Angeles courtroom of federal Judge Lawrence Lydick. Attendants wheeled the 77-year-old tycoon into the courtroom from Cedars of Lebanon Hospital, where, according to his doctors, he had languished in unstable condition since January. Frail but still handsome, Hammer looked to be the remains of a truly charismatic man. Throughout the court appearance, he stayed hooked up to monitoring machines watched closely by medical specialists in an adjoining room.

Hammer was present to plead to a charge of an illegal campaign contribution made four years earlier, during Watergate. Specifically, the federal government alleged that he had concealed $54,000 in donations to the reelection campaign of President Richard Nixon. Hammer seemed to believe he had done nothing wrong. . . .

Then I explained how, notwithstanding his deserved reputation for getting his way, Hammer feared that continuing the court battle would kill him. By pleading guilty, Hammer knew, he could face a three-year prison term. He hoped, however, that the judge would spare him incarceration, a hope perhaps bolstered by the fact that Judge Lydick had been affiliated in law practice with Richard Nixon. Moreover, the judge had received more than 100 letters on Hammer's behalf, from U.S. senators, billionaire industrialists, religious leaders, world-renowned entertainers, university presidents, and fellow jurists.

At the end of the lead, I asked whether the judge would send a guilty but influential, wealthy, famous, elderly, apparently dying man to prison. That was the tension. If you care about the resolution, you will have to read on.

Openings that don't disappoint

Writers for other media use the tension-resolution model as a matter of course. At the beginning of a movie, the director gives the audience a tight shot of a gun above the mantelpiece. Viewers can guess that some time during the movie, the gun will be fired, and quite likely kill somebody. But who will fire the gun? Why? Who will die as a result? The tension has been established.

The tension-resolution technique has been around for centuries, but lacked a book-length treatment until 1986, when Jon Franklin finished his book *Writing for Story: Craft Secrets of Dramatic Nonfiction by a Two-Time Pulitzer Prize Winner.* Franklin wrote that almost any interesting story can be described like this:

. . . A sequence of actions that occur when a sympathetic character encounters a complicating situation [the tension] that he confronts and solves [the resolution].

A typical tension-resolution story skeleton looks like this:

Tension: Company fires Ann.
Developmental stages: Depression paralyzes Ann; Ann regains confidence; Ann sues former employer.
Resolution: Ann gets her job back.

Although any type of article can benefit from the tension-resolution model, not all ideas lend themselves well to the technique. That's because they lack a resolution. Its absence makes telling a compelling story difficult. People hope to win lotteries, but never buy a winning ticket. No resolution there. Complications without resolutions make for weak stories.

Fortunately, there are many article ideas with resolutions to choose from: Police solve a crime. A kindergarten teacher falsely accused of child abuse is rehired. A corrupt politician is removed from office. A severely disabled person completes an around-the-world journey.

Writers frequently find such resolutions by reading brief hard-news items in newspapers or viewing television headline services. The items found there are usually endings without beginnings. During my Armand Hammer research, I found superficial items about his buying a multimillion-dollar painting for his art collection, his flying to Moscow on his customized jet to negotiate privately with Leonid Brezhnev at the height of the Cold War, his firing the president of Occidental Petroleum Corporation.

But I wanted to know the "why" and the "how" along with the who, what, when and where. Learning the "why" and the "how" provided the necessary tension leading up to the resolutions I already knew.

The magazine writer who recognizes the potential for transforming a superficial daily news story into an in-depth article will provide the beginning: the meticulous police work that resulted in apprehending the criminal, the whistle-blower who courageously decided to expose political corruption.

The climax does not have to be a complete surprise. Readers turning to a profile of John Hinckley would quite likely already know that he tried to assassinate President Ronald Reagan. But a Hinckley profile using the tension-resolution technique could explain *how* Hinckley managed to shoot Reagan, building the suspense through the chronology of the events, or it could revolve around whether Hinckley is ever likely to show sincere remorse.

Because the movement from tension to resolution is so important, it makes sense to draft the ending first. Before I set Armand Hammer in a Los Angeles courtroom, I knew the outcome of the criminal proceedings, so I knew what I needed to foreshadow. An interesting courtroom anecdote by itself would not have been enough for a successful lead. Rather, it had to promise readers an interesting journey to a resolution unknown to them until the end.

Getting the telling details

Discovering the ending means researching; researching means collecting details. Those details are essential in writing a tension-resolution article.

For the Hammer profile, I started with secondary sources (already published articles and books, transcripts of broadcast programs); moved on to primary sources (lawsuits, property ownership records, divorce files and the like). I then interviewed Hammer's current and former colleagues, social acquaintances, family members and government officials. After accumulating a large volume of details, I organized them chronologically. From that chronology I was able to select and shape my lead and ending.

The best writers are alert for details that might turn an acceptable lead into a memorable one. Near the beginning of her career, now successful magazine writer and book author Edna Buchanan wrote about the murder of a man dumped into the street by the driver of a pickup truck. It was only after publication that Buchanan learned that the dead man had been wearing a black taffeta cocktail dress and red high heels. When she questioned the detectives about why they never told her that, they replied, "You didn't ask." After that, she always asked. Frequently, the answer became grist for an opening.

But details can be dangerous if handled poorly. Writers who take detail-collecting seriously are sometimes undiscerning in selecting the right ones for the lead. In profile-writing, for example, detail-happy writers often open with physical descriptions of their subjects—hair

344

color, shape of nose and brand of shoes—making readers wonder, "What is the writer trying to convey?"

No detail should be included in the lead unless it simultaneously moves the narrative forward and creates tension.

Avoiding stereotypes

It's important to screen out inappropriate details from the lead; avoiding stereotypes is even more so. Before beginning my Hammer profile, I read hundreds of accounts based on clichéd themes: the big-hearted philanthropist, or the rapacious tycoon; the art collector who cherished every painting for its beauty, or who bought paintings only for the prestige they brought him; and so on.

Obviously, not all of these themes could have been correct, and, in fact, none was totally correct—in part because the writers made the details conform to their own views rather than letting the lead grow organically from the details.

In his book, *Writing for Your Readers,* Donald M. Murray warns against clichés of vision that produce misleading openings: "The reporter must be capable of seeing what is new. Clichés of language are significant misdemeanors, but clichés of vision are felonies. Too often editors punish each misdemeanor but advocate the commission of felonies."

An example of such a felony is the article about the model student who has opened fire in the neighborhood for no obvious reason, killing and maiming whoever came into his rifle's crosshairs. The writer describes the killer as quiet, good to his mother, neat—the last person in the world anybody would have expected to go berserk. He is the cliché killer.

The trouble here is that the writer of the article failed to look in the right places for information. The killer's teachers, fellow students, and neighbors generated the stereotype, not by consciously lying, but they felt guilty for having been so wrong about somebody they thought they knew well.

If the reader is fortunate, the free lancer trying to explain the murder will refuse to be blinded by such clichés of vision. As Murray says:

Some good, hard-edged reporting will discover that neighborhood pets have been disappearing for years, the nice young man was seen cooking pigeons

345

when he was three years old . . . that his father, two brothers and three sisters have refused to live at home with him; that the studious young man has the reading level of a nine-year-old; and that his mother has fought a guerrilla war against getting psychiatric help for him since he was three years old.

Getting to the resolution

In putting an apparently sick, guilty Hammer in a Los Angeles courtroom for my lead, I knew the resolution all along. Through individual words and phrases, I foreshadowed the resolution: that in Hammer's case, appearances were deceiving.

After the tension-filled opening, I chronicled Hammer's life as fully as I could, always keeping the ending in mind. One of the themes leading to the ending was his willingness to bend the truth in his quest for wealth, fame, and a role on the stage of world diplomacy. Those themes helped develop the tension in the lead, while driving the story toward its resolution, which read like this:

> When Judge Lydick sentenced Hammer in late March 1976, the penalty was one year of probation and a fine of $3,000. The letters from the rich, the famous, and the powerful may have helped, as the dire medical reports may have helped. Looking terminally ill, Hammer was wheeled out of the courtroom, upset at this blot on his reputation but, in the main, relieved.
>
> A week later, he was back at work. Two months later, he was running the annual meeting of Occidental Petroleum Corporation in his usual velvet-fisted manner. Shortly thereafter he flew in his personal Occidental luxury airplane to Moscow, where he met with Soviet leader Leonid Brezhnev. Louis Nizer, Hammer's lawyer, called his client's recovery "a miracle."
>
> Twelve years later, Armand Hammer celebrated his ninetieth birthday with gala parties on five continents.

No matter the type of article, good leads all have a common denominator: They move readers seamlessly through the article by making them eager to know what is going to happen (tension), then taking them along for a fascinating ride to the end (resolution).

≫ 74

MAKE YOUR OPINIONS COUNT

BY RON BEATHARD

THE RESPECTED NEWSPAPER TRADITION OF PROVIDING AN OPEN FO-
rum for ideas, opinions, and commentaries can mean a sale for you.
For the op-ed page, which runs opposite a newspaper's editorial page,
editors are looking for serious, fact-filled opinion pieces on local, national, and world issues, and informal, even humorous, personal essays. It's a writing opportunity with few constraints: No editor stands
over your shoulder, red pencil in hand, deleting with the remark,
"That's editorializing!" Of course it is; that's why you are writing it.
Your op-ed piece is your letter to the world.

There is strong competition from syndicated columnists and recognized authorities who cover the Big Topics of the Week—health care,
foreign relations, Supreme Court decisions, and scientific and technical
subjects (the ozone layer, space exploration, and economics)—but
there is a niche for you.

Op-ed writing is a stimulating challenge. Within a short space you
have to grab and hold the reader's attention, make your arguments
cogent, your writing style forceful, and leave the reader thinking—not
an effortless task, but certainly a rewarding one. In addition, writing
op-eds is an efficient use of your writing time. Articles are short, averaging 600 to 900 words. (Every word counts; no puffery here.) Although all your facts and quotes must be carefully documented, lengthy
research is not required, interviews are usually not needed, and the
editor provides whatever artwork is necessary to accompany your article.

Choosing subjects to write about is difficult, not because there are
few, but because there are so many. From heavy and serious questions
of global significance to warm and friendly themes, the field is limited
only by your imagination.

Make a list of all the areas in which you are knowledgeable or experienced. (You'll be surprised how many there are.) Determine what the reader wants and needs to know about the subject—facts, details, opinions, and experiences—then add your perspective and viewpoint. Use the writing style that best fits the tone and subject of your piece: formal or informal, journalistic or descriptive.

Write about the local angle of a national issue. What will be the consequences of a Congressional bill on your school district? How do government health policies influence the economics of your community? Should a military installation near your town be closed?

Describe your thoughts and observations about a season or holiday, the first day of school, or vacation recollections—everyday topics to which you can add a special touch. Your personal essay can be warm and entertaining, light and humorous, or serious and provocative. Editors are looking for material that is different from traditional syndicated columns.

One advantage you have over national columnists is that you can write on subjects of local interest and history. What is the impact of a local factory closing? Does the community need that new bond issue? Why is it important for your town to preserve its historical heritage, and what is the most desirable and feasible way to bring it about?

Use your personal experience. You are a scout leader; how does scouting have to change to meet the problems and needs of today's youth? If trees and flowers are among your interests, how do they affect the environment? If you do volunteer work at the hospital, how has the role of volunteers changed as a result of new medical practices?

Draw on your professional experience. As an English teacher, state your views on why Americans can't spell. As a pharmacist, write about your role and relation to the consumer, or your thoughts on the health care crisis. As a librarian, discuss the impact of illiteracy in the United States, and the effect of new technologies on Americans' reading habits.

Use a spinoff as a start-up. Perhaps you have written a major magazine article, so your interviews, research, and notes are completed. Take this background information, condense the facts and details, add your thoughts and observations, and you'll have an op-ed piece.

In general, editors believe strongly in and have a deep commitment to the First Amendment. They want to provide opportunities for discussion of controversial subjects on their op-ed pages, with solid opinion and viewpoints based on clear reason—not the "I've-got-something-to-get-off-my-chest" approach. (That's for the letters column.) Because many controversial subjects—abortion, gun control, health reform—are popular with both readers and writers, an editor may be overstocked, so query first.

Choose a subject that is timely, yet has a long shelf life. Today's front-page story may be old news by the time your article hits the editor's desk. Because many editors publish op-ed pieces on a space-available basis, it may be weeks or even months before your article is published.

As you read newspapers and magazines, be alert for both light and serious short items and news anecdotes that could spark an idea for an op-ed article. Start a file.

There are more than 9,000 daily and weekly newspapers in the United States, and marketing your articles to the right paper requires a little research. Read the op-ed pages of as many papers as you can. Many editors outline their free-lance or guest-column policies on the op-ed page and are anxious to publish well-written, thought-provoking articles.

Unless you have a specific question for the editor—subject matter, payment, rights, etc.—a query letter is not necessary. A cover letter should accompany your article, stating your qualifications if the subject is scholarly or technical, citing sources if appropriate, and listing your previous credits.

Payment varies—small local papers may pay nothing; major city dailies, $100 or more—and is usually made on publication.

Some editors prefer that a writer live in the paper's circulation area; others may want to buy exclusive rights, or will allow you to resell your article outside the paper's circulation area. Since editorial policies differ, query first if you have any questions or concerns.

Writing op-ed articles requires clarity, brevity, and succinctness—qualities that can improve *any* of your writing.

349

≫ 75

THE BUSINESS OF WRITING ABOUT BUSINESS

BY CHRISTINE M. GOLDBECK

WALL STREET REPORTERS AREN'T THE ONLY WRITERS MAKING MONEY from the business community. Most business journals and regional weekly or monthly publications dealing with issues and information important to business people depend on free-lance writers, and pay well for the articles they receive or assign.

Step one to breaking into this market is to tell yourself that business is not intimidating or boring. That you aren't an M. B. A., that you flunked high school economics, that you don't know the difference between a mutual fund and a certificate of deposit—none of this really matters. The business community is not an ogre, and all business people are not stuffed shirts who are too busy with the bottom line to talk about their industry or their enterprise. Nor is business writing non-creative and rigidly routine.

In fact, many business owners and operators like to share their expertise and experiences. So, not only will you get bylines and make money writing about business, you will learn a lot.

Call the local Chamber of Commerce or any other business support agency to inquire whether there is a business journal published in your area, and check your newspaper to see whether it has a business page. Bigger daily papers usually run such a page in each issue. Smaller dailies often publish a business page on a weekly basis.

Business story subjects run the gamut: new businesses, profiles of business people, the grand opening of a business, a store reopening a year after it was destroyed by fire, trends in an industry, affirmative action contracts, a bankrupt bagel shop, a new product sold in the area, college bookstores selling quarts of milk for continuing education students . . . as long as it relates to doing business and you can write it for business people, you're in.

A newspaper editor will want samples of your published works in order to assess your ability to write interesting business copy. Business journals usually have writer's guidelines and on request, will mail them to you, along with a sample issue. Therefore, that byline might be but a telephone call to an editor away.

Let's say you've received a go-ahead from a business editor on an article about a business in your community. Now what?

You will of course want to set up an appointment to interview the owner, and to be prepared for that interview by learning something about him or her, the company, and the industry. Your local community library, as well as area university libraries, are great places to obtain information on the businesses and types of industries in the area. Take time to familiarize yourself with all the information that is available.

These are some of the references you should consult for background information on a company or a business executive:

• **Annual reports.** A public company's annual report contains helpful information (in addition to the stuff they write for stockholders). Look for statistics that reveal financial information about the company.

• **Trade journals** (magazines and newspapers devoted to a specific industry)

• **Local chambers of commerce and business associations.** Staffs at such agencies are usually good about giving you some information about their member companies, many of which are small- to medium-size private enterprises. So, if you need to know the identity of the president of Aunt Mabel's Meatballs, call the Chamber of Commerce nearest to the location of the business.

• **Commercial on-line services, the Internet, and the World Wide Web.** Here you'll find a wealth of information about industry trends and specific companies and business leaders. (For a recent piece on how high paper prices are affecting profit in a number of industries, I went to an on-line newsstand, searched under the key words "paper," "costs," and "paper prices," and got more information than I was able to use. But, it certainly gave me a lot of background, which I used to formulate questions for my interviews.) Dun & Bradstreet and other business references can also be contacted via the Internet.

Like a typical newspaper or magazine article, a business feature is built on the five Ws (*who, what, where, when,* and *why*—and don't forget *how*), answering such questions as:

351

What is the business: What does it make or what services does it provide for sale? Where is it located? How long has the company been in business? How does it market its product or service?

Once you have that vital information, you will need to focus on the people who run the business, asking every interviewee from whom you need information the following kinds of questions:

• What is your business strategy?
• How are you marketing your product?
• How much did you invest to start the business? Did you get loans, and if so, what kind?
• Who is your competition and how do you try to stay ahead of them?
• How much do you charge for your product?
• Is this a sole proprietorship, a privately held company, or a public operation?
• What are your annual sales?
• How many employees do you have?

Let's say you're going to write about your neighbor who makes meatballs and sells them to local supermarkets. If your piece is for a mainstream newspaper, the editor will probably instruct you to take what is called a "general assignment approach," which simply means you will have to use a style the average newspaper reader will understand and find satisfying. You won't use business lingo, and you will find something interesting, even homey, about your subject or topic and center your story on that specific point.

You will ask your subject how, when, and where she got started, why she wanted to sell her meatballs, and what made her think this business could be profitable. What did she do before making meatballs?

Your lead might read:

Up to her elbows in ground beef, Susan Tucker fondly recalls the times she and her Aunt Mabel made meatballs for the Saint Mary's Church socials. A year ago, Tucker gave up her 7-to-3 job sewing collars on coats to sell "Aunt Mabel's Meatballs." "Too bad Mabel isn't here to see how good business has been," she says.

This type of human interest piece, extolling personal success, the local church, and good old Aunt Mabel, sells mainstream newspapers.

If your piece is for a business journal, you'll need to handle it a little differently, since you are writing for a different audience—business people.

Something like this might work:

An Olive County businesswoman last year used a recipe for homemade meatballs to launch a business that currently employs ten people. Susan Tucker, the owner of Aunt Mabel's Meatballs, started the business in the kitchen of her Brownsville home. Within six months, she had made enough money to purchase and renovate an old restaurant located in Brownsville's commercial district, where she and her employees now make meatballs for wholesale and retail sales. They package and ship their product to a number of supermarkets and restaurants in the region and sell hot meatball hoagies to downtown shoppers, as well.

"I started out making and selling meatballs wholesale to places like Acme Market and Joe's Spaghetti House," Tucker says. "After we moved into this building, I thought it would be a good idea to sell the product retail, so I started selling sandwiches and fresh meatballs from here. That proved to be a good decision, too."

Tucker invested no capital when she launched the business. She says there was little overhead cost, and she quickly recouped what she paid for beef, eggs, and the other ingredients by selling the meatballs for $2.99 per pound.

See the difference? It's the same story, but tailored for a different readership.

This method of getting the information and writing a business journal piece can be used for any type of business or industry. Here's another example, using a service industry executive as the source:

The president of Bridgetown Health Services Inc. says his company now sells medical insurance to small businesses that have fewer than five employees. Owen Johnson says that the small business health plan was created in order to stay competitive in the ever-evolving health industry. The new policy was put on the market October 1, and within two months, the company had signed up 500 small businesses.

"There are major competitors trying to break into this marketplace. We wanted to get a jump on them. By selling our 'Small Business Health Plan,' we believe we have entrenched ourselves in the Northeast Pennsylvania medical insurance field," Johnson said. "It proved to be a good business decision."

Reporting on business is not difficult when you know your subject, get the vital information, then ask those extra questions specific to doing business in a particular field. If you were writing a piece about a fire, a murder, a local church yard sale, a visit from the Pope, you would ask questions specific to that event or person. This is really all

353

you will do in business writing: You will write the story so that your readers—business people—will be informed and entertained. Also, you'll build up your publication credits, make new contacts, and learn interesting things about the people in your area.

Reference materials I recommend and which you may want to have on hand include *The Associated Press Stylebook and Libel Manual,* which contains a section on business writing, and *BusinessSpeak,* compiled by Dick Schaaf and Margaret Kaeter (Warner Books). Both should be available through a local bookstore or in a good public or business library.

Trade groups with information about business journals include the Association of Area Business Publications, 5820 Wilshire Blvd., Suite 500, Los Angeles, CA 90036, (213) 937-5514, and The Network of City Business Journals, 128 S. Tryon St., Suite 2350, Charlotte, NC 28202, (800) 433-4565.

There are also professional societies for business writers. Write the Society of American Business Editors and Writers, P. O. Box 838, Columbia, MO 65205, or the American Business Press, 675 Third Ave., Suite 415, New York, NY 10017.

➤➤ 76

AT LEAST TWO SIDES TO EVERY STORY

BY HARRIET WEBSTER

IMAGINE THIRTY CARRIER PIGEONS WINGING THROUGH THE UNIVERSE, each one looking for a congenial place to nest. That's how I envision my queries—a flock of message-bearing birds searching for just the right homes.

I support myself as a full-time free lancer, and I've discovered that in order always to have enough work, I need to keep 25–30 queries in circulation all the time, and to produce fresh ideas continually. That's not such a problem since I embraced what I call the at-least-two-sides-to-every-story approach, which basically involves treating one subject from several angles. It's a great way to refuel and increase the number of queries you have in circulation and consequently the number of positive responses you get back. You may not be able to locate a publication that wants to run your feature story on that fantastic children's museum you visited, but perhaps an editor will take the bait when you suggest a piece describing ten great children's museums across the country.

The more well-crafted queries you submit, the more likely you are to catch an editor's interest. By looking at your article idea through the prism of your imagination, you'll soon find you can generate several proposals from what began as a single subject. Ideally, your inquiries will result in an assignment or an encouraging although less committed "go ahead." Don't turn away if, as frequently happens, you are asked to do the piece on speculation—that is, when an editor expresses interest in seeing your article but does not make a firm commitment to publish it.

I've found that an important key to getting solid assignments is putting together clips of your published work to show editors the quality of writing you can do. In the best scenario, by writing on spec you will produce a published piece as evidence of your competence, which will lead to a productive working relationship with a satisfied editor who may publish more of your articles down the road. Beginning writers who refuse to work on spec are in effect slamming the door in their own faces. The truth is that there's a speculation aspect to any piece, even if it's assigned. After seeing one of your queries, an editor may ask you to write a specific piece based on it, but that doesn't mean he has to publish it. If he does not accept it, he may pay what is called a "kill fee" (usually no more than 25% of the previously agreed upon price), assuming that the publication does in fact pay "kill fees." Many publications do not.

Now, after nearly 25 years of free-lancing, most of my work is assigned. However, I still write an occasional piece on spec, usually when I want to break into a new publication and an editor there says to go ahead with the article even though he isn't willing to make a commitment in advance to buy it. I know that, having expressed interest, he will give my piece a thorough reading, particularly if I deliver it in a reasonable length of time, while it's still fresh in his memory.

Looking at one subject from several angles and fashioning several queries around it helps me get moving when I'm stuck for ideas and enables me to query several different publications at the same time. While one editor may be willing to assign a piece on one aspect of my subject, another might express interest in a different approach, on spec. For a couple of years now, I've wanted to write an article about adult sibling relationships, particularly between sisters and brothers. I still haven't found an interested editor, but I did get a go-ahead on a related piece, one centered on a new bride's relationship with her husband's siblings. *Bride's Magazine* accepted it.

Sometimes the fresh perspective comes from a magazine editor. If you're willing to envision the subject you've proposed through someone else's eyes, you may be able to place your manuscript. I queried *Family Circle* about a piece profiling a mother-daughter housecleaning business. Though the editors weren't interested in that angle, they asked me if I would interview the mother and daughter to get their hints for the magazine's annual spring cleaning feature.

Here are some other ways to use the at least-two-sides-to-every-story approach to boost your queries and, ultimately, your sales.

356

1. *Individualize your queries.* Personally disorganized, I used to worry that I'd pass my bad habits on to my children. To help me figure out ways to keep that from happening, I developed a piece for *Working Mother* on how to teach your child organizational skills. In the course of doing that, I also suggested a piece to *Seventeen* showing teens how to organize their time. The magazine took it.

The point is this: Ideas are adaptable. If you want to do a piece on how to create kitchen storage space for a home magazine, why not also submit a query to a craft magazine on storage options for a basement workroom? Or, a parenting publication might be interested in a piece on how to solve storage problems in a child's room.

2. *Vary the point of view.* To write about a magnificent new playground built by volunteers, why not write one query homing in on a key figure—perhaps a teenager or a group of teens who immersed themselves in the project. Then write another suggesting a piece from the point of view of the school principal or adults in the community who spearheaded the project.

I was fortunate enough to sell a piece on peer education to *Better Homes & Gardens* (how to start a program in your child's school) and another to *Seventeen* (focusing on some teenagers involved in such a program). The first piece was heavy on advice from guidance counselors and school administrators, while the second relied on the voices of teenagers who have been involved in such a program.

3. *Approach varied markets.* Let's say your child is an avid soccer fan and you want to write about soccer. Query a sports magazine about a piece on the enormous growth of the sport nationally. Try a parenting magazine with a query on what makes a good coach; what to do when parents act like poor sports; what it feels like to be a soccer parent (spending your weekends freezing your toes at remote fields). Then pitch an article on safety considerations in soccer to a health publication and a consumer-oriented piece to a newspaper sports section in which you focus on the type of equipment needed and how to buy it at bargain prices.

4. *Experiment with opposites.* Suppose you are interested in writing a human-interest piece about a single woman who adopted a baby

357

from China. You envision a warm, heartfelt article that chronicles her feelings from the moment the agency called and asked if she was interested in the little girl, right up to the present. You send your query off to the lifestyle section of a number of newspapers and also submit it to several women's magazines. Have you covered all the possible markets? Perhaps not.

How about writing a second query that deals with the problems single women encounter when they try to adopt a child? Or perhaps you could suggest a piece about the frustrations involved in international adoptions. By proposing an article targeting the *problems* involved, as well as one describing a successful *experience,* you'll multiply your number of queries.

5. *Take your specialty apart.* The idea here is to take your main idea and turn it inside out. Interested in travel writing? Find out what kinds of travel pieces various publications run. Flip through a few issues and note the titles that intrigue you. Also check the features and departments and even the ads. You may find that in addition to destination pieces, a magazine runs personality and business profiles, and features on food, sports, shopping, museums, environmental issues, celebrations, and dozens of other subjects.

When I visited Colorado with my teen-age son, I figured I might be able to sell a travel piece about our trip. I was delighted when *The Boston Globe* assigned one on Glenwood Springs, a town we discovered by mistake and loved. And I was also able to expand my sales by writing several special-interest queries. Out of these, *FamilyFun* bought a first-person essay describing what it felt like to watch my son undertake his first serious rock-climbing experience.

I'm still circulating a query describing our experiences camping and hiking in Rocky Mountain National Park. I'm also thinking of querying a magazine that does an annual roundup of family-friendly resorts to see if they might be interested in a short piece about a splendid Victorian era hotel we visited.

6. *Big picture, little picture.* If you are an avid researcher, you may well find yourself feeling frustrated when, in the course of preparing a query for a piece, you collect tons of exciting material that doesn't fit into the article you're planning to write. Don't let the leftover material

go to waste. I once wrote a piece for *Americana Magazine* describing the technique used by guides at the Plimouth Plantation, a Massachusetts living history museum, to bring visitors into the lives of the people who lived in the village in the 17th century: Each of the guides plays the role of a specific individual who inhabited the plantation.

I was so fascinated by it that by the time I'd finished writing it, I had a great deal of material that I just couldn't fit in. In particular, I wanted to write about the reenactment of a Wampanoag Indian wedding ceremony I had attended. It turned out the reenactment is held several times a year, so I was able to work up a "weekender" piece for *Newsday,* a Long Island, NY, newspaper with a Sunday travel section that usually features a timely event or activity within a day's drive of the city.

Another possible approach is to write a query geared to a local publication and then to expand it to create a version appropriate for a regional or national magazine or newspaper. The moral of the story is that looking at both the big picture and the little picture is a great way to increase your query inventory.

By increasing the number of proposals you submit and the number and types of publications you submit them to—ranging from well-known national magazines to regional periodicals, from special-interest magazines to trade journals to newspapers—you up your chances of finding editors who will encourage you and may eventually publish your work. By looking at your ideas from many different angles, you will discover that you need never run out of material for intriguing queries.

Ideas are waiting to be discovered by article writers every day. Remember that "conversation" you had with your daughter this morning as she ran out the door to catch the school bus without taking time for breakfast . . . again? Parents all over the country can identify with that. What kinds of queries can you generate from it? A piece on teenage nutrition issues. An article focusing on how skipping breakfast affects school performance. A food piece listing ready-to-grab-and-eat-on-the-run nutritious breakfasts for kids. A first-person piece about the difficulty of letting go as your child verges on adulthood and makes her own sometimes dubious decisions. A nostalgic piece on eating breakfast with the kids when they were little. Whom will you interview? Nutritionists, teachers, teens, other parents, a pediatrician. . . .

359

Where will you send the queries? Health and parenting publications, magazines for young women, op-ed pages. . . . Soon you'll find yourself armed with a substantial batch of queries ready to circulate. With patience, perseverance, and a pinch of good luck, some of them will find good markets.

➤➤ 77

WRITING THE FAMILIAR ESSAY

By Sharon Hunt

As a student in public school in the 1960s, I struggled through essays as dry and unappealing as the secret notes my best friend and I ate before the teacher could read them.

As a writing tutor in college in the 1980s, I struggled through equally dry and unappealing essays written by electronics students who never attended an English class.

Later, as a literary journal editor, I cringed when essays arrived in the mail, and buried them at the bottom of my reading pile. When I could no longer procrastinate, I was often happily surprised by the essays I read. Gone were the dry offerings of seventh graders and future electronics wizards. In their place were essays of such passion I began putting new arrivals at the top of the pile and soon began writing my own.

I hadn't realized earlier what a pleasure familiar essays could be, and how popular they were—and continue to be. They are regularly found in such magazines as *Harper's, The Atlantic Monthly,* and *The New Yorker,* as well as many other publications; in *The New York Times* and a host of other daily and weekly newspapers; and in literary journals and anthologies.

One of the advantages of being an essayist is the range of available—and salable—subject matter. You can write about anything: the seasons, holidays, favorite places; children, parents, companions, and friends; all aspects of life. I pick subjects I feel passionately about. Without that passion, you can't expect to evoke it, or other emotions, in a reader.

Whatever the subject, before I begin to write, I set aside time to think about it. During this germination period, I draw on the journal I keep, a simple, battered notebook that goes everywhere with me.

When lines of conversation or description come to me, I write them down immediately, under a suitable heading. If I don't, I may not recall them later. My working journal also holds essay ideas and research leads (if the topic requires it). In my journal, I also carry on a conversation with myself about the tone or style I want to use in the essay.

In writing essays, I'm very conscious of style, which is a vital part of a familiar essay. Not only does style reflect the writer's distinctive view of a subject, it can also help get specific emotional responses from a reader. If your style is inappropriate for your subject, you won't get the reader response you hoped for. An essay about a debilitating illness, for example, will not evoke reader sympathy if your style is flippant or irreverent. Humor in many instances may backfire, yet in others may work beautifully. If you're uncertain about the right style for an essay, try writing the first page in a couple of different styles, then compare them.

Also, compare the possible voices for writing your essay. Should it be written in the third person, with that omnipotent narrator? Or is the first person, presenting the writer's point of view, a better choice? If you're not sure about which to use, experiment until you find the right one.

I enjoy writing in the first-person voice and find it helpful to imagine I'm carrying on a conversation with someone special as I write. In an essay about my father, entitled "Tell Me," I begin:

Tell me about being a boy in Newfoundland, about going out into the middle of the Atlantic with those fishermen with paws for hands and you not even able to swim.
Tell me about the Lady in White and Mummers at Christmas, ghosts and the women who jumped off the cliff, their purple-blue bodies cradling the rocks that broke them.

Two additional "tell me" paragraphs complete an opening sequence meant to do two things: First, it sets the tone of an inquisitive child wanting to know all about her father before he became her father. Second, this sequence catches readers' attention quickly by offering them a variety of possible story lines. This variety, although narrowed to the limits of essay length, makes readers curious, makes them want to go on reading.

A question or series of questions or a tantalizing or startling fact at

362

the beginning of an essay can also attract readers, as can stating your subject immediately. For example, in an essay for a local newspaper, I wrote:

> I've been saving to buy a piece of land. Just an acre or two; I'm not a greedy person.

Here, there is no doubt about the subject of the essay.

Use short story techniques throughout an essay to keep your readers reading. One of my favorites is selective use of description. In "Tell Me," my father recounted a tragic ferry accident that killed many neighbors and friends. Instead of describing the entire tragedy and focusing on how many were killed and how long it took the ferry to sink, I described incidents following the tragedy:

> . . . barrels of apples floated up on the beach later; someone found a little girl's dress with the price tag still on it.

These selective details give the tragedy a more human dimension. Images of apples meant for a winter's baking, and a child's new dress, never to be worn, emphasize the uncertainty that greets us each day and connects us as human beings. Such connections strengthen an essay and a reader's response to it.

Dialogue can also hold a reader's attention if it sounds real but doesn't have all the real pauses and repetitions that often characterize everyday speech. How can you create such dialogue? Ask yourself if all the "huhs" and "ahs" in the dialogue you've written are necessary to make the person "real," or if they only slow the reader down and add no insight into the person's character. If you feel you can delete such interruptions, do, then read the dialogue aloud. Does it sound real? If it does, you have stayed true to the person's character while removing digressions.

Using anecdotes in an essay gives you an opportunity to "show" rather than "tell," and varying sentence lengths will help create different moods. A reflective essay will benefit from longer sentences, which give a thoughtful quality to the work. On the other hand, short sentences give the work a sense of immediacy. "Tell Me" has a mixture of both. When writing of my father as a teenager, I used sentences like these:

My father could fight. Two stronger, wilder brothers ensured that.

Later, when he and many of the community's men lost their jobs and way of life, longer sentences helped emphasize that more reflective time in his life.

> Then the Company closed the mine and put most of the island's men, including my father, out of work for the first time in their lives. The Company closed the mine and changed the island from a thriving community where people painted their houses in the spring and went visiting in the summer to a place mired in government dependence.

Don't overlook the different effects unconventional capitalization and punctuation (or the lack of it) can have. In the above example, I capitalized "Company" to stress the importance of this mining operation to my father's community. Whenever "Company" is mentioned in the essay, it's preceded by "the," further emphasizing its importance. Also, in the second sentence in that example, I didn't use any commas, wanting to give readers a sense of what the people affected felt. *They* had no time to pause, to take a breath and consider their next step. Without the pauses commas allow, readers have to move through that sentence without a pause to stop and reflect, until the sentence is finished.

Finishing a thought or paragraph in an essay requires a transition to the next. A smooth transition greatly improves the flow of an essay, so readers relate ideas to each other without losing the continuity.

Transitional words such as "first," "second," "earlier," "later," "now," and "before" can provide this smooth flow, as can sentence arrangement and word order. "Tell me" repeated at the beginning of the first four paragraphs of my essay is an example of the use of word order to move easily from thought to thought. Another way to accomplish this is to arrange information so that the item mentioned last in one paragraph is mentioned again at the beginning of the next. An essay I wrote about female mentors gave me an opportunity to do this.

> There are absolutes in her life. Honesty. Love. Belief. A helping hand.
> That hand has often been extended to me . . .

A short paragraph ends with the image of a helping hand, while the next continues and expands on that image.

One of the pluses of a familiar essay is the denouement, the point at which the essay's various thoughts are tied together to make it stand for something beyond selective description and realistic dialogue; interesting anecdotes and varying sentence lengths; omitted commas and unnecessary capital letters. In my land-hungry essay, the denouement comes near the end. After talking about the kind of land I'd like to buy and where that land might be, I explain my real urge to be a land owner:

I'll wallow in the delight of this being mine to take care of for a while.

Tips for Writing and Marketing Familiar Essays

• Every essay benefits from rewriting until the purpose and flow you want have been achieved.

• Read each essay aloud. Can you follow its logic easily? If not, clarify so that a reader will not be left behind.

• Be sensitive to any possible embarrassment and resentment when writing about relatives or friends.

• Local weeklies or small dailies are good places to start submitting your essays.

• Suggest a regular column to the editor of a local paper. Submit a selection of four to six essays of the same length (this varies depending on editorial requirements) to show you can deliver.

• Read essays in local and national magazines and newspapers to which you'd like to submit your essays. Study the style and subject matter. What is it about these essays that keeps you reading?

➢➢ 78

TRUE CRIME WRITING:
A DYNAMIC FIELD

BY PETER A. DEPREE

FEW GENRES IN JOURNALISM TODAY ARE AS EXCITING AND PROFITable as true crime, whether article or book. Although this piece focuses on the true crime article, many of the techniques and methods discussed in the following six steps are readily applicable to the true crime book.

STEP ONE: *Researching the field.* Buy several true crime magazines and spend a rainy afternoon getting a feel for the slant and depth of the articles. Jot down what you liked and didn't like about them. Then, dash off a request to the editorial office of one or two of the magazines for the writers guidelines (include the requisite SASE).

STEP TWO: *Finding a crime.* Visit your local library and look in the index of the biggest newspaper in your area under the heading Murder/ Manslaughter, going back about four years, and photocopy those index pages. (Most crimes more than four or five years old are too stale to fit the slant of true detective magazines.) Highlight the crimes that seem most likely to make interesting true crime pieces. The few sentences describing each article will give you a good feel for the highlights of the case. Select about half a dozen cases that look promising. As you peruse them, you will whittle down the group for one reason or another until you're left with one or two that have all the elements you need for an effective true crime piece. Most detective magazine guidelines will help you narrow them down: The crime is always murder; the "perp" (police parlance for perpetrator) has been convicted; there was a substantial investigation leading to the arrest; the crime took place reasonably near your area (important, since you'll have to go to the court to gather research); and photos are available for illustration.

STEP THREE: *Doing the research.* First, with the index as a guide, collect all available newspaper articles on the crime you've selected so you can make an outline before reading the trial transcript. Your library should have either back issues or microfilm (provided you followed Step One and picked a case no more than four years old). If there are two or more newspapers in your area that covered the crime, get copies of all of them. Often, pertinent details were printed by one paper but not the other.

STEP FOUR: *Reading the trial transcript.* Call the clerk's office of the court where the trial took place and ask for the case number on the crime and whether the transcript is available to the public (it usually is). By now you should have a three- or four-page outline based on all the articles you've read. Take your outline and a lot of paper and pens to the courthouse, and be prepared to spend a whole day reading the trial record; even a trial that lasted only three or four days can fill several bound volumes. (When I was doing research for a book on the Nightstalker serial killer case in Los Angeles, the court record was 100,000 pages long and filled three shopping carts!) Skim and make notes of the quotes and material you'll need; this will be a lot easier if you've prepared your outline carefully, since you'll already know the key names to watch for—the lead detective, prosecutor, defense attorney, victim, witnesses, responding officer, and so forth. You'll need to look for material on several different levels simultaneously: details for accuracy, dramatic quotes, colorful background, etc. There will usually be far more of these elements than you could possibly pack into an article, so you have the luxury of choosing only the very best. You may discover a brand-new form of writing frustration when you have to slash all those dramatic prosecutorial summations and subplots down to the required word count.

Use whatever form of research you're comfortable with. I find a combination of scribbling notes in my own pseudo-shorthand and dictating into a hand-held recorder suits me. (Pack enough spare batteries and tapes!) I can mumble into my recorder faster than I can write. Having photocopies made at the court is usually prohibitively expensive, so copy very selectively. As a rule of thumb, the parts of a transcript that yield the most important factual information are the opening remarks of both attorneys; the questioning of the lead detective; the testimony of expert witnesses such as forensic technicians; and the summing up of both attorneys. A couple of tips: Dates are especially important, and so are names.

Almost as important as the transcript is the court file. Specify to the court clerk that you would like that as well as the transcript.

STEP FIVE: *Writing the article.* Reread the writers guidelines for the magazine to which you're submitting your piece, then write the kind of article *you* would find exciting and surprising (or shocking) to read. Chances are that if a particular detail, scene, or quote piques your interest, it belongs in your piece. Don't get lost in boring minutiae, but do remember that sprinkling in telling details seasons the piece and sharpens the focus.

If your detective used a K9 dog to search for evidence, you might mention that it was a Rottweiler named Butch, with a mangled ear. If the ballistics expert test-fired the gun, you could throw in that detail, noting that he fired it into a slab of gel, then retrieved the bullet and viewed it under a comparison microscope for tell-tale striations, and so on. The trial transcript is packed with details like these that make your article stand out from a "made-up" detective story.

As you're writing, watch your length. Editors are not impressed with articles that run a few thousand words over their suggested length.

STEP SIX: *Secondary wrap-up research.* True crime editors are picky about certain details, especially names (check those writers guidelines again!). If you mention "Mr. Gordon," you should specify that he is Commissioner John Gordon of the Gotham City Police Department. Change the names of witnesses or family members, for obvious reasons. Go back to the library to check the details that will give your writing authority. For instance, if the crime was committed with a shotgun and you don't know a pump-action from an over-&-under, you need to do some minor research to find out. If your crime involves DNA fingerprinting, you'll need to spend no more than an hour in the library to find enough useful facts to give your article a little snap. I recently wrote an article on a killer who was suffering from paranoid schizophrenia. In just four pages in two college psych textbooks—

twenty minutes' investment of my time—I came up with more than enough facts for my piece.

What to watch out for

There are at least four articles in my computer that are almost completely written, but went nowhere. Why? Because I made stupid, unnecessary mistakes—mistakes that *you* would never make if you follow a few simple rules. The following three are non-negotiable:

1) *Never start on an article without querying the magazine first.* Nothing is quite as frustrating as writing twenty detailed pages on the Longbow rapist, only to discover that Joe Bland already sold that piece to your target magazine a year ago. You now have a pile of perfectly good kindling.

2) *Always make doubly sure the trial transcript is available.* You should never have to invest more than one or two full days in researching the transcript and court file, but that doesn't help when on the day you need it you learn that the whole file was shipped five hundred miles away so the appeals judges could study it at their leisure. (We're talking *months* here.)

3) *Never start an article without making sure photos are available.* Etch this in stone. No true crime magazine will run an article without *at least* three photos. The minimum basics are a photo of the perp; one of the victim; one of the crime scene. These can be what I call "documentary-grade"; sometimes, even a particularly sharp photo clipped from a newspaper will suffice. But query your target magazine first, and always make sure the picture is in the public domain (i.e., a high school yearbook photo of the killer, a photo of the victim distributed to all the papers, a snapshot of the bank building where an armed robbery took place).

True crime writing might be called entry-level journalism. If you can write a tightly researched and entertaining piece following these suggestions, you'll have a better chance of success.

➤➤ 79

WRITING THE FEATURE ARTICLE

BY RITA BERMAN

THERE IS A GOOD STEADY MARKET FOR FEATURE ARTICLES. READERS are always looking for ways to improve themselves. Pick up any magazine at the newsstands. What do you see? Articles on how to cope with a teenager or a baby, make tasty meals in 30 minutes, take off ten pounds. How to live longer, happier, wealthier, understand and buy art, learn word processing, or—how to write. All of these feature articles are aimed directly at the reader.

The content of a feature article is more important than the author's name, so the unknown writer has as good an opportunity as the well-known one to have an article accepted, provided that the manuscript is well done and meets the editor's needs.

"Find facts that are new and known by few," an editor told me when I began my writing career. Sounds gimmicky, but it's good advice. Remember that a feature article focuses on the human-interest angle of facts, but this is not a hard and fast rule. Many feature articles are instructive or informational: how-to, how-I, or how-you. The principles of these how-tos (also known as service articles) are that you state the problem, offer a solution, and end with a result. Your advice must guide the readers through the steps taken so that they, too, can recreate your success. Other features are based on interviewing an expert or recognized authority in the field you wish to write about, then in your article, sharing their experiences and knowledge with the reader.

You must do a lot of thinking and planning, as well as gathering and organizing facts. You need to consider the subject of the article; how much readers will be interested in that subject; possible markets; sources that could provide ideas and facts; who might be interviewed for the article; and whether illustrations or photographs may be needed.

By the time you have collected notes, material, photographs, or illustrations, the article may be taking shape in your mind. Before writing your feature, organize your thoughts and material. Know what you want to put into your article, but don't try to keep it all in your head. *Use an outline to get started and stay on track.*

1. On your worksheet, write the working title, which could change after you've written the piece, or as you go along.

Titles are the bait you use to attract editors and readers. Most magazine titles rarely exceed six to eight words. A good title should suggest the contents and tone of the story. Titles cannot be copyrighted, but avoid using one that might be confused with a previously published piece.

2. Jot down a list of words, phrases, or sentences to remind you of all the items and points you wish to cover in your feature.

3. Decide what kind of lead to use to attract the reader:

The question lead: What can you do to get a million dollars?
The controversial statement: It's easy to get a million dollars.
The case history or anecdotal lead: I made my first million—the easy way.
A statement of fact: There are more millionaires than ever.
A descriptive lead: A million dollars in gold lay gleaming in the vault.

A strong lead is crucial in feature writing because this is what draws the reader into the article, and immediately after the lead, you proceed in a way that will sustain that reader's interest and provide the reason or justification for your lead.

This transition from the lead to the text is sometimes referred to as the bridge, hook, angle, or peg of the story.

Example: For one feature, "How We Sold Our Home" (published in *Army, Navy, Air Force Times*), I used a grabber lead about military families being familiar with change-of-station orders, and how we had led a nomadic existence for 12 years.

4. After your lead, what kind of bridge will you use to hold readers' interest?

In my feature, a paragraph stating that about 7 million homes change hands each year provided the bridge; the rest of the piece was my personal story. I involved the readers by informing them that selling our house without using a real estate broker saved us thousands of dollars. That was my response to the reader's natural "what's in it for me?" question. No matter what the subject—going on a cruise, or trying to avoid paying more taxes—readers always ask, "What's in it for me?"

5. The body of your piece. What anecdotes, examples, or facts will you use to prove the point you want to make? For a how-to piece this is where you will describe the pitfalls, things that didn't work, as well as tips that will lead to a satisfactory conclusion.

I continued my home sale feature by describing a few simple steps that should be followed when selling without an agent. Then I was off into the body of the story, repeating and expanding the reasons for selling the house ourselves, and describing how we did it: preparing the house and grounds; pricing the house realistically; and how we saved time and money when we conducted the sale.

6. The conclusion. A final strong paragraph should wrap it all up effectively for the reader.

My last paragraph for "How We Sold Our Home" echoed my lead by referring to military families and their nomadic way of life. This helped reinforce the message to the military readers of *Army, Navy, Air Force Times* that they too might be moving and selling a house sometime in the future.

Do not try to write any of the sections in final form at this stage. The outline should be used as a guide to prompt the flow of thoughts and to keep you moving in the right direction. It will be particularly helpful if for any reason you have to put the article aside.

Writing the rough draft

With the outline to guide you, you will be ready to begin writing your feature. Write directly and simply, as if talking to your readers. Short paragraphs. Write to be understood, not to impress. As your piece begins to take shape, you will have to consider what transitions are needed to take the reader from example to example, and how you will tie the whole thing together. Keep the feature story flowing toward a strong closing paragraph to balance the hard-hitting lead.

Use subheads and a blurb so that readers can grasp the main idea quickly. A blurb is a summary of what the article is about. You need to know this yourself in order to write the feature. If you are unable to compress the scope of the feature into a sentence or two, perhaps you need to think about it some more.

For informational articles, sidebars and boxes keep the article tight and give it impact. In "How We Sold Our Home" I included a box headed "What do real estate terms mean?" listing key words and definitions such as *appraisal, closing costs, earnest money.*

Tell the reader how and where to get more information on the topic, including addresses and phone numbers, if available. If the how-to was based on interviews, give your sources credit for their remarks.

Accuracy is essential in how-to articles, so recheck your facts before you send out the manuscript.

Revision

You should spend almost as much time on revising and rewriting as you spent on thinking, planning, and writing your rough draft. Are the points in good logical order? The best possible words? It's fun to cross out words you have written and substitute new ones that are clearer and give sharper meaning to your story.

If a sentence sounds awkward on rereading, rephrase it. Chop a long sentence into two. Write in simple sentences rather than long, compound or complex ones.

Allow some time to elapse between the first and second draft. If I wait for a day or two, sentences or sections that need reworking seem to leap off the page. Try to read the article aloud, or better still, tape it. Listening to your words will uncover writing weaknesses.

Write to space

The only way you can cut a feature, if it ends up being too long, is to prune throughout. An alternative is to write to space from the outset. Do this by assigning a specific number of words to each section of your outline. As a guide, for a 1,500-word piece you might allot 50 words for the introduction, 150 words for the bridge, 1,200 words for the body of the piece, and 100 words for the conclusion. An average page of typing contains 250 words (25 lines of 10 words), so 1,500 words should run approximately six pages.

Getting the feature published

The usual publication outlet for features is in the monthly or quarterly magazines, thousands of which are published in all regions of the country. New magazines hit the newsstands every month, and the old ones change their formats. In addition, magazines sold by subscription only also have a constant need for steady, reliable writers who can write interesting features. Names and addresses of consumer, special interest, trade, and a host of other magazines can be found in the back of this book; select the best possible markets for your feature.

Many listings request that writers query instead of submitting a completed manuscript. By querying, you find out if—and where—there is interest in your piece. Make a list of markets to query, and send for writers guidelines before you write your query letter. Guidelines provide information on topics that are wanted, word length, preferred submission format, whether photographs are needed, the rights bought, pay scale, and other useful information about editorial needs.

Select one publication and submit a query letter. If you draw a negative response, revise the letter and work your way through the market list. After you get a go-ahead from an editor, you can prepare the article to meet the magazine's editorial needs, and thus increase your chances of being published.

>> 80

BIOGRAPHER AT WORK

BY GALE E. CHRISTIANSON

THE BIOGRAPHER BONDS HIMSELF TO HIS SUBJECT IN A UNION MORE symbiotic than matrimony. Almost never are the two separated during the long months and years of their association, for dreams and night-mares are as much the stuff of writing lives as the countless hours passed in airless archives or mornings wrestling with the blank page.

Thus your subject must be a companion whose character faults, which magnify in the glare of intense scrutiny, are offset by accom-plishments sufficiently redeeming to override skepticism and assuage doubt. Such was the case for me with the great Isaac Newton, the subject of my first biography. Though mean-spirited and given to with-ering tirades against those who challenged his scientific ideas, the in-ventor of calculus, the mortal who flung gravity across the void, is forever woven into my tapestry of the blessed.

My feelings for Loren Eiseley, the anthropologist, literary naturalist, and author of some of this century's most elegant and evocative essays, are rather more ambivalent. While writing Eiseley's life, I was gradu-ally overwhelmed by his tendency to cast events in conspiratorial hues and to blame everyone but himself for his sufferings. To put it simply: Had I known what I was getting into with Eiseley, I think I would have passed.

Yet the biographer should also be cautious when his prospective subject seems too companionable. Identifying too closely with the subject violates the constraints essential to writing biography. Psy-choanalysts term this process "co-creation" or the "commingling of consciousness." Setting out to write the life of another, the biographer is actually carrying on an interior dialogue with himself, while plying his own emotional terrain.

After choosing a subject, the real work begins. Almost every serious biographer (we are not here concerned with so-called celebrity biographies or what I call tabloidism) must face the daunting prospect of burrowing deep into one or more archives. But it is well to complete as much background reading as possible before immersing yourself in the primary sources. Since it is not only unwise but impossible to attempt to include everything about a life, however important, the researcher must be selective. The late Barbara Tuchman characterized biography as a prism of history, while others have likened it to fine portraiture. Leon Edel, best known for his multivolume life of Henry James, speaks of "the figure under the carpet," whose true identity can be resolved only by carefully scrutinizing the tea leaves of research. Whatever the method or the metaphor, the biographer must create a unique angle of vision by fitting keys to locks that yield only to the right questions.

Some biographers enter archives armed with little more than a pencil and a generous supply of 3″ by 5″ cards; others carry laptop computers whose clicking keyboards serve as a constant distraction to those with a sensitive ear. My preference is the portable archives made available via photocopying. With photocopies at one's fingertips, dates, quotations, and myriad other details can be rechecked as often as need be, thus minimizing the number of inadvertent errors that steal into a manuscript.

Moreover, the biographer's perspective is subject to change. This is especially true when dealing with letters, diaries, and notebooks, which may require several readings. Notes are inevitably incomplete and have a way of growing cold during the months or possibly years that may pass before the author returns to them.

But most important to me is that an exact copy recharges the atmosphere as the original did when I first viewed it in the archives. Photocopies are the catalysts of inspiration and of musing, and serve as a constant reminder of the responsibility one bears to one's subject.

Finally, the more quickly material is gathered the sooner one can return home. The costs of photocopying are but a fraction of what it takes to hole up in major cities, where archives tend to be found.

To my continual surprise, I am often asked if I research the *whole* life before I begin to write it. The answer is an emphatic "yes," for, to paraphrase Kierkegaard, a life must be lived forward but it can only be understood backward.

No writer can tell another when enough research is enough, when science must yield to art. This is a personal matter based on a hidden clock whose ticking is as individual as the human thumbprint. But one thing is certain: There will never be a book without writing, and without self-imposed deadlines, the writing will never begin.

To biographers of people who have only recently died, primary sources constitute more than words and images captured on paper. These include the house in which one's subject came into the world, and perhaps left it; the church in which he attended Sunday school; the neighborhood streets along which he bashfully walked hand in hand with his first love; and, if one is very lucky, the living memories of those who grew up with him and took his measure "way back when."

Interviewing friends, relatives, and colleagues of your subject is a tricky albeit rewarding business, best left until you are conversant with the archives. It is only at this point that the right questions can be asked. The web of memory is often very delicate, and responds most sympathetically when probed by a gentle and informed petitioner. And the more you address the same questions to various individuals, the sounder the process. Above all, listen. It is often the seemingly little things these people say that turn out to be the most important.

And what about writing the life of a living person? Having never done so, I can only say, *caveat emptor!* Since the life is not a finished thing, its telling will be superceded by future works based on a sounder perspective. Access to information may also be a problem, even if the subject is cooperative in the beginning. What is gladly given with one hand can be angrily snatched away by the other, especially if the subject's views and those of the biographer clash. With so many other wonderful subjects to choose from, why run the risk?

In her often cited account of Shakespeare's imagined sister, Virginia Woolf asserted that the writer must have "a room of one's own." What is true of the novelist and the poet is no less true of the biographer. "You must have a room, or a certain hour or so a day," wrote the mythographer Joseph Campbell, "where you don't know what was in the newspapers that morning, you don't know who your friends are, you don't know what you owe anybody, you don't know what anybody owes you." This is the place of creation where the writer brings forth what he or she is—and is to be.

Saturated with facts and documents, the writer confronts a ream of

377

blank pages. Do not be surprised or dispirited if nothing happens right away, for obviously a book never writes itself. Someone, presumably the author, must shape the narrative while deciding which details to retain or to cut, which gestures to play up or to play down, which lines to quote or to omit.

A biography can begin at any point in a subject's life, from birth to the deathbed, from the moment when lightning struck, to the transforming pain caused by the loss of a loved one. The tale begins by fitting one of those precious keys into a lock, turning it, and bidding the reader to enter. During my research on Loren Eiseley, for example, it became clear that he had idealized his father, an itinerant hardware salesman who reminded me of no one so much as Willy Loman. Thus the book begins with three-year-old Loren in the arms of Clyde Edwin Eiseley, gazing into the midnight sky of a chill and leafless Nebraska spring in 1910, an incident Loren recounted in an essay penned many years later. The two are transfixed by Halley's comet.

"If you live to be an old man," his father whispered, "you will see it again. It will come back in seventy-five years."

"Yes, Papa," the boy replied dutifully. Tightening his hold on his father's neck, he promised that when he grew old, he would gaze on the comet a second time and remember the person he would always care for more than any other.

Once you begin, set yourself a challenging yet reachable goal. Mine is some 1,000 words a day, the equivalent of about three typed pages. When the gods are kind, as happens on occasion, the total may double, but more often than not I fall a few paragraphs short. I also try to finish a day's writing at a point which will stimulate the creative flow the next morning, the psychological equivalent of priming the pump.

There is much to be gained by reading fine literature while trying to approximate it oneself. The genre does not matter: Novels and essays, short stories and narrative histories, poetry and plays all serve to deepen one's sensibilities.

Your actual voice can also help to locate your literary voice. At day's end, or night's if you are an owl, read your edited work back to yourself aloud. You will not find it easy to ignore dissonant sound waves. Take pleasure in selecting chapter titles as well as epigraphs, if you plan to use them. A copy of *Bartlett's Familiar Quotations* interleaved with scores of ragged markers is a positive sign that you are well on your way. As for the biography itself, keep in mind the fact that Hemingway had thirty titles in reserve, should his editor veto *For Whom the Bell Tolls*.

In time—if you have the determination and the talent—something will happen. You will experience one of those very special days when the narrative voice and the mind become one. It will not last; the days of the storm petrel must inevitably follow. Yet you will also find, when rereading your manuscript for the twentieth time, that you were not appreciably better on your best days than on your worst. Your mind has been operating at two levels, the one conscious but illusory, the other subconscious but real. You have subtly programmed yourself to remain within certain boundaries, both scholarly and aesthetic. You have found your own way of identifying with your subject, and mutual suspicion has yielded to trust. The pages, so pitifully few in the beginning, are piling up with satisfying regularity. You are a biographer.

➤➤ 81

Turn Your Travels into Sales

By Barbara Petoskey

Even if you have no interest in star ratings of hotels, there are many undiscovered opportunities for you to use your vacation or other out-of-town trips to increase your manuscript sales. Best of all you can capitalize on your experiences, whether you write nonfiction, fiction or poetry.

We're all familiar with the traditional travel piece, packed with food and lodging tips and a hearty dollop of local color. But there are many other ways to get extra mileage from your travel.

The facts

If you'd like to write just a brief piece about your journey without getting into "how to get there and where to stay," find a small niche market. Consider, for example:

- Annual events (such as the Garlic Festival/Gilroy, California)
- Historical events (battle of Tippecanoe/Indiana)
- Well-known people (Motown Records Museum/Detroit)
- Distinctive architecture (Baltimore rowhouses)
- A clustering of a particular art or business (Native American silver-smiths or Amish quiltmakers, antique malls or flea markets)
- Any regional specialty, sport, or style

Even an article that relies primarily on library research may benefit from in-person experience. For me, a half-day stop in Amherst, Massachusetts, on my way from Boston to Michigan enriched two differently focused biographical essays I wrote on Emily Dickinson: One sold to a literary magazine, the other to a book lover's newsletter.

Multiple slanting options abound. A tour of, say, Ernest Hemingway's home in Key West could yield salable pieces for fans of either literature or cats. And watch for the famous person in an unexpected spot: While we naturally link Samuel Clemens and Hannibal, Missouri, his final resting place is Elmira, New York, where he also wrote some of his finest novels. (Incidentally, his grave marker is "Two Fathoms"—or "mark twain"—high; could there be an article in that?)

When hunting for markets for these travel capsules, don't overlook regional, hobby, or trade publications. A magazine that wouldn't consider a standard travel piece may snap up an article about a place with a clever tie-in for its audience. So whether you choose to focus on the Trap Shooting Hall of Fame in Vandalia, Ohio, or the Tupperware Museum in Kissimmee, Florida, your mini-account of a place off the beaten track may capture an editor's imagination.

Facts plus

Fresh perceptions evoked by new surroundings can make travel the perfect springboard for the personal experience essay. Many magazines and newspaper Sunday supplements—a good weekly market—may buy such features if you have a unique story to tell, even if you're not a big-name byline. Only you can recount the unique experience of your drive to the Grand Canyon as a late-spring snowstorm howled out of the Rockies, or your reactions to visiting the village from which your ancestors came. I've turned twelve days in Maracaibo into three essays: Venezuelan cab drivers, celebrating Christmas in the tropics, and getting along in a foreign country whose language you don't know well. Also, consider writing an account of your unique situation: as a solo traveler after divorce; a visit to Disneyland *without* children or to Club Med *with* kids; travel using a wheelchair.

And don't overlook the absurd. The common denominator of most trips is something that goes wrong: That missed turn, lost key, or noisy hotel guest next door may provide you with anything from a humorous filler to a full-blown misadventure.

The flavor: fiction

Obviously, if you write fiction, your travels can provide you with authentic details to help you develop that vivid sense of place that pulls readers into your story. Scout sites for action: streets, landmarks, centers of activity. And, of course, such details must all be accurate. Just try writing that your heroine took the Lincoln Tunnel from Man-

381

hattan to Queens, and your credibility will plunge into the East River. (The Lincoln Tunnel goes to Jersey).

A good city map can give you the general geographic layout, so you'll want to watch for the unusual quirk, custom, or telling detail that captures the essence of the place or that can play a role in your fiction. When I set my comic-suspense short story "After Hours" in Chicago, I noted that "the lighted faces of the Tribune Tower clocks watched like eerie moons"—a point not featured in the average tourbook. While you don't have to go everywhere your characters do, if the events of your story or novel unfold in San Francisco, it can't hurt to have heard the clang of a cable car or your thumping heart as you scaled those hills.

Even if your fiction never mentions events that occurred before page one, the influence of the "backstory" on present action will help make your characters three-dimensional. Perhaps this shows up in a regional expression or taste or in a turn of phrase in your dialogue. If your Harvard-educated lawyer reveals her fondness for a breakfast of huevos rancheros, she may hint at Southwestern roots. Wherever you go, watch, listen, store it up, and jot it down. Such tidbits may later help define a character's personality.

The feeling: poetry

Travel broadens not only the mind, but stirs the soul as well. How can a poet fail to be touched by new sensations? Whether on a trip to the Great Wall or to your grandmother's house, your emotions and reactions may send you scrambling for paper.

Impressions come in all varieties. I've published descriptive poems about the New Orleans French Quarter, the rugged Oregon coast, and autumn in New England. I've also used an exotic place or experience as a metaphorical jumping-off point: the "fall" of returning from a brief get-away on an island aptly named Paradise; sensing kinship with a pair of dolphins sighted off a Gulf of Mexico beach. None of these poems would ever have come to me in my own backyard.

On site

Serendipity accounts for much of travel's pleasure. Whether you've pursued your plan or simply stumbled onto the unexpected, make notes for future writing; take photographs; pick up brochures, postcards, maps, newspapers, hotel "visitors' guides," matchbooks, or even those paper placemats found in mom-and-pop restaurants that highlight tourist attractions—anything that will help you later to recreate that local experience.

Also be sure to note:

• Food (local fruits and vegetables, spices, unusual preparation)
• Architecture (brick, frame, adobe, ranch-style, Cape Cod, high-rise)
• Fashions (conservative or trendy, formal or casual)
• Music (country, soul, reggae, jazz, bluegrass)
• Major ethnic influences (Asian, African, Scandinavian, Italian, Jewish)
• Regional words (*soda* vs. *pop*)
• Regional brands or store names
• Weather (sunny or cloudy, humid or dry)
• Vegetation, landscaping (deciduous, conifer, cactus, palm, fenced yards, no yards)

When you get back home, organize your notes and materials—by place, topic, plot, whatever works—so you don't find later that you "can't get there from here."

The next time you hit the road, for whatever reason, have a good time. Maybe soak up a little sun. And be sure to soak up some atmosphere to put into your writing.

383

➢➢ 82

WRITING FOR THE TRADES

BY MARY E. MAURER

THERE ARE THOUSANDS OF OPPORTUNITIES FOR WRITERS IN TRADE, technical, and professional journals. I stumbled upon the trade field quite by accident, when I agreed to write a profile about the business of a friend. Now half of my income is derived from trade magazines. These publications serve a readership united by occupation or industry, avocation or education. There are also many "trades" serving members of associations or unions.

Trade magazines typically carry business-related news of new products and trends, features on successful businesses and their owners or managers, and service pieces on solving management, employee, and/or customer problems. Within major occupations and industries, there are often magazines for specific aspects, such as marketing, buying, selling, design, production, and training.

Why write for the trades? It's an excellent way for you to hone your craft and be published regularly, thus building up your clip files. Writing for the trades also enables you to strengthen a relationship with an editor, since many have small staffs and are eager to find hard-working serious writers. Regular sales to the trades can provide you with a steady income; pay for trade articles averages $50 to $200 for 1,200 to 1,800 words.

Do you have what it takes? That depends on two things:

1. How serious are you about writing? Articles written for the trades are informative, instructional, technical; they are rarely just entertaining. That means your writing must be clear and focused for a specific purpose and audience.

2. Are you willing to become an "industry expert"? Writers wishing to break into the trade market need to have or develop a strong under-

standing of the occupation or industry. You *must* know your subject thoroughly.

To become a trade expert, first, examine your own profession or hobbies. What do you know? What skills do you have? What intrigues you? Next, look into the careers of friends or family members. Does anyone have an occupation you find fascinating? Consider your community. Is it rural or urban? Is your town or region famous for a particular product?

Next, review your current writing interests. Very often your *general* interests can be focused and developed so you can write for a trade publication in the same field. Interested in gardening? Become an expert in commercial gardening, and try to write for *GrowerTalks,* a publication catering to commercial greenhouse growers. Do you often write about health topics? Increase your knowledge of physical fitness, and aim a piece at *Fitness Management,* the magazine for commercial, corporate, and community fitness centers.

You may also want to specialize in a particular type of article: **profiles** (of successful owners, managers, businesses); **how to** (cut costs, increase production, stop shoplifters); **forecast** (technical trends, industry changes); **product reports** (what's new, what it does, and who is using it); **history** (profiles of those who helped shape the industry); and **health and safety** (tips on increasing worker productivity through healthy habits and accident prevention).

Once you decide on the area you wish to develop, you have several options. Of course, you'll do the kind of reading and research required for any article. However, for the trades you'll also need to follow those steps to become an "expert":

1. Develop contacts within the industry. Talk to people who are working in the trade. See how they work and ask them about their problems. Develop a list of technical people you can call on for information.

2. In addition to reading general magazines and books, read technical reports, manuals, and trade journals to determine where your knowledge fits into the "big picture" of the industry.

3. Attend trade shows and conferences related to your specialized field. You'll pick up useful information, see new products, meet new people.

4. Visit stores, manufacturing plants, farms, whatever is connected to your specialty.

Now you're ready to write, but you have to study the market. You *must* know and understand the trade journal readership: You can't fake it. Readers of trade publications have very specific expectations. A good list of selected trade magazines is included in this book, but you'll find the most extensive list in *Encyclopedia of Associations* (published by Gale Research), available in the reference department of most large public libraries. It lists trade, business, and commercial organizations, educational organizations, hobby and avocational organizations, and others. You'll find the name of the publication, address, year founded, circulation, size of staff, and other interesting bits of information.

You can sometimes find copies of trade publications at the library, as well as on large newsstands; if not, you can order sample copies. Study at least six different publications in your area of interest; read as many issues as you can. Begin by examining the contents. What is the purpose of the magazine? Study the style and format. Does the magazine use second or third person, active or passive voice? How is technical information offered? What about buzz words, jargon? Every occupation uses some "industry-specific" vocabulary. How does the magazine use graphics, photos? Read the advertising. What is being sold? Who is the target customer?

Write a brief letter of introduction to each editor, detailing your knowledge and background in the industry. Include your resumé and published clips, if they are pertinent. Ask for a copy of their writers guidelines and an editorial calendar if one is available.

Study the guidelines, and *follow* them. Write clearly, with your readers' needs in mind. The best way to be successful in the trades is to find your niche and be knowledgeable and dependable.

Your work, and your chances of being published regularly, will be enhanced by photos, charts, sidebars, and so forth. Editors of trade magazines are always pleased to find writers who are competent with a camera, though you need not be a professional photographer. Add to your article's visual impact by breaking it into clearly defined sections with bullets and headings.

Ready to write for the trades? Remember: Become an expert and know your readers, and your dreams of a byline will be fulfilled.

>> POETRY

Setting Free the Poems

By T. Alan Broughton

A FEW YEARS AGO, I FOUND MYSELF WRITING A LETTER TO MY thirty-five-year-old daughter reprimanding her for the messy condition of her house when my wife and I had visited it briefly on a fall afternoon. I won't go into the complicated reasons for taking exception to the piles of magazines, the clothes tossed here and there, the dishes stacked not just in the sink but wherever any space was left. I wrote the letter, she wrote back (in more temperate terms than I deserved), and I was left a week later with astonishment at my own behavior. Are we always doomed to be parents to our children? I remember saying firmly to my parents when I was in my thirties, "At a certain point, we have to decide whether we can get over the fact that you made me and helped to bring me up. Either you let go and we make a friendship, or we freeze in the past, struggling to be polite." That fall day I had been standing again at the doorway to my daughter's disheveled bedroom in her teenage years. But a few weeks after I had written that letter, I felt an immense relief. We were too old for that. She was on her own. I didn't have to burden myself any more with thinking that I knew who she was or what she ought to be. I thought I knew her because I had been in on the making of her existence. Now I could see her as a stranger whom I loved. The attachment was still there, but the freedom was far greater.

Poems aren't really the poet's children, of course. If we take that analogy too far, the writer in us may retreat too fully from the far less controllable and more surprising world of wordless reality. Art should never be a substitute for living. But we sometimes form relationships with what we write that are as fatally flawed as the pattern I've described above. The questions, then, are when do we need to cut loose from the poem we've made? How do we do that? Why is it necessary?

389

My experience in some thirty-five years of teaching writing is that very few writers are at a loss for ways to begin poems. We all have something to say, even if we make that beginning difficult by being overly self-critical. The difficulty is in letting the poem grow beyond its origins, in not limiting it to that impulsive moment when we began, a moment that tried to convince us that it must be honored and cherished, that *it* was the poem and ever will be. The hard part comes in setting the poem free to become what it needs to be, which is rarely what we first thought it had to be.

Here are two examples by poets whose accomplishments are sufficient to have earned our trust: Ezra Pound and William Carlos Williams.

In a Station of the Metro

> The apparition of these faces in the crowd;
> Petals on a wet, black bough.

Think of these as three lines because, even if the first is the title, it serves the function of a line in the poem as a whole. It is Pound's haiku—deft, suggestive, intense, full of a resonant silence. No time here to go into its layers of emotion and perception. I only want to glimpse its past to demonstrate how far this final version is from its origins. In a discussion of the poem, Pound says he stepped out of a subway train in Paris "and saw suddenly a beautiful face, and then another and another, and then a beautiful child's face, and then another beautiful woman, and I tried all that day to find words for what this had meant to me, and I could not find any words that seemed to me worthy, or as lovely as that sudden emotion. . . . I wrote a thirty-line poem, and destroyed it because it was what we call work 'of second intensity.' Six months later, I made a poem half that length; a year later I made the following hokku*-like sentence."

Of course, we've never seen a copy of that original version, because he destroyed it, but I'm sure I know what it suffered from. I've kept reams of my own worksheets, which I rarely look at again. But I keep them because they give me a certain sense of security; after all, I can

---

*Alternate spelling of *haiku*.

390

always go back to an earlier version if I really mess up. Any of you who suffer from the same slightly timorous approach to revisions might want to try that method. What Pound must have discarded were many lines, exploratory images, associations from times and places not immediately present in the experience itself—in short, all the detritus the mind spews out as it attempts to find its way, like the chips of marble gathering around the jut of stone that soon becomes a knee, a tensed thigh. The poem begins to insist on what it must become, whether we knew it or not when we began. At a certain point the poem stops being a collection of words that are serving the maker's needs and becomes a work the poet must serve with everything she or he has learned.

Note the insistence in Pound's statement on the beautiful faces, but in particular how it closes in on the phrase "another beautiful *woman*." If there is one thing that this poem is *not* about, it's the faces of beautiful *women* in the setting of a subway station—one which we know Pound could do very well, with that extraordinary mixture of irony and sensuality. He waits six months and tries again. I suspect he did not destroy the next version. Perhaps his interest in Fenellosa and Chinese poetry intervenes. Often what a poet needs in the search to distance a work sufficiently from himself or herself is that objective fascination with matters of syllables, line lengths, sounds, images, even the simple appearance of the shape on a page. Now he is ready for the "hokku-like sentence." Thirty lines have become three. What has happened is that the essence of the experience has insisted on being the poem. The passage of time is one of the poet's keenest instruments in the toil of revision. By the end, the poet's relationship to the work is *radically* different from what it was in the beginning, if that word can be taken to mean that the poet has found a way back to the deepest roots of the poem, something he did not know he knew when he began. The child becomes the father of the man?

Or try this equally famous poem by Williams:

so much depends
upon
a red wheel
barrow
glazed with rain
water
beside the white
chickens

391

This poem has been discussed, analyzed, anatomized, and chased around every classroom so often that it is miraculous how well it still survives. But even though many critics are aware that a personal experience is "behind" the poem, very rarely does this enter into discussions of the poem. Why? Primarily because that personal experience has been excluded from the finished poem. If it were essential, you can be certain Williams would have included it somehow.

For instance, what if the title of the poem were: *View from the Window of a Dying Child's Bedroom*. It could have been—if Williams were a much lesser poet. Apparently, the poem is derived from Williams's experience as the attending physician at the house where one of his patients, a child, was close to dying. In some pause while everyone was waiting, Williams gazed out the window. What else he saw in addition to the shiny, wet wheelbarrow and the chickens, we don't know. Any backyard contains more junk—to say nothing of trees, bushes, maybe a visible street, etc. I have no proof, but I can well imagine Williams beginning with the elegiac and intense combination of the child's toy, the indifferent chickens, the beauty of everything shining and renewed after a rainfall, the poignant awareness of death hovering in the room where he stands. Somewhere along the way, Williams jettisons the possible tones of bathos, the pathetic extensions of his own emotions into the images of the child's world, and gives us in their place a honed, clear combination of images that are focused outward into an immensely suggestive area that can never be filled with the words of our explanations—*so much depends upon*. Four words that have only the hint of image in the etymology of the word *de-pends*. The poem has been set free from its limiting circumstances.

These poems have served as good advisors to me over the years. I gladly take the beginnings of my poems from whatever source announces itself. Full of anxiety and a kind of joy, I watch those words start to mar the page or screen. I don't say it consciously, but even as they continue down the page, I can't help sensing that they are only the first cries of a poem that will grow into something quite different, growing away from me but taking me with it—finally to become something quite separate from me and what I thought the poem was, but blessed for the journey it has let me take in its presence.

>> 84

IN PRAISE OF RHYME

BY JENNIFER SHEPHERD

AFTER MY LACK OF SUCCESS IN RECEIVING PUBLICATION FOR RHYMED poetry, I decided to test the "audience" of real people out in the world, not just higher-ups in the literary community. Where I live, we have a lot of coffeehouses where there are regular poetry readings.

I read some of my work for an audience of about 100 people, and I found their response to be very warm. They didn't treat my poems as if they were less important or more superficial because they were in rhyme form. In fact, listeners that evening said that the rhyme actually helped them focus on the various pieces they heard, allowing them to analyze and retain the poems better.

This got me thinking about the exclusionary nature of many poetry editors, how rhyming is just not considered "cool" these days. I can't help wondering if, in the universal rebellion against rhyme, the literary community has been missing out on a heck of a lot of fun.

Ideas that pour forth naturally from a poet's brain in rhyme form do so for reasons of their own. Should rhyming poetry automatically be categorized as less profound, less worthy of consideration, than the non-rhyming kind? To do so excludes a large number of thoughtful rhymers from even receiving attention from both audience and peers.

Poetry used to be romantic and playful entertainment, conveyed primarily via storytellers' presentations. Anecdotes, songs, and tall tales anchored themselves more easily in the listener's mind when they were expressed through rhyme. Rhyme allowed people to carry the poet's sentiments home with them, because the words became fixed in their brains.

We now live in a much more literate age, and almost anyone can pick up a volume of poetry and begin to read. But we also live in an era of information and entertainment overload. Commercial jingles, news report sound bites, and the latest overplayed hit song on the radio flood us with far too much stimuli. Time seems to be speeding up, while our memories and attention spans get shorter. Most people remember very little of what they hear or see these days. And poetry, foremost among all artistic forms, is getting lost in the shuffle.

Meanwhile, poets from all over the world do their best to raise their voices above this cacophony. They continue to express ideas that they feel have value to an audience consisting of 1) themselves; 2) a hand-picked "worthy" few; or 3) as many people of the general public as possible.

All of them want essentially the same thing. The greatest poets of both past and present have sought to create doorways through which others can enter into a thought-provoking, reality-shifting experience.

Rhyme need not detract from creating this experience. Quite often, rhyme can actually enhance the balance and impact of a poem. Rhyme serves as a framing device for the poet's thoughts—the wooden beams, if you will, of a writer's doorway to reality. If the linguistic carpenter is at all skilled, rhyme can perform its task well.

Shakespeare's most affecting work still stimulates and captivates us, "in spite of" its iambic pentameter. And his work remains portable, readily available to the average memory, not just because of its age, but because it is structured in rhyme.

Yes, it's true—clumsy young poets sometimes fasten upon rhyme with a death grip, refusing to let go until they have created poetry destined to make readers (and listeners) scream with terror. But just because the occasional poem has imprinted itself indelibly upon your memory doesn't mean that you should greet each new rhymed poem with a visceral gasp, its very appearance causing you distress.

Don't berate rhyme. It has no power to harm you, in spite of the rumors circulating among many contemporary poets. Content that is vague or vacuous deserves blame; the rhyme form in itself does not.

So try stepping beyond the current literary norms. Be open to creating and enjoying poetry of all kinds. And the next time you encounter a rhyme, let it linger and possibly carve out a few neural pathways. That way, the piece might remain locked in your memory box and filed under "fun."

And who among us couldn't use a bit more fun?

394

➤➤85

To Make a Prairie

By Rita Dove

When I was inducted into Phi Beta Kappa at Miami University (Ohio) two decades ago, many of the presiding faculty were aghast when I answered their query concerning my career plans with "I want to be a poet." The implied sentiment was "How can you throw away your education?"—as if declaring one's intention to be a poet was analogous to putting on a dunce cap.

Phi Beta Kappa's motto, "philosophy or the love of knowledge is the guide of life," puts it well. Wisdom is the *guide* of life—not the goal. Intelligence is a desirable commodity, but, as one character in Madeleine L'Engle's book *A Wind in the Door* says, "The naked intellect is an extraordinarily inaccurate instrument." Intellectual achievement requires imagination.

I want to discuss here an activity which, although often smiled at or benevolently dismissed in children, is barely tolerated in adolescents, rarely commended in the boardroom, and, to the best of my knowledge, never encouraged in school—but without which no bridges would soar, no light bulbs burn, and no Greek warships set out upon Homer's "wine-dark sea." That activity is daydreaming—an activity so prevalent that we had to jerryrig a word, an oxymoron of sorts, because, so to speak, the default for dreaming is night. *Daydreaming*. There's a loftier expression for it, of course—reverie. But daydreaming is the word that truly sets us adrift. It melts on the tongue. The French phenomenologist Gaston Bachelard speaks of a "dreaming consciousness" and calls poetic reverie a "phenomenology of the soul," a condition in which "the mind is able to relax, but . . . the soul keeps watch, with no tension, calmed and active."

Many of you have heard the story of Thomas Edison's method for courting inspiration: Whenever he became stymied, he would take a nap, and often the solution to his problem would come to him in his sleep. Herbert Marcuse calls this kind of daydreaming the drive toward *Eros,* as opposed to—what else?—*Thanatos,* or death. And what is the ultimate expression of this drive toward Eros? Child's play, which Marcuse defines by saying that playing as a child plays is its own goal, its own contentment, whereas work serves a purpose that lies outside the self.

When I was a child, I loved math—the neatness of fractions, all those pies sliced into ever-diminishing wedges. I adored unraveling the messy narratives of story problems, reducing them to symbols. I did this with the singlemindedness of a census taker. However, there were two stumbling blocks in my mathematical education. The first occurred when I was forced to drill with flash cards; although there are absolute answers with flash cards, there is no end of the series: One correct solution merely prompts the next problem. Something about this procedure frightened me; I believe I recognized in it some metaphor for the numbing repetitions of daily existence—taking out the garbage, doing the dishes, washing laundry, driving to the office, working from 9 to 5. . . . Here's a poem I wrote on the subject:

Flash Cards

In math I was the whiz kid, keeper of oranges and apples.
What you don't understand, master, my father said; the faster
I answered, the faster they came.

I could see one bud on the teacher's geranium,
one clear bee sputtering at the wet pane.
The tulip trees always dragged after heavy rain
so I tucked my head as my boots slapped home.

My father put up his feet after work
and relaxed with a highball and *The Life of Lincoln.*
After supper we drilled and I climbed the dark

before sleep, before a thin voice hissed
numbers as I spun on a wheel. I had to guess.
Ten, I kept saying, *I'm only ten.*

I hit the second snag in 10th grade, a few weeks into geometry. My homework assignment was to prove a theorem. But how could I even begin if I had to use points and lines and planes in order to prove it—

points with no dimension, lines without thickness, and planes that had no length or width or area or perimeters, but stretched into infinity?

I asked my brother, who was two years older and had weathered geometry without a whimper, but his only advice was "You have to sit down and think about it until you get it." He let me use his desk to do this thinking. And so I sat for twenty minutes, for half an hour, trying to imagine what didn't exist. I began to daydream, and my eyes drifted to the ceiling . . . a plane. No, a representation of a plane; and, though I couldn't see it, the ceiling continued beyond the walls of my brother's room, into the hall and above my bedroom and my parents' bedroom— and if I could imagine the ceiling beyond that closed door, why not a ceiling that went on past the house and the neighborhood, all the way to Forever? Walls met ceiling, forming lines that did the same trick. Where ceiling and two walls met, a point . . .

Geometry

I prove a theorem and the house expands:
the windows jerk free to hover near the ceiling,
the ceiling floats away with a sigh.

As the walls clear themselves of everything
but transparency, the scent of carnations
leaves with them. I am out in the open

and above the windows have hinged into butterflies,
sunlight glinting where they've intersected.
They are going to some point true and unproven.

Some stereotypes

There are a thousand and one myths about artists in general, writers in particular, and specifically poets: Poets, the legend goes, are eccentric, not quite of this world; poets are blessed with imagination that the rest of us can never hope to approach. Poets lead wild—or at the very least, wildly disorganized—lives and say outrageous things in polite company. And lo, poets may even be the prophets of our time. The prevailing notions our society harbors about the creative arts make it difficult for artists, and especially that lofty breed of poets, to be taken seriously.

Oddly enough, there is the converse myth that poetry is difficult—

hermetic, cerebral stuff, impossible for the mere mortal to comprehend. I cannot tell you on how many occasions I have read poetry in a church basement or high school classroom, only to have someone come up afterwards and exclaim: "I never knew poetry could be like that—why, that was *fun!*"

What this tells us about our society is that we regard the creative arts with a degree of apprehension, perhaps even suspicion. We do not expect the arts to be accessible, nor do we see any reason to incorporate the arts into our everyday or professional lives. And so, unfortunately, for many students, the years at the university and the few years beyond, in graduate study, may be the last opportunity to live in an environment where intellectual discourse and artistic expression are acknowledged and considered essential.

Of course, stereotypes cut both ways. The flip side of the coin is the assumption that intellect and imagination do not mix. This might be, partly at least, a result of one of our century's most dangerous signs of progress—the concept of specialization.

Let me illustrate this point. In the winter of 1984, when I was giving a series of lectures on the East Coast, a severe storm closed many airports along the seaboard, forcing plane passengers to scramble for the trains. I was on my way to New York City from Providence, Rhode Island, with my husband and infant daughter. The train was so crowded that people were standing—even sitting—in the aisles and in the passageways between cars. In that situation there was no question of chivalry: No one stood up to give me a seat. After about an hour, a seat became free and the young man standing nearest to it—and therefore, according to the laws of survival of the fittest, entitled to it—sat down, then turned and motioned for me to take his place. After another half-hour of travel, the seat next to me became vacant, so I was able to scoot over and give my cavalier a chance to rest his feet.

We began a careful conversation: first about the weather, then my daughter's vital statistics (she was blissfully asleep), and finally, we turned to occupation. "What do you do?" I asked, and was puzzled by his obvious hesitation before the reply came: "I'm . . . I'm a microbiologist." Pause. Then he added, "I usually don't tell people that. It tends to stop conversation."

"So what do you usually tell people?" I asked.

"Oh, that I work in a lab. Or that I study diseases. And what about you?" He turned the tables: "What do you do?" Now it was my turn to hesitate before I answered: "I'm a poet."

"Oh!" he exclaimed. "That's wonderful!"

"And isn't microbiology wonderful, too?" I asked. "Sure," he conceded, "but when I tell people I'm a microbiologist, they're so afraid they won't understand anything I say, they never ask any further. It gets to be a bummer."

"Yeah," I said, "I know what you mean." And I did; many a time I had experienced that awkward silence toward me as a poet. I never knew, however, that there were scientists who suffered the same blues.

"So tell me," I went on, "what exactly *do* you do as a microbiologist?"

What followed was a fascinating account of this man's work with the molecular structure of DNA. He described how, aided by an electron microscope, he "walked" the length of a healthy DNA strand, taking notes along the way on the distinguishing traits of every cell. He then compared these observations with the reports from similar "walks" along DNA strands from people who had multiple sclerosis. By comparing these scientific diaries, he hoped to pinpoint the determining traits for one of the world's most devastating and mysterious diseases.

What impressed me especially about his account was the language he used to describe his work. In order to make this complicated process accessible to a layperson, he resorted to a vivid pictorial—even poetic—vocabulary. When I asked him whether he and his colleagues used the same metaphors in the lab, he seemed surprised. "Well," he replied, "we have specific technical terms of course, but we use some of these words, too. What else can you call it but taking a walk?"

Yes, what else could you call it? Here I was talking with a top-level scientist whose work was so specialized that it had to invent its own language in order to be able to imagine its own investigations. And at this point, when imagination enters, we also enter the domain of poetry.

Making a Prairie

To make a prairie,

Emily Dickinson wrote,

> it takes a clover and one bee,
> One clover, and a bee,
> And revery.
> The revery alone will do,
> If bees are few.

To make a prairie—or a light bulb, or the quantum theory of mechanics—you need revery. Daydreaming. The watchful soul in the relaxed mind.

A liberal education is intended to make people flexible, able to cope with the boundless changes that accelerating civilization will confront them with. So much of modern university education has become a closed society with privileged access to certain mysteries, a microcosm where palpable interaction with the physical world has been suspended in the interests of specialized knowledge. The Industrial Revolution, whose most poignant symbol is the assembly line, made specialization practical; now the Technological Revolution, whose symbol might be the silicon chip, makes specialization imperative.

But technological advances also de-emphasize the individual, reducing the grand gestures of the soul to so many impressions on a grain of sand. The humanities, with their insistence on communication and their willingness to admit paradox into the contemplation of truth, are too often silenced by the bully's club of empirical data. There's a Mother Goose rhyme that goes:

> If all the world were paper,
> And all the sea were ink;
> If all the trees were bread and cheese,
> What should we have to drink?

Yes, indeed—for if we assign a category to every wish and leave the fulfillment of these wishes to one discipline, we may be fed but not nourished; someone is sure to forget the lemonade. The groundwork laid in college stresses the connectedness of all learning. The task upon leaving college and entering into the intricacies of a chosen discipline is to avoid being narrowed into a mere functionary of a professional specialization.

How restless and curious the human mind is, how quickly the imagination latches onto a picture, a scene, something volatile and querulous and filled with living, mutable tissue! The mind is informed by the

400

spirit of play. The most fantastical doodles emerge from wandering ballpoint pens in both the classroom and the board meeting. Every discipline is studded with vivid terminology: In geometry various shapes are defined as "random slices of Swiss cheese," chains, or self-squared dragons. There are lady's slippers in botany and wingbacks in football games. There are onomatopoetic bushwhackers in the jungles of Nicaragua; there are doglegs on golf courses and butterfly valves in automobiles. The theory of quark confinement could be a quantum physicist's definition of the human soul. Astronomy has black holes with "event horizons"—the orbital path around a black hole where time stands still, the point beyond which one is drawn inextricably into the core of the imploding star. Every discipline craves imagination, and you owe it to yourself to keep yours alive.

In ancient Rome, every citizen possessed a genius. The genius was a personal spirit that came to every person at birth; it represented the fullness of one's potential powers. This genius was considered a birthright, but it needed to be nourished in order to survive. Now, in our narcissistic age children celebrating a birthday expect gifts to shower upon them from the outside, but the ancient Roman was expected to make a birthday sacrifice to his or her genius. If one served one's genius well during life, the genius became a *lars,* or household god, after one's death. If one neglected one's potential, the genius became a spook, a troublesome spirit who plagued the living.

Poets do not have a monopoly on imagination: the world will be ever unfolding, as long as one can imagine its possibilities, as long as one honors one's spirit—or, as the Romans would have said, one's "genius"—and lets the fresh air blow in, fragrant, from the flowering prairie.

401

➤➤ 86

POEMS AND MEANING

BY PETER MEINKE

POEMS DON'T HAVE TO MEAN ANYTHING. YOUNG POETS OFTEN MAKE the mistake of thinking they must have Something to Say. It's not that Saying Something is wrong, but it tends to distract from the main objective: saying something memorably, beautifully, permanently. Poetry is news that *stays* news. And what makes it stay news is how it's said, not what it says.

Think of your favorite poems. "Stopping By Woods On A Snowy Evening," by Robert Frost? Lovely description of an all-too-familiar scene, clear as a bell. Or is it? Is it really about death, or even suicide? Well, maybe. It's often what's *not* said that makes poems memorable. T. S. Eliot's "The Love Song of J. Alfred Prufrock"? We have lots of studies of indecisive men: What makes this one unforgettable? Is it about an entire repressed society? Is it about T. S. Eliot? It doesn't matter, does it? Lines like "I have heard the mermaids singing, each to each" will haunt you your entire life.

"O, my Luve's like a red red rose," wrote Robert Burns. This may or may not have been true, but who cares? Or more to the point, "As silent as a mirror is believed / Realities plunge in silence by . . ." is the beginning of Hart Crane's poem, "Legend." I'm not sure what it means (it *seems* to mean something), but I've always loved it. You will have your own examples.

There's a continuum of meaning on which poets position themselves: On one side are poets like Edward Field, who (typically) writes straightforward lines like, "My mother's family was made up of loving women," and on the other, John Ashbery writing "the unplanted cabbages stand tearful out of the mist." The Ashbery school takes the position that meaning is boring and bourgeois: Straight information is too easy. "Tell us something we don't know!" is their cry. The Field side takes the common-sense point of view that poetry belongs to the people, and if it doesn't make sense, who wants it? Surreal gibberish is also easy. (Both sides reflect a Puritan ethic they both deny: *What we do is hard work,* each says, and they're both right.)

Of course I'm exaggerating, but the point I want to make is that *you can station yourself anywhere along the meaning continuum and you will be "right"*: But for the sake of your poetry, let the words, the sounds, the rhythms, the images come first; and let the meaning follow.

And yet. And yet we want poems to mean something to us—and many of them do, but with this startling complication: *They mean different things to different people, and even different things to the same person at different times.* These are the best poems. But anyone who has done a lot of editing for magazines, or judging for contests, will testify to the mind-numbing experience of reading through piles of basically indecipherable poetry. Howard Nemerov, after wading through manuscripts for the lively periodical *Furioso,* most of which apparently followed Archibald MacLeish's dictum, "A poem should not mean / But be," once said: "Well, there they all were, and they didn't mean anything."

I think the best poems *tend* toward meaning, leaving space for us to move around, but at the same time giving us hints, pushing us in a general direction. This doesn't mean that a poem can mean *anything* ("Stopping By Woods," for example, is not about communism. There are no directional hints leading us that way).

To try to trace the development of meaning in a poem, I've chosen semi-randomly one of mine, called "Apples":

> The apple I see and the apple
> I think I see and the apple
> I say I see
> are at least three
> different apples . . .
>   One sympathizes with Dr. Johnson here
> when he kicked a stone
> to dispute the Bishop: such
> airy-fairy distinctions so much
> applesauce!
> And yet when you say
> what I think you say
> in a way that may
> or may not be final I can only hope

> that cold stone that white boulder that . . .
>   iceberg between us
> is not really there but is sliding
> like some titanic idea
> through the North Pole
> in the apple of my eye

What does this poem mean? I wrote it, and I'm not entirely sure! It seems to be a love poem that takes its time getting about its business. Perhaps—translated—it would go like this: Two lovers have had an argument (or something), and one of them is hoping that this coldness on his (or her) lover's part is not permanent but is just passing through. This isn't very interesting, unless you identify with the lovers (which readers of course sometimes do).

What's interesting are the apples.

The poem began, as most of mine do, with a phrase or sentence. I had been talking with a friend about memory, and more or less the first sentence "came out." So I wrote it down in the little notebook I carry around. This, I suppose, is the "inspiration" part of composition. (I visualize the composition of a poem as a series of little explosions, like Chinese firecrackers, each one setting the next one off.)

What I liked about the sentence was the repetition of "apple" four times and "see" three times. When (later, at home) I moved the lines around to emphasize the repetition, I also saw the rhyme of "see" and "three," so I wrote "I say I see" as a separate line, liking the sound and look of it by itself in a five-line stanza (the end words being "apple / apple / see / three / apples"—which is a nice little poem by itself).

While doing this (everything is happening simultaneously in poetry, which is one of the exciting things about writing it) I remembered the famous rebuttal on this general subject that Samuel Johnson made to the Idealist philosopher, Bishop Berkeley. Berkeley had theorized that matter was non-existent (it's all in our heads), and Johnson and Boswell were having a tough time refuting him, until Johnson "struck his foot against a large stone," saying "I refute it *thus*." And thus that old rascal Samuel Johnson entered this poem about apples.

This was a change in direction, so I indented it, and as I tinkered with the poem (the *possible* poem; I didn't know if it would work yet), I could see that "stone" went well with "Johnson" (and then "distinctions"). Dr. Johnson was being playful, so I became playful too—"such

404

airy-fairy distinctions"—and that led me, accidentally, to our slang word for too much fancy talk or overly sophisticated reasoning: "applesauce." *Voilà*! We're brought back to the original image of apples, but this time also thinking about language and the strange way that it works. Robert Frost, among many wonderful pronouncements, said the art of poetry involved "the taking advantage of happy accidents."

One question that this section brings up is how much knowledge to expect from a reader. The answer today seems to be—as our canon of required reading shifts, changes, and dwindles—not much. But our task as writers is not to avoid using learned or private references, only to use them clearly and to good effect. The reference to Dr. Johnson and Bishop Berkeley will be familiar to many readers, but those who have never heard of these eighteenth-century gentlemen won't have trouble following the poem. They'll only miss the little pleasure one gets from recognizing an apt illustration—and after all, if they're interested enough, they can look it up!

The poem, despite some rhyme, seemed destined to be in free verse: No set form was emerging. But I saw I could make a kind of loose pattern by making the Dr. Johnson section also five lines, to match the opening sentence; and then reinforce it by end-rhyming "such" and "much" to match "see" and "three" in the first section. Nobody much cares about this sort of thing, or even notices—but it's important that the writer care, trying his or her best to line up "the best words in the best order."

So now I had ten lines, a beginning of sorts, but where was I going? *What did it mean?* Frost said a poem, like a piece of ice, has to glide on its own melting; and as I sat thinking of the lines I had written— mostly about apples—I suddenly understood it was going to be a love poem. Why? I'm not sure, but I think "apple" suggested "Eve," the apple of knowledge, the apple of temptation. And, even closer to this poem, there's the golden apple, the Apple of Discord inscribed "to the fairest" and thrown out by Eris to make trouble among the beautiful goddesses. There are also love-apples (tomatoes) and apple-blossom time—there are so many different apples! I didn't reason all this out, but I'm trying to explain how poems, even little poems like this one, move toward meaning in associative ways.

And because I was also thinking about language, I began to write about how we talk to one another, how easy it is to misunderstand. I

405

had to match those apples verbally (words, like apples, are also different, depending on whether you're saying, hearing, or remembering them). I tried to reproduce the loose rhyme of the first stanza with the "say/say," "may/may" repetitions. I wanted to bring Dr. Johnson's stone back as a kind of metaphor for a lover's spat. That led to the final "idea" of the poem.

I like the "o" sound of "stone" because it went with "hope," and to emphasize it—and it fit emotionally—I made it "cold stone," then "white boulder" (maybe because we've had a driveway with white stones in it). The natural next step from cold stone and white boulder was to think of a glacier or an iceberg.

So the ingredients were all gathered. I hadn't known it when I began, but now I knew I was writing a love poem using apples and icebergs as metaphors for the difficulties of communication. A metaphor doesn't explain anything; rather, it creates a new situation that is in some ways the emotional and intellectual equivalent of an original feeling or thought. I think the appeal of poetry is that this feeling is orchestrated by the power of language to organize what is essentially disorganized experience, a temporary balancing act. *Let the language guide you, and the meaning will follow.* If you reverse that emphasis, you begin heading toward propaganda and advertisement: You're selling something.

What I had left to do in this poem was to tie the two images—apples and icebergs—together in some satisfying way. Is this always necessary? I doubt it, but I like to work that way, the way a musical composition fuses themes at the end. And language came to my rescue, as it tends to do if you're patient. The phrase "apple of my eye" can mean "my true love" or the actual pupil in the middle of my eye; so the most obvious reading of the poem (I think) is that the speaker hopes this misunderstanding is not there permanently but is passing through some cold part (the North Pole) of his lover's mind, and will soon be gone.

It can also mean, however—to hark back to the good Bishop Berkeley—that this idea is really in his own mind; it's something that he's seeing that may or may not be there, it depends where you're standing.

In addition, the word "titanic" darkens the poem considerably. It simply means (the denotation) "enormous," like the ancient Gods, the Titans. But in this context (the Titanic went down in the North Atlantic), we can't help but think (the connotation) of the doomed ship. So what began as a fairly lighthearted poem ends ambiguously on a darkening image.

This is a story that has been written about thousands and thousands of times: the progression of love from delight to disaster. I like the idea that this poem mirrors that lifelike situation, really recreates it. I don't think the meaning of the poem is very difficult; it's just that it's like life, a little slippery to get hold of. (What's the meaning of *your* life, or mine?) And yet linguistically it comes together—I hope—to give the reader a sense of closure usually missing from real-life experiences.

I'm not sure this poem is worth all this ink and heavy thinking. I thought I chose it randomly to illustrate the relation of meaning to poetry—and, thinking about it, I now see it's actually *about* meaning, so it may not have been as random as I thought. (I sometimes think *nothing* is random.) Mainly, I wanted to say, trust the language: If it wants to mean something to you, it will.

This is easy to say, and hard to do. We all have ideas that we want to inflict on other people, often very praiseworthy ideas: Love one other, take care of the trees, don't be a pig, etc. But my experience leads me to believe that your ideas are going to come through in spite of yourself, no matter what you do. You don't have to worry about this.

Instead, worry about whether you've used too many adverbs, or what word should end your line. Of course you should be passionate about your poems—there needs to be blood on the page (and tears and gravy, etc.)—but if you need to be told this (BE PASSIONATE!), you're in the wrong line of work, Charlie; get a real job.

Worry about the connotations of your words, and their sounds. Especially their sounds. People—friends, classmates, teachers, reviewers—will disagree on which words go best where. This makes things difficult, but it's the name of the game; it's what poets do.

On the "meaning continuum" I mentioned earlier, I know I'm on the side that favors a high degree of clarity. But I can't help that, and it's not important. Handling the language, with all its wonderful tricks and surprises, to the best of our ability: That's what's important. In a world where everything seems unrelated, chaotic, and fragmented, the language of poetry has this great innate ability to embody the interconnectedness of things: "O, my Luve's like a red red rose." Absolutely.

>> 87

WHEN LIGHT VERSE IS THE RIGHT VERSE

BY MURIEL LILKER

> Poems are made by fools like me,
> But only God can make a tree.
>
> "Trees," by Joyce Kilmer

OF COURSE, POEMS *ARE* EASIER TO PRODUCE THAN TREES, BUT THAT doesn't mean they're a cinch to dash off.

However—obviously—it can be done, and it can be fun—that is, if you observe certain basics.

For example, HOW do you rhyme? With care and precision. Just remember that light verse has a rhythm, or meter, all its own. It runs in a series of stressed syllables that bounce along in a discernible pattern. There's a beat to it, a catchy rhythm that you can jump to, sing to, and really feel. It's like keeping time to music, as in, da-DA da-DA da-DA da-DA.

When the rhythm is perfect, the poem scans. This is true of the two-liner (couplet), the four-liner (quatrain), or the longer poems that can run for six, eight, ten lines or more.

Let's see how we scan this two-liner of mine that appeared in *The New York Times:*

When Spirits Move

Even persons most laconic
Loosen under gin and tonic.

Got the beat? Go ahead and use it. It may be easier than you think. And fun. Especially when you can beat out your own observation on whatever you like—or dislike.

As far as subject matter is concerned, light verse is the perfect vehicle to sound off on anything that may puzzle you, worry you, exasperate you, or maybe even amuse you. Let off steam in rhyme—like my reaction to not taking enough of the right clothes along on vacation, which appeared in *The New York Times:*

Packing It In

It seems on vacation
Where I roam,
The most suitable clothes
Are those I've left home!

What are some of your own gripes? Think about what happens in the course of a day, or a week. Competition with a co-worker? A snafu at the car wash? Telephone pitches for aluminum siding at dinner time?

Look for a fresh approach to situations like these, or any others you might think of. Jot down some key words and try to build a poem around them. Don't get discouraged if it takes several attempts before you arrive at "it." It's worth the effort to find an original way of expressing your own reactions. The closer you can get to predicaments that others have, the better your chance of seeing them in print.

What else is ripe for the rhyming? All the holidays, ready for your own outlook on them. Are you tempted by the Halloween candy your kids bring home from trick-or-treating? Do you leave Christmas shopping for the last minute? Is Valentine's Day a basis for comparing gifts? Think about it.

And think about all the personal milestones, such as graduations, weddings, retirements, and birthdays. In the last category, I summed up a frustrated mother's reaction to a natal celebration in this way in *Good Housekeeping:*

And Many, Many More

Sing a happy birthday song
Havoc everywhere;
Soda on my brand-new rug,
Ice cream on the chair,
Children running all around
Celebrating when

409

Junior gains another year,
And Mother ages ten.

You'll find the topics can be endless. Can't stand seafood? Struggling to reconcile your bank statement? Bored with opera? Complain in a quatrain, and you may find that your own pet peeves are shared by many others. Better yet, an editor may recognize how widely held your opinions are, and agree to publish your sentiments.

Even an insomniac like me didn't mind losing sleep when the *Wall Street Journal* published:

A Rude Awakening

Insomnia wouldn't be so bad
If all the brilliant thoughts we had
While trapped in this awakened state
Would not, by dawn, evaporate!

Notice that the last line is the one that has the zinger. Build up to it. Save your wry comment or surprise or joke for the end. Then, sock it to them!

Where to send your poems? You might start by looking at magazines in a moderately large bookstore or in your local library. Riffle through them and look for poems on the bottoms of pages in "the back of the book." You may find them in *Good Housekeeping, McCall's,* and many others. If you do spot verse there, look for the editorial board on the masthead, get the name of the Features or Articles Editor, and send your poems off. Try also the "Post Scripts" page of *The Saturday Evening Post* and *Reader's Digest,* where I was delighted to find this poem of mine unexpectedly reprinted (from *Good Housekeeping*) in their "Toward More Picturesque Speech" feature:

June Bugged

With buds a-blooming on the trees
Awakening old allergies,
We greet thee, spring, all newly green
With tissues and antihistamine!

410

In your local newspaper, you may find a section that publishes light verse. It's also worth checking papers in surrounding suburban communities.

Some special tips

• Remember that most magazines have a lead time of at least three months. If you have an original idea for Halloween or Thanksgiving or June brides, you want to get it off well before that issue closes. While you're battling the high 80's in August, keep in mind that it is *not* too soon to send off that six-liner on Christmas shopping. In fact, the earlier the better for these "unseasonable" inspirations.
You might start up a tickler system on your calendar. Then, early in December, you'll realize it's time to send out that piece on your recalcitrant lawn.
• Send off just one poem at a time to an editor. You may indeed be prolific and have a lot to show for your efforts, but you want that one poem to stand out by itself as a meaningful submission. Type it up double-spaced, on one sheet of paper, with your name, address, and telephone number in the upper right-hand corner. Send it along with a short note to the Features or Articles Editor at the magazine or newspaper you've chosen. If you have been previously published, say where. Enclose the letter and poem in a 9x12 envelope, and *always* include an SASE (self-addressed stamped envelope) with enough postage to cover your poem's return.
Do steel yourself for rejections. Look at them as an opportunity to start all over again with a publication that might welcome—and publish!—your light verse.
• Yes, you can use a rhyming dictionary, and no, it is *not* a reflection on your lack of imagination. Suppose you already have your topic. You've even jotted down the key words you want to use, when suddenly one of them defies rhyming. What rhymes with calf? Well, you can think of laugh or staff or giraffe, none of which suits you. So you look in your rhyming dictionary under "aff" and find chaff, half, carafe, distaff, paragraph, and many more you'd never have thought of on your own. And neither might anyone else. So do feel free to use a rhyming dictionary to complete your efforts, and save your creative juices for the main course.

411

• Don't make things harder for yourself than you have to. It's not necessary to rhyme your key word. For instance, suppose you'd like to write about ice—how it has its positive side and isn't just a menace underfoot on wintry streets. Does that mean you have to rhyme the word ice itself? Not necessarily. You may have already thought of nice and rice and slice, and discarded them as useless. From the rhyming dictionary, you may have found twice, advice, entice, paradise, etc., which are equally worthless. I found all of these expendable, and worked out this ode to ice, as it appeared in *The New York Times:*

Cold Comfort

Ice has its place
Which is, I think
Not under foot,
But in a drink.

• Finally (or to start with), give some thought to an arresting title. The title is the first thing an editor sees, and your verse is more likely to be read when it's headed by a play on words, or a pun, or whatever original spin you can come up with. If it's clever enough, the title can sometimes be the best part of your poem.

Do try light verse. There *is* a market out there, so have fun looking for it.

Tell It—And Sell It!

Let's hear it now for odes that rhyme
Every stanza, every time,
Everything you like or curse
Paraphrase it in light verse.
Exert your level best to tell it,
Then, all you have to do is sell it!

412

➣➣ 88

POETRY AND MEMORY

BY JAMES APPLEWHITE

MEMORY IN THE WIDEST SENSE GOVERNS ALL I DO AS A WRITER, SINCE words, along with the skills acquired for relating them, are stored there. Yet, we aren't aware of the wonder of memory until it falters. Aging makes certain words, especially proper nouns, more difficult to access, in that organic computer-storage we call memory. We're surprised by any difficulty, because the vocabulary, syntax and formal skills we begin learning in childhood have always been spontaneously on hand for our use, as naturally as breathing or walking. Language with its rooting in memory, when we realize its scope and complexity, seems almost miraculous: this vast store to which we're continually adding and, if losing some, not much, in proportion to the total, which seems endlessly elastic.

The operation of memory was central to the argument of E.D. Hirsch's *Cultural Literacy*—a discussion highly relevant to the writer, who always was at first a reader. The words we're reading, apparently, remain only temporarily in a short-term memory, unless they're connected to some pre-existing network of things known. We remember by association, or linkage, and so reading with comprehension requires, in a sense, reading with recognition. We have to recognize the relatedness of what we're newly taking in, to what we already have stored, if there is to be significant understanding and retention. Hirsch argues, therefore, that the new knowledge acquired by the eyes and nerves from words must be connected into the networking of memory, things newly observed attaching themselves to things previously learned.

This means that our understanding of the present, this immediate, passing moment, is conditioned by, and contingent upon, memories from the past. Our eyes interpret not only the letters of words and sentences on the basis of previously acquired knowledge, but also the whole range of experience. We can't conceptualize things, or speak, or write, or take a walk, without using memory.

Writing a poem is therefore an act of memory. The process of arranging old and familiar words into a new order, to embody those conceptions and emotions that always seem different and individual, draws on the long-term storehouse of memory. Writing a poem dramatizes this almost imponderable relation of the present to the past: this moment of consciousness dependent on the deep reservoir of experience. This record of earlier time would lie mute and passive without the moment's articulation. And any current cognitive act would be thin and anonymous without the years' accumulated layers of memory— this basis of who we are. To see a tree as a tree is an act of pattern recognition requiring the past.

Certain poems feature memory explicitly, while all poems implicitly depend on its power. Perhaps such poems are especially moving (I had almost said *memorable*) because they remind us of the relation of the thoughts we think, this minute, to all those preceding thoughts that we cannot now particularly recall, but feel in their cumulative legacy. When the present mind feels the form and texture of a vast, earlier time-scale, one it cannot in detail recall or read, the result may be a profound aesthetic emotion. It is like looking at the ruined masonry of a Gothic abbey: You cannot know the exact history behind these walls and arches, yet you feel the resonance of the past beneath the fissured surface.

I don't think it profitable for a writer to try to *use* memory, directly. Memory is always allowing itself to be used, but won't be coerced; there are better strategies than head-on pressure. Memory has its own processes and its own selectivity. Scenes, faces, bits of story that rise up spontaneously are thus more likely to have an emotive significance than those memories we might deliberately call up.

Really to remember is often to reencounter a part of experience, perhaps distant from present life but still related to it. Profound memory can continue the assimilation of a part of our lives we'd thought we'd finished with, but hadn't. The poetic use of memory is therefore not really separate from that larger meditative attempt to make sense of our lives, of which poetry is part.

As poets, we can intensify this process by focused thinking, not so much on the past itself, as on those issues that *involve* the past: issues

414

of personal identity, confrontations with disappointment or loss, plans for the future that we see as completing long-cherished hopes and ambitions. Just as in keeping a dream-journal one learns to remember dreams better, so consistent meditation and writing can make the past and one's own buried emotions available for poetry. We don't always know how or what we really feel about certain matters—especially those areas of experience involving our childhood. My own experience has shown me that the driving force behind memory is not merely the desire to call up earlier days, but the deeply felt need to reencounter unresolved issues and emotions—the need to understand, to come to terms with, past time.

During the last several years, I've been working on an interrelated set of autobiographical and literary essays. My book of poems, *A History of the River* (Louisiana State University Press), presented a kind of cultural history of my region of the South, ranging from the curing rituals for bright leaf tobacco, through farm artifacts, such as Mason jars, sausage grinders, and mule-drawn plows, through patterns of farmhouse births and deaths and home burials. I was moved to portray the change of the world, as the time-order associated with these earlier objects and practices gave way to the more recent time, surrounding tractors, electrical appliances, mercury vapor farmyard lights, and television sets.

Last spring, I began to write a sequence of more formal poems focused directly on the experience of time. All of them seemed to involve streams, rivers, lakes or the ocean. I thought of them tentatively as *Meditations on Water*. Though my explicit subject was time and its river-like shapes as it flowed by, I was also trying to show how experiences accumulate in the mind, just as a lake holds water which is mostly out of sight. Here is a poem that began as I thought of boat rides on a lake as a child, and the home movies taken there, that extended and represented memory:

Remembering Home Movies on Water

My father cranks the outboard motor. His face
  looks tender
in the camera's fixed light. Beside me sits my
  mother
in her one-piece suit, peering ahead through time,

415

her face a sphinx-prediction of puzzlements to come:
my amazement at the world, uncertain identity,
courage against death and illness but inability
to assert my own need and course. That route
seemed plowed by the boat's expanding wake,
    the pout
of my mother's lips a judgment on his unwisdom:
this fated, accelerated design, the masculine
    momentum
she deplored and embraced. I also apparently wish
    not
to go on, though summers continued with another
    boat
and larger motor and myself at the helm, driver
so harshly one evening across the wave-cut river
that my girl in front carried bruises across her back
for a week. Her father cursed but she raised her neck
to my lips. I piled weight and muscle into this role
my mother derided, working in the concrete hole
beneath the cars, greasing as automatically as my
    parents
had inserted me into life: these disguises it permits,
these inherited expressions raised dumbly toward
    storm,
as we rush into the imitations from which we've
    come.
Now in this present so seemingly distanced, world-
    different,
I paddle across these circling mirrors to contemplate
their curious accumulation and reflection. Afternoon
sky changes blue into green. Clouds puff dryly
    in the sheen
that's liquid yet develops, a film to be viewed.
Gazing into depths I feel the years' dumb plunges
    flood
back and as Freud knew, that drowned world never
    will change.
I sit on its surface and suffer, accept, mourn,
    rearrange
myself in relation to this deadly dynamic I always
    take
to bed and don't escape: this lost ponderous hidden
    lake.

The lake's depth holds a reservoir of past time that is like the contents of the unconscious. The narrator, in sad recognition that this underwater world "never will change," is somewhat consoled by his sense that the present offers the possibility of new attitudes and relationships to this fixed past.

Other poems I'm working on grew out of recent experiences canoeing or sailing or running beside the Eno River near my house. It seemed that both through my writing and my involvement with water, I was trying to put the first part of my life and the second part together. In one of the poems that resulted, I used memory very centrally, though that had not been my original intention. The kind of writing and thought I'd recently been involved with apparently prepared the way for a spontaneous memory-event, which provided the narrative of the poem.

I had gotten back home almost too late for my customary run by the river, but went out anyway, along the dimming trails of the Eno State Park off Cole Mill Road. I ran deep into the forest and next to the river for a while, its slick quickness maintaining light on the surface, while the trees beside lost detail, becoming humps of shadow. On my way back to the parking area, I passed down into a vale where night had almost fallen. Lightning bugs winked, yellow-green and moving, and a sense of my childhood home came back, at first as a presence and tone without action or shape. A voice from the distant parking lot became a voice from a neighbor's porch. I felt the community gathered around me again and remembered the preacher's term, "communion of saints." When I'd made my slow way back out to the road, I had the shape of a poem in my head. I wrote it out the next day, in the slant-rhymed couplets I've been using lately for meditations. These rhymes, partial and less fully heard, let me say things more explicitly and deliberately, keeping the arguments and questions I want to voice now within the realm of the poetic. Here is the poem.

A Run with the Double River

I returned from the looping trail to Bobbitt's Hole,
finishing in darkness, walking a last half mile.
The footpath dimming among hardwoods angled
   down,
where air felt heavy as breath and a water shone.
Suddenly it was old summer, as lightning-sparks
of insects glowed near and large. A steepening
   of rocks

lay seamed with times like coal, under layers of
   noises.
An owl called, a vole rustled, a sighing like voices
came from trees toward the road. Deeply, I
   remembered:
a time without events, the shadow over a town that
   slumbered
into twilight as the lightning bugs like momentary
   sight
rose sparkling, the scene as if seeing itself in a
   night
wherein minds added up to an awareness and were
   calm.
It felt like our Sunday congregation singing a hymn.
Nothing had gone. Faces of friends, parents, old
   men
I hardly knew looked renewed, individual yet not,
   grown
together in this hum, this single continuing
   evening tone
that collected the drone of the electric fan and dove
   alone
on telephone wires into one thing—all made simple
   again,
as when a garden's leaves rise together after a rain.
But in what medium is this cloud of presences
   stored?
My church had told me of saints gathered unto the
   Lord.
It praised occasions when our single, ephemeral
moments melt together and we feel what is like the
   eternal:
the form within the flowing, shape where past years
   are.
I had entered this under-knowledge, like the river
   aware
of itself. We'd sat as static muttered in our porch's
   radio;
the stories of voices from the chairs around sounded
   low
and ceaselessly, like cicadas crowded into a single
   tree.
The stars pierced near and real. There was no TV.
Such memories seem transmitted by genes instead
   of by wires,
though the footage catalogued in archives aspires
to be this library of the blood. Two currents run
   together,

418

as clouds and stars paint these streams with passing
    glitter.
The TV in the house with its insistent, loud alarm
distracts from profounder dreaming, yet shows the
    charm
of the race. Its goddesses arouse us to love, and
    heroes kill.
This presentness seems a surface. The river's motion
    is still
though its depth holds a pressure of all early instants,
which roil and swerve and pulse. We run as water
    glints,
as it flashes into a consciousness, that the sky
    imprints
like a source. Each red leaf splashes upon it, come
into a mighty sequence, unique, subsumed in time.

Part of my life I've felt the past as a burden upon me, even as an oppression. I am a southerner, and share in the South's problem of history: the feeling I grew up with of having been anticipated by those fathers and grandfathers and greatgrandfathers who'd bequeathed me the world in which attitude and actions seemed already determined, or overdetermined. More recently however, I've felt my separation and freedom from a regional history which, not in the national consciousness (and sometimes in my own estimation), seems only a stereotypical relic—a formulaic reiteration—of exhausted prejudice, pride, and grievances.

What felt so fresh about this descent into a small ravine in the edge of night was the immediacy of a past that had neither gone stale nor dwindled into cliché—a past as the presences that inform one's identity, without obtruding their individual outlines. I experienced past time as a reunion of one part of the self with another. My current personality felt itself for a moment within a gathering of presences who had reappeared from deep in my earlier life. They were (and are) a part of who I am, though I'm not usually aware of that fact.

So as the poet sits writing, figures and images out of the past may sometimes crowd about. My schoolteacher uncle used to tell me of Odysseus in the land of the dead, and of how the spirits of the heroes and heroines of his land collected around him. Since he was still alive, they wanted him to hear their story, and perhaps to tell it again among the living. The prophet Tiresias also came forward, and told Odysseus how he was to get home again successfully. Odysseus may stand for

419

the poet in relation to deep memory. He or she gathers stories out of cultural and personal history: old stories that will be seen in the new form of their retelling. Like Odysseus, the poet learns from the past how to get back home to the present, how to live in it more vitally, how to proceed into the future. When we've come to the past as free persons, able to accept and internalize its mighty echo, it can send us along our way, abler and more confident, surer of our mission, and of who we are.

A poem is given shape by the poems remembered, collectively, from all the poet's earlier reading: sonnets, blank verse meditations, various kinds of free verse—by the sounds of emphasis and closure, the chiming of stanzas and of rhyme. Poetry is an old story that comes alive again with the new idea. The names and the events and the rhymes are similar but never quite the same. So I say again, the way to use time and memory as a writer is to let it use you. This involves respect toward the past, but not worship. *We* the living are the custodians of all record; we are the only minds of all history now able to reanimate its stories. Ours are the only voices through which the past can speak, in becoming the present and future. Ours is the equal of any time, because it has all times within it. But the empowerment of the past lies buried, unless we can find ways to experience it as alive. The poet occasionally needs to surrender some of his or her conscious intention, even some of the present sense of self, in order to be visited by the times and presences held in the deeper layers of memory. What we remember without usually being aware of it may help us become more truly ourselves as poets.

>> 89

POETS, LEARN YOUR TRADE

BY ROBERT MEZEY

I HAVE BEEN ASKED TO OFFER SOME USEFUL ADVICE TO BEGINNING writers and I shall address myself to young poets, since poetry is the art I know best. I confess that I feel a little uncomfortable in this role of wise old counselor, being neither particularly old nor particularly wise and, in fact, in want of advice myself. (What wouldn't I give for a conversation with Robert Frost or John Crowe Ransom or W. H. Auden. There are many things I should like to ask them about this beautiful and difficult art.) Also, I am all too aware that the precepts that immediately spring to mind are the ones that veteran writers always hand out to the young. Nevertheless I will mention a few of them; they are easily summarized, they are no less true for being clichés, and they bear repetition.

First of all, live. Experience, observe, reflect, remember—try to be one of those on whom nothing is lost (in Henry James' great phrase). It is not necessary that your experience be wide, only that it be deep. Think what Emily Dickinson managed to live without—sex, travel, drugs, a career, a lifestyle—and yet few Americans have ever lived as fully, as intensely as she. Live your life. One cannot write out of books.

Read, for after all, one does write out of books also, and poetry is made of poetry. Reading and writing are inseparable; if you are not a reader, you are not a writer. Read history, novels, science, whatever you like, and above all, poetry. As in life, so in reading: Deep is better than wide. And read the best—not your mostly dismal contemporaries, but what has lasted hundreds and thousands of years: Homer, Virgil, Dante, Shakespeare, the King James Bible. Read continually.

Revise what you have written, and then revise it again. You don't want to work all the life out of it, but precision and liveliness and an air of spontaneity are the fruit of long hours of writing and rewriting, of trial and error. First thought is *not* best thought, and poetry, unlike jazz, is not improvisation. In fact, first thoughts tend to be banal, unfocused, conventional, not quite coherent. Most poems require a number of drafts—maybe twenty; maybe fifty. Don't be too easily satisfied.

Those are perhaps the three essential commandments. (If they are not easily obeyed, it may be that you are not destined to be a poet.) But I want to tell you something that nowadays not many others would tell you or even assent to. You must learn to write verse. Not "free" verse, but verse—numbers, measures—call it what you will. It is what poetry has always been written in until the last century or so, and indeed it is only over the last few decades that nonmetrical verse has become the norm (if something which, by definition, violates the norm can *be* a norm). Before you break the rules, you need to know the rules; before you seek novelty, you ought to demonstrate that you know the ancient craft. That is no more than simple honesty and humility. You cannot properly call yourself a poet otherwise. A poet who cannot compose in verse is like a painter who cannot draw or a scientist who does not grasp the scientific method. Besides, as you acquire facility, you will find that verse-making supports your sentences, generates ideas, leads you where you might not otherwise have gone; and you will find what many poets have long known, that free verse is not easier than metrical verse, but much more difficult, and very few can write it well. As André Gide said, art is born of constraint and dies of too much freedom.

How can you go about learning to write in meter? As poets have always learned, by reading good verse and trying to imitate its sounds. You may need to count on your fingers at first, to be sure that you have the permitted number of syllables and the accents in the right positions, but soon you will be able to play by ear. It is useful to have some theoretical understanding, but in the end, an iambic pentameter is a line that sounds like an iambic pentameter, and you must know it the way you know the tune of an old familiar song. Be careful where you look for instruction: Many teachers don't know much about the meters, and these days most poets don't either, and the books can be misleading or flat out wrong. George Stewart's book *The Technique of English Verse* (Holt, Rinehart & Winston) is good; so is James McAuley's *Versification* (Michigan State University Press), the shortest and maybe the best; so is Derek Attridge's *The Rhythms of English Poetry* (Longman). (Remember that good prosodists, though they hear the verse much the same way, may use different terminology or different symbols of scansion.) Be sure you read good models; many contemporary poets who write in meter, or what they call meter, do it atrociously: It is obvious that they don't know how the game is played. You can't go wrong with Marlowe, Herbert, Jonson, Milton, Pope, Tennyson, or Frost, or a hundred others. If you want to read the best of your own times, look for Philip Larkin, Edgar Bowers, Donald Justice, Richard Wilbur, Anthony Hecht, the late distinguished American poet, Henri Coulette, and there are a few others.

All the good poets make up a great free university, which you can attend at any hour of the day or night, choosing whatever teacher you like. Whatever you do, read aloud, both the verse of your models and your own, and listen to it carefully. (It might help to listen to it on tape. It might help to listen to records or tapes of good poets who also read well: Frost, Justice, Larkin, Wilbur, Ransom.)

Once you get the tune fixed in your head, you will have it forever, and you will recognize it in all its many varied patterns. You should, at the very least, be able to write pentameters, tetrameters, and trimeters (the longer and shorter lines are more difficult), and in both strict iambic and loose; common measure and ballad meter; rhymed couplets, tercets, and quatrains; blank verse and passable sonnets. The better you can write in meter, the better you can hear the old verse, and, to some extent, vice versa. And it is essential that you hear the great English poems as they were meant to be heard and that you have some idea of what those poets were trying to do. Otherwise you will have a very imperfect understanding of the poetry of your own language, and that is a serious deficiency in a poet. (Not to say in any cultivated man or woman—after all, accentual-syllabic verse, its invention and development, is one of the glories of our civilization.)

Once you have achieved some mastery of your craft, you can have a go at free verse if you like. Having learnt something about making verse lines that are really lines, you are likelier to do better than if you had never written anything but free. And you may well discover that for all its charms, free verse cannot do nearly as much as metrical verse can, in expressing feeling, in clarifying thought, in varying tempo, in delineating nuances of tone or subtleties of meaning, in emphasizing, modulating, elevating, clinching both ideas and emotions, and above all, in bringing about that perhaps magical phenomenon that poetry alone is capable of: making us feel that the sounds of the words *are* what is being said, that the sounds somehow deepen, enlarge, enact, embody—in a sense, create—the reality behind them. As Henri Coulette once wrote, "Meter is thinking; it is the basis of intimacy between reader and writer."

These are some of the powers of meter and rhyme, and only the profoundest, sincerest, and most original poet can put them aside, and then only if he knows what he is putting aside. I am no Yeats, God knows, but I urge you, young poets, to do what he urged *his* young fellow poets to do: Learn your trade. Sing whatever is well made.

➤➤ 90

YESTERDAY'S NOISE: THE POETRY OF CHILDHOOD MEMORY

BY LINDA PASTAN

How sweet the past is, no matter how wrong, or how sad.
How sweet is yesterday's noise.
                    —Charles Wright, "The Southern Cross"

I WROTE AN ESSAY TEN YEARS AGO CALLED "MEMORY AS MUSE," AND looking back at it today I am struck by the fact that in the poems I write about childhood now the mood has changed from one of a rather happy nostalgia ("Memory as Muse") to a more realistic, or at least a gloomier, assessment of my own childhood and how it affects me as a writer ("Yesterday's Noise"). Let me illustrate with a poem called "An Old Song," from my most recent book.

An Old Song*

How loyal our childhood demons are,
growing old with us in the same house
like servants who season the meat
with bitterness, like jailers
who rattle the keys
that lock us in or lock us out.

Though we go on with our lives,
though the years pile up
like snow against the door,
still our demons stare at us
from the depths of mirrors
or from the new faces across a table.

And no matter what voice they choose,
what language they speak,
the message is always the same.
They ask "Why can't you do
anything right?" They say
"We just don't love you anymore."

425

As A. S. Byatt said about herself in an interview: "I was no good at being a child." My mother told me that even as a baby I would lie screaming in the crib, clearly terrified of the dust motes that could be seen circling in the sun, as if they were a cloud of insects that were about to swarm and bite me. By the time I was five or six, I had a series of facial tics so virulent that I still can't do the mouth exercises my dentist recommends for fear I won't be able to stop doing them. I'm afraid they'll take hold like the compulsive habits of childhood that led my second-grade teacher to send me from the room until I could, as she put it, control my own face. There was the isolating year (sixth grade) of being the one child nobody would play with, the appointed victim, and there was the even more isolating year (fourth grade) of being, alas, one of the victimizers. There was my shadowy room at bedtime, at the end of a dark hallway, and, until some worried psychologist intervened, no night light allowed.

I thought about calling my last book *Only Child* because something about that condition seemed to define not only me, but possibly writers in general who sit at their desks, necessarily alone, for much of the time. In some ways, of course, it defines all of us, born alone, dying alone, alone in our skins no matter how close we seem to be to others. I tried to capture my particular loneliness as a child, my difficulty in making friends, my search for approval, in what I thought would be the title poem of that book:

Only Child*

Sister to no one,
I watched
the children next door
quarrel and make up
in a code
I never learned
to break.

Go Play!
my mother told me.
Play! said the aunts,
their heads all nodding
on their stems,
a family of rampant
flowers

426

and I a single shoot.
At night I dreamed
I was a twin
the way my two hands,
my eyes,
my feet were twinned.
I married young.

In the fractured light
of memory—that place
of blinding sun or shade,
I stand waiting
on the concrete stoop
for my own children
to find me.

At a reading I gave before a group of Maryland PEN women, someone who had clearly not read beyond the tables of contents of my books introduced me as a writer of light verse. I remember thinking in a panic that I hardly had a single light poem to read to those expectant faces, waiting to be amused. Did I have such an unhappy life, then—wife, mother, grandmother, with woods to walk in, books to read, good friends, even a supportive editor?

I am, in fact, a more or less happy adult, suffering, thank God, from no more than the usual griefs age brings. But I think my poems are colored not only by a possibly somber genetic temperament, but also by my failure at childhood, even when I am not writing about childhood per se. And more and more, as I grow older, those memories themselves insist upon inserting themselves into my work. Perhaps it is the very way our childhoods change in what I called "the fractured light of memory" that make them such an inexhaustible source of poetry. For me, it is like the inexhaustible subject of the seasons that can be seen in the changeable light of the sun, or the versatile light of the imagination, as benign or malevolent or indifferent, depending upon a particular poet's vision at a particular moment.

I want to reflect a little then on those poems we fish up from the depths of our childhoods. And for any teachers reading this, I want to suggest that assigning poems to student writers that grow out of their childhoods can produce unusually good results, opening up those frozen ponds with what Kafka called the axe of poetry.

Baudelaire says that "genius is childhood recalled at will." I had a 19-year-old student once who was not a genius but who complained

427

that he couldn't write about anything except his childhood. Unfortunately, his memory was short, and as a result, all of his poems were set in junior high school. He had taken my course, he told me, in order to find new subjects. I admit that at first glance junior high doesn't seem the most fertile territory for poems to grow in. On the other hand, insecurity, awakening sexuality, fear of failure—many of the great subjects do exist there. It occurred to me that when I was 19, what I usually wrote about were old age and death. Only in my middle years did I start looking back into my own past for the subjects of poems. This started me wondering about the poetry of memory in general. Did other poets, unlike my young students, come to this subject relatively late, as I had? As I looked rather casually and unscientifically through the books on my shelves, it did seem to me that when poets in their twenties and thirties wrote about children, it was usually their own children that concerned them, but when they were in their late forties or fifties or sixties, the children they wrote about tended to be themselves.

Donald Justice, in an interview with *The Missouri Review,* gave as good an explanation of this as anyone. He said, "In the poems I have been thinking of and writing the last few years, I have grown aware that childhood is a subject somehow available to me all over again. The perspective of time and distance alter substance somewhat, and so it is possible to think freshly of things that were once familiar and ordinary, as if they had become strange again. I don't know whether this is true of everybody's experience, but at a certain point childhood seems mythical once more. It did to start with, and it does suddenly again."

There are, first of all, what I call "Poems of the Happy Childhood," Donald Justice's own poem "The Poet At Seven" among them. But for poets less skilled than Justice, there is a danger to such poems, for they can stray across the unmarked but mined border into sentimentality and become dishonest, wishful sort of recollections. When they are working well, however, these "Poems of the Happy Childhood" reflect the Wordsworthian idea that we are born "trailing clouds of glory" and that as we grow older we are progressively despiritualized. Even earlier than Wordsworth, in the mid-17th century, Henry Vaughan anticipated these ideas in his poem, "The Retreat."

I mention Wordsworth and Vaughan because in looking back over

428

the centuries at the work of earlier poets, I find more rarely than I expected poems that deal with childhood at all. Their poems are the exceptions, as are Shakespeare's 30th Sonnet and Tennyson's "Tears, Idle Tears." Perhaps it wasn't until Freud that people started to delve routinely into their own pasts. But nostalgia per se was not so rare, and in a book called *The Uses of Nostalgia: Studies in Pastoral Poetry,* the English critic Laurence Lerner comes up with an interesting theory. After examining pastoral poetry from classical antiquity on, he concludes that pastoral poems express the longing of the poets to return to a childhood arcadia, and that in fact what they longed to return to was childhood itself. He then takes his theory a step further and postulates that the reason poets longed for childhood is simply that they had lost it. He writes, "The list is varied of those who learned to sing of what they loved by losing it. . . . Is that what singing is? Is nostalgia the basis not only of pastoral but of other art too?" Or as Bob Hass puts it in his poem "Meditation at Lagunitas," "All the new thinking is about loss./ In this it resembles all the old thinking."

But though there are some left who think of childhood as a lost arcadia, for the most part Freud changed all of that.

We have in more recent times the idea of poetry as a revelation of the self to the self, or as Marge Perloff put it when describing the poems of Seamus Heaney, "Poetry as a dig."

The sort of poems this kind of digging often provides are almost the opposite of "Poems of the Happy Childhood," and they reflect a viewpoint that is closer to the childhood poems I seem to be writing lately. In fact, a poem like "Autobiographia Literaria" by Frank O'Hara actually consoles the adult by making him remember, albeit with irony in O'Hara's case, how much more unpleasant it was to be a child. If the poetry of memory can console, it can also expiate. In his well-known poem, "Those Winter Sundays," Robert Hayden not only recreates the past but reexamines his behavior there and finds it wanting. The poem itself becomes an apology for his behavior as a boy, and the act of writing becomes an act of repentance.

If you can't expiate the past, however, you can always revise it— and in various and occasionally unorthodox, ways. Donald Justice in the poem "Childhood" runs a list of footnotes opposite his poem, explaining and clarifying. Mark Strand in "The Untelling" reenters the childhood scene as an adult and warns the participants of what is to occur in the future.

Probably the most ambitious thing a poem of childhood memory can accomplish is the Proustian task of somehow freeing us from time itself. Proust is perfectly happy to use random, seemingly unimportant memory sensations as long as they have the power to transport him backwards. When he tastes his madeleine, moments of the past come rushing back, and he is transported to a plane of being on which a kind of immortality is granted. We can grasp for a moment what we can never normally get hold of—a bit of time in its pure state. It is not just that this somehow lasts forever, the way we hope the printed word will last, but that it can free us from the fear of death. To quote Proust: "A minute emancipated from the temporal order had recreated in us for its apprehension the man emancipated from the temporal order." Proust accomplished his journey to the past via the sense or taste, but any sense or combination of senses will do. In my poem "PM/AM," I used the sense of hearing in the first stanza and a combination of sight and touch in the second. Here is the second:

AM**

The child gets up
on the wrong side of the bed.
There are splinters
of cold light on the floor,
and when she frowns
the frown freezes on her face
as her mother has warned her it would.
When she puts her elbows roughly
on the table her father says:
you got up on the wrong side of the bed;
and there is suddenly
a cold river
of spilled milk.
These gestures are merely formal,
small stitches in the tapestry
of a childhood she will remember
as nearly happy. Outside
the snow begins again,
ordinary weather
blurring the landscape
between that time and this,
as she swings her cold legs
over the side of the bed.

430

But did I really say: "A childhood she will remember as nearly happy"? Whom are you to believe, the poet who wrote that poem years ago or the poet who wrote "An Old Song"? As you see, the past can be reinterpreted, the past can be revised, and the past can also be invented. Sometimes, in fact, one invents memories without even meaning to. In a poem of mine called "The One-Way Mirror Back," I acknowledge this by admitting: "What I remember hardly happened; what they say happened I hardly remember." Or as Bill Matthews put it in his poem "Our Strange and Lovable Weather"—

> . . . any place lies about its weather,
> just as we lie about our childhoods,
> and for the same reason: we can't
> say surely what we've undergone
> and need to know, and need to know.

This "need to know" runs very deep and is one of the things that fuels the poems we write about our childhoods.

But the simplest, the most basic thing such poems provide are the memories themselves, the memories for their own sakes. Here is the third stanza of Charles Simic's poem "Ballad": "Screendoor screeching in the wind/ Mother hobble-gobble baking apples/ Wooden spoons dancing, ah the idyllic life of wooden spoons/ I need a table to spread these memories on." The poem itself, then, can become such a table, a table to simply spread our memories on.

Looking back at some of my own memories, I sometimes think I was never a child at all, but a lonely woman camouflaged in a child's body. I am probably more childlike now. At least I hope so.

---

*"An Old Song" and "Only Child" appear in *Heroes In Disguise,* Norton, 1991.
**"AM" is from *PM/AM:New and Selected Poems,* Norton, 1982.

431

➢➢ 91

WRITING POETRY FOR CHILDREN AND YOUNG ADULTS

BY PAT LOWERY COLLINS

FOR YOUNG CHILDREN, A POEM IS A DEEPLY SATISFYING WAY OF LOOK-ing at the world. Fascinated at first by rhyme for its own sake, they soon begin to appreciate poetry that deals with simple concepts. They love slapstick, the wildly impossible, the ridiculous, word play, fanciful questions, clever and unexpected conclusions, twists and turns. They dote on repetition, used to great effect in *A Fine Fat Pig,* by Mary Anne Hoberman, in which the word abracadabra, used as an exclamation, precedes each line describing a zebra.

They revel in the action rhymes, finger play, and later, jump rope games, that depend on onomatopoeia, hyperbole and alliteration, as well as in such farcical verse as *Merry Merry FIBruary,* by Doris Orgel. Using these last two devices and the fun of a deliberate fib, the claim is made that "On the first of FIBruary/Setting out from Hacken-sack/ My Aunt Selma, in a seashell/ Sailed to Samarkand and back."

Poetry books for this age group are heavily illustrated, not only to complement the words, but also sometimes to explain them. And since poets are usually very visual writers, they will often provide the artist with exciting possibilities for illustrations without really trying.

The combined *Hector Protector* and *As I Went Over the Water* by Maurice Sendak is an unusual case in which poems and illustrations are all of one piece. Words emphasizing the text pepper the illustrations, and much of the action is in the pictures instead of the words. But in most cases, poems, even for the very young, rhymed or un-rhymed, should be able to stand on their own.

Sometimes a single poem is used as the entire text for a picture book, illustrated so as to enhance or help to develop a concept or story. The text of my nonfiction book, *I Am an Artist,* is actually one long poem conveying the concept, through the finely detailed paintings of Robin Brickman, that art is a process which begins with our experiences in the natural world.

It's been my observation that children in the middle grades (ages 9–12) are no longer as fascinated by rhyme. To some degree they want a poem to be as profound as what they are experiencing in life, something that takes them seriously. Yet, they still look for poetry that is simple and unlabored. *Haiku,* three unrhymed lines (in Japanese they must consist of 17 syllables) offering an unusual perspective on a spark of reality, is a perfect vehicle. Writing in this form is not as easy as it sounds. To provide an example, I struggled to produce: "Evening/is quietly stitching/the seam of night."

Children of this age are intrigued by the subtlety of haiku, and its shortness is irresistible to those just learning to put their own thoughts on paper.

But humorous, silly verse, either in such traditional forms as the limerick or in new and inventive ways, still holds great appeal. Thus the information that "Oysters/are creatures/without/any features," provided by John Ciardi in *Zoo Doings,* may be better remembered than the multiplication tables.

It is also a good time for books such as *Alice Yazzie's Year,* by Ramona Maher, in which unrhymed poems, each one complete in itself, taken together tell a story of a year in the life of a Navajo girl, a year that holds such mysteries as the birth of a lamb. We are told that "The new lamb sucks/The pinyon burns low/The lamb goes to sleep/His nose is a black star."

Poems about parents quarrelling or grandparents dying are often interspersed with poetry in a lighter vein in collections for this age group. One that does this effectively is *Knock at A Star,* collected by X. J. Kennedy and Dorothy M. Kennedy.

Language for its own sake becomes the focus again for readers about eleven to twelve, when communication with peers, intrigue, and secrets are important. Poetry is then a vehicle to express feelings without exposing them. Tools for this are found in nonsense sounds, obscure meanings, double meanings, rhyme, and, of course, humor. The mystery of nonsense—even an entire made-up language—seems to hold the same allure as it had for the four-year-old. Young readers are all too willing to accept the special logic of Lewis Carroll's "Jabberwocky"

433

and will have no trouble figuring out that when the Jabberwock "came whiffling through the tulgey wood/And burbled as it came," the "beamish boy" slays him as his "vorpal blade went snicker-snack!"

But these same children are also looking for poets able to look at life in the ways that they do. The poetry of Walter de la Mare has a timeless appeal because he affirms feelings that are universal. His book *Peacock Pie* was first published in 1913 and has been in print ever since. I'm currently illustrating a collection for Atheneum called *Sports, Power and Dreams of Glory, Poems Starring Girls,* edited by Isabel Joshlin Glaser, that affirms the dreams and aspirations of young women in such poems as "Abigail," by Kaye Starbird*, which ends by saying, "And while her mother said, 'Fix your looks,'/ Her father added, 'Or else write books.'/ And Abigail asked, 'Is that a dare?' And wrote a book that would curl your hair."

Teenagers may establish a passionate identification with one particular poet as they look for role models, a sense of history, a way to understand the world as it changes in and around them. By this time, they have probably been made aware of the mechanics and craft of poetry and are intrigued by experimentation. They can appreciate any poet whose vision is not too obscure. Because of the need of adolescents to deal with strong feelings and disturbing issues such as death and suicide, they are often attracted to poets with dysfunctional lives, for example, Sylvia Plath and Anne Sexton.

Most poetry for this age group appears in anthologies related to a single theme, to a city or to some historical period.

My own feeling is that even though the poetry you are compelled to write may turn out to have a special appeal for this age group, you will be competing with Shakespeare, T. S. Eliot, Walt Whitman, Emily Dickinson, and a cast of thousands. Of course, there is a lot of wonderful poetry out there for young children too, but not enough of it. And here I think the masters of today are a good match for those of yesterday and have an edge because they speak to the familiar.

But knowing your audience is only a beginning. There are a number of other things you should bear in mind in writing poetry for young people.

---

*Excerpted from "Abigail," in *The Pheasant on Route Seven,* by Kaye Starbird. Copyright ©1968 by Kaye Starbird. Reprinted by permission of Marian Reiner for the author.

Don't fall victim to the mistaken notion that writing poetry for children of any age is easier than writing for adults. Your perspectives and topics may be different, but the skills you must bring to task are the same, skills honed through years of reading good poetry and working to develop your craft. Your most important assets will be a good memory and a strong awareness of the child within you.

It is a common misconception that almost anyone can write poetry for children. It's true we can get away with serving them peanut butter sandwiches for dinner, but it better be creamy peanut butter or the kind with just the right amount of nuts. Just so, the quality of poetry we give our children should be the best available, from the very beginning of their awareness of language.

Another misconception is that almost any idea for a children's book should be written in rhymed verse. Quite the opposite is true. Although there are exceptions, even reasonably good verse will not necessarily make for a more compelling text, and bad verse can, in fact, be deadly. So many "first" manuscripts in verse are submitted to editors that there is almost a universal resistance to them. Here I must admit to being an offender myself with my first book for children, *My Friend Andrew*. Looking back, I realize that any advantage I may have had was somehow knowing enough to keep it simple.

Things I personally object to, not under the control of the poet, are anthologies that include bad poems simply because they're by "good" poets, and minor poems by major poets because they're short; uneven collections by one poet or many; and anthologists who completely overlook contemporary poems and poets. The inability of some editors to recognize good poetry or to appreciate a child's ability to understand abstract concepts is a real problem.

Besides being as meticulous when writing poetry for children as you would be in writing for adults, you should, under penalty of a one-way trip down the rabbit hole, avoid all of the following:

• Poetry that talks down to the reader or is used as a vehicle to deliver a moral or message, unless it is written with good humor, as when Shel Silverstein, in his *Where the Sidewalk Ends,* admonishes readers to "Listen to the Mustn'ts."

• Near rhymes. They stop children in their tracks and detract from the flow of the poem. An example would be "lion's" rhymed with

435

"defiance" and "cat" with "hate" in the poem "My Old Cat," by Hal Summers. *(Knock at A Star)*

• Rhymes that are too cute, convenient, or overused. "Rain" rhymed with "Spain" comes to mind.

• Lazy images. Even well-known poets sometimes do this, settling for the most obvious image, metaphor, or simile as in "wide as the sky."

• Rhyme for rhyme's sake, not because it will assist in saying what you want to say in the most interesting way. If, as with the book, *Madeline,* by Ludwig Bemelmans, it would be hard to imagine your own story being told in any other way, then, by all means, go for it. (I felt this way about *Andrew.*)

• Subject matter inappropriate for the intended age group, sometimes directed more to the parent than the child, or dealing with subjects outside the child's experience.

• Distorted rhyme that's hard to read aloud. Always read your own work aloud to avoid this.

• Poetry that is florid and old-fashioned, written in the accepted style of an earlier period.

• Poetry that is too complex or obscure. Young readers won't want to struggle to understand what may be very personal imagery.

• Writing presented in the form of a poem that isn't poetry by any stretch of the imagination and isn't even good prose.

• Writers who believe they must write like another poet in order to be published.

There was only one Dr. Seuss. If he had insisted on being another Edward Lear, we would have missed his unique vision and voice. If you aren't sure enough of your own voice, keep studying the work of poets you admire—their pace, rhyme schemes and structure—and keep writing until you find how to say what you want to in ways uniquely yours.

Like Valerie Worth, in her *All the Small Poems,* you may have won-derful, quiet perceptions to express about everyday objects and hap-

436

penings. Borrow her microscope if you must, but wear your prescription lenses and present the world through your observations and special talents, having in mind that building a poem is much like building a block tower: You will be balancing one word or line against another; arranging and rearranging; dropping one word, adding another, until the poem begins to say what you had in mind all along or what may never before have occurred to you. When a poem really comes together, really "happens," it is a moment like no other. You will feel like the child whose tower at long last has reached the sky.

Today, the market for children's poetry is quite different from what it was in the inhospitable 1980s. Then, there were a few poets who had cracked the barrier somewhat earlier and continued to be published, but a limited number of new names came on the scene. Thanks to the firmer financial footing of most book departments for young readers, to some editors who realize that poetry rounds out a list, and to the demand by teachers and librarians, there is currently greater opportunity for new poets. A number of publishing houses are actively seeking poetry for children, but they are highly selective and still apt to overlook a talented newcomer in favor of a poet more likely to turn a profit.

But the field of poetry has never been considered a lucrative one. There are exceptions, as with any art form, and for some poets, who continue to put their words down on paper napkins and laundry lists, there is really no escape.

⮞⮞ PLAYWRITING

➤➤ 92

CREATING EFFECTIVE STAGE CHARACTERS

BY DAVID COPELIN

ONE OF THE GREATEST REWARDS OF WRITING PLAYS LIES IN CRAFTING memorable characters. I love those wonderful moments in the process when characters you've invented start developing traits you never imagined for them, changing in ways that make them seem almost autonomous, creating *themselves.*

Although such moments can't be guaranteed, you can prepare for them by choosing those techniques of characterization that will help you jump-start the souls of the diverse citizens of your imagination.

How do you do this? Let's look at three areas of character creation: the *verbal,* the *non-verbal,* and the *relational.*

To dramatize the world is to unmask it. A novelist can describe characters at length, telling us who they are, what they look like, what they think and feel, and even how we should react to them. But a playwright's characters must unmask *themselves*—and quickly. Characters reveal who they are through their stage behavior: their words, their interaction with other characters, their strategic silences, their presence or absence in a particular scene. Stage characters also comment on each other. Some of that commentary is credible, some is not. Part of the role of the audience, part of their pleasure, is to figure out which part is which.

Since plays are so compressed in time and space, a little has to stand for a lot. So, to the extent that you can sketch a character's "character" with a few lines of dialogue, or through a minimal number of gestures, you will be a master of dramatic economy. In the most successful plays, such economy exposes both character and the world that surrounds that character in a theatrically involving way.

Dialogue is a primary means of communication in the theater. The first thing to remember about dialogue is that you can do quite a lot with very little. For example, take Tom Stoppard's provocative comedy *Travesties.* At one point in the play, mention is made of an imminent world-wide social revolution. A British Embassy bureaucrat inquires, "A *social* revolution? Unaccompanied women smoking at the opera, that sort of thing?"

We laugh, and we instantly understand who the character is, the nature of the society he's used to, and his utter incomprehension of a radically changing world. Stoppard tells us everything we need to know *in one line.*

Depending on who they are and what they want, characters will have different strategies of communication. In David Mamet's *Sexual Perversity in Chicago,* a young woman has just begun a love affair and has been with her new boyfriend for several days. When she returns to the apartment she shares with a woman friend, her roommate greets her laconically: "Your plants died."

In that brief moment, we learn a good deal about the roommate's personality, the women's relationship, the passage of time, domestic responsibility, jealousy, and cynicism. In performance, this moment is both funny and poignant.

Some characters don't talk much, but are devastatingly powerful. (Check out Ruth in Harold Pinter's *The Homecoming.*) Some characters chatter on and on, but are of little consequence in a play's power scheme. Such chatter can be quite useful as a source of comic relief, or it can be a convincing mannerism of disguise for a character who needs to conceal something from other characters and from the audience.

Audiences tend to believe whatever stage characters say. You can use this credulity in many ways. One of your most interesting options is to have characters *lie*—to themselves, to other characters, and to the audience. Moreover, characters who sometimes lie may also sometimes tell the truth! This is a situation ripe for dramatic exploitation.

Characters who reveal small truths win an audience's confidence; they can then conceal the larger truths you're *really* writing about until late in the play, and the audience will forgive you—and the characters—the deception.

Have you noticed that direct audience address has become quite commonplace in contemporary plays? Have you noticed how mixed

442

the results are? If you have one of your characters confide in the audience, make sure that the character *has* to do so. Don't use this technique simply because it appears to be easier than juxtaposing characters with different agendas. Such appearances deceive the audience.

It's usually unwise to have a character state the theme of your play. Focus instead on what the characters *want* and on what actions they take to get it. The audience will then have all the information they need to perceive the theme on their own.

Try not to have your characters explain their own or each other's motivations. Plays in which every character speaks as though she or he has had years of psychotherapy tend to be dramatically inert, because they do too much of the audience's work, too little of their own.

How do you choose one mode of verbal communication over another? Think of your cast of characters as an orchestra—whether chamber, full, or jug band doesn't matter. Much of your play's "music" comes from the permutations and combinations of characters as they speak and interact, so mixing speakers with different voices and rhythms automatically creates a theatrical "score." Of course, you may be writing a play in which all the characters *need* to sound alike. If so, go ahead. But this is not a choice to be made *unconsciously*. Your choice must reveal the *interplay* between plot and character, the *tension* between individual personalities and the situations they find themselves in. That's what's important dramatically.

As a play evolves, any kind of change in a character is permissible, as long as he or she behaves consistently within the parameters that you set. Altering a character's age, class or gender can have a positive impact on both the story and the other characters in the play, especially if the change makes your character less stereotypical, more idiosyncratic—and *raises the stakes*. This criterion also applies to adding, deleting and combining characters. Each such change will force you to review your dialogue, and probably to revise and tighten it.

Once your characters are established verbally, with their conflicting personalities revealed by their particular and unique ways of speaking, remember that, on stage, they also exist visually. That raises a whole different set of challenges—the *non-verbal*. Since you're writing for performance, you need to think about *people*, not just about words on a page; about non-verbal communication; and about communication in three dimensions.

443

Be aware that while words are important, visual elements, silence, and non-verbal sound all must be part of your playwriting strategy. Words express only what characters need to *say*. A character's tone of voice, body language, and the like express the emotions that underlie those words more complexly. This is what actors call "subtext." What's *between* the lines may reinforce what's being said out loud, or contradict it. In either case, what isn't spoken may well be more important to the persuasiveness of your play than what *is*.

The 18th-century diarist Samuel Pepys often wrote of going to the theater "to hear a play." We don't do that anymore; nowadays, we go to *see* a play. The difference is crucial. For modern people, seeing is believing. Therefore, in the theater, where the entire visual and aural context can be manipulated for effect, lighting and non-verbal sound can contribute to an audience's understanding of character as strongly as do your words. You need to appreciate what non-verbal communication can and cannot do to help you define your characters. How do they walk? What radio station do they listen to? Should the lighting make them look innocuous or sinister? Do they belch? And so on.

You can combine verbal and non-verbal means to present character far more effectively than you can express it with either mode alone. In Marie Irene Fornes's play, *The Conduct of Life,* an overworked, exploited domestic servant in the household of a Latin American fascist talks to us as she goes about her chores. She lists a number of things she does as soon as she wakes up, adding, "Then I start the day." After another list of chores, she repeats, "Then I start the day." After a third list, she says it again. And we're exhausted!

We understand, we *feel,* the dreariness of the character's life, and the oppression of her situation, even as we see her do her chores quickly and efficiently. The playwright's words and the actress's physicality combine to create an unforgettable character and theater with a powerful political sensibility.

You must also consider the *relational* aspects of character.

What do I mean by that?

I've been talking about character as if each personality in a play were an individual, distinct from other characters and more or less independent of them. But characters in plays are even less autonomous than human beings are in the "real" world. Whatever may be the rules of the dramatic universe you've created, chances are that *relationships* between characters are more important to the play's energy and forward motion than the individual characters you create one by one can ever be.

Try thinking about your characters in pairs, in triangles, in the context of their society, as well as individually. You can create character groupings that illustrate the workings of social forces without being too obvious about it, without losing the charm of the immediate and personal. If you need to, you can alter audience expectations of time, space, blood ties, cause and effect, or anything else that they usually take for granted. It's fun, and it stops conventional thinking in its tracks—one of the reasons we have theater in the first place.

For example, look at Caryl Churchill's *Cloud 9*. This justly celebrated play subverts commonplace notions of what character is in the theater and in the world. Churchill's highly economical method, which only a truly imaginative playwright could use so effectively, explodes received ideas about gender and its immutability. By having men play female characters and women play male characters, by having them interact in highly provocative ways, Churchill dramatizes complex issues that range from patriarchy and imperialism, to domestic violence and sexual pleasure. The play is exhilarating, because Caryl Churchill has the wit and the craft to turn our expectations of character upside down—and make us like it.

You will probably not want or be able to use every technique for presenting character that you run across, but your own arsenal of ways to make the people "work" is bound to grow, whether you write kitchen-sink realism, post-neo-futurist cabaret sketches, playlets for children, or any other dramatic form that puts human beings on a stage.

Remember, the wide variety of character-revealing techniques is there to serve your purposes. If you can't find contemporary techniques that fulfill your needs, feel free to invent (or revive!) those that do. Whatever makes your characters memorable makes *you* a better playwright.

➤➤93

Before You Try Broadway . . .

By Anna Coates

As a Los Angeles-based writer, script analyst, and devotee of community theater, I see a lot of plays that could have been a lot better, and I read a lot of scripts that probably should have been shredded at birth.

Which is not necessarily a bad thing.

One of the functions of little theater is to give the playwright a chance to see what works and what doesn't—not on the page, but on the stage, with living, fumbling, stumbling actors. The playwright's duty—alas, oft-neglected—is to figure out what doesn't work, and why, and if necessary to cut and chop or even to begin again.

And in a world that seems unjustly biased toward screenwriters—from Joe Eszterhas and his three-million-dollar *Basic Instinct* to Joe Schmoe and his twenty-thousand-dollar B-flick advance—the playwright has one wonderful advantage over the screenwriter. In addition to basic moral superiority, of course.

The playwright can learn as he goes.

The playwright may aspire to Broadway, but he has a crack at many lesser triumphs along the way. He can tinker with his work, tightening here and lengthening there. Even after he surrenders a script to a director's interpretation, he may continue to edit and rewrite, with or without the director's blessing.

Markets for a stage script can be divided into four categories: *community theater, experimental theater, "legitimate theater"* (aka, the Big Time), and *publication/TV*.

Of course, the categories aren't mutually exclusive. Community theater can mean a show performed on a makeshift stage in a church basement, or an elaborate and well-funded production staged as part of the regular "season" of a repertory house. (You understand, of

446

course, that the term "well-funded" is relative!) Student productions are another type of community theater, and in some college towns they are eagerly awaited as the only theater available.

Community theaters like to produce well-known plays by established playwrights. That gets a little tired when you're seeing *Our Town* or *Streetcar* for the fifth time in six years, but if you think about it, it makes sense. Working with tiny budgets, directors tend to pick shows that are proven winners with broad appeal. They keep in mind that audiences—not to mention casts—may be unseasoned, and will react most favorably to mainstream fare.

This doesn't mean your original light comedy or social drama can't find a home with a little theater—of course it can. But you may need extra patience to find the right house to handle its premiere.

And yes, local companies will occasionally get crazy and go for *experimental theater.* But you're more likely to come across it in a city like Los Angeles or New York with a heavy concentration of actors and writers, an abundance of venues, and a weird (whoops, I mean *varied*) range of tastes.

If you're slathering to do your play on the Great White Way, or at least on cable TV, back up and slow down.

The road to Broadway (and Off-, and off-Off) wends its way through many a community theater and college campus. Sure, your play might be one of the fifteen selected by the O'Neill Theatre Center's National Playwrights Conference. On the other hand, it might be one of the fifteen hundred they reject. And it's within the realm of possibility— just faintly, there at the border—that you'll zap out your first rough script to a cable television company and get a fat check and a contract by FedEx a week later. Certainly, if you're confident about the quality of your work you should try.

But for most mere mortals the way to earn a few credits and learn the ropes is to have their work produced by a small local theater or an undergraduate director.

And that should be pretty easy. After all, an undergraduate director is really just a college kid. And local theaters pay nothing—or maybe carfare—and ought to be happy to get what they can get. Right?

Well, no.

The great majority of scripts submitted to student directors, to little

447

theaters, and to contests will never be produced or optioned because they are badly written.

It's not because the writers are without talent. There is almost always—no, *always*—something positive I can say about a piece of writing, and I'll go out of my way to figure out what it is. Still, it's frustrating and annoying to read script after script in which plots are direct rip-offs from current movies or standard stage productions, down to characters' names and dialogue. Sure, we all know there are only three basic storylines. The trick is to make yours seem fresh.

What directors and readers and editors look for in a script is a storyline that flows and that is logical *within context*. Think about the eternal *Ten Little Indians*. Now, the idea of a disgruntled murderer gathering nine victims and bumping them off slowly and cleverly, one by one, is a bit preposterous, especially in this day of Uzi machine guns and other high tech timesavers. But so cleverly is this story crafted that contemporary audiences are able to lose themselves in the drama and the terror, and suspend disbelief—for ninety minutes, at least.

Realistic dialogue

Beyond plot, what you should be most concerned with is that your script be peopled by believable characters who use realistic, interesting dialogue. Trust me, if you write a terrific story and a potential producer thinks it needs a modified end, or an older main character, or a different setting, she will let you know. Those are very fixable flaws and an excellent piece of work won't remain homeless because of them.

What will get "no thanks" is a hackneyed plot, flat, stereotyped characters, and trite, wooden dialogue.

Stilted dialogue is a common problem. If you want to know how real people speak, listen to them.

Don't be afraid of contractions! You'll seldom hear a person say, "I do not know what I am going to do about it." Most people will say "I don't know what I'm going to do about it." (The exceptions might be a person speaking stiffly, for emphasis, or a non-native speaker. For instance, on the television series *Star Trek: the Next Generation,* Mr. Data's "un-contracted" speech helps define his android character. This device is effective because the other cast members speak naturally.)

When in doubt, read your dialogue aloud.

People sometimes—uh, pause, when they speak. And sometimes they begin sentences with *and* or *but*. But I find writers, are, well . . . reluctant to use hesitation in dialogue.

If you want your hero to say, "Gloria, I—I'm confused. This feeling is so strong. And I don't know what's happening between us," then don't write "Gloria, I am confused. This feeling is so strong. I do not know what is happening between us."

Remember that theoretically the actor should utter only the lines you write. Yes, he may get fed up and throw in an ad-lib and the director may decide to use it. In that case you, the playwright, have not done your job. Dialogue that *works* doesn't tempt actors to rewrite.

(As I'm chasing you with the hickory switch, remember that an early production of your play is your chance to cut and polish for later audiences. Maybe the church-basement director won't allow you to rewrite dialogue mid-production, but you certainly may do so before you resubmit your play to larger regional companies.)

The professional look

Budding playwrights I have found avoid commas although I'm not sure why. Without commas the actors may forget to breathe if you follow me or at least they'll be confused.

An occasional *tpyo* is no big deal, but when every other line of a script contains misspellings like "ocaissional," "privledge," "thier," and "perference," can you blame me for concluding that the writer was just too lazy to consult his dictionary?

Grammar mistakes are irksome, too. No, you don't need perfect diction to write a good script. On the other hand, a writer who aspires to be a professional should certainly know the difference between "lie" and "lay." Your heroine may choose to lay on the bed, but that's a pretty good trick if she's alone in the room. And anyway, isn't this a G-rated production?

The writer should know whether his characters are doing well or doing good (or both). He should know whether that cool rebel flaunts rules or flouts them, and why that kid's new puppy can't be a gift from Daddy and I.

He should know if it's proper to contract *it is* as *its* or if it's not.

Of course, people don't speak perfectly, and judiciously placed solecisms make dialogue ring true. But when *every* character confuses literal and figurative, and says fortuitous when he means fortunate, or infer when he means imply, I begin to suspect the blunders aren't the characters' but the writer's own.

Get the simple stuff straight: Split infinitives will continue to easily slip by me. Likewise sentence fragments.

Dialect trips up a lot of playwrights. No, you don't have to be African-American to create a character who speaks "Black English," and you don't have to be Chinese to write about a fellow from Beijing. But spare me your "G'wan, man, I be jivin' yo' funky sef'" and your "Solly, no speaky Engrish" and most of all, your Southern Belles who say "y'all" when they're speaking to only one person.

If you must indicate a dialect, do it like this:

BELLE

Why, I declare!
(Belle's thick Southern accent makes this sound like, "wha, ah declayuh.")

You need indicate this only once. The director will get the idea, and so will the actress. And both of them will thank you.

Try to keep your set directions to a minimum. Just tell us we're on a pretty beach at sunset, and let the set designer worry about the golden sun and the cry of the gulls and the sails like white wings against the horizon. And keep in mind that the more sets and props your play calls for, the more it will cost to produce.

Keep blocking—the stage directions that show the actors when and how to move—to a minimum. Entrances and exits must be indicated, of course, and long slow clinches are fun to write. But if Tom enters angry, the director will guess that he might slam the door. If Suzy is doing an audience aside, the director will definitely place her downstage. If the phone rings, he can figure out that Jan will need to cross to answer it. O.K.? So indicate movement when necessary to advance the story, and don't leave your actors rooted in place like young saplings. But do have mercy and let the poor director have something to do.

It's scary for a writer to pack up her work and send it out for strangers to peruse. Presumably the fledgling playwright reminds herself that stage companies—local to pro—*want* to like her work. They, like you, are in this biz for the love of the written and spoken word. And besides, who wouldn't like to discover the next Sam Shepard?

What amazes me is that with this in mind, so many scripts are sent out flawed not only in the ways we've discussed above, but badly typed and poorly photocopied.

Neatness counts. Your third-grade teacher told you that and you probably relearned it in college when your psych professor showed you a study indicating that of two term papers *identical* in content the one typed neatly earned higher grades than one full of typos and cross-outs.

So what's the trouble?

I know. It takes a long time to type a hundred pages, doesn't it? It hardly seems worthwhile to retype the whole thing every time you add a couple of paragraphs or take one away.

Stop! You're breaking my heart!

The fact is, if you want to be taken seriously, your script must look professional. That means $8\frac{1}{2}'' \times 11''$ white paper, black ink, margins at the top, bottom, and sides, numbered pages, and invisible corrections or none at all. Absolutely no strike-outs.

Submit a photocopy, never the original. If your script is returned to you clean, there's no reason not to send it out again, but spare us the dog-eared, coffee-ringed, penciled fourth-timers! No one likes to feel like last choice.

The standard format for a play script, adjusted according to number of acts and intended medium and audience, is available from many sources, including books from your local library. But you won't be penalized for indenting dialogue seventeen spaces instead of fifteen, or for numbering your pages at the top center instead of at the top right.

Cover letters

Whether you are submitting your work to a little theater, a contest committee, a cable television director, or a magazine editor, address your cover letter to a specific person *with whom you have spoken,* and who has agreed to look at your work. And I don't want to hear any

451

whining about the cost of toll calls. First of all, most of these people aren't going to want to sit and chat (until they've read your script and realize you're brilliant and incredibly talented). And secondly, are you interested in getting produced or in sitting around complaining about an unavoidable business expense?

If you're submitting your script to a contest or television company, write ahead to request specific instructions about format, formal copyright registration, and whether a signed release is required. But when you want a local theater director to look at your work, it's still necessary to call ahead. By calling in advance, you can make sure that you have the correct contact name and address and that the director is willing to consider your work. Why waste time if she's not? Many directors will look at new plays only between seasons, and if you mail your script to a college theater department in June, it's likely to gather dust at least until September. And remember that your work should *always* go out with the copyright symbol (©) that indicates "copyright protected" at the right-hand top of the cover page.

Like your call, your cover letter should be brief. "Here's the script we talked about, and thanks for your time" will do. If you want to, add a few lines to mention your credits, if you have any, or your credentials, if they're germane. If your script is a comedy about a dairy farmer, and you happen to live on a dairy farm, say so.

Don't send a script replete with four-letter words to a children's playhouse, no matter how the kids in your neighborhood talk. And keep in mind that an all-nude sex comedy isn't likely to play in Peoria.

If you've done your homework and kept set and prop requirements to a minimum, you can say so in your cover letter. But don't use your cover letter to sell the script; it must sell itself. Don't write, "This is a wonderful, rip-roaring comedy full of hilarious moments in the wacky life of a dairy farmer."

With all the pitfalls I've described, what's the worst mistake aspiring playwrights make?

It's not confused plotting or flat characterization or trite dialogue. It's not sloppy typing or garbled cover letters. It's not even forgetting to put your name and phone number somewhere it can be found.

The worst mistake budding playwrights make is *not trying*. Not writing that script, or not polishing it, or not sending it out. Or sending it out only once, then giving up.

You may place your first script its first time out. Or you may place your tenth, its tenth time out, then watch it move along through little theaters and repertory ensembles. And as you look back on all the rejections, you'll realize that you learned something from every one.

I'm rooting for you, so get busy. And, hey—see you on Broadway!

➤➤ 94

ACT ONE, SCENE ONE:
BEGINNING A PLAY

BY JEFFREY SWEET

NOT SO VERY LONG AGO, IT WAS COMMON PRACTICE TO START A PLAY
with a pair of secondary characters in a scene that ran along these
lines:

MARY: Young Gregory was out late last night. He finally came back at three
in the morning.
JOHN: Did he say anything about where he was or why there's such a big
dent in his car?
MARY: No, but he'd had too much to drink, I can tell you that.
JOHN: I wonder if this has anything to do with the letter he received yesterday. The one that made him turn so pale.
MARY: I couldn't say. But this morning at breakfast you could have cut the
tension between him and his parents with a knife.

All right, I'm exaggerating, but not by very much. The introductory
conversation between two servants, or two gossips in the neighborhood, or a character newly returned from travels asking about events
during his absence often kicked off the action. If you can call this
action.

The idea behind such scenes was to pump the audience full of the
information necessary to understand the subsequent events. Playgoers
used to sit patiently for the first ten minutes or so knowing that enduring this sort of exposition was the price they had to pay in order to
get to the good stuff. And I'm not talking only about plays by forgotten
hacks. The only reason for the lame passage between Camillo and
Archidamus in Act One, Scene One of Shakespeare's *The Winter's
Tale* is to help the audience get its bearings. (Just because Shakespeare
is the best doesn't mean he didn't make his share of mistakes.)

Generally speaking, plays start faster than they used to.

I think this is partially the result of television. Tune into a prime-time drama series, and you'll see something like this in the pre-credits action:

> *Stand-up comic onstage, telling jokes. Audience laughing. A woman in black carrying a purse slips in through the stage entrance. She moves to a door marked "Dressing Room," enters the room and closes the door behind her. Inside, she switches on the light, looks around, sees a framed photo of an attractive lady sitting on the make-up table. Suddenly, she smashes the photo onto the floor so that the glass from the frame breaks. Onstage, the comic says goodnight and takes his bows. In a cheerful mood, he goes to his dressing room. He switches on the light, takes a step and hears a crunch. He looks down on the floor and sees he has stepped on the glass from the smashed frame. Then he hears a voice: "You were really cooking tonight, Charley. You were killing them." He turns and sees the woman standing behind the door, pointing a small pistol at him. Sweat builds up on his lip. "And I always thought 'die laughing' was an expression," she says. Now she smiles. The camera pulls in on her finger on the trigger. Fade out. Bouncy music kicks in and the credits begin.*

Do you want to know who the woman is, why she smashed the picture and whether she's going to ventilate Charley? You've got to stay tuned past the credits and the opening batch of commercials. If you do, you'll probably be willing to sit through some less immediately compelling stuff setting up other characters till the story returns to Charley and his mysterious visitor. And then, odds are, having invested this much time, you'll stick around for the rest of the show. By beginning with a provocative but unexplained incident, the story has been launched, caught your attention and given you enough reason to take the ride to the last stop.

The craft of writing for television has necessarily been affected by the nature of the audience's relation to the medium. Aware that the audience, holding channel changers in their hands, can switch to a competing program at any time, the writers know they have to serve up immediate and pressing reasons for viewers to stick around. Obviously, few are likely to stick around if the show starts with the equivalent of two servants relating offstage events. So a TV script tends to start with a scene that builds to a pressing dramatic question.

Of course, audiences don't come to the theater with channel changers in hand. But, after years of watching the box in their living rooms and getting used to the pacing of tales told there, they come to the theater in the habit of being plunged into the heart of the story

455

quickly. To grab the playgoer fast, many contemporary playwrights have borrowed a leaf from television's book by beginning their plays with characters in the middle of high-energy sequences equivalent to the one introducing Charley's dilemma.

John Guare's remarkable play, *Six Degrees of Separation,* starts with two of the leading characters, Ouisa and Flan Kittredge, excitedly telling the audience about their narrow escape moments before from some unnamed threat, checking to see that none of their valuables has been stolen, savoring how close they may have come to death. Having established their hysteria, Guare then has them take us back several hours to a lower-key scene anticipating the arrival of a friend who is to join them for dinner. With the benefit of hindsight, we know that they will shortly be hyperventilating, and so we watch carefully to see what part this dinner will play in the chain of events that leads to their alarums.

Guare could very well have *started* with the Kittredges discussing their dinner plans and then proceeding with the rest of the play as written. Doing this would not have meant omitting any of his story. But, by kicking the play off with the two in such an agitated state and then flashing back, Guare makes the audience sit up and take notice from the first moment. No coy wooing of the playgoer here; he snares our interest instantly. Knowing that the flashback holds the answer to the question, "What's making the Kittredges so upset?," the audience pays closer attention to the lower-key scene that follows than they would have if the play had started with that scene.

I'm not suggesting that all plays should begin in the middle of action, but quite a few would be improved if they did. I asked the members of a playwriting workshop I run to bring in scripts they were working on, and, as an experiment, we read excerpts from them, each time starting on page ten. In all but two cases, the writers decided their plays actually began better on their tenth pages than on their firsts.

What information was contained in the missing pages? My students discovered that most of it was implicit in the scenes from page 10 on. By beginning in the *middle* of dramatic action—instead of setting up the circumstances in the first ten pages—the playwrights gave the audience the fun of figuring out the circumstances for themselves. Gone were the dull stretches of characters entering the stage, pouring drinks, and slipping in nuggets of self-introduction. Gone, too, were the one-way phone calls designed to sneak in exposition. Rather than switching on and warming up the scripts' motors and then coaxing them up to speed, the plays now had a sense of urgency from the word go, and that urgency made them compelling.

The opening of a play not only gets the story started, it also makes a contract with the audience. The first few minutes virtually announce, "This is the kind of play we're doing," and the audience sets its expectations accordingly. We watch different genres with different expectations. It is very important, then, for the opening of your script to set the audience's expectations correctly. If you break a promise to a friend in real life, you're likely to lose the trust and confidence of that friend. Break a promise to the people who have paid to see your play, and they will respond with confusion and irritation. If, for instance, you begin your play with a pair of bewigged fops trading quips in blank verse, you'd better not suddenly switch in the middle of the second act to a modern psychological thriller. Raising the curtain on a solo figure in black tights on a bare stage miming the life cycle would be a misleading introduction to a Neil Simon-style domestic comedy.

This may sound like very obvious advice, but some very savvy theatrical talents nearly lost a great musical because of such a miscalculation. *A Funny Thing Happened on the Way to the Forum* was trying out in a pre-Broadway engagement in Washington in 1962. According to all accounts, the show was substantially the one we've come to know, but the audiences weren't taking to it. The laughs were few and far between, and each night a dismaying chunk of the audience disappeared at intermission. The perplexed creative team—which included such celebrated figures as George Abbott, Larry Gelbart, Bert Shevelove and Stephen Sondheim—asked director-choreographer Jerome Robbins to take a look and tell them where they were going wrong.

After the performance, Robbins informed them that the problem was with the opening number, a light-hearted little tune called "Love is in the Air," which promised a romantic frolic. What followed instead, however, was an evening of broad jokes, slapstick, and farcical intrigue. Robbins said what was needed was an opening that *promised* broad jokes, slapstick, and farcical intrigue. An opening, he insisted, should promise the audience what in fact a show is going to deliver.

Composer-lyricist Stephen Sondheim went to his piano and wrote a

457

song entitled, "Comedy Tonight," which did just that. According to legend, as soon as it was put in, the reaction to the show turned around completely. What had previously played to indifference now brought cheers. *A Funny Thing Happened* went on to New York, where it received glowing reviews and was proclaimed a hit, all because the opening was changed. It is now counted a classic musical comedy.

Not only do you establish the genre of a show in the first few minutes, you also establish stylistic rights. At the beginning of *Six Degrees of Separation,* Guare swiftly signals the audience that he reserves the right to 1) have any of his characters, at the drop of a hat and without self-consciousness, address the audience directly, and 2) with the briefest of transitions, leap to any other time or place in the story. And, indeed, throughout the script, both major and minor characters feel no compunction about making eye contact with a theater full of playgoers and speaking their minds. What's more, scenes move abruptly back and forth in time and jump, without second thought, from the Kittredges' fancy apartment to Central Park to Greenwich Village and wherever else it is necessary to go to witness the essential events of the story. And, oh yes, the number of laughs at the show's beginning clearly indicates the audience is in for a comedy.

It is a truism among musical theater writers that the opening number is usually the one you write last, because it is only after you've finished the rest of the show that you know what the opening should prepare the audience for. Straight plays are structurally less complicated than musicals, but upon completing a draft, a smart dramatist looks closely at the opening few pages to see if they correctly establish the world and style of the two hours to follow. The audience isn't likely to go through your door if you don't offer them the key to unlock it.

➢➢ 95

BLUEPRINT FOR WRITING A PLAY

BY PETER SAGAL

IF I WEREN'T A PLAYWRIGHT, I'D BE AN ARCHITECT, WHICH ON CERtain days I think is the finest kind of artist there is, because architects create art that is indisputably useful, necessary: Architecture is the art that stitches together the seams of the physical environment. But since I can't draw, I can't do math, and I'm too lazy to undergo all that study, I have to settle for being a playwright. I comfort myself, though, by imagining plays as architecture: art defined by its function, articulated by structure, inspired by the truths about the people who are to use it. Plays, like architecture, are, or should be, useful; they should express their beauty through purpose sheathed with ornament.

So one should go about the business of writing a play with all the dedication, discipline, knowledge, etc. that any fine art requires, but something else, too—something shared again with architecture, and that is a sense of *responsibility*. The architect knows that his or her building may or may not be admired by passers-by, but most definitely it will be used; a mistake on the drawing board may result in discomfort and displeasure for unknown thousands whom the architect failed by making a building that may have been fashionable or pretty but did not *work*, though architects ask people to live and perform their professional and personal functions within such a building. We playwrights ask less but still something substantial: We ask for time. Give us two or three hours of your life, two or three hours that can never be replaced, and we will enclose you in a soundproof room, turn off the lights so you can't read, and forbid you to talk, and we promise that it will be worthwhile.

Your first responsibility as a playwright is to waste no one's time. Consider your audience's attention as a precious gift, a gem, and if you fumble, it's lost forever. Time is a sacred thing, because everyone has only a finite supply of it.

Your job as a playwright, then, is to create a series of events, conversations, and images so important that it's worth asking the audience to give up their lives for a while and listen. I think this is the most difficult task in all writing, with the possible exception of book-length epic poetry. You do not have the expansive freedom of the novelist, or the factual safety net of the journalist. There's no tolerance for sloppiness; writing a play is done with a gun to the head. Here's how to do it:

Love your art

The theater won't pay you, won't comfort you, will provide you with little reward, and for that reward will drain your blood. In the best case your writing will be subject to the whims and caprices of actors, technicians, directors, producers; in the worst case, it will be ignored. If very, very successful, it will reach a tiny fraction of the people who watch "Married With Children" on TV, and your financial remuneration will be an even tinier fraction of the amount received by the writers who produce that work and others like it. Don't write for the theater if you want to write for television or the movies, or even for Broadway, which is a fictional place, like the Big Rock Candy Mountain. Write for yourself; write because if you don't you'll go crazy. Write because nothing else in your life compares to the power of creating your own worlds. Write plays because you believe that the experience of people gathering in a theater to see a play is nothing less than sacred. If you don't have the strength of this quasi-religious conviction, then the trials ahead could well overwhelm you.

Study your art

I am continually amazed by how many aspiring playwrights are ignorant of dramatic writing outside of a narrow canon of recognized giants: Shakespeare, Tennessee Williams, Arthur Miller, David Mamet, Sam Shepard, etc. In many cases, the writer sets out to imitate one or more of them. One problem, of course, is that these writers are geniuses, and you can't just imitate their work.

The other problem is that they *aren't* geniuses at all; they were and are working writers who slogged away for years and years, and most of them did their slogging in the theater. There isn't a single great writer for the theater who did not spend a long apprenticeship: Shake-

460

speare, for example, started with the Lord Chamberlain's Men as an actor, writing plays himself only after he had performed uncounted dozens of other, now unknown works.

Such a lengthy servitude isn't necessary, but it is foolish not to recognize such problems as how to make the stage relevant to your life and the lives around you. If you live in a city with an active theater scene, go all the time, particularly to the new plays; the failures will be as educational as the few successes. If you don't have that luxury, then read as much as you can: Read your peers in American playwriting (Tony Kushner, Marlane Meyer, Neal Bell, Jose Rivera, Migdalia Cruz, Wendy Hammond, etc., etc.) and their counterparts in Great Britain; read plays from non-English speaking and non-Western traditions. You will come across hundreds of good ideas and save yourself from making thousands of mistakes. It is idiotic to try to invent the theater from scratch every time you sit down. Depart and rebel, by all means, but know what you are rebelling against.

I am very skeptical of books and articles that offer "rules" for writing, which is why I refuse to offer any specific suggestions to aspiring playwrights, such as, "start in the middle," "make the exposition active," etc. I have arrived at my own set of principles of dramatic writing, but they describe not so much how to write a play, as the kind of play I like. For every one of those rules, there's an exception, and in many cases, the exceptions are brilliant plays. For example, I don't like to have my characters address the audience, offering information about the other characters. That means I'll never write *The Glass Menagerie* or *The Marriage of Bette and Boo,* or even *Henry V,* among the many other plays I admire. The theater, more than any other form of writing, is a living thing: It grows and changes, departing from what just happened and pointing toward what's next. Rules hinder evolution. Further, when you sit down to write, you should be writing from an interior vision of what *your* play *is,* not some acquired idea of what *a* play is *like.* Television writers follow rules, because people who watch television know what they want and watch TV, expecting to get just that. This is the opposite of theater.

Practice your art

Writers in any form have to confront and control the hunger for acclaim. In the theater, this becomes even more difficult because, first,

461

you are collaborating with actors and other artists who are eager to make their mark, and more important, your work is read out loud to large groups of people who might very well make loud noises that indicate approval (or disapproval). It becomes very tempting to get those words out of the word processor, into the hands of actors, and up in front of the audience, and to let the magic of the moment make up for any shortcomings. However, if you remember what I said about responsibility, you will see that this is a pernicious urge to be avoided. The rules of discipline, writing, and constant revision hold as much in playwriting as in poetry—don't buy into the old adage that a playscript is a "blueprint" and can slide by on heart alone. It *is* a blueprint, and it had better be a perfect blueprint or this house won't stand.

So write, write, write; experiment with sound and language and vision and structure. Do not be indulgent. Do not be lazy. Do not put less than perfect words on a stage and hope that the audience will buy them. Don't try to dazzle. Don't coast. Whatever you put on a page, make it your own. Remember, when you sit down to write a play, you are taking the future of an ancient and fragile art form in your hands: A bad play strikes another blow at it, in these wounded and wounding times; a good play breathes new life into the theater, and sends it striding on into a few more hearts, which may, in turn, nourish it after us.

⪼ 96

ADVICE TO PLAYWRIGHTS

By Janet Neipris

WHEN I BEGIN A PLAYWRITING CLASS, THE FIRST LECTURE IS Fifty Rules to Follow When Writing a Play. Of the fifty rules, forty-nine are structural; only the fiftieth is practical. That rule is, "Make certain you love this project, that you have passion for this play, because you will be working on it for five to ten years, and it is passion that will sustain you." Talent is only one part of playwriting, craft is another, and the third, and perhaps most important, is perseverance.

Recently, I began to write a play at the suggestion of an artistic director of a theatre. The subject—the life and loves of an eminent American playwright—was fascinating, filled with opportunities for research, and eminently commercial. It would be hard to believe this project would not excite any living playwright.

So, I began. But, the more research I did, and the more I learned, the less I was in love with the subject. It remained a good idea, but not for me. The director, who had suggested the play and had promised a staged reading of it, called to ask, "Do you hear the play singing yet?" "No," I replied, "but that will come."

Well, it never did. So, after six months of work, many scenes outlined and written, but no fire from inside, I abandoned the project. It was the most courageous thing I've ever done as a playwright, and with it came the conviction that I was never going to write about something I didn't love. From that moment on, I was certain my actions matched the practical advice I always give young playwrights: WRITE FROM THE HEART.

WRITING YOUR PLAY

1. First, always write out of *passion*. Passion is what sustains perseverance. You have to believe that the play you are writing *must* be

463

written, and that you are the only one who could tell the story you want to tell in exactly this way.

2. Second, you should be convinced your play is worth developing *artistically,* that its subject matter is of significance and is identifiable to an audience. Always remember you are crafting a piece of dramatic literature. Significant doesn't necessarily mean recreating the Civil War on stage, but rather, that you are writing about a subject that is common to the human heart.

3. Then, you must be convinced your play is worth developing *commercially,* and that an audience will want to pay to come to see it. Your play should either entertain, question, or challenge, and at best, do all three.

4. Always write with the *practical* elements in mind—the set design, costumes, and props. For example, an action that involves fifty elephants or twenty minor characters or a waterfall is certainly impractical, both technically and financially. The writer can, however, be practical without compromising his or her art. For example, if a waterfall is integral to the plot, maybe slides could be suggested, or a backdrop, or sound.

5. Make sure your play is not exactly like this season's hit. The theatre traditionally honors quality, craft, and originality. To create, after all, means to make something where there once was nothing. To create suggests imagining.

6. Write a play that does more than simply mirror reality. Reality is never enough for a complete artistic piece. It is only a beginning. If the audience wanted simple reality, they could just open their windows and look out. Also, be certain never to use a real name for any of your characters. It is the playwright's job to *start* with reality, then *transform* it into a dramatic story.

7. Don't expect to get your script right the first time. You are trying to portray *unique* characters in *conflict,* which leads to *confrontation, resolution,* and *change.* The first draft serves to help you find out what you are writing about. The subsequent drafts, the *rewrites,* are about craft.

8. Before you send the manuscript out, make certain it is the best you can make it. Competition is high, but so is expectation when any publisher or theatre receives a new play. The first chance is the best

chance, so you want to give editors, artistic directors, literary managers, possible producers, and readers the best script possible.

HOW TO BREAK IN

Getting an agent

Do you need an agent in order to get a play produced? Not necessarily, as many theatres and contests do accept scripts that are not represented by an agent. However, having an agent will make it easier to ensure that your script gets a reading. In cases where a regional theatre does require representation, an agent is a necessity. In addition, an agent can be helpful in negotiating a contract with a theatre, a contract that represents you, the playwright, professionally and financially.

1. Get a list of drama agents from one of the following sources:

a. *Dramatists Sourcebook,* published by Theatre Communications Group (TCG), 355 Lexington Ave., New York, NY 10017.
b. *The Dramatists Guild Quarterly,* Summer Directory, published annually by the Dramatists Guild, 234 W. 44th St., Sardi Building, New York, NY 10036.

2. Research *which* agents represent *the kind of plays you write* by reading volumes of *The Best Plays* and *Short Plays* published annually and available in most public libraries. Additional sources include the general drama sections of large bookstores and libraries.

3. Write query letters to agents of interest to you, describing your play briefly and any possible readings or productions of the play. Also, if you have a recommendation from another writer, you can mention the name, but get permission from the writer first.

Then, ask the agent if you may send a script. If you've had no answer a month after sending your script, send a short polite letter asking about its status.

Getting a reading or production

1. Go to local productions in order to familiarize yourself with local directors and actors. Start a notebook listing actors and directors you are interested in working with in the future.

2. Subscribe to *The Dramatists Guild Quarterly,* which lists production possibilities and contests, many of which include production opportunities.

3. Purchase a copy of the *Theatre Directory* from Theatre Communications Group, 355 Lexington Ave., New York, NY 10017. This lists regional theatres and rules for submission of scripts.

4. Join a local theatre group that does play readings and productions. There are such groups in many communities, either attached to a regional theatre or working independently.

5. Try to set up a reading locally or even in your own home. First, discuss your script with a local professional director. Make a list of questions you want to ask about themes, tone, focus, possible cuts, and casting. If you can't make a connection with a local director, you might try to direct this first read-through yourself.

Then, cast the play with local actors or friends. The main purpose of this first reading is for the playwright to "hear" the play. This reading will serve both as an opportunity to plan your second draft of the play, and also for you to align yourself, if possible, with actors and directors in your community. It never hurts to have an actor or director interested in your script. A passionate actor or director who has a script he or she wants to perform or direct is a gift to any playwright.

Getting the play up and alive in any way you can means the project is *in process,* and the *process* of readings and workshop productions (limited rehearsal, staging, and performances) is what ultimately leads to productions.

Don't expect perfection from a reading or production. You are trying to master your craft and improve your playwriting skills. The purpose of early readings or productions is to do your best work, take notes, then rewrite.

Be patient. Playwriting is about talent, craft, and most of all, perseverance and patience. Remember that Beckett sent out the completed draft of *Waiting For Godot* thirty-two times before it was accepted for production.

Getting published

Publishers of plays are listed in the *Dramatists Sourcebook.* A play can only be published if it has been produced, has received good notices, and is deemed commercial, meaning that it will have a future life in regional, community, high school and college theatres. Plays also get published as part of contests.

So, in order to be published, you need either to have a production or win a contest. There are exceptions to these rules, but they are rare. The major publishers of plays are the Dramatists Play Service and the Samuel French Company, as well as Baker's Plays, which publishes children's plays. There are, however, a growing number of smaller and reputable dramatic publishing companies.

Also, there are many young playwrights' competitions throughout the country. If you are a student, consult your English or drama teacher for details. Many of these contests include publication.

Remember, the play belongs to you. Ultimately, if the work is good and you have the endurance of the long distance runner, you will write the play, rewrite, be produced and be published.

⥺ JUVENILE AND YOUNG ADULT

➤➤ 97

BEING THERE—AND OTHER KINDS OF RESEARCH

BY EVE BUNTING

I'VE DISCOVERED, WHEN I'M WRITING A STORY OR BOOK, THAT NOTH-ing beats "being there." By that I mean being in the place where your imaginary action takes place. This not only makes sure your setting is authentic, but it gives color and veracity to what you write. And there are often unexpected bonuses.

The idea for my young adult novel, *Jumping the Nail,* came from a newspaper article that told of a towering cliff in La Jolla, California. Below the cliff is a deep, deep pool, actually an inlet of the ocean that is circled by sharp, jagged rocks. The cliff, called the Bear Claw in real life but changed to be The Nail in my story, is an irresistible magnet to most local teen-agers. Although it is against the law to jump from the top of the Bear Claw into the water below, kids do it. They do it because of bravado, or to impress their peers, or because they are dared by others, or simply because it's there. Some have been killed; some have been disabled for life. Some have jumped safely and become local heroes and heroines. One of my editors sent me the clipping about it and suggested it might make a good story. I didn't think so. It sounded gruesome, and the thought of that jump made me instantly queasy.

"Why don't you drive down and take a look at it," my editor suggested. Well, it's a four-hour drive each way. I didn't believe I would be tempted, but I went. I looked and I was hooked!

A teen-ager jumped while I was there, possibly because he had three women spectators, one of whom was writing furiously on a yellow legal pad. He must have thought "Press," because afterwards he came over to me and told me his name and said, "Be sure you spell that right!"

471

I would never have done that book if I hadn't gone to see the cliff. Seeing it was what made the place and the book real. The way the seagulls rose, squawking from their nests in the cliff when the boy flung himself from the top; the way the wind made his hair stand straight up so he looked like a marionette as he dropped through the air.

After the boy told me his name, he invited me to come to the top of the Bear Claw and see how high it was. He had me inspect the metal notice board at the top that warned of danger. I saw the names scratched on it, and the dates that told when they'd jumped. One said, "I jumped and lived." Obviously it was a sort of roll of honor that he would now be able to join.

He also told me that once a car had gone over that cliff into the pool and that the skeletons of a boy and girl were down there, still trapped in their seats. True or not, it made for a great dramatic sense in my book and was an added bonus.

When I was writing *Someone is Hiding on Alcatraz Island,* I went to San Francisco for a week and took the ferry out to Alcatraz every day. I sat silently in the cell where Danny, my protagonist, would sit. I climbed the water tower that he would climb and saw from that vantage point what he would see. I felt the cold, chill, dank air of the island. Would I have ever known the way the morgue looked, that terrible heart-stopping stillness? Would I have really understood the labyrinth of dark corridors and passageways, if I hadn't drawn my own map? Since that book was published, I have had hundreds of letters from students and teachers telling of how they visited Alcatraz, with my book in hand, and went where Danny went. I have that comfortable confidence that the old warden's house is exactly where I said it was, that the cafeteria where the prisoners ate their meals was exactly as I described it. One day I went on a "tour" of Alcatraz with a park ranger and a group of tourists. This is the scene as I later wrote it:

The ranger stopped around the corner. This bottom row of cells was different. Six of them had solid metal doors.

"The prisoners called these 'the hole.' There were no lights, no beds. Just an empty box with metal walls and a metal floor." We craned to see past him. . . "If anyone would like to go see how it feels in the hole, I'll close the door for a few seconds. I promise you I won't forget and leave you behind."

I was one of the few who accepted his invitation to be locked in the hole.

The square of gray, half-light that lay across the metal floor grew narrower. There was a sound like a cork coming out of a bottle, a strange, sucking sound as the last light vanished and the door sealed tight. Darkness swelled around us.

This was how it was. This was how I described it in my book. I'd been there.

My bonus? The ranger told us that one of the reasons Alcatraz was phased out as a prison was that age made the walls at the back of the cells soft and crumbly. Prisoners began to realize this and try to "dig out." In *Someone is Hiding on Alcatraz Island,* the outlaws lock Danny in one of the cells. And he digs himself out through one of those crumbling back walls. He's in a long, dusty corridor that runs the entire length of the cell block. There's an old bucket, a couple of old ratty mops. I knew about all of that. I'd been there. I understood the damp, chill terror that Danny felt. I'd felt it, too, in that dark, ghostly place.

Sometimes luck plays a part in "being there." I am Irish and often visit Irish relatives. A few years ago, when I was writing my middle-grade novel, *S.O.S. Titanic,* my husband and I went "home" to Ireland for a few weeks. I had planned to visit the shipyard where the *Titanic* was built, not that what I saw figured in my book, but just so I could feel in my bones and blood the beginnings of that tragic voyage. What I didn't know was that there was a special traveling exhibit that just happened to be in Belfast when I was there. (Don't ever again laugh at the luck of the Irish!)

On display were dinner plates, silverware, ship's bells that had been retrieved from the ship on the ocean floor. I read menus, water-stained; splendid advertisements of the *Titanic*'s maiden voyage; press reports of this, the most gigantic and the safest steamship ever built. I saw shoes from a drowned passenger's recovered belongings. A man's watch. How quietly the people filed past the memorabilia; how reverently. Even the children holding their parents' hands were subdued. To my amazement there was another part of this display: I stepped into a room, completely dark except for a few pinpricks of light, stars above my head. The glass in front of me was so close to being invisible that I seemed to be standing in a lifeboat, the huge model of the *Titanic* in

473

front of me. It was nose down, dying silently in the ocean. All around me were other lifeboats. On the sea's surface were floating deck chairs, crates, planking, rubbish of all kinds, life jackets and people. They clung to the wreckage. They lay, inert. There were no shrieks or moans or screams. But I could hear them. It was so real that I felt I was there.

When I wrote *S.O.S. Titanic,* I had that memory. I think I will always have it. The ship has just hit the iceberg, and Barry is in the water:

As he watched, the stern rose even higher and the screams grew louder. The first funnel was under the water now. Orange sparks rose from it like embers from a bonfire. In the wash, a wooden chair flowed toward him, and he grabbed for it. . . . The ship's lights went out, and a great moaning rose from the people in the water. . . . The ship stood upright, as if on her head. Her three giant propellers, like arms, reached for the starlit sky.

It was almost too real to me.

My picture book *So Far From the Sea* is set in Manzanar, one of the camps in which Japanese American citizens were interned during World War II. I went to the long-abandoned camp, walked among the deserted huts, and found an old graveyard, way in the back. Some people had died in this camp and been buried here, so far from the sea. My research might have turned this up, but it couldn't have given me my feelings of sadness and desolation as I looked at those long-ago graves overgrown with weeds.

When I can't "be there" I depend on research that I do in various libraries, first in the children's department. I find that children's books are clear and focused and contain all the most important information, and they're usually easier to comprehend than books from the adult sections.

Once I researched a book in a rather unique way. I had read in our newspaper about blackbirds that stopped in the same trees each year, as they migrated across the country. They ate the crops, stripped the corn from its stalks, left devastation everywhere. Farmers were ruined. There was no way to get rid of the birds or to divert their flight from one year to the next. The farmers tried scaring them away with fireworks, shooting at them, banging utensils together to make a deafening noise. The birds would squawk off, circle, and come back to the trees where they'd been before. The farmers tried poisoning them. They cut down favorite trees so the birds couldn't find them when they returned.

The birds settled for other trees, equally comfortable. I immediately saw a story possibility: a child who loved the beauty of the birds, a father who saw only his year's work destroyed by these pests.

But here I was, in California. It was the middle of winter, and I wanted to write the book. Circumstances other than the weather made it impossible for me to go to Iowa or Ohio or Illinois, the states most affected by the migrating birds. The library, even the children's room, yielded little information. What to do?

Then I remembered something. I keep the letters that children write me, and I was sure I had quite a few from those midwestern states. I pulled out any that had an Iowa, an Ohio, or an Illinois postmark and wrote to my correspondents. I asked each one if he or she lived on a farm or had a friend who did. Did they know about this yearly invasion of the blackbirds? Would they write and tell me about it? Would they tell me their feelings about the birds? How did their fathers and mothers feel? I asked other peripheral questions: What's the weather like at the time the birds come? What chores did they themselves have to do on the farm? How did they spend their spare time? What were some of their favorite meals? On and on and on. List after list. It was fun to be writing to the letter writers, for me to be the one asking the questions for a change!

Maybe I sent off thirty letters.

Maybe I got three hundred back!

I had not given the teachers of America sufficient credit! Almost every child had brought my letter to school, and almost all the teachers had turned it into a class project.

Wow! I got boxes of letters, packages of letters, I even got audio tapes and photos of families and animals and landscapes. One boy recorded the grunts of an Iowa pig and the moos of an Iowa cow.

In the end, I had all I needed to write *Blackbird Singing*—and more. The book is dedicated to those classes with my deepest gratitude. They got books on publication day. And one of the teachers who helped me most wrote an article about the project from first request to published book. That article helped her win the "Teacher of the Year" award. In this case, I could safely say that "writing there" was even better than "being there." And my bonus? One of the children told me of going to pick blackberries. His letter was so rich and realistic that I had a blackberry-picking scene in the book.

If you can't experience your setting firsthand, try some other way to add depth to your setting. If you do make a "site visit," take photographs, take notes, not only of a specific kind, but notes that relate to your own feelings and emotions. You will probably use them verbatim in your book. Draw a map for yourself. Describe in detail the church you see with its lopsided gravestones, the railway station, the town square, the statue with the bayonet and the cocked hat. Go to the town library and look for local information. If there's a historical society, pay it a visit. Talk to the historians, show your interest and excitement, and they will respond. Look and listen. If you get that wonderful local color fixed in your mind, it will be there in your story.

And always, always be alert for bonuses.

➤➤ 98

Writing Biographies for Young People

By James Cross Giblin

There was a time when it was accepted practice for young people's biographies to whitewash their subjects to a certain extent. For example, juvenile biographies either ignored or gave a once-over-lightly treatment to personal failings like a drinking problem, and they scrupulously avoided any mention of complications in their subjects' sex lives.

Such whitewashing was intended to serve several different purposes. It protected the subject's reputation and made him or her a more suitable role model, one of the main goals of juvenile biographies in earlier periods. At the same time it shielded young readers from some of life's harsher realities.

All this has changed in the last twenty-five or thirty years as an increased openness in the arts and the media has spread to the field of children's literature. Young people who watch TV talk shows after school and dip into celebrity tell-all books expect more realism in the biographies that are written expressly for them. As a consequence, juvenile biographies of Franklin D. Roosevelt now acknowledge that he had a mistress, and young adult studies of John F. Kennedy frankly discuss his health problems and womanizing.

Today, the chief goal of a young people's biography is not to establish a role model but rather to provide solid, honest information about a man or woman worth knowing for one reason or another. However, a children's writer still has to make judgments about what facts to include in the biography and how much emphasis to give them. These judgments aren't always easy to arrive at, as I've discovered with the biographies I've written for young people. Each book presents its own unique problems, for which unique solutions must be found.

Much depends on the age of the intended audience. For example, when I was writing a picture book biography of George Washington for ages six to nine, I felt it was important to describe Washington's changing attitude toward slavery, from easy acceptance in youth to rejection as he grew older. With that background in place, I was confident even quite young readers could grasp the significance of Washington's will, which specified that his slaves would be freed after the death of his wife, Martha.

A picture book biography of Thomas Jefferson presented a much more complex set of problems. Although Jefferson had written in the Declaration of Independence that "all men are created equal," he never rejected the concept of slavery as Washington did. How could he? The very existence of his beloved Monticello depended on slave labor. After much thought, I decided there was no way I could avoid discussing Jefferson's conflicted position. But I tried to present it as clearly and simply as possible and was careful not to let the discussion overshadow Jefferson's many accomplishments.

The role of the slave Sally Hemings proved harder to deal with. Whenever I mentioned in talks with writers that I was doing a biography of Jefferson, African-Americans in the audience invariably asked how I was going to treat Sally. I told them I intended to incorporate items from the historical record in the main text—that Sally had come into Jefferson's household as part of his wife's inheritance from her father; had accompanied Jefferson's younger daughter to Paris when Jefferson was the American ambassador to France; and had become one of the most trusted house slaves at Monticello in her later years.

In the back matter, along with other additional information, I said I'd include the story that one of Sally's sons, Madison Hemings, told an Ohio journalist in the mid-19th century. According to Madison, Jefferson had made Sally his mistress after his wife's death and had fathered her seven children, five of whom lived to adulthood and three of whom "passed" as white.

My editor felt that the latter story, aside from being controversial, would be too complicated for six-to-nine-year-olds to absorb. She urged me to leave it out, and in the end I decided she was right. If the book had been directed toward an upper elementary or young adult readership, I would have insisted on the story's retention. But I decided it was probably too involved for a younger audience.

However, the references to Sally Hemings remain in the body of the book, letting readers know that a slave by that name figured in Thomas Jefferson's life. When those same readers grow older, they can read about Sally in greater detail in other books about Jefferson. Meanwhile, my book—while not going deeply into the matter—will at least have introduced Sally to them instead of pretending she didn't exist.

Biographies for older children confront the writer with a different set of difficulties. What sort of balance do you aim for between the subject's achievements and his failings? This question was brought home to me in a particularly vivid way when I was working on a biography of Charles A. Lindbergh for ages ten to fourteen. Rarely in American history has there been such a sharp dichotomy between a subject's accomplishments—in Lindbergh's case his almost incredible solo flight to Paris in 1927, along with his other contributions to aviation—and his errors, namely his flirtation with fascism in the 1930s and his open admiration of Nazi Germany.

If I'd been writing a biography for adults, I might well have focused more intently on the part Lindbergh played in bringing about the appeasement of Adolf Hitler at Munich and his subsequent speeches urging the United States to take an isolationist stand with regard to the war in Europe. But while I went into this phase of Lindbergh's life in some detail, I decided it was my duty as a biographer for young people to "accentuate the positive," as the old song lyric goes.

An adult biographer may choose to expose or debunk his subject, assuming that readers will be able to compare his version of the person's life with other, more favorable accounts. I don't believe that option is open to the juvenile biographer, whose readers will most likely have little or no prior knowledge of the subject and thus will be unable to make comparisons. Such readers deserve a more even-handed introduction to the person.

Of course, that wouldn't be possible if one were writing about a destructive personality like Adolf Hitler, Joseph Stalin, or Senator Joseph McCarthy. But even in the portrayal of someone as reviled as these men, the juvenile biographer would have the responsibility of trying to help young readers understand how a human being could be capable of such inhuman acts. In other words, the writer wouldn't simply wallow in the person's excesses, as some adult biographers might be tempted to do, but instead would do his best to offer a full-scale portrait and locate the sources of the person's evil actions.

If you're thinking about writing a biography for young people, here are a few questions you would do well to ask yourself. Having the answers in hand should save you time when you're researching and writing the project.

• Depending on the age group of the readers, how best can you convey an accurate, three-dimensional picture of the subject in ways that the intended audience can comprehend?

• If the book is for younger children, should you discuss the seamier aspects of the subject's life, or merely hint at them and leave a fuller treatment to biographers for older children?

• If you're writing for an older audience, how much space should you devote to the darker side of the subject's life and experience? In a biography of sports star Magic Johnson, for example, should you go into detail about the promiscuous behavior that, by Johnson's own account, was responsible for his becoming infected with the AIDS virus, or should you merely mention it in passing?

As you seek answers to these questions, you'll have to rely ultimately on your own good taste and judgment, combined with your knowledge of the prevailing standards in the children's book field. Perhaps the most decisive factor of all, though, will be your feeling for the subject.

Jean Fritz, the author of many award-winning biographies for young people, once said that she had to *like* a subject tremendously before she could write about the person. I'd amend that to say I must be *fascinated* by a subject in order to invest the time and energy needed to discover what makes the person tick.

The intensity of your fascination with your subject should be of great help as you decide how much weight to give the person's positive and negative aspects. It should also communicate itself to young people, making them want to keep on reading about the intriguing man or woman at the center of your biography.

➤➤ 99

SOME CLUES TO THE JUVENILE MYSTERY

BY ELOISE MCGRAW

MYSTERIES ARE POPULAR WITH YOUNG PEOPLE, AND OFFER AN INVITing possibility for a writer exploring the juvenile field. The question is, how do you write a mystery for children? What is one, exactly?

Recently, I read a sampling of such books from the library, then reviewed three I've written myself. I was struck by how totally unlike each was from the others, and how slippery the genre is to define. Juvenile mystery fiction, unlike the adult variety, does not fall into sharply defined categories with rigid rules, such as the thriller, the spy story, the detective novel, the classic puzzle. Nor do juveniles usually center on a murder or feature a professional investigator. In mood, they range from chilling drama to lighthearted comedy; on subject matter, from grit to fluff. Plotting, format, and all the other elements in juvenile mysteries seem to be a matter of author's choice.

But a closer look reveals three elements all juvenile mysteries have in common:

A secret—preferably a good, interesting, tantalizing one.

A child investigator—usually the viewpoint character, who wants to discover the secret, either for the fun of it or to help some friend or relative in danger or because he's in danger himself.

An opponent—This may be either (1) a rival trying to discover the secret, too, or (2) the secret-keeper, who is trying to keep the secret dark.

Let me illustrate with examples from my own books:

In *The Money Room,* the boy Scotty is the *investigator,* and the *opponent* is old Dorrie Suggs. The two are rivals; both, for entirely different reasons, are trying to find Great-Gramp's "money room." The *secret-keeper* (Great-Gramp himself) is long dead, so while he remains an important character, he is an offstage, enigmatic one.

481

In *Tangled Webb,* Juniper Webb is the *investigator,* and her step-mother Kelsey is the *secret-keeper,* desperately trying to forestall Juniper's efforts to discover anything about her past. The conflict is between those two.

In *A Really Weird Summer,* Nels is both *secret-keeper* and *investigator.* He is fleeing from a decision he cannot face, escaping from reality into an elaborate and dangerous fantasy that at the same time he can't help probing, testing, and trying to see through. The conflict is within himself.

A secret, an investigator, an opponent. When you plan your mystery, begin with those three basics. And here are three precepts to keep in mind:

(1) Make your secret the pivot of the book—the reason behind every development in the story.

(2) Be sure your child investigator, with whom (usually) the reader identifies, has a strongly motivated need to discover the secret.

(3) Be sure your opponent's motivations are equally strong.

You will then have two dogs and one bone, so to speak, and conflict is inevitable. It is an essentially simple plot, but sturdy enough to support whatever complexities and embellishments you want to give it.

So much for the design of the underlying structure of your juvenile mystery. The next step is to get the action underway—and keep it moving. You now start a process of cause and effect.

The cause: Begin with an *opening incident or situation* that will focus the investigator's (and reader's) attention on the secret and trigger his curiosity, suspicion, or concern.

The effect: The incident should prod the investigator to take action; he or she begins asking questions, spying, then trying to make sense of the "answers."

Here are some examples:

The Money Room. Opening incident: On Scotty's first day in the farmhouse inherited from Great-Gramp, two odd things happen: His sister finds in the attic a box of old bank notes, and a pushy old stranger walks in uninvited, claiming he knew Great-Gramp, and says he wants to buy the house. *Action:* Scotty decides the rumored "money room" may be more than rumor, and begins to search.

A Really Weird Summer. Opening incident: Nels, exploring the for-

482

mer hotel where he and his siblings are spending the summer, sees the reflection of an unknown boy in a mirror, but the room the mirror reflects is empty. *Action:* Nels searches the room and discovers a bookcase that swings open to reveal a secret closet.

Tangled Webb. Opening incident: Juniper, certain that her efforts to get to know her new young stepmother, Kelsey, are failing because Kelsey has something to hide, confides in her father, who pooh-poohs her fears. *Action:* She asks Kelsey where she grew up; Kelsey gives a nervous, evasive answer, and later offers a different one that Juniper discovers to be an elaborate lie.

Whatever action the investigator-character takes, it must produce a *reaction* in the opponent-character, who at once takes *defensive measures.* If your opponent's defense merely increases your investigator's suspicions—as Kelsey's lie increases Juniper's—the investigator is bound to probe further; the opponent is bound to throw up another defense.

This sequence of cause and effect—action producing reaction that triggers further action—will form the body of your story, each escalation adding urgency to the struggle. The escalation can go on as long as it takes for all your story's threads to be woven into the fabric. And there *should* be a number of threads. Together they will form a screen opaque enough to keep the reader from seeing the essential simplicity of the plot.

The story's threads may be secondary characters who influence the investigator, incidents that produce new questions, or guesses that seem logical but are merely false leads. Other threads could be true subplots having to do with various aspects of the investigator's life. In *Weird Summer,* Stevie's story—his growing desperation as he puzzles over his brother Nels's behavior—runs parallel to Nels's own, and the two threads twist together at the climax. In *The Money Room,* Scotty's problems in facing an unfamiliar town and a new school provide a number of story threads, as does his maturing attitude toward his mother. In *Tangled Webb,* Juniper's memories of her dead mother, her fear of estrangement from her father, and her growing fondness for her new two-year-old stepbrother, Preston, color the story; two friends who aid in the sleuthing advance the plot; her encounter with the unknown Blanche adds a secondary riddle.

These story lines give the author a good source of false clues to drag across the trail: misdirection to keep the audience from watching the magician's hands. Much of the action in *The Money Room* is generated by the puzzling attacks on the family or on the house; much of Scotty's detective work is aimed at discovering the attacker and his motivation. Only the author—the magician devising the tricks—knows that there are two attackers, with totally different motives. This is what makes the attacks puzzling, builds suspense, and keeps the reader reading until the truth comes out. But play fair: Be sure to plant some real clues among the false ones, so that when the mystery is finally solved the story will hang together and the outcome seem logical, inevitable, and satisfying.

Meanwhile, your investigator must keep ferreting. The closer he gets to the truth, the more reckless the opponent's defense tactics should become. Eventually the opponent panics and shows his hand. *This is the crisis.*

The investigator now challenges. This may mean an open challenge, as in *Tangled Webb,* when Juniper, in her father's presence, asks Kelsey if she knows Blanche. Or it may mean taking an all-or-nothing gamble, as Scotty does when he shows the "money room" to Suggs. Either way, the challenge works; the book's secret is revealed. *This is the climax.*

Denouement. This is the point at which the conflict is resolved, in whatever manner is right and inevitable for your story. Maybe the investigator wins as in *The Money Room.* Maybe, as in *Tangled Webb,* nobody wins until a further entangling is accomplished, after which everybody wins.

To make your story more than "just" a mystery, be sure that, along with the secret, your characters' personal problems are solved. In *Tangled Webb,* the deceits that have been undermining the family's security are cleared away, and all the relationships and attitudes shift. By the end of *The Money Room,* Scotty has broken free of the past, saved the family's home, found a friend and a new maturity. In *A Really Weird Summer,* Nels has faced reality and himself, and made a lifetime choice.

Above all, start with a first-rate secret. If you can devise what I think of as a *sleight-of-hand secret,* you will enhance the puzzle element of your mystery and make it much harder for the reader to guess the solution. You will also provide a satisfying bang at the end of your story.

Try to think just one step beyond whatever secret you have in mind. In *The Money Room,* the central question seems to be: *Will finding Great-Gramp's money room make the family rich?* But it is precisely the money room's lack of value that saves the family's home. The only financial gain comes unexpectedly from something assumed quite worthless throughout the book.

In *Tangled Webb,* Juniper's question is: *Who is Kelsey, really?* This is the one question to which she forces an answer. But the real question of the book, the one neither she nor the reader thinks it necessary to ask, is: *Who is Preston, really?* The answer to this springs a surprise that changes everything at the end.

So: how to invent a good secret?

Devise a situation that looks like one thing, but turns out to be quite another. Focus attention on one question, but let the climax answer a much more pertinent question that nobody had thought to ask.

>> 100

Is It Good Enough for Children?

By Madeleine L'Engle

A WHILE AGO WHEN I WAS TEACHING A COURSE ON TECHNIQUES OF fiction, a young woman came up to me and said, "I do hope you're going to teach us something about writing for children, because that's why I'm taking this course."

"What have I been teaching you?" I asked her.

"Well—writing."

"Don't you write when you write for children?"

"Yes, but—isn't it different?"

No, I assured her, it isn't different. The techniques of fiction are the techniques of fiction, and they hold as true for Beatrix Potter as they do for Dostoevsky.

But the idea that writing for children isn't the same as writing for adults is prevalent indeed, and usually goes along with the conviction that it isn't quite as good. If you're a good enough writer for adults, the implication is, of course, you don't write for children. You write for children only when you can't make it in the real world, because writing for children is easier.

Wrong, wrong, wrong!

I had written several regular trade novels before a publisher asked me to write about my Swiss boarding school experiences. Nobody had told me that you write differently when you write for children, so I didn't. I just wrote the best book I possibly could; it was called *And Both Were Young*. After that I wrote *Camilla,* which has been reissued as a young adult novel, and then *Meet the Austins*. It's hard today for me to understand that this simple little book had a very hard time finding a publisher because it's about a death and how an ordinary family reacts to that death. Death at that time was taboo. Children weren't supposed to know about it. I had a couple of offers of publication if I'd take the death out. But the reaction of the family—children as well as the parents—to the death was the core of the book.

Nowadays what we offer children makes *Meet the Austins* seem pale, and on the whole, I think that's just as well, because children know a lot more than most grown-ups give them credit for. *Meet the Austins* came out of my own family's experience with several deaths. To have tried to hide those deaths from our children would have been blind stupidity. All hiding does is confuse children and add to their fears. It is not subject matter that should be taboo, but the way it is handled.

A number of years ago—the first year I was actually making reasonable money from my writing—my sister-in-law was visiting us, and when my husband told her how much I had earned that year, she was impressed and commented, "And to think most people would have had to work so hard for that!"

Well, it is work, it's most certainly work; wonderful work, but work. Revision, revision, revision. Long hours spent not only in the actual writing, but in research. I think the best thing I learned in college was how to do research, so that I could go right on studying after I had graduated.

Of course, it is not *only* work; it is work that makes the incomprehensible comprehensible. Leonard Bernstein says that for him music is cosmos in chaos. That is true for writing a story, too. Aristotle says that what is plausible and impossible is better than what is possible and implausible.

That means that story must be *true*, not necessarily *factual*, but true. This is not easy for a lot of people to understand. When I was a school child, one of my teachers accused me of telling a story. She was not complimenting me on my fertile imagination; she was accusing me of telling a lie.

Facts are fine; we need facts. But story takes us to a world that is beyond facts, out on the other side of facts. And there is considerable fear of this world.

The writer Keith Miller told me of a young woman who was determined that her three preschool children were going to grow up in the real world. She was not, she vowed, going to sully their minds with myth, fantasy, fairy tales. They were going to know the truth—and for truth, read fact—and the truth would make them free.

487

One Saturday, after a week of rain and sniffles, the sun came out, so she piled the children into her little red VW bug and took them to the Animal Farm. The parking lot was crowded, but a VW bug is small, and she managed to find a place for it. She and the children had a wonderful day, petting the animals, going on rides, enjoying the sunshine. Suddenly, she looked at her watch and found it was far later than she realized. She and the children ran to where the VW bug was parked, and to their horror, found the whole front end was bashed in.

Outraged, she took herself off to the ranger's office. As he saw her approach, he laughed and said, "I'll bet you're the lady with the red VW bug."

"It isn't funny," she snapped.

"Now, calm down, lady, and let me tell you what happened. You know the elephant your children had such fun riding? She's a circus-trained elephant, and she was trained to sit on a red bucket. When she saw your car, she just did what she was trained to do and sat on it. Your engine's in the back, so you can drive it home without any trouble. And don't worry. Our insurance will take care of it. Just go on home, and we'll get back to you on Monday."

Slightly mollified, she and the kids got into the car and took off. But she was later than ever, so when she saw what looked like a very minor accident on the road, she didn't stop, but drove on.

Shortly, the flashing light and the siren came along, and she was pulled over. "Lady, don't you know that in this state it's a crime to leave the scene of an accident?" the trooper asked.

"But I wasn't in an accident," she protested.

"I suppose your car came that way," she said, pointing to the bashed-in front.

"No. An elephant sat on it."

"Lady, would you mind blowing into this little balloon?"

That taught her that facts alone are not enough; that facts, indeed, do not make up the whole truth. After that she read fairy tales to her children and encouraged them in their games of Make Believe and Let's Pretend.

I learned very early that if I wanted to find out the truth, to find out why people did terrible things to each other, or sometimes wonderful things—why there was war, why children are abused—I was more likely to find the truth in story than in the encyclopedia. Again and again I read *Emily of New Moon,* by Lucy Maud Montgomery, because Emily's father was dying of diseased lungs, and so was mine. Emily had a difficult time at school, and so did I. Emily wanted to be a writer, and so did I. Emily knew that there was more to the world that provable fact, and so did I. I read fairy tales, the myths of all nations, science fiction, the fantasies and family stories of E. Nesbit. I read Jules Verne and H. G. Wells. And I read my parents' books, particularly those with lots of conversation in them. What was not in my frame of reference went right over my head.

We tend to find what we look for. If we look for dirt, we'll find dirt, whether it's there or not. A very nice letter I received from a reader said that she found *A Ring of Endless Light* very helpful to her in coming to terms with the death of a friend, but that another friend had asked her how it was that I used dirty words. I wrote back saying that I was not going to reread my book looking for dirty words, but that as far as I could remember, the only word in the book that could possibly be construed as dirty was *zuggy,* which I'd made up to avoid using dirty words. And wasn't looking for dirty words an ugly way to read a book?

One of my favorite books is Frances Hodgson Burnett's *The Secret Garden.* I read it one rainy weekend to a group of little girls, and a generation later to my granddaughters up in an old brass bed in the attic. Mary Lennox is a self-centered, spoiled-rotten little heroine, and I think we all recognize at least a little of ourselves in her. The secret garden is as much the garden of Mary's heart as it is the physical walled garden. By the end of the book, warmth and love and concern for others have come to Mary's heart, when Colin, the sick boy, is able to walk and run again. And Dickon, the gardener's boy, looks at the beauty of the restored garden and says, "It's magic!" But "magic" is one of the key words that has become taboo to today's self-appointed censors, so, with complete disregard of content, they would add *The Secret Garden* to the pyre. I shudder. This attitude is extreme. It is also dangerous.

It comes down to the old question of separate standards, separate for adults and children. The only standard to be used in judging a children's book is: *Is it a good book?* Is it good enough for me? Because if a children's book is not good enough for all of us, it is not good enough for children.

489

>> 101

CHILDREN'S FICTION: A WORLD TURNED UPSIDE DOWN

BY PAT ZETTNER

IF YOU WANT TO WRITE FOR CHILDREN, THINK BACK TO THE STORIES you loved best when you were young. Did you fly away with Peter Pan and the Lost Boys? Perhaps you struggled with Anne of Green Gables to win the approval of her foster mother, Marilla; fought pirates with Jim Hawkins; or traveled the Yellow Brick Road with Dorothy.

Chances are that the characters who won your devotion were strong, self-sufficient youngsters facing trouble with little adult help or advice.

But you've grown up since you thrilled to those books. Maybe you're a parent or teacher now, or even a grandparent. If so, you've learned to see children as adult responsibilities. As you follow the frequently given advice to "write what you know," you probably fashion adult characters in your own image. They serve as nurturers, mentors, sometimes even judge and jury.

But to create stories that appeal to young readers, you must once again look at the world through the eyes of youth. From their earliest years on, children long to be older, stronger, freer than they really are. Small wonder, then, if they love to identify with young characters who struggle with their own problems, learn lessons on their own, and manage their own fates. Once you understand this principle, you'll hold an essential key to successful children's fiction: THE EMPOWERED CHILD.

Most children's books that have endured empower young main characters in one of two ways. The first might be called the *acceptance story*. In such a plot, a strong-minded child with an admirably independent spirit struggles to win an adult's approval. This young hero(ine) usually finds it difficult to meet adult standards without sacrificing his or her own individuality.

490

One of the best-loved examples of this approach is the Ramona series. Its author, Beverly Cleary, understands that to children, parents and teachers can seem as alien as if they came from Saturn, and that behavior condemned by older people as "bad" or "naughty" often seems quite innocent to the "wrongdoer," a fact that adults too often ignore.

Elementary schoolers usually prefer stories about older children, but they enjoy reading about Ramona's kindergarten mishaps because the stories are *funny* and because Ramona is a survivor. Though these readers have passed beyond the confusions of kindergarten, they find it reassuring to identify with a character whom nothing keeps down for long.

Eventually, the adults in Ramona's life do come to understand her needs. That's an important point. In books for young children, the child must clearly gain adult acceptance.

In some acceptance books for older readers, the protagonist is just as clearly a winner. Take L. M. Montgomery's *Anne of Green Gables* series. While Anne has plenty of problems with her no-nonsense foster mother, Marilla comes to love the imaginative girl unconditionally. For both Ramona and Anne, the conflicts are with attitudes rather than with uncaring people. There's room for adjustment on both sides, which results in a win/win situation for everybody.

In harder-edged teen-age acceptance novels, the victory can be ambiguous and bittersweet. For example, while the main characters of Katherine Paterson's *Jacob Have I Loved* and S. E. Hinton's *Tex* never receive the full measure of love they yearn for, they *do* develop the understanding and strength they need to deal with the lack of it.

An even more popular type of plot for children is the *achievement story,* in which a young protagonist meets and conquers a challenge on his or her own. While a major appeal of "acceptance" books is that readers may have faced similar problems with the adults in their own lives, the "achievement" story frequently describes experiences they are unlikely to encounter—and might not really want to!

Most of us like fiction that takes us beyond the limits of our daily routines. Since the boundaries of children's lives are usually narrower and stricter than those of adults, young readers particularly love to share the triumphs of an adventurer. You go a long way toward connecting with your young audience when you write about a self-sufficient child or one who finds the resources to become independent.

But once you set out to write about such a youngster, keep this in mind: The minute you put adults in your plot, they're apt to clamor for power. This take-charge tendency can be an advantage in the acceptance story by adding conflict to your plot. But in an achievement story, you're pitting your main character against nature or another child or entrapping him in a self-made dilemma, and the wise children's writer won't allow a helpful adult to grab center stage. Instead, he *empowers* the young character.

How?

The simplest tactic, of course, is to banish adult caregivers entirely. Oliver Twist and Jane Eyre began the long parade of young orphans who would star in novels. Think twice about disposing of parents entirely in stories for small children; adults must still be kept discreetly in the background.

Besides killing off hapless parents before the story begins, writers can neutralize adult interference in countless other ways. Children run away. They're abandoned, shipwrecked, or captured. They set off on treasure hunts in which pirates gain the upper hand. They're sucked up by a tornado and deposited in a magical but dangerous land. In many recent novels, they continue to live under the same roof with parents who, for whatever reason, have simply abdicated the caregiving role.

If you choose not to sidestep adults in any of these ways, how can you make them an asset rather than a liability? First of all, be careful how you set up child vs. adult conflicts. Plots work best when protagonist and antagonist are fairly evenly matched. An adult's power so outweighs that of a pre-adolescent that you must even the odds in some credible way for your young character to have a hope of succeeding.

In stories for teens, on the other hand, conflict with adult authority is almost a given—though it need not be the main focus of the plot. Adolescence is, after all, one long, bumpy shift from the comfortable dependence of childhood to ultimate self-rule. Adolescents—who are constantly admonished to "be mature" but are seldom trusted to do so, are apt to chafe under authority. Yet the down side of independence can be an uncomfortable degree of responsibility, making parental guidance feel almost desirable.

You can connect with your youthful readers simply by making your characters react believably in the face of adult control. Listen to my narrator in "Lady M. and the Reluctant Witch":

"Cathy," she [Mrs. Z.] called after me, "would you come into my office for a minute? Don't worry about being late—I'll give you a pass."
That's how it is when you're in authority. You can do whatever you want.

A resentful Cathy knows better than to talk back:

But I didn't say anything. That's how it is when you're *not* in authority.

Carol, the main character of another story, "A Perfect Day for Ice Cream," has all but agreed to coach her little sister's soccer team, when she has second thoughts:

"We'll have to see what Mom and Dad think. They may say," I hedged, "I'm doing too much already."
You might think that when people have been rearing kids for sixteen and one-half years, they'd know when *not* to be permissive. Right? Wrong.
"Coach a soccer team?" Mom raised her eyebrows. "What about your grades? Your own practices take a lot of time."
Dad fixed that. "Leave her alone, Anne," he said. "She's old enough to set her own schedule. That's part of growing up."

Any teen-ager who has longed for both independence *and* security can relate to Carol's ambivalence.

You can use adult authority figures to even greater advantage in plotting—*as long as their control paves the way for the story problem without affecting how your character deals with it.* When Mrs. Zinsemeyer of "Lady M." denies my heroine the lead in *Macbeth,* she sets Cathy up for envy, resentment, and the consequent problems. It's then up to my heroine to fumble her way to a solution.

But what if your character needs advice? A push in handling the central problem? Assign the job to another youngster. In this case, it's Cathy's best friend, Sue, who first persuades her to accept the part of First Witch and later lashes out at her bad attitude.

Do you suspect that a story or two of your own may suffer from the curse of adult control? How can you recognize it? And what can you do about it?

Check your manuscripts for the following symptoms:

1) **Adult as disciplinarian**: An anthropomorphic tale features Rascal, a feisty little squirrel who's stolen the rich and nutty surprise pie Granny baked for the Oakville Orphanage. He gets his comeuppance— a stomachache—for devouring it at one sitting. "I hope you've learned your lesson," Granny Squirrel scolds, as she spoons up something soothing and tucks him into bed. "But just to make sure, you can't have any pie for a month." "Oh no," promises the pea-green sufferer, "I'll never do it again!"

Now see what happens when we empower Rascal. Suppose he witnesses Granny's dismay and discovers his conscience for the first time. If of his own free will he offers to help gather nuts and make a new pie, he has learned to respect others' property and to accept responsibility. No need for a tummyache or for punishment imposed from outside. *His change has come from within.*

2) **Adult as fairy godmother**: Davey yearns to play in a city-wide baseball competition, but he needs a new catcher's mitt his family simply cannot afford. Our hero frets until, miraculously, the mitt arrives, the final gift of a beloved aunt.

This is a wish-fulfillment story, a type as old as Cinderella. Since we all like to have dreams come true, it *might* reach publication as is. But plots resolved by fairy godmothers (sometimes disguised as aunts or uncles, moms, dads, grandparents, kindly neighbors, teachers, or policemen—not to mention heroic dogs, cats, and pet frogs) are inherently weak. A variant in which Davey surmounts obstacles to earn the mitt on his own will have both a stronger main character and a more satisfying plot.

3) **Adult as achiever**: Lisa looks on anxiously, as Babe, the family's Shetland mare, goes into labor. Dad says reassuringly, "Don't worry, Lisa. The vet will soon be here. Everything's going to be all right." Afterward—when everything really *is* O.K.—it's time to choose a name for the new foal. "I know," says Mom. "He's such a beautiful red color. Let's call him Rusty." "Yea!" shouts Lisa. "Rusty!" That's a great name!"

Mom and Dad must surely leave the farm occasionally. What if the pony goes into labor while they're away? When Lisa has to handle the situation alone—either by tending to the birth herself or by bringing the vet—her achievement provides something for the reader to identify with, and she has unquestionably earned the right to name the foal herself.

4) **Adult as protector**: In a story idea for somewhat older readers, Teri and Mike have lost their parents in an automobile crash. These frightened, grief-stricken city kids are sent to live with Uncle Joe and Aunt Jane, whom they've never seen. They worry and ponder rebellion throughout the trip. No one will ever replace their parents. But when they're met at the airport, Teri sees the tenderness in her aunt's eyes. Clasped in a hug, she knows that, with Aunt Jane to take care of them, someday, somehow, everything will turn out all right.

Mike and Teri's struggles to adapt to a new life with their aunt and uncle might make a moving, readable acceptance novel. But their conflict can't be solved without struggle or in a sudden revelation, so it won't make a short story. File this under BOOK IDEAS TO EXPLORE.

If a story in your files is akin to one of these plots, then empowering its main character may well lead to a sale. Remember, in *successful* children's fiction adults play only bit parts, while independent young characters learn lessons and solve problems on their own. It's our world of adult control turned upside down.

➤➤ 102

MAKING YOUR STORY BREATHE

BY NORMA FOX MAZER

WHEN I PICK UP A BOOK IN THE LIBRARY OR THE BOOKSTORE, I ALWAYS want to know what it's about. Yet when I'm asked the same question about a story on which I'm working, I stumble anxiously over my words. I don't want to answer! I dislike taking the fascination of creating a world and characters and reducing it to a few phrases. All the same, answering this question is what I force myself to do for every book I write. Ideally, I know what the book is "about" (and can state it in a single sentence) *before* I start writing. Sometimes this actually happens.

One night years ago, while I was washing dishes, a sentence appeared in my head. I say "appeared" because it was so clear I seemed to see it: "A girl is kidnapped by her father." I knew at once that I'd been given a gift: a story in seven words. The hard work was over. All I had to do now was ask the myriad questions implicit in that sentence—and answer them by telling a good story. Those questions, beginning with *why? how? when?*, became *Taking Terri Mueller.*

More often, though, rather than a gift, what I have is a muddle. I hate to confess this, after so many years of writing. Doing it right seems simple: Decide what you're going to write about, work a story around it, and go to it. Yeeeaaah! I have written and rewritten hundreds of pages and found myself still sweating out what the story is really about. This happened with my novel, *Missing Pieces*. I began by wanting to write about a close-knit, self-sufficient female household: mother, daughter, and elderly aunt. Right away, I knew the odd house they live in (built on a hill, tiny black-and-white tiles in the hall, kitchen in the basement . . .), I knew Aunt Zis, with her pride and bony shoulders, and I knew a little about Jessie—fuzzy eyebrows and a mouth that worked overtime.

I developed Jessie, and a couple of friends for her, each with her own story (racism, shyness); threw in a boy; worked up a love life for her overweight mother, Maribeth; and in an escalating series of scenes went after the main story: the terrors of aging (beloved Aunt Zis) as seen through Jessie's eyes and heart. Early on, to explain this manless family, I wrote a few sentences abut Jessie's father, "the disappearing dude," as she jauntily called him, who'd taken off when she was small.

O.K. The usual rounds of writing and rewriting, and off to the editor at last. The manuscript came back with a three-page comment that boiled down to: too many stories, not enough focus. And, oh, by the way, I'm really interested in that father.

My initial reaction was a snappish, "Well, I'm not!" An attitude. It lasted overnight. But by morning the thought was, "Oh . . . actually, I'm kind of interested in the dude, myself."

I began to tell the same story, but in a new light, focusing on Jessie and her father. I threw out the old title, deleted scenes, recast others, created new ones. Still, it took at least one more major revision before I could put the story into this sentence: *A girl whose father left her years ago is tormented by her desire to know why he did it and who he really was.*

Once a premise is clear, it always seems obvious, and I'm amazed that it eluded me for so long. After it's nailed down, the story opens up for me, and I can go to work on making it breathe. That single sentence (sometimes paragraph) is the spine of the story; around it grows the flesh and blood. And this is where the tools of the trade come into play: *narrative, dialogue, characterization.*

I work to make my story live and breathe (or appear to, anyway; we are illusionists only) in a variety of ways, some hard to describe, others quite pragmatic. Let me get the hard-to-describe stuff out of the way. It has to do with getting to a place that I think of as the free place. In that place, there are no constraints. Scenes appear in my head, words appear on the screen. There is some level of truth or sight here that is exhilarating. It's like crossing a border. On this side, the usual side, I'm walking a path through a dim woods, moving along, but not seeing enough. There are shadows everywhere, and I'm anxious about getting where I'm going.

If I'm lucky and cross the border, everything changes, becomes lighter, vaster, more open. An endless meadow in which I romp and fly. How to get into that meadow, where I'd like to abide? It's not exactly sheer chance, but there's no map, either. Often enough, I'm stuck on the woodsy side, slogging along and devising little tricks and ways of doing things to keep me going forward.

Sculptors start with a lump of clay; writers, with nothing: It's all in the head. When I'm drafting, what I want is something malleable, something to work on—words, scenes, characters. My best trick is to sit in front of the computer wearing my drafting hat, a battered gray fedora, pulled down over my eyes, and type without stopping. The hat over the eyes keeps me from seeing anything but what's on the only screen that matters—the one in my mind.

The next day, before the hat goes on, I look at what I produced. A mess! My heart sinks. With a little effort, I can remember that I've done this 24 times before, and 24 times a novel emerged. But, of course, that was the past and it happened through sheer chance and good luck. This time, I can tell, it's the end of my life as a writer. I don't write stories, I make messes! Still, what are messes for, except to be cleaned up, so I might as well get to it. I start by putting in all the capitals and commas and correcting the spelling. This is soothing. I'm not doing real writing, which means I don't have to be anxious.

It never fails that while I'm doing this, ideas sprout on nearly every line, and one thing leads to another, which leads to a cheerful frame of mind and the possibility that I might still make it as a writer. I do another five or six messy pages. After several months of this routine, I come out from under the hat with a rough, but not impossible, draft.

I begin rewriting and revising. I love this part, but I can still use help. I'll do anything to give it to myself.

Here are a few of my tricks:

1. Eavesdrop. A sentence heard on the fly on a busy New York City street—"They destroyed my innocent childhood"—gave me a sudden insight into Diane, one of Jessie's friends in *Missing Pieces,* and was the basis for at least two important scenes I hadn't known I was going to write.

2. Free write, just as the kids do in school. In *After the Rain,* the letters Rachel writes her brother were never intended for the book. They began as a way for me to get to know more about her.

3. Switch from first person to third, or from third to first. If, for instance, you've written the draft in third person, rewrite your entire manuscript in first person. This doesn't mean merely changing all the "she said"s to "I said"s. It means seeing the story in a fresh way. Third person is the storytelling voice. It has greater freedom than the first person: It's a voice that can know more than the character knows; a voice that can give the viewpoint of more than one character. Transforming a third-person narrative into first person forces a sharper concentration on the character's views, thoughts, and feelings.

How about the reverse? First person is necessarily the narrower vision, but the voice is capable of drawing in the reader more swiftly. The first-person voice rarely stops to notice the scenery (those awful long paragraphs of description I used to think I had to master to be a *real* writer). Only as much of the story can be told as the first-person character is capable of understanding, noticing, and reporting. When your characters are adolescents, this is a severe limitation. First person can also be too talky: Somebody's always in your ear saying, I, I, I, I.

When I rewrite a manuscript into the third person, I always feel grateful for the new notes that are rung, the new details observed. In the third person, things leap out that I, as author, can write into the story but the close-in, first-person viewpoint couldn't notice and still remain a true first person.

4. Take another step with the voice and rewrite the manuscript once more, from third person back to first, or from first person back again to third. Yes, this seems like a lot of work, and it is. But for me, it never fails to add something new, fresh, and vital.

The third-person characters who spent their time in the first person would emerge opened up, with a more intimate tone, while the first-person characters, as a result of their brief third-person lives, now have steadier, quieter, more mature voices.

5. Use pictures. When I was writing *Taking Terri Mueller*, I had a problem with Terri's father; I hated him. He was a great dad, relaxed, loving, and attentive, but I hated him for kidnapping his daughter, and the emotion put me into writer's gridlock. I came across a magazine picture of a man holding a baby up toward his face and smiling with ecstatic love. I ripped the picture out and taped it over my typewriter. Every day, before I did anything else, I looked at that picture and thought, "This is the way Terri's father feels about her. This was how

much he loved her as an infant and has gone on loving her." Finally, I could comprehend how devastating it was for him to think he was going to lose Terri. After that I could write again.

6. Read out loud. The last thing I do is read the manuscript to someone else. The last two words in that sentence are crucial for me. I can read something out loud to myself and be quite satisfied, but when I read the same thing to my husband Harry, the blunders leap out at me. As for silent reading, it's amazing how often my eye skips over sentences on the screen that are awkward or unclear. Unheeding, I speed past the extra adjective, the unneeded adverb, but the moment I have to speak them, I stumble. Narrative holes loom bigger, too, when spoken.

7. Talk the talk. Dialogue is tricky. We all have verbal ticks, but putting them into dialogue rarely works. What do people really say when they get mad, when they're baffled, amused, amazed? I say what I would say, or what I'd like to say. (I'm not confrontational, but I love writing noisy, loud, decisive characters.) Then I write it, then I rewrite it, then I read it out loud.

8. Finally, when you think you have nothing left to do, do this: Go through each chapter as if you *must* cut it by ¼, and be merciless with anything that is repetitious, unclear, clichéd. Be on the lookout, too, for those bits that make you chuckle fondly or glow a little inwardly. Those are nearly always the ones that ought to come out, where the writer is working too hard at being a Wonderful Writer.

Did I say somewhere that when you get the premise, the hard work is over? Silly me. The most dazzling, dramatic idea to come down the pike in the last decade isn't worth much if not brought to life, if the characters don't (as one of my readers once so winningly said) walk alongside the reader. This is what I really want when I write and what all the work and revisions are about: creating a space and a place that is unique, a world the reader enters and might never want to leave.

➤➤ 103

Bringing History to Life for Young Readers

By Cheryl Zach

IF YOU WANT TO LURE A CHILD OR TEENAGER INTO READING YOUR historical novel or story, you must bring the history to life. A plot slowed by dull lists of facts and figures won't spark a young person's interest. An exciting story with well-researched background, on the other hand, will find eager readers and can impart information along the way.

The two main rules for juvenile historical fiction might seem contradictory—make sure the background is accurate, but don't allow the facts to slow or obscure the story—but both are essential ingredients for successful historical juvenile fiction.

Research begins at your local library. Check the computer listings and/or card files for books that will provide background on the historical period for your story. First, you may want to start with general histories, then narrow your search to specific areas, times, people, and places that you know your books will include. For my young adult historical romance series, *Southern Angels,* I began my research with histories of the Civil War. When I had a basic understanding of the overall conflict, I narrowed the scope and looked more closely at the places and events I planned to feature.

Don't try to cover too much in a juvenile novel. For instance, you can't include the entire Western expansion in a novel; better to chronicle one wagon train west through the eyes of a youthful voyager.

Whether for middle grade (roughly ages 8 to 12) or young adult readers (around 12 and up), the juvenile novel usually spans a fairly short period of time, often only a few weeks to a few months. In my case, it would have been difficult to cram a story that encompassed the whole Civil War into a short book. Each of my *Southern Angels* novels covers a year or less, the longest period of time desirable for readers of this age.

General histories will give you a broad overview of your period, but the bibliographies and footnotes you'll find in them can alert you to books on more specific topics that may be just what you need. Be sure to look for journals and diaries, published letters, and newspaper accounts that were written during the era in which your novel is set. These are known as primary sources—written or narrated by people who were at the scene, who lived the history while it was being made, as opposed to accounts written after the fact, called secondary sources.

Yet even primary sources have their drawbacks; you must allow for regional and personal biases that may be reflected in the first-person accounts. Because my novels focus on the lives of civilians, the women who also suffered hardships through the War, I was especially interested in journals by women alive at that time. These included famous and not-so-famous diarists such as Hannah Ropes and Louisa May Alcott (author of *Little Women*), both of whom were nurses during the conflict; and Sarah Morgan of Louisiana and Mary Chestnut of Virginia, who wrote detailed accounts of their lives during the War. Finding sources for my slave girl Hannah, who escapes to freedom during the War, was harder, but a few written accounts do exist, such as Harriet Jacob's *Incidents in the Life of A Slave Girl,* as well as oral histories and stories of former slaves that were recorded later. A medium-to-large library is likely to have a reference librarian on the staff who can help you locate promising sources. Even a small public library will have access to interlibrary loan, which can secure the books and articles you need. If you choose a historical incident that occurred close to where you live, don't forget to check privately published diaries, family chronicles, and local historical sites.

If time and money allow, traveling to the source of your fictional story can offer additional inspiration. When I went to Charleston to research my first Civil War book, *Hearts Divided,* I visited homes that pre-dated the Civil War, preserved for today's tourists to enjoy. I also discovered that Charleston had been home to a girls' boarding school, a setting I had already planned for my fictional southern belles.

But one detail intrigued me; a locally printed pamphlet on old homes informed me that the wall around the boarding school had been topped with broken bottles, to deter young men from climbing in to see the young ladies. As soon as I read this, I knew what the first scene of my novel would be: Elizabeth waiting in the school garden for her new beau. When he climbs over the wall, he scratches his hand on a piece of glass and she laughs. And I also knew that later in the book, the same young man would be gravely wounded in the first big battle of the War, and Elizabeth would remember with shame and regret how she had laughed. This is the kind of detail that sparks a writer's imagination and suggests new possibilities for a story.

If you can't travel to the site, you can still draw upon local sources. A footnote in a history book alerted me to the existence of a Confederate museum in New Orleans. I reached it by phone, and with the help of the museum staff, I ordered several locally published books that provided me with invaluable background for the second book in my series, *Winds of Betrayal.* Write or call local museums and historical societies, and you may discover treasure troves of information relevant to the book you are writing.

When the research is completed, how do you make your story sound authentic without overwhelming it with too many facts? Of course, you must establish your setting, but once the background has been sketched in, work in the details as subtly and unobtrusively as possible. As with any good story, remember to show, not tell. Use your five senses to make the scenes vibrate with life: the salty tang of a sea breeze, the clammy touch of fog slipping in from the docks, the clatter of horses' hooves on a cobblestone street, the cloying taste of "coffee" made from ground sweet potatoes (when the Union blockade made real coffee unobtainable), the stench of a bloody field hospital, window panes rattling from the force of cannon fire—the list is endless.

Remember that neither children nor teen readers want long stretches of description; even in a historical novel or story, young readers still prefer action and dialogue. So I work small period details into the action: The girls in my books may pull their long skirts away from the thorny clutches of a rose bush, or balance heavy hoop skirts as they walk down a staircase. Once you've established that they're wearing several petticoats and corsets so tightly laced that they can't run easily, go on with the story.

In addition to details about clothing, keep in mind details about their homes, the food they ate, the chores they were expected to do, the

503

schooling young people at that particular time would receive, the mode of transportation they would use. Remember that family structure and community mores were different in other times, that the attitudes and beliefs of your characters must be authentic for the time period, yet interesting to readers today. All this can keep you balanced on a thin line when it comes to moral or ethical issues.

I wanted to make the Southern girls in my books believable as products of their time and place, when the institution of slavery was acceptable to many Americans. Yet I couldn't care about—nor expect modern readers to care about—people who didn't recognize the inhumanity and injustice of such a system. So as part of her growth through the novels, each girl had to come to understand that slavery, though widespread at the time, is inherently evil.

Despite the special challenges of writing historical fiction, the rewards can be substantial. Teachers use historical novels as learning tools in the classroom, and most important of all, young readers will respond positively to vividly told stories of girls and boys who lived long ago.

>> 104

THE BIG "I" IN CHILDREN'S FICTION

BY BEVERLY J. LETCHWORTH

ACTIONS CAN DO IT. DIALOGUE CAN DO IT. BUT INTROSPECTION DOES it most accurately.

Introspection (a character's thoughts) has an important and definite place in children's fiction. No other method of expression accomplishes characterization so effectively, because introspection shows the character's exact reactions to circumstances. By using it you'll create characters who will live in your young readers' minds long after they finish reading the story.

> Erin looked away. She had wanted to impress Kelly, and now she looked like a stupid little kid. Might as well give up thinking about riding lessons, she thought dismally.

No doubt exists now in your young readers' minds about how Erin feels. She's failed and feels like a stupid child. Her hopes about lessons have dissolved, too, leaving her dejected.

Young readers feel upset about this turn of events and empathetic toward Erin. Adding introspection fully aroused their emotions—a "must" in fiction writing, whether for children or adults. Hooray! You've succeeded. Why? Because readers will want to read on to see how Erin remedies her depressing situation. Since they're in tune with her, they want her to achieve her goal and find happiness.

Introspection is vital in making your characters come alive because it adds to the readers' knowledge of the characters, and like actions and dialogue, reveals personality. The character's soul is what young readers want to know. Thoughts show precisely how a character feels about an event, a person or an idea. Physical action and dialogue express individuality, but what the character *thinks* as an event happens, reveals more.

Holly stopped drawing and leaned back in her chair. She heard her brother whistling in the kitchen.

This passage describes physical activity but reveals nothing about Holly's emotions. Is she angry, reassured, worried? Add her thoughts, and your readers will step into Holly's soul.

Holly stopped drawing and leaned back in her chair. She heard her brother whistling in the kitchen. He always whistles the same old song, she thought with a smile. Even after all the pain of the last few weeks, he still whistles. He's some guy!

Introspection also builds empathy and realization of feelings in your young readers. By reading about a character's inner thoughts, children not only recognize and understand their own feelings better, they acknowledge these feelings in others, too.

Kevin felt the others staring at him. He hated that. [Kids have experienced this embarrassment and will relate to this emotion.]
Stacy watched them leave. For a moment she felt tears burn her eyes. Then she marched back to the table. She'd show them. She wasn't giving up. [Kids will empathize with this rejection and feel stirred by Stacy's determination.]

Introspection also reveals changes as they occur in your characters and their relationships.

Bobby waved to Jason sprinting into the gym. Jason wore his red and orange tee shirt with the black arrow on the front.

This description shows action but doesn't reveal Bobby's attitudes or feelings. Add introspection and Bobby comes alive:

Bobby waved to Jason sprinting into the gym. Jason wore his red and orange tee shirt with the black arrow on the front. What a show-off, Bobby thought. He thinks he's so great now that he's on the track team and can wear the Arrow's tee shirt. He hardly even talks to me anymore. We won't be best friends at this rate.

Now readers really know how Bobby feels. He's hurt and angry about Jason's aloofness, and his once friendly feelings toward his best friend are fading because of Jason's callous treatment.

But won't readers know the character's reaction or thoughts by what they've already learned about him and what has gone before in the story? Not necessarily, and maybe not clearly enough. You don't want

506

to make the reader guess—one important reason for including intro-spection is so the reader will know for sure.

For example, suppose your character, Lisa, is caught in a storm. Thunder crashes. Rain slashes down. This event has not happened earlier in your story, so the reader is not certain how Lisa may react. Is she afraid? Actually, she feels exhilarated by the storm. Including her thoughts during the downpour will show exactly how she feels.

On the other hand, perhaps Lisa, who is impulsive and adventure-some, has one fear not previously divulged—thunderstorms. The reader, knowing Lisa's personality, expects Lisa to be excited by the storm. Lisa's thoughts will show otherwise.

Several rules dictate the use of introspection:

• Don't bog your reader down with paragraph after paragraph of thoughts, but don't include so few that the characters lack depth. As usual, rules for writing are never definite, never laid out so you use precisely two layers of this and one layer of that. But with practice you'll sense how much introspection to use, and where to use it.

• During intense action scenes, keep your character's thoughts brief so you won't slow the action. Several well-placed short sentences showing thoughts and feelings throughout a fast-paced scene will be enough to keep readers in tune with the character.

• In stories for young children under seven and eight, keep a charac-ter's thoughts at a minimum. Children this age usually don't analyze deeply, and they'll be bored by long passages of inaction. As they mature, however, they'll relish delving into a character's inner feelings.

Introspection is a natural element in fiction, but sometimes in the heat of creation writers overlook its value. Because we know we must keep the action and dialogue fast-paced to hold children's interest, we may whiz through page after page and forget about introspection. Fail-ure to pause to record thoughts and feelings reduces your story to a mechanical read—devoid of emotion and invigorating life.

On second thought, do writers ever *whiz* when they write? I, for one, usually *trudge,* occasionally *march,* but rarely *whiz.* I'm a slow writer—what can I say? There's so much to think about when you're writing: so many rules and techniques—vivid verbs, sentence varia-tion, show don't tell, character tags, motivation of protagonist, and that introspection thing!

507

➤➤ 105

LET YOUR THEME CHOOSE YOU

BY MARION DANE BAUER

SOME YEARS AGO, AFTER THE PUBLICATION OF MY FOURTH OR FIFTH novel for young people, I made a horrifying discovery: I was writing the same story . . . every time!

No matter that sometimes the main character was a girl, sometimes a boy. No matter that the settings changed with every book. No matter that the stories varied widely: one, a girl running away from home; another, a girl delivered into foster care; another, a young woman struggling with mental illness; another, a boy coming to terms with his brother's heroism—or lack of it—during service in World War II. My theme never changed. Every story began with a young person alienated from a parent or parent figure. Every story ended when my young character made a connection with that important person again.

My first thought upon facing this discovery was, "My career is over. I have nothing more to say!" Then I went on to write another book and another and another. I was still a writer, after all. Usually I wrote the kind of story that I was most comfortable with—realistic, hard-hitting family dramas. Sometimes I tried other forms—ghost stories and light fantasies. Those alienations and connections between parent and child kept right on happening.

Finally, I took the biggest step ever, a novella called *Ghost Eye*. "This will be entirely different," I told myself. The main character wasn't even a child. He was an odd-eyed white Cornish rex cat, haughty, disdainful, with no interest in connections of any kind. Yet, when he arrived at the concluding scene of the story, what happened? My haughty, independent cat turned, for the first time, to the girl who was supposed to be his mistress, the one he had been rejecting from the beginning, settled next to her, and rumbled into a contented purr. Parent-connection made, again! No matter how different my choice of genre and characters and style.

508

It was time, I decided, to accept this "truth" of mine, just as I accept the color of my eyes. And having accepted this theme, I realized that instead of trying to escape it, it was time to begin, consciously, to mine it. So in my next story, my main character was alienated from her beloved older sister. And in the next I had the mother run away instead of the child. It has been like stumbling into a gold mine. I know where to go looking for my stories now, and each one, when I find it, is totally mine.

None of us is limited to the facts of our own lives when we write our stories. Even if you've grown up on a farm, you can still gather the information and experience you need to write about a child growing up in the city. Even as an adult, by using your imagination and empathy, you can write from the point of view of a young girl . . . or for that matter, a mother raccoon. Though law-abiding, you can write a murder mystery; you can even write a murder mystery from the point of view of the murderer. The possibilities for creating characters, settings, plots are as wide as your imagination, as rich as your ability to learn. But your themes will, inevitably, emerge from your own psyche.

You don't choose your themes; they choose you. The meaning of your stories will rise out of your deepest longings, often out of longings so deep that you haven't admitted them even to yourself. Your convictions, your confusions, your most passionate dreams will be there whenever you begin a story, so you might as well learn to tap into them.

How can you do that? First, by recognizing inspiration when it comes. Inspiration is energy, pure and simple. When an idea has the ability to touch your center, it will carry a kind of excitement with it, a shimmer of vitality, of possibilities yet unexplored. The idea itself may have no discernible connection to your life, but if it has the potential to be the core of one of your stories, the excitement will be there.

To be a fiction writer is to keep your story sensors open all the time. Whether you are reading a newspaper, listening to a friend's complaints about her boss, or observing a stray dog, every piece of information you take in is sifted through your imagination for possible stories. But the stories for which you can, almost instantly, *feel* a resolution are the ones that are fully yours. They tie into your personal themes.

Every one of my stories begins with an emotion. Or perhaps it would be more accurate to say, each begins with a situation that evokes an emotion in me. A boy wanting to "show them all" with a .22 rifle draws on my own, mostly buried, rage. A girl feeling cut off from her much-loved older sister reaches into my loneliness, my longing for the sister I never had.

But if the story is mine to write, the resolution will arrive almost simultaneously with the idea. And the resolution will involve emotion, too. When I feel Michael's rage I know that when he finally turns to the stepfather he has always rejected, the rage will begin to heal. Touched by Caitlin's loneliness, I can at the same time imagine what a reconciliation with her sister will feel like. I may not yet know *how* she will arrive at that reconciliation, but I know exactly what the end of the story will be. And in knowing that, I know both why I am writing the story and what it will mean.

Understanding the emotional conflict that sets off your story and the emotional resolution that brings it to a conclusion gives you a framework; your task then is to fill in that framework with your character's struggle to resolve her conflict.

Can your themes or mine ever change? They can indeed, but only as we do, only as we discover new personal truths. I have recently written the text for a picture book called *Jason's Bears*. Actually, that small story took me five years and uncounted drafts before it was completed. The writing took that long because I had stumbled into a story problem for which my old "theme" could not provide a resolution.

Jason, who loves bears, is being tormented by a bullying older brother into thinking that the bears he loves are waiting in every corner of his house to eat him up. The solution was clearly that the little boy should not put himself further under his big brother's power; he had to find his own power before he could come to terms with those bears, and he finally did. But he found it only after I had discovered some of my own power as a writer and could believe in such an ending.

Every person has a unique set of longings, as well as a different set of resolutions to those longings. That is why no one can write *the* "story for all time." And yet the reason stories can be written at all is that nothing points more inevitably to the universal than the personal and unique. Each of us seeks another person's insights to understand our lives.

So if you find yourself repeating a single theme, or two or three themes, relax. You are in good company. Remember that Mark Twain

510

wrote of hope and disillusion in a thousand different guises. In story after story, Jane Austen tweaked homely commonplace. Edgar Allan Poe was obsessed with evil. Your gift, your need, your longing will also be your creative fire. And it will turn up again and again, whether you ask it to or not.

➤➤ 106

WRITING ABOUT NATURE FOR YOUNG PEOPLE

BY DOROTHY HINSHAW PATENT

WHEN I BEGAN WRITING ABOUT NATURE FOR YOUNG PEOPLE MORE than twenty years ago, it was enough to recount the facts in clear, uncomplicated prose sprinkled with active verbs and colorful adjectives. Not anymore. Nowadays, an author must compete with computers, video games, CDs, and exciting television dramas, including breathtaking footage of nature in action. There are also hundreds of nature books out there published in the last five years. How can you compete in such a challenging field?

The key is to think of nature writing as merely a subcategory of writing in general, not as a separate genre. Good writing can be recognized wherever you find it, and the same techniques work, no matter what your audience or your topic.

How can that be? you may ask. Nonfiction must stick to the facts, while fiction allows writers to use their imaginations to conjure up new, exciting worlds and cliff-hanging plots. Fortunately, the natural world and its relationships with human beings are full of stories that are just as exciting as anything our minds can create—it's up to the author to find them, figure out how to use them, and then to turn them into dramatic prose. Here's the first paragraph from my book *The Way of the Grizzly:*

The grizzly reared up on her hind legs, ears pricked and sensitive nose held high. She scanned the brush for signs of movement and glimpsed rustling grass ahead to her left. She wheeled around, dropped to all fours, and plunged forward, rushing to the spot; but the ground squirrel had already escaped into a well-hidden tunnel in the soft earth of the tundra. The bear reared again, turning her body this way and that as she concentrated her senses on the search for signs of the squirrel. Finding none, she went back to all fours and began to feed on the abundant grasses near the streambank. She walked slowly

512

forward with a swaying, toed-in saunter as she swung her head from side to side, grabbing clumps of the lush and tasty grass with her powerful jaws.

Grizzly bears are popularly portrayed as meat-hungry hunters. But in fact, these massive creatures are rarely fortunate enough to find meat. They spend most of their time feeding on plants. . . .

By now, I hope the reader is hooked, and I've managed to fit in some important facts about the grizzly along with the drama of the constant quest for food: the bear's acute senses, its way of moving, and the fact that it eats more plants than animals.

The incident described above is based on my experiences with grizzlies in Denali National Park in Alaska. One catch with this type of writing is that the author must have personal experience with the subject of the book, not just from thorough library research. This may present problems, especially since nature books in general do not command big advances or expense-paid research trips. Even an excursion to the zoo, with time spent just sitting and watching the animals and trying to put yourself into their sensory world, can bring life to your writing. The more your personal experience can infuse your prose, the more alive it will be to your readers.

How do you find out where you can have personal experience with your subject as well as the other information you'll need to write your book? Let's say your topic is the life of the wood duck. First off, you'll want to find out where wood ducks live (that's simple; just check a bird identification guidebook), then find out where you can visit to see these beautiful birds. National and state parks are familiar places for experiencing nature. But perhaps the most easily accessible places to see American wildlife are our National Wildlife Refuges. Run by the U.S. Fish and Wildlife Service, these public lands are managed for the benefit of wildlife. There's at least one refuge in each of the fifty states. The system was originally developed to provide habitats for migrating waterfowl, but in recent years, preserving the natural variety of species present in an area has also become a goal.

Once you find a refuge where you can see wood ducks, it's a good idea to contact the refuge manager. Phoning is better than writing; managers are busy people, and your letter could end up on the bottom of a pile, never to surface again. Besides, you want to make personal contact. I've been delighted to find that when a wildlife manager finds that I'm writing for children and that I've already done my homework, he or she is friendly, cooperative, and helpful. Besides letting you know how best to see the ducks on the refuge, the manager can give you ideas for additional sources of information, such as Ducks Unlimited, a private group involved in saving waterfowl habitat. Once you get going on the information search, one thing leads to another until you'll probably have more potential sources than you know what to do with.

In addition to personal experience, thorough research into primary sources is of utmost importance. Information from sources like encyclopedias and popular books for the layman is often out of date and just plain incorrect. Recent papers written by researchers in scientific journals are a great source for the most up-to-date, interesting, and accurate information. These days, there are many ways to find such articles. Your best bet is to check the reference department of a nearby university library. The reference librarian can steer you to the best database for your particular topic.

With a little practice and a scientific dictionary in hand, you should be able to understand the most important points in scientific papers. Each field of research has its own jargon, but once you catch on, you'll be able to extract the information you need. One key paper can provide you with a wealth of references, as each has a complete bibliography of related work. Just be aware that not everyone agrees on what's going on in the complicated natural world, so be sure to read the work of researchers with different opinions.

Once you've acquired some knowledge of your subject, you're bound to have some unanswered questions. I've found that those questions are often the same ones the scientists haven't yet answered—but you'd better check to find out. The address of the author of a paper is usually included with the article, so you can contact the experts yourself. Don't be shy. Like the rest of us, scientists are happy when others show interest in their work.

Another benefit of contacting experts is that they may be willing to read your manuscript for factual errors. Everyone gains from such a reading: The author can be confident of the facts; the expert knows that accurate information is being presented; and the young reader is provided with the best available information. I've found that these experts rarely tinker with my prose: They aren't professional writers, and they almost always limit their comments to matters of accuracy. Such a reading was especially invaluable with my book on alligators—

despite my care in choosing sources, an expert reader was able to point out numerous places in my manuscript where the information had not been scientifically verified, and I was able to correct it before sending it off to the publisher.

What about the actual writing of your book? How do you organize it, and how do you keep it interesting in between dramatic paragraphs? Now and then, a child who is especially interested in a topic will take your book out of the library, but the truth is most nature books for children are bought primarily by school libraries and are used by students in writing reports. For this reason, if your book is about a particular kind of animal or group of animals, you must present all the basic information—how big the animals get, how long they live, what they look like, where they live, and how they feed, reproduce, interact with one another, and protect themselves from predators. Finding ways to present all these facts in interesting ways can be a big challenge. I've found one useful technique is to find a general theme of importance that this animal can illustrate. For example, the theme of my book *Buffalo: The American Bison Today* was how to manage a wild species on a limited refuge. *Where the Bald Eagles Gather* was about the importance of scientific research, while *Where the Wild Horses Roam* discussed the problems of conflicts between the economic interests of ranchers and the romantic desire of other people to have horses running free in the American West.

Another approach is to focus the entire book on a key aspect of the animals' lives and tell the story from a fresh angle. *Feathers,* for example, gave me an opportunity to discuss a new perspective on how birds live, and the book has been one of my most successful.

Age level is another important consideration with children's books. If written for children 5 to 8, your book will be very different from one for ages 12 and up. Books for younger children are shorter, and their sentences and paragraphs are shorter as well. The information presented must be as concrete as possible, as in this example:

Killer whales are big. A male can grow as long as 32 feet. His dorsal fin can reach a height of 5 ½ feet, taller than an average woman. He can weigh up to 9 tons, as much as 140 persons together.

That paragraph from my book *Killer Whales* (for ages 4 to 8) is the extent of the text on a page; the rest of the space is taken up by a

515

photo illustrating the dorsal fin of a male. For one of my books on large mammals, I remember phoning the post office, U-Haul, and UPS in an effort to find a delivery truck of approximately the same size and weight as my subject!

Children 10 and up are better able to deal with abstract concepts not tied to concrete images. And if you're writing for the young adult market, you can have fun bringing out the controversies within a particular scientific discipline. Older children love to read about the pros and cons of vital issues. Here's the first paragraph of my young adult book *The Vanishing Feast,* which concerns the vanishing genetic diversity of our food crops and domesticated animals:

It was the winter of 1942, in the middle of World War II. The Germans were shelling Leningrad, Russia. No food could come in to feed the people, and there was no heat. Tens of thousands were dying from the cold and starvation. D. S. Ivanov was one of the casualties. But Ivanov was different from most of those who perished. At his death, he was surrounded by thousands of packets of rice—rice too precious to eat, even if it meant saving his own life. Ivanov was not the only one to die at the All Union Research Institute of Plant Industry. One of his colleagues died at his writing table, working until the last moment, while others starved slowly, protecting boxes of corn, wheat, peas, and other edible seeds. Altogether, ten dedicated workers starved at the institute in the process of saving the world's greatest collection of seeds and tubers.

The idea that seeds could be worth dying for is powerful and almost forces the reader to continue on: What could it be that made these people sacrifice their lives? What is the significance of their act for people today? The only way to find out is to read on!

Here are a few important miscellaneous points about nature books for young people. Generally, you don't need to submit a complete manuscript to get a contract from a publisher. Sending an outline, one or two sample chapters, and a cover letter that convinces the editor that you're the right person for the job usually suffices. When you write, even for the youngest children, don't be afraid to use appropriate vocabulary that may be unfamiliar to readers; one purpose of your book is to teach the correct names for things. Don't write down to children, and if your topic has depressing overtones, as do so many stories about the natural world today, find a way of giving your readers hope for the future. After all, the future depends on them, and they have the power to make positive changes in this often discouraging world.

516

One final matter concerns illustrating your book. The vast majority of nature books published today for children under age 12 are illustrated with copious photographs, preferably at least one per spread. I've been fortunate to have forged a partnership with William Muñoz, a fine photographer who lives nearby. And when it hasn't been practical for him to take the photos—as with subjects like whales—I've found a scientist who has taken publication-quality photos. But if you're new to this field, don't be concerned about the photos. Gain the attention of an editor first, then discuss how the book might be illustrated. Some publishers have photo research departments with access to a number of photo sources. Books for older children, such as *The Vanishing Feast,* may have only one or two black-and-white photos in each chapter.

So get your facts straight, acquire some personal experience with your subject, find a larger theme that makes your book more than just a life cycle presentation, keep the age level of your readers in mind, and respect your readers. By following these guidelines and writing interesting prose, you, too, can write nature books for children that will be successful.

≫ EDITING AND MARKETING

>> 107

NEGOTIATING THE BOOK CONTRACT

BY SHERRI L. BURR

YOUR DREAM IS ABOUT TO BE REALIZED. YOUR FIRST BOOK CONTRACT arrives in the mail. You go directly to the advance clause. It is exactly as you agreed. You look no further, sign the contract, and return it, confident of your great deal.

You are deliriously happy, until one day you run into an experienced writing friend. She's unhappy because she has not received a single royalty from her publisher since her advance.

"How could that happen?" you ask.

"I never read the fine print that said royalties were paid on net proceeds. I thought I'd be paid on the gross sales price. Instead, the publisher is paying me a percentage based on the amount that is received from booksellers, minus a few deductions for shipping costs and other overhead charges. My current statement says I owe the publisher money."

"That's terrible," you reply, secretly wondering if the same thing could happen to you. You rush home, take out your contract, and begin to read it. You are appalled by what you find and wonder what to do.

While this may never have happened to you, it serves as a reminder to review your contract carefully before signing. It is easy to understand why writers do not read their book contracts carefully. Contracts are usually written in "legal garbage-ese" and printed in the smallest type that the best computer scientists can design. The saying, "The big print giveth and the small print taketh away," is particularly appropriate to book contracts.

But don't despair; all contracts are negotiable. You just need to invest some time in determining what rights you should keep, and what rights the publisher will want. Here are some important issues to consider when reviewing your contract:

Manuscript clause

Many book contracts begin with a standard clause dealing with the specifics of the manuscript: the title, the name of the author, the length, the due date, how many copies you must deliver in hard copy and on disk. Sometimes, in this clause the publisher reserves the right to reject the final manuscript as unacceptable or unpublishable.

A savvy negotiator may be able to get the publisher to waive this clause, but don't count on it. Instead, try to insert that the publisher's right of rejection must be "reasonably exercised," which is often implied in the contract. Publishers rarely reject a manuscript at the final stages, unless they think that it is unpublishable.

What makes a manuscript unpublishable? The final draft may not be as well written as the initial proposal. Or the subject of the book has become dated: A psychological profile of George Bush that might have sold in 1987 would not be acceptable in 1989. Or the manuscript may contain damaging information about a prominent family, and the publisher becomes worried about potential libel suits. For these and other reasons, the publisher will insist on keeping an "out" clause in the contract, permitting the return of all rights to the author.

If a publisher does exercise its "out" clause, what happens to your advance? Often, the advance is tied to the production of an acceptable manuscript. Under most contracts, if the publisher deems your manuscript unacceptable, you must refund the advance.

In Joan Collins' well-publicized dispute with Random House, however, a jury ruled that she did not have to return her advance—even though Random House found her manuscript unacceptable—and that the company had to pay her part of the additional monies due on her contract. Instead of the usual clause that the author must produce an "acceptable" manuscript, Ms. Collins' contract merely required her to produce a "completed" manuscript. Although this case has been unusual for the publicity it generated, there have been other instances where the publisher, as an act of good will, has permitted the author to keep the advance.

Copyright issues

Ideally, the contract should provide that the publisher will register the copyright *in the name of the author*. Some contracts, particularly those from university and small presses, state that the publisher will register the copyright *in the name of the publisher,* but this clause is negotiable.

The "Rights and Royalties" clauses are critical for you to understand. If your publisher has only the capacity to publish your book in English and distribute it in Canada and the United States, why grant the publisher all the rights to your book, including the right to publish it in any translation throughout the world? Instead, tell the publisher that you want to sell the rights only to the English-language edition in specific countries. Also, consider selling the publisher audio and electronic rights only if the company has these divisions. If not, retain the rights for sales at a later date.

If your publisher is a major conglomerate with movie divisions and your book has movie potential, consider granting the publisher the movie rights, but only if you are sure that you or your agent could not sell the movie rights yourselves for more profit. Ask your agent about his contacts with Hollywood and whether he has sub-agency relations with Hollywood agents.

You should also be aware that the publisher may ask to split the movie rights 50–50. Try to negotiate to a more profitable (60–40, 75–25, 85–15) split, because the publisher will be acting as your agent.

Royalty provisions

Traditional publishers typically offer a royalty fee of 10% to 15% on the retail price for hardcover books, but less for paperback. On mass market paperback books, publishers may print 500,000 copies or more, offer authors a 5% royalty, and sell the books in discount markets such as K-Mart and Wal-Mart. Writers or their agents can propose a royalty schedule. For example, after the first 10,000 or 50,000 or 100,000 or so in sales, the royalty fee increases according to an agreed-upon scale.

Some smaller presses offer payment on net proceeds because they sell fewer copies and therefore receive less money. Make sure the term "net proceeds" is concretely defined in your contract; it is important to specify that net proceeds include the money that the publisher receives from its sales. In a net profit deal, you should be able to negotiate a higher royalty percentage payment, at least 10% to 15% or more.

Accounting provisions

Accounting provisions indicate when you can expect to receive royalty checks. Most trade publishers have semiannual accountings; most academic and small presses have annual accountings. Payments are made within 30 to 90 days following the close of the accounting period.

These provisions may be difficult to negotiate because they often depend on the publisher's overall accounting practices. However, trade publishers have been known to provide shorter accounting periods for their best-selling authors who are generating a great deal of revenue. You can ask for a similar arrangement, but if you do not yet fall into this category, do not be surprised if your publisher resists setting up a different system for you.

Warranties

Almost impossible to negotiate, these clauses require the author to guarantee to the publisher that:
- the author is the sole creator and owner of the work.
- the work has not been previously published.
- the work does not violate another work's copyright.
- the work does not violate anyone's right of privacy.
- the work does not libel or defame anyone.
- the work does not violate any government regulation.

If you or your work violates the above warranties, the publisher has a right to cancel the contract.

Warranty clauses are often accompanied by an indemnity provision, requiring the author to indemnify, or repay, the publisher, should the work violate a warranty provision. If the publisher is sued because of the author's work, the author must defend the lawsuit and reimburse the publisher for any related expenses.

Expenses, permissions, and fair use

Publishers may grant authors budgets to cover certain expenses, such as those connected with travel or interviews. This is obviously a negotiable point, though it may be difficult for a first-time book author to negotiate reimbursement for such expenses.

If you plan to quote from copyrighted works, you should get the permission of the copyright holder (usually either the author or the publisher) to do so. Sometimes the publisher will grant a budget for permission fees; other times, you must cover the cost of such permissions.

In some cases, authors claim a fair-use privilege to use other people's work, such as when critiquing it, in which case permission is not needed. Determining whether the fair-use privilege applies requires authors to use their best judgment. However, you should be aware that if the copyright owner sues, you have to pay to defend both yourself and the publisher.

New editions, author's copies, out of print

The contract may also specify that the publisher has the first right to publish further editions of the work. This should be a negotiable item. Authors of a continuing series (such as mysteries) and textbook publications should beware of such clauses, because they may give the publisher the right to name other writers to produce additional editions. Obviously, the original author would want to retain this right.

The author's copies clause specifies how many free copies of your book you will receive, and the cost of any additional copies you may want to purchase. Sometimes these clauses specify that you cannot resell reduced-price copies. Try to strike this portion of the clause or spell out circumstances where resale would be permitted, such as when you sell copies at a lecture, conference, or book signing.

Also, make sure that the contract provides that when the book goes out of print, all rights revert to the author.

Assignment

A clause that has become standard in the era of mergers and acquisitions is the assignment clause, granting the publisher the right to assign the contract to another publisher. You could easily sell your book to Publisher A only to have Publisher Q purchase or merge with Publisher A soon thereafter. With an assignment clause, Publisher Q would assume the responsibility for publishing your book. You would be protected because the book would still be published.

Your contract may contain fewer clauses than those mentioned here, or it may be more extensive. Whether it's long or short, in large or small print, you should read your contract carefully! You will not only avoid royalty payment shock, but also prevent your book contract dreams from becoming nightmares should some unforeseen disaster strike. Having read your contract, you will know that the price of a magnifying glass could prove a good investment!

525

$\succ\!\!\succ$ 108

CONFESSIONS OF A FIRST READER

BY ROY SORRELS

YOUR NOVEL, THE PRECIOUS MANUSCRIPT YOU'VE SLAVED OVER FOR months—years, maybe—the one you've revised and edited till it shines like gold, lovingly typed, checked and double-checked for typos, packaged for safety, and mailed off to an editor in a spirit of hopeful optimism, gets passed on by the editor to a free-lance "first reader."

It's every writer's nightmare, but it's also reality. Most manuscripts, even those sent to an editor by a well-known agent, are first read by the editor's in-office assistant, but more often by a first reader.

I was that first reader, for one of the biggest companies in the business. For two years, while writing my own first novel, I dropped by an editor's office once a week to pick up several manuscripts, mostly novels, took them home, read them, and prepared a "reader's report" including a brief plot summary and a paragraph giving my recommendation as to whether it was a "hit" or a "miss" and why.

I gave each manuscript a fair and conscientious read, often speeding up considerably after the first 30 or so pages, when it became abundantly and often painfully clear that what I was reading was unpublishable. Over 90 percent of what I read was, in my opinion, unpublishable, but I really wanted to go to my next meeting with my boss and be able to say, "*This* one is great. Read it! Buy it!"

In the process, I picked up a few extremely valuable tips that helped me write and sell my first novel and several more since. I'd like to share what I learned about any talented writer's chances of eventually getting published.

The first thing aspiring writers must remember is that the editor is their friend. Most writers imagine editors as barriers to their success whose main job is to reject their work. *Not so.* Editors get paid to find good, publishable manuscripts—stuffing form rejection slips into

SASEs is only a disappointing byproduct of that search. They want the manuscript they've just received from a writer to be something great! After all, if editors don't find enough excellent manuscripts, they lose their jobs.

Although it's true that agented material has a strong advantage, even the slush pile gets looked at eventually. Whether your unagented manuscript gets attention or not rests on these six crucial points:

1) Never—*never*—send a manuscript to a publisher unless you have an editor's name, and not just any editor but the right one for your type of book. A manuscript addressed to "Editor" or "To Whom It May Concern" may never reach the editor responsible for the type of book you're submitting. It's relatively simple to get the name of the right editor, but it does require some extra work. If you've written a police procedural, for example, go to your local bookstore or public library to find the name of a publisher who has brought out several police procedural novels. Consult the list of publishers in *Literary Market Place* (available in the reference department of most libraries) for the phone number of that publisher and call and ask for the editorial department. Request the name of the person who handles police procedurals (or whatever category your manuscript is).

I've done this with numerous publishers, and I've always been able to get the name of the appropriate person. If you're asked why you want to know, just tell the truth, and most of the time you'll get the name you're looking for. By addressing your manuscript to a specific editor, it will reach the person who is responsible for the type of material you've written, usually guaranteeing much better attention—even though it may not be accepted.

2) Include a cover letter that's informative, *well-written,* and succinct (rarely more than one page), since you want it to be read. Include brief biographical information, noting any credits or relevant information, and two or three lines about your book. As some wise person once said, "You never get a second chance to make a good first impression," and you want your first impression to show that even though you are perhaps unpublished, you've taken the trouble to learn how a pro acts.

3) As a first reader, I was shocked to see how often beginners reveal their ignorance of the basics of presenting a manuscript. *Neatness counts*—and not simply flawless typing and clean paper that doesn't

look as if it's already been shopped around to every publisher in town, but an overall professional presentation.

4) Once you've succeeded in getting an editor to open to page one of your manuscript, you absolutely must be sure you start with a powerfully effective opening line, first paragraph, and opening page. If what the editor reads on page one grabs or moves or amuses him, then he might read your entire manuscript, or at least pass it on to a reader—and at that point you'll have just as much chance as anybody else of having your manuscript accepted for publication.

5) I often saw the editor I worked for wander over to the slush pile table and riffle quickly through half a dozen manuscripts before handing me one to read. I was mystified: What could she possibly see from ten seconds of flipping pages? When I asked her, she answered, "I'm looking for lots of dialogue." Questioned further, she explained that one of the major flaws in novels from beginning writers was too much narration, not enough lively conversation between characters. Dialogue is vital in getting a reading for an unagented script, not just well-written dialogue, but plenty of it.

6) From slogging through countless bad novels and the occasional one that stood out above the others, I learned that there is absolutely no substitute for the combination of powerful storytelling and vibrant characters. A *story* that is strong and *characters* that come alive on the page will make up for all sorts of other flaws.

But the most important lesson I learned—and I unfailingly applied it to my own beginning novel-writing career—is not to be intimidated by the overwhelming number of submissions publishers receive. So what if Publisher X gets a thousand submissions a week, if 99 percent of them are weak and amateurishly presented? If you've written an excellent novel, and you present it in a professional manner, your chances are as good as any other writer's. Remember, the editor is hungry for good writing.

The motto of every aspiring and not-yet-published writer should always be, "If at first you don't succeed, try again." As a first reader I wrote negative reports on a few books that, a year or two later, I saw in bookstores. One was nominated for a prestigious award. I thought they were dreadful and said so in my reader's reports, but that was simply one person's opinion. Some other first reader, and an editor, obviously loved them. And bought them.

➤➤ 109

THE ALL-IMPORTANT QUERY LETTER

BY STEVE WEINBERG

ONE OF THE MOST IMPORTANT RULES FOR FREE-LANCE WRITERS TRY-ing to break into a magazine is too frequently violated: When trying to sell an article to an editor unfamiliar with your work, send a query letter. Do not send a complete manuscript.

A few editors buy nonfiction from writers unknown to them on the basis of a completed manuscript. But not many.

So let's discuss why it makes sense to query first, then discuss the elements of successful query letters.

Why query?

1. Time is money. Free lancers who want to make money should not invest months researching and writing a manuscript without an expression of interest from an editor. I have written successful queries after just a few hours of research. Time is precious for editors, too. They rarely want to invest in reading unsolicited manuscripts.

A query letter will help you focus your thoughts. The brevity of the form (one or two pages) will allow you to revise the letter until the phrasing is just right. When the letter reaches its destination, the editor can read it at a convenient moment, mull it over, reread it if necessary.

2. Query letters can avoid rejections based on the focus or the style, rather than the substance. The small percentage of editors who take time to read manuscripts because they like the idea frequently find they dislike the approach. Why did the writer use first person instead of omniscient third person? Why did the writer choose a question lead instead of an anecdotal opening? Rather than guide the unfamiliar writer through a major revision, the editor will just say no.

3. Editors are too distracted during their work day to hold lengthy conversations by telephone with unfamiliar writers. Trying to sell arti-

529

cles by telephone almost never works. Besides, editors want to see a writing sample—a query letter can serve as that sample.

The elements of successful query letters

1. Queries should be one or two single- or double-spaced pages. Brevity is mainly for the convenience of the editor, but it benefits writers, too, forcing them to distill their thoughts. A query is not the place for a writer to overwhelm an editor with mastery of the topic's detail. If editors are interested but want to know more, they will ask for more.

2. Within the brief query letter, the main idea should be described in one sentence if possible, certainly in no more than one paragraph. That description should be written compellingly, a grabber. It should not be written boringly, as in "This idea has to do with missing persons." Much better:

Murderers, thousands of them, are walking around free. That is scary enough. Even scarier is that police, prosecutors, and judges have no idea who they are. They are perpetrators of a type of homicide so common, yet so little discussed, that it lacks a commonly accepted label. Let's call it, for now, missing and presumed murdered.

When possible, it is best to write the main idea in the style of the proposed article, as in the previous paragraph from a query letter of mine. A proposed headline usually helps, too.

3. After the nutshell description, the letter should explain why readers of that magazine are likely to care. This should be subtle. Hype ("an irresistible topic") will turn off editors. So will preachiness. ("Your magazine must publish this article because of its importance to your readers.") Your query letter should make editors say, "This is irresistible" or "This is really important to my readers."

4. With the editor clued in to the "what" and "why," it is time to tell the editor the "how" of information gathering. What sources might consent to be interviewed? What documents can be consulted in libraries, government agencies or business archives? Are reference books available? If possible, work in a telling anecdote, a case history, or a

statistic already in hand—and simultaneously demonstrate your passion for the topic.

5. Now that the editor knows about the process of information gathering, she or he will be curious about the proposed structure, point of view, timing and tone.

Will the article be structured chronologically? In cinematic-type scenes? An outline is often the best way to convey the structure.

As for point of view, through whose eyes will the article be told? The author's, in either first person or omniscient third person? The person who is the main subject of the article? A query proposing an article about "capital punishment" is too vague. But telling an editor the article will talk about capital punishment through the executioner's point of view might produce a "go-ahead" or assignment.

About timing: If you include the fact that the number of death-row convicts executed has doubled over the last decade, you have provided the editor with the relevance of your proposed piece.

Moving on to tone, will the article be serious or light? Or downright humorous?

6. Include something about yourself, such as prior publications, if any; and where you can be contacted by mail, telephone, fax and/or electronic mail.

Novices worry that if they cannot include previously published articles, it will mean immediate rejection. Not so. Every published writer was at some point unpublished. Furthermore, some editors put little stock in clips, because they cannot tell how much is the result of revision by an editor. For clips, aspiring authors can substitute relevant personal experience, work experience or academic training.

A caution: Some editors and experienced writers suggest placing personal information in the first paragraph. I disagree. It is the idea that should be emphasized, not the writer who will be researching the idea. Well-known writers might receive assignments on the basis of their names; beginning and intermediate writers rarely do.

7. Address your query to a specific editor. Which editor? Perhaps the editor of a particular section or department. Perhaps the managing editor, articles editor, features editor or editor-in-chief.

You may find the name of the appropriate editor in the magazine's masthead. If not, try calling the magazine. (During that call, request a copy of the magazine's guidelines for writers.)

What to leave out of query letters

Omitted from my seven-point list is something that other writers suggest including in query letters—a paragraph about what the magazine's competitors have (or have not) published on the topic. The point is apparently to convince an editor that competing magazines have not run the same story.

I disagree. Most editors do not assume their readers also buy the competitors. So if I have an idea that I want to sell to *The Atlantic Monthly,* I search a few years of its back issues to make sure I am not duplicating. If I find nothing similar, I begin drafting the query. Sure, I will also search back issues of *Harper's, Mother Jones,* and other magazines that might be considered *The Atlantic Monthly*'s competitors. But if I find an article in those publications on my topic, I will not mention it in my query. What I will do is make sure my approach is different enough from what has appeared elsewhere so that my article is advancing knowledge, not duplicating knowledge.

In your query letter, don't mention article length; payment; deadlines (unless the topic is fresh for only a short time, or seasonal); artwork (unless it is a big part of why you should get the assignment); and other contractual terms such as rights.

Editors frequently reject query letters with mistakes in grammar, incorrect punctuation or misspellings—no matter how good the idea. They are usually unimpressed by college degrees (unless directly relevant to the proposed article), friends of theirs you claim to know, or language filled with pyrotechnics at the expense of clarity. They are not interested in what you think of their magazines, and are especially offended by mini-lectures on how you would improve those magazines.

Simultaneous submission of queries?

Whether to submit the same or similar query letters simultaneously to multiple magazines is a topic without one correct answer. Debates within writers' groups and editors' forums over the decades have failed to resolve the matter.

Some free lancers say they are uncomfortable sending multiple que-

532

ries. They do not want to risk having an editor remember that after making an assignment based on careful consideration, a competitor wound up with the article.

I disagree. Free lancers will starve if they wait for one editor after another to respond. Simultaneous query submissions are smart business. What if two or more editors want you to write for them? My reaction: You should be so lucky.

So now it is time to go forth and submit query letters, simultaneously.

A Sample Query Letter

Here are parts of the query letter—with brief explanations inserted—that sold my proposed article about missing persons. I addressed the query to the managing editor at the *ABA* [American Bar Association] *Journal,* based on a conversation with a writer who had already published in the magazine:

MISSING AND PRESUMED MURDERED

[The editor used the headline I suggested. He fleshed it out with this subheadline: When a young Texan vanished, he joined a phenomenon that bedevils prosecutors and police nationwide: How to find justice when they suspect homicide, but have no victim to help prove it.]

Murderers, thousands of them, are walking around free. That is scary enough. Even scarier is that police, prosecutors, and judges have no idea who they are.
[If that isn't a grabber, what is? Because I hoped it could also serve as the opening paragraph of the actual article, the editor immediately experienced the style I hoped to use.]

They are perpetrators of a type of homicide so common, yet so little discussed, that it lacks a commonly accepted label. Let's call it, for now, missing and presumed murdered.
[This paragraph expands on the grabber of a lead as well as further demonstrating my style and introducing my informal, but not flippant, tone.]

The best estimate, based on FBI statistics and anecdotal evidence, is that 21,000 children, teenagers, and adults are missing and presumed murdered. The common denominators are that their bodies remain hidden, with no conviction of perpetrators on the horizon.
[This defines an unfamiliar topic further, plus suggests some of my sources— the FBI and interviews with persons involved in such cases.]

Probably the best-known case is that of Jimmy Hoffa, who disappeared in 1975. Despite almost immediate notification of the disappearance, hundreds of

law enforcement officers, including the best the FBI could offer, failed to find the Teamsters Union leader. Twenty years later, Hoffa is presumed dead. But no body has surfaced, and those responsible remain at large.
[Here I make the unfamiliar familiar by referring to a well-known case. I also further hint at the depth and breadth of my research.]

In the remainder of the query letter, I explained:
• Why readers of that particular magazine would be likely to care (because these cases frustrate the participants in the legal system and cause the citizenry at large to lose faith in that system)
• How I planned to research the article (by gathering FBI and state police statistics; interviewing family members of missing persons, police officers, prosecutors, defense attorneys and judges; reading trial transcripts; narrating the case of my brother-in-law, missing since 1981, based on notes kept and documents gathered during 14 years of investigating)
• The likely structure of the article (told in sections, beginning with a disappearance, followed by the police investigation, the decision by a prosecutor whether to move forward, the defense strategy in cases involving a specific suspect, the trial and verdict. This is largely a chronological approach, with modifications. Furthermore, each section would begin and end with my brother-in-law's case, which would serve as the connecting thread)
• The point of view (through the thoughts of the investigators, as recounted by them in hindsight and through contemporaneous reports or diaries)

I ended the query with a paragraph about my credentials. I received the assignment soon thereafter. The article appeared in the September 1995 issue of the *ABA Journal*.

>> 110

WHAT YOU NEED TO KNOW ABOUT COPYRIGHT

BY HOWARD ZAHAROFF

"WORDS ARE JUST OUR CURRENCY, OUR MEDIUM OF EXCHANGE WITH our readers," says the writer-protagonist in Richard Ford's *The Sportswriter*. From a lawyer's perspective he's at best half-right. Although as a writer you are trading in your words, and trading on your talent, what you are selling to publishers and editors are your copyrights.

Therefore to plan your career, negotiate with publishers, even draw up your will, it is important that you understand the basics of copyright law. As a lawyer who practices in this field, I promise you that this isn't too hard. Let me prove it by answering a dozen questions that writers often ask.

Before doing so, a few comments. First, the answers I give are based on U.S. law, as it exists at the time of this writing. International issues are mostly ignored. Second, my focus is mainly on works first published or created after March 1, 1989, the last major revision of the Copyright Act (which I refer to below as the "Act"). Third, although the Copyright Office cannot provide legal advice, its Circulars and Public Information Office (call 202/707-3000) provide guidance on many of the following issues. (Start with Circular 1: "Copyright Basics.") There are also many excellent books available, such as Ellen Kozak's *Every Writer's Guide to Copyright & Publishing Law* (Owl, 1990) and *The Rights of Authors, Artists and Other Creative People: The Basic ACLU Guide to Author and Artist Rights,* by Kenneth Norwick and Jerry Chasen.

1. *What can be copyrighted?* Copyright protects nearly every original piece you write (or draw, compose, choreograph, videotape, sculpt, etc.): not just your novel, article, story or poem, but the software

program you create, the advertisements and greeting cards you published, and the love letters you wrote in college. But copyright does
not protect your ideas, only the way you *express* them.

2. *What protection does copyright law provide?* A "copyright" is
really a bundle of rights. The copyright owner (whom we'll call the
"proprietor") controls not only the right to copy the work, but also
the rights to perform or display the work publicly, to make the "first
sale" of each copy of the work, and to prepare "derivative works,"
that is, adaptations, translations, and versions in other media, such as
creating a screenplay or movie from a novel or play.

3. *How long do copyrights last and are they renewable?* For works
created or first published after 1977, copyright generally lasts 50 years
after the death of the author. However, for anonymous or pseudony-
mous works, or works made "for hire" (see below), the term expires
100 years from the creation or 75 years from publication. There are no
renewals. (For works published before 1978, special rules, including
rights of renewal, apply. See Circular 15: "Renewal of Copyright.") A
proposal is pending to increase the term by 20 years, a change already
adopted in many foreign countries.

4. *How do you obtain a copyright?* Copyright protection arises
automatically as soon as you put your ideas into tangible form. Thus,
once on paper, canvas, video, or computer disk, your creation is protected by law.

5. *Is a copyright notice required for protection?* No. Before March
1, 1989, a notice was required on all *published* copies of a work. ("Published" simply means distributed to the public; it does not require
printing in a periodical or book.) However, on that day the United
States joined the international copyright treaty known as the Berne
Convention and removed this requirement for works published after
that date.

Still, including a copyright notice alerts everyone to your claim and
prevents infringers from pleading "innocence" (that is, that they had
no idea your work was copyrighted). Thus, good reasons remain for
including notices on all published copies of your work, and for insisting
that your publisher do so.

If you are concerned that your *unpublished* work may be used or copied without permission (for example, you are circulating copies of your latest, highly marketable, piece within your newly formed writers group), you can't lose by including a notice.

6. *What should my copyright notice say?* A proper notice has three elements:

- The international copyright symbol © or the word "Copyright." Most publishers use both. (The abbreviation "Copr." is also acceptable.)
- The year in which the work is first published. (For unpublished works, you may omit a date.)
- Your name, or a recognizable abbreviation (e.g., International Business Machines Corporation may use "IBM").

In general, notices should be displayed prominently at the beginning of your work, although any reasonable location is acceptable. If your piece will appear in a magazine, anthology, or other collective work, a single notice in the publisher's name will preserve most of your rights. However, including a separate copyright notice in your own name will clarify that only you, *not* the publisher, has the right to authorize further uses of your work.

7. *Must I register my work with the Copyright Office?* Although registration is not required for copyright protection, it is a precondition to suing for infringement of the copyrights in any work first published in the U.S. (and in the unpublished works of U.S. citizens and residents), and enables you to recover both attorneys' fees and "statutory damages." (These are damages of up to $100,000, as determined by the judge, which the proprietor may elect to recover from the infringer in lieu of proving and recovering actual losses.)

You can register your copyrights at any time during the term of copyright. However, registration within three months of publication generally preserves your rights to all infringement remedies, including statutory damages, while registration within five years of publication provides special benefits in legal proceedings.

8. *How do you register a work?* Copyright Office Form TX is the basic form for nondramatic literary works. Form PA is used to register works of the performing arts, including plays and movies. These two-sided forms cost $20 to file and are fairly easy to complete (but only

if you read the accompanying instructions!). Adjunct Form GR/CP allows writers to reduce costs by making a single registration for all works published in periodicals within a 12-month period. In 1996 the Copyright Office issued new, simplified forms, including Short Form TX, a one-sided form which can now be used to register copyrights in new works of single authors. (You can order forms and circulars over the Copyright Office Hotline, 202/707-9100.)

When you apply you must submit one copy of the work, if unpublished, and two copies of the "best edition" of the work, if published. (Only one copy of the best edition is required for contributions to collective works.) The "best edition" is the published edition of highest quality, determined by paper quality, binding, and other factors listed by the Copyright Office (see Circular 7b: "'Best Edition' of Published Copyrighted Works for the Collections of Library of Congress"). For example, if the work was published in both hard and soft covers, the hard cover is normally the best edition.

9. *Should I register my work?* In most cases, no. If your work was published, your publisher may have registered it. If not, failure to register mainly loses you the option of *immediate* relief and statutory damages. Moreover, infringement is the exception and, where it occurs, often can be settled without lawsuits or registration. Besides, most writers earn too little to justify the cost of registration (certainly for articles, poems, and other short works).

10. *What is "public domain" and how can you find out what's there?* Works that are not protected by copyright are said to be in the "public domain"—that is, freely usable by the public, without the need to get permission or pay a fee. This includes works in which copyright has expired or been lost, works for which copyright is not available, and works dedicated to the public. Although there are many exceptions, in general the following are in the public domain:

- Works published more than 75 years ago.
- Works first published or copyrighted during 1920 to 1963, if the copyright was not renewed.
- Works published without a proper copyright notice before 1978.
- Works published without a prior notice between January 1, 1978 and February 28, 1989 (although the Act enables the proprietor to correct this failure).

• Works created by employees of the Federal government as part of their duties.

For a fee the Copyright Office will examine the status of a work. (See Circular 22: "How to Investigate the Copyright Status of a Work.")

11. *What is fair use?* The Act allows the limited use of others' works for research, teaching, news reporting, criticism, and similar purposes. These permitted uses are called "fair use." Although the Act never defines that term, it lists factors to consider, including the purpose and character of the use (e.g., for profit vs. teaching), the nature of the work (e.g., a science text vs. a poem), the amount and substantiality of the use, and its effect on the market for the work.

Here are some basic rules that should help you stay on the right side of the law (and help you recognize when someone's use of your work doesn't).

• Copying for noncommercial purposes, such as classroom teaching, is given a wider scope than copying for commercial use. For example, in general you may quote less of the published writings of a politician in a television docudrama than a history professor may quote in journal articles.

• Copying factual material gets more latitude than copying fiction. Fiction contains more of the "originality" protected by the Act: characters and events, sometimes even time and place, derive from the writer's imagination. Facts, on the other hand, are not "original" and cannot be copyrighted.

• Parody is a permissible use, as long as it does not appropriate too much of the original.

• Quoting or paraphrasing from unpublished works should be kept to a minimum. Until recently, copying from unpublished works without permission was almost always considered unfair. Although the latest cases, and a 1992 amendment to the Copyright Act, have made unpublished works subject to fair use, it remains difficult to prove fair use of an unpublished work.

• The Act permits certain uses of copyrighted works by libraries, archives, educators, charitable organizations, and others. See section 108–110 of the Act and Circular 21.

These rules are complex. Therefore, if you intend to copy more than

539

a negligible amount from another person's work, write to the publisher or copyright owner, or consult a copyright lawyer. Don't take a chance.

12. *What is a "work made for hire," and who owns the rights to these works?* The creator of a work generally owns the copyrights. There is an exception, however, for "works made for hire." Here it is the party who commissions and pays for the work, rather than the actual creator, who owns the copyrights. So when is a work "for hire"? First, unless expressly excluded by contract, all works created by employees within the scope of their employment are "for hire." (This will normally not include works created on your own time that are unrelated to your employment.) So if you are employed by a newspaper, or hired by a software publisher to write documentation, your employer owns the copyrights in the works you've been paid to create. If you use copies of these works at your next job, you are infringing your former employer's copyrights.

Second, certain specified categories of works (including translations, compilations, and parts of audiovisual works) are considered "for hire" if they have been specially commissioned and a signed writing identifies them as "for hire." Therefore, *if you are not an employee and you haven't agreed in writing that your work is "for hire" (or otherwise assigned your rights), you will generally continue to own the copyrights in your work* even if others paid you to create it (although they will have the right to use your work for the express purposes for which they paid you).

You may wonder about the division of rights when your article, story, or poem is published in a magazine (or other collective work) and there is no written agreement. The Act supplies the answer: The publisher acquires only the right to publish your piece as part of that collective work, of any revision of that work, and of any later collective work in the same series. You retain all other rights, so you are free to revise or remarket your piece.

The above is a *general* discussion of the copyright law as it applies to free lancers. Myriad qualifications and exceptions are not included here. Before making any important copyright decisions, consult a knowledgeable copyright lawyer, the Copyright Office, or a trusted publisher or agent who has an up-to-date understanding of the law.

Where to Sell

Where to Sell

All information in these lists concerning the needs and requirements of magazines, book publishing companies, and theaters comes directly from the editors, publishers, and directors, but personnel and addresses change, as do requirements. No published listing can give as clear a picture of editorial needs and tastes as a careful study of several issues of a magazine or a book catalogue, and writers should never submit material without first thoroughly researching the prospective market. If a magazine is not available in the local library or on the newsstand, write directly to the editor for the price of a sample copy; contact the publicity department of a book publisher for an up-to-date catalogue, or a theater for a current schedule. Many companies also offer a formal set of writers guidelines, available for an SASE (self-addressed, stamped envelope) upon request.

While some of the more established markets may seem difficult to break into, especially for the beginner, there are thousands of lesser-known publications where editors will consider submissions from first-time free lancers.

All manuscripts must be typed double-space and submitted with self-addressed envelopes bearing postage sufficient for the return of the material. If a manuscript need not be returned, note this with the submission, and enclose an SASE or a self-addressed, stamped postcard for editorial reply. Use good white paper; onion skin and erasable bond are not acceptable. *Always* keep a copy of the manuscript, since occasionally material is lost in the mail. Magazines may take several weeks, or longer, to read and report on submissions. If an editor has not reported on a manuscript after a reasonable length of time, write a brief, courteous letter of inquiry.

Some publishers will accept, and may in fact prefer, work submitted on computer disk, usually noting the procedure and type of disk in their writers guidelines.

ARTICLE MARKETS

The magazines in the following list are in the market for free-lance articles in many categories. Unless listings state otherwise, a writer should submit a query first, including a brief description of the proposed article and any relevant qualifications or credits. A few editors want to see samples of published work, if available.

Submit photos or slides *only* if the editor has specifically requested them. A self-addressed envelope with postage sufficient to cover the return of the manuscript or the answer to a query should accompany all submissions.

GENERAL-INTEREST PUBLICATIONS

AIR & SPACE/SMITHSONIAN—370 L'Enfant Promenade, 10th Fl., Washington, DC 20024–2518. George Larson, Ed. General-interest articles, 1,000 to 3,500 words, on aerospace experience, past, present, and future. Pays varying rates, on acceptance. Query.

AIR FORCE TIMES—See *Times News Service.*

AMERICAN HERITAGE— 60 Fifth Ave., New York, NY 10011. Richard F. Snow, Ed. Articles, 750 to 5,000 words, on U.S. history and background of American life and culture from the beginning to recent times. No fiction. Pays $300 to $1,500, on acceptance. Query.

AMERICAN JOURNALISM REVIEW— 8701 Adelphi Rd., Adelphi, MD 20783. Rem Rieder, Ed. Articles, 500 to 5,000 words, on print and electronic journalism. Pays 20¢ a word, on publication. Query.

THE AMERICAN LEGION—Box 1055, Indianapolis, IN 46206. Joe Stuteville, Ed. Articles, 750 to 2,000 words, on current world affairs, public policy, and subjects of contemporary interest. Payment is negotiable, on acceptance. Query.

AMERICAN VISIONS, THE MAGAZINE OF AFRO-AMERICAN CULTURE—1156 15th St. N.W., Suite 615, Washington, DC 20005. Joanne Harris, Ed. Articles, 1,500 words, and columns, 750 to 2,000 words, on African-American history and culture with a focus on the arts. Pays from $100 to $1,000, after publication. Query.

AMERICAS—OAS, 19th and Constitution Ave. N.W., Washington, DC 20006. Rebecca Read Medrano, Ed. Features, 2,500 to 4,000 words, on Latin America and the Caribbean. Wide focus: anthropology, the arts, travel, science, and development. "We prefer stories that can be well illustrated." No political material. Pays from $400, on publication. Query.

ARMY TIMES—See *Times News Service.*

THE ATLANTIC MONTHLY—77 N. Washington St., Boston, MA 02114. William Whitworth, Ed. Non-polemical, meticulously researched articles on public issues, politics, social sciences, education, business, literature, and the arts. Ideal length: 3,000 to 6,000 words, though short pieces, 1,000 to 2,000 words, are also welcome and longer text pieces will be considered. Pays excellent rates.

BLACK DIASPORA—298 5th Ave., 7th Fl., New York, NY 10001. Attn: Ed. General-interest articles, 1,000 to 2,500 words, of interest to "the entire black population." Timely, informative, sophisticated articles about culture, politics, arts and lifestyles; how-to pieces that cater to the needs to minority consumers. Pays 10¢ to 15¢ a word, made 45 days after publication.

CAPPER'S—1503 S.W. 42nd St., Topeka, KS 66609–1265. Nancy Peavler, Ed. Articles, 300 to 500 words: human-interest, personal experience for family section, historical. Payment varies, on publication.

CHANGE—1319 18th St. N.W., Washington, DC 20036. Attn: Ed. Dept. Well-researched features, 2,500 to 3,500 words, on programs, people, and institutions of higher education; and columns, 700 to 2,000 words. "We can't usually pay for unsolicited articles."

THE CHRISTIAN SCIENCE MONITOR—One Norway St., Boston, MA 02115. Jane A. Lampmann, Features Ed. Articles, 800 words, on arts and entertainment, education, lifestyle, family, science and technology, sports, travel, food, profiles; essays and poetry; "Home Forum Page"; guest columns for "Opinion Page." Pay varies, on acceptance. Original material only, exclusive rights for 90 days.

CHRONICLES—The Rockford Institute, 934 N. Main St., Rockford, IL 61103. Thomas Fleming, Ed. "A Magazine of American Culture." Articles and poetry that displays craftsmanship and a sense of form. "Read the magazine first to get a feel for what we do." No fiction, fillers or jokes. Payment varies.

COLUMBIA—1 Columbus Plaza, New Haven, CT 06510–3326. Richard McMunn, Ed. Journal of the Knights of Columbus. Articles, 500 to 1,500 words, on a wide variety of topics of interest to K. of C. members, their families, and the Catholic layman: current events, religion, education, art, etc., illustrated with color photos. Pays $250 to $500, including art, on acceptance.

THE COMPASS—365 Washington Ave., Brooklyn, NY 11238. J.A. Randall, Ed. True stories, to 1,500 words, on the sea, sea trades, and aviation. Pays to $1,000, on acceptance. Query with SASE.

CONSUMERS DIGEST—5705 N. Lincoln Ave., Chicago, IL 60659. John Manos, Ed. Articles, 500 to 3,000 words, on subjects of interest to consumers: products and services, automobiles, health, fitness, consumer legal affairs, and personal money management. Photos. Pays from 35¢ to 50¢ a word, extra for photos, on publication. Buys all rights. Query with resumé and published clips.

COSMOPOLITAN—224 W. 57th St., New York, NY 10019. Helen Gurley Brown, Ed. Guy Flatley, Man. Ed. Articles, to 3,000 words, and features, 500 to 2,000 words, on issues affecting young career women. Query.

COUNTRY JOURNAL— 4 High Ridge Park, Stamford, CT 06905. Peter V. Fossel, Ed. Articles, 500 to 1,500 words, for country and small-town residents. Helpful, authoritative pieces; how-to projects, small-scale farming, and gardening. Pays $75 to $500, on acceptance. Send SASE for guidelines. Query with SASE.

DIVERSION MAGAZINE—1790 Broadway, New York, NY 10019. Tom Passavant, Ed.-in-Chief. Articles, 600 to 2,000 words, on travel, sports, hobbies, entertainment, food, etc., of interest to physicians at leisure. Photos. Pays from $500, on acceptance. Query.

EBONY— 820 S. Michigan, Chicago, IL 60605. Lerone Bennett, Jr., Exec. Ed. "We do not solicit free-lance material."

THE ELKS MAGAZINE— 425 W. Diversey Parkway, Chicago, IL 60614. Judith L. Keogh, Man. Ed. Articles, 1,500 to 3,000 words, on technology, business, sports, and topics of current interest, for non-urban audience with above-average income. Pays 15¢ to 20¢ a word, on acceptance. Query with SASE.

EMERGE—BET Plaza, 1900 W. Place N.E., Washington, DC 20018. Florestine Purnell, Man. Ed. "Black America's Newsmagazine." Articles, 1,200 to 2,000 words, on current issues, ideas, or news personalities of interest to successful, well-informed African-Americans. Department pieces, 650 to 700 words, on a number of subjects. Pays 50¢ a word, on publication. Query.

ESQUIRE—250 W. 55th St., New York, NY 10019. Edward Kosner, Ed.-in-Chief. David Hirshey, Deputy Ed. Articles, 2,500 to 6,500 words, for intelligent adult audience. Pay varies, on acceptance. Query with published clips; complete manuscripts from unpublished writers. SASE required.

ESSENCE—1500 Broadway, New York, NY 10036. Susan L. Taylor, Ed.-in-Chief. Linda Villarosa, Exec. Ed. Provocative articles, 800 to 2,500 words, about black women in America today: self-help, how-to pieces, business and finance, work, parenting, health, celebrity profiles, and political issues. Pays varying rates, on acceptance. Query required.

FAMILY CIRCLE—110 Fifth Ave., New York, NY 10011. Nancy Clark, Deputy Ed. Articles, to 2,000 words, on "women who have made a difference," marriage, family, and child-rearing issues; consumer affairs, health and fitness, humor and psychology. Pays top rates, on acceptance. Query required.

GLAMOUR—350 Madison Ave., New York, NY 10017. Ruth Whitney, Ed.-in-Chief. Pamela Erens, Articles Ed. Editorial approach is "how-to" for women, 18 to 35. Articles on careers, health, psychology, interpersonal relationships, etc. Fashion, health, and beauty material staff-written. Pays from $1,000 for 1,500-to 2,000-word articles, from $1,500 for longer pieces, on acceptance.

GLOBE—5401 N.W. Broken Sound Blvd., Boca Raton, FL 33487. Robert Taylor, Man. Ed. Factual articles, 500 to 1,000 words, with photos: exposés, celebrity interviews, consumer and human-interest pieces. Pays $50 to $1,500.

GOOD HOUSEKEEPING— 959 Eighth Ave., New York, NY 10019. Evelyn Renold, Articles Ed. Articles, 2,500 words, on a unique or trend-setting event; family relationships; personal medical pieces dealing with an unusual illness, treatment, and result; personal problems and how they were solved. Short essays, 750 to 1,000 words, on family life or relationships. Pays first-time writers $500 to $750 for short, essay-type articles; $1,500 to $2,000 for full-length articles, on acceptance. "Payment scale rises for writers with whom we work frequently." Buys all rights, though the writer retains the right to use material from the article as part of a book project. Queries preferred. Guidelines.

GRIT—1503 S.W. 42nd St., Topeka, KS 66609. Michael Scheibach, Ed.-in-Chief. Articles, 500 to 1,200 words, on people, home, garden, lifestyle, friends and family, grandparenting, Americana, American history and traditions, travel. Short fiction, 1,000 to 2,000 words (must be addressed to Fiction

Ed.). SASE required. Pays 15¢ to 25¢ a word, extra for photos. Query. Guidelines and theme calendar.

HARPER'S BAZAAR—1700 Broadway, 37th Fl., New York, NY 10019. Elizabeth Tilberis, Ed.-in-Chief. Articles for sophisticated women on current issues, books, art, film, travel, fashion and beauty. Send queries with one- to three-paragraph proposal; include clips and SASE. Rarely accepts fiction. Payment varies.

HARPER'S MAGAZINE— 666 Broadway, New York, NY 10012. Attn: Ed. Articles, 2,000 to 5,000 words. Query with SASE required. Very limited market.

HISTORIC PRESERVATION—1785 Massachusetts Ave. N.W., Washington, DC 20036. Anne Elizabeth Powell, Ed. Feature articles from published writers, 1,500 to 4,000 words, on residential restoration, preservation issues, and people involved in preserving America's heritage. Mostly staff-written. Query.

HOUSE BEAUTIFUL—1700 Broadway, New York, NY 10019. Elaine Greene, Features Ed. Articles related to the home. Pieces on architecture, design, travel, and gardening. One personal memoir each month, "Thoughts of Home," with high literary standards. Pays varying rates, on acceptance. Query with detailed outline and SASE. Guidelines.

IDEALS—P.O. Box 305300, Nashville, TN 37230. Lisa Ragan, Ed. Articles, 800 to 1,000 words; poetry, 12 to 50 lines. Light, nostalgic pieces. Payment varies. SASE for guidelines.

INQUIRER MAGAZINE—*Philadelphia Inquirer,* P.O. Box 8263, 400 N. Broad St., Philadelphia, PA 19101. Ms. Avery Rome, Ed. Local-interest features, 500 to 7,000 words. Profiles of national figures in politics, entertainment, etc. Pays varying rates, on publication. Currently overstocked; not accepting any free-lance submissions at this time.

KIWANIS—3636 Woodview Trace, Indianapolis, IN 46268. Chuck Jonak, Man. Ed. Articles, 2,500 words, on home; family; international issues; the social, health, and emotional needs of youth (especially under age 6); career and community concerns of business and professional people. No travel pieces, interviews, profiles. Pays $400 to $1,000, on acceptance. Query. Send SASE for guidelines.

LADIES' HOME JOURNAL—125 Park Ave., New York, NY 10017. Susan Crandell, Exec. Ed. Articles on contemporary subjects of interest to women. "See masthead for specific-topic editors and address appropriate editor." Query with SASE required.

LISTEN MAGAZINE—55 W. Oak Ridge Dr., Hagerstown, MD 21740. Lincoln Steed, Ed. Articles, 1,000 to 1,200 words, on problems of alcohol and drug abuse, for teenagers; personality profiles; self-improvement articles, and drug-free activities. Photos. Pays 5¢ to 7¢ a word, extra for photos, on acceptance. Guidelines. Query.

LOS ANGELES TIMES MAGAZINE—Times Mirror Sq., Los Angeles, CA 90053. John Lindsay, Ed. Dir. Articles, to 5,000 words: general-interest news features, photo spreads, profiles, and narratives focusing on current events. Pays to $4,000, on acceptance. Query required.

MCCALL'S—110 Fifth Ave., New York, NY 10011. Attn: Articles Ed. Articles, 1,000 to 1,800 words, on current issues, human interest, family relationships. Payment varies, on acceptance. SASE.

MADEMOISELLE—350 Madison Ave., New York, NY 10017. Faye Haun, Man. Ed. Articles, 750 to 2,500 words, on subjects of interest to single, working women in their twenties. Reporting pieces, essays, first-person accounts, and humor; how-tos on personal relationships, work, and fitness. No fiction. Pays excellent rates, on acceptance. SASE required. Query with clips.

METROPOLITAN HOME—1633 Broadway, New York, NY 10019. Attn: Articles Dept. Service and informational articles for residents of houses, co-ops, lofts, and condominiums, on real estate, equity, wine and spirits, collecting, trends, travel, etc. Interior design and home furnishing articles with emphasis on lifestyle. Pay varies. Query with clips.

THE MOTHER EARTH NEWS—49 E. 21st St., 11th Fl., New York, NY 10010. Matthew Scanlon, Ed. Articles for rural and urban readers: home improvements, how-tos, indoor and outdoor gardening, family pastimes, health, food, ecology, energy, and consumerism. Pays varying rates, on acceptance.

MOTHER JONES—731 Market St., Suite 600, San Francisco, CA 94103. Jeffrey Klein, Ed. Investigative articles, political essays, cultural analyses, multicultural issues. "OutFront" pieces, 250 to 500 words. Query with SASE.

MS.—230 Park Ave., 7th Fl., New York, NY 10169. Attn: Manuscript Ed. Articles relating to feminism, women's roles, and social change; reporting, essays, theory, and analysis. No poetry or fiction. Pays market rates. Query with resumé, clips, and SASE.

NATIONAL ENQUIRER—Lantana, FL 33464. Attn: Ed. Dept. Articles, of any length, for mass audience: topical news, the occult, how-to, scientific discoveries, human drama, adventure, personalities. Photos. Pays from $325. Query or send complete manuscript. SASE.

NAVY TIMES—See *Times News Service.*

NEW WOMAN—215 Lexington Ave., New York, NY 10016. Attn: Manuscripts and Proposals. Articles on personal and professional relationships, health, fitness, lifestyle, money, and career issues. Editorial focus is on self-discovery, self-development, and self-esteem. "Read the magazine to become familiar with our needs, and request guidelines with SASE. We look for originality, solid research, and a friendly, accessible style." Pays varying rates, on acceptance.

THE NEW YORK TIMES MAGAZINE—229 W. 43rd St., New York, NY 10036. Attn: Articles Ed. Timely articles, approximately 3,000 words, on news items, forthcoming events, trends, culture, entertainment, etc. Pays to $2,500 for major articles, on acceptance. Query with clips.

THE NEW YORKER—20 W. 43rd St., New York, NY 10036. Send submissions to appropriate Editor (Fact, Fiction, or Poetry). Factual and biographical articles for "Profiles," "Reporter at Large," etc. Pays good rates, on acceptance. Query.

NEWSWEEK—251 W. 57th St., New York, NY 10019–1894. Attn: My Turn. Original opinion essays, 1,000 to 1,100 words, for "My Turn" column; must contain verifiable facts. Submit manuscript with SASE. Pays $1,000, on publication.

548

PARADE—711 Third Ave., New York, NY 10017. Articles Correspondent. National Sunday newspaper magazine. Factual and authoritative articles, 1,200 to 1,500 words, on subjects of national interest: social issues, common health concerns, sports, community problem-solving, and extraordinary acheivements of ordinary people. "We seek unique angles on all topics." No fiction, poetry, cartoons, games, nostalgia, quotes, or puzzles. Pays from $1,000. Query with two writing samples and SASE.

PENTHOUSE—277 Park Ave., 4th Fl., New York, NY 10172–0003. Peter Bloch, Ed. Lavada B. Nahon, Sr. Ed. General-interest or controversial articles, to 5,000 words. Pays to $1 a word, on acceptance.

PEOPLE WEEKLY—Time-Life Bldg., Rockefeller Ctr., New York, NY 10020. John Saar, Asst. Man. Ed. "Vast majority of material is staff-written." Will consider article proposals, 3 to 4 paragraphs, on timely, entertaining, and topical personalities. Pays good rates, on acceptance.

PLAYBOY—680 N. Lake Shore Dr., Chicago, IL 60611. Peter Moore, Articles Ed. Sophisticated articles, 4,000 to 6,000 words, of interest to urban men. Humor, satire. Pays to $3,000, on acceptance. Query.

PLAYGIRL—801 Second Ave., New York, NY 10017. Judy Cole, Ed.-in-Chief. Articles, 1,500 to 3,500 words, on sexuality, relationships, and celebrities for women ages 18 and up. Query with clips. Fiction and nonfiction. Pays negotiable rates, after acceptance.

PSYCHOLOGY TODAY—Sussex Publishing, 49 E. 21st St., New York, NY 10010. Lisa Liebman, Exec. Ed. Bimonthly. Articles, 2,000 words, on timely subjects relating to human behavior or the national psyche. Pays varying rates, on publication.

QUEEN'S QUARTERLY—Queens Univ., Kingston, Ont., Canada K7L 3N6. Boris Castel, Ed. Articles, to 5,000 words, on a wide range of topics, and fiction, to 5,000 words. Poetry; send no more than 6 poems. B&W art. Pays to $400, on publication.

READER'S DIGEST—Pleasantville, NY 10570. Kenneth Tomlinson, Ed.-in-Chief. Unsolicited manuscripts will not be read or returned. General-interest articles already in print and well-developed story proposals will be considered. Send reprint or query to any editor on the masthead.

REAL PEOPLE—450 7th Ave., Suite 1701, New York, NY 10123–0073. Alex Polner, Ed. True stories, to 500 words, on interesting people, strange occupations and hobbies, eye opening stories about people, places and odd happenings. Pays $25 to $50, on publication; send submissions to "Real Shorts," Brad Hamilton, Ed. Query for interviews, 1,000 to 1,800 words, with movie or TV actors, musicians, and other entertainment celebrities. Pays $150 to $350, on publication. SASE.

REDBOOK—224 W. 57th St., New York, NY 10019. Harriet Lyons, Sr. Ed. Toni Gerber Hope, Sr. Ed. Articles, 1,000 to 2,500 words, on subjects related to relationships, marriage, sex, current social issues, crime, human interest, health, psychology, and parenting. Payment varies, on acceptance. Query with clips.

ROLLING STONE—1290 Ave. of the Americas, 2nd Fl., New York, NY 10104. Attn: Ed. Magazine of American music, culture, and politics. No fiction. "We rarely accept free-lance material." Query.

THE ROTARIAN—1560 Sherman Ave., Evanston, IL 60201–3698. Willmon L. White, Ed. Articles, 1,200 to 2,000 words, on international social and economic issues, business and management, human relationships, travel, sports, environment, science and technology; humor. Pays good rates, on acceptance. Query.

THE SATURDAY EVENING POST—1100 Waterway Blvd., Indianapolis, IN 46202. Ted Kreiter, Exec. Ed. Family-oriented articles, 1,500 to 3,000 words: humor, preventive medicine, destination-oriented travel pieces (not personal experience), celebrity profiles, the arts, and sciences. Pieces on sports and home repair (with photos). Pays varying rates, on publication. Queries preferred.

SMITHSONIAN MAGAZINE—900 Jefferson Dr., Washington, DC 20560. Marlane A. Liddell, Articles Ed. Articles on history, art, natural history, physical science, profiles, etc. Query with clips.

SOAP OPERA DIGEST—45 W. 25th St., New York, NY 10010. Jason Bonderoff, Deputy Ed. Roberta Caploe, Carolyn Hinsey, Man. Eds. Investigative reports and profiles, to 1,500 words, about New York- or Los Angeles-based soaps. Pays from $250, on acceptance. Query with clips.

SPORTS ILLUSTRATED—1271 Ave. of the Americas, New York, NY 10020. Chris Hunt, Articles Ed. Query. Rarely uses free-lance material.

STAR—660 White Plains Rd., Tarrytown, NY 10591. Attn: Ed. Dept. Topical articles, 50 to 800 words, on show business and celebrities. Pays varying rates.

TIMES NEWS SERVICE—Army Times Publishing Co., Springfield, VA 22159. Attn: R&R Ed. Articles, 500 to 750 words, that are informative, helpful, entertaining, and stimulating to a military audience for "R&R" newspaper section. Pays $75 to $100, on acceptance. Also, 1,000-word articles on careers after military service, travel, finance, and education for *Army Times, Navy Times,* and *Air Force Times.* Address Supplements Ed. Pays $125 to $250, on acceptance. Guidelines.

THE TOASTMASTER—P.O. Box 9052, Mission Viejo, CA 92690. Suzanne Frey, Ed. Articles, 1,500 to 2,500 words, on decision making, leadership, language, interpersonal and professional communication, humor, logical thinking, rhetorical devices, public speaking in general, profiles of great orators, speaking techniques, etc. Pays $100 to $250, on acceptance.

TOWN & COUNTRY—1700 Broadway, New York, NY 10019. Pamela Fiori, Ed.-in-Chief. Considers one-page proposals for articles. Include clips and resumé. Rarely buys unsolicited manuscripts.

TRAVEL & LEISURE—1120 Ave. of the Americas, New York, NY 10036. Nancy Novogrod, Ed.-in-Chief. Articles, 800 to 3,000 words, on destinations and leisure-time activities. Regional pieces for regional editions. Pays varying rates, on acceptance. Query.

TROPIC—*The Miami Herald*, One Herald Plaza, Miami, FL 33132. Tom Shroder, Exec. Ed. Essays and articles, 1,000 to 4,000 words, on current trends and issues, light or heavy, for sophisticated audience. No short fiction (under 900 words) or poetry. Limited humor. Pays $200 to $1,000, on publication. SASE. Allow 4 to 6 weeks for response.

VANITY FAIR—350 Madison Ave., New York, NY 10017. Attn: Submissions (Specify News, Arts, or Culture). Pays on acceptance. Query.

VILLAGE VOICE—36 Cooper Sq., New York, NY 10003. Doug Simmons, Man. Ed. Articles, 500 to 2,000 words, on current or controversial topics. Pays $100 to $1,500, on acceptance. Query or send manuscript with SASE.

WASHINGTON POST MAGAZINE—*The Washington Post,* 1150 15th St. N.W., Washington, DC 20071. Liza Mundy, Man. Ed. Essays, profiles, and Washington-oriented general-interest pieces, to 5,000 words, on business, arts and culture, politics, science, sports, education, children, relationships, behavior, etc. Pays from $1,000, after acceptance.

WOMAN'S DAY—1633 Broadway, New York, NY 10019. Rebecca Greer, Articles Ed. Articles, 500 to 2,000 words, on subjects of interest to women: marriage, education, family health, child rearing, money management, interpersonal relationships, changing lifestyles, etc. Dramatic first-person narratives about women who have experienced medical miracles or other triumphs, or have overcome common problems, such as alcoholism. SASE required. Pays top rates, on acceptance. Query; unsolicited manuscripts not accepted.

WOMAN'S WORLD—270 Sylvan Ave., Englewood Cliffs, NJ 07632. Attn: Ed. Articles, 600 to 1,800 words, of interest to middle-income women between the ages of 18 and 60, on love, romance, careers, medicine, health, psychology, family life, travel; dramatic stories of adventure or crisis, investigative reports. Send SASE for guidelines. Pays $300 to $900, on acceptance. Query.

CURRENT EVENTS, POLITICS

THE AMERICAN LEGION—Box 1055, Indianapolis, IN 46206. Joe Stuteville, Ed. Articles, 750 to 2,000 words, on current world affairs, public policy, and subjects of contemporary interest. Pays $500 to $2,000, on acceptance. Query.

THE AMERICAN SCHOLAR—1811 Q St. N.W., Washington, DC 20009–9974. Joseph Epstein, Ed. Non-technical articles and essays, 3,500 to 4,000 words, on current affairs, the American cultural scene, politics, arts, religion, and science. Pays to $500, on acceptance.

THE AMICUS JOURNAL—Natural Resources Defense Council, 40 W. 20th St., New York, NY 10011. Kathrin Day Lassila, Ed. Investigative articles, profiles, book reviews, and essays, related to the environment, especially national and international environmental policy. Also poetry "rooted in nature." Pays varying rates, 30 days after publication. Queries required.

THE ATLANTIC MONTHLY—77 N. Washington St., Boston, MA 02114. William Whitworth, Ed. In-depth articles on public issues, politics, social sciences, education, business, literature, and the arts, with emphasis on information rather than opinion. Ideal length is 3,000 to 6,000 words, though short pieces, 1,000 to 2,000 words, are also welcome. Pays excellent rates, on acceptance.

BRIARPATCH—2138 McIntyre St., Regina, Saskatchewan, Canada S4P 2R7. George Manz, Man. Ed. "Saskatchewan's Independent Newsmagazine." Left-wing articles, 600 to 1,200 words, on politics, women's issues, environment, labor, international affairs for Canadian activists involved in social change issues. Pays in copies. Queries preferred.

551

CALIFORNIA JOURNAL—2101 K St., Sacramento, CA 95816. A.G. Block, Ed. "Independent analysis of politics and government." Balanced articles, 1,500 words, related to California government and politics. Advocacy pieces, 800 words. Pays $350 for articles, on publication. (No payment for advocacy pieces.) Query.

CAMPAIGNS & ELECTIONS—1511 K St. N.W., #1020, Washington, DC 20005. Ron Faucheaux, Ed. Feature articles, 700 to 4,000 words, related to the strategies, techniques, trends, and personalities of political campaigning. Campaign case studies, 1,500 to 3,000 words; how-to articles, 700 to 2,000 words, on specific aspects of campaigning; items, 100 to 800 words, for "Inside Politics"; and in-depth studies, 700 to 3,000 words, of public opinion, election results, and political trends that help form campaign strategy. Pays in subscriptions and free admission to certain public seminars.

CHURCH & STATE—1816 Jefferson Pl. N.W., Washington, DC 20036. Joseph L. Conn, Man. Ed. Articles, 600 to 2,600 words, on issues of religious liberty and church-state relations. Pays varying rates, on acceptance. Query.

COMMENTARY—165 E. 56th St., New York, NY 10022. Neal Kozodoy, Ed. Articles, 5,000 to 7,000 words, on contemporary issues, Jewish affairs, social sciences, community life, religious thought, culture. Serious fiction; book reviews. Pays on publication.

COMMONWEAL—15 Dutch St., New York, NY 10038. Margaret O'Brien Steinfels, Ed. Catholic. Articles, to 3,000 words, on political, social, religious, and literary subjects. Pays 3¢ a word, on acceptance.

COMMONWEALTH—55 Summer St., 9th Fl., Boston, MA 02110. Dave Denison, Ed. Articles, 2,000 to 4,500 words, on politics, government, and public policy issues affecting Massachusetts citizens. Payment varies, on acceptance. Query.

CONSERVATIVE REVIEW—1307 Dolley Madison Blvd., Rm. 203, McLean, VA 22101. Fred Smith, Ed. Articles, ideally 300 to 500 words (longer is O.K., if subject warrants), that offer information on topics, not just conservative sermons. "Writers should be intimately familiar with their subject." Pays in copies.

COUNTRY CONNECTIONS—P.O. Box 6748, Dept. TW, Pine Mountain Club, CA 93222–6748. Catherine R. Leach, Ed. Bimonthly. Articles, to 2,500 words, and fiction, to 1,500 words. Poetry. B&W photos. "Study magazine first. We serve as a forum for public discourse about ethics, politics, social justice, community, animal rights and environmental issues, and life in the country." Pays $25 for features, $15 for fiction and poetry, on publication.

CULTUREFRONT—198 Broadway, 10th Fl., New York, NY 10038. Attn: Ed. "A Magazine of the Humanities." Fiction and articles, 2,500 words, related to theme. "Presents news and a variety of views on the production, interpretation, and politics of culture." No payment. Query for current themes.

CURRENT HISTORY—4225 Main St., Philadelphia, PA 19127. William W. Finan, Jr., Ed. Country-specific political science and current affairs articles, to 20 pages. Hard analysis written in a lively manner. "We devote each issue to a specific region or country. Writers should be experts with up-to-date knowledge of the region." Queries preferred. Pays $300, on publication.

EMERGE—BET Plaza, 1900 W. Place N.E., Washington, DC 20018. Florestine Purnell, Man. Ed. "Black America's Newsmagazine." Articles, 1,200 to 2,000 words, on current issues, ideas, or news personalities of interest to successful, well-informed African-Americans. Department pieces, 650 to 700 words, on a number of subjects. Pays 50¢ a word, on publication. Query.

ENVIRONMENT—1319 18th St. N.W., Washington, DC 20036–1802. Barbara T. Richman, Man. Ed. Articles, 2,500 to 5,000 words, on environmental, scientific, and technological policy and decision-making issues, especially on a global scale. Pays $100 to $300, on publication. Query.

FOREIGN SERVICE JOURNAL—2101 E St. N.W., Washington, DC 20037. Articles of interest to the Foreign Service and the US diplomatic community. Pays to 20¢ a word, on publication. Query.

THE FREEMAN—Foundation for Economic Education, 30 S. Broadway, Irvington-on-Hudson, NY 10533. Beth Hoffman, Man. Ed. Articles, to 3,500 words, on economic, political, and moral implications of private property, voluntary exchange, and individual choice. Pays 10¢ a word, on publication.

IN THESE TIMES—2040 N. Milwaukee Ave., Chicago, IL 60647. James Weinstein, Ed. Biweekly. Articles, 1,500 to 2,500 words, on politics, labor, women's issues, etc. "A magazine with a progressive political perspective. Please read before querying us." Payment varies, on publication. Query.

IRISH AMERICA— 432 Park Ave. S., Suite 1000, New York, NY 10016. Patricia Harty, Ed. Articles, 1,500 to 2,000 words, of interest to Irish-American audience; preferred topics include history, sports, the arts, and politics. Pays 10¢ a word, after publication. Query.

LABOR'S HERITAGE—10000 New Hampshire Ave., Silver Spring, MD 20903. Stuart Kaufman, Ed. Quarterly journal of The George Meany Memorial Archives. Publishes 15- to 30-page documented articles of original research for labor scholars, labor union members, and the general public. Pays in copies.

MOMENT MAGAZINE— 4710 41st St. N.W., Washington, DC 20016. Hershel Shanks, Ed. Sophisticated articles, 2,500 to 5,000 words, on Jewish culture, politics, religion, and personalities. Columns, to 1,500 words, with uncommon perspectives on contemporary issues, humor, strong anecdotes. Book reviews, 400 words. Pays $40 to $600.

MOTHER JONES—731 Market St., Suite 600, San Francisco, CA 94103. Jeffrey Klein, Ed. Investigative articles and political essays. Pays $1,000 to $3,000 for feature articles, after acceptance. Query with clips and SASE required.

THE NATION—72 Fifth Ave., New York, NY 10011. Katrina Vanden Heuvel, Ed. Articles, 1,500 to 2,500 words, on politics and culture from a liberal/left perspective. Editorials, 750 to 1,000 words. Pays $75 per published page, to $300, on publication. Query.

THE NEW YORK TIMES MAGAZINE—229 W. 43rd St., New York, NY 10036. Attn: Articles Ed. Timely articles, approximately 4,000 words, on news items, trends, culture, etc. Pays $1,000 for short pieces, from $2,500 for major articles, on acceptance. Query with clips.

THE NEW YORKER—20 W. 43rd St., New York, NY 10036. Attn: Ed., "Comment." Political/social essays, 1,000 words. Payment on acceptance. Query.

ON THE ISSUES—Choices Women's Medical Ctr., Inc., 97–77 Queens Blvd., Forest Hills, NY 11374–3317. Ronni Sandroff, Ed. "The Progressive

Woman's Quarterly." Articles, up to 2,500 words, on political or social issues. Movie, music, and book reviews, 500 to 750 words. Query. Payment varies, on publication.

PEACE—2753 E. Broadway, S101–1969, Mesa, AZ 85204. Linda S. James, Ed. Quarterly. Articles and fiction, to 3,000 words, that center on the 1960s. Possible topics include life on the road; politics; interviews; and stories from those who fought in the Vietnam War and those who chose not to. Pays subscription and free extra copies (as available). Guidelines.

POLICY REVIEW—214 Massachusetts Ave. N.E., Washington, DC 20002. Attn: Articles Ed. Articles, 800 to 5,000 words, on reporting and analysis of domestic public policy issues. "We are the flagship journal of The Heritage Foundation, a conservative public policy research institute. We use articles that highlight private sector and local government alternatives to welfare state politics." Pays about $500, on publication.

THE PROGRESSIVE— 409 E. Main St., Madison, WI 53703. Matthew Rothschild, Ed. Articles, 1,000 to 3,500 words, on political and social problems. Pays $100 to $300, on publication.

REASON—3415 S. Sepulveda Blvd., Suite 400, Los Angeles, CA 90034. Brian Doherty, Ed. "Free Minds and Free Markets." Articles, 850 to 5,000 words, on politics, economics, and culture "from a dynamic libertarian's perspective." Pays varying rates, on acceptance. Query.

ROLL CALL: THE NEWSPAPER OF CAPITOL HILL— 900 2nd St. N.E., Washington, DC 20002. Susan Glasser, Ed. Factual, breezy articles with political or Congressional angle: Congressional history, human-interest subjects, political lore, etc. Political opinion or commentary on Congressional institutional issues. Pays on publication.

SATURDAY NIGHT—184 Front St. E., Suite 400, Toronto, Ont., Canada M5A 4N3. Kenneth Whyte, Ed. Canada's oldest magazine of politics, social issues, culture, and business. Features, 1,000 to 5,000 words, and columns, 800 to 1,000 words; fiction, to 3,000 words. Must have Canadian tie-in. Payment varies, on acceptance.

TIKKUN—251 W. 100th St., 5th Fl., New York, NY 10025. Michael Lerner, Ed. "A Bimonthly Jewish Critique of Politics, Culture & Society." Articles and fiction, 2,400 to 3,000 words. Poetry. "Read a copy to get a sense of what we publish. We are always interested in work pertaining to contemporary culture." Pays in copies.

VFW MAGAZINE— 406 W. 34th St., Kansas City, MO 64111. Richard K. Kolb, Ed. Articles, 1,000 words, related to current foreign policy and defense, American armed forces abroad, and international events affecting U.S. national security. Also, up-to-date articles on veteran concerns and issues affecting veterans. Pays to $500, on acceptance. Query. Guidelines.

THE WASHINGTON MONTHLY—1611 Connecticut Ave. N.W., Washington, DC 20009. Charles Peters, Ed. Helpful, informative articles, 1,000 to 4,000 words, on DC-related topics, including politics, and government and popular culture. Pays 10¢ a word, on publication.

WASHINGTON POST MAGAZINE—*The Washington Post,* 1150 15th St. N.W., Washington, DC 20071. Liza Mundy, Man. Ed. Essays, profiles, and general-interest pieces, to 5,000 words, on Washington-oriented politics and related issues. Pays from $1,000, after acceptance. SASE required.

WHO CARES: THE MAGAZINE FOR PEOPLE WHO DO—1511 K St. N.W., #412, Washington, DC 20005. Leslie Crutchfield, Heather McLeod, News and Features Eds. Rebecca Roth, Photo/Creative Ed. Articles, 1,000 words, on service programs throughout the country for "Partners in Change." Features, 1,500 to 2,500 words, on specific issues related to service and action. "Entrepreneur" pieces, 1,500 to 2,500 words, focus on the business of starting a successful nonprofit. "On Campus," 800 words, on unique service programs that involve college students. "Faith in Service," 1,000 to 1,500 words, on connections between service and spirituality. "Who's Who and What's What," 100- to 400-word news blurbs on service and action. Also, humorous essays, 800 words, and first-person narratives, related fiction, and other creative essays, 800 to 2,000 words. No payment for unsolicited articles. Payment for assigned pieces varies, on publication.

REGIONAL AND CITY PUBLICATIONS

ADIRONDACK LIFE—P.O. Box 97, Jay, NY 12941. Elizabeth Folwell, Ed. Features, to 5,000 words, on outdoor and environmental activities and issues, arts, wilderness, wildlife, profiles, history, and fiction; focus is on the Adirondack Park region of New York State. Pays to 25¢ a word, 30 days after acceptance. Query.

ALABAMA HERITAGE—The Univ. of Alabama, Box 870342, Tuscaloosa, AL 35487–0342. Suzanne Wolfe, Ed. Quarterly. Articles, to 5,000 words, on local, state, and regional history: art, literature, language, archaeology, music, religion, architecture, and natural history. Query, mentioning availability of photos and illustrations. Pays an honorarium, on publication, plus 10 copies. Guidelines.

ALASKA—808 E St., Suite 200, Anchorage, AK 99501. Tricia Brown, Ed. Articles, 2,000 words, on life in Alaska. Pays varying rates, on acceptance. Guidelines.

ALBERTA SWEETGRASS—Aboriginal Multi-Media Society of Alberta, 15001 112th Ave., Edmonton, Alberta, Canada T5M 2V6. R. John Hayes, Ed. Tabloid. Articles, 200 to 1,000 words (most often 500 to 800 words): features, profiles, and community-based articles all with an Alberta angle.

ALOHA, THE MAGAZINE OF HAWAII AND THE PACIFIC—P.O. Box 3260, Honolulu, HI 96801. Cheryl Chee Tsutsumi, Ed. Articles, 1,500 to 2,500 words, on the life, customs, and people of Hawaii and the Pacific. Poetry. Fiction. Pays $150 to $500 for full-length features, on publication. Query.

AMERICAN DESERT MAGAZINE—12289 Mint Ct., Rancho Cucamonga, CA 91730. Raymond Shadwick, Pub./Ed. Quarterly. Articles, 1,000 to 2,500 words, related to the southwest deserts: desert history, natural features, survival, Native American culture, profiles. Pays 3¢ a word, on publication. Guidelines.

555

APPELLATION—(formerly *Napa Valley Appellation*) P.O. Box 516, Napa, CA 94559. Antonia Allegra, Ed.-in-Chief. Quarterly. Articles, 900 to 1,500 words, on the lifestyles, wines, and gardens of the Napa Valley. Pays $200 to $500, on acceptance.

APPRISE—P.O. Box 2954, 1982 Locust Ln., Harrisburg, PA 17105. Jim Connor, Ed.-in-Chief. Articles, 1,500 to 3,500 words, of regional (central Pennsylvania) interest, including profiles of notable Pennsylvanians, and broadly based articles of social interest that "enlighten and inform." Pays 10¢ a word, on publication.

ARIZONA HIGHWAYS—2039 W. Lewis Ave., Phoenix, AZ 85009. Robert J. Early, Ed. First-person experience articles, 1,600 to 1,800 words, on travel in Arizona; pieces on adventure, humor, lifestyles, nostalgia, history, archaeology, nature, etc. Departments also using personal experience pieces include "Mileposts," "Focus on Nature," "Along the Way," "Back Road Adventures," "Hiking," "Legends of the Lost," and "Arizona Humor." Pays 35¢ to 55¢ a word, on acceptance. Query required. Guidelines.

ATLANTA—1360 Peachtree St., Suite 1800, Atlanta, GA 30309. Lee Walburn, Ed. Articles, 1,500 to 5,000 words, on Atlanta subjects or personalities. Pays $300 to $2,000, on publication. Query.

BACK HOME IN KENTUCKY—P.O. Box 681629, Franklin, TN 37068–1629. Nanci P. Gregg, Man. Ed. Articles on Kentucky history, travel, craftsmen and artisans, Kentucky cooks, and "colorful" characters; limited personal nostalgia specifically related to Kentucky. Pays $25 to $100 for articles with B&W or color photos. Queries preferred.

BALTIMORE MAGAZINE—16 S. Calvert St., Suite 1000, Baltimore, MD 21202. Ramsey Flynn, Ed. Articles, 500 to 3,000 words, on people, places, and things in the Baltimore metropolitan area. Consumer advice, investigative pieces, profiles, humor, and personal experience pieces. Payment varies, on publication. Query required.

THE BIG APPLE PARENTS' PAPER—36 E. 12th St., New York, NY 10003. Helen Rosengren Freedman, Man. Ed. Articles, 500 to 750 words, for New York City parents. Pays $35 to $50, on publication. Buys first NY-area rights.

BIG SKY JOURNAL—P.O. Box 1069, Bozeman, MT 59771. Brian Baise, Editorial Assoc. Published 5 times a year. Fiction, to 4,000 words, and articles, to 2,500 words, on Montana subjects or with Montana settings. Payment varies, on publication. Query.

BIRMINGHAM—2027 First Ave. N., Birmingham, AL 35203. Joe O'Donnell, Ed. Profiles, business articles, and nostalgia pieces, to 2,500 words, with Birmingham tie-in. Pays $50 to $175, on publication.

BLUE RIDGE COUNTRY—P.O. Box 21535, Roanoke, VA 24018. Kurt Rheinheimer, Ed. Bimonthly. Regional articles, 1,200 to 2,000 words, that "explore and extol the beauty, history, and travel opportunities in the mountain regions of VA, NC, WV, TN, KY, MD, SC, and GA." Color slides or B&W prints considered. Pays $200 for photo-features, on publication. Queries preferred.

BOCA RATON—JES Publishing, Amtec Ctr., Suite 100, 6413 Congress Ave., Boca Raton, FL 33487. Marie Speed, Ed. Articles, 800 to 3,000 words, on Florida topics, personalities, and travel. Pays $50 to $500, on acceptance. Query with clips required.

THE BOSTON GLOBE MAGAZINE—*The Boston Globe*, Boston, MA 02107. Evelynne Kramer, Ed. General-interest articles on regional topics and profiles, 2,500 to 5,000 words. Query and SASE required.

BOSTON MAGAZINE—300 Massachusetts Ave., Boston, MA 02115. Kerry Nugent-Wells, Ed. Asst. Informative, entertaining features, 1,000 to 3,000 words, on Boston-area personalities, institutions, and phenomena. Query. Pays to $2,000, on publication.

BOUNDARY WATERS JOURNAL—9396 Rocky Ledge Rd., Ely, MN 55731. Stuart Osthoff, Ed. Articles, 2,000 to 3,000 words, on wilderness, recreation, nature, and conservation in Minnesota's Boundary Waters Canoe Area Wilderness and Ontario's Quetico Provincial Park. Regular features include canoe-route journals, fishing, camping, hiking, cross-country skiing, wildlife and nature, regional lifestyles, history, and events. Pays $200 to $400, on publication; $50 to $150 for photos.

BUFFALO SPREE MAGAZINE—Box 38, Buffalo, NY 14226. Johanna Van De Mark, Ed./Pub. Articles, to 1,800 words, for readers in the western New York region. Pays $75 to $125, $25 for poetry, on publication.

BUSINESS IN BROWARD—P.O. Box 7375, Ft. Lauderdale, FL 33338–7375. Sherry Friedlander, Ed. Published 8 times a year. Articles, 1,000 words, on small business in eastern Florida county. Pay varies, on acceptance.

BUZZ: THE TALK OF LOS ANGELES—11835 W. Olympic Blvd., Suite 450, Los Angeles, CA 90064. Allan Mayer, Ed.-in-Chief. Articles, varying lengths, of particular relevance to readers in southern California. Query. Pays $1 a word, within 30 days of acceptance.

CANADIAN GEOGRAPHIC—39 McArthur Ave., Vanier, Ont., Canada K1L 8L7. Rick Boychuck, Ed. "Making Canada Better Known to Canadians and the World." Articles on interesting places, nature and wildlife in Canada. Payment varies, on acceptance. Query.

CAPE COD LIFE—P.O. Box 1385, Pocasset, MA 02559–1385. Brian F. Shortsleeve, Pub. Articles, to 2,000 words, on current events, business, art, history, gardening, and nautical lifestyle on Cape Cod, Martha's Vineyard, and Nantucket. Pays 10¢ a word, 30 days after publication. Queries preferred.

CARIBBEAN TRAVEL AND LIFE— 8403 Colesville Rd., Silver Spring, MD 20910. Veronica Gould Stoddart, Ed. Articles, 500 to 3,000 words, on all aspects of travel, recreation, leisure, and culture in the Caribbean, the Bahamas, and Bermuda. Pays $75 to $550, on publication. Query with published clips.

CAROLOGUE—South Carolina Historical Society, 100 Meeting St., Charleston, SC 29401–2299. Stephen Hoffius, Ed. General-interest articles, to 10 pages, on South Carolina history. Queries preferred. Pays in copies.

CHICAGO—500 N. Dearborn, Suite 1200, Chicago, IL 60610. Shane Tritsch, Man. Ed. Articles, 1,000 to 5,000 words, related to Chicago. Pays varying rates, on acceptance. Query.

CHICAGO HISTORY—Clark St. at North Ave., Chicago, IL 60614. Rosemary Adams, Ed. Articles, to 4,500 words, on Chicago's urban, political, social, and cultural history. Pays to $250, on publication. Query.

CHICAGO TRIBUNE MAGAZINE—*Chicago Tribune*, 435 N. Michigan Ave., Rm. 532, Chicago, IL 60611. Attn: Ed. Profiles and articles, to 6,000 words, on public, social, and cultural issues in the Midwest/Chicago area. Pays $250 to $1,500, on publication. Query.

CINCINNATI MAGAZINE— 409 Broadway, Cincinnati, OH 45202. Emily Foster, Ed. Articles, 1,000 to 3,000 words, on Cincinnati people and issues. Pays $75 to $100 for 1,000 words. Query with writing sample.

CITYLIMITS—325 N. Clippert St., Suite B, Lansing, MI 48912. Carole Eberly, Ed. Upbeat fiction, 1,500 to 2,500 words, of interest to Lansing, MI, area readers. Pays $150, on publication. Query preferred.

COLORADO BUSINESS—7009 S. Potomac, Englewood, CO 80112. Bruce Goldberg, Man. Ed. Articles, varying lengths, on business, business personalities, and economic trends in Colorado. Pays on publication. Query.

COMMON GROUND MAGAZINE—P.O. Box 99, McVeytown, PA 17051–0099. Ruth Dunmire and Pam Brumbaugh, Eds. Quarterly. General-interest articles, 500 to 5,000 words, related to central Pennsylvania's Juniata River Valley and its rural lifestyle. Related fiction, 1,000 to 2,000 words. Poetry, to 12 lines. Fillers, photos, and cartoons. Pays $25 to $200 for articles, $5 to $15 for fillers, and $5 to $25 for photos, on publication. Guidelines.

COMMONWEALTH—55 Summer St., 9th Fl., Boston, MA 02110. Dave Denison, Ed. Articles, 2,000 to 4,500 words, on politics, government, and public policy issues affecting Massachusetts citizens. Payment varies, on acceptance. Query.

CONNECTICUT—789 Reservoir Ave., Bridgeport, CT 06606. Charles Monagan, Ed. Articles, 1,500 to 3,500 words, on Connecticut topics, issues, people, and lifestyles. Pays $500 to $1,200, within 30 days of acceptance.

CONNECTICUT FAMILY—See *New York Family*.

DELAWARE TODAY—P.O. Box 2087, Wilmington, DE 19899. Ted Spiker, Ed. Service articles, profiles, news, etc., on topics of local interest. Pays $75 to $125 for department pieces, $50 to $500 for features, on publication. Queries with clips required.

DETROIT MONTHLY—1400 Woodbridge, Detroit, MI 48207. Megan Swoyer, Ed. Articles on Detroit-area people, issues, lifestyles, and business. Payment varies. Query required.

EASTSIDE PARENT—Northwest Parent Publishing, 2107 Elliott Ave., #303, Seattle, WA 98121. Ann Bergman, Ed. Articles, 300 to 2,500 words, for parents of children ages 12 and under. Pays $25 to $200, on publication. Queries preferred. Also publishes *Seattle's Child, Portland Parent* and *Pierce County Parent*.

ERIE & CHAUTAUQUA MAGAZINE—317 W. Sixth St., Erie, PA 16507. K. L. Kalvelage, Man. Ed. Feature articles, to 2,500 words, on issues of interest to upscale readers in the Erie, Warren, and Crawford counties (PA), and Chautauqua (NY) county. Pieces with regional relevance. Pays after publication. Query preferred, with writing samples. Guidelines.

FAMILY TIMES—P.O. Box 932, Eau Claire, WI 54702. Ann Gorton, Ed. Articles, from 800 words, for parents in the Chippewa Valley, WI. Pays $35 to $50, on publication. Queries preferred. Guidelines.

FLORIDA KEYS MAGAZINE—P.O. Box 6524, Key West, FL 33041. Gibbons Cline, Ed. Articles, 800 to 2,400 words, on the Florida Keys: history, environment, personality profiles, fishing, boating, diving, etc. Fillers, humor. Photos. Pays $2 per column inch, on publication.

FLORIDA TREND—Box 611, St. Petersburg, FL 33731–0611. John F. Berry, Ed. Articles on Florida business and businesspeople. Query with SASE required.

FLORIDA WILDLIFE— 620 S. Meridian St., Tallahassee, FL 32399–1600. Attn: Ed. Bimonthly of the Florida Game and Fresh Water Fish Commission. Articles, 800 to 1,500 words, that promote native flora and fauna, hunting, fishing in Florida's fresh waters, outdoor ethics, and conservation of Florida's natural resources. Pays $50 to $300, on publication. SASE for guidelines and how-to-submit memo.

GEORGIA JOURNAL—The Indispensable Atlanta Co., Inc., P.O. Box 1604, Decatur, GA 30031–1604. David Osier, Ed./Pub. Conoly Hester, Man. Ed. Articles, 200 to 5,000 words, on Georgia's natural and human history and environment; also outdoor adventures, people, historical figures, places, events, travel in Georgia. Poetry, to 20 lines, and fiction, to 5,000 words, with Georgia settings; Georgia writers preferred. Pays $50 to $500, on publication. Query for nonfiction.

GOLDENSEAL—The Cultural Ctr., 1900 Kanawha Blvd. E., Charleston, WV 25305–0300. Ken Sullivan, Ed. Articles, 1,000 and 3,000 words, on West Virginia history, folklife, folk art and crafts, and music of a traditional nature. Pays 10¢ a word, on publication. Guidelines.

GRAND RAPIDS—549 Ottawa N.W., Grand Rapids, MI 49503. Carole R. Valade, Ed. Service articles (dining guide, travel, personal finance, humor) and issue-oriented pieces related to Grand Rapids, Michigan. Pays $35 to $200, on publication. Query.

GULF COAST GOLFER—See *North Texas Golfer.*

HAMPSHIRE WEST—See *New Hampshire Editions.*

HAWAII—1400 Kapiolani Blvd., A25, Honolulu, HI 96814. Jim Borg, Ed. Bimonthly. Articles, 1,000 to 2,500 words, related to Hawaii. Pays 10¢ a word, on publication. Query.

HIGH COUNTRY NEWS—Box 1090, Paonia, CO 81428. Betsy Marston, Ed. Biweekly. Articles, 2,000 words, and roundups, 750 words, on western environmental issues, public lands management, energy, and natural resource issues; profiles of western innovators; pieces on western politics. "Writers must take regional approach." B&W photos. Pays $3 to $5 per column inch, on publication. Query.

HONOLULU—36 Merchant St., Honolulu, HI 96813. John Heckathorn, Ed. Features highlighting contemporary life in the Hawaiian islands: politics, sports, history, people, arts, events. Queries required. Pays $300 to $700, on acceptance.

ILLINOIS ENTERTAINER—124 W. Polk, Suite 103, Chicago, IL 60605. Michael C. Harris, Ed. Articles, 500 to 1,500 words, on local and national entertainment (emphasis on alternative music) in the greater Chicago area. Personality profiles; interviews; reviews. Photos. Pays varying rates, on publication. Query preferred.

INDIANAPOLIS MONTHLY—950 N. Meridian St., Suite 1200, Indianapolis, IN 46204. Sam Stall, Ed. Articles, 200 to 6,000 words, on health, sports, politics, business, interior design, personalities, controversy, and other topics. All material must have an Indianapolis/Indiana focus. Pays $50 to $500, on publication.

INQUIRER MAGAZINE—*Philadelphia Inquirer*, P.O. 8263, 400 N. Broad St., Philadelphia, PA 19101. Ms. Avery Rome, Ed. Articles, 1,500 to 2,000 words, and 3,000 to 7,000 words, on politics, science, arts and culture, business, lifestyles and entertainment, sports, health, psychology, education, religion, and humor. Pays varying rates. Query.

THE IOWAN MAGAZINE—108 Third St., Suite 350, Des Moines, IA 50309. Mark Ingebretsen, Ed. Articles, 1,000 to 3,000 words, on business, arts, people, and history of Iowa. Photos a plus. Payment varies, on acceptance. Query required.

ISLAND LIFE—P.O. Box 929, Sanibel Island, FL 33957. Joan Hooper, Ed. Articles, 500 to 1,200 words, with photos, on wildlife, flora and fauna, design and decor, the arts, shelling, local sports, historical sites, etc., directly related to the islands of Sanibel, Captiva, Marco, Estero, or Gasparilla. No first-person articles. Pays on publication.

JACKSONVILLE—White Publishing Co., 1650 Prudential Dr., Suite 300, Jacksonville, FL 32207. Larry Marscheck, Ed. Service pieces and articles, 1,500 to 2,500 words, on issues and personalities of interest to readers in the greater Jacksonville area. Department pieces, 1,200 to 1,500 words, on business, health, travel, personal finance, real estate, arts and entertainment, sports, dining out, food. Home and garden articles on local homeowners, interior designers, remodelers, gardeners, craftsmen, etc., 1,000 to 2,000 words. Pays $200 to $500, on publication. Query required. Guidelines.

JOURNAL OF THE WEST—1531 Yuma, Box 1009, Manhattan, KS 66505–1009. Robin Higham, Ed. Articles, to 20 pages, on the history and culture of the West, then and now. Pays in copies.

KANSAS!—Kansas Dept. of Commerce, 700 S.W. Harrison, Suite 1300, Topeka, KS 66603–3957. Andrea Glenn, Ed. Quarterly. Articles, 1,000 to 1,250 words, on the people, places, history, and events of Kansas. Color slides. Pays to $250, on acceptance. Query.

KANSAS CITY MAGAZINE—7007 College Blvd., Suite 430, Overland Park, KS 66211. Doug Worgul, Ed. Articles, 250 to 3,500 words, of interest to readers in Kansas City. Pays to 30¢ a word, on acceptance. Query.

KENTUCKY LIVING—P.O. Box 32170, Louisville, KY 40232. Paul Wesslund, Ed. Articles, 800 to 2,000 words, with strong Kentucky angle: profiles (of people, places, events), history, biography, recreation, travel, leisure or lifestyle, and book excerpts. Pays $125 to $350, on acceptance. Guidelines.

LAKE SUPERIOR MAGAZINE—P.O. Box 16417, Duluth, MN 55816–0417. Paul Hayden, Ed. Articles with emphasis on Lake Superior regional subjects: historical and topical pieces that highlight the people, places, and events that affect the Lake Superior region. Pictorial essays; humor and occasional fiction. Quality photos enhance submission. "Writers must have a thorough knowledge of the subject and how it relates to our region." Pays to $400, extra for photos, on publication. Query.

THE LOOK—P.O. Box 272, Cranford, NJ 07016–0272. John R. Hawks, Pub. Articles, 1,500 to 3,000 words, on fashion, student life, employment, relationships, and profiles of interest to local (NJ) readers ages 16 to 26. Also, beach stories and articles about the New Jersey shore. Pays $30 to $200, on publication.

LOS ANGELES MAGAZINE—11100 Santa Monica Blvd., 7th Fl., Los Angeles, CA 90025. Michael Caruso, Ed. Articles, to 3,000 words, of interest to sophisticated, affluent southern Californians, preferably with local focus on a lifestyle topic. Payment varies. Query.

LOS ANGELES READER—5550 Wilshire Blvd., Suite 301, Los Angeles, CA 90036. Erik Himmelsbach, Man. Ed. Articles, 750 to 5,000 words, on subjects related to the Los Angeles area; special emphasis on feature journalism, entertainment, and the arts. Pays $25 to $500, on publication. Query preferred.

LOUISVILLE—137 W. Muhammad Ali Blvd., Suite 101, Louisville, KY 40202. John Filiatreau, Ed. Articles, 1,000 to 2,000 words, on community issues, personalities, and entertainment in the Louisville area. Photos. Pays from $50, on acceptance. Query; articles on assignment only. Limited freelance market.

M MAGAZINE—P.O. Box 581, Hazard, KY 41702. Doug Crawford, Ed. Quarterly. "The Modern Magazine of the Mountains." Articles and stories, 2,000 to 3,000 words. Poetry, to 30 lines. Fillers and humor, 500 to 1,000 words. "Contemporary Appalachian material needed." Artist profiles, with samples of work, also used. Pays in copies.

MARYLAND—2503 Davidsonville Rd., Gambrills, MD 21054. D. Patrick Hornberger, Ed. Dir. Articles, 800 to 2,200 words, on Maryland subjects. Pay varies, on acceptance. Query preferred. Guidelines.

MEMPHIS—Contemporary Media, Box 256, Memphis, TN 38101. Tim Sampson, Ed. Articles, 1,500 to 4,000 words, on a wide variety of topics related to Memphis and the Mid-South region: politics, education, sports, business, history, etc. Profiles; investigative pieces. Pays $50 to $500, on publication. Query. SASE for guidelines.

METROKIDS—1080 N. Delaware Ave., Suite 702, Philadelphia, PA 19125. Nancy Lisagor, Ed. Tabloid. Features and department pieces, 500 to 1,000 words, on regional family travel, dining, and entertainment in the Delaware Valley. Pays $25 to $50, on publication.

MICHIGAN LIVING—1 Auto Club Dr., Dearborn, MI 48126–9982. Len Barnes, Ed. Travel articles, 300 to 2,000 words, on tourist attractions and recreational opportunities in the U.S. and Canada, with emphasis on Michigan: places to go, things to do, costs, etc. Color photos. Pays $55 to $500, (rates vary for photos), on acceptance.

MID-WEST OUTDOORS—111 Shore Dr., Hinsdale, IL 60521–5885. Gene Laulunen, Ed. Articles, to 1,500 words, with photos, on where, when, and how to fish and hunt, within 500 miles of Chicago. Pays $25, on publication.

MILWAUKEE MAGAZINE—312 E. Buffalo, Milwaukee, WI 53202. John Fennell, Ed. Profiles, investigative articles, and service pieces, 2,000 to 5,000 words; local tie-in a must. No fiction. Pays $400 to $900, on publication. Query preferred.

561

MINNESOTA MONTHLY—Lumber Exchange Bldg., 10 S. Fifth St., Suite 1000, Minneapolis, MN 55402. Laurie Hertzel, Sr. Ed. Articles, to 4,000 words, on people, places, events, and issues in Minnesota. Pays $50 to $800, on acceptance. Query.

MONTANA JOURNAL—1431 S. Higgins Ave., Missoula, MT 59801. Mike Haser, Ed. Articles, to 1,000 words, about the people, places, and events that helped build Montana. Pays 2¢ a word, on publication. Queries preferred.

MONTANA MAGAZINE—P.O. Box 5630, Helena, MT 59604. Beverly R. Magley, Ed. Recreation, travel, general interest, regional profiles, photo-essays. Montana-oriented only. B&W prints, color slides. Pays 15¢ a word, on publication.

MPLS. ST. PAUL—220 S. 6th St., Suite 500, Minneapolis, MN 55402–4507. Brian E. Anderson, Ed. In-depth articles, features, profiles, and service pieces about the Minneapolis-St. Paul area, 300 to 4,000 words. Pays to $2,000.

NAPA VALLEY APPELLATION—See *Appellation.*

NEBRASKA HISTORY—P.O. Box 82554, Lincoln, NE 68501. James E. Potter, Ed. Articles, 3,000 to 7,000 words, on the history of Nebraska and the Great Plains. B&W line drawings. Pays in copies. Cash prize awarded to one article each year.

NEVADA—1800 Hwy. 50 East, Suite 200, Carson City, NV 89710. David Moore, Ed. Articles, 500 to 700 or 1,500 to 1,800 words, on topics related to Nevada: travel, history, profiles, humor, and place. Special section on Nevada events. Photos. Pay varies, on publication.

NEW FRONTIERS OF NEW MEXICO—P.O. Box 1299, Tijeras, NM 87059. Wally Gordon, Ed./Pub. Fiction and in-depth nonfiction, to 3,000 words, related to New Mexico and the Southwest. Humor, to 1,000 words. Poetry, to 100 lines. Pays $25 to $200, on publication.

NEW HAMPSHIRE EDITIONS—100 Main St., Nashua, NH 03060. Rick Broussard, Ed. Dean Dexter, Man. Ed. Lifestyle, business, and history articles with a New Hampshire angle, with sources from all regions of the state, for the company's regional monthly and *New Hampshire Legacy* (formerly called *Hampshire West*). Query. Payment varies, on publication.

NEW HAMPSHIRE LEGACY—See *New Hampshire Editions.*

NEW JERSEY REPORTER—The Ctr. for Analysis of Public Issues, 16 Vandeventer Ave., Princeton, NJ 08542. Neil Upmeyer, Ed. Bob Narus, Man. Ed. In-depth articles, 1,000 to 4,000 words, on New Jersey politics and public affairs. Pays $100 to $600, on publication. Query required.

NEW MEXICO MAGAZINE—Lew Wallace Bldg., 495 Old Santa Fe Trail, Santa Fe, NM 87503. Attn: Ed. Articles, 250 to 2,000 words, on New Mexico subjects. No poetry or fiction. Pays about 30¢ a word, on acceptance. Query.

NEW YORK FAMILY—141 Halstead Ave., Suite 3D, Mamaroneck, NY 10543. Felice Shapiro, Susan Ross, Pubs. Betsy F. Woolf, Sr. Ed. Articles related to family life in New York City. Pays $50 to $200, on publication. Same requirements for *Westchester Family* and *Connecticut Family.*

NEWPORT LIFE—174 Bellevue Ave., Suite 207, Newport, RI 02840. Susan Ryan, Sr. Ed. Quarterly. Articles, 500 to 2,500 words, on the people and

562

places of Newport County: general-interest and historical articles, interviews, profiles, investigative pieces, and photo-features. Departments, 600 to 750 words, include "At the Helm" (on some aspect of boating), "Arts Marquee," "Food for Thought," and "Down to Business." Photos must be available for all articles. Pays 10¢ a word, on publication. Query.

NORTH DAKOTA HORIZONS—P.O. Box 2639, Bismarck, ND 58502. Lyle Halvorson, Ed. Quarterly. Articles, about 2,500 words, on people, places, and events in North Dakota. Photos. Pays $75 to $300, on publication.

NORTH GEORGIA JOURNAL—P.O. Box 127, Roswell, GA 30077. Olin Jackson, Pub./Ed. History, travel, and lifestyle features, 2,000 to 3,000 words, on north Georgia. History features need human-interest approach and must be written in first person; include interviews. Photos a plus. Pays $75 to $250, on acceptance. Query.

NORTH TEXAS GOLFER—9182 Old Katy Rd., Suite 212, Houston, TX 77055. Steve Hunter, Ed. Articles, 800 to 1,500 words, involving local golfers or related directly to north Texas. Pays from $50 to $425, on publication. Query. Same requirements for *Gulf Coast Golfer* (related to south Texas).

NORTHEAST MAGAZINE—*The Hartford Courant,* 285 Broad St., Hartford, CT 06115. Lary Bloom, Ed. Articles and short essays, 750 to 3,000 words, that reflect the concerns of Connecticut residents. Pays $250 to $1,000, on acceptance.

NORTHERN LIGHTS—Box 8084, Missoula, MT 59807–8084. Attn: Ed. Articles, 500 to 3,000 words, about the contemporary West. "We look for beautifully crafted personal essays that illuminate what it means to live in the Rocky Mountain West. We're looking to bust the Hollywood stereotypes." Pays 10¢ a word, on publication.

NORTHWEST REGIONAL MAGAZINES—P.O. Box 18000, Florence, OR 97439–0130. Attn: Jim Forst or Judy Fleagle. All submissions considered for use in *Oregon Coast, Oregon Outside* and *Northwest Travel.* Articles, 800 to 2,000 words, pertaining to the Pacific Northwest, on travel, history, town/city profiles, outside activities, and nature. News releases, 200 to 500 words. Articles with photos (slides) preferred. Pays $50 to $350, after publication. Guidelines.

NOW & THEN—CASS/ETSU, P.O. Box 70556, Johnson City, TN 37614–0556. Jane Harris Woodside, Ed. Fiction and nonfiction, 1,500 to 3,000 words: short stories, articles, interviews, essays, memoirs, book reviews. Pieces must be related to theme of issue and have some connection to the Appalachian region. Also photos and drawings. SASE for guideline and current themes. Pays $15 to $75, on publication.

OHIO MAGAZINE—62 E. Broad St., Columbus, OH 43215. Jean Kelly, Ed. Profiles of people, cities, and towns of Ohio; pieces on historic sites, tourist attractions, little-known spots. Lengths and payment vary. Query with clips.

OKLAHOMA TODAY—Box 53384, Oklahoma City, OK 73152–9971. Jeanne M. Devlin, Ed. Articles, 1,000 to 4,000 words: travel; profiles; history; nature and outdoor recreation; and arts. All material must have regional tie-in. Pays $75 to $750, on acceptance or publication. Queries preferred. Guidelines.

ORANGE COAST—245-D Fischer Ave., Suite 8, Costa Mesa, CA 92626. Martin J. Smith, Ed. Articles, 2,000 to 3,000 words, of interest to educated Orange County residents. Pieces, 1,000 to 1,500 words, for regular departments including "Coastwatch" (services and products), "Short Cuts" (local phenomena). Query with clips. Pays $400 to $800 for features; $100 to $200 for departments; $25 to $50 for "Short Cuts" and "Coastwatch," after acceptance. Guidelines.

OREGON COAST—See *Northwest Regional Magazines.*

OREGON OUTSIDE—See *Northwest Regional Magazines.*

ORLANDO MAGAZINE—P.O. Box 2207, Orlando, FL 32802. Brooke Lange, Ed. Locally based articles and department pieces, lengths vary, for residents of Central Florida. Query with clips.

OUT WEST: THE NEWSPAPER THAT ROAMS— 408 Broad St., Suite 11, Nevada City, CA 95959. Chuck Woodbury, Ed./Pub. Entertaining and informative articles, 150 to 750 words, and short pieces, 30 to 75 words, on the rural West (not the old West): interesting people, unusual places to stay, offbeat attractions. "Send for a sample of the paper before you submit." Pays about 5¢ a word, on publication. Web site is http://www.outwestnewspaper.com.

OUTDOOR TRAVELER, MID-ATLANTIC—WMS Publications, Inc., P.O. Box 2748, Charlottesville, VA 22902. Marianne Marks, Ed. Scott Clark, Assoc. Ed. Articles, 1,500 to 2,000 words, about outdoor recreation, travel, adventure, and nature in the Mid-Atlantic region (NY, PA, NJ, MD, DE, DC, WV, VA, and NC). Departments include "Destinations," 450 to 600 words, on practical and descriptive guides to sports destinations; book reviews, 200 words. Pays $375 to $500 for features; payment varies for departments, on publication. Guidelines.

PALM SPRINGS LIFE—Desert Publications, 303 N. Indian Canyon Dr., P.O. Box 2724, Palm Springs, CA 92263. Stewart Weiner, Ed. Articles, 1,000 to 3,000 words, of interest to "wealthy, upscale people who live and/or play in the desert." Pays $150 to $1,000 for features, $25 to $75 for short profiles, on publication. Query required.

PENNSYLVANIA HERITAGE—P.O. Box 1026, Harrisburg, PA 17108–1026. Michael J. O'Malley III, Ed. Quarterly of the Pennsylvania Historical Museum Commission. Articles, 3,000 to 4,000 words, on fine and decorative arts, architecture, archaeology, oral history, exhibits, industry and technology, travel, and folklore, written with an eye toward illustration. Photographic essays. Pieces should "introduce readers to the state's rich culture and historic legacy." Pays $300 to $500 for articles; up to $100 for photos and drawings, on acceptance.

PENNSYLVANIA MAGAZINE—Box 576, Camp Hill, PA 17001–0576. Matthew K. Holliday, Ed. General-interest features with a Pennsylvania focus. All articles must be accompanied by photocopies of possible illustrations. Guidelines.

PERSIMMON HILL—1700 N.E. 63rd St., Oklahoma City, OK 73111. M.J. Van Deventer, Ed. Published by the National Cowboy Hall of Fame. Articles, 1,500 to 2,000 words, on Western history and art, cowboys, ranching, and nature. Top-quality illustrations a must. Pays from $100 to $250, on publication.

PHILADELPHIA—1818 Market St., Philadelphia, PA 19103. Eliot Kaplan, Ed. Articles, 1,000 to 5,000 words, for sophisticated audience, relating to Philadelphia area. No fiction or poetry. Pays on acceptance. Query.

564

PHOENIX MAGAZINE—5555 N. 7th Ave., Suite B200, Phoenix, AZ 85013. Richard Vonier, Ed. Articles, 1,000 to 3,000 words, on topics of interest to Phoenix-area residents. Pays $300 to $1,000, on publication. Queries preferred.

PIERCE COUNTY PARENT—See *Eastside Parent.*

PITTSBURGH— 4802 Fifth Ave., Pittsburgh, PA 15213. Christopher Fletcher, Ed. Profiles (to 800 words), feature stories and service pieces (1,200 to 3,000 words), and in-depth news features (to 5,000 words) geared to western Pennsylvania, eastern Ohio, northern West Virginia, and western Maryland readers. Pays from $300, on publication. Query with outline preferred; send to Man. Ed.

PITTSBURGH POST-GAZETTE—34 Blvd. of the Allies, Pittsburgh, PA 15230. Mark S. Murphy, Ed. Sunday magazine. Well-written, well-organized, in-depth articles of local, regional, or national interest, 2,500 to 3,500 words, on issues, personalities, human interest, historical moments. No fiction, hobbies, how-tos or "timely events" pieces. Pays from $350, on publication. Query.

PORTLAND MAGAZINE—578 Congress St., Portland, ME 04101. Colin Sargent, Ed. "Maine's City Magazine." Articles on local people, legends, culture, and trends. Fiction, to 750 words. Pays on publication. Query preferred.

PORTLAND PARENT—See *Eastside Parent.*

RANGE MAGAZINE— 106 E. Adams, Suite 201, Carson City, NV 89706. Caroline Hadley, Ed. Quarterly. Articles, 500 to 1,200 words, on issues that threaten the West, its people, lifestyles, lands, and wildlife. "Our main purpose is to present public awareness of the positive presence of ranching operations on America's rangelands." Payment varies, on publication. Query preferred.

RECKON—Southern Culture Publications, Hill Hall, Room 301, The Univ. of Mississippi, University, MS 38677. Lynn McKnight, Ed. Quarterly. Fiction, 3,000 to 7,000 words, and articles, 1,000 to 5,000 words, on the contemporary American South. "Preference is given to prose with a distinct literary tone. Content must be informed, intelligent, and interpretive." No poetry or fillers. Pays 25¢ a word, on publication. Guidelines.

RECREATION NEWS—P.O. Box 32335, Washington, DC 20007–0635. Rebecca B. Heaton, Ed. Articles, 1,500 to 2,000 words, on recreation and travel for government workers in the Washington, DC area. Light, first-person accounts, 800 words, for "Sporting Life" column. "Articles should have a conversational tone that's lean and brisk." Pays $50 for reprints, to $300 for cover articles, on publication. Queries preferred. Guidelines.

RHODE ISLAND MONTHLY— 95 Chestnut St., Providence, RI 02903. Paula M. Bodah, Man. Ed. Features, 1,000 to 4,000 words, ranging from investigative reporting and in-depth profiles to service pieces and visual stories, on Rhode Island and southeastern Massachusetts. Seasonal material, 1,000 to 2,000 words. Fillers, 150 to 500 words, on Rhode Island places, customs, people, events, products and services, restaurants and food. Pays $250 to $1,000 for features; $25 to $50 for shorts, on publication. Query.

ROCKY MOUNTAIN GARDENER—P.O. Box 1230, Gunninson, CO 81230. Susan Martineau, Pub./Ed.-in-Chief. Quarterly. How-to articles, 1,000 to 1,200 words, on regional techniques and varieties; profiles of regional gardeners and gardens, 1,000 to 1,500 words; book reviews and production reviews, 800 to 1,000 words. "Articles must be focused on Rocky Mountain area from New Mexico to Montana. We prefer new, novel, or specific information, not just general gardening topics." Pays 10¢ a word, on publication.

RUNNER TRIATHLETE NEWS—P.O. Box 19909, Houston, TX 77224. Lance Phegley, Ed. Articles on running for road racing and multi-sport enthusiasts in TX, LA, OK, NM, and AR. Payment varies, on publication.

RURALITE—P.O. Box 558, Forest Grove, OR 97116. Attn: Ed. or Feature Ed. Articles, 800 to 2,000 words, of interest to a primarily rural and small-town audience in OR, WA, ID, WY, NV, northern CA, and AK. "Think pieces" affecting rural/urban interests, regional history and celebrations, self-help, profiles, etc. No fiction or poetry. No sentimental nostalgia. Pays $30 to $400, on acceptance. Queries required. Guidelines.

SACRAMENTO MAGAZINE— 4471 D St., Sacramento, CA 95819. Krista Hendricks Minard, Ed. Features, 2,500 words, on a broad range of topics related to the region. Department pieces, 1,200 to 1,500 words, and short pieces, 400 words, for "City Lights" column. Pays $75 to $300, on publication. Query.

SAN DIEGO MAGAZINE— 4206 W. Point Loma Blvd., P.O. Box 85409, San Diego, CA 92138. Virginia Butterfield, Exec. Ed. Articles, 1,500 to 3,000 words, on local personalities, politics, lifestyles, business, history, etc., relating to San Diego area. Photos. Pays $250 to $600, on publication. Query with clips.

SAN DIEGO READER—P.O. Box 85803, San Diego, CA 92186. Jim Holman, Ed. Literate articles, 2,500 to 10,000 words, on the San Diego region. Pays $500 to $2,000, on publication.

SAN FRANCISCO BUSINESS TIMES—275 Battery St., Suite 940, San Francisco, CA 94111. Mike Consol, Ed. Business-oriented articles, about 20 column inches. Limited free-lance market. Pays $75 to $100, on publication. Query.

SAN FRANCISCO EXAMINER MAGAZINE—*San Francisco Examiner*, 110 Fifth St., San Francisco, CA 94103. Attn: Ed. Articles, 1,200 to 3,000 words, on lifestyles, issues, business, history, events, and people in northern California. Query. Pays varying rates.

SAN FRANCISCO FOCUS—2601 Mariposa St., San Francisco, CA 94110–1400. Amy Rennert, Ed. Service features, profiles of local newsmakers, and investigative pieces of local issues, 2,500 to 3,000 words. News items, 250 to 800 words, on subjects ranging from business to arts to politics. Payment varies, on acceptance. Query required.

SAVANNAH MAGAZINE—P.O. Box 1088, Savannah, GA 31402. Georgia R. Byrd, Ed. Articles, 2,500 to 3,500 words, on people and events in and around Savannah and Chatham County. Historical articles, 1,500 to 2,500 words, of local interest. Reviews, 500 to 750 words, of Savannah-based books and authors. Short pieces, 500 to 750 words, on weekend getaways near Savannah. Pays $75 to $350, after acceptance. Submit complete manuscript. Guidelines.

SEATTLE—701 Dexter Ave. N., Suite 101, Seattle, WA 98109. Giselle Smith, Ed. City, local issues, home, and lifestyle articles, 500 to 2,000 words, relating directly to the greater Seattle area. Personality profiles. Pays $100 to $700, on publication. Guidelines.

566

SEATTLE WEEKLY—1008 Western, Suite 300, Seattle, WA 98104. David Brewster, Ed. Articles, 250 to 4,000 words, from a Northwest perspective. Pays $25 to $800, on publication. Query. Guidelines.

SEATTLE'S CHILD—Northwest Parent Publishing, 2107 Elliott Ave., #303, Seattle, WA 98121. Ann Bergman, Ed. Articles, 400 to 2,500 words, of interest to parents, educators, and childcare providers of children under 12, and investigative reports and consumer tips on issues affecting families in the Puget Sound region. Pays $75 to $400, on publication. Query required.

SENIOR MAGAZINE—3565 S. Higuera St., San Luis Obispo, CA 93401. Attn: Ed. Articles, 600 to 900 words: personality profiles, travel pieces, articles about new things, places, business, sports, movies, television, and health; book reviews (of new or outstanding older books) of interest to seniors. Pays $1.50 per inch; $10 to $25 for B&W photos, on publication.

SILENT SPORTS—717 10th St., P.O. Box 152, Waupaca, WI 54981. Attn: Ed. Articles, 1,000 to 2,000 words, on canoeing, bicycling, cross-country skiing, running, hiking, backpacking, and other "silent" sports, in the upper Midwest region. "Articles must focus on the upper Midwest. No articles about places, people, or events outside the region." Pays $40 to $100 for features; $20 to $50 for fillers, on publication. Query.

SMOKY MOUNTAIN MEMORIES—P.O. Box 4810, Sevierville, TN 37864. Sarah E. Myers, Ed. Published 8 times a year. Articles, 300 to 1,000 words, and poems on subjects of interest to "those who love the Smokies." No payment. Query.

SNOW COUNTRY—5520 Park Ave., Trumbull, CT 06611–0395. Kathleen Ring, Sr. Ed. Published 8 times a year. Features, 4,000 words, and articles, 1,000 to 2,000 words on skiing, mountain biking, in-line skating, camping, rafting and other year-round mountain sports as well as lifestyle issues. First-person adventure articles, travel pieces, service-oriented articles, profiles of snow country residents. "Mountain Living," 100- to 700-word pieces on people and points of view, anecdotes, trends, issues. Query with clips and resumé. Pays 80¢ a word, on acceptance.

SOUTH CAROLINA HISTORICAL MAGAZINE—South Carolina Historical Society, 100 Meeting St., Charleston, SC 29401-2299. Stephen Hoffius, Ed. Scholarly articles, to 25 pages with footnotes, on all areas of South Carolina history. Pays in copies.

SOUTH CAROLINA WILDLIFE—P.O. Box 167, Columbia, SC 29202–0167. Attn: Man. Ed. Articles, 1,000 to 2,000 words, with regional outdoors focus: conservation, natural history and wildlife, recreation. Profiles. Pays from 10¢ a word. Query.

SOUTH FLORIDA MAGAZINE— 800 Douglas Rd., Suite 500, Coral Gables, FL 33134. Nancy Moore, Ed. Features, 1,100 to 3,500 words, and department pieces, 900 to 1,300 words, on news, profiles, and hot topics related to south Florida. Short, bright items, 200 to 400 words. Pays $75 to $700, within 30 days of acceptance. Query.

SOUTHERN CULTURES—Ctr. for the Study of the American South, CB #3355, Manning Hall, UNC-CH, Chapel Hill, NC 27599-3355. Linda Haac, Man. Ed. Articles, 15 to 25 typed pages, on folk, popular, and high culture of the South. "We're interested in submissions from a wide variety of intellectual traditions that deal with ways of life, thought, belief, and expression in the United States South." Pays in copies.

SOUTHERN OUTDOORS—5845 Carmichael Rd., Montgomery, AL 36117. Larry Teague, Ed. How-to pieces, 800 to 1,200 words, and 2,000-word how-to and where-to articles on hunting and fishing, for fishermen and hunters in the Southern states. Pays 20¢ a word, on acceptance. Query.

SOUTHWEST ART—5444 Westheimer, Suite 1440, Houston, TX 77056. Susan McGarry, Ed. Articles, 1,200 to 1,800 words, on the artists, art collectors, museum exhibitions, gallery events and dealers, art history, and art trends west of the Mississippi River. Particularly interested in representational or figurative arts. Pays from $400, on acceptance. Query with at least 20 slides of artwork to be featured.

THE STATE: DOWN HOME IN NORTH CAROLINA—128 S. Tryon St., Suite 2200, Charlotte, NC 28202. Scott Smith, Man. Ed. Articles, 750 to 2,000 words, on people, history, and places in North Carolina. Photos. Pays on publication.

SUNSET MAGAZINE— 80 Willow Rd., Menlo Park, CA 94025. William Marken, Ed. Western regional. Limited free-lance market.

SUNSHINE: THE MAGAZINE OF SOUTH FLORIDA—*The Sun-Sentinel*, 200 E. Las Olas Blvd., Ft. Lauderdale, FL 33301–2293. John Parkyn, Ed. Articles, 1,000 to 3,000 words, on topics of interest to south Floridians. Pays $300 to $1,000, on acceptance. Query. Guidelines.

SWEAT—736 E. Loyola Dr., Tempe, AZ 85282. Joan Westlake, Ed. "South West Exercise And Training." Articles, 500 to 1,200 words, on sports or fitness with an Arizona angle. "No personal articles or tales. We want investigative pieces. Articles must relate specifically to Arizona or Arizonans." Pays $25 to $60 for articles; $12 to $70 for photos, on publication. Queries required; no unsolicited manuscripts.

TALLAHASSEE MAGAZINE—P.O. Box 1837, Tallahassee, FL 32302–1837. Kathy Grobe, Man. Ed. Andy Lindstrom, Ed.-at-Large. Articles, 800 to 1,500 words, on the life, people, and history of the north Florida-south Georgia area. Pays on acceptance. Query.

TEXAS HIGHWAYS MAGAZINE—P.O. Box 141009, Austin, TX 78714–1009. Jack Lowry, Ed. Texas travel, history, and scenic features, 200 to 1,800 words. Pays about 40¢ to 50¢ a word, $80 to $550 per photo. Query. Guidelines.

TEXAS MONTHLY—P.O. Box 1569, Austin, TX 78767–1569. Gregory Curtis, Ed. Features, 2,500 to 5,000 words, and departments, to 2,500 words, on art, architecture, food, education, business, politics, etc. "We like solidly researched pieces that uncover issues of public concern, reveal offbeat and previously unreported topics, or use a novel approach to familiar topics." Pays varying rates, on acceptance. Queries required.

TEXAS PARKS & WILDLIFE—Fountain Park Plaza, 3000 S. Interstate Hwy. 35, Suite 120, Austin, TX 78704. Jim Cox, Sr. Ed. Articles, 800 to 1,500 words, promoting the conservation and enjoyment of Texas wildlife, parks, waters, and all outdoors. Features on hunting, fishing, birding, camping, and the environment. Department pieces, to 1,000 words, for "Parks & Places to Go," "State of Nature," and "Woods and Waters." Photos a plus. Pays to $600, on acceptance; extra for photos.

TIMELINE—1982 Velma Ave., Columbus, OH 43211-2497. Christopher S. Duckworth, Ed. Articles, 1,000 to 6,000 words, on history of Ohio (politics, economics, social, and natural history) for lay readers in the Midwest. Pays $100 to $900, on acceptance. Queries preferred.

TORONTO LIFE—59 Front St. E., Toronto, Ont., Canada M5E 1B3. John Macfarlane, Ed. Articles, 1,500 to 4,500 words, on Toronto. Pays $1,500 to $3,500, on acceptance. Query.

TROPIC—*The Miami Herald,* One Herald Plaza, Miami, FL 33132. Tom Shroder, Exec. Ed. General-interest articles, 750 to 3,000 words, for south Florida readers. Pays $200 to $1,000, on acceptance.

TUCSON LIFESTYLE—Old Pueblo Press, 7000 E. Tanque Verde, Tucson, AZ 85715. Sue Giles, Ed.-in-Chief. Local slant to all articles on businesses, lifestyles, the arts, homes, fashion, and travel in the Southwest. Payment varies, on acceptance. Query preferred.

TWIN CITIES READER—10 S. Fifth St., Minneapolis, MN 55402. Claude Peck, Ed. Articles, ½ page to 4 printed pages, on local public affairs and arts for readers ages 25 to 44. Pays $25 to $150, on publication.

VALLEY MAGAZINE—11151 Laurel Canyon Blvd., San Fernando, CA 91340. Bonnie Steele, Ed. Articles, 1,000 to 1,500 words, on celebrities, issues, education, health, business, dining, and entertaining, etc., in the San Fernando Valley. Pays $100 to $350, within 8 weeks of acceptance.

VENTURA COUNTY & COAST REPORTER—1567 Spinnaker Dr., Suite 202, Ventura, CA 93001. Nancy Cloutier, Ed. Articles, 3 to 5 pages, on any locally slanted topic. Pays $10, on publication.

VERMONT—2 Maple St., Suite 40D, Middlebury, VT 05753. Julie Kirgo, Man. Ed. Articles on all aspects of contemporary Vermont: its people, culture, politics, and special places. Pays $100 to $800, on publication. Query.

VERMONT LIFE— 6 Baldwin St., Montpelier, VT 05602. Tom Slayton, Ed.-in-Chief. Articles, 500 to 3,000 words, on Vermont subjects only. Pays 20¢ a word, extra for photos. Query preferred.

VIRGINIA—The Country Publishers, Inc., P.O. Box 798, Berryville, VA 22611. Garrison Ellis, Ed. Quarterly. "Written for and about people, places, events, and activities in, around, and affecting Virginia." Features, 2,000 to 2,500 words; articles, 1,200 to 1,800 words; humor, folklore, and legend, to 2,000 words; fiction, 1,000 to 1,500 words, with regional setting or reference; related poetry, to 32 lines. Department pieces, 500 to 700 words. Photos. Pays $200 to $300, 30 days after publication.

VIRGINIA BUSINESS— 411 E. Franklin St., Suite 105, Richmond, VA 23219. James Bacon, Ed. Articles, 1,000 to 2,500 words, related to the business scene in Virginia. Pays varying rates, on acceptance. Query required.

VIRGINIA WILDLIFE—P.O. Box 11104, Richmond, VA 23230-1104. Attn: Ed. Articles, 1,500 to 2,000 words, with Virginia tie-in, on fishing, hunting, wildlife management, outdoor safety and ethics, etc. Articles may be accompanied by color photos. Pays from 15¢ a word, extra for photos, on publication. Query.

WASHINGTON POST MAGAZINE—*The Washington Post,* 1150 15th St. N.W., Washington, DC 20071. Liza Mundy, Man. Ed. Personal-experience essays, profiles, and general-interest pieces, to 6,000 words, on business, arts and culture, politics, science, sports, education, children, relationships, behavior, etc. Articles should be of interest to people living in Washington, DC, area. Pays from $750, on acceptance. Limited market.

THE WASHINGTONIAN—1828 L St. N.W., Suite 200, Washington, DC 20036. John Limpert, Ed. Helpful, informative articles, 1,000 to 4,000 words, on DC-related topics. Pays 50¢ a word, on publication.

WE ALASKANS MAGAZINE—*Anchorage Daily News*, Box 149001, Anchorage, AK 99514–9001. George Bryson, Ed. Articles, 500 to 1,000 words, and features, 3,000 to 4,000 words, mostly on Alaska topics. Profiles, narratives, essays, and humor. Pays $50 to $150 for short articles, $300 to $600 for features, on publication.

WESTCHESTER FAMILY—See *New York Family*.

WESTERN SPORTSMAN—140 Ave. F N., Saskatoon, Sask., Canada S7L 1V8. George Gruenefeld, Ed. Informative articles, to 2,500 words, on hunting, fishing, and outdoor experiences in British Columbia, Alberta, Saskatchewan, and Manitoba. How-tos, humor, cartoons. Photos. Pays $75 to $300, on acceptance.

WESTWAYS—2601 S. Figueroa St., Los Angeles, CA 90007. Attn: Ed. Articles, 1,000 to 3,000 words, and photo-essays, on California, western U.S., greater U.S., and overseas: history, contemporary living, travel, personalities, etc. Photos. Pays from 50¢ a word, extra for photos, on acceptance. Query.

WINDSPEAKER—Aboriginal Multi-Media Society of Alberta, 15001 112th Ave., Edmonton, Alberta, Canada T5M 2V6. Debora Lockyer, Ed. Tabloid. Features, news items, sports, op-ed pieces, columns, etc., 200 to 1,000 words, concerning Canada's Aboriginal peoples. Pays from $3 per published inch, after publication. Query. Guidelines.

WINDY CITY SPORTS—1450 W. Randolph, Chicago, IL 60607. Jeff Banowetz, Ed. Articles, to 1,000 words, on amateur sports in the Chicago area. Queries required. Pays $100, on publication.

WISCONSIN TRAILS—P.O. Box 5650, Madison, WI 53705. Lucy J. Rhodes, Assoc. Ed. Articles, 1,500 to 3,000 words, on regional topics: outdoors, lifestyle, events, history, arts, adventure, travel; profiles of artists, craftspeople, and regional personalities. Pays $150 to $500, on publication. Query.

WISCONSIN WEST MAGAZINE—2645 Harlem St., Eau Claire, WI 54701. Attn: Ed. Articles on current issues for residents of western Wisconsin: profiles of restaurants, weekend leisure activities and getaways, and famous people of western Wisconsin; historical pieces; short humor. Payment varies, on publication.

WYOMING RURAL ELECTRIC NEWS—P.O. Box 380, Casper, WY 82606–0380. Kris Wendtland, Ed. Articles, 500 to 900 words, on issues relevant to rural Wyoming. Articles should support Wyoming's personal and economic growth, social development, and education. Wyoming writers given preference. Pays $20 to $50, on publication.

YANKEE—Yankee Publishing Co., P.O. Box 520, Dublin, NH 03444. Judson D. Hale, Ed. Articles and fiction, 500 to 2,500 words, on New England and New England people. Pays $500 to $2,500 for features, on acceptance.

TRAVEL ARTICLES

ACCENT/TRAVELOG—Box 10010, Ogden, UT 84409. Attn: Eds. Articles, 1,000 words, on travel destinations, ways to travel, and travel tips. No budget trips. Pays 15¢ a word, $35 for color photos, on acceptance. Query with SASE.

ADVENTURE ROAD—See *Road Smart*.

ADVENTURE WEST—P.O. Box 3210, Incline Village, NV 89451. Michael Oliver, Assoc. Ed. Bimonthly. Travel articles, 1,500 to 2,000 words, on risky wild adventures; 1,500 to 2,000 words, on shorter trips; and 1,000 to 1,500 words on short excursions with information on where to stay and what to do. Profiles and essays also used. Emphasis must be on American West, including Alaska, Hawaii, western Canada, and western Mexico. Pays 30¢ a word, on publication.

AIR FAIR: THE MAGAZINE FOR AIRLINE EMPLOYEES— 6401 Congress, #100, Boca Raton, FL 33487. Debra Fredel, Ed. Travel articles, 1,800 words, with photos, on shopping, sightseeing, dining, and nightlife for airline employees. Prices, discount information, and addresses must be included. Pays $250, after publication.

AIR FORCE TIMES—See *Times News Service*.

ARIZONA HIGHWAYS—2039 W. Lewis Ave., Phoenix, AZ 85009. Richard G. Stahl, Man. Ed. Informal, well-researched personal-experience and travel articles, 1,600 to 1,800 words, focusing on a specific city or region in Arizona. Also articles dealing with nature, environment, flora and fauna, history, anthropology, archaeology, hiking. Departments for personal-experience pieces include "Focus on Nature," "Along the Way," "Back Road Adventures," "Hiking," and "Arizona Humor." Pays 35¢ to 55¢ a word, on acceptance. Query with published clips only. Guidelines.

ARMY TIMES—See *Times News Service*.

BIG WORLD—P.O. Box 21, Coraopolis, PA 15108. Jim Fortney, Ed. Bimonthly. Articles, 500 to 4,000 words, that offer advice on working and studying abroad, humorous anecdotes, first-person experiences, or other travel information. "For people who prefer to spend their traveling time responsibly discovering, exploring, and learning, in touch with locals and their traditions, and in harmony with their environment." Pays $10 to $20 for articles, $5 to $20 for photos, on publication.

BLUE RIDGE COUNTRY—P.O. Box 21535, Roanoke, VA 24018. Kurt Rheinheimer, Ed. Regional travel articles, 750 to 1,200 words, on destinations and backroads drives in the mountain regions of VA, NC, WV, TN, KY, MD, SC, and GA. Color slides and B&W prints considered. Pays to $200 for photofeatures, on publication. Queries preferred.

BREW—1120 Mulberry St., Des Moines, IA 50309. Beverly Walsmith, Ed. "Traveling America's Brewpubs and Microbreweries." Bimonthly. Articles, 1,500 to 1,800 words, on new brewpubs around the country. "Our focus is on the brewpub and the community where it is located." Pays 10¢ a word, on publication. Query preferred.

CALIFORNIA HIGHWAY PATROLMAN—2030 V St., Sacramento, CA 95818–1730. Carol Perri, Ed. Travel articles, to 2,000 words, focusing on places in California. "We prefer out-of-the-way stops instead of regular tourist destinations, with possibly a California Highway Patrol tie-in." Query or send complete manuscript with photos (or photo availability). SASE required. Pays 2½¢ a word, $5 for B&W photos, on publication.

CANADIAN DIVER & WATERSPORT—See *Diver Magazine.*

CAR & TRAVEL—1000 AAA Dr., Heathrow, FL 32746–5063. Douglas Damerst, Ed. Articles, 600 to 1,500 words, on consumer automotive and travel concerns. Pays $200 to $800, on acceptance. Query with writing samples required. Articles by assignment only.

CARIBBEAN TRAVEL AND LIFE— 8403 Colesville Rd., Suite 830, Silver Spring, MD 20910. Veronica Gould Stoddart, Ed. Lively, informative articles, 500 to 2,500 words, on all aspects of travel, leisure, recreation, and culture in the Caribbean, Bahamas, and Bermuda, for upscale, sophisticated readers. Photos. Pays $75 to $550, on publication. Query.

CHILE PEPPER—P.O. Box 80780, Albuquerque, NM 87196. Melissa Stock, Man. Ed. First-person food and travel articles, 1,000 to 1,500 words, about spicy world cuisine. Queries required. Payment varies, on publication.

CONDE NAST TRAVELER—360 Madison Ave., New York, NY 10017. Alison Humes, Features Ed. Uses very little free-lance material.

THE COOL TRAVELER—P.O. Box 273, Selinsgrove, PA 17870. Bob Moore, Pub./Ed. Bimonthly. Articles, 800 words, including excerpts from diaries and letters written while traveling. "We emphasize 'what happened' rather than 'what to see.'" Pays to $20, on publication.

CRUISE TRAVEL— 990 Grove St., Evanston, IL 60201. Robert Meyers, Ed. Charles Doherty, Man. Ed. Ship-, port-, and cruise-of-the-month features, 800 to 2,000 words; cruise guides; cruise roundups; cruise company profiles; travel suggestions for one-day port stops. "Photo-features strongly recommended." Payment varies, on acceptance. Query with sample color photos.

DIVER MAGAZINE—295–10991 Shellbridge Way, Richmond, B.C., Canada V6X 3C6. Stephanie Bold, Ed. Illustrated articles, 500 to 1,000 words, on dive destinations. Shorter pieces are also welcome. "Travel features should be brief and accompanied by excellent slides and/or prints and a map. Unsolicited articles will be reviewed only from August to October and will be considered for *Diver Magazine* and *Canadian Diver & Watersport.*" Guidelines. Limited market.

EARLY AMERICAN HOMES—Box 8200, Harrisburg, PA 17105–8200. Mimi Handler, Ed. Travel features about historic sites (pre-1850) and surroundings, 1,500 to 2,500 words. Pays $250 to $500, on acceptance. Query.

ENDLESS VACATION—Box 80260, Indianapolis, IN 46280. Laurie D. Borman, Ed. Travel features, to 1,500 words; primarily on North American destinations, some international destinations. Pays on acceptance. Query preferred. Send SASE for guidelines. Limited market.

FAMILY CIRCLE—110 Fifth Ave., New York, NY 10011. Sylvia Barsotti, Sr. Ed. Travel articles, to 1,500 words. Concept travel pieces should appeal to a national audience and focus on affordable activities for families; prefer service-filled, theme-oriented travel pieces or first-person family vacation stories. Payment varies, on acceptance. Query.

FRIENDLY EXCHANGE—P.O. Box 2120, Warren, MI 48090–2120. Adele Malott, Ed. Articles, 700 to 1,500 words, of interest to active midwestern and western families, on travel, lifestyle, and leisure. "Must have 'people' orientation." Photos. Pays $400 to $1,000, extra for photos. Query required. Guidelines.

GRAND TOUR: THE JOURNAL OF TRAVEL LITERATURE—P.O. Box 66, Thorofare, NJ 08086. Jennifer Fisher, Man. Ed. Quarterly. Travel-related memoirs, essays, and articles, 1,000 to 7,000 words, that "combine the sharp eye of the reporter with the craft of the short story writer and the rhythm of the poet." Pays $50 to $200, on publication.

INDIA CURRENTS—P.O. Box 21285, San Jose, CA 95151. Arvind Kumar, Submissions Ed. First-person accounts, 1,500 words, of trips to India or the subcontinent. Helpful tips for first-time travelers. Prefer descriptions of people-to-people interactions. Pays in subscriptions.

INTERNATIONAL LIVING—105 W. Monument St., Baltimore, MD 21201. Jane Francis Lears, Ed. Dir. Newsletter. Short pieces and features, 200 to 2,000 words, with useful information on investing, shopping, travel, employment, education, real estate, retirement, and lifestyles overseas. Pays $100 to $400, after publication.

ISLANDS—3886 State St., Santa Barbara, CA 93105. Joan Tapper, Ed.-in-Chief. Destination features, 2,500 to 4,000 words, on islands around the world as well as department pieces and front-of-the-book items on island-related topics. Pays from 50¢ a word, on acceptance. Query with clips required. Guidelines.

MICHIGAN LIVING—Automobile Club of Michigan, 1 Auto Club Dr., Dearborn, MI 48126. Len Barnes, Ed. Informative travel articles, 300 to 2,000 words, on U.S. and Canadian tourist attractions and recreational opportunities; special interest in Michigan. Pays $55 to $500 (rates vary for photos), on acceptance.

THE MIDWEST MOTORIST—12901 N. Forty Dr., St. Louis, MO 63141. Michael Right, Ed. Articles, 1,000 to 1,500 words, with color slides, on domestic and foreign travel. Pays from $150, on acceptance.

MOUNTAIN LIVING MAGAZINE—7009 S. Potomac, Englewood, CO 80112. Karen Coe, Ed. Travel articles, 1,200 to 1,500 words, on cities, regions, establishments in the mountainous regions of the U.S. Pays $200 to $300, on acceptance.

NATIONAL GEOGRAPHIC—1145 17th St. N.W., Washington, DC 20036. William Allen, Ed. First-person articles on geography, exploration, natural history, archaeology, and science: 40% staff-written; 60% written by published authors. Does not consider unsolicited manuscripts.

NATIONAL MOTORIST—Bayside Plaza, 188 The Embarcadero, San Francisco, CA 94105. Jane Offers, Ed. Quarterly. Illustrated articles, 500 to 1,100 words, for California motorists, on motoring in the West, domestic and international travel, car care, roads, personalities, places, etc. Color slides. Pays from 10¢ a word, on acceptance. Pays for photos on publication. SASE required.

NAVY TIMES—See *Times News Service.*

NEW WOMAN—215 Lexington Ave., New York, NY 10016. Attn: Manuscripts and Proposals. Travel features with self-growth angle. Pays $1 per word, on acceptance. Query required.

NEW YORK DAILY NEWS— 450 W. 33rd St., New York, NY 10001. Gunna Bitee Dickson, Travel Ed. Articles, 700 to 900 words, on all manner of travel. Price information must be included. B&W or color photos or slides. Pays $100 to $200 (extra for photos), on publication.

THE NEW YORK TIMES—229 W. 43rd St., New York, NY 10036. Nancy Newhouse, Travel Ed. Query with SASE required; include writer's background, description of proposed article. Pays on acceptance.

NORTHWEST REGIONAL MAGAZINES—P.O. Box 18000, Florence, OR 97439. Attn: Judy Fleagle or Jim Forst. All submissions considered for use in *Oregon Coast, Oregon Outside,* and *Northwest Travel..* Articles, 1,200 to 2,000 words, on travel, history, town/city profiles, outdoor activities, and nature. News releases, 200 to 500 words. Articles with slides preferred. Pays $50 to $300, after publication. Guidelines.

NORTHWEST TRAVEL—See *Northwest Regional Magazines.*

OREGON COAST—See *Northwest Regional Magazines.*

OREGON OUTSIDE—See *Northwest Regional Magazines.*

OUT WEST: THE NEWSPAPER THAT ROAMS— 408 Broad St., Suite 11, Nevada City, CA 95959. Chuck Woodbury, Ed./Pub. Entertaining and informative articles, 150 to 750 words, and short pieces, 30 to 75 words, on the rural West (not the old West): interesting people, unusual places to stay, offbeat attractions. "Send for a sample of the paper before you submit." Pays about 5¢ a word, on publication.

OUTDOOR TRAVELER, MID-ATLANTIC—WMS Publications, Inc., P.O. Box 2748, Charlottesville, VA 22902. Marianne Marks, Ed. Scott Clark, Assoc. Ed. Articles, 1,500 to 2,000 words, about outdoor recreation, travel, adventure, and nature in the mid-Atlantic region (NY, PA, NJ, MD, DE, DC, WV, VA, and NC). Departments include "Destinations," 450 to 600 words, on practical and descriptive guides to sports destinations; book reviews, 200 words. Pays $300 to $400 for features; payment varies for departments, on publication. Guidelines.

ROAD SMART—(formerly *Adventure Road*) The Aegis Group, 30400 Van Dyke Ave., Warren, MI 48093. Sallee Spencer, Ed. Official publication of the Amoco Motor Club. Articles, 1,500 words, on destinations in North America, Mexico, and the Caribbean. Photos. Pays $500 to $1,000, on acceptance. Query.

RV WEST MAGAZINE—Vernon Publications, 3000 Northup Way, Suite 200, Bellevue, WA 98009–9643. Sandi Becker, Ed. Travel and destination articles, 750 to 1,750 words, on where to go and what to do in the 13 western states with your recreational vehicle. Color slides or B&W prints must accompany articles. Pays $1.50 per column inch, on publication. Guidelines.

SACRAMENTO MAGAZINE— 4471 D St., Sacramento, CA 95819. Krista Hendricks Minard, Ed. Articles, 1,000 to 1,500 words, on destinations within a 6-hour drive of Sacramento. Pay varies, on publication. Query.

SPECIALTY TRAVEL INDEX—305 San Anselmo Ave., #313, San Anselmo, CA 94960. C. Steen Hansen, Co-Pub./Ed. Semiannual directory of adventure vacation tour companies, destinations, and vacation packages. Articles, 1,000 to 1,200 words, with how-to travel information, humor, and opinion. Pays 20¢ per word, on publication. Slides and photos considered. Queries preferred.

TEXAS HIGHWAYS MAGAZINE—P.O. Box 141009, Austin, TX 78714–1009. Jack Lowry, Ed. Travel, historical, cultural, scenic features on Texas, 200 to 1,800 words. Pays about 40¢ to 50¢ a word; photos $80 to $500. Guidelines.

TIMES NEWS SERVICE—Army Times Publishing Co., Springfield, VA 22159. Attn: R&R Ed. Travel articles, 700 words, on places of special interest to military people for use in "R&R" newspaper section. "We like travel articles to focus on a single destination but with short sidebar covering other things to see in the area." Pays $100, on acceptance. Pays $35 for original color slides or prints. Also, travel pieces, 1,000 words, for supplements to *Army Times*, *Navy Times*, and *Air Force Times*. Address Supplements Ed. Pays $125 to $200, on acceptance. Guidelines.

TRANSITIONS ABROAD—18 Hulst Rd., Box 1300, Amherst, MA 01004–1300. Jason Whitmarsh, Man. Ed. Articles for overseas travelers of all ages who seek an enriching, in-depth experience of the culture: work, study, travel, budget tips. Include practical, first-hand information. Emphasis on travel for personal enrichment. "Eager to work with inexperienced writers who want to share information not usually found in guidebooks. High percentage of material is from free-lancers." B&W photos a plus. Pays $1.50 per column inch, after publication. SASE required. Guidelines and editorial calendar.

TRAVEL AMERICA—World Publishing Co., 990 Grove St., Evanston, IL 60201–4370. Randy Mink, Man. Ed. Robert Meyers, Ed. Features, 800 to 1,200 words, on U.S. vacation destinations. Pays up to $300, on acceptance. Top-quality color slides a must. Query.

TRAVEL & LEISURE—1120 Ave. of the Americas, New York, NY 10036. Nancy Novogrod, Ed.-in-Chief. Articles, 800 to 3,000 words, on destinations and travel-related activities. Regional pieces for regional editions. Short pieces for "Fitness & Health" and "T&L Reports." Pays on acceptance: $2,500 to $5,000 for features; $750 to $1,500 for regionals; $50 to $300 for short pieces. Query; articles on assignment.

TRAVEL SMART—Dobbs Ferry, NY 10522. Attn: Ed. Short pieces, 250 to 1,000 words, about interesting, unusual and/or economical places. Give specific details on hotels, restaurants, transportation, and costs. Pays on publication. "Send manila envelope with 2 first-class stamps for copy and guidelines."

TRAVELERS' TALES, INC.—10 Napier Ln., San Francisco, CA 94133. Attn: Ed. Personal travel stories and anecdotes, to 20 pages, for book anthologies focused on a particular country or theme. Payment varies, on publication. Guidelines.

WESTWAYS—2601 S. Figueroa St., Los Angeles, CA 90007. Attn: Ed. Travel articles, 1,300 to 3,000 words, on where to go, what to see, and how to get there, with an emphasis on southern California and the West. Domestic and foreign travel articles are also of interest. Pays 75¢ a word, on acceptance.

INFLIGHT MAGAZINES

ABOARD—100 Almeria Ave., Suite 220, Coral Gables, FL 33134. Roberto Casin, Ed. Inflight magazine of 11 Latin American international airlines in Chile, Dominican Republic, Ecuador, Guatemala, El Salvador, Bolivia, Nicaragua, Honduras, Uruguay, and Paraguay. Articles, 1,200 to 1,500 words, with photos, on these countries and on science, sports, technology, adventure, wildlife, fashion, business, ecology, and gastronomy. No political stories. Pays $150, on acceptance and on publication. Query required.

ALASKA AIRLINES MAGAZINE—2701 First Ave., Suite 250, Seattle, WA 98121. Paul Frichtl, Ed. Articles, 250 to 2,500 words, on business, travel, and profiles of regional personalities for West Coast business travelers. Payment varies, on publication. Query.

AMERICA WEST AIRLINES MAGAZINE—Skyword Marketing Inc., 4636 E. Elwood St., Suite 5, Phoenix, AZ 85040–1963. Michael Derr, Ed. Business articles, destination pieces, arts and culture, 500 to 2,000 words; thoughtful but light essays. Pays from $250, on publication. Clips and SASE required. Guidelines. Very limited market.

AMERICAN WAY—P.O. Box 619640, DFW Airport, TX 75261–9640. John Ostdick, Ed. American Airlines' inflight magazine. No unsolicited material.

EXCURSIONS—SCG, Inc., 5110 N. 44th St., Suite 210-L, Phoenix, AZ 85018. Lisa Polacheck, Ed. Inflight magazine for Reno Air. Destination features, 600 to 1,600 words, with relevant, vibrant photos. Send SASE for current destinations and pay rates. Payment varies, on publication. Query required.

HEMISPHERES—1301 Carolina St., Greensboro, NC 27401. Kate Greer, Ed.-in-Chief. United Airlines inflight magazine. Articles, 1,200 to 1,500 words, on business, investing, travel, sports, family, food and wine, etc., that inform and entertain sophisticated, well-traveled readers. "The magazine strives for a unique global perspective presented in a fresh, strong, and artful graphic environment." Pays good rates, on acceptance. Query. Guidelines.

HORIZON AIR MAGAZINE—2701 First Ave., #250, Seattle, WA 98121–1123. Todd Powell, Ed. Business and travel articles on the companies, people, issues, and trends that define the Northwest. News items, 200 to 500 words, and profiles for "The Region" section. Other departments pieces, 1,600 words, cover corporate and industry profiles, regional issue analysis, travel, and community profiles. Pays $100 to $600, on publication.

IN-FLIGHT—SCG, Inc., 5110 N. 44th St., Suite 210-L, Phoenix, AZ 85018. Lisa Polacheck, Ed. Serves KIWI International Airlines and Air South Airlines. Destination-related features, 600 to 1,600 words, with photos. Columns cover trivia, self-improvement, poignant success stories, and whimsical compositions. Send SASE for current destinations. Payment varies, on publication.

SKYVIEW—SCG, Inc., 5110 N. 44th St., Suite 210-L, Phoenix, AZ 85018. Lisa Polacheck, Ed. Magazine of Western Pacific Airlines, serving Denver/Colorado Springs, and various West Coast and Midwest destinations. Destination-related articles, 600 to 1,600 words, with photos. Columns cover money, sports, fashion, and whimsy. Send SASE for current destinations. Payment varies, on publication.

USAIR MAGAZINE—New York Times Custom Publishing, 122 E. 42 St., 14th Fl., New York, NY 10168. Catherine Sabino, Ed. Kathy Passero, Man. Ed. Articles on travel, lifestyle trends, sports, personality profiles, food and wine, shopping, the arts and culture. "Our goal is to provide readers with lively and colorful, yet practical articles that will make their lives and their leisure time more rewarding." Pays good rates, within 60 days of acceptance. Query with clips and SASE; no unsolicited manuscripts or faxes.

WOMEN'S PUBLICATIONS

ASPIRE—107 Kenner Ave., Nashville, TN 37205. Jeanette Thomason, Ed.-in-Chief. Lifestyle magazine for Christian women. Articles, 500 to 2,000 words, on trends in health, career issues, parenting, and relationships, "inspiring and encouraging readers to incorporate faith into daily life." Pays 30¢ a word, on acceptance. Query with resumé and clips. SASE for guidelines.

BBW: BIG BEAUTIFUL WOMAN—8484 Wilshire Blvd., Suite 900, Beverly Hills, CA 90211. Janey Milstead, Ed.-in-Chief. Articles, 1,500 words, of interest to women ages 25 to 50, especially large-size women, including interviews with successful large-size women and personal accounts of how to cope with difficult situations. Tips on restaurants, airlines, stores, etc., that treat large women with respect. Payment varies, on publication. Query.

BRIDAL GUIDE—Globe Communications Corp., 3 E. 54th St., New York, NY 10022. Diane Forden, Ed.-in-Chief. Cherylann Coutts, Travel Ed. Bimonthly. Articles, 1,500 to 3,000 words, on relationships, sexuality, health and nutrition, psychology, travel, and finance. No wedding planning, beauty, fashion articles; no fiction, essays, poetry. Pays on acceptance. Query with SASE.

BRIDE'S—(formerly *Bride's & Your New Home*) 140 E. 45th St., New York, NY 10017. Sally Kilbridge, Man. Ed. Articles, 800 to 3,000 words, for engaged couples or newlyweds, on wedding planning, relationships, communication, sex, decorating, finances, careers, remarriage, health, birth control, religion, in-laws. Major editorial subjects: home, wedding, and honeymoon (send honeymoon queries to Travel Dept.). No fiction or poetry. Pays from 50¢ a word, on acceptance.

COMPLETE WOMAN—875 N. Michigan Ave., Suite 3434, Chicago, IL 60611. Bonnie L. Krueger, Ed. Martha Carlson, Assoc. Ed. Articles, 1,000 to 2,000 words, with how-to sidebars, giving practical advice to women on love, sex, careers, health, personal relationships, etc. Also interested in reprints. Pays varying rates, on publication. Query with clips.

COSMOPOLITAN—224 W. 57th St., New York, NY 10019. Helen Gurley Brown, Ed. Betty Nichols Kelly, Fiction and Books Ed. Articles, to 3,000 words, and features, 500 to 2,000 words, on issues affecting young career women, with emphasis on jobs and personal life. Fiction on male-female relationships: short shorts, 1,500 to 3,000 words; short stories, 3,000 to 4,000 words; condensed published novels, 25,000 words. SASE required. Payment varies.

COUNTRY WOMAN—P.O. Box 989, Greendale, WI 53129. Kathy Pohl, Man. Ed. Profiles of country women (photo-feature packages), inspirational, reflective pieces. Personal-experience, nostalgia, humor, service-oriented articles, original crafts, and how-to features, to 1,000 words, of interest to country women. Pays $25 to $75 for crafts, humor, nostalgia; pays $150 for photo-features, on acceptance.

THE CREATIVE WOMAN—TAPP Group, 126 E. Wing, Suite 288, Arlington Hts., IL 60004. Margaret Choudhury, Ed. Quarterly. Essays, fiction, poetry, criticism, graphic arts, and photography, from a feminist perspective. Send SASE for upcoming themes. Payment varies, on publication.

ELLE—1633 Broadway, New York, NY 10019. Amy Gross, Ed. Dir. Articles, varying lengths, for fashion-conscious women, ages 20 to 50. Subjects include beauty, health, fitness, travel, entertainment, and lifestyles. Pays top rates, on publication. Query required.

ESSENCE—1500 Broadway, New York, NY 10036. Susan L. Taylor, Ed.-in-Chief. Linda Villarosa, Exec. Ed. Provocative articles, 800 to 2,500 words, about black women in America today: self-help, how-to pieces, business and finance, work, parenting, health, celebrity profiles, art, travel, and political issues. Fiction, 800 to 2,500 words. Pays varying rates, on acceptance. Query for articles.

EXECUTIVE FEMALE—30 Irving Pl., New York, NY 10003. Gay Bryant, Ed.-in-Chief. Articles, 750 to 2,500 words, on managing people, time, money, companies, and careers, for women in business. Pays varying rates, on acceptance. Query.

FAMILY CIRCLE—110 Fifth Ave., New York, NY 10011. Nancy Clark, Deputy Ed. Articles, to 2,000 words, on "women who have made a difference," marriage, family, and child-care and elder-care issues; consumer affairs, psychology, humor, health, nutrition, and fitness. Pays top rates, on acceptance. Query required.

GLAMOUR—350 Madison Ave., New York, NY 10017. Pamela Erens, Articles Ed. Ruth Whitney, Ed.-in-Chief. Laurie Sprague, Man. Ed. Articles, from 1,500 words, on careers, health, psychology, politics, current events, interpersonal relationships, etc., for women ages 18 to 35. Fashion, entertainment, travel, food, and beauty pieces staff-written. Pays from $500, on acceptance. Query Articles Ed.

GOOD HOUSEKEEPING—959 Eighth Ave., New York, NY 10019. Evelyn Renold, Articles Ed. Lee Quarfoot, Fiction Ed. Articles, about 2,500 words, for married working women with children, 18 and under. Social issues, dramatic personal narratives, medical news, marriage, friendship, psychology, crime, finances, work, parenting, and consumer issues. Best places to break in: "Better Way" (short, advice-driven takes on health, money, safety, and consumer issues) and profiles (short takes on interesting or heroic women or families). No submissions on food, beauty, needlework, or crafts. Short stories, 2,000 to 5,000 words, with strong identification for women. Unsolicited fiction not returned; if no response in 6 weeks, assume work was unsuitable. Pays top rates, on acceptance. Guidelines. Query with SASE for nonfiction.

HARPER'S BAZAAR—1700 Broadway, 37th Fl., New York, NY 10019. Elizabeth Tilberis, Ed.-in-Chief. Articles, 1,500 to 2,500 words, for active, sophisticated women: the arts, world affairs, travel, families, education, careers, health, and sexuality. Payment varies, on acceptance. No unsolicited manuscripts; query with SASE.

IOWA WOMAN—P.O. Box 680, Iowa City, IA 52244. Joan Taylor, Ed. Fiction, poetry, creative nonfiction, book reviews, and personal essays; articles, to 6,500 words, on women in the arts and in midwestern history; interviews with prominent women; current social, economic, artistic, and environmental issues. Poems, any length (submit up to 5); photos and drawings. Pays $5 a page, $15 for illustrations, on publication. Queries preferred for articles. Guidelines.

578

THE JOYFUL WOMAN—P.O. Box 90028, Chattanooga, TN 37412. Joy Rice Martin, Ed. Joanna Rice, Ed. Asst. Fiction, 500 to 1,200 words, for women with a "Christian commitment." Also first-person inspirational true stories, profiles of Christian women, practical and Bible-oriented how-to articles. Pays 3¢ to 4¢ a word, on publication. Queries required.

LADIES' HOME JOURNAL—125 Park Ave., New York, NY 10017. Myrna Blyth, Pub. Dir./Ed.-in-Chief. Articles of interest to women. Send queries to: Susan Crandell, Articles Ed. (news/general interest); Debbie Pike, Ed. (health/medical); Melina Gerosa, Ed. (celebrity/entertainment); Pamela Guthrie O'Brien, Features Ed. (sex/psychology); Lois Johnson, Beauty Dir. (beauty/fashion/fitness); Jan Hazard, Food Ed.; Shana Aborn, Features Ed. (personal experience); Mary Mohler, Sr. Ed. (children and families). Fiction accepted through literary agents only. True, first-person accounts, 1,000 words, "about the most intimate aspects of our lives" for anonymous "Woman to Woman": Submit typed, double-spaced manuscript with SASE to Box WW, c/o address above; pays $750. Guidelines.

MCCALL'S—110 Fifth Ave., New York, NY 10011. Attn: Articles Ed. Human-interest, self-help, social issues, and popular psychology articles, 1,200 to 2,000 words. Also publishes "Love Lessons," first person essays, 1,400 words; "Families," how-to articles, 1,400 words; "Health Sense," short newsy items; and "Medical Report," health-related items, 1,200 words. Query with SASE. Payment varies, on acceptance.

MADEMOISELLE—350 Madison Ave., New York, NY 10017. Faye Haun, Man. Ed. Articles, 1,500 to 2,500 words, on work, relationships, health, and trends of interest to single, working women in their early to mid-twenties. Reporting pieces, essays, first-person accounts, and humor. No how-to or fiction. Submit query with clips and SASE. Pays excellent rates, on acceptance.

MODERN BRIDE—249 W. 17th St., New York, NY 10011. Mary Ann Cavlin, Exec. Ed. Articles, 1,500 to 2,000 words, for bride and groom, on wedding planning, financial planning, juggling career and home, etc. Pays $600 to $1,200, on acceptance.

MS.—230 Park Ave., 7th Fl., New York, NY 10169. Attn: Manuscript Ed. Articles relating to feminism, women's roles, and social change; national and international news reporting, profiles, essays, theory, and analysis. No fiction or poetry accepted, acknowledged, or returned. Query with resumé and published clips.

NA'AMAT WOMAN—200 Madison Ave., Suite 2120, New York, NY 10016. Judith A. Sokoloff, Ed. Articles on Jewish culture, women's issues, social and political topics, and Israel, 1,500 to 3,000 words. Short stories with a Jewish theme. Pays 10¢ a word, on publication.

NATURAL LIVING TODAY—175 Varick St., 9th Fl., New York, NY 10014. Attn: Ed. Dept. Bimonthly. Articles, 1,000 to 2,000 words, on all aspects of a natural lifestyle for women. Pays $75 to $200, on publication. Query.

NEW WOMAN—215 Lexington Ave., New York, NY 10016. Attn: Manuscripts and Proposals. Articles for women ages 25 to 49, on self-discovery, self-development, and self-esteem. Features: relationships, careers, health and fitness, money, fashion, beauty, food and nutrition, travel features with self-growth angle, and essays by and about women pacesetters. Pays about $1 a word, on acceptance. Query with SASE.

ON THE ISSUES—Choices Women's Medical Ctr., Inc., 97–77 Queens Blvd., Forest Hills, NY 11374–3317. Ronni Sandroff, Ed. "The Progressive Woman's Quarterly." Articles, to 2,500 words, on political or social issues. Movie, music, and book reviews, 500 to 750 words. Payment varies, on publication. Query.

PLAYGIRL— 801 Second Ave., New York, NY 10017. Judy Cole, Ed.-in-Chief. Erotic entertainment for women. Insightful articles on sexuality and romance; sizzling fiction, humor, and in-depth celebrity interviews of interest to contemporary women. Pays varying rates, after acceptance. Query with clips. Guidelines.

RADIANCE: THE MAGAZINE FOR LARGE WOMEN—P.O. Box 30246, Oakland, CA 94604. Alice Ansfield, Ed./Pub. Quarterly. Articles, 1,500 to 3,500 words, that provide information, inspiration, and resources for women all sizes of large. Features include information on health, media, fashion, and politics that relate to issues of body size. Fiction and poetry also welcome. Pays to $100, on publication.

REDBOOK—224 W. 57th St., New York, NY 10019. Harriet Lyons, Sr. Ed. Dawn Raffel, Fiction Ed. Toni Hope, Sr. Ed. For mothers, ages 25 to 45. Short stories, 10 to 15 typed pages; dramatic inspirational narratives, 1,000 to 2,000 words. SASE required. Pays on acceptance. Query with writing samples for articles. Guidelines.

SAGEWOMAN—P.O. Box 641, Point Arena, CA 95468–0641. Anne Newkirk Niven, Ed. Quarterly. Articles, 200 to 5,000 words, on issues of concern to pagan and spiritually minded women. Material which expresses an earth-centered spirituality: personal experience, scholarly research, Goddess lore, ritual material, interviews, humor, and reviews. Accepts material by women only. Pays 3¢ a word, from $10, on publication.

SELF—350 Madison Ave., New York, NY 10017. Attn: Ed. "We no longer accept unsolicited manuscripts or queries."

TODAY'S CHRISTIAN WOMAN— 465 Gundersen Dr., Carol Stream, IL 60188. Ramona Cramer Tucker, Ed. Articles, 1,500 to 1,800 words, that are "warm and personal in tone, full of real-life anecdotes that deal with marriage, parenting, friendship, spiritual life, single life, health, work, and self." Humorous anecdotes, 150 words, that have a Christian slant. Payment varies, on acceptance. Queries required. Guidelines.

VIRTUE— 4050 Lee Vance View, Colorado Springs, CO 80918–7102. Jeanette Thomason, Ed. Articles and fiction, 1,200 to 1,400 words, on family, marriage, self-esteem, working women, humor, women's spiritual journeys, issues, relationship with family, friends and God. "Provocative, meaningful stories, especially those with bold messages shown in gracious ways." Pays 15¢ to 25¢ a word for articles; $25 to $50 for poetry, on publication. Submit up to 3 poems at a time. Query with SASE required.

VOGUE—350 Madison Ave., New York, NY 10017. Attn: Features Ed. Articles, to 1,500 words, on women, entertainment and the arts, travel, medicine, and health. General features. Pays good rates, on acceptance. Query; no unsolicited manuscripts.

WOMAN'S DAY— 1633 Broadway, New York, NY 10019. Rebecca Greer, Sr. Articles Ed. Human-interest or helpful articles, to 2,000 words, on marriage, child-rearing, health, careers, relationships, money management. Dramatic first-person narratives of medical miracles, rescues, women's experiences, etc. "We respond to queries promptly; unsolicited manuscripts are returned unread." SASE. Pays top rates, on acceptance.

WOMAN'S OWN—1115 Broadway, New York, NY 10010. Estelle Sobel, Ed. Articles, 1,500 to 2,000 words, offering inspirational and practical advice on relationships and career and lifestyle choices for women 25 to 35. Common subjects: staying together, second marriages, working women, asserting yourself, meeting new men, "love-styles," sex, etc. Columns, 800 words, for "Suddenly Single," "Moving Up," "Round-Up," "Mindpower," "Dieter's Notes," "Fashion Advisor," and "Financial Advisor." Profiles, 250 to 500 words, of women who have overcome great odds for "Woman in the News." Fun, in-depth quizzes. Short pieces on trends and breakthroughs for "Let's Put Our Heads Together." Query. Pays $100 to $300, on acceptance.

WOMAN'S TOUCH—1445 Boonville, Springfield, MO 65802–1894. Peggy Musgrove, Ed. Aleda Swartzendruber, Assoc. Ed. Inspirational articles, 500 to 1,000 words, for Christian women. Pays on acceptance. Allow 3 months for response. Submit complete manuscript. Guidelines and editorial calendar.

WOMAN'S WORLD—270 Sylvan Ave., Englewood Cliffs, NJ 07632. Andrea Bien, Feature Ed. Articles, 600 to 1,800 words, of interest to middle-income women between the ages of 18 and 60, on love, romance, careers, medicine, health, psychology, family life, travel; dramatic stories of adventure or crisis, investigative reports. Fast-moving short stories, about 1,900 words, with light romantic theme. (Specify "short story" on outside of envelope.) Mini-mysteries, 1,200 words, with "whodunit" or "howdunit" theme. No science fiction, fantasy, horror, ghost stories, or gratuitous violence. Pays $300 to $900 for articles; $1,000 for short stories; $500 for mini-mysteries, on acceptance. Query for articles. Guidelines.

WOMEN IN BUSINESS—American Business Women's Assn., 9100 Ward Pkwy., Box 8728, Kansas City, MO 64114–0728. Dawn J. Grubb, Assoc. Ed. How-to business features, 1,000 to 1,500 words, for working women ages 35 to 55, business trends, small-business ownership, self-improvement, and retirement issues. Profiles of ABWA members only. Pays on acceptance. Query required.

WOMEN'S CIRCLE—P.O. Box 299, Lynnfield, MA 01940. Marjorie Pearl, Ed. Success stories on home-based female entrepreneurs. How-to articles on contemporary craft and needlework projects. Unique money-saving ideas and recipes. Pays varying rates, on acceptance.

WOMEN'S SPORTS + FITNESS—170 E. 61st St., 6th Fl., New York, NY 10021. Mary Duffy, Ed. Articles on fitness, nutrition, outdoor sports; how-tos; profiles; adventure travel pieces; and controversial issues in women's sports, 500 to 2,000 words. Pays on publication.

WORKING MOTHER—Lang Communications, 230 Park Ave., New York, NY 10169. Attn: Ed. Dept. Articles, to 2,000 words, that help women in their task of juggling job, home, and family. "We like pieces that solve or illuminate a problem unique to our readers." Payment varies, on acceptance.

WORKING WOMAN—230 Park Ave., New York, NY 10169. Articles, 350 to 2,500 words, on business and personal aspects of the lives of executive and managerial women and entrepreneurs. Pays from $300, on acceptance.

MEN'S PUBLICATIONS

ESQUIRE—250 W. 55th St., New York, NY 10019. Edward Kosner, Ed.-in-Chief. David Hirshey, Deputy Ed. Articles, 2,500 to 4,000 words, for intelligent audience. Pays varying rates, on acceptance. Query with clips and SASE.

GALLERY— 401 Park Ave. S., New York, NY 10016–8802. Barry Janoff, Ed.-in-Chief. Rich Friedman, Man. Ed. Articles, investigative pieces, interviews, profiles, to 2,500 words, for sophisticated men. Short humor, satire, service pieces, and fiction. Photos. Query. Guidelines.

GENRE—7080 Hollywood Blvd., Suite 1104, Hollywood, CA 90028. John Polly, Assoc. Ed. Fiction, 3,000 to 5,000 words, and articles, 750 to 3,000 words, of interest to gay men. "Feature articles should be national in scope and somehow related to the gay male experience." Pays to 50¢ a word, on publication.

GQ—350 Madison Ave., New York, NY 10017. No free-lance queries or manuscripts.

THE GREEN MAN—P.O. Box 641, Point Arena, CA 95468–0641. Diane Conn Darling, Ed. "Exploring Paths for Pagan Men." Articles, 1,500 to 5,000 words, exploring a theme. Future themes include: "The Goddess," "Service," "Wisdom of the Beasts," and "Man's Body." No payment. Query for more information.

MEN'S FITNESS—21100 Erwin St., Woodland Hills, CA 91367. Attn: Ed. Authoritative and practical articles, 1,500 to 1,800 words, and department pieces, 1,200 to 1,500 words, on sports, fitness, health, nutrition, and men's issues. Pays $500 to $1,000, on acceptance.

MEN'S HEALTH—Rodale Press, 33 E. Minor St., Emmaus, PA 18098. Steve Perrine, Articles Ed. Articles, 1,000 to 2,500 words, on fitness, diet, health, relationships, sports, and travel for men ages 25 to 55. Pays from 50¢ a word, on acceptance. Query.

NEW MAN— 600 Rinehart Rd., Lake Mary, FL 32746. Brian Peterson, Ed. Articles, to 2,000 words, that help men "in their quest for godliness and integrity." Profiles of everyday men who are doing something extraordinary, action-packed thrill and adventure articles, trend pieces that take an in-depth look at issues facing men today. Short items, 50 to 250 words, on unusual facts, motivational quotes, perspectives on news and events. Pays 10¢ to 35¢ per word, on publication.

PENTHOUSE—277 Park Ave., 4th Fl., New York, NY 10172–0003. Peter Bloch, Ed. Lavada B. Nahon, Sr. Ed. General-interest profiles, interviews, or investigative articles, to 5,000 words. No unsolicited fiction. Pays on acceptance.

PLAYBOY— 680 N. Lake Shore Dr., Chicago, IL 60611. Peter Moore, Stephen Randall, Eds. Articles, 3,500 to 6,000 words, and sophisticated fiction, 1,000 to 10,000 words (5,000 preferred), for urban men. (Address fiction to Attn: Fiction Ed.) Humor; satire. Science fiction. Pays to $5,000 for articles and fiction, $2,000 for short-shorts, on acceptance. SASE required.

ROBB REPORT—1 Acton Pl., Acton, MA 01720. Robert R. Feeman, Ed. Upscale lifestyle magazine for men. Feature articles and regular columns on investment opportunities, exotic cars, classic and collectible autos, yachts, fashion, travel, investibles and collectibles, technology, business profiles, etc., emphasizing luxurious lifestyles. Pays on publication. Query with SASE and clips.

SENIORS MAGAZINES

AARP BULLETIN— 601 E St. N.W., Washington, DC 20049. Elliot Carlson, Ed. Publication of the American Association of Retired Persons. Payment varies, on acceptance. Query required.

ANSWERS: THE MAGAZINE FOR ADULT CHILDREN OF AGING PARENTS—75 Seabreeze Dr., Richmond, CA 94804. Susan R. Keller, Ed./Pub. Features, 1,000 to 1,200 words, "written on specific topics with a step-by-step approach to improving an individual's caregiving experience." Columns, 800 words, on medication concerns, insurance, legal affairs, emotions, housing issues, products, and health and nutrition. News and book reviews, 50 to 100 words. Payment varies, on publication. Query with outline. Guidelines.

50 AND FORWARD—160 Mayo Rd., Suite 100, Edgewater, MD 21037. Debra Asberry, Ed./Pub. Fiction, 3,000 words, that can be serialized over 3 issues; articles, 800 to 1,200 words; fillers; and B&W art. "Readers are very active, 50 years old and over." Pays $25 and up, on acceptance.

FLORIDA RETIREMENT LIFESTYLES—Gidder House Publishing, Inc., P.O. Box 66, Mount Dora, FL 32757–0066. Mr. Kerry Smith, Ed. Concise and direct articles, 800 to 1,500 words, that address the issues and concerns of people contemplating a move to Florida for their retirement: financial strategies, retirement communities, recreation, sports, volunteer and educational opportunities, etc. Pays 10¢ a word (to $100), on publication.

GOOD TIMES—Senior Publications, Inc., 5148 Saint-Laurent Blvd., Montreal, Quebec, Canada H2T 1R8. Denise B. Crawford, Ed.-in-Chief. Judy Wayland, Asst. Ed. "The Canadian Magazine for Successful Retirement." Celebrity profiles as well as practical articles on health, beauty, cuisine, hobbies, fashion, leisure activities, travel, taxes, legal rights, consumer protection, etc. Payment varies. Query.

GRAND TIMES— 403 Village Dr., El Cerrito, CA 94530–3355. Kira Albin, Man. Ed. Articles and fiction, 600 to 1,800 words, for active retirees in the San Francisco Bay area. "We strive to inform, inspire, and entertain. No articles that play on ageist stereotypes." Pays $10 to $35, on acceptance. Guidelines.

LIFE LINES—129 N. 10th St., Rm. 241, Lincoln, NE 68508–3648. Dena Rust Zimmer, Ed. Short stories, "Sports and Hobbies," "Remember When . . . ," "Travels With . . . ," and "Perspectives on Aging," to 450 words. Poetry, to 50 lines. Fillers and short humor, "the shorter the better." No payment.

MATURE LIFESTYLES—15951 McGregor Blvd., #2D, Ft. Myers, FL 33908. Linda Heffley, Ed. Articles, 500 to 1,200 words, for readers over 50 in Florida. No fiction or poetry. Pays $45 to $75, on publication.

MATURE LIFESTYLES—P.O. Box 44327, Madison, WI 53744. Tracy Siemion, Ed. "South Central Wisconsin's Newspaper for the Active 50-Plus Population." Fillers, humor, jokes, and puzzles. No payment.

MATURE LIVING—127 Ninth Ave. N., Nashville, TN 37234–0140. Al Shackleford, Ed. Fiction and human-interest articles, to 1,200 words, for senior adults. Must be consistent with Christian principles. Payment varies, on acceptance.

MATURE OUTLOOK—Meredith Corp., 1912 Grand Ave., Des Moines, IA 50309–3379. Peggy Person, Assoc. Ed. Bimonthly. Upbeat, contemporary articles, varying lengths, for readers 50 and older, travel and leisure topics. Regular columns cover health, money, food, gardening, travel, and stories of real people, 300 to 1,000 words. Pays $125 to $1,000, on acceptance. Query required. Guidelines.

MATURE YEARS—201 Eighth Ave. S., P.O. Box 801, Nashville, TN 37202. Marvin W. Cropsey, Ed. Articles of interest to older adults: health and fitness, personal finance, hobbies and inspiration. Anecdotes, to 300 words, poems, cartoons, jokes, and puzzles for older adults. "A Christian magazine that seeks to build faith. We always show older adults in a favorable light." Include name, address, and social security number with all submissions. Allow 2 months for response.

MILESTONES—246 S. 22nd St., Philadelphia, PA 19103. Cathy Green, Ed. Robert Epp, Dir. Tabloid published 10 times a year. News articles and features, 750 to 1,000 words, on humor, personalities, political issues, etc., for readers 50 and older. Pays $25 for articles, $10 for photos, on publication.

MODERN MATURITY—3200 E. Carson St., Lakewood, CA 90712. J. Henry Fenwick, Ed. Articles, to 2,000 words, on careers, workplace, human interest, living, finance, relationships, and consumerism for readers over 50. Query. Pays $500 to $2,500, on acceptance.

NEW CHOICES FOR RETIREMENT LIVING—See *New Choices: Living Even Better After 50.*

NEW CHOICES: LIVING EVEN BETTER AFTER 50—(formerly *New Choices for Retirement Living*) 28 W. 23rd St., New York, NY 10010. David A. Sendler, Ed.-in-Chief. News and service magazine for people ages 50 to 65. Articles on planning for retirement, health and fitness, financial strategies, housing options, travel, profiles/interviews (celebrities and newsmakers), relationships, leisure pursuits, etc. Payment varies, on acceptance. Query or send complete manuscript.

NEW JERSEY 50+ PLUS—1830 US Rt. 9, Toms River, NJ 08755–1210. Pat Jasin, Ed. Articles on finance, health, travel, and social issues for older readers. Pays in copies. Query required.

RETIRED MILITARY FAMILY—169 Lexington Ave., New York, NY 10016. Stacy P. Brassington, Ed. Articles, 1,000 to 1,500 words, on travel, finance, food, hobbies, second careers, grandparenting, and other topics of interest to military retirees and their families. Pays to $200, on publication.

THE RETIRED OFFICER MAGAZINE—201 N. Washington St., Alexandria, VA 22314. Attn: Manuscripts Ed. Articles, 800 to 2,000 words, of interest to military members and their families. Current military/political affairs, recent military history (especially Vietnam and Korea), military family lifestyles, health, money, second careers. Photos a plus. Pays to $1,000, on acceptance. Queries required. Guidelines.

RX REMEDY—120 Post Rd. W., Westport, CT 06880. Val Weaver, Ed. Bimonthly. Articles, 600 to 2,500 words, on health and medication issues for readers 55 and older. Regular columns include "Housecall" and "The Nutrition Prescription." Query. Pays $1 to $1.25 a word, on acceptance.

584

SENIOR BEACON—P.O. Box 40126, Georgetown, TX 78628. Carolyn Keeling, Ed. Poetry, to 100 words, and short (one- or 2-line) fillers for seniors in Texas. No payment.

SENIOR HIGHLIGHTS—26081 Merit Cir., Suite 101, Laguna Hills, CA 92653. Julie Puckett, Asst. Ed. Articles, 800 words, on health, money, lifestyles, and travel. Responds within 3 months. No payment. Queries preferred. Responds within 3 months. Guidelines.

SENIOR MAGAZINE—3565 S. Higuera St., San Luis Obispo, CA 93401. Attn: Ed. Articles, 600 to 900 words, of interest to men and women 40+; personality profiles, travel pieces, articles about new things, places, business, sports, movies, television, and health. Reviews of new or outstanding older books. Pays $1.50 per inch; $10 to $25 for B&W photos, on publication.

SENIOR TIMES—Suite 814, 1102 Pleasant St., Worcester, MA 01602–1232. Edwin H. Gledhill, Ed. Short stories, historial or people oriented, 500 to 1,200 words. Articles, 500 to 1,200 words, on arts, travel, local interest, entertainment, and positive role models for aging. Poetry, 10 to 200 words. No payment.

SENIOR WORLD NEWSMAGAZINE—1000 Pioneer Way, El Cajon, CA 92020–1923. Laura Impastato, Ed. Articles, 800 to 1,000 words, for active, older adults (55+); focus is on Southern California. Articles on local, state and national news. Features about celebrities, remarkable seniors, consumer interest, finance and investment, housing, sports, hobbies, collectibles, trends, travel, etc. Health and medicine articles emphasizing wellness, preventive care, and the latest on medical treatments. Pays $75 to $100, on publication.

WESTCOAST REFLECTIONS—2604 Quadra St., Victoria, BC, Canada V8T 4E4. Jane Kezar, Assoc. Ed. Published 10 times a year "for those 39 and holding." Upbeat, humorous, positive articles, 700 to 1,200 words, on travel, recreation, health and fitness, hobbies, home and garden, cooking, finance, and continuing education. Occasionally uses more serious pieces on housing, finances, and health. Nothing political or religious. "The articles we publish are not necessarily about people over 50, but are for them. Writing style should reflect this; use terminology understood by the mature reader." Pays 10¢ a word, on publication. Queries preferred. Guidelines.

YESTERDAY'S MAGAZETTE—P.O. Box 18566, Sarasota, FL 34276. Ned Burke, Ed. Articles and stories, 500 to 1,000 words, set in the 1920s to '70s. Photos a plus. Traditional poetry, to 24 lines. Pays $5 to $25 for articles, on publication. Pays in copies for short pieces and poetry.

HOME & GARDEN/FOOD & WINE

AFRICAN VIOLET MAGAZINE—2375 North St., Beaumont, TX 77702. Ruth Rumsey, Ed. Articles, 700 to 1,400 words, on growing methods for African violets; history and personal experience with African violets. Violet-related poetry. No payment.

THE AMERICAN COTTAGE GARDENER—P.O. Box 22232, Santa Fe, NM 87502–2232. Rand B. Lee, Ed. Quarterly. Articles, 750 to 3,000 words for cottage gardeners: how-to; plant profiles of specific genera or cultivars; interviews with noted or experienced cottage gardeners, plant breeders, and other specialists. "Topics we're always interested in: regional and ethnic cot-

585

tage gardening, unusual plants adaptable to the cottage gardening style, fruits and vegetables in the ornamental plot." Pays in copies. Queries required.

THE AMERICAN GARDENER—(formerly *American Horticulturist*) 7931 E. Boulevard Dr., Alexandria, VA 22308–1300. Kathleen Fisher, Ed. Bimonthly. Articles, to 2,500 words, for American ornamental gardeners: profiles of prominent horticulturists, plant research and plant hunting, events and personalities in horticulture history, plant lore and literature, the politics of horticulture, etc. Humorous pieces for "Offshoots." "We run very few how-to articles." Pays $100 to $400, on publication. Query preferred.

AMERICAN HORTICULTURIST—See *The American Gardener.*

AMERICAN ROSE—P.O. Box 30,000, Shreveport, LA 71130. Beth Horstman, Man. Ed. Articles on home rose gardens: varieties, products, helpful advice, rose care, etc.

APPELLATION—(formerly *Napa Valley Appellation*) P.O. Box 516, Napa, CA 94559. Antonia Allegra, Ed.-in-Chief. Quarterly. Articles, 900 to 1,500 words, on the lifestyles, wines, and gardens of the international wine country regions. Pays $200 to $500, on acceptance.

BETTER HOMES AND GARDENS—1716 Locust St., Des Moines, IA 50309–3023. Jean LemMon, Ed. Articles, to 2,000 words, on money management, health, travel, and cars. Pays top rates, on acceptance. Query.

BON APPETIT—6300 Wilshire Blvd., Los Angeles, CA 90048. Barbara Fairchild, Exec. Ed. Articles on fine cooking (menu format or single focus), cooking classes, and gastronomically focused travel. Query with clips. Pays varying rates, on acceptance.

BRIDE'S—(formerly *Bride's & Your New Home*) 140 E. 45th St., New York, NY 10017. Sally Kilbridge, Man. Ed. Articles, 800 to 2,000 words, for engaged couples or newlyweds on wedding planning, home and decorating, and honeymoon. No fiction or poetry. Send travel queries to Travel Dept. Pay starts at 50¢ per word, on acceptance.

CANADIAN GARDENING—130 Spy Ct., Markham, Ont., Canada L3R 0W5. Rebecca Hanes-Fox, Man. Ed. Features, 1,200 to 2,500 words, that help avid home gardeners solve problems or inspire them with garden ideas. How-to pieces, to 1,000 words, on garden projects; include introduction and step-by-step instructions. Profiles of gardens, to 2,000 words. Department pieces, 200 to 400 words, for "Gardeners' Journal." Pays $75 to $700, on acceptance. Queries preferred.

CANADIAN SELECT HOMES MAGAZINE—25 Sheppard Ave. W., Suite 100, North York, Ont., Canada M2N 6S7. Barbara Dixon, Ed. How-to articles, profiles of Canadian homes, renovation, decor, and gardening features, 800 to 1,500 words. Canadian content and locations only. Pays from $400 to $900 (Canadian), on acceptance. Query with international reply coupons. Send SAE with international reply coupons for guidelines.

CANADIAN WORKSHOP MAGAZINE—130 Spy Ct., Markham, Ont., Canada L3R 5H6. Hugh McBride, Ed. Articles, 1,500 to 2,800 words, on do-it-yourself home renovations, energy saving projects, etc., with photos. Pays varying rates, on acceptance.

CAROLINA GARDENER—P.O. Box 4504, Greensboro, NC 27404. L.A. Jackson, Ed. Bimonthly. Articles, 1,200 to 1,500 words, specific to southeast gardening: profiles of gardens in the southeast and of new cultivars or "good ol' southern heirlooms." Slides and illustrations should be available to accompany articles. Pays $150, on publication. Query required.

CHILE PEPPER—P.O. Box 80780, Albuquerque, NM 87196. Melissa Stock, Man. Ed. Food and travel articles, 1,000 to 1,500 words. "No general and obvious articles, such as 'My Favorite Chile Con Carne.' We want first-person articles about spicy world cuisine." No fillers. Payment varies, on publication. Queries required.

COOKING LIGHT—P.O. Box 1748, Birmingham, AL 35201. Elle Barrett, Exec. Ed. Articles on fitness, exercise, health and healthful cooking, nutrition, and healthful recipes. Query.

COOK'S ILLUSTRATED—17 Station St., P.O. Box 569, Brookline, MA 02147. Mark Zanger, Exec. Ed. Bimonthly. Articles that emphasize techniques of home cooking with master recipes, careful testing, trial and error. Payment varies, within 60 days of acceptance. Query. Guidelines.

COUNTRY GARDENS—1716 Locust St., Des Moines, IA 50309-3023. LuAnn Brandsen, Ed. Quarterly. Garden-related how-tos and profiles of gardeners, 750 to 1,500 words. Department pieces, 500 to 700 words, on garden-related travel, food, projects, decorating, entertaining. "The gardens we feature are informal, lush, old-fashioned rather than formal and manicured." Pays $250 to $400 for columns; $350 to $800 for features, on acceptance. Query required.

COUNTRY LIVING—224 W. 57th St., New York, NY 10019. Marjorie E. Gage, Features Ed. Articles, 800 to 1,200 words, on decorating, antiques, cooking, travel, home building, crafts, and gardens. "Most material is written in-house; limited free-lance needs." Payment varies, on acceptance. Query preferred.

EATING WELL—Ferry Rd., P.O. Box 1001, Charlotte, VT 05445-1001. Marcelle DiFalco, Ed. Bimonthly. Feature articles, 2,000 to 5,000 words. Department pieces, 100 to 200 words, for "Nutrition News" and "Marketplace." "We look for strong journalistic voice; authoritative, timely coverage of nutrition issues; healthful recipes that emphasize good ingredients, simple preparation, and full flavor; and a sense of humor." Query. Payment varies, 45 days after acceptance.

ELLE DECOR—1633 Broadway, New York, NY 10019. Charles Bricker, Exec. Ed. Articles, 300 to 1,000 words, on designers and craftspeople (query with photos of the designers and their work) and on houses and apartments "notable for their quirkiness or their beauty, preferably an eclectic combination of the two." Pays $1.25 a word, on publication. Query.

FINE GARDENING—The Taunton Press, 63 S. Main St., Newtown, CT 06470-5506. Suzanne La Rosa, Pub. Bimonthly. Articles, 800 to 2,000 words, for readers with a serious interest in gardening: how-tos, garden profiles, as well as pieces on specific plants or garden equipment. Some poetry. "Our primary focus is on ornamental gardening and landscaping." Art-driven publication; picture possibilities are very important. Pays $150 per magazine page, part on acceptance, part on completed galley. Query. Guidelines.

FLOWER & GARDEN MAGAZINE—700 W. 47th St., Suite 310, Kansas City, MO 64112. Attn: Ed. Practical how-to articles, 1,000 words, on lawn and garden advice. Photos a plus. Pays varying rates, on acceptance (on publication for photos). Query.

FOOD & WINE—1120 Ave. of the Americas, New York, NY 10036. Dana Cowin, Ed.-in-Chief. Mary Ellen Ward, Man. Ed. No unsolicited material.

GARDEN DESIGN—100 Ave. of the Americas, 7th Fl., New York, NY 10013. Dorothy Kalins, Ed.-in-Chief. Garden-related features, 500 to 1,000 words, on private, public, and community gardens; articles on art and history as they relate to gardens.

GOURMET: THE MAGAZINE OF GOOD LIVING—Conde Nast, 360 Madison Ave., New York, NY 10017. Attn: Ed. No unsolicited manuscripts; query.

GROWERTALKS—P.O. Box 9, 335 N. River St., Batavia, IL 60510–0009. Debbie Hamrick, Ed. Dir. Articles, 800 to 2,600 words, that help commercial greenhouse growers (not florist/retailers or home gardeners) do their jobs better: trends, successes in new types of production, marketing, business management, new crops, and issues facing the industry. Payment varies, on publication. Queries preferred.

THE HERB COMPANION—Interweave Press, 201 E. Fourth St., Loveland, CO 80537. Kathleen Halloran, Ed. Trish Faubion, Man. Ed. Bimonthly. Articles, 1,500 to 3,000 words; fillers, 75 to 150 words. Practical horticultural information, original recipes illustrating the use of herbs, thoroughly researched historical insights, step-by-step instructions for herbal craft projects, profiles of notable individuals in the field, book reviews. Pays $125 per published page, on publication.

THE HERB QUARTERLY—P. O. Box 689, San Anselmo, CA 94960. Linda Sparrowe, Ed. Articles, 2,000 to 4,000 words, on herbs: practical uses, cultivation, gourmet cooking, landscaping, herb tradition, medicinal herbs, crafts ideas, unique garden designs; profiles of herb garden experts; practical how-tos for the herb businessperson. Include garden design when possible. Pays on publication. Guidelines; send SASE.

HOME GARDEN—1716 Locust St., Des Moines, IA 50309. Douglas A. Jimerson, Ed.-in-Chief. Gardening/lifestyle magazine. No unsolicited manuscripts. Query with resumé.

HOME MAGAZINE—1633 Broadway, 44th Fl., New York, NY 10019. Gale Steves, Ed.-in-Chief. Linda Lentz, Articles Ed. Articles of interest to homeowners: architecture, remodeling, decorating, products, project ideas, landscaping and gardening, financial aspects of home ownership, home offices, home-related environmental and ecological topics. Pays varying rates, on acceptance. Query, with 50- to 200-word summary.

HOME MECHANIX—2 Park Ave., New York, NY 10016. Paul Spring, Ed. Articles on home improvement and home-related topics including money management, home security, home care, home environment, home security, yard care, design and remodeling, tools, repair and maintenance, electronics, new products and appliances, building materials, lighting and electrical, home decor.

HOME POOL & BAR-B-QUE—P.O. Box 272, Cranford, NJ 07016–0272. John R. Hawks, Pub. Articles about pool maintenance, design, safety, products, bar-b-que recipes. Pays $30 to $100, on publication.

HORTICULTURE—98 N. Washington St., Boston, MA 02114. Thomas C. Cooper, Ed. Published 10 times a year. Authoritative, well-written articles, 500 to 2,500 words, on all aspects of gardening. Pays competitive rates, on publication. Query.

HOUSE BEAUTIFUL—1700 Broadway, New York, NY 10019. Elaine Greene, Features Ed. Elizabeth Hunter, Travel Ed. Service articles related to the home. Pieces on design, travel, and gardening. Query with detailed outline and photos if relevant. Guidelines.

LOG HOME LIVING—P.O. Box 220039, Chantilly, VA 22022. Janice Brewster, Exec. Ed. Articles, 1,000 to 1,500 words, on modern manufactured and handcrafted kit log homes: homeowner profiles, design and decor features. Pays $200 to $500, on acceptance.

THE MAINE ORGANIC FARMER & GARDENER—RR 2, Box 594, Lincolnville, ME 04849. Jean English, Ed. Quarterly. How-to articles and profiles, 100 to 2,500 words, for organic farmers and gardeners, consumers who care about healthful foods, and activists. Tips, 100 to 250 words. "Our readers want good solid information about farming and gardening, nothing soft." Pays about 6¢ a word, on publication. Queries preferred.

METROPOLITAN HOME—1633 Broadway, New York, NY 10019. Michael Lassell, Articles Dir. Service and informational articles for residents of houses, co-ops, lofts, and condominiums, on real estate, equity, wine and spirits, collecting, trends, travel, etc. Interior design and home furnishing articles with emphasis on lifestyle. Payment varies. Query.

THE MOTHER EARTH NEWS—49 E. 21st St., 11th Fl., New York, NY 10010. Matthew Scanlon, Ed. Articles on country living: home improvement and construction, how-tos, indoor and outdoor gardening, crafts and projects, etc. Also health, ecology, energy, and consumerism pieces; profiles. Pays varying rates, on acceptance.

NAPA VALLEY APPELLATION—See *Appellation.*

NATIONAL GARDENING MAGAZINE—180 Flynn Ave., Burlington, VT 05401. Michael MacCaskey, Ed.-in-Chief. Feature articles, 1,200 to 2,500 words, and departments, 800 to 1,000 words, for advanced and beginning gardeners: the latest on fruits, vegetables, and flowers; profiles of edible and ornmental plants; well-tested gardening techniques; news on how to use beneficial plants and creatures; information on soil improvement; and profiles of experienced gardeners. Include photos and slides if possible. Pay starts at 25¢ per word, on acceptance. Query.

ORGANIC GARDENING—33 E. Minor St., Emmaus, PA 18098. Sandra Weida, Office Coordinator. Published 9 times a year. How-to features, 1,000 to 2,000 words, for home gardeners, primarily vegetable gardeners; also, mini-profiles, 500 to 600 words; and tips, techniques, and news, 100 to 600 words. "Organic methods only! Features must include variety recommendations as well as how to grow." Pays 50¢ a word for features; $25 to $125 for departments. Time of payment varies. Queries preferred.

QUICK 'N EASY COUNTRY COOKIN—See *Quick 'n Easy Home Cooking.*

QUICK 'N EASY HOME COOKING—(formerly *Quick 'n Easy Country Cookin'*) Long Publications, 8393 E. Holly Rd., Holly, MI 48442. Michael J. Happy, Man. Ed. Family-oriented cooking articles, 400 to 500 words and articles with a human-interest/Christian perspective. Pays to $20 for articles, on publication. "We also accept short verse, puzzles, and humorous fillers, to 50 words."

ROCKY MOUNTAIN GARDENER—P.O. Box 1230, Gunnison, CO 81230. Susan Martineau, Pub./Ed.-in-Chief. Quarterly. How-to articles, 1,000 to 1,200 words, on regional techniques and varieties; profiles of regional gardeners and gardens, 1,000 to 1,500 words; book reviews and production reviews, 800 to 1,000 words. "Articles must be focused on Rocky Mountain area from New Mexico to Montana. We prefer new, novel, or specific information, not just general gardening topics." Pays 10¢ a word, on publication.

VEGGIE LIFE—1041 Shary Cir., Concord, CA 94518. Sharon Mikkelson, Ed. Bimonthly. Features, 1,500 to 2,000 words, for "people interested in lowfat, meatless cuisine, organic gardening, natural health, nutrition, and herbal healing." Food features (include 8 to 10 recipes); department pieces, 1,000 to 1,500 words. Payment varies, on acceptance. Queries preferred.

WINE SPECTATOR—387 Park Ave. S., New York, NY 10016. Jim Gordon, Man. Ed. Features, 600 to 2,000 words, preferably with photos, on news and people in the wine world, travel, food, and other lifestyle topics. Pays from $400, extra for photos, on publication. Query required.

WINES & VINES—1800 Lincoln Ave., San Rafael, CA 94901. Philip E. Hiaring, Ed. Articles, 2,000 words, on grape and wine industry, emphasizing marketing, management, and production. Pays 10¢ a word, on acceptance.

WORKBENCH—700 W. 47th St., Suite 310, Kansas City, MO 64112. A. Robert Gould, Exec. Ed. Illustrated how-to articles on home improvement and woodworking, with detailed instructions. Pays from $150 per printed page, on acceptance. Guidelines.

YOUR HOME/INDOORS & OUT —P.O. Box 10010, Ogden, UT 84409. Attn: Ed. Dept. Articles, 1,000 words, with good color transparencies and fresh ideas in all areas of home decor: the latest in home construction (exteriors, interiors, building materials, design); the outdoors at home (landscaping, pools, patios, gardening); home management, buying, and selling. No do-it-yourself pieces. Pays 15¢ a word, $35 for color photos, on acceptance. Query required.

FAMILY & PARENTING MAGAZINES

ADOPTIVE FAMILIES MAGAZINE—3333 Hwy. 100 N., Minneapolis, MN 55422. Linda Lynch, Ed. Bimonthly. Articles, 1,500 to 2,500 words, on living in an adoptive family and other adoption issues. Photos of families, adults, or children. Payment is negotiable. Query.

ALL ABOUT KIDS—1077 Celestial St., #101, Cincinnati, OH 45202–1629. Tricia Mullin, Ed. Articles and fiction, to 600 words, for parents in the greater Cincinnati area. Fillers, to 500 words. "Our mission is to reinforce the mental health of today's families by providing information and resources that make parenting less stressful and more fun." Pays about $30 to $40, on publication. Queries preferred.

AMERICAN BABY—KIII Family & Leisure Group, 249 W. 17th St., New York, NY 10011. Judith Nolte, Ed. Articles, 1,000 to 2,000 words, for new or expectant parents on prenatal and infant care. Personal experience, 900 to

1,200 words, (do not submit in diary format). Department pieces, 50 to 350 words, for "Crib Notes" (news and feature topics) and "Medical Update" (health and medicine). No fiction, fantasy pieces, dreamy musings, or poetry. Pays $500 to $1,000 for articles, $100 for departments, on acceptance. Guidelines.

ANSWERS: THE MAGAZINE FOR ADULT CHILDREN OF AGING PARENTS—75 Seabreeze Dr., Richmond, CA 94804. Susan R. Keller, Ed./Pub. Features, 1,000 to 1,200 words, written from product or how-to slant on caring for an elderly parent. Columns, 800 words, on medication concerns, insurance, legal affairs, emotions, housing issues, products, and health and nutrition. News and book reviews, 50 to 100 words. Payment varies, on publication. Query with outline; response time is 60 days. Guidelines.

BABY MAGAZINE—124 E. 40th St., Suite 1101, New York, NY 10016. Jeanne Muchnick, Ed. Bimonthly. Parenting articles, 400 to 750 words, geared toward women in the last trimester of pregnancy and the first year of baby's life. "We want how-to articles designed to smooth the transitions from pregnancy to parenthood." Payment varies, on acceptance. Query.

BABY TALK—301 Howard St., San Fransisco, CA 94105. Trisha Thompson, Ed. Articles, 1,000 to 1,500 words, by parents or professionals, on babies, baby care, etc. No poetry. Pays varying rates, on acceptance. SASE required.

BAY AREA PARENT—401 Alberto Way, Suite A, Los Gatos, CA 95032–5404. Mary Brence Martin, Ed. Articles, 1,200 to 1,400 words, on local parenting issues for readers in California's Santa Clara County and the South Bay area. Query. Mention availability of B&W photos. Pays 6¢ a word, $10 to $15 for photos, on publication. Also publishes *Valley Parent* for central Contra Costa County and the tri–valley area of Alameda County.

THE BIG APPLE PARENTS' PAPER—36 E. 12th St., New York, NY 10003. Helen Rosengren Freedman, Man. Ed. Articles, 500 to 750 words, for NYC parents. Pays $35 to $50, on publication. Buys first NY-area rights.

BLACK CHILD—2870 Peachtree Rd., Suite 264, Atlanta, GA 30355. Candy Mills, Ed. Bimonthly. Articles, 800 words, on parenting or child care issues for parents of African-descent children. No fiction. Pays 4¢ a word, on publication.

CATHOLIC PARENT—Our Sunday Visitor, Inc., 200 Noll Plaza, Huntington, IN 46750. Woodeene Koenig-Bricker, Ed. Features, how-tos, and general-interest articles, 800 to 1,000 words, dealing with the issues of raising children "with solid values in today's changing world. Keep it anecdotal and practical with an emphasis on values and family life." Payment varies, on acceptance. Guidelines.

CENTRAL CALIFORNIA PARENT—2037 W. Bullard, #131, Fresno, CA 93711. Sally Cook, Pub. Articles, 500 to 1,500 words, of interest to parents. Payment varies, on publication.

CHILDSPLAY—P.O. Box 60744, Longmeadow, MA 01116. Barbara M. Cohen, Ed. "The Parenting Publication for New England." Articles, 1,000 to 1,500 words, for "upwardly mobile, educated parents of children under 12." Payment varies, on publication.

CHRISTIAN HOME & SCHOOL—3350 E. Paris Ave. S.E., Grand Rapids, MI 49512. Gordon L. Bordewyk, Ed. Articles for parents in Canada and the U.S. who send their children to Christian schools and are concerned about the challenges facing Christian families today. Pays $75 to $150, on publication. Send SASE for guidelines or 9"x12" SASE with 4 first-class stamps for guidelines and sample issue.

CHRISTIAN PARENTING TODAY— 4050 Lee Vance View, Colorado Springs, CO 80918. Brad Lewis, Ed. Articles, 900 to 2,000 words, dealing with raising children with Christian principles. Departments: "Parent Exchange," 25 to 100 words, on problem-solving ideas that have worked for parents; "Life in our House," insightful anecdotes, 25 to 100 words, about humorous things said at home. Queries preferred for articles. Pays 15¢ to 25¢ a word, on publication. Pays $40 for "Parent Exchange," $25 for "Life in our House." Guidelines.

CONNECTICUT FAMILY—See *New York Family.*

EASTSIDE PARENT—Northwest Parent Publishing, 2107 Elliott Ave., #303, Seattle, WA 98121. Ann Bergman, Ed. Articles, 300 to 2,500 words, for parents of children under 12. Readers tend to be professional, two-career families. Queries preferred. Pays $25 to $200, on publication. Also publishes *Seattle's Child, Portland Parent*, and *Pierce County Parent.*

EXCEPTIONAL PARENT—209 Harvard St., Suite 303, Brookline, MA 02146–5005. Stanley D. Klein, Ed. Articles, 1,000 to 1,500 words, for parents raising children with disabilities. Practical ideas and techniques on parenting, as well as the latest in technology, research, and rehabilitation. Query. Pays $25, on publication.

EXPECTING— 685 Third Ave., New York, NY 10017. Maija Johnson, Ed. Not buying any new material in the foreseeable future.

FAMILY—169 Lexington Ave., New York, NY 10016. Stacy P. Brassington, Ed. Articles, 1,000 to 2,000 words, of interest to women with children. Topics include: military lifestyle, home decorating, travel, moving, food, personal finances, career, relationships, family, parenting, health and fitness. Pays to $200, on publication.

FAMILYFUN—Walt Disney Publishing Group, 244 Main St., Northampton, MA 01060. Clare Ellis, Ed. Read-aloud stories, to 750 words, and articles, to 1,500 words, on family activities and "creative parenting." Payment varies, on acceptance. Queries preferred.

FAMILY TIMES—P.O. Box 932, Eau Claire, WI 54702. Ann Gorton, Ed. Articles, from 800 words, on children and parenting issues: health, education, raising children, how-tos, new studies and programs for educating parents. "Information should be as specific to the Chippewa Valley, WI, as possible." Pays $35 to $50, on publication. Query preferred. Guidelines.

FULL-TIME DADS—P.O. Box 577, Cumberland, ME 04021. Stephen Harris, Ed. Fiction, articles, essays, and humor, 600 to 1,200 words, and short poems for fathers who are very involved with their children. "All material must relate to supportive fatherhood." Payment is one copy.

GROWING CHILD/GROWING PARENT—22 N. Second St., P.O. Box 620, Lafayette, IN 47902–0620. Nancy Kleckner, Ed. Articles, to 1,500 words, on subjects of interest to parents of children under 6. No personal experience pieces or poetry. Guidelines.

HOME LIFE— 127 Ninth Ave. N., Nashville, TN 37234. Charlie Warren, Ed.-in-Chief. Southern Baptist. Articles, to 1,500 words, on Christian marriage, parenting, and family relationships. Query with SASE required. Pays from $75 for articles, on acceptance.

JOYFUL CHILD JOURNAL—34 Russell Ave., Buffalo, NY 14214. Karen Spring Stevens, Exec. Ed. Quarterly. Fiction and nonfiction, 500 to 1,000 words, that "explore how society and education can more effectively nurture children (and adults) to express their fullest potential, thus releasing their inner joy. Articles on educating and parenting the whole child (body, mind, and spirit)." Some short poetry. Pays in copies. Queries preferred. Guidelines.

L.A. BABY—See *Wingate Enterprises, Ltd.*

L.A. PARENT—See *Wingate Enterprises, Ltd.*

LIVING WITH TEENAGERS—127 Ninth Ave. N., Nashville, TN 37234. Attn: Ed. Articles from a Christian perspective for parents of teenagers. Query, resumé, and writing sample preferred.

METROKIDS—1080 N. Delaware Ave., Suite 702, Philadelphia, PA 19125. Nancy Lisagor, Ed. Tabloid for Delaware Valley families. Features and department pieces, 500 to 1,000 words, on regional family travel, dining, and entertainment. Pays $25 to $50, on publication.

MOSAICA DIGEST—242 Fourth St., Lakewood, NJ 08701. Attn: Submission Dept. Joseph Ginberg, Pres. Fiction, 1,500 to 4,000 words; articles, 1,500 to 3,000 words; fillers, 100 to 300 words, of interest to Jewish families. First-person pieces, humor, travel, and history. Articles of Jewish interest are preferred (not articles about religion or religious issues). "We are a family-oriented magazine, and everything must be squeaky clean! No profanity, etc." Reprints are preferred. Pays to $50, on publication.

NEW YORK FAMILY—141 Halstead Ave., Suite 3D, Mamaroneck, NY 10543. Felice Shapiro, Susan Ross, Eds. Articles related to family life in New York City and general parenting topics. Pays $50 to $200. Same requirements for *Westchester Family* and *Connecticut Family.*

PARENTGUIDE NEWS—419 Park Ave. S., 13th Fl., New York, NY 10016. Jenine M. DeLuca, Ed.-in-Chief. Articles, 1,000 to 1,500 words, related to families and parenting issues: trends, profiles, health, education, special programs, products, etc. Humor and photos also considered.

PARENTING—See *Wingate Enterprises, Ltd.*

PARENTS—685 Third Ave., New York, NY 10017. Ann Pleshette Murphy, Ed. Articles, 1,500 to 2,500 words, on parenting, family, women's and community issues, etc. Informal style with quotes from experts. Pays from $1,000, on acceptance. Query.

PARENTS EXPRESS—P.O. Box 12900, Philadelphia, PA 19108. Sharon Sexton, Ed. Articles on children and family topics for Philadelphia-area parents. Pays $120 to $250 for first rights, $25 to $35 for reprints, on publication.

PENINSULA PARENT—See *Windmill Publishing, Inc.*

PIERCE COUNTY PARENT—See *Eastside Parent.*

PORTLAND PARENT—See *Eastside Parent.*

SAN DIEGO PARENT—See *Wingate Enterprises, Ltd.*

SEATTLE'S CHILD—Northwest Parent Publishing, 2107 Elliott Ave., #303, Seattle, WA 98121. Ann Bergman, Ed. Articles, 400 to 2,500 words, of interest to parents, educators, and childcare providers of children under 12, plus investigative reports and consumer tips on issues affecting families in the Puget Sound region. Pays $75 to $400, on publication. Query.

SESAME STREET PARENTS—One Lincoln Plaza, New York, NY 10023. Articles, 800 to 2,500 words, on children and violence; Susan Schneider, Exec. Ed. Articles on educational issues; Jonathan Small, Sr. Ed. Articles on health; Ziba Kashef, Assoc. Ed. "Covers parenting issues for families with young children (to 8 years old)." Pays $1 per word, up to 6 weeks after acceptance. SASE for guidelines.

STEPFAMILIES—Stepfamily Assn. of America, 215 Centennial Mall S., Suite 212, Lincoln, NE 68508–1834. Attn: Ed. Quarterly. Articles, 2 to 4 pages, relevant to stepfamily living. Fillers and poetry. No payment.

SUCCESSFUL BLACK PARENTING—P.O. Box 6359, Philadelphia, PA 19139. Marta Sanchez-Speer, Acting Ed. Bi-monthly. Features, 800 to 1,000 words; department pieces 500 to 700 words; and columns 150 to 200 words on black children and black families. Payment varies, on publication. Query.

TIDEWATER PARENT—See *Windmill Publishing, Inc.*

TWINS—6740 Antioch, Suite 155, Merriam, KS 66204. Jean Cerne, Ed.-in-Chief. Bimonthly. Features, 6 to 8 double-spaced pages; columns, 4 to 6 pages. "Twin-specific parenting information, from both the professional (research-based) and personal (hands-on experience) perspectives." Pays varying rates, on publication. Query.

VALLEY PARENT—See *Bay Area Parent.*

WESTCHESTER FAMILY—See *New York Family.*

WINDMILL PUBLISHING, INC.—Parenting Publications of America, 2753 Atwoodtown Rd., Virginia Beach, VA 23456. Peggy Sijswerda, Ed. Informational articles, 800 to 1,100 words, for regional parenting tabloids, including *Tidewater Parent* and *Peninsula Parent.* Pays $40 to $60, within 2 weeks of publication.

WINGATE ENTERPRISES, LTD.—P.O. Box 3204, 443 E. Irving Dr., Burbank, CA 91504. Attn: Eds. Publishes city-based parenting magazines with strong "service-to-parent" slant. Articles, 1,200 words, on child development, health, nutrition, and education. *San Diego Parent* covers San Diego area; *Parenting* covers the Orange County, CA, area; *L.A. Parent* is geared toward parents of children to age 10; *L.A. Baby* to expectant parents and parents of newborns. Pays $100 to $350, on acceptance. Query.

WORKING MOTHER—Lang Communications, 230 Park Ave., New York, NY 10169. Attn: Ed. Dept. Articles, to 2,000 words, that help women juggle job, home, and family. Payment varies, on acceptance.

LIFESTYLE MAGAZINES

AMERICAN HEALTH—28 W. 23rd St., New York, NY 10010. Attn: Ed. Dept. Lively, authoritative articles, 1,000 to 3,000 words, on women's health and lifestyle aspects of health and fitness; 100- to 500-word news reports. Pays $150 to $250 for news stories; payment varies for features, on acceptance. Query with clips.

AQUARIUS: A SIGN OF THE TIMES—984 Canton St., Roswell, GA 30075. Dan Liss, Ed. Articles, 800 words (with photos or illustrations), on New Age lifestyles and positive thought, holistic health, metaphysics, spirituality, environment. No payment.

ASPIRE—107 Kenner Ave., Nashville, TN 37205. Jeanette Thomason, Ed.-in-Chief Lifestyle magazine for Christian women. Articles, 500 to 2,000 words, on trends in health, career issues, parenting, and relationships, "inspiring and encouraging readers to incorporate faith into daily life." Pays 30¢ a word, on acceptance. Query with resumé and clips. Send SASE for guidelines.

AVATAR JOURNAL—237 N. Westmonte Dr., Altamonte Springs, FL 32714. Miken Chappell, Ed. Bimonthly. Articles, 500 to 1,000 words, on self-development, awakening consciousness, and spiritual enlightenment. "Spiritual in nature. Pieces that teach a lesson, paradigm shifts, epiphany experiences, anecdotes with theme of obtaining enlightenment, healing, inspiration, metaphysics." Pays $100 for articles; $50 for poems, on publication.

BACKHOME—P.O. Box 70, Hendersonville, NC 28793. Lorna K. Loveless, Ed. Articles, 800 to 2,500 words, on home schooling, recycling, home business, healthful cooking. "We hope to provide readers with ways to gain more control over their lives by becoming more self-sufficient: raising their own food, making their own repairs, using alternative energy, etc. We do not promote 'dropping out' of society, but ways to become better citizens and caretakers of the planet." Pays $25 per page; $20 for photos, on publication. Queries preferred.

BLACK DIASPORA—298 5th Ave., 7th Fl., New York, NY 10001. Attn: Ed. General-interest articles, 1,000 to 2,500 words, of interest to "the entire black population." Timely, informative, sophisticated articles about culture, politics, arts and lifestyles; how-to pieces that cater to the needs of minority consumers. Pays 10¢ to 15¢ a word, made 45 days after publication.

CAPPER'S—Editorial Dept., 1503 S.W. 42nd St., Topeka, KS 66609–1265. Nancy Peavler, Ed. Human-interest, personal-experience, historical articles, 300 to 700 words. Poetry, to 15 lines, on nature, home, family. Novel-length fiction for serialization. Letters on women's interests, recipes, and hints for "Heart of the Home." Jokes. Children's writing and art section. Pays varying rates, on publication.

THE CHRISTIAN SCIENCE MONITOR—One Norway St., Boston, MA 02115. Jane A. Lampmann, Features Ed. Newspaper. Articles on lifestyle trends, women's rights, family, and parenting. Pays varying rates, on acceptance.

COMMON BOUNDARY—5272 River Rd., Suite 650, Bethesda, MD 20816. Attn: Manuscript Ed. Bimonthly. Feature articles, 3,000 to 4,000 words, exploring the connections between psychotherapy, spirituality, and creativity. Essays, book reviews, department pieces (1,500 to 1,800 words), and 500-word news items. Readers are primarily mental health professionals, pastoral counselors, spiritual directors, and lay readers.

COUNTRY AMERICA—1716 Locust St., Des Moines, IA 50309–3023. Bill Eftink: general inquiries. Roberta Peterson: country people, country lifestyle, almanac, travel, comedy; Neil Pond: country entertainment, entertainers' lifestyles and events; Dick Sowienski: general interest, personalities, country essays, travel; Diane Yanney: foods, recipes, country crafts; Bob Ehlert: heritage and traditions, country places, country people. Articles should be light on copy with potential for several color photos. Queries preferred.

COUNTRY CONNECTIONS—P.O. Box 6748, Dept. TW, Pine Mountain Club, CA 93222–6748. Catherine R. Leach, Ed. Bimonthly. Articles, to 2,500 words, and fiction, to 1,500 words. Poetry. B&W photos. "Study magazine first. We serve as a forum for public discourse about ethics, politics, social justice, community, city rights, animal and environmental issues, and life in the country." Pays $25 for features, $15 for fiction and poetry, on publication.

CREATION SPIRITUALITY NETWORK MAGAZINE—P.O. Box 20369, Oakland, CA 94620. Rebecca Bier, Ed. Essays, 1,500 to 2,500 words, on life and the creation spirituality movement. Pays 2¢ to 5¢ a word, on publication.

DIALOGUE: A WORLD OF IDEAS FOR VISUALLY IMPAIRED PEOPLE OF ALL AGES—(formerly *Lifeprints*) P.O. Box 5181, Salem, OR 97304–0181. Carol McCarl, Ed. Quarterly. Articles, 800 to 1,200 words, and poetry, 20 lines, for visually impaired youth and adults. Career opportunities, educational skills, and recreational activities. "We want to give readers an opportunity to learn about interesting and successful people who are visually impaired." Payment varies, on publication. Queries are preferred. SASE.

EARTH STAR—P.O. Box 1033, Cambridge, MA 02140. Cody Bideaux, Ed. Bimonthly. Articles, 200 to 3,000 words, on health, metaphysical subjects, environment, celebrity interviews, music. Pieces on local Boston arts and entertainment. "Our readers are interested in spirituality, personal growth, social responsibility, contemporary social issues, and holistic health." Pays $50 to $200, on acceptance. Query.

FATE—P.O. Box 64383, St. Paul, MN 55164–0383. Attn: Ed. Factual fillers and true stories, to 3,000 words, on strange or psychic happenings and mystic personal experiences. Pays 10¢ a word.

FELLOWSHIP—Box 271, Nyack, NY 10960–0271. Richard Deats, Ed. Bimonthly published by the Fellowship of Reconciliation, an interfaith, pacifist organization. Features, 1,500 to 2,000 words, and articles, 750 words, "dealing with nonviolence, opposition to war, and a just and peaceful world community." Photo-essays (B&W photos, include caption information). SASE required. Pays in copies and subscription. Queries preferred.

FREE SPIRIT MAGAZINE—107 Sterling Pl., Brooklyn, NY 11217. Andrea Strudensky, Ed. Bimonthly. Articles, 4,000 words, on environmental issues, holistic health, political issues, and general interest for readers in Manhattan. Interviews. "We're a magazine of personal health and transformation." Pays 10¢ a word, on acceptance. Query preferred.

GENRE—7080 Hollywood Blvd., Suite 1104, Hollywood, CA 90028. John Polly, Assoc. Ed. Fiction, 3,000 to 5,000 words, and articles, 750 to 3,000 words, of interest to gay men. "Feature articles should be national in scope and somehow related to the gay male experience." Pays to 50¢ a word, on publication.

GERMAN LIFE—Zeitgeist Publishing, 1 Corporate Dr., Grantsville, MD 21536. Heidi Whitesell, Ed. Bimonthly. Articles, 500 to 2,500 words, on German culture, its past and present, and how America has been influenced by its German element: history, travel, people, the arts, and social and political issues. Fillers, 50 to 200 words. Pays $300 to $500 for full-length articles, to $80 for short pieces and for fillers, on publication. Queries preferred.

GOOD TIMES—1500 Market St., 12th Fl., Centre Sq. E., Philadelphia, PA 19102. Karen Detwiler, Ed.-in-Chief. Lifestyle magazine for mature Pennsylvanians 50 years and older. Articles, 1,500 to 2,000 words, on medical issues, health, travel, finance, fashion, gardening, fitness, legal issues, celebrities, lifestyles, and relationships. Guidelines. Payment varies, on publication. Query.

THE GREEN MAN—P.O. Box 641, Point Arena, CA 95468–0641. Diane Conn Darling, Ed. "Exploring Paths for Pagan Men." Articles, 1,500 to 5,000 words, exploring a theme. Future themes include: "The Goddess," "Service," "Wisdom of the Beasts," and "Man's Body." No payment. Query for more information.

HEALTH QUEST—200 Highpoint Dr., Suite 215, Chalfont, PA 18914. Valerie Boyd, Ed.-in-Chief. Tamara Jeffries, Man. Ed. "The Publication of Black Wellness." Articles, 700 to 1,500 words, on health issues of interest to African-American men and women. "We focus on total health, so articles cover mind, body, spirit, and cultural wellness." Payment varies, on publication. Query preferred.

HEART & SOUL—Rodale Press, Inc., 733 Third Ave., 15th Fl., New York, NY 10017. Stephanie Stokes Oliver, Ed.-in-Chief. Articles, 800 to 1,500 words, on health, beauty, fitness, nutrition, and relationships for African-American women. "We aim to be the African-American woman's ultimate guide to a healthy lifestyle." Payment varies, on acceptance. Queries preferred.

HOW ON EARTH!—P.O. Box 339, Oxford, PA 19363–0339. Sally Clinton, Ed.-in-Chief. Articles, 1,000 to 2,000 words, by writers ages 13 to 24 on vegetarian living, animals, the environment, social justice, youth empowerment, and activism; essays, personal pieces, interviews, and creative writing, 400 to 800 words, on related subjects; food reviews, 300 to 700 words; music and book reviews, 200 to 500 words. "Living Vegetarian," general essays, to 800 words, about being vegetarian in a meat eating society. Adult submissions are occasionally accepted for research/information articles and general interest articles, 1,000 to 2,000 words. Pays in copies. Query. Guidelines.

ILLYRIA: THE ALBANIAN-AMERICAN NEWSPAPER—2321 Hughes Ave., Bronx, NY 10458. Joseph Finora, Man. Dir. Articles on news, politics, people, sports, history, travel, food, and culture. All articles must relate to Albania or Albanians. Photos. Pays $50 to $70, on publication.

INSIDE MAGAZINE—226 S. 16th St., Philadelphia, PA 19102–3392. Jane Biberman, Ed. Jewish lifestyle magazine. Articles, 1,500 to 3,000 words, on Jewish issues, health, finance, and the arts. Pays $75 to $600, after publication. Queries required; send clips if available.

INTERRACE—2870 Peachtree Rd., Suite 264, Atlanta, GA 30335. Candy Mills, Ed. Articles, 800 words, with an interracial, intercultural, or interethnic theme: news event, commentary, personal account, exposé, historical, interview, etc. No fiction. "Not limited to black/white issues. Interaction between blacks, whites, Asians, Latinos, Native Americans, etc., is also desired." No payment.

INTUITION—2570 W. El Camino Real, Suite 308, Mountain View, CA 94040. Colleen Mauro, Ed. Bimonthly. Articles, 750 to 5,000 words, on intuition, creativity, and spiritual development. Departments, 750 to 2,000 words, include profiles; "Frontier Science," breakthroughs pertaining to parapsychology, creativity, etc.; "Intuitive Tools," history and application of a traditional approach to accessing information. Pays $25 for book reviews to $1,000 for cover articles.

JEWISH CURRENTS—22 E. 17th St., #601, New York, NY 10003. Morris U. Schappes, Ed. Articles, 2,400 to 3,000 words, on Jewish culture or history: Holocaust resistance commemoration, Black-Jewish relations, Yiddish literature and culture, Jewish labor struggles. "We are a secular Jewish magazine." No fiction. No payment.

THE JEWISH HOMEMAKER—705 Foster Ave., Brooklyn, NY 11230. Mayer Bendet, Ed. Bimonthly. Articles, 1,200 to 2,000 words, for a traditional/ Orthodox Jewish audience. Humor. Payment varies, on publication. Query.

LEFTHANDER MAGAZINE—P.O. Box 8249, Topeka, KS 66608–0249. Kim Kipers, Ed. Bimonthly. Articles, 1,500 to 1,800 words, related to left-handedness: profiles of left-handed personalities; performing specific tasks or sports as a lefty; teaching left-handed children. Personal experience pieces for "Perspective." SASE for guidelines. Pays $80 to $100, on publication. Buys all rights. Query.

LIFEPRINTS—See *Dialogue: A World of Ideas for Visually Impaired People of All Ages.*

LINK: THE COLLEGE MAGAZINE—The Soho Bldg., 110 Greene St., Suite 407, New York, NY 10012. Ty Wenger, Ed.-in-Chief. News, lifestyle, and issues for college students. Informational how-to and short features, 500 to 800 words, on education news, finances, academics, employment, lifestyles, and trends. Well-researched, insightful, authoritative articles. Queries preferred. Pays $100 to $500, on publication. Guidelines.

MOMENT MAGAZINE— 4710 41st St. N.W., Washington, DC 20016. Andrew Silow-Carroll, Sr. Ed. Sophisticated articles, 2,500 to 5,000 words, on Jewish culture, politics, religion, and personalities. Columns, to 1,500 words, with uncommon perspectives on contemporary issues, humor, strong anecdotes. Book reviews, 400 words. Pays $40 to $600.

MOUNTAIN LIVING MAGAZINE—7009 S. Potomac, Englewood, CO 80112. Karen Coe, Ed. Articles, 1,200 to 1,500 words, on topics related to the mountains of the U.S.: travel, home design, architecture, gardening, art, cuisine, sports, and people. Pays $125 to $300, on acceptance.

NATIVE PEOPLES MAGAZINE—5333 N. 7th St., Suite C-224, Phoenix, AZ 85014–2804. Gary Avey, Ed. Quarterly. Articles, 1,800 to 2,800 words, on the "arts and lifeways" of the native peoples of the Americas; authenticity and positive portrayals of present traditional and cultural practices necessary. Pays 25¢ a word, on publication. Query, including availability of photos.

NATURAL HEALTH—17 Station St., Box 1200, Brookline Village, MA 02147. Attn: Ed. Bimonthly. Features, 1,500 to 3,000 words: practical information, new discoveries, and current trends on natural health and living. Topics include natural goods and medicine, alternative health care, nutrition, wellness, personal fitness, and modern holistic teachings. Departments and columns, 250 to 1,000 words. Payment varies, on acceptance.

NEW AGE JOURNAL— 42 Pleasant St., Watertown, MA 02172–2312. Joan Duncan Oliver, Ed. Articles for readers who take an active interest in social change, personal growth, health, and contemporary issues. Features, 2,000 to 4,000 words; columns, 750 to 1,500 words; short news items, 50 words; and first-person narratives, 750 to 1,500 words. Pays varying rates, after acceptance.

NEW CHOICES: LIVING EVEN BETTER AFTER 50—28 W. 23rd St., New York, NY 10010. Allen J. Sheinman, Articles Ed. David A. Sendler, Ed.-in-Chief. News and service magazine for people ages 50 to 65. Articles on retirement planning, financial strategies, housing options, as well as health and fitness, travel, leisure pursuits, etc. Payment varies, on acceptance.

NEWPORT LIFE—174 Bellevue Ave., Suite 207, Newport, RI 02840. Susan Ryan, Sr. Ed. Quarterly. Articles, 500 to 2,500 words, on the people and places of Newport County: general-interest and historical articles, interviews, profiles, investigative pieces, and photo-features. Departments, 600 to 750 words, include "At the Helm" (on some aspect of boating), "Arts Marquee," "Food for Thought," and "Historical Newport." Photos must be available for all articles. Pays 10¢ a word, on publication. Query.

OUT—The Soho Bldg., 110 Greene St., Suite 600, New York, NY 10012. Sarah Pettit, Ed.-in-Chief. Articles, 50 to 8,000 words, on various subjects (current affairs, culture, fitness, finance, etc.) of interest to gay and lesbian readers. "The best guide to what we publish is to read previous issues." Payment varies, on publication. Query. Guidelines.

OUT YOUR BACKDOOR—4686 Meridian Rd., Williamston, MI 48895. Jeff Potter, Ed. Articles and fiction, 2,500 words, for thrifty, down-to-earth culture enthusiasts. "Budget travel, second-hand treasure, and homespun but high-quality culture all combine to yield an energetic, practical, folksy post-modern magazine." Study sample issue before submitting. Pays in copies.

PERCEPTIONS—10734 Jefferson Blvd., Suite 502, Culver City, CA 90230. Judi V. Brewer, Ed. Articles, to 2,500 words, on government, alternative health, metaphysics. Reviews, to 500 words. Cartoons. "Broad-spectrum focus crossing barriers that separate ideologies, politics, etc." Sections include Political Slant (relevant information focusing on what we have in common); Healing Spiral (little-known facts and remedies); Concepts (a forum to broaden, awaken, and tickle the intellect). Pays in copies.

THE PHOENIX—7152 Unity Ave. N., Brooklyn Ctr., MN 55429. Pat Samples, Ed. Tabloid. Articles, 800 to 1,500 words, on recovery, renewal, and growth. Department pieces for "Bodywise," "Family Skills," or "Personal Story." "Our readers are committed to physical, emotional, mental, and spiritual health and well-being. Read a sample copy to see what we publish." Pays 3¢ to 5¢ a word, on publication. Guidelines and calendar.

QUICK 'N EASY COUNTRY COOKIN'—See *Quick 'N Easy Home Cooking*.

QUICK 'N EASY HOME COOKING—(formerly *Quick 'N Easy Country Cookin'*) Long Publications, 8393 E. Holly Rd., Holly, MI 48442. Michael J. Happy, Man. Ed. Family-oriented articles, 400 to 500 words, on cooking, and articles with a human-interest/down-home perspective. Short verse, humorous fillers, to 50 words. Pays $20 for articles, on publication.

ROBB REPORT—1 Acton Pl., Acton, MA 01720. Robert R. Feeman, Ed. Consumer magazine for the high-end/luxury market. Features on lifestyles, home interiors, boats, travel, investment opportunities, exotic automobiles, business, technology, etc. Payment varies, on publication. Query with SASE and published clips.

SAGEWOMAN—P.O. Box 641, Point Arena, CA 95468–0641. Anne Newkirk Niven, Ed. Quarterly. Articles, 200 to 5,000 words, on issues of concern to pagan and spiritually minded women. Material which expresses an earth-centered spirituality: personal experience, scholarly research, Goddess lore, ritual material, interviews, humor, and reviews. Accepts material by women only. Pays 3¢ a word, from $10, on publication.

SCIENCE OF MIND—P.O. Box 75127, Los Angeles, CA 90075. Jim Shea, Asst. Ed. Articles, 1,500 to 2,000 words, that offer a thoughtful perspective on how to experience greater self-acceptance, empowerment, and meaningful life. "Achieving wholeness through applying Science of Mind principles is the primary focus." Inspiring first-person pieces, 1,000 to 2,000 words. Interviews with notable spiritual leaders, 3,500 words. Poetry, to 28 lines. Pays $25 per page. Queries required (except for poetry).

SWING—342 Madison Ave., #1402, New York, NY 10017. Megan Liberman, Sr. Ed. Articles, 1,500 to 3,000 words, on political and social issues of interest to readers in their 20s. Pays 75¢ to $1 a word, on publication. Query with clips.

T'AI CHI—P.O. Box 26156, Los Angeles, CA 90026. Marvin Smalheiser, Ed. Articles, 800 to 4,000 words, on T'ai Chi Ch'uan, other internal martial arts and related topics such as qigong, Chinese medicine and healing practices, Chinese philosophy and culture, health, meditation, fitness, self-improvement, as well as news about teachers and schools. Pays $75 to $500, on publication. Query required.

TURNING WHEEL—P.O. Box 4650, Berkeley, CA 94704. Susan Moon, Ed. Quarterly. Articles, poetry, fillers, and artwork. "Magazine is dedicated to the development of engaged Buddhism, engaged spirituality and spiritual politics." No payment.

USAIR MAGAZINE—NYT Custom Publishing, 122 E. 42nd St., 14th Fl., New York, NY 10168. Catherine Sabino, Ed. Kathy Passero, Man. Ed. USAir inflight magazine. Articles on travel, lifestyle trends, sports, personality profiles, food and wine, shopping, the arts and culture. "Our goal is to provide readers with lively and colorful, yet practical articles that will make their lives and their leisure time more rewarding." Payment made within 60 days of acceptance. Query with clips; no unsolicited manuscripts.

VEGETARIAN VOICE—P.O. Box 72, Dolgeville, NY 13329. Jennie Collura, Sr. Ed. Quarterly. Informative, well-researched and/or inspiring articles, 600 to 1,800 words, on lifestyles and consumer concerns, health, nutrition, animal rights, the environment, world hunger, etc. "Our underlying philosophy is total vegetarian; all our recipes are vegan and we do not support the use of leather, wool, silk, etc." Guidelines. Pays in copies.

VENTURE INWARD—67th and Atlantic Ave., P.O. Box 595, Virginia Beach, VA 23451. A. Robert Smith, Ed. Articles, to 4,000 words, on metaphysical and spiritual development subjects. Prefer personal experience. Opinion pieces, to 800 words, for "Guest Column." "Turning Point," to 800 words, on an inspiring personal turning point experience. "The Mystical Way," to 1,500 words, on a personal paranormal experience. "Holistic Health," brief accounts of success using Edgar Cayce remedies. Book reviews, to 500 words. Pays $30 to $300, on publication. Query.

VIRTUE: THE CHRISTIAN MAGAZINE FOR WOMEN— 4050 Lee Vance View, Colorado Springs, CO 80918–7102. Jeanette Thomason, Ed. Articles, 1,200 to 1,400 words, on family, marriage, self-esteem, working women;

women's relationships with family, friends, and God. Fiction and poetry. Pays 15¢ to 25¢ a word, $25 to $50 for poetry, on publication. Query with SASE required.

WEIGHT WATCHERS MAGAZINE—360 Lexington Ave., New York, NY 10017. Randi Rose, Health Ed. Articles on health, nutrition, fitness, and weight-loss motivation and success. Pays from $500, on acceptance. Query with clips required. Guidelines.

WHOLE LIFE TIMES—21225 Pacific Coast Hwy., Suite B, P.O. Box 1187, Malibu, CA 90265. S.T. Alcantara, Assoc. Ed. Tabloid. Feature articles, 2,000 words, with a holistic perspective. Departments and columns, 800 words. Well-researched articles on the environment, current political issues, women's issues, and new developments in health, as well as how-to, humor, new product information, personal experience, and interviews. Pays 5¢ a word, on publication.

WIRED—520 Third St., San Francisco, CA 94107–1427. Jessie Freund, Ed. Asst. Lifestyle magazine for the "digital generation." Articles, essays, profiles, fiction, and other material that discusses the "meaning and context" of digital technology in today's world. Guidelines. Payment varies, on publication.

YOGA JOURNAL—2054 University Ave., Berkeley, CA 94704. Rick Fields, Ed. Articles, 1,200 to 4,000 words, on holistic health, spirituality, yoga, and transpersonal psychology; New Age profiles; interviews. Pays $100 to $1,200, on acceptance.

SPORTS AND RECREATION

ADVENTURE CYCLIST—Adventure Cycling Assn., P.O. Box 8308, Missoula, MT 59807. Daniel D'Ambrosio, Ed. Articles, 1,200 to 2,500 words: accounts of bicycle tours in the U.S. and overseas, interviews, personal-experience pieces, humor, and news shorts. Pays $25 to $65 per published page.

ADVENTURE WEST—P.O. Box 3210, Incline Village, NV 89451. Michael Oliver, Assoc. Ed. Bimonthly. Recreational travel articles, 1,500 to 2,000 words, on risky wild adventures; 1,500 to 2,000 words, on shorter trips that offer a high degree of excitement; and service pieces, 1,000 to 1,500 words on short excursions. Profiles and essays also used. Emphasis must be on American West, including Alaska, Hawaii, western Canada, and western Mexico. Pays 30¢ a word, on publication.

AKC GAZETTE—(formerly *Pure-Bred Dogs/American Kennel Gazette*) 51 Madison Ave., New York, NY 10010. Mark Roland, Features Ed. "The official journal for the sport of purebred dogs." Articles, 1,000 to 2,500 words, relating to purebred dogs, for serious fanciers. Pays $200 to $450, on acceptance. Queries preferred.

AMERICAN HUNTER—NRA Publications, 11250 Waples Mill Rd., Fairfax, VA 22030. Tom Fulgham, Ed. Articles, 1,400 to 2,000 words, on hunting. Photos. Pays on acceptance. Guidelines.

AMERICAN MOTORCYCLIST—American Motorcyclist Assn., 33 Collegeview Rd., Westerville, OH 43081–1484. Greg Harrison, Ed. Articles and fiction, to 3,000 words, on motorcycling: news coverage, personalities, tours. Photos. Pays varying rates, on publication. Query with SASE.

THE AMERICAN RIFLEMAN—11250 Waples Mill Rd., Fairfax, VA 22030. Mark Keefe, Man. Ed. Factual articles on use and enjoyment of sporting firearms. Pays on acceptance.

BACKPACKER MAGAZINE—Rodale Press, 33 E. Minor St., Emmaus, PA 18098. John Viehman, Exec. Ed. Articles, 250 to 3,000 words, on self-propelled backcountry travel: backpacking, kayaking/canoeing, mountaineering; technique, nordic skiing, health, natural science. Photos. Pays varying rates. Query.

THE BACKSTRETCH—P.O. Box 7065, Louisville, KY 40257–0065. Barrett Shaw, Ed. United Thoroughbred Trainers of America. Feature articles, with photos, on subjects related to thoroughbred horse racing. Pays after publication. Sample issue and guidelines on request.

BACKWOODSMAN—P.O. Box 627, Westcliffe, CO 81252. Charlie Richie, Ed. Articles for the twentieth-century frontiersman: muzzleloading, primitive weapons, black powder cartridge guns, woodslore, survival, homesteading, trapping, etc. Historical and how-to articles. No payment.

BASEBALL FORECAST, BASEBALL ILLUSTRATED—See *Hockey Illustrated.*

BASKETBALL FORECAST—See *Hockey Illustrated.*

BASSIN'—NatCom, Inc., 5300 CityPlex Tower, 2448 E. 81st St., Tulsa, OK 74137–4207. Mark Chesnut, Exec. Ed. Articles, 1,200 to 1,400 words, on how and where to bass fish, for the amateur fisherman. Pays $350 to $500, on acceptance. Query.

BASSMASTER MAGAZINE—B.A.S.S. Publications, P.O. Box 17900, Montgomery, AL 36141. Dave Precht, Ed. Articles, 1,500 to 2,000 words, with photos, on freshwater black bass and striped bass. "Short Casts" pieces, 400 to 800 words, on news, views, and items of interest. Pays $200 to $400, on acceptance. Query.

BC OUTDOORS—1132 Hamilton St., #202, Vancouver, B.C., Canada V6B 2S2. Karl Bruhn, Ed. Articles, to 1,500 words, on fishing, hunting, conservation, and all forms of non-competitive outdoor recreation in British Columbia and Yukon. Photos. Pays from 20¢ to 27¢ a word, on publication.

BIRD WATCHER'S DIGEST—P.O. Box 110, Marietta, OH 45750. William H. Thompson, III, Ed. Articles, 600 to 2,500 words, for bird watchers: first-person accounts; how-tos; pieces on endangered species; profiles. Pays from $50, on publication. Submit complete manuscript. SASE for guidelines.

BLACK BELT—P.O. Box 918, Santa Clarita, CA 91380–9018. Attn: Ed. Articles related to self-defense: how-tos on fitness and technique; historical, travel, philosophical subjects. Pays $100 to $300, on publication. Guidelines.

BOUNDARY WATERS JOURNAL—9396 Rocky Ledge Rd., Ely, MN 55731. Stuart Osthoff, Ed. Articles, 2,000 to 3,000 words, on wilderness, recreation, nature, and conservation in Minnesota's Boundary Waters Canoe Area Wilderness and Ontario's Quetico Provincial Park. Regular features include canoe-route journals, fishing, camping, hiking, cross-country skiing, wildlife and nature, regional lifestyles, history, and events. Pays $200 to $400, on publication; $50 to $150 for photos.

BOW & ARROW HUNTING—Box 2429, 34249 Camino Capistrano, Capistrano Beach, CA 92624–0429. Roger Combs, Ed. Dir. Articles, 1,200 to 2,500 words, with B&W or color photos, on bowhunting; profiles and technical pieces, primarily on deer hunting. Pays $100 to $300, on acceptance. Same address and mechanical requirements for *Gun World.*

BOWHUNTER MAGAZINE—P.O. Box 8200, Harrisburg, PA 17105–8200. M.R. James, Ed. Informative, entertaining features, 500 to 2,000 words, on bow-and-arrow hunting. Fillers. Photos. "Study magazine first." Pays $100 to $400, on acceptance.

BOWLING—5301 S. 76th St., Greendale, WI 53129. Bill Vint, Ed. Articles, to 1,500 words, on all aspects of bowling, especially human interest. Profiles. "We're looking for unique, unusual stories about bowling people and places and occasionally publish business articles." Pays varying rates, on publication. Query required.

BUCKMASTERS WHITETAIL MAGAZINE—P.O. Box 244022, Montgomery, AL 36124–4022. Russell Thornberry, Exec. Ed. Semiannual. Articles and fiction, 2,500 words, for serious sportsmen. "Big Buck Adventures" articles capture the details and the adventure of the hunt of a newly discovered trophy. Fresh, new whitetail hunting how-tos; new biological information about whitetail deer that might help hunters; entertaining deer stories; and other department pieces. Photos a plus. Pays $250 to $400 for articles, on acceptance. Guidelines.

BUGLE—Rocky Mountain Elk Foundation, P.O. Box 8249, Missoula, MT 59807–8249. Jan Brocci, Asst. Ed. Quarterly. Fiction and nonfiction, 1,500 to 4,000 words, on elk and elk hunting. Department pieces, 1,000 to 3,000 words, for: "Thoughts and Theories"; "Situation Ethics"; and "Women in the Outdoors." Pays 20¢ a word, on acceptance.

CANADIAN DIVER & WATERSPORT—See *Diver Magazine.*

CANOE AND KAYAK MAGAZINE—(formerly *Canoe*) P.O. Box 3146, Kirkland, WA 98083. Paul Temple, Ed.-in-Chief Features, 1,100 to 2,000 words; department pieces, 500 to 1,000 words. Topics include canoeing or kayaking adventures, destinations, boat and equipment reviews, techniques and how-tos, short essays, camping, environment, humor, health, history, etc. Pays 12.5¢ a word, on publication. Query preferred. Guidelines.

CAR AND DRIVER—2002 Hogback Rd., Ann Arbor, MI 48105. Csaba Csere, Ed.-in-Chief. Articles, to 2,500 words, for enthusiasts, on new cars, classic cars, industry topics. "Ninety percent staff-written. Query with clips. No unsolicited manuscripts." Pays to $2,500, on acceptance.

CASCADES EAST—716 N.E. Fourth St., P.O. Box 5784, Bend, OR 97708. Geoff Hill, Ed./Pub. Articles, 1,000 to 2,000 words, on outdoor activities (fishing, hunting, golfing, backpacking, rafting, skiing, snowmobiling, etc.), history, special events, and scenic tours in central Oregon Cascades. Photos. Pays 5¢ to 10¢ a word, extra for photos, on publication.

CHESAPEAKE BAY MAGAZINE—1819 Bay Ridge Ave., Annapolis, MD 21403. Tim Sayles, Ed. Articles, to 1,500 words, on boating, fishing, destinations and people on the Chesapeake Bay. Photos. Pays $100 to $700, on acceptance. Query.

CURRENTS—212 W. Cheyenne Mountain Blvd., Colorado Springs, CO 80906. Greg Moore, Ed. Quarterly. "Voice of the National Organization for

Rivers." Articles, 500 to 2,000 words, for kayakers, rafters, and river canoe-ists, pertaining to whitewater rivers and/or river running. Fillers. B&W action photos. Pays from $40 for articles, $30 to $50 for photos, on publication. Queries preferred.

CYCLE WORLD—1499 Monrovia Ave., Newport Beach, CA 92663. David Edwards, Ed.-in-Chief. Technical and feature articles, 1,500 to 2,500 words, for motorcycle enthusiasts. Photos. Pays on publication. Query.

CYCLING U.S.A.—U.S. Cycling Federation, One Olympic Plaza, Colorado Springs, CO 80909. Frank Stanley, Ed. Articles, 500 to 1,000 words, on bicycle racing. Pays 10¢ to a word, on publication. Query.

THE DIVER—P.O. Box 54788, St. Petersburg, FL 33739. Bob Taylor, Ed. Articles on divers, coaches, officials, springboard and platform techniques, training tips, etc. Pays $15 to $35, extra for photos ($5 to $10 for cartoons), on publication.

DIVER MAGAZINE—230–11780 Hammersmith Way, Richmond, B.C., Canada V7A 5E3. Stephanie Bold, Ed. Illustrated articles, 500 to 1,000 words, on dive destinations. Shorter pieces are also welcome. "Travel features should be brief and accompanied by excellent slides and/or prints and a map. Unsolicited articles will be reviewed only from August to October and will be considered for *Diver Magazine* and *Canadian Diver & Watersport*." Pays $2.50 per column inch, on publication. Guidelines. Limited market.

EQUUS—Fleet Street Corp., 656 Quince Orchard Rd., Gaithersburg, MD 20878. Laurie Prinz, Exec. Ed. Articles, 1,000 to 3,000 words, on all breeds of horses, covering their health, care, the latest advances in equine medicine and research. "Attempt to speak as one horseperson to another." Pays $100 to $400, on publication.

FLY FISHERMAN—6405 Flank Dr., Box 8200, Harrisburg, PA 17105. Philip Hanyok, Man. Ed. Query.

FLY ROD & REEL—P.O. Box 370, Camden, ME 04843. James E. Butler, Ed. Fly-fishing pieces, 2,000 to 2,500 words, and occasional fiction; articles on the culture and history of the areas being fished. Pays on acceptance. Query.

FOOTBALL DIGEST—Century Publishing Co., 990 Grove St., Evanston, IL 60201. Kenneth Leiker, Ed. William Wagner, Assoc. Ed. Articles, 1,500 to 2,500 words, for the hard-core football fan: profiles of pro and college stars, nostalgia, trends in the sport. Pays on publication. Query.

FOOTBALL FORECAST—See *Hockey Illustrated.*

FUR-FISH-GAME—2878 E. Main St., Columbus, OH 43209. Mitch Cox, Ed. Illustrated articles, 800 to 2,500 words, preferably with how-to angle, on hunting, fishing, trapping, dogs, camping, or other outdoor topics. Some humorous or where-to articles. Pays to $150, on acceptance.

GAME AND FISH PUBLICATIONS—P.O. Box 741, Marietta, GA 30061. Attn: Ed. Dept. Publishes 30 monthly outdoor magazines for 48 states. Articles, 1,500 to 2,500 words, on hunting and fishing. How-tos, where-tos, and adventure pieces. Profiles of successful hunters and fishermen. No hiking, canoeing, camping, or backpacking pieces. Pays $125 to $175 for state-specific articles, $200 to $250 for multi-state articles, before publication. Pays $25 to $75 for photos.

GOLF DIGEST—5520 Park Ave., Trumbull, CT 06611. Jerry Tarde, Ed. Instructional articles, tournament reports, and features on players, to 2,500 words. Fiction, 1,000 to 2,000 words. Poetry, fillers, humor, photos. Pays varying rates, on acceptance. Query preferred.

GOLF FOR WOMEN—P.O. Box 951989, Lake Mary, FL 32795–1989. Pat Baldwin, Ed.-in-Chief. Golf-related articles of interest to women; fillers and humor. Instructional pieces are staff-written. Query.

GOLF JOURNAL—Golf House, P.O. Box 708, Far Hills, NJ 07931–0708. Brett Avery, Ed. Official publication of the United States Golf Association. A general-interest magazine on the game with articles on a variety of contemporary and historic topics. Pays varying rates, on publication.

GOLF TIPS—Werner Publishing Corp., 12121 Wilshire Blvd., #120, Los Angeles, CA 90025–1175. John Ledesma, Man. Ed. Articles, 500 to 1,500 words, for serious golfers: unique golf instruction, golf products, interviews with pro players. Fillers: short "shotmaking" instruction tips. Queries preferred. Pays $200 to $600, on publication.

THE GREYHOUND REVIEW—National Greyhound Assn., Box 543, Abilene, KS 67410. Tim Horan, Man. Ed. Articles, 1,000 to 10,000 words, pertaining to the greyhound racing industry: how-to, historical nostalgia, interviews. Pays $85 to $150, on publication.

GULF COAST GOLFER—See *North Texas Golfer.*

GUN DIGEST—4092 Commercial Ave., Northbrook, IL 60062. Ken Warner, Ed. Well-researched articles, to 5,000 words, on guns and shooting, equipment, etc. Photos. Pays from 10¢ a word, on acceptance. Query.

GUN DOG—P.O. Box 35098, Des Moines, IA 50315. Rick Van Etten, Man. Ed. Features, 1,000 to 2,500 words, with photos, on bird hunting: how-tos, where-tos, dog training, canine medicine, breeding strategy. Fiction. Humor. Pays $150 to $300 for fillers and short articles, $150 to $450 for features, on acceptance.

GUN WORLD—See *Bow & Arrow Hunting.*

HANG GLIDING—U.S. Hang Gliding Assn., P.O. Box 1330, Colorado Springs, CO 80901–1330. Gilbert Dodgen, Ed. Articles, 2 to 3 pages, on hang gliding. Pays to $50, on publication. Query.

HOCKEY ILLUSTRATED—Lexington Library, Inc., 233 Park Ave. S., New York, NY 10003. Stephen Ciacciarelli, Ed. Articles, 2,500 words, on hockey players and teams. Pays $125, on publication. Query. Same address and requirements for *Baseball Illustrated, Wrestling World, Pro Basketball Illustrated, Pro Football Illustrated, Baseball Forecast, Pro Football Preview, Football Forecast,* and *Basketball Forecast.*

HORSE & RIDER—12265 W. Bayaud Ave., Suite 300, Lakewood, CO 80228. Sue M. Copeland, Ed. Articles, 500 to 3,000 words, with photos, on western riding and general horse care geared to the performance horse: training, feeding, grooming, health, etc. Pays varying rates, on publication. Buys one-time rights. Guidelines.

HORSEMEN'S YANKEE PEDLAR—83 Leicester St., N. Oxford, MA 01537. Kelley R. Small, Pub. News and feature-length articles, about horses and horsemen in the Northeast. Photos. Pays $2 per published inch, on publication. Query.

HOT BOAT—Sport Publications, 8484 Wilshire Blvd., #900, Beverly Hills, CA 90211. Brett Bayne, Ed. Family-oriented articles, 600 to 1,000 words, on motorized water sport events and personalities: general-interest, how-to, and technical features. Pays $85 to $300, on publication. Query.

HUNTING—6420 Wilshire Blvd., Los Angeles, CA 90048–5515. Todd Smith, Ed. How-to/where-to articles on practical aspects of hunting. At least 15 photos required with articles. Query required. Guidelines. Pays $300 to $500 for articles with B&W photos, extra for color photos. Manuscripts are paid on acceptance; photos, on publication.

INSIDE SPORTS—990 Grove St., Evanston, IL 60201. Kenneth Leiker, Ed. In-depth, insightful sports articles, player profiles relating to baseball, football, basketball, hockey, auto racing, and boxing. Payment varies, on publication. Query.

KITPLANES—P.O. Box 6050, Mission Viejo, CA 92690. Dave Martin, Ed. Articles, 1,000 to 4,000 words, on all aspects of design, construction, and performance of aircraft built from kits and plans by home craftsmen. Pays $60 per page, on publication.

LAKELAND BOATING—1560 Sherman Ave., Suite 1220, Evanston, IL 60201–5047. Randall W. Hess, Ed. Articles for powerboat owners on the Great Lakes and other area waterways, on long-distance cruising, short trips, maintenance, equipment, history, regional personalities and events, and environment. Photos. Pays on publication. Query. Guidelines.

MEN'S HEALTH—Rodale Press, 33 E. Minor St., Emmaus, PA 18098. David Zinczenko, Sr. Ed. Articles, 1,000 to 2,500 words, on sports, fitness, diet, health, nutrition, relationships, and travel, for men ages 25 to 55. Pays from 50¢ a word, on acceptance. Query.

MICHIGAN OUT-OF-DOORS—P.O. Box 30235, Lansing, MI 48909. Dennis Knickerbocker, Ed. Features, 1,000 to 2,500 words, on hunting, fishing, camping, and conservation in Michigan. Pays $75 to $150, on acceptance.

MID-WEST OUTDOORS—111 Shore Dr., Hinsdale, IL 60521–5885. Gene Laulunen, Ed. Articles, 1,000 to 1,500 words, with photos, on where, when, and how to fish and hunt in the Midwest. No Canadian material. Pays $15 to $35, on publication.

MOTOR TREND—6420 Wilshire Blvd., Los Angeles, CA 90048–5515. C. Van Tune, Ed. Articles, 250 to 2,000 words, on autos, racing, events, histories, and profiles. Color photos. Pay varies, on acceptance. Query.

MOTORHOME MAGAZINE—2575 Vista Del Mar, Ventura, CA 93001. Barbara Leonard, Ed. Dir. Articles, to 2,000 words, with color slides, on motorhomes. Also travel and how-to pieces. Pays to $600, on acceptance.

MUSHING—P.O. Box 149, Ester, AK 99725–0149. Todd Hoener, Ed. Dog-driving how-tos, profiles, and features, 1,500 to 2,000 words; and department pieces, 500 to 1,000 words, for competitive and recreational dogsled drivers, weight pullers, dog packers, and skijorers. International audience. Photos. Pays $20 to $175, on publication. Queries preferred. Guidelines and sample issue on request.

NATIONAL PARKS MAGAZINE—1776 Massachusetts Ave. N.W., Washington, DC 20036. Sue E. Dodge, Ed. Articles, 1,500 to 2,000 words, on areas in the National Park System, proposed new areas, threats to parks or park wildlife, new trends in park use, legislative issues, and endangered species of plants or animals relevant to national parks. No fiction, poetry, personal narratives, "My trip to . . . ," or straight travel pieces to individual parks. Articles, 1,500 words, on "low-impact" travel to 4 or 5 national park sites. Pays $400 to $1,000, on acceptance. Query with clips (original slant or news hook is essential to successful query). Guidelines.

THE NEW ENGLAND SKIERS GUIDE—Box 1125, Waitsfield, VT 05673. Jill Jemison, Ed. Annual (June deadline for submissions). Articles on alpine and nordic skiing and snowboarding, equipment, and winter vacations at New England resorts. Rates vary.

NEW YORK OUTDOORS—51 Atlantic Ave., Floral Park, NY 11001. Scott Shane, Ed.-in-Chief. Features, to 1,500 words, with B&W prints or color transparencies, on any aspect of outdoor sports travel or adventure in northeast US. Pays to $250 for major features. Queries preferred.

NORTH TEXAS GOLFER—9182 Old Katy Rd., Suite 212, Houston, TX 77055. Bob Gray, Ed./Pub. Articles, 800 to 1,500 words, of interest to golfers in north Texas. Pays $50 to $250, on publication. Queries required. Same requirements for *Gulf Coast Golfer* (for golfers in south Texas).

NORTHEAST OUTDOORS—Woodall Publishing Corp., 13975 W. Polo Trail Dr., Lake Forest, IL 60045–5000. Ann Emerson, Man. Ed. Articles, 500 to 1,000 words, preferably with B&W photos, on camping and recreational vehicle (RV) touring in northeast U.S.: recommended private campgrounds, camp cookery, recreational vehicle hints. Stress how-to, where-to. Cartoons. Pays $20 to $80, on publication. Guidelines.

OFFSHORE—220 Reservoir St., Needham Heights, MA 02194. Peter Serratore, Ed. Articles, 1,200 to 2,500 words, on boats, people, places, maritime history, and events along the New England, New York, and New Jersey coasts. Writers should be knowledgeable boaters. Photos a plus. Pays $250 to $500.

OUTDOOR AMERICA—707 Conservation Ln., Gaithersburg, MD 20878–2983. Attn: Articles Ed. Quarterly publication of the Izaak Walton League of America. Articles, 1,250 to 2,000 words, on natural resource conservation issues and outdoor recreation, with emphasis on IWLA member/chapter tie-in; especially fishing, hunting, and camping. Also, short items, 500 to 750 words. Pays 20¢ a word. Query with clips.

OUTDOOR CANADA—703 Evans Ave., Suite 202, Toronto, Ont., Canada M9C 5E9. James Little, Ed. Published 8 times yearly. Articles, 1,500 to 2,000 words, on fishing, camping, hiking, canoeing, hunting, and wildlife. Pays $400 to $600, on publication.

OUTSIDE—Outside Plaza, 400 Market St., Santa Fe, NM 87501. No unsolicited material.

PADDLER MAGAZINE—P.O. Box 775450, Steamboat Springs, CO 80477. Eugene Buchanan, Ed. Dir. Articles on canoeing, kayaking, rafting, sea kayaking. "Best way to break in is to target a specific department, i.e. 'Hotlines,' 'Paddle People,' etc." Pays $5 an inch, on publication. Query preferred. Guidelines.

PENNSYLVANIA ANGLER—Pennsylvania Fish and Boat Commission, P.O. Box 67000, Harrisburg, PA 17106–7000. Attn: Art Michaels, Ed. Articles, 500 to 3,000 words, with photos, on freshwater fishing in Pennsylvania. Pays

$50 to $400, on acceptance. Must send SASE with all material. Query. Guidelines.

PENNSYLVANIA GAME NEWS—Game Commission, 2001 Elmerton Ave., Harrisburg, PA 17110–9797. Bob Mitchell, Ed. Articles, to 2,500 words, on outdoor subjects, except fishing and boating. Photos. Pays from 6¢ a word, extra for photos, on acceptance.

PETERSEN'S BOWHUNTING— 6420 Wilshire Blvd., Los Angeles, CA 90048–5515. Greg Tinsley, Ed. How-to articles, 2,000 to 2,500 words, on bowhunting. Also pieces on where to bowhunt, unusual techniques and equipment, and profiles of successful bowhunters will also be considered. Photos must accompany all manuscripts. Pays $300 to $400, on acceptance. Query.

PLANE & PILOT—12121 Wilshire Blvd., #1200, Los Angeles, CA 90025–1175. SteveWerner, Ed. Aviation related articles, 1,500 to 3,000 words, targeted to the single engine, piston powered recreational pilot. Training, maintenance, travel, equipment, pilot reports. Occasional features on antique, classic, and kit- or home-built aircraft. Payment varies, on publication. Query preferred.

POWER AND MOTORYACHT—249 W. 17th St., New York, NY 10011. Diane M. Byrne, Man. Ed. Articles, 1,000 to 2,000 words, for owners of powerboats, 24 feet and larger. Seamanship, ship's systems, maintenance, sportfishing news, travel destinations, profiles of individuals working to improve the marine environment. "For our readers, powerboating is truly a lifestyle, not just a hobby." Pays $500 to $1,000, on acceptance. Query required.

POWERBOAT—1691 Spinnaker Dr., Suite 206, Ventura, CA 93001. Eric Colby, Ed. Articles, to 2,000 words, with photos, for high performance powerboat owners, on outstanding achievements, water-skiing, competitions; technical articles on hull and engine developments; how-to pieces. Pays $300 to $1,000, on publication. Query.

PRACTICAL HORSEMAN—Box 589, Unionville, PA 19375. Mandy Lorraine, Ed. How-to articles conveying experts' advice on English riding, training, and horse care. Pays on acceptance. Query with clips.

PRO BASKETBALL ILLUSTRATED—See *Hockey Illustrated.*

PRO FOOTBALL ILLUSTRATED, PRO FOOTBALL PREVIEW—See *Hockey Illustrated.*

PURE-BRED DOGS/AMERICAN KENNEL GAZETTE—See *AKC Gazette.*

RIDER—2575 Vista Del Mar, Ventura, CA 93001. Mark Tuttle Jr., Ed. Articles, to 3,000 words, with slides, on travel, touring, commuting, and camping motorcyclists. Pays $100 to $750, on publication. Query.

ROCK + ICE MAGAZINE— 603A S. Broadway, Boulder, CO 80303. Marjorie McCloy, Ed. Bimonthly. Articles, 500 to 6,000 words, and fiction, 1,500 to 4,000 words, for technical rock and ice climbers: sport climbers, mountaineers, alpinists, and other adventurers. Slides and B&W photos considered. Query. Pays $300 per published page.

RUNNER'S WORLD—Rodale Press, 33 E. Minor St., Emmaus, PA 18098. Bob Wischnia, Sr. Ed. Articles for "Human Race" (submit to Eileen Shovlin), "Finish Line" (to Cristina Negron), and "Health Watch" (to Adam Bean) columns. Send feature articles or queries to Bob Wischnia. Payment varies, on acceptance. Query.

608

RV TRAVELER—Woodall Publishing Co., P.O. Box 5000, Lake Forest, IL 60045–5000. Debbie Harmsen, Ed. RV-related travel articles, 1,000 to 1,200 words, for Midwest camping families. Pay varies, on publication.

SAFARI— 4800 W. Gates Pass Rd., Tucson, AZ 85745. William Quimby, Publications Dir. Articles, 2,000 words, on worldwide big game hunting and/ or conservation projects of Safari Club International's local chapters. Pays $200, extra for photos, on publication.

SAIL—275 Washington St., Newton, MA 02158–1630. Patience Wales, Ed. Articles, 1,500 to 3,500 words, features, 1,000 to 2,500 words, with photos, on sailboats, equipment, racing, and cruising. How-tos on navigation, sail trim, etc. Pays $75 to $1,000 on publication. Guidelines.

SAILING—125 E. Main St., Port Washington, WI 53074. M. L. Hutchins, Ed. Features, 700 to 1,500 words, with photos, on cruising and racing; first-person accounts; profiles of boats and regattas. Query for technical or how-to pieces. Pays varying rates, 30 days after publication. Guidelines.

SALT WATER SPORTSMAN—77 Franklin St., Boston, MA 02110. Barry Gibson, Ed. Articles, 1,200 to 1,500 words, on how anglers can improve their skills, and on new places to fish off the coast of the U.S. and Canada, Central America, the Caribbean, and Bermuda. Photos a plus. Pays $350 to $700, on acceptance. Query.

SEA, AMERICA'S WESTERN BOATING MAGAZINE—17782 Cowan, Suite C, Irvine, CA 92614. Eston Ellis, Sr. Ed. Features, 800 to 1,500 words, and news articles, 200 to 250 words, of interest to West Coast power boaters: cruise destinations, analyses of marine environmental issues, technical pieces on navigation and seamanship, news from western harbors. No fiction, poetry, or cartoons. Pays varying rates, on publication.

SEA KAYAKER—P.O. Box 17170, Seattle, WA 98107–0870. Christopher Cunningham, Ed. Articles, 400 to 4,500 words, on ocean kayaking. Related fiction. Pays about 12¢ a word, on publication. Query with clips and international reply coupons.

SHOTGUN SPORTS—P.O. Box 6810, Auburn, CA 95604. Frank Kodl, Ed. Articles with photos, on trap and skeet shooting, sporting clays, hunting with shotguns, reloading, gun tests, and instructional shooting. Pays $25 to $200, on publication.

SILENT SPORTS—717 10th St., P.O. Box 152, Waupaca, WI 54981–9990. Attn: Ed. Articles, 1,000 to 2,000 words, on bicycling, cross country skiing, running, canoeing, hiking, backpacking, and other "silent" sports. Must have regional (upper Midwest) focus. Pays $50 to $100 for features; $20 to $50 for fillers, on publication. Query.

SKI MAGAZINE—2 Park Ave., New York, NY 10016. Andy Bigford, Ed. Articles, 1,300 to 2,000 words, for experienced skiers: profiles, and destination articles. Short, 100-to 300-word, news items for "Ski Life" column. Equipment and racing articles are staff-written. Query (with clips) for articles. Pays from $50, on acceptance.

SKI RACING INTERNATIONAL—Box 1125, Rt. 100, Waitsfield, VT 05673. Jill Jemison, Man. Ed. Articles by experts on race techniques and conditioning secrets. Coverage of World Cup, pro, collegiate, and junior ski and snowboard competition. Comprehensive results. Photos. Rates vary.

609

SKIN DIVER MAGAZINE— 6420 Wilshire Blvd., Los Angeles, CA 90048–5515. Bill Gleason, Pub./Ed. Illustrated articles, 500 to 2,000 words, on scuba diving activities, equipment, and dive sites. Pays $50 per published page, on publication.

SKYDIVING MAGAZINE—1725 N. Lexington Ave., DeLand, FL 32724. Michael Truffer, Ed. Timely news articles, 300 to 800 words, relating to sport and military parachuting. Fillers. Photos. Pays $25 to $200, extra for photos, on publication.

SNOW COUNTRY—5520 Park Ave., Trumbull, CT 06611–0395. Kathleen Ring, Sr. Ed. Published 8 times a year. Features, 2,500 to 4,000 words, and articles, 1,000 to 2,000 words on skiing, mountain biking, in-line skating, camping, rafting and other year-round mountain sports as well as lifestyle issues. First-person adventure articles, travel pieces, service-oriented articles, profiles of snow country residents. "Mountain Living," 100-to 700-word pieces on people and points of view, anecdotes, trends, issues. Query with clips and resumé. Pays 80¢ a word, on acceptance.

SNOWEST—520 Park Ave., Idaho Falls, ID 83402. Lane Lindstrom, Ed. Articles, 1,200 words, on snowmobiling in the western states. Pays to $100, on publication.

SOCCER JR.—27 Unquowa Rd., Fairfield, CT 06430. Joe Provey, Ed. Articles, fiction, and fillers related to soccer for readers in 5th and 6th grade. Pays $450 for features; $250 for department pieces, on acceptance. Query.

SOUTH CAROLINA WILDLIFE—P. O. Box 167, Columbia, SC 29202–0167. John E. Davis, Ed. Articles, 1,000 to 2,000 words, with state and regional outdoor focus: conservation, natural history, wildlife, and recreation. Profiles, how-tos. Pays on acceptance.

SPORT MAGAZINE— 6420 Wilshire Blvd., Los Angeles, CA 90048. Cam Benty, Ed. Dir. No fiction, poetry, or first person. Query with clips.

SPORTS ILLUSTRATED—1271 Ave. of the Americas, New York, NY 10020. Chris Hunt, Articles Ed. Query.

SPORTS ILLUSTRATED FOR KIDS—1271 Ave. of the Americas, New York, NY 10020–1393. Steve Malley, Asst. Man. Ed. Articles, 1,000 to 1,500 words, (submit to Amy Lennard Goehner) and short features, 500 to 600 words, (submit to Jon Scher) for 8-to 13-year-olds. "Most articles are staff-written. Department pieces are the best bet for free lancers." (Read magazine and guidelines to learn about specific departments.) Puzzles and games (submit to Erin Egan). No fiction or poetry. Pays $500 for departments, $1,000 to $1,250 for articles, on acceptance. Query required.

STOCK CAR RACING— 65 Parker St., #2, Newburyport, MA 01950. Dick Berggren, Feature Ed. Articles, to 6,000 words, on stock car drivers, races, and vehicles. Photos. Pays to $400, on publication.

SURFING—P. O. Box 3010, San Clemente, CA 92674. Nick Carroll, Ed. Skip Snead, Asst. Ed. Short newsy and humorous articles, 200 to 500 words. No first-person travel articles. "Knowledge of the sport is essential." Pays varying rates, on publication.

SWEAT—736 E. Loyola Dr., Tempe, AZ 85282. Joan Westlake, Ed. Articles, 500 to 1,200 words, on sports or fitness with an Arizona angle. "No personal articles or tales. We want investigative pieces. Articles must relate specifically to Arizona or Arizonans." Pays $25 to $60 for articles; $12 to $70 for photos, on publication. Queries required; no unsolicited manuscripts.

T'AI CHI—P.O. Box 26156, Los Angeles, CA 90026. Marvin Smalheiser, Ed. Articles, 800 to 4,000 words, on T'ai Chi Ch'uan, other internal martial arts and related topics such as qigong, Chinese medicine and healing practices, Chinese philosophy and culture, health, meditation, fitness, and self-improvement. Pays $75 to $500, on publication. Query required. Guidelines.

TENNIS—5520 Park Ave., P. O. Box 0395, Trumbull, CT 06611–0395. Donna Doherty, Ed. Instructional articles, features, profiles of tennis stars, grassroots articles, humor, 800 to 2,000 words. Photos. Payment varies, on publication. Query.

TENNIS WEEK—341 Madison Ave., #600, New York, NY 10017–3705. Eugene L. Scott, Pub. Kim Kodl, Cherry V. Masih, Merrill Chapman, Man. Eds. In-depth, researched articles, from 1,000 words, on current issues and personalities in the game. Pays $125, on publication.

TRAILER BOATS—20700 Belshaw Ave., Carson, CA 90746–3510. Randy Scott, Ed. Lifestyle, technical and how-to articles, 500 to 2,000 words, on boat, trailer, or tow vehicle maintenance and operation; skiing, fishing, and cruising. Fillers, humor. Pays $100 to $700, on acceptance.

TRAILER LIFE—2575 Vista Del Mar, Ventura, CA 93001. Barbara Leonard, Ed. Articles, to 2,000 words, with photos, on trailering, truck campers, motorhomes, hobbies, and RV lifestyles. How-to pieces. Pays to $600, on acceptance. Guidelines.

TRIATHLETE—121 Second St., San Francisco, CA 94105. Lisa Y. Park, Man. Ed. Published 12 times yearly. Articles, varying lengths, pertaining to the sport of triathlon. Color slides. Pays 15¢ a word, on publication. Query.

VELONEWS—1830 N. 55th St., Boulder, CO 80301. John Wilcockson, Ed. John Rezell, Sr. Ed. Articles, 500 to 1,500 words, on competitive cycling, training, nutrition; profiles, interviews. No how-to or touring articles. "We focus on the elite of the sport." Pay varies, on publication.

THE WALKING MAGAZINE—9–11 Harcourt, Boston, MA 02116. Seth Bauer, Ed. Articles, 1,500 to 2,000 words, on fitness, health, equipment, nutrition, travel, and adventure, famous walkers, and other walking-related topics. Shorter pieces, 500 to 1,500 words, and essays for "Ramblings" page. Photos welcome. Pays $750 to $2,500 for features, $100 to $600 for department pieces, on acceptance. Guidelines.

THE WATER SKIER—799 Overlook Dr., Winter Haven, FL 33884. Jonathan Cullimore, Man. Ed. Feature articles on waterskiing. Pays varying rates, on publication.

WATERSKI—World Publications, Inc., 330 W. Canton Ave., Winter Park, FL 32789. Rob May, Ed. Features, 1,250 to 2,000 words, on boating and water skiing. Instructional features, 1,350 words, including sidebars; quick tips, 350 words. (Travel pieces and profiles are done on assignment only.) Pays $35 for fillers; $125 to $500 for columns and features, after acceptance. Guidelines. Query.

THE WESTERN HORSEMAN—P.O. Box 7980, Colorado Springs, CO 80933–7980. Pat Close, Ed. Articles, about 1,500 words, with photos, on care and training of horses; farm, ranch, and stable management; health care and veterinary medicine. Pays to $400, on acceptance.

611

WESTERN OUTDOORS—3197-E Airport Loop, Costa Mesa, CA 92626. Attn: Ed. Timely, factual articles on fishing, 1,200 to 1,500 words, of interest to western sportsmen. Pays $400 to $500, on acceptance. Query. Guidelines.

WESTERN SPORTSMAN—140 Ave. F N., Saskatoon, Sask., Canada S7L 1V8. George Gruenefeld, Ed. Articles, to 2,500 words, on hunting and fishing in British Columbia, Alberta, Saskatchewan, and Manitoba; how-to pieces. Photos. Pays $75 to $300, on acceptance.

WINDSURFING—P.O. Box 2456, Winter Park, FL 32790. Tom James, Ed. Features, instructional pieces, and tips, by experienced boardsailors. Fast action photos. Pays $50 to $75 for tips, $250 to $300 for features, extra for photos. SASE for guidelines.

WINDY CITY SPORTS—1450 W. Randolph, Chicago, IL 60607. Jeff Banowetz, Ed. Articles, 1,000 words, on amateur sports in Chicago. Pays $100, on publication. Query required.

WOMEN'S SPORTS + FITNESS—170 E. 61st St., 6th Fl., New York, NY 10021. Mary Duffy, Ed. Articles on fitness, nutrition, outdoor sports; how-tos; profiles; adventure travel pieces; and controversial issues in women's sports, 500 to 2,000 words. Pays on publication.

WRESTLING WORLD—See *Hockey Illustrated.*

YACHTING—20 E. Elm St., Greenwich, CT 06830. Charles Barthold, Ed. Articles, 1,500 words, on upscale recreational power and sail boating. How-to and personal-experience pieces. Photos. Pays $350 to $1,000, on acceptance. Queries preferred.

AUTOMOTIVE MAGAZINES

AMERICAN MOTORCYCLIST—American Motorcyclist Assn., 33 Collegeview Rd., Westerville, OH 43081–1484. Greg Harrison, Ed. Articles and fiction, to 3,000 words, on motorcycling: news coverage, personalities, tours. Photos. Pays varying rates, on publication. Query with SASE.

CAR AND DRIVER—2002 Hogback Rd., Ann Arbor, MI 48105. Steve Spence, Man. Ed. Articles and profiles, to 2,500 words, on unusual people or manufacturers involved in cars, racing, etc. "Ninety percent staff-written. Query with clips. No unsolicited manuscripts." Pays to $2,500, on acceptance.

CAR & TRAVEL—1000 AAA Dr., Heathrow, FL 32746–5063. Douglas Damerst, Ed. Automobile and travel concerns, including automotive travel, purchasing, and upkeep, 750 to 1,500 words. Pays $300 to $600, on acceptance. Query with clips; articles are by assignment only.

CYCLE WORLD—1499 Monrovia Ave., Newport Beach, CA 92663. David Edwards, Ed.-in-Chief. Technical and feature articles, 1,500 to 2,500 words, for motorcycle enthusiasts. Photos. Pays $100 to $200 per page, on publication. Query.

MOTOR TREND—6420 Wilshire Blvd., Los Angeles, CA 90048–5515. C. Van Tune, Ed. Articles, 250 to 2,000 words, on autos, auto history, racing, events, and profiles. Photos required. Pay varies, on acceptance. Query.

OPEN WHEEL—See *Stock Car Racing.*

RESTORATION—P.O. Box 50046, Dept. TW, Tucson, AZ 85703–1046. W.R. Haessner, Ed. Articles, 1,200 to 1,800 words, on restoration of autos, trucks, planes, trains, etc., and related building (bridges, structures, etc.). Photos. Pays from $25 per page, on publication. Queries required.

RIDER—2575 Vista Del Mar Dr., Ventura, CA 93001. Mark Tuttle Jr., Ed. Articles, to 3,000 words, with color slides, on travel, touring, commuting, and camping motorcyclists. Pays $100 to $750, on publication. Query.

ROAD & TRACK—1499 Monrovia Ave., Newport Beach, CA 92663. Ellida Maki, Man. Ed. Short automotive articles, to 450 words, of a "timeless nature" for knowledgeable car enthusiasts. Pays on publication. Query.

ROAD KING—Hammock Publishing, 3322 W. End Ave., Suite 700, Nashville, TN 37203. Tom Berg, Ed. Bill Hudgins, Ed. Dir. Bimonthly. Articles, 300 to 1,500 words, on business of trucking from a driver's point of view; profiles of drivers and their rigs; technical aspects of trucking equipment; trucking history; travel destinations near major interstates; humor; fillers. No fiction. Include clips with submission. Pays negotiable rates, on acceptance.

STOCK CAR RACING—65 Parker St., #2, Newburyport, MA 01950. Dick Berggren, Ed. Features, technical automotive pieces, and profiles of interesting racing personalities, to 6,000 words, for oval track racing enthusiasts. Fillers. Pays $75 to $350, on publication. Same requirements for *Open Wheel*.

FITNESS MAGAZINES

AMERICAN FITNESS—15250 Ventura Blvd., Suite 200, Sherman Oaks, CA 91403. Peg Jordan, R.N., Ed. Rhonda Wilson, Man. Ed. Articles, 500 to 1,500 words, on exercise, health, research, trends, research, nutrition, alternative paths, etc. Illustrations, photos.

COOKING LIGHT—P.O. Box 1748, Birmingham, AL 35201. Melissa Aspell, Fitness Ed. Articles on fitness, exercise, health and healthful cooking, nutrition, and healthful recipes. Query.

FITNESS—Gruner & Jahr USA Publishing, 110 Fifth Ave., New York, NY 10011. Sally Lee, Ed. Articles, 500 to 2,000 words, on health, exercise, sports, nutrition, diet, psychological well-being, alternative therapies, sex, and beauty for readers around 30 years old. Queries required. Pays $1 per word, on acceptance.

IDEA TODAY—6190 Cornerstone Ct. E., Suite 204, San Diego, CA 92121–3773. Terese Hannon, Asst. Ed. Practical articles, 1,000 to 3,000 words, on new exercise programs, business management, nutrition, sports medicine, dance-exercise, and one-to-one training techniques. Articles must be geared toward the aerobics instructor, exercise studio owner or manager, or personal trainer. No consumer or general health articles. Payment is negotiable, on acceptance. Query preferred.

INSIDE TEXAS RUNNING—9514 Bristlebrook Dr., Houston, TX 77083–6193. Joanne Schmidt, Ed. Articles and fillers on running in Texas. Pays $35 to $100 for articles, $10 to $25 for photos and short fillers, on acceptance.

MEN'S FITNESS—21100 Erwin St., Woodland Hills, CA 91367. Peter Sikowitz, Ed.-in-Chief. Features, 1,500 to 1,800 words, and department pieces, 1,200 to 1,500 words: "authoritative and practical articles dealing with fitness, health, and men's issues." Pays $500 to $2,000, on acceptance. Limited market.

MEN'S HEALTH—Rodale Press, 33 E. Minor St., Emmaus, PA 18098. Jeff Csatari, Sr. Ed. Articles, 1,000 to 2,500 words, on fitness, diet, health, relationships, sports, and travel, for men ages 25 to 55. Pays from 50¢ a word, on acceptance. Query.

NATURAL HEALTH—17 Station St., Box 1200, Brookline Village, MA 02147. Bimonthly. Features, 1,500 to 3,000 words: practical information, new discoveries, and current trends about natural health and living. Topics include: natural goods and medicines, alternative health care, nutrition, wellness, personal fitness, and modern holistic teachings. Departments and columns, 250 to 1,000 words. Pays varying rates, on acceptance.

THE PHYSICIAN AND SPORTSMEDICINE— 4530 W. 77th St., Minneapolis, MN 55435. Terry Monahan, Exec. Ed. News and feature articles. Clinical articles must be co-authored by physicians. Sports medicine angle necessary. Pays $150 to $1,000, on acceptance. Query. Guidelines.

SHAPE—21100 Erwin St., Woodland Hills, CA 91367–3772. Elizabeth Turner, Assoc. Ed. Articles, 1,200 to 1,500 words, with new and interesting ideas on the physical and mental side of getting and staying in shape; reports, 300 to 400 words, on journal research. Payment varies, on publication. Guidelines. Limited market.

SWEAT—736 E. Loyola Dr., Tempe, AZ 85282. Joan Westlake, Ed. Articles, 500 to 1,200 words, on amateur sports, outdoor activities, wellness, or fitness with an Arizona angle. "No personal articles or tales. We want investigative pieces. Articles must relate specifically to Arizona or Arizonans." Pays $25 to $60 for articles; $15 to $70 for photos, on publication. Queries required; no unsolicited manuscripts.

TOTAL HEALTH—165 N. 100 E. #2, St. George, UT 84770. Katherine Hurd, Ed. Articles, 1,200 to 1,400 words, on fitness, diet, preventative health care, and mental health. Pays $50 to $75, on publication. Queries preferred.

VEGETARIAN TIMES—P.O. Box 570, Oak Park, IL 60303. Toni Apgar, Ed. Dir. Articles, 1,200 to 2,500 words, on vegetarian cooking, nutrition, health and fitness, and profiles of prominent vegetarians. "News Items" and "In Print" (book reviews), to 500 words. "Herbalist" pieces, to 1,800 words, on medicinal uses of herbs. Queries required. Pays $75 to $1,000, on acceptance. Guidelines.

VIM & VIGOR—1010 E. Missouri Ave., Phoenix, AZ 85014. Jake Poinier, Ed. Positive articles, with accurate medical facts, on health and fitness, 1,200 to 2,000 words, by assignment only. Writers may submit qualifications for assignment. Pays $500, on acceptance. Guidelines.

THE WALKING MAGAZINE— 9–11 Harcourt, Boston, MA 02116. Seth Bauer, Ed. Articles, 1,500 to 2,500 words, on fitness, health, equipment, nutrition, travel and adventure, famous walkers, and other walking-related topics. Shorter pieces, 150 to 800 words, and essays for "Ramblings" page. Photos welcome. Pays $750 to $1,800 for features, $100 to $500 for department pieces, within a week of acceptance. Guidelines.

WEIGHT WATCHERS MAGAZINE—360 Lexington Ave., New York, NY 10017. Randi Rose, Health Ed. Articles on health, nutrition, fitness, and weight-loss motivation and success. Pays from $500, on acceptance. Query with clips required. Guidelines.

WOMEN'S SPORTS + FITNESS—170 E. 61st St., 6th Fl., New York, NY 10021. Mary Duffy, Ed. Articles on fitness, nutrition, outdoor sports; how-tos; profiles; adventure travel pieces; and controversial issues in women's sports, 500 to 2,000 words. Pays on publication.

YOGA JOURNAL—2054 University Ave., Berkeley, CA 94704. Rick Fields, Ed. Articles, 1,200 to 4,000 words, on holistic health, meditation, consciousness, spirituality, and yoga. Pays $50 to $1,200, on publication.

YOUR HEALTH—1720 Washington Blvd., Box 10010, Ogden, UT 84409. Attn: Ed. Staff. Articles, 1,000 words, on individual health care needs: fitness, low-impact aerobics, nutrition, prevention and treatment, etc. Color photos required. Pays 15¢ a word, on acceptance.

CONSUMER/PERSONAL FINANCE

COMPLETE WOMAN— 875 N. Michigan Ave., Suite 3434, Chicago, IL 60611. Bonnie Krueger, Ed. Martha Carlson, Assoc. Ed. Articles, 1,000 to 2,000 words, with how-to sidebars, giving advice to women. Also interested in reprints. Pays varying rates, on publication. Query with clips.

FAMILY CIRCLE—110 Fifth Ave., New York, NY 10011. Nancy Clark, Deputy Ed. Ann Matturo, Celeste Mitchells, Assoc. Eds. Enterprising, creative, and practical articles, 1,000 to 1,500 words, on investing, smart ways to save money, secrets of successful entrepreneurs, and consumer news on smart shopping. Pays $1 a word, on acceptance. Query with clips.

GOOD HOUSEKEEPING— 959 Eighth Ave., New York, NY 10019. Lisa Benenson, Better Way Ed. Short advice-driven articles on money, finances, consumer issues, health, and safety for "Better Way" section. Pays good rates, on acceptance. Guidelines.

KIPLINGER'S PERSONAL FINANCE MAGAZINE—1729 H St. N.W., Washington, DC 20006. Attn: Ed. Dept. Articles on personal finance (i.e., buying insurance, mutual funds). Pays varying rates, on acceptance. Query required.

KIWANIS—3636 Woodview Trace, Indianapolis, IN 46468. Chuck Jonak, Man. Ed. Articles, 2,500 words, on financial planning for younger families and retirement planning for older people. Pays $400 to $1,000, on acceptance. Query required.

MODERN BRIDE—249 W. 17th St., New York, NY 10011. Mary Ann Cavlin, Exec. Ed. Articles, 1,500 to 2,000 words, for bride and groom, on wedding planning, financial planning, juggling career and home, etc. Pays $600 to $1,200, on acceptance.

MODERN MATURITY—3200 E. Carson St., Lakewood, CA 90712. Annette Winter, Sr. Ed. Articles, 300 to 2,000 words, on a wide range of financial topics of interest to people over 50. Pays from $1 a word, on acceptance. Queries required.

NEW CHOICES FOR RETIREMENT LIVING—See *New Choices: Living Even Better After 50.*

NEW CHOICES: LIVING EVEN BETTER AFTER 50—(formerly *New Choices for Retirement Living*) 28 W. 23rd St., New York, NY 10010. Allen J. Sheinman, Articles Ed. David A. Sendler, Ed.-in-Chief. News and service magazine for people ages 50 to 65. Articles on retirement planning, financial strategies, housing options, as well as health and fitness, travel, leisure pursuits, etc. Payment varies, on acceptance.

NEW WOMAN—215 Lexington Ave., New York, NY 10016. Attn: Manuscripts and Proposals. Articles for women ages 25 to 49, on careers, money, relationships, health and fitness, fashion, beauty, food and nutrition, travel with a self-growth angle. Pays about $1 a word, on acceptance. Query with SASE.

OUT—The Soho Bldg., 110 Greene St., Suite 600, New York, NY 10012. Sarah Pettit, Ed.-in-Chief. Articles, 50 to 8,000 words, on arts, politics, fashion, finance and other subjects for gay and lesbian readers. Guidelines. Query.

RETIRED MILITARY FAMILY—169 Lexington Ave., New York, NY 10016. Stacy P. Brassington, Ed. Articles, 1,000 to 1,500 words, on finance, second careers and other topics of interest to military retirees and their families. Pays up to $200, on publication.

ROBB REPORT—1 Acton Pl., Acton, MA 01720. Robert R. Feeman, Ed. Features on investment opportunities for high-end/luxury market. Lifestyle articles, home interiors, boats, travel, exotic automobiles, business, technology, etc. Payment varies, on publication. Query with SASE and clips.

SENIOR HIGHLIGHTS—26081 Merit Cir., Suite 101, Laguna Hills, CA 92653. Carol Folz, Man. Ed. Articles, 800 words, on money, lifestyles, health, and travel. No payment. Guidelines. Query with SASE.

SILVER CIRCLE—4900 Rivergrade Rd., Irwindale, CA 91706. Jay Binkly, Ed. National consumer-interest quarterly. Consumer service articles, 800 to 3,000 words, on careers, money, health, home, auto, gardening, food, travel, hobbies, etc. Pays $250 to $2,000, on acceptance. Query.

WOMAN'S DAY—1633 Broadway, New York, NY 10019. Rebecca Greer, Sr. Articles Ed. Articles, to 2,000 words, on financial matters of interest to a broad range of women. Pays top rates, on acceptance. Query with SASE. No unsolicited manuscripts.

WOMEN IN BUSINESS—American Business Women's Assn., 9100 Ward Pkwy., P.O. Box 8728, Kansas City, MO 64114–0728. Dawn J. Grubb, Man. Ed. How-to business features, 800 to 1,200 words, for working women. Business trends, small-business ownership, self-improvement, and retirement issues; all articles must include members of the American Business Women's Association. Pays on acceptance. Query.

YOUR MONEY—5705 N. Lincoln Ave., Chicago, IL 60659. Dennis Fertig, Ed. Informative, jargon-free personal finance articles, to 2,500 words, for the general reader, on investment opportunities and personal finance. Pays 40¢ a word, on acceptance. Query with clips for assignment. (Do not send manuscripts on disks.)

BUSINESS AND TRADE PUBLICATIONS

ABA JOURNAL—American Bar Assn., 750 N. Lake Shore Dr., Chicago, IL 60611. Gary A. Hengstler, Ed./Pub. Articles, to 3,000 words, on law-related topics: current events in the law and ideas that will help lawyers practice better and more efficiently. Writing should be in an informal, journalistic style. Pays from $1,000, on acceptance; buys all rights.

ACCESSORIES MAGAZINE—50 Day St., Norwalk, CT 06854. Karen Alberg, Ed. Dir. Articles, with photos, for women's fashion accessories buyers and manufacturers. Profiles of retailers, designers, manufacturers; articles on merchandising and marketing. Pays $75 to $200 for short articles, from $200 to $500 for features, on publication. Query.

ACROSS THE BOARD—845 Third Ave., New York, NY 10022. Karen Bodner, Asst. to the Ed. Articles, 1,000 to 4,000 words, on a variety of topics of interest to business executives; straight business angle not required. Payment varies, on publication.

ALTERNATIVE ENERGY RETAILER—P.O. Box 2180, Waterbury, CT 06722. John Florian, Ed. Dir. Feature articles, 1,000 words, for retailers of hearth products, including appliances that burn wood, coal, pellets, and gas, and hearth accessories and services. Interviews with successful retailers, stressing the how-to. B&W photos. Pays $200, extra for photos, on publication. Query.

AMERICAN DEMOGRAPHICS—P.O. Box 68, Ithaca, NY 14851–9989. Brad Edmondson, Ed.-in-Chief. Articles, 500 to 2,000 words, on the 4 key elements of a consumer market (its size, its needs and wants, its ability to pay, and how it can be reached), with specific examples of how companies market to consumers. Readers include marketers, advertisers, and strategic planners. Pays $100 to $500, on acceptance. Query.

AMERICAN MEDICAL NEWS—515 N. State St., Chicago, IL 60610. Ronni Scheier, Deputy Ed. Articles, 900 to 1,500 words, on socioeconomic developments in health care of interest to physicians across the country. No pieces on health, clinical treatments, or research. Pays $500 to $1,500, on acceptance. Query required. Guidelines.

AMERICAN SCHOOL & UNIVERSITY—P.O. Box 12901, 9800 Metcalf, Overland Park, KS 66212–2215. Joe Agron, Ed. Articles and case studies, 1,200 to 1,500 words, on design, construction, operation, and management of school and university facilities. Queries preferred.

ARCHITECTURE—1130 Connecticut Ave. N.W., Suite 625, Washington, DC 20036. Quincy Baldwin, Ed. Articles, to 3,000 words, on architecture, building technology, professional practice. Pays 50¢ a word.

AREA DEVELOPMENT MAGAZINE—400 Post Ave., Westbury, NY 11590. Geraldine Gambale, Ed. Articles for top executives of industrial companies on sites and facility planning. Pays 25¢ per work. Query.

ART BUSINESS NEWS—19 Old King's Hwy. S., Darien, CT 06820. Sarah Seamark, Ed. Articles, 1,000 words, for art dealers and framers, on trends and events of national importance to the art and framing industry, and relevant business subjects. Payment varies, on publication. Query preferred.

AUTOMATED BUILDER—P.O. Box 120, Carpinteria, CA 93014. Don Carlson, Ed. Articles, 500 to 750 words, on various types of home manufacturers and dealers with slides or color prints. Pays $300, on acceptance, for articles with photos. Query required.

BARRON'S—200 Liberty St., New York, NY 10281. Edwin A. Finn, Jr., Ed. Investment-interest articles. Query.

BEAUTY EDUCATION—3 Columbia Cir., Albany, NY 12212. Catherine Frangie, Pub. Articles, 750 to 1,000 words, that provide beauty educators, trainers, and professionals in the cosmetology industry with information, skills, and techniques on such topics as hairstyling, makeup, aromatherapy, retailing, massage, and beauty careers. Send SASE for editorial calendar and themes. Pays in copies. Query.

BICYCLE RETAILER AND INDUSTRY NEWS—502 W. Cordova Rd., Santa Fe, NM 87501. Marc Sani, Ed. Articles, to 1,200 words, on employee management, employment strategies, and general business subjects for bicycle manufacturers, distributors, and retailers. Pays 20¢ a word (higher rates for more complex articles), plus expenses, within 30 days of publication. Query.

BOOKPAGE—ProMotion, Inc., 2501 21st Ave. S., Suite 5, Nashville, TN 37212. Ann Meador Shayne, Ed. Book reviews, 500 words, for a consumer-oriented tabloid used by booksellers to promote new titles and authors. Query with writing samples and areas of interest; Editor will make assignments for reviews. Pays in copies. Guidelines.

BUILDER—Hanley-Wood, Inc., One Thomas Cir. N.W., Suite 600, Washington, DC 20005. Noreen S. Welle, Ed. Articles, to 1,500 words, on trends and news in home building: design, marketing, new products, etc. Pays negotiable rates, on acceptance. Query.

BUSINESS—P.O. Box 10010, Ogden, UT 84409. Beth McDaniel, Man. Ed. Informative articles, 1,000 words, on business concerns of the businessperson/entrepreneur in U.S. and Canada. Color photos. Pays 15¢ a word; $35 to $50 for photos. Query. Guidelines.

BUSINESS TIMES—P.O. Box 580, 315 Peck St., New Haven, CT 06513. Joel MacClaren, Ed. Articles on Connecticut-based businesses and corporations. Query.

CAMPGROUND MANAGEMENT—P.O. Box 5000, Lake Forest, IL 60045–5000. Mike Byrnes, Ed. Detailed articles, 500 to 2,000 words, on managing recreational vehicle campgrounds. Photos. Pays $50 to $200, after publication.

CHIEF EXECUTIVE—733 Third Ave., 21st Fl., New York, NY 10017. J.P. Donlon, Ed. CEO bylines. Articles, 2,500 to 3,000 words, on management, financial, or business strategies. Departments, 1,200 to 1,500 words, on investments, amenities, and travel. Features on CEOs at leisure, Q&A's with CEOs, other topics. Pays varying rates, on acceptance. Query required.

CHRISTIAN RETAILING—600 Rinehart Rd., Lake Mary, FL 32746. Carol Chapman Stertzer, Man. Ed. Features, 1,500 to 2,300 words, on new products, trends, or topics related to running a profitable Christian retail store. Pays $150 to $300, on publication.

CLEANING AND MAINTENANCE MANAGEMENT MAGAZINE—13 Century Hill Dr., Latham, NY 12110–2197. Anne Dantz, Ed. Articles, 500 to 1,200 words, on managing efficient cleaning and custodial/maintenance operations, profiles, photo-features, or general-interest articles directly related to the industry; also technical/mechanical how-tos. Photos encouraged. Pays to $200 for features, on publication. Query. Guidelines.

CLUB MANAGEMENT—8730 Big Bend Blvd., St. Louis, MO 63114. Tom Finan, Pub. The official magazine of the Club Managers Assn. of America. Features, to 2,000 words, and news items from 100 words, on management, budget, cuisine, personnel, government regulations, etc., for executives who run private clubs. "Writing should be tight and conversational, with liberal use of quotes." Color photos usually required with manuscript. Query preferred. Guidelines.

618

COMMERCIAL CARRIER JOURNAL—Chilton Way, Radnor, PA 19089. Paul Richards, Man. Ed. Thoroughly researched articles on private fleets and for-hire trucking operations. Pays from $50, on acceptance. Queries required.

COMPUTER GRAPHICS WORLD—10 Tara Blvd., Suite 500, Nashua, NH 03062–2801. Stephen Porter, Ed. Articles, 1,000 to 3,000 words, on computer graphics and multimedia technology and their use in science, engineering, architecture, film and broadcast, and interactive entertainment areas. Photos. Pays $600 to $1,000 per article, on acceptance. Query.

THE CONSTRUCTION SPECIFIER—Construction Specifications Institute, 601 Madison St., Alexandria, VA 22314. Jack Reeder, Ed. Technical articles, 1,000 to 3,000 words, on the "nuts and bolts" of commercial construction, for architects, engineers, specifiers, contractors, and manufacturers. Pays 15¢ per word, on publication.

CONVERTING MAGAZINE—1350 E. Touhy Ave., P.O. Box 5080, Des Plaines, IL 60017–5080. Mark Spaulding, Ed.-in-Chief. Business articles, 750 to 1,500 words, serving the technical, trends, and productivity information needs of flexible-packaging converting companies, as well as manufacturers of labels, paperboard cartons, and other converted products. Payment varies, on publication. Query required.

COOKING FOR PROFIT—P.O. Box 267, Fond du Lac, WI 54936–0267. Colleen Phalen, Pub./Ed.-in-Chief. Articles, of varying lengths, for foodservice professionals: profiles of successful restaurants, chains, and franchises, schools, hospitals, nursing homes, or other "institutional feeders"; also case studies on successful energy management within the foodservice environment. Business to business articles of interest to foodservice professionals. Payment varies, on publication.

CRAIN'S CHICAGO BUSINESS—740 Rush St., Chicago, IL 60611. Glenn Coleman, Man. Ed. Business articles about the Chicago metropolitan area exclusively.

DAIRY FOODS MAGAZINE —Cahners Publishing Co., 1350 E. Touhy Ave., Des Plaines, IL 60018. Ellen Mather, Ed. Articles, to 2,500 words, on innovative dairies, dairy processing operations, marketing successes, new products for milk handlers and makers of dairy products. Fillers, 25 to 150 words. Payment varies.

DENTAL ECONOMICS—P.O. Box 3408, Tulsa, OK 74101. Dick Hale, Ed. Articles, 1,200 to 3,500 words, on business side of dental practice, patient and staff communication, personal investments, etc. Pays $100 to $400, on acceptance.

DRAPERIES & WINDOW COVERINGS— 450 Skokie Blvd., Suite 507, Northbrook, IL 60062–7913. Katie Sosnowchik, Ed. Articles, 1,000 to 2,000 words, for retailers, wholesalers, designers, and manufacturers of draperies and window, wall, and floor coverings. Profiles, with photos, of successful businesses in the industry; management and marketing related articles. Pays $150 to $250, after acceptance. Query.

EMERGENCY— 6300 Yarrow Dr., Carlsbad, CA 92009–1597. Doug Fiske, Ed. Articles, to 3,000 words, of interest to paramedics, emergency medical technicians, flight nurses, and other pre-hospital personnel; disaster management, advanced and basic life support, assessment, treatment. Pays $100 to

$400 for features, $50 to $300 for departments. Photos are a plus. Guidelines and editorial calendar available.

EMPLOYEE SERVICES MANAGEMENT—NESRA, 2211 York Rd., Suite 207, Oak Brook, IL 60521–2371. Cynthia M. Helson, Ed. Articles, 1,200 to 2,500 words, for human resource and employee service professionals on work/life issues, employee services, wellness, management and personal development. Pays in copies.

THE ENGRAVERS JOURNAL—26 Summit St., P.O. Box 318, Brighton, MI 48116. Rosemary Farrell, Man. Ed. Articles, of varying lengths, on topics related to the engraving industry or small business. Pays $60 to $175, on acceptance. Query.

ENTREPRENEUR—2392 Morse Ave., Irvine, CA 92614. Rieva Lesonsky, Ed.-in-Chief. Articles for small business owners, on all aspects of running a business. Pay varies, on acceptance. Query required.

EXECUTIVE FEMALE—30 Irving Pl., New York, NY 10003. Gay Bryant, Ed.-in-Chief. Articles, 750 to 2,500 words, on managing people, time, money, companies, and careers, for women in business. Pays varying rates, on acceptance. Query.

FARM JOURNAL—Centre Sq. W., 1500 Market St., Philadelphia, PA 19102–2181. Earl Ainsworth, Ed. Practical business articles, 500 to 1,500 words, with photos, on growing crops and raising livestock. Pays 20¢ to 50¢ a word, on acceptance. Query required.

FITNESS MANAGEMENT—P.O. Box 1198, Solana Beach, CA 92075. Edward H. Pitts, Ed. Authoritative features, 750 to 2,500 words, and news shorts, 100 to 750 words, for owners, managers, and program directors of fitness centers. Content must be in keeping with current medical practice; no fads. Pays 8¢ a word, on publication. Query.

FLORIST—29200 Northwestern Hwy., Southfield, MI 48034. Barbara Koch, Man. Ed. Articles, to 1,500 words, with photos, on retail florist shop management.

FLOWERS &—Teleflora Plaza, Suite 118, 12233 W. Olympic Blvd., Los Angeles, CA 90064. Joanne Jaffe, Ed.-in-Chief. Articles, 500 to 1,500 words, with how-to information for retail florists. Pays 30¢ a word, on acceptance. Query with clips.

GARDEN DESIGN—100 Ave. of the Americas, 7th Fl., New York, NY 10013. Dorothy Kalins, Ed.-in-Chief. Garden-related features, 500 to 1,000 words, on private, public, and community gardens; articles on art and history as they relate to gardens. Pays from 50¢ a word, on acceptance. Guidelines.

GENERAL AVIATION NEWS & FLYER—P.O. Box 39099, Tacoma, WA 98439–0099. Dave Sclair, Pub. Articles, 500 to 2,500 words, of interest to "general aviation" pilots. Pays to $3 per column inch (approximately 40 words); $10 for B&W photos; to $50 for color photos; within a month of publication.

GOLF COURSE NEWS—38 Lafayette St., Yarmouth, ME 04096. Hal Phillips, Ed. Features and news analyses, 500 to 1,000 words, on all aspects of golf course maintenance, design, building, and management. Pays $200, on acceptance.

GOVERNMENT EXECUTIVE—1501 M St. N.W., Washington, DC 20005. Timothy Clark, Ed. Articles, 1,500 to 3,000 words, for civilian and military government workers at the management level.

GREENHOUSE MANAGEMENT & PRODUCTION—P.O. Box 1868, Fort Worth, TX 76101–1868. David Kuack, Ed. How-to articles, innovative production and/or marketing techniques, 500 to 1,800 words, accompanied by color slides, of interest to professional greenhouse growers. Pays $50 to $300, on acceptance. Query required.

GROWERTALKS—P.O. Box 9, 335 N. River St., Batavia, IL 60510–0009. Debbie Hamrick, Ed. Dir. Articles, 800 to 2,600 words, that help commercial greenhouse growers (not florist/retailers or home gardeners) do their jobs better: trends, successes in new types of production, marketing, business management, new crops, and issues facing the industry. Payment varies, on publication. Queries preferred.

HARDWARE AGE—Chilton Way, Radnor, PA 19089. James M. Cory, Ed.-in-Chief. Articles for home improvement retailers. Almost entirely staff-written; limited free-lance needs. Query.

HARDWARE TRADE—10510 France Ave. S., #225, Bloomington, MN 55431. Patt Patterson, Ed. Dir. Articles, 800 to 1,000 words, on unusual hardware and home center stores and promotions in the Northwest and Midwest. Photos. Query.

HEALTH FOODS BUSINESS—2 University Plaza, Suite 204, Hackensack, NJ 07601. Gina Geslewitz, Ed. "The Business Magazine for Natural Products Retailers." Profiles of health food stores, 5 to 7 double-spaced pages. Pays $100 to $150, on publication. Query.

HEALTH PROGRESS— 4455 Woodson Rd., St. Louis, MO 63134–3797. Judy Cassidy, Ed. Journal of the Catholic Health Association. Features, 2,000 to 4,000 words, on hospital and nursing home management and administration, medical-moral questions, health care, public policy, technological developments in health care and their effects, nursing, financial and human resource management for health-care administrators, and innovative programs in hospitals and long-term care facilities. Payment negotiable. Query.

HEATING/PIPING/AIR CONDITIONING—2 Prudential Plaza, 180 N. Stetson Ave., Suite 2555, Chicago, IL 60601. Robert T. Korte, Ed. Articles, to 5,000 words, on heating, piping, and air conditioning systems in industrial plants and large buildings; engineering information. Pays $60 per printed page, on publication. Query.

HOME OFFICE COMPUTING—Scholastic, Inc., 411 Lafayette St., New York, NY 10003. Cathy G. Brower, Exec. Ed. Articles, 3,000 words, that provide readers with practical information on how to run their businesses and use technology more effectively. Profiles of home-based entrepreneurs and small business owners. Departments, 1,200 words, on finance, legal issues, sales and marketing, communications, government. Writers must be familiar with microcomputers and software, home office products, and issues affecting small and home businesses. Payment varies, on acceptance.

HOSPITALS & HEALTH NETWORKS—737 N. Michigan Ave., Chicago, IL 60611. Mary Grayson, Ed. Articles, 800 to 900 words, for hospital administrators. Query.

621

HUMAN RESOURCE EXECUTIVE—LRP Publications Co., 747 Dresher Rd., Horsham, PA 19044–0980. David Shadovitz, Ed. Profiles and case stories, 1,800 to 2,200 words, of interest to people in the personnel profession. Pays varying rates, on acceptance. Queries required.

IN BUSINESS—419 State Ave., Emmaus, PA 18049–3097. Jerome Goldstein, Ed. Bimonthly. Articles, 1,500 words, for environmental entrepreneurs: reports on economically successful businesses that also demonstrate a commitment to the environment, advice on growing a "green" business, family-run businesses, home-based businesses, community ecological development, etc. Pays $100 to $250 for articles; $25 to $75 for department pieces, on publication. Query with clips.

INC.—38 Commercial Wharf, Boston, MA 02110. George Gendron, Ed. No free-lance material.

INCOME OPPORTUNITIES—1500 Broadway, Suite 600, New York, NY 10036–4015. Linda Molnar, Ed.-in-Chief. Articles on marketing, financing, and managing a small or home-based business, especially on a tight budget. Profiles of entrepreneurs who started their businesses on a shoestring. Pays varying rates, on acceptance. Query; no unsolicited manuscripts.

INDEPENDENT BUSINESS—125 Auburn Ct., Suite 100, Thousand Oaks, CA 91362. Maryann Hammers, Sr. Ed. Articles, 1,200 to 2,000 words, of practical interest and value to small business owners. Pays $550 to $1,500, on acceptance. Query. Guidelines.

INDEPENDENT LIVING PROVIDER—150 Motor Pkwy., Suite 420, Hauppauge, NY 11788–5145. Anne Kelly, Ed. Articles, 1,500 to 3,000 words, on the sales and services of home medical equipment dealers. Pays 15¢ a word, on publication. Query.

INSTANT & SMALL COMMERCIAL PRINTER—P.O. Box 7280, Libertyville, IL 60048. Anne Marie Mohan, Ed. Articles, 3 to 6 typed pages, for operators and employees of printing businesses specializing in retail printing and/or small commercial printing: case histories, how-tos, technical pieces, small-business management. Pays $150 to $250, extra for photos, on publication. Query.

INTERNATIONAL BUSINESS—9 E. 40th St., 10th Fl., New York, NY 10016. Lori Ioannou, Ed.-in-Chief. Articles, 1,000 to 1,500 words, on global marketing strategies. Short pieces, 500 words, with tips on operating abroad. Profiles, 750 to 3,000 words, on individuals or companies. Pays 80¢ to $1 a word, on acceptance and on publication. Query with clips.

JEMS, JOURNAL OF EMERGENCY MEDICAL SERVICES—P.O. Box 2789, Carlsbad, CA 92018. John Becknell, Ed.-in-Chief. Articles, 1,500 to 3,000 words, of interest to emergency medical providers (EMTs, paramedics, nurses, and physicians) who work in the EMS industry worldwide.

LLAMAS—P.O. Box 100, Herald, CA 95638. Cheryl Dal Porto, Ed. "The International Camelid Journal," published 7 times yearly. Articles, 300 to 3,000 words, of interest to llama and alpaca owners. Pays $25 to $300, extra for photos, on publication. Query.

MANAGING OFFICE TECHNOLOGY—1100 Superior Ave., Cleveland, OH 44114. Lura Romei, Ed. Articles, 3 to 4 double-spaced, typed pages, on new concepts, management techniques, technologies, and applications for management executives. Payment varies, on acceptance. Query preferred.

MIX MAGAZINE— 6400 Hollis St., Suite 12, Emeryville, CA 94608. Blair Jackson, Exec. Ed. Articles, varying lengths, for professionals, on audio, audio post-production, sound production, live sound, and music entertainment technology. Pay varies, on publication. Query.

MODERN HEALTHCARE—740 N. Rush St., Chicago, IL 60611. Clark Bell, Ed. News weekly covers management, finance, building design and construction, and new technology for hospitals, health maintenance organizations, nursing homes, and other health care institutions. Pays $200 to $400, on publication. Query; very limited free-lance market.

MODERN TIRE DEALER—P.O. Box 3599, Akron, OH 44309–3599. Lloyd Stoyer, Ed. Tire retailing and automotive service articles, 1,000 to 1,500 words, with photos, on independent tire dealers and retreaders. Pays $300 to $450, on publication. Query; articles by assignment only.

NATIONAL FISHERMAN—121 Free St., P.O. Box 7438, Portland, ME 04112. James W. Fullilove, Ed. Articles, 200 to 2,000 words, aimed at commercial fishermen and boat builders. Pays $4 to $6 per inch, extra for photos, on publication. Query preferred.

NATION'S BUSINESS—1615 H St. N.W., Washington, DC 20062–2000. Articles on small-business topics, including management advice and success stories. Pays negotiable rates, on acceptance. Guidelines.

NEPHROLOGY NEWS & ISSUES/NORTH AMERICA—15150 N. Hayden Rd., Suite 101, Scottsdale, AZ 85260. Mark Neumann, Ed. News articles, human-interest features, and opinion essays on dialysis, kidney transplants, and kidney disease.

THE NETWORK JOURNAL—333 Nostrand Ave., Brooklyn, NY 11216. Njeru Waithaka, Man. Ed. Monthly newspaper. Articles, 800 to 1,500 words, on small business, personal finance, and career management of interest to African American small business owners and professionals. Profiles of entrepreneurs; how-to pieces; articles on sales and marketing, managing a small business, personal fiance. Pays $35 to $75, on acceptance.

NEW CAREER WAYS NEWSLETTER— 67 Melrose Ave., Haverhill, MA 01830. William J. Bond, Ed. How-to articles, 1,500 to 2,000 words, on new ways to succeed at work in the 1990s. Pays varying rates, on publication. Query with outline and SASE. Same address and requirements for *Workskills Newsletter.*

NEW HAMPSHIRE EDITIONS—100 Main St., Nashua, NH 03060. Rick Broussard, Ed. Dean Dexter, Man. Ed. Lifestyle, business, and history articles with a New Hampshire angle, with sources from all regions of the state, for the company's statewide magazine and its specialty publication, *New Hampshire Legacy.* Payment varies, on publication.

NEW HAMPSHIRE LEGACY—See *New Hampshire Editions.*

THE NORTHERN LOGGER AND TIMBER PROCESSOR—Northeastern Logger's Assn., Inc., P.O. Box 69, Old Forge, NY 13420. Eric A. Johnson, Ed. Features, 1,000 to 2,000 words, of interest to the forest product industry. Photos. Pays varying rates, on publication. Query preferred.

NSGA RETAIL FOCUS—National Sporting Goods Assoc., 1699 Wall St., Suite 700, Mt. Prospect, IL 60056. Bob Nieman, Ed. Members magazine. Articles, 1,000 to 1,500 words, on sporting goods industry news and trends, the latest in new product information, and management and store operations. Payment varies, on publication. Query.

OPPORTUNITY MAGAZINE—18 E. 41st St., New York, NY 10017. I.J. Elsenstadter, Ed. How-to articles for people who work at home, small business owners, and people interested in franchising and distributorships. Payment varies, on publication. Query.

OPTOMETRIC ECONOMICS—American Optometric Assn., 243 N. Lindbergh Blvd., St. Louis, MO 63141–7881. Gene Mitchell, Man. Ed. Articles, 1,000 to 3,000 words, on private practice management for optometrists; direct, conversational style with how-to advice on how optometrists can build, improve, better manage, and enjoy their practices. Short humor and photos. Payment varies, on acceptance. Query.

PARTY & PAPER RETAILER—70 New Canaan Ave., Norwalk, CT 06850. Trisha McMahon Drain, Ed. Articles, 800 to 1,000 words, that offer employee, management, and retail marketing advice to the party or stationery store owner: display ideas, success stories, financial advice, legal advice. "Articles grounded in facts and anecdotes are appreciated." Pay varies, on publication. Query with published clips.

PET BUSINESS—7-L Dundas Cir., Greensboro, NC 27407. Rita Davis, Ed. Brief, documented articles on animals and products found in pet stores; research findings; legislative/regulatory actions; business and marketing tips and trends. Pays $4 per column inch, on publication; pays $20 for photos.

PHOTO MARKETING—3000 Picture Pl., Jackson, MI 49201. Gary Pageau, Exec. Ed. Business articles, 1,000 to 3,500 words, for owners and managers of camera/video stores or photo processing labs. Pays $150 to $500, extra for photos, on acceptance. Query; no unsolicited manuscripts.

PHYSICIAN'S MANAGEMENT—7500 Old Oak Blvd., Cleveland, OH 44130. Bob Feigenbaum, Ed. Articles, 1,500 words, on finance, investments, malpractice, and office management for primary care physicians. No clinical pieces. Pays $125 per printed page, on acceptance. Query.

PIZZA TODAY—P.O. Box 1347, New Albany, IN 47151. Bruce Allar, Ed. Articles, to 2,500 words, on pizza business management for pizza entrepreneurs. Pizza business profiles. Pays $75 to $150 per published page, on publication. Query.

P.O.B.—Business News Publishing Co., 755 W. Big Beaver Rd., Suite 100, Troy, MI 48084. Victoria L. Dickinson, Ed. Technical and business articles, 1,000 to 4,000 words, for professionals and technicians in the surveying and mapping fields. Technical tips on field and office procedures and equipment maintenance. Pays $150 to $400, on acceptance.

POLICE MAGAZINE— 6300 Yarrow Dr., Carlsbad, CA 92009–1597. Randall Resch, Ed. Articles and profiles, 1,000 to 3,000 words, on specialized groups, equipment, issues, and trends of interest to people in the law enforcement profession. Pays $100 to $300, on acceptance. Query.

POOL & SPA NEWS—3923 W. Sixth St., Los Angeles, CA 90020. News articles for the swimming pool, spa, and hot tub industry. Pays from 10¢ to 20¢ a word, on publication. Query.

PUBLISH—Integrated Media, Inc., 501 Second St., San Francisco, CA 94107. Jake Widman, Ed. Features, 1,500 to 2,000 words, and reviews, 400 to 800 words, on all aspects of computerized publishing. Pays $400 to $600 for reviews, $850 to $1,200 for full-length features, on acceptance.

PUBLISHERS WEEKLY—249 W. 17th St., New York, NY 10011. Daisy Maryles, Exec. Ed. Articles, 900 words, on a current issue or problem facing publishing and bookselling for "My Say" column. Articles for "Booksellers' Forum" may be somewhat longer.

QUICK PRINTING—PTN Publishing Co., 445 Broad Hollow Rd., Melville, NY 11747. Gerald Walsh, Ed. Jean Scott, Asst. Ed. Articles, 1,500 to 2,500 words, of interest to owners and operators of quick print shops, copy shops, and small commercial printers, on how to make their businesses more profitable; include photography/figures. Also, articles on using computers in graphic arts applications. Pays from $100, on publication.

REMODELING—Hanley-Wood, Inc., One Thomas Cir. N.W., Suite 600, Washington, DC 20005. Wendy A. Jordan, Ed. Articles, 250 to 1,700 words, on remodeling and industry news for residential and light commercial remodelers. Pays on acceptance. Query.

RESEARCH MAGAZINE—2201 Third St., P.O. Box 77905, San Francisco, CA 94107. Rebecca McReynolds, Ed. Articles of interest to stockbrokers, 1,000 to 3,000 words, on financial products, selling, how-tos, and industry trends. Pays from $600 to $1,200, on publication. Query.

RESTAURANTS USA—1200 17th St. N.W., Washington, DC 20036–3097. Jennifer Batty, Ed. Publication of the National Restaurant Assn. Articles, 1,000 to 1,500 words, on the foodservice and restaurant business. Restaurant experience preferred. Pays $350 to $800, on acceptance. Query.

ROOFER MAGAZINE—12734 Kenwood Ln., Bldg. 73, Ft. Myers, FL 33907. Angela Hutto, Ed. Technical and non-technical articles, human-interest pieces, 500 to 1,000 words, on roofing-related topics: new roofing concepts, energy savings, pertinent issues, roofing contractor profiles, industry concern. Humorous items welcome. No general business or computer articles. Include photos. Pays negotiable rates, on publication. Guidelines.

THE ROTARIAN—1560 Sherman Ave., Evanston, IL 60201–3698. Willmon L. White, Ed. Articles, 1,200 to 2,000 words, on international social and economic issues, business and management, environment, science and technology. "No political or religious subjects." Pays good rates, on acceptance. Query.

RV BUSINESS—2575 Vista Del Mar Dr., Ventura, CA 93001. Sherman Goldenberg, Ed.-in-Chief. Articles, to 1,500 words, on RV industry news and product-related features. Articles on legislative matters affecting the industry. General business features rarely used. Pays varying rates.

SAFETY COMPLIANCE LETTER—24 Rope Ferry Rd., Waterford, CT 06386. Michele Rubin, Ed. Interview-based articles, 800 to 1,250 words, for corporate safety managers, on successful safety and health programs and issues in the workplace. Pays to 17¢ a word, on acceptance. Query.

SAFETY MANAGEMENT—24 Rope Ferry Rd., Waterford, CT 06386. Heather Vaughn, Ed. Interview-based articles, 1,000 words, for safety professionals, on improving workplace safety and health. Pays to 15¢ a word, on acceptance. Query.

SIGN BUSINESS—P.O. Box 1416, Broomfield, CO 80038. Regan Dickinson, Man. Ed. Articles specifically targeted to the sign business. Prefer step-by-step how-to features. Pays $50 to $200, on publication.

SMALL PRESS REVIEW—Dustbooks, P.O. Box 100, Paradise, CA 95967. Len Fulton, Ed./Pub. Reviews, 200 words, of small literary books and magazines; tracks the publishing of small publishers and small-circulation magazines. Query.

SOFTWARE MAGAZINE—One Research Dr., Suite 400B, Westborough, MA 01581. Mike Bucken, Ed. Technical features, to 3,500 words, for computer-literate MIS audience, on how various software products are used. Pays about $750 to $1,000, on publication. Query required. Calendar of scheduled editorial features available.

SOUTHERN LUMBERMAN—P.O. Box 681629, Franklin, TN 37068–1629. Nanci P. Gregg, Man. Ed. Articles on sawmill operations, interviews with industry leaders, how-to technical pieces with an emphasis on increasing sawmill production and efficiency and new installations. "Always looking for 'sweetheart' mill stories; we publish one per month." Pays $100 to $250 for articles with B&W photos. Queries preferred.

SOUVENIRS AND NOVELTIES—7000 Terminal Sq., Suite 210, Upper Darby, PA 19082. Attn: Ed. Articles, 1,500 words, quoting souvenir shop managers on items that sell, display ideas, problems in selling, industry trends. Photos. Pays from $1 per column inch, extra for photos, on publication.

STONE WORLD—1 Kalisa Way, Suite 205, Paramus, NJ 07652. Michael Reis, Ed. Articles, 750 to 1,500 words, on new trends in installing and designing with stone. For architects, interior designers, design professionals, and stone fabricators and dealers. Pays $4 per column inch, on publication. Query.

TANNING TRENDS—3101 Page Ave., Jackson, MI 49203–2254. Joseph Levy, Ed. Articles on small businesses and skin care for tanning salon owners. Scientific pro-tanning articles and "smart tanning" pieces. Query for profiles. "Our aim is to boost salon owners to the 'next level' of small business ownership. Focus is on business principles with special emphasis on public relations and marketing." Payment varies, on publication.

TEA & COFFEE TRADE JOURNAL—130 W. 42nd St., New York, NY 10036. Jane P. McCabe, Ed. Articles, 3 to 5 pages, on trade issues of importance to the tea and coffee industry. Pays $5 per published inch, on publication. Query.

TEXTILE WORLD—6151 Powers Ferry Rd., Atlanta, GA 30339. Mac Isaacs, Ed. Articles, 500 to 2,000 words, with photos, on manufacturing and finishing textiles. Pays varying rates, on acceptance.

TODAY'S OR NURSE—See *Today's Surgical Nurse.*

TODAY'S SURGICAL NURSE—(formerly *Today's OR Nurse*) Slack, Inc., 6900 Grove Rd., Thorofare, NJ 08086. Frances R. DeStefano, Man. Ed. Clinical or general articles, from 2,000 words, of direct interest to operating room nurses.

TOURIST ATTRACTIONS AND PARKS—7000 Terminal Sq., Suite 210, Upper Darby, PA 19082. Articles, 1,500 words, on successful management of parks and leisure attractions. News items, 250 and 500 words. Pays 7¢ a word, on publication. Query.

TRAILER/BODY BUILDERS—P.O. Box 66010, Houston, TX 77266. Paul Schenck, Ed. Articles on engineering, sales, and management ideas for truck body and truck trailer manufacturers. Pays from $100 per printed page, on acceptance.

TRAINING MAGAZINE—50 S. Ninth St., Minneapolis, MN 55402. Jack Gordon, Ed. Articles, 1,000 to 2,500 words, for managers of training and development activities in corporations, government, etc. Pays to 30¢ a word, on acceptance. Query.

TREASURY & RISK MANAGEMENT—111 W. 57th St., New York, NY 10019. Anthony Baldo, Ed. Bimonthly. Articles, 200 to 3,000 words, on treasury management for corporate treasurers, CFOs, and vice presidents of finance. Pays 50¢ to $1 a word, on acceptance. Query.

TRUCKERS/USA—P.O. Box 323, Windber, PA 15963. David Adams, Ed. Articles, 500 to 1,000 words, on the trucking business and marketing. Trucking-related poetry and fiction. Payment varies, on publication.

UNIQUE OPPORTUNITIES— 455 S. 4th Ave., #1236, Louisville, KY 40202. Bett Coffman, Asst. Ed. Articles, 2,000 to 3,000 words, that cover the economic, business, and career-related issues of interest to physicians who are interested in relocating or entering new practices. Doctor profiles, 500 words. "Our goal is to educate physicians about how to evaluate career opportunities, negotiate the benefits offered, plan career moves, and provide information on the legal and economic aspects of accepting a position." Pays 50¢ a word for features; $100 to $200 for profiles, on acceptance. Query.

WINES & VINES—1800 Lincoln Ave., San Rafael, CA 94901. Philip E. Hiaring, Ed. Articles, 2,000 words, on grape and wine industry, emphasizing marketing, management, and production. Pays 10¢ a word, on acceptance.

WOODSHOP NEWS—35 Pratt St., Essex, CT 06426–1185. Ian C. Bowen, Ed. Features, one to 3 typed pages, for and about people who work with wood: business stories, profiles, news. Pays from $3 per column inch, on publication. Queries preferred.

WORKING WOMAN—230 Park Ave., New York, NY 10169. Articles, 350 to 2,500 words, on business and personal aspects of working women's lives. Pays from $300, on acceptance.

WORKSKILLS NEWSLETTER—See *New Career Ways Newsletter.*

WORLD OIL—Gulf Publishing Co., P.O. Box 2608, Houston, TX 77252–2608. Robert E. Snyder, Ed. Engineering and operations articles, 3,000 to 4,000 words, on petroleum industry exploration, drilling, or production. Photos. Pays from $50 per printed page, on acceptance. Query.

WORLD SCREEN NEWS—1123 Broadway, Suite 901, New York, NY 10010. George P. Winslow, Ed. Features and short pieces on trends in the business of international television programming (network, syndication, cable, and pay). Pays to $850, after publication.

WORLD WASTES— 6151 Powers Ferry Rd. N.W., Atlanta, GA 30339. Bill Wolpin, Ed./Pub. Case studies, market analysis, and how-to articles, 1,000 to 2,000 words, with photos of refuse haulers, recyclers, landfill operators, resource recovery operations, and transfer stations, with solutions to problems in the field. Pays from $125 per printed page, on publication. Query preferred.

IN-HOUSE/ASSOCIATION MAGAZINES

Publications circulated to company employees (sometimes called house magazines or house organs) and to members of associations and organizations are excellent, well-paying markets for writers at all levels of experience. Large corporations publish these magazines to promote good will, familiarize readers with the company's services and products, and keep them abreast of the issues and events concerning a particular cause or industry.

AARP BULLETIN— 601 E St. N.W., Washington, DC 20049. Elliot Carlson, Ed. Publication of the American Assn. of Retired Persons. Payment varies, on acceptance. Query required.

THE AMERICAN GARDENER—(formerly *American Horticulturist*) 7931 E. Boulevard Dr., Alexandria, VA 22308–1300. Kathleen Fisher, Ed. Bimonthly publication of the American Horticulture Society. Articles, to 2,500 words, for American ornamental gardeners: profiles of prominent horticulturists, plant research and plant hunting, events and personalities in horticulture history, plant lore and literature, the politics of horticulture, etc. Humorous pieces for "Offshoots." "We run very few how-to articles." Pays $100 to $400, on publication. Query preferred.

AMERICAN HORTICULTURIST—See *The American Gardener.*

AMERICAN HOW-TO—12301 Whitewater Dr., Suite 260, Minnetonka, MN 55343. Tom Sweeney, Ed. Bimonthly magazine for members of The Handyman Club of America. Articles, 1,000 to 1,500 words, for homeowners interested in do-it-yourself projects. Carpentry, plumbing, electrical work, landscaping, masonry, tools, woodworking, and new products. Payment is 50¢ a word, on acceptance. Send SASE for editorial calendar with upcoming themes. Queries preferred.

CALIFORNIA HIGHWAY PATROLMAN—2030 V St., Sacramento, CA 95818–1730. Carol Perri, Ed. Articles on transportation safety, California history, travel, consumerism, past and present vehicles, humor, special holidays, general items, etc. Photos a plus. Buys one-time rights; pays 2½¢ a word, $5 for B&W photos, on publication. Guidelines and/or sample copy with 9x11 SASE.

CATHOLIC FORESTER—355 Shuman Blvd., P.O. Box 3012, Naperville, IL 60566–7012. Dorothy Deer, Ed. Official publication of the Catholic Order of Foresters, a fraternal life insurance organization for Catholics. General-interest articles and fiction, to 1,500 words, that deal with contemporary issues; no moralizing, explicit sex or violence. "Need health and wellness, parenting, and financial articles." Pays 20¢ a word, on acceptance.

COLUMBIA—1 Columbus Plaza, New Haven, CT 06510–0901. Richard McMunn, Ed. Journal of the Knights of Columbus. Articles, 1,500 words, for Catholic families. Must be accompanied by color photos or transparencies. No fiction. Pays to $500 for articles and photos, on acceptance.

THE COMPASS—365 Washington Ave., Brooklyn, NY 11238. J.A. Randall, Ed. True stories, to 2,000 words, on the sea, sea trades, and aviation. Pays to $1,000, on acceptance. Query with SASE.

THE ELKS MAGAZINE— 425 W. Diversey Pkwy., Chicago, IL 60614. Judith L. Keogh, Man. Ed. Articles, 1,500 to 3,000 words, on technology, business, sports, and topics of current interest; for non-urban audience with above-average income. Pays 15¢ to 20¢ a word, on acceptance. Query.

FIREHOUSE—PTN Publishing Company, 445 Broad Hollow Rd., Melville, NY 11747. Harvey Eisner, Ed.-in-Chief. Articles, 500 to 2,000 words: on-the-scene accounts of fires, trends in firefighting equipment, controversial fire-service issues, and lifestyles of firefighters. Query.

THE FURROW—Deere & Co., John Deere Rd., Moline, IL 61265. George R. Sollenberger, Exec. Ed. Specialized, illustrated articles on farming. Pays to $1,200, on acceptance.

FUTURIFIC—Foundation for Optimism, 305 Madison Ave., #10B, New York, NY 10165. Charlotte Kellar, Ed. Forecasts of what will be. "Only optimistic material will get published. Solutions, not problems. We track all developments giving evidence to our increasing life expectancy, improving international coexistence, the global tendency toward peace, and improving economic trends. We also report on all new developments, economic, political, social, scientific, technical, medical or other that are making life easier, better and more enjoyable." Pays in copies. Queries preferred.

HARVARD MAGAZINE—7 Ware St., Cambridge, MA 02138-4037. John Rosenberg, Ed. Articles, 500 to 5,000 words, with a connection to Harvard University. Pays from $100, on publication. Query required.

IDEA PERSONAL TRAINER— 6190 Cornerstone Ct. E., Suite 204, San Diego, CA 92121-3773. Therese Hannon, Asst. Ed. For personal fitness trainers assn. Articles on exercise science; program design; profiles of successful trainers; business, legal, and marketing topics; tips for networking with other trainers and with allied medical professionals; client counseling; and training tips. "What's New" column includes industry news, products, and research. Payment varies, on acceptance. Query.

KIWANIS—3636 Woodview Trace, Indianapolis, IN 46268. Chuck Jonak, Man. Ed. Articles, 2,500 words (with sidebars, 250 to 350 words), on lifestyle, relationships, world view, education, trends, small business, religion, health, etc. No travel pieces, interviews, profiles. Pays $400 to $1,000, on acceptance. Query.

THE LION—300 22nd St., Oak Brook, IL 60521. Robert Kleinfelder, Sr. Ed. Official publication of Lions Clubs International. Articles, 800 to 2,000 words, and photo-essays, on club activities. Pays from $100 to $700, including photos, on acceptance. Query.

NEW HOLLAND NEWS—New Holland, Inc., P.O. Box 1895, New Holland, PA 17557. Attn: Ed. Articles, to 1,500 words, with strong color photo support, on agriculture and rural living. Pays on acceptance. Query.

OPTIMIST MAGAZINE— 4494 Lindell Blvd., St. Louis, MO 63108. Dennis R. Osterwisch, Ed. Articles, to 1,000 words, on activities of local Optimist Club, and techniques for personal and club success. Pays from $100, on acceptance. Query.

THE PRICECOSTCO CONNECTION—P.O. Box 34088, Seattle, WA 98124-1088. Anita Thompson, Man. Ed. Tabloid. Articles, 100 to 1,200 words, about small business and about PriceCostCo members. SASE for guidelines. Pays $300 to $400, on acceptance. Queries preferred.

629

RESTAURANTS USA—1200 17th St. N.W., Washington, DC 20036–3097. Jennifer Batty, Ed. Publication of the National Restaurant Assn. Articles, 1,000 to 1,500 words, on the foodservice and restaurant business. Restaurant experience preferred. Pays $350 to $800, on acceptance. Query.

THE RETIRED OFFICER MAGAZINE—201 N. Washington St., Alexandria, VA 22314. Address the Manuscripts Ed. Articles, 1,800 to 2,000 words, of interest to military retirees and their families. Current military/national affairs, recent military history, health/medicine, and second-career opportunities. No fillers. Photos a plus. Pays to $1,000, on acceptance. Query. Guidelines.

THE ROTARIAN—1560 Sherman Ave., Evanston, IL 60201–3698. Willmon L. White, Ed. Publication of Rotary International, world service organization of business and professional men and women. Articles, 1,200 to 2,000 words, on international social and economic issues, business and management, human relationships, travel, sports, environment, science and technology; humor. Pays good rates, on acceptance. Query.

SCULPTURE—International Sculpture Ctr., 1050 17th St. N.W., Suite 250, Washington, DC 20036. Suzanne Ramljak, Ed. Magazine of the International Sculpture Center. (Also available on newsstands.) Articles on sculpture, sculptors, collections of sculpture, books on sculpture, criticism, technical processes, etc. Payment varies, on publication. Query.

WOMEN IN BUSINESS—9100 Ward Pkwy., Box 8728, Kansas City, MO 64114–0728. Dawn J. Grubb, Assoc. Ed. Bimonthly publication of the American Business Women's Assn. How-to features, 1,000 to 1,500 words, for career women from 25 to 55 years old, on business trends, small-business ownership, self-improvement, and retirement issues. Profiles of ABWA members only. Guidelines. Pays 15¢ a published word, on acceptance. Query.

RELIGIOUS MAGAZINES

AMERICA—106 W. 56th St., New York, NY 10019–3893. George W. Hunt, S.J., Ed. Articles, 1,000 to 2,500 words, on current affairs, family life, literary trends. Pays $75 to $150, on acceptance.

AMERICAN JEWISH HISTORY—American Jewish Historical Society, 2 Thornton Rd., Waltham, MA 02154. Dr. Marc Lee Raphael, Ed. Academic articles, 15 to 30 typed pages, on the settlement, history, and life of Jews in North and South America. Queries preferred. No payment.

AMIT MAGAZINE— 817 Broadway, New York, NY 10003–4761. Micheline Ratzersdorfer, Rita Schwalb, Eds. Helen Teitelbaum, Managing Ed. Articles, 1,000 to 2,000 words, of interest to Jewish women: Middle East, Israel, history, holidays, travel.

ANGEL TIMES—Angelic Realms Unlimited, Inc., Suite 110, 22 Perimeter Park, Atlanta, GA 30341. Linda Whitmon Vephula, Pub. Quarterly. Articles, 1,500 words, on angels. No payment.

ANGLICAN JOURNAL— 600 Jarvis St., Toronto, Ont., Canada M4Y 2J6. Attn: Ed. National newspaper of the Anglican Church of Canada. Articles, to 1,000 words, on news of the Anglican Church across the country and around the world, including social and ethical issues and human-interest subjects in a religious context. Pays $50 to $300, on acceptance. Query required.

ANNALS OF ST. ANNE DE BEAUPRÉ—P.O. Box 1000, St. Anne de Beaupré, Quebec, Canada G0A 3C0. Roch Achard, C.Ss.R., Ed. Articles, 500 to 1,500 words, that promote devotion to St. Anne and Christian family values. "Write something inspirational, educational, objective, and uplifting." No poetry. Pays 3¢ to 4¢ a word, on acceptance.

BAPTIST LEADER—American Baptist Churches-USA, P.O. Box 851, Valley Forge, PA 19482–0851. D. Ng, Ed. Practical how-to or thought-provoking articles, 1,200 to 2,000 words, for local church lay leaders, pastors, and Christian education staff.

BIBLE ADVOCATE—P.O. Box 33677, Denver, CO 80233. Roy Marrs, Ed. Articles, 1,000 to 2,000 words, and fillers, 100 to 500 words, on Bible passages and Christian living. Poetry, 5 to 25 lines, on religious themes. Opinion pieces, to 700 words. "Be familiar with the doctrinal beliefs of the Church of God (Seventh Day). For example, they don't celebrate a traditional Easter or Christmas." Pays $15 per page (to $35) for articles, $10 for poetry, on publication. Guidelines.

BRIGADE LEADER—Box 150, Wheaton, IL 60189. Deborah Christensen, Man. Ed. Inspirational articles, 1,000 words, for Christian men who lead boys in Christian service brigade programs. "Most articles are written on assignment by experts; very few free lancers used. Query with clips and we'll contact you if we need you for an assignment." Pays $60 to $150.

CATECHIST—330 Progress Rd., Dayton, OH 45449. Patricia Fischer, Ed. Informational and how-to articles, 1,200 to 1,500 words, for Catholic teachers, coordinators, and administrators in religious education programs. Pays $25 to $100, on publication.

CATHOLIC DIGEST—P.O. Box 64090, St. Paul, MN 55164–0090. Attn: Articles Ed. Articles, 1,000 to 3,500 words, on Catholic and general subjects. Fillers, to 300 words, on instances of kindness rewarded, for "Hearts Are Trumps"; accounts of good deeds, for "People Are Like That." Pays from $200 for original articles, $100 for reprints, on acceptance; $4 to $50 for fillers, on publication. Guidelines.

CATHOLIC NEAR EAST MAGAZINE—1011 First Ave., New York, NY 10022–4195. Michael La Civita, Ed. Bimonthly publication of CNEWA, a papal agency for humanitarian and pastoral support. Articles, 1,500 to 2,000 words, on people of the Middle East, northeast Africa, India, and eastern Europe: their faith, heritage, culture, and present state of affairs. Special interest in Eastern Christian churches. Color photos for all articles. Pays 20¢ a word. Query.

CATHOLIC PARENT—Our Sunday Visitor, Inc., 200 Noll Plaza, Huntington, IN 46750. Woodeene Koenig-Bricker, Ed. Features, how-tos, and general-interest articles, 800 to 1,000 words, for Catholic parents. "Keep it anecdotal and practical with an emphasis on values and family life. Don't preach." Payment varies, on acceptance.

CATHOLIC TWIN CIRCLE—33 Rossotto Dr., Hamden, CT 06514. Loretta G. Seyer, Ed. Features, how-tos, and interviews, 1,000 to 2,000 words, of interest to Catholic families; include photos. Opinion or inspirational columns, 600 to 800 words. Strict attention to Catholic doctrine required. Enclose SASE. Pays from 10¢ a word for articles, $50 for columns, on publication.

631

CHARISMA & CHRISTIAN LIFE— 600 Rinehart Rd., Lake Mary, FL 32746. Lee Grady, Ed. Dir. Charismatic/evangelical Christian articles, 1,500 to 2,500 words, for developing the spiritual life. News stories, 300 to 1,500 words. Photos. Pays varying rates, on publication.

THE CHRISTIAN CENTURY— 407 S. Dearborn St., Chicago, IL 60605. James M. Wall, Ed. Ecumenical. Articles, 1,500 to 3,000 words, with a religious angle, on political and social issues, international affairs, culture, the arts. Poetry, to 20 lines. Photos. Pays about $50 per printed page, extra for photos, on publication.

CHRISTIAN EDUCATION COUNSELOR— 1445 Boonville Ave., Springfield, MO 65802–1894. Sylvia Lee, Ed. Articles, 600 to 800 words, on teaching and administrating Christian education in the local church, for local Sunday school and Christian school personnel. Pays 5¢ to 10¢ a word, on acceptance.

CHRISTIAN EDUCATION JOURNAL—Trinity Evangelical Divinity School, 2065 Half Day Rd., Deerfield, IL 60015. Dr. Perry G. Downs, Ed. Articles, 10 to 25 typed pages, on Christian education topics. Guidelines.

CHRISTIAN HOME & SCHOOL—3350 E. Paris Ave. S.E., Grand Rapids, MI 49512. Gordon L. Bordewyk, Ed. Articles for parents in Canada and the U.S. who send their children to Christian schools and are concerned about the challenges facing Christian families today. Pays $75 to $150, on publication. Send SASE for guidelines.

CHRISTIAN MEDICAL & DENTAL SOCIETY JOURNAL—See *Today's Christian Doctor.*

CHRISTIAN PARENTING TODAY— 4050 Lee Vance View, Colorado Springs, CO 80918. Brad Lewis, Ed. Articles, 900 to 2,000 words, dealing with raising children with Christian principles. Departments: "Your Child Today" and "Train Them Up," 300 to 400 words, on child development (emotional, spiritual, etc.); "Healthy & Safe," 300-to 400-word how-to pieces on keeping children emotional and physically safe, home and away; "Family Room," 600 to 700 words, on parent-child activities; "The Lighter Side," humorous essays on family life, 600 to 700 words; "Parent Exchange," 25 to 100 words on problem-solving ideas that have worked for parents; "Life in Our House," insightful anecdotes, 25 to 100 words, about humorous things said at home. (Submissions for "Parent Exchange" and "Life in our House" are not acknowledged or returned.) Pays 15¢ to 25¢ a word, on publication. Pays $25 to $125 for department pieces. Guidelines; send SASE.

CHRISTIAN SINGLE—127 Ninth Ave. N., Nashville, TN 37234–0140. Stephen Felts, Ed. Articles, 600 or 1,200 words, for single adults about leisure activities, issues related to single parents, inspiring personal experiences, humor, life from a Christian perspective. Payment varies, on acceptance. Query. Guidelines.

CHRISTIAN SOCIAL ACTION—100 Maryland Ave. N.E., Washington, DC 20002. Lee Ranck, Ed. Articles, 1,500 to 2,000 words, on social issues for concerned persons of faith. Pays $75 to $125, on publication.

CHRISTIANITY TODAY— 465 Gundersen Dr., Carol Stream, IL 60188. Michael G. Maudlin, Man. Ed. Doctrinal social issues and interpretive essays, 1,500 to 3,000 words, from evangelical Protestant perspective. No fiction or poetry. Pays $200 to $500, on acceptance. Query.

CHURCH & STATE—1816 Jefferson Pl. N.W., Washington, DC 20036. Joseph L. Conn, Man. Ed. Articles, 600 to 2,600 words, on issues of religious liberty and church-state relations. Pays varying rates, on acceptance. Query.

CHURCH EDUCATOR—Educational Ministries, Inc., 165 Plaza Dr., Prescott, AZ 86303. Robert G. Davidson, Ed. How-to articles, to 1,750 words, on Christian education: activity projects, crafts, learning centers, games, bulletin boards, etc., for all church school, junior and high school programs, and adult study group ideas. Allow 3 months for response. Pays 3¢ a word, on publication.

THE CHURCH MUSICIAN—127 Ninth Ave. N., Nashville, TN 37234. Jere Adams, Ed. Articles on choral techniques, instrumental groups, worship planning, music administration, directing choirs (all ages), rehearsal planning, music equipment, new technology, drama/pageants and related subjects, hymn studies, book reviews, and music-related fillers. Pays 5½¢ a word, on acceptance.

COLUMBIA—1 Columbus Plaza, New Haven, CT 06510–0901. Richard McMunn, Ed. Knights of Columbus. Articles, 1,500 words, for Catholic families. Must be accompanied by color photos or transparencies. No fiction. Pays to $500 for articles with photos, on acceptance.

COMMENTARY—165 E. 56th St., New York, NY 10022. Neal Kozodoy, Ed. Articles, 5,000 to 7,000 words, on contemporary issues, Jewish affairs, social sciences, religious thought, culture. Serious fiction; book reviews. Pays on publication.

COMMONWEAL—15 Dutch St., New York, NY 10038. Margaret O'Brien Steinfels, Ed. Catholic. Articles, to 3,000 words, on political, religious, social, and literary subjects. Pays 3¢ a word, on acceptance.

COMPASS: A JESUIT JOURNAL—Box 400, Sta. F, 50 Charles St. E., Toronto, Ont., Canada M4Y 2L8. Robert Chodos, Ed. Essays, 1,500 to 2,500 words, on current religious, political, and cultural topics. "We are ecumenical in spirit and like to provide a forum for lively debate and an ethical perspective on social and religious questions." Query preferred. Pays $100 to $500, on publication.

THE COVENANT COMPANION—5101 N. Francisco Ave., Chicago, IL 60625. John E. Phelan, Ed. Articles, 1,000 words, with Christian implications published for members and attenders of Evangelical Covenant Church, "aimed at gathering, enlightening, and stimulating devotion to Jesus Christ and the living of the Christian life." Poetry. Pays $15 to $35, on publication.

CRUSADER—P.O. Box 7259, Grand Rapids, MI 49510. G. Richard Broene, Ed. Fiction, 900 to 1,500 words, and articles, 400 to 1,000 words, for boys ages 9 to 14 that show how God is at work in their lives and in the world around them. Also, short fillers. Pays 4¢ to 6¢ a word, on acceptance.

DECISION—Billy Graham Evangelistic Assn., 1300 Harmon Pl., P.O. Box 779, Minneapolis, MN 55440–0779. Roger C. Palms, Ed. Christian testimonies and teaching articles on evangelism and Christian nurturing, 1,200 to 1,500 words. Vignettes, 400 to 1,000 words. Pays varying rates, on publication.

DISCOVERIES—WordAction Publishing Co., 6401 The Paseo, Kansas City, MO 64131. Attn: Asst. Ed. Weekly take-home paper designed to correlate with Evangelical Sunday school curriculum. Fiction, 500 to 700 words, for 8- to 10-year-olds. Stories should feature contemporary, true-to-life characters

633

and should illustrate character building and scriptural application. No poetry. SASE required. Pays 5¢ a word, on publication. Guidelines.

DREAMS & VISIONS—Skysong Press, 35 Peter St. S., Orillia, Ont., Canada L3V 5A8. Steve Stanton, Ed. New frontiers in Christian fiction. Eclectic fiction, 2,000 to 6,000 words, that "has literary value and is unique and relevant to Christian readers today." Pays ½¢ per word.

ENRICHMENT: A JOURNAL FOR PENTECOSTAL MINISTRY—1445 Boonville Ave., Springfield, MO 65802. Wayde I. Goodall, Ed. Articles, 1,200 to 1,500 words, slanted to ministers, on preaching, doctrine, practice; how-to features. Pays to 10¢ a word, on acceptance.

EVANGEL—Light and Life Press, Box 535002, Indianapolis, IN 46253–5002. Julie Innes, Ed. Free Methodist. Personal experience articles, 1,000 words; short devotional items, 300 to 500 words; fiction, 1,200 words, showing personal faith in Christ to be instrumental in solving problems. Guidelines. Pays 4¢ a word for articles, $10 for poetry, on publication.

EVANGELIZING TODAY'S CHILD—Box 348, Warrenton, MO 63383–0348. Attn: Ed. Articles, 1,200 to 1,500 words, for Sunday school teachers, Christian education leaders, and children's workers. Feature articles should include teaching principles, instruction for the reader, and classroom illustrations. "Impact" articles, 700 to 900 words, show the power of the Gospel in or through the life of a child; "Resource Center," 200- to 300-word teaching tips. Also short stories, 800 to 1,000 words, of contemporary children dealing with problems; must have a scriptural solution. Pays 10¢ to 12¢ a word for articles; $15 to $25 for "Resource Center" pieces; 7¢ a word for short stories, 60 days after acceptance. Guidelines.

FAITH TODAY—M.I.P. Box 3745, Markham, Ontario, Canada L3R 5J6. Brian C. Stiller, Ed. Articles, 1,500 words, on current issues relating to the church in Canada. Pays negotiable rates, on publication. Queries required.

THE FAMILY DIGEST—P.O. Box 40137, Fort Wayne, IN 46804. Corine B. Erlandson, Ed. Articles, 750 to 1,100 words, on family life, Catholic subjects, seasonal, parish life, prayer, inspiration, how-to, spiritual life, for the Catholic reader. Also publishes short humorous anecdotes drawn from personal experience and light-hearted cartoons. Pays 5¢ a word; $10 for personal anecdotes; $20 for cartoons, 6 weeks after acceptance.

FELLOWSHIP—Box 271, Nyack, NY 10960–0271. Richard Deats, Ed. Bimonthly published by the Fellowship of Reconciliation, an interfaith, pacifist organization. Articles, 750 and 1,500 to 2,000 words; B&W photo-essays, on active nonviolence, peace and justice, opposition to war. "Articles for a just and peaceful world community." SASE required. Pays in copies and subscription. Queries preferred.

FELLOWSHIP IN PRAYER—291 Witherspoon St., Princeton, NJ 08542. Articles, to 1,500 words, relating to prayer, meditation, and the spiritual life as practiced by men and women of all faith traditions. Pays in copies. Guidelines.

FOURSQUARE WORLD ADVANCE—1910 W. Sunset Blvd., Suite 200, P.O. Box 26902, Los Angeles, CA 90026. Ronald D. Williams, Ed. Official publication of the International Church of the Foursquare Gospel. Religious fiction and nonfiction, 1,000 to 1,200 words, and religious poetry. Pays $75, on publication. Guidelines.

FRIENDS JOURNAL—1501 Cherry St., Philadelphia, PA 19102–1497. Vinton Deming, Ed. Articles, to 2,000 words, reflecting Quaker life today: commentary on social issues, experiential articles, Quaker history, world affairs. Poetry, to 25 lines, and Quaker-related humor and crossword puzzles also considered. Pays in copies. Guidelines.

GLORY SONGS—127 Ninth Ave. N., Nashville, TN 37234. Jere V. Adams, Ed. For volunteer and part-time music directors and members of church choirs. Very easy music and accompaniments designed specifically for the small church (4 to 6 songs per issue). Includes 8-page pull-out with articles for choir members on leisure reading, music training, and choir projects. Pays 5½¢ per word, on acceptance.

GROUP, THE YOUTH MINISTRY MAGAZINE—Box 481, Loveland, CO 80539. Rick Lawrence, Ed. Interdenominational magazine for leaders of junior and senior high school Christian youth groups. Articles, 500 to 1,700 words, about practical youth ministry principles, techniques, or activities. Short how-to pieces, to 300 words. Pays to $200 for articles, $35 for department pieces, on acceptance. Guidelines.

GUIDE—Review and Herald Publishing Assn., 55 W. Oak Ridge Dr., Hagerstown, MD 21740. Carolyn Rathbun, Ed. Stories, to 1,200 words, for Christian youth, ages 10 to 14. Pays 3¢ to 7¢ a word, on publication.

GUIDEPOSTS—16 E. 34th St., New York, NY 10016. Celeste McCauley, Features Ed. True first-person stories, 250 to 1,500 words, stressing how faith in God helps people cope with life. Anecdotal fillers, to 250 words. Pays $100 to $400 for full-length stories, $25 to $100 for fillers, on acceptance.

HERALD OF HOLINESS—6401 The Paseo, Kansas City, MO 64131. Attn: Man. Ed. Church of the Nazarene. Articles, 800 to 2,000 words, about distinctive Nazarenes, Christian family life and marriage, a Christian approach to social issues, seasonal material, and short devotional articles. Pays 4¢ to 5¢ a word, within 30 days of acceptance. Guidelines.

HOME LIFE—127 Ninth Ave. N., Nashville, TN 37234. Attn: Ed.-in-Chief. Leigh Neely, Man. Ed. Southern Baptist. Fiction, personal experience, and articles on Christian marriage, parenthood, and family relationships. Human-interest pieces, 200 to 1,500 words; cartoons and short verse related to family. Query with SASE required. Pays on acceptance.

INDIAN LIFE—Box 3765, RPO Redwood Centre, Winnipeg, MB, Canada R2W 3R6. Attn: Acquisitions Ed. Christian teaching articles and testimonials of Native Americans, 1,000 to 1,200 words. "Our magazine is designed to help the North American Indian Church speak to the social, cultural, and spiritual needs of Native people." Writing should be at a seventh-grade reading level. "We prefer Native writers who write from within their culture. Read the magazine before submitting." Queries preferred.

INSIDE MAGAZINE—226 S. 16th St., Philadelphia, PA 19102–3392. Jane Biberman, Ed. Jewish lifestyle magazine. Articles, 1,500 to 3,000 words, on Jewish issues, health, finance, and the arts. Pays $75 to $600, after publication. Queries required; send clips if available.

JEWISH CURRENTS—22 E. 17th St., #601, New York, NY 10003. Morris U. Schappes, Ed. Articles, 2,400 to 3,000 words, on Jewish history, Jewish secularism, progressivism, labor struggle, Holocaust and Holocaust-resistance, Black-Jewish relations, Israel, Yiddish culture. "We are pro-Israel though non-Zionist and a secular magazine; no religious articles." Overstocked with fiction and poetry. No payment.

THE JEWISH HOMEMAKER—1372 Carroll St., Brooklyn, NY 11213. Michael Lozenik, Ed. Bimonthly. Articles, 1,200 to 2,000 words, for a traditional/Orthodox Jewish audience. Humor. Payment varies, on publication. Query.

THE JEWISH MONTHLY—B'nai B'rith International, 1640 Rhode Island Ave. N.W., Washington, DC 20036. Jeff Rubin, Ed. Articles, 500 to 3,000 words, on politics, religion, history, culture, and social issues of Jewish concern with an emphasis on people. Pays 10¢ to 25¢ a word, on publication. Query with clips.

JOURNAL OF CHRISTIAN NURSING—P.O. Box 1650, Downers Grove, IL 60515. Judy Shelly, Sr. Ed. Articles, 8 to 12 double-spaced pages, that help Christian nurses view nursing practice through the eyes of faith: spiritual care, ethics, values, healing and wholeness, psychology and religion, personal and professional ethics, etc. Priority given to nurse authors, though work by non-nurses will be considered. Opinion pieces, to 4 pages, for "The Last Word" section. Pays $25 to $80. Guidelines and editorial calendar.

THE JOYFUL WOMAN—P.O. Box 90028, Chattanooga, TN 37412. Joy Rice Martin, Ed. Articles and fiction, 500 to 1,200 words, for Christian women: first-person inspirational true stories, profiles of Christian women, practical and biblically oriented how-to articles. Pays 3¢ to 4¢ a word, on publication. Queries required; no unsolicited manuscripts.

LEADERSHIP—465 Gundersen Dr., Carol Stream, IL 60188. Kevin A. Miller, Ed. Articles, 500 to 3,000 words, on administration, finance, and/or programming of interest to ministers and church leaders. Personal stories of crisis in ministry. "We deal mainly with the how-to of running a church. We're not a theological journal but a practical one." Pays $50 to $350, on acceptance.

LIBERTY MAGAZINE—12501 Old Columbia Pike, Silver Spring, MD 20904–1608. Clifford R. Goldstein, Ed. Timely articles, to 2,500 words, and photo-essays, on religious freedom and church-state relations. Pays 6¢ to 8¢ a word, on acceptance. Query.

LIGHT AND LIFE—P.O. Box 535002, Indianapolis, IN 46253–5002. Doug Newton, Ed. Thoughtful articles about practical Christian living. Social and cultural analysis from an evangelical perspective. Pays 4¢ to 5¢ a word, on publication.

LIGUORIAN—Liguori, MO 63057–9999. Rev. Allan Weinert, Ed. Catholic. Articles and short stories, 1,500 to 2,000 words, on Christian values in modern life. Pays 10¢ to 12¢ a word, on acceptance.

THE LIVING LIGHT—U.S. Catholic Conference, Dept. of Education, Box 45, The Catholic Univ. of America, Washington, DC 20064. Berard L. Marthaler, Office of the Exec. Ed. Theoretical and practical articles, 1,500 to 4,000 words, on religious education, catechesis, and pastoral ministry.

LIVING WITH TEENAGERS—127 Ninth Ave. N., Nashville, TN 37234. Articles, 400 to 1,200 words, told from a Christian perspective for parents of teenagers; first-person approach preferred. Queries welcome; SASE required. Pay is negotiable and made on acceptance.

THE LOOKOUT—8121 Hamilton Ave., Cincinnati, OH 45231. David Faust, Ed. Articles, 500 to 1,800 words, on spiritual growth, family issues, applying Christian faith to current issues, and people overcoming problems with Christian principles. Inspirational or humorous shorts, 500 to 800 words; fiction, to 1,800 words. Pays 6¢ to 12¢ a word, on acceptance.

THE LUTHERAN— 8765 W. Higgins Rd., Chicago, IL 60631. Edgar R. Trexler, Ed. Articles, to 1,200 words, on Christian ideology, personal religious experiences, social and ethical issues, family life, church, and community. Pays $100 to $500, on acceptance. Query required.

MARRIAGE PARTNERSHIP—Christianity Today, Inc., 465 Gundersen Dr., Carol Stream, IL 60188. Ron Lee, Ed. Articles, 500 to 2,000 words, related to marriage, for men and women who wish to fortify their relationship. Cartoons, humor, fillers. Pays $50 to $300, on acceptance. Query required.

MATURE YEARS—201 Eighth Ave. S., P.O. Box 801, Nashville, TN 37202. Marvin W. Cropsey, Ed. Nondenominational quarterly. Articles, 1,500 to 2,000 words, on retirement or related subjects, inspiration. Humorous and serious fiction, 1,500 to 1,800 words. Travel pieces for seniors or with religious slant. Poetry, to 14 lines. Include social security number with manuscript. Guidelines.

THE MENNONITE—P.O. Box 347, Newton, KS 67114. Gordon Houser, Ed. Melanie Zuercher, Asst. Ed. Articles, 1,000 words, that emphasize Christian themes. Pays 5¢ a word, on publication. Guidelines.

MESSENGER OF THE SACRED HEART— 661 Greenwood Ave., Toronto, Ont., Canada M4J 4B3. Articles and short stories, about 1,500 words, for American and Canadian Catholics. Pays from 4¢ a word, on acceptance.

THE MIRACULOUS MEDAL— 475 E. Chelten Ave., Philadelphia, PA 19144–5785. Rev. William J. O'Brien, C.M., Ed. Dir. Catholic. Fiction, to 2,400 words. Religious verse, to 20 lines. Pays from 2¢ a word for fiction, from 50¢ a line for poetry, on acceptance.

MODERN LITURGY—160 E. Virginia St., #290, San Jose, CA 95112. Nick Wagner, Ed. Practical, imaginative how-to help for Roman Catholic liturgy planners. Pays in copies and subscription. Query required.

MOMENT MAGAZINE— 4710 41st St. N.W., Washington, DC 20016. Suzanne Singer, Man. Ed. Sophisticated, issue-oriented articles, 2,000 to 4,000 words, on Jewish topics. Nonfiction only. Pays $150 to $800, on publication.

MOMENTUM—National Catholic Educational Assn., 1077 30th St. N.W., Suite 100, Washington, DC 20007–3852. Patricia Feistritzer, Ed. Articles, 500 to 1,500 words, on outstanding programs, issues, and research in education. Book reviews. Pays $25 to $75, on publication. Query.

MOODY MAGAZINE— 820 N. La Salle Blvd., Chicago, IL 60610. Andrew Scheer, Man. Ed. Anecdotal articles, 1,200 to 2,000 words, on the evangelical Christian experience in the home, the community, and the workplace. Pays 15¢ to 20¢ a word, on acceptance. Query.

THE MUSIC LEADER—Baptist Sunday School Board, 127 Ninth Ave. N., Nashville, TN 37234. Anne Trudel, Ed. Quarterly. How-to articles, to 800 words, on organizing choir rehearsals for children; also time savers and other tips for choir directors. Inspirational poetry for challenge of teaching children. True (original) short pieces about funny or touching things that happened in preschool or children's choir. "Our readers are volunteer choir directors and teachers in evangelical churches. Articles should be encouraging, not too academic, and practical." Pays 5½¢ to 6½¢ a word, on acceptance. Submit complete manuscript; no queries.

NEW ERA—50 E. North Temple, Salt Lake City, UT 84150. Richard M. Romney, Man. Ed. Articles, 150 to 1,500 words, and fiction, to 2,000 words, for young Mormons. Poetry; photos. Pays 5¢ to 10¢ a word, 25¢ a line for poetry, on acceptance. Query.

NEW MAN—600 Rinehart Rd., Lake Mary, FL 32746. Brian Peterson, Ed. Articles, to 2,000 words, that help men "in their quest for godliness and integrity." Profiles of everyday men who are doing something extraordinary, action-packed thrill and adventure articles, trend pieces that take an in-depth look at issues facing men today. Short items, 50 to 250 words, on unusual facts, motivational quotes, perspectives on news and events. Pays 10¢ to 35¢ per word, on publication.

NEW WORLD OUTLOOK—475 Riverside Dr., Rm. 1333, New York, NY 10115. Alma Graham, Ed. Articles, 500 to 2,000 words, illustrated with color photos, on United Methodist missions and Methodist-related programs and ministries. Focus on national, global, and women's and children's issues, and on men and youth in missions. Pays on publication. Query.

OBLATES—15 S. 59th St., Belleville, IL 62223–4694. Mary Mohrman, Manuscripts Ed. Christine Portell, Man. Ed. Articles, 500 to 600 words, that inspire, uplift, and motivate through positive Christian values in everyday life. Inspirational poetry, to 16 lines. Pays $80 for articles, $30 for poems, on acceptance. Send 2 first-class stamps and SASE for guidelines and sample copy.

THE OTHER SIDE—300 W. Apsley, Philadelphia, PA 19144. Doug Davidson, Nonfiction Ed. Jennifer Wilkins, Fiction Ed. Rod Jellema, Poetry Ed. Independent, ecumenical Christian magazine devoted to issues of peace, justice, and faith. Fiction, 500 to 5,000 words, that deepens readers' encounter with the mystery of God and the mystery of ourselves. Nonfiction, 500 to 4,000 words (most under 2,000 words), on contemporary social, political, economic, or racial issues in the U.S. or abroad. Poems, to 50 lines; submit up to 3 poems. Payment is 2 copies plus $20 to $350 for articles; $75 to $250 for fiction; $15 for poems, on acceptance. Guidelines.

OUR FAMILY—Box 249, Battleford, Sask., Canada S0M 0E0. Nestor Gregoire, Ed. Articles, 1,000 to 3,000 words, for Catholic families, on modern society, family, marriage, current affairs, and spiritual topics. Humor; verse. Pays 7¢ to 10¢ a word for articles, 75¢ to $1 a line for poetry, on acceptance. SAE with international reply coupons required with all submissions. Guidelines.

PARENTLIFE—MSN 140, 127 Ninth Ave. N., Nashville, TN 37234. Attn: Ed. Informative articles and personal experience pieces, 400 to 1,200 words, relating to family and the preschool child, written with a Christian perspective. Payment varies, on acceptance.

PASTORAL LIFE—Box 595, Canfield, OH 44406–0595. Anthony L. Chenevey, Ed. Articles, 2,000 to 2,500 words, addressing the problems of pastoral ministry. Pays 4¢ a word, on publication. Guidelines.

PENTECOSTAL EVANGEL—1445 Boonville Ave., Springfield, MO 65802. Hal Donaldson, Ed. Assemblies of God. Religious, personal experience, and devotional articles, 400 to 1,000 words. Pays 6¢ a word, on acceptance.

PERSPECTIVE—Pioneer Clubs, Box 788, Wheaton, IL 60189. Rebecca Powell Parat, Ed. Articles, 750 to 1,500 words, that provide growth for adult club leaders in leadership and relationship skills and offer encouragement and practical support. Readers are lay leaders of Pioneer Clubs for boys and girls (age 2 to 12th grade). "Most articles written on assignment; writers familiar with Pioneer Clubs who would be interested in working on assignment should contact us." Queries preferred. Pays $40 to $90, on acceptance. Guidelines.

PIME WORLD—17330 Quincy St., Detroit, MI 48221. Paul W. Witte, Man. Ed. Articles, 600 to 1,200 words, on Catholic missionary work in Asia, West Africa, and Latin America. Color photos. No fiction or poetry. Pays 6¢ a word, extra for photos, on publication.

POWER AND LIGHT—6401 The Paseo, Kansas City, MO 64131. Beula J. Postlewait, Preteen Ed. Fiction, 400 to 800 words, for grades 5 and 6, defining Christian experiences and demonstrating Christian values and beliefs. Pays 5¢ a word for multi-use rights, on publication.

THE PREACHER'S MAGAZINE—10814 E. Broadway, Spokane, WA 99206. Randal E. Denny, Ed. Scholarly and practical articles, 700 to 2,500 words, on areas of interest to Christian ministers: church administration, pastoral care, professional and personal growth, church music, finance, evangelism. Pays 3½¢ a word, on publication. Guidelines.

PRESBYTERIAN RECORD—50 Wynford Dr., North York, Ont., Canada M3C 1J7. John Congram, Ed. Fiction and nonfiction, 1,500 words, and poetry, any length. Short items, to 800 words, of a contemporary and often controversial nature for "Vox Populi." The purpose of the magazine is "to provide news, not only from our church but the church-at-large, and to fulfill both a pastoral and prophetic role among our people." Queries preferred. SAE with international reply coupons required. Pays about $50 (Canadian), on publication. Guidelines.

PRESBYTERIANS TODAY—100 Witherspoon, Louisville, KY 40202–1396. Catherine Cottingham, Man. Ed. Articles, 1,200 to 1,500 words, of special interest to members of the Presbyterian Church (USA). Pays to $200, before publication.

PURPOSE—616 Walnut Ave., Scottdale, PA 15683–1999. James E. Horsch, Ed. Fiction, nonfiction, and fillers, to 750 words, on Christian discipleship and church-year related themes, with good photos; pieces of history, biography, science, hobbies, from a Christian perspective; Christian problem solving. First-person pieces preferred. Poetry, to 12 lines. "Send complete manuscript; no queries." Pays to 5¢ a word, to $2 a line for poetry, on acceptance.

QUAKER LIFE—Friends United Meeting, 101 Quaker Hill Dr., Richmond, IN 47374–1980. Johan Maurer, Ed. Ben Richmond, Man. Ed. News and analysis, devotional and study articles for members of Friends United Meeting, other Friends (Quakers), evangelical Christians, religious pacifists. Personal testimonies. Poetry. Guidelines. Pays in copies.

QUEEN OF ALL HEARTS—26 S. Saxon Ave., Bay Shore, NY 11706–8993. J. Patrick Gaffney, S.M.M., Ed. Publication of Montfort Missionaries. Articles and fiction, 1,000 to 2,000 words, related to the Virgin Mary. Poetry. Pay varies, on acceptance.

THE QUIET HOUR— 4050 Lee Vance View, Colorado Springs, CO 80919. Gary Wilde, Ed. Short devotionals. Pays $15, on acceptance. By assignment only; query.

RECONSTRUCTIONISM TODAY—30 Old Whitfield Rd., Accord, NY 12404. Lawrence Bush, Ed. Articles on contemporary Judaism and Jewish culture. No fiction or poetry. Pays in copies and subscription.

REVIEW FOR RELIGIOUS—3601 Lindell Blvd., St. Louis, MO 63108. David L. Fleming, S.J., Ed. Informative, practical, or inspirational articles, 1,500 to 5,000 words, from a Catholic theological or spiritual point of view. Pays $6 per page, on publication. Guidelines.

ST. ANTHONY MESSENGER—1615 Republic St., Cincinnati, OH 45210–1298. Norman Perry, O.F.M., Ed. Articles, 2,000 to 3,000 words, on personalities, major movements, education, family, religious and church issues, spiritual life, and social issues. Human-interest pieces. Humor; fiction, 2,000 to 3,000 words. Articles and stories should have religious implications. Query for nonfiction. Pays 14¢ a word, on acceptance.

ST. JOSEPH'S MESSENGER—P.O. Box 288, Jersey City, NJ 07303–0288. Sister Ursula Maphet, Ed. Inspirational articles, 500 to 1,000 words, and fiction, 1,000 to 1,500 words. Verse, 4 to 40 lines. Payment varies, on publication.

SEEK— 8121 Hamilton Ave., Cincinnati, OH 45231. Eileen H. Wilmoth, Ed. Articles and fiction, to 1,200 words, on inspirational and controversial topics and timely religious issues. Christian testimonials. Pays 5¢ to 7¢ a word, on acceptance. SASE for guidelines.

THE SENIOR MUSICIAN—127 Ninth Ave. N., Nashville, TN 37234. Jere V. Adams, Ed. Quarterly. For music directors, pastors, organists, pianists, choir coordinators. Easy choir music for senior adult choirs to use in worship, ministry, and recreation. Also includes leisure reading, music training, fellowship suggestions, and choir projects for personal growth. Pays 5½¢ a word, on acceptance.

SHARING THE VICTORY—Fellowship of Christian Athletes, 8701 Leeds Rd., Kansas City, MO 64129. John Dodderidge, Ed. Articles, interviews, and profiles, to 1,000 words, for co-ed Christian athletes and coaches in junior high, high school, college, and pros. Pays from $50, on publication. Query required.

SIGNS OF THE TIMES—P. O. Box 5353, Nampa, ID 83653–5353. Marvin Moore, Ed. Seventh-Day Adventists. Articles, 500 to 2,000 words: features on Christians who have performed community services; first-person experiences, to 1,000 words; health, home, marriage, human-interest pieces; inspirational articles. Pays to 20¢ a word, on acceptance. Send 9x12 SASE for sample and guidelines.

SISTERS TODAY—The Liturgical Press, St. John's Abbey, Collegeville, MN 56321–7500. Articles, 500 to 3,500 words, on theology, social justice issues, and religious issues for women and the Church. Poetry, to 34 lines. Pays $5 per printed page, $10 per poem, on publication; $50 for color cover photos and $25 for B&W inside photos. Send articles to: Sister Mary Anthony Wagner, O.S.B., Ed., St. Benedict's Monastery, St. Joseph, MN 56374–2099.

Send poetry to: Sister Virginia Micka, C.S.J.,1884 Randolph Ave., St. Paul, MN 55105.

SOCIAL JUSTICE REVIEW—3835 Westminster Pl., St. Louis, MO 63108–3409. Rev. John H. Miller, C.S.C., Ed. Articles, 2,000 to 3,000 words, on social problems in light of Catholic teaching and current scientific studies. Pays 2¢ a word, on publication.

SPIRITUAL LIFE—2131 Lincoln Rd. N.E., Washington, DC 20002–1199. Edward O'Donnell, O.C.D., Ed. Professional religious journal. Religious essays, 3,000 to 5,000 words, on spirituality in contemporary life. Pays from $50, on acceptance. Guidelines.

STANDARD— 6401 The Paseo, Kansas City, MO 64131. Articles and fiction, 300 to 1,700 words; true experiences; poetry, to 20 lines; fiction with Christian emphasis but not overtly preachy; cartoons in good taste. Pays 3½¢ a word, on acceptance.

TEACHERS INTERACTION—3558 S. Jefferson Ave., St. Louis, MO 63118. Rachael Hoyer, Ed. Practical articles, 800 to 1,200 words, for Christian teachers and how-to pieces, to 100 words, specifically for Lutheran Church-Missouri Synod volunteer church school teachers. Pays $20 to $100, on publication. Freelance submissions accepted.

THEOLOGY TODAY—Box 29, Princeton, NJ 08542. Thomas G. Long, Ed. Patrick D. Miller, Ed. Articles, 1,500 to 3,500 words, on theology, religion, and related social and philosophical issues. Literary criticism. Pays $75 to $200, on publication.

TODAY'S CHRISTIAN DOCTOR—(formerly *Christian Medical & Dental Society Journal*) P.O. Box 5, Bristol, TN 37621–0005. David B. Biebel, D. Min., Ed. Articles, 8 to 10 double-spaced pages, for Christian medical and dental professionals. Queries preferred. Guidelines.

TODAY'S CHRISTIAN WOMAN— 465 Gundersen Dr., Carol Stream, IL 60188. Ramona Cramer Tucker, Ed. Articles, 1,500 to 1,800 words, that are "warm and personal in tone, full of real-life anecdotes that deal with the following relationships: marriage, parenting, friendship, spiritual life, and self." Payment varies, on acceptance. Queries required. Guidelines.

THE UNITED CHURCH OBSERVER— 478 Huron St., Toronto, Ont., Canada M5R 2R3. Factual articles, 1,500 to 2,500 words, on religious trends, human problems, social issues. No poetry. Pays after publication. Query.

UNITED SYNAGOGUE REVIEW—155 Fifth Ave., New York, NY 10010. Lois Goldrich, Ed. Articles, 1,000 to 1,200 words, on issues of interest to Conservative Jewish community. Query.

UNITY MAGAZINE—1901 N.W. Blue Pkwy., Unity School of Christianity, Unity Village, MO 64065. Philip White, Ed. Religious and inspirational articles, 1,000 to 1,800 words, on health and healing, Bible interpretation, and the metaphysical. Poems. Pays 20¢ a word, on acceptance.

VIRTUE— 4050 Lee Vance View, Colorado Springs, CO 80918. Attn: Ed. Articles and fiction for Christian women. Journalistic reports on women's issues and women's lives and their spiritual journeys. Query for articles; SASE required. Guidelines.

THE WAR CRY—The Salvation Army, P.O. Box 269, Alexandria, VA 22313. Attn: Ed.-in-Chief. Inspirational articles, to 800 words, addressing modern life and issues. Color photos. Pays 15¢ to 20¢ a word for articles, $150 to $200 for photos, on acceptance.

WITH: THE MAGAZINE FOR RADICAL CHRISTIAN YOUTH—722 Main St., Box 347, Newton, KS 67114. Eddy Hall and Carol Duerksen, Eds. Fiction, 500 to 2,000 words; nonfiction, 500 to 1,600 words; and poetry, to 50 lines for Mennonite and Brethren teenagers. "Wholesome humor always gets a close read." B&W 8x10 photos accepted. Payment is 5¢ a word, on acceptance (3¢ a word for reprints).

WOMAN'S TOUCH—1445 Boonville, Springfield, MO 65802–1894. Peggy Musgrove, Ed. Aleda Swartzendruber, Assoc. Ed. Articles, 500 to 1,000 words, that provide help and inspiration to Christian women, strengthening family life, and reaching out in witness to others. Submit complete manuscript. Allow 3 months for response. Payment varies, on publication. Guidelines and editorial calendar.

WORLD VISION MAGAZINE—P.O. Box 9716, Federal Way, WA 98063–9716. Bruce Brander, Man. Ed. Thoroughly researched articles, 1,200 to 2,000 words, on worldwide poverty, evangelism, the environment, and justice. Include reputable sources and strong anecdotes. "Turning Points," first-person articles, 450 to 700 words, about a life-changing, spiritual experience related to serving the poor. "We like articles to offer positive ways Christians can make a difference." Query required. Payment negotiable, made on acceptance.

YOUNG SALVATIONIST—The Salvation Army, 615 Slaters Ln., P.O. Box 269, Alexandria, VA 22313. Attn: Lesa Davis, Prod. Mgr. Articles, 600 to 1,200 words, that teach the Christian view of everyday living, for teenagers. Short shorts, first-person testimonies, 600 to 800 words. Pays 15¢ a word (10¢ a word for reprints), on acceptance. SASE required. Send 8½x11 SASE (3 stamps) for theme list, guidelines, and sample copy.

YOUR CHURCH— 465 Gundersen Dr., Carol Stream, IL 60188. Richard Doebler, Ed. Articles, to 1,000 words, about church business administration. Pays about 15¢ a word, on acceptance. Query required. Guidelines.

HEALTH

ACCENT ON LIVING—P. O. Box 700, Bloomington, IL 61702. Raymond C. Cheever, Pub. Betty Garee, Ed. Articles, 250 to 1,000 words, about physically disabled people, including their careers, recreation, sports, self-help devices, and ideas that can make daily routines easier. Good photos a plus. Pays 10¢ a word, on publication. Query.

AMERICAN BABY—KIII Family & Leisure Group, 249 W. 17th St., New York, NY 10011. Judith Nolte, Ed. Articles, 1,000 to 2,000 words, for new or expectant parents on prenatal and infant care. Personal experience, 900 to 1,200 words (do not submit in diary format). Department pieces, 50 to 350 words, for "Crib Notes" (news and feature topics) and "Medical Update" (health and medicine). No fiction, fantasy pieces, dreamy musings, or poetry. Pays $500 to $1,000 for articles, $100 for departments, on acceptance. Guidelines.

AMERICAN FITNESS—15250 Ventura Blvd., Suite 200, Sherman Oaks, CA 91403. Peg Jordan, Ed. Rhonda Wilson, Man. Ed. Articles, 500 to 1,500 words, on exercise, health, trends, research, nutrition, alternative paths, etc. Illustrations, photos.

AMERICAN HEALTH—28 W. 23rd St., New York, NY 10010. Attn: Ed. Dept. Lively, authoritative articles, 1,000 to 3,000 words, on women's health and lifestyle aspects of health and fitness; 100- to 500-word news reports. Query with clips. Pays $250 ($50 kill fee) for news stories; 75¢ to $1 per word for features (kill fee is 25% of assigned fee), on acceptance.

AMERICAN JOURNAL OF NURSING—555 W. 57th St., New York, NY 10019. Santa J. Crisall, Clinical Dir. Articles, 1,500 to 2,000 words, with photos or illustrations, on nursing or disease processes. Query.

AQUARIUS: A SIGN OF THE TIMES—984 Canton St., Roswell, GA 30075. Dan Liss, Ed. Tabloid. Articles, 800 words (plus photo or illustration) on holistic health, metaphysics, spirituality, and the environment. "We are a great way for new writers to get clips." No payment.

ARTHRITIS TODAY—The Arthritis Foundation, 1330 W. Peachtree St., Atlanta, GA 30309. Cindy McDaniel, Ed. Research, self-help, how-to, general interest, general health, and lifestyle topics, and inspirational articles, 750 to 3,000 words, and short fillers, 100 to 250 words. "The magazine is written to help people with arthritis live more productive, independent, and pain-free lives." Pays $500 to $2,000 for articles, $75 to $250 for short fillers, on acceptance.

BABY TALK—301 Howard St., San Francisco, CA 94105. Trisha Thompson, Ed. Articles, 1,000 to 1,500 words, by parents or professionals, on babies and baby care, etc. No poetry. Pay varies, on acceptance. SASE required.

COPING: LIVING WITH CANCER—P.O. Box 682268, Franklin, TN 37068. Tricia Brown, Ed. Uplifting and practical articles for people living with cancer: medical news, lifestyle issues, and inspiring personal essays. No payment.

DIABETES SELF-MANAGEMENT—150 W. 22nd St., New York, NY 10011. James Hazlett, Ed. Articles, 2,000 to 4,000 words, for people with diabetes who want to know more about controlling and managing it. Up-to-date and authoritative information on nutrition, pharmacology, exercise physiology, technological advances, self-help, and other how-to subjects. "Articles must be useful, instructive, and must have immediate application to the day-to-day life of our readers. We do not publish personal experience, profiles, exposés, or research breakthroughs." Query with one-page rationale, outline, writing samples, and SASE. Pays from $500, on publication. Buys all rights.

EATING WELL—Ferry Rd., P.O. Box 1001, Charlotte, VT 05445–1001. Marcelle DiFalco, Ed. Bimonthly. "A food book with a health perspective." Feature articles, 2,000 to 5,000 words, for readers who "know that what they eat directly affects their well-being, and believe that with the right approach, one can enjoy both good food and good health." Department pieces, 100 to 200 words, for "Nutrition News" and "Eating Well in America." "We look for strong journalistic voice; authoritative, timely coverage of nutrition issues; healthful recipes that emphasize good ingredients, simple preparation, and full

643

flavor; and a sense of humor." Pays varying rates, 45 days after acceptance. Query.

FITNESS—Gruner & Jahr USA Publishing, 110 Fifth Ave., New York, NY 10011. Sally Lee, Ed. Articles, 500 to 2,000 words, on health, exercise, sports, nutrition, diet, psychological well-being, alternative therapies, sex, and beauty. Average reader is 30 years old. Query required. Pays $1 a word, on acceptance.

HEALTH—301 Howard St., 18th Fl., San Francisco, CA 94105. Paula Motte, Ed. Asst. Articles, 1,200 words, for "Food," "Fitness," "Vanities," "Mind," and "Relationships" departments. Query with clips and SASE required.

HEALTH QUEST—200 Highpoint Dr., Suite 215, Chalfont, PA 18914. Valerie Boyd, Ed.-in-Chief. Tamara Jeffries, Man. Ed. "The Publication of Black Wellness." Articles, 700 to 1,500 words, on health issues of interest to African-American men and women. "We focus on total health, so articles cover mind, body, spirit, and cultural wellness." Payment varies, on publication. Query preferred.

HEART & SOUL—Rodale Press, Inc., 733 Third Ave., 15th Fl., New York, NY 10017. Stephanie Stokes Oliver, Ed.-in-Chief. Articles, 800 to 2,000 words, on health, beauty, fitness, nutrition, and relationships for African-American readers. Pays varying rates, on acceptance. Queries preferred.

HERBALGRAM—P.O. Box 201660, Austin, TX 78720. Barbara Johnston, Man. Ed. Quarterly. Articles, 1,500 to 3,000 words, on herb and medicinal plant research, regulatory issues, market conditions, native plant conservation, and other aspects of herbal use. Pays in copies. Query.

IDEA TODAY—6190 Cornerstone Ct. E., Suite 204, San Diego, CA 92121–3773. Therese Hannon, Asst. Ed. Practical articles, 1,000 to 3,000 words, on new exercise programs, business management, nutrition, sports medicine, dance-exercise, and one-to-one training techniques. Articles must be geared toward the aerobics instructor, exercise studio owner or manager, or personal trainer. No consumer or general health pieces. Payment negotiable, on acceptance. Query preferred. Guidelines.

INDEPENDENT LIVING PROVIDER—150 Motor Parkway, Suite 420, Hauppauge, NY 11788–5145. Anne Kelly, Ed. Articles, 1,500 to 3,000 words, on sales and service by home medical equipment dealers. Topics: home health care business, managed care, health care reform, new products. Pays 15¢ a word, $15 per photo, on publication. Query.

LET'S LIVE—P.O. Box 74908, Los Angeles, CA 90004. Beth Salmon, Ed.-in-Chief. Articles, 1,000 to 1,500 words, on preventive medicine and nutrition, alternative medicine, diet, vitamins, herbs, exercise, recipes, and natural beauty. Pays $250, on publication. Query.

MEDIPHORS—P.O. Box 327, Bloomsburg, PA 17815. Dr. Eugene D. Radice, Ed. "A Literary Journal of the Health Professions." Short stories, essays, and commentary, 3,000 words, related to medicine and health. Poetry, to 30 lines. "We are not a technical journal of science. We do not publish research or review articles, except of a historical nature." Pays in copies. Guidelines.

NATURAL HEALTH—17 Station St., Box 1200, Brookline Village, MA 02147. Attn: Ed. Bimonthly. Features, 1,500 to 3,000 words, on holistic health, natural foods, herbal remedies, etc., and interviews. Departments and columns, 250 to 1,000 words. Photos. Pays varying rates, on acceptance.

NURSING 97—1111 Bethlehem Pike, P.O. Box 908, Springhouse, PA 19477–0908. Patricia Nornhold, Exec. Dir. Most articles are clinically oriented, and written by nurses for direct caregivers. Also covers legal, ethical, management, and career aspects of nursing; narratives about personal nursing experiences. No poetry, cartoons, or puzzles. Pays $25 to $300, on publication. Query.

NUTRITION HEALTH REVIEW—P.O. Box 406, Haverford, PA 19041. Frank Ray Rifkin, Ed. Quarterly tabloid. Articles on medical progress, information relating to nutritional therapy, genetics, psychiatry, behavior therapy, surgery, pharmacology, animal health; vignettes relating to health and nutrition. "Vegetarian-oriented; we do not deal with subjects that favor animal testing, animal foods, cruelty to animals or recipes that contain animal products." Humor, cartoons. Pays on publication. Query.

PATIENT CARE—5 Paragon Dr., Montvale, NJ 07645. Jeffrey H. Forster, Ed. Articles on medical care, for primary-care physicians; mostly staff-written. Pays varying rates, on publication. Query; all articles assigned.

PERCEPTIONS—10734 Jefferson Blvd., Suite 502, Culver City, CA 90230. Judi V. Brewer, Ed. Articles, to 2,500 words, on government, alternative health, metaphysics. Reviews, to 500 words. Cartoons. "Broad-spectrum focus crossing barriers that separate ideologies, politics, etc." Sections include Political Slant (relevant information focusing on what we have in common); Healing Spiral (little-known facts and remedies); Concepts (a forum to broaden, awaken, and tickle the intellect). Pays in copies.

THE PHOENIX—7152 Unity Ave. N., Brooklyn Ctr., MN 55429. Pat Samples, Ed. Tabloid. Articles, 800 to 1,500 words, on recovery, renewal, and growth. Department pieces for "12 Step," "Bodywise," "Family Skills," or "Personal Story." "Our readers are committed to physical, emotional, mental, and spiritual health and well-being. Read a sample copy to see what we publish." Pays 3¢ to 5¢ a word, on publication. Guidelines and calendar.

THE PHYSICIAN AND SPORTSMEDICINE— 4530 W. 77th St., Minneapolis, MN 55435. Terry Monahan, Exec. Ed. News and feature articles; clinical articles coauthored with physician. Sports medicine angle necessary. Pays $150 to $1,000, on acceptance. Query. Guidelines.

PREVENTION—33 E. Minor St., Emmaus, PA 18098. Lewis Vaughn, Man. Ed. Query required. No guidelines available. Limited market.

PSYCHOLOGY TODAY—Sussex Publishing, 49 E. 21st St., New York, NY 10010. Lisa Liebman, Exec. Ed. Bimonthly. Articles, 2,000 words, on timely subjects and news. Pays varying rates, on publication.

RX REMEDY—120 Post Rd. W., Westport, CT 06880. Val Weaver, Ed. Bimonthly. Articles, 600 to 2,500 words, on health and medication issues for readers 55 and older. Regular columns include "Housecall" and "The Nutrition Prescription." Query. Pays $1 to $1.25 a word, on acceptance.

TANNING TRENDS—3101 Page Ave., Jackson, MI 49203–2254. Joseph Levy, Ed. Articles on skin care and "smart tanning" for tanning salon owners. "We promote tanning clients responsibly and professionally." Payment varies, on publication.

TODAY'S OR NURSE—See *Today's Surgical Nurse.*

TODAY'S SURGICAL NURSE—(formerly *Today's OR Nurse*) Slack, Inc., 6900 Grove Rd., Thorofare, NJ 08086. Frances R. DeStefano, Man. Ed. Clinical or general articles, from 2,000 words, of direct interest to surgical nurses.

TOTAL HEALTH—165 N. 100 E. #2, St. George, UT 84770. Katherine Hurd, Ed. Articles, 1,200 to 1,400 words, on preventative health care, fitness, diet, and mental health. Color or B&W photos. Pays $50 to $75, on publication.

VEGETARIAN TIMES—P.O. Box 570, Oak Park, IL 60303. Toni Apgar, Ed. Dir. Articles, 1,200 to 2,500 words, on vegetarian cooking, nutrition, health and fitness, and profiles of prominent vegetarians. "News Items" and "In Print" (book reviews), to 500 words. "Herbalist" pieces, to 1,800 words, on medicinal uses of herbs. Queries required. Pays $75 to $1,000, on acceptance. Guidelines.

VEGETARIAN VOICE—P.O. Box 72, Dolgeville, NY 13329. Jennie Collura, Sr. Ed. Quarterly. Informative, well-researched and/or inspiring articles, 600 to 1,800 words, on health, nutrition, animal rights, the environment, world hunger, etc. Pays in copies. Guidelines.

VIBRANT LIFE—55 W. Oak Ridge Dr., Hagerstown, MD 21740. Attn: Ed. Features, 750 to 1,500 words, on total health: physical, mental, and spiritual. Upbeat articles on the family and how to live happier and healthier lives, emphasizing practical tips; Christian slant. Pays $80 to $250, on acceptance.

VIM & VIGOR—1010 E. Missouri Ave., Phoenix, AZ 85014. Jake Poinier, Ed. Positive health and fitness articles, 1,200 to 2,000 words, with accurate medical facts. By assignment only; no queries or unsolicited manuscripts. Writers with feature- or news-writing ability may submit qualifications for assignment. Pays $500, on acceptance. Guidelines.

THE WALKING MAGAZINE—9–11 Harcourt, Boston, MA 02116. Seth Bauer, Ed. Articles, 1,500 to 2,500 words, on fitness, health, equipment, nutrition, travel and adventure, famous walkers, and other walking-related topics. Shorter pieces, 150 to 800 words, and essays for "Ramblings" page. Photos welcome. Pays $750 to $1,800 for features, $100 to $500 for department pieces, on acceptance. Guidelines.

YOGA JOURNAL—2054 University Ave., Berkeley, CA 94704. Rick Fields, Ed. Articles, 1,200 to 4,000 words, on holistic health, meditation, consciousness, spirituality, and yoga. Pays $100 to $1,200, on acceptance.

YOUR HEALTH—5401 N.W. Broken Sound Blvd., Boca Raton, FL 33487. Susan Gregg, Ed.-in-Chief. Health and medical articles, 1,000 to 2,000 words, for a lay audience. Queries preferred. Pays $75 to $200, on publication.

YOUR HEALTH—1720 Washington Blvd., Box 10010, Ogden, UT 84409. Attn: Ed. Staff Articles, 1,000 words, on individual health care needs: prevention, treatment, low-impact aerobics, fitness, nutrition, etc. Color photos required. Pays 15¢ a word, on acceptance. Guidelines.

EDUCATION

ACTIVITY RESOURCES—P.O. Box 4875, Hayward, CA 94540. Mary Laycock, Ed. Math educational material only for books geared to mathematics for grades K through 8. Submit complete book manuscript. Royalty.

AMERICAN SCHOOL & UNIVERSITY—P.O. Box 12901, 9800 Metcalf, Overland Park, KS 66212–2215. Joe Agron, Ed. Articles and case studies, 1,200 to 1,500 words, on design, construction, operation, and management of school and university facilities. Queries preferred.

THE BOOK REPORT—Linworth Publishing, 480 E. Wilson Bridge Rd., Suite L, Worthington, OH 43085–2372. Carolyn Hamilton, Ed./Pub. "The Journal for Secondary School Librarians." Articles by school librarians or other educators about practical aspects of running a school library. Write for themes and guidelines. Also publishes *Library Talk,* "The Magazine for Elementary School Librarians," and *Technology Connection,* "The Magazine for Library and Media Specialists."

CAREERS & THE DISABLED—See *Minority Engineer.*

CHANGE—1319 18th St. N.W., Washington, DC 20036. Attn: Ed. Columns, 700 to 2,000 words, and in-depth features, 2,500 to 3,500 words, on programs, people, and institutions of higher education. "We can't usually pay for unsolicited articles."

THE CLEARING HOUSE—Heldref Publications, 1319 18th St. N.W., Washington, DC 20036. Judy Cusick, Man. Ed. Bimonthly for middle level and high school teachers and administrators. Articles, 2,500 words, related to education: useful teaching practices, research findings, and experiments. Some opinion pieces and satirical articles related to education. Pays in copies.

EQUAL OPPORTUNITY—See *Minority Engineer.*

GIFTED EDUCATION PRESS QUARTERLY—P.O. Box 1586, 10201 Yuma Ct., Manassas, VA 20108. Maurice Fisher, Pub. Articles, to 4,000 words, written by educators, laypersons, and parents of gifted children, on the problems of identifying and teaching gifted children and adolescents. "Interested in incisive analyses of current programs for the gifted and recommendations for improving the education of gifted students. Particularly interested in advocacy for gifted children, biographical sketches of highly gifted individuals, and the problems of teaching humanities, science, ethics, literature, and history to the gifted. Looking for highly imaginative and knowledgeable writers." Query required. Pays in subscription.

THE HISPANIC OUTLOOK IN HIGHER EDUCATION—17 Arcadian Ave., Paramus, NJ 07652. Attn: Ed. Articles, 1,500 to 2,000 words, on the issues, concerns, and potential models for furthering the academic results of Hispanics in higher education. Queries are preferred. Payment varies, on publication.

HOME EDUCATION MAGAZINE—P.O. Box 1083, Tonasket, WA 98855–1083. Helen E. Hegener, Man. Ed. Informative articles, 750 to 2,000 words, on all aspects of the growing homeschool movement. Send complete manuscript or detailed query with SASE. Pays 45¢ per column inch, on publication.

THE HORN BOOK MAGAZINE—11 Beacon St., Suite 1000, Boston, MA 02108. Roger Sutton, Ed.-in-Chief. Articles, 600 to 2,800 words, on books for young readers and related subjects for librarians, teachers, parents, etc. Payment varies, on publication. Query.

INDEPENDENT LIVING PROVIDER—See *Minority Engineer.*

INSTRUCTOR MAGAZINE—Scholastic, Inc., 555 Broadway, New York, NY 10012. Mickey Revenaugh, Ed. Articles, 300 to 1,500 words, for teachers in grades K through 8. Payment varies, on acceptance.

ITC COMMUNICATOR—International Training in Communication, P.O. Box 1809, Sutter Creek, CA 95685. JoAnn Levy, Ed. Educational articles, 200 to 800 words, on leadership, language, speech presentation, procedures for meetings, personal and professional development, written and spoken communication techniques. SASE required. Pays in copies.

LEADERSHIP PUBLISHERS, INC.—P.O. Box 8358, Des Moines, IA 50301–8358. Attn: Dr. Lois F. Roets. Educational materials for talented and gifted students, grades K to 12. Send SASE for catalogue and guidelines before submitting. Pays in royalty for books, and flat fee for booklets.

LEARNING—1607 Battleground Ave., Greensboro, NC 27408. Attn: Manuscript Ed. Articles that help teachers deal with issues such as stress, motivation, burnout, and other self-improvement topics; successful teaching strategies to reach today's kids; and ideas to get parents involved. SASE required. Pays $15 to $300. Allow 6 months for response.

LIBRARY TALK—See *The Book Report.*

MEDIA & METHODS—1429 Walnut St., Philadelphia, PA 19102. Michele Sokoloff, Ed. Dir. Articles, 800 to 1,000 words, on media, technologies, and methods used to enhance instruction and learning in K through 12th-grade classrooms. Pays $50 to $200, on publication. Query required.

MINORITY ENGINEER—1160 E. Jericho Turnpike, Suite 200, Huntington, NY 11743. James Schneider, Ed. Articles, 1,000 to 1,500 words, for college students, on career opportunities; techniques of job hunting, and role-model profiles of professional minority engineers. Interviews. Pays 10¢ a word, on publication. Query. Also publishes: *Equal Opportunity; Careers & the Dis-ABLED*, query James Schneider; *Woman Engineer* and *Independent Living Provider*, query Editor Anne Kelly.

MOMENTUM—National Catholic Educational Assn., 1077 30th St. N.W., Suite 100, Washington, DC 20007–3852. Patricia Feistritzer, Ed. Articles, 500 to 1,500 words, on outstanding programs, issues, and research in education. Book reviews. Query or send complete manuscript. No simultaneous submissions. Pays $25 to $75, on publication.

THE MUSIC LEADER—Baptist Sunday School Board, 127 Ninth Ave. N., Nashville, TN 37234. Anne Trudel, Ed. Quarterly. How-to articles, to 800 words, on organizing choir rehearsals for children; also time savers and other tips for choir directors. Inspirational poetry for challenge of teaching children. True (original) short pieces about funny or touching things that happened in preschool or children's choir. "Our readers are volunteer choir directors and teachers in evangelical churches. Articles should be encouraging, not too academic, and practical." Pays 5½¢ to 6½¢ a word, on acceptance. Send complete manuscript; no queries.

PHI DELTA KAPPAN—408 N. Union St., Box 789, Bloomington, IN 47402–0789. Pauline Gough, Ed. Articles, 1,000 to 4,000 words, on educational research, service, and leadership; issues, trends, and policy. Rarely pays for manuscripts.

SCHOOL ARTS MAGAZINE—50 Portland St., Worcester, MA 01608. Dr. Eldon Katter, Ed. Articles, 800 to 1,000 words, on art education with special application to the classroom: successful and meaningful approaches to teaching art, innovative art projects, uncommon applications of art techniques or equipment, etc. Photos. Pays varying rates, on publication. Guidelines.

SCHOOL SAFETY—National School Safety Ctr., 4165 Thousand Oaks Blvd., Suite 290, Westlake Village, CA 91362. Ronald D. Stephens, Exec. Ed. Published 8 times during the school year. Articles, 2,000 to 3,000 words, of use to educators, law enforcers, judges, and legislators on the prevention of drugs, gangs, weapons, bullying, discipline problems, and vandalism; also on-site security and character development as they relate to students and schools. No payment.

TEACHING K-8— 40 Richards Ave., Norwalk, CT 06854. Patricia Broderick, Ed. Dir. Articles, 1,200 words, on the profession of teaching children. Pays to $35, on publication. Queries are not necessary.

TECH DIRECTIONS—Box 8623, Ann Arbor, MI 48107. Paul J. Bamford, Man. Ed. Articles, one to 10 double-spaced typed pages, for teachers and administrators in industrial, technology, and vocational educational fields, with particular interest in classroom projects, computer uses, and legislative issues. Pays $10 to $150, on publication. Guidelines.

TECHNOLOGY CONNECTION—See *The Book Report.*

TODAY'S CATHOLIC TEACHER—330 Progress Rd., Dayton, OH 45449. Mary Noschang, Ed. Articles, 600 to 800 words, 1,000 to 1,200 words, and 1,200 to 1,500 words, on education, parent-teacher relationships, innovative teaching, teaching techniques, etc., of use to educators in Catholic schools. Pays $65 to $250, on publication. SASE required. Query. Guidelines.

WOMAN ENGINEER—See *Minority Engineer.*

FARMING AND AGRICULTURE

ACRES USA—P.O. Box 8800, Metairie, LA 70011. Fred C. Walters, Ed. Articles on sustainable agriculture: technology, case reports, "hands-on" advice. "Our emphasis is on commercial production of quality food without the use of toxic chemicals." Pays 5¢ a word, on publication.

AMERICAN BEE JOURNAL—51 N. Second St., Hamilton, IL 62341. Joe M. Graham, Ed. Articles on beekeeping, for professionals. Photos. Pays 75¢ a column inch, extra for photos, on publication.

BEE CULTURE— 623 W. Liberty St., Medina, OH 44256. Mr. Kim Flottum, Ed. Basic how-to articles, 500 to 2,000 words, on keeping bees and selling bee products. Slides or B&W prints. Payment varies, on acceptance and on publication. Queries preferred.

BUCKEYE FARM NEWS—Ohio Farm Bureau Federation, 2 Nationwide Plaza, Box 479, Columbus, OH 43216–0479. Lynn Echelberger, Copy Ed. Articles, to 600 words, related to agriculture. Pays on publication. Query. Limited market.

DAIRY GOAT JOURNAL—P.O. Box 10, Lake Mills, WI 53551. Dave Thompson, Ed. Articles, to 1,500 words, on successful dairy goat owners, youths and interesting people associated with dairy goats. "Especially interested in practical husbandry ideas." Photos. Pays $50 to $150, on publication. Query.

FARM AND RANCH LIVING—5400 S. 60th St., Greendale, WI 53129. Nick Pabst, Ed. Articles, 2,000 words, on rural people and situations; nostalgia pieces; profiles of interesting farms and farmers, ranches and ranchers. Pays $15 to $400, on acceptance and on publication.

FARM INDUSTRY NEWS—7900 International Dr., Minneapolis, MN 55425. Joe Degnan, Ed. Articles for farmers, on new products, machinery, equipment, chemicals, and seeds. Pays $350 to $500, on acceptance. Query required.

FARM JOURNAL—Centre Sq. W., 1500 Market St., Philadelphia, PA 19102–2181. Sonja Hillgren, Ed. Articles, 500 to 1,500 words, with photos, on the business of farming. Pays 20¢ to 50¢ a word, on acceptance. Query.

FARM SUPPLY RETAILING—P.O. Box 23536, Minneapolis, MN 55423–0536. Joseph Rydholm, Ed. Profiles, 1,400 words, of successful farm supply retailers and articles on running/managing a small business, preferably slanted to the farm supply retailer. Photos. Pays $150 to $200 for articles; $25 to $75 for photos, on publication.

THE FURROW—Deere & Co., John Deere Rd., Moline, IL 61265. George Sollenberger, Exec. Ed. Specialized, illustrated articles on farming. Pays to $1,200, on acceptance.

THE LAND—P.O. Box 3169, Mankato, MN 56002–3169. Randy Frahm, Ed. Articles on Minnesota agriculture and rural issues. Pays $25 to $45, on acceptance. Query required.

NEW HOLLAND NEWS—New Holland, Inc., P.O. Box 1895, New Holland, PA 17557–0903. Attn: Ed. Articles, to 1,500 words, with strong color photo support, on agriculture and rural living. Pays on acceptance. Query.

OHIO FARMER—1350 W. Fifth Ave., Columbus, OH 43212. Tim White, Ed. Technical articles on farming, rural living, etc., in Ohio. Pays $50 per column, on publication.

ONION WORLD—P.O. Box 9036, Yakima, WA 98909–9036. D. Brent Clement, Ed. Production and marketing articles, to 1,500 words (preferred length 1,200 words), for commercial onion growers and shippers. "Research oriented articles are of definite interest. No gardening articles." Pays about $125, on publication. Query preferred.

PEANUT FARMER—3000 Highwoods Blvd., Suite 300, Raleigh, NC 27604–1029. Mary Evans, Man. Ed. Articles, 500 to 2,000 words, on production and management practices in peanut farming. Pays $50 to $350, on publication.

PENNSYLVANIA FARMER—P.O. Box 4475, Gettysburg, PA 17325. John R. Vogel, Ed. Articles on farmers in PA, NJ, DE, MD, and WV; timely business-of-farming concepts and successful farm management operations. Short pieces on humorous experiences in farming. Payment varies, on publication.

PROGRESSIVE FARMER—2100 Lakeshore Dr., Birmingham, AL 35209. Toni Holifield, Ed. Asst. Articles, to 5 double-spaced pages (3 pages preferred), on farmers or new developments in agriculture; rural communities; and personal business issues concerning the farmstead, home office, relationships, worker safety, finances, taxes, and regulations. Pays $50 to $400, on publication. Query.

RURAL HERITAGE—281 Dean Ridge Ln., Gainesboro, TN 38562. Gail Damerow, Ed. How-to and feature articles, 800 to 1,200 words, related to the present-day use of work horses, mules, and oxen. Pays 5¢ a word, $10 for photos, on publication. SASE for guidelines.

SHEEP! MAGAZINE—P.O. Box 10, Lake Mills, WI 53551. Dave Thompson, Ed. Articles, to 1,500 words, on successful shepherds, woolcrafts, sheep raising, and sheep dogs. "Especially interested in people who raise sheep successfully as a sideline enterprise." Photos. Pays $80 to $150, extra for photos, on publication. Query.

SMALL FARM TODAY—3903 W. Ridge Trail Rd., Clark, MO 65243–9525. Paul Berg, Man. Ed. Agriculture articles, 800 to 1,800 words, on preserving and promoting small farming, rural living, and "agripreneurship." How-to articles on alternative crops, livestock, and direct marketing. Pays 3½¢ a word, on publication. Query.

SMALL FARMER'S JOURNAL—P.O. Box 1627, Dept. 106, Sisters, OR 97759. Address the Eds. How-tos, humor, practical work horse information, livestock and produce marketing, gardening information, and articles appropriate to the independent family farm. Pays negotiable rates, on publication. Query.

TOPICS IN VETERINARY MEDICINE—Pfizer Animal Health, 812 Springdale Dr., Exton, PA 19341. Kathleen Etchison, Ed. Technical articles, 1,200 to 1,500 words, and clinical features, 500 words, on veterinary medicine. Photos. Pays $300, $150 for shorter pieces, extra for photos, on publication.

WALLACES FARMER—6200 Aurora Ave., Suite 609E, Urbandale, IA 50322–2838. Frank Holdmeger, Ed. Features, 600 to 700 words, on farming in Iowa; methods and equipment; interviews with farmers. Query. Payment varies, on acceptance.

THE WESTERN PRODUCER—Box 2500, Saskatoon, Saskatchewan, Canada S7K 2C4. Address Man. Ed. Articles, to 800 words (prefer under 600 words), on agricultural and rural subjects, preferably with a Canadian slant. Photos. Pays from 15¢ a word; $20 to $40 for B&W photos; $35 to $100 for color photos, on acceptance.

WYOMING RURAL ELECTRIC NEWS—P.O. Box 380, Casper, WY 82606–0380. Kris Wendtland, Ed. Articles, 500 to 900 words, on issues relevant to rural Wyoming. Articles should support Wyoming's personal and economic growth, social development, and education. Wyoming writers given preference. Pays $20 to $50, on publication.

ENVIRONMENT AND CONSERVATION

AMERICAN FORESTS—1516 P St. N.W., Washington, DC 20005. Michelle Robbins, Ed. Looking for skilled science writers for well-documented articles on the use, enjoyment, and management of forests. Send clips. Query.

651

THE AMICUS JOURNAL—Natural Resources Defense Council, 40 W. 20th St., New York, NY 10011. Kathrin Day Lassila, Ed. Quarterly. Articles and book reviews on local, national and international environmental topics. (No fiction, speeches, or product reports accepted.) Pays varying rates, 30 days after acceptance. Query with SASE required.

ANIMALS—350 S. Huntington Ave., Boston, MA 02130. Joni Praded, Dir./Ed. Informative, well-researched articles, to 2,500 words, on animal protection, national and international wildlife, pet care, conservation, and environmental issues that affect animals. No personal accounts or favorite pet stories. Pays from $350, on acceptance. Query.

AUDUBON—700 Broadway, New York, NY 10003. Michael W. Robbins, Ed. Bimonthly. Articles, 300 to 4,000 words, on conservation and environmental issues, natural history, ecology, and related subjects. Payment varies, on acceptance. Query.

BIRD WATCHER'S DIGEST—P.O. Box 110, Marietta, OH 45750. William H. Thompson, III, Ed. Articles, 600 to 2,500 words, for bird watchers: first-person accounts; how-tos; pieces on endangered species; profiles. Pays from $50, on publication. Submit complete manuscript.

BUGLE—Rocky Mountain Elk Foundation, P.O. Box 8249, Missoula, MT 59807–8249. Jan Brocci, Asst. Ed. Quarterly. Fiction and nonfiction, 1,500 to 4,000 words, on elk and elk hunting. Department pieces, 1,000 to 3,000 words, for: "Thoughts and Theories"; "Situation Ethics"; and "Women in the Outdoors." Pays 20¢ a word, on acceptance.

E: THE ENVIRONMENTAL MAGAZINE—Earth Action Network, Inc., P.O. Box 5098, Westport, CT 06881. Jim Motavalli, Ed. Environmental features, 4,000 words, and news for departments: 400 words for "In Brief"; and 1,000 words for "Currents." Pays 20¢ a word, on publication. Query.

FLORIDA WILDLIFE— 620 S. Meridian St., Tallahassee, FL 32399–1600. Attn: Ed. Bimonthly of the Florida Game and Fresh Water Fish Commission. Articles, 800 to 1,200 words, that promote native flora and fauna, hunting, fishing in Florida's fresh waters, outdoor ethics, and conservation of Florida's natural resources. Pays $50 a page, on publication. SASE for "how to submit" memo.

IN BUSINESS— 419 State Ave., Emmaus, PA 18049–3097. Jerome Goldstein, Ed. Bimonthly. Articles, 1,500 words, for environmental entrepreneurs: reports on economically successful businesses that also demonstrate a commitment to the environment, advice on growing a "green" business, family-run businesses, home-based businesses, community ecological development, etc. Pays $100 to $250 for articles; $25 to $75 for department pieces, on publication. Query with clips.

NATIONAL GEOGRAPHIC—1145 17th St. N.W., Washington, DC 20036. William Allen, Ed. First-person, general-interest, heavily illustrated articles on science, natural history, exploration, and geographical regions. Written query required.

NATIONAL PARKS MAGAZINE—1776 Massachusetts Ave. N.W., Washington, DC 20036. Leslie Happ, Ed.-in-Chief. Articles, 1,500 to 2,000 words, on areas in the National Park System, proposed new areas, threats to parks or park wildlife, new trends in park use, legislative issues, and endangered species of plants or animals relevant to national parks. No fiction, poetry, personal narratives, "My trip to . . . ," or straight travel pieces to individual parks. Articles, 1,500 words, on "low-impact" travel to 4 or 5 national park sites. Pays $400 to $1,000, on acceptance. Query with clips (original slant or news hook is essential to successful query). Guidelines.

NATIONAL WILDLIFE— 8925 Leesburg Pike, Vienna, VA 22184. Mark Wexler, Ed. Articles, 1,000 to 2,500 words, on wildlife, conservation, environment; outdoor how-to pieces. Photos. Pays on acceptance. Query.

OUTDOOR AMERICA—707 Conservation Ln., Gaithersburg, MD 20878–2983. Attn: Articles Ed. Quarterly publication of the Izaak Walton League of America. Articles, 1,250 to 2,000 words, on natural resource conservation issues and outdoor recreation, with emphasis on IWLA member/chapter tie-in; especially fishing, hunting, and camping. Short items, 500 to 750 words. Pays 20¢ a word. Query with clips.

OUTDOOR TRAVELER, MID-ATLANTIC—WMS Publications, Inc., P.O. Box 2748, Charlottesville, VA 22902. Marianne Marks, Ed. Tom Gillespie, Assoc. Ed. Quarterly. Articles, 1,500 to 2,000 words, on hiking/backpacking, canoeing/kayaking/rafting, camping, mountain biking, road cycling, travel, nature, and the environment from New York state to North Carolina. Travel articles on destinations and areas that offer recreational opportunities. Departments include "Destinations," 450 to 600 words, on practical and descriptive guides to sports destinations; book and product reviews. Pays $300 to $400 for features; payment varies for departments, on publication. Guidelines.

PACIFIC DISCOVERY—California Academy of Sciences, Golden Gate Park, San Francisco, CA 94118–4599. Gordy Slack, Assoc. Ed. Quarterly. Well-researched articles, 1,500 to 3,000 words, on natural history and preservation of the environment. Pays 25¢ a word, before publication. Query.

SIERRA— 85 2nd St., San Francisco, CA 94105. Joan Hamilton, Ed.-in-Chief. Articles, 750 to 2,500 words, on environmental and conservation topics, travel, hiking, backpacking, skiing, rafting, cycling. Photos. Pays from $500 to $2,000, extra for photos, on acceptance. Query with clips.

SMITHSONIAN MAGAZINE— 900 Jefferson Dr., Washington, DC 20560. Marlane A. Liddell, Articles Ed. Articles on history, art, natural history, physical science, profiles, etc. Query with clips, SASE.

SPORTS AFIELD—250 W. 55th St., New York, NY 10019. Terry McDonell, Ed-in-Chief. Articles, 500 to 2,000 words, with quality photos, on hunting, fishing, nature, survival, conservation, ecology, personal experiences. How-to pieces; humor, fiction. Payment varies, on acceptance.

TEXAS PARKS & WILDLIFE—Fountain Park Plaza, 3000 S. Interstate Hwy. 35, Suite 120, Austin, TX 78704. Jim Cox, Sr. Ed. Articles, 800 to 1,500 words, promoting the conservation and enjoyment of Texas wildlife, parks, waters, and all outdoors. Features on hunting, fishing, birding, camping, and the environment. Department pieces, to 1,000 words, for "Parks & Places to Go," "State of Nature," and "Woods and Waters." Photos a plus. Pays to $600, on acceptance; extra for photos.

VIRGINIA WILDLIFE—P.O. Box 11104, Richmond, VA 23230–1104. Attn: Ed. Articles, 1,250 to 1,750 words, on fishing, hunting, wildlife management, outdoor safety, ethics, etc. All material must have Virginia tie-in and may be accompanied by color photos. Pays from 15¢ a word, extra for photos, on acceptance. Query.

WHOLE EARTH REVIEW—P.O. Box 38, Sausalito, CA 94966. Attn: Ed. Quarterly. Articles and book reviews. "Good article material is often found in passionate personal statements or descriptions of the writer's activities." Pays $40 for reviews; payment varies for articles, on publication.

WILDLIFE CONSERVATION—The Wildlife Conservation Society, Bronx, NY 10460. Nancy Simmons, Sr. Ed. First-person articles, 1,500 to 2,000 words, on "popular" natural history, "based on author's research and experience as opposed to textbook approach." Payment varies, on acceptance. Guidelines.

MEDIA AND THE ARTS

THE AMERICAN ART JOURNAL—730 Fifth Ave., Suite 205, New York, NY 10019–4105. Jayne A. Kuchna, Ed. Scholarly articles, 2,000 to 10,000 words, on American art of the 17th through the early 20th centuries. Photos. Pays $200 to $500, on acceptance.

AMERICAN INDIAN ART MAGAZINE—7314 E. Osborn Dr., Scottsdale, AZ 85251. Roanne P. Goldfein, Ed. Detailed articles, 10 to 20 double-spaced pages, on American Indian arts: painting, carving, beadwork, basketry, textiles, ceramics, jewelry, etc. Pays varying rates, on publication. Query.

AMERICAN JOURNALISM REVIEW— 8701 Adelphi Rd., Adelphi, MD 20783. Rem Rieder, Ed. Articles, 500 to 5,000 words, on print or electronic journalism, ethics, and related issues. Pays 20¢ a word, on publication. Query.

AMERICAN VISIONS, THE MAGAZINE OF AFRO-AMERICAN CULTURE—1156 15th St. N.W., Suite 615, Washington, DC 20005. Joanne Harris, Ed. Articles, 1,500 to 2,500 words, and columns, 1,000 words, on African-American culture with a focus on the arts. Pays from $100 to $600, on publication. Query.

THE ARTIST'S MAGAZINE—1507 Dana Ave., Cincinnati, OH 45207. Sandra Carpenter, Ed. Features, 1,200 to 2,500 words, and department pieces for the working artist. Poems, to 20 lines, on art and creativity. Single-panel cartoons. Pays $150 to $350 for articles; $65 for cartoons, on acceptance. Guidelines. Query.

ARTSATLANTIC—145 Richmond St., Charlottetown, P.E.I., Canada C1A 1J1. Joseph Sherman, Ed. Articles and reviews, 600 to 3,000 words, on visual, performing, and literary arts primarily in Atlantic Canada. Also, "idea and concept" articles of universal appeal. Query.

AT THE CROSSROADS MAGAZINE—P.O. Box 317, Sta. P, Toronto, Ontario, Canada M5S 2S8. Karen Augustine, Ed.-in-Chief. Published 3 times a year. "The only real source promoting black women's art." Fiction, to 6 typed pages, and nonfiction, to 16 pages: interviews and profiles; news; reviews of black cultural events, concerts, books, dance, theatre, and music. All forms of visual arts. "We are looking for fresh, challenging articles, columns, and opinion pieces. Get as creative and controversial as you want. No anti-black or homophobic material." Pays in honorarium or subscription.

BLUEGRASS UNLIMITED—Box 111, Broad Run, VA 20137–0111. Peter V. Kuykendall, Ed. Articles, to 3,500 words, on bluegrass and traditional country music. Photos. Pays 8¢ to 10¢ a word, extra for photos.

THE CHURCH MUSICIAN—127 Ninth Ave. N., Nashville, TN 37234. Jere V. Adams, Ed. Articles on choral techniques, instrumental groups, worship planning, music administration, directing choirs (all ages), rehearsal planning, music equipment, new technology, drama/pageants and related subjects, hymn studies, book reviews, and music-related fillers. Pays 5½¢ a word, on acceptance.

CLASSICAL MUSIC MAGAZINE—106 Lakeshore Rd. E., Suite 212, Mississauga, Ont., Canada L5G 1E3. Derek Deroy, Ed. Feature articles, 1,500 to 3,500 words, and short pieces, to 500 words. Interviews, personality profiles, book reviews, historical articles. "All articles should pertain to the world of classical music. No academic analysis. A solidly researched historical article with source references, or an interview with a famous classical personality are your best bets." Guidelines. Pays $100 to $500 (Canadian) for articles, $35 to $75 for short pieces, on publication.

DANCE MAGAZINE—33 W. 60th St., New York, NY 10023. Richard Philp, Ed.-in-Chief. Features on dance, personalities, techniques, health issues, and trends. Photos. Query; limited free-lance market.

DANCE TEACHER NOW—3101 Poplarwood Ct., Suite 310, Raleigh, NC 27604–1010. K.C. Patrick, Ed. Articles, 1,000 to 3,000 words, for professional dance educators, senior students, and other dance professionals on practical information for the teacher and/or business owner; economic and historical issues related to the profession. Profiles of schools, methods, and people who are leaving their mark on dance. Must be thoroughly researched. Photos a plus. Pays $200 to $350, on acceptance. Query.

DECORATIVE ARTIST'S WORKBOOK—1507 Dana Ave., Cincinnati, OH 45207. Anne Hevener, Ed. How-to articles, 1,000 to 1,500 words, on decorative painting. "Painting projects only, not crafts." Profiles, 500 words, of up-and-coming painters for "The Artist of the Issue" column. Pays $150 to $250 for features; $85 for profiles, on acceptance. Query required.

DOUBLETAKE—Ctr. for Documentary Studies at Duke Univ., 1317 W. Pettigrew St., Durham, NC 27705. Attn: Manuscript Ed. Quarterly. Realistic fiction, to 5,000 words, narrative poetry (submit up to 6 poems), book excerpts, personal experience, essays, humor, and cultural criticism. Color or B&W photo-essays, works in progress, and proposals "in the broadest definition of documentary work." (Submit up to 60 slides.) "We want to be a magazine where image and word have equal weight." Payment varies, on acceptance. Guidelines. Query for nonfiction. SASE.

DRAMATICS—Educational Theatre Assoc., 3368 Central Pkwy., Cincinnati, OH 45225–2392. Don Corathers, Ed. Articles, interviews, how-tos, 750 to 4,000 words, for high school students of the performing arts with an emphasis on theater practice: acting, directing, playwriting, technical subjects. Prefer articles that "could be used by a better-than-average high school teacher to teach students something about the performing arts." Pays $25 to $300 honorarium. Complete manuscripts preferred; graphics and photos accepted.

FILM QUARTERLY—Univ. of California Press Journals, 2120 Berkeley Way, Berkeley, CA 94720. Ann Martin, Ed. Historical, analytical, and critical articles, to 6,000 words; film reviews, book reviews. Guidelines.

FLUTE TALK—Instrumentalist Publishing Co., 200 Northfield Rd., Northfield, IL 60093. Kathleen Goll-Wilson, Ed. Articles, 6 to 12 double-spaced pages, on flute performance, music, and pedagogy; fillers; photos and line drawings. Thorough knowledge of music or the instrument a must. Pays honorarium, on publication. Queries preferred.

FORBES MEDIACRITIC—P.O. Box 762, Bedminster, NJ 07921. Terry Eastland, Ed. Quarterly. "The Best and Worst of America's Journalism." Articles, 5,000 words, on any aspect of our news media. Payment varies.

GLORY SONGS—127 Ninth Ave. N., Nashville, TN 37234. Jere V. Adams, Ed. For volunteer and part-time music directors and members of church choirs. Very easy music and accompaniments designed specifically for the small church (4 to 6 songs per issue). Includes 8-page pull-out with articles for choir members on leisure reading, music training, and choir projects. Pays 5½¢ per word, on acceptance.

GUITAR PLAYER MAGAZINE—411 Borel Ave., Suite 100, San Mateo, CA 94402. Attn: Ed. Articles, from 200 words, on guitars and related subjects. Pays $100 to $600, on acceptance. Buys one-time and reprint rights.

INDIA CURRENTS—P.O. Box 21285, San Jose, CA 95151. Arvind Kumar, Submissions Ed. Fiction, to 1,800 words, and articles, to 800 words, on Indian culture in the United States and Canada. Articles on Indian arts, entertainment, and dining. Also music reviews, 300 words; book reviews, 300 to 400 words; commentary on national or international events affecting the lives of Indians, 800 words. Pays in subscriptions.

INTERNATIONAL MUSICIAN—Paramount Bldg., 1501 Broadway, Suite 600, New York, NY 10036. Attn: Ed. Articles, 1,500 to 2,000 words, for professional musicians. Pays varying rates, on acceptance. Query.

KEYBOARD MAGAZINE—Suite 100, 411 Borel Ave., San Mateo, CA 94402. Tom Darter, Ed. Dir. Articles, 1,000 to 5,000 words, on keyboard instruments, MIDI and computer technology, and players. Photos. Pays $200 to $600, on acceptance. Query.

LIVING BLUES—Hill Hall, Room 301, Univ. of Mississippi, University, MS 38677. David Nelson, Ed. Articles, 1,500 to 10,000 words, about living African-American blues artists. Interviews. Occasional retrospective/historical articles or investigative pieces. Pays $75 to $200, on publication; $25 to $50 per photo. Query.

MODERN DRUMMER—12 Old Bridge Rd., Cedar Grove, NJ 07009. Ronald L. Spagnardi, Ed. Articles, 500 to 2,000 words, on drumming: how-tos, interviews. Pays $50 to $500, on publication.

NEW ENGLAND ENTERTAINMENT DIGEST—P.O. Box 88, Burlington, MA 01803. Julie Ann Charest, Ed. News and features on the arts and entertainment industry in New England. Pays $10 to $35, on publication.

PERFORMANCE—1101 University Dr., Suite 108, Fort Worth, TX 76107. Don Waitt, Pub./Ed.-in-Chief. Reports on the touring industry: concert promoters, booking agents, concert venues and clubs, as well as support services, such as lighting, sound, and staging companies.

PETERSEN'S PHOTOGRAPHIC—6420 Wilshire Blvd., Los Angeles, CA 90048–5515. Geoffrey B. Engel, Ed. Articles and how-to pieces, with photos, on travel, video, and darkroom photography, for beginners, advanced amateurs, and professionals. Pays $125 per printed page, on publication.

656

PHOTO: ELECTRONIC IMAGING MAGAZINE—57 Forsyth St. N.W., Suite 1600, Atlanta, GA 30303. E. Sapwater, Exec. Ed. Articles, 1,000 to 3,000 words, on electronic imaging, desktop publishing, pre-press, and multimedia. Material must be directly related to professional imaging trends and techniques. Query required; all articles on assignment only. Payment varies, on publication.

PLAYBILL—52 Vanderbilt Ave., New York, NY 10017. Judy Samelson, Ed. No unsolicited manuscripts.

POPULAR PHOTOGRAPHY—1633 Broadway, New York, NY 10019. Jason Schneider, Ed.-in-Chief. How-to articles, 500 to 2,000 words, for amateur photographers. Query with outline and photos.

ROLLING STONE—1290 Ave. of the Americas, 2nd Fl., New York, NY 10104. Attn: Ed. Magazine of American music, culture, and politics. No fiction. Query; no unsolicited manuscripts. Rarely accepts free-lance material.

SCULPTURE—International Sculpture Ctr., 1050 17th St. N.W., Suite 250, Washington, DC 20036. Glenn Harper, Ed. Articles on sculpture, sculptors, collections of sculpture, books on sculpture, criticism, technical processes, etc. Payment varies, on publication. Query.

THE SENIOR MUSICIAN—127 Ninth Ave. N., Nashville, TN 37234. Jere V. Adams, Ed. Quarterly music periodical. Easy choir music for senior adult choirs to use in worship, ministry, and recreation. Also includes leisure reading, music training, fellowship suggestions, and choir projects for personal growth. For music directors, pastors, organists, pianists, choir coordinators. Pays 5½¢ a word, on acceptance.

SOUTHWEST ART—5444 Westheimer, Suite 1440, Houston, TX 77056. Susan McGarry, Ed. Articles, 1,200 to 1,800 words, on the artists, art collectors, museum exhibitions, gallery events and dealers, art history, and art trends west of the Mississippi River. Particularly interested in representational or figurative arts. Pays from $400, on acceptance. Query with at least 20 slides of artwork to be featured.

STAGE DIRECTIONS—SMW Communications, Inc., 3101 Poplarwood Ct., Suite 310, Raleigh, NC 27604. Stephen Peithman, Ed. Neil Offen, Man. Ed. How-to articles, to 2,000 words, on acting, directing, costuming, makeup, lighting, set design and decoration, props, special effects, fundraising, and audience development for readers who are active in all aspects of community, regional, academic, or youth theater. Short pieces, 400 to 500 words, "are a good way to approach us first." Pays 10¢ a word, on publication. Guidelines.

STORYTELLING MAGAZINE—P.O. Box 309, Jonesborough, TN 37659. Attn: Eds. Features, 1,000 to 3,000 words, related to the oral tradition and stories, to 1,200 words, written in the oral tradition. News items, 200 to 400 words, and photos reflecting unusual storytelling events/applications. Themes for each issue; query first or send SASE to request topics. "We're looking for meaty free-lance work that reflects the ongoing dynamics of a reviving oral tradition." Pays 10¢ a word.

TCI—32 W. 18th St., New York, NY 10011. Jacqueline Tien, Pub. David Johnson, Ed. Articles, 500 to 2,500 words, on design, technical, and management aspects of theater, opera, dance, television, and film for those in performing arts and the entertainment trade. Pays on acceptance. Query.

TDR (THE DRAMA REVIEW): A JOURNAL OF PERFORMANCE STUDIES—721 Broadway, 6th Fl., New York, NY 10003. Richard Schechner, Ed. Eclectic articles on experimental performance and performance theory; cross-cultural, examining the social, political, historical, and theatrical contexts in which performance happens. Submit query or manuscript with SASE and disk. Pays $100 to $250, on publication.

U.S. ART—220 S. Sixth St., Suite 500, Minneapolis, MN 55402. Frank J. Sisser, Ed./Pub. Features and artist profiles, 2,000 words, for collectors of limited-edition art prints. Query. Pays $400 to $450, within 30 days of acceptance.

VIDEOMAKER—P.O. Box 4591, Chico, CA 95927. Stephen Muratore, Ed. Authoritative, how-to articles geared to hobbyist and professional video camera/camcorder users: instructionals, editing, desktop video, audio and video production, innovative applications, tools and tips, industry developments, new products, etc. Pays varying rates, on publication. Queries preferred.

WEST ART—P.O. Box 6868, Auburn, CA 95604–6868. Martha Garcia, Ed. Features, 350 to 700 words, on fine arts and crafts. No hobbies. Photos. Pays 50¢ per column inch, on publication. SASE required.

HOBBIES, CRAFTS, COLLECTING

AMERICAN HOW-TO—12301 Whitewater Dr., Suite 260, Minnetonka, MN 55343. Tom Sweeney, Ed. Bimonthly. Articles, 1,000 to 1,500 words, for homeowners interested in do-it-yourself projects. Carpentry, plumbing, electrical work, landscaping, masonry, tools, woodworking, and new products. Payment is 50¢ a word, on acceptance. Send SASE for editorial calendar with upcoming themes. Queries preferred.

AMERICAN WOODWORKER—Rodale Press, 33 E. Minor St., Emmaus, PA 18098. David Sloan, Ed. "A how-to bimonthly for the woodworking enthusiast." Technical or anecdotal articles, to 2,000 words, relating to woodworking or furniture design. Fillers, drawings, slides and photos considered. Pays from $150 per published page, on publication; regular contributors paid on acceptance. Queries preferred. Guidelines.

ANCESTRY—P.O. Box 476, Salt Lake City, UT 84110. Loretto Szucs, Acquisitions Ed. Bimonthly for genealogists and hobbyists who are interested in getting the most out of their research. Articles, 1,500 to 4,000 words, that instruct (how-tos, research techniques, etc.) and inform (new research sources, new collections, etc.). No family histories, genealogies, or pedigree charts. Pays $25 to $75, on publication. Guidelines.

THE ANTIQUE TRADER WEEKLY—Box 1050, Dubuque, IA 52004. Jon Brecka, Ed. Articles, 1,000 to 2,000 words, on all types of antiques and collectors' items. Photos. Pays from $25 to $200, on publication. Query preferred. Buys all rights.

ANTIQUES & AUCTION NEWS—P.O. Box 500, Mount Joy, PA 17552. Attn: Ed. Weekly newspaper. Factual articles, 600 to 1,500 words, on antiques, collectors, collections, and places of historic interest. Photos. Query required. Pays $5 to $20, after publication.

ANTIQUEWEEK—P.O. Box 90, Knightstown, IN 46148. Tom Hoepf, Ed., Central Edition; Connie Swaim, Ed., Eastern Edition. Weekly antique, auction, and collectors' newspaper. Articles, 500 to 1,500 words, on antiques, collectibles, restorations, genealogy, auction and antique show reports. Photos. Pays from $40 to $150 for in-depth articles, on publication. Query. Guidelines.

AQUARIUM FISH—P.O. Box 6050, Mission Viejo, CA 92690. Edward Bauman, Ed. Articles, 2,000 to 4,000 words, on freshwater, saltwater, and pond fish, with or without color transparencies. (No "pet fish" stories.) Payment varies, on publication.

AUTOGRAPH COLLECTOR MAGAZINE—510-A S. Corona Mall, Corona, CA 91719. Ev Phillips, Ed. Articles, 1,000 to 3,500 words, on all areas of autograph collecting: preservation, framing, and storage, specialty collections, documents and letters, collectors and dealers. Queries preferred. Payment varies.

BECKETT BASEBALL CARD MONTHLY—15850 Dallas Pkwy., Dallas, TX 75248. Tim Polzer, Ed. Articles, 500 to 2,000 words, geared to baseball card collecting, with an emphasis on the pleasures of the hobby. "We accept no stories with investment tips." Query. Pays $100 to $250, on acceptance. Guidelines.

BECKETT BASKETBALL MONTHLY—15850 Dallas Pkwy., Dallas, TX 75248. Mike Payne, Man. Ed. Articles, 400 to 1,000 words, on the sports-card hobby, especially basketball card collecting for readers 10 to 40. Query. Pays $100 to $250, on acceptance. Also publishes *Beckett Football Card Monthly, Beckett Focus on Future Stars, Beckett Hockey Monthly,* and *Beckett Racing Monthly.* SASE for guidelines.

BIRD TALK—Box 6050, Mission Viejo, CA 92690. Kathleen Samuelson, Ed.-in-Chief. Articles for pet bird owners: care and feeding, training, safety, outstanding personal adventures, exotic birds in their native countries, profiles of celebrities' pet birds, travel to bird parks or shows. Good transparencies a plus. Pays up to 10¢ a word, after publication. Query required.

BIRD WATCHER'S DIGEST—P.O. Box 110, Marietta, OH 45750. William H. Thompson III, Ed. Articles, 600 to 3,000 words, on bird-watching experiences and expeditions: information about rare sightings; updates on endangered species; interesting backyard topics and how-tos. Pays from $50, on publication. Allow 8 weeks for response.

BIRDER'S WORLD—44 E. 8th St., Suite 410, Holland, MI 49423. Eldon D. Greij, Ed. Bimonthly. Articles, 2,200 to 2,800 words, on all aspects of birding, especially on a particular species or the status of an endangered species. Tips on birding, attracting birds, or photographing them. Personal essays, 1,000 to 2,000 words. Book reviews, to 500 words. Pays $400 to $450, on publication. Query preferred.

BREW—1120 Mulberry St., Des Moines, IA 50309. Beverly Walsmith, Ed. "Traveling America's Brewpubs and Microbreweries." Bimonthly. Articles, 1,500 to 1,800 words, on new brewpubs around the country. "Our focus is on the brewpub and the community where it is located." Pays 10¢ a word, on publication. Query preferred.

CANADIAN STAMP NEWS—103 Lakeshore Rd., Suite 202, St. Catharines, Ont., Canada L2N 2T6. Ellen Rodger, Ed. Biweekly. Articles, 1,000 to

2,000 words, on stamp collecting news, rare and unusual stamps, and auction and club reports. Special issues throughout the year; send SASE for guidelines. Photos. Pays from $70, on publication.

CANADIAN WORKSHOP MAGAZINE—130 Spy Ct., Markham, Ont., Canada L3R 5H6. Hugh McBride, Ed. Articles, 1,500 to 2,800 words, on do-it-yourself home renovations, energy saving projects, etc., with photos. Pays varying rates, on acceptance.

CARD PLAYER—3140 S. Polaris #8, Las Vegas, NV 89102. Linda Johnson, Pub. "The Magazine for Those Who Play to Win." Articles on poker events, personalities, legal issues, new casinos, tournaments, and prizes. Also articles on strategies, theory and game psychology to improve poker play. Occasionally uses humor, cartoons, puzzles, or anecdotal material. Pays $35 to $100, on publication; $15 to $35 for fillers. Guidelines.

THE CAROUSEL NEWS & TRADER— 87 Park Ave. W., Suite 206, Mansfield, OH 44902. Attn: Ed. Features on carousel history and profiles of amusement park operators and carousel carvers of interest to band organ enthusiasts, carousel art collectors, preservationists, amusement park owners, artists, and restorationists. Pays $50 per published page, after publication. Guidelines.

CHESS LIFE—186 Rt. 9W, New Windsor, NY 12553–7698. Glenn Petersen, Ed. Articles, 500 to 3,000 words, for members of the U.S. Chess Federation, on news, profiles, technical aspects of chess. Features on all aspects of chess: history, humor, puzzles, etc. Fiction, 500 to 2,000 words, related to chess. Photos. Pays varying rates, on acceptance. Query; limited free-lance market.

CLASSIC TOY TRAINS—21027 Crossroads Cir., Waukesha, WI 53187. Attn: Ed. Articles, with photos, on toy train layouts and collections. Also toy train manufacturing history and repair/maintenance. Pays $75 per printed page, on acceptance. Query.

COLLECTING TOYS—21027 Crossroads Cir., Waukesha, WI 53187. Tom Hammel, Ed. Bimonthly. Articles of varying lengths for a "nostalgia/collecting magazine that celebrates the great toys of the 1940s through '90s." Profiles of toy collectors, designers, and manufacturers; articles for toy collectors. Color photos. Pays $75 to $100 per page.

COLLECTOR EDITIONS—170 Fifth Ave., New York, NY 10010. Joan Muyskens Pursley, Ed. Articles, 750 to 1,500 words, on collectibles, mainly contemporary limited-edition figurines, plates, and prints. Pays $150 to $350, within 30 days of acceptance. Query with photos.

COLLECTORS JOURNAL—P.O. Box 601, Vinton, IA 52349. Stephanie Schallau, Ed. Weekly tabloid. Features, to 2,000 words, on antiques and collectibles. Pays $10 for articles, $15 for articles with photos, on publication.

COLLECTORS NEWS—P.O. Box 156, Grundy Ctr., IA 50638. Linda Kruger, Ed. Articles, to 1,000 words, on private collections, antiques, and collectibles, especially modern limited-edition collectibles, 20th-century nostalgia, Americana, glass and china, music, furniture, transportation, timepieces, jewelry, farm-related collectibles, and lamps; include quality color or B&W photos. Pays $1 per column inch; $25 for front-page color photos, on publication.

660

COMBO—5 Nassau Blvd. S., Garden City S., NY 11530. Ian M. Feller, Ed. Articles, from 800 words, related to non-sports cards (comic cards, TV/movie cards, science fiction cards, etc.) and comic books; collecting and investing; fillers. Queries preferred. Pays to 10¢ a word, on publication.

COUNTRY FOLK ART MAGAZINE—8393 E. Holly Rd., Holly, MI 48442–8819. Michael Happy, Man. Ed. Articles on decorating, artisans, collectibles; how-to pieces, 750 to 1,000 words, with a creative slant on American folk art. Pays $150 to $300, on acceptance. Submit pieces on seasonal topics one year in advance.

CRAFTS 'N THINGS—2400 Devon, Suite 375, Des Plaines, IL 60018–4618. Julie Stephani, Ed. How-to articles on all kinds of crafts projects, with instructions. Send manuscript with instructions and photograph of the finished item. Pays $50 to $250, on acceptance.

CROSS-STITCH PLUS—306 E. Parr Rd., Berne, IN 46711. Lana Schurb, Ed. How-to and instructional counted cross-stitch. Pays varying rates.

CROSS-STITCH SAMPLER—See *Fine Lines.*

DOG FANCY—P.O. Box 6050, Mission Viejo, CA 92690. Kim Thornton, Ed. Articles, 1,500 to 2,000 words, on dog care, health, grooming, breeds, activities, events, etc. Photos. Payment varies, on publication.

DOLL WORLD—(formerly *International Doll World*) 306 E. Parr Rd., Berne, IN 46711. Cary Raesner, Ed. Informational articles about doll collecting.

FIBERARTS—50 College St., Asheville, NC 28801. Ann Batchelder, Ed. Published 5 times yearly. Articles, 400 to 2,000 words, on contemporary trends in fiber sculpture, weaving, surface design, quilting, stitchery, papermaking, felting, basketry, and wearable art. Query with photos of subject, outline, and synopsis. Pays varying rates, on publication.

FINE LINES—(formerly *Cross-Stitch Sampler*) P.O. Box 718, Ingomar, PA 15127. Deborah A. Novak, Ed. Publication of the Historic Needlework Guild. Articles, 500 to 1,500 words, about counted cross-stitch, drawn thread, or themes revolving around stitching (samplers, needlework tools, etc.). Pays varying rates, on acceptance. Queries required.

FINE WOODWORKING—63 S. Main St., Newtown, CT 06470. Scott Gibson, Ed. Bimonthly. Articles on woodworking: basics of tool use, stock preparation and joinery, specialized techniques and finishing, shop-built tools, jigs and fixtures; or any stage of design, construction, finishing and installation of cabinetry and furniture. "We look for high-quality worksmanship, thoughtful designs, safe and proper procedures." Departments: "Methods of Work," "Q&A," "Books," "Tool Forum," and "Notes and Comments." Pays $150 per page, on publication; pays from $10 for department pieces. Query.

FINESCALE MODELER—P.O. Box 1612, Waukesha, WI 53187. Bob Hayden, Ed. How-to articles for people who make nonoperating scale models of aircraft, automobiles, boats, figures. Photos and drawings should accompany articles. One-page model-building hints and tips. Pays from $40 per published page, on acceptance. Query preferred.

GAMES—P.O. Box 184, Ft. Washington, PA 19034. R. Wayne Schmittberger, Ed.-in-Chief. "The magazine for creative minds at play." Features and short articles on games and playful, offbeat subjects. Visual and verbal puzzles, pop culture quizzes, brainteasers, contests, game reviews. Pays top rates, on publication. Send SASE for guidelines; specify writer's, crosswords, variety puzzles, or brainteasers.

GOLD AND TREASURE HUNTER—P.O. Box 47, Happy Camp, CA 96039. Marcie Stumpf, Man. Ed. Bimonthly. Articles, 1,500 to 2,000 words, about people discovering gold, treasure, and outdoor adventure. First-person experiences, humorous pieces, profiles, and how-to as well as fiction. "We provide family recreation opportunities and explore old sites and travel sites." Pays 3¢ a word, on publication.

HERITAGE QUEST—American Genealogical Lending Library, P.O. Box 329, Bountiful, UT 84011. Leland Meitzler, Ed. Bimonthly. Genealogy how-to articles, 2 to 4 pages; national, international, or regional in scope. Pays $30 per published page, on publication.

THE HOME SHOP MACHINIST—2779 Aero Park Dr., Box 1810, Traverse City, MI 49685. Joe D. Rice, Ed. How-to articles on precision metalworking and foundry work. Accuracy and attention to detail a must. Pays $40 per published page, extra for photos and illustrations, on publication. Guidelines.

INTERNATIONAL DOLL WORLD—See *Doll World.*

KITPLANES—P.O. Box 6050, Mission Viejo, CA 92690. Dave Martin, Ed. Articles geared to the growing market of aircraft built from kits and plans by home craftsmen, on all aspects of design, construction, and performance, 1,000 to 4,000 words. Pays $60 per page, on publication.

LOST TREASURE—P.O. Box 1589, Grove, OK 74344. Patsy Beyer, Man. Ed. How-to articles, legends, folklore, and stories of lost treasures. Also publishes *Treasure Facts*: how-to information for treasure hunters (hunt strategies, techniques, pitfalls, how to increase finds, use equipment, locate treasure, etc.), club news, who's who in treasure hunting, tips, etc. *Treasure Cache* (annual): articles on documented treasure caches with sidebar telling how to search for cache highlighted in article. Pays 4¢ a word, $5 for photos, $100 for cover photos.

LOTTOWORLD MAGAZINE—2150 Goodlette Rd., Suite 200, Naples, FL 33940. Barry Miller, Man. Ed. Articles of interest to readers (over 18 years old) who play the lottery. Human-interest pieces on lottery winners and losers, winning systems, advice on predicting numbers and increasing your odds of winning, general information on state lotteries, etc. Payment varies, 30 days after publication.

THE MIDATLANTIC ANTIQUES MAGAZINE—P.O. Box 908, Henderson, NC 27536. Lydia Stainback, Ed. Articles, 500 to 2,000 words, on antiques, collectibles, and related subjects. "We need show and auction reporters." Queries are preferred. Payment varies, on publication.

MILITARY HISTORY—741 Miller Dr. S.E., #D2, Leesburg, VA 22075. Jon Guttman, Ed. Bimonthly. Features, 4,000 words with 500-word sidebars, on the strategy, tactics, and personalities of military history. Department pieces, 2,000 words, on intrigue, weaponry, and perspectives; book reviews. No fiction. Pays $200 to $400, on publication. Query. SASE for guidelines.

MINIATURE COLLECTOR—30595 Eight Mile Rd., Livonia, MI 48152–1761. Ruth Keessen, Pub. Articles, 800 to 1,200 words, with photos, on outstanding $\frac{1}{12}$-scale (dollhouse) miniatures and the people who make and collect them. Original, illustrated how-to projects for making miniatures. Pays varying rates, within 30 days of acceptance. Query with photos.

MINIATURE QUILTS—See *Traditional Quiltworks.*

MODEL RAILROADER—21027 Crossroads Cir., P.O. Box 1612, Waukesha, WI 53187. Andy Sperandeo, Ed. Articles on model railroads, with photos of layout and equipment. Pays $90 per printed page, on acceptance. Query.

MOTOR BOATING & SAILING—250 W. 55th St., 4th Fl., New York, NY 10019–3203. Peter A. Janssen Ed./Pub. Articles, 1,500 words, on buying, maintaining, and enjoying boats. "Appeal to the dreams, adventures, and the lifestyles of committed boat owners." Hard-core, authoritative how-to. Query. Payment varies, on acceptance.

NEW ENGLAND ANTIQUES JOURNAL— 4 Church St., Ware, MA 01082. Jody Young, Gen. Mgr. Jamie Mercier, Man. Ed. Well-researched articles, usually by recognized authorities in their field, 1,500 to 5,000 words, on antiques of interest to dealers or collectors; auction and antiques show reviews, from 1,000 words; antiques market news, to 500 words; photos required. Pays from $100, on publication. Query or send manuscript. Reports in 2 to 4 weeks.

NOSTALGIA WORLD—Box 231, North Haven, CT 06473. Richard Mason, Jr., Ed. Features, 3,000 words, and other articles, 1,500 words, on all kinds of collectibles: records, TV memorabilia (Munsters, Star Trek, Dark Shadows, Elvira, etc.), comics, gum cards, toys, sheet music, monsters, magazines, dolls, movie posters, etc. Pays $10 to $25, on publication.

NUTSHELL NEWS—21027 Crossroads Cir., P.O. Box 1612, Waukesha, WI 53187. Sybil Harp, Ed. Articles, 1,200 to 1,500 words, for dollhouse-scale miniatures enthusiasts, collectors, craftspeople, and hobbyists. Interested in artisan profiles, tours of collections, and how-to projects. "Writers must be knowledgeable miniaturists." Color slides or B&W prints required. Payment varies; part on acceptance, balance on publication. Query.

PETERSEN'S PHOTOGRAPHIC— 6420 Wilshire Blvd., Los Angeles, CA 90048. Geoffrey B. Engel, Ed. How-to articles on all phases of still photography of interest to the amateur and advanced photographer. Pays about $125 per printed page for article accompanied by photos, on publication.

POPULAR MECHANICS—224 W. 57th St., New York, NY 10019. Deborah Frank, Man. Ed. Articles, 300 to 1,500 words, on latest developments in mechanics, industry, science, telecommunications; features on hobbies with a mechanical slant; how-tos on home and shop projects; features on outdoor adventures, boating, and electronics. Photos and sketches a plus. Pays to $1,500; to $500 for short pieces, on acceptance. Buys all rights.

POPULAR WOODWORKING—1507 Dana Ave., Cincinnati, OH 45207. Steve Shanesy, Ed. Project articles, to 5,000 words; techniques pieces, to 1,500 words; anecdotes and essays, to 1,000 words, for the "modest production woodworker, small shop owner, wood craftsperson, intermediate hobbyist and woodcarver." Pays $500 to $1,000 for large, complicated projects; $100 to $500 for small projects and other features; pays on acceptance, half on publication. Query with brief outline and photo of finished project.

QUILTING TODAY—See *Traditional Quiltworks.*

RENAISSANCE MAGAZINE—Phantom Press Publications, 5A Green Meadow Dr., Nantucket, MA 02554. Kim Guarnaccia, Ed. Feature articles on jousting, history, costuming, Renaissance faires; interviews; and reviews of Renaissance books, music, movies, and games. Pays 3¢ a word, on publication.

RESTORATION—P.O. Box 50046, Dept. TW, Tucson, AZ 85703–1046. W.R. Haessner, Ed. Articles, 1,200 to 1,800 words, on restoring and building machines, boats, autos, trucks, planes, trains, buildings, toys, tools, etc. Photos and art required. Pays $50 per page, on publication. Query.

RUG HOOKING MAGAZINE—Stackpole Magazines, 500 Vaughn St., Harrisburg, PA 17110. Patrice Crowley, Ed. How-to and feature articles on rug hooking for beginners and advanced artists. Payment varies.

SCHOOL MATES—U.S. Chess Federation, 186 Rte. 9W, New Windsor, NY 12553–7698. Brian Bugbee, Ed. Articles and fiction, 250 to 800 words, and short fillers, related to chess for beginning chess players (primarily children, 8 to 16). "Primarily instructive material, but there's room for fun puzzles, cartoons, anecdotes, etc. All chess related. Articles on chessplaying celebrities are always of interest to us." Pays from $20, on publication. Query; limited free-lance market.

73 AMATEUR RADIO—WGI, 70 Rte. 202N, Peterborough, NH 03458. F.I. Marion, Assoc. Pub./Ed. Articles, 1,500 to 3,000 words, for electronics hobbyists and amateur radio operators. Pays $50 to $250.

SEW NEWS—P.O. Box 1790, News Plaza, Peoria, IL 61656. Linda Turner Griepentrog, Ed. Articles, to 3,000 words, "that teach a specific technique, inspire a reader to try new sewing projects, or inform a reader about an interesting person, company, or project related to sewing, textiles, or fashion." Emphasis is on fashion (not craft) sewing. Pays $25 to $400, on acceptance. Queries required; no unsolicited manuscripts accepted.

SPORTS CARD TRADER—5 Nassau Blvd., Garden City South, NY 11530. Attn: Ed. Office. Articles, from 1,000 words, related to all sports cards, autographs, video games, phone cards, starting lineups, especially baseball, football, basketball, and hockey cards; collecting and investing. Fillers. Queries preferred. Pays 10¢ a word, on publication.

SPORTS COLLECTORS DIGEST—Krause Publications, 700 E. State St., Iola, WI 54990. Tom Mortenson, Ed. Articles, 750 to 2,000 words, on old baseball card sets and other sports memorabilia and collectibles. Pays $50 to $100, on publication.

SUDS 'N STUFF—Bosak Publishing, 4764 Galicia Way, Oceanside, CA 92056. Bunny Bosak, Assoc. Ed. Bimonthly. Articles on breweries and beer. Pays varying rates, after publication. Queries preferred.

TEDDY BEAR REVIEW—Collector Communications Corp., 170 Fifth Ave., New York, NY 10010. Stephen L. Cronk, Ed. Articles on antique and contemporary teddy bears for makers, collectors, and enthusiasts. Pays $100 to $300, within 30 days of acceptance. Query with photos.

THREADS MAGAZINE—Taunton Press, 63 S. Main St., Box 5506, Newtown, CT 06470. Attn: Ed. Bimonthly. Technical pieces on garment construction by writers who are expert sewers, quilters, embellishers, and other needle workers. Pays $150 per published page, on publication.

TRADITIONAL QUILTWORKS—Chitra Publications, 2 Public Ave., Montrose, PA 18801. Attn: Ed. Team. Specific, quilt-related how-to articles, 700 to 1,500 words. Patterns, features, and department pieces. Queries preferred. Pays $75 per published page, on publication. Also publishes *Quilting Today* and *Miniature Quilts.*

TREASURE CACHE, TREASURE FACTS—See *Lost Treasure.*

WEST ART—Box 6868, Auburn, CA 95604–6868. Martha Garcia, Ed. Features, 350 to 700 words, on fine arts and crafts. No hobbies. Photos. Pays 50¢ per column inch, on publication. SASE required.

WESTERN & EASTERN TREASURES—P.O. Box 1598, Mercer Island, WA 98040–1598. Rosemary Anderson, Man. Ed. Illustrated articles, to 1,500 words, on treasure hunting and how-to metal-detecting tips. Pays 2¢ a word, extra for photos, on publication.

WILDFOWL CARVING AND COLLECTING—Stackpole Magazines, 500 Vaughn St., Harrisburg, PA 17110. Cathy Hart, Ed.-in-Chief. How-to and reference articles, of varying lengths, on bird carving; collecting antique and contemporary carvings. Query. Pays varying rates, on acceptance.

WIN MAGAZINE—120 S. San Fernando Blvd., Suite 439, Burbank, CA 91502. Joey Sinatra, Ed. Gambling-related articles. Pays on publication.

WOODENBOAT MAGAZINE—P.O. Box 78, Brooklin, ME 04616. Matthew Murphy, Ed. How-to and technical articles, 4,000 words, on construction, repair, and maintenance of wooden boats; design, history, and use of wooden boats; and profiles of outstanding wooden boat builders and designers. Pays $150 to $200 per 1,000 words. Query preferred.

WOODWORK—42 Digital Dr., Suite 5, Novato, CA 94949. John McDonald, Ed. Bimonthly. Articles for woodworkers on all aspects of woodworking (simple, complex, technical, or aesthetic). Pays $150 per published page; $35 for "Techniques," on publication. Queries or outlines (with slides) preferred.

WORKBASKET MAGAZINE—700 W. 47th St., Suite 310, Kansas City, MO 64112. Kay M. Olson, Ed. Instructions and models for original knit, crochet, and tat items. (Designs must fit theme of issue.) How-tos on crafts and gardening, 400 to 1,200 words, with photos. Pays on acceptance; negotiable rates for instructional items.

WORKBENCH—700 W. 47th St., Suite 310, Kansas City, MO 64112. A. Robert Gould, Exec. Ed. Articles on do-it-yourself home improvement and maintenance projects and general woodworking articles for beginning and expert craftsmen. Complete working drawings with accurate dimensions, step-by-step instructions, lists of materials, in-progress photos, and photos of the finished product must accompany submission. Pays from $150 per published page, on acceptance. Query.

YELLOWBACK LIBRARY—P.O. Box 36172, Des Moines, IA 50315. Gil O'Gara, Ed. Articles, 300 to 2,000 words, on boys'/girls' series literature (Hardy Boys, Nancy Drew, Tom Swift, etc.) for collectors, researchers, and dealers. "Especially welcome are interviews with, or articles by past and present writers of juvenile series fiction." Pays in copies.

YESTERYEAR—P.O. Box 2, Princeton, WI 54968. Michael Jacobi, Ed. Articles on antiques and collectibles for readers in WI, IL, IA, MN, and surrounding states. Photos. Will consider regular columns on collecting or antiques. Pays from $15, on publication. Limited market.

ZYMURGY—Box 1679, Boulder, CO 80306–1679. Dena Nishek, Ed. Articles appealing to beer lovers and homebrewers. Pays after publication. Guidelines. Query.

SCIENCE & COMPUTERS

AD ASTRA—National Space Society, 922 Pennsylvania Ave. S.E., Washington, DC 20003–2140. Pat Dasch, Ed.-in-Chief. Lively, non-technical features, to 3,000 words, on all aspects of international space exploration. Particularly interested in "Living in Space" articles; space settlements; lunar and Mars bases. Pays $150 to $200, on publication. Query. Guidelines.

AMERICAN HERITAGE OF INVENTION & TECHNOLOGY— 60 Fifth Ave., New York, NY 10011. Frederick Allen, Ed. Quarterly. Articles, 2,000 to 5,000 words, on history of technology in America, for the sophisticated general reader. Pays on acceptance. Query.

THE ANNALS OF IMPROBABLE RESEARCH—AIR, P.O. Box 380853, Cambridge, MA 02238. Marc Abrahams, Ed. Science humor, science reports and analysis, one to 4 pages. Brief science-related poetry. B&W photos. "This journal is the place to find the mischievous, funny, iconoclastic side of science." Guidelines. No payment.

ARCHAEOLOGY—135 William St., New York, NY 10038. Peter A. Young, Ed.-in-Chief. Articles on archaeology by professionals or lay people with a solid knowledge of the field. Pays $250 to $500, on publication. Query required.

ASTRONOMY—P.O. Box 1612, Waukesha, WI 53187. Jeff Kanipe, Man. Ed. Articles on astronomy, astrophysics, space programs, recent discoveries. Hobby pieces on equipment and celestial events; short news items. Pays varying rates, on acceptance.

C/C + + USERS JOURNAL—1601 W. 23rd St., Suite 200, Lawrence, KS 66046–4153. Marc Briand, Man. Ed. Practical, how-to articles, 2,500 words (including up to 250 lines of code) on C/C + + programming. Algorithms, class designs, book reviews, tutorials. No programming "religion." Pays $110 per published page of text, $90 per published page of code, on publication. Query. Guidelines.

COMPUTERSCENE MAGAZINE—3507 Wyoming Blvd. N.E., Albuquerque, NM 87111. Greg Hansen, Man. Ed. Laine Douglas Shomaker, Asst. Ed. Computer-related articles and fiction, 800 to 1,500 words. "We provide New Mexico computer users with entertaining and informative articles on all aspects of computers: hardware, software, technology, productivity, advice, personal experience, even computer-related fiction." Fillers, 400 to 800 words. Pays $40 to $75, on publication. Send SASE for guidelines and editorial calendar.

ELECTRONICS NOW—500 Bi-County Blvd., Farmingdale, NY 11735. Carl Laron, Ed. Technical articles, 1,500 to 3,000 words, on all areas related to electronics. Pays $50 to $500 or more, on acceptance.

ENVIRONMENT—1319 18th St. N.W., Washington, DC 20036–1802. Barbara T. Richman, Man. Ed. Factual and analytical articles, 2,500 to 5,000 words, on scientific, technological, and environmental policy and decision-making issues, especially on a global scale. Pays $100 to $300. Query.

FINAL FRONTIER—1017 S. Mountain Ave., Monrovia, CA 91016. George Hague, Ed. Articles, 1,500 to 2,500 words; columns, 800 words; and shorts, 250 words, about people, events, and new concepts of opening up the space frontier. Pays about 40¢ a word, on acceptance. Query.

FOCUS—Turnkey Publishing, Inc., P.O. Box 200549, Austin, TX 78720. J. Todd Key, Ed. Articles, 700 to 4,000 words, on Data General computers. Photos a plus. Pays to $50, on publication. Query required.

HOBSON'S CHOICE: SCIENCE FICTION AND TECHNOLOGY—The Starwind Press, P.O. Box 98, Ripley, OH 45167. Attn: Submissions Ed. Articles and literary criticism, 1,000 to 5,000 words, for readers interested in science and technology. Also science fiction and fantasy, 2,000 to 10,000 words. Pays 1¢ to 4¢ a word, on acceptance. Query for nonfiction.

HOMEPC—CMP Publications, 600 Community Dr., Manhasset, NY 11030–5772. Andrea Linne, Features Ed. Articles that help home computer users get the most out of their PCs. Payment varies, on acceptance. Query with clips and resumé required.

LINK-UP—2222 River Rd., King George, VA 22485. Loraine Page, Ed. Dir. Articles about online services, the Internet, and CD-ROM for the computer owner who uses this technology for business, home, and educational use. Pays $90 to $220 for articles, on publication. Photos a plus.

MACHOME JOURNAL—544 Second St., San Francisco, CA 94107. Sandra Anderson, Ed.-in-Chief. Jargon-free solutions to the information needs of Macintosh computer users. "Present technology in concise, factual, complete, non-condescending manner." Submissions on disk or over online services preferred; guidelines strongly recommended. Payment varies.

MACWORLD—50l Second St., Suite 500, San Francisco, CA 94107. Attn: Ed. Reviews, news, consumer, and how-to articles, of varying lengths, related to Macintosh computers. Query with clips only; no unsolicited manuscripts. Pays from $150 to $3,500, on acceptance. Guidelines.

NATURAL HISTORY—American Museum of Natural History, Central Park W. at 79th St., New York, NY 10024. Bruce Stutz, Ed.-in-Chief. Informative articles, to 3,000 words, on anthropology and natural sciences. "Strongly recommend that writers send SASE for guidelines and read our magazine." Pays from $1,000 for features, on acceptance. Query.

NETWORK NEWS—9710 S. 700 E., Bldg. A, Suite 206, Sandy, UT 84070. Linda Boyer, Ed. Humorous editorial articles, 600 to 800 words, on computing, especially networking. "Readers are computer professionals who are concerned with the multivendor network computing world." Submit with SASE for reply only; manuscripts will not be returned. Pays 30¢ a word, after acceptance.

OMNI—General Media International, 277 Park Ave., 4th Fl., New York, NY 10172–0003. Pamela Weintraub, Ed. Monthly on-line (electrical) version. Articles 750 to 1,000 words, on scientific aspects of the future: space colonies, cloning, machine intelligence, ESP, origin of life, future arts, lifestyles, etc. Address fiction, 2,000 to 10,000 words, to Ellen Datlow, Fiction Ed., *OMNI Internet* at above address. Pays $800 to $3,500 for articles; $150 for shorter items, on acceptance. Query.

POPULAR ELECTRONICS—500 Bi-County Blvd., Farmingdale, NY 11735. Dan Karagiannis, Ed. Features, 1,500 to 2,500 words, for electronics hobbyists and experimenters. "Our readers are science and electronics oriented, understand computer theory and operation, and like to build electronics projects." Fillers and cartoons. Pays $25 to $500, on acceptance.

667

POPULAR SCIENCE—2 Park Ave., New York, NY 10016. Fred Abatemarco, Ed.-in-Chief. Articles, with photos, on developments in science and technology. Short illustrated articles on new inventions and products; photo-essays, book excerpts. Payment varies, on acceptance.

PUBLISH—Integrated Media, Inc., 501 Second St., San Francisco, CA 94107. Jake Widman, Ed. Features, 1,500 to 2,000 words, and reviews, 400 to 800 words, on all aspects of computerized publishing. Pays $400 to $600 for reviews, $850 to $1,200 for full-length features, on acceptance.

RESELLER MANAGEMENT MAGAZINE—(formerly *Reseller Magazine*) 275 Washington St., Newton, MA 02158. John Russell, Ed. Articles, 500 to 1,200 words, that emphasize profitable strategies for value-added resellers, systems, integrators, software developers, and VAR-consultants. "Magazine sections include how-tos for selling, marketing, customer, technology, business, and verticals." Payment varies. Query.

RESELLER MAGAZINE—See *Reseller Management Magazine.*

THE SCIENCES—2 E. 63rd St., New York, NY 10021. Peter G. Brown, Ed. Essays and features, 2,000 to 4,000 words, and book reviews, on all scientific disciplines. Pays honorarium, on publication. Query.

SCIENCEWORLD—Scholastic, Inc., 555 Broadway, New York, NY 10012–3999. Karen McNulty, Ed. Science articles, 750 words, and science news articles, 200 words, on life science, earth science, physical science, environmental science and/or health for readers in grades 7 to 10 (ages 12 to 15). "Articles should include current, exciting science news. Writing should be lively and show an understanding of teens' perspectives and interests." Pays $100 to $125 for news items; $200 to $650 for features. Query with a well-researched proposal, suggested sources, 2 to 3 clips of your work, and an SASE.

SKY & TELESCOPE—Sky Publishing Corp., P.O. Box 9111, Belmont, MA 02178–9111. Timothy Lyster, Man. Ed. Articles for amateur and professional astronomers worldwide. Department pieces for "Amateur Astronomers," "Astronomical Computing," "Telescope Making," "Observer's Page," and "Gallery." Also, 1,000-word opinion pieces, for "Focal Point." Mention availability of diagrams and other illustrations. Pays 10¢ to 25¢ a word, on publication. Query required.

TECHNOLOGY REVIEW—MIT, W59–200, Cambridge, MA 02139. Steven J. Marcus, Ed. General-interest articles on technology and its implications. Payment varies, on acceptance. Query.

WORDPERFECT MAGAZINES—MS 7300, 270 W. Center St., Orem, UT 84057. Attn: Ed. Features, 1,400 to 1,800 words, and columns, 1,200 to 1,400 words, on how-to subjects with easy-to-follow instructions that familiarize readers with WordPerfect software. Avoid jargon. Pays $400 to $700, on acceptance. Query. Guidelines.

ANIMALS

ANIMAL PEOPLE—P.O. Box 960, Clinton, WA 98236–0906. Attn: Ed. "News for People Who Care About Animals." Tabloid published 10 times a year. Articles and profiles, "especially of seldom recognized individuals of unique and outstanding positive accomplishment, in any capacity that benefits animals or illustrates the intrinsic value of other species. No atrocity stories, essays on why animals have rights, or material that promotes animal abuse, including hunting, fishing, trapping, and slaughter." No fiction or poetry. Pays honorarium, on acceptance. Query.

AKC GAZETTE—(formerly *Pure-Bred Dogs/American Kennel Gazette*) 51 Madison Ave., New York, NY 10010. Mark Roland, Features Ed. "The official journal for the sport of purebred dogs." Articles, 1,000 to 2,500 words, relating to serious breeders of purebred dogs. Pays from $250 to $450, on acceptance. Query preferred.

ANIMALS—350 S. Huntington Ave., Boston, MA 02130. Joni Praded, Dir./Ed. Informative, well-researched articles, to 2,500 words, on animal protection, national and international wildlife, pet care, conservation, and environmental issues that affect animals. No personal accounts or favorite pet stories. Pays from $350, on acceptance. Query.

AQUARIUM FISH—P.O. Box 6050, Mission Viejo, CA 92690. Edward Bauman, Ed. Articles, 2,000 to 4,000 words, on freshwater, saltwater, and pond fish, with or without color transparencies. (No "pet fish" stories.) Payment varies, on publication.

BIRD TALK—Box 6050, Mission Viejo, CA 92690. Kathleen Samuelson, Ed.-in-Chief. Articles for pet bird owners: care and feeding, training, safety, outstanding personal adventures, exotic birds in their native countries, profiles of celebrities' birds, travel to bird parks or bird shows. Pays 7¢ to 10¢ a word, after publication. Query required; good transparencies a plus.

CAT FANCY—P.O. Box 6050, Mission Viejo, CA 92690. Debbie Phillips-Donaldson, Ed. Nonfiction, to 2,500 words, on cat care, health, grooming, etc. Pays 5¢ to 10¢ a word, on publication. Query with SASE required.

DAIRY GOAT JOURNAL—P.O. Box 10, Lake Mills, WI 53551. Dave Thompson, Ed. Articles, to 1,500 words, on successful dairy goat owners, youths and interesting people associated with dairy goats. "Especially interested in practical husbandry ideas." Photos. Pays $50 to $150, on publication. Query.

DOG WORLD—PJS Publishing Inc., 29 N. Wacker Dr., Chicago, IL 60606–3298. Donna L. Marcel, Ed. Articles, to 3,000 words, for breeders, pet owners, exhibitors, kennel operators, veterinarians, handlers, and other pet professionals on all aspects of pet care and responsible ownership: health care, training, legal rights, animal welfare, etc. Queries required. Allow 4 months for response. Pays $50 to $500, on acceptance. Queries required. Guidelines.

EQUUS—Fleet Street Corp., 656 Quince Orchard Rd., Gaithersburg, MD 20878. Laurie Prinz, Man. Ed. Articles, 1,000 to 3,000 words, on all breeds of horses, covering their health and care as well as the latest advances in equine medicine and research. "Attempt to speak as one horseperson to another." Pays $100 to $400, on publication.

THE FLORIDA HORSE—P.O. Box 2106, Ocala, FL 34478. F.J. Audette, Ed. Articles, 1,500 words, on Florida thoroughbred breeding and racing. Also veterinary articles, financial articles, and articles of general interest. Pays $100 to $200, on publication.

GOOD DOG!—P.O. Box 10069, Austin, TX 78766–1069. Judi Sklar, Ed. Bimonthly. "The Consumer Magazine for Dog Owners." Articles, one to 2 pages, that are informative and fun to read. No fiction. No material "written" by the dog. Small payment, on publication.

HORSE & RIDER—12265 W. Bayaud Ave., Suite 300, Lakewood, CO 80228. Sue M. Copeland, Ed. Articles, 500 to 3,000 words, with photos, on western training and general horse care: feeding, health, grooming, etc. Pays varying rates, on publication. Guidelines.

HORSE ILLUSTRATED—P.O. Box 6050, Mission Viejo, CA 92690. Moira C. Harris, Ed. Articles, 1,500 to 2,500 words, on all aspects of owning and caring for horses. Photos. Pays $200 to $300, on publication. Query.

HORSEMEN'S YANKEE PEDLAR— 83 Leicester St., N. Oxford, MA 01537. Kelley R. Small, Pub. News and feature-length articles, about horses and horsemen in the Northeast. Photos. Pays $2 per published inch, on publication. Query.

HORSEPLAY—P.O. Box 130, Gaithersburg, MD 20884. Lisa M. Kiser, Ed. Articles, 700 to 3,000 words, on eventing, show jumping, horse shows, dressage, driving, and fox hunting for horse owners and English riders. Profiles, instructional articles, occasional humor, and competition reports. Pays 10¢ a word or flat fee, after publication; buys all rights. Query with SASE. Guidelines.

LLAMAS—P.O. Box 100, Herald, CA 95638. Cheryl Dal Porto, Ed. "The International Camelid Journal," published 7 times yearly. Articles, 300 to 3,000 words, of interest to llama and alpaca owners. Pays $25 to $300, extra for photos, on publication. Query.

MUSHING—P.O. Box 149, Ester, AK 99725–0149. Todd Hoener, Pub. How-tos, innovations, history, profiles, interviews, and features related to sled dogs, 1,500 to 2,000 words, and department pieces, 500 to 1,000 words, for competitive and recreational dog drivers and skijorers. International audience. Photos. Pays $20 to $250, on publication. Queries preferred. Guidelines.

PRACTICAL HORSEMAN—Box 589, Unionville, PA 19375. Mandy Lorraine, Ed. How-to articles on English riding, training, and horse care. Payment varies, on acceptance. Query with clips.

PURE-BRED DOGS/AMERICAN KENNEL GAZETTE—See *AKC Gazette.*

SHEEP! MAGAZINE—P.O. Box 10, Lake Mills, WI 53551. Dave Thompson, Ed. Articles, to 1,500 words, on successful shepherds, woolcrafts, sheep raising, and sheep dogs. "Especially interested in people who raise sheep successfully as a sideline enterprise." Photos. Pays $15 to $150, extra for photos, on acceptance. Query.

THE WESTERN HORSEMAN—P.O. Box 7980, Colorado Springs, CO 80933–7980. Pat Close, Ed. Articles, 1,500 words, with photos, on care and training of horses; farm, ranch, and stable management; health care and veterinary medicine. Pays to $500, on acceptance.

WHISKERS— 9311 S.E. Foster Rd., #20, Portland, OR 97266. William Laing, Ed./Pub. Animal-related articles and stories, 250 to 1,000 words: how-to articles on pet care and health, new pet ownership, events, human/pet interest pieces, fiction, poetry, pet anecdotes, riddles. Pays in copies. Guidelines.

WILDLIFE CONSERVATION—The Wildlife Conservation Society, Bronx, NY 10460. Nancy Simmons, Sr. Ed. Articles, 1,500 to 2,000 words, that "probe conservation controversies to search for answers and help save threatened species." Payment varies, on acceptance. Guidelines.

TRUE CRIME

DETECTIVE CASES—See *Globe Communications Corp.*

DETECTIVE DRAGNET—See *Globe Communications Corp.*

DETECTIVE FILES—See *Globe Communications Corp.*

GLOBE COMMUNICATIONS CORP.—1350 Sherbrooke St. W., Suite 600, Montreal, Quebec, Canada H3G 2T4. Dominick A. Merle, Ed. Factual accounts, 3,500 to 6,000 words, of "sensational crimes, preferably sex crimes, either pre-trial or after conviction." All articles will be considered for *Startling Detective, True Police Cases, Detective Files, Headquarters Detective, Detective Dragnet*, and *Detective Cases*. Query with pertinent information, including dates, site, names, etc. Pays $250 to $350, on acceptance; buys all rights.

HEADQUARTERS DETECTIVE—See *Globe Communications Corp.*

P.I. MAGAZINE: AMERICA'S PRIVATE INVESTIGATION JOURNAL—755 Bronx Ave., Toledo, OH 43609. Bob Mackowiak, Ed. Profiles of professional investigators containing true accounts of their most difficult cases. Pays $50 to $75, plus copies, on publication.

STARTLING DETECTIVE—See *Globe Communications Corp.*

TRUE POLICE CASES—See *Globe Communications Corp.*

MILITARY

AIR FORCE TIMES—See *Times News Service.*

AMERICAN SURVIVAL GUIDE—774 S. Placentia Ave., Placentia, CA 92670. Jim Benson, Ed. Articles, 1,500 to 2,000 words, with photos, on human and natural forces that pose threats to everyday life, all forms of preparedness, food production and storage, self defense and weapons, etc. All text must be accompanied by photos (and vice versa). Pays $70 per published page, on publication. Query.

AMERICA'S CIVIL WAR—Cowles History Group, 741 Miller Dr. S.E., Suite D-2, Leesburg, VA 22075. Attn: Ed. Articles, 3,500 to 4,000 words, on the strategy, tactics, personalities, arms and equipment of the Civil War. Department pieces, 2,000 words. Query with illustration ideas. Pays from $100, on publication.

ARMY MAGAZINE—Box 1560, Arlington, VA 22210–0860. Mary B. French, Ed.-in-Chief. Features, 1,000 to 2,000 words, on military subjects. Essays, humor, history (especially World War II), news reports, first-person anecdotes. Pays 12¢ to 18¢ a word, $25 to $50 for anecdotes, on publication. Guidelines.

ARMY TIMES—See *Times News Service.*

COMMAND—P.O. Box 4017, San Luis Obispo, CA 93403. Ty Bomba, Ed. Bimonthly. Articles, 800 to 10,000 words, on any facet of military history or current military affairs. "Popular, not scholarly, analytical military history." Pays 5¢ a word, on publication. Query.

FAMILY—169 Lexington Ave., New York, NY 10016. Liz DeFranco, Ed. Articles, 1,000 to 2,000 words, of interest to military women with children. Pays to $200, on publication. Guidelines.

LEATHERNECK—Box 1775, Quantico, VA 22134–0776. William V. H. White, Ed. Articles, to 3,000 words, with photos, on U.S. Marines. Pays $50 per printed page, on acceptance. Query.

MARINE CORPS GAZETTE—Box 1775, Quantico, VA 22134. Col. John E. Greenwood, Ed. Military articles, 500 to 2,000 words and 2,500 to 5,000 words. "Our magazine serves primarily as a forum for active duty officers to exchange views on professional, Marine Corps-related topics. Opportunity for 'outside' writers is limited." Queries preferred.

MILITARY—2122 28th St., Sacramento, CA 95818. Lt. Col. Michael Mark, Ed. Articles, 600 to 2,500 words, on firsthand experience in military service: World War II, Korea, Vietnam, and all current services. "Our magazine is about military history by the people who served. They are the best historians." No payment.

MILITARY HISTORY—741 Miller Dr. S.E., #D2, Leesburg, VA 22075. Jon Guttman, Ed. Bimonthly. Features, 4,000 words with 500-word sidebars, on strategy and tactics of military history. Department pieces, 2,000 words, on intrigue, personality, weaponry, perspectives, and travel. Pays $200 to $400, on publication. Query. Guidelines.

NAVY TIMES—See *Times News Service.*

THE RETIRED OFFICER MAGAZINE—201 N. Washington St., Alexandria, VA 22314. Attn: Manuscripts Ed. Articles, 1,800 to 2,000 words, of interest to military retirees and their families. Current military/political affairs, recent military history (especially Vietnam and Korea), health, money, military family lifestyles, and second-career job opportunities. Photos a plus. Pays to $1,000, on acceptance. Queries required; no unsolicited manuscripts. Guidelines.

TIMES NEWS SERVICE—Army Times Publishing Co., Springfield, VA 22159. Attn: R&R Ed. Free-lance material for "R&R" newspaper section. Articles about military life and its problems, as well as interesting things people are doing. Travel articles, 700 words, on places of interest to military people. Profiles, 600 to 700 words, on interesting members of the military community. Personal-experience essays, 750 words. No fiction or poetry. Pays $75 to $100, on acceptance. Also articles, 1,200 words, for supplements to *Army Times*, *Navy Times*, and *Air Force Times*. Address Supplements Ed. Pays $125 to $250, on acceptance. Guidelines.

VFW MAGAZINE—406 W. 34th St., Kansas City, MO 64111. Richard K. Kolb, Ed. Articles, 1,000 words, related to current foreign policy and defense, American armed forces abroad, and international events affecting U.S. national security. Also, up-to-date articles on verteran concerns and issues affecting veterans. Pays to $500, on acceptance. Query. Guidelines.

VIETNAM—Cowles History Group, 741 Miller Dr. S.E., Suite D-2, Leesburg, VA 22075. Attn: Ed. Articles, 3,500 to 4,000 words, on the strategy, tactics, personalities, arms, and equipment of the Vietnam War. Pays from $100, on publication. Query with illustration ideas.

WORLD WAR II—Cowles History Group, 741 Miller Dr. S.E., Leesburg, VA 22075. Attn: Ed. Articles, 3,500 to 4,000 words, on the strategy, tactics, personalities, arms, and equipment of World War II. Pays from $100, on publication. Query with illustration ideas.

HISTORY

ALABAMA HERITAGE—The Univ. of Alabama, Box 870342, Tuscaloosa, AL 35487–0342. Suzanne Wolfe, Ed. Quarterly. Articles, to 5,000 words, on local, state, and regional history: art, literature, language, archaeology, music, religion, architecture, and natural history. Pays an honorarium, on publication, plus 10 copies. Query, mentioning availability of photos and illustrations. Guidelines.

AMERICAN HERITAGE— 60 Fifth Ave., New York, NY 10011. Richard F. Snow, Ed. Articles, 750 to 5,000 words, on U.S. history and background of American life and culture from the beginning to recent times. No fiction. Pays from $300 to $1,500, on acceptance. Query.

AMERICAN HERITAGE OF INVENTION & TECHNOLOGY— 60 Fifth Ave., New York, NY 10011. Frederick Allen, Ed. Quarterly. Articles, 2,000 to 5,000 words, on history of technology in America, for the sophisticated general reader. Query. Pays on acceptance.

AMERICAN HISTORY— 6405 Flank Dr., P.O. Box 8200, Harrisburg, PA 17105. Attn: Ed. Articles, 3,000 to 5,000 words, soundly researched. Style should be popular, not scholarly. No travelogues, fiction, or puzzles. Pays $300 to $650, on acceptance. Query.

AMERICAN JEWISH HISTORY—American Jewish Historical Society, 2 Thornton Rd., Waltham, MA 02154. Dr. Marc Lee Raphael, Ed. Articles, 15 to 30 typed pages, on American Jewish history. Queries preferred. No payment.

AMERICA'S CIVIL WAR—Cowles History Group, 741 Miller Dr. S.E., Suite D-2, Leesburg, VA 22075. Attn: Ed. Articles, 3,500 to 4,000 words, on the strategy, tactics, personalities, arms and equipment of the Civil War. Department pieces, 2,000 words. Query with illustration ideas. Pays from $100, on publication.

AVIATION HISTORY—Cowles History Group, 741 Miller Dr. S.E., Suite D-2, Leesburg, VA 22075. Attn: Eds. Bimonthly. Articles, 3,500 to 4,000 words with 500-word sidebars and excellent illustrations, on aeronautical history. Department pieces, 2,000 words. Pays $150 to $300, on publication. Query.

THE BEAVER—167 Lombard Ave., #478, Winnipeg, Manitoba, Canada R3B 0T6. C. Dafoe, Ed. Articles, 500 to 3,000 words, on Canadian history, "written to appeal to general readers as well as the expert in Canadian history." Payment varies, on publication. Queries preferred.

CAROLOGUE—South Carolina Historical Society, 100 Meeting St., Charleston, SC 29401–2299. Stephen Hoffius, Ed. General-interest articles, to 10 pages, on South Carolina history. Queries preferred. Pays in copies.

CHICAGO HISTORY—Clark St. at North Ave., Chicago, IL 60614. Rosemary Adams, Ed. Articles, to 4,500 words, on political, social, and cultural history of Chicago. Pays to $250, on publication. Query.

CIVIL WAR TIMES—P.O. Box 8200, Harrisburg, PA 17105–8200. James Kushlan, Ed. Articles, 3,000 to 4,000 words, on the Civil War. "Accurate, annotated stories with strong narrative relying heavily on primary sources and the words of eyewitnesses. We prefer gripping, top-notch accounts of battles in the Eastern Theater of the war, and Confederate eyewitness accounts (memoirs, diaries, letters) and common soldier photos." Pays $300 to $500, on acceptance. Query.

COMMAND—P.O. Box 4017, San Luis Obispo, CA 93403. Ty Bomba, Ed. Bimonthly. Articles, 800 to 10,000 words, on any facet of military history or current military affairs. "Popular, not scholarly, analytical military history." Pays 5¢ a word, on publication. Query.

EARLY AMERICAN HOMES—Box 8200, Harrisburg, PA 17105–8200. Mimi Handler, Ed. Illustrated articles, 1,000 to 3,000 words, on early American life: arts, crafts, furnishings, gardens, and architecture before 1850. Pays $50 to $500, on acceptance. Query.

EIGHTEENTH-CENTURY STUDIES—Dept. of English, CB 3520, Greenlaw Hall, Univ. of North Carolina, Chapel Hill, NC 27599. Attn: Eds. Quarterly. Articles, to 6,500 words, on all aspects of the eighteenth century, especially those that are interdisciplinary or that are of general interest to scholars working in other disciplines. Blind submission policy: Submit 2 copies of manuscript; author's name and address should appear only on separate title page. No payment.

GOLDENSEAL—The Cultural Ctr., 1900 Kanawha Blvd. E., Charleston, WV 25305–0300. Ken Sullivan, Ed. Features, 3,000 words, and shorter articles, 1,000 words, on traditional West Virginia culture and history. Oral histories, old and new B&W photos, research articles. Pays 10¢ a word, on publication. Guidelines.

THE HIGHLANDER—P.O. Box 397, Barrington, IL 60011. Angus Ray, Ed. Bimonthly. Articles, 1,300 to 1,900 words, related to Scottish history. "We do not use any articles on modern Scotland or current problems in Scotland." Pays $100 to $150, on acceptance.

HISTORIC PRESERVATION—1785 Massachusetts Ave. N.W., Washington, DC 20036. Robert Wilson, Ed. Feature articles from published writers, 1,500 to 4,000 words, on residential restoration, preservation issues, news, and people involved in preserving America's heritage. Partly staff-written. Query required.

HISTORIC TRAVELER— 6405 Flank Dr., Harrisburg, PA 17112. John Stanchak, Ed. Bimonthly. Articles, 800 to 1,500 words, for upscale readers with a strong interest in history and historic sites. "Accurate information on historic destinations. Possible topics: battlefields, museums, antique shows, events, hotels, inns, transportation, reenactments, preserved communities, and architectural wonders. No South Pacific Islands, Alpine skiing, or Mediterranean cruises." Pays $300 to $500, on acceptance. Query with SASE and clips. Guidelines.

HISTORY NEWS—AASLH, 530 Church St., Suite 600, Nashville, TN 37219–2325. Deanna Kerrigan, Ed. History-related articles, 2,500 to 3,500 words, about museums, historical societies and sites, libraries, etc.; "In My Opinion" pieces, 1,000 words; "Technical Leaflets," 5,000 words. B&W photos. Submit 2 copies of manuscript. No payment made. Guidelines.

JOURNAL OF THE WEST—1531 Yuma, Box 1009, Manhattan, KS 66505–1009. Robin Higham, Ed. Articles, to 20 pages, devoted to the history and the culture of the West, then and now. B&W photos. Pays in copies.

LABOR'S HERITAGE—10000 New Hampshire Ave., Silver Spring, MD 20903. Stuart Kaufman, Ed. Quarterly journal of The George Meany Memorial Archives. Articles, 15 to 30 pages, for labor scholars, labor union members, and the general public. Pays in copies.

MILITARY HISTORY—741 Miller Dr. S.E., #D2, Leesburg, VA 22075. Jon Guttman, Ed. Bimonthly. Features, 4,000 words with 500-word sidebars, on the strategy, tactics, and personalities of military history. Department pieces, 2,000 words, on espionage, weaponry, personalities, perspectives, and travel. Pays $200 to $400, on publication. Query. Guidelines.

MONTANA JOURNAL—1431 S. Higgins Ave., Missoula, MT 59801. Mike Haser, Ed. Bimonthly tabloid. Human-interest articles, to 1,000 words, about the people, places, and events that helped build Montana. Pays 2¢ a word, on publication. Query preferred.

MONTANA, THE MAGAZINE OF WESTERN HISTORY—225 N. Roberts St., Box 201201, Helena, MT 59620–1201. Charles E. Rankin, Ed. Authentic articles, 3,500 to 5,500 words, on the history of the American and Canadian West; new interpretive approaches to major developments in western history. Footnotes or bibliography must accompany article. "Strict historical accuracy is essential." No fiction. Queries preferred. No payment made.

NEBRASKA HISTORY—P.O. Box 82554, Lincoln, NE 68501. James E. Potter, Ed. Articles, 3,000 to 7,000 words, relating to the history of Nebraska and the Great Plains. B&W line drawings. Allow 60 days for response. Pays in copies. Cash prize awarded to one article each year.

NOW & THEN—CASS/ETSU, P.O. Box 70556, Johnson City, TN 37614–0556. Jane Harris Woodside, Ed. Fiction and nonfiction, 1,500 to 3,000 words: short stories, articles, interviews, essays, memoirs, book reviews. Pieces must be related to theme of issue and have some connection to the Appalachian region. Also photos and drawings. SASE for guidelines and current themes. Pays $15 to $75, on publication.

OLD WEST—P.O. Box 2107, Stillwater, OK 74076. John Joerschke, Ed. Thoroughly researched and documented articles, 1,500 to 4,500 words, on the history of the American West. B&W 5x7 photos to illustrate articles. Queries are preferred. Pays 3¢ to 6¢ a word, on acceptance.

PENNSYLVANIA HERITAGE—P.O. Box 1026, Harrisburg, PA 17108–1026. Michael J. O'Malley III, Ed. Quarterly of the Pennsylvania Historical and Museum Commission. Articles, 3,000 to 4,000 words, that "introduce readers to the state's rich culture and historic legacy." Pays $300 to $500, up to $100 for photos or drawings, on acceptance.

PERSIMMON HILL—1700 N.E. 63rd St., Oklahoma City, OK 73111. M.J. Van Deventer, Ed. Published by the National Cowboy Hall of Fame. Articles, 1,500 to 2,000 words, on Western history and art, cowboys, ranching, and nature. Top-quality illustrations with captions a must. Pays from $100 to $250, on publication.

PROLOGUE—National Archives, NECP, Washington, DC 20408. Quarterly. Articles, varying lengths, based on the holdings and programs of the National Archives, its regional archives, and the presidential libraries. Query. Pays in copies.

RENAISSANCE MAGAZINE—Phantom Press Publications, 5A Green Meadow Dr., Nantucket, MA 02554. Kim Guarnaccia, Ed. Feature articles on

Renaissance history, costuming, jousting. Also Renaissance faires, interviews, reviews of Renaissance books, music, movies, and games. Pays 3¢ a word, on publication.

SOUTH CAROLINA HISTORICAL MAGAZINE—South Carolina Historical Society, 100 Meeting St., Charleston, SC 29401–2299. Stephen Hoffius, Ed. Scholarly articles, to 25 pages including footnotes, on South Carolina history. "Authors are encouraged to look at previous issues to be aware of previous scholarship." Pays in copies.

SOUTHERN OREGON HERITAGE—106 N. Central Ave., Medford, OR 97501–5926. Marcia W. Somers, Man. Ed. Well-written, human stories (not fiction), 800 to 2,500 words, based on the history of the southern Oregon region: "its people, places, buildings, and events. Make sure there is a storyline, not just a reiteration of facts." Pays $50 to $250, on publication.

TRUE WEST—P.O. Box 2107, Stillwater, OK 74076–2107. John Joerschke, Ed. True stories, 500 to 4,500 words, with photos, about the Old West to 1930. Some contemporary stories with historical slant. Source list required. Pays 3¢ to 6¢ a word, extra for B&W photos, on acceptance.

VIETNAM—Cowles History Group, 741 Miller Dr. S.E., Suite D-2, Leesburg, VA 22075. Attn: Ed. Articles, 3,500 to 4,000 words, on the strategy, tactics, personalities, arms, and equipment of the Vietnam War. Pays from $100, on publication. Query with illustration ideas.

THE WESTERN HISTORICAL QUARTERLY—Utah State Univ., Logan, UT 84322–0740. Clyde A. Milner II, Ed. Original articles about the American West, the Westward movement from the Atlantic to the Pacific, twentieth-century regional studies, Spanish borderlands, Canada, northern Mexico, Alaska, and Hawaii. No payment made.

WORLD WAR II—Cowles History Group, 741 Miller Dr. S.E., Leesburg, VA 22075. Attn: Ed. Articles, 3,500 to 4,000 words, on the strategy, tactics, personalities, arms, and equipment of World War II. Pays from $100, on publication. Query with illustration ideas.

YESTERDAY'S MAGAZETTE—P.O. Box 18566, Sarasota, FL 34276. Ned Burke, Ed. Articles and fiction, to 1,000 words, on the 1920s through '70s, nostalgia and memories of people, places, and things. Traditional poetry, to 24 lines. Pays $5 to $25, on publication. Pays in copies for poetry and short pieces. Guidelines.

COLLEGE, CAREERS

THE BLACK COLLEGIAN—140 Carondelet St., New Orleans, LA 70130. Sonya Stinson, Ed. Articles, to 2,000 words, on experiences of African-American students, careers, and how-to subjects. Pays on publication. Query.

BYLINE—Box 130596, Edmond, OK 73013. Marcia Preston, Ed.-in-Chief. General fiction, 2,000 to 4,000 words. Nonfiction: 1,500- to 1,800-word features and 300- to 750-word special departments. Poetry, 10 to 30 lines preferred. Nonfiction and poetry must be about writing. Humor, 200 to 600 words, about writing. "We seek practical and motivational material that tells writers how they can succeed, not why they can't. Overdone topics: writers' block, the muse, rejection slips." Pays $5 to $10 for poetry; $15 to $35 for departments; $50 for features and $100 for short fiction, on acceptance.

676

CAMPUS LIFE— 465 Gundersen Dr., Carol Stream, IL 60188. Harold Smith, Exec. Ed. Fiction and humor reflecting Christian values, 1,000 to 3,000 words, for high school and college students. Pays from $150 to $400, on acceptance. Limited free-lance market. Published writers only. Queries required. SASE.

CAREER WORLD—GLC. 60 Revere Dr., Northbrook, IL 60062–1563. Carole Rubenstein, Sr. Ed. Published 7 times a year, September through April. Gender-neutral articles about specific occupations and career development for junior and senior high school audience. Query with clips and resumé. Payment varies, on publication.

CAREERS AND THE COLLEGE GRAD—260 Center St., Holbrook, MA 02343. Jennifer Most, Ed. Annual. Career-related articles, 1,500 to 2,000 words, for junior and senior liberal arts students. Career-related fillers, 500 words and line art or color prints. Queries preferred. No payment. Same address and requirements for *Careers and the MBA* (semiannual) for first- and second-year MBA students, and *Careers and the Engineer* (semiannual) for junior and senior engineering students.

CAREERS & THE DISABLED—See *Minority Engineer.*

CAREERS AND THE ENGINEER—See *Careers and the College Grad.*

CAREERS AND THE MBA—See *Careers and the College Grad.*

CIRCLE K—3636 Woodview Trace, Indianapolis, IN 46268–3196. Nicholas K. Drake, Exec. Ed. Serious and light articles, 1,500 to 1,700 words, on careers, college issues, trends, leadership development, self-help, community service and involvement. Pays $150 to $400, on acceptance. Queries preferred.

COLLEGE BROADCASTER—National Assn. of College Broadcasters, 71 George St., Providence, RI 02912–1824. Attn: Ed. Quarterly. Articles, 500 to 2,000 words, on student radio and TV station operations and media careers. Pays in copies. Query.

EQUAL OPPORTUNITY—See *Minority Engineer.*

FLORIDA LEADER—c/o Oxendine Publishing, P.O. Box 14081, Gainesville, FL 32604–2081. Kay Quinn, Man. Ed. Published 3 times a year. Articles, 800 to 1,000 words, for Florida college students. "Focus on leadership, career success, profiles of growth careers in Florida and the Southeast." Pays $35 to $50, on publication.

LINK: THE COLLEGE MAGAZINE—The Soho Building, 110 Greene St., Suite 407, New York, NY 10012. Ty Wenger, Ed.-in-Chief. News, lifestyle, and issues for college students. Informational how-to and short features, 500 to 800 words, on education news, finances, academics, employment, lifestyles, and trends. Well-researched, insightful, authoritative articles. Pays $100 to $500, on publication. Queries preferred. Guidelines.

MINORITY ENGINEER—1160 E. Jericho Turnpike, Suite 200, Huntington, NY 11743. James Schneider, Exec. Ed. Articles, 1,000 to 1,500 words, for college students, on career opportunities; techniques of job hunting; developments in and applications of new technologies. Interviews. Profiles. Pays 10¢ a word, on publication. Query. Same address and requirements for *Woman Engineer* (address Anne Kelly), and *Equal Opportunity* and *Careers & the DisABLED* (address James Schneider).

677

ONCE UPON A TIME—553 Winston Ct., St. Paul, MN 55118. Audrey B. Baird, Ed. "A 32-page magazine for Children's Writers and Illustrators." Quarterly. Articles, to 900 words: questions, insights, tips and experiences (no fiction) on the writing and illustrating life by published and unpublished writers. B&W artwork. No payment.

STUDENT LEADER—c/o Oxendine Publishing Inc., P.O. Box 14081, Gainesville, FL 32604–2081. Kay Quinn, Man. Ed. Semiannual. "The Magazine for America's Most Outstanding Students." Articles, 800 to 1,000 words, on leadership issues and career and college success. "Include quotes from faculty, corporate recruiters, current students, recent alumni." Pays $50 to $100, on publication.

STUDENT LEADERSHIP—P.O. Box 7895, Madison, WI 53707–7895. Jeff Yourison, Ed. Articles, to 2,000 words, and poetry for Christian college students. All material should reflect a Christian world view. Queries required.

UNIQUE OPPORTUNITIES—455 S. 4th Ave., #1236, Louisville, KY 40202. Bett Coffman, Asst. Ed. Articles, 2,000 to 3,000 words, that cover economic, business, and career-related issues of interest to physicians who are looking for their first practice or looking to make a career move. Doctor profiles, 500 words. "Our goal is to educate physicians about how to evaluate career opportunities, negotiate the benefits offered, plan career moves, and provide information on the legal and economic aspects of accepting a position." Pays 50¢ a word for features; $100 to $200 for profiles, on acceptance. Query.

WOMAN ENGINEER—See *Minority Engineer.*

OP-ED MARKETS

THE ATLANTA CONSTITUTION—P.O. Box 4689, Atlanta, GA 30302. Teresa Weaver, Op-Ed Ed. Articles related to the Southeast, Georgia, or the Atlanta metropolitan area, 200 to 800 words, on a variety of topics: law, economics, politics, science, environment, performing and manipulative arts, humor, education; religious and seasonal topics. Pays $75 to $125, on publication. Submit complete manuscript.

THE BALTIMORE SUN—P.O. Box 1377, Baltimore, MD 21278–0001. Hal Piper, Opinion-Commentary Page Ed. Articles, 600 to 1,500 words, on a wide range of topics: politics, education, foreign affairs, lifestyles, etc. Humor. Payment varies, on publication. Exclusive rights: MD and DC.

THE BOSTON GLOBE—P.O. Box 2378, Boston, MA 02107–2378. Marjorie Pritchard, Ed. Articles, to 700 words, on economics, education, environment, foreign affairs, and regional interest. Pays $100, on publication. Send complete manuscript. Exclusive rights: New England.

BOSTON HERALD—One Herald Sq., Boston, MA 02106. Attn: Editorial Page Ed. Pieces, 600 to 800 words, on economics, foreign affairs, politics, regional interest, and seasonal topics. Prefer submissions from regional writers. Payment varies, on publication. Exclusive rights: MA, RI, and NH.

THE CHARLOTTE OBSERVER—P.O. Box 30308, Charlotte, NC 28230–0308. Ed Williams, Ed. Well-written, thought-provoking articles, to 700 words.

"We are only interested in articles on local (Carolinas) issues or that use local examples to illustrate other issues." Pays $50, on publication. No simultaneous submissions in NC or SC.

THE CHICAGO TRIBUNE— 435 N. Michigan Ave., Chicago, IL 60611. Marcia Lythcott, Op-Ed Page Ed. Pieces, 800 to 1,000 words, on domestic and international affairs, environment, regional interest, and personal essays. SASE required.

THE CHRISTIAN SCIENCE MONITOR—One Norway St., Boston, MA 02115. Lisa Parney, Opinion Page Coordinator. Pieces, 750 to 900 words, on domestic and foreign affairs, economics, education, environment, law, media, and politics. Pays $100, on acceptance. Retains all rights for 90 days after publication.

THE CLEVELAND PLAIN DEALER—1801 Superior Ave., Cleveland, OH 44114. Gloria Millner, Assoc. Ed. Pieces, 700 to 900 words, on a wide variety of subjects. Pays $75, on publication.

DES MOINES REGISTER—P.O. Box 957, Des Moines, IA 50304. Attn: "Opinion" Page Ed. Articles, 500 to 750 words, on all topics. Prefer Iowa subjects. Pays $35 to $75, on publication. Exclusive rights: IA.

DETROIT FREE PRESS—321 W. Lafayette Blvd., Detroit, MI 48226. Attn: Op-Ed Ed. Opinion pieces, to 800 words, on domestic and foreign affairs, economics, education, environment, law, politics, and regional interest. Priority given to local writers or topics of local interest. Pays $50 to $100, on publication. Query. Exclusive rights: MI and northern OH.

THE DETROIT NEWS— 615 W. Lafayette Blvd., Detroit, MI 48226. Attn: Richard Burr. Pieces, 500 to 750 words, on a wide variety of subjects. Pays $75, on publication.

THE FLINT JOURNAL—200 E. First St., Flint, MI 48502–1925. Carlton Winfrey, Opinion Dept. Ed. Articles, 650 words, of regional interest by local writers. Non-local writers should query. No payment. Limited market.

INDIANAPOLIS STAR—P.O. Box 145, Indianapolis, IN 46206–0145. John H. Lyst, Ed. Articles, 700 to 800 words. Pays $40, on publication. Exclusive rights: IN.

LONG BEACH PRESS-TELEGRAM— 604 Pine Ave., Long Beach, CA 90844. Larry Allison, Ed. Articles, 750 to 900 words, on regional topics. Pays $75, on publication. Exclusive rights: Los Angeles area.

LOS ANGELES TIMES—Times Mirror Sq., Los Angeles, CA 90053. Bob Berger, Op-Ed Ed. Commentary pieces, 650 to 700 words, on many subjects. "Not interested in nostalgia or first-person reaction to faraway events. Pieces must be exclusive." Payment varies, on publication. Limited market. SASE required.

THE NEW YORK TIMES—229 W. 43rd St., New York, NY 10036. Attn: Op-Ed Ed. Opinion pieces, 650 to 800 words, on any topic, including public policy, science, lifestyles, and ideas, etc. Include your address, daytime phone number, and social security number with submission. "If you haven't heard from us within 2 weeks, you can assume we are not using your piece. Include SASE if you want work returned." Pays on publication. Buys first North American rights.

NEWSDAY—"Viewpoints," 235 Pinelawn Rd., Melville, NY 11747. Noel Rubinton, "Viewpoints" Ed. Pieces, 700 to 800 words, on a variety of topics. Pays $150, on publication.

THE ORANGE COUNTY REGISTER—P.O. Box 11626, Santa Ana, CA 92711. K.E. Grubbs, Jr., Ed. Articles on a wide range of local and national issues and topics. Pays $50 to $100, on publication.

THE OREGONIAN—1320 S.W. Broadway, Portland, OR 97201. Attn: Opinion & Commentary Ed. Articles, 900 to 1,000 words, of news analysis from Pacific Northwest writers or on regional topics. Pays $100 to $150, on publication. Send complete manuscript.

PITTSBURGH POST GAZETTE—34 Blvd. of the Allies, Pittsburgh, PA 15222. John Allison, Contributions Ed. Articles, to 1,000 words, on a variety of subjects. No whimsy. Pays $60 to $150, on publication. SASE required.

THE REGISTER GUARD—P.O. Box 10188, Eugene, OR 97440. Don Robinson, Editorial Page Ed. All subjects; regional angle preferred. Pays $25 to $50, on publication. Very limited use of non-local writers.

THE SACRAMENTO BEE—2100 Q St., Sacramento, CA 95852. William Kahrl, Opinion Ed. Op-ed pieces, to 750 words; state and regional topics preferred. Pays $150, on publication.

ST. LOUIS POST-DISPATCH—900 N. Tucker Blvd., St. Louis, MO 63101. Donna Korando, Commentary Ed. Articles, 700 words, on economics, education, science, politics, foreign and domestic affairs, and the environment. Pays $70, on publication. "Goal is to have half of the articles by local writers."

ST. PAUL PIONEER PRESS—345 Cedar St., St. Paul, MN 55101. Ronald D. Clark, Ed. Articles, to 750 words, on a variety of topics. Strongly prefer authors or topics with a connection to the area. Pays $75, on publication.

ST. PETERSBURG TIMES—Box 1121, 490 First Ave. S., St. Petersburg, FL 33731. Jon East, "Perspective" Section Ed. Authoritative articles, to 2,000 words, on current political, economic, and social issues. Payment varies, on publication. Query.

SAN FRANCISCO EXAMINER—110 5th St., San Francisco, CA 94103. Attn: Op-Ed Ed. Well-written articles, 500 to 650 words, double-spaced; preference given to local and state issues and to subjects bypassed by most news media. No sports. No first-run movies. Payment varies, on publication.

SEATTLE POST-INTELLIGENCER—P.O. Box 1909, Seattle, WA 98111. Charles J. Dunsire, Editorial Page Ed. Articles, 750 to 800 words, on foreign and domestic affairs, environment, education, politics, regional interest, religion, science, and seasonal material. Prefer writers who live in the Pacific Northwest. Pays $75 to $150, on publication. SASE required. Very limited market.

USA TODAY—1000 Wilson Blvd., Arlington, VA 22229. Juan J. Walte, Ed./Columns. Articles, 600 words, on current public policy issues. Very limited market. Pays $200, on publication. Query.

THE WALL STREET JOURNAL—Editorial Page, 200 Liberty St., New York, NY 10281. David B. Brooks, Op-Ed Ed. Articles, to 1,500 words, on politics, economics, law, education, environment, humor (occasionally), and foreign and domestic affairs. Articles must be timely, heavily reported, and of national interest by writers with expertise in their field. Pays $150 to $300, on publication.

WASHINGTON TIMES—3600 New York Ave. N.E., Washington, DC 20002. Frank Perley, Articles and Opinion Page Ed. Articles, 800 to 1,000 words, on a variety of subjects. No pieces written in the first-person. "Syndicated columnists cover the 'big' issues; find an area that is off the beaten path." Pays $150, on publication. Exclusive rights: Washington, DC, and Baltimore area.

ADULT MAGAZINES

CHIC— 8484 Wilshire Blvd., Suite 900, Beverly Hills, CA 90211. Scott Schalin, Lisa Jenio, Exec. Eds. Sex-related articles, interviews, erotic fiction, 2,500 words. Query for articles. Pays $500 for articles, $350 for fiction, on acceptance.

D-CUP—Swank Publications, Inc., 210 Rt. 4 E., Suite 401, Paramus, NJ 07652. Bob Rosen, Ed. Erotic fiction and interviews with large-breasted models, 2,000 to 2,500 words. Pays $100 to $250, on publication.

GALLERY— 401 Park Ave. S., New York, NY 10016–8802. Barry Janoff, Ed.-in-Chief. Rich Friedman, Man. Ed. Articles, investigative pieces, interviews, profiles, to 2,500 words, for sophisticated men. Short humor, satire, service pieces, and fiction. Photos. Pays varying rates, on publication. Query. Guidelines.

PENTHOUSE—277 Park Ave., 4th Fl., New York, NY 10172–0003. Peter Bloch, Ed. Lavada B. Nahon, Sr. Ed. Articles, to 5,000 words: general-interest profiles, interviews (with introduction), and investigative pieces. Pays on acceptance.

PLAYBOY— 680 N. Lake Shore Dr., Chicago, IL 60611. Peter Moore, Stephen Randall, Articles Eds. Articles, 3,500 to 6,000 words, and sophisticated fiction, 1,000 to 10,000 words (5,000 preferred), for urban men. Humor; satire. Science fiction. Pays to $5,000 for articles and fiction, $2,000 for short-shorts, on acceptance.

PLAYERS— 8060 Melrose Ave., Los Angeles, CA 90046. David Jamison, Ed. Articles, 2,500 to 3,500 words, for black men: politics, economics, travel, fashion, grooming, entertainment, sports, interviews, fiction, humor, satire, health, and sex. Photos a plus. Pays on publication.

PLAYGIRL— 801 Second Ave., New York, NY 10017. Judy Cole, Ed.-in-Chief. Articles, 1,500 to 4,000 words, for women 18 and older. Erotic fiction, 1,000 to 3,500 words. Pays varying rates, on acceptance.

VARIATIONS, FOR LIBERATED LOVERS—277 Park Ave., New York, NY 10172. V. K. McCarty, Ed. Dir./Assoc. Pub. First-person true narrative descriptions of "a couple's enthusiasm, secrets, and exquisitely articulated sex scenes squarely focused within one of the magazine's pleasure categories." Pays $400, on acceptance.

FICTION MARKETS

This list gives the fiction requirements of general- and special-interest magazines, including those that publish detective and mystery, science fiction and fantasy, romance and confession stories. Editors usually prefer to see complete manuscripts for fiction, rather than queries. Other good markets for short fiction are the *College, Literary, and Little Magazines* where, though payment is modest (usually in copies only), publication can bring the work of a beginning writer to the attention of editors at the larger magazines. Juvenile fiction markets are listed under *Juvenile, Teenage, and Young Adult Magazines*. Publishers of book-length fiction manuscripts are listed under *Book Publishers*.

GENERAL FICTION

ABORIGINAL SF—P.O. Box 2449, Woburn, MA 01888–0849. Charles C. Ryan, Ed. Stories, 2,500 to 7,500 words, with a unique scientific idea, human or alien character, plot, and theme of lasting value; "must be science fiction; no fantasy, horror, or sword and sorcery." Pays $200. Send SASE for guidelines.

AFRICAN VOICES—270 W. 96th St., New York, NY 10025. Carolyn A. Butts, Exec. Ed. Bimonthly. Humorous, erotic, and dramatic fiction, 500 to 2,500 words, by ethnic writers. Nonfiction, 500 to 1,500 words: investigative articles, artist profiles, essays, and first-person narratives. Poetry, to 50 lines. Pays $25 for fiction, on publication, plus 5 copies of magazine. (Payment varies for nonfiction.)

AIM MAGAZINE—P.O. Box 20554, Chicago, IL 60620. Myron Apilado, Ed. Short stories, 800 to 3,000 words, geared to proving that people from different backgrounds are more alike than they are different. Story should not moralize. Pays from $15 to $25, on publication. Annual contest.

ALFRED HITCHCOCK MYSTERY MAGAZINE—1270 Ave. of the Americas, New York, NY 10020. Cathleen Jordan, Ed. Well-plotted, plausible mystery, suspense, detection and crime stories, to 14,000 words; "ghost stories, humor, futuristic or atmospheric tales are all possible, as long as they include a crime or the suggestion of one." Pays 8¢ a word, on acceptance. Guidelines with SASE.

ALOHA, THE MAGAZINE OF HAWAII AND THE PACIFIC—P.O. Box 3260, Honolulu, HI 96801. Cheryl Tsutsumi, Ed. Fiction to 2,000 words, with a Hawaii focus. Pays $150 to $300, on publication. Query.

THE AMERICAN VOICE—332 W. Broadway, Suite 1215, Louisville, KY 40202. Frederick Smock, Ed. Avant-garde, literary fiction, nonfiction, and well-crafted poetry, any length (shorter works are preferred). "Please read our journal before attempting to submit." Payment varies, on publication.

ANALOG SCIENCE FICTION AND FACT—1270 Ave. of the Americas, New York, NY 10020. Stanley Schmidt, Ed. Science fiction, with strong characters in believable future or alien setting: short stories, 2,000 to 7,500 words; novelettes, 10,000 to 20,000 words; serials, to 70,000 words. Include SASE. Pays 5¢ to 8¢ a word, on acceptance. Query for novels.

ASIMOV'S SCIENCE FICTION MAGAZINE—1270 Ave. of the Americas, New York, NY 10020. Gardner Dozois, Ed. Short science fiction and fantasies, to 15,000 words. Pays 6¢ to 8¢ a word, on acceptance. Guidelines.

THE ATLANTIC MONTHLY—77 N. Washington St., Boston, MA 02114. William Whitworth, Ed. Short stories, 2,000 to 6,000 words, of highest literary quality, with "fully developed narratives, distinctive characterization, freshness in language, and a resolution of some kind." SASE. Pays $2,500, on acceptance.

THE BELLETRIST REVIEW—Marmarc Publications, P.O. Box 596, Plainville, CT 06062. Marlene Dube, Ed. Semiannual. Fiction, 1,500 to 5,000 words: adventure, contemporary, erotica, psychological horror, humor, literary, mainstream, suspense, and mystery. No fantasy, juvenile, westerns, overblown horror, or confessional pieces. Annual fiction contest; send SASE for guidelines. Pays in copies.

THE BOSTON GLOBE MAGAZINE—*The Boston Globe*, Boston, MA 02107. Evelynne Kramer, Ed. Short stories, to 3,000 words. Include SASE. Pays on acceptance.

BOYS' LIFE—1325 W. Walnut Hill Ln., P.O. Box 152079, Irving, TX 75015–2079. Shannon Lowry, Fiction Ed. Publication of the Boy Scouts of America. Humor, mystery, science fiction, adventure, 1,200 words, for 8- to 18-year-old boys; study back issues. Pays from $750, on acceptance. Send SASE for guidelines.

BUFFALO SPREE MAGAZINE—Box 38, Buffalo, NY 14226. Johanna Van De Mark, Ed./Pub. Fiction and humor, to 2,000 words, for readers in the western New York region. Pays $100 to $125, on publication.

BYLINE—Box 130596, Edmond, OK 73013. Marcia Preston, Ed.-in-Chief. Kathryn Fanning, Man. Ed. General fiction, 2,000 to 4,000 words. Nonfiction: 1,500-to 1,800-word features and 300-to 750-word special departments. Poetry, 10 to 30 lines preferred. Nonfiction and poetry must be about writing. Humor, 200 to 600 words, about writing. "We seek practical and motivational material that tells writers how they can succeed, not why they can't. Overdone topics: writers' block, the muse, rejection slips." Pays $5 to $10 for poetry; $15 to $35 for departments; $50 for features; and $100 for short fiction, on acceptance. SASE for guidelines.

CAPPER'S—1503 S.W. 42nd St., Topeka, KS 66609–1265. Nancy Peavler, Ed. Fiction, 7,500 to 40,000 words (12,000 to 20,000 words preferred), for serialization. No profanity, violence, or explicit sex. Pays $75 to $400, on publication.

CATHOLIC FORESTER—355 Shuman Blvd., P.O. Box 3012, Naperville, IL 60566–7012. Dorothy Deer, Ed. Official publication of the Catholic Order of Foresters. Fiction, to 1,500 words (prefer shorter); "looking for more contemporary, meaningful stories dealing with life today." No sex or violence or "preachy" stories; religious angle not required. Pays 20¢ a word, on acceptance.

CHESS LIFE—186 Rt. 9W, New Windsor, NY 12553–7698. Glenn Petersen, Ed. Fiction, 500 to 2,000 words, related to chess for members of the U.S. Chess Federation. Also, articles, 500 to 3,000 words, on chess news, profiles, technical aspects of chess. Pays varying rates, on acceptance. Query; limited market.

COBBLESTONE: THE HISTORY MAGAZINE FOR CHILDREN—7 School St., Peterborough, NH 03458–1454. Meg Chorlian, Ed. Fiction, 500 to 800 words, for children aged 8 to 14 years; must relate to theme. Pays 20¢ to 25¢ a word, on publication. Send SASE for guidelines.

COMMENTARY—165 E. 56th St., New York, NY 10022. Neal Kozodoy, Ed. Fiction, of high literary quality, on contemporary social or Jewish issues. Pays on publication.

COMMON GROUND MAGAZINE—P.O. Box 99, McVeytown, PA 17051–0099. Ruth Dunmire and Pam Brumbaugh, Eds. Quarterly. Fiction, 1,000 to 2,000 words, related to Central Pennsylvania's Juniata River Valley. Pays $25 to $200, on publication. Guidelines.

COSMOPOLITAN—224 W. 57th St., New York, NY 10019. Betty Kelly, Fiction Ed. Romance or mystery short stories and novel excerpts; submissions must be sent by a publisher or agent. Payment rates are negotiable. SASE.

COUNTRY WOMAN—P.O. Box 989, Greendale, WI 53129. Kathy Pohl, Man. Ed. Fiction, 750 to 1,000 words, of interest to rural women; protagonist must be a country woman. "Stories should focus on life in the country, its problems and joys, as experienced by country women; must be upbeat and positive." Pays $90 to $125, on acceptance.

CRICKET—P.O. Box 300, Peru, IL 61354–0300. Marianne Carus, Ed.-in-Chief. Fiction, 200 to 2,000 words, for 9-to 14-year-olds. Pays to 25¢ a word, on publication. SASE.

DISCOVERIES—WordAction Publishing Co., 6401 The Paseo, Kansas City, MO 64131. Attn: Asst. Ed. Weekly take-home paper designed to correlate with Evangelical Sunday school curriculum. Fiction, 500 to 700 words, for 8-to 10-year-olds. Stories should feature contemporary, true-to-life characters and should illustrate character building and scriptural application. No poetry. Pays 5¢ a word, on publication. Guidelines.

DOGWOOD TALES MAGAZINE—P.O. Box 172068, Memphis, TN 38187. Attn: Ed. Bimonthly "for the fiction lover in all of us." Short stories, 250 to 6,000 words (prefer no more than 3,000 words), in any genre except religion or pornography. "Stories should be fresh, well-paced, and have strong endings." Contests. SASE for guidelines.

ELLERY QUEEN'S MYSTERY MAGAZINE—1270 Ave. of the Americas, 10th Fl., New York, NY 10020. Janet Hutchings, Ed. High-quality detective, crime, and mystery stories, 1,500 to 10,000 words. Also "Minute Mysteries," 250 words, short verses, limericks, and novellas, to 17,000 words. "We like a mix of classic detection and suspenseful crime." "First Stories" by unpublished writers. Pays 3¢ to 8¢ a word, on acceptance.

ESQUIRE—250 W. 55th St., New York, NY 10019. Edward Kosner, Ed.-in-Chief. Send finished manuscript of short story; submit one at a time. No full-length novels. No pornography, science fiction, or "true romance" stories.

EVANGEL—Light and Life Press, Box 535002, Indianapolis, IN 46253–5002. Julie Innes, Ed. Free Methodist. Fiction and nonfiction, to 1,200 words, with personal faith in Christ shown as instrumental in solving problems. Pays 4¢ a word, on publication. SASE for guidelines.

FAMILY CIRCLE—110 Fifth Ave., New York, NY 10011. Kathy Sagan, Sr. Ed. Fiction is no longer being considered.

FAMILY FUN—Walt Disney Publishing Group, 244 Main St., Northampton, MA 01060. Alexandra Kennedy, Ed. Articles, to 1,500 words, on family activities and "creative parenting." Payment varies, on acceptance.

FICTION INTERNATIONAL—English Dept., San Diego State Univ., San Diego, CA 92182–8140. Harold Jaffe, Ed. Post-modernist and politically committed fiction and theory. Query for themes. Submit between September 1st and December 15th.

FLY ROD & REEL—P.O. Box 370, Camden, ME 04843. James E. Butler, Ed. Occasional fiction, 2,000 to 2,500 words, related to fly fishing. Special annual fiction issue published in summer. Payment varies, on acceptance.

GALLERY—401 Park Ave. S., New York, NY 10016–8802. Barry Janoff, Ed. Dir. Rich Friedman, Man. Ed. Fiction, to 3,000 words, for sophisticated men. "We are not looking for science fiction, mystery, 40s-style detective, or stories involving aliens from other planets. We do look for interesting stories that enable readers to view life in an off-beat, unusual, or insightful manner: fiction with believable characters and actions. We encourage quality work from unpublished writers." Pays $500, on publication. SASE for guidelines.

GENRE SAMPLER MAGAZINE—P.O. Box 6978, Denver, CO 80206. S. Wright, Ed. Quarterly plus two special issues (which feature novellas and high school students). Short stories, 2,500 to 4,000 words, in the following genres: mystery; suspense; thriller; romance; horror; literary; adventure; science fiction; fantasy; western; mainstream; and young adult. Pays $10 to $20, on publication.

GLIMMER TRAIN PRESS—710 S.W. Madison St., #504, Portland, OR 97205. Susan Burmeister-Brown, Ed. Fiction, 1,200 to 7,500 words. "Eight stories in each quarterly magazine." Pays $500, on acceptance. Submit material in January, April, July, and October; allow 3 months for response. "Send SASE for guidelines before submitting."

GOOD HOUSEKEEPING—959 Eighth Ave., New York, NY 10019. Lee Quarfoot, Fiction Ed. Short stories, 1,000 to 3,000 words, with strong identification figures for women, by published writers and "beginners with demonstrable talent." Novel condensations or excerpts from about-to-be-published books only. "Writers whose work interests us will hear from us within 4 to 6 weeks of receipt of manuscript. Please send inexpensive copies of your work; and do not enclose SASEs or postage. We can no longer return or critique manuscripts. We do accept multiple submissions." Pays top rates, on acceptance.

GRIT—1503 S.W. 42nd St., Topeka, KS 66609. Michael Scheibach, Ed.-in-Chief. Short stories, 1,500 to 2,500 words; occasionally shorter stories, 800 to 2,000 words. Articles, 500 to 1,200 words, on interesting people and topics. Should be upbeat, inspirational, wholesome; of interest to mature adults. No reference to drinking, smoking, drugs, sex, or violence. Also publishes some short poetry and true-story nostalgia. Pays 12¢ to 22¢ a word, extra for photos, on publication. All fiction submissions should be marked "Fiction Dept." Guidelines.

GUIDEPOSTS FOR KIDS—P.O. Box 538A, Chesterton, IN 46304. Mary Lou Carney, Ed. Value-centered bimonthly for 7- to 12-year-olds. Problem fiction, mysteries, historicals, 1,000 to 1,400 words, with "realistic dialogue and sharp imagery. No preachy stories about Bible-toting children." Pays $300 to $500 for all rights, on acceptance. No reprints.

HARDBOILED—Gryphon Publications, P.O. Box 209, Brooklyn, NY 11228–0209. Gary Lovisi, Ed. Hard, cutting-edge crime fiction, to 3,000 words, "with impact." "It's a good idea to read an issue before submitting a story." Payment varies, on publication. Query for articles, book and film reviews.

HARPER'S MAGAZINE— 666 Broadway, New York, NY 10012. Attn: Eds. Will consider unsolicited fiction manuscripts. Query for nonfiction (very limited market). No poetry. SASE required.

HIGHLIGHTS FOR CHILDREN— 803 Church St., Honesdale, PA 18431–1824. Christine French Clark, Man. Ed. Fiction on sports, humor, adventure, mystery, etc., 900 words, for 8-to 12-year-olds. Easy rebus form, 100 to 120 words, and easy-to-read stories, to 500 words, for beginning readers. "We are partial to stories in which the protagonist solves a dilemma through his or her own resources." Pays from 14¢ a word, on acceptance. Buys all rights.

HOMETOWN PRESS—2007 Gallatin St., Huntsville, AL 35801. Jeffrey C. Hindman, M.D., Ed.-in-Chief. Fiction, 800 to 2,500 words, well-crafted and tightly written, suitable for family reading. New and unpublished writers welcome. Guidelines.

THE JOYFUL WOMAN—P.O. Box 90028, Chattanooga, TN 37412. Joy Rice Martin, Ed. First-person inspirational true stories and sketches, 500 to 1,000 words; occasionally uses some fiction. Pays 3¢ to 4¢ a word, on publication.

LADIES' HOME JOURNAL— 125 Park Ave., New York, NY 10017. Fiction; only accepted through agents.

THE LOOKOUT— 8121 Hamilton Ave., Cincinnati, OH 45231. David Faust, Ed. Short-shorts, 1,000 to 1,800 words, with moral or Christian themes. No historical fiction, science fiction, or fantasy. Pays to 9¢ a word, on acceptance.

THE MAGAZINE OF FANTASY AND SCIENCE FICTION—Box 420, Lincoln City, OR 97367. Kristine Kathryn Rusch, Ed. Fantasy and science fiction stories, to 15,000 words. Pays 5¢to 7¢ a word, on acceptance.

MATURE LIVING—127 Ninth Ave. N., Nashville, TN 37234. Al Shackleford, Ed. Fiction, 900 to 1,200 words, for senior adults. Must be consistent with Christian principles. Pays $75, on acceptance.

MIDSTREAM—110 E. 59th St., New York, NY 10022. Joel Carmichael, Man. Ed. Fiction with a Jewish/Zionist reference, to 3,000 words. Pays 5¢ a word, after publication. Allow 3 months for response.

NA'AMAT WOMAN—200 Madison Ave., 21st Fl., New York, NY 10016. Judith A. Sokoloff, Ed. Short stories, approximately 2,500 words, with Jewish theme. Pays 10¢ a word, on publication.

NEW MYSTERY MAGAZINE—The Flatiron Bldg., 175 Fifth Ave., Suite 2001, New York, NY 10010–7703. Charles Raisch, Ed. Quarterly. Mystery, crime, detection, and suspense short stories, 2,000 to 6,000 words, with "sympathetic characters in trouble and visual scenes." Book reviews, 250 to 2,000 words, of upcoming or recently published novels. Pays 3¢ to 10¢ a word, on publication. No guidelines; study back issues.

THE NEW YORKER—20 W. 43rd St., New York, NY 10036. Attn: Fiction Dept. Short stories, humor, and satire. Payment varies, on acceptance.

PLAYBOY—680 N. Lake Shore Dr., Chicago, IL 60611. Alice K. Turner, Fiction Ed. Limited market.

PLAYGIRL—801 Second Ave., New York, NY 10017. Judy Cole, Ed.-in-Chief. Contemporary, erotic fiction, from a female perspective, 3,000 to 4,000 words. "Fantasy Forum," 1,000 to 2,000 words. Pays from $500; $25 to $100 for "Fantasy Forum," after acceptance.

POWER AND LIGHT—6401 The Paseo, Kansas City, MO 64131. Beula J. Postlewait, Preteen Ed. Fiction, 500 to 800 words, for grades 5 to 6, defining Christian experiences and values. Pays 5¢ a word for multiple-use rights, on publication.

PURPOSE—616 Walnut Ave., Scottdale, PA 15683–1999. James E. Horsch, Ed. Fiction, 750 words, on problem solving from a Christian point of view. Poetry, 3 to 12 lines. Pays to 5¢ a word for fiction; to $1 per line for poetry, on acceptance.

QUEEN'S QUARTERLY—Queens Univ., Kingston, Ont., Canada K7L 3N6. Attn: Fiction Ed. Fiction, to 5,000 words, in English and French. Pays to $300, on publication.

RANGER RICK—8925 Leesburg Pike, Vienna, VA 22184. Deborah Churchman, Fiction Ed. Action-packed nature- and conservation-related fiction, to 900 words, for 6- to 12-year-olds. No anthropomorphism. "Multicultural stories welcome." Pays to $550, on acceptance. Buys all rights. Guidelines.

REDBOOK—224 W. 57th St., New York, NY 10019. Dawn Raffel, Fiction Ed. Fresh, distinctive short stories, of interest to women. No unsolicited poetry, novellas, or novels accepted. Pays from $1,500 for short stories (to 25 pages), on acceptance. Allow 12 weeks for reply.

ST. ANTHONY MESSENGER—1615 Republic St., Cincinnati, OH 45210–1298. Norman Perry, O.F.M., Ed. Barbara Beckwith, Man. Ed. Fiction that makes readers think about issues, lifestyles, and values. Pays 14¢ a word, on acceptance. Queries or manuscripts accepted.

SCHOOL MATES—U.S. Chess Federation, 186 Rte. 9W, New Windsor, NY 12553–7698. Brian Bugbee, Ed. Fiction and articles, 250 to 800 words, and short fillers, related to chess for beginning chess players (primarily children, ages 6 to 16). "Instructive, but there's room for fun puzzles, anecdotes, etc. All chess related." Pays from $20, on publication. Query; limited free-lance market.

SEA KAYAKER—P.O. Box 17170, Seattle, WA 98107–0870. Christopher Cunningham, Ed. Short stories exclusively related to ocean kayaking, 1,000 to 3,000 words. Pays on publication.

SEVENTEEN—850 Third Ave., New York, NY 10022. Ben Shrank, Fiction Ed. High-quality, literary short fiction, to 4,000 words. Pays on acceptance.

SPORTS AFIELD—250 W. 55th St., New York, NY 10019. Terry McDonell, Ed-in-Chief. Occasional fiction, 1,500 words, on hunting, fishing, outdoor and nature-related topics. Humor. Payment varies, on acceptance.

STRAIGHT—8121 Hamilton Ave., Cincinnati, OH 45231. Heather E. Wallace, Ed. Well-constructed fiction, 1,000 to 1,500 words, showing Christian teens using Bible principles in everyday life. Contemporary, realistic teen characters a must. Most interested in school, church, dating, and family life stories. Pays 5¢ to 7¢ a word, on acceptance. Guidelines.

'TEEN— 6420 Wilshire Blvd., Los Angeles, CA 90048-5515. Attn: Fiction Dept. Short stories, 2,500 to 4,000 words: mystery, teen situations, adventure, romance, humor for teens. Pays from $200, on acceptance.

TEEN LIFE—1445 Boonville Ave., Springfield, MO 65802-1894. Tammy Bicket, Ed. Fiction, to 1,200 words, for 13- to 19-year-olds. Articles, 500 to 1,000 words. Strong evangelical emphasis a must: believable characters working out their problems according to biblical principles. Buys first rights; pays on acceptance. Reprints considered.

TQ/TEEN QUEST—2221 Walnut Hill Ln., Irving, TX 75038. Christopher Lyon, Ed. Fiction, 1,500 to 2,000 words, for Christian teens. Pays 10¢ to 15¢ a word, on publication. No queries.

TRUE CONFESSIONS—233 Park Ave. S., New York, NY 10003. Pat Byrdsong, Ed. Timely, emotional, first-person stories, 2,000 to 10,000 words, on romance, family life, and problems of today's young blue-collar women. Pays 5¢ a word, after publication.

VIRGINIA—The Country Publishers, Inc., P.O. Box 798, Berryville, VA 22611. Garrison Ellis, Ed. Quarterly. Fiction, 1,500 to 2,000 words, with Virginia setting or reference. Pays $200 to $300, 30 days after publication.

VIRTUE— 4050 Lee Vance View, Colorado Springs, CO 80918-7102. Jeanette Thomason, Ed. Fiction, 1,200 to 1,400 words, with a Christian slant; inspirational, women's spiritual journeys, women's perspectives. Pays 15¢ to 25¢ a word, on publication. Query with SASE for articles.

WESTERN PEOPLE—Box 2500, Saskatoon, Sask., Canada S7K 2C4. Attn: Ed. Short stories, 1,200 to 2,500 words, on subjects or themes of interest to rural readers in western Canada. Pays $100 to $200, on acceptance. Enclose international reply coupons and SAE.

WOMAN'S WORLD—270 Sylvan Ave., Englewood Cliffs, NJ 07632. Attn: Fiction Dept. Fast-moving short stories, about 1,700 words, with light romantic theme. (Specify "short story" on outside of envelope.) Mini-mysteries, 1,200 words, with "whodunit" or "howdunit" theme. No science fiction, fantasy, or historical romance and no horror, ghost stories, or gratuitous violence; no holiday themes. "Dialogue-driven romances help propel the story." Pays $1,000 for short stories, $500 for mini-mysteries, on acceptance. SASE for guidelines.

YANKEE—Yankee Publishing Co., P.O. Box 520, Dublin, NH 03444. Judson Hale, Ed. Edie Clark, Fiction Ed. High-quality, literary short fiction, to 3,000 words (shorter preferred), with New England setting; no sap buckets or lobster pot stereotypes. Pays $1,000, on acceptance.

DETECTIVE AND MYSTERY

ALFRED HITCHCOCK MYSTERY MAGAZINE—1270 Ave. of the Americas, New York, NY 10020. Cathleen Jordan, Ed. Well-plotted, previously unpublished mystery, detective, suspense, and crime short stories, to 14,000 words. Submissions by new writers strongly encouraged. Pays 8¢ a word, on acceptance. No multiple submissions, please. (Submissions sent to *AHMM* are not considered for, or read by, *Ellery Queen's Mystery Magazine*.) Guidelines with SASE.

ARMCHAIR DETECTIVE—129 W. 56th St., New York, NY 10019. Kate Stine, Ed.-in-Chief. Judi Vause, Man. Ed./Pub. Articles on mystery and detective fiction; biographical sketches, reviews, etc. No fiction. Pays $12 a printed page; reviews are unpaid.

ELLERY QUEEN'S MYSTERY MAGAZINE—1270 Ave. of the Americas, 10th Fl., New York, NY 10020. Janet Hutchings, Ed. Detective, crime, and mystery fiction, approximately 1,500 to 10,000 words. Occasionally publishes novelettes, to 20,000 words, by established authors and humorous mystery verse. No sex, sadism, or sensationalism. Particularly interested in new writers and "first stories." Pays 3¢ to 8¢ a word, on acceptance.

HARDBOILED—Gryphon Publications, P.O. Box 209, Brooklyn, NY 11228–0209. Gary Lovisi, Ed. Hard, cutting-edge crime fiction (suspense, noir, private eye) to 3,000 words. Payment varies, on publication. Query for articles, book and film reviews, and longer fiction (or novel excerpts).

MURDEROUS INTENT—P.O. Box 5947, Vancouver, WA 98668–5947. Margo Power, Ed./Pub. Quarterly. Mystery and suspense stories and mystery-related articles, 2,000 to 4,000 words; fillers, to 750 words; poems, to 30 lines. "We see way too many stories of husband and wife bumping each other off. We love humor in mysteries. Surprise us!" Pays $10, on acceptance. Query for nonfiction.

MYSTERY TIME—P.O. Box 2907, Decatur, IL 62524. Linda Hutton, Ed. Semiannual. Suspense, 1,500 words, and poems about mysteries, up to 16 lines. "We prefer female protagonists. No gore or violence." Pays $5, on acceptance.

NEW MYSTERY MAGAZINE—The Flatiron Bldg., 175 Fifth Ave., Suite 2001, New York, NY 10010–7703. Charles Raisch, Ed. Mystery, crime, detection, and suspense short stories, 2,000 to 6,000 words. No true crime. Book reviews, 250 to 2,000 words, of upcoming or recently published novels. Pays $15 to $300, on publication. No guidelines; study back issues.

OVER MY DEAD BODY!—P.O. Box 1778, Auburn, WA 98071–1778. Cherie Jung, Features Ed. Mystery, suspense, and crime fiction, to 4,000 words. Author profiles, interviews, and mystery-related travel, 750 to 1,500 words. Fillers, to 100 words. Include B&W photos. "We are entertainment for mystery fans, from cozy to hardboiled and everything in between." Pays 1¢ a word for fiction; $10 to $25 for nonfiction; $5 for fillers; $10 to $25 for illustrations, on publication.

RED HERRING MYSTERY MAGAZINE—P.O. Box 8278, Prairie Village, KS 66208. Attn: Eds. Quarterly. Mystery fiction, 2,500 to 6,000 words. Mystery-related poetry (to 30 lines), fillers, puzzles and B&W line drawings. No gratuitous sex or violence. No true crime. Pays $10 plus copy, on publication.

SCIENCE FICTION AND FANTASY

ABERRATIONS—P.O. Box 460430, San Francisco, CA 94146. Richard Blair, Man. Ed. Michael Andre-Driussi, Sr. Fiction Ed. Science fiction, horror, and fantasy, to 8,000 words. "Experimental, graphic, multi-genre is O.K. with science fiction/fantasy/horror tie-in." Pays ¼¢ a word, on publication. Guidelines.

ABORIGINAL SF—P.O. Box 2449, Woburn, MA 01888–0849. Charles C. Ryan, Ed. Short stories, 2,500 to 7,500 words, and poetry, one to 2 typed pages, with strong science content, lively, unique characters, and well-designed plots. No sword and sorcery, horror, or fantasy. Pays $200 for fiction, $15 for poetry, $4 for science fiction jokes, and $20 for cartoons, on publication.

ABSOLUTE MAGNITUDE—P.O. Box 13, Greenfield, MA 01302. Warren Lapine, Ed. Quarterly. Technical science fiction, 1,000 to 25,000 words. No fantasy, horror, satire, or funny science fiction. Pays 3¢ to 5¢ a word (1¢ a word for reprints), on publication. Guidelines.

ADVENTURES OF SWORD & SORCERY—P.O. Box 285, Xenia, OH 45385. Randy Dannenfelser, Ed. Quarterly. High fantasy and heroic fantasy, 1,000 to 8,000 words. Pays 3¢ to 6¢ a word, on acceptance.

ANALOG SCIENCE FICTION AND FACT—1270 Ave. of the Americas, New York, NY 10020. Stanley Schmidt, Ed. Science fiction with strong characters in believable future or alien setting: short stories, 2,000 to 7,500 words; novelettes, 10,000 to 20,000 words; serials, to 80,000 words. Also uses future-related articles. Pays to 7¢ a word, on acceptance. Query for serials and articles.

ASIMOV'S SCIENCE FICTION MAGAZINE—1270 Ave. of the Americas, New York, NY 10020. Gardner Dozois, Ed. Short, character-oriented science fiction and fantasy, to 15,000 words. Pays 5¢ to 8¢ a word, on acceptance. Guidelines.

CENTURY—Century Publishing, Inc., P.O. Box 150510, Brooklyn, NY 11215–0510. Robert K.J. Killheffer, Ed. Literary science fiction, fantasy, and magic realism, 1,000 to 20,000 words. Pays 4¢ to 6¢ a word, on acceptance.

DRAGON MAGAZINE—201 Sheridan Springs Rd., Lake Geneva, WI 53147. Anthony J. Bryant, Ed. Barbara G. Young, Fiction Ed. Articles, 1,500 to 7,500 words, on fantasy and science fiction role-playing games. Fantasy, 1,500 to 8,000 words. Pays 5¢ to 8¢ a word for fiction, on acceptance. Pays 4¢ a word for articles, on publication. All submissions must include a disclosure form. Guidelines.

FANTASY & TERROR—See *Fantasy Macabre.*

FANTASY MACABRE—P.O. Box 20610, Seattle, WA 98102. Jessica Salmonson, Ed. Fiction, to 3,000 words, including translations. "We look for a tale that is strong in atmosphere, with menace that is suggested and threatening rather than the result of dripping blood and gore." Pays 1¢ a word, to $30 per story, on publication. Also publishes *Fantasy & Terror* for poetry-in-prose pieces.

HAUNTS—Nightshade Publications, Box 8068, Cranston, RI 02920–0068. Joseph K. Cherkes, Ed. Horror, science/fantasy, and supernatural short stories with strong characters, 1,500 to 8,000 words. No explicit sexual scenes or gratuitous violence. Pays ½¢ to 1¢ a word, on publication. Manuscripts read January through June.

HOBSON'S CHOICE: SCIENCE FICTION AND TECHNOLOGY—The Starwind Press, P.O. Box 98, Ripley, OH 45167. Attn: Submissions Ed. Science fiction and fantasy, 2,000 to 10,000 words. Articles and literary criticism, 1,000 to 5,000 words, for readers interested in science and technology. Query for nonfiction. Pays 1¢ to 4¢ a word, on acceptance.

THE LEADING EDGE—3163 JKHB, Provo, UT 84602. Alex Grover, Ed. Semiannual. Science fiction and fantasy, 3,000 to 12,000 words; poetry, to 600 lines; and articles, to 8,000 words, on science, scientific speculation, and literary criticism. No excessive profanity, overt violence, or excessive sexual situations. No simultaneous submissions. Pays $10 to $100, on publication. Guidelines.

THE MAGAZINE OF FANTASY AND SCIENCE FICTION—P.O. Box 479, Lincoln City, OR 97367. Kristine Kathryn Rusch, Ed. Fantasy and science fiction stories, to 10,000 words. Pays 5¢ to 7¢ a word, on acceptance.

MAGIC REALISM—P.O. Box 922648, Sylmar, CA 91392–2648. C. Darren Butler, Ed. Julie Thomas, Man. Ed. Quarterly. Stories, to 7,500 words (4,000 words preferred), of magic realism, exaggerated realism, some genre fantasy/dark fantasy. Occasionally publish glib fantasy like that found in folktales, fairy tales, and myths. No occult, sleight-of-hand magicians, or wizards/witches. Pays ¼¢ per word for prose; $3 per page for poetry. SASE for guidelines.

MARION ZIMMER BRADLEY'S FANTASY MAGAZINE—P.O. Box 249, Berkeley, CA 94701. Marion Zimmer Bradley, Ed. Quarterly. Well-plotted stories, 3,500 to 4,000 words. Action and adventure fantasy "with no particular objection to modern settings." Send SASE for guidelines before submitting. Pays 3¢ to 10¢ a word, on acceptance.

NEXT PHASE—Phantom Press Publications, 5A Green Meadow Dr., Nantucket Island, MA 02554. Kim Guarnaccia, Ed. Science fiction, fantasy, experimental fiction, and commentary, to 3,000 words, and interviews with authors, poets, or artists. Poetry, any length. "We prefer environmentally or socially conscious fiction." Pays in copies.

OMNI—General Media International, 277 Park Ave., 4th Fl., New York, NY 10172–0003. Ellen Datlow, Fiction Ed. On-line magazine. Strong, realistic science fiction, 2,000 to 10,000 words, with good characterizations. "We want to intrigue our readers with mindbroadening, thought-provoking stories that will excite their sense of wonder." Some fantasy. No horror, ghost, or sword and sorcery tales. Pays $1,300 to $2,250, on acceptance. SASE.

PIRATE WRITINGS—P.O. Box 329, Brightwaters, NY 11718–0329. Edward J. McFadden, Pub./Ed. Tom Piccirilli, Assoc. Ed. Mystery, science fiction, fantasy, 250 to 6,000 words. Poetry, to 20 lines. Pays 1¢ to 5¢ a word, on publication.

PLOT MAGAZINE—Calypso Publishing, P.O. Box 1351, Sugar Land, TX 77487–1351. Christina C. Russell, Man. Ed. Fantasy, science fiction, horror, suspense, and speculative fiction, to 7,500 words. "We encourage new and emerging writers. If your story can give us gooseflesh, we want to see it." Pays $10 for stories, $5 for line drawings, on acceptance.

SCAVENGER'S NEWSLETTER—519 Ellinwood, Osage City, KS 66523. Janet Fox, Ed. Flash fiction, 1,200 words, in the genres of science fiction, fantasy, horror, and mystery. Articles, 1,000 words, pertaining to writing and art in those genres. Poems, to 10 lines, and humor, 500 to 700 words, for writers and artists. "Most of the magazine is market information." Pays $4 for fiction, articles, and cover art; $2 for humor, poems, and inside art, on acceptance.

SCIENCE FICTION CHRONICLE—P.O. Box 022730, Brooklyn, NY 11202–0056. Andrew Porter, Ed. News items, 200 to 500 words, for science fiction and fantasy readers, professionals, and booksellers. Interviews with authors, 2,500 to 4,000 words. No fiction. Pays 3½¢ to 5¢ a word, on publication. Query.

THE SCREAM FACTORY—Deadline Press, 16473 Redwood Lodge Rd., Los Gatos, CA 95030. Bob Morrish, Ed. Quarterly. Articles, 1,000 to 7,000 words, on horror fiction and film. Interviews, 750 to 4,000 words, with authors and directors; brief, analytical reviews, 100 to 400 words, of old and new books. No fiction. Query. Pays ½¢ a word, on publication.

TALEBONES—Fairwood Press, 12205 1st Ave. S., Seattle, WA 98168. Patrick J. Swenson, Ed. Science fiction and dark fantasy, to 5,000 words. Articles, to 3,000 words, on the state of speculative fiction. Poetry. Cartoons with science fiction or fantasy themes. "I'm looking for science fiction and dark fantasy with strong characters and entertaining story lines. Fiction should be more toward the darker side, without being pure horror." Pays 1¢ a word, on acceptance.

2AM MAGAZINE—P.O. Box 6754, Rockford, IL 61125–1754. Gretta M. Anderson, Ed. Fiction, of varying lengths. "We prefer dark fantasy/horror; great science fiction and sword and sorcery stories are welcome." Profiles and intelligent commentaries. Poetry, to 50 lines. Pays from ½¢ a word, on acceptance. Guidelines.

WORLDS OF FANTASY & HORROR—123 Crooked Ln., King of Prussia, PA 19406–2570. George Scithers, Pub. Darrell Schweitzer, Ed. Quarterly. Fantasy and horror (no science fiction), to 7,000 words. Pays about 3¢, on acceptance. Guidelines.

CONFESSION AND ROMANCE

BLACK CONFESSIONS—See *Black Romance.*

BLACK ROMANCE—233 Park Ave. S., New York, NY 10003. Marcia Y. Mahan, Ed. Romance fiction, 4,500 to 5,000 words, and relationship articles. Queries preferred. Pays $100 to $125, on publication. Also publishes *Black Secrets, Bronze Thrills, Black Confessions,* and *Jive.* Guidelines.

BLACK SECRETS—See *Black Romance.*

BRONZE THRILLS—See *Black Romance.*

INTIMACY—233 Park Ave. S., 7th Fl., New York, NY 10003. Marcia Y. Mahan, Ed. Fiction, 5,000 to 5,800 words, for black women ages 18 to 45; must have contemporary plot and contain 2 romantic and intimate love scenes. Pays $100 to $125, on publication. Guidelines.

JIVE—See *Black Romance.*

MODERN ROMANCES—233 Park Ave. S., New York, NY 10003. Eileen Fitzmaurice, Ed. Romantic and topical confession stories, 2,000 to 10,000 words, with reader-identification and strong emotional tone. Pays 5¢ a word, after publication. Buys all rights.

TRUE CONFESSIONS—233 Park Ave. S., New York, NY 10003. Pat Byrdsong, Ed. Timely, emotional, first-person stories, 2,000 to 10,000 words, on romance, family life, and problems of today's young blue-collar women. Pays 5¢ a word, after publication.

TRUE EXPERIENCE—233 Park Ave. S., New York, NY 10003. Rose Bernstein, Ed. Heather Young, Assoc. Ed. Realistic first-person stories, 1,000 to 12,000 words, on family life, single life, love, romance, overcoming hardships, mysteries. Pays 3¢ a word, after publication.

TRUE LOVE—233 Park Ave. S., New York, NY 10003. Kristina M. Kracht, Ed. Fresh, young, true-to-life stories, on love and topics of current interest. Must be written in the past tense and first person. Pays 3¢ a word, after publication. Guidelines.

TRUE ROMANCE—233 Park Ave. S., New York, NY 10003. Pat Vitucci, Ed. True or true-to-life, dramatic and/or romantic first-person stories, 2,000 to 9,000 words. All genres: tragedy, mystery, peril, love, family struggles, etc. Topical themes. Love poems. "We enjoy working with new writers." Reports in 3 to 5 months. Pays 3¢ a word, a month after publication.

POETRY MARKETS

As the following list attests, the market for poetry in general magazines is quite limited: There aren't many general-interest magazines that use poetry, and in those that do, the competition to break into print is stiff, since editors use only a limited number of poems in each issue. In addition to the magazines listed here, writers may find their local newspapers receptive to poetry.

While poetry may be scant in general-interest magazines, it is the backbone of a majority of the college, little, and literary magazines (see page 695). Poets will also find a number of competitions offering cash awards for unpublished poems in the *Literary Prize Offers* list.

ALOHA, THE MAGAZINE OF HAWAII AND THE PACIFIC—P.O. Box 3260, Honolulu, HI 96801. Cheryl Chee Tsutsumi, Ed. Poetry relating to Hawaii. Pays $30 per poem, on publication.

AMERICA—106 W. 56th St., New York, NY 10019. Patrick Samway, S.J., Literary Ed. Serious poetry, preferably in contemporary prose idiom, 10 to 25 lines. Occasional light verse. Submit 2 or 3 poems at a time. Pays $1.40 per line, on publication. Guidelines. SASE required.

POETRY MARKETS

THE AMERICAN SCHOLAR—1811 Q St. N.W., Washington, DC 20009–9974. Joseph Epstein, Ed. Highly original poetry for college-educated, intellectual readers. Pays $50, on acceptance.

THE ATLANTIC MONTHLY—77 N. Washington St., Boston, MA 02114. Peter Davison, Poetry Ed. Previously unpublished poetry of highest quality. Limited market; only 2 to 3 poems an issue. Interested in new poets. Occasionally uses light verse. "No simultaneous submissions; we make prompt decisions." Pays excellent rates, on acceptance.

CAPPER'S—1503 S.W. 42nd St., Topeka, KS 66609–1265. Nancy Peavler, Ed. Free verse, light verse, traditional, nature, and inspirational poems, 4 to 16 lines, with simple everyday themes. Submit up to 6 poems at a time, with SASE. Pays $10 to $15, on acceptance.

CHILDREN'S PLAYMATE—P.O. Box 567, Indianapolis, IN 46206. Terry Harshman, Ed. Poetry for children, 6 to 8 years old, on good health, nutrition, exercise, safety, seasonal and humorous subjects. Pays from $15, on publication. Buys all rights.

THE CHRISTIAN SCIENCE MONITOR—One Norway St., Boston, MA 02115. Elizabeth Lund, Poetry Ed. Finely crafted poems that celebrate the extraordinary in the ordinary. Seasonal material always needed. No violence, sensuality, racism, death and disease, helplessness, hopelessness. Short poems preferred; submit no more than 5 poems at a time. SASE required. Pays varying rates, on publication.

COMMONWEAL—15 Dutch St., New York, NY 10038. Rosemary Deen, Poetry Ed. Catholic. Serious, witty poetry. Pays 50¢ a line, on publication. SASE required. No submissions accepted June to September.

COMPLETE WOMAN—Dept. P, 875 N. Michigan Ave., Suite 3434, Chicago, IL 60611. Attn: Poetry Ed. Send poetry with SASE. Pays in one copy.

COUNTRY WOMAN—P.O. Box 989, Greendale, WI 53129. Kathy Pohl, Man. Ed. Traditional rural poetry and light verse, 4 to 30 lines, on rural experiences and country living; also seasonal poetry. Poems must rhyme. Pays $10 to $25, on acceptance.

EVANGEL—Light and Life Press, Box 535002, Indianapolis, IN 46253–5002. Julie Innes, Ed. Free Methodist. Devotional or nature poetry, 8 to 16 lines. Pays $10, on publication.

MATURE YEARS—201 Eighth Ave. S., P.O. Box 801, Nashville, TN 37202. Marvin W. Cropsey, Ed. United Methodist. Poetry, to 14 lines, on preretirement, retirement, Christianity, inspiration, seasonal subjects, aging. No "saccharine" poetry. Submit up to 6 poems at a time. Pays 50¢ to $1 per line.

MIDSTREAM—110 E. 59th St., New York, NY 10022. M.S. Solow, Poetry Ed. Poetry of Jewish interest. "Brevity highly recommended." Pays $25, on publication. Allow 3 months for response.

THE MIRACULOUS MEDAL—475 E. Chelten Ave., Philadelphia, PA 19144–5785. John W. Gouldrick, C.M., Ed. Catholic. Religious verse, to 20 lines. Pays 50¢ a line, on acceptance.

694

MODERN BRIDE—249 W. 17th St., New York, NY 10011. Mary Ann Cavlin, Exec. Ed. Short verse of interest to bride and groom. Pays $25 to $35, on acceptance.

THE NATION—72 Fifth Ave., New York, NY 10011. Grace Schulman, Poetry Ed. Poetry of high quality. Pays after publication. SASE requried.

NATIONAL ENQUIRER—Lantana, FL 33463. Kathy Martin, Fillers Ed. Short poems, with traditional rhyming verse, of an amusing, philosophical, or inspirational nature. No experimental poetry. Original epigrams, humorous anecdotes, and "daffynitions." Submit seasonal/holiday material at least 2 months in advance. Pays $25, after publication. Material will not be returned; do not send SASE.

THE NEW YORKER—20 W. 43rd St., New York, NY 10036. Attn: Poetry Ed. First-rate poetry. Pays top rates, on acceptance. Include SASE.

PATHWAYS—Christian Board of Publication, Box 179, St. Louis, MO 63166. Christine Hershberger Miner, Ed. Short poems by 12-to 15-year-olds. Pays 30¢ a line, on publication.

PURPOSE—616 Walnut Ave., Scottdale, PA 15683–1999. James E. Horsch, Poetry Ed. Poetry, to 8 lines, with challenging Christian discipleship angle. Pays 50¢ to $1 a line, on acceptance.

RADIANCE: THE MAGAZINE FOR LARGE WOMEN—P.O. Box 30246, Oakland, CA 94604. Alice Ansfield, Ed./Pub. Quarterly. Poetry for women. Payment varies, on publication.

ST. JOSEPH'S MESSENGER—P.O. Box 288, Jersey City, NJ 07303–0288. Sister Ursula Maphet, Ed. Light verse and traditional poetry, 4 to 40 lines. Pays $5 to $20, on publication.

THE SATURDAY EVENING POST—P.O. Box 567, Indianapolis, IN 46206. Steven Pettinga, Post Scripts Ed. Light verse and humor. No conventional poetry. SASE required. Pays $15, on publication.

THE UNITED METHODIST REPORTER—P.O. Box 660275, Dallas, TX 75266–0275. John Lovelace, Ed. Religious verse, 4 to 16 lines. Pays $2, on acceptance.

WESTERN PEOPLE—P.O. Box 2500, Saskatoon, Sask., Canada S7K 2C4. Michael Gillgannon, Man. Ed. Short poetry with Western Canadian themes. Pays on acceptance. Send international reply coupons.

YANKEE—Yankee Publishing Co., P.O. Box 520, Dublin, NH 03444. Jean Burden, Poetry Ed. Serious poetry of high quality, to 30 lines. Pays $50 per poem for all rights, $35 for first rights, on publication. SASE required.

YESTERDAY'S MAGAZETTE—P.O. Box 18566, Sarasota, FL 34276. Ned Burke, Ed. Traditional poetry, to 24 lines. Pays in copies for poetry and short pieces.

COLLEGE, LITERARY, AND
LITTLE MAGAZINES

The thousands of literary journals, little magazines, and college quarterlies published today welcome work from novices and pros alike; editors are always interested in seeing traditional and experimental fiction, poetry, essays, reviews, short articles, criticism, and satire, and as long as the material is well-written, the fact that a writer is a beginner doesn't adversely affect his or her chances for acceptance.

Most of these smaller publications have small budgets and staffs, so they may be slow in their reporting time; several months is not unusual. In addition, they usually pay only in copies of the issue in which published work appears and some (particularly college magazines) do not read manuscripts during the summer.

Publication in the literary journals can, however, lead to recognition by editors of large-circulation magazines, who read the little magazines in their search for new talent. There is also the possibility of having one's work chosen for reprinting in one of the prestigious annual collections of work from the little magazines.

Because the requirements of these journals differ widely, it is important to study recent issues before submitting work to one of them. Large libraries may carry a variety of journals, or a writer may send a postcard to the editor and ask the price of a sample copy.

For a complete list of literary and college publications and little magazines, writers may consult such reference works as *The International Directory of Little Magazines and Small Presses*, published annually by Dustbooks (P.O. Box 100, Paradise, CA 95967).

AFRICAN AMERICAN REVIEW—Dept. of English, Indiana State Univ., Terre Haute, IN 47809. Joe Weixlmann, Ed. Essays on African American literature, theater, film, art, and culture; interviews; poems; fiction; and book reviews. Submit up to 6 poems. Pays an honorarium and copies. Query for book review assignments; send 3 copies of all other submissions. Responds in 3 months.

AFRICAN VOICES—270 W. 96th St., New York, NY 10025. Carolyn A. Butts, Exec. Ed. Bimonthly. Humorous, erotic, and dramatic fiction, 500 to 2,500 words, by ethnic writers. Nonfiction, 500 to 1,500 words, including investigative articles, artist profiles, essays, and first-person narratives. Pays in copies.

AGNI—Dept. TW, Boston Univ., Creative Writing Program, 236 Bay State Rd., Boston, MA 02215. Askold Melnyczuk, Ed. Erin Belieu, Man. Ed. Short stories, poetry, and essays. Manuscripts read October 1 to April 30.

ALABAMA LITERARY REVIEW—Troy State Univ., Smith 253, Troy, AL 36082. Theron Montgomery, Chief Ed. Semiannual. Contemporary, literary fiction and nonfiction, 3,500 words, and poetry, to 2 pages. Thought-provoking B&W photos. Pays in copies (honorarium when available). Responds within 3 months.

ALASKA QUARTERLY REVIEW—Univ. of Alaska Anchorage, 3211 Providence Dr., Anchorage, AK 99508. Attn: Eds. Short stories, novel excerpts, short plays, and poetry (traditional and unconventional forms). Submit manuscripts between August 15 and May 15. Pays in copies (and honorarium when funding is available).

ALBATROSS—P.O. Box 7787, North Port, FL 34287–0787. Richard Smyth, Richard Brobst, Eds. High-quality poetry; especially interested in ecological and nature poetry written in narrative form. Interviews with well-known poets. Submit 3 to 5 poems at a time with brief bio. Pays in copies.

AMELIA—329 E St., Bakersfield, CA 93304. Frederick A. Raborg, Jr., Ed. Poetry, to 100 lines; critical essays, to 2,000 words; reviews, to 500 words; belles lettres, to 1,000 words; fiction, to 4,500 words; fine pen-and-ink sketches; photos. Pays $35 for fiction and criticism, $10 to $25 for other non-fiction and artwork, $2 to $25 for poetry. Annual contest.

THE AMERICAN BOOK REVIEW—Unit for Contemporary Literature, Illinois State Univ., Campus Box 4241, Normal, IL 61790–4241. Romayne C. Rubinas, Man. Ed. Literary book reviews, 700 to 1,200 words. Pays 2-year subscription and copies. Query with clips of published reviews.

AMERICAN LITERARY REVIEW—Univ. of North Texas, P.O. Box 13827, Denton, TX 76203–6827. Barbara Rodman, Ed. Short fiction, to 30 double-spaced pages, and poetry (submit 3 to 5 poems). Pays in copies.

THE AMERICAN POETRY REVIEW—1721 Walnut St., Philadelphia, PA 19103. Attn: Eds. Highest quality contemporary poetry. Responds in 10 weeks.

THE AMERICAN SCHOLAR—1811 Q St. N.W., Washington, DC 20009–9974. Joseph Epstein, Ed. Articles, 3,500 to 4,000 words, on science, politics, literature, the arts, etc. Book reviews. Pays to $500 for articles, $100 for reviews, on publication.

THE AMERICAN VOICE—332 W. Broadway, Suite 1215, Louisville, KY 40202. Frederick Smock, Ed. Published 3 times per year. Avant-garde, literary fiction, nonfiction, and well-crafted poetry, any length (shorter works are preferred). "Please read our journal before attempting to submit." Payment varies, on publication.

AMERICAN WRITING— 4343 Manayunk Ave., Philadelphia, PA 19128. Alexandra Grilikhes, Ed. Semiannual. "We encourage experimentation, new writing that takes risks with form, point of view, language, perceptions. We're interested in the voice of the loner, states of being, and initiation." Fiction and nonfiction, to 3,500 words, and poetry. Pays in copies.

AMHERST REVIEW—Box 1811, Amherst College, P.O. Box 5000, Amherst, MA 01002–5000. Molly Lyons, Ed. Fiction, to 6,000 words. Manuscripts read September through February only. Pays in copies.

ANOTHER CHICAGO MAGAZINE—3709 N. Kenmore, Chicago, IL 60613. Attn: Ed. Semiannual. Fiction, essays on literature, and poetry. "We want writing that's urgent, new, and lives in the world." Pays $5 to $50, on acceptance.

ANTIETAM REVIEW—7 W. Franklin St., Hagerstown, MD 21740. Susanne Kass and Ann Knox, Eds.-in-Chief. Fiction, to 5,000 words; poetry and photography. Submissions from natives or residents of MD, PA, WV, VA, DE, or DC only. Pays from $20 to $100. Guidelines. Manuscripts read September through January.

THE ANTIGONISH REVIEW—St. Francis Xavier Univ., P.O. Box 5000, Antigonish, N.S., Canada B2G 2W5. George Sanderson, Ed. Poetry; short stories, essays, book reviews, 1,800 to 2,500 words. Pays in copies.

ANTIOCH REVIEW—P.O. Box 148, Yellow Springs, OH 45387–0148. Robert S. Fogarty, Ed. Timely articles, 2,000 to 8,000 words, on social sciences, literature, and humanities. Quality fiction. Poetry. No inspirational poetry. Pays $10 per printed page, on publication. Poetry considered from September to May; other material considered year-round.

APALACHEE QUARTERLY—Apalachee Press, P.O. Box 10469, Tallahassee, FL 32302. Barbara Hamby, Rikki Clark, Kim MacQueen, Bruce Boehrer, Beth Meekin, Eds. Experimental fiction, to 30 manuscript pages; poems (submit 3 to 5). Pays in copies. Manuscripts read September to May.

APPALACHIA—5 Joy St., Boston, MA 02108. Parkman D. Howe III, Poetry Ed. Semiannual publication of the Appalachian Mountain Club. Oldest mountaineering journal in the country covers nature, conservation, climbing, hiking, canoeing, and ecology. Poems, to 30 lines. Pays in copies.

ARACHNE—2363 Page Rd., Kennedy, NY 14747–9717. Susan L. Leach, Ed. Semiannual. Fiction, to 1,500 words. Poems (submit up to 7). "We are looking for rural material and would like first publication rights." No simultaneous submissions. Pays in copies. Manuscripts read in January and July.

ARIZONA COWBOY CONNECTION MAGAZINE—(formerly *Arizona Cowboy Poets Magazine*) P.O. Box 498, Prescott, AZ 86302. Sally Harper Bates, Geri Davis, Eds. Cowboy and western poetry, any length. Articles, 250 to 500 words, on cowboy views, themes, lifestyles, and attitudes; articles about families involved in the Arizona livestock community. Pays in copies.

ARIZONA QUARTERLY—Univ. of Arizona, Main Library B-541, Tucson, AZ 85721. Edgar A. Dryden, Ed. Criticism of American literature and culture from a theoretical perspective. No poetry or fiction. Pays in copies.

ART TIMES—P.O. Box 730, Mt. Marion, NY 12456. Raymond J. Steiner, Ed. Cheryl A. Rice, Poetry Ed. Fiction, to 1,500 words, and poetry, to 20 lines, for literate, art conscious readers (generally over 40 years old). Feature essays on the arts are staff-written. Pays $25 for fiction, in copies for poetry, on publication.

ARTFUL DODGE—College of Wooster, Wooster, OH 44691. Daniel Bourne, Ed. Annual. Fiction, to 20 pages. Literary essays, especially those involving personal narrative, to 15 pages. Poetry, including translations of contemporary poets; submit 3 to 6 poems at a time; long poems encouraged. Pays $5 per page, on publication, plus 2 copies. Manuscripts read year-round.

THE ASIAN PACIFIC AMERICAN JOURNAL—The Asian American Writers' Workshop, 37 St. Marks Pl., New York, NY 10003–7801. Curtis Chin, Man. Dir. Short stories, excerpts from longer fiction works, plays, and essays, 2,000 to 3,000 words, by emerging or established Asian American writers. Poetry (submit 4 to 6 poems). Pays in copies. Query required for reviews and interviews; queries preferred for other articles.

AURA LITERARY/ARTS REVIEW—P.O. Box 76, Univ. Center, UAB, Birmingham, AL 35294. Steve Mullen, Ed. Fiction and essays on literature, to 5,000 words; book reviews, to 4,000 words; poetry; photos. Pays in copies. Guidelines.

BANEKE—P.O. Box 2417, Gainesville, FL 32602. Jorge Ibanez, Ed. Articles, book reviews, and interviews on Latino writers and artists. Pays in copies. Query preferred.

BELLES LETTRES—11151 Captain's Walk Ct., N. Potomac, MD 20878–0441. Janet Mullaney, Ed. Published 3 times a year; devoted to literature by or about women. Articles, 250 to 2,000 words: reviews, interviews, rediscoveries, and retrospectives; columns on publishing news, reprints, and nonfiction titles. Query required. Pays in copies (plus honorarium if funds available).

THE BELLINGHAM REVIEW—The Signpost Press, MS 9053, Western Washington Univ., Bellingham, WA 98225. Robin Hemley, Ed. Semiannual. Fiction and nonfiction, to 10,000 words, and poetry, any length. Pays in copies and subscription. Manuscripts read from September 15 to May 1. Contest.

BELLOWING ARK—P.O. Box 45637, Seattle, WA 98145. Robert R. Ward, Ed. Bimonthly. Short fiction, poetry, and essays of varying lengths, that portray life as a positive, meaningful process. B&W photos; line drawings. Pays in copies. Manuscripts read year-round.

THE BELOIT FICTION JOURNAL—Box 11, Beloit College, Beloit, WI 53511. Fred Burwell, Ed. Short fiction, one to 35 pages, on all themes. No pornography, political propaganda, religious dogma. Pays in copies. Manuscripts read September to May.

BELOIT POETRY JOURNAL—RFD 2, Box 154, Ellsworth, ME 04605. Attn: Ed. Strong contemporary poetry, of any length or in any mode. Pays in copies. Guidelines.

BIG SKY STORIES—P.O. Box 477, Choteau, MT 59422. Happy Jack Feder, Ed. Bimonthly. Fiction, 1,000 to 5,000 words and 600 to 800 words, set in Montana or Wyoming before 1950. "Know your history. Our readers know theirs." Payment varies, on publication.

BLACK BEAR REVIEW—Black Bear Publications, 1916 Lincoln St., Croydon, PA 19021–8026. Ave Jeanne, Ed. Semiannual. Book reviews and contemporary poetry. "We publish poems with social awareness, but any well-written piece is considered." Pays in one copy.

BLACK RIVER REVIEW—855 Mildred Ave., Lorain, OH 44052–1213. Deborah Gilbert and Kaye Coller, Eds. Contemporary poetry, fiction (to 4,000 words), essays, short book reviews, B&W artwork. No greeting card verse or slick magazine prose. Submit between January 1 and May 1. Pays in copies. Guidelines.

THE BLACK WARRIOR REVIEW—The Univ. of Alabama, P.O. Box 2936, Tuscaloosa, AL 35486–2936. Mindy Wilson, Ed. Fiction; poetry; translations; reviews and essays. Pays $75 to $90 for fiction; $35 to $40 for poetry, on publication. Annual awards. Manuscripts read year-round.

THE BLOOMSBURY REVIEW—1762 Emerson St., Denver, CO 80218. Tom Auer, Ed. Marilyn Auer, Assoc. Ed. Book reviews, publishing features, interviews, essays, poetry. Pays $5 to $25, on publication.

BLUE UNICORN—22 Avon Rd., Kensington, CA 94707. Attn: Ed. Published in October, February, and June. "We are looking for originality of image, thought, and music; we rarely use poems over a page long." Submit up to 5 poems. Artwork used occasionally. Pays in one copy. Guidelines. Contest.

BLUELINE—English Dept., SUNY, Potsdam, NY 13676. Anthony Tyler, Ed. Essays and fiction, to 3,500 words, on Adirondack region or similar areas. Poems, to 75 lines; submit no more than 5. Pays in copies. Manuscripts read September to November 30.

BORDERLANDS: TEXAS POETRY REVIEW—P.O. Box 49818, Austin, TX 78765. Attn: Ed. Semiannual. "Outward-looking" poetry of a political, spiritual, ecological, or social nature. Bilingual writers and writers from Texas and the Southwest given special attention. Send up to 5 pages of unpublished poetry. Essays, to 3,000 words, on contemporary poets, especially those from the Southwest. Pays one copy. Query for essays and contest.

BOSTON REVIEW—E53, Room 407, 30 Wadsworth, MIT, Cambridge, MA 02139. Betsy Reed, Man. Ed. Reviews and essays, 800 to 3,000 words, on literature, art, music, film, photography. Original fiction, to 5,000 words. Poetry. Pays $40 to $100. Manuscripts read year-round.

BOTTOMFISH—21250 Stevens Creek Blvd., Cupertino, CA 95014. David Denny, Ed. Annual. Short stories, short-shorts, poetry, creative nonfiction, interviews, photography. Pays in copies. Manuscripts read September to February. (Decisions made in March. Magazine published in April.)

BOULEVARD— 4579 Laclede Ave., #332, St. Louis, MO 63108-2103. Richard Burgin, Ed. Published 3 times a year. High-quality fiction and articles, to 30 pages; poetry. Pays to $250, on publication.

BRIAR CLIFF REVIEW—Briar Cliff College, 3303 Rebecca St., Sioux City, IA 51104. Tricia Currans-Sheehan, Ed. Prose, to 5,000 words: fiction, humor/satire, Siouxland history, thoughtful nonfiction. Also poetry, book reviews, and art. "We're an eclectic literary and cultural magazine focusing on, but not limited to, Siouxland writers and subjects." Pays in copies. Manuscripts read August through October.

BUCKNELL REVIEW—Bucknell Univ., Lewisburg, PA 17837. Attn: Ed. Interdisciplinary journal in book form. Scholarly articles on arts, science, and letters. Pays in copies.

CALLALOO—Univ. of Virginia, Dept. of English, 322 Bryan Hall, Charlottesville, VA 22903. Charles H. Rowell, Ed. Fiction, poetry, drama, and popular essays by, and critical studies and bibliographies on Afro-American, Caribbean, and African artists and writers. Payment varies, on publication.

CALLIOPE—Creative Writing Program, Roger Williams Univ., Bristol, RI 02809–2921. Martha Christina, Ed. Short stories, to 2,500 words; poetry. Pays in copies and subscription. No submissions April through July.

CALYX, A JOURNAL OF ART & LITERATURE BY WOMEN—P.O. Box B, Corvallis, OR 97339. M. Donnelly, Man. Ed. Fiction, 5,000 words; book reviews, 1,000 words (please query about reviews); poetry, to 6 poems. Include short bio. Pays in copies and subscription. Guidelines. Submissions accepted October 1 to November 15.

CANADIAN FICTION MAGAZINE—Box 1061, Kingston, Ontario, Canada K7L 4Y5. Attn: Ed. High-quality short stories, novel excerpts, and experimental fiction, to 5,000 words, by Canadians. Interviews with Canadian authors; translations. Pays $10 per page, on publication. Annual prize, $500. Manuscripts read year-round.

THE CANDLELIGHT POETRY JOURNAL—P.O. Box 3184, St. Augustine, FL 32085. Carl Heffley and Robin Sherwood, Eds. Quarterly. Poetry, to 30 lines. (Submit no more than 5 poems.) Articles, 1,000 to 1,500 words, about poetry. Pays in copies. Queries required for articles.

THE CAPE ROCK—Dept. of English, Southeast Missouri State Univ., Cape Girardeau, MO 63701. Harvey E. Hecht, Ed. Semiannual. Poetry, to 70 lines, and B&W photography. (One photographer per issue; pays $100.) Pays in copies and $200 for best poem in each issue. Manuscripts read August to April.

THE CARIBBEAN WRITER—Univ. of the Virgin Islands, RR 02, Box 10,000, Kingshill, St. Croix, USVI 00850. Erika J. Waters, Ed. Annual. Fiction, to 15 pages (submit no more than 2 stories at a time), poems (no more than 5), and personal essays (no more than 2); the Caribbean should be central to the work. Blind submissions policy: place title only on manuscript; name, address, and title of manuscripts on separate sheet. Pays in copies. Annual deadline is September 30.

THE CAROLINA QUARTERLY—Greenlaw Hall CB#3520, Univ. of North Carolina, Chapel Hill, NC 27599–3520. Amber Vogel, Ed. Fiction, to 7,000 words, by new or established writers. Poetry, to 300 lines. Manuscripts read year-round.

THE CENTENNIAL REVIEW—312 Linton Hall, Michigan State Univ., East Lansing, MI 48824–1044. R.K. Meiners, Ed. Articles, 3,000 to 5,000 words, on sciences, humanities, and interdisciplinary topics. Pays in copies.

CENTURY—Century Publishing, Inc., P.O. Box 150510, Brooklyn, NY 11215–0510. Robert K.J. Killheffer, Ed. Literary science fiction, fantasy, and magic realism, 1,000 to 20,000 words. Pays 4¢ to 6¢ a word, on acceptance.

THE CHARITON REVIEW—Truman State Univ., Kirksville, MO 63501. Jim Barnes, Ed. Highest quality poetry and fiction, to 6,000 words. Modern and contemporary translations. "The only guideline is excellence in all matters."

CHELSEA—Box 773, Cooper Sta., New York, NY 10276. Richard Foerster, Ed. Alfredo de Palchi and Andrea Lockett, Assoc. Eds. Fresh, original fiction and nonfiction, to 25 manuscript pages. Poems (submit 4 to 6). "We are an eclectic literary magazine serving a sophisticated international audience. No racist, sexist, pornographic, or romance material." Query for book reviews. Pays $15 per page, on publication.

CHICAGO REVIEW—5801 S. Kenwood Ave., Chicago, IL 60637. David Nicholls, Ed. Essays, interviews, reviews, fiction, translations, poetry. Pays in copies plus one year's subscription. Manuscripts read year-round; replies in 2 to 3 months.

CHIRON REVIEW—522 E. South Ave., St. John, KS 67576–2212. Michael Hathaway, Ed. Contemporary fiction, to 4,000 words; articles, 500 to 1,000 words; and poetry, to 30 lines. Photos. Pays in copies. Poetry and chapbook contests.

CICADA—329 E St., Bakersfield, CA 93304. Frederick A. Raborg, Jr., Ed. Quarterly. Single haiku, sequences, or garlands; essays about the forms; haibun, tanka, renga, and fiction (one story per issue) related to haiku or Japan. Pays in copies.

CIMARRON REVIEW—205 Morrill Hall, Oklahoma State Univ., Stillwater, OK 74078–0135. E. P. Walkiewicz, Ed. Poetry, fiction, essays. Seeks an individual, innovative style that focuses on contemporary themes. Pays $50 for stories and essays; $15 for poems, plus one-year subscription. Manuscripts read year-round.

CINCINNATI POETRY REVIEW—Humanities Dept., College of Mt. St. Joseph, Cincinnati, OH 45233. Jeffrey Hillard, Ed. Semiannual. Poetry of all types. Pays in copies.

CLOCKWATCH REVIEW—Dept. of English, Illinois Wesleyan Univ., Bloomington, IL 61702–2900. James Plath, Ed. Semiannual. Fiction, to 4,000 words, and poetry, to 36 lines. "Our preference is for fresh language, a believable voice, a mature style, and a sense of the unusual in the subject matter." Pays $25 for fiction, $5 for poetry, on acceptance, plus copies. Manuscripts read year-round.

COLLAGES & BRICOLAGES—P.O. Box 86, Clarion, PA 16214. Marie-José Fortis, Ed. Annual. Fiction and nonfiction, plays, interviews, book reviews, and poetry. Surrealistic, feminist, and expressionistic drawings in ink. "I seek innovation and honesty. The magazine often focuses on one subject; query for themes." B&W photos; photo-collages. Pays in copies. Manuscripts read August through October.

COLUMBIA: A MAGAZINE OF POETRY & PROSE— 404 Dodge, Columbia Univ., New York, NY 10027. Attn: Ed. Semiannual. Fiction and nonfiction; poetry; essays; interviews; visual art. Pays in copies. Guidelines. Manuscripts read September to May.

THE COMICS JOURNAL—Fantagraphics, Inc., 7563 Lake City Way, Seattle, WA 98115. Attn: Man. Ed. "Looking for free lancers with working knowledge of the diversity and history of the comics medium." Reviews, 2,500 to 5,000 words; domestic and international news, 500 to 7,000 words; "Opening Shots" editorials, 500 to 1,500 words; interviews; and features, 2,500 to 5,000 words. Query for news and interviews. Pays 2¢ a word, on publication. Guidelines.

CONFRONTATION—Dept. of English, C.W. Post of L. I. U., Brookville, NY 11548. Martin Tucker, Ed. Serious fiction, 750 to 6,000 words. Crafted poetry, 10 to 200 lines. Pays $10 to $150, on publication.

THE CONNECTICUT POETRY REVIEW—P.O. Box 818, Stonington, CT 06378. J. Claire White and Harley More, Eds. Poetry, 5 to 20 lines, and reviews, 700 words. Pays $5 per poem, $10 per review, on acceptance. Manuscripts read September to January and April to June.

CONNECTICUT RIVER REVIEW—35 Lindsley Pl., Stratford, CT 06497. Norah Christianson, Ed. Semiannual. Poetry. Submit 3 to 5 poems, to 40 lines. Pays in one copy. Guidelines.

THE COOL TRAVELER—P.O. Box 273, Selinsgrove, PA 17870. Bob Moore, Pub./Ed. Bimonthly. Articles, 800 words, including excerpts from diaries and letters written while traveling. "We are a literary newsletter about place and experience; we emphasize 'what happened' rather than 'what to see.'" Pays to $20, on publication.

CQ/CALIFORNIA STATE POETRY QUARTERLY—California State Poetry Society, Box 7126, Orange, CA 92613. Attn: Ed. Board. Poetry, to 60 lines. All poets welcome. Payment is one copy. Responds within 2 to 4 months.

CRAZY QUILT—P.O. Box 632729, San Diego, CA 92163–2729. Attn: Eds. Fiction, to 4,000 words, poetry, one-act plays, and literary criticism. Also B&W art, photographs. Pays in copies. Manuscripts read year-round.

CRAZYHORSE—English Dept., Univ. of Arkansas, Little Rock, AR 72204. Address Poetry Ed., Fiction Ed. or Criticism Ed. Mainstream poetry, short fiction, and criticism. Pays $10, on publication.

THE CREAM CITY REVIEW—English Dept., Box 413, Univ. of Wisconsin, Milwaukee, WI 53201. Andrew Rivera, Cynthia Belmont, and Matt Roberson, Eds. Semiannual. "We serve a national audience interested in a diversity of writing (in terms of style, subject, genre) and writers (gender, race, class, publishing history, etc.). Both well-known and newly published writers of fiction, poetry, and essays are featured, along with B&W artwork." Pays in copies. Manuscripts read September to June.

CREATIVE NONFICTION—P.O. Box 81536, Pittsburgh, PA 15217–0336. Lee Gutkind, Ed. Christian Gatti, Asst. Ed. Creative nonfiction. "No length requirements, although we are always searching for writers who can communicate a strong idea with drama and humor in a few pages." Pays $10 per published page.

THE CREATIVE WOMAN—TAPP Group, 126 East Wing, Suite 288, Arlington Hgts., IL 60004. Margaret Choudhury, Ed. Quarterly. Essays, fiction, poetry, criticism, graphic arts, and photography, from a feminist perspective. SASE for upcoming themes. Payment varies, on publication.

THE CRESCENT REVIEW—P.O. Box 15069, Chevy Chase, MD 20825. J.T. Holland, Ed. Short stories only. Pays in copies. Manuscripts read July through October and January through April.

CUMBERLAND POETRY REVIEW—P.O. Box 120128, Acklen Sta., Nashville, TN 37212. Attn: Eds. High-quality poetry and criticism; translations. Send up to 6 poems with brief bio. No restrictions on form, style, or subject matter. Pays in copies.

CUTBANK—English Dept., Univ. of Montana, Missoula, MT 59812. Attn: Eds. Semiannual. Fiction, to 40 pages, (submit one story at a time) and poems (submit up to 5 poems). All manuscripts are considered for the Richard Hugo Memorial Poetry Award and the A.B. Guthrie, Jr. Short Fiction Award. Pays in copies. Guidelines. Manuscripts read August 15 to March 15.

DENVER QUARTERLY—Univ. of Denver, Denver, CO 80208. Bin Ramke, Ed. Literary, cultural essays and articles; poetry; book reviews; fiction. Pays $5 per printed page, after publication. Manuscripts read September 15 to May 15.

DESCANT—Texas Christian Univ., T.C.U. Box 32872, Fort Worth, TX 76129. Stanley Trachtenberg, Neil Easterbrook, and Steve Sherwood, Eds. Fiction, to 6,000 words. Poetry, to 40 lines. No restriction on form or subject. Pays in copies. Frank O'Connor Award ($500) is given each year for best short story published in the volume. Submit material September through May only.

THE DEVIL'S MILLHOPPER—The Devil's Millhopper Press, USC/Aiken, 171 University Pkwy., Aiken, SC 29801–6309. Stephen Gardner, Ed. Poetry. Send SASE for guidelines and contest information. Pays in copies.

THE DISTILLERY—Motlow State Community College, P.O. Box 88100, Tullahoma, TN 37388. Stuart Bloodworth, Ed. Semiannual. Fiction, 4,000 words; poetry, 100 lines; critical essays, photos and drawings. Pays in copies.

DOUBLE DEALER REDUX— 632 Pirate's Alley, New Orleans, LA 70116. Rosemary Jams, Ed. Quarterly. Fiction, essays, and poetry. "We showcase the work of promising writers." No payment. Query required.

DREAMS & VISIONS—Skysong Press, 35 Peter St. S., Orillia, Ontario, Canada L3V 5A8. Steve Stanton, Ed. Eclectic fiction, 2,000 to 6,000 words, that is "in some way unique and relevant to Christian readers today." Pays ½¢ per word.

EARTH'S DAUGHTERS—P.O. Box 41, Central Park Sta., Buffalo, NY 14215. Attn: Ed. Published 3 times a year. Fiction, to 1,000 words, poetry, to 40 lines, and B&W photos or drawings. "Finely crafted work with a feminist theme." Pays in copies. SASE for guidelines and themes.

ECLECTIC RAINBOWS—1538 Tennessee Walker Dr., Roswell, GA 30075. Linda T. Dennison, Ed./Pub. Semiannual. Essays (no nostalgia), articles, humor, celebrity interviews, 1,000 to 4,000 words. Poetry, to 36 lines. Limited fiction (no science fiction or horror). "Emphasis is on personal and planetary growth and transformation." Pays to $25, on publication. Guidelines. Contest.

ELF: ECLECTIC LITERARY FORUM—P.O. Box 392, Tonawanda, NY 14150. C. K. Erbes, Ed. Fiction, 3,500 words. Essays on literary themes, 3,500 words. Poetry, to 30 lines. Allow 4 to 6 weeks for response. Pays in 2 copies.

EPOCH—251 Goldwin Smith Hall, Cornell Univ., Ithaca, NY 14853–3201. Michael Koch, Ed. Serious fiction and poetry. Pays $5 a page for fiction and poetry. No submissions between April 15 and September 21. Guidelines.

EUREKA LITERARY MAGAZINE—Eureka College, P.O. Box 280, Eureka, IL 61530. Loren Logsdon, Ed. Nancy Perkins, Fiction Ed. Semiannual. Fiction, 25 to 30 pages, and poetry, submit up to 4 poems at a time. "We seek to promote no specific political agenda or literary theory. We strive to publish the best of the fiction and poetry submitted to us." Pays in copies.

EVENT—Douglas College, Box 2503, New Westminster, BC, Canada V3L 5B2. David Zieroth, Ed. Short fiction, reviews, poetry. Pays $22 per printed page, on publication.

EXPRESSIONS—P.O. Box 16294, St. Paul, MN 55116. Sefra Kobrin Pitzele, Ed. Semiannual. Literature and art by people with disabilities and ongoing illnesses. Fiction and articles, to 2,500 words. Poetry, to 64 lines. B&W artwork. "We hope to be a place where talented people who may have limited energy, finances, or physical ability can be published." Pays in copies. Guidelines. Contests.

EXQUISITE CORPSE—P.O. Box 25051, Baton Rouge, LA 70894. Andrei Codrescu, Ed. Fiction, nonfiction, and poetry for "a journal of letters and life." B&W photos and drawings. Read the magazine before submitting. Payment is 10 copies and one-year subscription. Manuscripts read year-round.

FARMER'S MARKET—Elgin Community College, 1700 Spartan Dr., Elgin, IL 60123–7193. Attn: Ed. Short stories, to 30 pages, and poetry. Pays in copies and subscription.

FEELINGS—Anderie Poetry Press, P.O. Box 85, Easton, PA 18044–0085. Carl and Carole Heffley, Eds. "America's Beautiful Poetry Magazine." Quarterly. Submit up to 3 poems, 30 lines each, "that convey an immediate sense of recognition, intensity of thought, and heart-to-heart communication."

704

Awards 3 editor's choice prizes of $10, plus readers' choice award of $10, each issue.

FICTION—c/o English Dept., City College of New York, Convent Ave. at 138th St., New York, NY 10031. Mark Jay Mirsky, Ed. Semiannual. Short stories and novel excerpts, to 5,000 words. "Read the magazine before submitting." Payment varies, on acceptance. Manuscripts not read in the summer.

FICTION INTERNATIONAL—English Dept., San Diego State Univ., San Diego, CA 92182–8140. Harold Jaffe, Ed. Post-modernist and politically committed fiction and theory. Pays in copies. Manuscripts read from September 1 to December 15.

THE FIDDLEHEAD—Campus House, Univ. of New Brunswick, Fredericton, N.B., Canada E3B 5A3. Attn: Ed. Serious fiction, 2,500 words. Pays about $10 per printed page, on publication. SAE with international reply coupons required. Manuscripts read year-round.

FIELD—Rice Hall, Oberlin College, Oberlin, OH 44074. Stuart Friebert, David Young, Alberta Turner, David Walker, Eds. Serious poetry, any length, by established and unknown poets; essays on poetics by poets. Translations by qualified translators. Payment varies, on publication. Manuscripts read year-round.

FINE MADNESS—P.O. Box 31138, Seattle, WA 98103–1138. Attn: Ed. Poetry, to 10 pages. Fiction by invitation only. Pays in copies. No simultaneous submissions. Guidelines.

FLYWAY—203 Ross Hall, Iowa State Univ., Ames, IA 50011–1201. Stephen Pett, Ed. Poetry, fiction, creative nonfiction, and reviews. Pays in copies. Manuscripts read September through May.

FOLIO—Dept. of Literature, American Univ., Washington, DC 20016. Attn: Ed. Semiannual. Fiction, poetry, translations, and essays. Photos and drawings. Pays in 2 copies. Submissions read September through March. Contest.

FOOTWORK, THE PATERSON LITERARY REVIEW—Poetry Ctr., Passaic County Comm. College, College Blvd., Paterson, NJ 07505–1179. Maria Mazziotti Gillan, Ed. High-quality fiction and poetry, to 10 pages. Pays in copies. Manuscripts read January through May.

THE FORMALIST—320 Hunter Dr., Evansville, IN 47711. William Baer, Ed. Metrical poetry, to 2 pages, including blank verse, couplets, and traditional forms such as sonnets, ballads, villanelles, etc. "Sound and rhythm make poetry what it is." Howard Nemerov Sonnet Award ($1,000); SASE for details.

THE FRACTAL—George Mason Univ., 4400 University Dr., Fairfax, VA 22030–4444. Sean C. Newborn, Sr. Ed. Literary fiction and poetry and academic nonfiction. Science fiction, fantasy, and horror stories of varying lengths. Guidelines. Pays $25 for fiction; $50 for nonfiction; $5 for poetry, on publication. Contest.

FREE INQUIRY—P.O. Box 664, Buffalo, NY 14226. Paul Kurtz, Ed. Tim Madigan, Exec. Ed. Articles, 500 to 5,000 words, for "literate and lively readership. Focus is on criticisms of religious belief systems, and how to lead an ethical life without a supernatural basis." Pays in copies.

FUGUE—Univ. of Idaho, English Dept., Brink Hall, Room 200, Moscow, ID 83843. Address Exec. Ed. Literary digest of the Univ. of Idaho. Fiction, to

7,000 words. Nonfiction, to 2,000 words, on writing. Poetry, any style, 100 lines. "We try to give new writers in all classifications of fiction and poetry a chance at publication." Manuscripts not returned; include SASE for editorial reply. Guidelines. Pays in copies.

FULL-TIME DADS—P.O. Box 577, Cumberland, ME 04021. Stephen Harris, Ed. Fiction, articles, essays, and humor, 600 to 1,200 words, and short poems for fathers who are very involved with their children. "All material must relate to supportive fatherhood." Payment is one copy.

GEORGETOWN REVIEW—G&R Publishing, 400 E. College St., Box 227, Georgetown, KY 40327. John Fulmer, Man. Ed. Tracy Heinlen, Ed. Semi-annual. Good quality fiction and essays, to 20 pages. Poetry (submit up to 5 poems). "We're not afraid of genre fiction (adventure, science fiction, etc.) if it's done well. We are looking for new, exciting voices." Also book and movie reviews. Pays in copies and "possible payment," on publication.

THE GEORGIA REVIEW—Univ. of Georgia, Athens, GA 30602–9009. Stanley W. Lindberg, Ed. Short fiction; literary, interdisciplinary, and personal essays; book reviews; poetry; artwork. Translations and novel excerpts strongly discouraged. No simultaneous submissions. Manuscripts read September through May.

THE GETTYSBURG REVIEW—Gettysburg College, Gettysburg, PA 17325. Peter Stitt, Ed. Quarterly. Poetry, fiction, essays, and essay reviews, 1,000 to 20,000 words. "Review sample copy before submitting." Pays $2 a line for poetry; $25 per printed page for fiction and nonfiction. Allow 3 to 6 months for response. No simultaneous submissions.

GLIMMER TRAIN PRESS—710 S.W. Madison St., #504, Portland, OR 97205. Susan Burmeister-Brown, Ed. Quarterly. Fiction, 1,200 to 7,500 words. Eight stories in each issue. Pays $500, on acceptance. Submit material in January, April, July, and October. Allow 3 months for response. Short story award for new writers; SASE for details.

GOTHIC JOURNAL—P.O. Box 6340, Elko, NV 89802–6340. Kristi Lyn Glass, Pub. Bimonthly. News and reviews for readers, writers, and publishers of romantic suspense, romantic mystery, and gothic, supernatural, and woman-in-jeopardy romance novels. Articles, 1,000 to 2,000 words, on gothic and romantic suspense topics; author profiles, 3,000 to 4,000 words; book reviews, 250 to 500 words. Pays $20 for articles, $30 for author profiles, on publication.

GRAHAM HOUSE REVIEW—Box 5000, Colgate Univ., Hamilton, NY 13346. Peter Balakian, Ed. Bruce Smith, Ed. Poetry, translations, and essays on modern poets. Payment depends on grants. Manuscripts read year-round; responds within 8 weeks.

GRAIN—Box 1154, Regina, Sask., Canada S4P 3B4. J. Jill Robinson, Ed. Short stories, to 30 typed pages; poems, send up to 8; visual art. Pays $30 to $100 for stories and poems, $100 for cover art, $30 for other art. SAE with international reply coupons required. Manuscripts read year-round.

GRAND STREET—131 Varick St., #906, New York, NY 10013. Jean Stein, Ed. Quarterly. Poetry, any length. Pays $3 a line, on publication. Will not read unsolicited fiction or essays.

GRAND TOUR: THE JOURNAL OF TRAVEL LITERATURE—P.O. Box 66, Thorofare, NJ 08086. Jennifer Fisher, Man. Ed. Quarterly. Travel-related memoirs, essays, and articles, 1,000 to 7,000 words, that "combine the sharp eye of the reporter with the craft of the short story writer and the rhythm of the poet." Pays $50 to $200, on publication.

GREEN MOUNTAIN REVIEW—Johnson State College, Johnson, VT 05656. Neil Shepard, Poetry Ed. Tony Whedon, Fiction Ed. Fiction and creative nonfiction, including literary essays, book reviews, and interviews, to 25 pages. Poetry. Payment varies (depending on funding), on publication. Manuscripts read September through April.

GREEN'S MAGAZINE—P.O. Box 3236, Regina, Sask., Canada S4P 3H1. David Green, Ed. Fiction for family reading, 1,500 to 4,000 words. Poetry, to 40 lines. No simultaneous submissions. Pays in copies. International reply coupons must accompany U.S. manuscripts. Manuscripts read year-round.

THE GREENSBORO REVIEW—Dept. of English, Univ. of North Carolina, Greensboro, NC 27412–5001. Jim Clark, Ed. Semiannual. Poetry and fiction. Submission deadlines: September 15 and February 15. Pays in copies. Writer's guidelines and guidelines for literary awards issue available.

GULF COAST—English Dept., Univ. of Houston, Houston, TX 77204. Attn: Ed. Semiannual. Fiction (no genre fiction), nonfiction, poetry (submit up to 5), and translations. No payment.

HALF TONES TO JUBILEE—Pensacola Junior College, English Dept., 1000 College Blvd., Pensacola, FL 32504. Walter F. Spara, Ed. Fiction, to 1,500 words, and poetry, to 60 lines. Pays in copies. Manuscripts read August 15 to May 15. Contest.

HAPPY—240 E. 35th St., Suite 11A, New York, NY 10016. Bayard, Ed. Quarterly. Fiction, to 6,000 words. "No previously published work. No pornography. No racist/sexist pandering. No bourgeois boredom." Pays $5, on publication, plus one copy.

HARP-STRINGS—P.O. Box 640387, Beverly Hills, FL 34464. Madelyn Eastlund, Ed. Poems, 14 to 80 lines, on a variety of topics and in many forms. No light verse, "prose masquerading as poetry," confessions, or raw guts poems. Pays in copies.

HAUNTS—Nightshade Publications, Box 8068, Cranston, RI 02920–0068. Joseph K. Cherkes, Ed. Short stories, 1,500 to 8,000 words: horror, science-fantasy, and supernatural tales with strong characters. Pays ½¢ to 1¢ a word, on publication. Manuscripts read January 1 to June 1.

HAWAII REVIEW—Dept. of English, Univ. of Hawaii, 1733 Donagho Rd., Honolulu, HI 96822. Michelle Y. Viray, Ed.-in-Chief. Quality fiction, poetry, interviews, essays, and literary criticism reflecting both regional and global concerns. Manuscripts read year-round.

HAYDEN'S FERRY REVIEW—Box 871502, Arizona State Univ., Tempe, AZ 85287–1502. Attn: Ed. Semiannual. Fiction, essays, and poetry (submit up to 6 poems). Include brief bio and SASE. Deadline for Spring/Summer issue is September 30; Fall/Winter issue, February 28. Pays in copies.

THE HEARTLANDS TODAY—Firelands Writing Ctr. of Firelands College, Huron, OH 44839. Larry Smith and Nancy Dunham, Eds. Fiction, 1,000 to 4,500 words, and nonfiction, 1,000 to 3,000 words, about the contemporary Midwest. Poetry (submit 3 to 5 poems). "Writing must be set in the Midwest, but can include a variety of themes." B&W photos. Pays $10 to $20 honorarium, plus copies. Query for current themes. Contest.

HEAVEN BONE—P.O. Box 486, Chester, NY 10918. Steve Hirsch, Ed. Annual. "The Bridge Between Muse & Mind." Fiction, to 5,000 words. Magazine and book reviews, 250 to 2,500 words. Poetry (submit no more than 10 pages at a time). "If we have a bias in subject matter, it might tend toward the so called alternative-cultural, post-beat, and yogic/anti-paranoiac. Read a copy before submitting." Allow 6 months for response. Pays in copies.

HEROES FROM HACKLAND—1225 Evans, Arkadelphia, AR 71923. Mike Grogan, Ed. Quarterly. Nostalgic articles, 750 to 1,500 words, on B-movies (especially westerns and serials), comic books, grade school readers, juvenile series books, cartoons, vintage autos, country music and pop music before 1956, and vintage radio and television. "We believe in heroes, especially those popular culture icons that serious critics label 'ephemera.'" Pays in copies.

THE HIGHLANDER—P.O. Box 397, Barrington, IL 60011. Angus Ray, Ed. Bimonthly. Articles, 1,300 to 1,900 words, related to Scottish history. "We do not want articles on modern Scotland or current problems in Scotland." Pays $100 to $150, on acceptance.

THE HOLLINS CRITIC—P.O. Box 9538, Hollins College, Roanoke, VA 24020. John Rees Moore, Ed. Published 5 times a year. Features an essay on a contemporary fiction writer or poet, cover sketch, brief biography, and book list. Also, book reviews and poetry. Pays $25 for poetry, on publication.

HOME LIFE—127 Ninth Ave. N., Nashville, TN 37234. Charlie Warren, Ed.-in-Chief. Southern Baptist. Articles, 600 to 1,800 words: marriage and family, seasonal, humor and inspiration. Also uses one piece of fiction each month. Pays to $24 for poetry, from $75 for articles, on acceptance. Query.

THE HUDSON REVIEW— 684 Park Ave., New York, NY 10021. Frederick Morgan and Paula Deitz, Eds. Quarterly. Fiction, to 10,000 words. Essays, to 8,000 words. Poetry, submit up to 10 at a time. Payment varies, on publication. Guidelines. Reading periods: Nonfiction read January 1 through April 30. Poetry read April 1 through July 31. Fiction read June through November 30.

HURRICANE ALICE: A FEMINIST QUARTERLY—Dept. of English, Rhode Island College, Providence, RI 02908. Attn: Ed. Articles, fiction, essays, interviews, and reviews, 500 to 3,000 words, with feminist perspective. Pays in copies.

HYPHEN MAGAZINE—P.O. Box 10481, Chicago, IL 60610. Attn: Ed. Original fiction, poetry, interviews, articles, reviews, and columns, as well as artwork. Pays in copies.

IN THE COMPANY OF POETS—P.O. Box 10786, Oakland, CA 94610. Jacalyn Evone, Ed./Pub. Semiannual. Fiction and creative essays, to 2,500 words, for a wide multicultural range of readers. Poems of any length. Drawings and photos. Pays in 3 copies. Guidelines. Manuscripts read year-round.

INDIANA REVIEW—Ballantine 465, Indiana Univ., Bloomington, IN 47405. Shirley Stephenson, Ed. Geoffrey Pollock, Assoc. Ed. Fiction with an emphasis on storytelling and sophistication of language. Poems that are well-executed and ambitious. Pays $5 per page. Manuscripts read year-round.

INTERIM—Dept. of English, Univ. of Nevada, Las Vegas, NV 89154–5034. A. Wilber Stevens, Ed. Semiannual. Poetry, any form or length, and fiction, to 7,500 words (uses no more than 2 stories per issue). Pays in copies and 2-year subscription. Responds in 2 months.

708

THE IOWA REVIEW—EPB 308, Univ. of Iowa, Iowa City, IA 52242. David Hamilton, Ed. Essays, poems, stories, reviews. Pays $10 a page for fiction and nonfiction, $1 a line for poetry, on publication. Manuscripts read September 1 through April 15.

IOWA WOMAN—P.O. Box 680, Iowa City, IA 52244. Attn: Ed. Fiction, poetry, creative nonfiction, book reviews, and personal essays. Articles, to 6,500 words; interviews with prominent women; current social, economic, artistic, and environmental issues. Poems, any length (submit up to 5); photos and drawings. Queries preferred for articles. Pays $5 a page, $15 for illustrations, on publication. Guidelines.

JACARANDA—Dept. of English & Comparitive Literature, California State Univ., Fullerton, CA 92634. Cornel Bonca, Bruce Kijewski, Laurence Roth, Eds. Semiannual. Fiction, to 30 pages, and poetry (submit up to 3 poems). No payment. Guidelines.

THE JAMES WHITE REVIEW—P.O. Box 3356, Butler Quarter Sta., Minneapolis, MN 55403. Phil Willkie, Pub. "A Gay Men's Literary Quarterly." Short stories, to 9,000 words, and poetry, to 250 lines. Book reviews. Responds in 3 months.

JAPANOPHILE—Box 223, Okemos, MI 48864. Earl R. Snodgrass, Ed. Fiction, to 4,000 words, with a Japanese setting. Each story should have at least one Japanese character and at least one non-Japanese. Articles, 2,000 words, that celebrate Japanese culture. "We seek to promote Japanese-American understanding. We are not about Japan-bashing or fatuous praise." Pays to $20, on publication. Annual short story contest; deadline December 31.

JOURNAL OF NEW JERSEY POETS—County College of Morris, 214 Center Grove Rd., Randolph, NJ 07869–2086. Sander Zulauf, Ed. Semiannual. Serious contemporary poetry by current and former New Jersey residents. "Although our emphasis is on poets associated with New Jersey, we seek work that is universal in scope." Pays in copies.

JOYFUL NOISE: A JOURNAL OF CHRISTIAN POETRY—P.O. Box 401, Bowling Green, KY 42102. Jim Erskine, Ed. Christian-oriented poetry, to 30 lines. "Personal, 'small' subjects perferred over 'large' themes such as love, brotherhood, etc. No political, new age, or social issues." Pays in copies.

KALEIDOSCOPE—United Disability Services, 326 Locust St., Akron, OH 44302–1876. Darshan Perusek, Ph.D., Ed.-in-Chief. Semiannual. Fiction, essays, interviews, articles, and poetry relating to disability and the arts, to 5,000 words. Photos a plus. "We present balanced, realistic images of people with disabilities and publish pieces that challenge stereotypes." Submissions accepted from writers with or without disabilities. Pays $10 to $125. Guidelines recommended. Manuscripts read year-round; response may take up to 6 months.

KALLIOPE: A JOURNAL OF WOMEN'S ART—Florida Community College at Jacksonville, 3939 Roosevelt Blvd., Jacksonville, FL 32205. Attn: Ed. Fiction, to 2,500 words; poetry; interviews of women writers, to 2,000 words; and B&W photos of fine art. Query for interviews only. Pays $10 or in copies.

KANSAS QUARTERLY/ARKANSAS REVIEW—Dept. of English & Philosophy, P.O. Box 1890, Arkansas State Univ., State University, AR 72467. Norman Lavers, Ed. Fiction and creative nonfiction (essays, memoirs, travel to remote places, commentary on science or ecology). Limited poetry. Pays $10 per page.

KELSEY REVIEW—Mercer County Community College, P.O. Box B, Trenton, NJ 08690. Robin Schore, Ed. Fiction and nonfiction, to 2,000 words, and poetry by writers living or working in Mercer County, NJ. Pays in copies.

THE KENYON REVIEW—Kenyon College, Gambier, OH 43022. David H. Lynn, Ed. Published 3 times a year. Fiction, poetry, essays, literary criticism, and reviews. "We appreciate manuscripts from writers who read the magazine." Pays $10 a printed page for prose, $15 a printed page for poetry, on publication. Manuscripts read September through March.

KINESIS: THE LITERARY MAGAZINE FOR THE REST OF US—P.O. Box 4007, Whitefish, MT 59937. Leif Peterson, Ed./Pub. Fiction, essays, and reviews, 2,000 to 6,000 words; poetry, to 60 lines. "Make sure it moves!" Pays in copies and subscription.

KIOSK—c/o English Dept., 306 Clemens Hall, SUNY Buffalo, Buffalo, NY 14260. Lia Vella, Ed. Jonathan Pitts, Fiction Ed. Charlotte Pressler, Poetry Ed. Fiction, to 20 pages, with a "strong sense of voice, narrative direction, and craftsmanship." Poetry "that explores boundaries, including the formally experimental." Address appropriate editor. Pays in copies. Manuscripts read September 1 to December 1.

LAMBDA BOOK REPORT—1625 Connecticut Ave. N.W., Washington, DC 20009. Jim Marks, Ed. Reviews and features, 500 to 1,100 words, of gay and lesbian books. Pays $15 to $60, 30 days after publication. Queries preferred.

LATINO STUFF REVIEW—P.O. Box 440195, Miami, FL 33144. Nilda Cepero-Llevada, Ed./Pub. Short stories, 3,000 words; poetry, to one page; criticism and essays on literature, the arts, social issues. Bilingual publication focusing on Latino topics. Pays in copies.

THE LEADING EDGE—3163 JKHB, Provo, UT 84602. Alex Grover, Ed. Semiannual. Science fiction and fantasy, 3,000 to 12,000 words; poetry, to 600 lines; and articles, to 8,000 words, on science, scientific speculation, and literary criticism. No excessive profanity, overt violence, or excessive sexual situations. No simultaneous submissions. Pays $10 to $100, on publication. Guidelines.

LIGHT—Box 7500, Chicago, IL 60680. John Mella, Ed. Quarterly. Light verse. Also fiction, reviews, and essays, to 2,000 words. Fillers, humor, jokes, quips. "If it has wit, point, edge, or barb, it will find a home here." Cartoons and line drawings. Pays in copies. Query for nonfiction.

LILITH, THE INDEPENDENT JEWISH WOMEN'S MAGAZINE—250 W. 57th St., New York, NY 10107. Susan Weidman Schneider, Ed. Fiction, 1,500 to 2,000 words, on issues of interest to Jewish women.

THE LION AND THE UNICORN—Box 53, English Dept., Mankato State Univ., Mankato, MN 56002–8400. Louisa Smith, Ed. Articles, from 2,000 words, offering criticism of children's and young adult books, for teachers, scholars, artists, and parents. Query preferred. Pays in copies.

LITERAL LATTE—61 E. 8th St., Suite 240, New York, NY 10003. Jenine Gordon, Ed./Pub. Bimonthly distributed to cafés and bookstores in New York City. Fiction and personal essays, to 6,000 words; poetry, to 2,000 words; B&W art. Pays in subscription and copies. Contests.

THE LITERARY REVIEW—Fairleigh Dickinson Univ., 285 Madison Ave., Madison, NJ 07940. Walter Cummins, Ed.-in-Chief. Jill Kushner, Man. Ed. Martin Green, Harry Keyishian, William Zander, Eds. Serious fiction; poetry; translations; essays and reviews on contemporary literature. Pays in copies.

LONG SHOT—P.O. Box 6238, Hoboken, NJ 07030. Danny Shot and Nancy Mercado, Eds. Fiction, poetry, and nonfiction, to 10 pages. B&W photos and drawings. Pays in copies.

THE LONG STORY—18 Eaton St., Lawrence, MA 01843. Attn: Ed. Stories, 8,000 to 20,000 words; prefer stories with a moral/thematic core, particularly about poor and working class people. Pays in copies. Manuscripts read year-round.

THE LONGNECK—P.O. Box 659, Vermillion, SD 57069. J.D. Erickson, Ed. Essays and fiction, 2,000 words. Vignettes, nostalgia. Poetry; submit no more than 5 poems. No religious material. Deadline: February 1 annually. Payment is in copies.

LYNX EYE—c/o Scribblefest Literary Group, 1880 Hill Dr., Los Angeles, CA 90041. Pam McCully, Kathryn Morrison, Eds. Quarterly. Short stories, vignettes, novel excerpts, one-act plays, essays, belle lettres, satires, and reviews, 500 to 5,000 words; poetry, to 30 lines; and fillers, to 250 words. Pays $10, on acceptance.

MAGIC REALISM—Pyx Press, P.O. Box 922648, Sylmar, CA 91392–2648. C. Darren Butler, Ed. Quarterly. Stories, to 7,500 words (4,000 words preferred), and poetry, any length, of magic realism, exaggerated realism, some genre fantasy/dark fantasy. Occasionally publish glib fantasy like that found in folktales, fairy tales, and myths. No occult, sleight-of-hand magicians, or wizards/witches. Pays ¼¢ per word, plus copy. Contest; SASE for details.

THE MALAHAT REVIEW—Univ. of Victoria, P.O. Box 1700, Victoria, BC, Canada V8W 2Y2. Derk Wynand, Ed. Fiction and poetry, including translations. Pays from $25 per page, on acceptance.

MANOA—English Dept., Univ. of Hawaii, Honolulu, HI 96822. Frank Stewart, Ed. Ian MacMillan, Fiction Ed. Jodi Kilcup, Book Reviews Ed. Fiction, to 30 pages; essays, to 25 pages; book reviews, 4 to 5 pages; and poetry (submit 4 to 6 poems). "Writers are encouraged to read the journal carefully before submitting." Pays $25 for poetry and book reviews; $20 to $25 per page for fiction, on publication.

MANY MOUNTAINS MOVING— 420 22nd St., Boulder, CO 80302. Naomi Horii, Ed. Published 3 times yearly. Fiction, nonfiction, and poetry by writers of all cultures. Pays in copies.

MASSACHUSETTS REVIEW—Memorial Hall, Univ. of Massachusetts, Amherst, MA 01003. Attn: Ed. Literary criticism; articles on public affairs, scholarly disciplines. Essays. Short fiction, 15 to 25 pages. Poetry. Pays $50, on publication. Manuscripts read November through May. Guidelines.

MEDIPHORS—P.O. Box 327, Bloomsburg, PA 17815. Eugene D. Radice, MD, Ed. "A literary journal of the health professions." Short stories, essays, and commentary, 3,500 words. "Topics should have some relation to medicine and health, but may be quite broad." Poems, to 30 lines. Humor. Pays in copies. Guidelines.

MICHIGAN HISTORICAL REVIEW—Clarke Historical Library, Central Michigan Univ., Mt. Pleasant, MI 48859. Attn: Ed. Semiannual. Scholarly articles related to Michigan's political, social, economic, and cultural history; articles on American, Canadian, and Midwestern history that directly or indirectly explore themes related to Michigan's past. Manuscripts read year-round.

MICHIGAN QUARTERLY REVIEW—3032 Rackham Bldg., Univ. of Michigan, Ann Arbor, MI 48109. Laurence Goldstein, Ed. Scholarly essays on all subjects; fiction; poetry. Pays $8 a page, on publication. Annual contest for authors published in the journal.

MID-AMERICAN REVIEW—Dept. of English, Bowling Green State Univ., Bowling Green, OH 43403. George Looney, Ed. High-quality fiction, poetry, articles, translations, and reviews of contemporary writing. Fiction, to 5,000 words, (query for longer work). Reviews, articles, 500 to 2,500 words. Pays to $50, on publication (pending funding). Manuscripts read September through May.

MIDWEST QUARTERLY—Pittsburg State Univ., Pittsburg, KS 66762. James B. M. Schick, Ed. Scholarly articles, 2,500 to 5,000 words, on contemporary academic and public issues; poetry. Pays in copies. Manuscripts read year-round.

THE MINNESOTA REVIEW—Dept. of English, E. Carolina Univ., Greenville, NC 27858. Attn: Ed. Politically committed fiction, 1,000 to 6,000 words; nonfiction, 5,000 to 7,500 words; and poetry, 3 pages maximum, for readers committed to social issues, including feminism, neomarxism, etc. Pays in copies. Responds in 2 to 4 months.

MISSISSIPPI REVIEW—Ctr. for Writers, Univ. of Southern Mississippi, Southern Sta., Box 5144, Hattiesburg, MS 39406–5144. Frederick Barthelme, Ed. Serious fiction, poetry, criticism, interviews. Pays in copies.

THE MISSOURI REVIEW—1507 Hillcrest Hall, Univ. of Missouri-Columbia, Columbia, MO 65211. Greg Michalson, Man. Ed. Speer Morgan, Ed. Evelyn Somers, Nonfiction Ed. Poems, of any length. ("We do poetry features: 6 to 10 pages of poetry by 3 to 5 poets in each issue.") Fiction and essays. Book reviews. Pays $20 per printed page, on contract. Manuscripts read year-round.

MODERN HAIKU—P.O. Box 1752, Madison, WI 53701–1752. Robert Spiess, Ed. Haiku and articles about haiku. Pays $1 per haiku, $5 a page for articles. Manuscripts read year-round.

MONTHLY REVIEW—122 W. 27th St., New York, NY 10001. Paul M. Sweezy, Harry Magdoff, Eds. Analytical articles, 5,000 words, on politics and economics, from independent socialist viewpoint. Pays $25 for reviews, $50 for articles, on publication.

MOOSE BOUND PRESS—P.O. Box 111781, Anchorage, AK 99511–1781. Sonia Walker, Ed. Short stories, to 5,000 words. Poetry, to 30 lines. Essays, to 500 words. "Wholesome, energetic, and uplifting writing for quarterly journals." No payment.

MOVING OUT: A FEMINIST LITERARY AND ARTS JOURNAL—P.O. Box 21249, Detroit, MI 48221. Poetry, fiction, articles, and art by women. Submit 4 to 6 poems at a time. Pays in copies.

MUDDY RIVER POETRY REVIEW— 89 Longwood Ave., Brookline, MA 02146. Zvi A. Sesling, Ed. Semiannual. Poems. "While free verse is preferred, nothing will be rejected if it is quality." No previously published poems. Payment is one copy.

MYSTERY TIME—P.O. Box 2907, Decatur, IL 62524. Linda Hutton, Ed. Semiannual. Suspense, 1,500 words, and poems about mysteries, up to 16 lines. "We prefer female protagonists. No gore or violence." Pays $5, on acceptance.

NEBO: A LITERARY JOURNAL—Dept. of English and Foreign Languages, Arkansas Tech. Univ., Russellville, AR 72801–2222. Attn: Ed. Poems (submit up to 5); mainstream fiction, to 3,000 words; critical essays, to 10 pages. Pays in one copy. Guidelines. Offices closed May through August. "Best time to submit is September through February."

NEGATIVE CAPABILITY— 62 Ridgelawn Dr. E., Mobile, AL 36608. Sue Walker, Ed. Poetry, any length; fiction, essays, art. Contests.

NEW AUTHOR'S JOURNAL—1542 Tibbits Ave., Troy, NY 12180. Mario V. Farina, Ed. Fiction, to 3,000 words, and poetry. Topical nonfiction, to 1,000 words. Pays in copies. Manuscripts read year-round.

NEW DELTA REVIEW—c/o Dept. of English, Louisiana State Univ., Baton Rouge, LA 70803–5001. Attn: Eds. Semiannual. Fiction and nonfiction, to 5,000 words. Submit up to 4 poems, any length. Also essays, interviews, reviews, and B&W photos or drawings. "We want to see your best work, even if it's been rejected elsewhere." Pays in copies. Manuscripts read year-round.

NEW ENGLAND REVIEW—Middlebury College, Middlebury, VT 05753. Stephen Donadio, Ed. Jodee Stanley, Man. Ed. Fiction, nonfiction, and poetry of varying lengths. Also, speculative and interpretive essays, critical reassessments, statements by artists working in various media, interviews, testimonials, letters from abroad. "We are committed to exploration of all forms of contemporary cultural expresssion." Pays $10 per page ($20 minimum), on publication. Manuscripts read September to May.

NEW ENGLAND WRITERS' NETWORK—P.O. Box 483, Hudson, MA 01749–0483. Glenda Baker, Ed.-in-Chief. Short stories and novel excerpts, to 2,000 words. All genres except pornography. Personal and humorous essays, to 1,000 words. Upbeat, positive poetry, to 32 lines. Pays $10 for stories; pays in copies for other material. Guidelines. Submit fiction and essays June 1 to August 31 only. Poetry may be submitted year-round.

NEW LAUREL REVIEW— 828 Lesseps St., New Orleans, LA 70117. Lee Meitzen Grue, Ed. Annual. Fiction, 10 to 20 pages; nonfiction, to 10 pages; poetry, any length. Library market. No inspirational verse. International readership. Read journal before submitting. Pays in one copy.

NEW LETTERS—Univ. House, Univ. of Missouri-Kansas City, 5101 Rockhill Rd., Kansas City, MO 64110–2499. James McKinley, Ed.-in-Chief. Fiction, 3,500 to 5,000 words. Poetry, submit 3 to 6 poems at a time. SASE for literary awards guidelines. Manuscripts read October 15 to May 15.

NEW ORLEANS REVIEW—Loyola Univ., New Orleans, LA 70118. Ralph Adamo, Ed. Serious fiction and poetry, personal essays, interviews, and B&W art.

THE NEW PRESS LITERARY QUARTERLY— 63–44 Saunders St., Suite 3, Rego Park, NY 11374. Robert Balogh, Pub. Quarterly. Fiction and nonfiction, to 2,500 words. Poetry to 200 lines. Pays $15 for prose. Contests.

THE NEW YORK QUARTERLY—P.O. Box 693, Old Chelsea Sta., New York, NY 10113. William Packard, Ed. Published 3 times a year. Poems of any style and persuasion, well written and well intentioned. Pays in copies. Manuscripts read year-round. SASE required.

NEXUS—Wright State Univ., W016A Student Union, Dayton, OH 45435. Tara Miller, Man. Ed. Joanne Huist Smith, Asst. Ed. Poetry, hard-hitting fiction, photography. One-act plays. Essays on obscure poets, artists, and musicians. Pays in copies.

NIGHTMARES—Box 587, Rocky Hill, CT 06067–0587. Ed Kobialka, Ed. Quarterly. Horror fiction, to 7,000 words, including ghost stories, science fiction and fantasy, mystery, "even romance, as long as it's scary." Related poetry. No excessive blood and gore. Pays $10 for fiction; $5 a page for poetry, on acceptance.

NIGHTSUN—School of Arts & Humanities, Frostburg State Univ., Frostburg, MD 21532–1099. Douglas DeMars, Ed. Annual. Short stories, about 6 pages, and poems, to 40 lines. Payment is 2 copies. Manuscripts read September 1 to May 1.

NIMROD INTERNATIONAL JOURNAL—Univ. of Tulsa, 600 S. College Ave., Tulsa, OK 74104–3189. Dr. Francine Ringold, Ed.-in-Chief. Publishes 2 issues annually, one awards and one thematic. Quality poetry and fiction, experimental and traditional. Pays $5 a page (to $25) and copies. Annual awards for poetry and fiction. Guidelines.

96 INC.—P.O. Box 15559, Boston, MA 02215. Attn: Ed. Semiannual. Fiction, 1,000 to 7,500 words, interviews, and poetry of varying length. Pays $10 to $25, on publication.

THE NORTH AMERICAN REVIEW—Univ. of Northern Iowa, Cedar Falls, IA 50614–0516. Peter Cooley, Poetry Ed. Poetry of high quality. Pays from $20 per poem, on publication. Manuscripts read year-round.

NORTH ATLANTIC REVIEW—15 Arbutus Ln., Stony Brook, NY 11790–1408. John Gill, Ed. Annual. Fiction and nonfiction, to 5,000 words; fillers, humor, photographs and illustrations. A special section on social or literary issues is a part of each issue. No unsolicited poetry. Pays in copies. Responds in 5 or 6 months.

THE NORTH DAKOTA QUARTERLY—Univ. of North Dakota, Grand Forks, ND 58202–7209. Attn: Ed. Essays in the humanities and social sciences; fiction, reviews, and poetry. Limited market. Pays in copies and subscription.

NORTHEASTARTS—Boston Arts Organization, Inc., JFK Sta., P.O. Box 6061, Boston, MA 02114. Mr. Leigh Donaldson, Ed. Fiction and nonfiction, to 750 words; poetry, to 30 lines; and short essays and reviews. "Both published and new writers are considered. No obscene or offensive material." Payment is 2 copies.

NORTHEAST CORRIDOR—Beaver College, 450 S. Easton Rd., Glenside, PA 19038. Susan Balée, Ed. Semiannual. Literary fiction, personal essays, and interviews, 10 to 20 pages. Poetry, to 40 lines (submit 3 to 5). "We seek the work of writers and artists living in or writing about the Northeast Corridor of America." Pays $25 for stories or essays, $10 for poems, on publication.

714

THE NORTHERN READER—Savage Press, Box 115, Superior, WI 54880. Mike Savage, Ed. Quarterly. Fiction, to 2,000 words. Free verse and metrical poetry, essays, and fillers. Pays in copies. Guidelines.

NORTHWEST REVIEW—369 PLC, Univ. of Oregon, Eugene, OR 97403. Elizabeth Claman, Fiction Ed. Fiction, commentary, essays, and poetry. Reviews. Pays in copies. Guidelines.

NORTHWOODS JOURNAL—P.O. Box 298, Thomaston, ME 04861. Robert W. Olmsted, Ed. Articles of interest to writers and fiction, 2,500 words. Poetry, any length. "Do not submit anything until you've read guidelines." Pays $5 per page, on acceptance.

NOTRE DAME REVIEW—Creative Writing Program, English Dept., Univ. of Notre Dame, Notre Dame, IN 46556. Attn: Man. Ed. Semiannual. Fiction, 10 to 15 pages. Essays, reviews, and poetry, 3 to 5 pages. Manuscripts read September through April. Payment varies, on publication.

OASIS—P.O. Box 626, Largo, FL 33779–0626. Neal Storrs, Ed. Short fiction and literary essays, to 7,000 words, poetry, and translations from French, German, Italian, or Spanish. Any subject. "Style is paramount." Pays $15 to $50 for prose, $5 per poem, on publication. Guidelines. Responds quickly.

OFFERINGS—P.O. Box 1667, Lebanon, MO 65536. Velvet Fackeldey, Ed. Quarterly. Poetry, to 30 lines, traditional and free verse. No payment.

THE OHIO REVIEW—Ellis Hall, Ohio Univ., Athens, OH 45701-2979. Wayne Dodd, Ed. Short stories, poetry, essays, reviews. Pays $5 per page for prose, $1 a line for poetry, plus copies, on publication. SASE required. Submissions read September through May.

THE OLD RED KIMONA—Humanities Div., Floyd College, Box 1864, Rome, GA 30162. Jon Hershey and Jeff Mack, Eds. Annual. Fiction, to 1,200 words. Poetry, submit 3 to 5 poems. "Poems and stories should be concise and imagistic. Nothing sentimental or didactic." Pays in copies.

100 WORDS—473 EPB, Univ. of Iowa, Iowa City, IA 52242. Carolyn Brown, Ed. Semiannual. Prose, poetry, and nonfiction, no more than 100 words, that reflect in an original way the theme of the issue. No payment.

ONIONHEAD—Arts on the Park, Inc., 115 N. Kentucky Ave., Lakeland, FL 33801–5044. Attn: Ed. Council. Short stories, to 4,000 words; essays, to 2,500 words; and poetry, to 60 lines; on provocative social, political, and cultural observations and hypotheses. Pays in copies. Send SASE for Wordart poetry contest information. Manuscripts read year-round; responds in 12 weeks.

OSIRIS—Box 297, Deerfield, MA 01842. Andrea Moorhead, Ed. Multilingual poetry journal, publishing poetry in English, French, German, and other languages in a translation/original format. Pays in copies.

OTHER VOICES—Univ. of Illinois at Chicago, Dept. of English (M/C 162), 601 S. Morgan St., Chicago, IL 60607–7120. Lois Hauselman, Ruth Canji, Tina Peano, Eds. Semiannual. Fresh, accessible short stories, one-act plays, and novel excerpts, to 5,000 words. Pays in copies and modest honorarium. Manuscripts read October to April.

OUTERBRIDGE—College of Staten Island, English Dept. 2S-218, 2800 Victory Blvd., Staten Island, NY 10314. Charlotte Alexander, Ed. Annual.

Well-crafted stories, about 20 pages, and poetry, to 4 pages, "directed to a wide audience of literate adult readers." Pays in 2 copies. Manuscripts read September to June.

THE OXFORD AMERICAN—P.O. Box 1156, Oxford, MS 38655. Marc Smirnoff, Ed. Quarterly. Short fiction and nonfiction of a Southern nature. "Our interest in good nonfiction is strong." Cartoons, photos, and drawings. Pays from $50 for poetry and art; from $100 for nonfiction, on publication.

PAINTBRUSH: A JOURNAL OF CONTEMPORARY MULTICULTURAL LITERATURE—Language & Literature Div., Truman State Univ., Kirksville, MO 63501. Ben Bennani, Ed. Annual. No longer accepting freelance poetry, translations, or book reviews. Publishes special monograph issues highlighting the work of individual writers. Query.

PAINTED BRIDE QUARTERLY—230 Vine St., Philadelphia, PA 19106. Kathleen Volk-Miller, Marion Wrenn, Eds. Fiction and poetry of varying lengths. Pays $5, plus subscription.

PALO ALTO REVIEW—1400 W. Villaret, San Antonio, TX 78224–2499. Ellen Shull, Ed. Semiannual. Fiction and articles, 5,000 words. "We look for wide-ranging investigations of historical, geographical, scientific, mathematical, artistic, political, and social topics, anything that has to do with living and learning." Interviews; 200-word think pieces about almost anything for "Food for Thought"; poetry, to 50 lines (send 3 to 5 poems at a time); reviews, to 500 words, of books, films, videos, or software. "Fiction shouldn't be too experimental or excessively avant-garde." Pays in copies.

PARABOLA: THE MAGAZINE OF MYTH AND TRADITION—656 Broadway, New York, NY 10012. Attn: Eds. Quarterly. Articles, to 4,000 words, and fiction, 500 words, retelling traditional stories, folk and fairy tales. "All submissions must relate to an upcoming theme. We are looking for a balance between scholarly and accessible writing devoted to the ideas of myth and tradition." Send SASE for guidelines and themes. Payment varies, on publication.

THE PARIS REVIEW—541 E. 72nd St., New York, NY 10021. Attn: Fiction and Poetry Eds. Fiction and poetry of high literary quality. Pays on publication.

PARNASSUS—205 W. 89th St., Apt. 8F, New York, NY 10024–1835. Herbert Leibowitz, Ed. Critical essays and reviews on contemporary poetry. International in scope. Pays in cash and copies. Manuscripts read year-round.

PARTISAN REVIEW—Boston Univ., 236 Bay State Rd., Boston, MA 02215. William Phillips, Ed.-in-Chief. Edith Kurzweil, Ed. Serious fiction, poetry, and essays. Payment varies. No simultaneous submissions. Manuscripts read year-round.

PASSAGER: A JOURNAL OF REMEMBRANCE AND DISCOVERY—c/o Univ. of Baltimore, 1420 N. Charles St., Baltimore, MD 21201–5779. Mary Azrael, Kendra Kopelke, Ebby Malmgren, Eds. Fiction and essays, 4,000 words, of "remembrance and discovery." Poetry, to 40 lines. "We publish writers of all ages, but with an emphasis on new older writers." Pays in copies.

PASSAGES NORTH—Northern Michigan Univ., College of Arts & Sciences, Magers Hall, Marquette, MI 49855. Anne Ohman Youngs, Ed. Semiannual; published in December and June. Poetry, fiction, interviews. Pays in copies. Manuscripts read September to May.

PANGOLIN PAPERS—P.O. Box 241, Nordland, WA 98358. Pat Britt, Ed. Literary fiction, 100 to 7,000 words. Pays in copies

PEARL—3030 E. Second St., Long Beach, CA 90803. Marilyn Johnson, Ed. Fiction, 500 to 1,200 words, and poetry, to 40 lines. "We are interested in accessible, humanistic poetry and fiction that communicates and is related to real life. Along with the ironic, serious, and intense, humor and wit are welcome." Pays in copies.

PEQUOD—New York Univ., English Dept., 19 University Pl., 2nd Fl., New York, NY 10003. Mark Rudman, Ed. Semiannual. Short stories, essays, and literary criticism, to 10 pages; poetry and translations, to 3 pages. Pays honorarium, on publication.

PIEDMONT LITERARY REVIEW—Bluebird Ln., Rt. #1, Box 1014, Forest, VA 24551. Evelyn Miles, Man. Ed. Quarterly. Poems, any length and style (partial to rhyme and meter); submit up to 5 poems to William R. Smith, Poetry Ed., 3750 Woodside Ave., Lynchburg, VA 24503. Submit Asian verse to Dorothy McLaughlin, 10 Atlantic Rd., Somerset, NJ 08873. Submit prose, to 2,500 words, to Dr. Olga Kronmeyer, 25 W. Dale Dr., Lynchburg, VA 24501. No pornography. Pays one copy.

PIG IRON PRESS—P.O. Box 237, Youngstown, OH 44501-0237. Jim Villani, Ed. Fiction and nonfiction, to 8,000 words. Poetry, to 100 lines. Write for upcoming themes. Pays $5 per published page or poem, on publication. Manuscripts read year-round. Responds in 3 months.

PIVOT—250 Riverside Dr., #23, New York, NY 10025. Martin Mitchell, Ed. Annual. Poetry, to 75 lines. Pays 2 copies. Manuscripts read Jan. 1 to June 1.

PLEIADES—English Dept., Central Missouri State Univ., Warrensburg, MO 64093. R. M. Kinder, Exec. Ed. Traditional and experimental fiction, 3,000 to 6,000 words. Literary criticism, reviews, and belle lettres. Poetry. "We like to explore cultural diversity." Pays $10 for prose; $3 for poetry, on publication.

PLOT MAGAZINE—Calypso Publishing, P.O. Box 1351, Sugar Land, TX 77487-1351. Christina C. Russell, Man. Ed. Fantasy, science fiction, horror, suspense, and speculative fiction, to 7,500 words. "We encourage new and emerging writers. If your story can give us gooseflesh, we want to see it." Pays $10 for stories, $5 for line drawings, on acceptance.

PLOUGHSHARES—Emerson College, 100 Beacon St., Boston, MA 02116-1596. Attn: Ed. Serious fiction, to 6,000 words. Poetry (submit up to 3 poems at a time). Pays $10 per page ($40 to $200), on publication, plus 2 copies and subscription. Manuscripts read August through March. Guidelines.

THE PLUM REVIEW—P.O. Box 1347, Philadelphia, PA 19105. Mike Hammer, Ed.-in-Chief. Semiannual. Short stories, to 5,000 words, and poems "in all styles, subjects matters, and lengths." Essays relating to poetry as well as interviews with prominent poets. Pays in copies.

POEM—c/o English Dept., U.A.H., Huntsville, AL 35899. Nancy Frey Dillard, Ed. Serious lyric poetry. Pays in copies. Manuscripts read year-round (best times to submit are December to March and June to September).

POET MAGAZINE—P.O. Box 54947, Oklahoma City, OK 73154. Attn: Ed. Quarterly. Broad spectrum of poetry and how-to articles. "Dedicated to publishing poets at all levels. New and experienced poets encouraged to submit." Submit copies (not originals) of up to 5 poems, any form, and articles of any length on subjects related to poetry. Include one loose first-class stamp (not SASE) for guidelines, contest information, or editorial reply; manuscripts will not be returned. Payment is one copy.

POETRY— 60 W. Walton St., Chicago, IL 60610. Joseph Parisi, Ed. Poetry of highest quality. Submit 3 to 4 poems. Allow 10 to 12 weeks for response. Pays $2 a line, on publication.

POETRY EAST—DePaul Univ., English Dept., 802 W. Belden Ave., Chicago, IL 60614–3214. Elizabeth Sloan, Man. Ed. Semiannual. Poetry, essays, and translations. "Please send a sampling of your best work. Do not send book-length manuscripts without querying first." Pays in copies.

THE POET'S PAGE—P.O. Box 372, Wyanet, IL 61379. Ione K. Pence, Ed./Pub. Quarterly. Poetry, any length, any style, any topic. Articles and essays on poetry and poetic forms, poets, styles, etc. Pays in copies.

PORTLAND REVIEW—c/o Portland State Univ., P.O. Box 751, Portland, OR 97207. Aaron Mahony, Ed. Semiannual. Short fiction, essays, poetry, one-act plays (to 5 pages), photography, and artwork. "Please include a bio." Payment is one copy.

POTOMAC REVIEW—P.O. Box 354, Port Tobacco, MD 20677. Eli Flam, Ed. Quarterly. Fiction and literary essays, to 2,500 words. Poetry, to 2 pages. Pays in copies.

POTPOURRI—P.O. Box 8278, Prairie Village, KS 66208. Polly W. Swafford, Ed. Quarterly. Short stories, to 3,500 words. Literary essays, travel pieces, and humor, to 2,500 words. Poetry and haiku, to 75 lines. "We like clever themes that avoid reminiscence, depressing plots and violence." Pays in one copy.

PRAIRIE SCHOONER—201 Andrews Hall, Univ. of Nebraska, Lincoln, NE 68588–0334. Hilda Raz, Ed. Short stories, poetry, essays, book reviews, and translations. Pays in copies. SASE required. Manuscripts read September through May; responds in 3 months. Annual contests.

PRESS QUARTERLY—125 W. 72nd St., Suite 3-M, New York, NY 10023. Daniel Roberts, Ed. Short stories and poems that "deliver an invigorating dose of clear, humanized storytelling." Articles on the creative process itself. Payment varies, on publication.

PRIMAVERA—Box 37-7547, Chicago, IL 60637. Attn: Editorial Board. Annual. Fiction and poetry that focus on the experiences of women; author need not be female. B&W photos and drawings. No simultaneous submissions. Pays in 2 copies. Responds within 3 months.

PRISM INTERNATIONAL—E462–1866 Main Mall, Dept. of Creative Writing, Univ. of British Columbia, Vancouver, B.C., Canada V6T 1Z1. Attn: Ed. High-quality fiction, poetry, drama, creative nonfiction, and literature in translation, varying lengths. Include international reply coupons. Pays $20 per published page. Annual short fiction contest.

THE PROLIFIC FREELANCER—(formerly *Prolific Writer's Magazine*) P.O. Box 543, Oradell, NJ 07649. Brian Konradt, Ed. Bimonthly. Articles, 2,500 words, on managing, marketing, and making money as a freelance writer and publisher. No fiction. Pays to $200, on publication. Guidelines.

PROOF ROCK—P.O. Box 607, Halifax, VA 24558. Don Conner, Fiction Ed. Serena Fusek, Poetry Ed. Fiction, to 2,500 words. Poetry, to 32 lines. Reviews. Pays in copies.

THE PROSE POEM—English Dept., Providence College, Providence, RI 02198. Peter Johnson, Ed. Prose poems. Book reviews, 4 to 6 pages. Pays in copies. Query for book reviews. Manuscripts read January 1 to April 1.

PUCK—Permeable Press, 2336 Market St., #14, San Francisco, CA 94114. Brian Clark, Ed. "The Unofficial Journal of the Irrepressible." Annual. Non-genre fiction, to 15,000 words; essays and "speculative" nonfiction, to 10,000 words. "Fiery editorial range. Fiction should provoke but not be dogmatic. We especially welcome un/under-published writers. Read a sample first." Pays in copies and honorarium.

PUCKERBRUSH REVIEW—76 Main St., Orono, ME 04473–1430. Constance Hunting, Ed. Semiannual. Literary fiction, criticism, and poetry of various lengths, "to bring literary Maine news to readers." Pays in 2 copies. Manuscripts read year-round.

PUDDING MAGAZINE: THE INTERNATIONAL JOURNAL OF APPLIED POETRY—c/o Pudding House Writers Resource Ctr., Bed & Breakfast for Writers, Johnstown, OH 43031. Jennifer Bosveld, Ed. Poems on popular culture, social concerns, personal struggle; poetry therapy that has been revised for art's sake; articles/essays on poetry in the human services. Manuscripts read year-round.

PUERTO DEL SOL—New Mexico State Univ., Box 3E, Las Cruces, NM 88003–0001. K. West, Kevin McIlvoy, and Antonya Nelson, Eds. Short stories and personal essays, to 30 pages; novel excerpts, to 65 pages; articles, to 45 pages, and reviews, to 15 pages. Poetry, photos. Pays in copies. Manuscripts read September 1 to April 1.

QUARTER AFTER EIGHT—Ellis Hall, Ohio Univ., Athens, OH 45701. Attn: Eds. Annual. Avant-garde short fiction, novel excerpts, essays, criticism, investigations, and interviews, to 10,000 words. Submit no more than 2 pieces. Prose poetry (submit up to 5 prose poems); no traditional poetry. Pays in copies. Manuscripts read September through February.

QUARTERLY WEST—317 Olpin Union, Univ. of Utah, Salt Lake City, UT 84112. M.L. Williams and Lawrence Coates, Eds. Fiction, short-shorts, poetry, translations, and reviews. Pays $25 to $50 for stories, $15 to $50 for poems. Manuscripts read year-round. Biennial novella competition in even-numbered years.

RAG MAG—P.O. Box 12, Goodhue, MN 55027–0012. Beverly Voldseth, Ed. Semiannual. Eclectic fiction and nonfiction, art, photos. Poetry, any length. Must be related to theme. No religious writing. Pays in copies. SASE for guidelines and themes.

RAMBUNCTIOUS REVIEW—1221 W. Pratt Blvd., Chicago, IL 60626. Mary Alberts, Richard Goldman, Nancy Lennon, Beth Hausler, Eds. Fiction, to 12 pages; poems, submit up to 5 at a time. Pays in copies. Manuscripts read September through May. Contests.

READER'S BREAK—Pine Grove Press, P.O. Box 40, Jamesville, NY 13078. Gertrude S. Eiler, Ed. Semiannual. Fiction, to 3,500 words. "We welcome stories about relationships, tales of action, adventure, science fiction and fantasy, romance, suspense, and mystery. Themes and plots may be historical,

719

contemporary, or futuristic. Our emphasis is on fiction, but we will read non-fiction in story form." Poems, to 75 lines. Pays in one copy.

RED CEDAR REVIEW—Dept. of English, 17-C Morrill Hall, Michigan State Univ., E. Lansing, MI 48824–1036. Laura Klynstra, Poetry Ed. Tom Bissell, Fiction Ed. Fiction, to 5,000 words, and poetry (submit up to 5 poems). Pays in copies. Manuscripts read year-round.

RESPONSE: A CONTEMPORARY JEWISH REVIEW—27 W. 20th St., 9th Fl., New York, NY 10011–3707. David R. Adler and Michael Steinberg, Eds. Pearl Gluck, Fiction and Poetry Ed. Fiction, to 25 double-spaced pages, in which Jewish experience is explored in an unconventional fashion. Articles, to 25 pages, with a focus on Jewish issues. Poetry, to 80 lines, and book reviews. Pays in copies.

REVIEW: LATIN AMERICAN LITERATURE AND ARTS—Americas Society, 680 Park Ave., New York, NY 10021. Alfred J. MacAdam, Ed. Semiannual. Work in English translation by and about young and established Latin American writers; essays and book reviews considered. Send queries for 1,000-to 1,500-word manuscripts, and short poem translations. Payment varies, on acceptance.

RIVER CITY—Dept. of English, Univ. of Memphis, Memphis, TN 38152. Paul Naylor, Ed. Poems, short stories, essays, and interviews. No novel excerpts. Pay varies according to grants. Manuscripts read September through April. Guidelines. Contests.

RIVER STYX—3207 Washington Ave., St. Louis, MO 63103. Attn: Ed. Published 3 times a year. Poetry, fiction, personal essays, literary interviews, and B&W photos. Payment is $8 per printed page and 2 copies. Manuscripts read May to November.

RIVERSIDE QUARTERLY—Box 12085, San Antonio, TX 78212. Leland Sapiro, Ed. Science fiction and fantasy, to 3,500 words; reviews, criticism, any length; poetry and letters. "Read magazine before submitting." Send poetry to Sheryl Smith, 515 Saratoga, #2, Santa Clara, CA 95050. Pays in copies.

ROANOKE REVIEW—Roanoke College, Salem, VA 24153. Robert R. Walter, Ed. Quality short fiction, to 5,000 words, and poetry, to 100 lines. Pays in copies.

ROCKFORD REVIEW—P.O. Box 858, Rockford, IL 61105. David Ross, Ed.-in-Chief. Published 3 times a year. Fiction, essays, and satire, 250 to 1,300 words. Experimental and traditional poetry, to 50 lines (shorter works preferred). One-act plays and other dramatic forms, to 10 pages. "We prefer genuine or satirical human dilemmas with coping or non-coping outcomes that ring the reader's bell." Submit up to 3 works at a time. Pays in copies; 2 $25 Editor's Choice Prizes awarded each issue.

ROSEBUD—P.O. Box 459, Cambridge, WI 53523. Rod Clark, Ed. Quarterly. Fiction, articles, profiles, 1,200 to 1,800 words, and poems; love, alienation, travel, humor, nostalgia, and unexpected revelation. Pays $45 plus copies, on publication. Guidelines.

SAN FERNANDO POETRY JOURNAL—18301 Halstead St., Northridge, CA 91325. Richard Cloke, Ed. Quality poetry, 20 to 100 lines, with social content; scientific, philosophical, and historical themes. Pays in copies.

SANSKRIT LITERARY/ART PUBLICATION— Cone Ctr., Univ. of North Carolina/Charlotte, Charlotte, NC 28223–0001. Attn: Ed. Annual. Poetry, short fiction, photos, and fine art.

SANTA BARBARA REVIEW—104 La Vereda Ln., Santa Barbara, CA 93108. P.S. Leddy, Ed. Short stories, novellas, and occasionally plays. Biographies and essays, to 6,500 words. Poems. Translations. B&W art and photos. Pays in copies.

SCANDINAVIAN REVIEW—725 Park Ave., New York, NY 10021. Attn: Ed. Published 3 times a year. Essays on contemporary Scandinavia: arts, sciences, business, politics, and culture of Scandinavia. Fiction and poetry, translated from Nordic languages. Pays from $100, on publication.

SCRIVENER—McGill Univ., 853 Sherbrooke St. W., Montreal, Quebec, Canada H3A 2T6. Ursula Hines, Ed. Poems, submit 5 to 15; prose, to 20 pages; reviews, to 5 pages. Photography and graphics. Pays in copies.

SENECA REVIEW—Hobart & William Smith Colleges, Geneva, NY 14456. Deborah Tall, Ed. Poetry, translations, and essays on contemporary poetry. Pays in copies. Manuscripts read September 1 to May 1.

SHENANDOAH—Washington and Lee Univ., Troubadour Theatre, 2nd Fl., Lexington, VA 24450–0303. R.T. Smith, Ed. Quarterly. Highest quality fiction, poetry, criticism, essays and interviews. "Please read the magazine before submitting!" Pays $25 per page for prose; $2.50 per line for poetry, on publication. Annual contests.

SHOOTING STAR REVIEW—7123 Race St., Pittsburgh, PA 15208. Sandra Gould Ford, Pub. Fiction and folktales, to 3,000 words, essays, to 2,000 words, and poetry, to 50 lines, on the African-American experience. Query for book reviews only. Pays $5 for poems; $10 for essays; $10 to $20 for fiction. Send SASE for topic deadlines. Responds to queries in 3 weeks; manuscripts in 4 months.

SHORT FICTION BY WOMEN—Box 1254, Old Chelsea Sta., New York, NY 10113. Rachel Whalen, Ed. Semiannual. Short stories, novellas, and novel excerpts, to 20,000 words, by women writers. No horror, romance, or mystery fiction. Payment varies, on publication. Manuscripts read year-round. Guidelines.

SING HEAVENLY MUSE! WOMEN'S POETRY & PROSE—P.O. Box 13320, Minneapolis, MN 55414. Attn: Ed. Short stories and essays, to 5,000 words. Poetry. Query for themes and reading periods. Pays in copies.

SKYLARK—2200 169th St., Hammond, IN 46323–2094. Pamela Hunter, Ed. "The Fine Arts Annual of Purdue Calumet." Fiction and articles, to 4,000 words. Poetry, to 21 lines. B&W prints and drawings. Pays in one copy. Manuscripts read November 1 through April 30 for fall publication.

THE SLATE—P.O. Box 581189, Minneapolis, MN 55458–1189. Rachel Fulkerson, Chris Dall, Patty Delaney, Jessica Morris, Kari Andruscavage, Eds. Published 3 times a year. Short fiction, poetry, nonfiction, and essays. "We are dedicated to reviving a cultural interest in the written word and to nourishing the relationship between writer and reader." Pays in copies. Manuscripts read year-round.

SLIPSTREAM—Box 2071, Niagara Falls, NY 14301. Attn: Ed. Contemporary poetry, any length. Pays in copies. Query for themes. Guidelines. Annual poetry chapbook contest ($500 prize) has December 1 deadline; send SASE for details. Fiction overstocked; query.

THE SMALL POND MAGAZINE—P.O. Box 664, Stratford, CT 06497–0664. Napoleon St. Cyr, Ed. Published 3 times a year. Fiction, to 2,500 words; poetry, to 100 lines. Pays in copies. Query for nonfiction. Include short bio. Manuscripts read year-round.

SMALL PRESS REVIEW—Box 100, Paradise, CA 95967. Len Fulton, Ed. Reviews, 200 words, of small literary books and magazines; tracks the publishing of small publishers and small-circulation magazines. Query.

SNAKE NATION REVIEW—Snake Nation Press, 110 #2 W. Force, Valdosta, GA 31601. Roberta George, Ed. Quarterly. Short stories, novel chapters, and informal essays, 5,000 words, and poetry, to 60 lines. Pays in copies and prizes.

SNOWY EGRET—P.O. Box 9, Bowling Green, IN 47833. Philip Repp, Ed. Poetry, fiction, and nonfiction, to 10,000 words. Natural history from artistic, literary, philosophical, and historical perspectives. Pays $2 per page for prose; $2 to $4 for poetry, on publication. Manuscripts read year-round.

SONORA REVIEW—Dept. of English, Univ. of Arizona, Tucson, AZ 85721. Attn: Fiction, Poetry, or Nonfiction Ed. (Address appropriate genre editor.) Annual contests; send for guidelines. Simultaneous submissions accepted (except for contest entries). Manuscripts read year-round.

THE SOUTH CAROLINA REVIEW—Dept. of English, Clemson Univ., Clemson, SC 29634–1503. Frank Day, Man. Ed. Semiannual. Fiction, essays, reviews, and interviews, to 4,000 words. Poems. Send complete manuscript plus diskette. Send SASE or E-mail address for guidelines. Pays in copies. Response time is 6 to 9 months. Manuscripts read September through May (but not in December).

SOUTH DAKOTA REVIEW—Box 111, Univ. Exchange, Vermillion, SD 57069–2390. Brian Bedard, Ed. Exceptional fiction, 3,000 to 5,000 words, and poetry, 10 to 25 lines. Critical articles, especially on American literature, Western American literature, theory and esthetics, 3,000 to 5,000 words. Pays in copies. Manuscripts read year-round; slower response time in the summer.

THE SOUTHERN CALIFORNIA ANTHOLOGY—c/o Master of Professional Writing Program, WPH 404, Univ. of Southern California, Los Angeles, CA 90089–4034. James Ragan, Ed.-in-Chief. Fiction, to 20 pages, and poetry, to 5 pages. Pays in copies. Manuscripts read September to January.

SOUTHERN EXPOSURE—P.O. Box 531, Durham, NC 27702. Pat Arnow, Ed. Quarterly forum on "Southern movements for social change." Short stories, to 3,600 words, essays, investigative journalism, and oral histories, 500 to 3,600 words. Pays $25 to $250, on publication. Query.

SOUTHERN HUMANITIES REVIEW—9088 Haley Ctr., Auburn Univ., AL 36849. Dan R. Latimer, Virginia M. Kouidis, Eds. Short stories, essays, and criticism, 3,500 to 15,000 words; poetry, to 2 pages. Responds within 3 months. No simultaneous submissions. SASE required.

SOUTHERN POETRY REVIEW—Advancement Studies, Central Piedmont Community College, Charlotte, NC 28235. Ken McLaurin, Ed. Poems. No restrictions on style, length, or content. Manuscripts read September through May.

THE SOUTHERN REVIEW— 43 Allen Hall, Louisiana State Univ., Baton Rouge, LA 70803–5005. James Olney and Dave Smith, Eds. Emphasis on contemporary literature in United States and abroad with special interest in southern culture and history. Fiction and essays, 4,000 to 8,000 words. Serious poetry of highest quality. Pays $12 a page for prose, $20 a page for poetry, on publication. No manuscripts read in the summer.

SOUTHWEST REVIEW—307 Fondren Library W., Box 374, Southern Methodist Univ., Dallas, TX 75275. Elizabeth Mills, Sr. Fiction Ed. "A quarterly that serves the interests of the region but is not bound by them." Fiction, essays, poetry, and interviews with well-known writers, 3,000 to 7,500 words. Pays varying rates. Manuscripts read September 1 through May 31.

SOU'WESTER—Southern Illinois Univ. at Edwardsville, Edwardsville, IL 62026–1438. Fred W. Robbins, Ed. Allison Funk, Assoc. Ed. Nancy Avdoian, Poetry Ed. Roger Ridenour, Fiction Ed. Fiction, to 8,000 words. Poetry, any length. Pays in copies. Manuscripts not read in August.

THE SOW'S EAR POETRY REVIEW—19535 Pleasant View Dr., Abingdon, VA 24211–6827. Attn: Ed. Quarterly. Eclectic poetry and art. Submit one to 5 poems, any length, plus a brief biographical note. Interviews, essays, and articles, any length, about poets and poetry are also considered. B&W photos and drawings. Payment is one copy. Poetry and chapbook contests. Guidelines.

SPARROW MAGAZINE—Sparrow Press, 103 Waldron St., W. Lafayette, IN 47906. Felix Stefanile, Ed./Pub. Contemporary (14-line) sonnets, and occasionally formal poems in other structures. Submit up to 5 poems. Pays $3 per poem, on publication. A $25 sonnet prize is awarded to a contributor in each issue.

THE SPOON RIVER POETRY REVIEW—Dept. of English, Stevenson Hall, Illinois State Univ., Normal, IL 61790–4240. Lucia Cordell Getsi, Ed. Poetry, any length. Pays in copies. Editors' Prize Contest; SASE for details.

SPSM&H—329 E St., Bakersfield, CA 93304. Frederick A. Raborg, Jr., Ed. Single sonnets, sequences, essays about the sonnet form, short fiction in which the sonnet plays a part, books, and anthologies. Pays $10, plus copies, for fiction and essays.

THE STABLE COMPANION—P.O. Box 6485, Lafayette, IN 47903. Susanna Brandon, Pub. Quarterly. "The Literary Magazine for Horse Lovers." Fiction and nonfiction, to 5,000 words, on horse-related topics, recent or historical, humorous or serious. No how-to pieces on riding or horse care. Poetry, to 40 lines. "We're looking for dramatic tension, high interest, character development, and dialogue in both fiction and nonfiction." Special children's issue published each December. Pays in copies. Guidelines.

STAND MAGAZINE—122 Morris Rd., Lacey's Spring, AL 35754. Daniel Schenker and Amanda Kay, U.S. Eds. (179 Wingrove Rd., Newcastle upon Tyne NE4 9DA UK) British quarterly. Fiction, 2,000 to 5,000 words, and poetry to 100 lines (submit up to 6 poems). No formulaic verse.

STATE STREET REVIEW—FCCJ North Campus, 4501 Capper Rd., Jacksonville, FL 32218–4499. John Hunt, Exec. Ed. Vickie Swindling, Man. Ed. Semiannual. Fiction, to 6,000 words. Nonfiction, 2,000 words, on writers, poets, or on writing itself. Poetry. Pays in copies.

STORY QUARTERLY—P.O. Box 1416, Northbrook, IL 60065. Anne Brashler, Diane Williams, Eds. Short stories and interviews. Pays in copies. Manuscripts read year-round.

THE STYLUS—9412 Huron Ave., Richmond, VA 23294. Roger Reus, Ed. Annual. Articles on writers ("no scholarly/heavily footnoted/dull literary theses"). Original fiction and author interviews. Pays in copies.

THE SUN—The Sun Publishing Co., 107 N. Roberson St., Chapel Hill, NC 27516. Sy Safransky, Ed. Essays, interviews, and fiction, to 7,000 words; poetry; photos, illustrations, and cartoons. "We're interested in all writing that makes sense and enriches our common space." Pays to $300 for fiction, to $500 for nonfiction, $75 for poetry, on publication.

SUN AND SHADE—4205 Quail Ranch Rd., New Smyrna Beach, FL 32168. Kim M. Nicastro, Ed. Semiannual. Fiction, 500 to 5,000 words. Preference given to Florida writers. Pays $15 to $35, on publication.

SYCAMORE REVIEW—Purdue Univ., Dept. of English, West Lafayette, IN 47907. Rob Davidson, Ed.-in-Chief. Semiannual. Poetry, short fiction (no genre fiction), personal essays, drama, and translations. Pays in copies. Manuscripts read September to April.

TAMAQUA—Humanities Dept., Parkland College, 2400 W. Bradley Ave., Champaign, IL 61821. Bruce Morgan, Ed. Semiannual. Fiction, to 12,000 words; intelligent, well-written essays, to 10,000 words; poetry. Pays $10 to $75, on publication.

TAR RIVER POETRY—Dept. of English, East Carolina Univ., Greenville, NC 27834. Peter Makuck, Ed. Poetry and reviews. "Interested in skillful use of language, vivid imagery. Less academic, more powerful poetry preferred." Pays in copies. Submit from September through April.

THE TEXAS REVIEW—English Dept., Sam Houston State Univ., Huntsville, TX 77341. Paul Ruffin, Ed. Fiction, poetry, articles, to 20 typed pages. Reviews. Pays in copies and subscription.

THEMA—Box 74109, Metairie, LA 70033–4109. Virginia Howard, Ed. Fiction, to 20 pages, and poetry, to 2 pages, related to theme. Pays $25 per story; $10 per short-short; $10 per poem; $10 for B&W art/photo, on acceptance. Send SASE for themes and guidelines.

360 DEGREES: ART & LITERARY REVIEW—980 Bush St., Suite 200, San Francisco, CA 94109. Karen Kinnison, Ed. Quarterly art and literary review, featuring fiction and poetry (any length), artwork, graphic imagery, and "art-text," words mixed with images. Send photocopies and photographs only. Pays in copies.

THE THREEPENNY REVIEW—P.O. Box 9131, Berkeley, CA 94709. Wendy Lesser, Ed. Fiction, to 5,000 words. Poetry, to 100 lines. Essays, 1,500 to 3,000 words, on books, theater, film, dance, music, art, television, and politics. Pays to $200, on acceptance. Limited market. Guidelines. Manuscripts read September through May.

TIGHTROPE—323 Pelham Rd., Amherst, MA 01002. Ed Rayher, Ed. Limited-edition, letterpress semiannual. Poetry, any length. Pays in copies. Manuscripts read year-round.

TOMORROW MAGAZINE—P.O. Box 148486, Chicago, IL 60614–8486. Tim W. Brown, Ed. Poetry with an underground sensibility. Pays in copies.

TOMORROW: SPECULATIVE FICTION—P.O. Box 6038, Evanston, IL 60204. Algis Budrys, Ed. Bimonthly. Fiction, to 20,000 words, including science fiction, fantasy, and horror. No poetry, cartoons, or nonfiction. Pays 4¢ to 7¢ a word, on publication.

TOUCHSTONE—P.O. Box 8308, Spring, TX 77387. Bill Laufer, Pub. Annual. Fiction, 750 to 2,000 words: mainstream, experimental. Interviews, essays, reviews. Poetry, to 40 lines. Pays in copies. Manuscripts read year-round.

TOYON—English Dept., Humboldt State Univ., Arcata, CA 95521. Attn: Eds. Fiction, nonfiction, poetry, jokes, photos, and artwork. Queries preferred. No payment.

TREASURE HOUSE—Treasure House Publishing, 1106 Oak Hill Ave., #3A, Hagerstown, MD 21742. Attn: Ed.-in-Chief. Fiction, 1,500 to 3,000 words, and poetry. Submit poems (up to 10) to: Poetry Ed., *Treasure House,* c/o 709 Graydon Ave., #3, Norfolk, VA 23507. (Submit fiction to Hagerstown address.) Pays in copies. Guidelines.

TRIQUARTERLY—Northwestern Univ., 2020 Ridge Ave., Evanston, IL 60208–4302. Attn: Ed. Serious, aesthetically informed and inventive poetry and prose, for an international and literate audience. Pays $20 per page for prose, $1.50 per line for poetry. Manuscripts read October through March. Allow 10 to 12 weeks for reply.

TRIVIA—P.O. Box 9606, N. Amherst, MA 01059–9606. Kay Parkhurst, Ed. Semiannual journal of radical feminist writing. Literary essays, experimental prose, translations, interviews, and reviews. "After-readings": personal accounts of the writer's reaction to books or other writings by women. Pays in copies. Guidelines. Manuscripts read year-round.

2AM MAGAZINE—P.O. Box 6754, Rockford, IL 61125–1754. Gretta Anderson, Ed. Poetry, articles, reviews, and personality profiles, 500 to 2,000 words, as well as fantasy, horror, and some science fiction/sword-and-sorcery short stories, 500 to 5,000 words. Pays ½¢ a word, on acceptance. Manuscripts read year-round.

URBANUS MAGAZINE—P.O. Box 192921, San Francisco, CA 94119. P. Drizhal, Ed. Semiannual. Fiction and nonfiction, 1,000 to 5,000 words, and poetry, to 40 lines, that reflect post-modernist influences for a "readership generally impatient with the mainstream approach." B&W photos and drawings. Pays 1¢ to 2¢ a word; $10 a page for poetry, on acceptance. Query for reading periods.

VERMONT INK—P.O. Box 3297, Burlington, VT 05401. Donna Leach, Ed. Quarterly. Short stories, 2,000 words, that are well-written, entertaining, and "basically G-rated": adventure, historical, humor, mainstream, mystery and suspense, regional interest, romance, science fiction, and westerns. Poetry, to 25 lines, should be upbeat and humorous. Pays $25 for stories; $10 for poetry, on acceptance.

VERVE—P.O. Box 3205, Simi Valley, CA 93093. Ron Reichick, Ed. Contemporary fiction and nonfiction, to 1,000 words, that fit the theme of the issue. Poetry, to 2 pages; submit up to 5 poems. Pays in one copy. Query for themes.

VIGNETTE—P.O. Box 109, Hollywood, CA 90078–0109. Dawn Baillie, Ed. Fiction, to 5,000 words, based on one-word concepts. Send SASE for current themes. Pays $100 to $300, on publication.

THE VILLAGER—135 Midland Ave., Bronxville, NY 10708. Amy Murphy, Ed. Mary Hazzah, Fiction/Articles Ed. Mrs. Joseph Aiello, Poetry Ed. Fiction, 900 to 1,500 words, "in good taste": mystery, adventure, humor, romance. Short, preferably seasonal poetry. Pays in copies.

VINCENT BROTHERS REVIEW—4566 Northern Cir., Riverside, OH 45424–5733. Kimberly Willardson, Ed. Published 3 times a year. Fiction, nonfiction, poetry, fillers, and B&W art. "Read back issues before submitting." Pays from $10 for fiction and nonfiction; $10 for poetry used in "Page Left" feature. Guidelines.

VIRGINIA QUARTERLY REVIEW—One W. Range, Charlottesville, VA 22903. Attn: Ed. Quality fiction and poetry. Serious essays and articles, 3,000 to 6,000 words, on literature, science, politics, economics, etc. Pays $10 per page for prose, $1 per line for poetry, on publication.

VISIONS INTERNATIONAL—1007 Ficklen Rd., Fredericksburg, VA 22405. Bradley R. Strahan, Ed. Published 3 times a year. Poetry, to 30 lines, and B&W drawings. (Query first for art.) "Nothing amateur or previously published. Read magazine before submitting." Pays in copies (or honorarium when funds available). Manuscripts read year-round.

WASCANA REVIEW—c/o Dept. of English, Univ. of Regina, Regina, Sask., Canada S4S 0A2. Kathleen Wall, Ed. Short stories, 2,000 to 6,000 words; critical articles on short fiction and poetry; poetry. Pays $3 per page for prose, $10 for poetry, after publication.

WASHINGTON REVIEW—P.O. Box 50132, Washington, DC 20091–0132. Clarissa Wittenberg, Ed. Poetry; articles on literary, performing and fine arts in the Washington, D.C., area. Fiction, 1,000 to 2,500 words. Area writers preferred. Pays in copies. Responds in 3 months.

WEBSTER REVIEW—English Dept., SLCC—Meramec, 11333 Big Bend Rd., St. Louis, MO 63122. Robert Boyd, Greg Marshall, Eds. Fiction; poetry; interviews; essays; translations. Pays in copies. Manuscripts read September through May.

WEST BRANCH—Bucknell Hall, Bucknell Univ., Lewisburg, PA 17837. Karl Patten, Robert Taylor, Eds. Poetry and fiction. Pays in copies and subscriptions.

WESTERN HUMANITIES REVIEW—Univ. of Utah, Salt Lake City, UT 84112. Amanda Pecor, Man. Ed. Quarterly. Fiction and essays, to 30 pages, and poetry. Pays $50 for poetry, $150 for short stories and essays, on publication. Manuscripts read October through June; responds in 3 to 6 months.

WHETSTONE—P.O. Box 1266, Barrington, IL 60011. Attn: Eds. Fiction, personal essays, and creative nonfiction, to 20 pages. Poems, submit up to 7. Payment varies, on publication.

THE WILLIAM AND MARY REVIEW—P.O. Box 8795, College of William and Mary, Williamsburg, VA 23187–8795. Forrest Pritchard, Ed. Annual. Fiction, critical essays, and interviews, 2,500 to 7,500 words; poetry, all genres (submit 4 to 6 poems). Pays in copies. Manuscripts read September through April. Responds in 3 months.

WILLOW SPRINGS—MS-1, Eastern Washington Univ., Cheney, WA 99004–2496. Attn: Ed. Fiction, poetry, translation, and art. Length and subject matter are open. No payment. Manuscripts read September 15 to May 15.

726

WIND MAGAZINE—P.O. Box 24548, Lexington, KY 40524. Steven R. Cope and Charlie G. Hughes, Eds. Semiannual. Short stories, poems, and essays. Reviews of books from small presses and news of interest to the literary community. Pays in copies. Manuscripts read year-round.

THE WINDLESS ORCHARD—Dept. of English, Indiana-Purdue Univ., Ft. Wayne, IN 46805. Robert Novak, Ed. Contemporary poetry; submit up to 3 poems. Pays in copies. SASE required. Manuscripts read year-round.

WINDSOR REVIEW—Dept. of English, Univ. of Windsor, Windsor, Ont., Canada N9B 3P4. Attn: Ed. Short stories, poetry, and original art. Pays $15 for poetry; $50 for fiction, on publication. Responds in one to 3 months.

WITHOUT HALOS—Ocean County Poets Collective, P.O. Box 1342, Point Pleasant Beach, NJ 08742. Frank Finale, Ed. Submit 3 to 5 poems (to 2 pages) between January 1 and June 30. Pays in copies.

WITNESS—Oakland Community College, 27055 Orchard Lake Rd., Farmington Hills, MI 48334. Peter Stine, Ed. Thematic journal. Fiction and essays, 5 to 20 pages, and poems (submit up to 3). Pays $6 per page for prose, $10 per page for poetry, on publication.

WOMAN OF POWER—P.O. Box 2785, Orleans, MA 02653. Charlene McKee, Ed. A magazine of feminism, spirituality, and politics. Nonfiction, to 5,000 words. Send SASE for issue themes and guidelines. Pays in copies and subscription. Manuscripts read year-round.

THE WORCESTER REVIEW—6 Chatham St., Worcester, MA 01609. Rodger Martin, Ed. Poetry (submit up to 5 poems at a time), fiction, critical articles about poetry, and articles and reviews with a New England connection. Pays in copies. Responds within 6 months.

THE WORMWOOD REVIEW—P.O. Box 4698, Stockton, CA 95204–0698. Marvin Malone, Ed. Quarterly. Poetry and prose-poetry, 4 to 400 lines. "We encourage wit and conciseness." Pays 3 to 20 copies or cash equivalent.

WRITERS FORUM—Univ. of Colorado, 1420 Austin Bluffs Pkwy., Colorado Springs, CO 80933–7150. C. Kenneth Pellow, Ed. Annual. Mainstream and experimental fiction, 1,000 to 8,000 words. Poetry (one to 5 poems per submission). Emphasis on western themes and writers. Pays in copies. Manuscripts read year-round, but best time to submit is July through November.

WRITERS' INTERNATIONAL FORUM—(formerly *Writers' International Open Forum*) P.O. Box 516, Tracyton, WA 98393–0516. Sandra Haven, Ed. Dir. Fiction, 500 to 2,000 words, all genres except horror. "We help writers improve skills and marketability through the exchange of ideas and responses to our published stories by our subscribers." *Special Juniors Edition*: Stories, to 2,000 words, and essays, to 1,200 words, written by and for children 8 to 16 years old. *Special Seniors Edition*: Fiction, to 2,000 words, and essays to 1,200 words, written for and by seniors. Pays from $5, on acceptance.

XANADU—Box 773, Huntington, NY 11743–0773. Mildred Jeffrey, Weslea Sidon, Lois V. Walker, Sue Kain, Eds. Poetry on a variety of topics; no length restrictions. Articles on poetry. Pays in copies. Manuscripts read September through June.

YALE REVIEW—Yale Univ., P.O. Box 208243, New Haven, CT 06520–8243. J.D. McClatchy, Ed. Serious poetry, to 200 lines, and fiction, 3,000 to 5,000 words. Pays average of $300.

THE YALOBUSHA REVIEW—P.O. Box 186, University, MS 38677–0186. Attn: Ed. Annual. Short stories, to 35 pages. Creative essays, to 20 pages. Poetry, any length. "We seek a balance of local, regional, and national writers. We publish new as well as established writers." Pays in copies. (Editor's Choice in fiction and poetry receives $100.)

YARROW—English Dept., Lytle Hall, Kutztown State Univ., Kutztown, PA 19530. Harry Humes, Ed. Semiannual. Poetry. "Just good, solid, clear writing. We don't have room for long poems." Pays in copies. Manuscripts read year-round.

ZYZZYVA—41 Sutter, Suite 1400, San Francisco, CA 94104. Howard Junker, Ed. Publishes work of West Coast writers only: fiction, essays, and poetry. Pays $50 to $250, on acceptance. Manuscripts read year-round.

GREETING CARDS & NOVELTY ITEMS

Companies selling greeting cards and novelty items (T-shirts, coffee mugs, buttons, etc.) often have their own specific requirements for the submission of ideas, verse, and artwork. In general, however, each verse or message should be typed double-space on a 3x5 or 4x6 card. Use only one side of the card, and be sure to put your name and address in the upper left-hand corner. Keep a copy of every verse or idea you send. (It's also advisable to keep a record of what you've submitted to each publisher.) Always enclose an SASE, and do not send out more than ten verses or ideas in a group to any one publisher. Never send original artwork unless a publisher indicates a definite interest in using your work.

AMBERLEY GREETING CARD COMPANY—11510 Goldcoast Dr., Cincinnati, OH 45249–1695. Ned Stern, Ed. Humorous ideas for cards: birthday, illness, friendship, anniversary, congratulations, "miss you," etc. Send SASE for market letter before submitting ideas. Pays $150. Buys all rights.

AMERICAN GREETINGS—One American Rd., Cleveland, OH 44144. Kathleen McKay, Ed. Recruitment. Study current offerings and query before submitting.

BLUE MOUNTAIN ARTS, INC.—P.O. Box 1007, Boulder, CO 80306. Attn: Editorial, Dept. TW. Poetry and prose about love, friendship, family, philosophies, etc. Also material for special occasions and holidays: birthdays, get well, Christmas, Valentine's Day, Easter, etc. Submit seasonal material 5 months in advance of holiday. No artwork or rhymed verse. Include SASE. Pays $200 per poem.

BRILLIANT ENTERPRISES—117 W. Valerio St., Santa Barbara, CA 93101–2927. Ashleigh Brilliant, Ed. Illustrated epigrams. Send SASE for the price of a catalogue and samples. Pays $40, on acceptance.

COMSTOCK CARDS—600 S. Rock, Suite 15, Reno, NV 89502–4115. David Delacroix, Ed. Adult humor, outrageous or sexual, for greeting cards. SASE for guidelines. Payment varies, on publication.

CONTEMPORARY DESIGNS—P.O. Box 60, Gilbert, IA 50105–0060. Sallie Abelson, Ed. Short, positive, humorous sayings for coffee mugs, T-shirts, memo pads, etc. "We are in need of sayings that fit into the following categories: college students, Jewish, camp, teacher, working world. We are not interested in puns, gross ideas, poetry, or prose. No need to enclose artwork; however, if you have a picture of your idea, you may draw it out or describe it." Submit each idea separately on 3x5 cards. Include writer's name and address on each card. Responds in 6 weeks. Pays from $35, on acceptance. Guidelines.

CONTENOVA GIFTS—879 Cranberry Ct., Oakville, Ont., Canada L6L 6J7. Jeff Sinclair, Creative Dir. Catchy, humorous, and sentimental one-liners for ceramic gift mugs. Submit on 3x5 cards; up to 15 ideas at a time. Payment varies, on acceptance. Guidelines.

DAYSPRING GREETING CARDS—P.O. Box 1010, Siloam Springs, AR 72761. Ann Woodruff, Ed. Religious/Christian cards. Uses unrhymed (preferred) and rhymed messages, traditional and light verse (various lengths) for humorous, inspirational, juvenile, and religious cards: anniversary, birthday, holidays, congratulations, friendship, get well, graduation, keep in touch, love, miss you, new baby, please write, sympathy, thank you, wedding, etc. Submit holiday/seasonal material one year ahead. Pays $35 to $50, on acceptance. SASE for guidelines.

DESIGN DESIGN, INC.—P.O. Box 2266, Grand Rapids, MI 49501–2266. Tom Vituj, Creative Dir. Humorous and sentimental ideas for greeting cards. Everyday (birthday, get well, just for fun, etc.) and seasonal (Christmas, Valentine's Day, Easter, Mother's Day, Father's Day, Graduation, Halloween, Thanksgiving) material. Flat fee payment on publication.

DUCK & COVER—P.O. Box 21640, Oakland, CA 94620. Jim Buser, Ed. Outrageous, off the wall, original one-liners for buttons and magnets. SASE for guidelines. Pays $25, on publication.

EPHEMERA, INC.—P.O. Box 490, Phoenix, OR 97535. Attn: Ed. Provocative, irreverent, and outrageously funny slogans for novelty buttons and magnets. Submit typed list of slogans with an SASE. Pays $25 per slogan, on publication. SASE for Guidelines.

HALLMARK CARDS, INC.—Box 419580, Mail Drop 216, Kansas City, MO 64141. No unsolicited submissions.

KATE HARPER DESIGNS—1526 Francisco St., Berkeley, CA 94703. Attn: Writer's Guidelines. Quotes, to 20 words, about work, life, technology, political themes, current social issues, etc., from everyday people for hand-assembled "quotation" cards that take a lighthearted look at life in the 90s. Submit original quotes on index card, one quote per card. No drawings, artwork, or visuals. Send SASE for guidelines before submitting. Pays $25, on acceptance.

OATMEAL STUDIOS—Box 138 TW, Rochester, VT 05767. Attn: Ed. Humorous, clever, and new ideas needed for all occasions. Send legal-size SASE for guidelines.

PANDA INK—P.O. Box 5129, West Hills, CA 91308–5129. Ruth Ann Epstein, Ed. Judaica, metaphysical, cute, whimsical, or beautiful sentiment for greeting cards, bookmarks, clocks, and pins. Submit ideas typed on 8½ x 11 paper, include SASE. "Best time to submit is beginning of the year; decisions are made in January." Payment varies, on acceptance.

PARAMOUNT CARDS—P.O. Box 6546, Providence, RI 02940–6546. Attn: Editorial Freelance. Humorous card ideas for birthday, relative's birthday, friendship, romance, get well, Christmas, Valentine's Day, Easter, Mother's Day, Father's Day, and Graduation. Submit each idea (5 to 10 per submission) on 3x5 card with name and address on each. Payment varies, on acceptance.

PLUM GRAPHICS—P.O. Box 136, Prince Station, New York, NY 10012. Yvette Cohen, Ed. Editorial needs change frequently; write for guidelines (new guidelines 3 to 4 times per year). Queries required. Pays $40 per card, on publication.

RED FARM STUDIO—1135 Roosevelt Ave., P.O. Box 347, Pawtucket, RI 02862. Attn: Production Coord. Traditional cards for birthday, get well, wedding, anniversary, friendship, new baby, sympathy, congrats, and Christmas; also light humor. Pays $4 a line.

REGENCY THERMOGRAPHERS— 64 N. Conahan Dr., P.O. Box 2009, Hazelton, PA 18201. Burt Dolgin, Ed. Quotations for wedding invitations; clever invitation verses for birthday parties and other special occasions. Pays $25 per quote/verse, on acceptance.

ROCKSHOTS, INC.— 632 Broadway, New York, NY 10012. Bob Vesce, Ed. Adult, provocative, humorous gag lines for greeting cards. Submit on 4x5 cards with SASE. Pays $50 per line, on acceptance. SASE for guidelines.

SANGAMON COMPANY—Route 48 W., P.O. Box 410, Taylorville, IL 62568. Attn: Ed. Dept. "We will send writer's guidelines to experienced free lancers before reviewing any submissions. We work on assignment." Pays competitive rates, on acceptance.

SUNRISE PUBLICATIONS, INC.—P.O. Box 4699, Bloomington, IN 47402–4699. Attn: Text Ed. Original copy for holiday and everyday cards. "Submit up to 15 verses, one to 4 lines, on 3x5 cards; simple, to-the-point ideas that could be serious, humorous, or light-hearted, but sincere, without being overly sentimental. Rhymed verse not generally used." Allow 3 months for response. SASE for guidelines. Pays standard rates.

VAGABOND CREATIONS, INC.—2560 Lance Dr., Dayton, OH 45409. George F. Stanley, Jr., Ed. Greeting cards with graphics only on cover (no copy) and short punch line inside: birthday, everyday, Valentine's Day, Christmas, and graduation. Mildly risqué humor with double entendre acceptable. Ideas for illustrated theme stationery. Pays $15, on acceptance.

WARNER PRESS PUBLISHERS—P.O. Box 2499, Anderson, IN 46018. Robin Fogle, Sr. Product Ed. "Writers must send SASE for guidelines before submitting." Religious themes, sensitive prose, and inspirational verse for boxed cards, posters, and calendars. Pays $20 to $35, on acceptance. Also accepts ideas for coloring and activity books.

WEST GRAPHICS PUBLISHING—385 Oyster Point Blvd., #7, S. San Francisco, CA 94080. Attn: Production Dept. Outrageous humor concepts, all occasions (especially birthday) and holidays, for photo and illustrated card lines. Submit on 3x5 cards: concept on one side; name, address, and phone number on other. Pays $100, 30 days after publication.

HUMOR, FILLERS, AND SHORT ITEMS

Magazines noted for their filler departments, plus a cross-section of publications using humor, short items, jokes, quizzes, and cartoons, follow. However, almost all magazines use some type of filler material from time to time, and writers can find dozens of markets by studying copies of magazines at a library or newsstand.

THE AMERICAN FIELD—542 S. Dearborn, Chicago, IL 60605. B.J. Matthys, Man. Ed. Short fact items and anecdotes on hunting dogs and field trials for bird dogs. Pays varying rates, on acceptance.

AMERICAN SPEAKER—Attn: Current Comedy, 1101 30th St. N.W., Washington, DC 20007. Aram Bakshian, Ed.-in-Chief. Original, funny, performable jokes on news, fads, topical subjects, business, etc., for "Current Comedy" section of *American Speaker* Magazine. Jokes for roasts, retirement dinners, and for speaking engagements. Humorous material specifically geared for public speaking situations such as microphone feedback, introductions, long events, etc. Also interested in longer original jokes and anecdotes that can be used by public speakers. No poems, puns, ethnic jokes, or sexist material. Pays $12, on publication. Guidelines.

AMERICAN WOODWORKER—Rodale Press, 33 E. Minor St., Emmaus, PA 18098. Ellis Walentine, Ed. Fillers relating to woodworking or furniture design. Guidelines.

THE ANNALS OF IMPROBABLE RESEARCH—AIR, P.O. Box 380853, Cambridge, MA 02238. Marc Abrahams, Ed. Science humor, science reports and analysis, one to 4 pages. B&W photos. "This journal is the place to find the mischievous, funny, iconoclastic side of science. An insider's journal that lets anyone sneak into the company of wonderfully mad scientists." Guidelines. No payment.

ARMY MAGAZINE—2425 Wilson Blvd., Arlington, VA 22210–0860. Mary B. French, Ed.-in-Chief. True anecdotes on military subjects. Pays $25 to $50, on publication.

THE ATLANTIC MONTHLY—77 N. Washington St., Boston, MA 02114. Attn: Ed. Sophisticated humorous or satirical pieces, 1,000 to 3,000 words. Some light poetry. Pays from $500 for prose, on acceptance.

BICYCLING—33 E. Minor St., Emmaus, PA 18098. Attn: Eds. Anecdotes, helpful cycling tips, and other items for "Bike Shorts" section, 150 to 250 words. Pays $25 to $50, on acceptance.

BYLINE—Box 130596, Edmond, OK 73013. Marcia Preston, Ed.-in-Chief. Humor, 200 to 400 words, about writing. Pays $15 to $20 for humor, on acceptance.

CAPPER'S—1503 S.W. 42nd St., Topeka, KS 66609–1265. Nancy Peavler, Ed. Letters, to 300 words, sharing heartwarming experiences, nostalgic accounts, household hints, poems, and recipes, for "Heart of the Home." Pieces, to 600 words, on people or groups who are making a difference, for "Community Heartbeat." Jokes, submit up to 6 at a time. Pays varying rates (and in gift certificates), on publication.

CASCADES EAST—716 N. E. 4th St., P. O. Box 5784, Bend, OR 97708. Kim Hogue, Ed. Fillers related to travel, history, and recreation in central Oregon. Pays 5¢ to 10¢ a word, extra for photos, on publication.

CATHOLIC DIGEST—P.O. Box 64090, St. Paul, MN 55164–0090. Attn: Filler Ed. Articles, 200 to 500 words, on instances of kindness, for "Hearts Are Trumps." Stories about conversions, for "Open Door." Reports of tactful remarks or actions, for "The Perfect Assist." Accounts of good deeds, for "People Are Like That." Humorous pieces, 50 to 300 words, on parish life, for "In Our Parish." Amusing signs, for "Signs of the Times." Jokes; fillers. No fiction. Pays $4 to $50, on publication.

CHICKADEE—179 John St., Suite 500, Toronto, Ont., Canada M5T 3G5. Catherine Jane Wren, Man. Ed. Juvenile poetry, 10 to 15 lines. Fiction, 800 words. Pays on acceptance. Enclose international reply coupons.

CHILDREN'S PLAYMATE—1100 Waterway Blvd., P.O. Box 567, Indianapolis, IN 46206. Terry Harshman, Ed. Articles and fiction, puzzles, games, mazes, poetry, crafts, and recipes for 6- to 8-year-olds, emphasizing health, fitness, sports, safety, and nutrition. Pays to 17¢ a word (varies on puzzles), on publication.

THE CHURCH MUSICIAN—127 Ninth Ave. N., Nashville, TN 37234. Jere V. Adams, Ed. Humorous fillers with a music slant for church music leaders, pastors, organists, pianists, and members of the music council or other planning groups. (No clippings.) Pays 5½¢ a word, on publication.

COLUMBIA JOURNALISM REVIEW—Columbia Univ., 700 Journalism Bldg., New York, NY 10027. Gloria Cooper, Man. Ed. Amusing mistakes in news stories, headlines, photos, etc. (original clippings required), for "Lower Case." Pays $25, on publication.

COMBO—5 Nassau Blvd. S., Garden City South, NY 11530. Ian M. Feller, Ed. Fillers related to non-sports cards (comic cards, TV/movie cards, science fiction cards, etc.) and comic books. Pays 10¢ a word, on publication.

COUNTRY WOMAN—P. O. Box 989, Greendale, WI 53129. Kathy Pohl, Man. Ed. Short rhymed verse, 4 to 20 lines, seasonal and country-related. All material must be positive and upbeat. Pays $10 to $15, on acceptance.

CRACKED—Globe Communications, Inc., 3 E. 54th St., 15 Fl., New York, NY 10022–3108. Lou Silverstone, Andy Simmons, Eds. Cartoon humor, one to 5 pages, for 10- to 15-year-old readers. "Queries are not necessary, but read the magazine before submitting material!" Pays from $100 per page, on acceptance.

FACES—Cobblestone Publishing, 7 School St., Peterborough, NH 03458–1454. Carolyn P. Yoder, Ed. Puzzles, mazes, crosswords, and picture puzzles for children. Send SASE for list of monthly themes before submitting.

FAMILY CIRCLE—110 Fifth Ave., New York, NY 10011. Uses some short humor, 750 words. No fiction. Payment varies, on acceptance.

THE FAMILY DIGEST—P.O. Box 40137, Fort Wayne, IN 46804. Corine B. Erlandson, Ed. Family- or Catholic parish-oriented humor. Anecdotes, 25 to 250 words, of funny or unusual real-life parish and family experiences. Pays $10, on acceptance.

FARM AND RANCH LIVING—5400 S. 60th St., Greendale, WI 53129. Nick Pabst, Ed. Fillers on rural people and living, 200 words. Pays from $15, on acceptance and publication.

FATE—P.O. Box 64383, St. Paul, MN 55164–0383. Attn: Ed. Factual fillers, to 300 words, on strange, psychic, or paranormal happenings. True personal stories, to 500 words, on proof of mystic experiences. Pays 10¢ a word for fillers, $25 for personal accounts. SASE for guidelines.

FIELD & STREAM—2 Park Ave., New York, NY 10016. Duncan Barnes, Ed. Fillers on hunting, fishing, camping, etc., to 500 words. Cartoons. Pays $75 to $250, sometimes more, for fillers; $100 for cartoons, on acceptance.

FINESCALE MODELER—P.O. Box 1612, Waukesha, WI 53187. Bob Hayden, Ed. One-page hints and tips on building nonoperating, scale models. Payment varies, on acceptance.

GERMAN LIFE—Zeitgeist Publishing, 1 Corporate Dr., Grantsville, MD 21536. Heidi Whitesell, Ed. Fillers, 50 to 200 words, on German culture, its past and present, and how America has been influenced by its German element: history, travel, people, the arts, and social and political issues; also humor and cartoons. Articles, 500 to 2,000 words. Pays to $80 for fillers; $300 to $500 for articles, on publication. Queries preferred for articles.

GLAMOUR—350 Madison Ave., New York, NY 10017. Attn: Viewpoint Ed. Articles, 1,000 words, for "Viewpoint" section: opinion pieces for women. Pays $500, on acceptance.

GUIDEPOSTS—16 E. 34th St., New York, NY 10016. Celeste McCauley, Features Ed. Inspirational anecdotes, to 250 words. Pays $10 to $50, on acceptance.

THE HERB COMPANION—Interweave Press, 201 E. Fourth St., Loveland, CO 80537. Kathleen Halloran, Ed. Trish Faubion, Man. Ed. Bimonthly.

Fillers, 75 to 150 words, for herb enthusiasts: practical horticultural tips, original recipes using herbs, etc. Payment varies, on publication.

MAD MAGAZINE—1700 Broadway, 5th Fl., New York, NY 10019. Attn: Eds. Humorous pieces on a wide variety of topics. Two- to 8-panel cartoons (not necessary to include sketches with submission). Pays top rates, on acceptance. Guidelines strongly recommended.

MATURE LIVING—127 Ninth Ave. N., MSN 140, Nashville, TN 37234. Attn: Ed. Brief, humorous, original items; 25-line profiles with action color photos; "Grandparents Brag Board" items; Christian inspirational pieces for senior adults, 125 words. Pays $10 to $20.

MATURE YEARS—201 Eighth Ave. S., P.O. Box 801, Nashville, TN 37202. Marvin W. Cropsey, Ed. Poems, cartoons, puzzles, jokes, anecdotes, to 300 words, for older adults. Allow 2 months for manuscript evaluation. "A Christian magazine that seeks to build faith. We always show older adults in a favorable light." Include name, address, social security number with all submissions.

MID-WEST OUTDOORS—111 Shore Dr., Hinsdale, IL 60521–5885. Gene Laulunen, Man. Ed. Where to and how to fish and hunt in the Midwest, 700 to 1,500 words, with 2 photos. Pays $15 to $30, on publication.

MODERN BRIDE—249 W. 17th St., New York, NY 10011. Mary Ann Cavlin, Exec. Ed. Humorous pieces, 500 to 1,000 words, for brides. Pays on acceptance.

NATIONAL ENQUIRER—Lantana, FL 33463. Kathy Martin, Fillers Ed. Short, humorous or philosophical fillers, witticisms, anecdotes, jokes, tart comments. Original items only. Short poetry with traditional rhyming verse, amusing, philosophical, or inspirational in nature. No obscure or artsy poetry. Submit seasonal/holiday material at least 3 months in advance. Pays $25, after publication.

THE NEW HUMOR MAGAZINE—Box 216, Lafayette Hill, PA 19444. Edward Savaria, Jr., Ed. Quarterly. Fiction, "from observations in life to the absurd" and reviews of funny books; to 1,000 words. Also short poetry, jokes, and fillers. Pays $40 to $250 for stories and reviews, $5 to $35 for jokes and fillers, on acceptance.

THE NEW YORKER—20 W. 43rd St., New York, NY 10036. Attn: Newsbreaks Dept. Amusing mistakes in newspapers, books, magazines, etc. Pays from $10, extra for headings and tags, on acceptance.

OPTOMETRIC ECONOMICS—American Optometric Assn., 243 N. Lindbergh Blvd., St. Louis, MO 63141. Gene Mitchell, Man. Ed. Short humor for optometrists; writers should have some knowledge of optometry. Payment varies, on acceptance.

OUTDOOR LIFE—2 Park Ave., New York, NY 10016. Stephen Byers, Ed. Short instructive items, 900 to 1,100 words, on hunting, fishing, boating, and outdoor equipment; regional pieces on lakes, rivers, specific geographic areas of special interest to hunters and fishermen. Photos. No fiction or poetry. Pays $300 to $350, on acceptance.

PLAYBOY—680 N. Lake Shore Dr., Chicago, IL 60611. Attn: Party Jokes Ed. or After Hours Ed. Jokes; short original material on new trends, lifestyles, personalities; humorous news items. Pays $100 for jokes; $50 to $350 for "After Hours" items, on publication.

PLAYGIRL— 801 Second Ave., New York, NY 10017. Attn: Man. Ed. Humorous pieces, 800 to 1,500 words, on romance and relationships with a sexual twist, from male or female perspective, 800 to 1,000 words, for "Playgirl Punchline." Pays varying rates, after acceptance. Query.

READER'S DIGEST—Pleasantville, NY 10570. Consult "Contributor's Corner" page for guidelines. No submissions acknowledged or returned.

REAL PEOPLE— 450 7th Ave., Suite 1701, New York, NY 10123–0073. Brad Hamilton, Ed. True stories, to 500 words, about interesting people for "Real Shorts" section: strange occurrences, everyday weirdness, etc.; may be funny, sad, or hair-raising. Also humorous items, to 75 words, taken from small-circulation magazines, newspapers, etc. Pays $25 to $50, on publication.

RHODE ISLAND MONTHLY—95 Chestnut St., Providence, RI 02903. Paula M. Bodah, Man. Ed. Short pieces, to 500 words, on Rhode Island and southeastern Massachusetts: places, customs, people and events. Pays $50 to $150. Query.

ROAD & TRACK—1499 Monrovia Ave., Newport Beach, CA 92663. El-lida Maki, Man. Ed. Short automotive articles, to 450 words, of "timeless nature" for knowledgeable car enthusiasts. Pays on publication. Query.

ROAD KING—Hammock Publishing, 3322 W. End Ave., Suite 700, Nash-ville, TN 37203. Attn: Fillers Ed. Trucking-related cartoons and fillers. Pay-ment is negotiable, on publication.

THE ROTARIAN—1560 Sherman Ave., Evanston, IL 60201–3698. Will-mon L. White, Ed. Occasional humor articles. Payment varies, on acceptance. No payment for fillers, anecdotes, or jokes.

SACRAMENTO MAGAZINE— 4471 D St., Sacramento, CA 95819. Krista Minard, Ed. "City Lights," interesting and unusual people, places, and behind-the-scenes news items, to 400 words. All material must have Sacra-mento tie-in. Payment varies, on publication.

SKI MAGAZINE—2 Park Ave., New York, NY 10016. Lisa Gosselin, Exec. Ed. Short, 100- to 300-word items on news, events, and people in skiing for "Ski Life" department. Pays on acceptance.

SLICK TIMES—P.O. Box 1710, Valley Center, CA 92082. Ken Gammage, Ed. Political humor, 1,000 to 2,000 words, "poking fun at the Clintons." Pays $250 to $375, on publication.

SOAP OPERA UPDATE—270 Sylvan Ave., Englewood Cliffs, NJ 07632. Dawn Mazzurco, Exec. Ed. Soap-opera oriented fillers, to 500 words. Payment varies, on publication.

SPORTS AFIELD—250 W. 55th St., New York, NY 10019. Attn: Almanac Ed. Unusual, useful tips, anecdotes, 100 to 300 words, for "Almanac" section: hunting, fishing, camping, boating, etc. Photos. Pays on publication.

SPORTS CARD TRADER—5 Nassau Blvd., Garden City South, NY 11530. Douglas Kale, Ed. Fillers related to collecting and investing in sports cards, especially baseball, football, basketball, and hockey cards. Also articles on investing in sports cards or memorabilia and interviews with athletes. Pays 10¢ a word, on publication.

STAR— 660 White Plains Rd., Tarrytown, NY 10591. Attn: Ed. Topical articles, 50 to 800 words, on show business and celebrities. Pays varying rates.

735

STITCHES, THE JOURNAL OF MEDICAL HUMOUR—16787 Warden Ave., R.R. #3, Newmarket, Ont., Canada L3Y 4W1. Simon Hally, Ed. Humorous pieces, 250 to 2,000 words, for physicians. "Most articles have something to do with medicine." Short humorous verse and original jokes. Pays 30¢ to 40¢ (Canadian) a word; $50 (Canadian) for cartoons, on publication.

TECH DIRECTIONS—Box 8623, Ann Arbor, MI 48107. Paul J. Bamford, Man. Ed. Cartoons, puzzles, brainteasers, and humorous anecdotes of interest to technology and industrial education teachers and administrators. Pays $20 for cartoons; $25 for puzzles, brainteasers, and other short classroom activities; $5 for humorous anecdotes, on publication.

THOUGHTS FOR ALL SEASONS: THE MAGAZINE OF EPIGRAMS—478 N.E. 56th St., Miami, FL 33137. Michel P. Richard, Ed. Epigrams and puns, one to 4 lines, and poetry, to one page. "Writers are advised not to submit material until they have examined a copy of the magazine." Payment is one copy.

TOUCH—Box 7259, Grand Rapids, MI 49510. Carol Smith, Man. Ed. Puzzles based on the NIV Bible, for Christian girls ages 8 to 14. Pays $10 to $15 per puzzle, on publication. Send SASE for theme update.

TRAVEL SMART—Dobbs Ferry, NY 10522. Attn: Ed. Interesting and useful travel-related tips. Practical information for vacation or business travel. Fresh, original material. Pays $5 to $150. Query for over 250 words.

TRUE CONFESSIONS—233 Park Ave. S., New York, NY 10003. Pat Byrdsong, Ed. Warm, inspirational first-person fillers, to 300 words, about love, marriage, family life, prayer for "Woman to Woman," "My Moment with God," "My Man," and "Incredible But True." Also, short stories, 1,000 to 2,000 words. Pays after publication. Buys all rights.

WISCONSIN TRAILS—P.O. Box 5650, Madison, WI 53705. Attn: Ed. Short fillers, 300 words, about Wisconsin: places to go, things to do, etc. Pays $50, on publication.

JUVENILE AND YOUNG ADULT MAGAZINES

JUVENILE MAGAZINES

AMERICAN GIRL—8400 Fairway Pl., P.O. Box 998, Middleton, WI 53562–0998. Attn: Magazine Dept. Asst. Bimonthly. Articles, to 800 words, and contemporary or historical fiction, to 3,000 words, for girls ages 8 to 12. "We do not want 'teenage' material, i.e. articles on romance, make-up, dating, etc." Payment varies, on acceptance. Query for articles; include photo leads with historical queries.

BABYBUG—P.O. Box 300, Peru, IL 61354. Marianne Carus, Ed.-in-Chief. Stories, to 4 sentences; poems, and action rhymes, to 8 lines, for infants and toddlers, 6 months to 2 years. Pays from $25, on publication. Guidelines.

BOYS' QUEST—P.O. Box 227, Bluffton, OH 45817–4610. Attn: Ed. Bimonthly. Fiction and nonfiction, 500 words, for boys ages 6 to 12. "We are looking for articles, stories, and poetry that deal with timeless topics such as pets, nature, hobbies, science, games, sports, careers, simple cooking, etc." B&W photos a plus. Pays 5¢ a word, on publication. Guidelines.

CALLIOPE: WORLD HISTORY FOR YOUNG PEOPLE—Cobblestone Publishing, Inc., 7 School St., Peterborough, NH 03458. Rosalie Baker and Charles Baker, Eds. Theme-based magazine, published 5 times yearly. Articles, 750 words, with lively, original approach to world history (East/West) through the Renaissance. Shorts, 200 to 750 words, on little-known information related to issue's theme. Fiction, to 1,200 words: historical, biographical, adventure, or retold legends. Activities for children, to 800 words. Poetry, to 100 lines. Puzzles and games. Pays 20¢ to 25¢ a word, on publication. Guidelines and themes.

CHICKADEE—Owl Communications, 179 John St., Suite 500, Toronto, Ont., Canada M5T 3G5. Catherine Jane Wren, Ed. Adventure, folktale, and humorous stories and poems for 3- to 9-year-olds. Also puzzles, activities, and observation games. No religious material. Pays varying rates, on acceptance. Submit complete manuscript with $1.50 check or money order for return postage. Guidelines available.

CHILD LIFE—1100 Waterway Blvd., P.O. Box 567, Indianapolis, IN 46206. Lise Hoffman, Ed. Articles, 600 to 800 words, for 9- to 11-year-olds. Fiction and wacky humor, to 1,000 words. Emphasis on sports, fitness, and health. General interest. Puzzles. Photos. Pays 12¢ a word, extra for professional-quality photos, on publication. Buys all rights.

CHILDREN'S DIGEST—1100 Waterway Blvd., P.O. Box 567, Indianapolis, IN 46206. Layne Cameron, Ed. Health and general-interest publication for preteens. Informative articles, 500 to 1,200 words, and fiction (especially realistic, adventure, mystery, and humorous), 500 to 1,500 words. Historical and biographical articles. Poetry and activities. Pays from 12½¢ a word, from $15 for poems, on publication.

CHILDREN'S PLAYMATE—1100 Waterway Blvd., P.O. Box 567, Indianapolis, IN 46206. Terry Harshman, Ed. General-interest and health-related short stories (health, fitness, nutrition, safety, and exercise), 500 to 600 words, for 6- to 8-year-olds. Simple science articles and how-to crafts pieces with brief instructions. Poems, puzzles, easy recipes, dot-to-dots, mazes, hidden pictures. Pays to 17¢ a word, from $15 for poetry, on publication. Buys all rights.

CLUBHOUSE—Box 15, Berrien Springs, MI 49103. Krista Phillips, Ed. Action-oriented Christian stories, 800 to 1,200 words. Children in stories should be wise, brave, funny, kind, etc. Pays $25 to $35 for stories.

COBBLESTONE: THE HISTORY MAGAZINE FOR CHILDREN—7 School St., Peterborough, NH 03458–1454. Meg Chorlian, Ed. Theme-related articles, biographies, plays, and short accounts of historical events, 700 to 800 words, for 8- to 15-year-olds; also supplemental nonfiction, 300 to 600 words. Fiction, 700 to 800 words. Activities (crafts, recipes, etc.) that can be done

737

either by children alone or with adult supervision. Poetry, to 100 lines. Crossword and other word puzzles using the vocabulary of the issue's theme. Pays 20¢ to 25¢ a word, on publication. (Payment varies for activities and poetry.) Guidelines and themes.

CRAYOLA KIDS—Meredith Custom Publishing, 1912 Grand Ave., Des Moines, IA 50309–3379. Deborah Gore Ohrn, Ed. Bimonthly for readers 3 to 8 years old. Stories, 150 to 250 words; hands-on crafts and activities, one to 4 pages. Interviews. Pays $100 to $250, on publication. Query with resumé and work samples.

CRICKET—P.O. Box 300, Peru, IL 61354–0300. Marianne Carus, Ed.-in-Chief. Articles and fiction, 200 to 2,000 words, for 9- to 14-year-olds. (Include bibliography with nonfiction.) Poetry, to 30 lines. Pays to 25¢ a word, to $3 a line for poetry, on publication. Guidelines.

DISCOVERIES—WordAction Publishing Co., 6401 The Paseo, Kansas City, MO 64131. Attn: Asst. Ed. Weekly designed to correlate with Evangelical Sunday school curriculum. Fiction, 500 to 700 words, for 8- to 10-year-olds should feature contemporary, true-to-life characters and illustrate character building and scriptural application. No poetry. Pays 5¢ a word, on publication. Guidelines.

THE DOLPHIN LOG—The Cousteau Society, 777 United Nations Plaza, New York, NY 10017. Lisa Rao, Ed. Articles, 400 to 600 words, on a variety of topics related to our global water system: marine biology, ecology, natural history, and water-related subjects, for 7- to 13-year-olds. No fiction. Pays $50 to $200, on publication. Query.

FACES—Cobblestone Publishing, 7 School St., Peterborough, NH 03458–1454. Carolyn P. Yoder, Asst. Pub. In-depth feature articles, 800 words, with an anthropology theme. Shorts, 300 to 600 words, related to themes. Fiction, to 800 words, on legends, folktales, stories from around the world, etc., related to theme. Activities, to 700 words, including recipes, crafts, games, etc., for children. Pays 20¢ to 25¢ a word. Guidelines and themes.

FIELD & STREAM—2 Park Ave., New York, NY 10016. Duncan Barnes, Ed. Articles, to 500 words, on hunting and fishing, real-life adventure, how-to projects, natural phenomena and history, conservation, and sporting ethics for *Field and Stream Jr.*, a special section aimed at 8- to 12-year-olds. Puzzles and fillers, 25 to 100 words. Pays from $75 to $650, on acceptance. Queries preferred.

THE FLICKER MAGAZINE—P.O. Box 660544, Vestavia Hills, AL 35266–0544. Lynn Christmas, Submissions Ed. Bimonthly. Features, to 1,000 words; articles, 600 to 800 words; and short pieces, to 300 words, for elementary age children. Positive fiction, articles on real-life role models, and activities that provide hands-on fun. "Avoid magic, ghosts, space fantasies, and supernatural happenings not involving God." Pays 8¢ to 12¢ a word, on acceptance.

THE FRIEND—50 E. North Temple, 23rd Fl., Salt Lake City, UT 84150. Vivian Paulsen, Man. Ed. Stories and articles, 1,000 to 1,200 words. Stories, to 250 words, for younger readers and preschool children. Pays from 9¢ a word, from $25 per poem, on acceptance. Prefers completed manuscripts. Guidelines.

GIRLS' LIFE—Monarch Avalon, Inc., 4517 Harford Rd., Baltimore, MD 21214. Kelly White, Michelle Silver, Sr. Eds. Features of various lengths and one-page fillers that will entertain and educate girls ages 7 to 14. Payment varies, on publication. Query with resumé and clips. Guidelines.

GUIDEPOSTS FOR KIDS—P.O. Box 538A, Chesterton, IN 46304. Mary Lou Carney, Ed. Issue-oriented, thought-provoking articles, 1,000 to 1,500 words. "Things kids not only need to know, but want to know." Fiction: historicals and mysteries, 700 to 1,300 words, and contemporary stories, 1,000 words. "Not preachy. Dialogue-filled and value-driven." Pays competitive rates, on acceptance. Query for articles.

HIGHLIGHTS FOR CHILDREN— 803 Church St., Honesdale, PA 18431–1824. Beth Troop, Manuscript Coord. Stories and articles, to 900 words, for 8- to 12-year-olds: humorous pieces, sports stories, stories that treat holidays in unusual ways (overstocked with Halloween material), retellings of legends and myths, and articles about children who are engaged in the arts. Fiction should have strong plot, believable characters, story line that holds reader's interest from beginning to end. No crime or violence. For articles, cite references used and qualifications. Easy rebus-form stories. Easy-to-read stories and articles, 300 to 600 words. Pays from 14¢ a word, on acceptance. Guidelines.

HOPSCOTCH, THE MAGAZINE FOR GIRLS—P.O. Box 164, Bluffton, OH 45817–0164. Marilyn Edwards, Ed. Bimonthly. Articles and fiction, 600 to 1,000 words, and short poetry for girls ages 6 to 12. Special interest in articles, with photos, about girls involved in worthwhile activities. "We believe young girls deserve the right to enjoy a season of childhood before they become young adults; we are not interested in such topics as sex, romance, cosmetics, hairstyles, etc." Pays 5¢ a word, on publication. Guidelines.

HUMPTY DUMPTY'S MAGAZINE—1100 Waterway Blvd., P.O. Box 567, Indianapolis, IN 46206. Sandy Grieshop, Ed. General-interest publication with an emphasis on health and fitness for 4- to 6-year-olds. Easy-to-read fiction, to 500 words, some with health and nutrition, safety, exercise, or hygiene as theme; humor and light approach preferred. Creative nonfiction, including photo stories. Crafts with clear, brief instructions. No-cook recipes using healthful ingredients. Short verse, narrative poems. Pays to 22¢ a word, from $15 for poems, on publication. Buys all rights.

JACK AND JILL—1100 Waterway Blvd., P.O. Box 567, Indianapolis, IN 46206. Daniel Lee, Ed. Articles, 500 to 800 words, for 7- to 10-year-olds, on sports, fitness, health, nutrition, safety, exercise. Features, 500 to 700 words, on history, biography, life in other countries, etc. Fiction, to 700 words. Short poems, games, puzzles, projects, recipes. Photos. Pays 10¢ to 20¢ a word, extra for photos, on publication.

JUNIOR SCHOLASTIC—Scholastic, Inc., 555 Broadway, New York, NY 10012. Lee Baier, Ed. On-the-spot reports from countries in the news. Payment varies, on acceptance. Query.

JUNIOR TRAILS—1445 Boonville Ave., Springfield, MO 65802–1894. Sinda Zinn, Ed. Fiction, 1,000 to 1,500 words, with a Christian focus, believable characters, and moral emphasis. Articles, 300 to 500 words, on science, nature, biography. Pays 3¢ to 5¢ a word, on acceptance.

KID CITY—Children's Television Workshop, 1 Lincoln Plaza, New York, NY 10023. We do not accept any free-lance work.

KIDS TRIBUTE—900A Don Mills Rd., Suite 1000, Don Mills, Ont., Canada M3C 1V6. Kim Green, Sr. Ed. Quarterly. Movie- or entertainment-related articles, 500 words, for 8- to 13-year-olds. Pays $50 to $75 (Canadian), on acceptance. Query required.

KIDS WORLD MAGAZINE—108–93 Lombard Ave., Winnipeg, Manitoba, Canada R3B 3B1. Stuart Slayen and Leslie Malkin, Eds. Published 6 times a year. Humorous, empowering fiction, 650 to 750 words; and contemporary, educational nonfiction, 750 to 1,200 words, for readers ages 9 to 12. (Magazine is distributed in elementary schools.) Pays $75 to $400 (Canadian), on publication. Queries preferred.

LADYBUG—P.O. Box 300, Peru, IL 61354–0300. Marianne Carus, Ed.-in-Chief. Paula Morrow, Ed. Picture stories and read-aloud stories, 300 to 750 words, for 2- to 6-year-olds; poetry, to 20 lines; songs and action rhymes; crafts, activities, and games. Pays to 25¢ a word for stories; to $3 a line for poetry, on publication. Guidelines.

MY FRIEND—Pauline Books & Media, Daughters of St. Paul, 50 St. Pauls Ave., Boston, MA 02130. Sister Anne Joan Flanagan, Ed. "The Catholic Magazine for Kids." Readers are 6 to 12 years old. Catholic-focused articles, media literacy, lives of saints, etc., 150 to 600 words. Buys first rights. Fiction overstocked. Pays $35 to $100 for articles, $5 for fillers. Query for artwork. Guidelines.

NATIONAL GEOGRAPHIC WORLD—1145 17th St. N.W., Washington, DC 20036–4688. Susan Tejada, Ed. Picture magazine for young readers, ages 8 and older. Natural history, adventure, archaeology, geography, science, the environment, and human interest. Proposals for picture stories only. No unsolicited manuscripts.

NEW MOON, THE MAGAZINE FOR GIRLS AND THEIR DREAMS—P.O. Box 3620, Duluth, MN 55803–3620. Joe Kelly, Man. Ed. "Our goal is to celebrate girls and support their efforts to hang on to their voices, strengths, and dreams as they move from being girls to becoming women." Profiles of girls and women, 300 to 1,000 words. Science and math experiments, 300 to 600 words. Submissions from both girls and adults. Queries preferred. Pays 5¢ to 8¢ a word, on publication. Also publishes companion letter, *New Moon Parenting: For Adults Who Care About Girls*.

ODYSSEY: SCIENCE THAT'S OUT OF THIS WORLD—Cobblestone Publishing, 7 School St., Peterborough, NH 03458–1454. Elizabeth Lindstrom, Ed. Features, 750 words, on astronomy, space science, and other related physical sciences for 8- to 14-year-olds. Science-related fiction, myths, legends, and science fiction stories. Experiments and games. Pays 20¢ to 25¢ a word, on publication. Guidelines and themes.

ON THE LINE—616 Walnut, Scottdale, PA 15683–1999. Mary Clemens Meyer, Ed. Weekly paper for 10- to 14-year-olds. Nature, general nonfiction, and how-to articles, 350 to 500 words; fiction, 900 to 1,200 words; poetry, puzzles, cartoons. Pays to 4¢ a word, on acceptance.

OWL—Owl Communications, 179 John St., Suite 500, Toronto, Ont., Canada M5T 3G5. Nyla Ahmad, Ed. Articles, 500 to 1,000 words, for 8- to 12-year-olds, about animals, science, people, technology, new discoveries, activities. Pays varying rates, on acceptance. Guidelines.

740

PLAYS, THE DRAMA MAGAZINE FOR YOUNG PEOPLE—120 Boylston St., Boston, MA 02116–4615. Elizabeth Preston, Man. Ed. Wholesome one-act comedies, dramas, skits, satires, farces, and creative dramatic material suitable for school productions at junior high, middle, and lower grade levels. Plays with modern settings preferred. Also uses dramatized classics, folktales and fairy tales, puppet plays. No religious plays or musicals. Pays good rates, on acceptance. Buys all rights. Query for classics, folk and fairy tales. Guidelines.

POCKETS—1908 Grand Ave., Box 189, Nashville, TN 37202–0189. Janet Knight, Ed. Ecumenical magazine for 6- to 12-year-olds. Fiction and scripture stories, 600 to 1,500 words; short poems; games and family communication activities; role model stories; and stories about children involved in justice and environmental projects. Pays from 12¢ a word, $25 to $50 for poetry, on acceptance. Guidelines and themes. Annual fiction contest; send SASE for details.

POWER AND LIGHT—6401 The Paseo, Kansas City, MO 64131. Beula J. Postlewait, Preteen Ed. Fiction, 500 to 800 words, for grades 5 and 6, with Christian emphasis. Cartoons and puzzles. Pays 5¢ a word for multi-use rights, 1¾¢ a word for reprints. Pays $15 for cartoons and puzzles.

R-A-D-A-R—Standard Publishing, 8121 Hamilton Ave., Cincinnati, OH 45231. Elaina Meyers, Ed. Weekly Sunday school take-home paper. Articles, 400 to 500 words, on nature, hobbies, crafts. Short stories, 900 to 1,000 words: mystery, sports, school, family, with 12-year-old as main character; serials, 2,000 words. Christian emphasis. Poems. Pays to 7¢ a word, to 50¢ a line for poetry, on acceptance.

RANGER RICK—National Wildlife Federation, 8925 Leesburg Pike, Vienna, VA 22184. Gerald Bishop, Ed. Articles, to 900 words, on wildlife, conservation, natural sciences, and kids in the outdoors, for 6- to 9-year-olds. Nature-related fiction, mysteries, fantasies, and science fiction welcome. Games (no crosswords or word-finds), crafts, humorous poems, outdoor activities, and puzzles. For nonfiction, query with sample lead, list of references, and names of experts you plan to contact. Guidelines. Pays to $550, on acceptance.

SCHOLASTIC DYNAMATH—555 Broadway, New York, NY 10012–3999. Attn: Manuscript Ed. Articles, games, and puzzles for 5th and 6th grade math students. Send 9x12 SASE for free sample of magazine. Query.

SCIENCEWORLD—Scholastic, Inc., 555 Broadway, New York, NY 10012–3999. Karen McNulty, Ed. Science articles, 750 words, and science news articles, 200 words, on life science, earth science, physical science, environmental science and/or health for readers in grades 7 to 10 (ages 12 to 15). "Articles should include current, exciting science news. Writing should be lively and show an understanding of teens' perspectives and interests." Pays $100 to $125 for news items; $200 to $650 for features. Query with a well-researched proposal, suggested sources, 2 to 3 clips of your work, and an SASE.

SESAME STREET MAGAZINE—One Lincoln Plaza, New York, NY 10023. Anne Heller, Exec. Ed. Articles on children and violence: Susan Schneider, Articles Ed. Articles on educational issues: Nadia Zonis, Medical/Health Ed. Articles, 800 to 2,500 words, on medical, psychological, and educational issues for families with young children (up to 8 years old). Pays 50¢ to $1 per word, up to 6 weeks after acceptance.

SHOFAR—43 Northcote Dr., Melville, NY 11747. Gerald H. Grayson, Ed. Short stories, 500 to 750 words; articles, 250 to 750 words; poetry, to 50 lines; short fillers, games, puzzles, and cartoons for Jewish children, 8 to 13. All material must have a Jewish theme. Pays 10¢ a word, on publication. Submit holiday pieces at least 6 months in advance.

SKIPPING STONES—P.O. Box 3939, Eugene, OR 97403. Arun N. Toké, Exec. Ed. "A Multicultural Children's Magazine." Articles, approximately 500 to 750 words, relating to community and family, religions, culture, nature, traditions, and cultural celebrations in other countries, for 7- to 15-year-olds. "Especially invited to submit are children from cultural backgrounds other than European-American and/or those with physical challenges. We print art, poetry, songs, games, stories, and photographs from around the world and include many different languages (with English translation)." Payment is one copy, on publication. Guidelines.

SOCCER JR.—27 Unquowa Rd., Fairfield, CT 06430. Joe Provey, Ed. Fiction and fillers about soccer for readers ages 8 and up. Pays $450 for a feature or story; $250 for department pieces, on acceptance. Query.

SPIDER—P.O. Box 300, Peru, IL 61354. Attn: Submissions Ed. Fiction, 300 to 1,000 words, for 6- to 9-year-olds: realistic, easy-to-read stories, fantasy, folk and fairy tales, science fiction, fables, myths. Articles, 300 to 800 words, on nature, animals, science, technology, environment, foreign culture, history (include short bibliography with articles). Serious, humorous, or nonsense poetry, to 20 lines. Puzzles, activities, and games, to 4 pages, also considered. Pays 25¢ a word, $3 per line for poetry, on publication.

SPORTS ILLUSTRATED FOR KIDS—Time & Life Bldg., 1271 Ave. of the Americas, New York, NY 10020–1393. Stephen Malley, Sr. Ed. Articles, 1,000 to 1,500 words, (submit to Amy Lennard Goehner) and short features, 500 to 600 words, (submit to Jon Scher) for 8- to 13-year-olds. "Most articles are staff-written. Department pieces are the best bet for free lancers." (Read magazine and guidelines to learn about specific departments.) Puzzles and games (submit to Erin Egan). No fiction or poetry. Pays $500 for departments, $1,000 to $1,250 for articles, on acceptance. Query required.

STONE SOUP, THE MAGAZINE BY YOUNG WRITERS AND ARTISTS—Box 83, Santa Cruz, CA 95063–0083. Gerry Mandel, Ed. Stories, free-verse poems, plays, book reviews by children under 14. "Preference given to writing based on real-life experiences." Pays $10.

STORY FRIENDS—Mennonite Publishing House, Scottdale, PA 15683. Rose Stutzman, Ed. Stories, 350 to 800 words, for 4- to 9-year-olds, on Christian faith and values in everyday experiences. Poetry. Pays to 5¢ a word, to $10 per poem, on acceptance.

3-2-1 CONTACT—Children's Television Workshop, 1 Lincoln Plaza, New York, NY 10023. Curtis Slepian, Ed. Entertaining and informative articles, 600 to 1,000 words, for 8- to 14-year-olds, on all aspects of science, computers, scientists, and children who are learning about or practicing science. Pays $75 to $500, on acceptance. No fiction. Query.

TOUCH—Box 7259, Grand Rapids, MI 49510. Carol Smith, Man. Ed. Upbeat fiction and features, 500 to 1,000 words, for Christian girls ages 8 to 14; personal life, nature, crafts. Poetry, puzzles. Pays 2½¢ a word, extra for photos, on acceptance. Query with SASE for theme update.

TURTLE MAGAZINE FOR PRESCHOOL KIDS—1100 Waterway Blvd., Box 567, Indianapolis, IN 46206. Nancy S. Axelrad, Ed. Heavily illustrated articles with an emphasis on health and nutrition for 2- to 5-year-olds. Humorous, entertaining fiction. Also, crafts, pencil activities, and simple science experiments. Simple poems. Action rhymes and read-aloud stories, to 300 words. Pays to 22¢ a word for stories; from $15 for poems; payment varies for activities, on publication. Buys all rights. Guidelines.

U.S. KIDS—1100 Waterway Blvd., P.O. Box 567, Indianapolis, IN 46206. Beth Struck, Health/Fitness Ed. Articles, to 1,000 words, on issues related to kids ages 5 to 10, fiction, true-life adventures, science and nature topics. Special emphasis on health and fitness. Fiction with real-world focus; no fantasy.

VENTURE—Christian Service Brigade, P.O. Box 150, Wheaton, IL 60189. Deborah Christensen, Ed. Fiction and nonfiction, 1,000 words, for 8- to 11-year-old boys involved in Stockade. "Think like a boy this age. They want action, adventure, and humor. They also need to see how faith in God affects every area of life and is more than just a prayer to get out of trouble." Humor and fillers; color photos also accepted. Pays 5¢ to 10¢ a word, on publication.

WONDER TIME— 6401 The Paseo, Kansas City, MO 64131. Lois Perrigo, Ed. Stories, 250 to 350 words, for 6- to 8-year-olds, with Christian emphasis to correlate with Sunday school curriculum. Pays $25 for stories, on production. Send SASE for guidelines, themes, and sample issue.

YOUNG JUDEAN—50 W. 58th St., New York, NY 10019. Jonathan Mayo, Ed. Quarterly. Articles, 500 to 1,000 words, with photos, for 9- to 12-year-olds, on Israel, Jewish holidays, Jewish-American life, Jewish history. Fiction, 800 to 1,000 words, on Jewish themes. Fillers, humor, reviews. No payment.

YOUTH UPDATE—*St. Anthony Messenger Press,* 1615 Republic St., Cincinnati, OH 45210. Attn: Ed. "Articles for Catholic teens that address timely topics. Avoid cuteness, glib phrases and cliches, academic or erudite approaches, preachiness." Pays on acceptance, 14¢ a word. Query with outline and SASE.

ZILLIONS—Consumers Union of the United States, 101 Truman Ave., Yonkers, NY 10703–9925. Moye Thompson, Man. Ed. Bimonthly. Articles, 1,000 to 1,500 words, on consumer education (money, product testing, health, etc.), for kids ages 9 to 14. "We are the *Consumer Reports* for kids." Pays $500 to $2,000, on publication. Guidelines.

YOUNG ADULT MAGAZINES

ALIVE NOW!—P.O. Box 189, Nashville, TN 37202. Attn: Ed. Short essays, 250 to 400 words, with Christian emphasis for adults and young adults. Poetry, one page. B&W photos. Pays $20 to $30, on publication. Query with SASE for themes.

ALL ABOUT YOU— 6420 Wilshire Blvd., Los Angeles, CA 90048–5515. Roxanne Camron, Ed. Dir. Articles, 1,000 to 1,500 words, on issues of interest to young women. Payment varies, on acceptance. Queries.

BLUE JEAN MAGAZINE—P.O. Box 90856, Rochester, NY 14609. Sherry S. Handel, Pub./Ed.-in-Chief. Articles "for teen girls who dare." Profiles, 1,000 to 3,000 words, on women business owners. Articles on nonprofit groups, environmental action, teen adventurers, careers, college information. Fiction and poetry. "About 75% of magazine is written by teen writers. You won't find supermodels, tips on dieting, or fashion spreads in our magazine." Pays in copies.

BOYS' LIFE—1325 W. Walnut Hill Ln., P.O. Box 152079, Irving, TX 75015–2079. Attn: Ed. Publication of Boy Scouts of America. Articles and fiction, 500 to 1,500 words, for 8- to 18-year-old boys. Pays from $350 for major articles, $750 for fiction, on acceptance. Query for articles; send complete manuscript for fiction.

CAMPUS LIFE— 465 Gundersen Dr., Carol Stream, IL 60188. Harold Smith, V.P./Ed. Articles reflecting Christian values and world view, for high school and college students. Humor, general fiction, and true, first-person experiences. "If we have a choice of fiction, how-to, and a strong first-person story, we'll go with the true story every time." Photo-essays, cartoons. Pays 10¢ to 15¢ a word, on acceptance. Query.

CHALLENGE—1548 Poplar Ave., Memphis, TN 38104–2493. Jeno Smith, Ed. Southern Baptist. Articles, to 800 words, for 12- to 18-year-old boys, on teen issues, current events. Photo-essays on Christian sports personalities. Pays 5¢ a word, extra for photos, on acceptance.

CRACKED—Globe Communications, Inc., 3 E. 54th St., 15 Fl., New York, NY 10022–3108. Lou Silverstone, Andy Simmons, Eds. Humor, one to 5 pages, for 10- to 15-year-old readers. Cartoons/comic book style work; no short stories or poetry. "Read magazine before submitting." Pays $100 per page, on acceptance.

EDGE, THE HIGH PERFORMANCE ELECTRONIC MAGAZINE FOR STUDENTS—(formerly *Young Scholar*) 4905 Pine Cone Dr., Suite 2, Durham, NC 27707. Greg Sanders, Ed. Electronic-only magazine for bright high school students, available on the World Wide Web at http://www.jayi.com/jayi/Fishnet/Edge. Features, 1,200 to 1,500 words. Departments include "News to Use," 400 to 500 words; "Performance," 750 words; "Mindstuff," 500-word reviews of older books; "What's Hot Now," 250 to 400 words, on interesting, worthwhile products. "The magazine is not about school; it's about teenagers living the learning lifestyle. Our readers are sophisticated. Don't write anything elementary, preachy, or thoughtless. Especially interested in literary journalism/creative nonfiction." Pays $400 to $500 for features, $25 to $300 for department pieces, on acceptance. Queries preferred. Guidelines available on Web site.

EXPLORING—P.O. Box 152079, 1325 W. Walnut Hill Ln., Irving, TX 75015–2079. Scott Daniels, Exec. Ed. Publication of Boy Scouts of America. Articles, 500 to 1,500 words, for 14- to 21-year-old boys and girls, on teenage trends, college, computer games, music, education, careers, "Explorer" activities (hiking, canoeing, camping), and program ideas for meetings. No controversial subjects. Pays $150 to $750, on acceptance. Query. Guidelines.

HOW ON EARTH!—P.O. Box 339, Oxford, PA 19363–0339. Sally Clinton, Ed.-in-Chief. Articles, 1,000 to 2,000 words, by writers ages 13 to 24 on vegetarian living, animals, the environment, social justice, youth empowerment, and activism; essays, personal pieces, interviews, and creative writing, 400 to 800 words, on related subjects; food reviews, 300 to 700 words; music and book reviews, 200 to 500 words. "Living Vegetarian," general essays, to 800 words, about being vegetarian in a meat eating society. Adult submissions are occasionally accepted for research/information articles and general interest articles, 1,000 to 2,000 words. Pays in copies. Query. Guidelines.

KEYNOTER—3636 Woodview Trace, Indianapolis, IN 46268. Julie A. Carson, Exec. Ed. Articles, 1,500 to 1,800 words, for high school leaders: general-interest features; self-help; contemporary teenage problems. No fillers, poetry, first-person accounts, or fiction. Pays $150 to $350, on acceptance. Query preferred.

LISTEN MAGAZINE—55 W. Oak Ridge Dr., Hagerstown, MD 21740. Lincoln Steed, Ed. Articles, 1,200 to 1,500 words, providing teens with "a vigorous, positive, educational approach to the problems arising from the use of tobacco, alcohol, and other drugs." Pays 5¢ to 7¢ a word, on acceptance.

THE LOOK—P.O. Box 272, Cranford, NJ 07016–0272. John R. Hawks, Pub. Articles, 1,500 to 3,000 words, on fashion, student life, employment, relationships, and profiles of interest to local (NJ) readers ages 16 to 26. Also, beach stories and articles about the New Jersey shore. Pays $30 to $200, on publication.

MERLYN'S PEN: THE NATIONAL MAGAZINES OF STUDENT WRITING—P.O. Box 1058, Dept. WR, East Greenwich, RI 02818. R. James Stahl, Ed. *Intermediate Edition*: writing by students in grades 6 through 9. Short stories, to 3,500 words; reviews; travel pieces; and poetry, to 100 lines. *Senior Edition*: for writers in grades 9 through 12. Fiction, 3,500 words. Poetry, to 200 lines. Responds with a brief critique in 10 weeks. Pays $5 to $25, plus copies. Guidelines.

NEW ERA—50 E. North Temple, Salt Lake City, UT 84150. Richard M. Romney, Ed. Articles, 150 to 1,500 words, and fiction, to 2,000 words, for young Mormons. Poetry. Photos. Pays 5¢ to 20¢ a word, 25¢ a line for poetry, on acceptance. Query.

SCHOLASTIC UPDATE—555 Broadway, New York, NY 10012–3999. Steve Manning and Herbert Buchsbaum, Eds. Biweekly. News articles, 500 words or 1,000 to 1,500 words, for teenagers. Pays $150 to $1,000, on acceptance. Send SASE for guidelines before querying.

SEVENTEEN—850 Third Ave., New York, NY 10022. Joe Bargmann, Features Ed. Articles, to 2,500 words, on subjects of interest to teenagers. Sophisticated, well-written fiction, 1,000 to 4,000 words, for young adults. Personal essays, to 1,200 words, by writers 21 and younger for "Voice." Pays varying rates, on acceptance.

SISTERS IN STYLE—233 Park Ave. S., 5th Fl., New York, NY 10003. Cynthia Marie Horner, Ed. Dir. Bimonthly. "For Today's Young Black Woman." Articles. No fiction or poetry. Beauty, fashion, quizzes, and advice for African-American teens. Payment varies, on publication. Query.

STRAIGHT—8121 Hamilton Ave., Cincinnati, OH 45231. Heather E. Wallace, Ed. Articles on current situations and issues for Christian teens. Humor. Well-constructed fiction, 1,000 to 1,500 words, showing teens using Christian principles. Poetry by teenagers. Photos. Pays about 5¢ to 7¢ a word, on acceptance. Guidelines.

'TEEN—6420 Wilshire Blvd., Los Angeles, CA 90048–5515. Attn: Ed. Short stories, 2,500 to 4,000 words: mystery, teen situations, adventure, romance, humor for teens. Pays from $200, on acceptance. Buys all rights.

745

TEEN LIFE—1445 Boonville Ave., Springfield, MO 65802–1894. Tammy Bicket, Ed. Articles, 500 to 1,000 words, and fiction, to 1,200 words, for 13- to 19-year-olds; strong evangelical emphasis. Interviews with Christian athletes and other well-known Christians; true stories; up-to-date factual articles. Send SASE for current topics. Pays on acceptance.

TEEN POWER—Box 632, Glen Ellyn, IL 60138. Sarah M. Peterson, Ed. Take-home Sunday school paper. True-to-life fiction or first-person (as told to), true teen experience stories with Christian insights and conclusion, 700 to 1,000 words. Pays 8¢ to 12¢ a word, extra for photos, on acceptance.

TEEN VOICES—316 Huntington Ave., Boston, MA 02115. Alison Amoroso, Ed.-in-Chief. Quarterly. Fiction, 200 to 350 words; nonfiction, 200 to 400 words; and poetry, to 100 words. Submissions by teenaged girls only. Pays in copies.

TIGER BEAT—Sterling/MacFadden Partnership, 233 Park Ave. S., New York, NY 10003. Louise Barile, Ed. Articles, to 4 pages, on young people in show business and the music industry. Pays varying rates, on acceptance. Query.

TQ/TEEN QUEST—2221 W. Walnut Hill Ln., Irving, TX 75038. Christopher Lyon, Ed. Articles and well-crafted fiction, to 2,000 words, for Christian teens. Cartoons and color slides. Pays 10¢ to 15¢ a word, on publication.

WHAT! A MAGAZINE—108–93 Lombard Ave., Winnipeg, Manitoba, Canada R3B 3B1. Stuart Slayen and Leslie Malkin, Eds. Published 5 times a year. Articles, 650 to 2,000 words, on contemporary issues for teenaged readers. (Magazine is distributed in high schools.) Pays $100 to $500 (Canadian), on publication.

YM—685 Third Ave., New York, NY 10017. Maria Baugh, Man. Ed. Articles, to 2,500 words, on entertainment, lifestyle, fashion, beauty, relationships, health, for women ages 14 to 19. Payment varies, on acceptance. Query with clips.

YOUNG AND ALIVE—4444 S. 52nd St., Lincoln, NE 68506. Richard J. Kaiser, Man. Ed. M. Marilyn Brown, Ed. Quarterly. Feature articles, 800 to 1,400 words, for blind and visually impaired young adults on adventure, biography, camping, careers, health, history, hobbies, holidays, marriage, nature, practical Christianity, sports, and travel. Photos. Pays 3¢ to 5¢ a word, $5 to $20 for photos, on acceptance. Guidelines.

YOUNG SALVATIONIST—The Salvation Army, 615 Slaters Ln., P.O. Box 269, Alexandria, VA 22313. Attn: Youth Ed. Articles for teens, 800 to 1,200 words, with Christian perspective; fiction, 800 to 1,200 words; short fillers. Pays 10¢ a word, on acceptance.

YOUNG SCHOLAR—See *Edge*.

ZELOS—Box 632, Glen Ellyn, IL 60138. Sarah M. Peterson, Ed. First-person true stories, personal experience, how-tos, humor, fiction, to 1,000 words, for 15- to 20-year-olds. Send photos, if available. Must have Christian emphasis. Pays 8¢ to 20¢ a word.

THE DRAMA MARKET

Community, regional, and civic theaters and college dramatic groups offer the best opportunities today for playwrights to see their work produced, whether on the stage or in dramatic readings. Indeed, aspiring playwrights will be encouraged to hear that many well-known playwrights received their first recognition in the regional theaters. Payment is generally nominal, but regional and university theaters usually buy only the right to produce a play, and all further rights revert to the author. Since most directors like to work closely with authors on any revisions necessary, theaters will often pay the playwright's expenses while in residence during rehearsals. The thrill of seeing your play come to life on the stage is one of the pleasures of being on hand for rehearsals and performances. In addition to producing plays and giving dramatic readings, many theaters also sponsor competitions or new play festivals.

Aspiring playwrights should query college and community theaters in their region to find out which ones are interested in seeing original scripts. Dramatic associations of interest to playwrights include the Dramatists Guild (234 W. 44th St., New York, NY 10036), and Theatre Communications Group, Inc. (355 Lexington Ave., New York, NY 10017), which publishes the annual *Dramatists Sourcebook. The Playwright's Companion*, published by Feedback Theatrebooks (305 Madison Ave., Suite 1146, New York, NY 10165), is an annual directory of theaters and prize contests seeking scripts. See the *Organizations for Writers* list for details on dramatists' associations.

Some of the theaters on this list require that playwrights submit all or some of the following with scripts—cast list, synopsis, resumé, recommendations, return postcard—and with scripts and queries, SASEs must always be enclosed.

While the almost unlimited television offerings on commercial, educational, and cable TV stations, in addition to the hundreds of films released yearly, may lead free-lance writers to believe that opportunities to sell movie and television scripts are infinite, unfortunately, this is not true. With few exceptions, TV and film producers and programmers will read scripts and queries submitted only through recognized agents. (For a list of agents, see page 862.) Writers who nonetheless want to try their hand at writing directly for this very limited market should be prepared to learn the special techniques and acceptable format of scriptwriting, either by taking a workshop through a university or at a writers conference, or by reading one or more of the many books on this subject. Also, experience in playwriting and a knowledge of dramatic structure gained through working in amateur, community, or professional theaters can be helpful.

REGIONAL AND UNIVERSITY THEATERS

ACTORS THEATRE OF LOUISVILLE—316 W. Main St., Louisville, KY 40202. Michael Bigelow Dixon, Lit. Mgr. Ten-minute comedies and dramas, to 10 pages. Longer one-act and full-length plays accepted from literary agents, and from playwrights with letter of recommendation from another professional theatre. SASE. Annual contest. Guidelines.

A. D. PLAYERS—2710 W. Alabama, Houston, TX 77098. Attn: Lit. Mgr. Jeannette Clift George, Artistic Dir. Full-length or one-act comedies, dramas, musicals, children's plays, and adaptations with Christian world view. Submit resumé, cast list, and synopsis with SASE. Readings. Pays negotiable rates.

ALABAMA SHAKESPEARE FESTIVAL—The State Theatre, #1 Festival Dr., Montgomery, AL 36117–4605. Eric Schmiedl, Lit. Assoc. Full-length scripts with southern and/or African-American themes, issues, or history; and scripts with southern and/or African-American authors. One work per author; query.

ALLEY THEATRE— 615 Texas Ave., Houston, TX 77002. Travis Mader, Dramaturg. Full-length plays, including translations and adaptations. No unsolicited scripts; agent submissions or professional recommendations only.

ALLIANCE THEATRE COMPANY—1280 Peachtree St. N.E., Atlanta, GA 30309. Attn: Lit. Dept. Full-length comedies and dramas especially those that "deal with moral/spiritual questions of life in multicultural America." Query with synopsis and up to ten pages of sample dialogue; no unsolicited scripts. Pay varies.

AMERICAN LITERATURE THEATRE PROJECT—Fountain Theatre, 5060 Fountain Ave., Los Angeles, CA 90029. Simon Levy, Prod. Dramaturg. One-act and full-length stage adaptations of classic and contemporary American literature. Sets and cast size are unrestricted. Send synopsis and SAS postcard. Rate of payment is standard, as set by the Dramatists Guild.

AMERICAN LIVING HISTORY THEATER—P.O. Box 752, Greybull, WY 82426. Dorene Ludwig, Artistic Dir. One-act, (one or 2 characters preferred) historically accurate (primary source materials only) dramas dealing with marketable or known American historical and literary characters and events. Submit treatment and letter with SASE. Responds within 6 months. Pays varying rates.

AMERICAN STAGE COMPANY—FDU, Box 336, Teaneck, NJ 07666. James Vagias, Exec. Prod. Full-length comedies, dramas, and musicals for cast of 5 or 6 and single set. No unsolicited scripts.

ARENA STAGE—Sixth and Maine Ave. S.W., Washington, DC 20024. Cathy Madison, Lit. Mgr. No unsolicited manuscripts; send synopsis, first 10 pages of dialogue, and bio.

ARKANSAS REPERTORY THEATRE COMPANY— 601 S. Main, P.O. Box 110, Little Rock, AR 72203–0110. Brad Mooy, Lit. Mgr. Full-length comedies, dramas, and musicals; prefer up to 8 characters. Send synopsis, cast list, resumé, and return postage; do not send complete manuscript. Reports in 3 months.

ARTREACH TOURING THEATRE—3074 Madison Rd., Cincinnati, OH 45209. Kathryn Schultz Miller, Artistic Dir. One-act dramas and adaptations for touring family theater; up to 3 cast members, simple sets. Submit script with synopsis, cast list, resumé, recommendations, and SASE. Payment varies.

BARTER THEATER—P.O. Box 867, Abingdon, VA 24210. Richard Rose, Artistic Dir. Full-length dramas, comedies, adaptations, and children's plays.

Submit synopsis, dialogue sample, and SASE. Allow 6 to 8 months for report. Payment rates negotiable.

BERKSHIRE THEATRE FESTIVAL—Box 797, Stockbridge, MA 01262. Arthur Storch, Artistic Dir. Full-length comedies, musicals, and dramas; cast to 8. Submit through agent only.

BOARSHEAD THEATER— 425 S. Grand Ave., Lansing, MI 48933. John Peakes, Artistic Dir. Full-length comedies and dramas with simple sets and cast of up to 10. Send precis, 5 to 10 pages of dialogue, cast list with descriptions. SAS postcard for reply.

BRISTOL RIVERSIDE THEATRE—Box 1250, Bristol, PA 19007. Susan D. Atkinson, Producing/Artistic Dir. Full-length plays with up to 15 actors and a simple set.

CALIFORNIA UNIVERSITY THEATRE—California, PA 15419. Dr. Richard J. Helldobler, Chairman. Unusual, avant-garde, and experimental one-act and full-length comedies and dramas, children's plays, and adaptations. Cast size varies. Submit synopsis with short, sample scene(s). Payment available.

CENTER STAGE—700 N. Calvert St., Baltimore, MD 21202. James Magruder, Resident Dramaturg. Full-length comedies, dramas, translations, adaptations. No unsolicited manuscripts. Send synopsis, a few sample pages, resumé, cast list, and production history. Allow 8 to 10 weeks for reply.

CHILDSPLAY, INC.—Box 517, Tempe, AZ 85280. David Saar, Artistic Dir. Multigenerational plays running 45 to 120 minutes: dramas, musicals, and adaptations for family audiences. Productions may need to travel. Submissions accepted July through December. Reports in 2 to 6 months.

CIRCLE IN THE SQUARE/UPTOWN—1633 Broadway, New York, NY 10019–6795. Michael Breault, Artistic Assoc. Accepts agented material only. SASE.

CITY THEATRE COMPANY—57 S. 13th St., Pittsburgh, PA 15203. John Henning, Lit. Dir. Full-length cutting-edge comedies and dramas; especially interested in women and minorities. Cast to 10; simple sets. Query September to May. Royalty.

CLASSIC STAGE COMPANY—136 E. 13th St., New York, NY 10003. Mary Esbjornson, Exec. Dir. David Esbjornson, Artistic Dir. Full-length adaptations and translations of existing classic literature. Submit synopsis with cast list and 12 pages of sample dialogue, September to May. Offers readings. Pays on royalty basis.

THE CONSERVATORY THEATRE ENSEMBLE—c/o Tamalpais High School, 700 Miller Ave., Mill Valley, CA 94941. Daniel Caldwell, Artistic Dir. Comedies, dramas, children's plays, adaptations, and scripts addressing high school issues for largely female cast (about 3 women per man). "One-act plays of approximately 30 minutes are especially needed, as we produce 40 short plays each season using teenage actors." Send synopsis and resumé.

CROSSROADS THEATRE CO.—7 Livingston Ave., New Brunswick, NJ 08901. Ricardo Khan, Artistic Dir. Sydné Mahone, Dir. of Play Development. Full-length and one-act dramas, comedies, musicals, and adaptations; issue-oriented experimental plays that offer honest, imaginative, and insightful examinations of the African-American experience. Also interested in African

749

and Caribbean plays and plays exploring cross-cultural issues. No unsolicited scripts; queries only, with synopsis, cast list, resumé, and SASE.

DELAWARE THEATRE COMPANY—200 Water St., Wilmington, DE 19801–5030. Cleveland Morris, Artistic Dir. Full-length comedies, dramas, and musicals dealing with interracial dynamics in America. Contemporary or historical settings. Prefer cast of no more than 10. Send synopsis or complete script; SASE required. Reports in 6 months. Write for details of Connections competition.

DENVER CENTER THEATRE COMPANY—1050 13th St., Denver, CO 80204. Attn: Lit. Dir. Readings and productions of new works presented throughout the year. Send letter of inquiry, synopsis, 10 pages of dialogue, and resumé of writing experience. Stipend and housing provided for workshops.

DETROIT REPERTORY THEATRE—13103 Woodrow Wilson Ave., Detroit, MI 48238. Barbara Busby, Lit. Mgr. Full-length comedies and dramas. Scripts accepted October to April. Enclose SASE. Pays royalty.

STEVE DOBBINS PRODUCTIONS—650 Geary Blvd., San Francisco, CA 94102. Alan Ramos, Lit. Dir. Full-length comedies, dramas, and musicals. Cast of up to 12. Query with synopsis and resumé. No unsolicited manuscripts. Reports in 6 months. Offers workshops and readings. Pays 6% of gross.

DORSET THEATRE FESTIVAL—Box 519, Dorset, VT 05251. Jill Charles, Artistic Dir. Full-length comedies, musicals, dramas, and adaptations for up to 8 cast members; simple set preferred. Query with synopsis, cast size, and SAS postcard. Pays varying rates. Residencies at Dorset Colony House for Writers available September to June, March to May; inquire.

EAST WEST PLAYERS—4424 Santa Monica Blvd., Los Angeles, CA 90029. Tim Dang, Artistic Dir. Ken Narasaki, Lit. Mgr. Produces 4 to 5 new plays annually. Original plays, translations, adaptations, musicals, and youth theater, "all of which must illuminate the Asian or Asian-American experience, or resonate in a significant fashion if cast with Asian-American actors." Readings. Prefer to see query letter with synopsis and 10 pages of dialogue; complete scripts also considered. Reports in 5 to 6 weeks for query; 6 months for complete script.

FLORIDA STUDIO THEATRE—1241 N. Palm Ave., Sarasota, FL 33577. Chris Angermann, New Play Development. Innovative plays with universal themes. Query with synopsis and SASE. Also accepting musicals.

WILL GEER THEATRICUM BOTANICUM—Box 1222, Topanga, CA 90290. Attn: Lit. Dir. All types of scripts for outdoor theater, with large playing area. Submit synopsis with SASE. Pays varing rates.

EMMY GIFFORD CHILDREN'S THEATER—See *Omaha Theater Company for Young People.*

THE GOODMAN THEATRE—200 S. Columbus Dr., Chicago, IL 60603. Susan V. Booth, Lit. Mgr. Queries from recognized literary agents or producing organizations required for full-length comedies or dramas. No unsolicited scripts.

THE GROUP, SEATTLE'S MULTICULTURAL THEATRE—305 Harrison St., Seattle, WA 98109. Attn: Lit. Dir. Full-length satires, dramas, musicals, and translations, with no more than 10-person cast and simple set. Special interest in plays suitable for multi-ethnic cast; serious plays on social/cultural

750

issues; satires and comedies with bite. Query with synopsis, sample dialogue, resumé, and SASE required. Reporting time: 6 to 12 weeks.

THE GUTHRIE THEATER—725 Vineland Pl., Minneapolis, MN 55403. Attn: Lit. Dept. Full-length dramas and adaptations of world literature, classic masterworks, oral traditions, and folktales. No unsolicited scripts; professional recommendation or letter of inquiry from playwright/agent. SASE. Reports in 3 to 4 months.

HIPPODROME STATE THEATRE—25 S.E. Second Pl., Gainesville, FL 32601. David Boyce, Dramaturg. Full-length plays with unit sets and casts of up to 8. Agent submissions and professional recommendations only.

HOLLYWOOD THESPIAN COMPANY—12838 Kling St., Studio City, CA 91604–1127. Rai Tasco, Artistic Dir. Full-length comedies and dramas for integrated cast. Include cast list and SAS postcard with submission.

HORIZON THEATRE COMPANY—P. O. Box 5376, Station E, Atlanta, GA 30307. Jeff and Lisa Adler, Artistic Dirs. Full-length comedies, dramas, and satires. Encourages submissions by women writers. Cast of no more than 10. Submit synopsis with cast list, resumé, and recommendations. Pays percentage. Readings. Reports in 6 months.

HUNTINGTON THEATRE COMPANY—252 Huntington Ave., Boston, MA 02115. Jayme Koszyn, Dramaturg. Full-length comedies and dramas. Query with synopsis, cast list, resumé, recommendations, and SAS postcard.

ILLINOIS THEATRE CENTER— 400 Lakewood Blvd., Park Forest, IL 60466. Steve S. Billig, Artistic Dir. Full-length comedies, dramas, musicals, and adaptations, for unit/fragmentary sets, and up to 8 cast members. Send summary and SAS postcard. No unsolicited manuscripts. Pays negotiable rates. Workshops and readings offered.

ILLUSTRATED STAGE COMPANY—Box 640063, San Francisco, CA 94164–0063. Steve Dobbins, Artistic Dir. Full-length comedies, dramas, and musicals for a cast of up to 18. Query with synopsis and SASE. No unsolicited manuscripts. Offers workshops and readings.

INVISIBLE THEATRE—1400 N. First Ave, Tucson, AZ 85719. Deborah Dickey, Lit. Mgr. Letter of introduction from theatre professional must accompany submissions for full-length comedies, dramas, musicals, and adaptations. Submit after September '97. Cast of up to 10; simple set. Also one-act plays. Pays royalty.

JEWISH REPERTORY THEATRE—1395 Lexington Ave., New York, NY 10128. Ran Avni, Artistic Dir. Full-length comedies, dramas, musicals, and adaptations, with up to 10 cast members, relating to the Jewish experience. Pays varying rates. SASE.

KUMU KAHUA THEATRE, INC.— 46 Merchant St., Honolulu, HI 96813. Dennis Carroll, Artistic Dir. Full-length plays especially relevant to life in Hawaii. Prefer simple sets for arena and in-the-round productions. Submit resumé and synopsis January through April. Pays $35 per performance. Readings. Contests.

LOS ANGELES DESIGNERS' THEATRE—P.O. Box 1883, Studio City, CA 91614–0883. Richard Niederberg, Artistic Dir. Full-length comedies, dramas, musicals, fantasies, or adaptations. Religious, political, social, and controversial themes encouraged. Nudity, "adult" language, etc., O.K. "Please

751

detail in the cover letter what the writer's proposed involvement with the production would be beyond the usual. Do not submit material that needs to be returned." Payment varies.

THE MAGIC THEATRE—Fort Mason Ctr., Bldg. D, San Francisco, CA 94123. Kent Nicholson, Lit. Mgr. Comedies and dramas. "Special interest in poetic, non-linear, and multicultural work for mainstage productions." Query with synopsis, resumé, first 10 to 20 pages of script, and SASE; no unsolicited manuscripts. Pays varying rates.

MANHATTAN THEATRE CLUB— 453 W. 16th, New York, NY 10011. Attn: Kate Loewald. Full-length and one-act comedies, dramas, and musicals. No unsolicited manuscripts or queries; agent submissions only.

METROPOLITAN THEATRICAL SOCIETY, INC.—(formerly *Takoma Players, Inc.*) Box 56512, Washington, DC 20012. Gaynelle Reed Lewis, Lit. Dir. Realistic, full-length dramas, comedies, and musicals. Special interest in plays suitable for multi-ethnic casts. Submit manuscript with SASE.

MILL MOUNTAIN THEATRE—One Market Sq., Second Fl., Roanoke, VA 24011–1437. Jo Weinstein, Lit. Mgr. One-act comedies and dramas, 25 to 35 minutes. For full-length plays, send letter, resumé, and synopsis. Payment varies.

MISSOURI REPERTORY THEATRE— 4949 Cherry St., Kansas City, MO 64110. Felicia Londré, Dramaturg. Full-length comedies and dramas. Query with synopsis, cast list, resumé, and SAS postcard. Royalty. Allow 6 months for response.

MUSICAL THEATRE WORKS— 440 Lafayette St., New York, NY 10003. Andrew Barrett, Lit. Mgr. Full-length musicals, for a cast of up to 15. Submit manuscript and cassette score with SASE. Responds in 4 to 6 months.

NATIONAL BLACK THEATRE—2033 Fifth Ave., Harlem, NY 10035. Attn: Tunde Samuel. Drama, musicals, and children's plays. "Scripts should reflect African and African-American lifestyle. Historical, inspirational, and ritualistic forms appreciated." Workshops and readings.

NATIONAL PLAYWRIGHTS CONFERENCE, EUGENE O'NEILL THEATRE CENTER—234 W. 44th St., Suite 901, New York, NY 10036. Mary F. McCabe, Conference Administrator. Annual competition to select new stage plays and teleplays/screenplays for development during the summer at organization's Waterford, CT, location. Submission deadline: December 1. Send #10-size SASE in the fall for guidelines. Pays stipend, plus travel/living expenses during conference.

NEW THEATRE, INC.—169 Massachusetts Ave., Boston, MA 02115. Attn: NEWorks Submissions Program. New full-length scripts for readings, workshop, and main stage productions. Include SASE.

NEW TUNERS/PERFORMANCE COMMUNITY—1225 W. Belmont Ave., Chicago, IL 60657. Allan Chambers, Artistic Dir. of Development. Full-length musicals only, for cast to 15; no wing/fly space. Send query with brief synopsis, cassette tape of score, cast list, resumé, SASE, and SAS postcard. Pays on royalty basis.

NEW YORK STATE THEATRE INSTITUTE—155 River St., Troy, NY 12180. Attn: Patricia Di Benedetto Snyder, Producing Artistic Dir. Emphasis on new, full-length plays and musicals for family audiences. Submit complete

752

script (with tape for musicals) or query with synopsis and cast list. Payment varies.

ODYSSEY THEATRE ENSEMBLE—2055 S. Sepulveda Blvd., Los Angeles, CA 90025. Ron Sossi, Artistic Dir. Full-length comedies, dramas, musicals, and adaptations: provocative subject matter, or plays that stretch and explore the possibilities of theater. Query Jan Lewis, Lit. Mgr., with synopsis, 8 to 10 pages of sample dialogue, and resumé. Pays variable rates. Allow 2 to 6 months for reply to script; 2 to 4 weeks for queries. Workshops and readings.

OLDCASTLE THEATRE COMPANY—Bennington Center for the Arts, P.O. Box 1555, Bennington, VT 05201. Eric Peterson, Dir. Full-length comedies, dramas, and musicals for a small cast (up to 10). Submit synopsis and cast list in the winter. Reports in 6 months. Offers workshops and readings. Pays expenses for playwright to attend rehearsals. Royalty.

OMAHA THEATER COMPANY FOR YOUNG PEOPLE—(formerly *Emmy Gifford Children's Theater*) 2001 Center St., Omaha, NE 68102. James Larson, Artistic Dir. Theatre for young audiences. Referrals only.

PENGUIN REPERTORY COMPANY—Box 91, Stony Point, Rockland County, NY 10980. Joe Brancato, Artistic Dir. Full-length comedies and dramas with cast size to 5. Submit script, resumé, and SASE. Payment varies.

PEOPLE'S LIGHT AND THEATRE COMPANY—39 Conestoga Rd., Malvern, PA 19355. Alda Cortese, Lit. Mgr. Full-length comedies, dramas, adaptations. No unsolicited manuscripts; query with synopsis, 10 pages of script required. Reports in 6 months. Payment negotiable.

PIER ONE THEATRE—Box 894, Homer, AK 99603. Lance Petersen, Lit. Dir. Full-length and one-act comedies, dramas, musicals, children's plays, and adaptations. Submit complete script; include piano score with musicals. "We are now concentrating on plays by Alaskan playwrights or of special significance to the Alaskan experience." Pays 8% of ticket sales for mainstage musicals; other payment varies.

PLAYHOUSE ON THE SQUARE—51 S. Cooper in Overton Sq., Memphis, TN 38104. Jackie Nichols, Artistic Dir. Full-length comedies, dramas; cast of up to 15. Contest deadline is April for fall production. Pays $500.

PLAYWRIGHTS HORIZONS—416 W. 42nd St., New York, NY 10036. Address Literary Dept. Full-length, original comedies, dramas, and musicals by American authors. No one-acts or screenplays. Synopses discouraged; send resumé and SASE, include tape for musicals. Off Broadway contract.

PLAYWRIGHTS' PLATFORM—164 Brayton Rd., Boston, MA 02135. Attn: Lit. Dir. Script development workshops and public readings for New England playwrights only. Full-length and one-act plays of all kinds. No sexist or racist material. Residents of New England send scripts with short synopsis, resumé, SAS postcard, and SASE. Readings conducted at Massachusetts College of Art (Boston).

POPLAR PIKE PLAYHOUSE—7653 Old Poplar Pike, Germantown, TN 38138. Frank Bluestein, Artistic Dir. Full-length and one-act comedies, dramas, musicals, and children's plays. Submit synopsis with SAS postcard and resumé. Pays $300.

PORTLAND STAGE COMPANY—Box 1458, Portland, ME 04104. Attn: Lit. Dir. Not accepting unsolicited material at this time.

PRINCETON REPERTORY COMPANY— 44 Nassau St., Suite 350, Princeton, NJ 08542. Victoria Liberatori, Artistic Dir. One-act and full-length comedies and dramas for a cast of up to 10. "We are dedicated to the production of unusual plays, new and reinterpreted, which promote a greater awareness of contemporary issues especially those focusing on women." Submit synopsis with resumé, cast list, and 3-page dialogue sample. Consideration for reading and/or production. Responds within one year.

THE REPERTORY THEATRE OF ST. LOUIS—Box 191730, St. Louis, MO 63119. Attn: Lit. Dir. Query with brief synopsis, technical requirements, and cast size. Unsolicited manuscripts will be returned unread.

ROUND HOUSE THEATRE—12210 Bushey Dr., Silver Spring, MD 20902. Attn: Production Office Mgr. Full-length comedies, dramas, and adaptations; cast of up to 10; prefer simple set. Send one-page synopsis. No unsolicited manuscripts.

SALT AND PEPPER MIME COMPANY/NEW ENSEMBLE ACTORS THEATRE—320 E. 90th St., #1B, New York, NY 10128. Ms. Scottie Davis, Dir. One-acts, under 5 minutes, conducive to "nontraditional" casting, surreal sets, and mimetic concept. One-or 2-person cast. Send resumé, SAS postcard, cast list, and synopsis to 250 W. 65th St., New York, NY 10023. Scripts reviewed from May to December. Works also considered for readings, critiques, storyplayers, and experimental development.

SEATTLE REPERTORY THEATRE—155 Mercer St., Seattle, WA 98109. Daniel Sullivan, Artistic Dir. Full-length comedies, dramas, and adaptations. Submit synopsis, 10-page sample, SAS postcard, and resumé to Kurt Beattie, Artistic Assoc. New plays series with workshops each spring.

SOCIETY HILL PLAYHOUSE—507 S. 8th St., Philadelphia, PA 19147. Walter Vail, Dramaturg. Full-length dramas, comedies, and musicals with up to 6 cast members and simple set. Submit synopsis and SASE. Reports in 6 months. Nominal payment.

SOUTHERN APPALACHIAN REPERTORY THEATRE—P.O. Box 620, Mars Hill, NC 28754. James W. Thomas, Artistic Dir. Full-length comedies, dramas, musicals, and plays including (but not limited to) scripts with Appalachian theme. Submit resumé, recommendations, full script, and SASE. Send SASE for information on Southern Appalachian Playwright's Conference (held in April each year). Pays $500 royalty if play is selected for production during the summer season. Deadline for submissions is October 1 each year.

THE SPUYTEN DUYVIL THEATRE CO.—P.O. Box 1024, New York, NY 10024. Attn: Lit. Dir. Full-length comedies and dramas with single set and cast size to 10. "Good women's roles needed." SASE required.

STAGE ONE: THE LOUISVILLE CHILDREN'S THEATRE— 425 W. Market St., Louisville, KY 40202. Attn: Lit. Dir. Adaptations of classics and original plays for children ages 4 to 18. Submit script with resumé and SASE. Reports in 4 months.

STAGES REPERTORY THEATRE—3201 Allen Pkwy., #101, Houston, TX 77019. Beth Sanford, Assoc. Artistic Dir. Unproduced new works by women for Women's Repertory Project; accepts plays October 1 through December 31; full-length dramas, comedies, translations, and adaptations. Submit synopsis; no unsolicited scripts. Send for guidelines for Texas playwrights' festival held in the spring.

754

THE TEN MINUTE MUSICALS PROJECT—Box 461194, W. Hollywood, CA 90046. Michael Koppy, Prod. One-act musicals. Include audio cassette, libretto, and lead sheets with submission. "We are looking for complete short musicals." Pays $250.

THEATER ARTISTS OF MARIN—Box 150473, San Rafael, CA 94915. Charles Brousse, Artistic Dir. Full-length comedies, dramas, and musicals for a cast of 2 to 8. Submit complete script with SASE. Reports in 4 to 6 months. Three showcase productions each year.

THEATER MU—3010 Hennepin Ave. S., #290, Minneapolis, MN 55419. Rick Shiomi, Artistic Dir. Luu Pham, Lit. Dir. Full-length and one-act comedies and dramas for primarily Asian-American cast. Submit synopsis with cast list, return post card, resumé, recommendations, and SASE. Allow 6 months for response. Also sponsors New Eyes Festival with staged readings for selected scripts. No payment.

THEATRE AMERICANA—Box 245, Altadena, CA 91003. Attn: Lit. Dir. Full-length comedies and dramas, preferably with American theme. No children's plays. Language and subject matter should be suitable for a community audience. Send bound manuscript with cast list, resumé, and SASE, by February 1. No payment. Allow 3 to 6 months for reply. Submit no more than 2 entries per season.

THEATRE/TEATRO—Bilingual Foundation of the Arts, 421 N. Ave., #19, Los Angeles, CA 90031. Guillermo Reyes, Lit. Mgr. Margarita Galban, Artistic Dir. Full-length plays about the Hispanic experience; small casts. Submit manuscript with SASE. Pays negotiable rates.

THEATREWORKS/USA— 890 Broadway, 7th Fl., New York, NY 10003. Barbara Pasternack, Lit. Mgr. One-hour children's musicals and plays with music for 5-person cast. Playwrights must be within commutable distance to New York City. Submit outline or treatment, sample scenes, and music in spring, summer. Pays royalty and commission.

WALNUT STREET THEATRE COMPANY—9th and Walnut Sts., Philadelphia, PA 19107. Beverly Elliott, Lit. Mgr., Main Stage. Full-length comedies, dramas, musicals, and popular, upbeat adaptations; also, one-to 4-character plays for studio stage. Submit 20 sample pages with SAS postcard, cast list, and synopsis. Musical submissions must include an audio tape. Reports in 5 months. Payment varies.

WOOLLY MAMMOTH THEATRE COMPANY—1401 Church St. N.W., Washington, DC 20005. Jim Byrnes, Lit. Mgr. Looking for offbeat material, unusual writing. Unsolicited scripts accepted. Payment varies.

GARY YOUNG MIME THEATRE—23724 Park Madrid, Calabasas, CA 91302. Gary Young, Artistic Dir. Comedy monologues and vignettes, for children and adults, one to 90 minutes; casts of one man or one man and one woman, and portable set. Pays varying rates. Enclose SAS postcard, resumé, recommendations, cast list, and synopsis.

PLAY PUBLISHERS

ALABAMA LITERARY REVIEW—Troy State Univ., 253 Smith Hall, Troy, AL 36082. Theron Montgomery, Ed. Full-length and one-act comedies and dramas, to 50 pages. Query preferred. Responds to queries in 2 weeks; 2

to 3 months for complete manuscripts. Do not submit material in August. Payment is in copies; honorarium when available.

AMELIA—329 E St., Bakersfield, CA 93304. Frederick A. Raborg, Jr., Ed. One-act comedies and dramas; no longer than 45 minutes running time. Responds in 2 to 3 months. Payment is $35, on acceptance.

ANCHORAGE PRESS—Box 8067, New Orleans, LA 70182. Attn: Ed. Plays and musicals that have been proven in multiple production, for children ages 6 to 18. "We publish 8 to 10 new playbooks and one to 3 new hardcover books each year." Royalty.

ART CRAFT PUBLISHING COMPANY—P.O. Box 1058, Cedar Rapids, IA 52406. Attn: Geri Stonebraker. Two-and 3-act comedies, mysteries, farces, and musicals and one-act comedies or dramas, with one interior setting and a large cast for production by middle, junior, and senior high school students. Pays royalty or flat fee.

BAKER'S PLAYS—100 Chauncy St., Boston, MA 02111. Raymond Pape, Assoc. Ed. Scripts for amateur production: full-length plays, one-act plays, children's plays, musicals, religious dramas; plays for high school, community theatre, and regional theatre production. Allow 4 months for response.

BLIZZARD PUBLISHING—73 Furby St., Winnipeg, Manitoba, Canada R3C 2A2. Anna Synenko, Acquisitions Ed. One-act and full-length dramas, children's plays, and adaptations. Queries preferred. Responds in 3 to 4 months. Royalty.

CHICAGO PLAYS, INC.—2632 N. Lincoln Ave., Chicago, IL 60614. Jill Murray, Pres. Full-length and one-act comedies, dramas, musicals, children's plays, and adaptations. "Submissions must have received a professional production in the Chicago area." Responds in 4 to 6 months. Royalty.

I. E. CLARK PUBLICATIONS—P.O. Box 246, Schulenburg, TX 78956. Donna Cozzaglio, Ed. One-act and full-length plays and musicals, for children, young adults, and adults. Serious drama, comedies, classics, fairytales, melodramas, and holiday plays. "We seldom publish a play that has not been produced." Responds in 2 to 6 months. Royalty.

COLLAGES & BRICOLAGES—P.O. Box 86, Clarion, PA 16214. Marie-José Fortis, Ed. One-act avant-garde comedies and dramas. Manuscripts read August through November; responds in one to 3 months. Payment is in copies.

CONFRONTATION—Dept. of English, C.W. Post of L.I.U., Greenvale, NY 11548. Martin Tucker, Ed. One-act comedies, dramas, and adaptations. Manuscripts read September through May. Responds in 6 to 8 weeks. Pays, $25 to $100, on publication.

CONTEMPORARY DRAMA SERVICE—Meriwether Publishing Co., Box 7710, 885 Elkton Dr., Colorado Springs, CO 80903. Arthur Zapel, Ed. Easy-to-stage comedies, skits, one-acts, musicals, puppet scripts, and full-length plays for schools and churches. (Junior high through college level; no elementary level material.) Adaptations of classics and improvised material for classroom use. Comedy monologues and duets. Chancel drama for Christmas and Easter church use. Enclose synopsis. Books on theater arts subjects, scene books, and anthologies. Textbooks for speech and drama. Pays by fee arrangement or royalty.

756

DRAMATIC PUBLISHING —311 Washington St., Woodstock, IL 60098. Sarah Clark, Ed. Full-length and one-act plays and musicals for the stock, amateur, and children's theater market. Royalty. Responds within 16 weeks.

DRAMATICS—Educational Theatre Assoc., 3368 Central Pkwy., Cincinnati, OH 45225–2392. Don Corathers, Ed. One-act and full-length plays for high school production. Pays $100 to $400 for one-time, non-exclusive publications rights, on acceptance.

ELDRIDGE PUBLISHING COMPANY—P. O. Box 1595, Venice, FL 34284. Nancy Vorhis, Ed. Dept. One-act and full-length plays and musicals suitable for performance by schools, churches, and community theatre groups. Comedies, tragedies, dramas, skits, spoofs, and religious plays (all holidays). Submit complete manuscript with cover letter, biography, and SASE. Responds in 2 months. Flat fee for one-act and religious plays, paid on publication; royalties for full-length plays.

SAMUEL FRENCH, INC.— 45 W. 25th St., New York, NY 10010. William Talbot, Ed. Full-length plays for dinner, community, stock, college, and high school theaters. One-act plays, 30 to 45 minutes. Children's plays, 45 to 60 minutes. Royalty.

HEUER PUBLISHING COMPANY—Drawer 248, Cedar Rapids, IA 52406. C. Emmett McMullen, Ed. One-act comedies and dramas for contest work; two-and three-act comedies, mysteries, or farces, and musicals, with one interior setting, for middle school and high school production. Pays royalty or flat fee.

LYNX EYE— c/o Scribblefest Literary Group, 1880 Hill Dr., Los Angeles, CA 90041. Pam McCully, Kathryn Morrison, Co-Eds. One-act plays, 500 to 5,000 words, for thoughtful adults who enjoy interesting reading and writing. Also, short stories, vignettes, novel excerpts, essays, belle lettres, satires, and reviews; poetry, to 30 lines. Pays $10, on acceptance.

NATIONAL DRAMA SERVICE—MSN 170, 127 Ninth Ave. N., Nashville, TN 37234. Attn: Ed. Scripts, 2 to 7 minutes long: drama in worship, puppets, clowns, Christian comedy, mime, movement, readers theater, creative worship services, and monologues. "We publish dramatic material that communicates the message of Christ. We want scripts that will give even the smallest church the opportunity to enhance their ministry with drama." Payment varies, on acceptance. Guidelines.

PIONEER DRAMA SERVICE—P. O. Box 4267, Englewood, CO 80155. Attn: Ed. Full-length and one-act plays as well as musicals, melodramas, and children's theatre. No unproduced plays or plays with largely male casts or multiple sets. Query preferred. Royalty.

PLAYERS PRESS, INC.—P.O. Box 1132, Studio City, CA 91614–0132. Robert W. Gordon, Ed. One-act and full-length comedies, dramas, and musicals. "No manuscript will be considered unless it has been produced." Query with manuscript-size SASE and 2 #10 SASEs for correspondence. Include resumé and/or biography. Responds in 3 to 12 months. Royalty.

PLAYS, THE DRAMA MAGAZINE FOR YOUNG PEOPLE—120 Boylston St., Boston, MA 02116–4615. Elizabeth Preston, Man. Ed. One-act plays, with simple contemporary sets, for production by young people, 7 to 17: comedies, dramas, farces, skits, holiday plays. Also adaptations of classics, biography plays, puppet plays, and creative dramatics. No musicals or plays with religious themes. Maximum lengths: lower grades and skits, 10 double-spaced pages; middle grades, 15 pages; junior and senior high, 20 pages. Guidelines. Pays good rates, on acceptance. Query for adaptations of folk tales and classics. Buys all rights.

PRISM INTERNATIONAL—Dept. of Creative Writing, Univ. of British Columbia Buch E462–1866 Main Mall, Vancouver, BC, Canada V6T 1Z1. Attn: Ed. One-act plays. Responds in 2 to 3 months. Pays $20 per page, on publication.

THE RADIO PLAY—The Public Media Foundation, 100 Boylston St., Suite 230, Boston, MA 02116. Valerie Henderson, Exec. Prod. Original radio plays and radio dramatizations of American classics in the public domain, 28 to 29 pages, to fit a 30-minute program format. Query for dramatizations only. Send SASE for style sheet.

RAG MAG—P.O. Box 12, Goodhue, MN 55027. Beverly Voldseth, Ed. Semiannual. Full-length and one-act comedies and dramas. SASE for guidelines and themes. Query with 3 to 7 pages of play. Pays in copies.

ROCKFORD REVIEW—P.O. Box 858, Rockford, IL 61105. David Ross, Ed. One-act comedies, dramas, and satires, to 1,300 words. "We prefer genuine or satirical human dilemmas with coping or non-coping outcomes that illuminate the human condition." Pays in copies (plus invitation to attend reading-reception in the summer). Two $25 Editor's Choice Prizes awarded each issue.

SINISTER WISDOM—P.O. Box 3252, Berkeley, CA 94703. Akiba Onada-Sikwoia, Ed. Quarterly. One-act (no longer than 15 pages) lesbian drama. "We are particularly interested in work that reflects the diversity of our experiences: as lesbians of color, ethnic lesbians, Jewish, old, young, working class, poor, disabled, fat. Only material by born-woman lesbians is considered." Responds in 3 to 9 months; write for upcoming themes. Payment is in 2 copies, on publication. SASE.

BOOK PUBLISHERS

The following list includes the major book publishers for adult and juvenile fiction and nonfiction and a representative number of small publishers from across the country, as well as a number of university presses.

Before submitting a complete manuscript to an editor, it is advisable to send a brief query letter describing the proposed book, and an SASE. The letter should also include information about the author's special qualifications for dealing with a particular topic and any previous publication credits. An outline of the book (or a synopsis for fiction) and a sample chapter may also be included.

While it is common practice to submit a book manuscript to only one publisher at a time, it is becoming more and more acceptable to submit the same query or proposal to more than one editor simultaneously. When sending multiple queries, *always* make note of it in each submission.

Book manuscripts may be packaged in typing paper boxes (available from a stationery store) and sent by first-class mail, or, more common and less expensive, by "Special Fourth Class Rate—Manuscript." For rates, details of insurance, and so forth, inquire at your local post office. With any submission to a publisher, be sure to enclose sufficient postage for the manuscript's return.

Royalty rates for hardcover books usually start at 10% of the retail price of the book and increase after a certain number of copies have been sold. Paperbacks generally have a somewhat lower rate, about 5% to 8%. It is customary for the publishing company to pay the author a cash advance against royalties when the book contract is signed or when the finished manuscript is received. Some publishers pay on a flat-fee basis.

While most of the publishers on this list consider either unsolicited manuscripts or queries, an increasing number now read only agented submissions. Since finding an agent is not an easy task, especially for newcomers, writers are advised to try to sell their manuscripts directly to the publisher first.

Writers seeking publication of their book-length poetry manuscripts are encouraged to enter contests that offer publication as the prize (see *Literary Prize Offers,* page 804); many presses that once considered unsolicited poetry manuscripts by emerging or unpublished writers now limit their reading of such manuscripts to those entered in their contests for new writers.

ABBEVILLE PRESS— 488 Madison Ave., New York, NY 10022. Attn: Submissions Ed. Illustrated adult nonfiction books on art, architecture, gardening, fashion, interior design, decorative arts, cooking, and travel. Submit outline and sample chapters to Meredith Wolf. Art-related juvenile books or those with an educational component. For juveniles, submit complete manuscript to Thomas Sand. All submissions must include sample illustrations; do not send original art or transparencies. Royalty.

ABINGDON PRESS—P.O. Box 801, Nashville, TN 37202. Mary Catherine Dean, Sr. Ed. General-interest books: mainline, social issues, marriage/family, self-help, exceptional people. Query with outline and one or 2 sample chapters. Guidelines.

ACADEMIC PRESS—Div. of Harcourt Brace, 525 B St., Suite 1900, San Diego, CA 92101. Attn: Ed. Dept. Scientific and technical books and journals for research-level scientists, students, and professionals; upper-level undergraduate and graduate science texts. Query.

ACADEMY CHICAGO PUBLISHERS—363 W. Erie St., Chicago, IL 60610. Anita Miller, Ed. General adult fiction; classic mysteries with emphasis on character and/or puzzle. History; biographies; travel; books by and about women; no explicit sex. Also interested in reprinting books dropped by other houses, including academic titles and anthologies. Query with 4 sample chapters. SASE required. Royalty.

ACCENT PUBLICATIONS—Box 36640, 4050 Lee Vance View, Colorado Springs, CO 80936. Mary Nelson, Man. Ed. Nonfiction church resources facilitating Christian education for the local church; evangelical Christian perspective; no trade books. "Request guidelines before querying." Query with sample chapters and SASE. Royalty. Paperback only.

ACE BOOKS —200 Madison Ave., New York, NY 10016. Susan Allison, V.P., Ed.-in-Chief. Science fiction and fantasy. Query with first 3 chapters and outline to Laura Anne Gilman, Ed. Royalty.

ACTIVITY RESOURCES—P.O. Box 4875, Hayward, CA 94540. Mary Laycock, Ed. Math educational material only. "Our main focus is on grades K through 8." Submit complete manuscript. Royalty.

ADAMA BOOKS—See *Modan Publishing*.

ADAMS-BLAKE PUBLISHING— 8041 Sierra St., Fair Oaks, CA 95628. Monica Blane, Ed. Books on business, careers, and technology. Query or send complete manuscript. Multiple submissions accepted. Royalty.

ADAMS-HALL PUBLISHING—11661 San Vicente Blvd., Suite 210, Los Angeles, CA 90049. Sue Ann Bacon, Marketing Dir. Business and personal finance books. Query with outline and sample chapters. Royalty.

ALASKA NORTHWEST BOOKS—2208 N.W. Market St., Suite 300, Seattle, WA 98107. Marlene Blessing, Ed.-in-Chief. Nonfiction, 50,000 to 100,000 words, with an emphasis on natural world and history of Alaska and the Pacific Northwest: travel books; cookbooks; field guides; children's books; outdoor recreation; natural history; native culture; lifestyle. Send query or sample chapters with outline. Guidelines.

ALGONQUIN BOOKS OF CHAPEL HILL—Box 2225, Chapel Hill, NC 27515. Shannon Ravenel, Ed. Dir. Trade books, fiction and nonfiction, for adults.

ALPINE PUBLICATIONS—225 S. Madison Ave., Loveland, CO 80537. B.J. McKinney, Pub. Nonfiction books, 35,000 to 60,000 words, on dogs, horses, cats, and companion animals. Submit outline and sample chapters or complete manuscript. Royalty.

ALYSON PUBLICATIONS—P.O. Box 4371, Los Angeles, CA 90078. Attn: Ed. Gay and lesbian adult fiction and nonfiction books, from 65,000 words. *Alyson Wonderland* imprint: Children's picture books with gay and lesbian themes; young adult titles, from 65,000 words. Query with outline and sample chapters. Royalty.

ALYSON WONDERLAND—See *Alyson Publications*.

AMERICAN EDUCATION PUBLISHING—150 E. Wilson Bridge Rd., Suite 145, Columbus, OH 43085. Attn: Ed. Dir. Children's books, 32 to 64 pages. Submit complete manuscript. Royalty.

AMERICAN PARADISE PUBLISHING—P.O. Box 37, St. John, USVI 00831. Gary M. Goodlander, Ed. "We are interested in 'hopelessly local' books, between 80 and 300 pages. We need useful, practical books that help our Virgin Island readers lead better and more enjoyable lives." Guidebooks, cookbooks, how-to books, books on sailing, yacht cruising, hiking, snorkeling, sportfishing, local history, and West Indian culture, specifically aimed at Caribbean readers/tourists. Query with outline and sample chapters. Royalty.

THE AMERICAN PSYCHIATRIC PRESS—1400 K St. N.W., Washington, DC 20005. Carol C. Nadelson, M.D., Ed.-in-Chief. Books that interpret scientific and medical aspects of psychiatry for a lay audience and that address specific psychiatric problems. Authors must have appropriate credentials to write on medical topics. Query required. Royalty.

AMPERSAND PRESS—Creative Writing Program, Roger Williams Univ., Bristol, RI 02809. Martha Christina, Dir. Fiction and poetry, chapbooks and full-length. Query only. Royalty.

ANCHOR BOOKS—Imprint of Doubleday and Co., 1540 Broadway, New York, NY 10036. Martha K. Levin, Pub. Adult trade paperbacks and hardcovers. Nonfiction, multicultural, sociology, psychology, philosophy, women's interest, etc. No unsolicited manuscripts.

ANCHORAGE PRESS—Box 8067, New Orleans, LA 70182. Attn: Acquisitions Ed. Dramatic publishers. Plays for children ages 4 to 18. "We publish 8 to 10 new playbooks and one to 3 new hardcover books each year." Royalty.

AND BOOKS—702 S. Michigan, South Bend, IN 46601. Janos Szebedinsky, Ed. Adult nonfiction. Topics include computers, fine arts, health, philosophy, regional subjects, and social justice.

ANHINGA PRESS—P.O. Box 10595, Tallahassee, FL 32302–0595. Rick Campbell, Ed. Poetry books. (Publishes 3 books a year.) Query or send complete manuscripts. Flat fee. Annual poetry prize of $2,000 plus publication; send #10 SASE for details.

APPALACHIAN MOUNTAIN CLUB BOOKS—5 Joy St., Boston, MA 02108. Attn: Ed. Dept. Regional (New England) and national nonfiction titles, 250 to 400 pages, for adult audience; juvenile and young adult nonfiction. Topics include guidebooks on non-motorized backcountry recreation, nature, mountain history/biography, search and rescue, conservation, and environmental management. Query with outline and sample chapters. Multiple queries considered. Royalty.

ARCADE PUBLISHING—141 Fifth Ave., New York, NY 10010. Richard Seaver, Pub./Ed. Timothy Bent, Ed. Fiction and nonfiction. No unsolicited manuscripts. Query.

ARCHWAY PAPERBACKS—Pocket Books, 1230 Ave. of the Americas, New York, NY 10020. Patricia MacDonald,V.P./ Ed. Dir. Young adult contemporary fiction (suspense thrillers, romances) and nonfiction (popular current topics), for ages 12 to 16. *Minstrel Books*: young reader fiction including thrillers, adventure, fantasy, humor, animal stories, for ages 6 to 11. Send query, outline, sample chapters to Attn: Manuscript Proposals.

ASTARTE SHELL PRESS—P.O. Box 3648, Portland, ME 04104. Sapphire, Ed. Books on theology, politics, and social issues from a feminist/woman's/multicultural perspective. No poetry. Send sample chapters or complete manuscripts. Royalty.

AUGUST HOUSE—P.O. Box 3223, Little Rock, AR 72203. Liz Parkhurst, Ed.-in-Chief. Adult books pertaining to folklore, folktales, and storytelling. Illustrated children's books featuring traditional folktales are published under the *August House LittleFolk* imprint. Submit proposal with sample chapters (at least 40 pages) and a descriptive outline or table of contents. Royalty.

AVALON BOOKS—401 Lafayette St., New York, NY 10003. Wilhelm H. Mickelsen, Pres. Marcia Markland, VP/Pub. Hardcover books, 40,000 to 50,000 words: romances, mysteries, and westerns. No explicit sex. Query with first 3 chapters and outline; nonreturnable. SASE for guidelines.

AVERY PUBLISHING GROUP—120 Old Broadway, Garden City Park, NY 11040. Attn: Man. Ed. Nonfiction, from 40,000 words, on health, childbirth, child care, healthful cooking. Query. Royalty.

AVON BOOKS—1350 Ave. of the Americas, New York, NY 10019. Robert Mecoy, Ed.-in-Chief. Genre fiction, general nonfiction, historical romance, 60,000 to 200,000 words. *Avon Hardcover*: Adult commercial fiction and nonfiction. Send one-or 2-page query letter describing book (including its length) with SASE. *AvoNova*: science fiction, 75,000 to 100,000 words. Query with synopsis and sample chapters. Ellen Edwards, Historical Romance; John Douglas, Science Fiction; Chris Miller, Fantasy. *Camelot Books*: Ellen Krieger, Ed. Fiction and nonfiction for 7-to 10-year-olds. Query. *Flare Books*: Ellen Krieger, Ed. Fiction and nonfiction for 12-year-olds and up. Query. Royalty. Paperback only.

AVONOVA—See *Avon Books*.

BAEN BOOKS—Baen Publishing Enterprises, P.O. Box 1403, Riverdale, NY 10471–1403. Jim Baen, Pres./Ed.-in-Chief. Strongly plotted science fiction; innovative fantasy. Query with synopsis and manuscript. Advance and royalty. Guidelines available for letter-sized SASE.

BAKER BOOK HOUSE—P. O. Box 6287, Grand Rapids, MI 49516–6287. Jane Schrier, Asst. to the Dir. of Pub. Religious nonfiction: books for trade, clergy, seminarians, collegians. Religious fiction. Royalty.

BALBOA—See *Tiare Publications*.

BALLANTINE BOOKS—201 E. 50th St., New York, NY 10022. Attn: Ed.-in-Chief. General fiction and nonfiction. Query.

BALSAM PRESS—36 E. 22nd St., 9th Fl., New York, NY 10010. Barbara Krohn, Exec. Ed. General and illustrated adult nonfiction. Query. Royalty.

BANKS CHANNEL BOOKS—P.O. Box 4446, Wilmington, NC 28406. Attn: Book Ed. Books of regional interest by North Carolina writers only. Query with sample chapters, SASE. Royalty.

BANTAM BOOKS—1540 Broadway, New York, NY 10036. Irwyn Applebaum, Pres./Pub. Adult fiction and nonfiction. Mass-market titles, submit queries to the following imprints: *Crime Line*, crime and mystery fiction; *Domain*, frontier fiction, historical sagas, traditional westerns; *Spectra*, science fiction and fantasy; *Bantam Nonfiction*, wide variety of commercial nonfiction, including true crime, health and nutrition, sports, reference. Agented queries and manuscripts only.

BANTAM, DOUBLEDAY, DELL—See *Bantam Books, Doubleday and Co.* and *Dell Books*.

BARRICADE BOOKS—150 Fifth Ave., New York, NY 10011. Lyle Stuart, Pub. General nonfiction, celebrity biographies, controversial subjects. No fiction. Send synopsis only with SASE. Modest advances against royalties.

BARRON'S EDUCATIONAL SERIES, INC.—250 Wireless Blvd., Hauppauge, NY 11788. Grace Freedson, Acquisitions Dir. Juvenile nonfiction (science, nature, history, hobbies, and how-to) and picture books for ages 3 to 6. Adult nonfiction (business, pet care, childcare, sports, test preparation, cookbooks, foreign language instruction). Query with SASE. Guidelines.

BAUHAN, PUBLISHER, WILLIAM L.—Box 443, Dublin, NH 03444. William L. Bauhan, Ed. Biographies, fine arts, gardening, architecture, and history books with an emphasis on New England. Submit query with outline and sample chapter.

BAYLOR UNIVERSITY PRESS—P.O. Box 97363, Baylor Univ., Waco, TX 76798–7363. Janet L. Burton, Academic Publications Coordinator. Scholarly nonfiction, especially oral history and church-state issues. Query with outline. Royalty.

BEACH BOOKS—See *National Press Books, Inc.*

BEACON PRESS—25 Beacon St., Boston, MA 02108. Attn: Sharon Rice. General nonfiction: world affairs, women's studies, anthropology, history, philosophy, religion, gay and lesbian studies, environment, nature writing, African-American studies, Asian-American studies, Native-American studies. Series: "Concord Library" (nature writing); "Barnard New Women Poets"; "Black Women Writers" (fiction); "Men and Masculinity" (nonfiction). Query. SASE required.

BEAR & COMPANY, INC.—P.O. Drawer 2860, Santa Fe, NM 87504. Barbara Clow, Ed. Nonfiction "that will help transform our culture philosophically, environmentally, and spiritually." Query with outline, sample chapters, and SASE. Royalty.

BEHRMAN HOUSE—235 Watchung Ave., W. Orange, NJ 07052. Adam Siegel, Projects Ed. Adult and juvenile nonfiction, varying lengths, in English and in Hebrew, on Jewish subject matter. Query with outline and sample chapters. Flat fee.

BENCHMARK BOOKS—99 White Plains Rd., Tarrytown, NY 10591–9001. Judith Whipple, Ed. Dir. Books, 3,000 to 30,000 words, for young readers (grades 3 up) on science, sports, the arts, wildlife, math, and health. Series include: "Cultures of the World," "Cultures of the Past," "Biomes of the World," "Life Issues," "Discovering Math," and others. Query with outline. Royalty or flat fee.

THE BESS PRESS—P.O. Box 22388, Honolulu, HI 96823. Revé Shapard, Ed. Nonfiction books about Hawaii, Asia, and the Pacific for adults, children, and young adults. Submit outline with sample chapters or complete manuscript. Royalty.

BETHANY HOUSE PUBLISHERS—11300 Hampshire Ave. S., Minneapolis, MN 55438. Attn: Ed. Dept. Religious fiction and nonfiction. Query with sample chapters. Royalty.

BETTER HOMES AND GARDENS BOOKS—See *Meredith Corp. Book Publishing*.

BINFORD & MORT PUBLISHING—1202 N.W. 17th Ave., Portland, OR 97209. J.F. Roberts, Ed. Books on subjects related to the Pacific Coast and the Northwest. Lengths vary. Query. Royalty.

BIRCH LANE PRESS—See *Carol Publishing Group.*

BLACK BUTTERFLY CHILDREN'S BOOKS—Writers and Readers Publishing, 625 Broadway, New York, NY 10012. Patricia Allen, Ed. Titles featuring black children and other children of color, ages 9 to 13, for Young Beginners series. Picture books for children up to 11; board books for toddlers; juvenile fiction for all ages. Query. Royalty.

BLACK BUZZARD PRESS—1110 Seaton Ln., Falls Church, VA 22046. Bradley R. Strahan, Ed. Poetry manuscripts, to 80 pages. Query. Royalty.

BLAIR, PUBLISHER, JOHN F.—1406 Plaza Dr., Winston-Salem, NC 27103. Carolyn Sakowski, Pres. Books from 50,000 words: biography, history, folklore, and guidebooks, with southeastern tie-in. Query. Royalty.

BLUE DOLPHIN PUBLISHING, INC.—P.O. Box 8, Nevada City, CA 95959. Paul M. Clemens, Ed. Books, 200 to 300 pages, on comparative spiritual traditions, lay and transpersonal psychology, self-help, health, healing, and "whatever helps people grow in their social awareness and conscious evolution." Query with outline, sample chapters, and SASE. Royalty.

BLUE HERON PUBLISHING—24450 N.W. Hansen Rd., Hillsboro, OR 97124. Dennis Stovall, Ed. Adult nonfiction for series on writing/reference. Also literary nonfiction. Query. Royalty.

BLUE MOON BOOKS, INC.—61 Fourth Ave., New York, NY 10003. Barney Rosset, Pub. Erotic fiction and nonfiction on a variety of topics. Send synopsis and sample chapters; SASE.

BOB JONES UNIVERSITY PRESS—1700 Wade Hampton Blvd., Greenville, SC 29614. Gloria Repp, Ed. Books for young readers, ages 6 to 12, that reflect "the highest Christian standards of thought, feeling, and action." Fiction, 8,000 to 40,000 words. Nonfiction, 10,000 to 30,000 words. Young adult books, 40,000 to 60,000 words. Read guidelines, then submit sample chapters. Pays on royalty or flat fee basis.

BONUS BOOKS—160 E. Illinois St., Chicago, IL 60611. Deborah Flapan, Man. Ed. Nonfiction; topics vary widely. Query with sample chapters and SASE. Royalty.

BOTTOM DOG PRESS, INC.—c/o Firelands College, Huron, OH 44839. Larry Smith, Dir. Collections of personal essays, stories, 50 to 200 pages, and poetry for chapbook publication (30 to 50 poems). "Interested writers should query with SASE for information on current anthology projects." Royalty.

BOYDS MILLS PRESS—815 Church St., Honesdale, PA 18431. Beth Troop, Manuscript Coord. Hardcover trade books for children. Fiction: picture books; middle-grade fiction with fresh ideas and involving story; young adult novels of literary merit. Nonfiction should be "fun, entertaining, and informative." Send outline and sample chapters for young adult novels and nonfiction, complete manuscripts for all other categories. Royalty.

BRANDEN PUBLISHING COMPANY—17 Station St., Box 843, Brookline Village, MA 02147. Attn: Ed. Dept. Novels, biographies, and autobiographies. Especially books by or about women, 250 to 350 pages. Also considers queries on history, computers, business, performance arts, and translations. Query only with SASE. Royalty.

BRASSEY'S BOOKS—1331 Dolley Madison Blvd., Suite 401, McLean, VA 22101-3926. Don McKeon, Ed. Nonfiction books, 75,000 to 130,000 words: national and international affairs, history, foreign policy, defense, military and political biography, sports. No fiction. Query with outline and sample chapters. Royalty.

BRAZILLER PUBLISHERS, GEORGE—60 Madison Ave., New York, NY 10010. Attn: Ed. Dept. Fiction and nonfiction. Mostly art, art history; some profiles of writers, collections of essays and short stories, anthologies. Send art history manuscripts to Adrienne Baxter, Ed.; others to Fiction Editor. Send outline with sample chapters. Payment varies.

BREAKAWAY BOOKS—336 W. 84th St., #4, New York, NY 10024. Garth Battista, Pub. Literary sports novels and single stories and poems, any length, for anthology series. "Our goal is to bring to light literary writing on the athletic experience." Royalty.

BRETT BOOKS, INC.—P.O. Box 290–637, Brooklyn, NY 11229–0011. Barbara J. Brett, Pres./Pub. Nonfiction for adult trade market. "Submit a query letter of no more than 2 pages, stating your professional background and summarizing your book proposal in 2 to 4 paragraphs." SASE. Royalty.

BRIDGE WORKS—Box 1798, Bridgehampton, NY 11932. Barbara Phillips, Pres./Ed. Dir. Mainstream adult literary fiction and nonfiction, 50,000 to 75,000 words. Royalty.

BRIDGEWATER BOOKS—Imprint of Troll Communications, 100 Corporate Dr., Mahwah, NJ 07430. Attn: Ed. Dept. Hardcover picture books and anthologies.

BRISTOL PUBLISHING ENTERPRISES—P.O. Box 1737, San Leandro, CA 94577. Patricia J. Hall, Ed. Cookbooks. Query with outline, sample chapters, resumé, and SASE. Royalty.

BROADMAN AND HOLMAN PUBLISHERS—127 Ninth Ave. N., Nashville, TN 37234. Richard P. Rosenbaum, Jr., Ed. Dir. Religious and inspirational nonfiction. Query with SASE. Royalty. Guidelines.

BROADWAY BOOKS—1540 Broadway, New York, NY 10036. John Sterling, Ed.-in-Chief. Adult nonfiction; small and very selective fiction list. Query with outline, sample chapters, and SASE. Royalty.

BROWNDEER PRESS—Imprint of Harcourt Brace & Co. Children's Books, 9 Monroe Pkwy., Suite 240, Lake Oswego, OR 97035–1487. Linda Zuckerman, Ed. Dir. Picture books, humorous middle-grade fiction, and young adult material written from an unusual perspective or about an unusual subject. Considers submissions from agents, published authors, or members of SCBWI only. Query for nonfiction with cover letter, resumé, and sample chapter; send complete manuscript for picture books (avoid rhyming text). For longer fiction, send first 3 chapters, synopsis, and short cover letter including list of published works. SASE required for all correspondence.

BUCKNELL UNIVERSITY PRESS—Bucknell Univ., Lewisburg, PA 17837. Mills F. Edgerton, Jr., Dir. Scholarly nonfiction. Query. Royalty.

BULFINCH PRESS—34 Beacon St., Boston, MA 02108. Attn: Ed. Dept. Books on fine arts and photography. Query with outline or proposal and vita.

BYRON PREISS VISUAL PUBLICATIONS—24 W. 25th St., New York, NY 10010. Attn: Ed. Dept. Book packager. "We are primarily interested in seeing samples from established authors willing to work to specifications on firm deadlines." Genres: science fiction, fantasy, horror, juvenile, young adult, nonfiction. Pays competitive advance against royalties for commissioned work.

C&T PUBLISHING—5021 Blum Rd., #1, Martinez, CA 94553. Todd Hensley, Pres. Quilting books, 64 to 200 finished pages. "Our focus is how-to, although we will consider picture, inspirational, or history books on quilting." Send query, outline, or sample chapters. Multiple queries considered. Royalty.

CALYX BOOKS—P.O. Box B, Corvallis, OR 97339. Margarita Donnelly, Micki Reaman, Eds. Feminist publisher. Novels, short stories, poetry, nonfiction, translations, and anthologies by women. Currently overstocked; query for anthologies and creative nonfiction. Send SASE for guidelines before submitting. Limited market.

CAMELOT BOOKS—See *Avon Books.*

CANDLEWICK PRESS—2067 Massachusetts Ave., Cambridge, MA 02140. Attn: Ed. Dept. No unsolicited material.

CAPSTONE PRESS, INC.—P.O. Box 669, N. Mankato, MN 56001–0669. Attn: Ed. Dept. High interest/low-reading level nonfiction for children, specifically, reluctant and new readers. Send SASE for catalogue of series themes. Query required. Flat fee.

CAROL PUBLISHING GROUP—600 Madison Ave., New York, NY 10022. Allan J. Wilson, Ed. General nonfiction. *Citadel Press*: biography (celebrity preferred), autobiography, film, history, and self-help, 70,000 words. *Birch Lane Press*: adult nonfiction, 75,000 words. *Lyle Stuart*: adult nonfiction, 75,000 words, of a controversial nature, gaming, etc.; address Hillel Black, Ed. Also *University Books*. Query with SASE required. Royalty.

CAROLRHODA BOOKS—241 First Ave. N., Minneapolis, MN 55401. Rebecca Poole, Ed. Complete manuscripts for ages 4 to 12: biography, science, nature, history, photo-essays; historical fiction. Guidelines. Hardcover.

CAROUSEL PRESS—P.O. Box 6061, Albany, CA 94706–0061. Stephanie Dillon, Ed. Travel guides, especially family-oriented. Send letter, table of contents, and sample chapter. "We publish one or 2 new books each year and will consider out-of-print books that the author wants to update." Modest advance and royalty.

CARROLL AND GRAF PUBLISHERS, INC.—260 Fifth Ave., New York, NY 10001. Kent E. Carroll, Exec. Ed. General fiction and nonfiction. No unagented submissions.

CARTWHEEL BOOKS—555 Broadway, New York, NY 10012. Tina Lynch, Asst. to Ed. Dir. Picture books, fiction, and nonfiction, to about 1,000 words, for children, preschool to third grade. Royalty or flat fee. Query; no unsolicited manuscripts.

CASSANDRA PRESS—P.O. Box 150868, San Rafael, CA 94915. Attn: Ed. Dept. New age, holistic health, metaphysical, and psychological books. Query with outline and sample chapters, or complete manuscript. Include SASE. Royalty (no advance).

THE CATHOLIC UNIVERSITY OF AMERICA PRESS—620 Michigan Ave. N.E., Washington, DC 20064. David J. McGonagle, Dir. Scholarly nonfiction: American and European history (both ecclesiastical and secular); Irish studies; American and European literature; philosophy; political theory; theology. Query with prospectus, annotated table of contents, or introduction and resumé. Royalty.

CHAPTERS PUBLISHING LTD.—2031 Shelburne Rd., Shelburne, VT 05482. Alesia Rowley, Ed. Nonfiction books on gardening, nature, and cooking. Query with outline, sample chapters, and resumé; include SASE. Royalty.

CHATHAM PRESS—P. O. Box A, Old Greenwich, CT 06870. Roger H. Lourie, Man. Dir. Books on the Northeast coast, gardening, New England maritime subjects, and the ocean. Large photography volumes. Query with outline, sample chapters, illustrations, and SASE. Royalty.

CHELSEA GREEN PUBLISHING CO.—P.O. Box 428, White River Junction, VT 05001. Jim Schley, Ed. Nonfiction: natural history, environmental issues, energy and shelter, organic agriculture, and ecological lifestyle books with strong backlist potential. Query with outline and SASE. Not considering any unsolicited manuscripts at this time. Royalty.

CHICAGO REVIEW PRESS— 814 N. Franklin St., Chicago, IL 60610. Cynthia Sherry, Ed. Nonfiction: activity books for young children, project books for ages 10 to 18, general nonfiction, architecture, pregnancy, how-to, popular science, and regional gardening and other regional topics. Query with outline and sample chapters.

CHILDREN'S BOOK PRESS—246 First St., Suite 101, San Francisco, CA 94105. Submissions Ed. Bilingual and multicultural picture books, 750 to 1,500 words, for children in grades K through 6. "We publish folktales and contemporary stories reflecting the traditions and culture of the emerging majority in the U.S. and worldwide. Ultimately, we want to help encourage a more international, multicultural perspective on the part of all young people." Query. Pays advance on royalties.

CHILDREN'S PRESS—Sherman Turnpike, Danbury, CT 06813. Attn: Ed. Dir. Juvenile nonfiction and picture books. Currently overstocked; not accepting unsolicited manuscripts.

CHILDREN'S LIBRARY PRESS—P.O. Box 1919, Joshua Tree, CA 92252. Attn: Acquisitions Ed. Texts for picture books. Submit complete manuscript. Royalty.

CHILTON BOOK CO.— One Chilton Way, Radnor, PA 19089. Christopher J. Kuppig, Gen. Mgr. *Wallace-Homestead Books.* Antiques and collectibles, sewing and crafts, professional/technical, and automotive topics. Query with outline, sample chapter, and SASE.

CHINA BOOKS—2929 24th St., San Francisco, CA 94110. Wendy K. Lee, Sr. Ed. Books relating to China or Chinese culture. Adult nonfiction, varying lengths. Juvenile picture books, fiction, nonfiction, and young adult books. Query. Royalty.

CHRONICLE BOOKS— 85 Second St., San Francisco, CA 94105. Attn: Ed. Dept. Topical nonfiction, history, biography, fiction, art, photography, architecture, design, nature, food, giftbooks, regional topics. Children's books. Send proposal with SASE.

CITADEL PRESS—See *Carol Publishing Group.*

CLARION BOOKS—215 Park Ave. S., New York, NY 10003. Dorothy Briley, Ed.-in-Chief/Pub. Fiction, nonfiction, and picture books: short novels and lively stories for ages 6 to 10 and 8 to 12, historical fiction, humor; picture books for infants and children to age 7; biography, natural history, social studies, American and world history for readers 5 to 8, and 9 up. Royalty. Hardcover.

CLARK CITY PRESS—P.O. Box 1358, Livingston, MT 59047. Attn: Ed. Dept. Collections of poems, short stories, and essays; novels, biographies. No unsolicited manuscripts. Royalty.

CLEIS PRESS—P.O. Box 14684, San Francisco, CA 94114. Frédérique Delacoste, Ed. Fiction and nonfiction, 200 pages, by women. No poetry. Send SASE with 2 first-class stamps for catalogue before querying. Royalty.

COBBLEHILL BOOKS—375 Hudson St., New York, NY 10014. Joe Ann Daly, Ed. Dir. Rosanne Lauer, Exec. Ed. Fiction and nonfiction for preschoolers through junior high school. Query for manuscripts longer than picture books; send complete manuscript with SASE for picture books. Royalty.

COFFEE HOUSE PRESS—27 N. 4th St., Suite 400, Minneapolis, MN 55401. Attn: Chris Fischbach. Literary fiction (no genres). Query with SASE.

COLLIER BOOKS—See *Macmillan Reference USA.*

CONARI PRESS—2550 Ninth St., Suite 101, Berkeley, CA 94710. Claudia Schaab, Ed. Assoc. Adult nonfiction: women's issues, personal growth, relationships, and spirituality. Submit outline, sample chapters, and SASE. Royalty.

CONCORDIA PUBLISHING HOUSE—3558 S. Jefferson Ave., St. Louis, MO 63118. Attn: Ed. Dept. Practical nonfiction with explicit religious content, conservative Lutheran doctrine. Children's fiction with explicit Christian content. No poetry. Query. Royalty.

CONFLUENCE PRESS—Lewis Clark State College, 500 8th Ave., Lewiston, ID 83502–2698. James Hepworth, Dir. Fiction, nonfiction, and poetry, of varying lengths, "to promote and nourish young writers, in particular, to achieve literary and artistic excellence." Send query, outline, and sample chapters. Flat fee or royalty.

CONSUMER REPORTS BOOKS—101 Truman Ave., Yonkers, NY 10703. Mark Hoffman, Ed. Medicine/health, food/nutrition, personal finance, retirement planning, automotive, home maintenance. Submit complete manuscript or send contents, outline, 3 chapters, and resumé.

CONTEMPORARY BOOKS, INC.—2 Prudential Plaza, Suite 1200, Chicago, IL 60601–6790. Nancy Crossman, Ed. Dir. Trade nonfiction, 100 to 400 pages, on health, fitness, sports, cooking, humor, business, popular culture, biography, real estate, finance, women's issues. Query with outline, sample chapters, and SASE. Royalty.

COPPER BEECH BOOKS—The Millbrook Press, 2 Old New Milford Rd., Brookfield, CT 06804. Sheilah Holmes, Ed. Nonfiction books for children, preschool to age 12. Series include books based on words, on "what if" scenarios, and world mysteries and "fact or fiction" issues. Query with outline and sample chapter. Royalty.

COPPER CANYON PRESS—P.O. Box 271, Port Townsend, WA 98368. Sam Hamill, Ed. Poetry books only. No multiple submissions. Query with SASE. Royalty.

CORNELL UNIVERSITY PRESS—Box 250, Sage House, 512 E. State St., Ithaca, NY 14851. John G. Ackerman, Dir. Scholarly nonfiction, 80,000 to 120,000 words. Query with outline. Royalty.

COTLER BOOKS, JOANNA—See *HarperCollins Children's Books.*

COUNTERPOINT—P.O. Box 65793, Washington, DC 20035–5793. Jack Shoemaker, Ed.-in-Chief. Adult literary nonfiction, including art, religion, history, biography, science, and current affairs; some literary fiction. Submit sample chapters and synopsis. Royalty.

CRAFTSMAN BOOK COMPANY—6058 Corte del Cedro, P.O. Box 6500, Carlsbad, CA 92018. Laurence D. Jacobs, Ed. How-to construction and estimating manuals and software for professional builders, 450 pages. Query. Royalty. Paperback.

CREATIVE ARTS BOOK CO.— 833 Bancroft Way, Berkeley, CA 94710. Donald S. Ellis, Pub. Adult nonfiction: women's issues, music, African-American and Asian, and California topics. Query with outline, sample chapters, SASE. Royalty.

CRIME LINE—See *Bantam Books.*

THE CROSSING PRESS—P.O. Box 1048, Freedom, CA 95019. Elaine Goldman Gill, Pub. Health and nutrition, holistic health, women's interests, spiritual growth, alternative parenting, cookbooks, pets. Royalty.

CROWN BOOKS FOR YOUNG READERS—201 E. 50th St., New York, NY 10022. Simon Boughton, Pub. Dir. Arthur Levine, Ed.-in-Chief. Children's nonfiction (science, sports, nature, music, and history) and picture books for ages 3 and up. Query. Guidelines.

DALKEY ARCHIVE PRESS—Illinois State Univ., Campus Box 4241, Normal, IL 61790–4241. John O'Brien, Sr. Ed. Avant-garde, experimental fiction, 200 to 300 manuscript pages, "of the highest literary quality." Royalty.

DANIEL AND COMPANY, JOHN—P.O. Box 21922, Santa Barbara, CA 93121. John Daniel, Pub. Books, to 200 pages, in the field of belles lettres and literary memoirs; stylish and elegant writing; essays and short fiction dealing with social issues; one poetry title per year. Send synopsis or outline with no more than 50 sample pages and SASE. Allow 6 to 8 weeks for response. Royalty.

DAVIES-BLACK PUBLISHING—3803 E. Bayshore Rd., Palo Alto, CA 94303. Melinda Adams Merino, Acquisitions Ed. Books, 250 to 400 manuscript pages, on career planning, organization development, and personal growth. Royalty.

DAVIS PUBLICATIONS, INC.—50 Portland St., Worcester, MA 01608. Books, 100 to 300 manuscript pages, for the art education market; mainly for teachers of art, grades K through 12. Must have an educational component. Grades K through 8, address Claire M. Golding; grades 9 through 12, address Helen Ronan. Query with outline and sample chapters. Royalty.

DAW BOOKS, INC.—375 Hudson St., 3rd Fl., New York, NY 10014–3658. Elizabeth R. Wollheim, Ed.-in-Chief. Sheila E. Gilbert, Sr. Ed. Peter Stampfel, Submissions Ed. Science fiction and fantasy, 60,000 to 120,000 words. Royalty.

DAWN PUBLICATIONS—14618 Tyler Foote Rd., Nevada City, CA 95959. Glenn J. Hovemann, Ed. Dept. Nature awareness books for children. Children's picture books with a positive, uplifting message to awaken a sense of appreciation and kinship with nature. For children's works, submit complete manuscript and specify intended age. SASE for guidelines. Royalty.

DEARBORN FINANCIAL PUBLISHING, INC.—155 N. Wacker Dr., Chicago, IL 60606–1719. Anita A. Constant, Sr. V.P. Books on financial services, real estate, banking, small business, etc. Query with outline and sample chapters. Royalty and flat fee.

DEL REY BOOKS—201 E. 50th St., New York, NY 10022. Shelly Shapiro, Exec. Ed. Veronica Chapman, Sr. Ed. Science fiction and fantasy, 60,000 to 120,000 words; first novelists welcome. Fantasy with magic basic to plotline.

Send manuscript, or query with outline with 3 sample chapters. Include manuscript-size SASE. Royalty.

DELACORTE PRESS—1540 Broadway, New York, NY 10036. Leslie Schnur, Jackie Farber, Maureen O'Neal, Jackie Cantor, Eds. Adult fiction and nonfiction. Accepts fiction (mystery, young adult, romance, fantasy, etc.) from agents only.

DELANCEY PRESS—P.O. Box 40285, Philadelphia, PA 19106. Wesley Morrison, Ed. Dir. All types of nonfiction, 60,000 words. No fiction. Query. Royalty.

DELL BOOKS—1540 Broadway, New York, NY 10036. Attn: Editorial Dept., Book Proposal. Commercial fiction and nonfiction, family sagas, historical romances, war action, general fiction, occult/horror/psychological suspense, true crime, men's adventure. Send narrative synopsis for fiction (to 4 pages) or outline (also to 4 pages) for nonfiction. Enclose SASE. No poetry. Allow 2 to 3 months for response.

DELTA BOOKS—1540 Broadway, New York, NY 10036. Attn: Ed. Dept., Book Proposal. General-interest nonfiction: psychology, feminism, health, nutrition, child care, science, self-help, and how-to. Send an outline with SASE.

DEVIN-ADAIR PUBLISHERS, INC.—6 N. Water St., Greenwich, CT 06830. J. Andrassi, Ed. Books on conservative affairs, Irish topics, photography, Americana, self-help, health, gardening, cooking, and ecology. Send outline, sample chapters, and SASE. Royalty.

DI CAPUA BOOKS, MICHAEL—See *HarperCollins Children's Books.*

DIAL PRESS—1540 Broadway, New York, NY 10036. Susan Kamil, Ed. Dir. Quality fiction and nonfiction. No unsolicited material.

DIMI PRESS—3820 Oak Hollow Ln. S.E., Salem, OR 97302–4774. Dick Lutz, Pres. How-to books, 35,000 words. "Books that help people live better lives." Query. Royalty.

DK PUBLISHING, INC.—95 Madison Ave., New York, NY 10016. Illustrated nonfiction for adults and children. Query. Royalty.

DOMAIN—See *Bantam Books.*

DOUBLEDAY AND CO.—1540 Broadway, New York, NY 10036. Arlene Friedman, Pub./Pres. Proposals from literary agents only. No unsolicited material.

DOWN HOME PRESS—P.O. Box 4126, Asheboro, NC 27204. Jerry Bledsoe, Ed. Nonfiction books related to the Carolinas and the South. Query or send complete manuscript. Royalty.

DUNNE BOOKS, THOMAS—175 Fifth Ave., New York, NY 10010. Thomas L. Dunne, Ed. Adult fiction (mysteries, trade, etc.) and nonfiction (history, biographies, science, politics, etc.). Query with outline, sample chapters, and SASE. Royalty.

DUQUESNE UNIVERSITY PRESS—600 Forbes Ave., Pittsburgh, PA 15282–0101. Attn: Ed. Dept. Scholarly publications in the humanities and social sciences; creative nonfiction (book-length only) by emerging writers. Guidelines.

DUTTON ADULT—375 Hudson St., New York, NY 10014. Arnold Dolin, Sr. V.P./Assoc. Pub. Fiction and nonfiction books. Manuscripts accepted only from agents or on personal recommendation.

770

DUTTON CHILDREN'S BOOKS—375 Hudson St., New York, NY 10014. Lucia Monfried, Ed.-in-Chief. Picture books, easy-to-read books; fiction and nonfiction for preschoolers to young adults. Submit outline and first 3 chapters with query for fiction and nonfiction, complete manuscripts for picture books and easy-to-read books. Manuscripts should be well written with fresh ideas and child appeal. Include SASE.

EAKIN PRESS—P.O. Drawer 90159, Austin, TX 78709–0159. Melissa Roberts, Sr. Ed. Adult nonfiction, 60,000 to 80,000 words: Texana, regional cookbooks, Mexico and the Southwest, WWII, military. Children's books: history, culture, geography, etc., of Texas and the Southwest. Juvenile picture books, 5,000 to 10,000 words; fiction, 20,000 to 30,000 words; young adult fiction, 25,000 to 40,000 words. Currently overstocked; query. Royalty.

EASTERN WASHINGTON UNIVERSITY PRESS—Mail Stop 14, Eastern Washington Univ., 526 5th St., Cheney, WA 99004–2431. Attn: Eds. Literary essays, history, social commentary, and other academic subjects. Limited fiction (one title every 2 years or so). One or 2 books of poetry, 60 to 150 pages, each year. "We are a small regional university press, publishing titles that reflect regional service, our international contacts, our strong creative writing program, and research and interests of our exceptional faculty." Send complete manuscript, query with outline, or Mac-compatible diskette. Royalty.

EERDMANS PUBLISHING COMPANY, INC., WM. B.—255 Jefferson Ave. S.E., Grand Rapids, MI 49503. Jon Pott, Ed.-in-Chief. Protestant, Roman Catholic, and Orthodox theological nonfiction; American religious history; ethics; philosophy; history; spiritual growth. For children's religious books, query Amy Eerdmans, Children's Book Ed. Royalty.

ELEMENT BOOKS—P.O. Box 830, 21 Broadway, Rockport, MA 01966. Paul Cash, Acquisitions Ed. Books on world religions, ancient wisdom, astrology, meditation, women's studies, and alternative health and healing. Study recent catalogue. Query with outline and sample chapters. Royalty.

EMC CORP.—300 York Ave., St. Paul, MN 55101. Eileen Slater, Ed. Vocational, career, and consumer education textbooks. Royalty. No unsolicited manuscripts.

ENSLOW PUBLISHERS, INC.—P.O. Box 605, 44 Fadem Rd., Springfield, NJ 07081. Brian D. Enslow, Ed./Pub. Nonfiction books for young people. Areas of emphasis are children's and young adult books for ages 10 to 18 in the fields of social studies, science, and biography. Also reference books for all ages and easy reading books for teenagers.

EPICENTER PRESS—P.O. Box 82368, Kenmore, WA 98028. Kent Sturgis, Pub. Quality nonfiction trade books, contemporary western art and photography titles, and destination travel guides emphasizing Alaska and the West Coast. "We are a regional press whose interests include but are not limited to the arts, history, environment, and diverse cultures and lifestyles of the North Pacific and high latitudes." Flat fee.

ERIKSSON, PUBLISHER, PAUL S.—P.O. Box 62, Forest Dale, VT 05745. Attn: Ed. Dept. General nonfiction (send outline and cover letter); some fiction (send 3 chapters with query). Royalty.

EVANS & CO., INC., M.—216 E. 49th St., New York, NY 10017. Attn: Ed. Dept. Books on health, self-help, popular psychology, and cookbooks.

Limited list of commercial fiction. Query with outline, sample chapter, and SASE. Royalty.

EVENT HORIZON PRESS—P.O. Box 867, Desert Hot Springs, CA 92240. Joseph Cowles, Pub. Adult fiction and nonfiction. Poetry books, from 50 pages. Not accepting any new material at this time.

EXCALIBUR PUBLICATIONS—Box 36, Latham, NY 12110–0036. Alan M. Petrillo, Ed. Books on military history, firearms history, antique arms and accessories, military personalities, tactics and strategy, history of battles. Query with outline and 3 sample chapters. SASE. Royalty or flat fee.

FABER AND FABER—53 Shore Dr., Winchester, MA 01890. Attn: Ed. Dept. Novels, anthologies, and nonfiction books on topics of popular culture and general interest. Query with SASE. Royalty.

FACTS ON FILE PUBLICATIONS—11 Penn Plaza, New York, NY 10001. Reference and trade books on science, health, literature, language, history, the performing arts, ethnic studies, popular culture, sports, etc. (No fiction, poetry, computer books, technical books or cookbooks.) Query with outline, sample chapter, and SASE. Royalty. Hardcover.

FAIRVIEW PRESS—2450 Riverside Ave. S., Minneapolis, MN 55454. Julie Odland Smith, Sr. Ed. (Adult). Robyn Hansen, Children's Book Ed. Adult books, 80,000 words, that offer advice and support on relationships, parenting, domestic violence, divorce, family activities, aging, health, self-esteem, social issues, addictions, etc. Children's picture books, about 1,000 words, for readers 4 to 9, on related subjects. Query with outline and sample chapters for adult books. Submit complete manuscript for picture books. Royalty.

FANFARE—1540 Broadway, New York, NY 10036. Beth de Guzman, Wendy McCurdy, Sr. Eds. Shawna Summers, Ed. Historical and contemporary adult women's fiction, about 90,000 to 150,000 words. Study field before submitting. Query. Paperback and hardcover.

FARRAR, STRAUS & GIROUX—19 Union Sq. W., New York, NY 10003. Adult and juvenile literary fiction and nonfiction. No guidelines or catalogue available.

FAWCETT/IVY BOOKS—201 E. 50th St., New York, NY 10022. Barbara Dicks, Exec. Ed. Adult mysteries, regencies, and historical romances, 75,000 to 120,000 words. "In the last year, all our acquisitions have been through agents." Query with outline and sample chapters. Average response time is 3 to 6 months. Royalty.

THE FEMINIST PRESS AT THE CITY UNIVERSITY OF NEW YORK—311 E. 94th St., New York, NY 10128. Florence Howe, Pub. Reprints of significant "lost" fiction, original memoirs, autobiographies, biographies; multicultural anthologies; handbooks; bibliographies. "We are especially interested in international literature, women and peace, women and music, and women of color." Royalty.

FINE, BOOKS, DONALD I.—Penguin U.S.A., Inc., 375 Hudson, New York, NY 10014. Attn: Ed. Dept. Literary and commercial fiction. General nonfiction. No queries or unsolicited manuscripts. Submit through agent only.

FIREBRAND BOOKS—141 The Commons, Ithaca, NY 14850. Nancy K. Bereano, Ed. Feminist and lesbian fiction and nonfiction. Royalty. Paperback and library edition cloth.

772

FIRESIDE BOOKS—1230 Ave. of the Americas, New York, NY 10020. No unsolicited manuscripts.

FLARE BOOKS—See *Avon Books.*

FODOR'S TRAVEL GUIDES—201 E. 50th St., New York, NY 10022. Karen Cure, Ed. Dir. Travel guides for both foreign and US destinations. "We hire writers who live in the area they will write about." Books follow established format; send writing sample and details about your familiarity with a given area.

FONT & CENTER PRESS—P.O. Box 95, Weston, MA 02193. Ilene Horowitz, Ed./Pub. Cookbooks. How-to books. Alternative history for adults and young adults. Send proposal, outline, and sample chapter(s). Responds in 3 months. SASE. Royalty.

FORTRESS PRESS—426 S. Fifth St., Box 1209, Minneapolis, MN 55440. Dr. Marshall D. Johnson, Dir. Books in the areas of biblical studies, theology, ethics, professional ministry, and church history for academic and professional markets, including libraries. Query.

FORUM—c/o Prima Publishing, 3875 Atherton Rd., Rocklin, CA 95765. Steven Martin, Ed. Serious nonfiction books on current affairs, public policy, libertarian/conservative thought, high level management, individual empowerment, and historical biography. Submit outline and sample chapters. Royalty.

THE FREE PRESS—See *Macmillan Reference USA.*

FREE SPIRIT PUBLISHING—400 First Ave. N., Suite 616, Minneapolis, MN 55401–1730. Elizabeth H. Verdick, Acquisitions Ed. Nonfiction self-help for kids, with an emphasis on school success, self-awareness, self-esteem, creativity, social action, lifeskills, and special needs. Creative classroom activities for teachers; adult books on raising, counseling, or educating children. Queries, sample chapters, or complete manuscripts. "Request free catalogue and guidelines." Royalty.

FRONT STREET BOOKS, INC.—P.O. Box 280, Arden, NC 28704. Stephen Roxburgh, Pres./Pub. Fiction, poetry, and picture books for children. Query with sample chapters. Royalty.

FULCRUM PUBLISHING—350 Indiana St., Suite 350, Golden, CO 80401. Attn: Submissions Dept. Adult trade nonfiction: travel, nature, American history, biography, women's topics, and gardening. No fiction. Send cover letter, sample chapters, table of contents, author credentials, and market analysis. Royalty.

FULL COURT PRESS BOOKS—See *National Press Books, Inc.*

GARLIC PRESS—See *National Press Books, Inc.*

GARRETT PARK PRESS—P.O. Box 190, Garrett Park, MD 20896. Robert Calvert, Jr., Pub. Reference books on career education, occupational guidance, and financial aid only. Query required. Multiple queries discouraged. Royalty.

GERINGER BOOKS, LAURA—See *HarperCollins Children's Books.*

GIBBS SMITH PUBLISHER—P.O. Box 667, Layton, UT 84401. Madge Baird, Ed. Dir. Adult nonfiction. Query. Royalty.

GINIGER CO. INC., THE K.S.—250 W. 57th St., Suite 519, New York, NY 10107. Attn: Ed. Dept. General nonfiction. Query with SASE; no unsolicited manuscripts. Royalty.

GLENBRIDGE PUBLISHING LTD.—6010 W. Jewell Ave., Lakewood, CO 80232. James A. Keene, Ed. Nonfiction books on a variety of topics, including business, history, and psychology. Query with sample chapter. Royalty.

GLOBE PEQUOT PRESS, THE—6 Business Park Rd., Box 833, Old Saybrook, CT 06475. Laura Strom, Acquisitions Ed. Nonfiction with national and regional focus; travel; outdoor recreation; personal finance; home-based business; cooking. Query with sample chapter, contents, and one-page synopsis. SASE required. Royalty or flat fee.

GOLD EAGLE—See *Worldwide Library.*

GOLDEN BOOKS FAMILY ENTERTAINMENT—(formerly *Western Publishing Co., Inc.*) 850 Third Ave., New York, NY 10022. Willa Perlman, Pres./ Pub. Robin Warner, Exec. V.P/Pub. children's publishing group. Children's fiction and nonfiction: picture books, storybooks, concept books, novelty books. Adult nonfiction. No unsolicited manuscripts. Royalty or flat fee.

GOLDEN WEST PUBLISHERS—4113 N. Longview, Phoenix, AZ 85014. Hal Mitchell, Ed. Cookbooks and nonfiction Western history and travel books. Query. Royalty or flat fee.

GOODFELLOW PRESS—16625 Redmond Way, Suite M20, Redmond, WA 98053–4499. Pamela R. Goodfellow, Pub. Strongly character-based fiction novels, 90,000 to 150,000 words. Send for guidelines. Royalty.

GRAYWOLF PRESS—2402 University Ave., Suite 203, St. Paul, MN 55114. Attn: Ed. Dept. Literary fiction (short story collections and novels), poetry, and essays.

GREAT QUOTATIONS—1967 Quincy Ct., Glendale Heights, IL 60139. Patrick Caton, Ed. General adult titles, 80 to 200 pages, with strong, clever, descriptive titles and brief, upbeat text. "We publish small, quick-read gift books." Query with outline and sample chapters or send complete manuscript. Royalty.

GREENWILLOW BOOKS—1350 Ave. of the Americas, New York, NY 10019. Susan Hirschman, Ed.-in-Chief. Children's books for all ages. Picture books.

GROSSET AND DUNLAP, INC.—200 Madison Ave., New York, NY 10016. Jane O'Connor, Pub. Mass-market children's books. Query. Royalty.

GROVE/ATLANTIC MONTHLY PRESS—841 Broadway, 4th Fl., New York, NY 10003–4793. Morgan Entrekin, Pub. Distinguished fiction and nonfiction. Query; no unsolicited manuscripts. Royalty.

GULLIVER BOOKS—See *Harcourt Brace & Co. Children's Book Div.*

HACHAI PUBLISHING—156 Chester Ave., Brooklyn, NY 11218. Dina Rosenfeld, Ed. Full-color children's picture books, 32 pages, for readers ages 2 to 8; Judaica, Bible tales. Query or send complete manuscript. Flat fee.

HANCOCK HOUSE PUBLISHERS, LTD.—1431 Harrison Ave., Blaine, WA 98230. Attn: Ed. Dept. Adult nonfiction: guidebooks, biographies, natural history, popular science, conservation, animal husbandry, falconry, and sports. Some juvenile nonfiction. Query with outline and sample chapters or send complete manuscript. Multiple queries considered. Royalty.

HARCOURT BRACE & CO.—525 B St., Suite 1900, San Diego, CA 92101. Attn: Ed. Dept. Adult trade nonfiction and fiction. No unsolicited manuscripts or queries.

HARCOURT BRACE & CO. CHILDREN'S BOOK DIV.—525 B St., Suite 1900, San Diego, CA 92101–4495. Attn: Manuscript Submissions. Juvenile fiction and nonfiction for beginning readers through young adults under the following imprints: *HB Children's Books, Browndeer Press, Gulliver Books, Red Wagon Books, Odyssey Paperbacks,* and *Voyager Paperbacks.* Query; manuscripts accepted from agents only.

HARCOURT BRACE PROFESSIONAL PUBLISHING—525 B St., Suite 1900, San Diego, CA 92101. Attn: Ed. Dept. Professional books for practitioners in accounting, auditing, tax. Query. Royalty.

HARDSCRABBLE BOOKS—See *University Press of New England.*

HARLEQUIN BOOKS/CANADA—225 Duncan Mill Rd., Don Mills, Ont., Canada M3B 3K9. Randall Toye, Ed. Dir. *Mira Books*: Dianne Moggy, Sr. Ed. Contemporary women's fiction, 100,000 words. Query. *Harlequin Superromance*: Paula Eykelhof, Sr. Ed. Contemporary romance, 85,000 words, with a mainstream edge. Query. *Harlequin Temptation*: Birgit Davis-Todd, Sr. Ed. Sensuous, humorous contemporary romances, 60,000 words. *Love and Laughter*: Malle Vallik, Assoc. Sr. Ed. The lighter side of love, 55,000 words. Query.

HARLEQUIN BOOKS/U.S.—300 E. 42nd St., 6th Fl., New York, NY 10017. Debra Matteucci, Sr. Ed. Contemporary romances, 70,000 to 75,000 words. Send for tip sheets. *Harlequin American Romances*: bold, exciting romantic adventures, "where anything is possible and dreams come true." *Harlequin Intrigue*: set against a backdrop of mystery and suspense, worldwide locales. Query. Paperback.

HARPER SAN FRANCISCO—1160 Battery St., San Francisco, CA 94111–1213. Attn: Acquisitions Ed. Books on spirituality and religion. No unsolicited manuscripts; query required.

HARPERCOLLINS CHILDREN'S BOOKS—10 E. 53rd St., New York, NY 10022–5299. Katrin Magnusson, Admin. Coord. Picture books, chapter books, and fiction and nonfiction for middle-grade and young adult readers. "Our imprints (*HarperTrophy* paperbacks, *Joanna Cotler Books, Michael di Capua Books*, and *Laura Geringer Books*) are committed to producing imaginative and responsible children's books. All publish from preschool to young adult titles." Guidelines. Royalty.

HARPERCOLLINS PUBLISHERS—10 E. 53rd St., New York, NY 10022–5299. Adult Trade Department: Address Man. Ed. Fiction, nonfiction (biography, history, etc.), reference. Submissions from agents only. College texts: Address College Dept. No unsolicited manuscripts; query only.

HARPERPAPERBACKS—HarperCollins, 10 E. 53rd St., New York, NY 10022. Carolyn Marino, Ed. Dir. John Silbersack, Science Fiction/Fantasy Ed.-in-Chief. John Douglas, Exec. Ed. Jessica Lichtenstein, Sr. Ed. Abigail Kamen-Holland, Gretchen Young, Caitlin Blasdell, Eds.

HARPERPRISM—10 E. 53rd St., New York, NY 10022–5299. John Silbersack, Ed.-in-Chief. Caitlin Blasdell, Ed. Science fiction/fantasy. No unsolicited manuscripts; query.

HARPERTROPHY—See *HarperCollins Children's Books.*

775

HARVARD COMMON PRESS—535 Albany St., Boston, MA 02118. Bruce Shaw, Ed. Adult nonfiction: cookbooks, travel guides, books on family matters, health, small business, etc. Send outline and sample chapters or complete manuscript. SASE. Royalty.

HARVARD UNIVERSITY PRESS—79 Garden St., Cambridge, MA 02138–1499. No free-lance submissions: "We hire no writers."

HARVEST HOUSE PUBLISHERS—1075 Arrowsmith, Eugene, OR 97402. LaRae Weikert, Ed. Mgr. Nonfiction with evangelical theme: how-tos, marriage, women, contemporary issues. Fiction. No biographies, autobiographies, history, music books, or poetry. Query with SASE.

HAWORTH PRESS, INC.—10 Alice St., Binghamton, NY 13904–1580. Bill Palmer, Ed. Scholarly press interested in research-based adult nonfiction: psychology, social work, gay and lesbian studies, women's studies, family and marriage; some recreation and entertainment. Send outline with sample chapters or complete manuscript. Royalty.

HAY HOUSE—P.O. Box 5100, Carlsbad, CA 92018–5100. Attn: Ed. Dir. Self-help books on health, self-awareness, spiritual growth, astrology, psychology, philosophy, metaphysics, and the environment. Query with outline and sample chapters. Royalties.

HAZELDEN EDUCATIONAL MATERIALS—Box 176, Center City, MN 55012. Betty Christiansen, Assoc. Ed. Self-help books, 100 to 400 pages, relating to addiction, recovery, spirituality, and wholeness. Query with outline and sample chapters. Multiple queries considered. Royalty.

HEALTH COMMUNICATIONS, INC.—3201 S.W. 15th St., Deerfield Beach, FL 33442. Christine Belleris, Ed. Dir. Books, 250 pages, on self-help, recovery, and personal growth for adults. Query with outline, 2 sample chapters, and SASE. Royalty.

HEALTH PRESS—P.O. Box 1388, Santa Fe, NM 87504. K. Schwartz, Ed. Health-related adult and children's books, 100 to 300 pages. "We're seeking cutting-edge, original manuscripts that will excite, educate, and help readers." Author must have credentials, or preface/intro must be written by M.D., Ph.D., etc. Controversial topics are desired; must be well researched and documented. Submit outline, table of contents, and first chapter with SASE. Royalty.

HEARST BOOKS and HEARST MARINE BOOKS—See *William Morrow and Co., Inc.*

HEINEMANN—361 Hanover St., Portsmouth, NH 03801. Attn: Trade Dept. Practical theatre, world literature, and literacy education. Query.

HEMINGWAY WESTERN STUDIES SERIES—Boise State Univ., 1910 University Dr., Boise, ID 83725. Tom Trusky, Ed. Artists' and eccentric format books (multiple editions) relating to Rocky Mountain environment, race, religion, gender and other public issues. Guidelines.

HERALD PRESS—616 Walnut Ave., Scottdale, PA 15683. Attn: Ed. Dept. Christian books for adults and children: inspiration, Bible study, self-help, devotionals, current issues, peace studies, church history, missions, evangelism, family life, fiction, and personal experience. Send one-page summary and 2 sample chapters. Royalty.

HIGHSMITH PRESS—P.O. Box 800, Fort Atkinson, WI 53538–0800. Donald Sager, Pub. Adult books, 80 to 360 pages, on professional library science, education, and reference. Teacher activity and curriculum resource books, 48 to 240 pages, for pre-K through 12. Query with outline and sample chapters. Royalty.

HIPPOCRENE BOOKS—171 Madison Ave., New York, NY 10016. George Blagowidow, Ed. Dir. Language instruction books and foreign language dictionaries, travel guides, and military history of Polish interest. Send outline and sample chapters with SASE for reply. Multiple queries considered. Royalty.

HOLIDAY HOUSE, INC.— 425 Madison Ave., New York, NY 10017. Regina Griffin, V. P. Ashley Mason, Assoc. Ed. General juvenile fiction and nonfiction. Submit complete manuscript or 3 sample chapters and summary; enclose SASE. Royalty. Hardcover only.

HOLT AND CO., HENRY—115 W. 18th St., New York, NY 10011. Michael Naumann, Pub. "Virtually all submissions come from literary agents or from writers whom we publish. We do not accept unsolicited submissions."

HOME BUILDER PRESS—National Assoc. of Home Builders, 1201 15th St. N.W., Washington, DC 20005–2800. Doris M. Tennyson, Sr. Ed. How-to and business management books, 150 to 200 manuscript pages, for builders, remodelers, and developers. Writers should be experts in homebuilding, remodeling, land development, sales, marketing, and related aspects of the building industry. Query with outline and sample chapter. Royalty. For author's packet TW, call John Tuttle (800) 368–5242, ext. 222.

HOMESTEAD PUBLISHING—P.O. Box 193, Moose, WY 83012. Carl Schreier, Pub. Regional books as well as fiction and nonfiction with more national appeal. Royalty.

HOUGHTON MIFFLIN COMPANY—222 Berkeley St., Boston, MA 02116–3764. Attn: Ed. Dept. Fiction: literary, historical. Nonfiction: history, biography, psychology. No unsolicited submissions. Children's book division, address Children's Trade Books: picture books, fiction, and nonfiction for all ages. Query. Royalty.

HOWARD UNIVERSITY PRESS—1240 Randolph St. N.E., Washington, DC 20017. Ed Gordon, Dir. Nonfiction books, 300 to 500 manuscript pages, on African diaspora, history, political science, literary criticism, biography, women's studies. Query with outline and sample chapters. Royalty.

HP BOOKS—200 Madison Ave., New York, NY 10016. Attn: Ed. Dept. Illustrated how-tos on cooking, automotive topics. Query with SASE.

HUMANICS PUBLISHING GROUP—P.O. Box 7400, Atlanta, GA 30357. W. Arthur Bligh, Acquisitions Ed. Inspiring trade books, 100 to 300 pages: self-help, spiritual, instructional, and health for body, mind, and soul. "We are interested in books that people go to for help, guidance, and inspiration." Query with outline required. Royalty.

HUNGRY MIND PRESS—57 Macalester St., St. Paul, MN 55105. David Unowsky, Ed. Gail See, Ed. Biographies and memoirs; contemporary affairs; cultural criticism; nature writing; spiritual reflection; travel essays; nonfiction. "Books that examine the human experience, encourage reflection, and enrich everyday life. We want to involve writers in the planning and marketing of their books and build a strong relationship with booksellers." Query with outline. Royalty.

HUNTER PUBLISHING, INC.—300 Raritan Center Pkwy., Edison, NJ 08818. Kim André, Acquisitions Dept. Adventure travel guides to the U.S., South America, and the Caribbean.

HYPERION—114 Fifth Ave., New York, NY 10011. Material accepted from agents only. No unsolicited manuscripts or queries considered.

IMPACT PUBLISHERS, INC.—P.O. Box 1094, San Luis Obispo, CA 93406. Attn: Acquisitions Ed. Popular psychology books, from 200 pages, on personal growth, relationships, families, communities, and health for adults. Children's books for "Little Imp" series on issues of self-esteem. "Writers must have advanced degrees and professional experience in human-service fields." Query with outline and sample chapters. Royalty.

INDIANA UNIVERSITY PRESS—601 N. Morton St., Bloomington, IN 47404–3797. Attn: Ed. Dept. Scholarly nonfiction, especially cultural studies, literary criticism, music, history, women's studies, African-American studies, science, philosophy, African studies, Middle East studies, Russian studies, anthropology, regional, etc. Query with outline and sample chapters. Royalty.

INSTRUCTOR BOOKS—See *Scholastic Professional Books.*

INTERNATIONAL MARINE—Box 220, Camden, ME 04843. Jonathan Eaton, Ed. Dir. John Kettlewell, Acquisitions Ed. Books on boating (sailing and power).

INTIMATE MOMENTS—See *Silhouette Books.*

ISLAND PRESS—1718 Connecticut Ave. N.W., Suite 300, Washington, DC 20009. James Jordan, V.P./Pub. Nonfiction focusing on natural history, literary science, the environment, and natural resource management. "We want solution-oriented material to solve environmental problems. For our imprint, *Shearwater Books*, we want books that express new insights about nature and the environment." Query or send manuscript. SASE required.

JAI PRESS, INC.—55 Old Post Rd., #2, P.O. Box 1678, Greenwich, CT 06836. Herbert Johnson, Ed. Research and technical reference books on such subjects as business, economics, management, sociology, political science, computer science, life sciences, and chemistry. Query or send complete manuscript. Royalty.

JALMAR PRESS—2625 Skypark Dr., Suite 204, Torrance, CA 90505. Dr. Bradley L. Winch, Pub. Nonfiction books for parents, teachers, and caregivers. "Our emphasis is on helping children and adults live from the inside/out so that they become personally and socially responsible." Multiple queries considered. Submit outline. Royalty.

JAMES BOOKS, ALICE—Univ. of Maine at Farmington, 98 Main St., Farmington, ME 04938. Jean Amaral, Program Dir. "Shared-work cooperative" publishes books of poetry (72 to 80 pages) by writers living in New England and New York. Manuscripts read in September and January. "We emphasize the publication of poetry by women and poets of color, but also welcome and publish manuscripts by men." Authors paid with 100 copies of their books. Write for guidelines. Holds national competition for Beatrice Hawley Award.

JESUIT WAY—See *Loyola Press.*

THE JOHNS HOPKINS UNIVERSITY PRESS—2715 N. Charles St., Baltimore, MD 21218. No unsolicited poetry or fiction considered.

JOHNSON BOOKS, INC.—1880 S. 57th Ct., Boulder, CO 80301. Barbara Mussil, Pub. Nonfiction: environmental subjects, archaeology, geology, natural history, astronomy, travel guides, outdoor guidebooks, fly fishing, regional. Query. Royalty.

JONATHAN DAVID PUBLISHERS, INC.— 68–22 Eliot Ave., Middle Village, NY 11379. Alfred J. Kolatch, Ed.-in-Chief. General nonfiction (how-to, sports, cooking and food, self-help, etc.) and books on Judaica. Query with outline, sample chapter, resumé, and SASE. Royalty or outright purchase.

JOVE BOOKS—200 Madison Ave., New York, NY 10016. Fiction and nonfiction. No unsolicited manuscripts.

JUST US BOOKS—356 Glenwood Ave., East Orange, NJ 07017. Cheryl Hudson, Ed. Children's books celebrating African-American heritage. Picture books, 24 to 32 pages. Chapter books and biographies, from 2,500 words. Queries with SASE required; no unsolicited manuscripts. Royalty or flat fee.

KALMBACH BOOKS—21027 Crossroads Cir., Waukesha, WI 53187. Terry Spohn, Sr. Acquisitions Ed. Adult nonfiction, 18,000 to 50,000 words, on scale modeling, model railroading, miniatures, and amateur astronomy. Send outline with sample chapters. Accepts multiple queries. Royalty.

KAR-BEN COPIES— 6800 Tildenwood Ln., Rockville, MD 20852. Judye Groner, Ed. Books on Jewish themes for preschool and elementary children (to age 9): picture books, fiction, and nonfiction. Complete manuscript preferred; SASE. Royalty.

KEATS PUBLISHING, INC.—27 Pine St., Box 876, New Canaan, CT 06840. Norman Goldfind, Pub. Health, nutrition, alternative and complementary medicine, and preventive health care. Royalty.

KENSINGTON PUBLISHING CORP.— 850 Third Ave., New York, NY 10022. Ann LaFarge, Exec. Ed. No unagented, unsolicited submissions.

KENT PRESS—P.O. Box 1169, Stamford, CT 06904–1169. Michelle Lostaglio, Man. Ed. Books on legal issues relating to intellectual property and licensing. Query with outline. Royalty.

KENT STATE UNIVERSITY PRESS—Kent State Univ., Kent, OH 44242. John T. Hubbell, Dir. Julia Morton, Sr. Ed. Interested in scholarly works in history and literary studies of high quality, any titles of regional interest for Ohio, scholarly biographies, archaeological research, the arts, and general nonfiction.

KNOPF BOOKS FOR YOUNG READERS, ALFRED A.—201 E. 50th St., New York, NY 10022. Attn: Ed. Distinguished juvenile fiction and nonfiction. Query; no unsolicited manuscripts. Royalty. Guidelines.

KNOPF, INC., ALFRED A.—201 E. 50th St., New York, NY 10022. Attn: Sr. Ed. Distinguished adult fiction and general nonfiction. Query. Royalty.

KODANSHA AMERICA, INC.—114 Fifth Ave., New York, NY 10011. Attn: Ed. Dept. Books, 50,000 to 200,000 words, on cross-cultural, Asian and other international subjects. Query with outline, sample chapters, and SASE. Royalty.

LADYBIRD BOOKS, INC.—Imprint of Penguin USA, 375 Hudson St., New York, NY 10014–3657. Attn: Ed. Dept. Books for toddlers, preschoolers, and older children. Fairy tales, classics, science and nature, and novelty items. Rarely accepts unsolicited manuscripts. Query required.

LAREDO PUBLISHING— 8907 Wilshire Blvd., Beverly Hills, CA 90211. Sam Laredo, Ed. Bilingual and ESL (English as a second language) titles in Spanish and English. Children's fiction and young adult titles. Query with outline. Royalty.

LARK BOOKS—50 College St., Asheville, NC 28801. Rob Pulleyn, Pub. Distinctive books for creative people in crafts, how-to, leisure activities, and "coffee table" categories. Query with outline. Royalty.

LAUREL-LEAF—1540 Broadway, New York, NY 10036. Attn: Ed. Dept. Unsolicited young adult manuscripts are accepted only for the Delacorte Press Prize for a first young adult novel. This must be a work of fiction written for ages 12 to 18, by a previously unpublished author. Send SASE for rules and guidelines.

LEADERSHIP PUBLISHERS, INC.—P.O. Box 8358, Des Moines, IA 50301–8358. Dr. Lois F. Roets, Ed. Educational materials for talented and gifted students, grades K to 12, and teacher reference books. No fiction or poetry. Send SASE for catalogue and writer's guidelines before submitting. Query or send complete manuscript. Royalty for books; flat fee for booklets.

LEE & LOW BOOKS—95 Madison Ave., New York, NY 10016. Philip Lee, Pub. Elizabeth Szabla, Ed.-in-Chief. Focus is on fiction and nonfiction picture books for children ages 4 to 10. "Our goal is to meet the growing need for books that address children of color and to provide books on subjects and stories they can identify with. Of special interest are stories set in contemporary America. Folklore and animal stories discouraged." Include SASE. Advance/royalty.

LIFETIME BOOKS, INC.—2131 Hollywood Blvd., Hollywood, FL 33020. Brian Feinblum, Sr. Ed. Nonfiction (200 to 300 pages): general interest, how-to, self-help, cooking, hobby, business, health, and inspiration. Query with letter or outline and sample chapter, SASE. Royalty. Send 9x12 SASE with 5 first-class stamps for catalogue.

LIMELIGHT BOOKS—See *Tiare Publications.*

LINCOLN-HERNDON PRESS, INC.— 818 S. Dirksen Pkwy., Springfield, IL 62703. Shirley A. Buscher, Asst. Pub. American humor that reveals American history. Humor collections. Query.

LITTLE, BROWN & CO.—1271 Ave. of the Americas, New York, NY 10020. Attn: Ed. Dept. Fiction, general nonfiction, sports books; divisions for law and medical texts. Query only.

LITTLE, BROWN & CO. CHILDREN'S BOOK DEPT.—34 Beacon St., Boston, MA 02108. Attn: Ed. Dept. Juvenile fiction and nonfiction and picture books. No unsolicited manuscripts. Accepts submissions from authors with previous credits in children's book or magazine publishing and agented material only.

LLEWELLYN PUBLICATIONS—P.O. Box 64383, St. Paul, MN 55164–0383. Nancy J. Mostad, Acquisitions Mgr. Books, from 75,000 words, on subjects of self-help, how-to, alternative health, astrology, metaphysics, new age, and the occult. Metaphysical/occult fiction. "We're interested in any kind of story (mystery, historical, gothic, occult, metaphysical adventure), just as long as the theme is authentic occultism." Query with sample chapters. Multiple queries considered. Royalty.

LODESTAR—375 Hudson St., New York, NY 10014. Virginia Buckley, Ed. Dir. Fiction (picture books to young adult, mystery, fantasy, western) and nonfiction (science, contemporary issues, nature, history) considered for ages 9 to 11, 10 to 14, and 12 up. Also fiction picture books for ages 4 to 8. "We are not accepting submissions at this time, but writers may query."

LOTHROP, LEE & SHEPARD BOOKS—1350 Ave. of the Americas, New York, NY 10019. Susan Pearson, Ed.-in-Chief. Juvenile fiction and nonfiction, picture books. Does not review unsolicited material. Royalty.

LOUISIANA STATE UNIVERSITY PRESS—P.O. Box 25053, Baton Rouge, LA 70894–5053. Attn: Acquisitions Ed. Scholarly adult nonfiction, dealing with the U.S. South, its history and its culture. Query with outline and sample chapters. Royalty.

LOVE AND LAUGHTER—See *Harlequin Books/Canada.*

LOVESWEPT—1540 Broadway, New York, NY 10036. Beth de Guzman, Sr. Ed. Shauna Summers, Ed. Adult contemporary romances, approximately 55,000 to 60,000 words. Study field before submitting. Query required. Paperback only.

LOYOLA PRESS—3441 N. Ashland Ave., Chicago, IL 60657–1397. Joseph F. Downey, S.J., Ed. Dir. Jeremy Langford, Man. Ed. Religious and ethics-related material for college-educated Christian readers. "Loyola Press Series": art, literature, and religion; contemporary Christian concerns. Imprints include *Jesuit Way*: Ignatian spiritual exercises and commentaries, related biographies; *Wild Onion Books*: Chicago-area interests and personalities, including churches, art, history. Nonfiction, 200 to 400 pages. Query with outline. Royalty.

LUCENT BOOKS—P.O. Box 289011, San Diego, CA 92198–9011. Bonnie Szumski, Man. Ed. Lori Shein, Ed. Books, 18,000 to 25,000 words, for junior high/middle school students. "Overview" series: current issues (political, social, historical, environmental topics). Other series include "World History," "Great Battles," "The Way People Live" (exploring daily life and culture of communities worldwide, past and present). No unsolicited material; work is by assignment only. Flat fee. Query for guidelines and catalogue.

LYLE STUART—See *Carol Publishing Group.*

LYONS & BURFORD, PUBLISHERS—31 W. 21st St., New York, NY 10010. Peter Burford, Ed. Books, 100 to 300 pages, related to the outdoors (camping, gardening, natural history, etc.) or sports. Query with outline. Royalty.

MCCLANAHAN BOOK CO.—23 W. 26th St., New York, NY 10010. Elise Donner, Ed. Dir. Mass-market books for children, preschool to third grade. "Most books published as part of a series." Submit complete manuscript. Flat fee.

MCELDERRY BOOKS, MARGARET K.—1230 6th Ave., New York, NY 10020. Margaret K. McElderry, V.P./Pub. Emma Dryden, Ed. Picture books; quality fiction; fantasy; beginning chapter books; humor; realism; and non-fiction.

MCFARLAND & COMPANY, INC., PUBLISHERS—Box 611, Jefferson, NC 28640. Robert Franklin, Pres./Ed.-in-Chief. Scholarly and reference books, from 225 manuscript pages, in many fields, except mathematical sciences. No new age, inspirational, children's, poetry, fiction, or exposés. Submit complete manuscripts or query with outline and sample chapters. Royalty.

MACMILLAN REFERENCE USA—(formerly *Prentice Hall Press*) 1633 Broadway, 5th Fl., New York, NY 10019. Attn: Ed. Dept. General Book Division: Religious, sports, science, travel, and reference books. No fiction. Paperbacks: *Collier Books.* History, psychology, contemporary issues, sports, popular information, childcare, health. *The Free Press.* College texts and professional books in social sciences, humanities. Query. Royalty.

MACMURRAY & BECK, INC.—P.O. Box 150717, Lakewood, CO 80215. Frederick Ramey, Exec. Dir. Quality fiction and nonfiction. Royalty. No unsolicited manuscripts; query.

MADISON BOOKS—4720 Boston Way, Lanham, MD 20706. James E. Lyons, Pub. Full-length nonfiction: history, biography, contemporary affairs, trade reference. Query required. Royalty.

MADLIBS—See *Price Stern Sloan, Inc.*

MAGINATION PRESS—19 Union Sq. W., New York, NY 10003. Susan Kent Cakars, Ed. Children's picture books dealing with the psychotherapeutic treatment or resolution of serious childhood problems. Picture books for children 4 to 8; nonfiction for children 8 to 13. Most books are written by mental health professionals. Submit complete manuscript. Royalty.

MARKOWSKI INTERNATIONAL PUBLISHERS—One Oakglade Cir., Hummelstown, PA 17036. Marjorie L. Markowski, Ed. Nonfiction, from 30,000 words: popular health and fitness, marriage and human relations, personal and career development, self-help, sales and marketing, leadership training, network marketing, motivation, success, and Christian topics. Also various aviation and model aviation topics. "We are interested in how-to, motivational, and instructional books of short to medium length that will serve recognized and emerging needs of society." Query with outline and 3 sample chapters. Royalty.

MCGREGOR HILL PUBLISHING—118 S. Westshore Blvd., Suite 233, Tampa, FL 33609. Lonnie Herman, Pub. Fiction and nonfiction, especially biography, sports, self-help. Query with outline and sample chapters or send complete manuscript. Royalty.

MEADOWBROOK PRESS—18318 Minnetonka Blvd., Deephaven, MN 55391. Attn: Submissions Ed. Upbeat, useful books, 60,000 words, on pregnancy, childbirth, and parenting; shorter works of humor, party planning, and children's activities; fiction anthologies and humorous poetry for children. Send for guidelines. Royalty or flat fee.

MEGA-BOOKS, INC.—116 E. 19th St., New York, NY 10003. Carol Gilbert, Man. Ed. Book packager. Young adult books, 150 pages, children's books. Query for guidelines. Flat fee.

MENTOR BOOKS—375 Hudson St., New York, NY 10014. Attn: Eds. Nonfiction for the college and high school market. Query required. Royalty.

MEREDITH CORP. BOOK PUBLISHING—(*Better Homes and Gardens Books*) 1716 Locust St., Des Moines, IA 50309–3023. James D. Blume, Ed.-

in-Chief. Books on gardening, crafts, decorating, do-it-yourself, cooking; mostly staff-written. "Interested in free-lance writers with expertise in these areas." Limited market. Query with SASE.

MESSNER, JULIAN—Simon & Schuster Educational Group, Silver Burdett Press, 299 Jefferson Rd., P.O. Box 480, Parsippany, NJ 07054–0480. John Dooling, Pub. Curriculum-oriented nonfiction. General nonfiction, for ages 8 to 14: science, nature, biography, history, social issues, and hobbies. Lengths vary. Royalty.

THE MICHIGAN STATE UNIVERSITY PRESS—1405 S. Harrison Rd., Suite 25, E. Lansing, MI 48823–5202. Attn: Ed. Dept. Scholarly nonfiction, with concentrations in history, regional history, African sources, business, and Civil War. Submit prospectus, table of contents, and sample chapters to Acquisitions Ed. Authors should refer to *The Chicago Manual of Style, 14th Edition*, for formats and styles.

MIDDLE PASSAGE PRESS—5517 Secrest Dr., Los Angeles, CA 90043–2029. Barbara Bramwell, Ed. Small press. Nonfiction that focuses on African-American experience in the historical, social, and political context of American life. Query with sample chapters. Royalty.

MILKWEED EDITIONS— 430 First Ave. N., Suite 400, Minneapolis, MN 55401–1743. Emilie Buchwald, Ed. "We publish excellent award-winning fiction, poetry, essays, and nonfiction, the kind of writing that makes for good reading." Publishes about 15 books a year. Submit complete manuscript. Royalty. Also publishes *Milkweeds for Young Readers*: high quality novels and biographies for middle grades.

THE MILLBROOK PRESS—2 Old New Milford Rd., Brookfield, CT 06804. Dottie Carlson, Manuscript Coord. Nonfiction for early elementary grades through grades 7 and up, appropriate for the school and public library or trade market, encompassing curriculum-related topics and extracurricular interests. Some picture books. Query with outline and sample chapter. Royalty.

MILLS & SANDERSON, PUBLISHERS—P.O. Box 833, Bedford, MA 01730–0833. Jan H. Anthony, Pub. Books, 200 pages, for series on family problem solving/psychotherapy or contemporary American biographies. Not considering any new material at this time.

MINSTREL BOOKS—See *Archway Paperbacks.*

MIRA BOOKS—See *Harlequin Books/Canada.*

THE MIT PRESS—55 Hayward St., Cambridge, MA 02142. Larry Cohen, Ed.-in-Chief. Books on computer science/artificial intelligence; cognitive sciences; economics; architecture; aesthetic and social theory; linguistics; technology studies; environmental studies; and neuroscience.

MODAN PUBLISHING—P.O. Box 1202, Bellmore, NY 11710. Bennett Shelkowitz, Man. Dir. Adult nonfiction. Young adult fiction and nonfiction. Children's picture books. Books with international focus or related to political or social issues. *Adama Books*: Judaica and Hebrew books from Israel.

MONDO PUBLISHING—One Plaza Rd., Greenvale, NY 11548. Attn: Submissions Ed. Picture books, nonfiction, and early chapter books for readers ages 4 to 10. "We want to create beautiful books that children can read on their own and find so enjoyable that they'll want to come back to them time and time again." Query or send complete manuscript. Royalty.

MOON HANDBOOKS—Moon Publications, Inc., P.O. Box 3040, Chico, CA 95927–3040. Taran March, Exec. Ed. Travel guides, 400 to 600 pages. Will consider multiple submissions. Query. Royalty.

MOREHOUSE PUBLISHING—871 Ethan Allen Hwy., Suite 204, Ridgefield, CT 06877. Deborah Grahame-Smith, Ed. E. Allen Kelley, Pub. Theology, pastoral care, church administration, spirituality, Anglican studies, history of religion, books for children, youth, elders, etc. Query with outline, contents, and sample chapter. SASE required. Royalty.

MORRIS, JOSHUA —See *Reader's Digest Young Families, Inc.*

MORROW AND CO., INC., WILLIAM—1350 Ave. of the Americas, New York, NY 10019. Attn: Eds. Adult fiction and nonfiction: no unsolicited manuscripts. *Mulberry Books* (children's paperbacks), Amy Cohn, Ed. Dir.; *Hearst Books* (general nonfiction) and *Hearst Marine Books*, Ann Bramsom, Ed. Dir.

MOUNTAIN PRESS PUBLISHING—1301 S. 3rd W., P.O. Box 2399, Missoula, MT 59806. Attn: John Rimel. Nonfiction, 300 pages: natural history, field guides, geology, horses, Western history, Americana, outdoor guides, and fur trade lore. Query with outline and sample chapters; multiple queries considered. Royalty.

THE MOUNTAINEERS BOOKS—1001 S.W. Klickitat Way, Suite 201, Seattle, WA 98134. Margaret Foster, Ed.-in-Chief. Nonfiction books on noncompetitive aspects of outdoor sports such as mountaineering, backpacking, walking, trekking, canoeing, kayaking, bicycling, skiing; independent adventure travel. Field guides, how-to and where-to guidebooks, biographies of outdoor people; accounts of expeditions. Natural history and conservation. Submit sample chapters and outline. Royalty.

MOYER BELL—Kymbolde Way, Wakefield, RI 02879. Jennifer Moyer, Pub. Adult fiction, nonfiction, and poetry. Query with sample chapter or send complete manuscript. Royalty.

MUIR PUBLICATIONS, JOHN—P.O. Box 613, Santa Fe, NM 87504–0613. Steven Cary, Pres. Travel guidebooks for adults. Nonfiction for children, 6 to 12. Health topics for adults and children. Send manuscript or query with sample chapters. No fiction. Royalty or work for hire.

MULBERRY BOOKS—See *William Morrow and Co., Inc.*

MUSTANG PUBLISHING CO., INC.—Box 3004, Memphis, TN 38173. Rollin A. Riggs, Ed. Nonfiction for 18-to 40-year-olds, specializing in travel, humor, and how-to. Send queries for 100-to 300-page books, with outlines and sample chapters. Royalty. SASE required.

THE MYSTERIOUS PRESS—Time and Life Bldg., 1271 Ave. of the Americas, New York, NY 10020. William Malloy, Ed.-in-Chief. Mystery/suspense novels. Agented manuscripts only.

NAIAD PRESS, INC.—Box 10543, Tallahassee, FL 32302. Barbara Grier, Ed. Adult fiction, 52,000 to 55,000 words, with lesbian themes and characters: mysteries, romances, gothics, ghost stories, westerns, regencies, spy novels, etc. Query with letter and one-page précis only. Royalty.

NATIONAL PRESS BOOKS, INC.—7200 Wisconsin Ave., Suite 212, Bethesda, MD 20814. Talia Greenberg, Ed. Nonfiction: history, criminology, reference and health; parenting; business, management, and automotive titles. Imprints include *Beach Books, Full Court Press Books, Garlic Press, Pande-*

monium Books, Plain English Press, and *Zenith Editions.* Query with outline and sample chapters. Royalty.

NATUREGRAPH PUBLISHERS—P.O. Box 1075, Happy Camp, CA 96039. Barbara Brown, Ed. Nonfiction: Native-American culture, natural history, outdoor living, land, gardening, Indian lore, and how-to. Query. Royalty.

THE NAVAL INSTITUTE PRESS—Annapolis, MD 21402. Attn: Acquisitions Dept. Nonfiction, 60,000 to 100,000 words: military histories; biographies; ship guides; how-tos on boating and navigation. Occasional fiction, 75,000 to 110,000 words. Query with outline and sample chapters. Royalty.

NELSON, INC., THOMAS—Thomas Nelson Trade Book Division, P.O. Box 141000, Nashville, TN 37214–1000. Rick Nash, Acquisitions Ed. Nonfiction: adult inspirational, motivational, devotional, self-help, Christian living, prayer, and evangelism. Fiction: commercial, from a Christian perspective. Query with resumé, sample chapter, synopsis, and SASE. Allow 12 weeks for response.

NEW HORIZON PRESS—P.O. Box 669, Far Hills, NJ 07931. Joan Dunphy, Ed.-in-Chief. True stories, 96,000 words, dealing with contemporary issues, especially true crime, that revolve around a hero or heroine. Royalty. Query.

NEW LEAF PRESS, INC.—P.O. Box 726, Green Forest, AR 72638. Jim Fletcher, Acquisitions Ed. Nonfiction, 100 to 400 pages, for Christian readers: how to live the Christian life, devotionals, gift books. Query with outline and sample chapters, or submit complete manuscript. Royalty.

THE NEW PRESS— 450 W. 41st St., New York, NY 10036. Andre Schiffrin, Dir. Serious nonfiction: history, economics, education, politics. Fiction in translation. Query required.

NEW RIVERS PRESS— 420 N. 5th St., Suite 910, Minneapolis, MN 55401. C.W. Truesdale, Ed./Pub. Collections of short stories, essays, and poems from emerging writers in upper Midwest. Query.

NEW VICTORIA PUBLISHERS—P.O. Box 27, Norwich, VT 05055. ReBecca Béguin, Ed. Lesbian feminist fiction and nonfiction, including mystery, biography, history, fantasy; some humor and education. Guidelines. Query with outline and sample chapters; SASE. Royalty.

NEW WORLD LIBRARY—14 Pamaron Way, Novato, CA 94949. Attn: Submissions Ed. Nonfiction, especially leading-edge inspirational/self-help books, enlightened business, Native American studies, classic wisdom, African-American studies, women's studies. "Aim for intelligent, aware audience, interested in personal and planetary transformation." Query with outline and SASE. Multiple queries accepted. Royalty.

NEWCASTLE PUBLISHING—13419 Saticoy St., N. Hollywood, CA 91605. Al Saunders, Pub. Nonfiction manuscripts, 200 to 250 pages, for older adults on personal health, health care issues, and relationships. "We are not looking for fads or trends. We want books with a long shelf life." Multiple queries considered. Royalty.

NEWMARKET PRESS—18 E. 48th St., New York, NY 10017. Esther Margolis, Pub. Nonfiction on health, psychology, self-help, child care, parenting, music, and film. Query required. Royalty.

NORTH COUNTRY PRESS—RR 1, Box 1395, Unity, ME 04988. Patricia Newell, Mary Kenney, Eds. Nonfiction with a Maine and/or New England tie-in with emphasis on the outdoors; also limited fiction (Maine-based mystery). "Our goal is to publish high-quality books for people who love New England." Query with SASE, outline, and sample chapters. No unsolicited manuscripts. Royalty.

NORTHEASTERN UNIVERSITY PRESS—360 Huntington Ave., 416 CP, Boston, MA 02115. Scott Brassart, Ed. Nonfiction, 50,000 to 200,000 words: trade and scholarly titles in music, criminal justice, women's studies, ethnic studies, law, sociology, environmental studies, American history, and literary criticism. Submit query with outline and sample chapter or complete manuscript. Royalty.

NORTHERN ILLINOIS UNIVERSITY PRESS—DeKalb, IL 60115. Mary L. Lincoln, Dir. Books, 250 to 450 pages, for scholars and informed general readers. Submit history and Russian studies topics to Mary Lincoln; politics, philosophy, anthropology, economics, and literature to Robert Anthony. "Regional topics are our special interest." Query with outline. Royalty.

NORTHLAND PUBLISHING—P.O. Box 1389, Flagstaff, AZ 86002. Erin Murphy, Ed. Nonfiction books on natural history; fine arts; Native American culture, myth, art, and crafts; and cookbooks. Unique children's picture books, 350 to 1,500 words, and middle reader chapter books, approximately 20,000 words, with American West/Southwest regional themes. Potential market for proposed adult and middle reader books. Query with outline, sample chapters. For children's books, send complete manuscript. "Include SASE with all submissions and queries. No queries by phone or fax." Royalty.

NORTHWORD PRESS, INC.—Box 1360, 7520 Highway 515, Minocqua, WI 54548. Barbara K. Harold, Man. Ed. Nonfiction nature and wildlife books for children and adults. Send for catalogue and guidelines. Royalty or flat fee.

NORTON AND CO., INC., W.W.—500 Fifth Ave., New York, NY 10110. Liz Malcolm, Ed. High-quality fiction and nonfiction. No occult, paranormal, religious, genre fiction (formula romance, science fiction, westerns), cookbooks, arts and crafts, young adult, or children's books. Query with synopsis, 2 to 3 chapters (including first chapter), and resumé. Return postage and packaging required. Royalty.

ODYSSEY PAPERBACKS—See *Harcourt Brace & Co. Children's Book Div.*

OHIO UNIVERSITY PRESS/SWALLOW PRESS—Scott Quadrangle, Athens, OH 45701. David Sanders, Dir. Scholarly nonfiction, 350 to 450 manuscript pages, especially literary criticism, regional studies, African studies. *Swallow Press*: general interest and western Americana. Query with outline and sample chapters. Royalty.

THE OLIVER PRESS—Charlotte Square, 5707 W. 36th St., Minneapolis, MN 55416. Teresa Faden, Assoc. Ed. Collective biographies for young adults. Submit proposals for books, 20,000 to 25,000 words, on people who have made an impact in such areas as history, politics, crime, science, and business. Flat fee (approximately $1,000).

OPEN COURT PUBLISHING CO.—Box 599, Peru, IL 61354. Attn: Gen. Books Acquisitions Dept. Scholarly books on philosophy, psychology, personal stories of development, religion, eastern thought, history, public policy, feminist thought, education, science, social issues, contemporary culture, and related topics. Send sample chapters with outline and resumé. Royalty.

ORCHARD BOOKS—95 Madison Ave., New York, NY 10016. No unsolicited manuscripts.

ORCHISES PRESS—P.O. Box 20602, Alexandria, VA 22320. Roger Lathbury, Ed. Nonfiction books, 128 to 500 pages; and intellectually sophisticated, technically expert poetry books, 48 to 128 pages. No fiction. Query with sample chapters. Royalty.

OREGON STATE UNIVERSITY PRESS—101 Waldo Hall, Corvallis, OR 97331. Attn: Ed. Dept. Scholarly books in a limited range of disciplines and books of particular importance to the Pacific Northwest, especially dealing with the history, natural history, culture, and literature of the region or with natural resource issues. Query with summary of manuscript.

OSBORNE/MCGRAW HILL—2600 Tenth St., Berkeley, CA 94710. Scott Rogers, Exec. Ed. Microcomputer books for general audience. Query. Royalty.

OUR SUNDAY VISITOR PUBLISHING—200 Noll Plaza, Huntington, IN 46750. Jacquelyn M. Lindsey, Jim Manney, Acquisitions Eds. Catholic-oriented books of various lengths. No fiction. Query with outline and sample chapters. Royalty.

THE OVERLOOK PRESS—149 Wooster St., New York, NY 10012. Tracy Carns, Ed. Dir. Literary fiction, some fantasy/science fiction, foreign literature in translation, general nonfiction, including art, architecture, design, film, history, biography, crafts/lifestyle, martial arts, Hudson Valley regional interest, and children's books. Query with outline, sample chapters and SASE. Royalty.

OWEN PUBLISHERS, INC., RICHARD C.—Dept. TW, P.O. Box 585, Katonah, NY 10536. Janice Boland, Ed. Fiction and nonfiction. Brief storybooks, approximately 45 to 100 words, suitable for 5-, 6-, and 7-year-old beginning readers for the "Books for Young Learners" collection. Royalties for writers. Flat fee for illustrators. Writers must send SASE for guidelines before submitting.

OXFORD UNIVERSITY PRESS—198 Madison Ave., New York, NY 10016. Attn: Ed. Dept. Authoritative books on literature, history, philosophy, etc.; college textbooks, medical, scientific, technical and reference books. Query. Royalty.

PANDEMONIUM BOOKS—See *National Press Books, Inc.*

PANTHEON BOOKS—201 E. 50th St., New York, NY 10022. Attn: Ed. Dept. Quality fiction and nonfiction. Query required. Royalty.

PAPIER-MACHE PRESS—135 Aviation Way, #14, Watsonville, CA 95076. Sandra Martz, Ed. Fiction, poetry, and nonfiction books; 6 to 8 books annually. "We emphasize, but are not limited to, the publication of books and related items for midlife and older women." Write for guidelines. Query. Royalty.

PARA PUBLISHING—P.O. Box 8206–238, Santa Barbara, CA 93118–8206. Dan Poynter, Ed. Adult nonfiction books on parachutes and skydiving only. Author must present evidence of having made at least 1,000 jumps. Query. Royalty.

PARAGON HOUSE—370 Lexington Ave., New York, NY 10017. Michael Giampaoli, Pub. Serious nonfiction, including philosophy, religion, and current affairs. Query. Royalty.

PAULIST PRESS—997 Macarthur Blvd., Mahwah, NJ 07430. Donald Brophy, Man. Ed. Adult nonfiction, 100 to 400 pages; and picture books, 8 to 10 pages, for readers 5 to 7 or 8 to 10. For adult books, query with outline and sample chapters. For juvenile books, submit complete manuscript to Karen Scialabba, Ed. Royalty.

PEACHPIT PRESS—2414 Sixth St., Berkeley, CA 94710. Roslyn Bullas, Ed. Books on computer and graphic-design topics. Query with outline and sample chapters for manuscripts 100 to 1,100 words. E-mail address is roslyn-@peachpit.com. Web site is http://www.peachpit.com.

PEACHTREE PUBLISHERS, LTD.—494 Armour Cir. N.E., Atlanta, GA 30324. Attn: Ed. Dept. Wide variety of children's books, fiction and nonfiction. No religious material, science fiction/fantasy, romance, mystery/detective, historical fiction; no business, scientific, or technical books. Send outline and sample chapters. SASE required. Royalty.

PELICAN PUBLISHING CO., INC.—1101 Monroe St., Gretna, LA 70053. Nina Kooij, Ed.-in-Chief. General nonfiction: Americana, regional, architecture, travel, politics, business, cookbooks. Children's books. Query with outline or synopsis and resumé. Royalty.

PENGUIN BOOKS—375 Hudson St., New York, NY 10014. Attn: Ed. Dept. Adult fiction and nonfiction paperbacks. Royalty.

PEREGRINE SMITH BOOKS—P.O. Box 667, Layton, UT 84041. Theresa Desmond, Ed. Juvenile books: western/cowboy; activity; how-to; nature/environment; and humor. Fiction picture books, to 2,000 words; nonfiction books, to 10,000 words, for readers 5 to 11. Royalty.

THE PERMANENT PRESS—Noyac Rd., Sag Harbor, NY 11963. Judith Shepard, Ed. Original and arresting novels. Query. Royalty.

PERSPECTIVES PRESS—P.O. Box 90318, Indianapolis, IN 46290–0318. Pat Johnston, Pub. Books on infertility, adoption, closely related reproductive health and child welfare issues (foster care, etc.). Also picture books, 32 pages, for children to 10 years old. "Writers must read our guidelines before submitting." Query. Royalty.

PETERSON'S/PACESETTER BOOKS—202 Carnegie Ctr., P.O. Box 2123, Princeton, NJ 08543–2123. Andrea Pedolsky, Exec. Ed. Books that bring a new point of view to perennial business topics or identify new issues and developments in the business world. "We want books that can bring something new to businesspeople's lives, that show the human side of the business world." Submit proposal with one sample chapter. Royalty.

PHILOMEL BOOKS—200 Madison Ave., New York, NY 10016. Patricia Lee Gauch, Ed. Dir. Juvenile picture books, young adult fiction, and some biographies. Fresh, original work with compelling characters and "a truly childlike spirit." Query required.

PINEAPPLE PRESS—P.O. Box 3899, Sarasota, FL 34230. June Cussen, Ed. Serious fiction and nonfiction, Florida-oriented, 60,000 to 125,000 words. Query with outline, sample chapters, and SASE. Royalty.

PINNACLE BOOKS— 850 Third Ave., New York, NY 10022. Paul Dinas, Exec. Ed. Nonfiction books: true crime, celebrity biographies, and humor. Unsolicited material not accepted.

PIPPIN PRESS—229 E. 85th St., Gracie Sta., Box 1347, New York, NY 10028. Barbara Francis, Pub. Small chapter books for children ages 7 to 10, emphasizing humor and fantasy, humorous mysteries; imaginative nonfiction for children of all ages; high-quality picture books. Query with SASE only; no unsolicited manuscripts. Royalty.

PLAIN ENGLISH PRESS—See *National Press Books, Inc.*

PLANET DEXTER—Addison-Wesley Publishing Co., One Jacob Way, Reading, MA 01867–3999. Beth Wolfensberger, Ed. Nonfiction educational books for children ages 5 to 12. "Our goal is to create book-based products with an accompanying toy, electronic gadget, craft item, or learning tool." No fiction or poetry. No textbook-style academic writing. SASE required.

PLAYERS PRESS, INC.—P.O. Box 1132, Studio City, CA 91614. Robert Gordon, Ed. Plays and musicals for children and adults; juvenile and adult nonfiction related to theatre, film, television, and the performing arts. Lengths vary. Query. Royalty.

PLENUM PUBLISHING CORP.—233 Spring St., New York, NY 10013. Linda Greenspan Regan, Exec. Ed. Trade nonfiction, approximately 300 pages, on popular science, criminology, psychology, social science, anthropology, and health. Query required. Royalty. Hardcover.

PLUME BOOKS—375 Hudson St., New York, NY 10014. Attn: Ed. Dept. Nonfiction: hobbies, business, health, cooking, child care, psychology, history, popular culture, biography, and politics. Fiction: serious literary and gay. Query.

POCKET BOOKS—1230 Ave. of the Americas, New York, NY 10020. Emily Bestler, VP/ Ed. Dir. Gina Centrello, Pub./Pres. Adult and young adult fiction and nonfiction. Mystery line: police procedurals, private eye, and amateur sleuth novels, 60,000 to 70,000 words. Royalty.

POPULAR PRESS—Bowling Green State Univ., Bowling Green, OH 43403. Ms. Pat Browne, Ed. Nonfiction, 250 to 400 pages, examining some aspect of popular culture. Query with outline. Flat fee or royalty.

POTTER, CLARKSON —201 E. 50th St., New York, NY 10022. Lauren Shakely, Ed. Dir. General trade books. Submissions accepted through agents only.

POWER PUBLICATIONS—56 McArthur Ave., Staten Island, NY 10312. Elizabeth Wallace, Exec. Dir. Adult nonfiction books on women's issues, nursing, the health field, and gender issues. Royalty.

POWERKIDS PRESS—See *Rosen Publishing Group, Inc.*

PRAEGER PUBLISHERS— 88 Post Rd. W., Westport, CT 06880–4232. James Dunton, Pub. General nonfiction; scholarly and textbooks. Query with outline. Royalty.

PRENTICE HALL PRESS—See *Macmillan Reference USA.*

PRESIDIO PRESS—505B San Marin Dr., Suite 300, Novato, CA 94945–1340. Attn: Ed. Dept. Nonfiction: military history and military affairs, from 90,000 words. Fiction: selected military and action-adventure works and mysteries, from 100,000 words. Query. Royalty.

PRICE STERN SLOAN, INC.—11835 Olympic Blvd., Los Angeles, CA 90064. Attn: Submissions Ed. Adult trade nonfiction, calendars, and novelty juvenile titles. Imprints include *Troubador Press, Wee Sing, MadLibs.* Query with SASE required. Royalty.

PRIMA PUBLISHING—P.O. Box 1260, Rocklin, CA 95677. Ben Dominitz, Pub. Jennifer Basye, Ed. Nonfiction on variety of subjects, including business, health, and cookbooks. "We want books with originality, written by highly qualified individuals." Royalty.

PROMPT PUBLICATIONS—2647 Waterfront Pkwy. E. Dr., Suite 300, Indianapolis, IN 46214–2041. Attn: Acquisitions Ed. Nonfiction softcover technical books on electronics, how-to, troubleshooting and repair, electrical engineering, video and sound equipment, cellular technology, etc., for all levels of technical experience. Query with outline, sample chapters, author bio, and SASE. Royalty.

PRUETT PUBLISHING COMPANY—2928 Pearl St., Boulder, CO 80301. Jim Pruett, Pub. Nonfiction: outdoors and recreation, western U.S. history, travel, natural history and the environment, fly fishing. Query. Royalty.

PUTNAM'S SONS, G.P.—200 Madison Ave., New York, NY 10016. Attn: Ed. Dept. General trade nonfiction, fiction. Query Nancy Paulson, Pres. and Pub., for children's books. No unsolicited manuscripts. Royalty.

QED PRESS—155 Cypress St., Fort Bragg, CA 95437. Cynthia Frank, Ed. Health, gerontology, and psychology books. Query with outline and sample chapters. Royalty.

QUEST BOOKS—Theosophical Publishing House, 306 W. Geneva Rd., P. O. Box 270, Wheaton, IL 60189–0270. Brenda Rosen, Exec. Ed. Nonfiction books on Eastern and Western religion and philosophy, holism, healing, transpersonal psychology, men's and women's spirituality, Native-American spirituality, meditation, yoga, ancient wisdom. Query. Royalty.

QUIXOTE PRESS—615 Ave. H, Fort Madison, IA 52627. Bruce Carlson, Pres. Adult fiction and nonfiction including humor, folklore, and regional cookbooks; some juvenile fiction. Query with sample chapters and outline. Royalty.

RAGGED MOUNTAIN PRESS—Box 220, Camden, ME 04843. Jonathan Eaton, Ed. Dir. John Kettlewell, Acquisitions Ed. Books on outdoor recreation.

RAINTREE STECK-VAUGHN PUBLISHERS—National Education Corp., 466 Southern Blvd., Chatham, NJ 07928. Walter Kossmann, Ed. Nonfiction books, 5,000 to 30,000 words, for school and library market: biographies for grades 3 and up; and science, social studies, and history books for primary grades through high school. Query with outline and sample chapters; SASE required. Flat fee and royalty.

RANDOM HOUSE, INC.—201 E. 50th St., New York, NY 10022. Attn: Ed. Dept. General fiction and nonfiction. Agented material only.

RANDOM HOUSE JUVENILE DIV.—201 E. 50th St., New York, NY 10022. Kate Klimo, Pub. Dir. Fiction and nonfiction for beginning readers; paperback fiction line for 7-to 9-year-olds. No unsolicited manuscripts. Agented material only.

READER'S DIGEST YOUNG FAMILIES, INC.—355 Riverside Ave., Westport, CT 06880–4810. Willy Derraugh, Pub. Children's books for readers ages 2 to 11. Imprints include: *Reader's Digest Kids,* high-quality, fully illustrated information and reference books; *Joshua Morris,* imaginative and uniquely formatted novelty books and book kits, with an emphasis on information and learning; *Wishing Well,* novelty formats. Address submissions to an imprint's Acquisitions Ed.

READER'S DIGEST KIDS—See *Reader's Digest Young Families, Inc.*

RED WAGON BOOKS—Harcourt, Brace & Co. Children's Books, 525 B St., Suite 1900, San Diego, CA 92101–4495. Attn: Acquisitions Ed. No unsolicited material.

REGNERY PUBLISHING, INC.— 422 First St. S.E., Suite 300, Washington, DC 20003. Attn: Ed. Dept. Nonfiction books. Query. Royalty.

RENAISSANCE HOUSE—541 Oak St., P. O. Box 177, Frederick, CO 80530. Eleanor H. Ayer, Ed. Regional guidebooks. Guidebooks on CO, AZ, CA, and the Southwest. "We use only manuscripts written to our specifications for new or ongoing series." Submit outline and short bio. Royalty.

REPUBLIC OF TEXAS PRESS—See *Wordware Publishing.*

RISING TIDE PRESS—5 Kivy St., Huntington Sta., New York, NY 11746. Lee Boojamra, Ed. Books for, by, and about lesbians. Fiction, 60,000 to 80,000 words: romance, mystery, and science fiction/fantasy. Nonfiction, 40,000 to 60,000 words. Royalty. Reports in 3 months. SASE for guidelines.

RIZZOLI INTERNATIONAL PUBLICATIONS, INC.—300 Park Ave. S., New York, NY 10010. Manuela Soares, Children's Book Ed. Original manuscripts that introduce children to fine art, folk art, and architecture of all cultures for a small list. Nonfiction and fiction for all ages. Query with SASE or response card. Royalty.

ROC—375 Hudson St., New York, NY 10014. Amy Stout, Exec. Ed. Jennifer Smith, Assoc. Manuscript Ed. Science fiction, fantasy. Query.

ROCKBRIDGE PUBLISHING—P.O. Box 351, Berryville, VA 22611. Katherine Tennery, Ed. Book-length nonfiction on the Civil War, Virginia history, and travel guides to Virginia. Query. Royalty.

RODALE PRESS—33 E. Minor St., Emmaus, PA 18098. Pat Corpora, Pub. Books on men's health, women's health, gardening, cookbooks, inspirational/spiritual, sewing, quilting, woodworking. Query with outline and sample chapter. Royalty and outright purchase. "We're always looking for truly competent free lancers to write chapters for books conceived and developed in-house." Payment on a work-for-hire basis; address Lois Hazel, Asst. Acquisitions Ed.

ROSEN PUBLISHING GROUP, INC.—29 E. 21st St., New York, NY 10010. Roger Rosen, Pres. Patra Sevastiades, Ed. Dir. Nonfiction, young adult books, 8,000 to 40,000 words, on multicultural, substance-abuse prevention, and career-guidance topics in multi–volume series. *PowerKids Press:* social and personal problems for children K through 4. Pays varying rates.

ROYAL FIREWORKS PRESS—1 First Ave., Unionville, NY 10988. Charles Morgan, Ed. Adult science fiction and mysteries. Juvenile and young adult fiction, biography, and educational nonfiction. Submit complete manuscripts with a brief plot overview. No multiple queries. Royalty.

RUNNING PRESS—125 S. 22nd St., Philadelphia, PA 19103. Attn: Exec. Ed. Trade nonfiction: art, craft, how-to, self-help, science, lifestyles. Young adult books and interactive packages. Query. Royalty.

RUTGERS UNIVERSITY PRESS—P.O. Box 5062, New Brunswick, NJ 08903. Paula Kantenwein, Editorial Asst. Nonfiction, 70,000 to 120,000 words. Query with outline and sample chapters. Royalty.

RUTLEDGE HILL PRESS—211 Seventh Ave. N., Nashville, TN 37219. Kirsten Hanson, Ed. Market-specific nonfiction. Query with outline and sample chapters. Royalty.

ST. ANTHONY MESSENGER PRESS—1615 Republic St., Cincinnati, OH 45210–1298. Lisa Biedenbach, Man. Ed. Inspirational nonfiction for Catholics, supporting a Christian lifestyle in our culture; prayer aids, scripture, church history, education, practical spirituality, parish ministry, liturgy resources. Query with 500-word summary. Royalty.

ST. MARTIN'S PRESS—175 Fifth Ave., New York, NY 10010. Attn: Ed. Dept. General adult fiction and nonfiction. Query. Royalty.

SAINT MARY'S PRESS—702 Terrace Heights, Winona, MN 55987–1320. Stephan Nagel, Ed.-in-Chief. Progressive Catholic publisher. Fiction, to 40,000 words, for young adults ages 14 to 17, "that gives insight into the struggle of teens to become healthy, hopeful adults and also sheds light on Catholic experience, history, or cultures." Query with outline and sample chapter. Royalty.

SANDLAPPER PUBLISHING, INC.—P.O. Drawer 730, Orangeburg, SC 29116–0730. Amanda Gallman, Book Ed. Nonfiction books on South Carolina history, culture, cuisine. Query with outline, sample chapters, and SASE.

SASQUATCH BOOKS—1008 Western Ave., #300, Seattle, WA 98104. Attn: Ed. Dept. Regional books by West Coast authors on a wide range of nonfiction topics: travel, natural history, gardening, cooking, history, and public affairs. Books must have a West Coast angle. Query with SASE. Royalty.

SCARECROW PRESS—4720 Boston Way, Lanham, MD 20706. Shirley Lambert, Ed. Dir. Reference works and bibliographies, from 150 pages, especially in the areas of cinema, TV, radio, and theater, mainly for use by libraries. Query or send complete manuscript; multiple queries considered. Royalty.

SCHOCKEN BOOKS—201 E. 50th St., New York, NY 10022. Attn: Ed. Dept. General nonfiction: Judaica, women's studies, education, history, religion, psychology, cultural studies. Query with outline and sample chapter. Royalty.

SCHOLASTIC, INC.—555 Broadway, New York, NY 10012. No unsolicited manuscripts.

SCHOLASTIC PROFESSIONAL BOOKS—411 Lafayette St., New York, NY 10003. Attn: Shawn Richardson. Books by and for teachers of kindergarten through eighth grade. *Instructor Books*: practical, activity/resource books on teaching reading and writing, science, math, etc. *Teaching Strategies Books*: 64 to 96 pages on new ideas, practices, and approaches to teaching. Query with outline, sample chapters or activities, contents page, and resumé. Flat fee or royalty. Multiple queries considered. SASE for guidelines.

SCHWARTZ BOOKS, ANNE—1230 Ave. of the Americas, New York, NY 10020. Anne Schwartz, Ed. Picture books through juvenile fiction and nonfiction as well as illustrated collections. Query; no unsolicited manuscripts.

SCOTT, FORESMAN AND CO.—See *Scott Foresman/Addison Wesley*.

792

SCOTT FORESMAN/ADDISON WESLEY—1900 E. Lake Ave., Glenview, IL 60025. Pat Donaghy, Pres. Elementary and secondary textbooks. Royalty or flat fee.

SCRIBNER—1230 Ave. of the Americas, New York, NY 10020. Attn: Ed. Dept. No unsolicited manuscripts.

SEAL PRESS—3131 Western Ave., Suite 410, Seattle, WA 98121–1041. Holly Morris, Ed. Dir. Feminist/women's studies books: popular culture and lesbian studies; parenting; domestic violence; health and recovery; sports and outdoors. Fiction, poetry, and young adult and children's books also published. Query. Royalty.

SEASIDE PRESS—See *Wordware Publishing.*

SEVEN STORIES PRESS— 632 Broadway, 7th Fl., New York, NY 10012. Dan Simon, Ed.-in-Chief. Small press. Fiction and nonfiction. Submit sample chapters, no more than 20 pages total. Royalty.

SHAW PUBLISHERS, HAROLD—388 Gunderson Dr., Box 567, Wheaton, IL 60189. Joan L. Guest, Man. Ed. Nonfiction, 120 to 320 pages, with an evangelical Christian perspective. Some fiction and literary books. Query. Flat fee or royalty.

SHEARWATER BOOKS—See *Island Press.*

THE SHEEP MEADOW PRESS—P.O. Box 1345, Riverdale-on-Hudson, NY 10471. Rob Giannetto, Ed. Mostly book-length poetry; some fiction, essays, and memoirs. Send complete manuscript. Royalty.

SIERRA CLUB BOOKS— 85 Second St., San Francisco, CA 94105. Attn: Ed. Dept. Nonfiction: environment, natural history, the sciences, outdoors and regional guidebooks, nature photography; juvenile nonfiction. Query with SASE. Royalty.

SIGNAL HILL PUBLICATIONS—1320 Jamesville Ave., Box 131, Syracuse, NY 13210. Jennifer Lashley, Ed. Fiction and nonfiction, 5,000 to 9,000 words, and poetry for adults who read at low levels, for use in adult basic education programs, volunteer literacy organizations, and job training programs. Query with outline, synopsis, and one to 3 sample chapters. "Read guidelines first. Do not submit material for juvenile or teenage readers." Royalty or flat fee.

SIGNATURE BOOKS, INC.—564 W. 400 North, Salt Lake City, UT 84116–3411. Attn: Board of Dirs. Adult fiction and nonfiction, from 100 pages. Adult poetry from 80 pages. Royalty.

SILHOUETTE BOOKS—300 E. 42nd St., New York, NY 10017. Isabel Swift, Ed. Dir. *Silhouette Romances*: Melissa Senate, Sr. Ed. Contemporary romances, 53,000 to 58,000 words. *Special Edition*: Tara Gavin, Sr. Ed. Sophisticated contemporary romances, 75,000 to 80,000 words. *Silhouette Desire*: Lucia Macro, Sr. Ed. Sensuous contemporary romances, 53,000 to 60,000 words. *Intimate Moments*: Leslie Wainger, Sr. Ed./Ed. Coord. Sensuous, exciting contemporary romances, 80,000 to 85,000 words. *Silhouette Yours Truly*: Leslie Wainger, Ed. Contemporary, fun romances with written word hook. Historical romance: 95,000 to 105,000 words, and more; query with synopsis and 3 sample chapters to Tracy Farrell, Sr. Ed. Query with synopsis and SASE to appropriate editor. Tipsheets available.

SILVER MOON PRESS—126 Fifth Ave., Suite 803, New York, NY 10011. Juvenile titles for a multicultural audience, ages 6 to 9 and 8 to 12. Historical fiction, 64 to 80 pages, and books on science also considered. Query with outline; multiple queries accepted. Payment varies.

SILVERCAT PUBLICATIONS— 4070 Goldfinch St., Suite C, San Diego, CA 92103–1865. Robert Outlaw, Acquisitions Ed. Nonfiction trade books, 100,000 to 120,000 words, that deal with consumer and quality-of-life issues. Query. Royalty.

SIMON & SCHUSTER—1230 Ave. of the Americas, New York, NY 10020. Adult books: No unsolicited material.

SIMON & SCHUSTER BOOKS FOR YOUNG READERS—1230 Ave. of the Americas, New York, NY 10020. Stephanie Owens Lurie, V.P./Ed. Dir. Books for ages preschool through high school: picture books to young adult; nonfiction for all age levels. Hardcover only. Send query letters only for picture books, fiction, and nonfiction for older readers. SASE required for reply.

SINGER MEDIA CORP.—Seaview Business Park, 1030 Calle Cordillera, #106, San Clemente, CA 92673. Helen J. Lee, V.P. Kristy Lee, Acquisitions Ed. International literary agency and syndicate specializing in licensing foreign rights to books in the fields of business, management, celebrity biographies, self-help, occult, and fiction in all genres. No poetry. Query first with SASE.

SKYLARK BOOKS—See *Yearling Books.*

THE SMITH— 69 Joralemon St., Brooklyn, NY 11201. Harry Smith, Ed. Fiction and nonfiction, from 64 pages, and poetry, 48 to 112 pages. "While publishing at a high level of craftsmanship, we have pursued the increasingly difficult, expensive and now relatively rare policy of keeping our titles in print over the decades." Query with outline and sample chapters. Royalty.

SMITH AND KRAUS, INC.—P.O. Box 127, Main St., Lyme, NH 03768. Marisa Smith, Pres. Books related to theater, including anthologies of monologues, works by modern playwrights, translations, and development books for young actors ages 7 to 22. Send query and synopsis. Response time is 3 months. Pays on acceptance and on publication.

SOHO PRESS— 853 Broadway, New York, NY 10003. Juris Jurjevics, Ed. Mysteries, thrillers, and contemporary fiction and nonfiction, from 60,000 words. Send SASE and complete manuscript. Royalty.

SOUNDPRINTS—165 Water St., Norwalk, CT 06854. Dierdre Langeland, Ed. Asst. Factual children's books, 800 words, about oceanic and backyard animals for young readers in preschool through fifth grade. No anthropomorphism. "Read one of our current stories in the relevant series before submitting." Pays flat fee.

SOUTHERN ILLINOIS UNIVERSITY PRESS—P.O. Box 3697, Carbondale, IL 62902–3697. James Simmons, Ed. Dir. Nonfiction in the humanities, 200 to 300 pages. Query with outline and sample chapters. Royalty.

SOUTHERN METHODIST UNIVERSITY PRESS—Box 415, Dallas, TX 75275. Kathryn Lang, Sr. Ed. Literary fiction. Nonfiction: scholarly studies in religion, medical ethics (death and dying); film, theater; scholarly works on Texas or Southwest. No juvenile material, science fiction, or poetry. Query. Royalty.

SPECIAL EDITION—See *Silhouette Books.*

SPECTACLE LANE PRESS—Box 34, Georgetown, CT 06829. Attn: Ed. Dept. Humor books, 500 to 5,000 words, on subjects of strong, current interest, illustrated with cartoons. Buys text or text/cartoon packages. Occasional non-fiction, non-humor books on provocative subjects of wide concern. Royalty.

SPECTRA BOOKS—1540 Broadway, New York, NY 10036. Anne Groell, Assoc. Ed. Tom Dupree, Sr. Ed. Science fiction and fantasy, with emphasis on storytelling and characterization. Query with SASE; no unsolicited manuscripts. Royalty.

STACKPOLE BOOKS—5067 Ritter Rd., Mechanicsburg, PA 17055. Judith Schnell, Ed. Dir. Books on the outdoors, nature, fishing, carving, woodworking, sports, sporting literature, cooking, gardening, history, and military reference. Query. Royalty; advance. Unsolicited materials will not be returned.

STANDARD PUBLISHING— 8121 Hamilton Ave., Cincinnati, OH 45231. Attn: Acquisitions Coord. Fiction for children based on Bible or with moral tone. Christian education. Conservative evangelical. Guidelines.

STANFORD UNIVERSITY PRESS—Stanford Univ., Stanford, CA 94305–2235. Norris Pope, Ed. "For the most part, we publish academic scholarship." No original fiction or poetry. Query with outline and sample chapters. Royalty.

STARBURST PUBLISHERS—Box 4123, Lancaster, PA 17604. Ellen Hake, Ed. Dir. Health, inspiration, Christian, new age, and gay and lesbian books. Query with outline for nonfiction book, synopsis for fiction book, and 3 sample chapters. Royalty.

STEERFORTH PRESS—105–106 Chelsea St., Box 70, S. Royalton, VT 05068. Michael Moore, Ed. Adult nonfiction and some literary fiction. Fifteen books a year: serious works of history, biography, politics, current affairs. Query with SASE. Royalty.

STEMMER HOUSE PUBLISHERS, INC.—2627 Caves Rd., Owings Mills, MD 21117. Barbara Holdridge, Ed. Juvenile picture books and adult nonfiction. Specializes in art, design, cookbooks, children's, and horticultural titles. Query with SASE. Royalty.

STERLING PUBLISHING CO., INC.—387 Park Ave. S., New York, NY 10016. Sheila Anne Barry, Acquisitions Dir. How-to, hobby, woodworking, alternative health and healing, fiber arts, crafts, dolls and puppets, ghosts, wine, nature, oddities, new consciousness, puzzles, juvenile humor and activities, juvenile nature and science, medieval history, Celtic topics, gardening, alternative lifestyle, business, pets, recreation, sports and games books, reference, and home decorating. Query with outline, sample chapter, and sample illustrations. Royalty.

STONEYDALE PRESS—523 Main St., Box 188, Stevensville, MT 59870. Dale A. Burk, Ed. Adult nonfiction, primarily how-to, on outdoor recreation with emphasis on big-game hunting. "We're a very specialized market. Query with outline and sample chapters essential." Royalty.

STOREY COMMUNICATIONS—Schoolhouse Rd., Pownal, VT 05261. Gwen Steege, Ed. Dir. How-to books for country living. Adult books, 100 to 350 pages, on gardening, animals, crafts, building, cooking, beer, and how-to. Juvenile nonfiction, 64 to 160 pages, on gardening, crafts, and cooking. Royalty or flat fee.

795

STORY LINE PRESS—Three Oaks Farm, Brownsville, OR 97327–9718. Robert McDowell, Ed. Fiction, nonfiction, and poetry of varying lengths. Query. Royalty.

STRAWBERRY HILL PRESS—3848 S.E. Division St., Portland, OR 97202–1641. Carolyn Soto, Ed. Nonfiction: biography, autobiography, history, cooking, health, how-to, philosophy, performance arts, and Third World. Query with sample chapters, outline, and SASE. Royalty.

SUNDANCE PUBLISHING—P.O. Box 1326, Taylor Rd., Littleton, MA 01460. M. Elizabeth Strauss, Pub. Curriculum materials to accompany quality children's, young adult, and adult literature. *Sundance Big Books* feature multicultural characters and themes. Royalty or flat fee.

TAB BOOKS—Professional Book Group, McGraw-Hill, Inc., Blue Ridge Summit, PA 17294. Ron Powers, Ed. Dir. Nonfiction: electronics, computers, vocational how-to, aviation, science fair projects, business start up, science and technology, juvenile science, technician-level automotive, marine and outdoor life, military history, and engineering. Royalty or flat fee.

TAYLOR PUBLISHING CO.—1550 W. Mockingbird Ln., Dallas, TX 75235. Macy Jaggers, Ed. Adult nonfiction: gardening, sports, health, popular culture, celebrity biographies, parenting, home improvement. Query with outline, sample chapter, author bio, and SASE. Royalty.

TEACHING STRATEGIES BOOKS—See *Scholastic Professional Books.*

TEN SPEED PRESS—P.O. Box 7123, Berkeley, CA 94707. Attn: Ed. Dept. Self-help and how-to on careers, recreation, etc.; natural science, history, cookbooks.Query with outline, sample chapters, and SASE. Paperback. Royalty.

THUNDER'S MOUTH PRESS—632 Broadway, 7th Fl., New York, NY 10012. Neil Ortenberg, Ed. Mainly nonfiction: current affairs, popular culture, memoirs, and biography, to 300 pages. Royalty.

TIARE PUBLICATIONS—P.O. Box 493, Lake Geneva, WI 53147. Gerry L. Dexter, Ed. Books of interest to radio hobbyists, 60,000 to 100,000 words: jazz discographies and commentaries, *Balboa* imprint; general nonfiction, *LimeLight* imprint. Query with outline and sample chapters. Royalties.

TILBURY HOUSE—132 Water St., Gardiner, ME 04345. Attn: Acquisitions Ed. Children's books that deal with cultural diversity or the environment; appeal to children and parents as well as the educational market; and offer possibilities for developing a separate teacher's guide. Adult books: nonfiction books about Maine or the Northeast. Query with outline and sample chapters.

TIME-LIFE FOR CHILDREN—777 Duke St., Alexandria, VA 22314. Mary Saxton, Submissions Coord. Juvenile books. Publishes series of 12 to 36 volumes (no single titles), so author must have a series concept. Send SASE for required release form before submitting material. Payment is flat fee.

TIMES BOOKS—201 E. 50th St., New York, NY 10022. Steve Wasserman, Ed. Dir. No unsolicited manuscripts or queries accepted.

TOPAZ—375 Hudson St., New York, NY 10014. Constance Martin, Ed. Historical romance. Query.

TOR BOOKS—175 Fifth Ave., 14th Fl., New York, NY 10010. Patrick Nielsen Hayden, Sr. Ed., science fiction and fantasy. Melissa Ann Singer, Sr.

Ed., general fiction. Books from 60,000 words. Query with outline and sample chapters. Royalty.

TOUCHSTONE—1230 Ave. of the Americas, New York, NY 10020. Attn: Ed. No unsolicited manuscripts.

TRICYCLE PRESS—Ten Speed Press, P.O. Box 7123, Berkeley, CA 94707. Nicole Geiger, Ed. Children's books: Picture books, submit complete manuscripts. Activity books, submit about 20 pages and complete outline. "Real life" books that help children cope with issues. SASE required. Do not send original artwork. Responds in 10 weeks. Royalty.

TROUBADOR PRESS—See *Price Stern Sloan, Inc.*

TSR, INC.—201 Sheridan Springs Rd., Lake Geneva, WI 53147. Attn: Manuscript Ed. Epic high fantasy, gritty, action-oriented fantasy, Gothic horror, some science fiction, about 100,000 words. Query. Advance royalty.

TUDOR PUBLISHERS, INC.—P.O. Box 38366, Greensboro, NC 27438. Pam Cox, Ed. Helpful nonfiction books for senior citizens, teenagers, and minorities. Young adult biographies and occasional young adult novels. Reference library titles. Occasional high-quality adult fiction. Send proposal or query with sample chapters. Royalty.

TURTLE POINT PRESS—103 Hog Hill Rd., Chappaqua, NY 10514. Jonathan D. Rabinowitz, Pres. Forgotten literary fiction, historical and biographical; some contemporary fiction, 200 to 400 typed pages. Also publishes imprint *Books & Co.* Query with sample chapters. Multiple queries considered. Royalty.

TWENTY-FIRST CENTURY BOOKS—115 W. 18th St., New York, NY 10011. Attn: Submissions Ed. Juvenile nonfiction, 20,000 to 30,000 words, for use in school and public libraries. Science, history, health, and social studies books for grades 5 and up. No textbooks, workbooks, or picture books. Also accepts single titles for middle-grade and young adult readers. "Books are published primarily in series of 4 or more; not all titles are necessarily by the same author." Submit outline and sample chapters. Royalty.

TYNDALE HOUSE—351 Executive Dr., Box 80, Wheaton, IL 60189. Ron Beers, V.P. Juvenile and adult fiction and nonfiction on subjects of concern to Christians. Picture books with religious focus for preschool and early readers. No unsolicited manuscripts. Send 9 x 12 SASE with 9 first-class stamps for catalogue and guidelines.

UAHC PRESS—838 Fifth Ave., New York, NY 10021. Aron Hirt-Manheimer and Bennett Graff, Eds. Religious educational titles on or related to Judaism. Adult nonfiction; juvenile picture books, fiction, nonfiction, and young adult titles. Query with outline. Royalty.

UNIVERSE PUBLISHING—300 Park Ave. S., New York, NY 10010. Bonnie Eldon, Man. Ed. Fine arts, photography, popular culture. Query with SASE. Royalty.

UNIVERSITY BOOKS—See *Carol Publishing Group.*

UNIVERSITY OF ARIZONA PRESS—1230 N. Park Ave., Suite 102, Tucson, AZ 85719–4140. Stephen Cox, Dir. Joanne O'Hare, Sr. Ed. Christine R. Szuter, Acquiring Ed. Amy Chapman Smith, Acquiring Ed. Scholarly and popular nonfiction: Arizona, American West, anthropology, archaeology, environmental science, Latin America, Native Americans, natural history, space sciences, women's studies. Query with outline and sample chapters or send complete manuscript. Royalty.

UNIVERSITY OF ARKANSAS PRESS—Div. of The Univ. of Arkansas, McIlroy House, 201 Ozark Ave., Fayetteville, AR 72701. Miller Williams, Dir. Short stories, nonfiction, and poetry. Query. Royalty.

UNIVERSITY OF CALIFORNIA PRESS—2120 Berkeley Way, Berkeley, CA 94720. Attn: Acquisitions Dept. Scholarly nonfiction. Query with cover letter, outline, sample chapters, curriculum vitae, and SASE.

UNIVERSITY OF GEORGIA PRESS—330 Research Dr., Athens, GA 30602–4901. Karen Orchard, Dir. Short story collections and poetry, scholarly nonfiction and literary criticism, Southern and American history, regional studies, biography and autobiography. For nonfiction, query with outline and sample chapters. Poetry collections considered in Sept. and Jan. only; short fiction in June and July only. A $10 fee is required for all poetry and fiction submissions. Royalty. SASE for competition guidelines.

UNIVERSITY OF HAWAII PRESS—2840 Kolowalu St., Honolulu, HI 96822. Patricia Crosby, Pam Kelley, and Sharon Yamamoto, Eds. Scholarly books on Asian, Asian American, and Pacific studies from disciplines as diverse as the arts, history, language, literature, natural science, philosophy, religion, and the social sciences. Query with outline and sample chapters. Royalty.

UNIVERSITY OF ILLINOIS PRESS—1325 S. Oak St., Champaign, IL 61820. Richard L. Wentworth, Ed.-in-Chief. Short story collections, 140 to 180 pages; nonfiction; and poetry, 70 to 100 pages. Rarely considers multiple submissions. Query. Royalty. "Not accepting unsolicited manuscripts at this time."

UNIVERSITY OF MINNESOTA PRESS—111 Third Ave. S., Suite 290, Minneapolis, MN 55401–2520. Biodun Iginla, Ed. Janaki Bakhle, Ed. Nonfiction: media studies, literary theory, critical aesthetics, philosophy, cultural criticism, regional titles, 50,000 to 225,000 words. Query with detailed prospectus or introduction, table of contents, sample chapter, and resumé. Royalty.

UNIVERSITY OF MISSOURI PRESS—2910 LeMone Blvd., Columbia, MO 65201–8227. Beverly Jarrett, Dir./Ed.in-Chief. Mr. Clair Wilcox, Acquisitions Ed. Scholarly books on American and European history; American, British, and Latin American literary criticism; political philosophy; intellectual history; regional studies; and short fiction.

UNIVERSITY OF NEBRASKA PRESS—312 N. 14th St., Lincoln, NE 68588–0484. Attn: Eds. Specializes in the history of the American West, Native-American studies, and literary criticism. Send proposals with summary, 2 sample chapters, and resumé. Write for guidelines for annual North American Indian Prose Award.

UNIVERSITY OF NEW MEXICO PRESS—Univ. of New Mexico, Albuquerque, NM 87131. Elizabeth C. Hadas, Ed. Dir. David V. Holtby, Larry Ball, Dana Asbury, and Barbara Guth, Eds. Scholarly nonfiction on social and cultural anthropology, archaeology, Western history, art, and photography. Query. Royalty.

UNIVERSITY OF NORTH CAROLINA PRESS—P.O. Box 2288, Chapel Hill, NC 27515–2288. David Perry, Ed.-in-Chief. General-interest books (75,000 to 125,000 words) on the lore, crafts, cooking, gardening, travel, and natural history of the Southeast. No fiction or poetry. Query preferred. Royalty.

UNIVERSITY OF NORTH TEXAS PRESS—P.O. Box 13856, Denton, TX 76203–6586. Frances B. Vick, Dir. Charlotte M. Wright, Assoc. Dir. Books on Western Americana, Texan culture, women's studies, multicultural studies, and folklore. Series include: "War and the Southwest" (perspectives, histories, and memories of war from authors living in the Southwest); "Western Life Series"; "Philosophy and the Environment Series"; and "Texas Writers" (critical biographies of Texas writers). Send manuscript or query with sample chapters; no multiple queries. Royalty.

UNIVERSITY OF OKLAHOMA PRESS—1005 Asp Ave., Norman, OK 73019–0445. John Drayton, Asst. Dir. Books, to 300 pages, on the history of the American West, Indians of the Americas, congressional studies, classical studies, literary criticism, natural history, and women's studies. Query. Royalty.

UNIVERSITY OF PENNSYLVANIA PRESS—Blockley Hall, 418 Service Dr., Philadelphia, PA 19104–6097. Timothy R. Clancy, Ed. Dir. Scholarly nonfiction. Query. Royalty.

UNIVERSITY OF PITTSBURGH PRESS—127 N. Bellefield Ave., Pittsburgh, PA 15260. Attn: Eds. Scholarly nonfiction; poetry. Query.

UNIVERSITY OF TEXAS PRESS—Div. of Univ. of Texas, Box 7819, Austin, TX 78713–7819. Joanna Hitchcock, Dir. Nonfiction books, 75,000 to 100,000 words. "Our press is located in the heart of Texas, but our books know no regional or even national boundaries." Query with outline. Royalty.

UNIVERSITY OF WISCONSIN PRESS—114 N. Murray St., Madison, WI 53715–1199. Attn: Acquisitions Ed. Scholarly nonfiction and regional books. Offers Brittingham Prize in Poetry and Pollak Prize in Poetry; query for details.

UNIVERSITY PRESS OF COLORADO—P.O. Box 849, Niwot, CO 80544. Attn: Ed. Dept. Scholarly books in the humanities, social sciences, and applied sciences. Fiction for new series.

UNIVERSITY PRESS OF FLORIDA—15 N.W. 15th St., Gainesville, FL 32611–2079. Walda Metcalf, Ed.-in-Chief/Assoc. Dir. Nonfiction, 150 to 350 manuscript pages, on regional studies, Native Americans, folklore, women's studies, Latin-American studies, contemporary literary criticism, sociology, anthropology, archaeology, international affairs, labor studies, and history. Poetry. Royalty.

THE UNIVERSITY PRESS OF KENTUCKY—663 S. Limestone St., Lexington, KY 40508–4008. Nancy Grayson Holmes, Ed.-in-Chief. Scholarly books in the major fields. Serious nonfiction of general interest. Books related to Kentucky and the Ohio Valley, the Appalachians, and the South. No fiction, drama, or poetry. Query.

UNIVERSITY PRESS OF MISSISSIPPI—3825 Ridgewood Rd., Jackson, MS 39211–6492. Seetha Srinivasan, Ed.-in-Chief. Scholarly and trade titles in American literature, history, and culture; southern studies; African-American, women's and American studies; social sciences; popular culture; folklife; art and architecture; natural sciences; and other liberal arts.

UNIVERSITY PRESS OF NEW ENGLAND—23 S. Main St., Hanover, NH 03755–2048. Attn: Ed. Dept. General and scholarly nonfiction. American,

British, and European history, literature, literary criticism, creative fiction and nonfiction, and cultural studies. Jewish studies, women's studies, studies of the New England region, environmental studies, and other policy issues. *Hardscrabble Books* imprint: New England fiction.

VAN NOSTRAND REINHOLD—115 Fifth Ave., New York, NY 10003. Brian D. Heer, Pres./CEO, Marianne Russell, VP-Editorial. Business, professional, scientific, and technical publishers of applied reference works. Hospitality, culinary, architecture, graphic and interior design, industrial and environmental health and safety, computer science, engineering, and technical management.

VANDAMERE PRESS—P.O. Box 5243, Arlington, VA 22205. Jerry Frank, Assoc. Acquisitions Ed. General trade, fiction and nonfiction, including history, military, parenting, career guides, and travel. Also books about the nation's capital for a national audience. Prefer to see outline with sample chapter for nonfiction; for fiction send 4 or 5 sample chapters. Multiple queries considered. Royalty. SASE required.

VIKING—375 Hudson St., New York, NY 10014. Barbara Grossman, Pub. Fiction and nonfiction. Nonfiction: psychology, sociology, child-rearing and development, cookbooks, sports, and popular culture. Query. Royalty.

VIKING CHILDREN'S BOOKS—375 Hudson St., New York, NY 10014. Attn: Ed. Dept. Fiction and nonfiction, including biography, history, and sports, for ages 7 to 14. Humor and picture books for ages 2 to 6. Query Children's Book Dept. with outline and sample chapter. SASE required. Royalty.

VILLARD BOOKS—201 E. 50th St., New York, NY 10022. Craig Nelson, V.P./Exec. Ed. Fiction, sports, inspiration, how-to, biography, humor, etc. "We look for authors who are promotable and books we feel we can market well." Royalty.

VINTAGE BOOKS—201 E. 50th St., New York, NY 10022. Attn: Ed. Dept. Quality fiction and serious nonfiction. Query with sample chapters for fiction; query for nonfiction.

VOYAGER PAPERBACKS—See *Harcourt Brace & Co. Children's Book Div.*

VOYAGEUR PRESS—123 N. Second St., Stillwater, MN 55082. Todd R. Berger, Editorial Assoc. Books, 15,000 to 100,000 words, on wildlife, travel, calendars, and children's books related to such subjects. Also nonfiction on Americana, collectibles, natural history, hunting and fishing, regional topics; and Native American fiction, any length. "Photography is very important for most of our books." Guidelines. Query with outline and sample chapters. Royalty.

WALKER AND COMPANY—435 Hudson St., New York, NY 10014. Attn: Ed. Dept. Adult fiction: mysteries, westerns. Adult nonfiction: Americana, biography, history, science, natural history, medicine, psychology, parenting, sports, outdoors, reference, popular science, self-help, business, and music. Juvenile nonfiction, including biography, science, history, music, and nature. Juvenile fiction: Middle grade and young adult novels. Query with synopsis and SASE. Guidelines. Royalty.

WALLACE-HOMESTEAD BOOKS—See *Chilton Book Co.*

WARNER BOOKS—1271 Ave. of the Americas, New York, NY 10020. Mel Parker, Pub., Warner Paperbacks. No unsolicited manuscripts or proposals.

WASHINGTON SQUARE PRESS—1230 Ave. of the Americas, New York, NY 10020. Amy Einhorn, Ed. Agented work only.

WASHINGTON STATE UNIVERSITY PRESS—Cooper Publications Bldg., P.O. Box 645910, Pullman, WA 99164–5910. Keith Petersen, Acquisitions Ed. Glen Lindeman, Ed. Books on northwest history, prehistory, and culture, 200 to 350 pages. Query. Royalty.

WASHINGTON WRITERS PUBLISHING HOUSE—P.O. Box 15271, Washington, DC 20003. Attn: Ed. Dept. Poetry books, 50 to 60 pages, by writers in the greater Washington, DC area only. Send SASE for guidelines.

WATTS, FRANKLIN—Sherman Turnpike, Danbury, CT 06813. Curriculum-oriented nonfiction for grades 4 to 12, including science, history, social studies, and biography. No unsolicited submissions.

WEE SING—See *Price Stern Sloan, Inc.*

WEISS ASSOCIATES, DANIEL—33 W. 17th St., New York, NY 10011. Michael Fitzgerald, Ed. Asst. Book packager. A few parenting and self-help books. Young adult books, 45,000 words; middle grade books, 33,000 words; elementary books, 10,000 to 12,000 words. Query with outline and 2 sample chapters. Royalty and flat fee.

WESLEYAN UNIVERSITY PRESS—110 Mt. Vernon St., Middletown, CT 06459–0433. Eileen McWilliam, Dir. Wesleyan Poetry series: 64 to 80 pages. Query. Royalty.

WESTMINSTER JOHN KNOX PRESS—100 Witherspoon St., Louisville, KY 40202. Davis Perkins, Dir. Stephanie Egnotovich, Man. Ed. Books that inform, interpret, challenge, and encourage Christian faith and living. Royalty. Send SASE for guidelines.

WHISPERING COYOTE PRESS—300 Crescent Ct., Suite 860, Dallas, TX 75201. Ms. Lou Alpert, Ed. Picture books, 32 pages, for readers ages 4 to 12. Submit complete manuscript with SASE. Royalty.

WHITE PINE PRESS—10 Village Sq., Fredonia, NY 14063. Elaine La-Mattina, Ed. Novels, books of short stories, and essay collections, 250 to 350 pages. Query with outline and sample chapters. Royalty.

WHITECAP BOOKS—351 Lynn Ave., N. Vancouver, BC, Canada V7J 2C4. Colleen MacMillan, Pub. Juvenile books, 72 to 84 pages, and adult books, varying lengths, on such topics as natural history, gardening, cookery, parenting, history and regional subjects. Query with table of contents, synopsis, and one sample chapter. Flat fee or royalty.

WHITMAN, ALBERT—6340 Oakton, Morton Grove, IL 60053. Kathleen Tucker, Ed. Picture books for preschool children; novels, biographies, mysteries, and nonfiction for middle-grade readers. Send complete manuscript for picture books, 3 chapters and outline for longer fiction; query for nonfiction. Royalty.

WILD ONION BOOKS—See *Loyola Press.*

WILDERNESS PRESS—2440 Bancroft Way, Berkeley, CA 94704. Thomas Winnett, Ed. Nonfiction: outdoor sports, recreation, and travel in the western U.S. Royalty.

WILEY & SONS, JOHN— 605 Third Ave., New York, NY 10158–0012. Attn: Ed. Dept. Nonfiction: science/technology; business/management; real estate; travel; cooking; biography; psychology; computers; language; history; current affairs; health; finance. Send proposals with outline, author vita, market information, and sample chapter. Royalty.

WILLIAMSON PUBLISHING CO.—P.O. Box 185, Charlotte, VT 05445. Attn: Nonfiction Ed. Activity books for children; adult hands-on books for country living. No children's picture books. Writers must send annotated table of contents, 2 sample chapters, and SASE.

WILLOW CREEK PRESS—Number 1, Fifty One Centre, P.O. Box 881, Minocqua, WI 54548. Tom Petrie, Ed. Books, 25,000 to 50,000 words, on nature, wildlife, and outdoor sports. Query with sample chapters. No fiction. Royalty.

WILSHIRE BOOK COMPANY—12015 Sherman Rd., N. Hollywood, CA 91605–3781. Melvin Powers, Pub. Nonfiction: self-help, motivation/inspiration/spiritual, psychology, recovery, how-to, entrepreneurship, mail order, horsemanship, and how to make money on the Internet; minimum, 60,000 words. Fiction: allegories that teach principles of psychological/spiritual growth. Send synopsis/detailed chapter outline, 3 chapters, and SASE. Royalty.

WINDSWEPT HOUSE PUBLISHERS—Mt. Desert, ME 04660. Jane Weinberger, Pub. Children's picture books; young adult novels; adult fiction and nonfiction. Query.

WISHING WELL—See *Reader's Digest Young Families, Inc.*

WOODBINE HOUSE— 6510 Bells Mill Rd., Bethesda, MD 20817. Susan Stokes, Ed. Books for or about people with disabilities only. No personal accounts, poetry, or books that can be marketed only through bookstores. Query or submit complete manuscript with SASE. Guidelines. Royalty.

WORDWARE PUBLISHING—1506 Capital Ave., Plano, TX 75074. Russell A. Stultz, Ed., *Wordware Computer Books*. Mary Goldman, Ed., *Republic of Texas Press*. Texana, Southwest regional, historical nonfiction including tales and legends of the old west and "legendary" characters, military history, women of the west and country humor. *Seaside Press*: history/guidebooks for cities, pet care, religion, humor. Query with sample chapters, manuscript completion date, and author experience. Royalty.

WORKMAN PUBLISHING CO., INC.—708 Broadway, New York, NY 10003. Attn: Ed. Dept. General nonfiction. Normal contractual terms based on agreement.

WORLDWIDE LIBRARY—225 Duncan Mill Rd., Don Mills, Ont., Canada M3B 3K9. Randall Toye, Ed. Dir. Feroze Mohammed, Sr. Ed. Action adventure series for *Gold Eagle* imprint; mystery fiction reprints only. No unsolicited manuscripts or queries.

YEARLING BOOKS—1540 Broadway, New York, NY 10036. Attn: Ed. Dept. Books for K through 6. Manuscripts accepted from agents only. Same address and requirements for *Skylark Books*.

ZENITH EDITIONS—See *National Press Books, Inc.*

Z-FAVE— 850 Third Ave., 16th Fl., New York, NY 10022. Elise Donner, Exec. Ed. Series and single titles for 8-to 16-year-olds. Send complete synopsis and sample chapters or complete synopsis and complete manuscript. Royalty.

ZONDERVAN PUBLISHING HOUSE—5300 Patterson S.E., Grand Rapids, MI 49530. Attn: Manuscript Review. Christian titles. General fiction and nonfiction; academic and professional books. Query with outline, sample chapter, and SASE. Royalty. Guidelines.

SYNDICATES

Syndicates buy material from writers and artists to sell to newspapers all over the country and the world. Authors are paid either a percentage of the gross proceeds or an outright fee. Of course, features by people well known in their fields have the best chance of being syndicated. In general, syndicates want columns that have been popular in a local newspaper or magazine. Since most syndicated fiction has been published previously in magazines or books, beginning fiction writers should try to sell their stories to magazines before submitting them to syndicates.

Always query syndicates before sending manuscripts, since their needs change frequently, and be sure to enclose SASEs with queries and manuscripts.

ARKIN MAGAZINE SYNDICATE—500 Bayview Dr., Suite G, N. Miami Beach, FL 33160. Joseph Arkin, Ed. Dir. Articles, 750 to 2,200 words, for trade and professional magazines. Must have small-business slant, be written in layman's language, and offer solutions to business problems. Articles should apply to many businesses, not just a specific industry. No columns. Pays 3¢ to 10¢ a word, on acceptance. SASE required; query not necessary.

CONTEMPORARY FEATURES SYNDICATE—P. O. Box 1258, Jackson, TN 38302–1258. Lloyd Russell, Ed. Articles, 1,000 to 10,000 words: how-to, money savers, business, etc. Self-help pieces for small business. Pays from $25, on acceptance. Query.

HARRIS & ASSOCIATES FEATURES—350 Sharon Park Dr., Q-1, Menlo Park, CA 94025. Dick Harris, Ed. Sports-and family-oriented features, to 1,200 words; fillers and short humor, 500 to 800 words. Queries preferred. Pays varying rates.

HISPANIC LINK NEWS SERVICE—1420 N St. N.W., Washington, DC 20005. Charles A. Ericksen, Ed. Trend articles, opinion and personal experience pieces, and general features with Hispanic focus, 650 to 700 words; editorial cartoons. Pays $25 for op-ed columns and cartoons, on acceptance. Send SASE for guidelines.

THE HOLLYWOOD INSIDE SYNDICATE—Box 49957, Los Angeles, CA 90049–0957. John Austin, Dir. Feature articles, 750 to 2,500 words, on TV and film personalities with B&W photo(s). Article suggestions for 3-part series. Pieces on unusual medical and scientific breakthroughs. Pays on percentage basis for features, negotiated rates for ideas, on publication.

KING FEATURES SYNDICATE—235 E. 45th St., New York, NY 10017. Paul Eberhart, Exec. Ed. Columns, comics. "We do not consider or buy individual articles. We are interested in ideas for nationally syndicated columns." Submit cover letter, six sample columns of 650 words each, bio sheet and any additional clips, and SASE. No simultaneous submissions. Query with SASE for guidelines.

LOS ANGELES TIMES SYNDICATE—Times Mirror Sq., Los Angeles, CA 90053. Commentary, features, columns, editorial cartoons, comics, puzzles and games; news services. Send SASE for submission guidelines.

NEW YORK TIMES SYNDICATION SALES—122 E. 42nd St., New York, NY 10168. Gloria Brown Anderson, Exec. Ed. Previously published health, lifestyle, and entertainment articles only, to 1,500 words. Query with published article or tear sheet and SASE. Pays 50% royalty on collected sales.

NEWSPAPER ENTERPRISE ASSOCIATION—200 Madison Ave., 4th Fl., New York, NY 10016. Robert Levy, Exec. Ed. Ideas for new concepts in syndicated columns. No single stories or stringers. Payment by contractual arrangement.

SINGER MEDIA CORP.—#106, 1030 Calle Cordillera, San Clemente, CA 92673. Helen J. Lee, V.P. International syndication, some domestic. Subjects must be of global interest. Features: celebrity interviews and profiles, women's, health, fitness, self-help, business, computer, etc., all lengths; psychological quizzes; puzzles (no word puzzles) and games for children or adults. Pays 50%.

TRIBUNE MEDIA SERVICES— 435 N. Michigan Ave., #1500, Chicago, IL 60611. Mark Mathes, Man. Ed. Continuing columns, comic strips, features, electronic databases. Query with clips.

UNITED PRESS INTERNATIONAL—1400 Eye St. N.W., Washington, DC 20005. Robert A. Martin, Man. Ed., International. Tobin Beck, Man. Ed., North America. No free-lance material.

LITERARY PRIZE OFFERS

Writers seeking the thrill of competition should review the extensive list of literary prize offers, many of them designed to promote the as yet unpublished author. All of the competitions listed here are for unpublished manuscripts and usually offer publication in addition to a cash prize. The prestige that comes with winning some of the more established awards can do much to further a writer's career, as editors, publishers, and agents are likely to consider the future work of the prize winner more closely.

There are hundreds of literary contests open to writers in all genres, and the following list covers a representative number of them. The summaries given below are intended merely as guides; since submission requirements are more detailed than space allows, writers should send SASE for complete guidelines before entering any contest. Writers are also advised to check the monthly "Prize Offers" column of *The Writer* Magazine (120 Boylston St., Boston, MA 02116–4615) for additional contest listings and up-to-date contest requirements. Deadlines are annual unless otherwise noted.

ACADEMY OF AMERICAN POETS—Walt Whitman Award, 584 Broadway, Suite 1208, New York, NY 10012–3250. An award of $5,000 plus publication and a one-month residency at the Vermont Studio Center is offered for a book-length poetry manuscript by a poet who has not yet published a volume of poetry. Deadline: November 15. Entry fee.

ACADEMY OF MOTION PICTURE ARTS AND SCIENCES—The Nicholl Fellowships, Dept. WR, 8949 Wilshire Blvd., Beverly Hills, CA 90211–1972. Up to five fellowships of $25,000 each are awarded for original screenplays that display exceptional craft and engaging storytelling. Deadline: May 1. Entry fee.

ACTORS THEATRE OF LOUISVILLE—Ten-Minute Play Contest, 316 W. Main St., Louisville, KY 40202–4218. A prize of $1,000 is offered for a previously unproduced ten-page script. Deadline: December 1.

AMERICAN ACADEMY OF ARTS AND LETTERS—Richard Rogers Awards, 633 W. 155th St., New York, NY 10032. Offers subsidized productions or staged readings in New York City by a nonprofit theater for a musical, play with music, thematic review, or any comparable work. Deadline: November 1.

AMERICAN ANTIQUARIAN SOCIETY—Fellowships for Historical Research, 185 Salisbury St., Worcester, MA 01609–1634. Attn: John B. Hench. At least three fellowships are awarded to creative and performing artists, writers, film makers, and journalists for research on pre-20th century American history. Residencies are four-to eight-weeks; travel expenses and stipends of $1,200 per month are offered. Deadline: October 1.

AMERICAN FICTION/NEW RIVERS PRESS—Fiction Awards, P.O. Box 229, Moorhead State Univ., Moorhead, MN 56563. Attn: Alan Davis, Ed. Prizes of $1,000, $500, and $250 are awarded for short stories, to 10,000 words. The stories of up to 20 finalists are published in the *American Fiction* anthology. Deadline: May 1. Entry fee.

THE AMERICAN-SCANDINAVIAN FOUNDATION—Translation Prize, 725 Park Ave., New York, NY 10021. A prize of $2,000 is awarded for an outstanding English translation of poetry, fiction, drama, or literary prose originally written in Danish, Finnish, Icelandic, Norwegian, or Swedish. Deadline: June 1.

ANHINGA PRESS—Anhinga Prize for Poetry, P.O. Box 10595, Tallahassee, FL 32302–0595. A $2,000 prize will be awarded for an unpublished full-length collection of poetry, 48 to 72 pages, by a poet who has published no more than one full-length collection. Deadline: March 15. Entry fee.

ARMY MAGAZINE—Essay Contest, Box 1560, Arlington, VA 22210. Prizes of $1,000, $500, and $250 plus publication are awarded for essays on a given theme. Deadline: May 31.

ASSOCIATION OF JEWISH LIBRARIES—Sydney Taylor Manuscript Competition, 1327 Wyntercreek Ln., Dunwoody, GA 30338. Attn: Paula Sandfelder, Coordinator. Offers $1,000 for the best fiction manuscript, 64 to 200 pages, by an unpublished book author, writing for readers 8 to 11. Stories must have a positive Jewish focus. Deadline: January 15.

BAKER'S PLAYS—High School Playwriting Contest, 100 Chauncy St., Boston, MA 02111. Plays about the high school experience, written by high school students, are eligible for awards of $500, $250, and $100. Deadline: January 31.

BANTAM DOUBLEDAY DELL BOOKS FOR YOUNG READERS—Marguerite de Angeli Prize, Dept. BFYR, 1540 Broadway, New York, NY 10036. A prize of $1,500 and a $3,500 advance against royalties is awarded for a middle-grade fiction manuscript that explores the diversity of the American experience. Open to U.S. and Canadian writers who have not previously published a novel for middle-grade readers. Deadline: June 30.

BARNARD COLLEGE—New Women Poets Prize, Women Poets at Barnard, Columbia Univ., 3009 Broadway, New York, NY 10027–6598. Attn: Directors. A prize of $1,500 and publication by Beacon Press is offered for an unpublished poetry manuscript, 50 to 100 pages, by a female poet who has never published a book of poetry. Deadline: October 15.

THE BELLETRIST REVIEW—Fiction Contest, Marmarc Publications, P.O. Box 596, Plainville, CT 06062–0596. Prize of $200 plus publication is awarded for an unpublished short story, 2,500 to 5,000 words. Deadline: July 15. Entry fee.

THE BELLINGHAM REVIEW—Tobias Wolff Award in Fiction/49th Parallel Poetry Award, MS-9053, Western Washington Univ., Bellingham, WA 98225. Tobias Wolff Award in Fiction: Offers prizes of $500 plus publication, $250, and $100 for a short story or novel excerpt. Deadline: March 1. Annie Dillard Award in Nonfiction: Offers prizes of $500 plus publication, $250, and $100 for previously unpublished essays. Deadline: March 1. 49th Parallel Poetry Award: Offers publication and prizes of $500, $250, and $100 for individual poems. Deadline: November 30. Entry fees.

BEVERLY HILLS THEATRE GUILD/JULIE HARRIS PLAYWRIGHT AWARD—2815 N. Beachwood Dr., Los Angeles, CA 90068. Attn: Marcella Meharg. Offers prize of $5,000, plus possible $2,000 for productions in Los Angeles area, for previously unproduced and unpublished full-length play. A $2,000 second prize and $1,000 third prize are also offered. Deadline: November 1.

BIRMINGHAM-SOUTHERN COLLEGE—Hackney Literary Awards, BSC A-3, Birmingham, AL 35254. A prize of $2,000 is awarded for an unpublished novel, any length. Deadline: September 30. Also, a $2,000 prize is shared for the winning short story, to 5,000 words, and poem of up to 50 lines. Deadline: December 31. Entry fees.

BLUE MOUNTAIN CENTER—Richard J. Margolis Award, 101 Arch St., 9th Floor, Boston, MA 02110. A prize of $1,000 is awarded annually to a promising journalist, poet, or essayist whose work combines warmth, humor, wisdom, and a concern with social issues. Applications should include up to 30 pages of published or unpublished work. Deadline: June 1.

BOISE STATE UNIVERSITY—Eccentric Format Book Competition, Hemingway Western Studies Center, Boise, ID 83725. Tom Trusky, Ed. A prize of $500 and publication is awarded for up to 3 books; manuscripts (text and/or visual content) and proposals are considered for the short-run printing of books on public issues, especially the Inter-Mountain West. Deadline: December 1.

BOSTON REVIEW—Short Story Contest, E53–407, MIT, Cambridge, MA 02139. A prize of $300 plus publication is awarded for the best previously unpublished story of up to 4,000 words. Deadline: October 1. Entry fee.

BUCKNELL UNIVERSITY—The Philip Roth Residence in Creative Writing, Stadler Center for Poetry, Bucknell Univ., Lewisburg, PA 17837. Attn: Cynthia Hogue, Dir. The fall residency may be used by a writer, over 21, not currently enrolled in a university, to work on a first or second book. The residency is awarded in odd-numbered years to a fiction writer, and in even-numbered years to a poet. Deadline: March 1.

CASE WESTERN RESERVE UNIVERSITY—Marc A. Klein Playwriting Award, Dept. of Theater Arts, 10900 Euclid Ave., Cleveland, OH 44106-7077. A prize of $1,000 plus production is offered for an original, previously unproduced full-length play by a student currently enrolled at an American college or university. Deadline: May 15.

CENTER FOR BOOK ARTS—Poetry Chapbook Prize, Center for Book Arts, 626 Broadway, 5th Floor, New York, NY 10012. Offers $1,000, publication and a public reading for poetry manuscript, to 500 lines. Deadline: December 31. Entry fee.

CHELSEA AWARD COMPETITION—P.O. Box 1040, York Beach, ME 03910. Attn: Ed. Prizes of $750 plus publication are awarded for the best unpublished short fiction and poetry. Deadlines: June 15 (fiction); December 15 (poetry). Entry fees.

THE CHICAGO TRIBUNE—Nelson Algren Awards, 435 N. Michigan Ave., Chicago, IL 60611. A first prize of $5,000 and three runner-up prizes of $1,000 are awarded for outstanding unpublished short stories, 2,500 to 10,000 words, by American writers. Deadline: February 1.

CLAREMONT GRADUATE SCHOOL—Kingsley Tufts Poetry Awards, 160 E. 10th St., Claremont, CA 91711. An award of $50,000 is given an American poet whose work is judged most worthy. An award of $5,000 is given an emerging poet whose work displays extraordinary promise. Books of poetry published or manuscripts completed in the calendar year are considered. Deadline: September 15.

CLEVELAND STATE UNIVERSITY POETRY CENTER—Poetry Center Prize, Dept. of English, Rhodes Tower, Rm. 1815, 1983 E. 24th St., Cleveland, OH 44115-2440. Publication and $1,000 are awarded for a previously unpublished book-length volume of poetry. Deadline: March 1. Entry fee.

COALITION FOR THE ADVANCEMENT OF JEWISH EDUCATION—David Dornstein Memorial Creative Writing Contest, 261 W. 35th St., Floor 12A, New York, NY 10001. A prize of publication and $1,000 is awarded for the best original, previously unpublished short story, to 5,000 words, on a Jewish theme or topic, by a writer age 18 to 35. Deadline: December 31.

COLONIAL PLAYERS, INC.—Promising Playwright Award, 98 Tower Dr., Stevensville, MD 21666. Attn: Fran Marchano. A prize of $750 plus possible production will be awarded for the best full-length play by a resident of MD, DC, VA, WV, DE, or PA. Deadline: December 31 (of even-numbered years).

COLORADO STATE UNIVERSITY—Colorado Prize for Poetry, Colorado Review, Dept. of English, Fort Collins, CO 80523. Attn: David Milofsky, Ed. Offers $1,000 plus publication for collection of original poems. Deadline: January 15. Entry fee.

COMMUNITY CHILDREN'S THEATRE OF KANSAS CITY—8021 E. 129th Terrace, Grandview, MO 64030. Attn: Mrs. Blanche Sellens, Dir. A prize of $500, plus production, is awarded for the best play, up to one hour long, to be performed by adults for elementary school audiences. Deadline: January 31.

COMMUNITY WRITERS ASSOCIATION—CWA Writing Contest, P.O. Box 12, Newport, RI 02840–0001. A prize of $250 plus free conference tuition is offered for short stories, to 2,000 words, and poetry, any length. Deadline: June 1. Entry fee.

EUGENE V. DEBS FOUNDATION—Bryant Spann Memorial Prize, Dept. of History, Indiana State Univ., Terre Haute, IN 47809. Offers a prize of $1,000 for a published or unpublished article or essay on themes relating to social protest or human equality. Deadline: April 30.

DEEP SOUTH WRITERS CONFERENCE—Contest Clerk, Drawer 44691, Univ. of Southwestern Louisianna, Lafayette, LA 70504–4691. Prizes ranging from $50 to $300 are offered for unpublished manuscripts in the following categories: short fiction, novel, nonfiction, poetry, drama, and French literature. Deadline: July 15. Miller Award: offers $500 for a play dealing with some aspect of the life of Edward de Vere (1550–1604), the 17th Earl of Oxford. Deadline: July 15 (of odd-numbered years). Entry fee.

DELACORTE PRESS—Prize for First Young Adult Novel, Bantam Doubleday Dell BFYR, 1540 Broadway, New York, NY 10036. A writer who has not previously published a young adult novel may submit a book-length manuscript with a contemporary setting suitable for readers ages 12 to 18. The prize is $1,500, a $6,000 advance, and hardcover and paperback publication. Deadline: December 31.

DRURY COLLEGE—Playwriting Contest, 900 N. Benton Ave., Springfield, MO 65802. Attn: Sandy Asher, Writer-in-Residence. Prizes of $300 and two $150 honorable mentions, plus possible production, are awarded for original, previously unproduced one-act plays. Deadline: December 1 (of even-numbered years).

DUBUQUE FINE ARTS PLAYERS—One-Act Playwriting Contest, 1321 Tomahawk Dr., Dubuque, IA 52003. Attn: Jennifer G. Stabenow, Coordinator. Prizes of $600, $300 and $200 plus possible production are awarded for unproduced, original one-act plays of up to 40 minutes. Deadline: January 31. Entry fee.

DUKE UNIVERSITY—Dorothea Lange-Paul Taylor Prize, Prize Committee, Center for Documentary Studies, Box 90802, Duke Univ., Durham, NC 27708–0802. A grant of up to $10,000 is awarded to a writer and photographer working together in the formative stages of a documentary project that will ultimately result in a publishable work. Deadline: January 31. Entry fee.

ELF: ECLECTIC LITERARY FORUM—Ruth Cable Memorial Prize, P.O. Box 392, Tonawanda, NY 14150. Awards of $500 and three $50 prizes are given for poems up to 50 lines. Short Fiction Prize awards $500 plus publication and two $50 prizes for stories, to 3,500 words. Deadline: March 31. Fiction deadline: August 31. Entry fee.

EMPORIA STATE UNIVERSITY—Bluestem Award, English Dept., Emporia State Univ., Emporia, KS 66801–5087. A prize of $1,000 plus publication is awarded for a previously unpublished book of poems by a U.S. author. Deadline: March 1. Entry fee.

THE FLORIDA REVIEW—Short Fiction Contest, Dept. of English, Univ. of Central Florida, Orlando, FL 32816–0001. Attn: Russell Kesler, Ed. Prizes of $500 and $200 plus publication are offered for short stories of up to 7,500 words. Deadline: June 15. Entry fee.

FLORIDA STUDIO THEATRE—Shorts Contest, 1241 N. Palm Ave., Sarasota, FL 34236. Attn: Christian Angermann. Short scripts, songs, and other performance pieces on a given theme are eligible for a prize of $500. Deadline: February 15.

THE FORMALIST—Howard Nemerov Sonnet Award, 320 Hunter Dr., Evansville, IN 47711. A prize of $1,000 plus publication is offered for a previously unpublished, original sonnet. Deadline: June 15. Entry fee.

FOUR WAY BOOKS—Poetry Contests, P.O. Box 535 Village Sta., New York, NY 10014. Attn: M. Barrett. Intro Series in Poetry: A prize of $1,500 plus publication is awarded for a book-length collection of poems by a poet who has not previously published a book of poetry. Award Series in Poetry: A prize of $2,000 plus publication is awarded for a book-length collection of poems by a poet who has published at least one collection of poetry. Deadline: May 1. Entry fee.

GEORGE MASON UNIVERSITY—Greg Grummer Award in Poetry, *Phoebe: A Journal of Literary Arts*, 4400 Univ. Dr., Fairfax, VA 22030. A prize of $500 plus publication is offered for an outstanding previously unpublished poem. Deadline: December 15. Entry fee.

GEORGE WASHINGTON UNIVERSITY—Jenny McKean Moore Writer-in-Washington, Dept. of English, Washington, DC 20052. Attn: Prof. Christopher Sten. A salaried teaching position for two semesters is offered to a creative writer (of various mediums in alternate years) having "significant publications and a demonstrated commitment to teaching. The writer need not have conventional academic credentials." The 1997–98 position was awarded to a fiction writer. Deadline: November 15.

GLIMMER TRAIN PRESS—Semiannual Short Story Award for New Writers, 812 S.W. Washington St., #1205, Portland, OR 97205. Writers whose fiction has never appeared in a nationally distributed publication are eligible to enter their stories of 1,200 to 7,500 words. Prizes are $1,200 plus publication, $500, and $300. Deadlines: March 31; September 30. Entry fee.

GREENFIELD REVIEW LITERARY CENTER—North American Native Authors First Book Awards, P.O. Box 308, 2 Middle Grove Rd., Greenfield Center, NY 12833. Attn: Joseph Bruchac, Dir. Native Americans of American Indian, Aleut, Inuit, or Metis ancestry who have not yet published a book are eligible to enter poetry, 48 to 100 pages, and prose, 120 to 240 pages (fiction or nonfiction) for $500 prizes plus publication. Deadline: May 1.

GROLIER POETRY PRIZE—6 Plympton St., Cambridge, MA 02138. Two $150 honorariums are awarded for poetry manuscripts of up to 10 double-spaced pages, including no more than five previously unpublished poems, by writers who have not yet published a book of poems. Deadline: May 1. Entry fee.

HEEKIN GROUP FOUNDATION—Fiction Fellowships Competition, 68860 Goodrich Rd., Sisters, OR 97759. Awards the following fellowships to beginning career writers: two $1,500 Tara Fellowships in Short Fiction; two $3,000 James Fellowships for a Novel in Progress; one $2,000 Mary Molloy Fellowship for a Juvenile Novel in Progress; and one $2,000 Siobhan Fellowhip for a Nonfiction Essay. Writers who have never published a novel, a children's novel, more than five short stories in national publication, or an essay are eligible to enter. Deadline: December 1. Entry fee.

HELICON NINE EDITIONS—Literary Prizes, 3607 Pennsylvania, Kansas City, MO 64111. Marianne Moore Poetry Prize: offers $1,000 for an original unpublished poetry manuscript of at least 48 pages. Willa Cather Fiction Prize: offers $1,000 for an original novella or short story collection, from 150 to 300 pages. Deadline: May 1. Entry fee.

KEY WEST HEMINGWAY DAYS FESTIVAL—Writing Contests, P.O. Box 4045, Key West, FL 33041. First Novel Contest: $1,000 plus literary representation for an unpublished first novel. Deadline: May 1. Young Writers' Scholarships: $1,000 prize for six pages of fiction, nonfiction, or poetry by college-bound high school juniors or seniors. Deadline: May 1. Short Story Contest: $1,000 plus festival airfare, and two $500 prizes for short stories, 3,000 words or fewer. Deadline: June 1. Entry fee.

HIGHLIGHTS FOR CHILDREN—Fiction Contest, 803 Church St., Honesdale, PA 18431. Three $1,000 prizes plus publication are offered for stories on a given subject, up to 900 words. The theme for 1997: mysteries. Deadline: February 28.

HILTON-LONG POETRY FOUNDATION—Naomi Long Madgett Poetry Award, c/o Lotus Press, Inc., P.O. Box 21607, Detroit, MI 48221. A prize of $500 plus publication will be awarded to an African-American writer for a previously unpublished collection of poems, 60 to 80 pages. Deadline: April 1.

RUTH HINDMAN FOUNDATION—H.E. Francis Award, Dept. of English, Univ. of Alabama, Huntsville, AL 35899. A prize of $1,000 plus publication is awarded for a short story of up to 5,000 words. Deadline: December 31. Entry fee.

L. RON HUBBARD'S WRITERS OF THE FUTURE CONTEST—P.O. Box 1630, Los Angeles, CA 90078. Unpublished fiction writers are eligible to enter science fiction or fantasy short stories under 10,000 words, or novellas under 17,000 words. Quarterly prizes: $1,000, $750, and $500. Annual prize: $4,000. Deadlines: March 31; June 30; September 30; December 31.

HUMBOLDT STATE UNIVERSITY—Raymond Carver Short Story Contest, English Dept., Arcata, CA 95521-8299. Offers a $1,000 first prize, plus publication in the literary journal *Toyon*, and a $300 second prize and $100 third prize, for an unpublished short story, to 25 pages, by an American writer. Deadline: November 1. Entry fee.

ICS BOOKS, INC.—"No S——! There I Was . . ." Contest, P.O. Box 10767, 1370 E. 86th Pl., Merrillville, IN 46410. Prizes of $2,000 and $500 plus publication are offered for humorous, tall tales. Deadline: October 15.

INSTITUTE OF HISPANIC CULTURE—José Martı Award, 3315 Sul Ross, Houston, TX 77098. Prizes of $1,000, $600, and $400 are awarded for essays, 15 to 20 pages, on a given theme. Deadline: August 31.

IUPUI CHILDREN'S THEATRE—Playwriting Competition, Indiana University-Purdue University at Indianapolis, 525 N. Blackford St., Indianapolis, IN 46202–3120. Offers four $1,000 prizes plus staged readings for plays for young people. Deadline: September 1 (of even-numbered years).

ALICE JAMES BOOKS—Beatrice Hawley Award, Univ. of Maine at Farmington, 98 Main St., Farmington, ME 04938. A prize of publication plus 100 free copies is offered for the best poetry manuscript, 60 to 70 pages. Deadline: January 15. Entry fee.

JOE JEFFERSON PLAYERS ORIGINAL PLAY COMPETITION—P.O. Box 66065, Mobile, AL 36660. A prize of $1,000 plus production is offered for an original, previously unproduced play. Deadline: March 1.

JEWISH COMMUNITY CENTER THEATRE—Dorothy Silver Playwriting Competition, 3505 Mayfield Rd., Cleveland Heights, OH 44118. Attn: Elaine Rembrandt, Dir. Offers $1,000 and a staged reading for an original, previously unproduced full-length play, on some aspect of the Jewish experience. Deadline: December 15.

CHESTER H. JONES FOUNDATION—National Poetry Competition, P. O. Box 498, Chardon, OH 44024. Prizes of $1,000, $750, $500, and $250, as well as several $50 and $10 prizes are awarded for original, unpublished poems of up to 32 lines. Deadline: March 31. Entry fee.

JAMES JONES SOCIETY—First Novel Fellowship, c/o Dept. of English, Wilkes Univ., Wilkes-Barre, PA 18766. An award of $2,500 is offered for a first novel-in-progress by an American. Deadline: March 1. Entry fee.

THE JOURNAL: THE LITERARY MAGAZINE OF O.S.U.—The Ohio State Univ. Press, 180 Pressey Hall, 1070 Carmack Rd., Columbus, OH 43210–1002. Attn: David Citino, Poetry Ed. Awards $1,000 plus publication for at least 48 pages of original, unpublished poetry. Deadline: September 30. Entry fee.

KALLIOPE: A JOURNAL OF WOMEN'S ART—Sue Saniel Elkind Poetry Contest, Florida Community College at Jacksonville, 3939 Roosevelt Blvd., Jacksonville, FL 32205. Publication and $1,000 are awarded for the best poem, under 50 lines, written by a woman. Deadline: October 30. Entry fee.

KEATS/KERLAN MEMORIAL FELLOWSHIP—The Ezra Jack Keats Memorial Fellowship Committee, 109 Walter Library, 117 Pleasant St. S.E., Univ. of Minnesota, Minneapolis, MN 55455. A $1,500 fellowship is awarded to a talented writer and/or illustrator of children's books who wishes to use the Kerlan Collection for furtherance of his or her artistic development. Deadline: May 1.

KENT STATE UNIVERSITY PRESS—Stan and Tom Wick Poetry Prize, P.O. Box 5190, Kent, OH 44242–0001. Publication and $1,000 are offered for a book of poems, 48 to 68 pages, by a writer who has not previously published a collection of poetry. Deadline: May 1. Entry fee.

JACK KEROUAC LITERARY PRIZE—Lowell Celebrates Kerouac! Festival, P.O. Box 8788, Lowell, MA 01853. A prize of $500 and festival reading are awarded for an unpublished work of fiction, nonfiction, or poetry relating to themes expressed in Kerouac's work. Deadline: August 1. Entry fee.

LA JOLLA FESTIVAL—International Imitation Raymond Chandler Writing Competition, c/o Friends of the La Jolla Library, 6632 Avenida Manana, La Jolla, CA 92037. Prizes of $500, $300, and $200 will be awarded for manuscripts, 500 words, that imitate or parody Raymond Chandler's writing style and subject matter. Deadline: August 1.

LIVE OAK THEATRE—New Play Award, 200 Colorado St., Austin, TX 78701. Attn: Michael Hankin. Offers $1,000 plus possible production for the best full-length, unproduced, unpublished play. Deadline: April 1.

LODI ARTS COMMISSION—Drama Festival, 125 S. Hutchins St., Suite D, Lodi, CA 95240. A prize of $1,000 plus production is awarded for a full-length play; a prize of $500 plus production is awarded for a children's play. Deadline: April 1 (of odd-numbered years).

LOVE CREEK PRODUCTIONS—One-Ace Play Festivals, 79 Liberty Pl., Weehawken, NJ 07087–7014. One-act plays and theme-based plays are awarded production or staged readings. Deadlines vary.

THE MADISON REVIEW—Dept. of English, 600 N. Park St., Helen C. White Hall, Univ. of Wisconsin-Madison, Madison, WI 53706. Phyllis Smart Young Prize in Poetry: awards $500 plus publication for a group of three unpublished poems. Chris O'Malley Prize in Fiction: awards $500 plus publication for an unpublished short story. Deadline: September 30. Entry fees.

MARTIN FOUNDATION FOR THE CREATIVE ARTS—Frank Waters Southwest Writing Award, P.O. Box 1357, Ranchos de Taos, NM 87529. Attn: Mag Dimond. A first prize of $2,000 plus publication, and two $2,000 honorable mentions, are offered for novels on a designated theme. Writers from the following states are eligible: NM, AZ, NV, UT, CO, TX. Deadline: August 31. Entry fee.

MIDDLEBURY COLLEGE—Katharine Bakeless Nason Prizes, c/o Bread Loaf Writers' Conference, Middlebury College, Middlebury, VT 05753. Attn: Carol Knauss. Publication and fellowships to the Bread Loaf Writers' Conference are offered for previously unpublished first books of poetry, fiction, and nonfiction. Deadline: March 1. Entry fee.

MID-LIST PRESS—First Series Awards, 4324 12th Ave. S., Minneapolis, MN 55407–3218. Publication and an advance against royalties are awarded for first books in the following categories: a novel in any genre, from 50,000 words; poetry, from 65 pages; short fiction, from 50,000 words; creative nonfiction, from 50,000 words. Deadline: February 1 (novel and poetry); July 1 (short fiction and creative nonfiction). Entry fees.

MIDWEST RADIO THEATRE WORKSHOP—MRTW Script Contests, 915 E. Broadway, Columbia, MO 65201. Workshop Script Contest: offers $800 in prizes, to be divided among two to four winners, and free workshop participation for contemporary radio scripts, 25 to 30 minutes long. Deadline: November 15. Entry fee.

MIDWEST THEATRE NETWORK—Biennial Rochester Playwright Festival, 5031 Tongen Ave. N.W., Rochester, MN 55901. Five to eight scripts of various lengths and types are chosen for festival production. Deadline: November 30 (of odd-numbered years).

MILL MOUNTAIN THEATRE—New Play Competition, 2nd Floor, One Market Square, Roanoke, VA 24011–1437. Attn: Jo Weinstein. Offers a $1,000 prize and staged reading, with possible full production, for an unpublished, unproduced, full-length or one-act play or musical. Cast size to ten. Deadline: January 1.

MISSISSIPPI REVIEW—Prize for Short Fiction, The Center for Writers, Univ. of Southern Mississippi, Box 5144, Hattiesburg, MS 39406–5144. Attn: R. Fortenberry. Publication and $1,000 are offered for the best short story; runner-up stories will be published. Deadline: March 31. Entry fee.

THE MISSOURI REVIEW—Editors' Prize, 1507 Hillcrest Hall, UMC, Columbia, MO 65211. Publication plus $1,500 is awarded for a short fiction manuscript (25 pages); $1,000 for an essay (25 pages); and $750 for poetry (10 pages). Deadline: October 15. Entry fee.

THE MOUNTAINEERS BOOKS—The Barbara Savage/"Miles from Nowhere" Memorial Award, 1001 S. W. Klickitat Way, Suite 201, Seattle, WA 98134. Offers a $3,000 cash award, plus publication and a $12,000 guaranteed advance against royalties for an outstanding unpublished, book-length manuscript of a nonfiction, personal-adventure narrative. Deadline: October 1 (of even-numbered years).

NATIONAL ENDOWMENT FOR THE ARTS—Nancy Hanks Center, 1100 Pennsylvania Ave. N.W., Room 720, Washington, DC 20506. Attn: Dir., Literature Program. Offers fellowships to writers and translators of poetry, fiction, plays, and creative nonfiction. Deadline: varies.

NATIONAL FEDERATION OF STATE POETRY SOCIETIES—Poetry Manuscript Contest, 3520 St. Rd. 56, Mechanicsburg, OH 43044. Attn: Amy Zook, Chairman. A prize of $1,000 is awarded for the best manuscript of poetry, 35 to 60 pages. Deadline: October 15. Entry fee.

NATIONAL POETRY SERIES—P.O. Box G, Hopewell, NJ 08525. Attn: Emily Wylie, Coordinator. Sponsors Annual Open Competition for unpublished book-length poetry manuscripts. Five manuscripts are selected for publication, and each winner receives a $1,000 award. Deadline: February 15. Entry fee.

NEW ENGLAND POETRY CLUB—Annual Contests, 11 Puritan Rd., Arlington, MA 02139. Attn: Virginia Thayer. Prizes range from $100 to $500 in various contests for members, nonmembers, and students. Deadline: April 15. Entry fee.

NEW ENGLAND THEATRE CONFERENCE—John Gassner Memorial Playwriting Award, c/o Dept. of Theatre, Northeastern Univ., 360 Huntington Ave., Boston, MA 02115. A $500 first prize and a $250 second prize are offered for unpublished, unproduced full-length plays written by New England residents or members of the NETC. Deadline: April 15. Entry fee.

NEW LETTERS—University of Missouri-Kansas City, 5100 Rockhill Rd., Kansas City, MO 64110–2499. Offers $750 for the best short story, to 5,000 words; $750 for the best group of three to six poems; $500 for the best essay, to 5,000 words. The work of each winner and first runner-up will be published. Deadline: May 15. Entry fee.

NIMROD/HARDMAN AWARDS—*Nimrod International Journal*, 600 S. College Ave., Tulsa, OK 74104–3189. Katherine Anne Porter Prize: offers prizes of $2,000 and $1,000 for fiction, to 7,500 words. Pablo Neruda Prize: offers prizes of $2,000 and $1,000 for one long poem or a selection of poems. Deadline: April 15. Entry fees.

NORTH CAROLINA WRITERS' NETWORK—International Literature Prizes, 3501 Hwy. 54 West, Studio C, Chapel Hill, NC 27516. Thomas Wolfe Fiction Prize: offers $500 for a previously unpublished short story or novel excerpt. Deadline: August 31. Paul Green Playwrights Prize: offers $500 for a previously unproduced, unpublished play. Deadline: September 30. Randall Jarrell Poetry Prize: offers $500 for a previously unpublished poem. Deadline: November 1. Entry fees.

NORTHEASTERN UNIVERSITY PRESS—Samuel French Morse Poetry Prize, English Dept., 406 Holmes, Northeastern Univ., Boston, MA 02115. Attn: Prof. Guy Rotella, Chairman. Offers $500 plus publication for a full-length poetry manuscript by a U.S. poet who has published no more than one book of poems. Deadline: August 1 (for inquiries); September 15 (for entries). Entry fee.

NORTHERN KENTUCKY UNIVERSITY—Y.E.S. New Play Festival, Dept. of Theatre, FA 227, Nunn Dr., Highland Hts., KY 41099–1007. Attn: Mike King, Project Dir. Awards three $400 prizes plus production for previously unproduced full-length plays and musicals. Deadline: October 15 (of even-numbered years).

NORTHERN MICHIGAN UNIVERSITY—Mildred & Albert Panowski Playwriting Competition, Forest Roberts Theatre, Northern Michigan Univ., 1401 Presque Isle Ave., Marquette, MI 49855–5364. Awards $2,000, plus production for an original, full-length, previously unproduced and unpublished play. Deadline: November 15.

O'NEILL THEATER CENTER—National Playwrights Conference, 234 W. 44th St., Suite 901, New York, NY 10036. Attn: Mary F. McCabe. Offers stipend, staged readings, and room and board at the conference, for new stage and television plays. Deadline: December 1. Entry fee.

OFF CENTER THEATER—Women Playwright's Festival, Tampa Bay Performing Arts Center, P.O. Box 518, Tampa, FL 33601. A $1,000 prize, production, and travel are offered for the best play about women, written by a woman; runner up receives staged reading. Deadline: September 15. Entry fee.

OHIO UNIVERSITY PRESS—Hollis Summers Poetry Prize, Scott Quadrangle, Athens, OH 45701. A $500 prize plus publication is awarded for an original collection of poetry, 60 to 95 pages. Deadline: November 15. Entry fee.

PEN CENTER USA WEST—Grants for Writers with HIV/AIDS, 672 S. Lafayette Park Pl., #41, Los Angeles, CA 90057. Grants of $1,000 are awarded to writers with HIV/AIDS to continue and/or finish a current literary project. Writers living in the western U.S. who have been actively involved in creating literary work during the past three years are eligible to apply. Deadline: October 1.

PEN/JERARD FUND AWARD—PEN American Center, 568 Broadway, New York, NY 10012. Attn: John Morrone, Programs & Publications. Offers $4,000 to beginning female writers for a work-in-progress of general nonfiction. Applicants must have published at least one article in a national magazine or major literary magazine, but not more than one book of any kind. Deadline: January 1 (of odd-numbered years).

PEN WRITERS FUND—PEN American Center, 568 Broadway, New York, NY 10012. Attn: India Amos, Writers Fund Coordinator. Grants and interest-free loans of up to $500 are available to published writers or produced playwrights facing unanticipated financial emergencies. If the emergency is due to HIV-and AIDS-related illness, professional writers and editors qualify

814

through the Fund for Writers and Editors with AIDS; all decisions are confidential. Deadline: year-round.

PEN WRITING AWARDS FOR PRISONERS—PEN American Center, 568 Broadway, New York, 10012. County, state, and federal prisoners are eligible to enter one unpublished manuscript, to 5,000 words, in each of these categories: fiction, drama, and nonfiction. Prisoners may submit up to 10 poems (any form) in the poetry category (to 20 pages total) in the poetry category. Prizes of $100, $50, and $25 are awarded in each category. Deadline: September 1.

PEREGRINE SMITH POETRY SERIES—Gibbs Smith, Publisher, P.O. Box 667, Layton, UT 84041. Offers a $500 prize plus publication for a previously unpublished 64-page poetry manuscript. Deadline: April 30. Entry fee.

PETERLOO POETS—Open Competition, 2 Kelly Gardens, Calstock, Cornwall PL18 9SA, U.K. Prizes totalling 5,100 British pounds, including a grand prize of £3,000 plus publication, are awarded for poems of up to 40 lines. Deadline: March 1. Entry fee.

PHILADELPHIA FESTIVAL OF WORLD CINEMA—"Set in Philadelphia" Screenwriting Competition, 3701 Chestnut St., Philadelphia, PA 19104. A $5,000 prize is awarded for the best screenplay, 85 to 130 pages, set primarily in the greater Philadelphia area. Deadline: January 1. Entry fee.

PIG IRON PRESS—Kenneth Patchen Competition, P.O. Box 237, Youngstown, OH 44501. Awards paperback publication, $100, and 50 copies of the winning manuscript of fiction (in even-numbered years) and poetry (in odd-numbered years). Deadline: December 31. Entry fee.

PIONEER DRAMA SERVICE—Shubert Fendrich Memorial Playwriting Contest, P.O. Box 4267, Englewood, CO 80155–4267. A prize of publication plus a $1,000 advance is offered for a previously produced, though unpublished, full-length play suitable for community theater. Deadline: March 1.

PIRATE'S ALLEY FAULKNER SOCIETY—William Faulkner Creative Writing Competition, 632 Pirate's Alley, New Orleans, LA 70116. Prizes are $7,500 for an unpublished novel of over 50,000 words; $2,500 for a novella of under 50,000 words; $1,500 for a short story of under 15,000 words; and $1,500 for a personal essay under 2,500 words. All awards include additional prize money to be used as an advance against royalties to encourage publisher interest. Deadline: April 1. Entry fees.

PLAYBOY—College Fiction Contest, 680 N. Lakeshore Dr., Chicago, IL 60611. Prizes of $3,000 plus publication, and $500, are offered for a short story, up to 25 pages, by a college student. Deadline: January 1.

PLAYHOUSE-ON-THE-SQUARE—New Play Competition, 51 S. Cooper, Memphis, TN 38104. Attn: Mr. Jackie Nichols, Exec. Dir. A stipend plus production is awarded for a full-length, previously unproduced play or musical. Deadline: April 1.

THE PLAYWRIGHTS' CENTER—Jerome Fellowships, 2301 Franklin Ave. E., Minneapolis, MN 55406. Five emerging playwrights are offered a $7,000 stipend and 12-month residency; housing and travel are not provided. Deadline: September 15.

POCKETS—Fiction Contest, c/o Lynn W. Gilliam, Assoc. Ed., P.O. Box 189, Nashville, TN 37202–0189. A $1,000 prize goes to the author of the winning 1,000-to 1,600-word story for children in grades 1 to 6. Deadline: August 15.

PRISM INTERNATIONAL—Short Fiction Contest, Creative Writing Dept., Univ. of B.C., E462–1866 Main Mall, Vancouver, B.C., V6T 1Z1. Publication, a $2,000 first prize, and 5 $200 prizes are awarded for stories of up to 25 pages. Deadline: December 1. Entry fee.

PURDUE UNIVERSITY PRESS—Verna Emery Poetry Award, 1532 S. Campus Courts-E, W. Lafayette, IN 47907–1532. Unpublished collections of original poetry, 60 to 90 pages, are considered for an award of publication plus royalties. Deadline: April 15. Entry fee.

QUARTERLY REVIEW OF LITERATURE—Poetry Awards, 26 Haslet Ave., Princeton, NJ 08540. Four to six prizes of $1,000, publication, and 100 books are awarded for 60-to 100-page manuscripts of poetry, poetic plays, long poems, or poetry in translation. Deadlines: May 31; November 30. Entry fee.

RANDOM HOUSE JUVENILE BOOKS—Dr. Seuss Picturebook Award Contest, 201 E. 50th St., New York, NY 10022. A prize of $25,000 plus publication is awarded for a picturebook manuscript by an author/illustrator who has not published more than one book. Deadline: December 1 (of even-numbered years).

RIVER CITY—Writing Awards in Fiction, Dept. of English, Memphis State Univ., Memphis, TN 38152. Awards of $2,000 plus publication, $500, and $300 are offered for previously unpublished short stories, to 7,500 words. Deadline: December 1. Entry fee.

ROME ART & COMMUNITY CENTER—Milton Dorfman Poetry Prize, 308 W. Bloomfield St., Rome, NY 13440. Offers prizes of $500, $200, and $100 plus publication for the best original, unpublished poems. Deadline: November 1. Entry fee.

IAN ST JAMES AWARDS—P.O. Box 60, Cranbrook, Kent TN17 2ZR, England. Attn: Merric Davidson. Offers 20 prizes of 200 to 2,000 British pounds plus publication for short stories. Deadline: April 30. Entry fee.

ST. MARTIN'S PRESS/MALICE DOMESTIC CONTEST—Thomas Dunne Books, 175 Fifth Ave., New York, NY 10010. Offers publication plus a $10,000 advance against royalties, for a best first traditional mystery novel. Deadline: October 15.

ST. MARTIN'S PRESS/PRIVATE EYE NOVEL CONTEST—PWA Contest, 175 Fifth Ave., New York, NY 10010. Co-sponsored by Private Eye Writers of America. The writer of the best first private eye novel, from 60,000 words, receives publication plus $10,000 against royalties. Deadline: August 1.

SARABANDE BOOKS—Poetry and Short Fiction Prizes, P.O. Box 4999, Louisville, KY 40204. Prizes are $2,000, publication, and a standard royalty contract in the competition for the Kathryn A. Morton Prize in Poetry (for a collection of poems, from 48 pages) and the Mary McCarthy Prize in Short Fiction (for a collection of short stories or novellas, 150 to 300 pages). Deadline: February 15. Entry fee.

SHENANARTS—Shenandoah International Playwrights Retreat, Rt. 5, Box 167-F, Staunton, VA 24401. Full fellowships are offered to playwrights to attend the four-week retreat held each August. Each year the retreat focuses on plays having to do with a specific region of the world. Deadline: February 1.

SIENA COLLEGE—International Playwrights' Competition, Siena College, 515 Loudon Rd., Loudonville, NY 12211–1462. Offers $2,000 plus campus residency expenses for the winning full-length script; no musicals. Deadline: June 30 (of even-numbered years).

SIERRA REPERTORY THEATRE—Taylor Playwriting Award, P. O. Box 3030, Sonora, CA 95370. Attn: Dennis Jones, Producing Dir. Offers $500, plus possible production, for a full-length play or musical that has received no more than two productions or staged readings. Deadline: August 31.

SNAKE NATION PRESS—Fiction and Poetry Contests, 110 #2 W. Force St., Valdosta, GA 31601. Attn: Nancy Phillips. Violet Reed Haas Prize: Offers publication plus $500 for a previously unpublished book of poetry, 50 to 75 pages. Deadline: January 15. *Snake Nation Review* Contest Issues: Prizes are publication plus $300, $200, and $100 for short stories; $100, $75, and $50 for poems. Deadlines: April 1; September 1. Entry fee.

SONORA REVIEW—Contests, Univ. of Arizona, Dept. of English, Tucson, AZ 85721. Poetry Contest: offers $500 plus publication for the best poem. Deadline: July 1. Short Story Contest: offers $500 plus publication for the best short story. Deadline: December 1. Entry fees.

SONS OF THE REPUBLIC OF TEXAS—Summerfield G. Roberts Award, 1717 8th St., Bay City, TX 77414. A prize of $2,500 is awarded for published or unpublished creative writing on the Republic of Texas, 1836–1846. Deadline: January 15.

THE SOUTHERN ANTHOLOGY—The Southern Prize, 2851 Johnston St., #123, Lafayette, LA 70503. A prize of $600 and publication are awarded for the best original, previously unpublished short story or novel excerpt, up to 7,500 words, or poem. Deadline: May 30. Entry fee.

SOUTHERN APPALACHIAN REPERTORY THEATRE—Playwrights' Conference, P.O. Box 620, Mars Hill, NC 28754–0620. Attn: Ms. Gaynelle M. Caldwell, Jr. Unproduced, unpublished scripts will be considered; up to 5 playwrights are selected to attend the conference and hear their plays read by professional actors; full production is possible. Deadline: October 1.

SOUTHERN POETRY REVIEW—Guy Owen Poetry Prize, Southern Poetry Review, Advancement Studies Dept., Central Piedmont Community College, Charlotte, NC 28235. Attn: Ken McLaurin, Ed. A prize of publication plus $500 is awarded for the best original, previously unpublished poem. Deadline: April 30. Entry fee.

THE SOW'S EAR PRESS—19535 Pleasant View Dr., Abingdon, VA 24211–6827. Chapbook Competition: offers a prize of $500 plus 50 published copies for the best poetry manuscript, as well as two $100 prizes. Deadline: April 30. Poetry Competition: offers prizes of $500, $100, and $50 for a previously unpublished poem of any length. Deadline: October 31. Entry fees.

SPOON RIVER POETRY REVIEW—Editors' Prize, 4240 Dept. of English, Illinois State Univ., Normal, IL 61790–4240. Publication and a $500 prize, as well as two $50 prizes, are awarded for single poems. Deadline: May 1. Entry fee.

STAND MAGAZINE—Short Story Competition, 179 Wingrove Rd., Newcastle upon Tyne, NE4 9DA, U.K. Prizes totalling 2,500 British pounds, including a £1,500 first prize, are awarded for previously unpublished stories under

8,000 words. Winning stories are published in *Stand Magazine*. Deadline: June 30 (of odd-numbered years). Entry fee.

STATE UNIVERSITY OF NEW YORK AT STONY BROOK—Short Fiction Prize, Dept. of English, Humanities Bldg., State Univ., Stony Brook, NY 11794–5350. Attn: Carolyn McGrath. A prize of $1,000 is offered for the best short story, up to 5,000 words, written by an undergraduate currently enrolled fulltime in an American or Canadian college. Deadline: February 28.

STORY LINE PRESS—Nicholas Roerich Prize, Three Oaks Farm, Brownsville, OR 97327–9718. A prize of $1,000 plus publication is awarded for an original book of poetry by a poet who has never before published a book of poetry. Deadline: October 15. Entry fee.

SUNY FARMINGDALE—Paumanok Poetry Award, Visiting Writers Program, Knapp Hall, SUNY Farmingdale, Farmingdale, NY 11735. Prizes of $1,000 and two $500 prizes are offered for entries of three to five poems. Deadline: September 15. Entry fee.

SYRACUSE UNIVERSITY PRESS—John Ben Snow Prize, 1600 Jamesville Ave., Syracuse, NY 13244–5160. Attn: Dir. Awards a $1,500 advance, plus publication, for an unpublished book-length nonfiction manuscript about New York State, especially upstate or central New York. Deadline: December 31.

TEN MINUTE MUSICALS PROJECT—Box 461194, W. Hollywood, CA 90046. Attn: Michael Koppy, Prod. Musicals of 7 to 14 minutes are eligible for a $250 advance against royalties and musical anthology productions at theaters in the U.S. and Canada. Deadline: August 31.

TENNESSEE MOUNTAIN WRITERS—The Tennessee Literary Awards, P.O. Box 4895, Oak Ridge, TN 37831–4895. Offers $250, $150, and $75 in each of three categories: Fiction, Essays, Poetry. Deadline: September 30. Entry fee.

DAVID THOMAS CHARITABLE TRUST—Open Competitions, P.O. Box 4, Nairn IV12 4HU, Scotland, UK. The trust sponsors a number of theme-based poetry and short story contests open to beginning writers, with prizes ranging from £25 to £1,200. Deadline: varies. Entry fee.

THE THURBER HOUSE—Thurber House Residencies, 77 Jefferson Ave., Columbus, OH 43215. Attn: Michael J. Rosen, Lit. Dir. Three-month residencies and stipends of $5,000 each are awarded in the categories of writing, playwriting, and journalism. Winners have limited teaching responsibilities with The Ohio State University. Deadline: December 15.

TRITON COLLEGE—Salute to the Arts Poetry Contest, 2000 Fifth Ave., River Grove, IL 60171. Winning original, unpublished poems, to 60 lines, on designated themes, are published by Triton College. Deadline: April 1.

UNICO NATIONAL—Ella T. Grasso Literary Award Contest, 72 Burroughs Pl., Bloomfield, NJ 07003. A prize of $1,000 is awarded for the best essay or short story, 1,500 to 2,000 words, on the Italian-American experience. Deadline: April 1.

U.S. NAVAL INSTITUTE—Arleigh Burke Essay Contest, *Proceedings Magazine*, 118 Maryland Ave., Annapolis, MD 21402–5035. Attn: Bert Hubinger. Awards prizes of $3,000, $2,000, and $1,000 plus publication, for essays on the advancement of professional, literary, or scientific knowledge in the naval or maritime services, and the advancement of the knowledge of sea power. Deadline: December 1. Also sponsors several smaller contests; deadlines vary.

UNIVERSITIES WEST PRESS—Emily Dickinson Award in Poetry, P.O. Box 697, Williams, AZ 86046–0697. A prize of $500 plus publication is awarded for an unpublished poem. Deadline: July 31. Entry fee.

UNIVERSITY OF AKRON PRESS—The Akron Poetry Prize, 374B Bierce Library, Akron, OH 44325–1703. Publication and $500 are offered for a previously unpublished collection of poems. Deadline: June 30. Entry fee.

UNIVERSITY OF CALIFORNIA IRVINE—Chicano/Latino Literary Contest, Dept. of Spanish and Portuguese, UCI, Irvine, CA 92717. Attn: Alejandro Morales, Dir. A first prize of $1,000 plus publication, and prizes of $500 and $250 are awarded in alternating years for poetry, drama, novels, and short stories. Deadline: April 30.

UNIVERSITY OF COLORADO—Nilon Award for Excellence in Minority Fiction, FC2, English Dept. Publications Ctr., Campus Box 494, Boulder, CO 80309–0494. Awards $1,000 plus joint publication for original, unpublished, book-length fiction, in English, by a U.S. citizen. Open to writers of the following ethnic minorities: African American, Hispanic, Asian, Native American or Alaskan Native, and Pacific Islander. Deadline: November 30.

UNIVERSITY OF GEORGIA PRESS—Flannery O'Connor Award for Short Fiction, Univ. of Georgia Press, 330 Research Dr., Athens, GA 30602–4901. Two prizes of $1,000 plus publication are awarded for book-length collections of short fiction. Deadline: July 31. Entry fees.

UNIVERSITY OF GEORGIA PRESS CONTEMPORARY POETRY SERIES—Athens, GA 30602–4901. Offers publication of manuscripts from poets who have published at least one volume of poetry. Deadline: January 31. Publication of book-length poetry manuscripts is offered to poets who have never had a book of poems published. Deadline: September 30. Entry fee.

UNIVERSITY OF HAWAII AT MANOA—Kumu Kahua Playwriting Contest, Dept. of Drama and Theatre, 1770 East-West Rd., Honolulu, HI 96822. Awards $500 for a full-length play, and $200 for a one-act, set in Hawaii and dealing with some aspect of the Hawaiian experience. Also conducts contest for plays written by Hawaiian residents. Deadline: January 1.

UNIVERSITY OF IOWA—Iowa Publication Awards for Short Fiction, Dept. of English, 308 English Philosophy Bldg., Iowa City, IA 52242–1492. The John Simmons Short Fiction Award and the Iowa Short Fiction Award, both for unpublished full-length collections of short stories, offer publication under a standard contract. Deadline: September 30.

UNIVERSITY OF MASSACHUSETTS PRESS—Juniper Prize, Amherst, MA 01003. Offers a prize of $1,000 plus publication for a book-length manuscript of poetry; awarded in odd-numbered years to writers who have never published a book of poetry, and in even-numbered years to writers who have published a book or chapbook of poetry. Deadline: September 30. Entry fee.

UNIVERSITY OF NEBRASKA-OMAHA—Awards in Poetry and Fiction, *The Nebraska Review*, Univ. of Nebraska-Omaha, Omaha, NE 68182–0324. Offers $500 each plus publication to the winning short story (to 5,000 words) and the winning poem (or group of poems). Deadline: November 30. Entry fee.

UNIVERSITY OF NEBRASKA PRESS—North American Indian Prose Award, 312 N. 14th St., Lincoln, NE 68588–0484. Previously unpublished book-length manuscripts of biography, autobiography, history, literary criticism, and essays will be judged for originality, literary merit, and familiarity with North American Indian life. A $1,000 advance and publication are offered. Deadline: July 1.

UNIVERSITY OF PITTSBURGH PRESS—127 N. Bellefield Ave., Pittsburgh, PA 15260. Agnes Lynch Starrett Poetry Prize: offers $2,500 plus publication in the Pitt Poetry Series for a book-length collection of poems by a poet who has not yet published a volume of poetry. Deadline: April 30. Entry fee. Drue Heinz Literature Prize: offers $10,000 plus publication and royalty contract for an unpublished collection of short stories or novellas, 150 to 300 pages, by a writer who has previously published a book-length collection of fiction or at least three short stories or novellas in nationally distributed magazines. Deadline: August 31.

UNIVERSITY OF SOUTHERN CALIFORNIA—Ann Stanford Poetry Prize, Master of Professional Writing Program, WPH 404, Univ. of Southern California, Los Angeles, CA 90089–4034. Publication plus prizes of $750, $250, and $100 are awarded; submit up to five poems. Deadline: April 15. Entry fee.

UNIVERSITY OF WISCONSIN PRESS POETRY SERIES—114 N. Murray St., Madison, WI 53715. Attn: Ronald Wallace, Ed. Previously unpublished manuscripts, 50 to 80 pages, are considered for the Brittingham Prize in Poetry and the Felix Pollak Prize in Poetry, each offering $1,000 plus publication. Deadline: October 1. Entry fee.

VETERANS OF FOREIGN WARS—Voice of Democracy Audio Essay Competition, VFW National Headquarters, 406 W. 34th St., Kansas City, MO 64111. Several national scholarships totalling $118,000 are awarded to high school students for short, tape-recorded essays. Themes change annually. Deadline: November 1.

VILLA MONTALVO—Biennial Poetry Competition, P.O. Box 158, Saratoga, CA 95071. Residents of CA, NV, OR, and WA are eligible to enter poems in any style for prizes of: $1,000 plus an artist residency at Villa Montalvo, $500, and $300, as well as eight prizes of $25. Deadline: October 1 (of odd-numbered years). Entry fee.

WAGNER COLLEGE—Stanley Drama Award, Dept. of Humanities, 631 Howard Ave., Staten Island, NY 10301. Awards $2,000 for an original, previously unpublished and unproduced full-length play or musical or thematically related one-acts. Deadline: September 1.

WASHINGTON PRIZE FOR FICTION—1301 S. Scott St., #424, Arlington, VA 22204–4656. Attn: Larry Kaltman, Dir. Offers $5,000, $2,500, and $1,000 for unpublished novels or short story collections, at least 65,000 words. Deadline: November 30. Entry fee.

WHITE-WILLIS THEATRE—New Playwrights Contest, 5266 Gate Lake Rd., Ft. Lauderdale, FL 33319. Offered are a $500 prize plus production for the winning unpublished, unproduced full-length play. Deadline: September 15. Entry fee.

TENNESSEE WILLIAMS/NEW ORLEANS LITERARY FESTIVAL—University of New Orleans, Lakefront, New Orleans, LA 70148. A $1,000 prize plus a staged reading and full production are offered for an original, unpublished one-act play. Deadline: December 1.

WRITERS AT WORK—Fellowship Competition, P.O. Box 1146, Centerville, UT 84014–5146. Prizes of $1,500 plus publication, and $500, in fiction and poetry categories, are awarded for excerpts of unpublished short stories, novels, essays, or poetry. Open to any writer who has not yet published a book-length volume of original work. Deadline: March 15. Entry fee.

YALE UNIVERSITY PRESS—Yale Series of Younger Poets Prize, Box 209040, Yale Sta., New Haven, CT 06520–9040. Attn: Ed. Series publication is awarded for a book-length manuscript of poetry written by a poet under 40 who has not previously published a volume of poems. Deadline: February 29. Entry fee.

YOUNG PLAYWRIGHTS, INC.—Young Playwrights Festival, Dept. T, 321 W. 44th St., Suite 906, New York, NY 10036. Festival productions and readings are awarded for the best plays by writers 18 or younger. Deadline: October 15.

WRITERS COLONIES

Writers colonies offer solitude and freedom from everyday distractions so that writers can concentrate on their work. Though some colonies are quite small, with space for just three or four writers at a time, others can provide accommodations for as many as thirty or forty. The length of a residency may vary, too, from a couple of weeks to five or six months. These programs have strict admissions policies, and writers must submit a formal application or letter of intent, a resumé, writing samples, and letters of recommendation. As an alternative to the traditional writers colony, a few of the organizations listed offer writing rooms for writers who live nearby. Write for application information first, enclosing a stamped, self-addressed envelope. Residency fees are subject to change.

THE EDWARD F. ALBEE FOUNDATION, INC.
14 Harrison St.
New York, NY 10013
(212) 266–2020
David Briggs, *Foundation Secretary*
Located on Long Island, "The Barn," or the William Flanagan Memorial Creative Persons Center, is maintained by the Albee Foundation. "The standards for admission are, simply, talent and need." Ten to 12 writers are accepted each season for one-month residencies, available from June 1 to October 1; applications, including writing samples, project description, and resumé, are accepted from January 1 to April 1. There is no fee, though residents are responsible for their own food and travel expenses.

ALTOS DE CHAVÒN
c/o Parsons School of Design
2 W. 13th St., Rm. 707
New York, NY 10011
(212) 229–5370
Stephen D. Kaplan, *Arts/Education Director*

Altos de Chavòn is a nonprofit center for the arts in the Dominican Republic committed to education, design innovation, international creative exchange, and the promotion of Dominican culture. Residencies average 12 weeks and provide the emerging or established artist an opportunity to live and work in a setting of architectural and natural beauty. All artists are welcome to apply, though writers should note there are no typewriters, the library is oriented more toward the design profession, and the apartments housing writers also accommodate university students. Two to three writers are chosen each year for the program. The fee is $300 per month for an apartment with kitchenette; linen and cleaning services are available at an extra cost. Applications include a letter of interest, writing sample, and resumé; artists are chosen in July.

MARY ANDERSON CENTER FOR THE ARTS
101 St. Francis Dr.
Mount St. Francis, IN 47146
(812) 923–8602
Sarah Roberson Yates, *Executive Director*

Founded in 1989, the artists' residency and retreat is situated on the grounds of a Franciscan friary. Space is available for seven residents at a time, including private rooms, working space, and a visual artists' studio; meals are provided. Two-week to three-month residencies are available and are granted based on project proposal and the artist's body of work; applications are accepted year-round. Fees are $30 per day, plus $15 to apply.

ATLANTIC CENTER FOR THE ARTS
1414 Art Center Ave.
New Smyrna Beach, FL 32168
(904) 427–6975
Nicholas Conroy, *Program Director*

The center is located on the east coast of central Florida, with 67 acres of pristine hammockland on a tidal estuary. All buildings, connected by raised wooden walkways, are handicapped accessible and air conditioned. The center provides a unique environment for sharing ideas, learning, and collaborating on interdisciplinary projects. Master artists meet with mid-career artists for readings and critiques, with time out for individual work. Residencies are three weeks. Fees are $100 a week for tuition and $25 a day for housing; off-site, tuition-only plans are available; financial aid is limited. Application deadlines vary.

BERLINER KÜNSTLERPROGRAM
Artists-in-Berlin Program
950 Third Ave.
New York, NY 10022
(212) 758–3223
Dr. Rolf Hoffmann, *Director*

One-year residencies are offered to well-known and emerging writers, sculptors, and composers to promote cultural exchange. Up to 20 residencies are offered for periods beginning between January 1 and June 30. Room, board, travel, and living expenses are awarded. Residents may bring spouse and children. Application, project description, and copies of publications are due by January 1 of the year preceding the residency.

BLUE MOUNTAIN CENTER
Blue Mountain Lake, NY 12812–0109
(518) 352–7391
Harriet Barlow, *Director*

Hosts month-long residencies for artists and writers from mid-June to late October. Established fiction and nonfiction writers, poets, and play-wrights whose work evinces social and ecological concern are eligible; 14 residents are accepted per session. Residents are not charged for their time at Blue Mountain, although all visitors are invited to contribute to the studio construction fund. There is no application form; apply by sending a brief biographical sketch, a plan for work at Blue Mountain, five to 10 slides or a writing sample of any length, an indication of preference for an early summer, late summer, or fall residence, and a $20 application fee, attention: *Admissions Committee.* Applications are due February 1.

BYRDCLIFFE ARTS COLONY
Artists' Residency Program
Woodstock Guild
34 Tinker St.
Woodstock, NY 12498
(914) 679–2079
Attn: *Director*

The Villetta Inn, located on the 400-acre arts colony, offers private rooms, a communal kitchen, and a peaceful environment for fiction writ-ers, poets, playwrights, and visual artists. Residencies from one to four months are offered from June to September. Fees are $400 to $500 per month. Submit application, resumé, writing sample, reviews, and refer-ences; the deadline is in mid-April.

THE CAMARGO FOUNDATION
W-1050 First National Bank Bldg.
332 Minnesota St.
St. Paul, MN 55101–1312
Ricardo Bloch, *Administrative Assistant*

The Camargo Foundation maintains a center of studies in France for the benefit of nine scholars and graduate students each semester who wish to pursue projects in the humanities and social sciences relative to France and Francophone culture. In addition, one artist, one composer, and one writer are accepted each semester. The foundation offers furnished apart-ments and a reference library in the city of Cassis. Research should be at an advanced stage and not require resources unavailable in the Marseilles-Aix-Cassis region. Fellows must be in residence at the foundation; the award is exclusively a residential grant. Application materials include: application form, curriculum vitae, three letters of recommendation, and project description. Writers, artists, and composers are required to send work samples. Applications are due February 1.

CENTRUM
P.O. Box 1158
Port Townsend, WA 98368
(360) 385–3102
Writers are awarded one-month residencies between September and May. Applicants selected by a peer jury receive free housing and a $300 stipend. Previous residents may return on a space-available basis for a fee of $300 a month. Applications are due October 1. The application fee is $10.

CHATEAU DE LESVAULT
Writers Retreat Program
Onlay
58370 Villapourìon
France
(33)-03–86–84–32–91; fax: (33)-03–86–84–35–78
Bibbi Lee, *Director*
This French country residence is located in western Burgundy, in the national park of Le Morvan. Five large rooms, fully equipped for living and working, are available October through April, for one month or longer. Residents in this small artists' community have access to the entire chateau, including the salon, library, and grounds. The fee is 4,500 francs (approximately $900) per month, or 2,500 francs for two weeks, and includes room, board, and utilities. Apply by writing to the selection committee, including project description, two references, writing samples, and publications list, if available. Applications are handled on a first-come basis.

CURRY HILL/GEORGIA
c/o 404 Crestmont Ave.
Hattiesburg, MS 39401–7211
(601) 264–7034
Mrs. Elizabeth Bowne, *Director*
This one-week retreat for eight fiction and nonfiction writers is offered for two sessions each spring by writer/teacher Elizabeth Bowne. "I care about writers and am delighted and enthusiastic when I can help develop talent." Interested persons should contact Mrs. Bowne early in October to learn exact dates. A $500 fee covers meals and lodging at Curry Hill, a family plantation home near Bainbridge, Georgia. Applicants are accepted on a first-come basis.

DJERASSI RESIDENT ARTISTS PROGRAM
2325 Bear Gulch Rd.
Woodside, CA 94062–4405
(415) 747–1250; fax: (415) 747–0105; e-mail: residency@djerassi.org
Charles Amirkhanian, *Executive Director*; Carol Law, *General Manager*
The Djerassi Program offers living and work spaces in a rural, isolated setting to playwrights, screenwriters, poets, translators, composers, librettists, and lyricists seeking undisturbed time for creative work. Residencies usually last one month; 60 artists are accepted each year. There are no fees other than the $25 application fee. Applications, with resumé and documentation of recent creative work, are due February 15. SASE for application.

824

DORLAND MOUNTAIN ARTS COLONY
Box 6
Temecula, CA 92593
(909) 676–5039
Attn: *Admissions Committee*

Dorland is a nature preserve and "primitive retreat for creative people" located in the Palomar Mountains of Southern California. "Without electricity, residents find a new, natural rhythm for their work." Novelists, playwrights, poets, nonfiction writers, composers, and visual artists are encouraged to apply for residencies of one to two months. The fee of $300 a month includes cottage, fuel, and firewood. Send SASE for application; deadlines are March 1 and September 1.

DORSET COLONY HOUSE
Box 519
Dorset, VT 05251
(802) 867–2223
John Nassivera, *Director*

Writers and playwrights are offered low-cost room with kitchen facilities at the historic Colony House in Dorset, Vermont. Residencies are one week to two months, and are available between September 15 and June 1. Applications are accepted year-round, and up to eight writers stay at a time. The fee is $95 per week; financial aid is limited. For more information, send SASE.

FINE ARTS WORK CENTER IN PROVINCETOWN
24 Pearl St.
Provincetown, MA 02657
Michael Wilkerson, *Executive Director*

Fellowships, including living and studio space and monthly stipends, are available at the Fine Arts Work Center on Cape Cod, for fiction writers, poets, and playwrights to work independently. Residencies are for seven months, October through May; apply before February 1 deadline. Five poets, five fiction writers, and one playwright are accepted. Send SASE for details; indicate that you are a writer in the request.

THE GELL WRITERS CENTER
Writers & Books
740 University Ave.
Rochester, NY 14607
(716) 473–2590
Joe Flaherty, *Director*

The Center, on Canandaigua Lake, is found in the Finger Lakes region of New York, and includes 24 acres of woodlands. Two separate living quarters, with private bath and work area, are available for $35 per night. All serious writers are welcome; reservations made on a first-come basis.

GLENESSENCE WRITERS COLONY
1447 W. Ward Ave.
Ridgecrest, CA 93555
(619) 446–5894
Allison Swift, *Director*

Glenessence is a luxury villa located in the Upper Mojave Desert, offering private rooms with bath, pool, spa, courtyard, shared kitchen,

825

fitness center, and library. Children, pets, and smoking are prohibited. Residencies are offered at $565 per month; meals are not provided. Reservations are made on a first-come basis.

THE TYRONE GUTHRIE CENTRE
Annaghmakerrig, Newbliss
County Monaghan
Ireland
(353) 47–54003; fax: (353) 47–54380
Bernard Loughlin, *Director*

Set on a 400-acre country estate, the center offers peace and seclusion to writers and other artists to enable them to get on with their work. All art forms are represented. One-to three-month residencies are offered throughout the year, at the rate of 1,200 to 1,600 pounds (about $1,920 to $2,560) per month, depending on the season; financial assistance is available to Irish citizens only. A number of longer term self-catering houses in the old farmyard are also available at £300 per week. Writers may apply for acceptance year-round.

THE HAMBIDGE CENTER
P.O. Box 339
Rabun Gap, GA 30568
(706) 746–5718
Judy Barber, *Director*

The Hambidge Center for Creative Arts and Sciences is located on 600 acres of quiet woods in the north Georgia mountains. Seven private cottages are available for fellows, who are asked to contribute $125 per week. Two-week to two-month residencies, from May to October, and limited winter residencies are offered to serious artists from all disciplines. Send SASE for application form. Application deadlines: October 30 and April 30.

HEADLANDS CENTER FOR THE ARTS
944 Fort Barry
Sausalito, CA 94965
(415) 331–2787

Programs for 1998 at the Headlands Center, located on 13,000 acres of open coastal space, are available to residents of Ohio, North Carolina, and California. Application requirements vary by state. The application deadline for the 1998 program is June 6, 1997. Decisions are announced in October for residencies beginning in February. Send SASE for more information.

HEDGEBROOK
2197 E. Millman Rd.
Langley, WA 98260
(360) 321–4786
Attn: *Director*

Hedgebrook provides women writers, published or not, of all ages and from all cultural backgrounds, with a natural place to work. Established in 1988, the retreat is located on 30 acres of farmland and woods on Whidbey Island in Washington State. Each writer has her own cottage, equipped with electricity and woodstove. A bathhouse serves all six cottages. Writers gather for dinner in the farmhouse every evening and frequently read in the living room/library afterwards. Limited travel scholarships are available. Residencies range from one week to two months. April 1 is the application deadline for residencies from mid-June to mid-December; October 1 for mid-January to late May. Applicants are chosen by a selection committee composed of writers. There is a $15 fee to apply; send SASE for application.

KALANI ECO-RESORT, INSTITUTE FOR CULTURE AND WELLNESS
Artist-in-Residence Program
RR2, Box 4500
Kehena Beach, HI 96778
(808) 965–7828; (8 00) 800 6886
Richard Koob, *Program Coordinator*
Located in a rural coastal setting of 113 botanical acres, Kalani Eco-Resort hosts and sponsors educational programs "with the aloha experience that is its namesake: harmony of heaven and earth." Residencies range from two weeks to two months and are available throughout the year. Fees range from $30 to $43 per day, meals available at additional fee. Applications accepted year-round.

LEIGHTON STUDIOS
Office of the Registrar
The Banff Centre for the Arts
Box 1020, Station 28
107 Tunnel Mountain Dr.
Banff, Alberta T0L 0C0
Canada
(403) 762–6180; (800) 565–9989; fax: (403) 762–6345; e-mail: arts info@banffcentre.ab.ca; internet: http://www.banffcentre.ab.ca
Theresa Boychuck, *Registrar*
The Leighton Studios are open year-round, providing time and space for artists to produce new work. Established writers, composers, musicians, and visual artists of all nationalities are encouraged to apply. Artists working in other mediums at the conceptual state of a project will also be considered. Weekly fees (Canadian dollars): $301 studio; $265 single room; $98.00 meals (optional). Reductions in the studio fee are available to applicants demonstrating financial need. Applications are accepted at any time. Space is limited; apply at least six months prior to preferred starting date. Write for application form.

THE MACDOWELL COLONY
100 High St.
Peterborough, NH 03458
(603) 924–3886; Internet: http://www.macdowellcolony.org
Pat Dodge, *Admissions Coordinator*
Studios, room, and board are available for writers to work without interruption in a woodland setting. Selection is competitive. Apply by January 15 for stays May through August; April 15 for September through December; and September 15 for January through April. Residencies last up to eight weeks, and 80 to 90 writers are accepted each year. Send SASE for application.

THE MILLAY COLONY FOR THE ARTS
P.O. Box 3
Austerlitz, NY 12017–0003
(518) 392–3103
Gail Giles, *Assistant Director*

At Steepletop, the former home of Edna St. Vincent Millay, writers are provided studios, living quarters, and meals at no cost. Residencies last one month. Application deadlines are February 1, May 1, and September 1. Send SASE for more information and application. Applications can also be accessed by e-mail (application@millaycolony.org).

MOLASSES POND WRITERS' RETREAT AND WORKSHOP
RR 1, Box 85C
Milbridge, ME 04658
(207) 546–2506
Martha Barron Barrett and Sue Wheeler, *Coordinators*

Led by published authors who teach writing at the University of New Hampshire. The one-week workshop is held in June and includes time set aside for writing, as well as manuscript critique and writing classes. Up to 10 writers participate, staying in five lakeside cottages with private work space and kitchen. Classes and communal dinner held in the main lodge. The $350 fee covers lodging, dinners, and tuition. Applicants must be serious about their work. No children's literature or poetry. Submit statement of purpose and 15 to 20 pages of fiction or nonfiction between March 1 and April 1.

JENNY McKEAN MOORE WRITER-IN-WASHINGTON
Dept. of English
The George Washington University
Washington, DC 20052
Attn: Prof. Christopher Sten

The fellowship allows for a writer to teach two paid semesters at The George Washington University. Teaching duties include a fiction workshop each semester for students from the metropolitan community who may have had little formal education; and one class each semester for university students. Applications include letter, indicating publications and other projects, extent of teaching experience, and other qualifications. The application must also include a resumé and a ten to 15 page sample of your work. The application deadline is November 15.

THE N.A.L.L. ASSOCIATION
232, Boulevard de Lattre
06140 Vence
France
(33) 93–58–13–26; fax: (33) 93–58–09–00
Attn: *Director*

This international center for writers and artists is located on eight acres of the Mediterranean village of Vence. Residents stay in cottages equipped with kitchen, bath, and private garden. One afternoon a week is set aside for residents to discuss their work with local artists over tea. Six-month residencies are encouraged. Cottages are rented at various rates, to members of the N.A.L.L. (Nature, Art, and Life League); membership is 500 francs (about $100) per year. Meals are not included. Submit resumé, writing sample, and project description. Applications are accepted year-round.

NEW YORK MILLS ARTS RETREAT AND REGIONAL CULTURAL CENTER
24 N. Main Ave.
P.O. Box 246
New York Mills, MN 56567
(218) 385–3339
Kent Scheer, *Retreat Coordinator*

The Cultural Center, housed in a restored 1895 general store, is an innovative non-profit organization offering gallery exhibits, musical performances, theater, literary events, educational programs, the Great American Think-Off philosophy competition, and the Continental Divide Film and Music Festival. The Arts Retreat provides housing at the Whistle Stop Inn, a bed and breakfast located in an old, Victorian style home. Each artist receives financial assistance through a stipend, ranging from $750 for a two-week residency to $1,500 for four weeks, provided by the Jerome Foundation. Five to seven emerging artists, writers, filmmakers, or musicians are accepted throughout the year. There is a review process twice a year (April and October), and the deadlines are April 1 for July to December and October 1 for January to June.

THE NORTHWOOD UNIVERSITY
Alden B. Dow Creativity Center
3225 Cook Rd.
Midland, MI 48640–2398
(517) 837–4478
Carol B. Coppage, *Director*

The Fellowship Program allows individuals time away from their on-going daily routines to pursue their project ideas without interruption. A project idea should be innovative, creative, and have potential for impact in its field. Four eight-week residencies, lasting from early-June to early-August, are awarded yearly. There is a $10 application fee. A $750 stipend plus room and board are provided. No spouses or families. Applications are due December 31.

PALENVILLE INTERARTS COLONY
2 Bond St.
New York, NY 10012
(518) 678–3332
Joanna Sherman, *Artistic Director*
The Palenville residency program has been suspended.

RAGDALE FOUNDATION
1260 N. Green Bay Rd.
Lake Forest, IL 60045
(847) 234–1063
Sonja Carlborg, *Director*

Uninterrupted time and peaceful space allow writers a chance to finish works in progress, to begin new works, to solve thorny creative problems, and to experiment in new genres. The foundation is located 30 miles north of Chicago, on 55 acres of prairie. Residencies of two weeks to two months are available for writers, artists, and composers. The fee is $15 a day; some full and partial fee waivers available, based solely on financial need. Send SASE for deadline information. Late applications considered when space is available. Application fee: $20.

SASKATCHEWAN WRITERS GUILD
Writers/Artists Colonies and Individual Retreats
P.O. Box 3986
Regina, Saskatchewan S4P 3R9
Canada
(306) 757-6310
Attn: *Director*

The Saskatchewan Colonies are at two locations: St. Peter's Abbey, near Humboldt, provides a six-week summer colony (July-August) and a two-week winter colony in February, for up to eight writers and artists at a time; applicant stays vary. Individual retreats of up to a month are offered year-round at St. Peter's, for up to three residents at a time. Emma Lake, near Prince Albert, is the site of a two-week residency in August. A fee of $100 a week includes room and board. Submit application form, resumé, project description, two references, and a 10-page writing sample. Saskatchewan residents are given preference. Apply two to three months in advance.

THE JOHN STEINBECK ROOM
Long Island University
Southampton Campus Library
Southampton, NY 11968
(516) 287-8382
Robert Gerbereux, *Library Director*

The John Steinbeck Room at Long Island University provides a basic research facility to writers who have either a current contract with a book publisher or a confirmed assignment from a magazine editor. The room is available for a period of six months with one six-month renewal permissible. Send SASE for application.

THE THURBER HOUSE RESIDENCIES
c/o Thurber House
77 Jefferson Ave.
Columbus, OH 43215
(614) 464-1032; fax: (614) 228-7445
Michael J. Rosen, *Literary Director*

Residencies in the restored home of James Thurber are awarded to journalists, poets, and playwrights. Residents work on their own writing projects, and in addition to other duties, teach one class at the Ohio State University. A stipend of $5,000 per quarter is provided. A letter of interest and curriculum vitae must be received by December 15, at which time applications are reviewed for the upcoming academic year.

UCROSS FOUNDATION
Residency Program
2836 U.S. Hwy. 14-16 East
Clearmont, WY 82835
(307) 737-2291
Elizabeth Guheen, *Executive Director*

Residencies, two to eight weeks, in the foothills of the Big Horn Mountains in Wyoming, allow writers, artists, and scholars to concentrate on their work without interruption. Two residency sessions are scheduled annually: February to June and August to December. There is no charge for room, board, or studio space. Application deadlines are March 1 for the fall session and October 1 for the spring session. Send SASE for more information.

VERMONT STUDIO CENTER
P.O. Box 613NW
Johnson, VT 05656
(802) 635–2727; fax: (802) 635–2730; e-mail: vscvt@pwshift.com
Attn: *Registrar*
The Vermont Studio Center offers two-week studio sessions for up to 12 writers from February through April, led by prominent writers and teachers focusing on fiction, creative nonfiction, and poetry. Independent writers' retreats from two to 12 weeks are available year-round for those seeking more solitude. Room, working studio, and meals are included in all programs. Fees are $1,300 for the two-week Writing Retreat and $2,600 for a month-long Residency. Financial assistance is available based on both merit and need. Applications are accepted year-round.

VILLA MONTALVO ARTIST RESIDENCY PROGRAM
P.O. Box 158
Saratoga, CA 95071
(408) 741–3421
Judy Moran, *Artist Residency Program Director*
Villa Montalvo, in the foothills of the Santa Cruz Mountains, offers one-to three-month, free residencies to writers and artists. Several merit-based fellowships are available. The application deadlines are September 1 and March 1; call for brochure and application form. Application fee is $20.

VIRGINIA CENTER FOR THE CREATIVE ARTS
Sweet Briar, VA 24595
(804) 946–7236
William Smart, *Director*
A working retreat for writers, composers, and visual artists in Virginia's Blue Ridge Mountains. Residencies from one week to two months are available year-round. Application deadlines are the 15th of January, May, and September; about 300 residents are accepted each year. A limited amount of financial assistance is available. Send SASE for more information.

THE WRITERS ROOM
10 Astor Pl., 6th Fl.
New York, NY 10003
(212) 254–6995; fax: (212) 533–6059
Donna Brodie, *Executive Director*
Located in Greenwich Village, the Writers Room provides highly subsidized work space to all types of writers at all stages of their careers. "We offer urban writers a quiet place to escape from noisy neighbors, children, roommates, and other distractions of city life." The room holds 30 desks separated by partitions, a typing room with five desks, a kitchen, and a library. Open 24 hours a day, 365 days a year. There is a $50 initiation

fee; fees for the three-month period include $350 for "project" desk and $175 for "floater" desk. Call, fax or write for application (no visits without appointment).

THE WRITERS STUDIO
The Mercantile Library Association
17 E. 47th St.
New York, NY 10017
(212) 755–6710
Harold Augenbraum, *Director*
The Writers Studio is a quiet place in which writers can rent space conducive to the production of good work. A carrel, locker, small reference collection, electrical outlets, and membership in the Mercantile Library of New York are available at the cost of $200 per three-month residency. Submit application, resumé, and writing samples; applications are considered year-round.

HELENE WURLITZER FOUNDATION OF NEW MEXICO
Box 545
Taos, NM 87571
(505) 758–2413
Rent-free and utility-free studios in Taos are offered to writers and creative artists in all media. "All artists are given the opportunity to be free of the shackles of a 9-to-5 routine." Length of residency varies from three to six months. The foundation is open from April 1 through September 30. Residencies are assigned into 2000, but cancellations do occur.

YADDO
Box 395
Saratoga Springs, NY 12866–0395
(518) 584–0746; fax: (518) 584–1312
Candace Wait, *Program Coordinator*
Visual artists, writers, choreographers, film/video artists, performance artists, composers, and collaborators are invited for stays from two weeks to two months. Room, board, and studio space are provided. No stipends. Deadlines are January 15 and August 1. There is a $20 application fee; send SASE for form.

WRITERS CONFERENCES

Each year, hundreds of writers conferences are held across the country; the following list, arranged by state, represents only a sampling. Each listing includes the location of the conference, the month during which it is usually held, and the name and address of the person from whom specific information may be received. Conferences are also listed annually in the

May issue of *The Writer* Magazine (120 Boylston St., Boston, MA 02116–4615).

ALABAMA

WRITING TODAY—Birmingham, AL. March 14–15. Write Martha Andrews, Dir., Birmingham-Southern College, Box 549003, Birmingham, AL 35254.

UNIVERSITY OF NORTH ALABAMA WRITERS' CONFERENCE—Florence, AL. April. Write Ron Smith, Dir., Dept. of English, Univ. of North Alabama, Florence, AL 35632–0001.

SOUTHERN CHRISTIAN WRITERS CONFERENCE—Birmingham, AL. June. Write Joanne Sloan, Dir., SCWC, P.O. 1106, Northport, AL 35476.

SCBWI "WRITING AND ILLUSTRATING FOR KIDS"—Birmingham, AL. October 18. Send SASE to Joan Broerman, Reg. Advisor, SCBWI, 1616 Kestwick Dr., Birmingham, AL 35226.

ALASKA

SITKA SYMPOSIUM ON HUMAN VALUES & THE WRITTEN WORD—Sitka, AK. June. Write Carolyn Servid, Dir., Island Institute, P.O. Box 2420, Sitka, AK 99835.

ARIZONA

PIMA WRITERS' WORKSHOP—Tucson, AZ. May. Write Meg Files, Dir., Pima College, 2202 W. Anklam Rd., Tucson, AZ 85709.

AMERICAN CHRISTIAN WRITERS CONFERENCE—Phoenix, AZ. October 23–25. Write Reg A. Forder, Dir., American Christian Writers, P.O. Box 110390, Nashville, TN 37222.

ARKANSAS

WHITE RIVER WRITERS' WORKSHOP: "INTENSIVES FOR POETS IN POETRY AND PRESENTATION"—Batesville, AR. June 15–22. Write Andrea Hollander Budy, Dir., White River Writers' Workshop, Lyon College, P.O. Box 2317, Batesville, AR 72503–2317.

CALIFORNIA

WRITERS' FORUM—Pasadena, CA. March 8. Write Meredith Brucker, Dir., Community Education, Pasadena City College, 1570 E. Colorado Blvd., Pasadena, CA 91106.

MOUNT HERMON CHRISTIAN WRITERS CONFERENCE—Mount Hermon, CA. March 21–25. Write David R. Talbott, Dir., Mount Hermon Assn. Inc., P.O. Box 413, Mount Hermon, CA 95041–0413.

PALM SPRINGS WRITERS' CONFERENCE—Palm Springs, CA. April 10–13. Write Arthur Lyons, Dir., PSWC, 646 Morongo Rd., Palm Springs, CA 92264.

SANTA BARBARA WRITERS CONFERENCE—Santa Barbara, CA. June 20–27. Write Barnaby Conrad, Dir., SBWC, Box 304, Carpinteria, CA 93014.

FOOTHILL COLLEGE WRITERS' CONFERENCE—Los Altos Hills, CA. June 26-July 1. Write Kim Wolterbeek, Dir., Foothill College, 12345 El Monte Rd., Los Altos Hills, CA 94022.

ROUND TABLE COMEDY WRITERS CONVENTION—Palm Springs, CA. July. Write Linda Perret, Dir., 30941 W. Agoura Rd., Suite 228, Westlake Village, CA 91361.

SQUAW VALLEY COMMUNITY OF WRITERS—Squaw Valley, CA. July, August, October. Write Brett Hall Jones, Dir., Squaw Valley Community of Writers, P.O. Box 2352, Olympic Valley, CA 96146.

FICTION INTENSIVE—Berkeley, CA. July 13–19. Write James N. Frey, Dir., UC Berkeley Extension, The Writing Program, 1995 University Ave., Berkeley, CA 94120–7002.

FOURTH ANNUAL BOOK PASSAGE MYSTERY WRITERS' CONFER-ENCE—Corte Madera, CA. July 17–20. Write Cecilia McGuire, Dir., 51 Tamal Vista Blvd., Corte Madera, CA 94925.

BOOK PASSAGE TRAVEL WRITERS' CONFERENCE—Corte Madera, CA. August. Write Mary Lou Miller, Dir., 51 Tamal Vista Blvd., Corte Madera, CA 94925.

WRITERS AND ILLUSTRATORS CONFERENCE IN CHILDREN'S LIT-ERATURE—Los Angeles, CA. August. Write Lin Oliver, Dir., SCBWI, 345 N. Maple Dr., Beverly Hills, CA 90210.

AMERICAN CHRISTIAN WRITERS CONFERENCE—Fullerton, CA. October 16–18. Write Reg A. Forder, Dir., American Christian Writers, P.O. Box 110390, Nashville, TN 37222.

COLORADO

1997 NATIONAL WRITERS ASSOCIATION SUMMER CONFER-ENCE—Denver, CO. June 13–15. Write Sandy Whelchel, Dir., National Writers Assn., 1450 S. Havana, Suite 424, Aurora, CO 80224.

STEAMBOAT SPRINGS WRITERS CONFERENCE—Steamboat Springs, CO. August 9. Write Harriet Freiberger, Dir., P.O. Box 774284, Steamboat Springs, CO 80477.

WRITERS IN THE ROCKIES TV & FILM SCREENWRITING CONFER-ENCE—Boulder, CO. August 23–24. Write Carolyn Hodges, Dir., 1980 Glenwood Dr., Boulder, CO 80304.

FLORIDA

KEY WEST LITERARY SEMINAR: "LITERATURE IN THE AGE OF AIDS"—Key West, FL. January 9–12. Write Miles Frieden, Dir., Key West Literary Seminar, 419 Petronia St., Dept. TW, Key West, FL 33040.

SOUTHWEST FLORIDA WRITERS' CONFERENCE—Fort Myers, FL. February 21–22. Write Joanne Hartke, Dir., Edison Community College, P.O. Box 60210, Fort Myers, FL 33906–6210.

SLEUTHFEST '97 MYSTERY/SUSPENSE/TRUE CRIME CONFER-ENCE—Fort Lauderdale, FL. April 11–13. Write James Neal Harvey Dir., Mystery Writers of America, 225 Barton Ave., Palm Beach, FL 33480.

OUTDOOR WRITERS ASSOCIATION OF AMERICA ANNUAL CON-FERENCE—Haines City, FL. June 22–26. Write James W. Rainey, Dir., 2017 Cato Ave., Suite 101, State College, PA 16801–2768.

HEMINGWAY DAYS WRITERS' WORKSHOP & CONFERENCE—Key West, FL. July 20–23. Write Dr. James Plath, Dir., Hemingway Days Festival, P.O. Box 4045, Key West, FL 33041.

17TH ANNUAL ROMANCE WRITERS OF AMERICA CONFERENCE—Orlando, FL. July 30-August 3. Write Allison Kelly, Dir., RWA, 13700 Veterans Memorial, #315, Houston, TX 77014.

FLORIDA REGION SCBWI CONFERENCE—Palm Springs, FL. September 14. Write Barbara Casey, Dir., 2158 Portland Ave., Wellington, FL 33414.

XVII SPACE COAST WRITERS GUILD ANNUAL CONFERENCE—Melbourne, FL. November. Write Dr. Edwin J. Kirschner, Pres., Space Coast Writers Guild, Box 804, Melbourne, FL 32902.

AMERICAN CHRISTIAN WRITERS CONFERENCE—Ft. Lauderdale, FL. November 14–15. Write Reg A. Forder, Dir., American Christian Writers, P.O. Box 110390, Nashville, TN 37222.

GEORGIA

AMERICAN CHRISTIAN WRITERS CONFERENCE—Atlanta, GA. March 14–15. Write Reg A. Forder, Dir., American Christian Writers, P.O. Box 110390, Nashville, TN 37222.

SPRINGMINGLE '97—Columbus, GA. March 14–16. Write Joan Broerman, Reg. Advisor, SCBWI, 1616 Kestwick Dr., Birmingham, AL 35226.

CURRY HILL PLANTATION WRITERS' RETREAT—Bainbridge, GA. March, April. Write Elizabeth Bowne, Dir., 404 Crestmont Ave., Hattiesburg, MS 39401–7211.

SOUTHEASTERN WRITER'S CONFERENCE—St. Simons Island, GA. June 15–21. SASE to Pat Laye, Secretary, Rt. 1, Box 102, Cuthbert, GA 31740.

MOONLIGHT AND MAGNOLIAS CONFERENCE—Atlanta, GA. September. Send SASE to Lillian Richey, Dir., Georgia Romance Writers, P.O. Box 941187, Atlanta, GA 31141–0187.

HAWAII

FIRST HAWAII BIENNIAL CONFERENCE FOR WRITERS & ILLUS-TRATORS OF CHILDREN'S LITERATURE—Honolulu, HI. June 27–30. Write Mede Stephens, Dir., "Children's Literature Hawaii," c/o Dept. of English, Univ. of Hawaii-Manoa, 1733 Donaghho Rd., Honolulu, HI 96822.

IDAHO

SUN VALLEY WRITERS' CONFERENCE—Sun Valley, ID. August. Write Reva Tooley, Dir., P.O. Box 957, Ketchum, ID 83340.

ILLINOIS

NORTHERN ILLINOIS WRITERS CONFERENCE—Rockford, IL. June. Write Elizabeth Flygare, Dir., Rockford Public Library, 215 N. Wyman St., Rockford, IL 61101.

WRITE-TO-PUBLISH CONFERENCE—Wheaton, IL. June 3–7. Write Lin Johnson, Dir., 9731 Fox Glen Dr., #6F, Niles, IL 60714–5861.

"OF DARK AND STORMY NIGHTS" WRITERS CONFERENCE—Rolling Meadows, IL. June 7. Write W.W. Spurgeon Jr., Dir., P.O. Box 1944, Muncie, IN 47308–1944.

MISSISSIPPI VALLEY WRITERS CONFERENCE—Rock Island, IL. June 8–13. Write David R. Collins, Dir., 3403— 45 St., Moline, IL 61265.

MIDWEST MYSTERY WRITERS' CONFERENCE—Normal, IL. August. Write Mary Adams, Dir., Lincoln College, 715 W. Raab Rd., Normal, IL 61761.

AMERICAN CHRISTIAN WRITERS CONFERENCE—Chicago, IL. August 14–16. Write Reg A. Forder, Dir., American Christian Writers, P.O. Box 110390, Nashville, TN 37222.

INDIANA

BUTLER UNIVERSITY MIDWINTER CHILDREN'S LITERATURE CONFERENCE—Indianapolis, IN. February 1. Send SASE to Shirley Daniell, Butler Univ. Midwinter Children's Literature Conference, 4600 Sunset Ave., Indianapolis, IN 46208.

INDIANA UNIVERSITY WRITERS' CONFERENCE—Bloomington, IL. June 22–27. Write Maura Stanton, Dir., Indiana Univ. Writers' Conference, BH 464, Bloomington, IN 47405.

KANSAS

WRITERS WORKSHOP IN SCIENCE FICTION—Lawrence, KS. June 30-July 13. Write James Gunn, Dir., English Dept., Univ. of Kansas, Lawrence, KS 66045.

KENTUCKY

GREEN RIVER WRITERS NOVELS-IN-PROGRESS WORKSHOP—Louisville, KY. March 15–21. Write Mary E. O'Dell, Dir., Green River Writers, Inc., 11906 Locust Rd., Middletown, KY 40243.

GREEN RIVER WRITERS ANNUAL WORKSHOP & RETREAT—Louisville, KY. July. Write Mary E. O'Dell, Dir., Green River Writers, Inc., 11906 Locust Rd., Middletown, KY 40243.

20TH ANNUAL APPALACHIAN WRITERS WORKSHOP—Hindman, KY. July 27-August 2. Write Mike Mullins, Dir., Box 844, Hindman, KY 41822.

LOUISIANA

DO WRITE!—Lafayette, LA. March. Write Rosalind Foley, Dir., Writers' Guild of Acadiana, 220 Doucet Rd., 164H, Lafayette, LA 70503.

MAINE

WELLS WRITERS' WORKSHOP 1997—Wells, ME. May 18–23. September 7–12. Write Mary Hill, Dir., 69 Broadway, Concord, NH 03301–2736.

IN CELEBRATION OF CHILDREN'S LITERATURE—Gorham, ME. July. Joyce Martin, Dir., 301A Bailey Hall, Univ. of Southern Maine, Gorham, ME 04038.

STONECOAST WRITERS' CONFERENCE—Freeport, ME. July. Write Barbara Hope, Dir., Summer Session Office, Univ. of Southern Maine, 96 Falmouth St., Portland, ME 04103.

DOWNEAST MAINE WRITER'S WORKSHOPS—Stockton Springs, ME. July. August. October. Write Janet J. Barron, Dir., P.O. Box 446, Stockton Springs, ME 04981.

STATE OF MAINE WRITERS' CONFERENCE—Ocean Park, ME. August 19–22. Write Richard F. Burns, Dir., P.O. Box 7146, Ocean Park, ME 04063–7146.

MARYLAND

MARYLAND WRITERS ASSOCIATION 10TH ANNUAL CONFERENCE—Bethesda, MD. September. Write Judith Reveal, Dir., 301 Wood Duck Dr., Greensboro, MD 21639.

SANDY COVE CHRISTIAN WRITERS CONFERENCE—North East, MD. October 5–9. Write Gayle Roper, Dir., 251 Water Works Rd., Coatesville, PA 19320.

MASSACHUSETTS

AMERICAN CHRISTIAN WRITERS CONFERENCE—Boston, MA. June 20–21. Write Reg A. Forder, Dir., American Christian Writers, P.O. Box 110390, Nashville, TN 37222.

HARVARD SUMMER SCHOOL WRITING PROGRAM—Cambridge, MA. June 23-August 15. Write David Gewanter, Dir., Harvard Summer School, 51 Brattle St., Cambridge, MA 02138.

CAPE COD WRITERS' CONFERENCE—Craigville, MA. August. Write Arlene Joffe Pollack, Dir., Cape Cod Writers' Center, P.O. Box 186, Barnstable, MA 02630.

MICHIGAN

MIDLAND WRITER'S CONFERENCE—Midland, MI. June 15. Write Katherine T. Redwine, Dir., 1710 W. St. Andrews, Midland, MI 48640.

MARANATHA CHRISTIAN WRITERS SEMINAR—Muskegon, MI. August 18–22. Write Leona Hertel, Dir., 4759 Lake Harbor Rd., Muskegon, MI 49441–5299.

MINNESOTA

YOUNG PLAYWRIGHTS SUMMER CONFERENCE—St. Paul, MN. July. Write Director of Community Programming, The Playwrights' Center, 2301 Franklin Ave., E. Minneapolis, MN 55406.

UNIVERSITY OF MINNESOTA SPLIT ROCK ARTS PROGRAM—Duluth, MN. July 6-August 9. Write Andrea Gilats, Dir., 306 Wesbrook Hall, Univ. of Minnesota, 77 Pleasant St. S.E., Minneapolis, MN 55455.

AMERICAN CHRISTIAN WRITERS CONFERENCE—Minneapolis, MN. August 8–9. Write Reg A. Forder, Dir., American Christian Writers, P.O. Box 110390, Nashville, TN 37222.

"WRITING TO SELL"—Minneapolis, MN. August 9. Write Minneapolis Writers' Workshop, P.O. Box 24356, Minneapolis, MN 55424.

MISSOURI

THE WRITING CAMP (For Young People in Grades 6–12)—Springfield, MO. June 5–9. Write Sandy Asher, Coord., Drury College, 900 N. Benton Ave., Springfield, MO 65802.

AMERICAN CHRISTIAN WRITERS CONFERENCE—St. Louis, MO. September 12–13. Write Reg A. Forder, Dir., American Christian Writers, P.O. Box 110390, Nashville, TN 37222.

SENIOR WRITERS RETREAT—Springfield, MO. October. Write Sandy Asher, Coord., Drury College, 900 N. Benton, Springfield, MO 65802.

SCBWI "WRITING FOR CHILDREN" WORKSHOP—Springfield, MO. October. Write Sandy Asher, Dir., Drury College, 900 N. Benton Ave., Springfield, MO 65802.

MONTANA

ENVIRONMENTAL WRITING INSTITUTE—Corvallis, MT. May. Write Richard Nelson, Dir., Environmental Studies Program, Univ. of Montana, Missoula, MT 59812.

SAGEBRUSH WRITERS NOVELS & ESSAYS WORKSHOP—Big Timber, MT. May 16–18. Write Gwen Petersen, Dir., Sagebrush Writers, Box 1255, Big Timber, MT 59011.

YELLOW BAY WRITERS' WORKSHOP—Flathead Lake, MT. August 10–16. Write Annick Smith, Dir., Ctr. for Cont. Education, Univ. of Montana, Missoula, MT 59812.

NEVADA

READING AND WRITING THE WEST—Reno, NV. July 13–25. Write Stephen Tchudi, Dir., Dept. of English, (098) Univ. of Nevada, Reno, NV 89557–0031.

NEW HAMPSHIRE

SCBWI NEW ENGLAND CONFERENCE—Manchester, NH. April 12. Write Jennifer A. Ericsson, Dir., 58 Knox Rd., Bow, NH 03304.

19TH ANNUAL FESTIVAL OF POETRY—Franconia, NH. July 27-August 2. Write Donald Sheehan, Dir., The Frost Place, Box 74, Franconia, NH 03580.

WHITE PINES CONFERENCE FOR CHILDREN'S BOOKWRITERS—Chester, NH. August 3–9. Write V.A. Levine, Dir., Childworks, 26 So. Main St., Concord, NH 03301.

SEACOAST WRITERS ASSOCIATION CONFERENCE—Chester, NH. October. Write Paula Flanders, Dir., Seacoast Writers Assoc., P.O. Box 6553, Portsmouth, NH 03802–6553.

NEW JERSEY

TRENTON STATE COLLEGE WRITERS CONFERENCE—Trenton, NJ. April. Write Jean Hollander, Dir., Writers Conference, English Dept., Hillwood Lakes CN 4700, Trenton, NJ 08650–4700.

NEW MEXICO

TAOS SCHOOL OF WRITING—Taos Ski Valley, NM. July. Write Norman Zollinger, Dir., P.O. Box 20496, Albuquerque, NM 87154.

SOUTHWEST WRITERS WORKSHOP 15TH ANNUAL CONFERENCE—Albuquerque, NM. August 15–17. Write Kris Conover, Dir., Southwest Writers Workshop, 1338-B Wyoming Blvd. N.E., Albuquerque, NM 87112.

NEW YORK

MEET THE AGENTS & BIG APPLE WRITING WORKSHOPS—New York, NY. April 19–20. Write Hannelore Hahn, Dir., International Women's Writing Guild, P.O. Box 810, Gracie Station, New York, NY 10028.

HOFSTRA UNIVERSITY CHILDREN'S LITERATURE CONFERENCE—Hempstead, NY. April 26. Write Lewis Shena, Dir., UCCE (Liberal Arts), 375 Hofstra Univ., Hempstead, NY 11550–1009.

PUBLISH AND PROSPER: ASJA ANNUAL WRITER'S CONFERENCE—New York, NY. May 3–4. Write Alexandra Cantor Owens, Dir., ASJA, 1501 Broadway, Suite 302, New York, NY 10036.

BUFFCON—Buffalo, NY. June. Write Douglas Anderson, Dir., Medaille College, Agassiz Circle, Buffalo, NY 14214.

CATSKILL POETRY WORKSHOP—Oneonta, NY. June-July. Write Carol Frost, Dir., Special Programs Office, Hartwick College, Oneonta, NY 13820.

VASSAR COLLEGE INSTITUTE OF PUBLISHING AND WRITING: CHILDREN'S BOOKS IN THE MARKETPLACE—Poughkeepsie, NY. June 15–20. Write Maryann Bruno, Assoc. Dir., Vassar College, Box 300, 124 Raymond Ave., Poughkeepsie, NY 12601.

THE WRITERS' CENTER AT CHAUTAUQUA—Chautauqua, NY. June 21-August 24. Write Mary Jean Irion, 149 Kready Ave., Millersville, PA 17551.

MANHATTANVILLE'S WRITERS' WEEK—Purchase, NY. June 23–27. Write Dean Ruth Dowd, RSCJ, Manhattanville College, 2900 Purchase St., Purchase, NY 10577.

HIGHLIGHTS FOUNDATION WRITERS WORKSHOP—Chautauqua, NY. July. Write Jan Keen, Dir., Highlights Foundation, 814 Court St., Honesdale, PA 18431.

ROBERT QUACKENBUSH'S CHILDREN'S BOOK WRITING AND ILLUSTRATING WORKSHOPS—New York, NY. July 7–11. Write Robert

Quackenbush, Dir., Quackenbush Studios, 460 E. 79th St., New York, NY 10021–1445.

HOFSTRA UNIVERSITY SUMMER WRITERS' CONFERENCE— Hempstead, NY. July 7–18. Write Lewis Shena, Dir., UCCE (Liberal Arts), 375 Hofstra Univ., Hempstead, NY 11550–1009.

NORTH CAROLINA

DUKE UNIVERSITY WRITERS' WORKSHOP—Durham, NC. June. Write Georgann Eubanks, Dir., Box 90700, Durham, NC 27708.

THE ASHEVILLE POETRY FESTIVAL—Asheville, NC. July 11–13. Write Allan Wolf, Dir., P.O. Box 9643, Asheville, NC 28815.

OHIO

SELF-PUBLISHING YOUR OWN BOOK—Kirtland, OH. February 13, May 14, July 14, October 19. Write Lea Leever Oldham, Dir., 34200 Ridge Rd., #110, Willoughby, OH 44094.

WRITING FOR MONEY—Kirtland, OH. February 22, April 19, July 26, September 27; Mayfield, OH. March 8, May 17, October 18. Write Lea Leever Oldham, Dir., 34200 Ridge Rd., #110, Willoughby, OH 44094.

6TH ANNUAL WESTERN RESERVE WRITERS MINI CONFERENCE— Kirtland, OH. April 5. Write Lea Leever Oldham, Dir., 34200 Ridge Rd., #110, Willoughby, OH 44094.

THE HEIGHTS WRITER'S CONFERENCE—Beachwood, OH. May 3. Write Lavern Hall, Dir., Writer's World Press, P.O. Box 24684, Cleveland, OH 44124–0684.

READERS AND WRITERS HOLIDAY—Columbus, OH. May 3. Write Central Ohio Fiction Writers, Box 292106, Columbus, OH 43229.

IMAGINATION—Cleveland, OH. July. Write Neal Chandler, Dir., English Dept., Cleveland State Univ., Cleveland, OH 44115.

ANTIOCH WRITERS' WORKSHOP—Yellow Springs, OH. July 19–26. Write Gilah Rittenhouse, Dir., Antioch Writers' Workshop, P.O. Box 494, Yellow Springs, OH 45387.

SKYLINE WRITERS CONFERENCE—North Royalton, OH. August. Write Mildred Claus, Dir., Skyline Writers Club, P.O. Box 33343, North Royalton, OH 44133.

14TH ANNUAL WESTERN RESERVE WRITERS & FREELANCE CONFERENCE—Kirtland, OH. September 6. Write Lea Leever Oldham, Dir., 34200 Ridge Rd., #110, Willoughby, OH 44094.

THE COLUMBUS WRITERS CONFERENCE—Columbus, OH. September 27. Write Angela Palazzolo, Dir., The Columbus Writers Conference, P.O. Box 20548, Columbus, OH 43220.

MIDWEST WRITERS' CONFERENCE—Canton, OH. October. Write Debbie Ruhe, Dir., Midwest Writers' Conference, Kent State Univ. Stark Campus, 6000 Frank Ave. N.W., Canton, OH 44720.

OKLAHOMA

OPPORTUNITY '97 WRITERS AND ARTISTS WORKSHOPS—Norman, OK. March 23. Write Betty Culpepper, Dir., 734 Westridge Terrace, Norman, OK 73069.

NORTHWEST OKLAHOMA WRITER'S WORKSHOP—Enid, OK. Spring. Write Dr. Earl Mabry, Dir., P.O. Box 1308, Enid, OK 73702.

THE OKLAHOMA FALL ARTS INSTITUTE'S WRITING WORKSHOP—Lone Wolf, OK. October. Write Mary Gordon Taft, Dir., Oklahoma Arts Institute, P.O. Box 18154, Oklahoma City, OK 73154.

OREGON

FISHTRAP GATHERING: WINTER & SUMMER—Wallowa Lake, OR. February, July. Write Rich Wandschneider, Dir., Fishtrap Inc., P.O. Box 38, Enterprise, OR 97828.

HAYSTACK WRITING PROGRAM—Cannon Beach, OR. June 1-August 9. Write Maggie Herrington, Dir., P.S.U. Extended & Summer Programs, P.O. Box 1491, Portland, OR 97207.

THE FLIGHT OF THE MIND—McKenzie Bridge, OR. June 13–20 & 22–29. SASE Judith Barrington, Dir., Flight of the Mind, 622 S.E. 29th Ave., Portland, OR 97214.

PENNSYLVANIA

PENNWRITER ANNUAL CONFERENCE—Pittsburgh, PA. May. Write C.J. Houghtaling, Dir., R.R. 2, Box 241, Middlebury Center, PA 16935.

PHILADELPHIA WRITER'S CONFERENCE—Philadelphia, PA. June. Write Jim McGowan, Dir., 107 Lincoln Dr., West, Ambler, PA 19002.

ST. DAVID'S CHRISTIAN WRITERS CONFERENCE—Beaver Falls, PA. June 15–20. Write Audrey Stallsmith, Registrar, 87 Pines Road East, Hadley, PA 16130.

MONTROSE CHRISTIAN WRITERS' CONFERENCE—Montrose, PA. July 7–11. Write Jill Meyers, Dir., Montrose Bible Conference, 5 Locust St., Montrose, PA 18801.

LIGONIER VALLEY WRITERS CONFERENCE—Ligonier, PA. July 11–13. Write Kay Myers, Box G, Ligonier, PA, 15658.

MID-ATLANTIC MYSTERY BOOK FAIR & CONVENTION—Philadelphia, PA. October 3–5. Write Deen Kogan, Dir., 507 S. 8th St., Philadelphia, PA 19147.

RHODE ISLAND

NEWPORT WRITERS CONFERENCE—Newport, RI. Fall. Write Eleyne Austen Sharp, Dir., Community Writers Assoc., P.O. Box 12, Newport, RI 02840.

SOUTH CAROLINA

SOUTH CAROLINA CHRISTIAN WRITERS CONFERENCE—Conestee, SC. September 20. Write Betty Robertson, Dir., P.O. Box 12624, Roanoke, VA 24027.

TENNESSEE

RHODES WRITING CAMP—Memphis, TN. June. Write Dr. Beth Kamhi, Dir., Dept. of English, Rhodes College, 2000 North Pkwy., Memphis, TN 38112.

SEWANEE WRITERS' CONFERENCE—Sewanee, TN. July 15–27. Write Wyatt Prunty, Dir., 310 St. Luke's Hall, 735 University Ave., Sewanee, TN 37383–1000.

AMERICAN CHRISTIAN WRITERS CONFERENCE—Nashville, TN. August 29-September 1. Write Reg A. Forder, Dir., American Christian Writers, P.O. Box 110390, Nashville, TN 37222.

TEXAS

AUSTIN WRITERS' LEAGUE SPRING & FALL CONFERENCES—Austin, TX. Ongoing. Write Angela Smith, Dir., Austin Writers' League, 1501 W. 5th St., Suite E-2, Austin, TX 78703.

AUSTIN WRITERS' LEAGUE FICTION & NONFICTION WORKSHOPS—Austin, TX. April. November. Write Angela Smith, Dir., Austin Writers' League, 1501 W. 5th St., Suite. E-2, Austin, TX 78703.

AGENTS! AGENTS! AGENTS!—Austin, TX. April. November. Write Angela Smith, Dir., Austin Writers' League, 1501 W. 5th St., Suite E-2, Austin, TX 78703.

AMERICAN CHRISTIAN WRITERS CONFERENCE—Dallas, TX. May 16–17. Write Reg Forder, Dir., American Christian Writers, P.O. Box 110390, Nashville, TN 37222.

CRAFT OF WRITING CONFERENCE—Richardson, TX. September 19–20. Write Janet Harris, Dir., Univ. of Texas, P.O. Box 830688, MS CN1.1, Richardson, TX 75083–0688.

UTAH

WRITERS AT WORK—Park City, UT. July 13–18. Write Dawn Marano, Dir., Writers at Work, P.O. Box 1146, Centerville, UT 84014–5146.

VERMONT

THE OLDERS' CHILDREN'S WRITING WORKSHOP—Albany, VT. Summer & Fall. Write Effin & Jules Older, Dirs., Box 163, Albany, VT 05820.

DOROTHY CANFIELD FISHER CONFERENCE—Burlington, VT. June 27–29. Write Kitty Werner, Dir., P.O. Box 1058, Waitsfield, VT 05673–1058.

BENNINGTON SUMMER WRITING WORKSHOPS—Bennington, VT. June 29-July 12 & July 13–26. Write Liam Rector, Dir., Bennington Summer Workshops, Bennington College, Bennington, VT 05201.

NEW ENGLAND WRITERS CONFERENCE—Windsor, VT. July 26. Write Frank & Susan Anthony, Dirs., Box 483, Windsor, VT 05089.

BREAD LOAF WRITERS' CONFERENCE—Ripton, VT. August 12–24. Write Michael Collier, Dir., Bread Loaf Writers' Conference, Middlebury College, Middlebury, VT 05753.

VIRGINIA

SHENANDOAH VALLEY WRITERS' GUILD—Middletown, VA. Spring. Write Prof. F.H. Cogan, Dir., Lord Fairfax Community College, P.O. Box 47, Middletown, VA 22645.

NORTHERN VIRGINIA CHRISTIAN WRITERS ANNUAL CONFERENCE—Fairfax, VA. March 15. Write Jennifer Ferranti, Dir., Nova Christian Writers Fellowship, P.O. Box 629, Dunn Loring, VA 22027.

CHRISTOPHER NEWPORT UNIVERSITY WRITERS' CONFERENCE—Newport News, VA. April 4–5. Write Terry Cox-Joseph, Dir., Office of Cont. Education, Christopher Newport Univ., 50 Shoe Ln., Newport News, VA 23606.

VIRGINIA CHRISTIAN WRITERS CONFERENCE—Roanoke, VA. April 12. Send SASE to Betty Robertson, CCM Publishing, Box 12624, Roanoke, VA 24027.

20TH HIGHLAND SUMMER CONFERENCE—Radford, VA. June. Write Joann Asbury, Assoc., HSC, Appalachian Regional Studies Ctr., P.O. Box 7014, Radford Univ., Radford, VA 24142.

HURSTON/WRIGHT WRITERS WEEK AT U.C.U.—Richmond, VA. July 20–27. Write Michele Bowen-Spencer, English Dept., P.O. Box 842005, Virginia Commonwealth Univ., Richmond, VA 23284.

SHENANDOAH INTERNATIONAL PLAYWRIGHTS RETREAT—Staunton, VA. August. Write Robert Graham Small, Dir., Pennyroyal Farm, Rt. 5, Box 167F, Staunton, VA 24401.

WASHINGTON

WRITERS INFORMATION NETWORK: THE PROFESSIONAL ASSOCIATION FOR CHRISTIAN WRITERS—Seattle WA. January, April, September, November. Write Elaine Wright Colvin, Dir., W. I. N., P.O. Box 11337, Bainbridge Island, WA 98110.

WRITER'S WEEKEND AT THE BEACH—Ocean Park, WA. February 21–23. Write Pat Rushford, Co-Dir., P.O. Box 877, Ocean Park, WA 98640.

AMERICAN CHRISTIAN WRITERS CONFERENCE—Seattle, WA. April 4–5. Write Reg Forder, Dir., American Christian Writers, P.O. Box 110390, Nashville, TN 37222.

CLARION WEST SCIENCE FICTION & FANTASY WRITERS WORKSHOP—Seattle, WA. June 15-July 25. Write Leslie Howle, Dir., 340 15th Ave. E., Suite 350, Seattle, WA 98112.

PACIFIC NORTHWEST WRITERS CONFERENCE—Seattle, WA. July. Write Judy Bodmer, Dir., PNWC, 2033 6th Ave., #804, Seattle, WA 98121–2546.

PORT TOWNSEND WRITERS' CONFERENCE—Port Townsend, WA. July 10–20. Write Carol Jane Bangs, Dir., Centrum, Box 1158, Port Townsend, WA 98368.

WISCONSIN

THE WRITE TOUCH X—Oconomowoc, WI. May 17–18. Write Sharon Antoniewicz, Dir., Wisconsin Romance Writers, 15417 W. National Ave., Suite 200, New Berlin, WI 53151.

GREEN LAKE WRITERS CONFERENCE—Green Lake, WI. July 5–12. Write Jan DeWitt, Dir., Green Lake Conference Ctr., W2511 State Hwy. 23, Green Lake, WI 54941–9300.

SCBWI-WISCONSIN 6TH ANNUAL FALL RETREAT—Madison, WI. October 4–6. Send SASE to Patricia Curtis Pfitsch, Dir., Rt. 1, Box 137, Gays Mills, WI 54631.

WYOMING

THE 6TH JACKSON HOLE WRITERS CONFERENCE—Jackson, WY. July 4–7. Write Susan Powel, Dir., Attn: Conferences, P.O. Box 3972, Univ. Station, Laramie, WY 82071.

INTERNATIONAL

BERMUDA NATURE & SCIENCE WRITING—Biological Station, Bermuda. March-April. Write Bill Sargent, Dir., 7 Lawnwood Pl., Charlestown, MA 02129–3031.

VANCOUVER SUMMER PUBLISHING INTENSIVES—Vancouver, B.C. July. Write Ann Cowan, Dir., Simon Fraser Univ. at Harbor Centre, 515 West Hastings St., Vancouver, B.C., V6B 5K3, Canada.

HOLLYWOOD NORTH FILM & TELEVISION CONFERENCE—Charlottetown, P.E.I. July 25–27. Write Evie Davidson, Coord., H.N.F.T.C., Canadian Screen Writers Alliance, 24 Watts Ave., West Royalty Ind. Park, Charlottetown, P.E.I., C1E 1B0, Canada.

VICTORIA SCHOOL OF WRITING—Victoria, B.C. July. Write Victoria School of Writing, c/o Write Away!, 607 Linden Ave., Victoria, B.C., V8V 4G6, Canada.

PRAGUE SUMMER WRITERS WORKSHOP—Prague, Czech Republic. July. Write Trevor Top, Dir., Univ. of New Orleans, Box 1171, New Orleans, LA 70148.

POETRY WORKSHOP—Galway, Ireland. July. Write Billy Collins, Dir., Dept. of English, Lehman College, Bronx, NY 10468.

CHRISTIAN WRITERS HOLY LAND TOUR—Israel. January 21–30. Write Reg Forder, Dir., American Christian Writers, P.O. Box 110390, Nashville, TN 37222.

LATIN AMERICA WRITERS' GROUP—Taxco, Mexico. Write Trevor Top, Dir., Univ. of New Orleans, Box 1171, New Orleans, LA 70148.

STATE ARTS COUNCILS

State arts councils sponsor grants, fellowships, and other programs for writers. To be eligible for funding, a writer *must* be a resident of the state in which he is applying. Write or call for more information; 1–800 numbers are toll free for in-state calls only; numbers preceded by TDD indicate Telecommunications Device for the Deaf; TTY indicates Teletypewriter.

ALABAMA STATE COUNCIL ON THE ARTS
One Dexter Ave.
Montgomery, AL 36130
(334) 242–4076; fax: (334) 240–3269
Albert B. Head, *Executive Director*

ALASKA STATE COUNCIL ON THE ARTS
411 W. 4th Ave., Suite 1E
Anchorage, AK 99501–2343
(907) 269–6610; fax: (907) 269–6601
Shannon Planchon, *Grants Officer*
Nancy Pearson, *Contact Person*

ARIZONA COMMISSION ON THE ARTS
417 W. Roosevelt
Phoenix, AZ 85003
(602) 255–5882; fax: (602) 256–0282
Attn: Presenting/Touring/Literature Director

ARKANSAS ARTS COUNCIL
1500 Tower Bldg.
323 Center St.
Little Rock, AR 72201
(501) 324–9766; fax: (501) 324–9154
James E. Mitchell, *Executive Director*

CALIFORNIA ARTS COUNCIL
1300 I St., Suite 930
Sacramento, CA 95814
(916) 322–6555; fax: (916) 322–6575; TDD: (916) 322–6569
Gay Carroll, *Public Information Officer*

COLORADO COUNCIL ON THE ARTS
750 Pennsylvania St.
Denver, CO 80203–3699
(303) 894–2617; fax: (303) 894–2615
Fran Holden, *Executive Director*

CONNECTICUT COMMISSION ON THE ARTS
1 Financial Plaza
Hartford, CT 06103
(860) 566–4770; fax: (860) 566–6462
John Ostrout, *Executive Director*

DELAWARE DIVISION OF THE ARTS
Carvel State Bldg.
820 N. French St.
Wilmington, DE 19801
(302) 577–3540; fax: (302) 577–6561
Barbara King, *Artist Services Coordinator*

FLORIDA ARTS COUNCIL
Dept. of State
Div. of Cultural Affairs
The Capitol
Tallahassee, FL 32399–0250
(904) 487–2980; fax: (904) 922–5259; TTY: (904) 488–5779
Attn: Ms. Peyton Fearington

GEORGIA COUNCIL FOR THE ARTS
530 Means St. N.W., Suite 115
Atlanta, GA 30318
(404) 651–7920; fax: (404) 651–7922
Caroline Ballard Leake, *Executive Director*
Ann R. Davis, *Grants Manager, Literature*

HAWAII STATE FOUNDATION ON CULTURE AND THE ARTS
44 Merchant St.
Honolulu, HI 96813
(808) 586–0300; fax: (808) 586–0308
Wendell P.K. Silva, *Executive Director*

IDAHO COMMISSION ON THE ARTS
Box 83720
Boise, ID 83720–0008
(208) 334–2119; fax (208) 334–2488
Attn: Diane Josephy Peavey

ILLINOIS ARTS COUNCIL
James R. Thompson Center
100 W. Randolph, Suite 10–500
Chicago, IL 60601
(312) 814–4990; (800) 237–6994; fax: (312) 814–1471
Richard Gage, *Director of Communication Arts*

INDIANA ARTS COMMISSION
402 W. Washington St., Rm. 072
Indianapolis, IN 46204–2741
(317) 232–1268; TDD: (317) 233–3001; fax: (317) 232–5595
Dorothy Ilgen, *Executive Director*

INSTITUTE OF PUERTO RICAN CULTURE
P.O. Box 4184
San Juan, PR 00902–4184
Luis E. Diaz Hernandez, *Executive Director*

IOWA ARTS COUNCIL
600 E. Locust
Des Moines, IA 50319–0290
(515) 281–4006; fax: (515) 242–6498
Attn: Bruce Williams

KANSAS ARTS COMMISSION
Jayhawk Tower
700 S.W. Jackson, Suite 1004
Topeka, KS 66603–3758
(913) 296–3335; fax: (913) 296–4989; TTY: (800) 766–3777
Robert T. Burtch, *Editor*

KENTUCKY ARTS COUNCIL
31 Fountain Pl.
Frankfort, KY 40601
(502) 564–3757; fax: (502) 564–2839; TDD: (502) 564–3757
Attn: *Executive Director*

LOUISIANA STATE ARTS COUNCIL
Box 44247
Baton Rouge, LA 70804
(504) 342–8180; fax: (504) 342–8173
James Borders, *Executive Director*

MAINE ARTS COMMISSION
25 State House Station
Augusta, ME 04333–0025
(207) 287–2724; fax: (207) 287–2335; TDD: (207) 287–6740
Alden C. Wilson, *Director*

MARYLAND STATE ARTS COUNCIL
Artists-in-Education
601 N. Howard St.
Baltimore, MD 21201
(410) 333–8232; fax: (410) 333–1062
Linda Vlasak, *Program Director*
Pamela Dunne, *AIE Program Assistant*

MASSACHUSETTS CULTURAL COUNCIL
120 Boylston St., 2nd Floor
Boston, MA 02116–4802
(617) 727–3668; (800) 232–0960; TTY: (617) 338–9153
Attn: Robert Ayres

MICHIGAN COUNCIL FOR ARTS AND CULTURAL AFFAIRS
1200 Sixth St., Suite 1180
Detroit, MI 48226–2461
(313) 256–3731; fax: (313) 256–3781
Betty Boone, *Executive Director*

MINNESOTA STATE ARTS BOARD
Park Square Court
400 Sibley St., Suite 200
St. Paul, MN 55101–1949
(612) 215–1600; (800) 8MN-ARTS; fax: (612) 215–1602
Karen Mueller, *Artist Assistance Program Associate*

847

COMPAS: WRITERS & ARTISTS IN THE SCHOOLS
304 Landmark Center
75 W. Fifth St.
St. Paul, MN 55102
(612) 292–3254; fax: (612) 292–3258
Daniel Gabriel, *Director*

MISSISSIPPI ARTS COMMISSION
239 N. Lamar St., Suite 207
Jackson, MS 39201
(601) 359–6030; fax: (601) 359–6008
Betsy Bradley, *Executive Director*

MISSOURI ARTS COUNCIL
Wainwright Office Complex
111 N. 7th St., Suite 105
St. Louis, MO 63101–2188
(314) 340–6845; fax: (314) 340–7215
Michael Hunt, *Program Administrator for Literature*

MONTANA ARTS COUNCIL
316 N. Park Ave., Suite 252
Helena, MT 59620–2201
(406) 444–6430; fax: (406) 444–6548
Fran Morrow, *Director of Artists Services*

NEBRASKA ARTS COUNCIL
3838 Davenport St.
Omaha, NE 68131–2329
(402) 595–2122; fax: (402) 595–2334
Jennifer Severin, *Executive Director*

NEVADA STATE COUNCIL ON THE ARTS
Capitol Complex
602 N. Curry St.
Carson City, NV 89710
(702) 687–6680; fax: (702) 687–6688
Susan Boskoff, *Executive Director*

NEW HAMPSHIRE STATE COUNCIL ON THE ARTS
Phenix Hall
40 N. Main St.
Concord, NH 03301–4974
(603) 271–2789; fax: (603) 271–3584; TDD: (800) 735–2964
Audrey Sylvester, *Artist Services Coordinator*

NEW JERSEY STATE COUNCIL ON THE ARTS
Grants Office, Artist Support & Services
CN 306
Trenton, NJ 08625
(609) 292–6130; fax: (609) 989–1440
S. Runk, *Grants Coordinator*

848

NEW MEXICO ARTS DIVISION
228 E. Palace Ave.
Santa Fe, NM 87501
(505) 827–6490; fax: (505) 827–6043
Randy Forrester, *Local Arts Coordinator*

NEW YORK STATE COUNCIL ON THE ARTS
915 Broadway
New York, NY 10010
(212) 387–7028; fax: (212) 387–7164
Kathleen Masterson, *Director, Literature Program*

NORTH CAROLINA ARTS COUNCIL
Dept. of Cultural Resources
Raleigh, NC 27601–2807
(919) 733–2111 ext. 22; fax: (919) 733–4834; e-mail:
dmcgill@ncacmail.dcr.state.nc.us
Deborah McGill, *Literature Director*

NORTH DAKOTA COUNCIL ON THE ARTS
418 E. Broadway, Suite 70
Bismarck, ND 58501–4086
(701) 328–3954; fax: (701) 328–3963
Patsy Thompson, *Executive Director*

OHIO ARTS COUNCIL
727 E. Main St.
Columbus, OH 43205–1796
(614) 466–2613; fax: (614) 466–4494
Bob Fox, *Literature Program Coordinator*

OKLAHOMA ARTS COUNCIL
P.O. Box 52001–2001
Oklahoma City, OK 73152–2001
(405) 521–2931; fax: (405) 521–6418
Betty Price, *Executive Director*

OREGON ARTS COMMISSION
775 Summer St. N.E.
Salem, OR 97310
(503) 986–0084; fax: (503) 986–0260; e-mail: billflood@state.or.us;
internet: http://www.das.state.or.us/oac/
Attn: Bill Flood

PENNSYLVANIA COUNCIL ON THE ARTS
Room 216, Finance Bldg.
Harrisburg, PA 17120
(717) 787–6883; fax (717) 783–2538
Amy Gabriel, *Literature Program*
Diane SidenerYoung, Ph.D., *Artists-in-Education Program*

RHODE ISLAND STATE COUNCIL ON THE ARTS
95 Cedar St., Suite 103
Providence, RI 02903
(401) 277–3880; fax: (401) 521–1351
Randall Rosenbaum, *Executive Director*

849

SOUTH CAROLINA ARTS COMMISSION
1800 Gervais St.
Columbia, SC 29201
(803) 734–8696; fax: (803) 734–8526
Steven Lewis, *Director, Literary Arts Program*

SOUTH DAKOTA ARTS COUNCIL
800 Governors Dr.
Pierre, SD 57501–2294
(605) 773–3131; fax: (605) 773–6962
Attn: Dennis Holub, *Executive Director*

TENNESSEE ARTS COMMISSION
404 James Robertson Pkwy., Suite 160
Nashville, TN 37243–0780
(615) 741–1701; fax: (615) 741–8559; e-mail: aswanson@mail.state.tn.us
Attn: Alice Swanson

TEXAS COMMISSION ON THE ARTS
P.O. Box 13406
Austin, TX 78711–3406
(512) 463–5535; fax: (512) 475–2699

UTAH ARTS COUNCIL
617 E. South Temple
Salt Lake City, UT 84102–1177
(801) 533–5895; fax: (801) 533–6196
Guy Lebeda, *Literary Coordinator*

VERMONT ARTS COUNCIL
136 State St., Drawer 33
Montpelier, VT 05633–6001
(802) 828–3291; fax: (802) 828–3363
Anne Sarcka *Grants Officer*

VIRGINIA COMMISSION FOR THE ARTS
223 Governor St.
Richmond, VA 23219
(804) 225–3132; fax: (804) 225–4327
Peggy J. Baggett, *Executive Director*

WASHINGTON STATE ARTS COMMISSION
234 E. 8th Ave.
P.O. Box 42675
Olympia, WA 98504–2675
(206) 753–3860
Bitsy Bidwell, *Community Arts Development Manager*

WEST VIRGINIA DEPT. OF EDUCATION AND THE ARTS
Culture and History Division
The Cultural Center, Capitol Complex
1900 Kanawha Blvd. E.
Charleston, WV 25305
(304) 558–0220
Lakin Ray Cook, *Executive Director*

850

WISCONSIN ARTS BOARD
101 E. Wilson St., 1st Floor
Madison, WI 53702
(608) 266–0190; fax: (608) 267–0380
Dean Amhaus, *Executive Director*

WYOMING ARTS COUNCIL
2320 Capitol Ave.
Cheyenne, WY 82002
(307) 777–7742; fax: (307) 777–5499
Michael Shay, *Literature Program Manager*

ORGANIZATIONS FOR WRITERS

ACADEMY OF AMERICAN POETS
584 Broadway, Suite 1208
New York, NY 10012
(212) 274–0343; fax: (212) 274–9427
Jonathan Galassi, *President*
      The Academy was founded in 1934 to support American poets at all stages of their careers and to foster the appreciation of contemporary poetry. The largest organization in the country dedicated specifically to the art of poetry, the academy sponsors a number of prizes and programs: an annual fellowship for distinguished poetic achievement; the Tanning prize, the largest annual literary award in the U.S.; the Lenore Marshall Poetry Prize; the James Laughlin Award; the Walt Whitman Award; the Harold Morton Landon Translation Award; poetry prizes at colleges and universities; and the American Poets Fund and the Atlas Fund, which provide financial assistance to poets and publishers of poetry. Readings, lectures, and regional symposiums take place in New York City and throughout the United States. Membership is open to all. Annual dues: $25 and up.

AMERICAN CRIME WRITERS LEAGUE
455 Crescent Ave.
Buffalo, NY 14214
e-mail: dougand@aol.com
Joan Hess, *President*
Douglas Anderson, *Membership Chair*
      A national organization of working professional mystery authors. To be eligible for membership in ACWL you must have published at least one of the following: one full-length work of crime fiction or nonfiction; three short stories; or three nonfiction crime articles. The bimonthly

851

ACWL BULLETin features articles by reliable experts and an exchange of information and advice among professional writers. Annual dues: $35.

AMERICAN SOCIETY OF JOURNALISTS AND AUTHORS, INC.
1501 Broadway, Suite 302
New York, NY 10036
(212) 997–0947
Alexandra Owens, *Executive Director*
   A nationwide organization of independent writers of nonfiction dedicated to promoting high standards of nonfiction writing through monthly meetings, annual writers' conferences, etc. The ASJA offers extensive benefits and services including referral services, numerous discount services, and the opportunity to explore professional issues and concerns with other writers. Members also receive a monthly newsletter with confidential market information. Membership is open to professional freelance writers of nonfiction; qualifications are judged by the membership committee. Call or write for application details.

THE ASSOCIATED WRITING PROGRAMS
Tallwood House, Mail Stop 1E3
George Mason University
Fairfax, VA 22030
(703) 993–4301; fax: (703) 993–4302
Attn: *Membership*
   The AWP seeks to serve writers and teachers in need of community, support, information, inspiration, contacts, and ideas. Provides publishing opportunities, job listings, and an active exchange of ideas on writing and teaching, including an annual conference. Members receive six issues of *AWP Chronicle* and eight issues of *AWP Job List*. Publications include *The AWP Official Guide to Creative Writing Programs*. Annual dues: $50, *individual*; $30, *student*.

THE AUTHORS GUILD, INC.
330 W. 42nd St., 29th Fl.
New York, NY 10036–6902
(212) 563–5904; fax: (212) 564–5363; e-mail: Authors@pipeline.com
Attn: *Membership Committee*
   As the largest organization of published writers in America, membership offers writers of all genres legal advice, reviews of publishing and agency contracts, and access to seminars and symposiums around the country on subjects of concern to authors. The Authors Guild also lobbies on behalf of all authors on issues such as copyright, taxation, and freedom of expression. A writer who has published a book in the last seven years with an established publisher, or has published three articles in periodicals of general circulation within the last eighteen months is eligible for active voting membership. An unpublished writer who has just received a contract offer may be eligible for associate membership. All members of the Authors Guild automatically become members of its parent organization, the Authors League of America. Annual dues: $90.

THE AUTHORS LEAGUE OF AMERICA, INC.
330 W. 42nd St.
New York, NY 10036–6902
(212) 564–8350; fax: (212) 564–5363; e-mail: Authors@pipeline.com
Attn: *Membership Committee*

A national organization representing over 14,000 authors and dramatists on matters of joint concern, such as copyright, taxes, and freedom of expression. Membership is restricted to authors and dramatists who are members of the Authors Guild and the Dramatists Guild. Matters such as contract terms and subsidiary rights are in the province of the two guilds.

BLACK THEATRE NETWORK
Box 11502
Fisher Bldg. Station
Detroit, MI 48211
(419) 372–2350
Lundeana Thomas, *President*

The Black Theatre Network is a national non-profit organization devoted to exposing all people to the beauty and complexity of black theater, and to preserving the art form for future generations. The BTN sponsors an annual national conference, the Randolph Edmonds Young Scholars Competition, and the Judy Ann Dearing Student Design Competition. Publications include the quarterly *BTNews*, *The Black Theatre Directory* (dissertations on Black Theatre), and *Black Voices*, a guide to plays by black authors. Annual dues: $25, *student & retiree*; $60, *individual*; $95, *organization*.

THE DRAMATISTS GUILD
234 W. 44th St.
New York, NY 10036–3909
(212) 398–9366
Peter Stone, *President*; Richard Garmise, *Executive Director*

The national professional association of playwrights, composers, and lyricists, the guild was established to protect dramatists' rights and to improve working conditions. Services include use of the guild's contracts; a toll-free number for members in need of business counseling; a discount ticket service; access to two health insurance programs and a group term life insurance plan; a reference library; and numerous seminars. Publications include *The Dramatists Guild Quarterly*, *The Dramatists Guild Resource Directory*, and *The Dramatists Guild Newsletter*. All playwrights, produced or not, are eligible for membership. Annual dues: $125, *active*; $75, *associate*; $35, *student*.

THE GENRE WRITER'S ASSOCIATION
P.O. Box 6301
Concord, CA 94524
(510) 254–7053
Bobbi Sinha-Morey, *Editor*

An international service organization, GWA is dedicated to the promotion of excellence in the fields of science fiction, fantasy, mystery, western, and horror writing. Members receive *The Genre Writer's News* plus market supplements, *Horror: The News Magazine of the Horror &*

853

Fantasy Field, a membership roster, and discounts on certain products. The association also sponsors awards. Membership is open to any writer, poet, artist, editor, publisher, or calligrapher who participates in these literary genres. Annual dues are $25 for US members; $30 for others.

INTERNATIONAL ASSOCIATION OF CRIME WRITERS
(NORTH AMERICAN BRANCH)
JAF Box 1500
New York, NY 10116
(212) 243–8966
J. Madison Davis, *President*

This international association was founded in 1987 to promote communications among crime writers worldwide, encourage translation of crime writing into other languages, and defend authors against censorship and other forms of tyranny. The IACW sponsors a number of conferences, publishes a quarterly newsletter, *Border Patrol,* and annually awards the Hammett prize for literary excellence in crime writing to a work of fiction by a US or Canadian author. Membership is open to published authors of crime fiction, nonfiction, and screenplays. Agents, editors, and booksellers in the mystery field are also eligible to apply. Annual dues: $50.

INTERNATIONAL ASSOCIATION OF THEATRE FOR CHILDREN
AND YOUNG PEOPLE
Box 22365
Seattle, WA 98122–0365
(206) 392–2147
Jen Marlowe, *Office Manager*

The development of professional theater for young audiences and international exchange are the organization's primary mandates. Provides a link between professional theaters, artists, directors, training institutions, and arts agencies; sponsors festivals and forums for interchange among theaters and theater artists. Annual dues: $50, *individual*; $25, *student and retiree.*

THE INTERNATIONAL WOMEN'S WRITING GUILD
Box 810, Gracie Station
New York, NY 10028–0082
(212) 737–7536; fax: (212) 737–9469; e-mail: http://www.iwwg.com
Hannelore Hahn, *Executive Director & Founder*

Founded in 1976, serving as a network for the personal and professional empowerment of women through writing. Services include six issues of a 32-page newsletter, a list of literary agents and publishing services, access to health insurance plans at group rates, access to writing conferences and related events throughout the U.S., including the annual "Remember the Magic" summer conference at Skidmore College in Saratoga Springs, NY, regional writing clusters, and year-round supportive networking. Any woman may join regardless of portfolio. Annual dues: $35; $45 *international.*

MIDWEST RADIO THEATRE WORKSHOP
KOPN
915 E. Broadway
Columbia, MO 65201
(314) 874–5676; fax: (314) 499–1662; e-mail: mrtw@mrtw.org
Debbie Karwoski, *Interim Director*

Founded in 1979, the MRTW is the only national resource for American radio dramatists, providing referrals, technical assistance, educational materials, and workshops. MRTW coordinates an annual national radio script contest, publishes an annual radio scriptbook, and distributes a script anthology with primer. Send SASE for more information.

MYSTERIES FOR MINORS—(See *Sisters in Crime*)

MYSTERY WRITERS OF AMERICA, INC.
17 E. 47th St., 6th Floor
New York, NY 10017
(212) 888–8171; fax: (212) 888–8107
Priscilla Ridgway, *Executive Director*
    The MWA exists for the purpose of raising the prestige of mystery and detective writing, and of defending the rights and increasing the income of all writers in the field of mystery, detection, and fact crime writing. Each year, the MWA presents the Edgar Allan Poe Awards for the best mystery writing in a variety of fields. The four classifications of membership are: *active*, open to any writer who has made a sale in the field of mystery, suspense, or crime writing; *associate*, for professionals in allied fields; *corresponding*, for writers living outside the U.S.; *affiliate*, for unpublished writers. Annual dues: $65; $32.50 *corresponding members*.

NATIONAL ASSOCIATION OF SCIENCE WRITERS, INC.
P.O. Box 294
Greenlawn, NY 11740
(516) 757–5664
Diane McGurgan, *Administrative Secretary*
    The NASW promotes the dissemination of accurate information regarding science through all media, and conducts a varied program to increase the flow of news from scientists, to improve the quality of its presentation, and to communicate its meaning to the reading public. Anyone who has been actively engaged in the dissemination of science information is eligible to apply for membership. Active members must be principally involved in reporting on science through newspapers, magazines, TV, or other media that reach the public directly. Associate members report on science through limited-circulation publications and other media. Annual dues: $60.

NATIONAL CONFERENCE OF EDITORIAL WRITERS
6223 Executive Blvd.
Rockville, MD 20852
(301) 984–3015
    A nonprofit professional organization established in 1947, NCEW exists to improve the quality of editorial pages and broadcast editorials, and to promote high standards among opinion writers and editors in North America. The association offers members networking opportunities, regional meetings, page exchanges, foreign tours, educational opportunities and seminars, an annual convention, and a subscription to the quarterly journal *The Masthead*. Membership is open to opinion writers and editors for general-circulation newspapers, radio or television stations, and syndicated columnists; teachers of journalism; and others who determine editorial policy. Annual dues are based on circulation or broadcast audience and range from $60 to $125.

THE NATIONAL LEAGUE OF AMERICAN PEN WOMEN, INC.
The Pen Arts Building
1300 17th St. N.W.
Washington, DC 20036–1973
(202) 785–1997
Elaine Waidelich, *National President*
Founded in 1897, the league promotes development of the creative talents of professional women in the arts. Membership is through local branches, available by invitation from current members in the categories of Art, Letters, and Music.

THE NATIONAL WRITERS ASSOCIATION
1450 S. Havana, Suite 424
Aurora, CO 80012
(303) 751–7844
Sandy Whelchel, *Executive Director*
New and established writers, poets, and playwrights throughout the U.S. and Canada may become members of the NWA, a full-time, customer-service-oriented association founded in 1937. Members receive a bimonthly newsletter, *Authorship*, and may attend the annual June conference. Annual dues: $60, *professional*; $50, *regular*; add $25 outside the U.S., Canada, and Mexico.

NATIONAL WRITERS UNION
113 University Place, 6th Fl.
New York, NY 10003
(212) 254–0279
Jonathan Tasini, *President*
Dedicated to bringing about equitable payment and fair treatment of free-lance writers through collective action. Membership is over 4,200 and includes book authors, poets, cartoonists, journalists, and technical writers in 14 chapters nationwide. The union offers its members contract and agent information, group health insurance, press credentials, grievance handling, a quarterly magazine, and sample contracts and resource materials. It sponsors workshops and seminars across the country. Membership is open to writers who have published a book, play, three articles, five poems, one short story or an equivalent amount of newsletter, publicity, technical, commercial, government, or institutional copy, or have written an equivalent amount of unpublished material and are actively seeking publication. Annual dues: $80 to $180.

NEW DRAMATISTS
424 W. 44th St.
New York, NY 10036
(212) 757–6960
Elana Greenfield, *Director of Artistic Programs*
New Dramatists is dedicated to finding gifted playwrights and giving them the time, space, and tools to develop their craft. Services include readings and workshops; a director-in-residence program; national script distribution for members; artist work spaces; international playwright exchange programs; script copying facilities; and a free ticket program. Membership is open to residents of New York City and the surrounding tri-state area. National memberships are offered to those outside the area

856

who can spend time in NYC in order to take advantage of programs. Apply between July 15 and September 15. No annual dues.

NORTHWEST PLAYWRIGHTS GUILD
Box 9218
Portland, OR 97207–9218
(503) 222–7010
Bill Johnson, *Office Manager*
The guild supports and promotes playwrights living in the Northwest through play development, staged readings, and networking for play competitions and production opportunities. Members receive monthly and quarterly newsletters. Annual dues: $25.

OUTDOOR WRITERS ASSOCIATION OF AMERICA, INC.
2017 Cato Ave., Suite 101
State College, PA 16801–2768
(814) 234–1011
James W. Rainey, *Executive Director*
A non-profit, international organization representing professional communicators who report and reflect upon America's diverse interests in the outdoors. Membership, by nomination only, includes a monthly publication, *Outdoors Unlimited*; annual conference; annual membership directory; contests. The association also provides scholarships to qualified students.

PEN AMERICAN CENTER
568 Broadway
New York, NY 10012
(212) 334–1660
Karen Kennerly, *Executive Director*
PEN American Center is one of more than 120 centers worldwide that compose International PEN. The 2,800 members of the American Center are poets, playwrights, essayists, editors, and novelists, as well as literary translators and those agents who have made a substantial contribution to the literary community. PEN American headquarters is in New York City, and branches are located in Boston, Chicago, New Orleans, Portland, Oregon, and San Francisco. Among the activities, programs, and services sponsored are literary events and awards, outreach projects to encourage reading, assistance to writers in financial need, and international and domestic human rights campaigns on behalf of many writers, editors, and journalists censored or imprisoned because of their writing. Membership is open to writers who have published two books of literary merit, as well as editors, agents, playwrights, and translators who meet specific standards; apply to membership committee.

THE PLAYWRIGHTS' CENTER
2301 Franklin Ave. E.
Minneapolis, MN 55406
(612) 332–7481
Carlo Cuesta, *Executive Director*
The Playwrights' Center fuels the contemporary theater by providing services that support the development and public appreciation of playwrights and playwriting. Members receive applications for all programs,

857

a calendar of events, eligibility to participate in special activities, including classes, outreach programs, and PlayLabs. For membership information, contact Lisa Stevens, Director of Communication and Membership. Annual dues: $35.

POETRY SOCIETY OF AMERICA
15 Gramercy Park
New York, NY 10003
(212) 254–9628; e-mail: http://www.poetrysociety.com
Elise Paschen, *Executive Director*
Founded in 1910, the PSA seeks to raise the awareness of poetry, to deepen the understanding of it, and to encourage more people to read, listen to, and write poetry. To this end, the PSA presents national series of readings including "Tributes in Libraries" and "Poetry in Public Places," mounts poetry posters on mass transit vehicles through "Poetry in Motion," and broadcasts an educational poetry series on cable television. The PSA also offers annual contests for poetry, seminars, poetry festivals, and publishes a newsletter. Annual dues: $40.

POETS AND WRITERS, INC.
72 Spring St.
New York, NY 10012
(212) 226–3586; fax: (212) 226–3963: internet: http://www.pw.org
Elliot Figman, *Executive Director*
Poets & Writers, Inc., was founded in 1970 to foster the development of poets and fiction writers and to promote communication throughout the literary community. A non-membership organization, it offers a nationwide information center for writers; *Poets & Writers Magazine* and other publications; as well as support for readings and workshops at a wide range of venues.

PUBLICATION RIGHTS CLEARINGHOUSE
National Writers Union/National Office West
337 17th St., Suite 101
Oakland, CA 94612
(510) 839–0110; fax: (510) 839–6097; e-mail: nwu@nwu.org
Irvin Muchnick, *Director*
Publication Rights Clearinghouse, the collective-licensing agency of the National Writers Union, was created in 1996 to help writers license and collect royalties for the reuse of their works in electronic databases and other new digital media. It is modeled after similar organizations that have long existed in the music industry. Enrollment is open to both NWU members and non-members. One-time enrollment fee is $20 for NWU members, or members of other writers' organizations that are associate sponsors of PRC; $40 for others.

ROMANCE WRITERS OF AMERICA
13700 Veterans Memorial Dr., Suite 315
Houston, TX 77014
(713) 440–6885; fax: (713) 440–7510
Allison Kelley, *Executive Manager*
An international organization with over 150 local chapters across the U.S., Canada, Europe, and Australia; membership is open to any writer,

published or unpublished, interested in the field of romantic fiction. Annual dues of $60, plus $10 application fee for new members; benefits include annual conference, contest, market information, and monthly newsmagazine, *Romance Writers' Report*.

SCIENCE-FICTION AND FANTASY WRITERS OF AMERICA, INC.
5 Winding Brook Dr., #1B
Guilderland, NY 12084
Peter Dennis Pautz, *Executive Secretary*

An organization whose purpose it is to foster and further the professional interests of science fiction and fantasy writers. Presents the annual Nebula Award for excellence in the field and publishes the *Bulletin* for its members (also available to non-members).

Any writer who has sold a work of science fiction or fantasy is eligible for membership. Annual dues: $50, *active* ; $35, *affiliate*; plus $10 installation fee; send for application and information.

SISTERS IN CRIME
P.O. Box 442124
Lawrence, KS 66044–8933
Elaine Raco Chase, *President*

Sisters in Crime was founded in 1986 to combat discrimination against women in the mystery field, educate publishers and the general public as to inequalities in the treatment of female authors, and raise the level of awareness of their contribution to the field. Membership is open to all and includes writers, readers, editors, agents, booksellers, and librarians. Publications include a quarterly newsletter and membership directory. Annual dues: $25, U.S.; $30, foreign. Members interested in mysteries for young readers may join Mysteries for Minors (Patricia Elmore, Chair, P.O. Box 442124, Lawrence, KS 66044–8933) with no additional dues.

SOCIETY FOR TECHNICAL COMMUNICATION
901 N. Stuart St., #904
Arlington, VA 22203–1854
(703) 522–4114
William C. Stolgitis, *Executive Director*

A professional organization dedicated to the advancement of the theory and practice of technical communication in all media. The 21,000 members in the U.S. and other countries include technical writers and editors, publishers, artists and draftsmen, researchers, educators, and audiovisual specialists. Annual dues: $95.

SOCIETY OF AMERICAN TRAVEL WRITERS
4101 Lake Boone Trail, Suite 201
Raleigh, NC 27607
(919) 787–5181
Michael S. Olson, CAE, *Executive Director*

The Society of American Travel Writers represents writers and other professionals who strive to provide travelers with accurate reports on destinations, facilities, and services. Membership is by invitation. Active membership is limited to salaried travel writers and free lancers who have a steady volume of published or distributed work about travel. Initiation fees: $200, *active*; $400, *associate*. Annual dues: $120, *active*; $240, *associate*.

SOCIETY OF CHILDREN'S BOOK WRITERS & ILLUSTRATORS
22736 Vanowen St., Suite 106
West Hills, CA 91307
(818) 888–8760
Lin Oliver, *Executive Director*

A national organization of authors, editors, publishers, illustrators, filmmakers, librarians, and educators, the SCBWI offers a variety of services to people who write, illustrate, or share an interest in children's literature. Full memberships are open to those who have had at least one children's book or story published. Associate memberships are open to all those with an interest in children's literature. Annual dues: $50.

SOCIETY OF ENVIRONMENTAL JOURNALISTS
P.O. Box 27280
Philadelphia, PA 19118
(215) 836–9970; fax: (215) 836–9972; e-mail: SEJOffice@aol.com
WWW: http://www.tribnet.com/environ/env—home.htm
Beth Parke, *Executive Director*

Dedicated to improving the quality, accuracy, and visibility of environmental reporting, the society serves 1,200 members with a quarterly newsletter, the *SEJournal*, national and regional conferences, computer online services on AOL, Compuserve, and the World Wide Web, and an annual directory. Annual dues: $35; $30, *student.*

SOCIETY OF PROFESSIONAL JOURNALISTS
16 S. Jackson St.
Greencastle, IN 46135–0077
(317) 653–3333
Greg Christopher, *Executive Director*

With 13,500 members and 300 chapters, the Society seeks to serve the interests of print, broadcast, and wire journalists. Services include legal counsel on journalism issues, jobs-for-journalists career search newsletter, professional development seminars, and awards that encourage journalism. Members receive *Quill*, a monthly magazine that explores current issues in the field. SPJ promotes ethics and freedom of information programs. Annual dues: $68, *professional*; $34, *student.*

THEATRE COMMUNICATIONS GROUP
355 Lexington Ave.
New York, NY 10017
(212) 697–5230
John Sullivan, *Executive Director*

TCG, a national organization for the American theater, provides services to facilitate the work of playwrights, literary managers, and other theater professionals and journalists. Publications include the quarterly bulletin *PlaySource*, which circulates information on new plays, translations, and adaptations to more than 300 TCG constituent theaters and to potential producers. Also publishes the annual *Dramatists Sourcebook* and a line of theater books including plays and translations. Individual members receive *American Theatre* Magazine. Annual dues: $35, *individual.*

860

WESTERN WRITERS OF AMERICA, INC.
1012 Fair St.
Franklin, TN 37064
(615) 791–1444
James A. Crutchfield, *Secretary/Treasurer*

Membership is open to qualified professional writers of fiction and nonfiction related to the history and literature of the American West. Its chief purpose is to promote a more widespread distribution, readership, and appreciation of the West and its literature. Holds annual convention in the last week of June. Sponsors annual Spur Awards, Owen Wister Award, and Medicine Pipe Bearer's Award for published work and produced screenplays. Annual dues: $60.

WRITERS GUILD OF AMERICA, EAST, INC.
555 W. 57th St.
New York, NY 10019
(212) 767–7800
Mona Mangan, *Executive Director*

WRITERS GUILD OF AMERICA, WEST, INC.
7000 W. 3rd St.
Los Angeles, CA 90048
(310) 550–1000
Brian Walton, *Executive Director*

The Writers Guild of America (East and West) represents writers in motion pictures, broadcast, cable and new media industries, including news and entertainment. In order to qualify for membership, a writer must fulfill current requirements for employment or sale of material in one of these fields.

The basic dues are $25 per quarter for both organizations. In addition, there are quarterly dues based on percentage of the member's earnings in any one of the fields over which the guild has jurisdiction. The initiation fee is $1,500 for WGAE, for writers living east of the Mississippi, and $2,500 for WGAW, for those living west of the Mississippi.

WRITERS INFORMATION NETWORK
P.O. Box 11337
Bainbridge Island, WA 98110
(206) 842–9103; fax: (206) 842–0536
Elaine Wright Colvin, *Director*

W.I.N. was founded in 1983 to provide a link between Christian writers and the religious publishing industry. Offered are a bimonthly newsletter, market news, editorial services, advocacy and grievance procedures, referral services, and conferences. Annual dues: $25; $35, *foreign.*

LITERARY AGENTS

As the number of book publishers that will consider only agented submissions grows, more writers are turning to agents to sell their manuscripts. The agents on the list that follows handle literary, and in some cases, dramatic material. Included in each listing are such important details as type of material represented, submission procedure, and commission. Since agents derive their income from the sales of their clients' work, they must represent writers who are selling fairly regularly to good markets. Nonetheless, many of the agents listed here note they will consider unpublished writers. Always query an agent first, and enclose a self-addressed, stamped envelope; most agents will not respond without it. Do not send any manuscripts until the agent has asked you to do so; and be wary of agents who charge fees for reading manuscripts. All of the following agents have indicated they do *not* charge reading fees, and those who pass on postage, phone, or photocopying fees to their clients have indicated such.

To learn more about agents and their role in publishing, the Association of Authors' Representatives, Inc., publishes a code of ethics as well as an up-to-date list of AAR members, available for $5 (check or money order) and a 55¢ legal-size SASE. Write to: Association of Authors' Representatives, Inc., 10 Astor Pl., 3rd Floor, New York, NY 10003.

Other lists of agents and their policies can be found in *Literary Market Place*, a directory found in most libraries, and in *Literary Agents of North America* (Author Aid/Research Associates International, 340 E. 52nd St., New York, NY 10022).

BRET ADAMS LTD.— 448 W. 44th St., New York, NY 10036. Attn: Bruce Ostler. Screenplays, teleplays, and stage plays. Unproduced writers considered. Query with synopsis, bio, resumé, and SASE. Commission: 10%. Fees: none.

JAMES ALLEN LITERARY AGENT—538 East Hartford St., P.O. Box 278, Milford, PA 18337. Attn: James Allen. Adult fiction. Query with 2- to 3-page synopsis; no multiple queries, requires exclusive. Commission: 10% domestic; 20% foreign. "My list is quite full; so these days, I'm mainly interested in taking on only people with previous booklength fiction publishing credits."

MICHAEL AMATO AGENCY—1650 Broadway, Rm. 307, New York, NY 10019. Attn: Michael Amato. Screenplays. Send query or complete manuscript. Commission: 10%. Fees: none.

MARCIA AMSTERDAM AGENCY— 41 W. 82nd St., #9A, New York, NY 10024. Attn: Marcia Amsterdam. Adult and young adult fiction; mainstream nonfiction. Screenplays and teleplays: comedy, romance, psychological suspense. Query with resumé; multiple queries O.K.; three-week exclusive for requested submissions. Commission: 15% domestic; 10% screenplays. Fees: photocopying and shipping.

THE AUTHOR'S AGENCY—3355 N. Five Mile Rd., Suite 332, Boise, ID 83713–3925. Attn: R.J. Winchell. Adult fiction and nonfiction. Screenplays, teleplays, stage plays. Unpublished and unproduced writers considered. Query with three sample chapters for fiction or nonfiction, complete manuscript for drama; include SASE. Commission: 15% books; 10% scripts. Fees: none. "Our interests are broad."

THE AXELROD AGENCY—54 Church St., Lenox, MA 01240. Adult fiction and nonfiction. Unpublished writers considered. Query; multiple queries O.K. Commission: 10% domestic; 20% foreign. Fees: photocopying.

MALAGA BALDI LITERARY AGENCY, INC.—2112 Broadway, Suite #403, New York, NY 10023. Attn: Malaga Baldi. Adult fiction and nonfiction. Unpublished writers considered. Query first; "if I am interested, I ask for proposal, outline, and sample pages for nonfiction, complete manuscript for fiction." Multiple queries O.K. Commission: 15%. Fees: none. Response time: 10 weeks minimum.

THE BALKIN AGENCY—P.O. Box 222, Amherst, MA 01004. Attn: Rick Balkin. Adult nonfiction. Unpublished writers considered. Query with outline; no multiple queries. Commission: 15% domestic; 20% foreign. Fees: none. "Most interested in serious nonfiction."

VIRGINIA BARBER AGENCY—101 Fifth Ave., New York, NY 10003. Adult fiction and nonfiction. No unsolicited manuscripts. Query with outline, sample pages, bio/resumé and SASE. No multiple queries. Commission: 15% domestic; 20% foreign. Fees: photocopying.

LORETTA BARRETT BOOKS—101 Fifth Ave., New York, NY 10003. Attn: Loretta Barrett. Adult fiction and nonfiction. Unpublished writers considered. Query with outline and bio/resumé; no multiple queries. Commission: 15%. Fees: telephone. Response time: 4 weeks; "Please do not call before then."

BERMAN, BOALS, & FLYNN, INC.—225 Lafayette St., #1207, New York, NY 10012. Attn: Lois Berman, Judy Boals, or Jim Flynn; Charles Grayauskie, Assistant. Screenplays, teleplays, and stage plays. Unpublished, unproduced writers considered. Query with SASE, bio, and resumé. Commission: 10%. Fees: photocopying.

REID BOATES LITERARY AGENCY—Box 328, 69 Cooks Crossroad, Pittstown, NJ 08867–0328. Attn: Reid Boates. Adult mainstream fiction and nonfiction. Unpublished writers considered. Query; no multiple queries. Commission: 15%. Fees: none.

BOOK DEALS, INC.—65 E. Scott St., Suite 16N, Chicago, IL 60610. Caroline Carney, Pres. Andrew Seagren, Assoc. Lit. Agent. General-interest adult fiction and nonfiction. Query with outline, 2 sample chapters, bio, and resumé. Unpublished writers considered. Commission: 15% domestic; 20% foreign. Fees: professional expenses.

BOOKSTOP LITERARY AGENCY—67 Meadow View Rd., Orinda, CA 94563. Attn: Kendra Marcus. Juvenile fiction only. Unpublished writers considered. No queries; send complete manuscript only with SASE. Commission: 15%. Fees: photocopying, shipping.

GEORGES BORCHARDT, INC.—136 E. 57th St., New York, NY 10022. Adult fiction and nonfiction. Unpublished writers considered by recommendation only. No unsolicited queries or submissions. Commission: 15%. Fees: photocopying, shipping.

BRANDT & BRANDT LITERARY AGENTS—1501 Broadway, New York, NY 10036. Adult fiction and nonfiction. Unpublished writers considered occasionally. Unsolicited query by letter only; no multiple queries. Commission: 15%. Fees: photocopying.

JANE JORDAN BROWNE—Multimedia Product Development, Inc., 410 S. Michigan Ave., Rm. 724, Chicago, IL 60605. Attn: Jane Jordan Browne. Adult fiction and nonfiction; juvenile, all ages. Query with SASE; multiple queries O.K. Commission: 15% domestic; 20% foreign. Fees: photocopying; foreign fax, telephone, and postage.

KNOX BURGER ASSOCIATES, LTD.—39½ Washington Square S., New York, NY 10012. Adult fiction and nonfiction. No science fiction, fantasy, or romance. Unpublished writers considered. Query with SASE; no multiple queries. Commission: 15%. Fees: photocopying.

SHEREE BYKOFSKY ASSOCIATES, INC.—11 East 47th St., New York, NY 10017. Adult nonfiction. Unpublished writers considered. Query with outline, up to 3 sample pages or proposal, and SASE. Multiple queries O.K. if indicated as such. Commission: 15%. Fees: none.

MARTHA CASSELMAN—P.O. Box 342, Calistoga, CA 94515–0342. Nonfiction, especially interested in cookbooks. Unpublished writers considered. Query with outline, sample pages, bio/resumé, and SASE for return. Multiple queries O.K. if noted as such. Commission: 15%. Fees: photocopying, overnight and overseas mail, phone, fax.

JULIE CASTIGLIA AGENCY—1155 Camino del Mar, Suite 510, Del Mar, CA 92014. Attn: Julie Castiglia. Fiction: mainstream, ethnic and literary. Nonfiction: psychology, health, finance, women's issues, science, biography, business, outdoors, and niche books. Query letter; no unsolicited manuscripts. No multiple queries. Commission: 15%. No reading fees. "Please do not query on the phone. Attend workshops and writers' conferences before approaching an agent."

HY COHEN LITERARY AGENCY, LTD.—P.O. Box 43770, Upper Montclair, NJ 07043. Attn: Hy Cohen. Adult fiction, nonfiction, and juvenile. Unpublished writers considered. Unsolicited queries and manuscripts O.K., "with SASE, please!" Multiple submissions considered. Commission: 10% domestic; 20% foreign. Fees: phone, photocopying, postage. "I rarely respond well to first-person narrative. Good luck!"

RUTH COHEN, INC.—P.O. Box 7626, Menlo Park, CA 94025. Attn: Ruth Cohen. Adult mysteries and women's fiction; quality juvenile fiction and nonfiction. Unpublished writers seriously considered. Query with first 10 pages, synopsis, bio and resumé, and SASE. Commission: 15%. Fees: some shipping, photocopying, and foreign agents.

DON CONGDON ASSOCIATES, INC.—156 Fifth Ave., Suite 625, New York, NY 10010. Adult fiction and nonfiction. Query with outline; no multiple queries. Commission: 10% domestic. Fees: photocopying.

THE DOE COOVER AGENCY—58 Sagamore Ave., Medford, MA 02155. Attn: Doe Coover, Colleen Mohyde. Adult fiction and general nonfiction. Unpublished writers considered. Query with outline, sample pages, bio/resumé, and SASE; multiple queries O.K. Commission: 15%. Fees: photocopying.

CURTIS BROWN LTD.—10 Astor Pl., New York, NY 10003. General trade fiction and nonfiction; also juvenile. Unpublished writers considered. Query; no multiple queries. Commission: unspecified. Fees: photocopying; express mail.

RICHARD CURTIS ASSOCIATES, INC.—171 E. 74th St., New York, NY 10021. Adult nonfiction. Unpublished writers considered. Query with bio/ resumé; no multiple queries. Commission: 15% domestic; 20% foreign. Fees: photocopying, shipping, purchase of author copies.

DARHANSOFF & VERRILL LITERARY AGENCY—179 Franklin St., New York, NY 10013. Adult fiction and nonfiction. Unpublished writers considered. Unsolicited queries "only with recommendations." Commission: 15% domestic; 20% foreign. Fees: none.

ELAINE DAVIE LITERARY AGENCY—620 Park Ave., Rochester, NY 14607. Attn: Elaine Davie. Adult fiction and nonfiction; "we specialize in popular/commercial novels by and for women, especially romance." Unpublished writers considered. Query with outline, and sample pages or synopsis and first 100 pages. SASE required. Multiple submissions O.K. Commission: 15%. Fees: none.

ANITA DIAMANT AGENCY, INC.—310 Madison Ave, # 1105, New York, NY 10017. Attn: R. Rue. Adult fiction: literary, mystery, romance. Also nonfiction "anything not technical." Query with outline or sample pages, and bio/resumé. No multiple queries. Commission: 15%. Fees: none.

SANDRA DIJKSTRA LITERARY AGENCY—1155 Camino del Mar, Suite 515C, Del Mar, CA 92014. Attn: Debra Ginsberg. Adult and children's fiction and nonfiction. Query with outline and bio/resumé. For fiction, submit first 50 pages and synopsis; for nonfiction, submit proposal. Commission: 15% domestic; 20% foreign. Fees: none. SASE.

THE JONATHAN DOLGER AGENCY—49 E. 96th St., 9B, New York, NY 10128. Attn: Tom Wilson. Adult trade fiction and nonfiction. Considers unpublished writers. Query with outline and SASE. Commission: 15%. Fees: photocopying, shipping. "No category mysteries, romance, or science fiction."

DOUGLAS, GORMAN, ROTHACKER & WILHELM, INC.—1501 Broadway, Suite 703, New York, NY 10036. Screenplays and full-length teleplays. Query with synopsis, bio/resumé; multiple queries O.K. Commission: 10%. Fees: none.

DWYER & O'GRADY, INC.—P.O. Box 239, East Lempster, NH 03605. Attn: Elizabeth O'Grady. Branch office: P.O. Box 790, Cedar Key, FL 32625. Specialize in children's picture books for ages 6 to 12. Require strong story line, dialogue, and character development. Unpublished writers considered. Query with bio/resumé; no multiple queries. Commission: 15%. Fees: photocopying, shipping. "Our primary focus is the representation of illustrators who also write their own stories; however, we represent several adult authors who write for the children's market."

JANE DYSTEL LITERARY MANAGEMENT—One Union Square W., Suite 904, New York, NY 10003. Attn: Jane Dystel, Miriam Goderich. Adult fiction and nonfiction. Unpublished writers considered. Query with bio/re-sumé; no multiple queries. Commission: 15%. Fees: shipping.

EDUCATIONAL DESIGN SERVICES—P.O. Box 253, Wantaugh, NY 11793. Attn: Bertram L. Linder. Educational texts only. Unpublished writers considered. Query with outline, sample pages or complete manuscript, bio/resumé, and SASE. No multiple queries. Commission: 15%. Fees: none.

ETHAN ELLENBERG LITERARY AGENCY—548 Broadway, Suite #5E, New York, NY 10012. Ethan Ellenberg, Agent. John Cintron, Assoc. Agent. Commercial and literary fiction and nonfiction. Specialize in first novels, thrillers, children's books, romance, science fiction, and fantasy. Nonfiction: health, new age/spirituality, pop-science, biography. No poetry or short stories. Query with first 3 chapters, synopsis, and SASE. "We respond within 2 weeks if interested." Commission: 15% domestic; 20% foreign. Fees: photocopying, shipping.

ANN ELMO AGENCY— 60 E. 42nd St., New York, NY 10165. Attn: Lettie Lee. Adult fiction, nonfiction, and plays. Juvenile for middle grades and up. No picture books. Unpublished writers considered. Please query first with outline, sample pages, and bio/resumé. No multiple queries. Commission: 15%. Fees: none.

FELICIA ETH—555 Bryant St., Suite 350, Palo Alto, CA 94301. Attn: Felicia Eth. Small list of adult fiction, "highly selective, mostly contemporary." Also issue-oriented, provocative nonfiction. Unpublished writers considered. Query with outline, sample pages, and bio/resume. Multiple queries O.K. if noted. Commission: 15% domestic; 20% foreign. Fees: photocopying. "I am a small, highly personal agency, not right for everyone but very committed to those I work with. I tend to work with writers based either on the West Coast or at least west of the Mississippi."

FARBER LITERARY AGENCY—14 E. 75th St., New York, NY 10021. Attn: Ann Farber. Adult fiction, nonfiction, and stage plays; juvenile books. Considers unpublished writers. Query with outline, sample pages, and SASE. Commission: 15% "with services of attorney." Fees: photocopying.

JOYCE FLAHERTY— 816 Lynda Ct., St. Louis, MO 63122. Attn: Joyce Flaherty. "We accept only the work of currently published authors of book-length manuscripts, who continue to write in their specialties." Adult fiction and nonfiction. Query with outline, sample chapter (first chapter for nonfiction), and bio. Commission: 15% domestic; 30% foreign. Fees: none.

FLANNERY LITERARY—34–36 28th St., #5, Long Island City, NY 11106–3516. Attn: Jennifer Flannery. Fiction and nonfiction; juvenile, all ages. Unpublished writers considered. Query by letter only (no phone or fax queries); multiple queries O.K. Commission: 15%. Fees: none.

FOGELMAN LITERARY AGENCY—7515 Greenville Ave., Suite 712, Dallas, TX 75231. Attn: Linda M. Kruger. Adult romance. Commerical books of pop-culture. Query with SASE. Commission: 15% domestic; 10% foreign. Fees: none.

ROBERT A. FREEDMAN DRAMATIC AGENCY, INC.—1501 Broadway, Suite 2310, New York, NY 10036. Attn: Robert A. Freedman or Selma Luttinger. Screenplays, teleplays, and stage plays. Send query only; multiple queries O.K. Commission: standard. Fees: photocopying.

SAMUEL FRENCH, INC.— 45 W. 25th St., New York, NY 10010. Attn: William Talbot, Editor. Stage plays. Unpublished writers considered. Query with complete manuscript; unsolicited and multiple queries O.K. Fees: none.

JAY GARON-BROOKE ASSOCIATES—101 W. 55th St., #5K, New York, NY 10019. Attn: Dick Duane or Robert Thixton. Adult fiction and nonfiction. Unpublished writers considered. Query with outline, bio/resumé, and SASE; no multiple queries. Commission: 15% domestic; 30% foreign. Fees: photocopying.

GELFMAN SCHNEIDER—250 W. 57th St., Suite 2515, New York, NY 10107. Attn: Jane Gelfman. Adult fiction and nonfiction. Unpublished writers only considered if recommended by other writers or teachers. Query with outline, sample pages, and bio; no multiple queries. Commission: 15% domestic; 20% foreign. Fees: none.

GOLDFARB & GRAYBILL—918 16th St. N.W., Suite 400, Washington, DC 20006. Attn: Nina Graybill. Adult fiction and nonfiction. No poetry, romance, science fiction, or children's books. Query with bio/resumé; for fiction, include a synopsis, sample chapter. Multiple queries O.K. Commission: 15%. Fees: photocopying, shipping. "We appreciate succinct, grammatical query letters and samples."

GOODMAN ASSOCIATES—500 West End Ave., New York, NY 10024. Attn: Elise Simon Goodman. Adult fiction and nonfiction. Unpublished writers considered. Query with outline, sample pages, and bio/resumé. Multiple queries O.K. Commission: 15% domestic; 20% foreign. Fees: photocopying, long-distance telephone, overseas postage.

SANFORD J. GREENBURGER—55 Fifth Ave., 15th Fl., New York, NY 10003. Attn: Faith Hornby Hamlin: Adult fiction (no science fiction, fantasy, or romance) and nonfiction, including sports books; juvenile picture books. Attn: Elyse Cheney: Thrillers, mysteries, women's fiction, African-American fiction. Literary nonfiction, memoirs, journalism, psychology, politics, nature writing, sports. Unpublished writers considered. Query with outline, sample pages, bio and resumé, and SASE; multiple queries O.K. Commission: 15% domestic; 20% foreign. Fees: photocopying.

MAIA GREGORY ASSOCIATES—311 East 72nd St., New York, NY 10021. Adult nonfiction only. Unpublished writers considered. Query with sample pages and bio/resumé. No multiple queries. Commission: 15%. Fees: none.

THE CHARLOTTE GUSAY LITERARY AGENCY—10532 Blythe, Los Angeles, CA 90064. Screenplays. Query only, bio/resumé, and SASE; no multiple queries. Commission: 10%.

HARDEN CURTIS ASSOCIATES— 850 Seventh Ave., Suite 405, New York, NY 10019. Attn: Mary Harden. Stage plays. Query with bio and resumé; no multiple queries. Commission: 10%. Fees: none.

HEACOCK LITERARY AGENCY, INC.—1523 Sixth St., Suite 14, Santa Monica, CA 90401. Attn: Rosalie Heacock, Pres. Adult fiction and nonfiction. Published and unpublished writers welcome to query with outline, bio/resumé, and SASE. Multiple queries O.K. if mentioned. Commission: 15%. Fees: out-of-pocket expenses. "The agency offers thoughtful representation and provides sounding board for new book ideas for established clientele. Please write your query letter as well as you write your original manuscript, for it is the first sample of your writing that the agent will see and evaluate. Good luck!"

FREDERICK HILL ASSOCIATES—1842 Union St., San Francisco, CA 94123. Attn: Bonnie Nadell. Branch office: 8446½ Melrose Pl., Los Angeles, CA 90069. Adult fiction and nonfiction. Unpublished writers considered. Query with outline and bio/resumé; multiple queries O.K. Commission: 15%. Fees: photocopying, postage.

JOHN L. HOCHMANN BOOKS—320 E. 58th St., New York, NY 10022. Attn: John L. Hochmann. Nonfiction: biography, social history, health and food, college textbook. Unpublished writers considered, "provided they present evidence of substantial expertise in the field they are writing about." Query with outline, sample pages, and bio/resumé. No multiple queries. Commission: 15% for domestic/Canadian; plus 15% foreign language and U.K. Fees: photocopying. "Do not submit jacket copy. Submit outlines and proposals that include evaluations of competing books." SASE.

BARBARA HOGENSON AGENCY—19 W. 44th St., Suite 1000, New York, NY 10036. Attn: Barbara Hogenson. Adult fiction and nonfiction. Screenplays, teleplays, and stage plays. Query; multiple queries O.K. Commission: 15% books; 10% dramatic. Fees: none.

HULL HOUSE LITERARY AGENCY—240 E. 82nd St., New York, NY 10028. Attn: David Stewart Hull, Pres. New writers contact Lydia Mortimer, Associate. Nonfiction: true crime, biography, military, general history. Fiction, especially crime fiction. Query with outline and bio/resumé; include sample pages with nonfiction queries only. Multiple queries O.K. Commission: 15% domestic; 10% foreign. Fees: photocopying, overseas fax and postage.

IMG LITERARY —22 E. 71st St., New York, NY 10021. Attn: Julian Bach, Carolyn Krupp. Adult fiction and nonfiction. Unpublished writers considered. Query with outline, sample pages, and bio/resumé. No multiple queries. Commission: 15%. Fees: photocopying.

INTERNATIONAL PUBLISHER ASSOCIATES, INC.—304 Guido Ave., Lady Lake, FL 32159. Attn: J. DeRogatis, Exec. Vice Pres. Adult fiction and nonfiction. Unpublished writers considered. Query with outline, sample pages, and SASE; multiple queries O.K. Commission: 15% domestic; 20% foreign. Fees: photocopying, shipping.

SHARON JARVIS & CO.—Toad Hall, Inc., RR2, Box 16B, Laceyville, PA 18623. Adult fiction and nonfiction. Unpublished writers considered. Query with bio or resumé, and outline or synopsis. No unsolicited manuscripts. Commission: 15%. Fees: photocopying. "Pay attention to what's selling and what's commercial."

JCA LITERARY AGENCY, INC.—27 W. 20th St., Suite 1103, New York, NY 10011. Adult fiction and nonfiction. Unpublished writers considered. Query with sample pages; multiple queries O.K. Commission: 15% domestic; 20% foreign. Fees: photocopying, shipping. "Be as straightforward and to-the-point as possible. Don't try to hype us or bury us in detail."

NATASHA KERN LITERARY AGENCY, INC.—P.O. Box 2908, Portland, OR 97208–2908. Attn: Natasha Kern. Adult fiction and nonfiction. Query. Commission: 15% domestic; 10% foreign. Fees: none.

LOUISE B. KETZ AGENCY—1485 First Ave., Suite 4B, New York, NY 10021. Attn: Louise B. Ketz. Adult nonfiction on science, business, sports, history, and reference. Considers unpublished writers "with proper credentials." Query with outline and bio/resumé; multiple queries occasionally considered. Commission: 10% to 15%. Fees: photocopying, shipping.

KIDDE, HOYT & PICARD—335 E. 51st St., New York, NY 10022. Attn: Katharine Kidde, Laura Langlie. General interest/trade nonfiction on current affairs, social sciences, and the arts. Adult mainstream fiction; some literary, mysteries, romances, thrillers. No science fiction, horror, or poetry. Unpublished writers not considered, "but we'll consider writers who have published short fiction or nonfiction—a published book is not necessary." Query with 2 or 3 chapters and synopsis; also include past writing experience. Multiple queries O.K. Commission: 15%. Fees: photocopying, postage.

KIRCHOFF/WOHLBERG, INC.—866 United Nations Plaza, Suite 525, New York, NY 10017. Attn: Liza Voges. Juvenile fiction and nonfiction only. Unpublished writers considered. Query; multiple submissions O.K. Commission: 15%. Fees: none.

HARVEY KLINGER, INC.—301 W. 53rd St., New York, NY 10019. Attn: Harvey Klinger. Adult fiction and nonfiction. Unpublished writers considered. Query with outline, sample pages, and bio/resumé. No multiple queries. Commission: 15% domestic; 25% foreign. Fees: photocopying, shipping.

BARBARA S. KOUTS—P.O. Box 560, Bellport, NY 11713. Attn: Barbara S. Kouts. Adult fiction, nonfiction, and juvenile. Unpublished writers considered. Query with bio/resumé. Multiple queries O.K. Commission: 10%. Fees: photocopying. "Send your best work always!"

OTTO R. KOZAK LITERARY AGENCY—P.O. Box 152, Long Beach, NY 11561. Screenplays and teleplays only. Unpublished and unproduced writers considered. Query with outline or treatment; no multiple queries. Commission: 10%. Fees: none. SASE required.

EDITE KROLL—12 Grayhurst Pk., Portland, ME 04102. Attn: Edite Kroll. Feminist non-fiction; humor; children's fiction and picture books written and illustrated by artists. Unpublished writers considered. Query with outline, sample pages, a brief note about the author, and SASE; multiple queries O.K. Commission: 15% domestic; 20% foreign. Fees: photocopying. "Keep queries brief. No phone or fax queries."

PETER LAMPACK AGENCY, INC.—551 Fifth Ave., Suite 1613, New York, NY 10176. Attn: Sandra Blanton, Agent. Loren Soeiro, Assoc. Agent. Literary and commercial fiction; "We like contemporary relationship and historical fiction in addition to thrillers, psychological suspense, mystery, action-adventure. We do not handle romance, science fiction, or horror." Also handle biography/autobiography, nonfiction on politics, finance, and law written by experts in the fields. Unpublished writers considered. Query with synopsis/outline and bio/resumé. Sample pages will be solicited after queries. Multiple queries O.K. Commission: 15%. Fees: photocopying.

THE ROBERT LANTZ-JOY HARRIS AGENCY—156 Fifth Ave., Suite 617, New York, NY 10010. Adult fiction and nonfiction. Unpublished writers considered. Query with outline, sample pages, and bio/resumé. No multiple queries. Commission: 15%. Fees: photocopying, shipping.

THE LANTZ OFFICE—888 Seventh Ave., New York, NY 10106. Attn: Robert Lantz. Adult fiction and nonfiction. Stage plays. Query with bio and resumé; no multiple queries. Commission: not specified. Fees: none.

MICHAEL LARSEN/ELIZABETH POMADA—1029 Jones St., San Francisco, CA 94109. Attn: M. Larsen, nonfiction; E. Pomada, fiction. Fiction: literary, commercial, and genre. Nonfiction: general, including pop psychology and science, biography, business, nature, health, history, arts, travel. Unpublished writers welcome. Query for fiction with first 30 pages, synopsis, SASE, and phone number; send #10 SASE for brochure. For nonfiction, query by phone: (415) 673–0939. Multiple queries O.K., "as long as we're told." Commission: 15%. Fees: none.

THE MAUREEN LASHER AGENCY—P.O. Box 888, Pacific Palisades, CA 90272. Attn: Ann Cashman. Adult fiction and nonfiction. Unpublished writers considered. Query with outline, sample pages, and bio/resumé. No multiple queries. Commission: 15%. Fees: none.

LEVANT & WALES, INC.—108 Hayes St., Seattle, WA 98109. Attn: Elizabeth Wales, Adrienne Reed. Adult fiction and nonfiction. Unpublished writers considered. Query with outline, sample pages, and bio/resumé. Multiple queries O.K. Commission: 15%. Fees: photocopying.

ELLEN LEVINE LITERARY AGENCY, INC.—15 E. 26th St., Suite 1801, New York, NY 10010. Adult fiction and nonfiction; juvenile material. Unpublished writers considered. Query with SASE. Commission: 15% domestic; 20% foreign. Fees: photocopying, shipping.

LICHTMAN, TRISTER, SINGER & ROSS—1666 Connecticut Ave. N.W., Suite 500, Washington, DC 20009. Attn: Gail Ross, Howard Yoon. Adult non-fiction. Unpublished writers considered. Query with outline, sample pages, resumé, and SASE. Multiple queries O.K. Commission: 15%. Fees: none.

THE LITERARY BRIDGE—P.O. Box 10593, Sedona, AZ 86339. Attn: Genero Capshaw. Adult fiction and nonfiction, all genres, from 125 pages. Young adult fiction and nonfiction, all genres, to 250 pages. Query or send complete manuscript. Commission: 10% to 12½%. Fees: none.

NANCY LOVE LITERARY AGENCY—250 E. 65th St., New York, NY 10021. Mostly nonfiction, including medical, alternative health care, parenting, spiritual and inspirational books, social issues, current affairs, crime, self-help; some fiction, but no genre except mysteries and thrillers. Unpublished writers considered. Query; no multiple submissions on novels. Commission: 15%. Fees: photocopying.

DONALD MAASS LITERARY AGENCY—157 W. 57th St., Suite 703, New York, NY 10019. Attn: Donald Maass, Pres. Jennifer Jackson, Associate. Adult fiction, specializing in science fiction, fantasy, mystery, suspense, historical, romance, mainstream, literary. Unpublished writers considered. Query; multiple queries O.K. if noted as such. Commission: 15% domestic; 20% foreign. Fees: none.

870

GERARD MCCAULEY AGENCY, INC.—P.O. Box 844, Katonah, NY 10536. Attn: Gerard F. McCauley. Adult nonfiction. Unpublished writers considered. Query; no multiple queries. Commission: 15%. Fees: postage.

GINA MACCOBY LITERARY AGENCY—P.O. Box 60, Chappaqua, NY 10514. Adult fiction and nonfiction; juvenile for all ages. Unpublished writers considered. Query; multiple queries O.K. Commission: 15%. Fees: photocopying, overseas postage, bank charges for converting foreign currencies. No unsolicited manuscripts, please.

CAROL MANN LITERARY AGENCY—55 Fifth Ave., New York, NY 10003. Attn: Carol Mann. Gail Feinberg, subs rights. 10% fiction; 90% nonfiction. Query; multiple queries O.K. Commission: 15%. Fees: photocopying, shipping.

MANUS ASSOCIATES, INC.— 417 E. 57th St., Suite 5D, New York, NY 10022. Attn: Janet Manus. Branch office: 430 Cowper St., Palo Alto, CA 94301. Adult fiction and nonfiction. No science fiction, category romance, or military books. Unpublished writers considered. Query with outline, sample pages, and bio/resumé. Multiple queries O.K. "on occasion." Commission: 15%. Fees: photocopying, shipping.

ELISABETH MARTON AGENCY— One Union Square W., Rm. 612, New York, NY 10003–3303. Attn: Tonda Marton. Plays only. Unproduced playwrights considered. Query; multiple queries O.K. Commission: 10%. Fees: none.

JED MATTES, INC.—2095 Broadway, #302, New York, NY 10023–2895. Adult fiction and nonfiction. Unpublished writers considered. Query; multiple queries O.K. Commission: 15% domestic; 20% foreign. Fees: none.

HELMUT MEYER LITERARY AGENCY—330 E. 79th St., New York, NY 10021. Attn: Helmut Meyer, Literary Agent. Adult fiction and nonfiction. Telephone queries preferred: (212) 288–2421. For letter queries, include outline, sample pages, and bio/resumé. No multiple queries. Commission: 15%. Fees: none.

HENRY MORRISON, INC.—Box 235, Bedford Hills, NY 10507. Adult fiction and nonfiction; booklength only. Unpublished writers considered. Query with outline; multiple queries O.K. Commission: 15% domestic; 20% foreign. Fees: photocopying, shipping. "We are concentrating on a relatively small list of clients, and work toward building them in the U.S. and international marketplaces. We tend to avoid autobiographical novels and extremely literary novels, but always seek good nonfiction on major political and historical subjects."

MULTIMEDIA PRODUCT DEVELOPMENT— 410 Michigan Ave., Suite 724, Chicago, IL 60605. Jane Jordan Browne, Pres. Danielle Egan-Miller, Agent. Adult fiction and nonfiction, as well as juvenile fiction and nonfiction. "We are interested in commercial, overnight sellers in the areas of mainstream fiction and nonfiction." No short stories, poems, screenplays, articles, or software. Query with bio and SASE. Commission: 15% domestic; 20% foreign. Fees: photocopying, foreign postage.

JEAN V. NAGGAR LITERARY AGENCY, INC.—216 E. 75th St., New York, NY 10021. Attn: Jean Naggar, Frances Kuffel, or Anne Engel (nonfic-

871

tion). Adult mainstream fiction and nonfiction; no romance or formula science fiction; stage plays. Signs on "hardly any" new writers. Query with outline, SASE, bio, and resumé; query for completed novels only; no multiple queries. Commission: 15%. Fees: long-distance calls, galleys, etc.; no reading fee.

RUTH NATHAN AGENCY— 80 Fifth Ave., Suite 706, New York, NY 10011. Decorative arts, show business, biography. Selected historical fiction, pre-1500. No unsolicited queries. Commission: 15%. Fees: photocopying, shipping. "To writers seeking an agent: Please note what my specialties are. Do not send science fiction, fantasy, children's books, or business books."

NEW ENGLAND PUBLISHING ASSOCIATES—P.O. Box 5, Chester, CT 06412. Attn: Elizabeth Frost Knappman, Edward W. Knappman. Adult nonfiction, especially women's studies, minority issues, literature, business, and reference. Unpublished writers considered. Query; "send a carefully thought-out proposal with concept statement, market analysis, competitive survey, author bio, annotated chapter outline, and 50–70 pages of sample chapters." Commission: 15% domestic; 20% foreign. Fees: none.

BETSY NOLAN LITERARY AGENCY—224 W. 29th St., 15th Fl., New York, NY 10001. Attn: Betsy Nolan. Adult nonfiction, especially popular psychology, child care, cookbooks, gardening, music books, African-American and Jewish issues. Query. Commission: 15%. Fees: none.

THE RICHARD PARKS AGENCY—138 E. 16th St., 5B, New York, NY 10003. Adult nonfiction; fiction by referral only. Unpublished writers considered. Query with SASE; multiple queries O.K. if noted as such. Commission: 15% domestic; 20% foreign. Fees: photocopying. "No phone calls or faxed queries, please."

P. PERKINS ASSOCIATES—5800 Arlington Ave., Suite 18J, Riverdale, NY 10471. Attn: Lori Perkins or Peter Rubie. Adult fiction and nonfiction. No romance or children's books. Unpublished writers considered. Query with outline, sample pages, bio, and resumé; multiple queries O.K. Commission: 15% domestic; 20% foreign. Fees: photocopying, shipping. "No unprofessional presentation or behavior; keep queries simple, direct, and to the point."

JAMES PETER ASSOCIATES, INC.—P.O. Box 772, Tenafly, NJ 07670. Attn: Bert Holtje. Adult nonfiction. Unpublished writers considered. Query with outline, sample pages, and bio/resumé. No multiple queries. Commission: 15%. Fees: none.

ALISON PICARD, LITERARY AGENT—P.O. Box 2000, Cotuit, MA 02635. Attn: Alison Picard Adult fiction, nonfiction, and juvenile. Unpublished writers considered. Query; multiple queries O.K. Commission: 15%. Fees: none.

SUSAN ANN PROTTER—110 W. 40th St., Suite 1408, New York, NY 10018. Adult fiction and nonfiction only, specializing in mysteries, contemporary thrillers and science fiction, health, psychology, self-help, popular science, medicine, and parenting. Query by mail only, with description, bio/resumé, synopsis, and SASE. Commission: unspecified. Fees: $10 handling fee for requested manuscripts to cover cost of return.

ROBERTA PRYOR, INC.—288 Titicus Rd., North Salem, NY 10560. Attn: Roberta Pryor. Adult fiction, nonfiction, current affairs, biographies, ecology. Unpublished writers considered. Query with outline, sample pages, and bio/resumé. Multiple queries O.K. Commission: 15% domestic; 10% foreign and film. Fees: photocopying, Federal Express. "When submitting book proposals, taboo is the coy refusal to give away any plot resolution. How do we know the author can resolve his plot, take care of loose ends? Some applicants feel a copywriter's approach, i.e. jacket copy come-on, will tickle our fancy. Not so."

RAINES & RAINES—71 Park Ave., Suite 4A, New York, NY 10016. Attn: Keith Korman, Joan Raines, Theron Raines. Adult fiction, nonfiction, and juvenile for all ages. Query; no multiple queries. Commission: 15% domestic; 20% foreign. Fees: photocopying and copies of books. "Keep query to one page."

HELEN REES LITERARY AGENCY—308 Commonwealth Ave., Boston, MA 02115. Literary fiction and nonfiction. No short stories, science fiction, or poetry. Unpublished writers considered. Query with outline, bio/resumé, and sample, to 50 pages. No multiple queries. Commission: 15%. Fees: none.

JODY REIN BOOKS, INC.—7741 S. Ash Ct., Littleton, CO 80122. Attn: Sandra Bond. Literary and mainstream adult fiction and nonfiction by writers who have been published in some format (magazines, newspapers, etc.). Query with bio and resumé. Commission: not specified. Fees: shipping.

JANE ROTROSEN AGENCY—318 E. 51st St., New York, NY 10022. Attn: Ruth Kagle, Andrea Cirillo, Meg Ruley. Adult fiction and nonfiction. Unpublished writers considered. Query; multiple queries O.K. Commission: 15% domestic and Canada; 20% foreign. Fees: none.

PESHA RUBINSTEIN LITERARY AGENCY—1392 Rugby Rd., Teaneck, NJ 07666. Attn: Pesha Rubinstein. Commercial fiction and nonfiction. Contemporary women's fiction. Juvenile books. No poetry, short stories, or fantasy. Unpublished writers considered. Query with first 10 pages; multiple queries O.K. Commission: 15% domestic; 20% foreign. Fees: photocopying. "Don't tell me you'll make me rich. Do tell me the ending of the story in the synopsis."

RUSSELL-SIMENAUER LITERARY AGENCY, INC.—P.O. Box 43267, Upper Monclair, NJ 07043. Attn: Jacqueline Simenauer, Margaret Russell. Nonfiction: pop psych, self-help; medical, nutrition, sexuality, new-age spirituality; women's and men's issues, investigative journalism, true crime, adventure, business, celebrities. Fiction: literary, commercial, mysteries, historical novels, first novels. Query with outline, sample pages, bio/resumé. Multiple queries O.K. Commission: 15% domestic; 25% foreign. Fees: shipping, phone, photocopying.

RUSSELL & VOLKENING, INC.—50 W. 29th St., New York, NY 10001. Adult and juvenile fiction and nonfiction. Unpublished writers considered. Query with letter and SASE. No multiple queries. Commission: 10%. Fees: none.

SANDUM & ASSOCIATES—144 E. 84th St., New York, NY 10028. Attn: Howard E. Sandum. Primarily nonfiction. Query with sample pages and bio/resumé. Multiple queries O.K. Commission: 15% domestic; 10% when foreign or TV/film subagents are used. "We do not consider manuscripts in genres such as science fiction, romance, or horror unless surpassing literary qualities are present."

SEBASTIAN AGENCY—333 Kearny St., Suite 708, San Francisco, CA 94108. Attn: Laurie Harper. Adult nonfiction only. "We have a full and active client list, so we must be very selective. We continue to look at proposals, mainly in the areas of psychology, consumer reference, health and beauty, or business books." Query with outline and bio. Commission: 15% domestic; 20% to 25% foreign. Fees: $100 annual administrative fee to all clients.

THE SHUKAT COMPANY, LTD.—340 W. 55th St., Suite 1A, New York, NY 10019. Attn: Scott Shukat, Pat McLaughlin. Screenplays and stage plays. Unpublished, unproduced writers occasionally considered. Query with outline, sample pages, and bio; no multiple queries. Commission: 15%. Fees: none. "Since this is a small office, we will reply only if we are interested in the material. SASE not necessary."

BOBBE SIEGEL, RIGHTS LITERARY AGENT— 41 West 83rd St., New York, NY 10024, NY 10024. Attn: Bobbe Siegel. Adult fiction and nonfiction. Unpublished writers considered. Query; multiple queries O.K. SASE required. Commission: 15%. Fees: photocopying and faxes. "Keep query short, to the point, and literate. Don't sing your own praises; manuscript should speak for itself."

F. JOSEPH SPIELER LITERARY AGENCY—154 W. 57th St., Rm. 135, New York, NY 10019. Attn: F. Joseph Spieler, Lisa M. Ross, John F. Thornton, Literary Agents. Branch office: Victoria Shoemaker, Agent, The Spieler Agency West, 1760 Solano Ave., Suite 300, Berkeley, CA 94707. Adult fiction and nonfiction; also juvenile for all ages. Unpublished writers considered. Query with outline; no multiple queries. Commission: 15%. Fees: third-party charges (e.g., messengers, photocopying) will be billed back at discretion, regardless of sale of project. No material will be returned if no SASE.

PHILIP G. SPITZER LITERARY AGENCY—50 Talmage Farm Ln., East Hampton, NY 11937. Attn: Philip Spitzer. Adult fiction and nonfiction. Query. Commission: 15% domestic; 20% foreign. Fees: photocopying.

GLORIA STERN AGENCY—2929 Buffalo Speedway, #2111, Houston, TX 77098. Attn: Gloria Stern. Adult nonfiction. Query with short outline, bio/resume, and one chapter. Multiple queries O.K. Commission: 15%. Fees: photocopying.

GUNTHER STUHLMANN, AUTHOR'S REPRESENTATIVE—P.O. Box 276, Becket, MA 01223. Attn: Barbara Ward. Literary fiction and nonfiction, especially biography, letters, and history. No mysteries, romance, science fiction, or adventure. Unpublished writers sometimes considered. Query with letter and SASE; no multiple queries. Commission: 10% North America; 15% Britain and Commonwealth; 20% foreign. "We take on few new clients at this time."

THE TANTLEFF OFFICE—375 Greenwich St., Suite 700, New York, NY 10013. Attn: John Santoianni, stage plays. Jill Back, film and television. Anthony Gardner, books. Adult fiction and nonfiction; stage plays, screenplays, teleplays. Unpublished writers considered. Query with synopsis, up to 10 sample pages, bio/resumé; multiple queries O.K. Commission: 10% plays; 15% books. Fees: none.

SUSAN P. URSTADT, INC.—P.O. Box 1676, New Canaan, CT 06840. Attn: Susan Urstadt. Adult nonfiction, specializing in art, antiques, architec-

874

ture, popular reference, crafts, travel, health, careers, regional books, etc. Unpublished writers considered. Query with outline, sample pages, overview of the market and competition, bio/resumé, and SASE. No multiple queries. Commission:15%. Fees: none. "We look for dedicated, cheerful, long-term authors of high quality who want to build writing careers with care."

JOHN A. WARE LITERARY AGENCY—392 Central Park W., New York, NY 10025. Attn: John Ware. Adult fiction and nonfiction. "Literate, accessible, noncategory fiction, plus thrillers and mysteries." Nonfiction: biography, history, current affairs, investigative journalism, social criticism, Americana and folklore, science, medicine, sports, memoir. Unpublished writers considered. Query letter only, with SASE; multiple queries O.K. Commission: 15% domestic; 20% foreign. Fees: photocopying. "No telephone queries, please, without referral."

WATKINS/LOOMIS AGENCY—133 E. 35th St., Suite One, New York, NY 10016. Attn: Lily Oei. Adult fiction and nonfiction. Unpublished writers considered. Query with SASE; no multiple queries. Commission: 15%. Fees: none.

SANDRA WATT & ASSOCIATES—8033 Sunset Blvd., Suite 4053, Los Angeles, CA 90046. Attn: Sandra Watt. Adult fiction and nonfiction. Unpublished writers considered. Query with bio/resumé; multiple submissions O.K. Commission: 15%. Fees: marketing fees for shipping, telephone, faxes, for new writers only. "We're old fashioned. We love good writing."

WIESER & WIESER, INC.—118 E. 25th St.,7th Fl., New York, NY 10010. Attn: Olga Wieser. Adult fiction and nonfiction. Unpublished writers considered. Query with outline and bio/resumé. No multiple queries. Commission: 15%. Fees: photocopying, shipping.

WITHERSPOON ASSOCIATES—157 W. 57th St., Suite 700, New York, NY 10019. Adult fiction and nonfiction. Unpublished writers considered. Query with sample pages; no multiple queries. Commission: 15%. Fees: none.

RUTH WRESCHNER, AUTHORS' REPRESENTATIVE—10 W. 74th St., New York, NY 10023. Attn: Ruth Wreschner. Adult fiction (mainstream novels, genre books, mysteries, romance) and nonfiction (by experts in a particular field); also young adult. No pornography, incest, or sexual abuse. Unpublished writers considered. Query with outline, sample pages, and bio/resumé. Multiple queries O.K. Commission: 15% domestic; 20% foreign. Fees: photocopying and postage.

ANN WRIGHT REPRESENTATIVES—165 W. 46th St., Suite 1105, New York, NY 10036–2501. Attn: Dan Wright. Screenplays and teleplays. Adult fiction must have strong film potential. Unpublished writers considered. Query with bio/resumé; no multiple queries. Commission: 10% to 20%. Fees: photocopying, shipping.

WRITERS HOUSE—21 W. 26th St., New York, NY 10010. Attn: Christian Finnegan, fiction. John Hodgeman, nonfiction; Alexa Lichtenstein, juvenile and young adult. Liza Landsman, multimedia. Adult fiction and nonfiction; juvenile for all ages; and young adult. Unpublished writers considered. "Query with one-page letter on why your project is excellent, what it's about, and why you're the wonderful author to write it." No multiple queries. Commission: 15% domestic; 20% foreign. Fees: out-of-pocket expenses only.

WRITERS' PRODUCTIONS—P.O. Box 630, Westport, CT 06881. Attn: David L. Meth. Adult fiction and nonfiction, both of literary quality. Children's books that fit into multimedia fantasies. Unpublished writers considered. Query with SASE. Multiple queries considered, but not preferred. Commission: 15% domestic; 25% foreign, dramatic, multimedia, software sales, licensing, and merchandising. Fees: photocopying, shipping. "Send your best, most professional written work. Research your market, know your field."

ZACHARY SHUSTER LITERARY AGENCY— 45 Newbury St., Boston, MA 02116. Attn: Lane Zachary or Todd Shuster. Adult fiction and nonfiction. Juvenile fiction and nonfiction. Screenplays. Query with sample pages or submit complete manuscript. Commission: 15% domestic; 20% foreign. Fees: none.

SUSAN ZECKENDORF ASSOCIATES, INC.—171 W. 57th St., New York, NY 10019. Attn: Susan Zeckendorf. Fiction: literary fiction; mysteries; thrillers; women's commercial fiction. Nonfiction: science; music; biography; social history. Unpublished writers considered. Query with outline and bio/resumé. Commission: 15% domestic; 20% foreign. Fees: photocopying. "Keep your description of the work brief."

Glossary

Advance — The amount a publisher pays a writer before a book is published; it is deducted from the royalties earned from sales of the finished book.

Agented material — Submissions from literary or dramatic agents to a publisher. Some publishing companies accept agented material only.

All rights — Some magazines purchase all rights to the material they publish, which means that they can use it as they wish, as many times as they wish. They cannot purchase all rights unless the writer gives them written permission to do so.

Assignment — A contract, written or oral, between an editor and writer, confirming that the writer will complete a specific project by a certain date, and for a certain fee.

B&W — Abbreviation for black-and-white photographs.

Book outline — Chapter-by-chapter summary of a book, frequently in paragraph form, allowing an editor to evaluate the book's content, tone, and pacing, and determine whether he or she wants to see the entire manuscript for possible publication.

Book packager — Company that puts together all the elements of a book, from initial concept to writing, publishing, and marketing it. Also called **book producer** or **book developer.**

Byline — Author's name as it appears on a published piece.

Clips — Copies of a writer's published work, often used by editors to evaluate the writer's talent.

Column inch — One inch of a typeset column; often serves as a basis for payment.

Contributor's copies — Copies of a publication sent to a writer whose work is included in it.

Copy editing — Line-by-line editing to correct errors in spelling, grammar, and punctuation, and inconsistencies in style. Differs from **content editing,** which evaluates flow, logic, and overall message.

Copy — Manuscript pages before they are set into type.

Copyright — Legal protection of creative works from unauthorized use. Under the law, copyright is secured automatically when the work is set down for the first time in written or recorded form.

Cover letter — A brief letter that accompanies a manuscript or book proposal. A cover letter is *not* a query letter (see definition of query).

Deadline — The date on which a written work is due at the editor's office, agreed to by author and editor.

Draft — A complete version of an article, story, or book. **First drafts** are often called **rough drafts.**

Fair use — A provision of the copyright law allowing brief passages of copyrighted material to be quoted without infringing on the owner's rights.

Feature — An article that is generally longer than a news story and whose main focus is an issue, trend, or person.

Filler — Brief item used to fill out a newspaper or magazine column; could be a news item, joke, anecdote, or puzzle.

First serial rights — The right of a magazine or newspaper to publish a work for the first time in any periodical. After that, all rights revert to the writer.

Galleys — The first typeset proofs of a manuscript, before they are divided into pages.

Ghostwriter — Author of books, articles, and speeches that are credited to someone else.

Glossy — Black-and-white photo with a shiny, rather than a matte, finish.

Hard copy — The printed copy of material written on a computer.

Honorarium — A modest, token fee paid by a publication to an author in gratitude for a submission.

International reply coupon (IRC) — Included with any correspondence or submission to a foreign publication; allows the editor to reply by mail without incurring cost.

Kill fee — Fee paid for an article that was assigned but subsequently not published; usually a percentage of the amount that would have been paid if the work had been published.

Lead time — Time between the planning of a magazine or book and its publication date.

Libel — A false accusation or published statement that causes a person embarrassment, loss of income, or damage to reputation.

Little magazines — Publications with limited circulation whose content often deals with literature or politics.

Mass market — Books appealing to a very large segment of the reading public and often sold in such outlets as drugstores, supermarkets, etc.

Masthead — A listing of the names and titles of a publication's staff members.

Ms — Abbreviation for manuscript; mss is the plural abbreviation.

Multiple submissions — Also called **simultaneous submissions.** Complete manuscripts sent simultaneously to different publications. Once universally discouraged by editors, the practice is gaining more acceptance, though some still frown on it. **Multiple queries** are generally accepted, however, since reading them requires less of an investment in time on the editor's part.

On speculation — Editor agrees to consider a work for publication "on speculation," without any guarantee that he or she will ultimately buy the work.

One-time rights — Editor buys manuscript from writer and agrees to publish it one time, after which the rights revert to the author for subsequent sales.

Op-ed — A newspaper piece, usually printed opposite the editorial page, that expresses a personal viewpoint on a timely news item.

Over-the-transom — Describes the submission of unsolicited material by a free-lance writer; the term harks back to the time when mail was delivered through the open window above an office door.

Payment on acceptance — Payment to writer when manuscript is submitted.

Payment on publication — Payment to writer when manuscript is published.

Pen name — A name other than his or her legal name that an author uses on written work.

Public domain — Published material that is available for use without permission, either because it was never copyrighted or because its copyright term is expired. Works published at least 75 years ago are considered in the public domain.

Q-and-A format — One type of presentation for an interview article, in which questions are printed, followed by the interviewee's answers.

Query letter — A letter — usually no longer than one page — in which a writer proposes an article idea to an editor.

Rejection slip — A printed note in which a publication indicates that it is not interested in a submission.

Reporting time — The weeks or months it takes for an editor to evaluate a submission.

Reprint rights — The legal right of a magazine or newspaper to print an article, story, or poem after it has already appeared elsewhere.

Royalty — A percentage of the amount received from retail sales of a book, paid to the author by the publisher. For hardcovers, the royalty is generally 10% on the first 5,000 copies sold; 12½% on the next 5,000 sold; 15% thereafter. Paperback royalties range from 4% to 8%, depending on whether it's a trade or mass-market book.

SASE — Self-addressed, stamped envelope, required with all submissions that the author wishes returned — either for return of material or (if you don't need material returned) for editor's reply.

Slush pile — The stack of unsolicited manuscripts in an editor's office.

Tear sheet — The pages of a magazine or newspaper on which an author's work is published.

Unsolicited submission — A manuscript that an editor did not specifically ask to see.

Vanity publisher — Also called **subsidy publisher.** A publishing company that charges author all costs of printing a book. No reputable book publisher operates on this subsidy basis.

Work for hire — When a work is written on a "for hire" basis, all rights in it become the property of the publisher. Though the work-for-hire clause applies mostly to work done by regular employees of a company, some editors offer work-for-hire agreements to free lancers. Think carefully before signing such agreements, however, since by doing so you will essentially be signing away your rights and will not be able to try to resell your work on your own.

Writers guidelines — A formal statement of a publication's editorial needs, payment schedule, deadlines, and other essential information.

INDEX TO MARKETS

883

890

897

907